VEGETARIAN RESTAURANTS

&

NATURAL FOOD STORES

First Printing 2002

Cover design by Kurma Rupa

Published simultaneously in the United States of America and Canada by Torchlight Publishing, Inc.

Library of Congress Cataloging-in-Publication Data

Howely, John
    Vegetarian restaurants and natural food stores in the US : a
comprehensive guide to over 2500 vegetarian eateries / John Howley.
      p.   cm.
  ISBN 1-887089-44-6 (paperback)
  1. Vegetarian restaurants—United States—Guidebooks. 2. Natural food
restaurants—United States—Guidebooks. I. Title
TX907.2 .H69 2002
647.9573—dc21   200200809

Torchlight Publishing
P.O. Box 52
Badger, CA 93603
www.torchlight.com

VEGETARIAN RESTAURANTS

&

NATURAL FOOD STORES

A Comprehensive Guide
to Over 2,500 Vegetarian Eateries

JOHN HOWLEY

TORCHLIGHT
PUBLISHING

John Howley

John Howley was born in Pennsylvania and grew up in Atlantic City. For a few years he lived and worked part time in the hotel that his mother operated. He also spent some time working in some restaurants. He studied to be an accountant at Drexel and Rutgers Universities. He became a member of ISKCON to study the Vedic (Indian) scriptures and became a pure vegetarian. He has been a vegetarian for over 20 years and has visited many vegetarian restaurants and natural food store during his extensive travel around the US.

Spiritual Guides Publisher

Started in 1993, Spiritual Guides was established to publish practical travel books on India, vegetarian subjects and spiritual subject matter. Spiritual Guides specializes just on these subjects in order to do the best job possible.

Warning and Request

Nothing stays the same. Places change and close, a good place can become bad, and phone numbers or addresses change. If you find something that is changed please write me and let me know. If you know some information about a place that I don't know, please inform me so I can add it to the edition of this book and our Web site at www.vegetarian-restaurants.net. I really appreciate any letters that are sent in. Thank you for your help.
Our email address is veggierestaurants@hotmail.com.

Acknowledgments

I would like to thank several people who help me with this book. I would like to thank some of the people who were very helpful with information about various restaurants and natural food store: Raymond Kissane (who gave me a good amount of information about vegetarian restaurants and did some editing in this book), Sravana Mangala (who called some of the places in this book and gave me some excellent practical advise to me), Garga Muni, RS Belokapi, Dennis Manairi, Garga Muni, Jaya Govinda, Noel Dela Merced and the many other people that I talked to. I would like to thank Kurma Rupa for doing a great job with the cover, Rsabdeva Dasa for doing an excellent job of editing this book, Sujana Dasi for helping with the back cover and marketing, and Manu Dasa who did such a great job on our Web site: www.vegetarian-restaruants.net. I would especially like to thank my mother who taught me what is a first-class restaurant and excellent service. I would like to thank AC Bhaktivedanta Swami Prabhupada for informing me about the importance of being a vegetarian and also he gave me an excellent path to become one, which is to chant the Hare Krishna mantra: Hare Krishna, Hare Krishna, Krishna, Krishna, Hare, Hare; Hare Rama, Hare Rama, Rama Rama, Hare, Hare.

How to Use This Book

An explanation of the coding used in this book.

**	Vegetarian restaurant
***	Vegan restaurant
$	under $10 for a meal
$$	between $10 and $20 for a meal
$$$	between $20 and $30 for a meal
$$$$	over $30 for a meal, not including alcohol
AMEX	American Express
DC	Dinner's Club
DIS	Discover
MC	MasterCard
VISA	Visa

If it says "at 77th Street" in the address, this means that it is at or near the junction of 77th Street.

A supermarket-type place is a large store with an excellent selection of vegetarian, vegan and organic items.

In the comment section, "recommended" means that it is an excellent place. To be highly recommended, the place almost certainly is pure vegetarian.

Full service means that a waiter or waitress comes to the table and the food is brought to you. Counter service means that you order at a counter and usually the food is then given to you at the counter, but sometimes the food may be brought to you. Delivery means that the food can be delivered to your home or office within a certain area.

In the direction section, a slant right means not a total turn, but at an angle (less than 90°). ⎯⎯⎯⎯⎯＼

TABLE OF CONTENTS

How I Became a Vegetarian

For a good part of my life I considered the reasoning behind eating animals for food, but could not bring myself to stop eating animals and becoming a vegetarian.

When I was going to Rutgers University studying accounting, a friend of mine gave me a book called *Nectar of Devotion* by His Divine Grace AC Bhaktivedanta Swami Prabhupada, Founder-Acharya of the International Society for Krishna Consciousness (commonly known as the Hare Krishna Movement). I read the book and Swami Prabhupada talked about becoming a devotee of Krishna (God) and that a person who was a true devotee of God was a vegetarian who did not kill animals to eat. I though this made a lot of sense but could not quite consider how I could become a vegetarian.

He also talked about the glories of chanting Hare Krishna (the names of God) and gave a *mantra* to chant, Hare Krishna, Hare Krishna, Krishna, Krishna, Hare, Hare; Hare Rama, Hare Rama, Rama Rama, Hare Hare. He said a devotee of Krishna did not have to make an independent effort to follow religious principles (which includes being a vegetarian), but by chanting Hare Krishna with sincerity that religious principles would naturally follow.

Considering that my life wasn't quite idea (to say the least), I decided to experiment and chant Hare Krishna. Swami Prabhupada said that you should count the mantras that you chant and that you should try to chant a set amount of rounds of 108 mantras of Hare Krishna, Hare Krishna, Krishna Krishna, Hare Hare, Hare Rama, Hare Rama, Rama Rama, Hare Hare. At first when I chanted I used a comb to keep track of the amount of mantras that I chanted. Then I started chanting on beads, as is suggested by the acharya (religions leaders).

To my amazement after about two months I had no interest in eating meat and naturally became a vegetarian with no separate effort. Over the last 23 years I continue to chant Hare Krishna and do not remember a time where I seriously considered eating meat, quite the contrary I have become fanatically against it.

I also consider the other reasons for being a vegetarian to be important such as why commit violence to another living creature that is not absolutely necessary, the health benefits and other moral considerations to be important reasons for being a vegetarian. So I can personally recommend both the benefits of being a vegetarian and chanting the mantra Hare Krishna, Hare Krishna, Krishna Krishna, Hare Hare; Hare Rama, Hare Rama, Rama Rama, Hare Hare in attaining a more peaceful and happy life.

Introduction

The idea to write this book came about five years ago. As I do a lot of traveling, I often found it difficult to find pure vegetarian restaurants or good natural food stores. At that time, I thought it would be a good idea to compile a detailed vegetarian restaurant book. I believe following a vegetarian regimen to be extremely important for a person to be properly situated in a moral life style, as I am sure many of the readers will agree.

About three years ago I decided to do this book. I then started saving the cards and take-out menus from the restaurants and natural food stores that I visited. I also started going out of my way to visit vegetarian restaurants and health food stores. At that time, I was living in Long Island and started making special trips into New York City to visit vegetarian restaurants.

Whenever I visited a city, I would pick up the local alternative newspaper, as they often list the vegetarian restaurants. I started checking the yellow pages for vegetarian restaurants. I got whatever books, magazines or newspapers I could find about vegetarian restaurants or natural food stores.

My friend had a really good collection of books about alternative subjects and vegetarian restaurants. He also had issues of Vegetarian Times dating back several years, so I went through these magazines and checked their listings of vegetarian restaurants and reviews on vegetarian restaurants. Also I checked out back issues of The Vegetarian Journal. Being a regular reader of Vegetarian Times and The Vegetarian Journal, I consider both these publications to be valuable assets for vegetarians or prospective vegetarians.

I also asked my friends to collect whatever information they could about vegetarian restaurants that they visited. As most of the people I know are vegetarian, I had many people collecting information for me. These people helped me get up-to-date information

of newly opened or closed restaurants.

My one friend, Raymond Kissane, spent years traveling and would go out of his way for hours sometimes to eat in a good vegetarian restaurant. He gave me information on over 50 restaurants listed in this book.

When I met vegetarians from various parts of the country, I would ask them their opinion on the various vegetarian restaurants that I had listed in their area and which ones they considered the best.

I then went onto the Internet and started to go through the various sites that contained information on vegetarian restaurants. Listed in the Internet section in the back of this book are some of the sites that I looked at to get information about vegetarian restaurants. I spent about two months on the Internet looking at every site I could find on the subject. Some sites, like Vegetarian in Paradise Yellow Pages, have some great information which includes really good reviews on many restaurants in the Los Angeles area. Another really good site is MSN's City Search, which lists restaurants according to how vegetarian-friendly they are, with a review of many of the restaurants. They also have a list of reviews of the restaurants from individuals writing into the site. I basically read everything I could find on the subject.

At this point I had a good list of vegetarian restaurants with a good amount of information about the various restaurants. The problem with this information was that much of the sources of this information were years out-of-date. So I then proceeded to call every restaurant and natural food store I had listed. I asked what times they were open, whether they were vegetarian or how vegetarian-friendly they are, some sample vegetarian dishes they served, what credit cards they accepted and several other questions. I also would often ask at the natural food stores what vegetarian restaurants were in their areas.

From this calling I found many restaurants to be closed and at least 50% of the listed opening hours to be wrong. I also found some extra vegetarian restaurants that were not listed anywhere. For instance, for one restaurant in New Hampshire the only information I had on it was the name of the restaurant, a phone number and the words "vegetarian-friendly." I then found out that this restaurant was a vegan restaurant and that the lady running the place was extremely friendly, helpful and dedicated to having a first-class vegan restaurant. She also told me that a health food store that I had earlier attempted to call and believed was closed was now a vegan restaurant that she also owned.

While calling I met some fantastic people and really got a great understanding of how nice vegetarian people often are. Many people were very willing to tell me about other vegetarian or vegetarian-friendly restaurants in their area.

I then went onto Whitepages.com on the Internet to find phone numbers that had been changed. In many cases I had the correct phone number, but the area code had changed.

Then I went onto Map Quest and got directions for many of the restaurants and natural food stores in this book. When I visited places, I would write down the directions to those places. These directions will make it much easier for the reader of this book to find many of these locations. Especially in big cities, when you ask directions for many vegetarian restaurants you could ask ten people where a restaurant is located and no will know. Having some general directions can really help one find the place and save much time.

Over the years, I had worked several times in restaurants. My mother spent a good part of her life in the restaurant business. From her I learned some valuable practical information on how a first-class restaurant should be run. She never lost her cool on the job, always acted extremely polite with her customers, always had time to be personal with her customers, would remember what they ordered and how it should be cooked and would always go out of her way to keep the customer happy.

One summer my brothers and I did a thorough weekly cleaning of my mother's restaurant. Also I sometimes would do some basic work in her restaurant such as washing the dishes, cutting up potatoes and general cleaning. Another time my mother got me a job as a busboy at one of the highest class restaurants in Atlantic City, where I got some firsthand experience in working in a fancy restaurant. Over the years I have helped managed some catering events.

I have added information in this book to give the reader extra sight on the vegetarian subject. There is information on reasons to be vegetarian, health benefits of being a vegetarian, disadvantages of eating meat, benefits of eating organic produce, a list of vegetarian organizations and some interesting vegetarian links on the Internet.

There is also a section on the vegetarian options at international cuisine restaurants and some things you should be careful of in these restaurants. There is a list of fast food restaurants and what vegetarian dishes they have. There is also a list of dishes that would appear to be vegetarian in restaurants that may contain meat products, so should be avoided.

There is a section that has a list of ingredients that may be found in various dishes that may be made using animal products.

I have tried to have the information in this book as detailed, accurate and up-to-date as possible. I am sure that future editions of this book will greatly improve with the help of the readers of this book. Please feel free to email me at veggierestaurants@hotmail.com with any updated information or reviews on vegetarian-friendly restaurants.

Along with this book we are also doing a web site at www.vegetarian-restaurants.net with an up-to-date list of vegetarian-friendly restaurants and natural food stores. There is a section on this Web site where there are updates since this book was written. You can print out these updates and take them with you when you travel. This site also has a good list of links to various alternative subjects.

GENERAL VEGETARIAN INFORMATION

At the present time approximately 5% of the population of the United States, or around 12 million people, consider themselves to be vegetarian. But a high percentage of these people occasionally eat meat. According to a Roper Poll done by the Vegetarian Resource Group in 1994 and 1997, only 1% of the population in the US is a Pure Vegetarian. This definition of pure vegetarian is to never consciously eat meat, fish or poultry, but eggs and dairy can be eaten.

The definition of **Pure Vegetarian** in this book is a person who does not consciously eat meat, fish, poultry or eggs; dairy can be eaten, which is the Hindu definition. A pure vegetarian will never eat meat under any circumstances. They will also avoid products that have meat products in them such as cheese made with the rennet of a cow's stomach, yogurt or pudding that contains gelatin, refried beans with lard in them, candy that contains eggs and other ingredients derived from meat products, and marshmallows and baked goods that contain eggs. Many people consider eating eggs to be vegetarian but according to our definition eating eggs is not pure vegetarian because it means eating what would eventually become a chicken. There are often animal products hidden in food and non-food items such as in medicines, cosmetics, toothpastes, soaps, etc. These products should also be avoided for a person to be considered a pure vegetarian.

Lacto Ovo Vegetarian

A lacto ovo vegetarian does not eat meat, fish or poultry, but eats eggs and milk. They eat eggs and products made with eggs in them, yogurt, cheese, milk and ice creams.

Lacto Vegetarian

A lacto vegetarian does not eat meat, fish, poultry or eggs, but includes dairy products in their diet. They will eat milk, ice cream (that does not include eggs), yogurt and cheese. They would avoid ice creams, baked goods, pancakes and veggie burgers that contain eggs.

Vegan

A vegan does not eat any fish, meat, poultry, eggs, dairy products or foods that contain any of these products. They also do not use any non-food items that contain products from animals, including wool from sheep, leather and silk. Vegans often do not eat honey, because bees may be killed while harvesting it.

According to many vegans, it is pronounced VEE-gun. A vegan diet consists of vegetables, grains, beans, nuts, fruits and seeds. This diet tends to be high in fiber and moderate in protein and fat.

A vegan will not use margarine that has casein, a milk product, in it and they do not use shoes that are made from leather. Vegans do not eat white granulated sugar because it is often processed by using char derived from animal bones to whiten the sugar. They also do not use products that are tested on animals, as are many cosmetics.

Macrobiotics

A macrobiotic diet is mainly vegetarian, but macrobiotic diets often include seafood. In this diet all other meat products are excluded, as are eggs and dairy products. They also do not eat "nightshade vegetables" (potato, pepper and eggplant), refined sugar and tropical fruits. This diet contains many foods found in Asian countries such as miso soup, root vegetables (daikon and lotus) and sea vegetables (seaweed, kelp, arame).

It emphasizes eating locally grown foods that are in season. Meals consist of 50% to 60% grains, 25% locally grown produce, and the rest of the diet mainly consists of beans and soups. In lesser amounts fruits, nuts and seeds are eaten.

This diet is based on the Chinese principles of yin and yang. Some people follow this diet as a philosophy of life and others follow it for health reasons.

Fruitarian

A fruitarian is a person who only eats fruits and vegetables that are actually classified as fruits such as avocados, nuts, seeds, eggplant, zucchini and tomatoes.

Raw or Living Food Diet

One who follows a raw food diet is a person who for the most part only eats raw foods that are not cooked. One who follows this type of diet believes that cooking changes food in a negative way and makes it less nutritious, diminishing the vitamin and mineral contents of the food. Most people who follow a raw-food diet only eat between 50% to 80% of their food raw. There is some logic to a raw food diet in the fact that cooking food destroys nutrients. But cooking food on the other hand makes foods easier to digest, which often offsets the anti-nutritional factors.

Several Reasons to be a Vegetarian

1. Because of the extreme mistreatment that animals have to go through while being raised for slaughter.
2. Health reasons.
3. Moral reasons. People don't want to kill animals in order to eat, when they can survive by eating vegetables, fruits, grains, nuts and milk.
4. Religious reasons. Certain religions prohibit the eating of meat. Seventh Day Adventists do not eat meat and Hindus often do not eat meat.
5. Some people just don't like the taste of meat.
6. Some people don't like the idea that meat sometimes contains diseases, such as Salmonella, Mad Cow (Creutzfeldt-Jakob Disease – CJD) or Listeria. Salmonella and Listeria are bacterias that can be found in meats and meat products. In heavy doses they can cause severe illness and maybe even death. A minor case of either disease may be over within 24 hours and appears like a flu. Mad Cow Disease can cause damage to the brain and cause death. It can cause a person to go crazy.

Health Benefits of Being a Vegetarian

According to studies, vegetarians have better health than people that eat meat. They have lower rates of coronary artery disease, gallstones, cancer (particularly lung and colon cancer), kidney stones, colon disease, diabetes and high blood pressure. It has been shown that sometimes a vegetarian diet can help cure these diseases. A vegetarian is also less likely to be overweight than a non-vegetarian.

In 1961, the Journal of the American Medical Association stated that ninety to ninety-seven percent of heart disease, the cause of more than half the deaths in the United States, could be prevented by a vegetarian diet.

The American Heart Association report states, "In well-documented population studies using standard methods of diet and coronary disease assessment…evidence suggests that a high-saturated-fat diet is an essential factor for a high incidence of coronary heart disease."

In 1990, the British Medical Journal Lancet reported on a study by Dr Dean Ornish of the University of California. Dr Ornish found that a vegetarian diet reversed clogging of the arteries in patients with serious heart disease.

In 1990, Dr Walter Willet, who conducted a study of diet and colon cancer, said, "If you step back and look at the data, the optimum amount of red meat you eat should be zero."

The National Academy of Science reported in 1983 that "people may be able to prevent many common cancers by eating less fatty meats and more vegetables and grain."

The USDA recommends that people reduce saturated fat and cholesterol, which are in high amounts in animal products, and low in vegetarian diets.

In his Notes on the Causation of Cancer, Rollo Russell writes, "I have found of twenty-five nations eating flesh largely, nineteen had a high cancer rate and only one had a low rate, and that of thirty-five nations eating little or no flesh, none had a high rate."

Various studies have shown that vegetarians have lower blood pressure than non-vegetarians. Vegetarians have much lower cholesterol levels than people that eat meat. Heart disease is found much less in vegetarians. Studies have also shown that vegetarians have up to half the cancer rate than those of non-vegetarians. Cases of breast cancer are much lower in countries that have low meat diets.

Vegetarians eat more antioxidants such as vitamin C, vitamin E, beta-carotenes and phytochemicals. Phyotochemicals are components in plants that help to prevent disease. Antioxidants decrease the chance of getting heart disease, cancer and other diseases.

Eating red meat increases the chance of dying from cancer of the breast and colon, heart disease and strokes. Meat eaters have much higher rates of cancer than vegetarians. Cancer and cardiovascular diseases are linked to diets with a high amount of saturated fat (meat) and with a low amount of fiber (meat).

Animal products are high in sodium, which causes the blood to retain water and also causes plaque to build up in the arteries, lowering the flow of blood, which are major causes of high blood pressure.

According to a study done in England for 12 years of 5,015 meat eaters and 6,115 vegetarians, it was found that vegetarians had 40% less chance of getting cancer.

According to William Castelli, MD, director of the Framingham Heart Study, vegetarians live three to six years longer than meat eaters. He said, "vegetarians have the best diet. They have the lowest rate of coronary disease of any group in the country and they have a fraction of our heart attack rate and they have only 40% of our cancer rate."

Grains and plant foods contain fiber, while animal products contain almost none. Because fiber is necessary for proper stool production, lack of proper fiber accounts for societies with meat-based diets to have higher cases of colon cancer. The main reasons why people need to take laxatives is because of lack of fiber in their diet and not drinking enough water.

There were guidelines published in Circulation: Journal of the American Heart Association (AHA). These guidelines were compiled by members of the AHA's Nutrition Committee with the cooperation of the American Cancer Society, National Institutes of Health, and the American Academy of Pediatrics.

Richard J Deckelbaum, MD, a co-author of the journal article, is a professor of nutrition at Columbia University and a member of the AHA Nutrition Committee. Edward A Fisher, MD, PhD, a co-author of the article, is director of lipoprotein research at New York's Mount Sinai Cardiovascular Institute.

Their recommendations are that a healthy diet consists of getting 30% of total calories from fat and no more than 10% of total calories from saturated fat, and 55% of total calories should come from complex carbohydrates such as grains, cereals, vegetables and fruits. It is also recommended that a person eat only enough calories to maintain their body weight. Problems come from eating too much fat, especially saturated fats from meat and eggs, eating too many calories, and getting too much calories from salt and sugar.

Because people in the US eat good amounts of meat, Americans eat five times as much protein as is recommended. An excess of protein can leach calcium from the bones, which is major cause of bone disorder.

It is important to get enough leafy vegetables that are high in antioxidants, which are good for overall health.

Some Important Guidelines

1. Eat a variety of foods.
2. Mainly eat foods from plant sources.
3. Don't eat too much salt or sugar.
4. Eat at least six servings of grains, breads and pastas.
5. Eat at least five servings of vegetables and fruits.
6. Avoid foods high in fat, especially those coming from animal sources.

Vegetarian Nutritional Considerations

A question that may be asked is whether a vegetarian gets the correct nutritional requirements that the human body needs. This next section discusses this mater.

The body has the ability to better absorb needed nutrients. For instance, if your body needs more calcium it will naturally absorb more from your food. If it needs less of a particular nutrient it will naturally absorb less.

Protein

An optimal diet gets around 10 to 15 percent of its calories from protein. It is usually best for a person to eat less than 70 grams of protein a day.

Proteins are nitrogen-containing compounds that when digested become amino acids. Amino acids make up protein, and they make up antibodies, enzymes, hormones and are the basic structure of every cell. Amino acids make up the proteins in muscles. They are also found in body fluids, bones, blood and the teeth.

Vegetarians usually eat enough protein but not too much. If a person eats too much protein, especially those from animal sources, it causes the kidneys to allow extra calcium to pass out in the urine. This is one of the reasons the recommended amount of calcium is high for Americans. These recommendations are increased because of the high intake of meat by many Americans. Eating too much protein increases blood pressure levels and increases the possibilities of coronary artery disease; it is also believed to increase the risk of kidney disease, kidney stone and osteoporosis.

Eating less protein helps to cause less kidney problems. Vegetarians tend to have less kidney diseases and kidney stones.

In most proteins there are 20 amino acids. When these amino acids link together, they form protein. Individual amino acids have certain functions in the body and can combine with other non-protein substances in the body to do things within the body. Glycine helps to make toxic substances harmless. Tryptophan helps in making the vitamin niacin. Histidine helps defend against a runny nose when you have hay fever or other allergies.

Essential amino acids are ones that are not produced by the body, and they have to be gotten from food. There are nine essential amino acids, which are: Histidine, Isoleucine, Leucine, Lysine, Methoonine, Phenylalanine, Threonine, Tryptophan and Valine. Plants contain all the nine essential amino acids that the body needs.

Meat contains high levels of protein. So much so that they can cause the body to receive excessively high amounts of protein. It is possible to get more than enough proteins from plant foods. Soybean has a good amount of the essential amino acids. It can be the only source of protein for a person.

In the past there was a concept of complementary proteins. This concept is that to get the proper amount of proteins that the body needs, during each meal you have to combine different foods in such a way as to get all the essential amino acids in the same meal. It was thought that by combining amino acids in a certain way that this would form a superior quality protein.

At the present time the concept of complementary proteins is not generally accepted. It is now believed that the body can get complement proteins in its own way. To be able to do this properly it is necessary to eat enough calories and to eat a selection of healthy foods (not junk food).

Some vegetarian foods high in protein are beans, lentil soup, oatmeal, bean burrito, vegetarian chili, tempeh, veggie burgers, falafel (chick pea balls), tofu, stir-fry vegetables, soy milk, pasta primavera and cereal.

Fats

There are three types of fats: saturated fat, polyunsaturated fat and monounsaturated fat. Most fat-containing foods contain all three types of fats. Saturated fat is found in meats, eggs, dairy and some vegetable oils such as coconut oil and palm oil. Monounsaturated fat is found in avocados, nuts, olives, olive oil and canola oil. Polyunsaturated fats are found in vegetable oils, soyfoods, seeds and nuts, and in less amounts in beans, grains and vegetables.

Saturated fats and trans fatty acids are the fats most likely to cause heart disease. Trans fatty acids are in foods that contain hydrogenated fats. To reduce the chance of heart disease it is a good idea to reduce all kinds of fats and especially to avoid hydrogenated and saturated fats.

The optimal diet will receive no more than 25 percent of its calories from fat, the majority of which should be either monounsaturated or polyunsaturated fat. The normal American gets 37% of their calories from fat. Vegetarians eat less fat and less saturated fats than meat eaters. A diet based on vegetables, fruits, grains, nonfat milk products and dried beans is low in fat.

Calcium

Vegetarians can better absorb calcium than non-vegetarians, so they usually don't need as much. It is a good idea for vegetarians to eat at least two servings of calcium-rich foods a day. As a class, most Americans eat less calcium than the minimum recommended amount set by the National Academy of Sciences.

Some foods high in calcium are milk, cheese, yogurt, broccoli, almonds, garbanzo beans (chick-peas), molasses, kidney beans, dried figs, sesame seeds, pinto beans, lentils, bok choy, navy beans, Chinese cabbage, calcium-fortified soymilk, tofu processed with calcium sulfate and dark green leafy vegetables such as collard greens, turnip greens, kale and mustard greens.

When a person eats meat their blood becomes more acidic. The body then takes calcium from the bones to neutralize this acid in the blood. In this way calcium is lost through the kidneys. The protein derived from plant foods has less sulfur in it, which causes the bones to lose less calcium. Amino acids that contain sulfur found in meat proteins cause the body to lose more calcium when taken in excess.

Sodium or salt can cause the body to lose calcium. Drinks such as coffee, tea and soft drinks that contain caffeine cause the body to lose calcium.

Substances such as oxalates and phytates can diminish the body's ability to absorb calcium. Because spinach contains oxalates, the body cannot properly absorb the calcium that it contains.

By exercising and walking you naturally keep more calcium in the body. If a person has exposure to the sun they produce vitamin D, which helps the body with the absorption of calcium.

Milk is a good source of calcium, protein, riboflavin and calories. Not everyone can eat milk, because many people in the world can't digest it. Young children produce an enzyme called lactase, which helps the body digest lactose, the sugar found in milk. As babies become older their bodies produce less lactase, as they need less of their mothers' milk. By the time a baby become three to five years old, much of the production of lactase has stopped as the child stops breast-feeding.

When the production of lactase stops, many adults can no longer digest milk from any species. If a person cannot digest milk, they get lactose intolerance. When the milk reaches the intestines, it cannot be digested and a person may get diarrhea, gas, abdominal cramps and bloating.

People from Northern Europe and many of the people in the United States do not tend to be lactose intolerant. But many people from Asia, Africa, Native Americans, South America and the Mediterranean tend to be lactose intolerant.

A possible replacement for cow's milk is soymilk, which is often calcium fortified. Rice milk can also be substituted.

Iron

Usually vegetarians have no problem getting enough iron in their diet. Eating foods rich in vitamin C enables the body to better absorb iron by as much as 20 times. The substance tannic acid in tea can reduce the absorption of iron, which can harm people in poorer countries who do not get enough food.

Iron forms part of the hemoglobin in red blood cells. Hemoglobin carries oxygen to the blood cells and to the muscles of the body. People who do not get enough iron, may not get enough oxygen to their blood cells and muscles, which makes them feel exhausted.

Some good sources of iron are cereals, whole breads, brown rice, beans, apricots, prune juice, Brussels sprout, broccoli, bok choy, cantaloupe, tofu, figs, tempeh, soybean, nuts, watermelon, dark green leafy vegetables, legumes, kidney beans, tahini, peas, dried fruits, raisins and nuts.

Vitamin C

Foods rich in vitamin C are broccoli, Brussels sprouts, cabbage, cantaloupe, cauliflower, citrus fruits, green pepper, honeydew melon, kiwi fruit, papaya, potatoes, strawberry and tomato.

Vitamin B12

The body only needs two micrograms of vitamin B12 per day. If you get a supplement that contains 50 micrograms of vitamin B12, most likely the body will only use 2 micrograms of it. A deficiency of B12 can lead to severe permanent nerve damage.

There may be a problem with a vegetarian in reference to getting enough vitamin B12 because it is only present in animal foods. Therefore a vegan may have a problem with a B12 deficiency. More than enough vitamin B12 can be gotten from eating milk products. Vegans can get the proper amount of B12 that the body needs by taking vitamin pills, fortified cereals or fortified soymilk. It is usually a good idea for vegan mothers to take a B12 supplement.

The bodies of humans and animals produce B12 in their intestines. But it is produced in such a place in the human body that it cannot be used by it.

The body stores B12 and also recycles it. There is usually enough B12 stored in the liver and tissues of the body to last for three years, and for some people over ten years.

There are many forms of B12, but Cyanocobalamin is the form that the body can use. Therefore even if some foods are high in other forms of B12, they are usually of no value for a person. Some foods that may appear to be good sources of B12 are not and these include nutritional yeast, bean sprouts, tempeh, sea vegetables, tamari (fermented soy sauce) and miso (fermented soy).

Most forms of nutritional yeast contain B12 that has no value, but the brand Red Star T-6635+ contains B12 that can be utilized. It has been made to contain Cyanocobalimin.

Riboflavin (B2)

The best sources of B2 come from milk or meat products. It can also be gotten from seaweed, cereals, legumes, green leafy vegetables and other sources.

Saturated Fat and Cholesterol

A diet with a low level of saturated fats and cholesterol is healthiest. If there is too much cholesterol in the body, there may be a hardening of the arteries that can cause heart disease. Eating a low amount of saturated fats and cholesterols can help reduce coronary artery disease, high blood pressure, diabetes and cancer.

Saturated fat causes the body to produce cholesterol. The body needs cholesterol, but the body makes enough by itself. Cholesterol is not needed from foods that we eat. American meat eaters take in about 500 milligrams of cholesterol each day, lacto-ovo vegetarians take in about 200 milligrams of cholesterol daily and a vegan does not take in any.

Plant foods do not contain cholesterol. Cholesterol is made by the liver and is only found in animal foods. The highest source of saturated fat comes from red meat. Certain dairy products such as cheese, sour cream, butter, ice creams, milk and the skin of poultry are also high in saturated fats. Chicken and fish have less saturated fat than red meat but also contain the type of saturated fat that can cause health problems. Intake of saturated fat raises the cholesterol level.

Saturated fat is usually solid like a stick of butter at room temperature. Cholesterol is a waxy substance and can often be found in the arteries of a person who is diseased.

Fiber

If a person has a good amount of fiber in the system and drinks plenty of water, they will have better bowel movement.

Fiber in plant food is material that is not totally digested after eating. Fiber in a person's food causes the food to pass quicker through the system, which reduces the possibility of harmful substances coming in contact with the intestine lining. Contaminants in the system can bind with fiber to take them out of the body. Since fibers are bulky, by eating foods high in fiber one tends to eat less, which may cause one to take in less calories, which can help one avoid becoming overweight.

If a person gets enough fiber, they tend to have less problems with constipation, varicose veins and hemorrhoids. Getting a good amount of fiber in a diet helps to control the blood sugar levels in diabetics, and helps to lower cancer and coronary artery diseases.

The current recommended amount of fiber in a person's diet is 30 grams per day, but if a person gets 40 or 50 grams this is better. Vegetarians can easily get the required amount of fiber. The average American gets only 12 grams of fiber daily in their diet, but a typical vegetarian gets two to four times this amount. It is important to get a good amount of water with the fiber.

A cup of vegetarian chili contains 14 grams of fiber, a cup of oatmeal 8 grams, a slice of whole-wheat bread 2 grams and a pear with its skin has 4 grams of fiber.

Free Radicals

Free radicals are molecules that are produced when the body is exposed to impuri-

ties from the environment such as from pollution, ozone, and by eating certain foods that contain things such as fat and meat. They can damage the immune system and cause a person to be more prone to illnesses and diseases.

Meat has a high amount of oxidants that cause the body to make free radicals, while on the other hand, vegetables have many antioxidants that help the body get rid of free radicals. A vegetarian diet is strong in phytochemicals that help a person have good health.

Potentially Dangerous Chemicals and Natural Products

Many of the over 25,000 chemicals used in cosmetic and personal care products have not been tested properly for danger to humans. Many of these products are toxins or contain toxic products.

Some things that can be dangerous in cosmetic and personal care products are alcohol (isopropyl), DEA, DMDM hydantoin, FD & C color, fluoride, fragrance, MEA, mineral oil, parabens, polyethylene glycol (PEG), propylene glycol (PG), sodium laureth sulfate (SLES), sodium lauryl sulfate (SLS), triclosan and urea hydantoin. Many of these products can be serious carcinogens and hormone-disrupting chemicals.

Because there are no regulations in regard to what is considered to be a "Natural Product," this term is often abused. Often the so-called natural products contain the same dangerous chemicals that they propound that they are replacing.

Dangerous Chemicals in Meat

Many potentially hazardous chemicals are often present in meat products. In the book **Poisons in Your Body**, by Gary and Steven Null, state some of the things happening in animal factories. "The animals are kept alive and fattened by the continuous administration of tranquilizers, hormones, antibiotics, and 2,700 other drugs. The process starts even before birth and continues long after death. Although these drugs will still be present in the meat when you eat it, the law does not require that they be listed on the package."

Arsenic is often used as a growth stimulant. The Department of Agriculture (USDA) found that arsenic exceeded the legal limit in 15% of the poultry in the US.

Sodium nitrite and sodium nitrate are chemicals used as preservatives to slow down putrefaction in cured meat, giving meat its bright-red color by reacting with pigments in the blood and muscles. If they are not used, then the meat will have its natural gray-brown color, which wouldn't be good for sales. These chemicals when taken in excess can poison humans, and many people have been poisoned by these chemicals. These chemicals can be especially dangerous to babies and young children. The United Nations' joint FAO/WHO Expert Committee of Food Additives warned, "Nitrate should on no account be added to baby food." AJ Lehman of the FDA pointed out that "only a small margin of safety exists between the amount of nitrate that is safe and that which may be dangerous."

Because of the horrible conditions that the animals to be slaughtered are put through, often they are given vast amounts of antibiotics, which can often create antibiotic-resistant bacteria that can be passed to persons who eat the meat. The FDA estimates that penicillin and tetracycline save the meat industry $1.9 billion a year.

Vegetarian Babies

Breast milk is the best food for a newly born child. Breast-feeding is best for a child for the first six months. Breast milk contains substances that protect the baby from disease. If a baby is breast fed as a child, they are less likely to develop allergies when they get older. Breast-feeding is also best for the mother, because it helps the uterus go back to its normal size faster.

Vegetarian woman usually have less contaminants in their breast milk than non-vegetarian women. This is because contaminants are often found in higher levels in the fat and tissues of animals. These contaminants are then past onto the baby in the milk.

Babies less than six months old should only drink breast milk, water or formula. They should not be fed anything else. They should not be given drinks that contain sugar, juices or baby cereal.

Baby formula is usually made from cow milk that has been altered to make it more digestible. Some are made of animal by-products and are often not vegetarian. Some are soy-based and do not contain any animal products. Brands that can be used by vegans include Prosobee, Soyalac and Isamil. Babies should not use regular soy milk, but should use infant formula soy milk.

Usually the first food a baby starts eating is iron-fortified rice cereal, which is easy for a baby to take. At the same time it is best to continue to breast feed the baby. Breast-feeding should be gradually discontinued over a period of time.

When children get older, it is usually best to give them food that is high in fat. This is because their stomachs are smaller than adults, so they may need more dense food. In this way infants get the correct amount of calories. Fat can be added to the diet by adding nut and seed butters to sandwiches. Avocado is also a food high in fat.

Children who are vegetarians are less likely to be overweight because their diet contains more fibers and less fats, saturated fat and cholesterol.

Diseases Found In Meat

Crammed together in unclean conditions, force-fed, and inhumanely treated, animals set to be slaughtered contract more diseases than is normal. Meat inspectors attempt to filter out bad meat, but because there is not sufficient time for examination and pressures from the industry, sometimes bad meat gets through to the consumer.

A report by the USDA in 1972 lists carcasses that passed inspection after the diseased parts were removed. Examples included nearly 100,000 cows with eye cancer and 3,596,302 cases of abscessed liver.

Meat and poultry are the primary sources of food borne pathogens, which cause over 10 million cases of human illnesses and 9,000 deaths a year in the US. Microbial pathogens are microorganisms that cause diseases from bacteria, viruses, fungi and parasites. Campylobacter and salmonella are not regulated and account for 80% of illnesses and 75% of diseases derived from meat or poultry. One infected animal can contaminate 16 tons of beef.

Raw meat often contains dangerous bacteria, which is often not regulated by either the USDA or FDA. It is expected that the consumers themselves kill dangerous pathogen bacteria. It is often found that meat is still raw and is not totally cooked when eaten; therefore it still contains dangerous bacteria.

The government allows the sale of chickens with airsacculitis, a pneumonia-like disease that causes pus-laden mucus to collect in the lungs. In order to meet federal standards, the chicken's chest cavities are cleaned out with air-suction guns. But during this process, diseased air sacs sometimes burst and pus seeps into the meat.

Many chickens are infected with campylobacter, a bacterial infection that causes bloody diarrhea, cramps and fever, and can lead to death (up to 800 a year in the US). Twenty percent of chickens with this disease were found to be resistant to quinolones (an antibiotic). This resistance was caused by FDA approval of use of this antibiotic for therapeutic use in chickens.

Chickens contaminated with salmonella, campylobacter and other diseased organisms are sold to people. The amount of salmonella and campylobacter is not tested. The US Code of Federal Regulations allows for birds with tumors and other disease manifestation to be sold after cutting out the infected sites.

Many of the seafood companies break the food safety regulations. Inspectors from the FDA only visit seafood-processing plants once a year, and often this only entails visiting their office and asking them what they are doing to insure food safety. Half the fish consumed in the US are imported and their processing plants are rarely inspected by US inspectors.

E coli O157:H7, which causes humans to get sick according to the USDA, may infect half the cattle that are used for ground beef. Each year over 73,000 people become sick from it and 600 die from it in the US. Mild symptoms cause diarrhea and abdominal cramps, and red-blood-cell destruction. Worst cases may cause kidney failure, paralysis and blindness, and a partial removal of the bowel.

Around 20% of US herds of cows are believed to be infected with Johne's disease. This disease has been linked to Crohn's disease, which causes a chronic case of diarrhea, and may cause the victim to have part of their intestines removed.

Hoof-and-mouth disease is a disease that causes infected animals to get blisters on their hooves and lips, and causes the animals to have problems with eating because of the blisters, loss of appetite and fever. Rarely is this disease fatal to the animals. Recently over two million animals were destroyed in the UK because of it, though only 1,400 actually had the disease. The rest were killed to supposedly keep the disease from spreading. Even though the government eventually decided that the best way to eradicate the disease was by using antibiotics (which easily kills the disease), many of the farmers requested that their animals be destroyed because they received payment from the government for these destroyed animals. Some farmers figured that if their infected animals were treated instead of killed, then the value of their herds would be highly reduced, because people would not want to purchase meat from cattle located anywhere near where there were infected cattle.

Often cooked meat contains benzenes and carcinogenic compounds.

Often meat eating can cause long-term digestive problems. Animal products can often putrefy the colon. If food is not properly digested, it can remain in the intestine and cause general health problems; and this often happens with meat.

In 1996, nine people in the United Kingdom died of a degenerative brain disease linked to bovine spongiform encephalopathy, popularly known as mad cow disease. Medical experts suspected that the victims contracted the disease by eating contaminated beef.

Terrible Treatment of Animals that are Slaughtered

Over 100,000 cattle are killed each day in the US. They are killed by being hung by their feet and having their throats cut, killed with a stun-gun, or shocked by electric prods. While being slaughtered, they are often beaten and kicked.

Factory hens are forced to live through totally outrageous living conditions. Chickens are kept crammed with four to eight chickens in a small cage. Each hen is kept confined in about 48 to 86 square inches of space. When egg production of chickens are reduced to almost nothing, they can be induced to resume egg production by forced molt, which is done by water deprivation and starvation for up to two weeks. Most hens are molted at least once in their lives. This practice is so bad that even McDonald's won't purchase eggs from suppliers that engage in this procedure.

There is no sell-by date for chickens, so it is unknown how long a dead chicken has been sitting around in a processing plant, trucks, storage, on the road, or a meat case before being sold.

In the production of veal, male calves are put in cramped cages and chained by their necks to keep them from turning around. They are fed a diet without roughage and iron to cause the meat of an almost fully-grown animal to be whitest and tender, like a newborn calf. They are injected with hormones and antibiotics to make them grow and to stay alive.

Drugs in Animals

Over 20,000 different drugs are used on animals, such as antibiotics, sterols and growth hormones. These drugs in animals are consumed when meat products are eaten. This could lead to a problem with secondary consumption of antibiotics.

How Meat Eating Destroys the Environment

At the present time, 70% of the grains in the US and 40% of the grains in the world are fed to livestock. It takes up to 16 pounds of soybeans and grains to produce one pound of beef and three to six pounds to produce one pound of turkey or eggs. The World Health Organization says that 1.2 billion people in the world do not get enough to eat. If less grains were fed to livestock, this would highly reduce that number.

A disproportionate amount of the resources of the earth are used to produce meat products. About half the water used by the US is used for cattle production. It takes 3 to 15 times as much water to produce animal protein as it does plant protein. A cow needs to eat 7 pounds of protein derived from soybeans or grains to make a pound of beef.

Around 390 gallons of water are used to produce a pound of beef and just 25 gallons of water to produce one pound of wheat.

Many trees are being cut down throughout the world so more cattle can be grazed. Much of this deforestation takes place in the tropical rain forests in Central and South America. Cattle production is the main reason for the destruction of the rain forests in Central and South America. More than 25% of the forests in Central America have been destroyed because of cattle production. For every quarter pound of hamburger exported from the region, there is a loss of 55 square feet of rain forest.

When livestock grazes on land this tends to cause erosion of the topsoil and the land to dry out. The US has lost about one-third of its topsoil. Good topsoil helps to keep land more cultivable.

Cattle production causes soil depletion. Around 685 million acres, 85 percent of the US western rangeland, is being degraded because of overgrazing.

Tens of millions of tons of methane are released into the atmosphere by the 1.3 billion cattle. Hundreds of millions of tons of CO_2 go into the atmosphere by burning forests to make pastures for cattle, which causes global warning.

It takes 78 calories of fossil fuel to produce 1 calorie of beef protein; 35 calories for 1 calorie of pork; 22 calories for 1 of poultry; but just 1 calorie of fossil fuel for 1 calorie of soybeans.

Livestock Organic Waste Helps Destroy the Environment

Cattle production produces a billion tons of organic waste each year. The waste from animals, fertilizers and pesticides is the main source of water pollution in the US. According to the EPA, field agricultural runoff is the main source of 60% of river and stream pollution.

A 1997 Senate report documents that livestock produces 10,000 pounds of solid manure for every person in the US. The waste from livestock is 130 times that produced by humans. When it rains, phosphorous and nitrogen from the manure seep into rivers and streams, which causes algae blooms (red tides). It also causes the increase of dinoflagellates, which are a one-celled entity that has killed millions of fish. If a human comes in contact with them, they experience sores on their skin and may experience memory loss.

Free-Range Chickens

Defining a chicken as "free-range," as sold in natural food store, insinuates that free range chickens are better treated and therefore morally alright to eat them. The government's definition of "free-range" just means that the poultry from which this meat is derived have had access to the outdoors. This could mean just a small area outside for thousands of birds. This does not mean that all the other tortuous techniques being inflicted on factory-farmed birds are not inflicted on free range chickens also.

According to *Consumer Report* (March 1998), it found that free-range poultry was more contaminated by salmonella and campylobacter than non free-range poultry. 63% of the tested chickens had salmonella, 16% had campylobacter and 8% had both.

Dangers of Meat & Fishing Industry

The meat industry is often found guilty of health, environmental and labor violations. Each year over 20,000 men are killed worldwide in the fishing industry according to the Agriculture Organization of the UN. This makes it the most dangerous profession.

A fisherman in the US is sixteen times more likely to be killed on the job than a policeman or fireman.

Why Hindus Don't Eat Meat by Bhaktivedanta Swami Prabhupada

The Vaishnava philosophy teaches that we should not even kill plants unnecessarily. In the *Bhagavad-gita* (9.26) Krishna (God) says: "If someone offers Me with love and devotion a leaf, a flower, a fruit, or a little water, I will accept it." We offer Krishna only the kind of food He demands, and then we eat the remnants. If offering vegetarian food to Krishna were sinful, then it would be Krishna's sin, not ours. But God is *apapaviddha*—sinful reactions are not applicable to Him. Eating food first offered to the Lord is also something like a soldier's killing during wartime. In a war, when the commander orders a soldier to attack, the obedient soldier who kills the enemy will get a medal. But if the same soldier kills someone on his own, he will be punished. Similarly, when we eat only *prasadam* (the remnants of food offered to Krishna or God), we do not commit any sin. This is confirmed in the *Bhagavad-gita* (3.13). "The devotees of the Lord are released from all kinds of sins because they eat food that is first offered for sacrifice. Others, who prepare food for personal sense enjoyment, verily eat only sin." The civilized human being, the religious human being, is not meant to kill and eat animals.

Eating vegetables is violence, and vegetarians are also committing violence against other living entities because vegetables also have life. Nondevotees are killing cows, goats, and so many other animals for eating purposes, and one who is vegetarian is also killing. That is the law of nature. *Jiva jivasya jivanam*: one living entity is the life for another living entity. But for a human being that violence should be committed only as much as necessary.

If one kills many thousands of animals in a professional way so that other people can purchase the meat to eat, one must be ready to be killed in a similar way in his next life and in life after life. There are many rascals who violate their own religious principles. According to Judeo-Christian scriptures, it is clearly said, "Thou shalt not kill." Nonetheless, giving all kinds of excuses, even the heads of religions indulge in killing animals while trying to pass as saintly persons. This mockery and hypocrisy in human society brings about unlimited calamities: therefore occasionally there are great wars. Masses of such people go out onto battlefields and kill themselves. Presently they have discovered the atomic bomb, which is simply awaiting wholesale destruction.

Some people say, "We believe that animals have no soul." That is not correct. They believe animals have no soul because they want to eat the animals, but actually animals do have a soul.

Here is the scientific proof; the animal is eating, you are eating: the animal is sleeping, you are sleeping; the animal is defending, you are defending; the animal is having sex, you are having sex; the animals have children, you have children; they have a living place, you have a living place. If the animal's body is cut, there is blood; if your body is cut, there is blood. So, all these similarities and not the presence of the soul? That is not logical. In logic there is something called analogy. Analogy means drawing a conclusion by finding many points of similarity. If there are so many points of similarity between human beings and animals, why deny one similarity? That is not logic. That is not science.

Some rascals put forward the theory that an animal has no soul or is something like dead stone. In this way they rationalize that there is no sin in animal-killing. Actually animals are not dead stone, but the killers of animals are stone-hearted. Consequently no reason or philosophy appeals to them. They continue keeping slaughterhouses and killing animals in the forest.

By killing animals, not only will we be bereft of the human form but we will have to take an animal form and somehow or other be killed by the same type of animal we have killed. This is the law of nature. The Sanskrit word *mamsa* means "meat." It is said: *mam sah khadanti mamsah.* That is, "I am now eating the flesh of an animal who will some day in the future be eating my flesh."

The purpose of food is to increase the duration of life, purify the mind, and aid bodily strength. This is its only purpose. In the past, great authorities selected those foods that best aid health and increase life's duration, such as milk products, sugar, rice, wheat, fruits and vegetable.

Animal fat is available in the form of milk, which is the most wonderful of all foods. Milk, butter, cheese, and similar products give animal fat in a form which rules out any need for the killing of innocent creatures. Protein is amply available through split peas, dal, whole wheat, etc.

The best food is the remnant of what is offered to the Supreme Personality of Godhead. In *Bhagavad-gita*, the Supreme Lord says that He accepts preparations of vegetables, flour and milk when offered with devotion. Of course, devotion and love are the chief things which the Supreme Personality of Godhead accepts.

Therefore to make food antiseptic, eatable, and palatable for all persons, one should offer food to the Supreme Personality of Godhead.

Meat Eater	Herbivore	Human
Has claws	No claws	No claws
No skin pores, perspires through tongue	Perspires through skin pores	Perspires through skin pores
Sharp front teeth for tearing, no flat molar teeth	No sharp front teeth, has flat rear molars	No sharp front teeth, has flat rear molars

Apparent Vegetarian Foods that May Contain Meat

Often ingredients in processed foods can contain meat, fish or egg products. Many people define vegetarian dishes to include just no meat or fish, while eggs are considered to be vegetarian. Therefore if you ask if a product that contains egg is vegetarian, you may be told that it is vegetarian.

Often, even though a dish may appear to be vegetarian, it may contain ingredients that are not vegetarian. When a food contains natural favors, it may be derived from meat. Different chemicals and additives such as mono- and diglycerides may be derived from either meat or vegetarian sources. Cheeses may be made with an enzyme that is derived from either meat (cow's stomach) or a vegetarian source.

Vegetarian foods may be cooked on a surface that may also be used to cook meat. So if you are interested in maintaining strict vegetarian principles, it is important to ask what surface grilled dishes such as veggie burger are cooked on, and whether the grilled dish is cooked on the same surface as meat. Often meat is cooked on the same grill as what a veggie burger or grilled cheese are cooked on.

Also foods that are cooked in oil may have meat cooked in the same oil. So it is a good idea to ask when ordering French fries or other such dishes, whether meat, chicken or some other non-vegetarian item has been cooked in the same oil.

Table sugar is made from either sugar cane or sugar beet. About half of the sugar used in the United States is made from cane sugar. Cane sugar is passed through charcoal, which can be made from animal, mineral or plant origin. About half the plants that process sugar use animal products to process the sugar. Since it is not usually possible to tell how the sugar was processed, vegans usually will not eat processed sugar.

Brown sugar, granulated sugar made from cane sugar, and confectioner's sugars are acceptable for vegetarians because they are not processed. Other satisfactory sugars are maple syrup, turbinado (raw) sugar, date sugar and sugar derived from fruit juice.

Often kosher gelatin is kosher but is not vegetarian (derived from meat or fish). Some gelatin is derived from fish products. To be kosher a product cannot mix meat and milk, but if gelatin is derived from fish and then mixed with milk, the product would be considered to be kosher because fish and milk can be mixed together and be kosher, but of course this product is not suitable for vegetarians.

Chinese stir-fry sauces may contain oyster sauce. Even in so-called Chinese vegetarian restaurants, oyster sauce (real, not just in name only) may be in the food. As some Chinese consider oysters to be vegetarian, therefore even when you ask if the food that contains oyster sauce is vegetarian, you may be told that it is vegetarian. Therefore you should ask if the food in question contains real oyster, not just that it is vegetarian.

Kosher symbols cannot always be used to tell if a food is vegetarian. To have the "K" or "Kosher" symbol on foods means that a rabbi overlooked the manufacturing process, and that it meets Hebrew dietary laws. Kosher food cannot contain both dairy products and meat together. A possible problem could be that an ingredient like gelatin made from a meat product can be considered kosher, if it is not mixed with milk. The manufacturers can add this kosher gelatin to yogurt and state on the label that it is kosher gelatin, and one could be fooled into thinking that this product is kosher, which means that meat and milk are not mixed, while in fact they are mixed together. The gelatin is kosher but the yogurt product is not.

"P" or "Parve" means that a food product does not contain meat or dairy products, but may contain eggs or fish.

"D," as in "Kosher D," means that the food product contains dairy or is made on a machine that was also used to process dairy products.

Many companies do not put the word "animal" on the ingredient label in order to not lose customers.

Good books in reference to ingredients are the *Consumer's Dictionary of Cosmetic Ingredients* and the *Consumer's Dictionary of Food Additives*.

Some Apparent Vegetarian Foods that May Contain Meat

Rice and vegetables may be cooked in chicken stock.

Soups may contain beef or chicken stock.

Wax made from animal products may be put on fruit.

Veggie burgers and veggie hot dogs may contain eggs.

Pudding and custard often contain eggs.

Gello often contains gelatin.

Potato salad may contain bacon or eggs.

Coleslaw and macaroni usually contains eggs (in the mayonnaise).

Baked beans often contain pork.

Green beans may contain bacon.

Flour tortillas, refried beans, biscuits and piecrust may contain lard.

Bean or split pea soups may contain ham or bacon.

Caesar salad dressing may contain anchovies.

Stir-fry vegetables may contain oyster sauce.

Sautéed vegetables may contain chicken stock or pork.

Cooked greens may contain salt pork in the South.

Spinach may contain eggs or bacon.

Baked goods, including cakes, cookies, pies and baked desserts, usually contain eggs.

Breads may contain eggs.

Quiche often contains eggs.

Fast Food Restaurants

The Internet is a great resource for getting information about ingredients in fast food joints. Many of the places list the ingredients for all items that they sell. Most of the sites have a nutritional section, which lists a contact email address. I found that by emailing this contact address that I usually got a quick, efficient, detailed response. Often I was sent a full ingredient list within 24 hours. Plus I was able to get a response on questions such as whether listed mono- and diglycerides are derived from a vegetarian source.

Applebee's (www.applebees.com)

There are some good selections for vegetarians here. It is a full-scale type restaurant, so service can take a while. They usually have good baked potatoes, mashed potatoes and New Potatoes. Most places have a side of steamed vegetables. Also have cheese nachos, onion peels, pizza and mozzarella sticks. Most like the only vegetarian salad dressings are Fat Free Honey Mustard Dressing (contains whey) and Reduced Calorie Italian. Bread sticks with marinara (breadsticks contain milk fat) are vegetarian.

Some places have a Vegetarian Plate (really good and a good value), which is steamed broccoli, cauliflower, zucchini and potatoes and a good salad. Most likely the dressing that comes with the salad is non-vegetarian.

Applebee's uses vegetable oil to cook fried dishes. They usually use the same surface to cook both meat and vegetarian dishes, so you should ask about this before ordering anything cooked on the grill or the French fries and mozzarella cheese sticks. The refried beans usually do not contain lard, but it changes from restaurant to restaurant, so you may want to ask about this.

Some places have the Sizzling Vegetable Skillet, grilled cheese and cheese quesadilla, but most likely they are cooked on the same grill as meat.

The Caesar dressing contains anchovies and is the standard dressing for the salad that comes with the Vegetarian Plate. The guacamole contains gelatin. The Garden Burger (served with guacamole that contains gelatin) may contain eggs, as some varieties of Garden Burgers contain eggs.

The rice dishes and soups usually contain meat stock. The Garden Vegetable Soup may not contain meat stock.

The cheese may contain animal enzymes, but usually vegetable enzymes are used. The baked goods and sauces may contain animal products so this should be checked. The waffles, croissants, French toast and cinnamon rolls usually contain eggs. The French fries may contain beef fat. The pastas all contain lactic acid and almost all their desserts contain gelatin.

Arby's (www.arbys.com)

There is not much of a selection here for vegetarians. They list the ingredients of the products they sell on their web site.

There are some salads and baked potatoes (plain or broccoli & cheese, not usually very good because they often sit for a long time). The turnovers are vegan (apple, cherry, blueberry), but there is a good chance they are cooked in the same oil as meat products. The Arby's sauce and barbeque sauce, lite Italian Dressing, French and sub dressing are most likely suitable for vegan. Some other options are the Mozzarella Cheese-stick and Jalapeño Bites.

The potato dishes such as the curly fries and home-style fries are usually cooked in the same oil as meat. The gravies and some of the sauces contain animal derived flavorings. The milkshakes and sour cream contain gelatin. Their buns and biscuits contain egg or milk derivatives. Thousand Island, Caesar, Ranch and Blue Cheese dressings contain eggs. The Parmesan Cheese Sauce contains Worcestershire Sauce (anchovies).

Au Bon Pain (www.aubonpain.com)

They list some of the ingredients of their products on their web site and they mark the vegetarian dishes. The salads and some of the bagels are vegan such as the cinnamon raisin, everything, Dutch apple, chocolate chip, plain and sesame bagels.

Has vegetarian cream cheese. The breads do not usually contain eggs. Have some vegetarian soups such as Garden Vegetarian and Vegetarian Chili. Mozzarella sandwich.

The French Onion soup contains chicken broth. Most of the baked goods contain eggs such as the Braided Roll, cookies, croissants, Danish, muffins and shortbread.

Auntie Anne's (www.auntieannes.com)
Have really good pretzels with an assortment of dips. The marinara dip contains gelatin.

Baskin-Robbins
(www.baskinrobbins.com)
They list their ingredients on their web site. Most of their ice creams are vegetarian. The sorbets and ices are vegetarian. The sugar cones and plain cones are vegan.

The ice creams that contain marshmallows are non-vegetarian because they contain gelatin. The Vanilla, French Vanilla and the one with cookie pieces ice creams contain eggs.

Bob's Big Boy
Bob's Big Boy usually has a good size large salad bar and hot bar with a decent selection for vegetarians and limited vegan items. Some vegetarian items are French Fries, onion rings and baked potato.

Bojangles (www.bojangles.com)
There are few things to get here for vegetarians. Some vegan dishes are corn-on-the-cob, green beans, Cajun Pinto beans and marinated coleslaw.

Vegetarian dishes are Macaroni & Cheese (vegetable enzymes), biscuits and multi-grain rolls.

The seasoned fries and hash browns contain animal products. The creamy coleslaw contains eggs. It is unknown what the natural favoring in the mashed potatoes is derived from.

Boston Market (www.bostonmarket.com)
Some vegan dishes are Tossed Salad (with no dressing or croutons), steamed vegetables, cranberry walnut relish, fruit salad and zucchini marinara. Apple cobbler, apple cinnamon apples and cinnamon applesauce. The vegetarian items are not cooked in animal oil or are any animal product cooked in this oil.

The macaroni & cheese and cornbread have eggs in them. The mash potatoes have gelatin and mono- and diglycerides from an unknown source. The pastas have eggs in them.

Bruegger's Bagel Bakery
(www.brueggers.com)
This place is a vegetarian-friendly place. They have good cheap bagels and make really good veggie bagel sandwiches. They also have really good soups, and indicate which ones are vegetarian. They have 3 or 4 soups a day, 2 of which are usually vegetarian. I really like this place. Great place for a good, cheap, quick meal with consistently good service. On their web site they list some of the ingredients of what they sell.

All the bagels are vegetarian. Some vegan bagels are: rosemary olive oil, chocolate chip, pumpernickel, blueberry, cranberry, orange and cinnamon sugar. Vegan soups are Garden Split Pea soup, Roasted Roma Tomato soup, Ratatouille, Chile Cilantro soup, Gazpacho, Marcello Minestrone and Tucson Minestrone soup. Good hummus spread and basic salads. Most of the cream cheeses are vegetarian except the smoked salmon and bacon scallion. The American, Muenster, Swiss, cheddar and provolone cheeses are made with microbial (vegetarian) rennet. The Bruegger's Bar contains milk, but no eggs.

The honey mustard, brownies and cookies contain eggs.

Burger King (http://www.burgerking.com/nutrition/ingredients.htm)
To ask about what is vegetarian call 305-378-7011. They list the ingredients of what they make on their web site.

The French fries contain natural favorings derived from meat products and are cooked separate from any meat products. Has basic salads. The Reduced Calorie Light Italian Dressing and the Olive Oil & Vinegar Dressing are vegan. The French dressing is vegan, but it does contain some natural flavors from an unknown source.

Some places carry veggie burger, but they are usually cooked in the same oil that is used to cook meat.

Not much else that they sell is vegetarian. The bagels usually contain egg whites, but some places may sell eggless bagels. The onion rings and hash browns are cooked in the same oil that meat products are cooked in. There is egg in the croissants. The cheeses may contain animal rennet. The honey mustard sauce, Ranch dressing, King Sauce, Thousand Island dressing and tartar sauce contain eggs and natural flavoring from an unknown source. The Ice Cream bars sold in some Burger Kings contain gelatin. The Spicy Bean Burger contains eggs, and the ones sold in Canada are usually cooked in the same oil that is used to cook meats.

California Pizza Kitchen

The pizza crusts are not vegan. They contain dairy but not eggs. The Tuscan Bean Soup is made without meat stock.

Carl's JR (www.carlsjr.com)

Carl has a list of ingredients that are used at each of its places that are available at the restaurants.

Has a salad bar and baked potatoes.

English muffin and cornmeal roll are both vegan. The flour tortilla, breadsticks and plain buns are vegan except that they contain mono- and diglycerides from an unknown source. The croutons contain milk and Parmesan cheese that contain enzymes from an unknown source.

The honey wheat bun contains honey but not eggs. The Sunrise Sandwich without the meat and chow mien noodles are vegetarian. The cheese served on the baked potato and broccoli is made with vegetarian rennet. The Jack and shredded cheddar contains vegetable rennet. The American and Swiss cheeses may contain vegetable rennet.

The margarine usually contains whey, but sometimes it is possible to request a margarine that doesn't contain whey.

The Thousand Island dressing contains anchovies and eggs. The House, Bleu Cheese and Fat-Free Italian dressings contain eggs. The French-Fat-Free contains sugar and starch that may contain animal products.

Carl's strawberry swirl cheesecake and raspberry parfait contains gelatin. The French fries, onion rings and other fried items are cooked in the same oil as meat products. The raisin bran muffin contains eggs.

The sour cream may contain gelatin but usually does not contain animal products, so you might want to ask about this. The hash browns contain natural flavoring from an unknown source.

Most of the baked desserts contain eggs or other non-vegetarian ingredients. The shakes contain mono- and diglycerides and other ingredients from unknown sources.

Checker's Drive-in Restaurant

There is not much of a reason to come here. The French fries may contain beef tallow, but either way are fried in oil that meat products are cooked in. The apple nuggets contain animal shortening and are cooked in oil that meat products are cooked in.

Chi-Chi's Mexican Restaurant (www.chichis.com)

Some vegan dishes are guacamole, salad, refried beans and chips & salsa.

Cheese nachos, Vegetable Quesadilla and Chile Con Queso are vegetarian. The cheeses are usually made with vegetable rennet, but may be made with animal rennet. The vegetables are cooked in a pan that is only used to cook vegetables. The margarine that is used in cooking contains whey (derived from milk).

The enchilada sauce contains chicken fat and the Spanish rice contains chicken fat. The Mexican fried ice cream contains eggs. The Apple Chimi is cooked in the same oil that is usually used to cook meat.

Chili's (www.chilis.com)

Some vegetarian and vegan dishes are Garden salad, Tortilla with Beans. Steamed Vegetables (such as broccoli, corn and squash) and baked potato. There is butter in the mashed potatoes.

The French fries are cooked in the same oil that meat products are cooked in. The Ranch dressing contains eggs. The House Vinaigrette contains natural flavors from unknown sources.

Chick-Fil-A (www.chickfila.com)

This place does not have much of a selection for vegetarians. Tossed salad. The cheesecake, fudge nut brownie and ice cream may contain eggs. The waffle potatoes contain beef fat.

Chuck E. Cheese's (www.chuckecheeses.com)

The pizza crust and sauce are vegan. The cheddar, Parmesan and mozzarella cheeses are made with vegetarian rennet. The Italian and fat-free Catalina dressings are vegan.

The blue cheese and Ranch dressings contain cheese.

The three-bean and pasta salad contain mayonnaise made from eggs. The Thousand Island dressing contains eggs.

Church's Fried Chicken (www.churchs.com)

Some vegetarian dishes are corn-on-the-cob, apple turnover (vegan), mashed potatoes (contains natural flavors and mono-and diglycerides from unknown sources), fried okra and biscuits. The okra contains whey and is cooked in vegetable oil.

The collard greens contain animal products.

The white and brown gravies contain beef fat and chicken. The French fries may contain beef fat, but is usually cooked in its own oil with no meat (but this oil may be mixed with oil that had meat cooked in it). Cajun rice and fried rice contain a meat stock. The coleslaw contains eggs. The lemon merinque pie contains eggs.

Country Kitchen International

Some vegetarian dishes are salads and side vegetables (frozen and then cooked in a micro-wave). The French fries are cooked in vegetable oil, but meat may be cooked in the same oil. Sour cream is purchased locally so its ingredients change from place to place.

The rice pilaf contains chicken broth. The pancakes, French toast, fruit pies and cake contain eggs.

Cracker Barrel

This place does not have much to offer for vegetarians. Fried foods are cooked with the meat. The baked potatoes are cooked with a meat sauce on them. There is no reason to come here.

Dairy Queen/Brazier

Their fries are vegan and they fry no other foods. Side salad is vegan. Garden salad has eggs.

Del Taco (www.deltaco.com)

They do not use lard. The French fries are cooked in vegetarian oil and are not cooked in oil that meat is cooked in. The pepperjack and ched-dar cheese are made with vegetable rennet. The red, green and secret sauces are vegetarian.

The shell in the tostada salad may be cooked with meat. The rice contains chicken broth. The beans may contain natural flavoring made from meat. The shakes contain milk and mono- and diglycerides from an unknown source.

Damon's

There is no real reason to come here. They have salads. The Blue Cheese, Thousand Island and Parmesan cheese dressings all contain eggs. The Caesar dressing contains anchovies. The Wholesome & Henry's Gardenburger contains eggs. The French fries are fried in the same oil that chicken is cooked in. The vegetables in the vegetable fettuccini may be cooked in the same pan that meat is cooked in.

Denny's (www.dennys.com)

There is not much of a vegetarian selection here. Denny's customer service phone number is 800 7-DENNYS, and you can request vegetarian information.

Some Denny's have Gardenburgers. They have baked potatoes and Sautéed Mushrooms (where they are cooked is questionable). Has oat-meal, English muffins, bagel and grits (which are most likely vegan). Some other vegan items are guacamole, boule bread, light rye bread, side salad, sauerkraut, applesauce and Dutch Apple Pie. Ve-gan dressings and sauces are Oriental, barbecue sauce, salsa, reduced French, oil & vinegar and Light Italian.

Some vegetarian dishes are cold cereals with milk, baby carrots, garden salad, cottage cheese, onion rings, corn, mozzarella sticks and the Blue Cheese Dressing.

Some places may have a Boca Burger, cheese pizza and a Vegetable Plate. The hash browns are vegan but may be cooked on a grill that meat is cooked on.

French fries contain beef fat and the rice pi-laf contains chicken broth. Cheese sticks, fries and onion rings are fried in oil that meat is cooked in. The lemon meringue pie contains gelatin. Breads that contain eggs are dinner rolls, cakes, French bread, Texas toast and all the pies except the Dutch apple pie. Honey mustard, Caesar, Thousand Is-land and French dressings contain eggs. There is gelatin in the Parmesan cheese.

Domino's

The Salads and the Marzetti, Italian and Lite Italian dressings are suitable for vegans.

The pizza crusts contain whey and the pizza sauce is vegan. One of their four pizza crusts is vegan, but only a select amount of stores have it. The enzymes used in the cheese are of a micro-bial origin (non-meat).

The hand-tossed crust contains mono- and diglycerides and natural flavoring from an un-known source. L-cysteine is an amino acid that is used in the crusts, in which its source is un-known. The Ranch dressing contains eggs. The French dressing contains natural flavoring from an unknown source.

Dunkin' Donuts
(www.dunkindonuts; ingredients list:, http://www.dunkindonuts.com/nutrition/?id=9)

Ingredients of all their products are listed on their web site. Most of the bagels are vegetarian.

Some of the donuts are free of eggs such as Apple Crumb Donut, Apple Fritter, Apple N' Spice Donut, Bavarian Kreme Donut, Black Raspberry Donut, Blueberry Crumb Donut, Bow Tie Donut, Chocolate Kreme Filled Donut, Coffee Roll, Glazed Donut, Glazed Fritter, Jelly Filled Donut, Lemon Donut, Strawberry Donut, Sugar Raised Donut and Vanilla Kreme Filled Donut. Most of the other donuts do contain eggs.

All the cookies contain eggs.

Eat'N Park (www.eatnpark.com)

Has a salad bar and a fruit cup. They have a Garden Burger (contains cheese), but it is usually cooked on the same grill as meat. Can sometimes get a vegetarian stir-fry, but it may be cooked on the same grill as meat.

Pasta salad contains mayonnaise that contains eggs. The French fries may be cooked in the same oil that meat is cooked in. The baked sweets usually contain eggs, but the bread is usually egg-free.

El Chico's (www.elchico.com)

There is not much reason to come here considering they have lard in many of their dishes including the tortillas, the refried beans contain bacon fat and the rice contains a chicken stock. The cheddar and Monterey Jack cheeses contain rennet derived from meat.

French fries are cooked in canola oil that no meat products are cooked in. The House Hot Sauce and guacamole are vegetarian.

El Pollo Loco (www.elpolloloco.com)

Some vegan dishes are corn-on-the-cob, guacamole, cucumber salad, BRC burrito with no cheese and spiced apples. Also vegan is Italian dressing, pinto beans, salsa and hot sauce.

Vegetarian dishes are Pina Colada Bang, Orange Bang, BRC burrito, spinach-flavored and tomato-flavored tortillas and honey-glazed carrots (dairy and honey). Most likely the Fiesta Corn and Spanish rice are vegan.

The margarine may contain whey. The mashed potatoes contain milk.

The instant stuffing and Baja Glaze contain chicken. The Caesar dressing contains gelatin and anchovies. Crispy Green Beans contains bacon and the BBZ baked beans contains ham. The cranberry walnut, Lime Parfait, the lite sour cream and raspberry marble cheesecake contain gelatin. The tortilla chips, tostada shells and French fries are cooked in the same oil as the chicken. The cheese may have either vegetarian or meat-derived rennet. Except for the El Pollo Loco salad dressing all the rest contain eggs. The Smokey black beans contain ham.

The macaroni and cheese, coleslaw, rainbow pasta salad, potato salad and broccoli slaw contains eggs. The Fiesta Cornbread Stuffing contains chicken. The churros are cooked in oil that is used to cook chicken taquitos.

Fazoli's (www.fazolis.com)

Has a good selection of vegetarian dishes and marks the dishes that are vegetarian on their menu. Have pastas, pizzas, salads and a veggie sub. They say there are no eggs in the pastas. The Baked Spaghetti with cheese is really good. Baked ziti with tomato sauce. Veggie submarine sandwich and pizza come with or without cheese. You order at the counter and then the dishes are prepared and your number is called. Has unlimited bread sticks with the meal. Very good place for a quick meal.

Fresh Choice

All-you-can-eat salad bar, pasta bar, fresh fruit and desserts. All pastas contain eggs and the marinara sauce is not vegan. Their nutritional info pamphlet lists all menu items and which are vegan.

Fuddruckers (www.fuddruckers.com)

The tortillas are vegan. The Vegetarian Fuddwrapper (may not be offered at all restaurants) contains rice, mozzarella cheese (contains an unknown enzyme) and grilled vegetables. The vegetables are usually grilled on a surface away from where meat is cooked. Has a Caesar salad and Garden salad.

The enzymes that are in the cheeses come from an unknown source. The French fries and onion rings are fried in oil separate from meat. The sandwich bun contains eggs.

Godfather's Pizza (www.godfatherspizza.com)

The pizza sauce and pizza dough are vegan.

Golden Fried Chicken (www.goldenfriedchicken.com)

Basically nothing in this place does not contain meat or eggs, so there isn't much reason to come here. The French fries and apple turnovers are cooked in oil that contains animal products.

The Carrot raisin salad is vegan. The biscuits contain buttermilk.

Gold Star Chili (www.goldstarchili.com)

This chain is located in Indiana, Ohio and Kentucky. Some vegetarian dishes are spaghetti, pizza, French fries, cheese fries, Husman's nacho chips, garlic bread and bread sticks. The pizza sauces, tossed salad, red beans and streusel dessert are vegan. The cheddar and mozzarella cheeses are made with microbial (vegetarian) enzymes. The waffle fries may contain beef fat.

Hardee's (www.hardees.com)

There is not much of a reason to come here, except to get a salad or a sandwich without the burger (or cheese). The cheese contains enzymes derived from both vegetable and animal. The fat-free French dressing contains milk products. The specialty bun and sourdough bread are vegan. The breakfast biscuits, seeded bun and Crispy Curls contain whey.

The pancakes contain eggs. The hash browns contain natural flavoring from an unknown source and are cooked in the same oil as meat. The French fries are fried in the same oil that meat is cooked in. The house dressing and Thousand Island dressing contain eggs.

Hot Stuff Pizza (www.hotstuffpizza.com)

Has pizzas. The Breadsticks and pizza sauce are vegan. The pizza dough has butter on it. Egg rolls have pork in them.

Jack in the Box (www.jackinthebox.com)

Has a pamphlet that lists the ingredients of all their products. As a rule they fry French fries and onion rings separately from the meats, but this is not strictly followed.

Vegan items are French fries, potato wedges, guacamole, salsa, side salad, English muffin, hamburger bun, sesame breadsticks, tortilla bowl, pita bread, gyro bread and Apple turnover. Hot sauce, malt vinegar, soy sauce and taco sauce are vegan.

Seasoned curly fries and stuffed jalapeno with cheese stuffing are vegetarian. The croutons contain butter flavoring and unknown natural flavoring. The Italian Low Calorie dressing contains unknown natural flavoring. The onion rings batter contains milk products and sulfites.

The secret sauce contains anchovies and eggs, cheesecake contains gelatin and egg rolls contains pork. The Caesar dressing contains anchovies. The Thousand Island dressing, blue cheese dressing, Tatar sauce and buttermilk sauce contain eggs. The French dressing contains honey and flavoring from an unknown source.

The hash browns contain natural flavoring from an unknown source, but otherwise are vegan. The cheesecake contains gelatin. The carrot cake contains eggs and ingredient from an un-

known source. The fudge cake contains eggs. Most of the breads contain chemicals and ingredients from unknown sources. The croissants contain enzymes and mono- and diglycerides from an unknown source.

The shortening on their griddle is vegetable based but contains natural butter flavor. The shortening for the deep fryers contains no animal products.

Kentucky Fried Chicken (www.kfc.com)

Some vegetarian dishes are the Three Bean Salad (vegan), Garden Salad (not all stores have), cornbread, corn-on-the-cob and biscuits. The mashed potatoes contain milk and butter. The macaroni and cheese contains unknown enzymes.

Meat flavoring are often used in various dishes in the all-you-can-eat buffet. The following dishes contain either meat or meat flavoring: red beans and rice, gravy, greens, barbecue baked beans and green beans. The chocolate parfait contains lard. The French fries and potato wedges are cooked in the same oil as the chicken is cooked in. The bread, potato salad and coleslaw contain eggs. The parfaits desserts contain eggs and some contain lard.

Krispy Kreme (www.krispykreme.com)

Because of the chemicals in the dough it is not possible to ascertain if any of the dough used in the doughnuts do not contain meat products.

Little Caesar's (www.littlecaesars.com)

Can view the ingredients of dishes on their web site. You can view the Little Caesars Vegetarian Guide on their web site or get it from the Corporate Communications, 2211 Woodward Avenue, Detroit, MI 48201-3400. They are definitely vegetarian friendly and have a good attitude towards vegetarians.

The pizza cheese is vegetarian. Vegan items are Crazy Bread, Crazy Sauce, pizza dough, tomato pizza sauce, veggie sandwich (without cheese), tossed salad and Greek salad (without cheese). Italian, Lite Italian dressing and Greek dressings are vegan.

Long John Silver's (www.longjohnsilvers.com)

There isn't much reason to come here except to get some corn-on-the-cob or salad (Lite Italian dressing is vegan). The Corn Clobbettes (with no butter) and rice is vegan.

The green beans contain meat flavoring. Most of the dressings including Ranch, Thousand Island and Caesar dressings and the white sauce in the wraps contain eggs. The buns and coleslaw contain eggs. The French fries and hushpuppies are fried in the same oil used to cook meat products.

Manchu Wok (www.manchuwok.com)

The steamed rice and Stir-fried Vegetables (cooked in canola oil) are vegan. The lo mein can be made vegetarian. Basically everything else contains meat or eggs. The noodles in the chow mein and the egg rolls contain eggs.

These items can contain pork: wonton soup, sweet & sour wontons and hot & sour soup. The fried rice has a sauce, but the ingredients are unknown.

Manhattan Bagel Co (www.manhattanbagel.com)

The bagels, except the egg bagel and the jalapeno cheddar, are vegan. They make good bagel sandwiches. The cheeses and cream cheeses are made with microbial (vegetarian) enzymes. The pizza bagel is made with mozzarella cheese and vegetarian tomato sauce. Sometime the bagels here can be a rubbery and you can really tire out your jaws chewing them.

Mazzio's Pizza (www.mazziospizza.com)

Has pizzas, breadsticks and pastas. This place has a salad bar. Some varieties of pastas contain eggs. The original and thin crusts, and the pizza sauce are vegan. A cheeseless pizza can be ordered. French and Italian dressings are vegan. Mozzarella, Monterey Jack, cheddar and provolone cheeses are made with vegetarian enzymes. Deep pan crust contains non-fat dry milk. The Alfredo sauce contains milk products.

McDonald's (http://www.mcdonalds.com)

On their web site they have a full list of ingredients. There aren't many reasons for a vegetarian to go to McDonald's especially consisting that their French Fries contain beef flavoring. Some vegetarian items are Granola, shakes, Butter Biscuit (but not the biscuit dressing), McDonaldland ® Cookies (contain honey and sugar) and McSalad Shaker salad. The hash browns seem to be vegetarian, but may be cooked in the same oil as the fries.

Most of the salad dressings contain eggs (some contain anchovies) except the Fat-free Herb Vinaigrette and Fat Free Ranch Dressing, which are vegetarian. The cheeses contain enzymes from an unknown source. The company states that they do not use beef or pork flavoring in India or Muslim countries.

Miami Subs

This place specializes in subs and sandwiches. The Garden Salad and House Dressing are vegan. The Caesar salad contains cheese. The Greek salad contains feta cheese. The enzymes in the cheeses are unknown.

The sub rolls contain eggs. The pita bread contains milk and enzymes from an unknown source. The Caesar dressing contains anchovies. The French fries and onion rings are cooked in the same oil as meat and fish products. The lime pie and cheesecake contain eggs. The onion rings batter contains whey and dry milk. The ingredients of the salad dressings are on the packets.

Nathan's (www.nathans.com)

The French fries are cooked in corn oil and are fairly good tasting.

Olive Garden (www.olivegarden.com)

If you don't eat eggs there is not much reason to come here, as almost all the dishes contain meat and eggs. The pastas are made with eggs and the breading for the Eggplant Parmigiana contains eggs.

Papa John's (www.papajohns.com)

Lists the ingredients of some of their dishes on their web site. The original pizza dough, the breadsticks and the pizza sauce (tomatoes, olive and canola oils) are vegan.

The mozzarella cheese used on the pizzas contains microbial (vegetarian) rennet. The thin pizza crust contains Parmesan cheese and olive oil. The Parmesan cheese contains animal rennet.

Pizza Hut (www.pizzahut.com)

There are both a meat-free and meat based marinara sauce for the pasta dishes. You should very clearly ask for the vegetarian sauce, and even then you should check it when it comes to make sure that you have received the correct sauce.

The pizza crust, regular pizza sauce and marinara pasta sauce are vegetarian. The French, Italian, Fat Free Ranch and Creamy Cucumber dressings are vegetarian (don't contain eggs).

The Creamy Caesar and Thousand Island dressings contain anchovies, eggs and cheese. White Pasta sauce contains chicken flavor (also milk, cream and cheese) and the fajita sauce contain chicken or chicken fat. The Taco Beans contains beef flavoring. The Honey Mustard, ranch, blue cheese, Romano and buttermilk dressings contain eggs. The desserts often contain natural flavors, so these desserts may be in question.

Pizzeria Uno Chicago Bar & Grill (www.pizzeriauno.com)

The regular and Uno pizza sauce, breadsticks and the pizza crust (except the deep-pan one), Marinara Sauce Pasta and the House Salad are all vegan

The Muenster, cheddar, Romano and mozzarella cheeses do not contain animal rennet. Has a broccoli and spinach topped pizza.

The asiago cheese in the Triple Mushroom pizza contains enzymes derived from animal products. The grilled vegetables are cooked on the same grill that meat is grilled on. The Lasagna contains a meat sauce. The Cheese sticks are served with a meat sauce. The Parmesan cheese is made with an enzyme derived from animals. The Pizza skins contain bacon.

Popeye's (www.popeyes.com)

They list their ingredients on their web site. There is not much of a reason to come here, as all they have is corn-on-the-cob and apple pie (vegan).

The French fries and onion rings have a batter with eggs and dairy and are cooked in an oil containing beef tallow and soybean oil. The biscuits contain eggs. There is mayonnaise in the coleslaw.

Rally's (www.rallys.com)

There is no real reason to come here and the only vegetarian choice is a cheese (from unknown enzymes) sandwich. The French fries have a batter that contains beef tallow and are cooked in oil that chicken is cooked in. The onion rings contain whey and natural flavoring from an unknown source, and are fried in oil that chicken is cooked in.

Rita's Italian Ices (www.ritasice.com)

The ices and plain pretzels are vegan. The custards and gelati contain eggs.

Round Table Pizza (www.roundtablepizza.com)

Some restaurants have a salad bar. The pizza sauce and pizza crust contain dry milk. Garden salad sandwich, green side salad, tortilla chips, pesto sauce and Guinevere's Garden Delight are vegan. Toppings include: artichoke hearts, pine-

apple, jalapeno peppers, tomatoes, mushrooms, zucchini, black olives and garlic.

The Parmesan cheese is made with an animal enzyme. The Gourmet Veggie Pizza contains eggs and natural flavors. Garden Pesto pizza contains Parmesan cheese. Macaroni salad, potato salad and the creamy garlic sauce contain eggs. The pre-made salads usually are made with mayonnaise. The Garlic Parmesan Twists contain eggs.

Shakey's (www.shakeys.com)

Shakey's has a good size salad bar. The pizza crust and pizza sauce are vegan. The Garden Ranch Pizza is cheeseless. Vegan toppings are green peppers, roasted red peppers, mushrooms and tomatoes. Some of the pastas and also the marinara sauce and Pomodora tomato sauce are vegan.

The mozzarella, provolone, fontina, asiago and Parmesan cheeses are not made with any animal ingredients. The Pasta Fresca dish is pasta with several types of vegetables. The vegetables are grilled in a pan that is washed and dried between each cooking.

The roasted red pepper sauce has chicken stock in it. The Pasta Fresca has a white sauce that contains white wine and milk. The mojo-potatoes are fried in the same oil that meat products are cooked in.

Sonic Drive-in Restaurant (www.sonicdrivein.com)

There is not really much reason to come here. The French fries are usually cooked separately from any meat product, but this may not always be true in every restaurant. The onion rings contain whey.

The sheet cake contains eggs. The American cheese may contain enzymes derived from animals. The buns are made locally, so you may want to ask the manager what they contain.

Souplantation and Sweet Tomatoes

This place has a large salads bar and soups. The pastas contain eggs. When I contacted their main office they wrote me back and told me that what they serve changes from place to place and that each place has a list of ingredients of all the dishes that they sell, which customers can ask to view.

Some non-vegan dishes are Artichoke Rice Salad, Pesto Salads, Thai Noodle Salad with Peanut Sauce, Sweet Tomato Onion Soup (margarine) and Vegetarian Harvest Soup (butter) Some vegan dishes are Aunt Doris Red pepper slaw, Baja Bean & Cilantro Salad, Spicy Southwestern Pasta Salad, Poppy Seed Coleslaw, three bean marinade salad, Banana Royal, vegetarian Marinara Sauce, Cabbage Coconut Slaw, Herbed Barley Salad, Fat-Free Italian Dressing, Thousand Island Dressing, Tropical Fruit Salad, Vegetarian Minestrone Soup, Spicy 4 Bean Minestrone Soup, Spicy Southwestern Pasta Salad, Santa Fe Black Bean Chili and Apple Medley, .

Steak Escape (www.steakescape.com)

Has salads, smashed potatoes, French fries and specially made veggie subs. The French fries are cooked separate from any meat products. The multi-grain roll and white roll are vegan.

Sautéed vegetables are cooked on the same grill as meat. Kraft Ranch and Italian dressings are vegetarian.

The baked cookies all contain eggs. The Swiss and provolone cheeses contain rennet derived from animal products.

Subway (www.subway.com)

Has their ingredients listed on their web site. It is a good idea to ask the preparer to change their plastic gloves and to wash the knife they use to cut the sandwiches, as residue from previous sandwiches may be on it.

Some of the Subways have a soy turkey sub and Boca Burgers. Also some of the branches have Gardenburger or Veggie Max, which may contain eggs (depends on the variety they are using). The soy-cheese offered at some places contains casein (a milk product).

The Italian dressing and olive & vinegar are vegetarian. Vegetarian breads are Italian Bread, Wheat Bread (contains honey), Hearty Italian Bread and Sesame Italian Bread. The Parmesan/Oregano and Deli Style Roll (contain eggs) contain enzymes from an unknown source. The bread products contain vegetable-derived mono- and diglycerides and L-cysteine.

Various types of cheese may be offered at various Subways, and they may contain either vegetarian or animal derived rennet. The salad dressings come in packages with the ingredients listed on them. The Asiago Caesar dressing contains anchovies. There are eggs in the honey mustard and Southwest Ancho sauces. The cookies contain eggs.

Swiss Chalet

There is not much reason to visit this place as the French fries are fried in beef tallow and the soups contain animal stock.

Taco Bell

They don't use lard. You should make sure to ask that nothing you order contains meat, as many of the dishes can be served with or without meat. Their phone number is 1-800-TACO-BELL.

Vegan dishes are bean taco, nachos without cheese, Cinnamon Twist, Border Ices and the Veggie Fajita Wrap. Vegan sauces are mild, red, salsa, hot and Pico de Gallo. Corn tortillas (hard tacos), burritos tortillas and wheat tortilla (soft tacos) are vegan.

The soft burrito tortillas are not vegan, they contain non-fat dry milk. The hard corn tortillas however are vegan, as are the refried beans.

Vegetarian dishes are pintos n' cheese, tostada, Mexican Pizza without meat, taco salad without meat, Breakfast Quesadilla, Country Breakfast without the sausage, Chalupa shell, Veggie Fajita Wrap, tortilla chips, Gordita flatbread, Seven-Layer Burrito with no sour cream and tostada shells.

Seasoned rice contains a chicken stock. The Fire Sauce contains natural flavor from an unknown source.

The guacamole is made with sour cream and the sour cream contains gelatin. The Fajita sauce contains chicken flavoring.

The enzymes in the cheeses are derived from an unknown source. The Ranch dressing usually contains eggs and milk.

Taco John's (www.tacojohns.com)

Lard is not used in cooking. Animal rennet is not used in the cheeses. Two different companies supply the wheat tortillas. Both types contain whey and one contains mono- and diglycerides from an unknown source. You can ask to have the cheese removed from some of the sandwiches, or have meat replaced with beans.

The bean burritos, corn tortilla and guacamole are vegan. Vegetarian sauces are chunky salsa, mild, hot and Pico de Gallo. The enchilada is vegetarian.

The Potato Olés, nachos, fajito shells and tacos are cooked in the same oil where meat is cooked. The sour cream may contain gelatin in some places, so it best to ask the manager if this is true.

Taco Time

Has a company policy against using beans with lard but some stores break this policy. The rice that comes with the Veggie Burrito is cooked with beef fat, so you should ask that it is not added.

TCBY (www.tcby.com) 800-688-8229, 800-343-5377)

Has really good frozen yogurts, sundaes, sorbets and hand-dipped ice creams. Has non-sugar-added ice creams and yogurts. The sorbet contains mono- and diglycerides derived from a vegetarian source. They say that none of the soft yogurts or ice creams contain eggs or any meat products.

T.G.I. Fridays (www.tgifridays.com)

Has good baked potatoes. Vegan dishes are the House Salad and Fresh Vegetable Medley (normally served with a non-vegetarian rice, but a plain baked potato can be substituted instead).

Some vegetarian dishes are Veggie Wrapper, Fettuccine Alfredo, Cheddar Cheese Nachos, Broken Noodles, Spinach & Feta Pizzadilla and Friday's Gardenburger. The cheese contains rennet from an unknown source.

All the soups contain some meat products. The brown rice pilaf has chicken stock. The Friday's Mushrooms are cooked in the same oil as meat and fish dishes. Fried beans contain bacon grease.

How the croutons are made is unknown. Whether any of the dressings contain eggs is unknown.

Tony Roma's, A Place For Ribs
(www.tonyromas.com)

Has baked potatoes and salads.

The onion ring loaf has milk and egg in its coating, and it is fried in oil that also meat is cooked in. The French fries are cooked in oil that also meat is cooked in. The Caesar dressing contains eggs.

Wendy's (www.wendys.com)

Some dishes have their ingredients listed on their web site. You can request a nutritional brochure by calling 614-764-3100.

The baked potatoes and some of the salads (side salad & deluxe garden salad) are suitable for vegetarians. The baked potatoes are fairly good and are cheap. Taco chips, applesauce and French fries. The French, Italian and Reduced Cal Italian dressings are vegetarian. Fat-free French dressing contains honey.

None of the cheeses contain rennet derived from animal products. Sandwich and kaiser buns contain whey. Cottage cheese. The pita bread contains L-cysteine (an amino acid) and enzymes from an unknown source.

The Frosty contains mono- and diglycerides

from an unknown source, but don't contain eggs. The Caesar vinaigrette and Italian Caesar dressings contain anchovies. The French fries are normally cooked in their own oil, but if demand is high for them they may be cooked in the same oil that chicken or fish is also cooked in. The potato salad and pasta salad contain eggs. The sour cream seems to be vegetarian (according to their web page) but has many chemicals so it is hard to tell. It may contain gelatin. The bleu cheese, Garden Ranch and reduced fat Hidden Valley Ranch dressings contain eggs. All the sauces normally put on the pita sandwiches are non-vegetarian. The Honey Mustard Nugget Sauce contains eggs.

Western Sizzlin's
(www.westernsizzlins.com)

Has a salads bar and baked potatoes. There are vegan and vegetarian dishes in the salad bar.

Mashed potatoes contain milk. The Ranch dressing contains buttermilk. The cheeses come from a variety of sources, so whether they contain animal products is unknown.

The vegetable soup contains beef broth and the green beans contain pork flavoring. The potato salad, coleslaw, Thousand Island dressing and Blue Cheese dressing contain eggs. The bread products may contain eggs, so it is best to ask about this.

Western Steer Family Restaurants
(www.westernsteer.com)

Has a large buffet that contains both cold and hot dishes. There is a good selection of raw vegetables in the salad bar. Some vegan dishes are steamed carrots and squash, French fries (cooked in oil separately), three-bean salad and the tomato vinaigrette dressing. What the other dressings contain is unknown.

Mashed potatoes contain milk and butter. The wheat buns contain milk (lactose), honey and mono- and diglycerides from an unknown source. The white buns contain milk and diglycerides from an unknown source.

The chocolate cookies contain eggs. The broccoli, turnip greens and green beans contain a bacon stock. The Caesar dressing does not contain anchovies.

Whataburger (www.whataburger.com)

There is not much reason for a vegetarian to come here.

The French fries are not fried in oil that meat is cooked in. Low-fat vinaigrette dressing is vegan. Apple turnovers are fried in a vegetable oil that only vegetarian products are cooked in. They contain natural flavoring from unknown source.

Texas toast (can be served with cheese). The cinnamon rolls contain milk products and enzymes and mono- and diglycerides from an unknown source.

The batter that covers the onion rings contains egg. The Ranch, low-fat Ranch and Thousand Island dressings contain eggs. The pancakes contain eggs. The blueberry muffins and cookies contain eggs and milk. The milk shakes contain milk products and mono- and diglycerides from an unknown source.

Alabama

1. Birmingham
2. Decatur
3. Gadsden
4. Hoover
5. Huntsville
6. Mobile
7. Rainbow City
8. Tuscaloosa

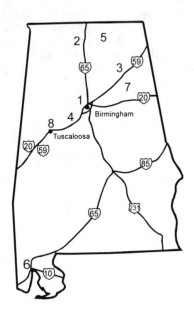

BIRMINGHAM

Five Point South district is an interesting alternative area with many restaurants, nightclubs and hotels.

Andy's Farm Market

2498 Rocky Ridge Road, Vestavia Hills; 205-824-0300. High quality fruits and vegetables.

Birmingham Farmers' Market

334 Findley Avenue W; 205-251-8737
Hours: Daily 24 hours a day.

**Golden Temple Natural Grocery

1901 11th Avenue South; 205-933-6333
Store Hours: Monday to Friday 8:30 am to 7 pm; Saturday 9:30 am to 5:30 pm; Sunday 12 noon to 5:30 pm; closed Sunday.
Rainbow Springs Cafe Hours: Monday to Saturday 11:30 am to 2 pm
3309 Lorna Road, Hoover; 205-823-7002
Store Hours: Mon to Fri 8:30 am to 7 pm; Sat 9:30 am to 5:30 pm; Sun 12 noon to 5:30 pm.
Natural Food Store and Vegetarian Café. Juice Bar. Organic produce. Vegan options.
Menu: Vegetarian sandwiches, salads and daily veg specials. Soups, rice dishes, salads, veggie burgers, Golden Temple Sandwich (guacamole, hummus, Swiss cheese, olives, mushrooms), Grilled Cheese, Quesadillas, Black Bean Burrito, Mexican Pizza, nachos, Mega GT Stack (brown basmati rice, black beans, cheese and guacamole) and other dishes. Fresh juices.
Comments: Fast service. Seating for around 75 people. Has a selection of sandwiches in the cooler. Low-fat and low-salt items. Has Birkenstock sandals.
Other Info: Limited service, take-out. Accepts MC, VISA. Price: $.
Directions: Located in the Five Points South area of Birmingham, which is a center for the arts and entertainment. From I-65 north, take the University Blvd exit (#259) (south exit) and go northeast on University. Then make a right on 8th Ave and go about a half-mile, then make a right on 19th St. Store is on the left at the junction with 11th Ave. From I-65 south, take 4th Ave (south exit) about 1¼ mile. Turn left at 4th Ave and go about a mile, then turn right at 19th St and go about a mile and this place on left.

The Green Door

2843 Culver Road; 205-871-2651
Hours: Monday to Friday 9:30 am to 5:30 pm; Saturday 10 am to 5 pm; closed Sunday.
Natural Food Store. No organic produce.
Comment: Has vitamins and nutritional items.
Directions: Going north on I-280, take Hollywood Blvd exit. Then take a right and go about a half-mile to the light. At the light take a right and go a quarter-mile, then take a left at Culver. The store is on the right.

The Pita Shop
1106 South 12th Street
205-328-2749
Hours: Monday to Friday 11 am to 9:30 pm
Saturday & Sunday 11 am to 2:30 pm, 5 pm to
10 pm
Middle Eastern and Lebanese. Not pure veg.
Menu: Hummus, falafel, tabbouleh and baba
ghanouj.
Other Info: Limited service, take-out. Price: $-
$$.

The Purple Onion
1717 10th Avenue S   205-933-2424
Hours: Sunday to Thursday 9 am to 2 am
Friday 9 am to 6 am
1931 North 2nd Avenue   205-252-4899
Hours: Daily for 24 hours
1550 Montgomery Highway   205-823-1069
Hours: Sunday to Thursday 9 am to 2 am
Friday 9 am to 6 am
Middle Eastern and Greek. Vegan options. Not
pure vegetarian.
Menu: Hummus, falafel, tabbouleh and baba
ghanouj.
Other Info: Counter service, take-out. Price: $-
$$.

Planet Smoothie
1100 20th Street S   205-933-7200
2000 Riverchase Galleria   205-987-4421
1851 Montgomery Highway S 205-982-6980
135 Inverness Plaza   205-991-7232
1926 28th Avenue S   205-870-9771
Web site: www.planetsmoothie.com
Hours: Monday to Saturday 10 am to 5 pm
Closed Sunday.
Smoothie Bar.
Menu: Serves good fruit juices.
Other Info: Accepts AMEX, DIS, MC, VISA.

Taj India
2226 Highland Avenue South
205-939-3805
Hours: Monday to Friday 11 am to 2 pm, 5 pm
to 10 pm; Saturday & Sunday 11:30 am to 2
pm, 5 pm to 10 pm
Indian. Not pure vegetarian.
Menu: Has a good selection of vegetarian dishes.
Comments: Plays classical Indian music. Relaxed, quiet place. Good, quick service. Décor is
lacking.
Other Info: Full service, take-out. Accepts
AMEX, DIS, MC, VISA. Price: $$.

DECATUR

Gloria's Good Health
1820 6th Avenue SE; 256-355-2439
Hours: Monday to Friday 10 am to 6 pm; Satur-
day 10 am to 5 pm; closed Sunday.
Natural Food Store.
Directions: This place is in the south section of
Decatur. This place is on Highway 31, about a
mile north of Rte 67.

GADSDEN

Apple-A-Day
Food max in Midtown Plaza, 280 North 3rd
205-546-845
Hours: Monday to Saturday 8:30 am to 8 pm
Sunday 12:30 am to 6 pm
Natural Food Store in a Regular Supermarket
called Gregerson's. Organic produce.
Directions: From I-59, take I-759 (spur), then
take Rte 411 (Rte 25) north and go about two
miles into Gadsden. Then at Rte 278 turn left
and go about 5 blocks. This place is then on the
left in the Midtown Plaza.

HOOVER

B & C Nutrition
1615 Montgomery Highway; 205-979-8307
Hours: Monday to Friday 10 am to 6:30 pm;
Saturday 10 am to 5 pm; closed Sunday.
Natural Food Store. Organic produce.
Directions: From I-65, take Exit #252 and get
on Hwy 31 going south and drive one mile and
the store is on the left. From I-459, take Mont-
gomery Hwy/Hwy 31 (#13) exit, then drive one
mile north and the store is on the right.

Golden Temple Natural Grocery & Cus-
tom Food International Restaurant
3309 Lorna Road, Hoover; 205-823-7002
Hours: Monday to Friday 10 am to 6:30 pm
Saturday 10 am to 6 pm
Natural Food Store and Restaurant. No organic
produce.
Menu: Has a good menu. Fresh juices.
Comments: The restaurant is in the Golden
Temple Natural Store.
Other Info: Cafeteria style, take-out. Price: $.
Directions: From I-65, exit at Montgomery Hwy
(Hwy 31). From north (on I-65) come straight
off the exit and turn right (from I-65 south turn
left) at Hwy 31 and go about 1½ miles, then turn

right at Patton Chapel Rd and this store is one mile down on the junction of Lorna Rd.

HUNTSVILLE

The happening area in town is near the University of Alabama at Huntsville campus.

Garden Cove Produce Center

628 Meridian Street, North; 256-534-2683
Hours: Monday to Wednesday 10 am to 7 pm; Thursday 9 am to 7 pm; Friday 9 am to 3 pm; Sunday 12 noon to 5 pm; closed Saturday.
Natural Food Store. A good Juice Bar. Organic produce and bulk food.
Directions: From Memorial Parkway (Hwy 231), go east on Pratt St. This place is on the right at the intersection of Meridian and Pratt.

Jamo's Juice & Java and More

413 Jordan Lane; 205-837-7880
Hours: Monday to Saturday 7 am to 10 pm Closed Sunday.
Middle Eastern Restaurant and Juice Bar. Not pure vegetarian.
Comments: Has mainly a vegetarian menu. Typical late night place. Live music on the weekends.
Other Info: Accepts AMEX, MC, VISA.
Directions: From I-565, take Exit #17 for Jordan Lane NW, then go north on Jordan Lane and this place is about a half-mile down on left.

Pearly Gates Natural Foods

2308 Memorial Parkway SW; 256-534-6233
Hours: Monday to Saturday 10 am to 6:30 pm Closed Sundays.
Natural Food Store. Organic foods. Has soups.
Directions: This place is about a mile southwest of the downtown, on Memorial Parkway, which is Highway 231. Take Exit #19 B or C on I-565 and go a mile south on Rte 231.

MOBILE

Jerusalem Café

5773 Airport Boulevard, Regency Shopping Center; 334-304-1155
Hours: Monday, Wednesday to Saturday 11 am to 8 pm; Tuesday 11 am to 2 pm; closed Sunday.

Middle Eastern. Not pure vegetarian.
Comments: Has a good amount of vegetarian foods.
Other Info: Accepts AMEX, MC, VISA.

Organic Foods

444B Azalea Road; 251-342-9554
Hours: Monday to Saturday 10 am to 6 pm Closed Sunday.
Natural Food Store.
Directions: From I-65, take Airport Blvd exit, and go west about 1¼ mile. Take a left at Azalea Rd and the store in on the right after about a mile.

RAINBOW CITY

Apple-A-Day

115 West Grand Avenue, Suite 63; 256-413-1300
Hours: Monday to Saturday 9:30 am to 6 pm Closed Sunday.
Natural Food Store.
Directions: It is about a mile northwest of downtown Rainbow City. From I-59, take Rainbow City exit, then take Rte 77 south for 4 miles. This place is at the intersection of Hwy 411 (Steele Station Rd) and Hwy 77.

TUSCALOOSA

The main street in town is University Boulevard.

Manna Grocery Natural Gourmet & Ethnic Foods

Meadowbrook Shopping Center, 2300 McFarland Boulevard #12; 205-752-9955
Store Hours: Monday to Saturday 9 am to 7 pm; closed Sunday. Deli Hours: Monday to Saturday 11 am to 2:30 pm
Natural Food Store and Deli. Bakery. Juice Bar. Vegan options. Not pure vegetarian.
Menu: Soups, salads, sandwiches and vegetarian specials.
Directions: From 1-20/59, take the McFarland Blvd exit (#73). From north, at the ramp take a right. From south, exit right and then bear left onto McFarland. Then go north on McFarland (Rte 82) about 2 miles and the store is in the Meadowbrook Shopping Center.

Alaska

1. Anchorage
2. Fairbank
3. Homer
4. Juneau
5. Palmer

A choice of eating places in Alaska can be found on the Internet at www.akdining.com.

ANCHORAGE

Safeway and Fred Meyers supermarkets often have fairly big health food sections.

Alladdin's
4240 Old Seward Highway
907-561-2373
Hours: Tuesday to Thursday 5 pm to 9 pm Friday & Saturday 5 pm to 10 pm
Middle Eastern. Not pure vegetarian.
Menu: Has many vegetarian dishes.
Other Info: Accepts AMEX, MC, VISA.

Anna's Health Foods
1403 Hyder Street; 907-277-2662
Hours: Monday to Friday 10 am to 6 pm Saturday & Sunday 10 am to 5 pm
Natural Food Store.
Comments: Owned by certified nutritionist.
Directions: This place is about one mile northeast of the main downtown area. From Rte 1 going north into town, when road splits go to the right a quarter mile, then at 14th St turn left and go a block, then at Hyder St turn left and this place is right at corner.

Enzyme Express
1330 East Huffman Road, Suite C
907-345-1330

Hours: Monday to Friday 10 am to 7 pm; Saturday 10 am to 5 pm; closed Sunday.
Raw Organic Juice Bar and Deli. Vegan Buffet.
Menu: Has good veggie burgers and soups. Buffet with smoothies and fresh juices along with health products. Healthy teas.
Other Info: Limited service, take-out. Accepts MC, VISA. Price: $-$$.
Directions: From Rte 1 south of town, take Huffman Rd exit and then go west on Huffman and this place is a half-mile down.

The Marx Brothers Café
627 West 3rd Avenue
907-278-2133
Summer Hours: Monday to Saturday 6 pm to 9:30 pm; Friday & Saturday 5:30 pm to 10 pm. Open on Sunday in summer. Closed Sunday during winter.
Regional, American. Not pure vegetarian
Comments: Will prepare special vegetarian meals. During the summer time they grow their own herbs, spices and lettuce. Romantic, elegant place. Has a fireplace. Upscale. The food and service gets high ratings.
Other Info: Full service, take-out. Banquet facilities. Reservations are suggested. Accepts AMEX, DIS, MC, VISA. Price: $$$.

Mexico in Alaska
730 Old Seward Highway; 907-349-1528
Hours: Monday to Friday 11 am to 3 pm, 5 pm

to 10 pm; Saturday 12 noon to 3 pm, 5 pm to 10 pm; Sunday 4 pm to 9 pm
Mexican. Vegan options. Not pure vegetarian.
Menu: Has a large selection of vegetarian dishes.
Comments: Casual, family place. Authentic, good food. Friendly, helpful service.
Other Info: Accepts MC, VISA. Price: $.

***Middleway Café
1200 West Northern Light Boulevard, next to REI outfitters; 907-272-6433
Hours: Daily 7 am to 6:30 pm
International, American. Mostly Pure Vegetarian. Juice Bar.
Menu: Has a large amount of vegetarian and vegan dishes. Has good cheap sandwiches, soups, soy burgers, hummus sandwiches, salads, whole-grain tortillas and wraps. Has vegan specials. Fresh juices and smoothies. Espresso.
Comments: Uses mostly organic ingredients. Friendly place. They grow their own herbs and spices.
Other Info: Counter service, take-out. Order at counter and they call out your name. Does not accept reservations. Cash only; no credit cards. Price: $$.
Directions: Take Hwy 1 into town. When the highway ends continue north onto Rte 1 and go north a quarter-mile, then turn left onto Benson Blvd and go west (becomes W Northern Light Blvd) and this place is 1¼ mile down.

Moose's Tooth
3300 Old Seward Highway   907-258-2537
2021 Spar Avenue   907-278-4999
Hours: Daily 11 am to 11 pm
Pizza. Not pure vegetarian.
Menu: Has really good pizzas. Whole-wheat ones.
Comments: Casual atmosphere. Price: $$.

Natural Pantry
601 East Diamond Boulevard; 907-522-4330
Hours: Monday to Friday 10:30 am to 9 pm; Saturday 10:30 am to 6 pm; closed Sunday.
Natural Food Store. Organic produce.
Menu: Has a daily vegetarian special.
Comments: Largest place and the best selection in the area. Casual place. Price: $.
Directions: From Hwy 1, take Diamond Blvd exit and go west on Diamond Blvd ¾ mile down.

Organic Oasis Health Foods & Juice Bar
2610 Spenard Road
907-277-7882
Hours: Monday 11:30 am to 7 pm; Tuesday 11:30 am to 10:30 pm; Wednesday 11:30 am to

9 pm; Thursday 11:30 am to 9 pm; Friday & Saturday 11:30 am to 10 pm
Gourmet Organic Natural Food Restaurant. Bakery, Smoothie Bar.
Comments: The food is good. Often has live music in the evening.
Directions: This place is in west Anchorage. Going north on Minnesota Dr from the airport, turn right onto W 27th Ave and go a half-mile, then turn left at Spenard Rd and this place is a block down.

Roy's Health Foods
501 East Northern Lights; 907-277-3226
Hours: Monday to Saturday 10 am to 6 pm
Natural Food Store.

Sacks Café
328 G Street, between 3rd and 4th Streets
907-274-4022
Hours: Sunday to Thursday 11 am to 3 pm, 5 pm to 9 pm; Friday & Saturday 11 am to 3 pm, 5 pm to 10:30 pm
West Coast Gourmet. Asian & Southwest. Vegan options. Not pure vegetarian.
Menu: Salads, sandwiches, Baked Penne Pasta, Roasted Vegetable Au Gratin and other dishes.
Comments: Romantic, casual, quiet. Nice décor. Good atmosphere. Very friendly.
Other Info: Full service, take-out. Accepts AMEX, DC, DIS, MC, VISA. Price: $$-$$$.

Snow City
1034 West 4th Avenue; 907-272-2489
Hours: Daily 7 am to 4:30 pm
Vegan and Vegetarian-friendly Restaurant. Not pure vegetarian (serves seafood).
Menu: Soups, salads, gourmet sandwiches and pastas. Has a breakfast cereal bar. Sometimes has vegan soups.
Comments: Cool, casual atmosphere.
Other Info: Non-smoking. Reservations not necessary. Accepts AMEX, DIS, MC, VISA.
Directions: This place is in the main downtown area in northwest Anchorage, about a quarter-mile from the water. Coming into town on the main street, when it ends at L St turn right and go one block, then turn right at W 4th Ave and this place is a half-block down.

Thai Kitchen
3405 East Tudor Street; 907-561-0082
Hours: Monday to Friday 11 am to 3 pm, 5 pm to 9 pm; Saturday & Sunday 5 pm to 8:30 pm
Thai. Not pure vegetarian.
Menu: The Tofu Eggplant is good.

Other Info: Full service, take-out. Does not take reservations. Accepts AMEX, DC, MC, VISA. Price: $$.

Thai Village

954 Muldoon Road; 907-337-9559
Hours: Monday to Saturday 11 am to 10 pm
Closed Sunday.
Thai. Not pure vegetarian.
Menu: Spicy Tofu and Garlic Tofu are popular dishes.
Comments: Gets good recommendations.

FAIRBANKS

Gambardella's Pasta Bella

706 2nd Avenue; 907-456-3417
Hours: Monday to Thursday 11 am to 9 pm; Friday & Saturday 11 am to 10 pm; Sunday 4 pm to 9 pm
Pizza and Pasta Italian. Not pure vegetarian.
Menu: Traditional Italian items such as Fettuccini Alfredo, gourmet pizza, Pasta Marinara, Eggplant Parmesan and Pesto Pasta. Vegetarian dishes are marked on the menu. Espresso and cappuccino.
Other Info: Full service, take-out. Accepts MC, VISA. Price: Lunch $, Dinner $$.

HOMER

Fresh Sourdough Express Bakery & Café

1316 Ocean Drive (Rte 1); 907-235-7571
Web site: www.freshsourdoughexpress.com
In-season Hours: Daily 7 am to 10 pm
Off-season Hours: 8 am to 3 pm
Bakery & Café. Not pure vegetarian.
Menu: Pizza, falafel, nachos, salads, Veggie Stir-fry and Home Fry Potatoes. Many baked goods. Organic breads baked daily. Organic coffee and tea.
Comments: Often uses organic produce.
Other Info: Non-smoking. Reservations not necessary. Accepts DIS, MC, VISA.
Directions: From downtown Homer go southeast on Rte 1 about a mile and this place, near Douglas Pl.

Smoky Bay Co-op

248 West Pioneer
907-235-7252

Hours: Monday to Saturday 9 am to 7 pm
Sunday 10 am to 6 pm
Natural Food Store and Deli. Organic produce.
Other Info: Accepts MC, VISA.

JUNEAU

El Sombrero

157 South Franklin Street; 907-586-6770
Hours: Monday to Thursday 11 am to 9 pm; Friday & Saturday 11 am to 10 pm; closed Sun.
Vegan-friendly Mexican. Not pure vegetarian.
Comments: Has good Mexican food. Friendly service.
Other Info: Accepts AMEX, MC, VISA.

Fiddlehead Restaurant

429 West Willoughby Avenue; 907-586-3150
Hours: Monday to Friday 7 am to 9 pm
Saturday & Sunday 8 am to 9 pm
Natural Food Gourmet International Restaurant. Not pure vegetarian. Vegan options.
Menu: Uses some native plants. Soups, sandwiches, salads, bean burgers and entrees. Fresh juices.
Comments: A good place. Live piano music in evenings. Local artwork displayed. Good atmosphere.
Other Info: Full service, take-out. Non-smoking. Accepts AMEX, MC, VISA. Price: $$.
Directions: From Rte 7 coming southwest into Juneau, turn right at Whittier St and go a quarter-mile, then at Willoughby Avenue turn left and this place is a block down.

Rainbow Foods

200 Seward Avenue; 907-586-6476
Hours: Monday to Friday 9 am to 7 pm
Sunday 9 am to 6 pm
Natural Food Store and Deli. Vegan options. Not pure vegetarian. Organic produce.
Menu: Has a good selection of vegetarian. Has a weekly dinner with dishes from cuisines from around the world.
Comments: Efficient staff. Accepts AMEX, MC, VISA.
Directions: From Rte 7 coming southwest into Juneau, turn left onto Main St and go 2 blocks and turn right onto W 2nd St. This place is then a block down at the corner of Seward Ave and 2nd St.

Arizona

1. Apache Junction
2. Bisbee
3. Chandler
4. Cottonwood
5. Flagstaff
6. Glendale
7. Mesa
8. Phoenix
9. Prescott
10. Scottsdale
11. Sedona
12. Sun City
13. Tempe
14. Tucson

BISBEE

Artists community. Happening town for 6,000 people.

Bisbee Food Co-op
72 Erie Street; 520-432-4011
Hours: Monday to Friday 9 am to 6 pm; Saturday 9 am to 5 pm; Sunday 12 noon to 4 pm
Natural Food Store and Vegetarian Café. Deli and Bakery. Organic produce.
Menu: Soups, veggie chili, sandwiches (makes them fresh 11 am to 2 pm), salads and baked goods.
Comments: Has around 20 seats.
Directions: This place is 2 miles east of downtown Bisbee on Rte 80, near the junction with Rte 92, near the Lavender pit.

CHANDLER

Pita Jungle
1949 West Ray Road; 480-855-3232
Hours: Sunday to Thursday 11 am to 9 pm
Friday & Saturday 11 am to 9:30 pm
Pita Sandwich Place. Not pure vegetarian.
Menu: Falafels, hummus, veggie burgers and other pita sandwiches.
Other Info: Accepts AMEX, DC, DIS, MC, VISA.

COTTONWOOD (SEDONA SUBURB)

Mount Hope Foods Naturally
853 South Main Street; 928-634-8251
Hours: Monday to Saturday 9 am to 7 pm
Sunday 10 am to 5 pm
Natural Food Store. Organic produce.
Menu: Has some ready-made sandwiches such as hummus or cheese and salads such as Greek Salad.
Directions: From I-17, take Camp Verde/Cottonwood exit. Head towards Cottonwood and go about 10 miles. At Main St turn left and this place is 1½ mile down on the right. This place is 1½ mile northwest of the main downtown area.

FLAGSTAFF

You can pick up the Flagstaff Live to get a list of vegetarian friendly restaurants. This college town has hiking and winter sports.

Café Express
16 North San Francisco Street; 928-774-0541
Hours: Sunday to Thursday 7 am to 3 pm, 5 pm to 8 pm; Fri & Sat 7 am to 3 pm, 5 pm to 9 pm
Coffeehouse and Café. Salad Bar and Bakery. Espresso Bar. Vegan options. Not pure veg.
Menu: Has over twenty vegetarian dishes and five vegan dishes. Has good natural food and vegan options. Soups, salads, chili, Spinach Enchiladas,

Black Bean Corn Salad, sandwiches and hot main dishes. Fresh baked breads and desserts. Fresh juices.

Comments: One of the largest natural food stores in Arizona.

Other Info: Full service, take-out. Has outdoor seating. Reservations not necessary. Non-smoking. Accepts AMEX, MC, VISA. Price: $.

Directions: This place is in the center of town. From I-17/I-40, take S Milton Rd exit (#185) and go straight (north) onto S Milton Rd and go 1¾ mile (becomes US-89A, then Hwy 40 Bus), then its becomes W Santa Fe Ave (bears sharply right and then this place is after a quarter-mile down).

Dara Thai Restaurant

14 South San Francisco Street; 928-774-0047
Hours: Monday to Saturday 11 am to 10 pm
Closed Sunday.
Southeast Asia. Vegan options. Not pure veg.
Menu: Most of the main courses can be made vegetarian. Has a separate vegetarian section on the menu. Has tofu dishes and will make most of the meat dishes vegetarian.
Comments: Food gets good rating. Good service.
Other Info: Full service, take-out. Accepts MC, VISA. Price: $$.

Delhi Palace

2700 South Woodland Village Boulevard, Suite 640; 928-556-0019
Indian. See Tempe, AZ.

**Macy's European Coffee House Bakery & Vegetarian Restaurant

14 South Beaver Street
520-774-2243; **Web site:** www.macyscoffee.com
Hours: Sunday to Thursday 6 am to 8 pm
Friday to Saturday 6 am to 10 pm
Fully Vegetarian International and Italian. Coffeehouse and Bakery. Vegan options.
Menu: Has some vegan and vegetarian dishes. Salads, soups and sandwiches. Has freshly made pastas, baked goods and sauces. Vegan cakes and cookies. Cappuccino, espresso, European coffee.
Comments: Live music, poetry night, chess night, opera night and story telling on Sunday mornings.
Other Info: Full service. Non-smoking. No credit cards; cash only. Price: $.
Directions: This place is in the center of town. From I-17/I-40, take S Milton Rd exit (#185) and go straight (north) onto S Milton Rd and go 1¾ mile (becomes US-89A, then Hwy 40 Bus), then its becomes W Santa Fe Ave (bears sharply

right) and go a quarter-mile, then at S Beaver St turn right and go a half-block down.

Morning Glory Café

115 South San Francisco Street, south of the tracks
928-774-3705
Hours: Monday to Friday 11 am to 4 pm
Mexican. Not pure vegetarian.
Menu: Has a variety of vegetarian soups, sandwiches and salads. Blue corn tamales. Has soy cheese.

Mountain Harvest

6 West Phoenix Avenue, between Beaver & San Francisco; 928-779 -9456
Hours: Monday to Saturday 8 am to 8 pm
Sunday 9 am to 7 pm
Natural Food Store and Deli. Juice Bar. Vegetarian-friendly. Not pure veg. Organic produce.
Menu: Has a good selection of vegan dishes in the deli. Only uses organic produce in dishes.
Comments: Has a good selection of organic produce. Very friendly, nice people. Was told that they serve some meat products, but none of the employees eat meat.

Mountain Oasis

11 East Aspen Street; 928-214-9270
Hours: Sunday to Thursday 11 am to 9 pm
Friday & Saturday 11 am to 10 pm
International, Southwestern and Mediterranean. Not pure vegetarian.
Menu: Has a good selection of vegetarian dishes. Tofu dishes, vegan and vegetarian soups, Corn and Tempeh Chowder, Miso Soup, Grilled Vegetarian Penne, Roast Red Pepper Pasta and shakes.
Other Info: Full service, take-out. Accepts AMEX, DC, DIS, MC, VISA. Price: $-$$.

New Frontiers Natural Foods

1000 South Milton Road; 520-774-5747
Hours: Monday to Saturday 9 am to 8 pm
Sunday 10 am to 7 pm
Natural Food Store and Deli. Bakery and Café. Vegan friendly. Organic produce. Not pure veg.
Menu: Has a good selection of vegetarian dishes. Vegetarian soups, sandwiches, salads, veggie chili, pasta dishes and much more.
Comments: Knowledgeable staff in supplement department. Large place with a good selection. Seating for 30.
Other Info: Accepts MC, VISA.
Direction: Directions: This place is in the center of town. From I-17/I-40, take S Milton Rd exit (#185) and go straight (north) onto S Milton Rd (becomes US-89A) and this place is 1 mile down.

Pasto
19 East Aspen Street; 928-779-1937
Hours: Sunday to Thursday 5 pm to 9 pm
Friday & Saturday 5 pm to 10 pm
Italian. Upscale. Not pure vegetarian.
Menu: Has a good selection of vegetarian dishes.
Comments: Has an outdoor and indoor dining area. Casual setting. Friendly place. Good food.
Other Info: Accepts AMEX, MC, VISA.

MESA

Nature's Health
2665 East Broadway; 480-649-6145
Hours: Monday to Friday 9 am to 7 pm; Saturday 9 am to 6 pm; closed Sunday.
Natural Food Store.
Directions: From Hwy 60, take the Gilbert Rd exit (#182) and go north about 2 miles. Turn right at Broadway (fifth light) and go 1 mile, then a few blocks after the canal, turn right into the strip mall parking lot (at corner of Broadway and Lindsey). This place is 2½ miles northeast of downtown Mesa.

PHOENIX

Bamboo House
502 East Thunderbird; 602-843-4243
Hours: Daily 11 am to 10 pm
Chinese. Vegan friendly. Not pure vegetarian.
Menu: The Sizzling Tofu in orange sauce is good.
Comments: Family owned and operated. Friendly, quick service.
Other Info: Accepts AMEX, MC, VISA.

The Farm at South Mountain
6106 South 32nd Street; 602-276-6360
Hours: Tuesday to Sunday 8 am to 3 pm
Closed Monday.
Mostly Vegetarian Natural and Raw Foods.
Menu: Salads, sandwiches, Grilled Eggplant Sandwich (recommended) and fresh baked goods.
Comments: Has outdoor seating (only) in their pecan grove. Often gets their cooking ingredients from their own garden. Has organic dishes. Gets good recommendations.
Directions: The place is in south Phoenix. From I-10, take University Dr exit (#151) and go south on E University Dr (becomes 32nd St) and this place is about 1½ mile down on 32nd.

Green Leaf Café's
4426 North 19th Avenue, in the Camelback and Indian School Road areas; 602-265-5992

Hours: Monday to Saturday 11 am to 4 pm
Closed Sunday.
Middle Eastern, Persian and some American. Not pure vegetarian.
Menu: Vegetarian Sampler, Veggie Stir-fry, Steamed Vegetables, Tofu Delight and Vegetable Stew. Purple Shoots is grilled eggplant and steamed asparagus with feta cheese.
Comments: Gourmet food. The Spudburger has eggs in it. Has live piano music on Friday.
Other Info: Full service, take-out, delivery, catering. Accepts AMEX, MC, VISA. Price: $$.
Directions: This place is in northwest Phoenix. From I-17 coming north from I-10, take Exit #203 towards Camelback Rd, then go straight onto N Black Canyon Hwy and go a few blocks, at W Camelback Rd turn right and go ¾ mile, then at N 19th Ave turn right and this place is a half-mile down.

Health Hut Natural Foods
8841 North 19th Avenue; 602-943-1171
Hours: Monday to Friday 9:30 am to 6 pm; Saturday 10 am to 5 pm; closed Sunday.
Natural Food Store.
Directions: In a shopping center.

India Palace
16842 North 7th St, at Bell Rd; 602-942-4224
Hours: Daily 11 am to 2:30 pm, 5 pm to 10 pm
Indian. Daily lunch buffet. Vegan options. Not pure vegetarian.
Menu: Has a selection of vegetarian dishes.
Other Info: Full service, take-out, delivery. Accepts AMEX, DC, DIS, MC, VISA. Price: $-$$.

India Delhi Palace
5050 East McDowell Road; 602-244-8181
Hours: Monday to Friday 11:30 pm to 2:30 pm (lunch buffet), 5 pm to 10 pm; Saturday & Sunday 11:30 am to 4:30 pm, 5 pm to 10 pm
Indian. Not pure vegetarian.
Menu: Has a wide selection of vegetarian dishes. Samosas, Indian breads, chickpeas dishes, Cauliflower & Potatoes, Eggplant and rice dishes.
Other Info: Full service, take-out. Accepts AMEX, DC, DIS, MC, VISA. Price: $$.

**International Vegetarian House (also known as Supreme Master Ching Hai Vegetarian House)
3239 East Indian School Road, at 32nd Street
602-264-3480
Hours: Tuesday to Saturday 11 am to 2:30 pm, 5 pm to 9 pm; closed Sunday & Monday.
Fully Vegetarian Chinese Buddhist. Mostly Vegan.

Menu: Pastas, salads, soups and baked goods. Selection of Chinese dishes such as Spring Rolls, Heaven Rice Rolls, brown rice, Broccoli and Chinese Mushrooms and Rice Soup. Serves all-vegan mock meat dishes that taste like the real thing.

Comments. Gets really high recommendations. Live music, poetry night, chess night, opera night, and story telling on Sunday mornings. Friendly service. Dishes containing dairy are marked on the menu. Has plenty of parking.

Other Info: Full service, take-out. Non-smoking. Accept reservations but not necessary. Accepts MC, VISA. **Price:** $-$$.

Directions: This place is in northeast Phoenix. From Hwy 51 coming north from downtown, take Indian School Rd exit (#3) and keep right at the fork in the ramp and merge on E Indian Rd and this place is 2 miles down.

Jamba Juice

4302 East Ray Road; 480-706-8500
Juice Bar.

Juice Works

10895 North Tatum Boulevard
480-922-5337
Hours: Monday to Thursday 7 am to 8 pm; Friday & Saturday 7 am to 9 pm; Sun 9 am to 7 pm
Juice Bar and Café. Vegan-friendly. Not pure vegetarian. **Price:** $.
Menu: Fresh juices and smoothies.
Directions: From Hwy 51, take exit #3 and go east on Indian School Rd for 2 miles, then at N 32nd St turn left (go north) and go 1½ mile, then at Camelback Rd turn left and this place is 2 blocks down.

Main Street Café

4426 North 19th Avenue
602-265-5992
Hours: Monday to Saturday 11 am to 4 pm
Closed Sunday.
Middle Eastern, International. Vegan-friendly. Not pure vegetarian.
Menu: Falafel, hummus, Veggie Stir-fry, veggie burgers, Jambalaya and other dishes. The Eggplant Lasagna is very good. Fresh juices and smoothies.
Other Info: Full service, take-out. Accepts AMEX, MC, VISA. **Price:** $-$$.
Directions: From I-17, take exit #202, then go east on W Indian School Rd for 1 mile, then at N 19th Ave turn left and this place is ¾ mile down.

Mediterranean House

1588 East Bethany Home Road; 602-248-8460
Hours: Monday to Fri 11 am to 2:30 pm, 4:30 pm to 9 pm; Sat 4:30 pm to 9 pm; closed Sun.
Middle Eastern. Not pure vegetarian.
Comments: Good size portions.
Other Info: Accepts MC, VISA. Full service, take-out.

Middle Eastern Bakery and Deli

3052 North 16th Street; 602-277-4927
Hours: Tuesday to Friday 9:30 am to 5 pm; Saturday 9:30 am to 4 pm; closed Sunday & Mon.
Middle Eastern. Not pure vegetarian.
Menu: Falafel, hummus, tabbouleh and other dishes. Freshly baked pita bread.
Other Info: Limited service, take-out, catering. Accepts MC, VISA. **Price:** $$.

Mitierra Super Juice

1617 North 3rd Street; 602-629-0923
Juice Bar.

Tarbell's

3213 East Camelback Road
602-955-8100; **Web site:** www.tarbells.com
Hours: Monday to Saturday 5 pm to 11 pm
Sunday 5 pm to 10 pm
American Restaurant. Not Pure Vegetarian.
Menu: Menu changes monthly. Has Organic Vegetable Plate, pastas, pizzas, Smoked Portobello, Arizona Grown Organic Vegetable Place, Grilled Portobello Mushroom and Sage Risotto.
Comments: White tablecloths on tables. Seats 120. Good place for a special event. Menu is on their web site.
Other Info: Full service, take-out. Accepts AMEX, DC, DIS, MC, VISA. **Price:** $$-$$$.
Directions: From I-10, take AZ Hwy 51/AZ 202 Loop exit (#147) and get on Hwy 51 going north for 3 miles, then exit towards Highland Ave, then stay straight onto N 18th St for 1 block, then at E Highland Ave turn right and go ¾ mile west, then at 22nd St turn left and go a half-mile north, then at E Camelback Rd turn right and go east and this place is 1½ mile down.

Taste of India

1609 East Bell Road #B4; 602-788-3190
Hours: Daily 11:30 am to 2:30 pm, 5 pm to 10 pm
Indian. Vegan options. Not pure vegetarian.
Menu: Has a large amount of vegetarian dishes.
Comments: Has outdoor dining.
Other Info: Full service, take-out. Accepts AMEX, DC, MC, VISA. **Price:** $-$$.

Trader Joe's (two locations)
Town & Country Plaza, 20th Street
at Camelback Road
Metro Power Center (second location)

Wild Oats Market
3933 East Camelback Road
602-954-0584; fax: 602-954-7435
Directions: From I-10, take Hwy 51/AZ 202
Loop exit (#147) and get on Hwy 51 going north
for 3 miles, then exit towards Highland Ave, then
stay straight onto N 18th St for 1 block, then at
E Highland Ave turn right and go ¾ mile west,
then at 22nd St turn left and go a half-mile north,
then at E Camelback Rd turn right and go east
and this place is 1¾ miles down. From I-17,
take Camelback Rd exit. Drive east about 7 miles.
This place is at the southwest corner of 40th and
Camelback on the right (before the light).
13823 North Tatum Boulevard; 602-953-7546
Directions: From Hwy 51, take Cactus Rd exit
(#10), then go east on E Cactus Rd for 1¾ mile,
then at N Tatum Blvd turn left for 1 mile and it
is a block past E Thunderbird Rd.
Hours: Daily 7 am to 10 pm
Natural Food Store and Cafe. Deli, Bakery,
Salad Bar and Juice Bar. Organic produce. Supermarket-type place. See Wild Oats Market
information.

Yusef's
15236 North Cave Creek Road; 602-867-2957
Hours: Monday to Saturday 10 am to 8 pm; Res-
taurant closes at 7 pm; closed Sunday.
Middle Eastern Restaurant, Deli and Grocery.
Vegan options. Not pure vegetarian.
Menu: Has a selection of vegetarian dishes such
as falafel, hummus, tabbouleh and grape leaves.
Other Info: Full service, take-out. Accepts
AMEX, DC, MC, VISA. Price: $.

PRESCOTT

New Frontiers Natural Foods
1112 Iron Springs Road; 928-445-7370
Hours: Monday to Saturday 8 am to 8 pm
Sunday 10 am to 6 pm
Natural Food Store and Deli. Bakery and Juice
Bar. Not pure vegetarian. Organic produce.
Comments: Seats 25.
Directions: Thus place is about 1½ mile north-
west of the center of town. From Hwy 69, take
US 89 S (E Sheldon St) west and go 1 mile (be-
come N Montezuma St/US 89), when US 89
turns to go south continue straight on Gurley St

a half-mile, then turn right at Grove Ave and go
north a half-mile, then take the left fork onto
Miller Valley Rd, then go 1 mile north, then at
Iron Spring Road turn slight right (go northwest)
and this place is a half-mile down.

**Prescott Natural Foods
330 West Gurley Street; 928-778-5875
Hours: Monday to Saturday 8 am to 8 pm
Sunday 10 am to 6 pm
Natural Food Store and Vegetarian Café. Deli
and Juice Bar. Not pure vegetarian. Organic
produce.
Comments: Seats 50.
Directions: Hwy 69, which becomes Gurley.
Gurley (Hwy 69, Hwy 89) is the main west-east
road going through town. This place is a block
past the town square on the east side of the road.

SCOTTSDALE (7 miles north of Phoenix)

Wild Oats Market
7129 East Shea Boulevard; 480-905-1441
Hours: Daily 7 am to 10 pm
Natural Food Store and Cafe. Deli, Bakery,
Salad Bar and Juice Bar. Organic produce. Supermarket-type place. See Wild Oats Market
informationon.
Comments: Seats 50.
Directions: From I-10, take Squaw Peak Freeway (Hwy 51) north 7 miles to Shea Blvd (#9),
then go east on Shea Blvd miles and this place is
about 3 miles down, at the corner of Scottsdale
Rd and Shea.

SEDONA

Heartline Café
1610 West Highway 89A; 928-282-0785
Hours: Thursday to Monday 11 am to 3 pm, 5
pm to 9 pm; Tues & Wed 5 pm to 9 pm
Continental. Not pure vegetarian.
Menu: Has a selection of vegetarian and vegan
dishes.
Comments: Upscale, romantic place. Is a well-
designed place with candlelit dining. Has tropi-
cal flowers and orchids.
Other Info: Reservations suggested. Accepts
AMEX, DC, DIS, MC, VISA. Price: $$-$$$.

India Palace
1910 West Hwy 89A, Suite 102; 928-204-2300
Hours: Daily 11 am to 2:30 pm (buffet lunch),
5 pm to 10 pm
Indian. See Phoenix, AZ.

New Frontiers National Foods

1420 West Highway 89A; 928-282-6311
Hours: Monday to Saturday 8 am to 8 pm
Sunday 10 am to 6 pm
Natural Food Store and Deli. Organic produce.
Vegan options. Not pure vegetarian.
Menu: Has a wide selection of vegetarian dishes.
Comments: Has around 15 tables.
Directions: In west Sedona on north side of Hwy
89A.

Oaxaca Restaurant

231 North Highway 89A, in the old downtown
520-282-4179
Hours: Sunday to Thursday 8 am to 8 pm
Friday & Saturday 8 am to 9 pm
Mexican, Southwestern. Not pure vegetarian.
Menu: Blue-corn and whole-wheat tortillas, burritos, tacos, enchiladas and salads. Cappuccino,
espresso.
Comments: It is a big place. Only vegetable oil is
used in cooking. Has healthy dishes that are
marked on the menu. Everything is made without any animal products in the bases or sauces.
Other Info: Full service, take-out. Accepts
AMEX, DIS, MC, VISA.

Rinzai's Market

West Sedona, next to Harkin's Theater
928-204-2185
Hours: Monday to Saturday 10 am to 7 pm
Closed Sunday.
Natural Food Store.

Sedona Salad Co.

2370 W Hwy 89A
520-282-0299
Hours: Daily 5:30 am to 10 pm
American. Juice and Soup Bar. Not pure veg.
Menu: Has a salad bar with over 50 items. Has
potatoes, soups and other dishes.
Comments: Has some organic items in the salad
bar.
Other Info: Limited service, take-out. Accepts
AMEX, MC, VISA. Price: $.
Directions: This place is in West Sedona, about
1½ mile west of downtown Sedona on Hwy 89A,
the main road going east-west through Sedona.

TEMPE

Boxed Greens Organic Produce

PO Box 1509; 480-577-7060; 888-588-8107;
Web site: www.boxedgreens.com
Delivers organic fruits and vegetables door to door.

Byblos Restaurant

3332 South Mill Avenue; 480-894-1945
Hours: Tuesday to Saturday 11 am to 3:30 pm, 5
pm to 10 pm; Sunday 4 am to 9 pm
Middle Eastern, Mediterranean, Greek. Not pure
vegetarian.
Menu: Falafel, hummus, stuffed grape leaves, tabbouleh and other dishes. Non-alcoholic beer and
wine.
Comments: Good service and food.
Other Info: Full service, take-out. Accepts
AMEX, DC, DIS, MC, VISA. Price: $$.

Delhi Palace

933 East University Drive, Suite 103; 520-921-
2200
Hours: Daily 11:30 am to 2:30 pm, 5 pm to 10 pm
Indian. Vegan options. Not pure vegetarian.
Menu: Has a wide selection of vegetarian dishes.
Other Info: Full service, take-out. Accepts
AMEX, DC, DIS, MC, VISA. Price: $$.

Gentle Strength Co-op and Desert Greens Café

234 West University, corner of Ash and University; 480-968-4831; 480-968-0081
Web site: www.gentlestrength.com
Store Hours: Daily 9 am to 9 pm
Café Hours: Monday to Friday 7 am to 7 pm;
Sat 9 am to 7 pm; Sunday Brunch 10 am to 2 pm
Natural Food Store and Vegetarian-friendly
Restaurant. Many vegan dishes. Organic.
Macrobiotic options.
Menu: Soups, sandwiches, Saguaro Sesame Tofu,
rice dishes, pastas, Artichoke Linguine, salads,
vegetable dishes, muffins and desserts. Has daily
specials.
Comments: Has good food in the casual café.
Has indoor and outdoor dining on the patio. The
store is well-stocked with organic produce and
other items.
Other Info: Counter service, take-out. Accepts
AMEX, MC, VISA. Price: $.
Directions: From I-10/I-17 coming east into
Tempe, take AZ Hwy 202 North Loop, then take
Exit #6 and go south on N Lake View Rd/S Mill
Rd for 1½ mile, then turn right onto University
and go west and this place is a third-mile down.
From I-10/I-17 going north (west), take Hwy 143
(#152) and go north to Exit #2, then go east on
University Drive and this place is 1½ mile down.

Haji Baba

1513 East Apache Boulevard; 480-894-1905
Hours: Monday to Saturday 10 am to 8 pm

Sunday 12 noon to 6 pm
Middle Eastern. Vegan options. Not pure veg.
Menu: Falafel, hummus and a Vegetarian Plate.
Other Info: Full service, take-out. Accepts DIS, MC, VISA.
Directions: Across from the fire station. Price: $.

Pita Jungle
1250 East Apache Boulevard; 480-804-0234
Hours: Daily 10 am to 10 pm
International Natural Foods. Middle Eastern, Mediterranean, American. Macrobiotic options. Vegan friendly. Not pure vegetarian.
Menu: Has a wide selection of vegetarian dishes and pita sandwiches. Falafel, hummus, Middle Eastern salads, tabbouleh and other dishes. Smoothies (can use soy milk) are good. Fresh-squeezed orange and grapefruit juice.
Comments: The food gets good ratings. Can substitute soy cheese or seitan sausage. Casual, friendly place. Good value. Quick service. Generous portions.
Other Info: Full service, take-out. Price: $.
Directions: From AZ Hwy 202 Loop, take Scottsdale Rd exit (#7) towards Arizona State U, get on N Scottsdale Rd (becomes S Rural Rd) going south for 1¼ mile, then at Apache Blvd turn left and go a half-mile, then make a U-turn and this place is a block down.

Sahara Middle Eastern Restaurant
808 South Mill Avenue; 480-966-1971
Hours: Monday to Saturday 11 am to 3 pm, 5 pm to 9 pm; closed Sunday.
Middle Eastern. Vegan options. Not pure veg.
Menu: Falafel, salads, hummus, baba ghanouj, tabbouleh, stuffed grape leaves and other dishes.
Other Info: Full service, take-out, catering. Cash only. Price: $-$$.

Saigon Healthy Cuisine
820 South Mill Avenue; 480-967-4199
Hours: Monday to Saturday 11 am to 2:30 pm, 4:30 pm to 9 pm; closed Sunday.
Vietnamese. Vegan options. Not pure vegetarian.
Menu: Spring Rolls, Sesame & Rice Noodles, Vegetable Soup, Vegetable Stew, rice dishes and other dishes.
Comments: Good value. Friendly service.
Other Info: Limited service, take-out. Accepts MC, VISA. Price: $.

Whole Foods Market
5120 South Rural, at Baseline; 480-456-1400
Hours: Daily 8 am to 10 pm

Natural Food Store and Cafe. Deli, Bakery, Salad Bar and Juice Bar. Organic produce. Supermarket-type place. See Whole Foods Market information.
Directions: From I-10, take US 60 exit (#154) towards Mesa Globe and go 2 miles, then take the Rural Rd exit (#174) towards Scottsdale, then turn right at S Rural Rd (go south) and this place is a half-mile down. This place is a couple miles southwest of downtown Tempe.

TUCSON

Aqua Vita Natural Foods Market
3225 North Los Altos, 1 block west of 1st Avenue (north side of road); 520-293-7770
Hours: Monday to Saturday 9 am to 7 pm
Closed Sunday
Natural Food Store. Has over 400 types of herbs. Organic produce.

**Casbah Tea House
628 North Fourth Avenue; 520-740-0393
Web site: www.casbahteahouse.com
Hours: Daily 11 am to 11 pm
Fully Vegetarian International, Middle Eastern, American. Mostly Vegan. Organic. Good buffet. Middle Eastern tea-house.
Menu: Has a wide selection of vegetarian and vegan dishes. Tempeh Burgers, Seitan Cheese Steak Sandwich, Seitan with Brown Basmati Rice & Cashew Gravy and Gypsy Stew (vegetable, red lentil, coconut curry). Has a daily special. Vegan cakes.
Comments: Excellent décor. Low hand-carved Afghani chairs. Egyptian tent, pillows and brass trays.
Other Info: Full service, take-out, catering. Non-smoking. Reservations recommended. Accepts MC, VISA. Price: $-$$.
Directions: Two blocks south of University, near 4th Street. Behind Creative Spirit Gallery. From I-10, take Exit #258 towards Congress St/Broadway, then go east on W Congress St a third-mile, then at W Broadway Blvd make a slight right and go a half-mile east, then at S 4th Ave turn left and go 1 block, then at E Broadway Blvd turn slight left and go 1 block, then at N 4th Ave turn right and this place is a half-mile down.

Delectables
533 North 4th Avenue; 520-884-9289
Web site: http://www.brainlink.com/~delectab
Hours: Sunday to Thursday 11 am to 9 pm
Friday & Saturday 11 am to 11 pm

Gourmet Food. Vegan friendly. Not pure veg.
Menu: Tabbouleh Salad, Green Garden Salad, Fresh Fruit Platter, Avocado Swiss Sandwich, basmati rice, hummus, artichoke hearts, Greek Salad, fresh fruit and Marinated Artichoke Hearts.
Comments: Has discount coupons on their site.
Other Info: Full service, take-out. Accepts AMEX, DC, DIS, MC, VISA. Price: $$.
Directions: From I-10, take Exit #258 towards Congress St/Broadway, then go east on W Congress St a third-mile, then at W Broadway Blvd make a slight right and go a half-mile east, then at S 4th Ave turn left and go 1 block, then at E Broadway Blvd turn slight left and go 1 block, then at N 4th Ave turn right and this place is a 4/10 mile down.

Food Conspiracy Co-op

412 North 4th Avenue, near the Univ of Arizona
520-624-4821; **fax:** 520-792-2703
email: natural@foodconspiracy.org
Web site: www.foodconspiracy.org
Hours: Monday to Saturday 9 am to 8 pm
Sunday 9 am to 7 pm
Natural Food Store and Deli. Organic produce.
Menu: Has deli items in the cooler.
Comments: Pleasant atmosphere. Arranges cooking classes. Large bulk section (over 600 items). Has a good selection of items.
Directions: From I-10, take Exit #258 towards Congress St/Broadway, then go east on W Congress St a third-mile, then at W Broadway Blvd make a slight right and go a half-mile east, then at S 4th Ave turn left and go 1 block, then at E Broadway Blvd turn slight left and go 1 block, then at N 4th Ave turn right and this place is a third-mile down.

Garland

119 East Speedway Boulevard; 520-792-4221
Hours: Daily 8 am to 10 pm
Southwestern, American and International Restaurant. Mainly vegetarian. Not pure vegetarian.
Menu: About 50% of the menu is vegetarian. Soups, salads, sandwiches and appetizers. Steamed Vegetables with Brown Rice, Veggie Fried Rice with Baked Tofu, Spinach Lasagna, Eggplant Parmesan with Baked Tofu, Veggie Sauté, pastas, Grilled Cheese Sandwiches, Enchiladas, Cheese and Beans Burritos, and Mushroom Sauté.
Other Info: Full service, take-out. Accepts AMEX, DIS, MC, VISA. Price: $$.
Directions: From I-10, take Exit #257 towards Speedway Blvd/U of Arizona and then get east on W Speedway Blvd and this place is 1 mile down.

**Govinda's

711 East Blacklidge Drive, between Glenn & Ft Lowell, in north Tucson; 520-792-0630
Hours: Tuesday (Indian Night) 5 pm to 9 pm Wednesday to Saturday 11:30 am to 2:30 pm, 5 to 9 pm; closed Sunday to Monday.
Fully Vegetarian International and Indian. Salad Bar. Mostly Vegan. Mostly organic.
Special Nights: Tuesday nights are East Indian nights. Wednesday is wheat-free night. Thursday is all vegan. On Sunday there is an eight-course meal for $3. On this night there is chanting, dancing and a brief Bhagavad-gita class.
Menu: The menu changes daily. Eggplant Medallions with Cashew Paté, sandwiches, mock meat dishes, Spinach Filo, Spinach Lasagna, Taco Salad, samosas, Veggie Burgers, steamed vegetables, dal, vegetable soups, salads, rice dishes and breads. Fresh juices. Buffet bar has two soups, two rice dishes, two vegetable dishes and bread.
Comments: Outdoor dining on beautiful patio with fountains, a garden, exotic birds, a small pond and waterfall. Spiritual, peaceful atmosphere. Excellent vegetarian buffet. Excellent restaurant. Well-managed, friendly place. "Govindas' may be the most unique eatery in Tucson." USA Today
Other Info: Cafeteria-style, take-out, catering. Non-smoking. Accepts reservations but not necessary. Accepts MC, VISA. Price: $9 for Lunch buffet, $10 for Dinner Buffet.
Directions: East off 1st Avenue, two blocks south of Ft Lowell. From I-10, take exit #255 towards Rte 77/Miracle Mile, then get on W Miracle Mile Strip (Rte 77 N) and go east 1½ mile, then continue straight east onto W Blacklidge Dr and this place is 1 mile down.

Health Hut

2561 East Fort Lowell Road; 520-327-4116
Natural Food Store. Very limited organic produce.

La Indita

622 North 4th Avenue, between 4th & 5th Street, near the university; 520-792-0523
Hours: Monday to Friday 11 am to 9 pm; Saturday 6 pm to 9 pm; Sunday 9 am to 9 pm
Mexican and Indian. Vegetarian friendly. Vegan options. Not pure vegetarian.
Menu: Vegetarian dishes are marked on the menu. Walnut-Spinach Enchiladas and vegetarian tamales. The Indian fried bread is popular. Fresh juices.
Comments: Has outdoor patio dining. Run by Maria Carcia, a Tarasean Indian from Michoacan, Mexico, and some of the dishes are her own reci-

pes. Does not use lard in cooking.

Other Info: Full service, take-out. Accepts AMEX, MC, VISA. Price: $.

Directions: From I-10, take Exit #258 towards Congress St/Broadway, then go east on W Congress St a third-mile, then at W Broadway Blvd make a slight right and go a half-mile east, then at S 4th Ave turn left and go 1 block, then at E Broadway Blvd turn slight left and go 1 block, then at N 4th Ave turn right and this place is a half-mile down.

Magpies (three locations)

4654 East Speedway	528-795-5977
603 North 4th Avenue	528-628-1661
7315 North Oracle	528-297-2712

Italian, Pizza. Vegan friendly.

Menu: Whole-wheat crusts with herbs mixed in. Vegan pizzas.

Maya Quetzal

429 North 4th Avenue, near the university
520-622-8207

Hours: Monday to Thursday 11 am to 2 pm, 5 pm to 9 pm; Friday & Saturday 11 am to 9 pm; closed Sunday.

Guatemalan. Not pure vegetarian.

Menu: Has several vegetarian main dishes. Guatemalan Black Beans, Stuffed Masa, rice and salads. Tamales with spinach, rice, corn and red pepper sauce. Vegetarian Taquitos (potatoes, carrots, cheese and salsa). Plato Vegetariano is a corn meso stuffed with spinach or walnuts with baked rice, corn and cheese.

Comments: Good service. Unique food.

Other Info: Full service, take-out, catering. Accepts MC, VISA. Price: $-$$.

Directions: See directions above for 4th Avenue.

New Delhi Palace

6751 East Broadway Boulevard; 520-296-8585

Hours: Daily 5 pm to 10 pm

North Indian. Daily Lunch Buffet. Vegan options. Not pure vegetarian.

Menu: Has a page of vegetarian main dishes on the menu. Fresh juices.

Other Info: Full service. Accepts AMEX, MC, VISA. Price: $$.

New Life Health Food Center

4841 East Speedway Boulevard; 520-795-7862

Hours: Monday to Friday 8 am to 8 pm; Saturday 8 am to 7 pm; Sunday 9 am to 6 pm

Natural Food Store. Organic produce.

Menu: Has ready-made sandwiches and salads.

Directions: From I-10, take Exit #257 towards Speedway Blvd/U of Arizona and then go east on W Speedway Blvd 5½ miles.

New Life Health Center

1745 West Ajo Way, Tucson; 520-294-4926

Hours: Monday to Friday 8 am to 6 pm; Saturday 8 am to 5 pm; Sunday 9 am to 4:30 pm

Natural Food Store. Organic produce.

Menu: Has ready-made sandwiches and salads.

New Life Health Center

4012 North Oracle Road; 520-888-4830

Hours: Monday to Saturday 8 am to 7 pm Sunday 8 am to 5 pm

Natural Food Store.

New Life Health Center

5612 East Broadway Boulevard; 520-747-0209

Hours: Monday to Friday 9 am to 7:30 pm; Saturday 9 am to 7 pm; Sunday 9 am to 5 pm

Natural Food Store.

Directions: Two blocks south of University, near 4th Street. Behind Creative Spirit Gallery. From I-10, take Exit #258 towards Congress St/Broadway, then go east on W Congress St a third-mile, then at W Broadway Blvd make a slight right and this place is on Broadway.

The Oasis Vegetarian Experience

216 East Congress; 520-884-1616

Hours Monday to Thursday 11 am to 8 pm; Friday & Saturday 11 am to 9 pm; closed Sunday.

Mainly Vegan. Has milk and cheese in some dishes.

Menu: Soups, salads and sandwiches. Specialty is the Hemp Burger (with hemp seeds).

Comments: Hippie, pleasant atmosphere. Small, cozy place. Sometimes has live bands on Saturday evenings. New restaurant. No alcohol.

Other Info: No credit cards; cash only. Price: $.

Trader Joe's

7133 Oracle Road; 520-297-5394; **fax:** 520-742-1761

Tucson Community Market

350 South Toole Avenue; 520-622-3911

Hours: Monday to Saturday 8 am to 7 pm Sunday 11 am to 6 pm

Natural Food Store.

Comments: Division of Tucson Cooperative Warehouse.

Directions: Located between 22nd and Broadway.

Wild Oats (three locations)
3360 East Speedway Boulevard; 520-795-9844;
fax: 520-795-8567 (seats 30)
Hours: Daily 7 am to 10 pm
Directions: From I-10, take Speedway exit (#257)
and go east 3 miles. This place is about a block
past Tucson Blvd on the right in a strip mall.
7133 N Oracle Road
520-297-5394 (has only around 10 seats)
Hours: Daily 7 am to 9 pm
Directions: From I-10, take Ina Rd exit (#248).
Then go east on E Ina Rd for 3½ miles, then at
Oracle Rd turn right and this place is half way
down the block.

4751 E Sunrise Drive
520-299-8858; fax: 520-299-0130 (seats 40)
Hours: Daily 7 am to 10 pm
Directions: From I-10, take Ina Rd exit (#248)
and then to east on Ina Rd for 7 miles. Then it
becomes E Skyline Dr for 2 miles, then it becomes Sunrise Dr and then this place is two more
miles down on the right.
Hours: Daily 7 am to 10 pm
Natural Food Store and Cafe. Deli, Bakery,
Salad Bar and Juice Bar. Organic produce. Supermarket-type place. See Wild Oats Market
information.
Comments: Has seating.

Arkansas

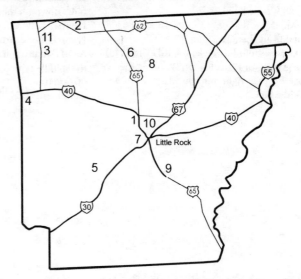

1. Conway
2. Eureka Springs
3. Fayetteville
4. Fort Smith
5. Hot Springs
6. Leslie
7. Little Rock
8. Mountainview
9. Pine Bluff
10. Sherwood
11. Springdale

CONWAY

Los Amigos
2850 Prince Street
501-329-7919
Hours: Sunday to Thursday 11 am to 9 pm; Friday 11 am to 10 pm; Saturday 11 am to 9:30 pm
Mexican. Not pure vegetarian.
Menu: Has several vegetarian Mexican dishes.
Other Info: Accepts AMEX, DIS, MC, VISA.
Price: $.

EUREKA SPRINGS

Horizon Restaurant
On County Road 187, just outside Eureka Springs
501-253-5525
Hours: Thursday to Saturday 5 pm to 9 pm; Sunday 10 am to 2 pm; closed Monday.
Restaurant. Not pure vegetarian.
Menu: Grassy Knob Vegetarian Delight sandwich is roasted red peppers, marinated artichoke hearts, sprouts and sun-dried tomatoes.

FAYETTEVILLE
This is a beautiful area in the Ozarks. This was the first place that Bill & Hillary Clinton lived after getting married.

Ozark Cooperative Warehouse
205 West Dickson Street, Box 1528; 501-521-7558 521-(COOP); **email:** info@ozarkcoop.com
Web site: www.ozarkcoop.com
Hours: Monday to Saturday 9 am to 8 pm
Sunday 10 am to 6 pm
Natural Food Store and Deli. Juice Bar. Organic produce.
Menu: Has a good selection of vegetarian and vegan options and daily hot specials.
Comments: Has a large selection of organic produce. Has a nutritional consultant and naturopathic doctor. This is the only coop in Arkansas. Web Site and great mail order site. It is definitely worth checking out their web site. Their mail order has bulk goods and many books in reference to vegetarian cooking.
Directions: From Business Route 71, go west on Dickson St a half-mile and this store is on the left.

The Village Epicureans
440 Mission
501-444-0010
Hours: Tuesday to Friday 11 am to 2:30 pm; Wednesday & Thursday 5:30 pm to 9 pm; Friday & Saturday 5:30 pm to 10 pm
International Vegetarian Natural Foods. Vegan

and Macrobiotic options. Mostly organic.

Menu: Soups, sandwiches, salads and fresh juices. The Moroccan Couscous and Nori Rolls (vegan sushi) are good.

Comments: Organic produce is used when possible. Friendly place. Mostly organic. Everything freshly made.

Other Info: Counter service, take-out, catering. Non-smoking. Accepts MC, VISA. Price: $.

Directions: From Bus Rte 71, go east on E Maple St a half-mile (5 blocks), then turn left onto Rte 45, and this place is one block down.

FORT SMITH

Olde Fashioned Foods
123 North 18th Street; 501-782-6183
Hours: Monday to Saturday 9 am to 6 pm
Closed Sundays.
Natural Food Store. Has some organic produce.
Direction: From I-540, take Exit #8 (#8A) (Rte 22 W) Rogers Ave exit, then go northwest on Rogers Ave for 3.25 miles. At 18th St turn right and this store is a yellow house a half block down on the left.

Old Fashioned National Foods Market
4900 Towson Avenue
501-649-8200
Hours: Monday to Saturday 9 am to 6 pm
Closed Sunday.
Natural Food Store. Has a good selection of organic produce.
Other Info: Accepts AMEX, MC, VISA.
Direction: From I-40, take Phoenix Ave exit (#10). Go west on Phoenix, at Towson Ave (Bus-71) turn left and this place is two block down at the corner of Phoenix Village Square (on the left in the back) and is hard to see from the street.

HOT SPRINGS

The Old Country Store
455 Broadway; 501-624-1172
Hours: Monday to Friday 9 am to 5:30 pm
Closed Saturday & Sunday.
Natural Food Store and Deli. Juice Bar. Organic produce.
Menu: Has many sandwiches and a Taco Bean Salad.
Comment: Makes own alfalfa sprouts. Friendly people.
Other Info: Accepts DIS, MC, VISA.
Directions: From Hwy 70, drive one block west (north) of Broadway and this place is on the right.

LESLIE

The Ozark Heritage Art Center is here.

Cove Creek Exchange
421 Main Street
870-447-2724
Hours: Monday to Friday 9 am to 5 pm; Saturday 10 am to 4 pm; closed Sundays.
Natural Food Store. Some organic produce.
Directions: From Hwy 65, turn east onto Oak. At Main turn left and the store is on the left in the middle of the downtown.

LITTLE ROCK

El Portion
12111 West Markham Street; 501-223-8588
Hours: Monday to Friday 11 am to 10 pm
Mexican. Has several vegetarian dishes. Uses 100% vegetable oil for cooking.
Other Info: Accepts AMEX, MC, VISA. Price: $.

Star of India
301 North Shackleford, C-4; 501-227-9900
Hours: Monday to Thursday 11:30 am to 3 pm, 5:30 pm to 10 pm
Saturday & Sunday 11:30 am to 3 pm, 5:30 pm to 10:30 pm
Indian Café. All-you-can-eat buffet.
Price: $$.
Comments: Has many vegetarian dishes and several vegan dishes. Reasonable prices.

Wild Oats
Village Shopping Center
10700 North Rodney Parham, Bldg 10
501-312-2326; **Web site:** www.wildoats.com
Hours: Daily 8 am to 9 pm
Natural Food Store and Café. Deli and Juice Bar. Organic produce.
Comments: Has automatic shopping carts for the handicapped.
Directions: From I-430, take Rodney Parham Rd (#8) exit. Go north (west) on Rodney Parham Rd and this place is a quarter-mile down on the right in the Village Shopping Center. This place is behind Chili's.

MOUNTAINVIEW

Stone Ground Natural Foods
Hwy 5, 9 & 14, Mountainview
870-269-8164
Natural Food Store. No produce.

PINE BLUFF

Sweet Clover Health Foods
Old Village Shopping Center
2624 West 28th Street
870-536-0107
Hours: Monday to Friday 10 am to 5 pm; Saturday 10 am to 4 pm; closed Sunday.
Natural Food Store. No produce.
Directions: From I-65, take Exit #35 for Pine Bluff/Dumas. Get on the south I-65 Spur and go about 3 miles, then take Bus-65 exit and go northeast on Bus-65, then make a slight right onto W 28th Ave and this place is a mile down in Old Village Shopping Center behind a bank.

SHERWOOD

Ann's Health Food Store
9800 Highway 107
501-835-6415
Hours: Monday to Friday 8:30 am to 6 pm
Closed Saturday & Sunday.
Natural Food Store. Has a limited amount of organic produce.
Directions: From I-630, take Kiehl exit. Get on Kiehl and at second traffic light (a half-mile down) turn right onto Hwy 107. This place is 2.5 miles down on the right.

SPRINGDALE

Mary's Natural Foods
220 South Thompson
501-751-4224
Hours: Monday to Saturday 9 am to 5:30 pm
Closed Sunday.
Natural Food Store. Organic carrots only.
Directions: From 1-71, take the exit for Rte 412 and then go east on Rte 412 about 2.5 miles, at Business 71, turn left (go north) and this place is a mile down on the left. Business 71 becomes Thompson.

Squash Blossom
5005 Dora Road
501-474-1147
Hours: Monday to Friday 9 am to 6 pm; Saturday 9 am to 5 pm; closed Sundays.
Natural Food Store and basic Deli.
Menu: Has cheese and vegetable sandwiches. Doesn't have much else. No juice bar.
Directions: From I-40 west, take the Dora/Forsmith exit and get on Dora Rd. This store is then about a mile down on the left. From I-40 coming east, take Dora/Ft Smith exit (#330). Make a left at Dora Rd, cross interstate and the store is on the right a quarter-mile down.

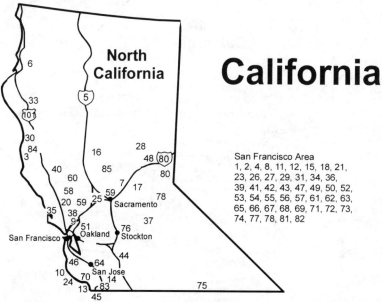

California

North California

San Francisco Area
1, 2, 4, 8, 11, 12, 15, 18, 21,
23, 26, 27, 29, 31, 34, 36,
39, 41, 42, 43, 47, 49, 50, 52,
53, 54, 55, 56, 57, 61, 62, 63,
65, 66, 67, 68, 69, 71, 72, 73,
74, 77, 78, 81, 82

1. Alamo
2. Albany
3. Albion
4. Angwin
5. Aptos
6. Arcata
7. Auburn
8. Benicia
9. Berkeley
10. Boulder Creek
11. Burlingame
12. Campbell
13. Capitola
14. Carmel
15. Castro Valley
16. Chico
17. Citrus Heights
18. Concord
19. Corte Madera
20. Cotati
21. Cupertino
22. Daly City
23. Danville
24. Davenport
25. Davis
26. El Cerrito
27. Emeryville
28. Eureka
29. Fairfax

30. Fort Bragg
31. Foster City
32. Fremont
33. Grass Valley
34. Greenbrae
35. Guerneville
36. Half Moon Bay
37. Jackson
38. Los Gatos
39. Menlo Park
40. Middletown
41. Mill Valley
42. Milbrae
43. Milpitas
44. Modesto
45. Monterey
46. Mountain View
47. Napa
48. Nevada City
49. Newark
50. Novato
51. Oakland
52. Pacifica
53. Palo Alto
54. Petaluma
55. Pleasant Hill
56. Redwood City
57. Richmond

58. Roseville
59. Sacramento
60. Saint Helena
61. San Anselmo
62. San Bruno
63. San Carlos
64. San Jose
65. San Leandro
66. San Mateo
67. San Rafael
68. San Ramon
69. Santa Clara
70. Santa Cruz
71. Santa Rosa
72. Sausalito
73. Sebastopol
74. Sonoma
75. Squaw Valley
76. Stockton
77. Suisun
78. Sunnyvale
79. Tahoe City
80. Truckee
81. Vacaville
82. Walnut Creek
83. Watsonville
84. Willits
85. Yuba City

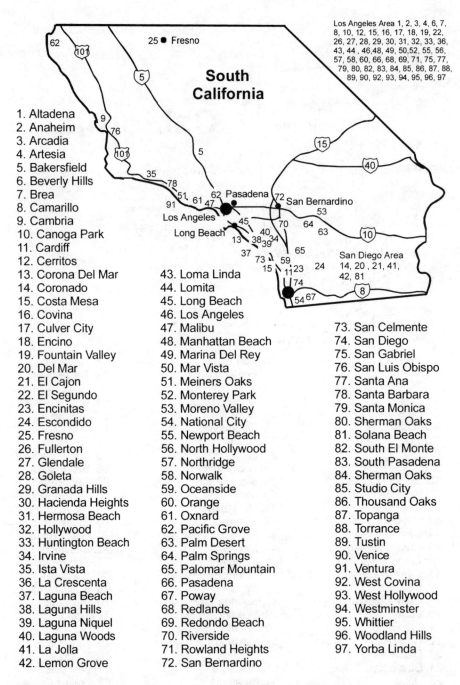

Los Angeles Area 1, 2, 3, 4, 6, 7,
8, 10, 12, 15, 16, 17, 18, 19, 22,
26, 27, 28, 29, 30, 31, 32, 33, 36,
43, 44 , 46,48, 49, 50,52, 55, 56,
57, 58, 60, 66, 68, 69, 71, 75, 77,
79, 80, 82, 83, 84, 85, 86, 87, 88,
89, 90, 92, 93, 94, 95, 96, 97

South California

San Diego Area
14, 20 , 21, 41,
42, 81

1. Altadena
2. Anaheim
3. Arcadia
4. Artesia
5. Bakersfield
6. Beverly Hills
7. Brea
8. Camarillo
9. Cambria
10. Canoga Park
11. Cardiff
12. Cerritos
13. Corona Del Mar
14. Coronado
15. Costa Mesa
16. Covina
17. Culver City
18. Encino
19. Fountain Valley
20. Del Mar
21. El Cajon
22. El Segundo
23. Encinitas
24. Escondido
25. Fresno
26. Fullerton
27. Glendale
28. Goleta
29. Granada Hills
30. Hacienda Heights
31. Hermosa Beach
32. Hollywood
33. Huntington Beach
34. Irvine
35. Ista Vista
36. La Crescenta
37. Laguna Beach
38. Laguna Hills
39. Laguna Niquel
40. Laguna Woods
41. La Jolla
42. Lemon Grove

43. Loma Linda
44. Lomita
45. Long Beach
46. Los Angeles
47. Malibu
48. Manhattan Beach
49. Marina Del Rey
50. Mar Vista
51. Meiners Oaks
52. Monterey Park
53. Moreno Valley
54. National City
55. Newport Beach
56. North Hollywood
57. Northridge
58. Norwalk
59. Oceanside
60. Orange
61. Oxnard
62. Pacific Grove
63. Palm Desert
64. Palm Springs
65. Palomar Mountain
66. Pasadena
67. Poway
68. Redlands
69. Redondo Beach
70. Riverside
71. Rowland Heights
72. San Bernardino

73. San Celmente
74. San Diego
75. San Gabriel
76. San Luis Obispo
77. Santa Ana
78. Santa Barbara
79. Santa Monica
80. Sherman Oaks
81. Solana Beach
82. South El Monte
83. South Pasadena
84. Sherman Oaks
85. Studio City
86. Thousand Oaks
87. Topanga
88. Torrance
89. Tustin
90. Venice
91. Ventura
92. West Covina
93. West Hollywood
94. Westminster
95. Whittier
96. Woodland Hills
97. Yorba Linda

ALAMO (Contra Costa County)

Natural Temptations
Alamo Square Shopping
Next door to Safeway
925-820-0606
Hours: Monday to Friday 10 am to 6 pm
Saturday 10 am to 6 pm
Natural Food Store. Organic produce. No deli.
Has freshly-made pre-made sandwiches and
burritos. Knowledgeable staff.
Directions: From Hwy 680, take Stone Valley
Rd west, then at Danville Blvd turn right and
this place on left next to Safeway.

ALBION (Mendocino Country)

The Ledford House
3000 North Highway 1
707-937-0282;
Web site: www.ledfordhouse.com
Restaurant. Not pure vegetarian.
Menu: Salads, bread, a vegetarian soup and often a vegetarian main dish.
Comments: Has an ocean view.

ANGWIN (Napa County)

Angwin Community Market
Angwin Plaza; 707-965-6321
Hours: Sunday to Thursday 8 am to 7:30 pm; Friday 9 am to 5 pm; closed Saturday.
Natural Food Store and Vegan-friendly Deli. No meat products.
Comments: Run by the Seventh Day Adventist Church.
Directions: From Hwy 29 going north, at Deer Park turn right towards Pacific Union College and this place is at the top of hill on Pacific Union College campus.

ARCATA
Humboldt State University is here.

Arcata Co-op and Spoons Take-Out Kitchen
811 "I" Street, downtown; 707-822-5947
Hours: Daily 10 am to 6 pm
Natural Food Store and Deli. Vegan options. Not pure vegetarian.
Menu: Salads, International dishes and other vegetarian dishes. Uses organic grown produce when possible. Fresh juices.
Comments: Spoons Take-Out Kitchen is in the Arcata Co-op.
Other Info: Deli style, take-out. Price: $. Accepts MC, VISA.
Directions: From Hwy 101, take Samoa Blvd exit and then go west on Samoa Blvd about 4 blocks. At "I" St turn right and this place is 4 blocks down on the left.

Daybreak Café
768 18th Street, at "G" Street; 707-826-7543
Hours: Sunday to Thursday 7 am to 3 pm; Friday and Saturday 7 am to 9 pm; closed Sunday.
Natural Foods. Vegan options. Not pure vegetarian.
Menu: Has a large selection of vegetarian dishes. Uses locally grown organic produce when possible. Full service, take-out. Organic cappuccino, espresso.
Comments: Displays art from local artists.
Other Info: Full service, take-out, catering. Accepts credit cards. Price: $.
Directions: From Hwy 101, take Sunset Ave exit and then go west on Sunset Ave 1 block, then turn left onto H St and this place is a third-mile down at corner of 18th St.

**Wildflower Café & Bakery
1604 G Street; 707-822-0360
Hours: Daily 11 am to 9 pm
Sunday Brunch 10 am to 2 pm
Vegetarian. Vegan options.
Menu: Has gourmet vegetarian and macrobiotic foods. Curry vegetables, salads, soups, Mushroom Stroganoff, sandwiches and other vegetarian dishes. Has freshly baked breads and desserts. Fresh juices.
Comments: Gets good recommendations. Uses organic grown produce when possible.
Other Info: Full service, take-out, catering. No credit cards. Price: $.
Directions: From Hwy 101, take 14th St exit towards Humboldt State Univ, then go west on 14th St 1 block, then turn right onto G St and this place is 2 blocks down.

AUBURN (Sacramento area)

Latitudes
130 Maple St #11; 530-885-9535
Hours: Wednesday to Saturday 11:30 am to 3 pm, 5 pm to 9 pm (Friday & Saturday until 10 pm); Sunday 10 am to 3 pm, 5 pm to 9 pm; Closed Monday & Tuesday.
Natural Foods. Vegan options. Mainly vegetarian (some meat dishes).
Menu: Has a large selection of vegetarian dishes. Fresh juices.
Comments: Has indoors and outdoors seating. Tropical décor. Has monthly themes (Thai, etc)
Other Info: Full service, take-out, catering. Accepts AMEX, DC, MC, VISA. Reservations suggested on Friday & Saturday nights. Price: Brunch and Lunch: $$. Dinner: $$$.
Directions: Downtown, across from the Courthouse.

BAKERSFIELD

Cone's Health Foods
1002 Wible Street; 661-832-5669
Hours: Monday to Friday 9 am to 8 pm; Saturday 10 am to 8 pm; Sunday 11 am to 6 pm
Natural Food Store.

Directions: From CA Hwy 99, take Ming Ave exit, then go east on Ming Ave 1 block, then at Wible Rd turn left (go north) and this place is a third-mile down.

BOULDER CREEK

**Blue Sun
13070 Highway 9; 831-338-2105
Hours: Daily 6 am to 2:30 pm
Vegetarian. Mainly vegan.
Menu: Vegan fruit turnovers, muffins, Tofu Scramble, salads, soups and Grilled Cheese Sandwiches. Excellent coffee.
Comments: There is a good view of the town from the restaurant. This is a good place.
Other Info: Counter service, take-out. Order at counter and food is brought to you. Cash or checks only; no credit cards. Price: $.
Directions: Boulder Creek is in the Santa Cruz Mountains. This place is south of the downtown.

New Leaf Market
13159 Highway 9; 831-338-7211
Natural Food Store and Deli. Organic produce.
Menu: Has a good selection of vegetarian dishes.
Other Info: Counter service, take-out.
Directions: This place is south of the downtown.

CAMARILLO

Lassen's Health Foods
2207 Pickwick Drive; 805-482-3287
Hours: Monday to Saturday 9 am to 6:30 pm Closed Sunday.
Natural Food Store and Café. Deli.
Directions: From Hwy 101 south, take Lewis Rd exit, at Daily Drive turn left, then at Arneill Rd turn right and go a half-mile, at Pickwick turn left and this place is halfway down the block. From Hwy 101 north, take Carmen Rd exit, at Ventura Blvd turn left, at Arneill Rd turn left and go a half-mile, at Pickwick turn left and store on right.

CAMBRIA
Many artist stay here. It is a vegetarian friendly town.

Robin's
4095 Burton Drive, at Main St; 805-927-5007
Hours: Daily 11 am to 9 pm
International Restaurant. Vegan options. Not pure vegetarian.
Menu: Has several vegetarian options including stir-fry, sandwiches and salads. Pasta had eggs in it.

Comments: Can eat here after visiting Hearst Castle. Very casual, relaxed type place. Excellent service. Has indoor and outdoor seating.
Other Info: Full service, take-out. Accepts MC, VISA. Price: $$-$$$.

CAPITOLA

**Dharma's Natural Foods Restaurant
4250 Capitola Road, just east of Santa Cruz
831-462-1717; **Web site:** www.dharmaland.com
Hours: Daily 8 am to 9 pm
Fully Vegetarian International. American, Thai, Italian, Mexican, Indonesian, Japanese, Chinese. Mostly Vegan.
Menu: Soups, salads and rice dishes are reasonably priced. Lasagna, Vegetable Turnover (no margarine crust, but vegan), Ruben sandwich (tempeh and sour cabbage) and non-dairy shakes. The Brahma Burger is made of grains and soy (cheese can be added). Vegetable Turnover is vegetables in a whole-wheat pastry covered with mushroom cashew gravy.
Comments: Most of the food is organic.
Other Info: Counter service, take-out. Non-smoking. Does not take reservations. No credit cards. Price: $.
Directions: This place is a few blocks east of Capitola Mall. From Highway 1, take the 41st Ave exit, then go south on 41st Ave for ¾ mile, then turn left, and this place is 1½ block down on the right. There is a parking lot in front.

New Leaf Community Market
Begonia Plaza, 1210 41st Avenue
408-479-7987; **Web site:** www.newleaf.com
Store Hours: Daily 8 am to 9 pm
Café Hours: Daily 7 am to 9 pm
Natural Food Store and Café. Deli, Bakery and Juice Bar. Organic produce.
Menu: Has a good selection of vegetarian dishes.
Comments: Friendly place.
Other Info: Accepts AMEX, DIS, MC, VISA.
Directions: From Hwy 1, take 41st Avenue exit and go south and this place is 1 mile down on the left in the Begonia Plaza.

CARDIFF

Ki's Restaurant
2591 South Coast Highway 101, Cardiff
760-436-5236; **Catering:** 760-434-5544
Web site: www.kisrestarant.com
Hours: Sunday to Thursday 8 am to 9 pm; Friday & Saturday 8 am to 9:30 pm
American. Mostly Vegetarian. Vegan options.

Menu: Breakfast Burrito, Tofu Scramble, granola, hot organic oats, veggie stew, salads, spinach salad, veggie burger, Roasted Tofu, Marinated Tempeh, Grilled Veggie Sandwich, Tofu Burrito, Basil Pasta, Veggie Lasagna, Stir-fry Vegetables, Roast Tofu Skewers, homemade soups, Squash Enchilada, Broccoli Penne and Stuffed Roasted Eggplant. Plenty of fresh juices.

Comments: On the beach in Cardiff with an ocean view. Local organic produce used when possible. Casual. Has entertainment on the weekends. Has a kid's menu. Gets highly recommended.

Other Info: Full service, take-out, catering. Accepts AMEX, MC, VISA.

Directions: From I-5, take the Lomas Santa Fe Drive exit, then go west 1 miles, then turn north onto Hwy 101 and this place is 1½ mile down. It is located in the middle of the restaurant area.

CARMEL

Cornucopia Community Market
Carmel Rancho Shopping Center
26135 Carmel Rancho Blvd, at Carmel Valley Road; 831-625-1454
Hours: Daily 9 am to 7 pm
Natural Food Store and Deli. Organic produce.
Menu: Soups, sandwiches, salads and hot dishes.
Comments: The deli gets good recommendation. Well-designed store according to Feng Shui principles. One of the best natural food stores in the country.
Other Info: Counter service, take-out.
Directions: From Hwy 1, take Carmel Valley Rd exit and go east a quarter-mile. At Carmel Ranch Blvd turn left and this place is 1 block down on left in Carmel Rancho Shopping Center.

Power Juice Company
Crossroads Shopping Center, 173 The Crossroads
831-626-6577
Hours: Monday to Friday 8 am to 7 pm; Saturday 9 am to 7 pm; Sunday 10 am to 5 pm
Juice and Sandwich Bar.
Menu: A good selection of juices. Has baked potatoes and soups. Local organic produce used when possible.

CHICO
Located here is California State University of Chico.

Chico Natural Foods
818 Main Street, at 8th; 530-891-1713
Hours: Monday to Saturday 8 am to 9 pm

Sunday 10 am to 6 pm
Natural Food Store and Vegetarian take-out Deli. Organic produce.
Menu: Soups (only thing that is hot), salads and sandwiches.
Comments: Bulk foods, whole grains, etc.
Other Info: Accepts AMEX, MC, VISA.
Directions: From Hwy 99, take Hwy 32 exit, then go west on Hwy 32 (8th St) and this place is 1 mile down on the left at junction of Main St and 8th.

**Shade Tree
817 Main Street; 530-894-6515
Hours: Monday to Saturday 11 am to 9 pm; Saturday Brunch 10 am to 2 pm; closed Sunday.
Vegetarian International and Mexican. Vegan options. Organic.
Menu: Has a good selection of vegetarian dishes. Has the "Today's Tamales," black bean burrito, soups, Tequila Tempeh, Spicy Tofu, basmati rice, Tostadas, South African Stir-fry, quesadillas, Sundried Tomato Pesto Fettuccini, salads and hibiscus punch. Fresh juices, organic coffee.
Comments: Good food. Pleasant atmosphere. Uses organic grown produce when possible. Uses unrefined olive and canola oils.
Other Info: Full service, take-out. Accepts AMEX, DIS, MC, VISA. Price: $-$$.
Directions: Located on the edge of the downtown. From Hwy 99, take Hwy 32 exit, then go west on Hwy 32 (8th St) for 1 mile, then at Main St turn left and this place is a little down the block.

S&S Organic Produce & Natural Foods
1924 Mangrove Road; 530-343-4930
Hours: Monday to Saturday 6 am to 9 pm
Sunday 8 am to 8 pm
Natural Food Store. Organic produce.

CITRUS HEIGHTS (Sacramento County)

Elliott's Natural Foods No 2
Greenback Square Shopping Center
8063 Greenback Lane
916-726-3033
Web site: www.elliotsnaturalfoods.com
Hours: Monday to Saturday 9:30 am to 6 pm (until 8 pm Thursday); Sunday 11 am to 5 pm
Natural Food Store. Juice Bar.
Comments: Manager has a degree in Oriental Medicine.
Directions: From I-80, take Greenback Lane, then go east on Greenback Lane 4 miles and this place is on the left in Greenback Square Shopping Center.

Fresh Choice
5419 Sunrise Boulevard; 916-863-5680
Hours: Sunday to Thursday 9 am to 9 am
Friday & Saturday 9 am to 10 pm

CORONA DEL MAR

Mayur
2931 East Coast Highway; 949-675-6622
Hours: Sunday to Friday 11 am to 2:30 pm, 5 pm to 10 pm; Saturday 5 pm to 10 pm
Indian. Vegan options. Not pure vegetarian.
Menu: Has several vegetarian dishes including Spinach & Paneer (cheese), dal, eggplant, rice dishes and other options.
Other Info: Full service, take-out. Accepts AMEX, MC, VISA. Price: $$.

CORONADO

Stretch's Coronado Café
943 Orange Avenue; 619-435-8886
Hours: Monday to Friday 7 am to 7 pm; Saturday 7:30 am to 7 pm; Saturday 7:30 am to 6 pm
Restaurant. Vegetarian-friendly. Not pure veg.
Menu: Salads, sandwiches, veggie burgers, pastas and other dishes. Fresh juices and smoothies.
Other Info: Counter service, take-out.

Viva Nova
1138 Orange Avenue; 619-437-2134
Hours: Monday to Friday 9 am to 5 pm; Saturday 10 am to 5 pm; closed Sunday.
Natural Food Store and Deli. Vegan options. Not pure vegetarian. Juice Bar.
Menu: Veggie burgers, soups, enchiladas, quiche, salads, vegetarian chili, baked potatoes, burritos and other dishes. Fresh juices and smoothies.
Comments: Good atmosphere. Friendly place.
Other Info: Limited service, take-out. Price: $.
Directions: From I-5, take Rte 75 exit towards Coronado, then go southwest on Rte 75 for 2 miles, then make a slight right onto Pomona Ave (Rte 282) and go 2 blocks, at 3rd St turn left and go 2 blocks, at Orange Ave turn left and this place is about 1 mile down, a few blocks from the ocean.

DAVENPORT

Davenport Cash Store
On coastal Highway 1; 831-425-1818
Hours: Daily 7:30 am to 9 pm
Restaurant and Bed-and-Breakfast. Has a sea view where you can often see whales.
Menu: Lasagna, salads, veggie Ravioli, pastas, veggie burgers and tofu dishes.

DAVIS

Davis Food Coop
620 G Street, at Sixth Street
530-758-2667; **email:** dwalter@daviscoop.com
Web site: www.daviscoop.com
Hours: Daily 8 am to 10 pm
Natural Food Store and Deli. Supermarket-type place. Coffee Bar and Bakery. Has a large amount of food products and some clothes, cards and gift items.
Menu: The deli has salads, jasmine rice and Thai noodles.
Comments: Charges about 20% off regular natural food store price. Working members get an additional 15% off the price. Seniors over 62 get the same discounts as members. Homeopathic remedies and a large bulk food section. Has over 5,000 customers. Organizes cooking classes and other classes. Lists a schedule on their web site.
Other Info: Accepts AMEX, DIS, MC, VISA.
Directions: From I-80, take Davis/Richards Blvd exit, then go north on Richards Blvd (becomes E St) a half-mile. At 6th St turn right and this place is 2 blocks down on the right, at corner of 6th and G.

Delta of Venus
122 B Street; 530-753-8639
Hours: Monday to Friday 7:30 to 10
Saturday & Sunday 8 am to 2 pm
Coffee House. Mainly vegetarian. Vegan-friendly.
Menu: Soups, salads, sandwiches, Curry Tofu Sandwiches and hot dishes.
Comments: In a converted old house. Pleasant atmosphere. Price: $.
Directions: From I-80, take Davis exit, then go north on Richards Blvd a quarter-mile, turn slight left onto 1st St and go 3 blocks, at B St turn right and this place is 1 block down.

Ding How
Lucky's Shopping Center, 640 Covell Boulevard
530-753-3590
Hours: Monday to Saturday 11:30 am to 2:30 pm, 4:30 pm 9:30 pm; Sun 12 noon to 9:30 pm
Mandarin Chinese. Vegan-friendly. Not pure vegetarian.
Menu: Has a vegetarian menu and a separate cooking area designated for cooking vegetarian food separate from the non-veg dishes.
Comments: Sunday nights are busy.

Pluto's
500 First Street, Davis; 530-758-8676
Hours: Daily 11 am to 10 pm

American. Health food. Not pure vegetarian.
Menu: Large salads, soups, sandwiches, Portobello Mushroom Sandwich, veggie burger, mashed potatoes and baked potatoes. A variety of toppings for the salads including candied walnuts.
Comments: Outdoor dining. Has magazines and books to read. Pleasant, cool atmosphere.
Other Info: Accepts MC, VISA.
Directions: In a little shopping center with the Gap. From I-80, take Davis exit, then go north on Richards Blvd a quarter-mile, turn slight left onto 1st St and this place is 1 block down.

DEL MAR

Jimbo's Naturally
Del Mar Highlands Town Center; 12853 El Camino Real; 858-793-7755
Web site: www.jimbos.com
Store Hours: 9 am to 8 pm
Deli Hours: 11 am to 8 pm
Natural Food Store and Vegan-friendly Cafe. Deli, Bakery, Salad Bar and Juice Bar. Organic produce.
Menu: Has salads, soups, sandwiches and daily specials such as Sea Veggie Stuffed Tofu or Macaroni and Cheese. Some vegetarian sandwiches are avocado and vegetables, Veggie Burger, Baked Tofu & fake Bacon sandwich, Super Sub, Mama's Eggplant sandwich and a cheese sandwich. Vegan desserts. Fresh juices and smoothies.
Comments: Has a large selection of organically grown food products. Very friendly atmosphere. The special is often a meat-based dish.
Other Info: Accepts MC, VISA.
Directions: From I-5, take Del Mar Heights exit and go east. At Camion Real turn right, then turn left into Del Mar Highlands Town Center.

EL CAJON (San Diego County)

Henry's Marketplace
152 N 2nd Street
619-579-8251
Natural Food Store and Deli. Organic produce. Bakery. Supermarket-type place.

EL SEGUNDO

PF Chang's China Bistro
2041 Rosecrans Avenue Ste 120; 310-607-9062
Hours: Sunday to Thursday 11 am to 11 pm Friday & Saturday 11 am to 12 midnight
Chinese and American. Not pure vegetarian. See Los Angeles.

ENCINITAS

Melodia
1002 North Coast (Highway 101)
760-942-8380
email: contact@cefemelodia.com
Web site: www.cafemelodia.com
Hours: Tuesday to Saturday 11 am to 3 pm, 5 pm to 10 pm; Sunday 11 am to 3 pm, 5 pm to 9 pm; closed Monday.
Brazilian. Mostly Vegetarian (some seafood). Vegan options. Not pure vegetarian.
Other Info: Accepts AMEX, MC, VISA.
Directions: From I-5, take Leucadia Blvd exit, then go west on Leucadia Blvd for a half-mile, then turn right at N Coast Hwy 101 and this place is 1½ block down.

Henry's Marketplace
1327 Encinitas Boulevard
760-633-4747 **fax:** 760-633-4748
Hours: Daily 8 am to 9 pm
Natural Food Store and Deli. Organic produce.
Directions: From I-15, take the Encinitas Blvd exit, then go east on Encinitas Blvd and this place is 1¾ mile down.

Roxy Restaurant & Ice Cream
517 First Street (South Coast Hwy)
760-436-5001
Hours: Monday to Saturday 11 am to 10 pm Sunday 11 am to 9 pm
International Natural Foods. Not pure vegetarian.
Menu: Good amount of vegetarian options. Squash enchiladas, veggie burgers, falafel, artitacos (cheddar cheese, black olives & artichoke hearts on a corn tortilla), quesadillas, vegetarian burritos and veggie tortillas. Homemade granola and 100% natural ice cream. The baklava is an eggless dessert. Fresh juices. Has specials.
Comments: Has live bands on Thursday to Sunday nights. Has indoor and outdoor seating in the front
Other Info: Full service, take-out. Accepts AMEX, MC, VISA. Price: $$.
Directions: From I-15, take the Encinitas Blvd exit, then go west on Encinitas Blvd a half-mile, then turn left on South Coast Hwy and this place is a third-mile down.

Siamese Basil
527 South 1st (Coast Highway 101)
760-753-3940
Hours: Daily 11 am to 3 pm, 5 pm to 9 pm
Thai. Vegan options. Not pure vegetarian.

Comments: No MSG. Fresh produce used when possible. Dishes are made to order. Food gets good ratings.
Other Info: Accepts AMEX, MC, VISA.

Swami's Café and Juice Bar
1163 First Street (South Coast Highway)
760-944-0612
Hours: Monday to Friday 7:30 am to 5 pm
Saturday & Sunday 7:30 am to 4 pm
Vegetarian-friendly Café. Juice Bar. Vegan options.
Menu: Burritos, Vegetable Curries, mock "meat" dishes, salad and other dishes. Fresh juices and smoothies.
Other Info: Counter service, catering, take-out. Price: $-$$.
Directions: From I-15, take the Encinitas Blvd exit, then go west on Encinitas Blvd a half-mile, then turn left on South Coast Hwy and this place is 1 mile down.

Trader Joe's
Encinitas Plaza, 115 N El Camino Real
760-634-2114

ESCONDIDO

Henry's (Wild Oats)
510 W 13 Street, at Centre City Parkway
760-745-2141
Hours: Daily 8 am to 9 pm
Natural Food Store and Cafe. Deli, Bakery, Salad Bar and Juice Bar. Organic produce. Supermarket-type place. See Wild Oats Market information.
Comments: Has a large alternative medicine and vitamin section. The prices are very reasonable. Has another branch at Oceanside, CA.
Directions: From CA Hwy 78, take the Centre City Parkway exit, then go south 1½ mile on N Centre City Pkwy, then turn left at W 13th Ave and this place is 50 yards down.

Jimbo's Naturally
1633 South Centre City Parkway
760-489-7755; **Web site:** www.jimbos.com
Store Hours: 8 am to 9 pm
Deli Hours: 9 am to 8 pm
Natural Food Store and Café. Deli, Bakery, Salad Bar and Juice Bar. Organic produce. See Del Mar for details.
Menu: Has salads, soups, sandwiches and daily specials.
Other Info: Accepts AMEX, MC, VISA.
Directions: From I-15, take Felicita exit. If going south turn right, if going north turn left. At stop sign turn right. Store winds and this place behind Sav-On on left. From CA Hwy 78, take the Centre City Parkway exit, then go south 1½ mile on N Centre City Pkwy.

**The Vegetarian Oasis
431 W 13th Avenue, at Centre City Parkway
760-740-9596
Hours: Monday to Friday 7 am to 5:30 pm; Saturday 9:30 pm to 6 pm; closed Sunday.
Vegetarian. Salad Bar. Salad Bar and Juice Bar. Vegan options. Take-out Deli.
Menu: Great salad bar using organic produce. Homemade soups, sandwiches, brown rice, veggie burgers, veggie tamales, burritos, chili and other dishes. Fresh juices and smoothies.
Comments: Local organic produce used when possible.
Other Info: Counter service, take-out, self-serve place. Price: $-$$.
Directions: From CA Hwy 78, take the Centre City Parkway exit, then go south 1½ mile on N Centre City Pkwy.

EUREKA

Eureka Co-op
1036 Fifth Street, at L Street; 707-443-6027
Hours: Monday to Saturday 7 am to 8 pm
Sunday 10 am to 8 pm
Natural Food Store and Deli. Bakery. Organic and local produce. Bulk goods.
Directions: Has a cow on roof and a painting of fruits and vegetables. This place on 5th Street (Hwy 101 north) and L, a block south of the county courthouse.

Eureka Natural Foods
1626 Broadway Street, at Wabash
707-442-6325
Hours: Monday to Friday 8 am to 8 pm; Saturday 9 am to 6 pm; Sunday 10 am to 6 pm
Natural Food Store, Deli and Café. Smoothie Bar. Vegetarian meals. Macrobiotic options. Fairly large place.
Menu: Soups, sandwiches, salads and hot dishes.
Comments: Sit down area. The owner is a vegetarian and is helpful.
Other Info: Limited service. Reservations are required. Price: $$. Accepts MC, VISA.
Directions: On Hwy 101 (becomes Broadway in Eureka) in front of Costco.

**Sunflower Natural Foods Drive In
10344 Fair Oaks Boulevard; 916-967-4331
Hours: Monday 10:30 am to 4 pm; Tuesday to

Saturday 10:30 am to 8 pm; Sun 11 am to 5 pm
Vegetarian Fast Food type place.
Menu: Burritos, nachos, veggie burgers and chili sandwiches. The Nutburger is really good. Everything is made on the premises. Emphasis on raw foods.
Comments: Gets some really good recommendations. Next to a park.
Other Info: Limited service, take-out. Accepts DIS MC, VISA. Price: $.
Directions: From US 50, take the Sunrise Blvd exit towards Fair Oaks, then merge onto Sunrise Blvd and go north 2½ miles, at California Ave turn right and go 1 block, at Fair Oak Blvd turn left and go 2 blocks.

Trader Joe's
Quail Pointe Shopping Center, 5307 Sunrise Blvd
916-863-1744

FELTON (Santa Cruz County)

New Leaf Community Market
6240 Highway 9; 831-335-7322
Hours: Daily 9 am to 9 pm
Natural Food Store and Café. Deli and Juice Bar. Organic produce. Supermarket-type place.
Directions: In downtown Felton. From 17 going north, take Big Basin exit. Go a few miles northwest on Mount Herman Rd. Make a right at Grahman Hill Rd (at light) and go a quarter-mile, then turn left at Hwy 9 (first traffic light) and this store is 1 block down on the left.

FORT BRAGG

Samratt
546 South Main Street; 707-964-0386
Hours: Monday to Saturday 11:30 am to 2:30 pm, 5 pm to 9 pm; Sunday 5 pm to 9 pm
Indian. Vegan options.
Menu: Vegetarian dishes include good curried dishes, lentil dishes and rice dishes.
Comments: Gets really high recommendations. Good service.
Other Info: Full service, take-out. Accepts AMEX, MC, VISA. Price: $$.

Viroporn's Thai Café
500 Chestnut, at Main Street; 707-964-7931
Hours: Mon to Fri 11:30 am to 2:30 pm, 5:30 pm to 8:30 pm; Sat & Sun 5:30 pm to 8:30 pm
Thai. Vegan options. Not pure vegetarian.
Menu: Vegetarian Curry, Spring Rolls, Thai salads, soups, Fried Rice and other dishes. Non-alcoholic beer.

Comments: In a converted streetcar. Popular in the evening.
Other Info: Full service, take-out. Cash or check; no credit cards. Price: $$.

FRESNO (Fresno County)

Christina's
Headline Shopping Center, 761 East Barstow
209-224-2222
Hours: Monday to Friday 9 am to 7 pm; Saturday 9 am to 6 pm; Sunday 11 am to 5 pm
Natural Food Store.
Directions: From Rte 41, take Shaw Ave exit, then go east on Shaw Ave for 1 mile, at 1st turn left and go ¾ mile, then make a left at Barstow Ave and this place is 1 block down in the Headline Shopping Center on the left.

Whole Foods Market
650 West Shaw Avenue; 559-241-0300
Hours: Daily 8 am to 9 pm
Natural Food Store and Cafe. Deli, Bakery, Salad Bar and Juice Bar. Organic produce. Supermarket-type place. See Whole Foods Market information.
Directions: From CA Hwy 41, take Shaw Ave exit and then go west on Shaw Ave and this place is 1½ mile down next to the Fig Garden Shopping Center.

FULLERTON

Chautauqua Natural Foods
436 Church Street; 707-923-2452
Hours: Monday to Saturday 10 am to 6 pm Closed Sunday.
Natural Food Store. Organic produce.
Menu: Has ready-made sandwiches and salads.
Other Info: Accepts AMEX, MC, VISA.
Directions: From 101, take Garberville exit. Get on Redwood Rd and at Church turn right. This place on right a half-block down.

Chin Ting
1939 Sunnycrest Drive; 714-738-1978
Hours: Mon to Fri 11:30 am to 2:30 pm, 5 pm to 9 pm; Sat 4:30 pm to 10 pm; Sun 4:30 pm to 9 pm
Chinese. Vegan options. Not pure vegetarian.
Menu: Has several vegetarian options.
Other Info: Full service, take-out. Accepts AMEX, DIS, MC, VISA. Price: $$.

Rutabegorz
211 N Pomona, near Chapman

714-871-1632
Hours: Monday to Thursday 11 am to 9:30 pm; Friday & Saturday 11 am to 10:30 pm; Sunday 4 pm to 9 pm
International Healthy Food. Vegan options. Not pure vegetarian.
Menu: Spinach Lasagna, sandwiches, stuffed mushrooms, pastas and veggie burritos. A wide variety of coffee. Has some vegetarian soups. Fresh juices.
Comments: Bohemian-style coffeehouse. Egyptian paintings on the walls. Good size portions. Friendly service. Food gets good recommendations.
Other Info: Full service, take-out. Accepts AMEX, DIS, MC, VISA. Price: $$.
Directions: From CA Hwy 91, take the Lemon St exit towards Anaheim Blvd/Harbor Blvd, then go north on S Harbor Blvd for 1 mile, at E Commonwealth Ave turn right and go 1 block, at N Pomona Ave turn left and this place is 1 block down.

Soulplantation
5939 Chapman Avenue; 714-895-1314
Hours: Sunday to Thursday 11 am to 9 pm
Friday & Saturday 11 am to 10 pm
All-you-can-eat Salad Bar with over 50 items. Soups, breads, fruits and more.

GOLETA (Santa Barbara County)

Good Earth
5955 Calle Real; 805-683-6101
Hours: Daily 7:30 am to 9:30
Natural Foods. Not pure vegetarian. Part of a national chain.
Menu: Has soups, salads, Mexican dishes, stir-fries and casseroles.
Other Info: Full service, take-out. Accepts AMEX, DIS, MC, VISA. Price: $$.

Henry's Marketplace
1295 South State Street; 909-766-6746
Hours: Daily 8 am to 8 pm
Natural Food Store and Deli. Organic produce. Supermarket-type place.
Directions: From Hwy 101, take the Carrillo St exit, then go on Carrillo St northeast a half-mile, at State St turn left and this place is a quarter-mile down.

Isla Vista's Food Co-op
6575 Seville Road; 805-968-1401
Hours: Monday to Friday 9 am to 10 pm
Closed Saturday & Sunday

Natural Food Store and Deli.
Directions: This place is a few blocks northeast of Isla Vista County Park and the ocean. From Hwy 101, take CA Rte 217 towards the Airport, then go southwest on Ward Memorial Blvd for 2½ miles, at Mesa Rd turn slight right and go a half-mile, at Ocean Rd turn left and go a half-mile, at El Colegio Rd turn slight right and go a third-mile, at Embarcadero Del Mar turn left and go a third-mile, at Seville Rd turn right and this place is a half-block down.

GRASS VALLEY

Natural Valley Health Foods
11562 Sutton Way; 530-273-6525
Hours: Monday to Saturday 9 am to 6 pm
Closed Sunday.
Natural Food Store.
Comments: This place is over 25 old.
Directions: From I-80, take Hwy 49 exit toward Grass Valley and then take Brunswick exit. This place at corner of Sutton and Brunswick.

JACKSON (Amador County)

Gold Trail Natural Foods
Mother Lode Plaza, 625 South Highway 49
209-223-1896
Hours: Monday to Friday 10 am to 6 pm
Saturday & Sunday 10 am to 5 pm
Natural Food Store and Café. Deli and Juice Bar.
Comments: Has a chiropractor.
Directions: On east side of Hwy 49 in Mother Lode Plaza.

LA JOLLA

Ashoka
8008 Girard Avenue, Floor 2; 858-454-6263
Hours: Tuesday to Sunday 5:30 pm to 9:30 pm
Closed Monday.
Indian. Not pure vegetarian.
Comments: Good views.
Other Info: Full service, take-out, delivery. Accepts AMEX, DC, DIS, MC, VISA.

**Che Café
9500 Gilman Drive; 858-534-2311
Web site: www.checafe.org
Hours: Open nights there are events. Best to check their web site when they have events and meals. Open on Wednesday 5 pm to 7 pm and most Fridays and Saturday 8 pm to 1 am.
Mainly Vegan Buffet. All-you-can-eat buffet.

Menu: All-you-can-eat vegan buffet for $5. The menu changes daily. Has veggie burgers, Indian curries, soups, salads and more.
Comments: It is located right on the campus. Non-profit vegetarian collective. Has live music weekend evenings. Straight-edge punk rockers come here, dead-heads and students. Has live music events and serves vegan foods at these events.
Other Info: Limited service, take-out. Price: $.
Directions: Corner of Scholars Drive and York Lane, off Gilman Drive at the University of California at San Diego.

Co-op on UCSD Campus
Student Center, Corner of Gilman Drive and Eucalyptus Grove UCSD campus
Hours: Monday to Thursday 8am to 5pm; Friday 8 am to 4 pm; closed Saturday & Sunday
Small Natural Food Store.
Menu: Has vegan sandwiches and a daily soup.
Comments: Organic produce, cruelty-free cosmetics, bulk foods, vitamins & supplements.
Comments: Metered parking available right in front of the student center.

Daily's Fit and Fresh
8915 Towne Center Drive; 619-453-1112
Hours: Monday to Saturday 10:30 am to 9 pm
Sunday 11 am to 8 pm
Natural Foods. Vegan options. Not pure veg.
Menu: Veggie pizza, Grilled Eggplant & Zucchini, Thai Noodle Salad, veggie burgers, Three-bean Chili and other dishes. Fresh juices and smoothies.
Comments: This restaurant has several branches in Southern California. All items on the menu contain 10 grams of fat or less.
Other Info: Limited service, take-out. Price: $.

House of Natural Foods
7521 Fay Ave, at Pearl & Fay; 858-454-4515
Hours: Monday to Saturday 9 am to 6 pm
Closed Sunday.
Natural Food Store. Organic produce.
Menu: Has a selection of good ready-made dishes in their coolers. Sandwiches, salads and hummus.
Other Info: Accepts AMEX, MC, VISA.

Jamba Juice
Villa La Jolla Shopping Center, 8657 Villa La Jolla Drive #101; 619-625-2582
9500 Gilman Drive Suite 1149
858-622-2020; Web site: www.jambajuice.com
Hours: Monday to Friday 7:30 am to 8 pm; Saturday 9 am to 4 pm; closed Sunday.
Juice Bar.

Star of India
1820 Garnet Avenue
858-459-3355; **fax:** 858-551-0851
Hours: Monday to Thursday 11:30 am to 10 pm
Friday to Sunday 12 noon to 10 pm
Indian. Not pure vegetarian.
Menu: Large vegetarian selection.
Comments: Pleasant atmosphere. One of San Diego's top ten rated restaurants, and one the best Indian restaurants in San Diego County.
Other Info: Full service, take-out, catering. Reservations suggested. Accepts AMEX, DC, DIS, MC, VISA. Price: $$.

Whole Foods Market
8825 Villa La Jolla Drive, La Jolla; 858-642-6700
Hours: Daily 8 am to 10 pm; Bakery open 7 am
Natural Food Store and Cafe. Deli, Bakery, Salad Bar and Juice Bar. Organic produce. Supermarket-type place. See Whole Foods Market information.
Directions: At the corner of Villa La Jolla & Noble Drive. From I-5, take the La Jolla Village Dr exit, then go west of La Jolla Village Dr for a quarter-mile, at Villa La Jolla Dr turn left and this place is 2 blocks down.

LA MESA

Henry's (Wild Oats Market)
4630 Palm Avenue, La Mesa
619-460-7722; **fax:** 619-460-8403
Hours: Daily 8 am to 9 pm
Natural Food Store and Cafe. Deli, Bakery, Salad Bar and Juice Bar. Organic produce. Supermarket-type place. See Wild Oats Market information.
Directions: From I-8, take Spirng St exit towards downtown, then go south a third-mile on Spring St, at La Mesa Blvd turn left and go 1 block, at Palm Ave turn right and this place is 1½ block down.

Souplantation
9158 Fletcher Parkway; 619-462-4232
Hours: Daily 11 am to 9 pm
Soup and Salad Place. Not pure vegetarian.
Menu: All-you-can-eat salad bar with more than 60 items. Soup, fruits and muffins.

LEMON GROVE (just east of San Diego)

Henry's Marketplace
3205 Lemon Grove Avenue; 619-667-8686
Hours: Daily 8 am to 9 pm.
Natural Food Store and Cafe. Deli, Bakery, Salad

Bar and Juice Bar. Organic produce. Supermarket-type place. See Wild Oats Market information.
Directions: From Hwy 94, take Lemon Grove Ave exit, then go south on Lemon Grove Ave and this place is a third-mile down.

LOMA LINDA

Loma Linda University
Medical Center Cafeteria, At Anderson St and Barton Road; 909-558-4000
Hours: Daily 22 hours a day
Vegetarian-friendly Hospital Cafeteria. Vegan options.
Menu: Has vegetarians soups, salads, mock meat dishes and casseroles.
Other Info: Cafeteria style, take-out. Non-smoking. Price: $.
Directions: From I-10, take Waterman Ave exit, then go south on S Waterman Ave for ¾ mile, at Barton Rd turn left and go 1¼ mile to the corner of Anderson St.

MENDOCINO

Corners Of The Mouth
45015 Ukiah Street; 707-937-5345
Hours: Daily 9 am to 7 pm
Natural Food Store. Organic produce. Popular, friendly place.
Directions: From Hwy 1, take Main St exit. At Main go west a half-mile, then at Lansing turn right and go 2 blocks, at Ukiah turn left and this place is a half-block down on the left in a red church.

Lu's Kitchen
45013 Ukiah Street; 707-937-4939
Hours: Monday to Friday 11:30 am to 5:30 pm Closed Saturday & Sunday
Mexican and American. Vegan options. Not pure vegetarian.
Menu: Quesadillas, tacos, Portobello Mushrooms, vegan pasta, Beans & Rice, large burritos and other dishes. Non-alcoholic beer.
Comments: Courtyard seating. It is next to a health food store. Local organic produce used when possible. Does not use lard in beans.
Other Info: Limited service, take-out. Price: $$.

Mendocino Café
10451 Lansing Street; 707-937-2422
Hours: Daily for lunch and dinner
California Style. Vegan options. Not pure vegetarian.

Menu: Their Thai Burrito (brown basmati rice and vegetables) is good. Asian noodle and tofu dish. Cappuccino, espresso. Non-alcoholic beer.
Comments: Indoor and outdoor seating.
Other Info: Full service, take-out. Price: $$.

**The Ravens/Stanford Inn by the Sea
Coast Highway One & Comptche Ukiah Road
707-937-5615; **Reservations:** 800-331-8884; **email:** stanford@stanfordinn.com
Web site: www.stanfordinn.com
Hours: Breakfast begins at 8 am
Dinner begins at 5:30 pm
Vegetarian and Vegan Gourmet Dining. Italian dishes. Bed & Breakfast.
Menu: Multi-grain Walnut Vegan pancakes, grilled red potatoes, sautéed vegetables, Sesame Granola, Taos Burrito, Citrus Polenta in Cashew-tahini sauce with sautéed greens, Seapalm Strudel, Calzone and German Chocolate Cake. For dinner has pizzas, salads, soups, Calzone and vegetarian main dishes such as Grilled Polenta, Shitake Tart, Pasta, Pistachio Encrusted Tofu, Grilled Portabella Burger, Lasagna and Forbidden Moroccan Curry. Very good desserts. Has a special vegan three-course meal, including soup or salad, a special weekly entree and dessert for $27.95.
Comments: Food gets high ratings. Most of the produce is organically grown in their own gardens. Rooms have a four-poster bed and a fireplace and have a view of either the ocean or the organic garden. High class place. The Stanford Inn gets a great rating from AAA. Their full menu is on their Web site.
Other Info: Reservations not necessary. Non-smoking. Accepts AMEX, DIS, MC, VISA. Price: $$$.
Directions: Northern California coast, just south of the town of Mendocino.

MIDDLETOWN

Stonefront Restaurant
Harbin Hot Spirngs, 18424 Harbin Springs Road
707-987-2477
Hours: Daily for breakfast and dinner
Natural Foods. Macrobiotic and Vegan options. Not pure vegetarian.
Menu: Soups, salads and hot dishes. Daily dinner special. Non-alcoholic beer.
Comments: Located in the Harbin Hot Springs Resort. Local organic produce used when possible.
Other Info: Counter service, take-out. Price: $-$$.

MODESTO

Trader Joe's
3250 Dale Road, at Standiford Road
209-491-0445

Tresetti's World Caffe
927 11th Street, downtown; 209-572-2990
Hours: Monday to Saturday 11 am to 10 pm
Closed Sunday.
International, American Natural & Raw Foods.
Vegan-friendly. Not pure vegetarian.
Comments: Good vegetarian dishes. Small, pleasant place.
Other Info: Full service, take-out. Reservations suggested. Accepts AMEX, MC, VISA. Price: $$-$$$.
Directions: From CA Hwy 99, take Central Modesto/CA-132, then go northwest (along highway) on 6th St for 0.65 mile, at I St (Rte 132) turn right and this place is 5 blocks down.

MORENO VALLEY

Dragon House Restaurant
22456 Alessandro Boulevard; 909-653-1442
Hours: Sun to Thur 11:30 am to 9:30 pm
Friday & Saturday 11:30 am to 9:30 pm
Chinese. Vegan options. Not pure vegetarian.
Menu: Has a vegetarian menu. Has mock "meats" (made from soybean).
Other Info: Full service, take-out. Accepts AM, MC, VISA. Price: $$.

Maharajah India Cuisine
23750 Alessandro Blvd; 909-653-6043
Indian. Not pure vegetarian. See Colton for details.

MOUNT SHASTA

Berryvale Grocery
305 S Mount Shasta Boulevard; 530-926-1576
Hours: Daily 8:30 am to 7:30 pm (closed 1 hour later in Summer)
Natural Food Store. Organic produce.
Directions: From I-5 north, take Central exit in Mt Shastra. Go east on West Lake Street 3 blocks, then at Mount Shasta Blvd (at traffic light) turn right and this place is 2 blocks down on the right.

NATIONAL CITY

Café Paradise
Paradise Valley Hospital, 2400 East 4th Street

619-470-4264
Hours: Daily for three meals
Mainly Vegetarian Cafeteria. Vegan options. Not pure vegetarian.
Menu: Menu changes weekly. Soups, salads and international dishes.
Comments: Cafeteria located in the Paradise Valley Hospital that is open to the public.
Other Info: Counter service, take-out. Price: $.
Directions: From I-805, take Palm Ave exit towards National City, then go a half-mile east on E Division St, at Euclid Ave turn right and go third-mile, at E 4th St turn left and this place is 1 block down on the right.

NEVADA CITY (Nevada County)

**Earth Song Market & Café
135 Argail Way #A 530-265-9392
Store Hours: Daily 8 am to 9 pm
Café Hours: 11:30 am to 8 pm (until 9 pm in summer); Sunday Brunch
Natural Food Store and Vegetarian Cafe. Deli, Salad Bar and Juice Bar. Macrobiotic and Vegan options.
Menu: Salads, soups, sandwiches, veggie burger, daily specials and hot main dishes. Fresh juices.
Comments: In the Sierra Nevada foothills. Local organic produce used when possible.
Other Info: Full service, take-out. Can eat in your car or outside. Accepts AMEX, MC, VISA. Price: $.
Directions: From Hwy 49, take Goldflat Rd exit, then go west on Goldflat 1 block. Then at Searls Ave turn right and go 3 blocks, at Argall turn left and this place is a half-block down on the left.

NEWARK (Alameda County)

Fresh Choice
1029 New Park Mall; 510-791-6096
Hours: Sunday to Thursday 11 am to 9 pm
Friday & Saturday 11 am to 10 pm

NEWPORT BEACH

PF Chang's China Bistro
1145 Newport Center Drive Floor 2
949-759-9007
Hours: Sunday to Thursday 11 am to 11 pm
Friday & Saturday 11 am to 12 midnight
Asian, Chinese. Not pure vegetarian. See Los Angeles.
Other Info: Accepts AMEX, DC, DIS, MC, VISA. Price: $.

Royal Thai Cuisine
4001 West Pacific Coast Highway
949-650-3322
Hours: Daily 11 am to 3 pm, 5 pm to 11 pm
Sunday Brunch 11 am to 3 pm
Thai. Not pure vegetarian.
Menu: Has a good selection of vegetarian dishes.
Has soups, salads, appetizers and ten vegetarian
main dishes.
Other Info: Full service, take-out. Accepts
AMEX, DIS, MC, VISA. Price: $$.

SAGE
2531 Eastbluff Drive; 949-718-9650
Hours: Monday to Thursday 11:30 am to 9:30
pm; Friday & Saturday 11:30 am to 10 pm; Sun-
day 10:30 am to 9:30 pm
American. Vegan options. Not pure vegetarian.
Menu: Has a wide selection of vegetarian dishes
such as pizzas, Sage salad (leeks, mixed greens,
corn, summer squash, tomatoes, roasted aspara-
gus, and Dijon vinaigrette), Sweet Potato Fries,
Chinese Noodles with vegetables and vegetable
pizza.
Other Info: Reservations required. Price: $$$.
Directions: From CA Hwy 73, take the Bison
Ave exit, then go west on Bison Ave for 1 mile.
Road bends to the left and becomes Bamboo St
and goes another quarter-mile, then at Bixia St
turn right and go 1 block, at Eastbluff Dr turn
right and this place is 1 block down.

**Veg a Go-Go
401 Newpoint Center Drive
Atrium Court Fashion Island
949-721-4088
Hours: Monday to Friday 11 am to 9 pm; Satur-
day 11 am to 8 pm; Sunday 11 am to 7 pm
Vegetarian International. Vegan options.
Menu: Hummus, chickpea in whole-wheat tor-
tilla, Thai vegetables, Indian curry, veggie burgers,
falafel and many other dishes.
Other Info: Counter service, take-out, catering.
Price: $. Cash only.

OCEANSIDE (San Diego County)

Boney's Marketplace
1820 Oceanside Boulevard
760-754-6555
Hours: Daily 9 am to 8
Natural Food Store.

Trader Joe's
2570 Vista Way
760-433-9994

OXNARD

Fresh Choice
1720 Ventura Boulevard; 988-8975

Lassen's Health Foods
3471 Saviors Road; 805-486-8266
Hours: Monday to Saturday 9 am to 8 pm
Closed Sunday.
Natural Food Store. Organic produce.
Menu: Has ready-made sandwiches.
Other Info: Accepts AMEX, MC, VISA.
Directions: This place is in south Oxnard. From
Hwy 101, take Vineyard Ave/Rte 232 towards
Oxnard, then go south on Vineyard Ave (Rte 232)
for a half-mile, then turn left at N Oxnard Blvd
(Rte 1) and go 2½ miles, then continue straight
onto Saviers and this place is 1½ mile down.

PACIFICA

Good Health Natural Foods
80 West Manor Drive; 650-355-5936
Hours: Monday to Thursday 9:30 am to 8 pm;
Friday 9:30 am to 7 pm; Saturday 9:30 am to 6
pm; Sunday 12 noon to 6 pm
Natural Food Store.
Directions: From Hwy 1, take Manor Drive exit
and go toward ocean. This place on left.

PACIFIC GROVE

Tillie Gort's Café
111 Central; 831-373-0335
Hours: Monday to Friday 11 am to 10 pm
Saturday & Sunday 9 am to 10:30 pm
Natural Foods. Vegan options. Not pure veg.
Menu: Pasta, Eggplant Parmesan and veggie Meat
Loaf. Has some organic dishes. Fresh juices,
cappuccino, espresso.
Comments: Coffeehouse type place. Displays art
here.
Other Info: Full service, take-out. Accepts MC,
VISA. Price: $$.
Directions: From CA Rte 1, take Monterey exit,
then go west on Camino Aguajita for a half-mile,
at Del Monte Ave turn left and go a half-mile,
then keep going straight onto Lighthouse Ave for
1½ mile, road becomes Central Ave and this place
is near the corner of Eardfey Ave.

PALM SPRINGS

Harvest Health Foods
73952 US Highway 111, Palm Springs
760-346-3215

Hours: Monday to Saturday 9 am to 6 pm Sunday 10 am to 4 pm
Natural Food Store and Deli. Juice Bar. Organic produce. Not pure vegetarian.
Menu: Sandwiches, Tempeh Sandwich, a variety of salads, soups and hot dishes.
Other Info: Accepts MC, VISA for grocery items. Cash only at deli.

**Native Foods
1775 E Palm Canyon Drive, Smoke Tree Village 760-416-0070; **Web site:** www.nativefoods.com
Hours: Monday to Saturday 11 am to 9 pm Closed Sunday.
Natural Food Store and Fully Vegan Restaurant. Organic produce. Macrobiotic options. Kosher certified.
Menu: Hollywood Bowl (steamed organic vegetable on top of brown rice, baked tofu, and Thai peanut sauce), Yakisoba (stir-fry noodles), Jerk Burger (made from seitan), Indonesian Tempeh Chips, BBQ Love Burger (seitan with BBQ sauce), reuben and hoagie sandwiches, mock "fish" dish and MadCowboy's Delight (soy chicken with BBQ sauce, corn & avocado). Cappuccino, espresso.
Comments: Specializing in homemade textured vegetable protein (TVP), tempeh and seitan.
Other Info: Full service, counter service, take-out, catering. Non-smoking. Does not take reservations. No credit cards. Price: $ or $$.

**Nature's Express
144 East Tahquitz Canyon Way (Palm Canyon and Indian Canyon); 760-318-9240; **fax:** 760-318-9241; **Web site:** www.nutures-express.com
Hours: Monday to Saturday 11 am to 8 pm Sunday 11 am to 6 pm
Vegetarian. Vegan options. Juice Bar. Fast food.
Menu: Pizzas, Mock Egg Salad, veggie burgers, Vegetarian Sushi, Baked Fries, chili, veggie dogs, baked potatoes, Rice & Bean and more. Fresh juices and smoothies.
Other Info: Limited service, take-out. Price: $ or $$.
Directions: From CA Hwy 111, go south on N Palm Canyon Dr for 1½ mile, then at E Tahquitz Canyon Way turn left and this place is 50 yards down.

PALOMAR MOUNTAIN (near San Diego)

**Mother Kitchen
33120 Canfield Road, Junction of highways S6 and S7; 760-742-4233

Hours: Monday, Thursday, Friday 11 am to 4 pm; Saturday & Sunday 8:30 am to 5 pm; closed Tuesday and Wednesday.
Vegetarian Restaurant. Juice Bar.
Menu: Salads, soups, sandwiches and veggie burgers. Fresh juices and smoothies.
Comments: It is a rustic cabin on top of Mount Palomar. You have to drive past this restaurant to visit the Mt Palomar telescope near San Diego. It is the only restaurant on this mountain. Pleasant little place with good views.
Other Info: Full service, take-out. Price: $$. Accepts MC, VISA.

PARADISE

Feather River Hospital Cafeteria
5974 Pentz Road
530-877-9361
Hours: Daily for lunch and dinner.
Vegetarian International. Salad Bar. Pizza Bar.
Menu: Mushroom Loaf, veggie burgers, salads, pizza, spaghetti, salads and enchiladas.
Comments: Seventh Day Adventist Hospital.
Other Info: Counter service, take-out. Price: $.

Paradise Natural Foods
5729 Almond Street; 530-877-5164
Hours: Monday to Thursday 9 am to 6 pm; Friday 9 am to 4 pm; Sunday 10 am to 3 pm (until 6 pm in Summer)
Natural Food Store. Organic produce (limited in winter).
Directions: Take Hwy 99 Skyway from Chico to Paradise. At Pearson Rd turn right, then at Almond (2 blocks down) turn left and this place on left. From Hwy 70, take Clark Rd (Hwy 191) to Paradise, then at Pearson Rd turn left, then at Almond turn right and this place on left.

PLEASANT HILL

Thai Village Restaurant
670-I Gregory Lane
925-256-0289
Hours: Monday to Friday 11 am to 2:30 pm, 5 pm to 9:30 (until 10 pm Friday); Saturday 5 pm to 10 pm; Sunday 5 pm to 9 pm
Thai. Not pure vegetarian.
Menu: Has several vegetarian dishes. Vegetable stir-fries, vegetable curries and other dishes. Can substitute tofu for meat in many of the dishes. Non-alcoholic beer and wine.
Other Info: Full service, take-out. Accepts MC, VISA. Price: $-$$.

POWAY (just northeast of San Diego)

Henry's Marketplace (Wild Oats)
13536 Poway Road; 858-486-7851
Hours: Daily 8 am to 9 pm.
Natural Food Store and Cafe. Deli, Bakery, Salad Bar and Juice Bar. Organic produce. Supermarket-type place. See Wild Oats Market information.
Directions: From I-15, go 2 miles east on Camino Del Norte, road becomes Twin Peaks Rd and go another 1½ mile, at Community Rd turn slight right and go 1¼ mile, at Poway Rd turn left and this place is a quarter-mile down on the left.

Potato Place
Target/Lucky Shopping Center, 14873 Pomerodo Place; 858-679-3343
Hours: Monday to Saturday 11 am to 8 pm Closed Sunday.
American Fast Food. Potato dishes with vegetables and vegetarian chili.

QUINCY

Quincy Natural Foods
30 Harbinson Street
530-283-3528; **fax:** 530-283-1537
Hours: Monday to Friday 9 am to 6:30 pm; Saturday 10 am to 5 pm; Sunday 10 am to 4 pm
Natural Food Store and Deli (ready-made sandwiches). Organic produce.
Directions: Take Hwy 70 into Quincy on Harbinson (one way) from Oroville or Chico and this place on left opposite the library. From Reno or Truckee, take Hwy 89 into Quiny and at the Court House loop around this place to corner with Harbinson.

RICHMOND (Contra Costa County)

William's Health Food Store
12249 San Pablo Avenue; 510-232-1911
Hours: Monday to Friday 9:30 am to 7 pm; Saturday 9:30 to 6 pm; Sunday 11 to 6 pm
Natural Food Store. Organic produce. Has the lowest prices of any natural food store in the area. Large bulk section.
Menu: Has ready-made sandwiches and wraps in their cooler.
Directions: Between Barrett Avenue and McDonald. From I-80, take the San Pablo Dam Road exit, then go a third-mile west on San Pablo Dam Rd, then at San Pablo Ave turn left and this place 1 block down.

ROSEVILLE (Sacramento area)

PF Chang's
1180 Galleria Blvd; 916-788-2800
Hours: Sunday to Thursday 11 am to 11 pm Friday & Saturday 11 am to 12 midnight
Chinese. Vegan options. Not pure vegetarian.
Menu: Has a good tofu appetizer and will substitute tofu in meat dishes.
Comments: A popular place and there can be a wait of more than an hour on Saturday nights.

SACRAMENTO

All Seasons All Reasons Fine Catering
2791 24th Street; 916-451-9393
Vegan and Vegetarian Catering. Caters events of 100 people or more.
Menu: Can do almost any vegetarian menu, and also has set menus. Braised Seitan Roll with apricots, Eggplant & Ginger Sauce and Yogurt Phyllo Tart.
Comments: Reasonably priced. The owner, Dave Pucilowshi, has been doing catering for over 15 years.
Cost: A $200 deposit at reservations. Hors d'oeuveres range from $11 to $20 dollar per guest. Full buffet from $15 to $35 per guest. Includes plates, forks, knives, cloth napkins and wine glasses. Other things can be rented at additional costs.

Cafe Europa
Arden Fair Mall Food Court
1689 Arden Way, Suite 2016
916-929-4140
Hours: Open during mall hours.
Greek. Not vegan-friendly. Price: $.
Menu: Falafel pita sandwich. Choice of tahini or ztatziki.

Elliott's Natural Foods
3347 El Camino Avenue
916-481-3173
Hours: Monday to Friday 9 am to 6 pm; Saturday 9 am to 5 pm; Sunday 11 am to 4 pm
Natural Food Store.
Comments: Friendly place.
Directions: From Business 80, take El Camino exit, then at El Camino turn right and this place is 5 miles down on the left between Watt and Fulton. From I-80, take Watt Ave exit, then go south on Watt Ave 3 miles, then at El Camino turn right and this place is one block down on right.

Farah's Sacramento Joy Restaurant

2052 Auburn Blvd; 916-920-3500
Hours: Sunday to Thursday 11 am to 9 pm; Friday 11 am to 3 pm; closed Sundays.
Restaurant. Kosher, Health food. Vegetarian and vegan options.
Menu: Hummus, tabbouleh salad and falafel.
Comments: Has large rooms for banquets.
Other Info: Full service, take-out, catering. Accepts AMEX, MC, VISA.

Gyro Supreme

545 Downtown Plaza, Suite 2109, food court in Downtown Plaza Mall; 916-444-6014
Hours: Monday to Saturday 10 am to 9 pm
Sunday 10 am to 6 pm
Mediterranean and Greek. Not pure vegetarian. Price: $.
Menu: Vegetarian Combo Plates and falafel sandwiches. Combo includes choice of 2 or 3 of the following: tabbouleh, hummus, baba ghanouj or falafel.

Henry Nguyen

1537 Howe Avenue, Curtis Park
916-927-1014
Hours: Sunday to Thursday 10:30 am to 9:30 pm; Friday & Saturday 10:30 am to 10:30 pm
Vietnamese and Asian. Vegan options. Not pure vegetarian.
Menu: Has around 25 vegetarian dishes. No MSG.
Other Info: Full service, take-out. Accepts AMEX, MC, VISA. Price: $$.

Juliana's Kitchen

1401 G Street; 916-444-0966
Hours: Daily Monday to Thursday 10 am to 7 pm; Friday 10 am to 3 pm; closed Saturday & Sunday.
Middle Eastern Natural Foods. Vegan options. Not pure vegetarian. The vegetable combination special is a bargain.
Menu: Middle Eastern specials, salads, hummus, falafel, pita sandwiches and desserts. Fresh juices.
Other Info: Limited service, take-out. Price: $.
Accepts AMEX, MC, VISA.

Luna's Café and Juice Bar

1414 16th Street; 916-441-3931
Hours: Monday & Tuesday 8 am to 5 pm; Wednesday & Friday 8 am to 11 pm; Saturday 10 am to 3 pm; closed Sundays.
Café and Juice Bar. Not pure vegetarian.
Menu: Bagels, quesadilla, chips and salsa. Fresh juices and smoothies. Makes smoothies with milk or orange juice. Light, health-oriented meals.
Comments: Has live music and weekly poetry readings (Thursday at 8 pm). Displays artwork from local California artists (for sale).
Other Info: Full service, take-out. Price: $.
Directions: From I-5, take US 50/I-80 Business exit, then go east on the Capital City Freeway a half-mile, then take 15th Street (Rte 160) exit, then go north on 16th St (Rte 160) and this place is ¾ mile down.

Mother India

1030 J Street, downtown Sacramento
916-491-4072
Hours: Monday to Wednesday 11 am to 2:30 pm; Thursday to Saturday 11 am to 2:30 pm, 5 pm to 9 pm; closed Sunday.
Indian. Vegan options. All-you-can-eat Lunch Buffet. Not pure vegetarian.
Menu: Channa Masala, rice dishes, Naan, chai and lassis.
Comments: Has outdoor dining. Popular for lunch.
Other Info: Full service, take-out, catering. Accepts MC, VISA.

Piccadilly Circus

5104 Arden Way, Carmichael
916-481-1955
Hours: Daily 9 am to 9 pm
Natural Food Store and Cafe. Deli, Bakery, Salad Bar and Juice Bar. Organic produce. Supermarket-type place.
Other Info: Counter service, take-out. Has seating. Accepts MC, VISA.
Directions: From Hwy 50, take Watt Ave Exit, then go north on Watt Ave 1 mile, then at Fair Oaks Blvd turn right and this place is 2½ miles down, at corner of Arden and Fair Oaks.

Sacramento Natural Foods Coop

1900 Alhambra Boulevard;
916-455-2667 (COOP)
Hours: Daily 9 am to 10 pm
Deli Hours: 9 am to 9 pm
Natural Food Store and Café. Deli and Juice Bar. Vegan options. Not pure vegetarian. Organic produce section is the size of a normal supermarket's produce section. Has both organic and regular produce. Small Bakery and coffee bar. All-you-can-eat vegetarian buffet.
Menu: Has a large variety of salads, soups, sandwiches, Black Bean Enchilada, Mexican braised Tofu, Polenta Torta, vegetable calzones, Black

Bean Chili and baked goods.

Comments: Biggest natural food store in Sacramento. Arranges classes on cooking, natural medicine, homeopathy and other subjects. You do not have to be a member to shop here. Food gets high ratings, but some people don't like the place (especially the staff).

Other Info: Accepts MC, VISA. Has seating. Price: $.

Directions: Near the junction of S Street and 30th Street. From CA 99 get on Capital City Freeway going towards Reno, then go a third-mile and take the T Street exit, then go north 1 block on 30th St, then turn right at S St and this place is 1 block down.

Taj Mahal

2355 Arden Way; 916-924-8378
Hours: Daily 11:30 am to 2:30 pm, 5:30 pm to 10 pm
Indian. Not pure vegetarian.
Menu: Has several vegetarian dishes including rice dishes, tandoori dishes and curried vegetables.
Other Info: Full service, take-out. Price $$. Accepts AMEX, DC, MC, VISA.

Trader Joe's

Town & Country Village, 2601 Marconi Avenue, at Fulton; 916-481-8797

SAINT HELENA

**Saint Helena Health Center Cafeteria

650 Sanitarium Road; 707-963-6214
Hours: Daily
Vegetarian.
Comments: Meals are mainly for people at the health center, but also non-residents can come if they make a reservation.
Other Info: Counter service, take-out. Reservations required.

SAN BERNARDINO

Kool Kactus Café

24957 Redlands Boulevard; 909-796-1545
Hours: Monday to Saturday 11 am to 8 pm
Sunday 11 am to 7:30 pm
Mexican. Not pure vegetarian.
Menu: Has a good selection of vegetarian dishes.
Other Info: Limited service, take-out, catering. Accepts DIS, MC, VISA. Price: $.

Lotus Garden

111 East Hospitality Lane; 909-381-6171
Hours: Sunday to Thursday 11:30 am to 9:30

pm; Friday & Saturday 11:30 am to 10:30 pm
Chinese. Vegan options. Not pure vegetarian.
Menu: Has a large selection of vegetarian dishes including Bok Choy, tofu dishes, Chinese noodles and mock "meat" dishes.
Other Info: Full service, take-out. Accepts AMEX, DIS, MC, VISA. Price: $$.

SAN CLEMENTE (Orange County)

Trader Joe's

Ocean View Plaza, 638 Camino de los Mares
714-240-9996

SAN DIEGO

Ashoka the Great

9474 Black Mountain Road; 858-695-9749
Hours: Daily 11 am to 3 pm, 5 pm to 10 pm
Indian. Not pure vegetarian. Lunch buffet.
Menu: Has a large amount of vegetarian Indian dishes that include pakoras, baked eggplant, rice dishes, samosas, an okra dish and Masala Dosa.
Other Info: Full service, take-out. Accepts AMEX, DIS, MC, VISA. Price: $-$$.

Café Athena

1846 Garnet Avenue, between Lamont and Ingraham; 858-274-1140; **fax:** 858-274-1145
Hours: Sunday to Thursday 11 am to 9:30 pm
Friday & Saturday 11 am to 10 pm
Mediterranean, Greek, American. Vegan options. Not pure vegetarian.
Menu: Has a good selection of vegetarian dishes. Marinated Artichoke Salad, hummus, Iman Bayaldi (eggplant dish), lentil soup and other dishes. This place has a good amount of vegan dishes that are marked with a "V". Non-alcoholic beer. The Greek Salad and Lentil Soup are good.
Comments: Many people believe this is the best Greek food in town. Good service. Casual. Has some outdoor seating. Has some oil paintings of whitewashed villas on the Aegean.
Other Info: Full service, take-out, catering. Reservations suggested for groups. Accepts AMEX, DIS, MC, VISA. Price: $-$$.

Café India

3760 Sports Arena Boulevard #5, at Hancock Street; 619-224-7500
Hours: Tuesday to Saturday 11 am to 10 pm; Sunday 12 noon to 10 pm; closed Monday.
Indian. Vegan options. Not pure vegetarian.
Menu: Has a daily all-you-can-eat vegetarian buffet that contains Indian and Italian dishes. Vegetable curries, lentil soup, rice dishes and

Indian bread.
Other Info: Full service, take-out, catering. Accepts AMEX, DC, DIS, MC, VISA. Price: $$.
Directions: It is near the Sports Arena in a shopping strip, behind Red Lobster.

Café Lulu

419 F Street, between Fourth and Fifth Avenues
619-238-0114
Hours: Sunday to Thursday 8 am to 1 am
Friday & Saturday 8 am to 9 am
Natural Foods. American. Not pure vegetarian, but most of the dishes are. Vegan options.
Menu: Soup, salads, sandwiches, grilled vegetable sandwiches, Lasagna, Gardenburgers and other dishes. Cappuccino, espresso.
Comments: Has blues and jazz music during the day and dance music at night. Has an interesting modern décor.
Other Info: Limited service, take-out. Cash only. Price: $.
Directions: From I-5, take the Front St exit towards Civic Center, then go south on 4th Ave and this place is a half-mile down.

Casa De Pico

2754 Calhoun Street; 619-296-3267
Hours: Sunday to Thursday 10 am to 9 pm; Friday & Saturday 10 am to 9:30 pm; open an hour later in the summer.
Mexican. Not pure vegetarian.
Menu: Has many vegetarian options including enchiladas, burritos, tacos and guacamole.
Comments: Has outdoor seating on the patio. Has live mariachi music at night. Has foods that are low in cholesterol, salt and fat. May have to wait an hour or two for a table.
Other Info: Full service, take-out. Accepts AMEX, DC, DIS, MC, VISA. Price: $$.
Directions: In the Bazaar Del Mundo Shopping Complex in the historic state park of Old Town San Diego.

Daily's

8915 Towne Centre Drive
858-453-1112; fax: 858-453-1393
Hours: Monday to Saturday 9 am to 9 pm
Sunday 10 am to 8 pm
Natural Foods. Emphasis on vegetarian dishes. Vegan options. Not pure vegetarian. Juice Bar.
Menu: Veggie pizza, grilled eggplant & zucchini, Thai Noodle Salad, garden vegetable burger, soups, Corn Chili and other dishes. Fresh juices and smoothies.
Comments: This restaurant has several branches

in Southern California. Has a children menu. All items on the menu contain 10 grams of fat or less and no more that 20% of calorie from any dish comes from fat. Health conscious meals.
Other Info: Limited service, semi-cafeteria, take-out. Accepts AMEX, MC, VISA. Price: $.
Directions: From I-5, take Genesee Ave exit, then go 2 miles southeast on Genesse Ave, at Nobel Dr turn left and go a third-mile, at Towne Centre Dr turn left and this place is 2 blocks down.

***Formosa Chinese Restaurant

16769 Bernardo Center Drive Suite K8 (Rancho Bernardo in northern San Diego County)
858-487-8999
Hours: Tuesday to Sunday 11 am to 2 pm, 5 pm to 8:30 pm; closed Monday
Vegan, Organic, Gourmet Chinese.
Menu: Hot & Sour Soup (really good), Snow Peas, Sweet & Sour "Chicken," mock beef and Orange Flavored Mock Chicken. Good green tea ice cream.
Comments: Makes own organic soy milk, tofu and imitation meats. Gets good recommendations. Local organic produce used when possible.
Other Info: Price: $$. Accepts AMEX, MC, VISA.
Directions: From I-15, take Rancho Bernardo Rd exit, then go west on Rancho Bernardo Rd for 1 block, at W Bernardo Dr turn left and this place is a half-mile down.

**Galoka

5662 La Jolla Boulevard
858-551-8610
Web site: www.galoka.com
Hours: Thursday to Sunday 5 pm to 12 midnight; closed Monday to Wednesday.
Fully Vegetarian Gourmet. Mostly Vegan. Mostly North Indian. Some Italian, Peruvian and Ethiopian.
Menu: Shrimp Jal Favazi, Keema (veggie ground beef with spices), Chicken Biryani, Warm Spinach Salad with roasted walnuts, samosas and other mock "meat" dishes.
Comments: Romantic, nice atmosphere. Located inside an art gallery. Has live jazz nightly. The food is good, especially the appetizers. Local organic produce used when possible. Has mahogany walls and flowers and candles on the tables.
Other Info: Full service, catering, buffet and take-out. Non-smoking. Reservations recommended. Accepts AMEX, MC, VISA. Price: $$-$$$.
Directions: About 2 minutes north of Pacific Beach.

**Govinda's
1030 Grand Avenue; 858-483-2500
Hours: 6 pm to 8 pm
Fully Vegetarian Indian and International.
Dinner Buffet.
Menu: Has rice dishes, vegetable dishes, soups,
salads and desserts.
Comments: Has very good food.
Directions: This place is 2 blocks from the beach.
From I-5, take Balboa Ave/Garnet Ave exit, then
go west on Garnet Ave and go a half-mile, then
continue straight onto Balboa Ave for a half mile,
then the road becomes Grand Ave and then this
place is 1 mile down.

Henry's Marketplace
4439 Genesee Avenue, Clairemont area
858-268-2400
Hours: Daily 8 am to 9 pm
Natural Food Store and Cafe. Deli, Bakery, Salad
Bar and Juice Bar. Organic produce. Supermarket-
type place. See Wild Oats Market information.
Directions: Across from the DMV. From I-5, take
the Genesse Ave exit, then go east on Genesee
Ave and this place is 5½ miles down. Or from I-
5, take Balboa Ave/Garnet Ave exit, then go east
on Balboa for 2 miles, at Genesse Ave turn left
and this place is a half-mile down.

Henry's Marketplace
4175 Park Boulevard, North Park
619-291-8287
Hours: Monday to Friday 7 am to 10 pm
Saturday & Sunday 8 am to 9 pm
Natural Food Store and Cafe. Deli, Bakery, Salad
Bar and Juice Bar. Organic produce. Supermarket-
type place. See Wild Oats Market information.
Directions: From Hwy 163, take the Washington St East/BUS Rte 8, then go east on Washington St a half-mile, at North St take a slight
left and go 1 long block, then take a sharp right
onto Park Blvd and this place is 50 yards down.

Henry's Marketplace
1260 Garnet Avenue, Pacific Beach
858-270-8200
Hours: Daily 8 am to 9 pm
Natural Food Store and Cafe. Deli, Bakery,
Salad Bar and Juice Bar. Organic produce. Supermarket-type place. See Wild Oats Market
information.
Directions: This place is 2 blocks from the beach.
From I-5, take Balboa Ave/Garnet Ave exit, then
go west on Garnet Ave a half-mile, then continue straight onto Balboa Ave for a half mile,

then the road becomes Grand Ave and go ¾ mile,
then at Fanuel St turn right and go 2 blocks, at
Garnet Ave turn left and this place is 1 block
down.

Henry's Marketplace
3315 Rosecrans Street, Point Loma
619-523-3640
Hours: Daily 8 am to 9 pm
Natural Food Store and Cafe. Deli, Bakery,
Salad Bar and Juice Bar. Organic produce. Supermarket-type place. See Wild Oats Market
information.
Directions: From I-5, take the CA Hwy 209/I-
8 E exit towards Rosecrans St, then go south on
Camino Del Rio (Rte 209) for a quarter-mile,
then Camino Del Rio becomes Rosecrans St and
then this place is a quarter-mile down.

Henry's Marketplace
3332 Sandrock Boulevard, Serra Mesa
858-565-1714
Hours: Daily 8 am to 9 pm
Natural Food Store and Cafe. Deli, Bakery,
Salad Bar and Juice Bar. Organic produce. Supermarket-type place. See Wild Oats Market
information.
Directions: From I-805, take the Balbao Ave/
CA Rte 274 exit, then go east on Balboa Ave for
a half-mile, at Convoy St turn right and go ¾
mile, at Aero Dr turn left and go ¾ mile, then at
Sandrock Rd turn slight right and this place is a
third-mile down.

Henry's Marketplace
3358 Governor Drive; 858-457-5006
Hours: Daily 8 am to 9 pm
Natural Food Store and Cafe. Deli, Bakery, Salad
Bar and Juice Bar. Organic produce. Supermarket-
type place. See Wild Oats Market information.
Directions: From I-5, take the Genesee Ave exit,
then go southeast on Genesee Ave for 3 miles, at
Governor Dr turn right and this place is a half-
mile down. Or from I-5, take Hwy 52 east and
go 1 mile, then take Regents Rd exit, then go
northeast on Regents Rd 1 mile, then turn right
at Governor Dr and this place is a third-mile
down.

Jamba Juice
510 Robinson Avenue, Hillcrest   619-683-2582
5638 Mission Center Road #106   619-785-5800
Hours: Sunday to Thursday 7 am to 9 pm
Friday & Saturday 8 am to 10 pm
Juice Bar.

**Jyoti Bihanga

3351 Adams Avenue, Normal Heights
619-282-4116
Hours: Monday, Tuesday, Thursday, Friday 11
am to 9 pm; Wednesday 11 am to 3 pm, closed
Wednesday night; Saturday 12 noon to 9 pm;
Saturday All-you-can-eat Breakfast Buffet 7:30 am
to 12 noon; closed most Sundays, but sometime
open 9 am to 1 pm
Fully Vegetarian. American and International.
Vegan and Macrobiotic options.
Menu: Salads, homemade soups, special of the
day, veggie burgers and desserts. All-you-can-eat
breakfast buffet on Saturday (some Sundays)
mornings. Tofu Scramble, granolas, Mushroom
Gravy on Home Fries, dairyless blueberry pancakes and fresh fruit for breakfast. BBQ Seitan
Sandwich. The "Infinite Blue" is a popular dish.
Has vegan main dishes and vegan dessert such as
vegan chocolate mousse and apple pie. Fresh
juices.
Warning: The Neatloaf" and the tofu burger may
contain eggs.
Comments: Has a fountain, 15-foot window and
high arched ceilings. Good restaurant run by the
devotees of Sri Chinmoy. Has a peaceful atmosphere. The brunch is very reasonably priced.
Service may be a bit slow.
Other Info: Full service, take-out. Accepts
AMEX, MC, VISA. Price: $-$$.
Directions: From I-805 coming south, take the
Madison Ave exit towards Adams Ave, then go
north on Ohio 1 block, at Adams Ave turn right
and this place is a little more than a half-mile
down, at Felton St. From I-805 coming north,
take Madison Ave exit, then go east on Madison
Ave for 3 blocks, then at Felton St turn left and
this place is 1 block down, at Adams Ave.

**Madras Café

9484 Black Mountain Road, at Miramar Road
858-695-6229
Hours: Monday to Thursday 11 am to 2:30 pm,
5:30 pm to 9 pm; Friday & Saturday 11:30 am
to 4 pm, 5:30 pm to 10 pm; closed Monday
Vegetarian Indian. Vegan options. Has a buffet.
Menu: Has South Indian dishes such as dosas and
idly. Have a reasonably priced buffet.
Other Info: Accepts AMEX, MC, VISA. Price:
$$.
Directions: This place is in Miramar, north of
University City in northeast San Diego. From I-
15, take Miramar Rd exit, then go west on
Miramar Rd a half-mile, at Black Mountain Rd
turn right and this place is 150 yards down.

Mandarin Plaza

3760 Sports Arean Boulevard Suite 3
619-224-4222
Hours: Daily 11 am to 10 pm
Mandarin and Cantonese Chinese. Not pure
vegetarian. Vegan options.
Menu: Has a vegetarian section on the menu.
Does not use MSG.
Other Info: Full service, take-out. Accepts
AMEX, DIS, MC, VISA. Price: $-$$.

New Seed Nutrition

946 Garnet, Pacific Beach; 858-270-7620
Natural Food Store.

**Ocean Beach People's Natural Foods

4765 Voltaire Street, at Sunset Cliffs (Ocean
Beach); 619-224-1387
Hours: Monday to Friday 8 am to 9 pm
Saturday & Sunday 9 am to 8 pm
Natural Food Store and take-out Vegetarian Deli.
Features raw and vegan foods. Vegan options.
Large selection of organic produce. Bakery. Not
pure vegetarian.
Menu: Has a good selection of raw foods and
organic salads. Cold and hot soups, sandwiches,
baked goods, main dishes and desserts. Fresh
juices.
Other Info: Counter service, take-out. Has seat-
ing outside. Accepts DIS, MC, VISA. Price: $.
Directions: Take Hwy 8W until it ends. At Sun-
set Cliff's Blvd turn left and go to Ocean Beach.
At Voltaire St turn left and this place on right.
From I-5, take Sea World Dr exit, then go east
on Sea World Dr for 1¾ mile, stay straight and
go onto Sunset Cliffs Blvd for 1 mile, at Voltaire
St turn left and this place is halfway down the
block.

Pokez Mexican Restaurant

947 E Street, downtown; 619-702-7160
Hours: Monday to Friday 9 am to 8 pm; Satur-
day 9 am to 6 pm; Sunday 9 am to 4 pm
Vegetarian-friendly Mexican. Vegan options. Not
pure vegetarian.
Menu: Has around 30 vegetarian dishes on the
menu. Vegetarian tacos, tofu burritos, enchiladas,
quesadillas and Tofu Tostada Salad. A basket of
chips and salsa come with the meal.
Comments: Beans, tortillas, chips and rice are
vegetarian. Cooks with canola olive and not lard.
Meat and tofu are not cooked in the same place.
A casual, hip place. Pokey is pronounced po-keys.
Happening place popular with musicians and artists. Many of the vegetarian dishes can be made

vegan. Usually has friendly and quick service. Reasonably priced. Recommended.

Other Info: Non-smoking. Reservations not necessary. Accepts MC, VISA (over $10). Price: $-$$.

Directions: This place is about a half-mile due south of the southeast corner of Balboa Park in downtown San Diego. From I-5, take CA Hwy 163/10th Ave exit to the downtown, then go straight south on 10th Ave for 5 blocks, at F St turn right and go 1 block, at 9th Ave turn right and go 1 block, at E St turn right and this place is 50 yards down.

Souplantation

6171 Mission Gorge Road	619-280-7087
3960 W Point Loma Boulevard	619-222-7404
17210 Bernardo Center Drive	619-675-3353
3804 Valley Centre Drive	619-481-3225
8105 Mira Mesa Boulevard	858-566-1172

Hours: Monday to Thursday, Sunday 11 am to 9 pm; Friday & Saturday 11 am to 10 pm

Web site: www.gardenfresh.com

Salad and Soup Bar. American Not pure vegetarian.

Menu: Has an all-you-can-eat salad bar with over 50 dishes. Soups, cornbread, desserts, fruits, pastas and much more.

Comments: Good service.

Other Info: Accepts DC, DIS, MC, VISA. Price: $$.

Soup Exchange

1840 Garnet Avenue, Pacific Beach
858-272-7766

Hours: Monday to Thursday 11 am to 9 pm; Friday & Saturday 11 am to 9:30 pm; Sunday 11 am to 9 pm

Soup and Salad Place. All-you-can-eat Soup and Salad Bar. Not pure vegetarian.

Menu: One or two vegetarian soups each day. Has a few dozens items in the salad bar. Fresh breads, nachos and muffins.

Other Info: Accepts AMEX, DC, DIS, MC, VISA. Price: $.

Sunshine Organic Foods

3918 30th Street, at University; 619-294-8055

Hours: Monday to Saturday 9 am to 8 pm
Sunday 10 am to 7 pm

Natural Food Store and Vegetarian Deli. Bakery. Organic produce (largest selection in San Diego).

Menu: The deli is vegan friendly and has vegan desserts. Grilled vegetable subs, soups, salads,

Seitan dishes and more.

Other Info: Accepts AMEX, DC, DIS, MC, VISA. Counter service, take-out. Has seating on the back patio.

Directions: From I-805, take University Ave exit and go west a half-mile, then at 30th St turn right and this place is 100 yards down on the left.

Taste of Thai

527 University Avenue, Hillcrest; 619-291-7525
15770 San Andreas Drive, Delmar (second branch); 858-793-9695

Hours: Monday to Saturday 11:30 am to 3 pm, 5 pm to 10:45 pm; Sunday 5 pm to 11:45 pm

Thai. Vegan options. Not pure vegetarian.

Menu: Any dish can be made vegetarian. Mock duck is good.

Comments: Service is excellent. Gets good recommendations. Very popular place. University Avenue branch has outdoor dining.

Other Info: Full service, take-out. Accepts AMEX, MC, VISA. Price: $-$$.

Trader Joe's

Carmel Mountain Ranch, 11955 Carmel Mt. Road; 619-673-0526
Pacific Beach, 1211 Garnet Avenue
619-272-7235

**Vegetarian Zone

2949 5th Avenue, 619-298-7302;
Web site: http://thevegetarianzone.com

Hours: Monday to Thursday 11:30 am to 3 pm, 5:30 pm to 9 pm; Friday 11:30 am to 3 pm, 5:30 pm to 10 pm; Saturday 9:30 am to 10 pm; Sunday 9:30 am to 9 pm; Saturday & Sunday Brunch

Full Vegetarian International and American. Vegan-friendly. Serves eggs. Bakery. New Age Shop next door.

Menu: Separate lunch and dinner menus. Greek Spinach Pie, salads, soups, sandwiches, Curried Vegetables over Brown Rice, Golden Tofu Nuggets, Sesame Vegetarian Chicken, Stuffed Grape Leaves, Nacho Supreme, Roast Vegetable Sandwich, Greek Spinach Pie, Spicy Tempeh Bake, Tofu Tacos, Spinach Mushroom Lasagna, steamed vegetables, veggie burgers, homemade dressings, Tofu Balls appetizer, homemade dressings and mushrooms Aphrodite (fresh mushrooms stuffed with walnuts, spinach and sunflower seeds).

Comments: The food gets high recommendations. Inside and outside garden patio dining. This place was formally called Kung Food. Open since 1975. Pleasant, friendly atmosphere.

Other Info: Full service, deli service, take-out,

catering, private parties. Non-smoking. Reservations not necessary. Accepts DIS, MC, VISA. Price: $-$$.
Directions: This place is located a block west of Balboa Park (near the northeast corner). From CA Hwy 163 going south, take the University Ave exit, then go on 6th Ave for 1¼ mile, then at Palm St turn right and go 1 block, then at 5th Ave turn right and this place is a half-block down. From I-5, take CA 163 exit, keep left at fork in ramp, merge onto CA 163 and go a third-mile, take the Quince St exit towards Balboa Park, then go on Quince St a quarter-mile, at 6th Ave turn left and go 1 block, at Palm St turn right and go 1 block, then at 5th Ave turn right and go a half-block.

Whole Foods Market
711 University Avenue; 619-294-2800
Hours: Daily 8 am to 10 pm
Natural Food Store and Cafe. Deli, Bakery, Salad Bar and Juice Bar. Organic produce. Supermarket-type place. See Whole Foods Market information.
Directions: This place is in north (central) San Diego. From CA Hwy 163, take the Washington St exit, then go a block west on Washington St, then turn left at 9th Ave and go 1 block, then turn right at University Avenue and this place is 1 block down.

SAN LUIS OBISPO

Big Sky
1121 Broad Street; 805-545-5401
Hours: Monday to Saturday 7 am to 10 pm Sunday 8 am to 9 pm
Restaurant. Vegan options. Not pure vegetarian.
Menu: Soups, salads, sandwiches, pastas, Mushroom Sandwich, Eggplant Sandwich, baba ghanouj, Spring Rolls, veggie chili and more.
Other Info: Accepts AMEX, MC, VISA.

Blazing Blenders Juice Bar
1108 Broad Street; 805-546-8122
Hours: Daily 8 am to 6 pm
Juice Bar.

Hobee's
1443 Calle Joaquin; 805-549-9186
Hours: Monday to Friday 7:30 am to 2:30 pm Saturday & Sunday 7:30 am to 3 pm

Jewel of India Restaurant
2115 Broad Street; 805-543-3558
Hours: Monday to Saturday 11:30 am to 3 pm,

5 pm to 9:30 pm; Sunday 5 pm to 9:30 pm
Indian. Vegan options. Not pure vegetarian.
Menu: Has many vegetarian dishes such as Channa Masala, Mung Dal, samosas and Malai Kofta.
Other Info: Full service, take-out. Accepts DIS, MC, VISA. Price: $$.

New Frontiers Natural Foods
896 Foothill Boulevard #896C
805-785-0194
Hours: Monday to Saturday 9 am to 7 pm Sunday 10 am to 5 pm
Natural Food Store and Deli. Organic produce.
Menu: Has a good selection of vegetarian dishes in the deli.
Other Info: Counter service, take-out.
Directions: This place is a half-mile southwest California Polytechnic University. From US 101, take CA Rte 1 exit towards Morro Bay/Hearst Castle, then go northwest on Santa Rosa St (Rte 1) for 0.65 mile, at Foothill Blvd turn left and this place is 1 block down.

Questa Co-op Natural Foods
745 Francis Street
805-544-7928; **email:** questa-coop@slonet.org
Hours: Daily 9 am to 9 pm
Natural Food Store. Organic produce.
Comments: Friendly place.
Directions: About 5 miles from the highway. From Hwy 101, take Marsh St exit and drive around the bend. At Broad St turn right (follow signs to airport). At Francis turn left. This place at corner of Francis and Broad, behind the Circle K Market.

Taj Palace
795 Foothill Boulevard, Suite A; 805-543-0722
Hours: Daily 11:30 am to 3 pm, 5 pm to 10 pm
Indian. Vegan options. Not pure vegetarian.
Menu: Has a good selection of vegetarian dishes.
Other Info: Full service, take-out. Accepts MC, VISA. Price: $$.

SANTA ANA

Niki's Tandoori Express
3705 S Bristol   714-838-7615
2031 E 1st Street   714-542-2969
Hours: Daily 11 am to 10 pm
Indian. Not pure vegetarian.
Menu: Has several vegetarian dishes.
Other Info: Counter service, take-out. Price: $-$$.

SANTA CLARA (Santa Clara County)

Dahlakl
735 Franklin Street
408-243-2384
Hours: Sunday to Thursday 11 am to 10 pm
Friday & Saturday 11 am to 12 midnight
Eritrean (East African). Not pure vegetarian.

**Dasaprakash
2636 Homestead Road, Santa Clara
408-246-8292; **fax:** 408-246-8293
email: dasaprakash@dasaprakash.com
Hours: Monday to Thursday 11:30 am to 2:30 pm, 5:30 pm to 9:30 pm; Friday 11:30 am to 2:30 pm, 5:30 pm to 10 pm; Saturday & Sunday 11:30 am to 10 pm
Vegetarian Indian. Mainly South Indian. Vegan-friendly.
Menu: Has a great selection of vegetarian dishes including soup, idly, dosas, vada, bondas, pakoras, samosas, poories, Indian curries, special rice dishes, Indian thali meals, Indian sweets and ice cream. Has a good web site with their full menu on it. Got good reviews in *LA Weekly* and the *Los Angeles Times*.
Comments: This is the branch of the famous Dasaprakash chain in India, which always has high quality great tasting food. Recommended. Good place to go for South Indian vegetarian dishes. Excellent service. Friendly place. Price: $$.
Directions: Across from the Santa Clara library. From US 101, take San Tomas Exwy/Montaque Exwy exit, then go south on San Tomas Exwy for 3 miles, at Homestead Rd turn right and this place is 2 blocks down.

Pasand India Cuisine
3701 El Camino Real, at Lawrence Expressway
408-241-5150
Web site: http://waiter.com/PASAND/pindex.html
Hours: Daily 11:30 am to 10 pm
Indian. Vegan options. Not pure vegetarian.
Menu: Authentic South Indian food. About half the dishes on the menu are vegetarian.
Comments: Has live classical Indian music on Friday and Saturday evenings. Can order food at their Web page. Exotic décor. Pleasant atmosphere.
Other Info: Full service, take-out, catering. Non-smoking. Accepts AMEX, DC, DIS, MC, VISA. Price: $$.
Directions: Next to Orchard Hardware at Lawrence Expressway.

**Real Ice Cream
3077 El Camino Real; 408-984-6601
Hours: Tuesday to Friday 12 noon to 3 pm, 5 pm to 9 pm; Saturday & Sunday 12 pm to 9 pm; closed Monday.
Vegetarian Ice Cream and Indian Snacks.
Menu: Has Indian flavored ice creams such as mango, leeches, chiccoo, almond pista saffron, badam pista kesar, kesar pista, masala chai, ginger, cardamom and saffron rose. Has Indian snack such as raj kachori, masala mix, papdi chat, phav bhaji, bhel puri, samosas and pani puri.
Directions: From US 101, take the San Tomas Expy/Montaque Exwy exit, then go south on the San Tomas Exwy for 2 miles, at El Camino Real/Rte 82 turn right and this place is a half-mile down.

Truya Sushi
3431 El Camino Real; 408-244-4534
Hours: Daily 11 am to 2 pm, 5 pm to 10 pm
Karaoke Hours: 10 pm to 2 am
Japanese. Vegetarian options. Not pure vegetarian.
Other Info: Full service, take-out. Accepts AMEX, DC, DIS, MC, VISA. Price: $$.

SANTA CLARITA

India's Tandoori
23360 Valencia Boulevard; 661-288-1200
Hours: Daily 11:30 am to 3 pm, 5 pm to 10 pm
Indian. Vegan options. Not pure vegetarian.
Menu: Has a vegetarian section on the menu that includes samosas, rice and curried vegetables.
Comments: Bakes with a traditional clay-oven.
Other Info: Full service, take-out. Accepts MC, VISA. Price: $.

Lassen's Health Foods
26861 Bouquet Canyon Road; 661-263-6935
Hours: Daily 9 am to 8 pm
Natural Food Store. Macrobiotic and Vegan options. Organic produce.
Comments: Local organic produce used when possible. Price: $$.

SANTA CRUZ

Asian Rose
1547 Pacific Avenue; 831-458-3023
Directions: Follow Rte 1 into town and the road becomes Chestnut St, then turn left 2 blocks down at Locust St and go 2 blocks, then turn left at Cedar St, then turn right then right again onto Pacific Ave and this place is 1 block down.

Hours: Monday to Saturday 11:30 am to 5 pm;
Closed Sunday
1116 Soquel (2nd branch); 831-423-7906
Directions: This place is in northeast Santa Cruz.
From Rte 1, go south on Morrissey Blvd for a
half-mile, then turn slight right at Soquel Ave
and this place is a quarter-mile down.
Hours: Monday to Thursday 5:30 pm to 9 pm;
Friday & Saturday 5 pm to 9:30 pm; closed Sun.
Vegetarian. Mainly Vegan. Salad Bar. Ceylon,
Balinese, Sri Lanka, Indian and Chinese.
Menu: You choose one, two, or three dishes from
around ten choices. Lemon Grass, Vegetable
Pakoras, organic tofu, spring beans, Sri Lankan
Spring Rolls, stir-fry dishes and Middle Eastern
dishes. Sri Lankan Curry Sampler Platter is a good
sampler of the dishes that they serve. Rice is served
with all meals. All vegan (except spring roll).
Comments: There are two branches of Asian Rose
in Santa Cruz, which both have the same owner.
The Pacific Ave branch is mainly open for lunch.
The food is served out buffet-style. The other
branch on Soquel is open for dinner. Family run
restaurant. Casual place.
Other Info: Soquel branch is full service. Cash
or check; no credit cards. Price: $$. Limited ser-
vice, take-out.

The Bagelry

320 A Cedar Street   831-429-8049
1636 Seabright Avenue   831-425-8550
Hours: Daily 6:30 to 5:30
Bagel Shop and Juice Bar. Vegan options. Not
pure vegetarian.
Menu: Has twenty types of bagels with tofu and
hummus spreads. Vegan soups, salads, sandwiches
and vegan cookies. Fresh juices.
Comments: Has outdoor seating.
Other Info: Counter service, take-out. Price: $.

Black Beach Café

2-1490 East Cliff Drive, East Santa Cruz
831-475-2233
Hours: Tuesday to Sunday 5 pm to 9 pm
Saturday and Sunday Brunch 9 am to 2 pm
American. Not pure vegetarian. Uses organic veg-
etables sometimes.
Menu: Hearts of romaine, baked portobello, goat
cheese and garlic salad with a special dressing.
Main dishes can come with tofu instead of meat.
Roasted potatoes and root vegetables such as beets,
bok choy and sweet potatoes. BBC Potato Ra-
violi with pumpkin sauce and Parmesan cheese.
For dessert there are Asian pears with an orange
sauce and Vanilla Ice Cream with plums in a

chocolate sauce.
Comments: Upscale place. Hip atmosphere.
Price: $$-$$$.

Eco-Goods

1130 Pacific Avenue
831-429-5758
Eco-friendly Place. Does not sell food. Sells hemp
clothing and non-toxic cleaners.

Emily's

1129 Mission Street, west Santa Cruz
831-429-9866
Bakery. Has really good vegan cookies and cakes.

Falafel of Santa Cruz

1501 Mission Street, on the Hwy 1 strip in west
Santa Cruz
831-459-0486
Hours: Daily 11 am to 9:30 pm
Falafel sandwiches. Not pure vegetarian.

The Food Bin

1130 Mission Street, west Santa Cruz
831-423-5526
Hours: Daily 9 am to 12 midnight
Natural Food Store. Organic produce.
Menu: Has a good selection of ready-made sand-
wiches and salads in the cooler.
Comments: It is a small place. Has a large selec-
tion of organic produce and an excellent selec-
tion of herbs. Opposite Emily's restaurant.
Directions: Take Hwy 1 into Santa Cruz and it
becomes Mission Street (take right fork). This
place at corner of Laurel and Mission about 7
blocks down.

Gabriella Café

910 Cedar Street
831-457-1677
Hours: Sunday to Thursday 11:30 am to 3 pm,
5:30 pm to 9:30 pm; Friday & Saturday 11:30
am to 3 pm, 5:30 pm to 10 pm; Weekend Brunch
International. Californian, Italian. Not pure veg-
etarian. Often uses organic produce.
Menu: Has a selection of vegetarian dishes. Pump-
kin Ravioli. The menu changes seasonally
Comments: Has candle-lit dining. Romantic at-
mosphere. Local organic produce used when pos-
sible. Got some good reviews in local publica-
tions.
Other Info: Full service, take-out. Reservations
required. Accepts AMEX, DIS, MC, VISA. Price:
$$-$$$.

Hobee's Restaurant

The Galleria de Santa Cruz
740 Front Street (Galleria)
831-458-1212
Hours: Sunday to Thursday 8 am to 9 pm
Friday & Saturday 8 am to 9:30 pm

**Jahva House

120 Union Street, at Cedar Street
831-459-9876
Hours: Daily 6:30 am to 5:30 pm
Vegetarian Café. Vegan options.
Menu: Soups, salads, sandwiches, veggie Lasagna, Tamale Pies and vegan desserts. Does not have much of a selection for eating.
Comments: Great atmosphere. Cash and local checks only.
Directions: Take Hwy 1 into Santa Cruz and keep going straight (take left fork) to first left turn, turn left at Locust St and go 2 blocks, at Cedar St turn left and go 1 block, then at Union St turn left and this place is near the corner.

Kresge Food Co-op

600 Kresge Counter service, take-out, Kresge College UCSC; 408-426-1506; **email:** coop@dv8.org; **Web site:** http://k9.dv8.org/~coop/
Natural Food Store.

Linda's Seabreeze Café

542 Seabright Avenue, East side of Santa Cruz
831-427-9713
Hours: Monday to Saturday 6 am to 2 pm
Sunday 7 am to 1 pm
American Breakfasts. Vegan options. Not pure vegetarian
Menu: Has different scrambled meals for breakfast, which are served with homemade muffins, Tofu Scramble and home fried potatoes. Greek Scramble (feta cheese, potatoes, spinach, black olive). Tofu Fun (tofu cooked with tomatoes, mushrooms and salsa).
Comments: Friendly place. Especially busy on Sunday morning, when you may have to wait an hour to be served.
Other Info: Full service, take-out. Cash and check only; no credit cards. Price $.

New Leaf Community Market

1134 Pacific Avenue, downtown
831-425-1793
Web site: www.newleaf.com
Hours: Daily 9 am to 9 pm
Natural Food Store and Vegan-friendly Deli.
Organic produce. Large store with good variety.

Directions: From Hwy 1 drive into Santa Cruz, then take Mission (or Chestnut), then turn left at Lincoln and this place is several blocks down at Pacific Avenue.

New Leaf Community Market

2351 Mission Street
408-426-1306; **fax:** 831-426-3257
email: newleaf@livingnaturally.com
Web site: www.newleaf.com
Hours: Daily 8 am to 9 pm
Natural Food Store and Vegan-friendly Deli.
Vegan options. Not pure vegetarian. Organic produce. Large store with a good variety.
Menu: A large selection of sandwiches, salads, soups and hot dishes. Fresh juices.
Comments: Outdoor dining. Counter service, take-out. Accepts MC, VISA. Price: $.
Directions: This place is in west Santa Cruz. Take Hwy 1 south into town, then bear right onto Mission St. (Follow signs for UCSC). Cross Bay St and continue down Mission St. Turn left at Fair Ave, turn right at MacPherson St and then turn right into the back parking lot of Mission Center. Entrance on MacPherson.

Pizza My Heart

1116 Pacific Avenue, Unit B; 831-426-2511
Hours: Sunday 11 am to 11 pm
Friday & Saturday 11 am to 2 am
Pizza Place. Not pure vegetarian.
Menu: Marks vegetarian pizzas in green on menu board.

Royal Taj

270 Soquel Avenue
831-427-2400
Hours: Daily 11:30 am to 2:30 pm, 5:30 pm to 10 pm
Indian. Not pure vegetarian. See Campbell.
Menu: Has a decent selection of vegetarian dishes.
Comments: The outside of the building is a bit run down, but it looks good inside.
Other Info: Accepts AMEX, DC, DIS, MC, VISA. Price: $-$$.

Saturn Café

145 Laurel Street;
831-429-8505; **fax:** 831-429-9069
email: info@saturncafe.com
Web site: www.saturncafe.com
Hours: Sunday to Thursday 11:30 am to 3 am
Friday & Saturday 11:30 am to 4 am
Delivers: 11:30 am to 2 pm in downtown Santa Cruz. Can phone or fax in order.

American Café and Bakery. Vegan and Vegetarian-friendly. Not pure vegetarian (serves tuna). **Menu:** Has a great selection of vegetarian dishes. Soups, salads, sandwiches, veggie burgers, Ratatouille, Veggie Chili Cheese Burger, chili, Fakin Bakin Cheeseburger, Grilled Mushroom Burger, pasta, organic salad, homemade soups, chips, vegan nachos, hummus sandwich, a daily special and desserts. Espresso. Features organic Nub Chai.
Comments: Has a good atmosphere. The food is really good. Very reasonably priced. Popular place for the students. Gets high recommendations.
Other Info: Counter service, take-out. Non-smoking. Reservations not necessary. Accepts MC, VISA. Price: $.
Directions: This place is in downtown Santa Cruz, about a half-mile from the beach. Take Rte 17 into town and road becomes Ocean St, at Broadway turn right and go a half-mile (road becomes Laurel St).

**Staff of Life Natural Foods
1305 Water Street, East Santa Cruz
831-423-8632, 831-423-8147
Café: 831-423-8041
Hours: Daily 9 am to 9 pm
Natural Food Store and Vegetarian Café. Deli, Salad bar and Juice Bar. Vegan options.
Menu: Has a good selection of vegetarian and vegan dishes. Soups, Vegan Succotash, salads, sandwiches, falafels, burritos, and a daily main dish special (usually rice or pasta based). Has vegan baked items including a Tofu Fruit Pie. The ingredients of the dressings are listed and they are marked whether they are vegan or organic. Salad items are marked whether they are organic or not. Fresh juices and smoothies.
Comments: Sells oils and body lotions by the ounce. The natural food store has a large selection of organic produce. Accepts MC, VISA.
Other Info: Counter service, take-out. Has outside dining. Price: $. Accepts MC, VISA.
Directions: From Hwy 1, take Morrissey exit and go south. At Water turn right. This place on right.

SANTEE (just north of San Diego)

Henry's Marketplace
9751 Mission Gorge Road
619-258-4060
Hours: Daily 8 am to 9 pm
Natural Food Store and Deli. Organic produce. Bakery. Supermarket-type place.

SOLANA BEACH (just north of San Diego, San Diego County)

Henry's Marketplace
659 Lomas Santa Fe Drive; 858-350-7900
Hours: Daily 8 am to 9 pm
Natural Food Store and Deli. Organic produce.
Directions: Solana Beach is on the coast, just north of San Diego. From I-5, take Lomas Santa Fe Dr exit, then go west on Lomas Santa Fe Dr and this place is 100 yards down.

**Zinc Café
132 South Cedros, Solana Beach
858-793-5436; Web site: www.zinccafe.com
Hours: Daily 7 am to 5 pm
Vegetarian. Californian and American.
Menu: Soups, salads, Baked Eggplant Pizza, Mushroom Medley Pizza, Zinc Salad (mixed greens, feta cheese, croutons, pine nuts, olives), Mexican Pizza, Mixed Vegetable Sandwich, Zinc Veggie Burger, Vegetarian Chili, baked goods, breads and desserts. For breakfast there is Roasted Herbed Potatoes, granola, oatmeal and fruit. Southwestern Pizzette is chipotle, mozzarella cheese, smoked Gouda, roasted corn, tomato and black beans.
Comments: Indoors and outdoors seating. Has a cozy outdoor patio with a fountain and trees.
Other Info: Counter service, take-out, catering. Accepts AMEX, DIS, MC, VISA. Price: $-$$.
Directions: South Cedros runs parallel with Hwy 101. From I-5, take Lomas Santa Fe Dr exit, then go west on Lomas Santa Fe Dr and go ¾ mile, then at South Cedros turn left and this place is 100 yards down.

SOQUEL

Tortilla Flats
4616 Soquel Drive; 831-476-1754
Hours: Daily for lunch and dinner
Mexican. Not pure vegetarian.
Menu: Beans, rice and "Flatland Mix" (a nut mixture) can be put on the burritos and tostadas.
Other Info: Full service, take-out. Accepts MC, VISA. Price: $-$$.

SOUTH LAKE TAHOE (El Dorado County)

Grass Roots
2040 Dunlap, just off Hwy 50; 530-541-7788
Hours: Monday to Saturday 10 am to 7 pm
Sunday 11 am to 6 pm

Natural Food Store and Bakery. Organic produce.
Menu: Baked goods and pizzas.
Other Info: Counter service, take-out.
Directions: Store at junction of Hwy 50 and Hwy 89, by the Y.

Sprouts Café
3123 Harrison Avenue (Hwy 50 & Alameda Avenue); 530-541-6969
Hours: Daily 8 am to 10 pm
Natural Foods. Not pure vegetarian.
Menu: Has a large selection of vegetarian dishes including soups, salads, sandwiches, quesadillas, tempeh burgers and tostadas. Fresh juices, cappuccino, espresso.
Other Info: Limited service, take-out. Cash only; no credit cards. Price: $.
Directions: This place is on the west side of South Lake Tahoe Recreation Area, 3 blocks from the lake.

SQUAW VALLEY

Squaw Valley Community Market
1600 Squaw Valley Road; 530-581-2014
Hours: Monday to Saturday 10 am to 8 pm
Sunday 11 am to 6 pm
Natural Food Store.
Directions: At the foot of Squaw Mountain. After entering Squaw Valley, at Squaw Valley Rd turn right and this place is two miles down on the right. It is in a strip mall next to the post office.

STOCKTON (San Joaquin county)

Trader Joe's
Lincoln Center South, 6535 Pacific Avenue, at Benjamin Holt Drive
209-951-7597

SUISUN (Solano County)

Raley's
270 Sunset Avenue; 707-426-1023
Hours: Daily 6 am to 11 pm
Supermarket with a large natural foods section.

TRUCKEE

New Moon Natural Foods
Donner Plaza, 11357C Donner Pass Road
530-587-7426
Hours: Monday to Saturday 9 am to 7 pm

Sunday 10 am to 6 pm
Natural Food Store.
Directions: From I-80, take Squaw Valley (Hwy 89) exit. From west turn left and from east turn right at exit. Take first left into Donner Plaza.

UKIAH (Mendocino County)

Earthly Delight (Arlene's)
415 Talmage Road; 707-462-4970
Hours: Monday to Saturday 9:30 am to 5:30 pm
Sunday 10 am to 4:30
Natural Food Store.
Directions: Located in the Pear Tree Shopping Center.

Ellie's Mutt Hutt & Vegetarian
732 South State Street; 707-468-5376
Hours: Monday to Saturday 6:30 am to 8 pm
Closed Sunday.
American. Vegan-friendly. Healthy food.
Menu: Has a wide selection of vegetarian dishes. Soups, salads, sandwiches, Mexican food and other dishes.
Other Info: Full service until 11 am. Counter service after 11 am. Accepts MC, VISA.
Directions: From Hwy 101, take the Gobbi St exit, then go west a half-mile on Gobbi St, at State St turn left and this place is 1 bock down.

Ukiah Natural Foods Co-op
721 South State Street; 707-462-4778
Hours: Monday to Friday 9 am to 7 pm; Saturday 10 am to 6 pm; Sunday 10 am to 6 pm
Natural Food Store. Organic produce.
Other Info: Full service until 11 am. Counter service after 11 am. Accepts MC, VISA.
Directions: From Hwy 101, take the Gobbi St exit, then go west a half-mile on Gobbi St, at State St turn left and this place is 1 bock down.

UPLAND

**Veggie Panda Wok
903-B West Foothill Boulevard; 909-982-3882
Hours: Tuesday to Saturday 11 am to 9 pm
Sunday & Monday 4 pm to 9 pm
Vegetarian Chinese. Has a buffet and full service.
Directions: It is between LA and Palm Springs about a mile from Interstate 10.
Other Info: Accepts AMEX, MC, VISA. Price: $.
Directions: Foothill is the main street going east–west through Upland.

VACAVILLE (Solano County)

The Nutrition Shoppe

Golden Hills Plaza, 983 Alamo Drive
707-447-2306
Hours: Monday to Friday 9 am to 7 pm
Saturday & Sunday 10 am to 6 pm
Natural Food Store and Juice Bar. Organic
produce & coffee.
Comments: Pretty good selection of items. Relatively good selection of foods. Large vitamin selection. Will special order items. Discount for case
purchases. Friendly place.
Other Info: Accepts AMEX, MC, VISA.
Directions: From I-80 east, take Alamo exit, then
head south on Alamo and this place is a quarter-mile down in same plaza as Food for Less.

Raley's

3063 Alamo Drive; 707-426-1092
Supermarket with a large natural foods section.

WATSONVILLE

Five Mile House

2904 Freedom Boulevard; 831-722-5700
Hours: Monday to Saturday 6:30 am to 5:30 pm
Sunday 6:30 am to 3 pm
Natural Food Store and Cafe. Organic produce.
Menu: Soups, sandwiches, salads and Mexican
dishes. Many of the dishes are organic.
Other Info: Counter service, take-out. Has seating. Accepts AMEX, DIS, MC, VISA.
Directions: From CA Hwy 1, go west on Freedom Blvd and this place is 5 miles down. This
place is about 3 mile northwest of downtown
Watsonville.

WILLITS

**Harvest Bounty

212 South Main Street, #23, on Highway 101
707-459-9647
Hours: Monday, Tuesday, Thursday, Friday 11
am to 5 pm; closed Wednesday, Saturday, Sun.
Vegetarian Restaurant.

Menu: Organic salads, fresh baked cornbread,
sandwiches, soups and main dishes. Fresh juices.
Other Info: Full service, take-out. Price: $.

Tsunami Restaurant

50 S Main Street, on Highway 101
707-459-4750
Hours: Sunday, Tuesday to Thursday 4:30 pm to
8 pm; Fri & Sat 4:30 to 9 pm; closed Mon.
Japanese and International. Not pure veg.
Menu: Salads, veggie sushi, 3 tofu dishes, mock
meat dishes and often has a vegetarian special.
Local organic produce used when possible. Some
of the desserts contain no eggs, dairy or sugar.
Comments: There is patio dining surrounded by
Japanese flowers, maple trees and plum trees.
Other Info: Full service, take-out. Reservations
recommended. Price: $$.

YORBA LINDA

Henry's Marketplace

17482 Yorba Linda Boulevard; 714-572-3535
Hours: Daily 8 am to 9 pm
Natural Food Store and Cafe. Deli, Bakery,
Salad Bar and Juice Bar. Organic produce. Supermarket-type place. See Wild Oats Market
information.
Directions: This place is about 5 miles due northeast of where Hwy 57 and Hwy 91 meet.

YUBA CITY (Sutter County)

Sunflower Natural Foods Market

726 Sutter Street; 530-671-9511
Store Hours: Monday to Saturday 10 am to 6
pm; closed Sunday.
Deli Hours: Monday to Saturday 10 am to 2:30
pm
Natural Food Store and Café. Deli, Bakery and
Juice Bar. Vegan options.
Comments: Next to Feather River, which is a
good place for swimming and boating.
Directions: From Hwy 20, take Sutter St exit,
then go south on Sutter St and this place is on
the right a quarter-mile down.

Los Angeles Area

To get some detailed up-to-date reviews about vegetarian restaurants in the Los Angeles area check out the Vegetarians in Paradise Web site (www.vegparadise.com). The reviews are detailed and interesting.

ALTADENA

**Oh Happy Days'
2283 North Lake Avenue; 626-797-0383
Hours: Monday to Friday 11 am to 6:30 pm; Saturday 11 am to 6 pm; closed Sunday.
Natural Food Store and Vegetarian Restaurant. Cafeteria Style. Vegan-friendly.
Menu: The menu changes daily. Soups, sandwiches, veggie Lasagna, curry, Asian dishes, Mexican dishes and salads.
Other Info: Counter service, take-out. Has seating. Accepts MC, VISA.
Directions: From I-210, take Arroyo Blvd exit towards Windsor Ave, then go east on W Woodbury Rd for 2¼ miles, at N Lake Ave turn left and this place is a half-mile down.

ANAHEIM
Anaheim is the home of Disney Land.

Disneyland
Bengal Barbecue, In Adventureland. Fruit plate (with yogurt), pretzels, Vegetarian Shishkabob has potatoes, bell pepper, zucchini, mushroom and onions.
Goofy's Kitch has a buffet with a good amount of vegetarian dishes. Eggless pasta with marinara sauce, salads, fruits, breads and juices. Potatoes with onion and green peppers, good selection of fruits and bagels for breakfast. Set price for the buffet. Price: $$.
River Belle Terrace, entrance of Adventureland and Frontierland, has Vegetable Stew.
Ville Verde, At Disneyland Hotel. Some of the homemade pastas do not contain eggs (some do, so check). Tomato Angel Hair Pasta and Basil. Fettuccine with Roasted Vegetables (Eggplant, zucchini, tomato, onion).

**Pooja
2751 West Lincoln Avenue; 714-527-3800
Hours: Tuesday to Sunday 11:30 am to 8:30 pm Closed Monday.
Vegetarian Gujarati Indian. Specializes in Gujarati cuisine. Lunch Buffet. Has good food.
Menu: Has a wide selection of vegetarian dishes.
Other Info: Accepts MC, VISA. Price: $.
Directions: From I-5, take Beach Blvd/Rte 39, then go south on Beach Blvd (Rte 39) and go 2¼ miles, then at W Lincoln Ave turn left and this place is a half-mile down.

**Yogiraj Vegetarian Restaurant
3107 West Lincoln Avenue ; 714-995-5900
Hours: Tuesday to Sunday 11 am to 9 pm Closed Monday
Fully Vegetarian Indian. Mostly Vegan.
Menu: Specializes in vegetarian Gujarati cooking. Has Bajri Rotis, homemade butter, dal, rice dishes, curried vegetables and Gujarati sweet rice.
Comments: Family run and operated.
Other Info: Full service, buffet service, take-out, catering. Non-smoking. Reservations are recommended. Cash only; no credit cards.
Directions: From 91 E or W take the Beach South exit and then make a right on Lincoln. From I-5, take Beach Blvd/Rte 39, then go south on Beach Blvd (Rte 39) and go 2¼ miles, then at W Lincoln Ave turn right and this place is a quarter-mile down.

ARCADIA (near Pasadena)

**Wonton
815 West Naomi Avenue, Unit A, Arcadia
626-445-5688
Hours: Daily 11 am to 10 pm
Vegetarian Chinese.
Menu: Noodle and rice dishes are specialties.
Other Info: Cash only; no credit cards.
Directions: From I-210, take the Baldwin Ave exit, then go south on Baldwin Ave for 1¾ miles and then this place is at the junction with W Naomi Ave.

ARTESIA

Ashoka the Great

18614 South Pioneer Boulevard; 562-809-4229
Hours: Mon to Fri 11 am to 3 pm, 5 pm to 10 pm; Sat & Sun 11 am to 10 pm; Lunch Buffet 11 am to 3 pm
Indian. Not pure vegetarian.
Menu: Has a large amount of vegetarian Indian dishes that include pakoras, baked eggplant, rice dishes, samosas, an okra dish and Masala Dosa.
Other Info: Full service, take-out. Accepts MC, VISA. Price: $-$$.
Directions: It is located near the Anaheim Convention Center and close to Disneyland. It is a mile southeast of the junction of Hwy 91 & I-605. From I-605, take the South St exit, then go east on South St for a half-mile, at Pioneer Blvd turn left and this place is a quarter-mile down.

Jay Bharat Restaurant

18701 Pioneer Boulevard
562-924-3310; **Web site:** www.jaybharat.com
Hours: Tuesday to Sunday 11 am to 8 pm
Closed Monday.
Indian. Not pure vegetarian.
Menu: Is very reasonably priced. South Indian snacks such as dosa and homemade sweets.
Comments: Popular place. In an Indian neighborhood with plenty of Indian grocery stores and sari shops in the area.
Other Info: Accepts MC, VISA. Price: $.
Directions: It is located near the Anaheim Convention Center and close to Disneyland. It is a mile southeast of the junction of Hwy 91 & I-605. From I-605, take the South St exit, then go east on South St for a half-mile, then at Pioneer Blvd turn left and this place is a quarter-mile down.

Udupi Palace

18635 Pioneer Boulevard; 562-860-1950
Hours: Tuesday to Sunday 11:30 to 10 pm
Closed Monday.
South Indian Vegetarian Restaurant.
Menu: Has South Indian foods such as dosa, Masala Dosa, idly and uttama (cream-of-wheat and cashews, recommended).
Other Info: Accepts MC, VISA.
Directions: It is located near the Anaheim Convention Center and close to Disneyland. It is a mile southeast of the junction of Hwy 91 & I-605. From I-605, take the South St exit, then go east on South St for a half-mile, then at Pioneer Blvd turn left and this place is a quarter-mile down.

***Woodlands

11833 Artesia Boulevard
562-860-8690
Hours: Tuesday to Sunday 11:30 am to 10 pm; Lunch Buffet 11:30 am to 3 pm; closed Monday.
Pure Vegetarian South Indian. Also has North Indian dishes.
Menu: Has a large selection of South Indian dishes. Dosa, Masala Dosa, Idly and thalis.
Comments: This is a branch of the Woodlands chain from South India, which are often the best (high class) vegetarian restaurants in India. Recommended.
Directions: From the Hwy 91 Artesia Freeway, take Pioneer Blvd exit towards Artesia, then go south on Pioneer a quarter-mile, then turn left at Artesia Blvd and this place is 100 yards down.

BEVERLY HILLS

A Votre Sante

242 South Beverly Drive
310-860-9441
Hours: Monday to Friday 8 am to 9:30 pm
Saturday: 9 am to 9 pm
Sunday: 9 am to 9 pm
Natural Foods Restaurant. Mostly Vegetarian (also serves fish and chicken). Vegan options. Organic foods.
Menu: Tofu Curry Wrap with Broccoli, brown rice, Mediterranean cuisine, pastas, salads, Asparagus Soup, Chow Mein, Falafel Platter, Tempeh Burgers, chapatti, Asparagus Risotto, Cornbread Muffins, veggie burgers, Caesar Pasta Salad, Black Bean Fettuccini, Vegetarian Burrito, Eggplant Lasagna (can be made with soy cheese), Hummus Quesadilla, Boca Burger, Blue Tortilla Chips with Salsa and Spinach Enchiladas with spinach and soy cheese. Two vegan soups daily. Has good soy cheese. For breakfast they have Scrambled Tofu, Fresh Fruit Bowl, Hot Cereal, Black Beans, Rosemary Potatoes & Asparagus and Hummus in a whole-wheat chapatti. Fresh juices.
Comments: A Votre Sante means in French "to your health." Popular place. Pleasant happening atmosphere. Has good soy cheese. Can request to get food oil free. A good part of the menu is non-dairy.
Other Info: Reservations requested for 6. Smoking allowed outside only. Accepts AMEX, MC, VISA. Price: $$.
Directions: From I-405, take the Wilshire Blvd East exit towards UCLA, then go east on Wilshire Blvd for 3¼ miles, at S Beverly Drive turn right and this place is 1½ block down.

Whole Foods Market

239 North Crescent Drive
310-274-3360
Hours: Daily 8 am to 9 pm
Natural Food Store and Cafe. Deli, Bakery, Salad Bar and Juice Bar. Organic produce. Supermarket-type place. See Whole Foods Market information.
Directions: From I-405, take the Wilshire Blvd Exit towards UCLA, then go east on Wilshire Blvd for 3½ miles, then at N Crescent Drive turn left and this place is 1½ block down.

BRENTWOOD (near Los Angeles)

A Votre Sante

13016 San Vicente Blvd; 310-451-1813
Hours: Monday 11 am to 10 pm; Tuesday to Friday 8:30 am to 10 pm; Saturday: 9 am to 10 pm; Sunday: 9 am to 9 pm
International Natural Foods. Vegan options. Organic foods. See Beverly Hills for details.
Directions: From I-405, take Sunset Blvd exit, then go southwest 1¼ mile on Sunset Blvd, at S Kenter Ave turn left (road becomes S Bundy Dr) and go a half-mile, at San Vicente Blvd turn right and this place is 1 mile down on the left.

Beverly Falafel

8508 3rd Street, In a mini-mall, a little south of the Beverly Center
310-652-1670
Hours: Daily 11 am to 9:30
Middle Eastern. Not pure vegetarian. Vegan options. Price: $.
Menu: Good falafel, hummus and eggplant.

Whole Foods – Brentwood

11737 San Vicente Boulevard; 310-826-4433
Hours: Daily 8 am to 10 pm; Café and Juice Bar opens at 7 am on the weekdays
Natural Food Store and Cafe. Deli, Bakery, Salad Bar and Juice Bar. Organic produce. Supermarket-type place. See Whole Foods Market information.
Directions: From I-405, take the Wilshire Blvd exit, then go west on Wilshire Blvd a half-mile, at San Vicente Blvd turn slight right and this place is a half-mile down.

BREA (Orange County)

Trader Joe's

Brea Imperial Center, 2500 Imperial Hwy, at Kraemer; 714-257-1180

CANOGA PARK

Delhi Sweet and Snacks

7257 Topanga Canyon Boulevard; 818-340-7500
Hours: Daily 11 am to 10 pm
Indian. Vegan options. Not pure vegetarian.
Menu: Has an inexpensive buffet with basmati rice dishes, salads, pakoras, naan, curry vegetables, raita, chutney and a dessert. Has a good selection of a la carte dishes including rice, Tandoori Roti, Bengan Bhartha (roasted eggplant and tomatoes), Okra Subji, Channa Masala and Gobhi Paratha
Comments: Popular, casual, friendly, basic place. Place order at counter and sit down and eat. Very reasonably priced.
Other Info: Accepts DIS, MC, VISA. Price: $.
Directions: This place is about 200 yards north of Sherman Way in the San Fernando Valley.

**Follow Your Heart

21825 Sherman Way
818-348-3240;
Web site: www.followyourheart.com
Hours: Daily 8 am to 9 pm
Breakfast Monday to Friday 8 am to 11:30 am
Saturday & Sunday brunch 8 am to 3pm
Natural Food Store and Fully Vegetarian (no eggs) **International Restaurant.** Vegan options.
Menu: Has a large selection of vegetarian dishes including several salads, a variety of pizzas, stuffed potatoes, ten sandwiches and ten main dishes. Salads, excellent soups (five daily, comes with whole-wheat roll), lentil soup, tofu dishes and main dishes. Pastas, mock "Chicken Fajita," burritos, FYH Burger, falafel, Zorro Burrito (huge, black beans, tofu chunks, rice, lettuce, salsa), large organic salads, multigrain mushroom burger with non-dairy mayo and cheese (soy optional), Nutburger and Vanilla Cake with sweet vanilla cream filling. The club sandwich is good. Popeye Split Pea Yam Soup is recommended. Menu is labeled for dairy and non-dairy. Has homemade tofu cottage cheese. Has vegetarian (rennetless) cheese. Fresh juices, raw milk, smoothies and shakes. Some desserts are Root Beer Float, Tofu Pumpkin Pie, Chocolate Torte and non-dairy milkshakes. Has a good selection (over 10) of nondairy homemade salad dressings.
Comments: Gets really high recommendations. Thirty-year-old natural foods market that is well stocked. The restaurant is in back of the natural food store. Indoor seating is fairly cramped, but there is usually more room at the counter and patio. Pleasant atmosphere. Knowledgeable and helpful staff. Ingredients used in cooking are free

of refined sugars and harmful additives. Generous portions. Has a cookbook that they sell. Friday night is Pizza Night, with dairy cheese or soy cheese pizza. Good desserts.

Other Info: Limited service, take-out. Has front patio seating that is open during the day and on Friday night. Non-smoking. Reservations not necessary. Accepts AMEX MC, VISA. Price: $$.

Directions: From Hwy 101, take Topanga Canyon exit north. Go north on Topanga Canyon Blvd (Rte 27) for 5½ miles, then at Sherman Way turn right and this place on left 1 block down.

Trader Joe's
Topanga Plaza
818-883-4134

CERRITOS

**Madras Tiffin
11321 East 183rd Street
310-924-0879

Hours: Tuesday to Sunday 11:30 am to 2:30 pm, 5 pm to 9:30 pm; closed Monday.

Vegetarian South Indian. Vegan options.

Menu: Has many vegetarian dishes including samosas, pakoras, dosa, puris, rice dishes and curried vegetables.

Comments: A bit upscale.

Other Info: Full service, take-out. Accepts MC, VISA. Price: $.

Directions: This place is next to the Los Cerritos Mall. From I-605, take South St Exit, then go west on South St 1 block, at Studebaker Rd turn right and go a half-mile, at 183rd St turn right and this place is a third-mile down.

***The Vegi Wokery
11329 183rd Street
562-809-3928

Hours: Monday to Saturday 11:30 am to 2:30 pm, 4:30 pm to 9 pm; closed Sunday.

Fully Vegan Chinese.

Menu: Has around 100 dishes on the menu. Special Vegetarian Pork Ribs, Steaming Vegetarian Fish, Vegetarian Honey Ham, Vegetarian Chicken Delight, Bean Curd Feast, Tofu Special, Vegetarian Carnival and Hot Bean Curd with Vegetables. Fresh juices.

Comments: Good atmosphere. Has good food. Reasonably priced. No MSG, eggs or dairy.

Other Info: Full service, catering. Non-smoking. Accepts reservations but aren't necessary.

Directions: From 91 Fwy take the Pioneer Blvd exit, then go south on Pioneer for 1 mile, then turn right at 183rd St (west) and go ¾ mile. Just past intersection of Gridley Rd, turn right into shopping center.

COSTA MESA

Country Store Nutrition
1775 Newport Boulevard, Costa Mesta
949-548-7751

Mother's Market & Kitchen
225 East 17th Street, near Newport; 949-631-4741; Web site: www.mothersmarket.com
email: customerservice@mothersmarket.com

Hours: Daily 9 am to 10 pm

Restaurant Hours: 9 am to 9:30 pm

Natural Food Store and Deli. International cuisine including Chinese, Middle Eastern, Mexican, Greek and Italian. Juice Bar. Fully vegetarian except tuna. Supermarket type place with a large organic produce section.

Menu: Has a large amount of vegetarian dishes including salads, soups, rice dishes, appetizers, sandwiches, pastas, Lasagna, Veggie Meatloaf, Veggie Pot Roast and entrees. Has weekly specials. Fresh juices, cappuccino, espresso. Non-alcoholic beer and wine. Has a kid's menu.

Other Info: Full service, take-out. Price: $.

Directions: From I-405, take Hwy 55 southwest, the highway ends and becomes Newport Blvd, and go ¾ mile. At 17th St turn left and this place is 2 blocks down on right.

Trader Joe's
103 East 17th; 714-642-5134

Whole Foods Market
1870 Harbor Boulevard, Costa Mesa
949-574-3800

Hours: Daily 9 am to 9 pm

Natural Food Store and Cafe. Deli, Bakery, Salad Bar and Juice Bar. Organic produce. Supermarket-type place. See Whole Foods Market information

Directions: From I-405, take Hwy 55 southwest, the highway ends and becomes Newport Blvd, and go a half-mile. At Harbor Blvd turn right and this place is 1 block down.

COVINA

Covina Tasty
1063 North Citrus Avenue; 626-332-8816

Hours: Daily 11 am to 11 pm

Mexican. Not pure vegetarian.

CULVER CITY

**Chandni Vegetarian Cuisine of India
3808 Bagley Avenue; 310-839-0482
Hours: Daily 11:30 am to 2:30 pm, 5 pm to 10 pm
Vegetarian Indian. Vegan options. All-you-can-eat buffet.
Menu: Has a large selection of vegetarian goods. Soups, breads, appetizers and other dishes.
Comments: Friendly service. Reasonably priced.
Other Info: Full service, take-out. Accepts MC, VISA. Price: $-$$.
Directions: From I-10, take the Robertson Blvd/Culver City exit, then go southeast on Exposition Blvd (or Robertson Blvd) a few blocks, at Venice Blvd turn right and this place is a third-mile down.

**Govinda's
3764 Watseka Avenue, just off Venice Blvd
310-836-1269; **Temple Number;** 310-836-2676
Hours: Monday to Saturday 11 am to 3 pm, 5 pm to 8:30 pm
Closed Sunday for feast that begins at 5:30 pm
Pure Vegetarian Indian and American. Many of the dishes contain dairy. Juice Bar
Menu: Has reasonably priced excellent lunch and dinner buffets. Veggie burgers, pizzas, curried vegetables, steam vegetables, rice dishes and excellent desserts.
Comments: Managed by the Hare Krishnas. The food is great and very reasonably priced. Recommended. Laid-back, casual, spiritual atmosphere. Has a good Indian Gift shop upstairs selling books, clothing, incense, religious items, deities and gift items.
Other Info: Cafeteria style, take-out, catering. Non-smoking. Reservations not necessary. Accepts MC, VISA. Price: $-$$.
Directions: This place is located next to a Hare Krishna Temple, just off Venice Blvd, at the border of Culver City and Los Angeles. Between Motor & Robertson. From I-10, take the Robertson Blvd/Culver City exit, then go southeast on Exposition Blvd (or Robertson Blvd) a few blocks, at Venice Blvd turn right and go a half-mile, at Watseka Ave turn right and this place is in the second building down on the right. Street parking.

Rainbow Acres
13208 Washington Boulevard; 310-306-8330
Hour: Monday to Friday 8:30 am to 9 pm
Saturday & Sunday 9 am to 8 pm
Natural Food Store and Deli. Salad Bar and Hot
Bar. Organic produce.
Menu: Salads, sandwiches, soups and hot dishes.
Other Info: Accepts AMEX, MC, VISA.
Directions: From I-405, take the Venice Blvd exit, and this place is a half-mile south of the exit on Washington Blvd.

Trader Joe's
10011 Washington Boulevard; 310-202-1108

ENCINO (LOS ANGELES COUNTY)

Trader Joe's
17640 Burbank Boulevard; 818-990-7751

FOUNTAIN VALLEY

***Alisan
17201 Brookhurst Street; 714-962-0055,
Hours: Daily 11 am to 2:30 pm, 4 pm to 9 pm
Sunday 12 noon to 8 pm
Fully Vegan, Organic, Chinese Vegetarian Restaurant.
Menu: Menu is extensive and has a great variety.
Comments: Run by a nice lady named Joanne and her husband. Good food and large portions. Friendly, efficient staff. Warm, inviting atmosphere,
Other Info: Full service, take-out. Non-smoking. Accepts AMEX, DIS, MC and VISA. Price: $$.
Directions: From I-405, take the Warner Ave East exit, then go east on Warner Ave for ¾ mile, at Brookhurst St turn right and this place is 2 blocks down.

**Au Lac Gourmet Vegetarian Rest.
16563 Brookhurst Street
714-418-0658
Web site: www.aulac.com
Hours: Tuesday to Sunday 10:30 am to 9 pm
Closed Monday.
Fully Vegetarian Vietnamese and Chinese. Mostly Vegan. Gourmet menu.
Menu: Vietnamese Crepes, Steamed Jicama Rolls, Wonton Soup, Vegetable Soup, Royal Noodle Soup, Tofu & Bamboo Shoots, Sautéed Green Beans, Shredded Tofu Vermicelli, Clay Pot Soy "Fish," Soy "Seafood" Hot Plate, "Chicken" with Lemon Grass, Grilled "Fish", Korean BBQ Vermicelli, Pepper Soy "Shrimp", Sweet and Sour Soy "Chicken", Claypot Sensation, mock "beef" and mock "seafood".
Comments: Has booth seating. The food is good. The staff is friendly. Friendly owner. Gives a cooking class. Has beautiful flowers that hang from

ceiling.
Other Info: Full service, take-out, catering. Non-smoking. Reservations recommended. Accepts AMEX, DIS, MC, VISA.
Directions: Located north of I-405 Freeway in Mile Square Park Plaza. From I-405, take the Brookhurst exit north, then go north on Brookhurst and this place is 1½ mile down on the left in the Mile Square Plaza, at the corner of Brookhurst and Heil.

GLENDALE (near Pasadena)

Adventist Book & Health Food Center
1501 East Chevy Chase Drive; 818-546-8552
Hours: Monday to Thursday 9 am to 7 pm; Friday 8:30 am to 2 pm; Sunday 10 am to 4 pm; closed Saturday.
Natural Food Store and Deli. Has a huge selection of items. Prices are the cheapest in the Los Angeles area.
Directions: From I-5, take Hwy 2/Glendale Fwy North exit towards Glendale, then go north on Hwy 2 for 3½ miles, take the Holly Dr exit, then go east on Holly Dr for 1 block, then turn right at Harvey Dr and go 2 blocks, at E Glenoaks Blvd turn left and go 2 blocks, then take a slight left on E Chevy Chase Dr and this place is a quarter-mile down.

Glendale Adventist Medical Center
1509 Wilson Terrace; 818-409-8090
Hours: Daily 6 am to 7:30 pm for hot food
Vegetarian Cafeteria and Salad Bar.
Menu: The menu changes daily.
Other Info: Cafeteria-style, take-out. Price: $.
Directions: This place is next to the Adventist Health Food Center above.

Sesame Donut
1506 Glenoaks Boulevard; 818-546-1300
Hours: Daily 24 hours
Donut Shop with Vegan Donuts. Vegan-friendly.
Menu: Donuts do not contain eggs, but some of the muffins do. Donuts are cooked in vegetable oil.
Comments: Say that none of the donuts contain eggs.
Other Info: Cash only; no credit cards.

Whole Foods Market (Mrs Gooch's)
826 North Glendale; 818-240-9350
Hours: Daily 8 am to 9 pm
Natural Food Store and Cafe. Deli, Bakery, Salad Bar and Juice Bar. Organic produce. Supermar-

ket-type place. See Whole Foods Market information. Has a decent selection of books.
Directions: From I-5, take Hwy 134 E/Ventura Fwy exit towards Pasadena, then go 2 miles, then take the Glendale Ave exit, then go north on N Glendale Ave and this place is a quarter-mile down.

GRANADA HILLS (Los Angeles County)

Trader Joe's
11114 Balboa Boulevard; 818-368-6461

**Vegetable Delight
17823 Chatsworth Street; 818-360-3997
Hours: Monday to Friday 11:30 am to 9:30 pm Saturday and Sunday 4 pm to 9:30 pm
Fully Vegetarian Chinese. Mainly Vegan.
Menu: Has a comprehensive menu with over 100 dishes from every part of China. Makes really good mock meat dishes from gluten and soy products. Has complete dinners. Hot & Sour Soup, Spring Rolls (gluten, cabbage, carrots, mushrooms), Veggie Shark Fin Soup, mock chicken (made of gluten), Crispy Wontons, Mock Shrimp, Szechuan Broccoli, Sesame Veg Beef (fried Chinese black mushrooms), Broccoli Veggie Chicken, Veggie Fish, Fried veg Shrimp, Vegetarian Squid, Fried Chinese Mushrooms, Eggplant with Basil, Lemon Veggie Chicken, Beef with Broccoli, Veggie Roast Duck and Sweet & Sour Pork. Has a dipping sauce for the Spring Rolls made of applesauce, plum sauce and ginger. Also has a veggie burger. The Green Tea Ice Cream is good. Non-alcoholic beer and wine.
Comments: Gets good recommendations. One of the better Chinese restaurants in the country. Family owned. Good service. Interesting atmosphere with walls covered with mirrors. Banquet room seats 60.
Other Info: Full service, take-out. Accepts AMEX, MC, VISA. Price: $$.
Directions: In the San Fernando valley area. From I-405, take the Devonshire St exit, then go ¾ mile west on Devonshire St, at Woodley Ave turn right and go a half-mile, at Chatsworth St turn left and this place is 2 miles down.

HACIENDA HEIGHTS (Los Angeles County)

**Garden Fresh Vegetarian Food
16034 Gale Avenue, at Stimson; 626-968-2279
Hours: Daily 11 am to 8 pm
Vegetarian Chinese.

Comments: Local organic produce used when possible.
Other Info: Full service, take-out. Cash only; no credit cards.
Directions: From Hwy 60, take Hacienda Blvd exit, then go north on S Hacenda Blvd for a half-mile, at Gale Ave turn right and this place is a half-mile down.

**Hsi Lai Temple

3456 South Glenmark Drive; 626-961-9697
Hours: Daily 11:30 am to 1:30 pm
Vegetarian Chinese, Buddhist. Salad Bar.
Comments: At the Hsi Lai Temple they serve a vegetarian lunch buffet for a suggested $5 donation. The temple is worth seeing and they have a museum. Price: $.
Directions: From CA Hwy 60, take Hacienda Blvd Exit, then go south on S Hacienda Blvd 1¾ mile, at Colima Rd turn left and go a third-mile, at S Allenton Ave turn right and go 1 block, at E Leander Dr turn left and go 2 blocks, at S Glenmark Dr turn right and this place is 1 block down.

HERMOSA BEACH

**The Spot Natural Food Restaurant

110 Second Street; 310-376-2355
Hours: Daily 11 am to 10 pm
Vegetarian Natural Food Restaurant. Many Vegan options.
Menu: Daily soup special, homemade breads, veggie burgers, sandwiches, burritos (huge), Tempeh Burger, tofu dishes, steamed vegetables with brown rice, Almond Rice, Steamed Vegetable Plate, Baked Eggplant (can be served with cheddar cheese) and vegetarian Lasagna. The Mushroom Walnut Loaf is a specialty. Has good Mexican-style dishes. Dinner meal comes with salad and whole-wheat bread. The Hunza Pie is good. Specials change daily. Has homemade Herb Dressing and Tahini Dressing. Bakes their own bread. Fresh juices.
Comments: A cozy, friendly, little place by the beach. Relaxed atmosphere. Friendly, efficient service. Good size portions. Has outdoor patio seating.
Other Info: Full service, take-out. Reservations not necessary. Non-smoking. Accepts AMEX, MC, VISA. Price: $$.
Directions: At the junction of Hermosa Avenue and Second Street. This place is at the north end of town near Manhattan Beach, a block from the ocean.

HOLLYWOOD

**Paru's Indian Vegetarian Restaurant

5140 Sunset Boulevard, Los Angeles
323-661-7600
Vegetarian Indian.
Comments: This restaurant is actually in Los Angeles, near Hollywood. See details on this restaurant in the Los Angeles section.

Toi On Sunset

7505½ West Sunset Boulevard; 323-874-8062
Hours: Daily 11 am to 4 am
Thai and American. Not pure vegetarian. Vegan friendly.
Menu: Has some vegetarian options. The menu says that any dish can be made vegetarian. Vegetarian Curry, brown rice, Wonton Soup, Tofu Pad Ciw (ask to be made without egg), Thai Black Rice and Eggplant with Pumpkin & Tofu.
Comments: Formal place. It is one of the highest rated Thai restaurants in the LA area. Plays rock music. Toi means "young one." No MSG or preservatives. Large Rock & Roll posters on the walls. There is another location in Santa Monica on Wilshire.
Other Info: Accepts AMEX, DIS, MC, VISA.

Trader Joe's

7304 Santa Monica Boulevard; 213-851-9772

Urth Café

8565 Melrose Ave
310-659-0628; **Web site:** www.urthcafe.com
Hours: Monday to Thursday 6:30 am to 11 pm
Friday, Saturday, Sunday 6:30 am to 12 midnight
Coffee Shop. Vegan-friendly. Not pure veg.
Menu: Organic coffee and soymilk. Has some vegan soups and desserts. Veggie Lasagna, veggie chili, soups, salads and sandwiches.
Comments: Celebrities sometimes come here.
Directions: This place is in West Hollywood near Beverly Hills. From Hwy 101 coming south, take Highland Ave/Hollywood Bowl exit, then go south on Cahuenga Blvd for a mile (becomes N Highland Ave), at Hollywood Blvd (if going north on 101, exit at Hollywood Blvd and go west) turn right and go 1¼ mile, at Fairfax Ave turn left and go 1¼ mile, at Melrose Ave turn right and this place is 1 mile down.

**Vegan Express

3217 Cahuenga Boulevard West; 323-851-8837
Hours: Daily 9 am to 9 pm
Fully Vegan. Thai, Chinese, American. Fast food.

Menu: Pepper "Steak" sandwich, Shrimp Fried Rice, Fish Filet, Crab Curry, Potato Salad, vegan-wraps, Cowboy Burgers and fully vegan desserts. Soups, salads, sandwiches and Spring Rolls. Uses seitan veggie meats.

Comments: Relaxed, friendly, little place. Pleasant outdoor patio. Family owned and operated. Reasonable prices. Local organic produce used when possible.

Other Info: Full service, catering, buffet, take-out, delivery. Non-smoking. Accepts AMEX, MC, VISA, personal cheques. Price: $-$$.

Directions: From 101 Freeway North get off at the Barham and Cahuenga exit. This place is a block west of the exit. There is parking at the rear of the restaurant. Near Universal Studios, at Barham.

HUNTINGTON BEACH

**Happy Veggie

7251 Warner Avenue; 714-375-9505
Hours: Monday to Saturday 11 am to 9 pm
Closed Sunday.
Vegetarian Chinese, Vietnamese. Vegan-friendly.
Menu: Has soups, noodle & rice dishes and curry vegetables.
Comments: This is a new place.
Other Info: Accepts AMEX, MC, VISA.
Directions: From I-405, take the Beach Blvd/Rte 39 exit towards Huntington Beach, then go south on Beach Blvd for 1 mile, at Warner Ave turn right and this place is ¾ mile down.

Juice For You

3801 Warner Avenue, at Pacific Coast Highway Unit B; 562-592-4494
Hours: Daily 7:30 am to 6 pm
Café and Juice Bar. Not pure vegetarian.
Menu: Sandwiches, burritoes and taco breakfast burrito The Garden Nut burger and Western Garden Nut burgers are good. The Vegi-Turkey sandwich contains egg-white. Fresh juices and smoothies.
Comments: At the beach.
Directions: Opposite from Sunset Beach and the Bolsa Chica Wetlands wildlife reserve

Linda's Mexican Restaurant

16446 Bolsa Chica Road
714-840-7374
Mexican. Not pure vegetarian.
Menu: Has a good amount of vegetarian dishes. The take-out menu is mainly vegetarian. Fries dishes in Canola oil.

Mother's Market & Kitchen

19770 Beach Boulevard, near Adams
714-963-6667
email: customerservice@mothersmarket.com;
Web site: www.mothersmarket.com
Store Hours: Daily 9 am to 10 pm
Restaurant Hours: Daily 9 am to 9:30 pm
Natural Food Store and Restaurant. International cuisine including Chinese, Middle Eastern, Mexican, Greek and Italian. Deli and Juice Bar. Fully vegetarian except tuna. Large supermarket-type place with organic produce.
Menu: Has a large amount of vegetarian dishes including salads, soup, rice, appetizers, sandwiches, pastas, Lasagna, Veggie Meatloaf, Veggie Pot Roast and entrees. Has weekly specials. Fresh juices. Cappuccino, espresso. Non-alcoholic beer and wine. Has a kid's menu.
Other Info: Full service, take-out. Accepts AMEX, DIS, MC, VISA. Price: $.
Directions: From I-405, take the Beach Blvd/Rte 39 exit towards Huntington Beach, then go south on Beach Blvd and this place is about 4 miles down.

Trader Joe's

18681A Main Street; 714-848-9640

**Vien Huong

19171 Magnolia Avenue, Suite 7; 714-964-5411
Hours: Monday to Friday 3 pm to 10 pm
Saturday & Sunday 11 am to 10 pm
Vegetarian Gourmet Vietnamese and Chinese. Vegan options.
Menu: Has many vegetarian options including dim sum, soups, appetizers and mock "meat" dishes.
Comments: Has free delivery within three miles from the restaurant.
Other Info: Full service, take-out. Accepts AMEX, MC, VISA. Price: $-$$.
Directions: At Magnolia Ave and Garfield. From I-405, take the Magnolia St exit towards Warner Ave West, then go south on Magnolia St and this place is 2½ miles down.

IRVINE

Jama Juice

17595 Harvard Avenue, Suite F; 949-250-3348
Hours: Monday to Friday 7 am to 9 pm
Saturday & Sunday 8 am to 9 pm
Juice and Smoothie Bar. Vegan options.
Menu: Has a large selection of juices.
Other Info: Counter service, take-out. Price: $.

Mother's Market and Kitchen

2963 Michelson Drive, Jamboree; 949-752-6667
Email: customerservice@mothersmarket.com
Web site: www.mothersmarket.com
Hours: Daily 9 am to 10 pm
Restaurant Hours: 9 am to 9:30 pm
Natural Food Store and International Restaurant. Chinese, Middle Eastern, Mexican, Greek and Italian. Juice Bar. Fully vegetarian except tuna.
Menu: Has a large amount of vegetarian dishes including salads, soup, rice, appetizers, sandwiches, pastas, Lasagna, Veggie Meatloaf, Veggie Pot Roast, and entrees. Has weekly specials. Fresh juices, cappuccino, espresso. Non-alcoholic beer and wine. Has a kid's menu.
Other Info: Full service, take-out. Accepts AMEX, DIS, MC, VISA. Price: $.
Directions: From I-405, take the Jamboree Road exit, then go southwest on Jamboree Rd for a quarter-mile, at Michelson Dr turn left and this place is 50 yards down.

Soup Exchange

3988 Barranca Parkway, at Culver
949-551-2113
Hours: Monday to Saturday 11 am to 9:30 pm
Sunday 10 am to 9:30 pm
Soups and Salad Place. Not pure vegetarian.
Menu: Soups, salads, breads, baked potatoes, fresh fruit and desserts.
Other Info: Cafeteria style, take-out.

Trader Joe's

Walnut Village Center, 14443 Culver Drive
714-857-8108

**The Wheel of Life

Heritage Plaza Shopping Center
14370 Culver Drive #2G, between Ralphs & Savon; 949-551-8222
Hours: Mon to Fri 11 am to 3 pm, 5 pm to 9 pm (until 9:30 pm Fri); Sat 11 am to 9:30 pm; Sun 11 am to 9 pm
Vegetarian Chinese and Thai Restaurant. Mainly Vegan.
Menu: Has many veggie mock "meats," mock "seafood" dishes, curry dishes, noodles dishes, Orange Peel Tofu, Pad Thai, vegetable curries, Thai salads, and great vegan coconut and lichi ice cream. Tempeh and tofu dishes.
Comments: Gets good recommendations. Friendly owner. Informal.
Other Info: Non-smoking. Accepts MC, VISA.
Directions: From I-5, take the Culver Dr exit, then go southwest on Culver Dr and this place is a quarter-mile down.

Wild Oats

18040 Culver Drive; 949-651-8880
Hours: Daily 7 am to 10 pm
Natural Food Store and Cafe. Deli, Bakery, Salad Bar and Juice Bar. Organic produce. Supermarket-type place. See Wild Oats Market information.
Directions: From I-5, take the Culver Dr exit, then go southwest on Culver Dr and this place is a third-mile down. It is just east of Rancho San Joaquin Golf Course.

ISLA VISTA (near Santa Barbara)

Isla Vista Food Co-op

6575 Seville Road; 805-968-1401
Hours: Daily 9 am to 10 pm
Natural Food Store. Really good selection of organic produce. Has ready-made sandwiches.
Other Info: Accepts AMEX, MC, VISA.
Directions: From Hwy 101, take the Glen Annie Rd/Storke Rd exit, then go south on Storke Rd 1¼ miles, turn right (road actually turn right) at El Colegio Rd and go ¾ mile, at Camino Pescadero turn right and go a third-mile, at Seville Rd turn left and this place is 1 block down. This place is about 1 mile southwest of Santa Barbara Airport.

LA CRESCENTA (Los Angeles County)

Trader Joe's

3433 Foothill Boulevard
818-249-3693

LAGUNA BEACH

Café Zinc

350 Ocean Avenue
949-494-6302; Web site: www.zinccafe.com
Store Hours: Monday to Friday 7 am to 6 pm
Saturday & Sunday: 8 am to 5 pm
Restaurant Hours: Monday to Friday 7 am to 4:30 pm; Saturday & Sunday 7 am to 5 pm
Natural Food Store and Vegetarian Restaurant.
Menu: Soups, salads, Baked Eggplant Pizza, Mushroom Medley Pizza, Mexican Pizza, Mixed Vegetable Sandwich, Zinc Veggie Burger, Vegetarian Chili, baked good, breads and desserts. For breakfast there is Roasted Herbed Potatoes, granola, oatmeal and fruit.
Comments: Indoor and outdoor seating. A good place to hangout. Sometimes run out of popular dishes on the weekends.
Other Info: Counter service, take-out, catering. Price: $-$$.

Directions: A little south of the main downtown area, a few blocks from beach. From Coast Highway, turn onto Broadway (in front of the main beach) and go 2 blocks, turn right at Forest Avenue (second light), then make another immediate right onto Ocean Avenue and this place is a half-block down.

Gauranga's Vegetarian Buffet

285 Legion Street; 949-494-7029
Hours: Monday to Saturday 12 am to 2 pm
Closed Sunday for feast.
Pure Vegetarian Indian and International. Vegan options. All-you-can-eat buffet. No meat, fish or eggs are used in any of the dishes.
Menu: Brown and basmati rice, two soups, pasta, Indian-style vegetables, steamed vegetables, entrees and desserts.
Comments: Recommended. Reasonably prices. This restaurant is in a Hare Krishna temple.
Other Info: Cafeteria style, take-out. Non-smoking. Reservations not necessary. Accepts MC, VISA.
Directions: Around three blocks south of the downtown, a few blocks east of the ocean. From Coastal Highway go east on Legion St and this place is 2 short blocks east, at Glenneyre.

***The Stand Natural Foods Restaurant

238 Thalia Street; 949-494-8101
Hours: Daily 7 am to 8 pm
Natural Food Store and Vegan Restaurant. Mexican and International. Juice Bar.
Menu: Has a big selection of salads, sandwiches, burritos and main dishes.
Comments: Has very good vegan food. Does not use salt, refined sugars or artificial ingredients. Has outdoors seating. Order at window.
Other Info: Limited service, take-out. Smoking allowed outside only. Reservations not necessary. Accepts AMEX, DIS, MC, VISA. Price: $.
Directions: This place is about 5 blocks south of the main downtown area. From Coastal Hwy, go east on Thalia St and this place is a half-block down.

LAGUNA NIQUEL

Henry's Marketplace (Wild Oats)

27271 La Paz Road; 949-349-1994
Hours: Daily 8 am to 9 pm
Natural Food Store and Cafe. Deli, Bakery, Salad Bar and Juice Bar. Organic produce. Supermarket-type place. See Wild Oats Market information.

Directions: From I-5, take the Alicia Pkwy exit and go southwest on Alicia Pkwy for 1½ mile, at Moulton Pkwy turn left and go a half-mile, at La Paz Rd (go south) turn right and this place is ¾ mile down.

LAGUNA WOODS

Mother's Market & Kitchen

24165 Paseo De Valencia; 949-768-6667
email: custemerservice@mothersmarket.com
Web site: www.mothersmarket.com
Hours: Daily 9 am to 10 pm
Restaurant Hours: 9 am to 9:30 pm
Natural Food Store and Restaurant. International cuisine including Chinese, Middle Eastern, Mexican, Greek and Italian. Juice Bar. Fully vegetarian except tuna.
Menu: Has a large amount of vegetarian dishes including salads, soup, rice, appetizers, sandwiches, pastas, Lasagna, Veggie Meatloaf, Veggie Pot Roast and entrees. Has weekly specials. Fresh juices. Cappuccino, espresso. Non-alcoholic beer and wine. Has a kid's menu.
Other Info: Full service, take-out. Price: $.
Directions: This place is a half-mile west of Laguna Hills Mall. From I-5, take El Toro Rd exit, then go south on Paseo De Valencia and this place is a quarter-mile down. Or from I-5, take El Toro Rd exit, then go southwest on Toro Rd and go a half-mile, at Paseo De Valencia turn left and this place is 50 yards down.

LOMITA

***House of Vege

2439 Pacific Coast Highway; 310-530-1180
Web site: www.gohouseofvege.com
Hours: Sunday to Thursday 11 am to 9 pm
Friday & Saturday 11 am to 9:30 pm
Fully Vegan, Vegetarian Chinese. Gourmet.
Menu: Chinese Soups, Corn & Tofu Soup, Deep Fried Seaweed Roll with Taro, mock "fish" and "pork", Szechuan Style Tofu, House Special Veggie Chicken (Soy Protein), very good Dry Sautéed String Bean, General Tsao Veggie Chicken (Mushroom), Eggplant with Basil, Veggie Pork & Broccoli, Fried Seaweed Roll with Toro, several varieties of rice and an excellent sticky rice pudding for dessert. A good dessert is the Red Bean Cakes.
Comments: Has really good service. Can get busy. Does private parties in the banquet room. Has an all-you-can-eat "tasting" platter for $11. You can choose from the over 50 items on the menu,

and you can eat as much as you want as long as you eat everything.
Other Info: Full service, catering, take-out. Non-smoking. Accepts reservations but are not necessary. Accepts AMEX, DIS, MC, VISA. Price: $$.
Directions: From I-110, get off at Pacific Coast Highway, then go west about 5 minutes, and this place is on the right hand side. Ample parking. It is near the border of Torrance and Lomita.

LONG BEACH

The Original Park Pantry
2104 East Broadway
562-434-0451; **Web site:** www.parkpantry.com
Hours: Monday to Friday 6 am to 10 pm
Friday & Saturday 6 am to 11 pm
American. Not pure vegetarian.
Menu: Vegetarian chili, pasta of the day, vegetable plate and other dishes.
Other Info: Full service, counter service, take-out. Accepts MC, VISA. Price: $-$$.

**Papa Jon's Natural Foods & Café
5006 East 2nd Street; 562-439-3444
Hours: Sunday to Thursday 8 am to 9 pm
Friday & Saturday 9 am to 9:30 pm
Vegetarian Restaurant and Natural Food Store. American and Mexican. Café and Deli. Very Vegan-friendly.
Menu: Split pea soup, Potato Corn Chowder, Vegetable Lentil Soup, sandwiches, burritos, tacos, Spinach Lasagna, vegetarian Sushi Rolls, Sheppard's Pie, Teriyaki Tofu (very good), Tempeh Burgers, TLT (Tofu, Lettuce and Tomato), Steamed Vegetables, Spinach Lasagna, Black Beans, Spinach & Mushroom Pasta, bagels, Cabbage Rolls with Mashed Potatoes and Spaghetti with Tofu Balls. Has around twenty vegan dishes. Has daily specials such as Tofu Fajitas, Spinach & Tofu Cannelloni and Black Bean Enchiladas. Soups change daily. Fresh juices, wheatgrass juice, smoothies and herbal teas.
Comments: Very reasonably priced. Serves dishes with eggs in them. Has good size portions. Has a large selection of dishes. Casual, informal setting. Popular place. Brightly lit. Has a deli counter where salad can be ordered for take-out. Fast service. Uses recycled paper napkins. Vegan dishes marked on the menu with an asterisk (*).
Other Info: Full service, take-out. Accepts MC, VISA. Price: $.
Directions: In a trendy small strip of stores in the middle of Belmont Shores. From Pacific Coast Hwy (Rte 1) going south, go on south Park Ave

for a quarter-mile, at E Anaheim St turn right and go a fifth-mile, at Park Ave turn left and go 1½ mile, at E 2nd St turn left and this place is 2 blocks down. From Rte 1 going north, go west on 7th St 1 mile, then turn left at Park Ave and go 1 mile, then turn left at 2nd St.

Trader Joe's
Marina Pacifica Mall, 6378 East Pacific Coast Highway; 310-598-3740

LOS ANGELES

Alaine's Bakery
2366 Pelham Avenue, West Los Angeles
310-470-1094
Hours: Monday to Friday 7 am to 6 pm
Saturday 8 am to 6 pm
Bakery and Deli. Has 100% vegan cakes, pies, cookies and muffins. Certified kosher.
Menu: Makes over 50 baked dishes. Rainforest Cake (their first product), a firm fruitcake loaf made with nuts and dried fruits, is very popular. Chocolate Mousee, Chocolate Chip Muffins, Orange Almond Cookies, Apple Pie, Carrot Cake, Banana Raspberry Muffins, Blueberry Uncheesecake and Chocolate Cake. Mixed Fruit, Apple, Lemon, Pear and Peach Tarts. Has several good sandwiches such as The Deli (vegan mock "meat" deli slices, sprouts, tomatoes, kosher dill pickles), Millet No-Meat-Loaf sandwich and The Veggie (avocado, sprouts, cucumber, tomato). The sandwiches are made with a sprouted whole grain blend. Better Than Egg (an eggless egg salad made with tofu and vegan mayonnaise) and blue corn chips. Has several types of teas and regular and organic coffee.
Comments: Has two small tables outside and indoor seating. Some baked goods are made with Xylitol, a sweetener from Finland that is made with the bark of birth trees. It has half the calories of regular sugar and does not contain any sugar.
Directions: It is one block east of Overland, close to Westside Pavilion. A half-mile west of Rancho Park Golf Course. Has a large green awning. From I-405, take the Olympic Blvd/Pico Blvd exit, then go on Sawtelle Blvd for 1 block, at Pico Blvd turn left and go 1 mile, at Pelham Ave turn left and this place is 1 block down.

Beverly Hills Juice Club
8382 Beverly Boulevard; 323-655-8300
Hours: Monday to Friday 8 am to 6 pm; Saturday 10 am to 6 pm; closed Sunday.

Juice Bar.

Menu: Vegetarian sushi and dairy-free ice cream. Fresh juices and smoothies.

Comments: Local organic produce used when possible.

Other Info: Counter service, take-out. Price: $.

**Café Luna Tierra Sol

2501 West Sixth Street

213-380-4754; Web site: www.lunatierrasol.com

Hours: Daily 7 am to 10 pm

Vegetarian Mexican and Central American. Juice Bar. Vegan options.

Menu: Cocido Soup, Eipotle Bowl (tofu and beans), Tofu Taco, Chilaquiles, chimichanga, and sweet potato and kiwi lime empandada.

Other Info: Full service, take-out. No credit cards. Price: $.

Directions: From US 101, take the Benton Way exit, then go southwest on N Rampart Blvd 1 mile, at W 6th St turn left and this place is 2 blocks down at S Carondelet St.

Don's Fountain of Health

3606 W 6th Street, in mid-Wilshire

213-387-6621

Hours: Monday to Friday 8 am to 3 pm

Closed Saturday & Sunday.

Natural Foods.

Menu: Soups, chili, veggie burgers and baked goods. Fresh organic juices.

Other Info: Full service, take-out, catering. Price: $.

Directions: Near the downtown. From Hwy 101, take the Melrose Ave/Normandie Ave exit, then go south on N Normandie Ave for 1¼ mile, then turn right at W 6th St and this place is at the corner.

**Dr. J's Health & Tasty

1303 Westwood Boulevard, Westwood

310-477-2721

Hours: Monday to Saturday 11 am to 8:30 pm

Sunday 11 am to 3 pm

Organic Vegetarian Asian and International. Has a Buffet. Mainly Vegan. Many organic items. Pay by the pound.

Menu: Rice Noodle Delight, veggie meatballs, rice dishes, Sweet & Sour Vegetables, Vegetable Delight, Veggie Chicken Nuggets, Curry Potatoes, Tofu Supreme (scrambled tofu with vegetables), Grilled Tofu, Brown Rice Medley, Veggie Chicken Meatballs, Veggie Ham, Veggie Fish Steak, Garden Fresh and organic desserts. Has a detoxifying tea. Barley Soup and Tofu Seaweed Vegetable Soup. Desserts such as Banana Cake, Oat Bran Muffins, Carob Brownies and Super Snack (cookie made from sunflower seeds, carob chips, dates, oats and herbal seasonings). Dr. J's Cleansing Balance Tea to end meal.

Comments: Local organic produce used when possible. Small place with three tables and counter seating. Basic place with Styrofoam plates and plastic forks and spoons. No MSG, sugar, dairy, wheat, chemical or yeast.

Other Info: Cafeteria-style, take-out. Price: $$.

Directions: Two blocks from Wilshire Blvd. From I-405, take the Wilshire Blvd East exit towards UCLA, then go northeast on Wilshire Blvd for a half-mile, then at Westwood Blvd turn right and this place is 2 blocks down.

Eat a Pita

465 North Fairfax Avenue; 323-651-0188

Hours: Sunday to Thursday 11 am to 10

Friday & Saturday 11 am to 11 pm

Greek. Not pure vegetarian.

Menu: Falafel, hummus, baba ghanouj and tabbouleh.

Comments: Casual, friendly. Outdoors seating.

Other Info: Counter service, take-out. Accepts MC, VISA. Price: $.

Erewhon Natural Foods

7660 Beverly Boulevard, between Fairfax & La Brea; 323-937-0777

Hours: Mon to Fri 8 am to 10 pm; Sunday 9 am to 9 pm; deli closes one hour before store.

Natural Food Store and Deli. Salad Bar and Juice Bar. Organic produce. Vegan-friendly.

Menu: Steamed vegetables, Spinach Lasagna, Stir-fried Vegetables and other dishes.

Comments: Has bulk items, supplements and many other items. Community bulletin board. Recycles.

Other Info: Counter service. Accepts MC, VISA. Price: $$.

Directions: From US 101 going south, take the Highland Ave/Hollywood Bowl exit, then go south on Cahuenga Blvd (becomes Highland Ave) for 2½ miles, at Beverly Blvd turn right and this place is 1 mile down. From US 101 going north, take Beverly Blvd exit and go west on Beverly Blvd and this place is 2½ miles down.

**The Good Life Health Food Center

3631 South Crenshaw Boulevard, at Exposition, northwest corner; 323-731-0588

Hours: Monday to Saturday 10 am to 9 pm

Sunday and Holidays 11 am to 7 pm

Natural Food Store and Vegetarian Café. Juice Bar. Vegan options.

Menu: Sandwiches, Soy Vegetable Patty with potatoes, quesadillas, pizzas, burritos and other dishes. Fresh juices, wheatgrass. Barley and oat juices.

Comments: Local organic produce used when possible.

Directions: In a strip mall in south central Los Angeles. From I-10, take the Crenshaw Blvd exit, then go south on Crenshaw Blvd and this place is 1 mile down.

Inaka Natural Foods Restaurant

131 South La Brea Avenue; 323-936-9353

Hours: Monday to Friday 12 noon to 2:30 pm, 6 pm to 10 pm; Saturday 5:30 pm to 10 pm; Sunday 5:30 pm to 9 pm

Macrobiotic. Vegan options. Not pure vegetarian (serves fish).

Menu: Steamed vegetables, brown rice and beans.

Comments: No dairy or eggs are used. Almost entirely vegetarian except some fish dishes.

Other Info: Full service, take-out. Accepts MC, VISA. Price: $$.

Directions: From US 101, take Highland Ave/Hollywood Bowl exit, then go south on Cahuenga Blvd (becomes Highland Ave) for 2½ miles, at Beverly Blvd turn right and go a third-mile, at N La Brea Ave turn left and this place is a quarter-mile down.

India's Tandoori

5947 West Pico Boulevard; 323-936-2050

Hours: Sunday to Tuesday 11:30 am to 10 pm Friday & Saturday 11:30 am to 11 pm

Indian. Vegan options. Not pure vegetarian.

Menu: Has a vegetarian section on the menu that includes samosas, rice and curried vegetables.

Comments: Bakes with a traditional clay-oven.

Other Info: Full service, take-out. Accepts AMEX, MC, VISA. Price: $.

Indo Café

10428½ National Boulevard; 310-815-1290

Hours: Tuesday to Thursday 11:30 am to 9:30 pm; Fri to Sun 11 am to 10 pm; closed Mon.

Indonesian. Vegan options. Not pure vegetarian.

Menu: Has a vegetarian menu with around 25 dishes. Sayur Asem (a spicy tamarind soup), Tempeh Goreng (an appetizer with a dipping sauce), Nasi Goreng (Indonesian style fried rice), Emping (deep-fried bean crisps), Bayam Hot Plate (spinach, tofu and garlic) and Kripik Singkong (yucca root chips)

Comments: Has a menu with full-color photos of the dishes. Has some Indonesian artifacts such as colorfully painted wooden masks, Indonesian style paintings, wooden tables and wooden chairs, colorful traditional designed tablecloths and painted wooden puppets. Popular place.

Other Info: Accepts MC, VISA. Seats around 50 persons.

Literati Café

12081 Wilshire Boulevard; 310-231-7484

Hours: Daily 8 am to 10 pm

Coffee Shop. Vegan options. Not pure veg.

Comments: Has some vegan desserts (cookies and chocolate cake) and soy milk for coffee.

Lydia Taylor's Vegetarian Affair

3715 Santa Rosalia Drive, near King and Crenshaw; 323-292-8664

Web site: www.lydia taylors.com

Hours: Monday to Thursday 10:30 am to 8:30 pm; Sunday 11 am to 8:30 pm; Friday 10:30 am to 4 pm; closed Saturday.

Fully Vegetarian Cafe. Juice Bar. Fast foods. Mostly Vegan.

Menu: Bab-Be-Que Burrito and Chicken Chop sandwiches are both really good.

Comments: 50's style diner. Excellent food. Reasonable prices. Friendly service. Very friendly people. "If it has a face or mother they don't serve it."

Directions: From I-10, take the La Brea Ave exit, then go south on S La Brea Ave 1 mile, at Rodeo Rd turn left and go a fifth-mile, at W ML King JR Blvd turn slight right and go 1 mile, at Marlton Ave turn right and go a fifth-mile, at Santa Rosalia Drive turn left and this place is a fifth-mile down.

**Mani's Bakery

519 South Fairfax Avenue; 323-938-8800

Hours: Daily 6:30 am to 12 midnight

Vegetarian Bakery and Coffeehouse. Vegan baked goods.

Menu: Sandwiches, fresh baked breads, desserts, baked goods, cakes, chocolate chip cookies, pies, truffles, turnovers and breakfasts. You can get soy milk for your coffee.

Comments: Has dairy-free, vegan and egg-free baked goods. Vegan baked goods are marked on the menu.

Other Info: Counter service, take-out. Accepts AMEX, DIS, MC, VISA. Price: $.

Directions: From US 101 coming south, take the Highland Ave/Hollywood Bowl exit, then go south on Cahuenga Blvd (becomes Highland Ave)

for ¾ mile, at Hollywood Blvd turn right and go 1¼ mile, at N Fairfax Ave turn left and this place is 2¼ miles down.

Messob Ethiopian Restaurant
1041 South Fairfax Avenue; 323-938-8827
Hours: Monday to Friday 11 am to 10 pm
Saturday & Sunday 11 am to 11 pm
Ethiopian. Has vegan options. Not pure veg.
Menu: Ethiopian style cooking includes several well-cooked spicy stews called wots. They are served with injera, a flat pancake type bread. The teff (a native grain of Ethiopia) injera gets some high recommendations. They serve another injera made of teff, millet, corn and barley. Has Vegetarian Dinner Combination, which is tomato salad, spicy potatoes, collard greens, lentils and pumpkin. Yemiser Wot is a spiced lentil stew. Vegetarian Delight has over seven varieties of Ethiopian dishes including Salad (lettuce and tomato), Pumpkin Wot (pumpkin stew), Tomato Fit-Fit (cold tomato stew), Yemisir Wot (spiced red pepper sauce and lentil stew), Yatakilt Alitcha (steamed vegetables), Collard Greens and Yater Alitcha (yellow split pea stew with ginger and garlic). The meal ends with a cup of spiced tea (cloves).
Comments: Plays Ethiopian music. Pleasant service. Has an Ethiopian type décor with a little hut at the window made of bamboo and seagrass. Has low tables. There are some African style umbrellas with a messob (Ethiopian serving table with African patterns) underneath them. Baklava is an Ethiopian dessert.
Other Info: Accepts AMEX, DIS, MC, VISA.
Directions: From I-10, take the Fairfax Ave exit, then go north on Fairfax Ave and this place is 1½ mile down.

**Native Foods
1110 1/2 Gayley Avenue, near the UCLA campus, in Westwood
310 209-1055; **Web site:** www.nativefoods.com,
Hours: Daily 11 am to 10 pm
Vegetarian International and American. Mainly Vegan. Fast Food-style Place. Mainly organic
Menu: The menu changes regularly. Soups, salads, sandwiches, Middle Eastern dishes, desserts, and other dishes. Has a good assortment of mock "meat" dishes and vegetable dishes. Sandwiches, Philly Cheese Steak (sliced seitan and vegan "Native Cheese"), Thai Slaw and chili "cheese" fries. Chinese "save the" Chicken. White Bean Leek, Jasmine Rice, Iron Yam, Bali Surf Burger, California Caesar, Tanya's Tempeh, Tuno Zuma, Na-

tive Cobb (club sandwich using vegetarian Native meats), Native Nachos, Farrah's Fattoush (Middle Eastern bread salad), Indonesian Tempeh Chips, Jamaican Jerk Salad, Spike's BBQ and Warm & Wild Mushroom Salad. The Neatloaf Special made of tofu and brown rice comes with mash potatoes and mushroom gravy. Fresh juices and smoothies.
Comments: Gets really high recommendations. Quick service restaurant. Has three branches in Westwood, Palm Desert and Palm Springs. Local organic produce used when possible. Has a small dinning area seating around 40. Makes their own soy cheese. Pleasant dining area. Has a skylight and a large window. Comfortable place. Reasonably priced.
Cooking Classes: Holds classes at the Palm Desert branch for $50 per class. You can reserve a spot by calling 760-836-9396.
Other Info: Counter service, take-out, catering. Accepts MC, VISA. Price: $$.
Directions: From I-405, take Wilshire Blvd exit, then go east on Wilshire Blvd for a third-mile, at Gayley Ave turn left and this place is 2 blocks down. It is about a block and a half from the UCLA campus, near the Mann's Theatre.

Nature Mart
2080 Hillhurst Avenue; 323-667-1677
Hours: Daily 8 am to 10 pm
Large Natural Food Store. Has a good size bulk section.
Directions: From I-580, take the Los Feliz Blvd, then go southwest on Los Feliz Blvd and go 1¼ mile, at Hillhurst Ave turn left and this place is 2 blocks down.

Newsroom Café
120 North Robertson Boulevard, West Hollywood, near Beverly Hills; 310-652-4444
email: newsroomcafe@yahoo.com
Winter Hours: Monday to Thursday 8 am to 9 pm; Friday 8 am to 10 pm; Saturday 9 am to 10 pm; Sunday 9 am to 9 pm; Stays open an hour latter during the summer.
International. Organic Juice Bar. Great Salad Bar. Vegan options. Use organic ingredients. Not pure vegetarian.
Menu: Homemade vegetarian soups, pastas, salads, sandwiches, Mexican dishes, homemade breads, Mushroom Ravioli, spicy cornbread with salsa and dairy-free desserts. Westsider (baked Japanese eggplant, melted mozzarella, red pepper with homemade mustard on a multigrain roll), NuMex Caesar salad, Indonesian Gado Gado

Salad and the Ultimate Maui Veggie Burger. The Ravioli is good. Has a large amount of creative drinks. Grasshopper is an ounce of wheatgrass, mint and pineapple juice. Immune Rocket Booster is beet, carrot, and celery juice with ginger, flaxseed oil, Echinacea and golden seal. Chinese herbal tonics.
Comments: Relaxed atmosphere and you can dress casually. Serves chicken and fish, but no red meats. Has a magazine rack and a Mac to hit the Internet. Often frequented by movie and rock stars.
Other Info: Accepts AMEX, MC, VISA. Price: $$.
Directions: From I-10, take the La Brea Ave exit, then go north on S La Brea Ave for 1 mile, then turn left (go northwest) at San Vicente Blvd for 2½ miles, then stay straight (bear left) onto Burton Way and go a half-mile, at S Robertson Blvd turn right and this place is 2 blocks down.

Nyala Restaurant
1076 South Fairfax Avenue; 323-936-5918
Hours: Monday to Friday 11:30 am to 10 pm
Saturday & Sunday 12 noon to 11 pm
Ethiopian. Vegan options. Not pure vegetarian.
Menu: Has a good selection of vegetarian Ethiopian food. Has an all-you-can-eat vegetarian buffet, Monday to Friday for lunch. Cappuccino, espresso.
Other Info: Full service, take-out. Accepts AMEX, DC, DIS, MC, VISA. Price: $$.

**Paru's Indian Vegetarian Restaurant
5140 West Sunset Boulevard, near Hollywood
323-661-7600
email: kannan@parusrestaurant.com;
Website: www.parurestaurant.com
Hours: Monday to Friday 12 noon to 3 pm, 6 pm to 10 pm; Sat & Sun 1 pm to 10 pm
Fully Vegetarian Authentic South Indian. Mostly Vegan.
Menu: Has a brunch on Saturday and Sunday. Most of the main dishes don't contain dairy. Good samosas, Vegetable Cutlet, Masala Dosa, Coconut Chutney, Mango Chutney, Uttapam, Idly, Paratha, sambar, Puri, Basmati Rice, Peas Pulao and Raita. Vegetable Curries such as Cauliflower with potato, Spinach with lentils, Mixed Vegetables and Potato with Eggplant. Indian Thali (Rice, poori (2), curry (2), Sambar, Rasam, Papad, yogurt, pickle, dessert). Desserts such as Almond Halava, Cream of Wheat Halava, Rice Pudding and Gulabjamun. Yogi's Delight is recommended.
Comments: Has a great outdoor patio with tropi-

cal plants. Open since 1979. Little on the expensive side, but not unreasonable. Warm, sociable experience. Well-decorated little dinning room. Oil is used for cooking.
Reviews: Paru's is perhaps the first exclusively vegetarian restaurant that doesn't cause carnivores to holler, "Where's the beef?!" It's difficult to know what to specifically recommend—everything we've tried has been uniformly delectable. Our favorite, however, remains the *dosa*, a kind of deep-fried Indian *crêpe roulée* filled with scintillatingly spiced potatoes and other vegies. B.L., L.A. Weekly
Other Info: Full service, take-out. Reservations not necessary. Non-smoking. Accepts AM, MC, VISA. Price: $$.
Directions: From the Hollywood Freeway (Hwy 101) take Sunset Blvd exit, then go east on Sunset Blvd and this place is ¾ mile down. Can also take exits Santa Monica or Normandie from Hwy 101. Or take MTA bus lines # 2 or 3, or take the Hollywood & Western or Sunset & Vermont stops on the Red Line subway.

P F Chang's China Bistro
121 North La Cienega Boulevard, #117 Beverly Center; 310-854-6467
Hours: Sunday to Thursday 11 am to 11 pm
Friday & Saturday 11 am to 12 midnight
Chinese. Vegan options. Not pure vegetarian. A national chain with three locations in the Los Angeles area.
Menu: Has several main dishes and several side vegetarian dishes. Vegetarian dishes are prepared separately in the kitchen from the non-vegetarian dishes. Ma Po Tofu (fried crispy tofu with broccoli) (really good), Vegetable Chow Fun, Coconut Curry Vegetables, brown rice, Temple Long Beans, Garlic Snap Peas, Poached Baby Bok Choy, Stir-Fried Spicy Eggplant, Lettuce Wraps, Singapore Noodles, Vegetable Chow Fun, rice noodles and brown rice. Jasmine Tea. Has various sauces such as Chinese chili sauce, pot sticker sauce and Chinese mustard (can be mixed together).
Comments: They prepare the vegetarian dishes in a separate area of the kitchen than the rest of the menu. Cleans wok (frying pan for cooking) at high temperatures, but do not use separate woks just for vegetarian dishes. For vegetarian dishes they use a vegetarian oyster sauce (mushroom base) that contains no animal products. Usually very busy during lunchtime. Intimate atmosphere. Interesting décor with excellent taste. Rosewood floors and chairs. Has a few stone pillars topped

with replicas of Xian warriors from China. Attentive service.

Warning: Make sure that you ask them to use the vegan oyster sauce.

Other Info: Accepts AMEX, DIS, MC, VISA. Price: $$.

Simply Wholesome

4508 West Slauson Avenue; 323-294-2144
Hours: Sunday to Friday 10 am to 8:30 pm
Saturday 8:30 am to 9 pm
Natural Food Store and Restaurant. Organic produce.
Menu: Has a good selection of vegetarian dishes.
Other Info: Counter service, take-out. Accepts AMEX, MC, VISA.
Directions: From I-405, take the La Tijera Blvd exit, then go east on La Tijera Blvd 0.65, turn slight left at S La Cienega Blvd and go a third-mile, turn slight right onto ramp, then turn right at Slauson Ave and this place is 1 mile down.

Trader Joe's (several locations)

2738 Hyperion Avenue, Silverlake
213-665-6774
8645 South Sepulveda Boulevard, Westchester
310-338-9238
10850 National Boulevard; 310-470-1917

Vegetarian Affair

3715 Santa Rosalia Drive; 323-292-8664
Vegetarian International. Same place as Lydia Taylor's Vegetarian Affair above.

VP Discounts

8001 Beverly Boulevard; 323-658-6506
Hours: Daily 8:30 am to 10 pm; Saturday 9 am to 9 pm; Sunday 10 am to 8 pm
Deli Hours: Monday to Friday 9 am to 6 pm; Saturday 9 am to 5 pm; deli closed Sunday.
Natural Food Store and Deli. Organic produce.
Other Info: Counter service, take-out. Has seating outside. Accepts AMEX, MC, VISA.
Directions: From I-10, take the La Brea Ave exit, then go north on La Brea Ave for 1 mile, at San Vicente Blvd turn left and go 1¼ mile west, at S Fairfax Ave turn right and go 1¼ mile, at Beverly Blvd turn left and this place is 2 blocks down at N Edinburgh Ave.

VP Discounts

11665 Santa Monica Boulevard; 310-444-7949
Hours: Daily 10 am to 7:30 pm; Saturday 9 am to 9 pm; Sunday 10 am to 8 pm
Natural Food Store.
Other Info: Accepts AMEX, MC, VISA.

White Memorial Medical Center Cafeteria

1720 Brooklyn Avenue; 323-265-5035
Hours: Daily
Hospital Cafeteria.
Menu: This cafeteria is in a Seven-Day Adventist hospital.
Other Info: Cafeteria style, take-out. Price: $$.
Directions: This place is near where I-10, I-5 and Hwy 101 meet. From I-5, take the C Chavez Ave exit, then go west on C Chavez Ave and this place is a quarter-mile down on the left.

Whole Foods Market

11666 National Boulevard, West Los Angeles
310-996-8840
Hours: Daily 8 am to 10 pm; Café and Juice Bar opens at 7 am on the weekdays.
Natural Food Store and Cafe. Deli, Bakery, Salad Bar and Juice Bar. Organic produce. Supermarket-type place. See Wild Oats Market information.
Directions: From I-405, take the National Blvd exit, then go west on National Blvd and this place is a half-mile down at the corner of Barrington and National.

Wild Oats Community Market

3476 South Centinela Avenue, Los Angeles
310-391-6333
Hours: Daily 8 am to 10 pm; Café and Juice Bar opens at 7 am on the weekdays.
Natural Food Store and Cafe. Deli, Bakery, Salad Bar and Juice Bar. Organic produce. Supermarket-type place. See Wild Oats Market information.
Directions: From I-405, take the Washington Blvd/Venice Blvd exit, then turn left at Sepulveda (if coming from south) and go 2 blocks (either way get on Venice Blvd going west toward ocean), at Venice Blvd turn left and go 1 mile, at S Centinela Ave turn right and this place is a half-mile down.

MALIBU

John's Garden Fresh

3835 South Cross Creek Road
310-456-8377
Hours: Monday to Saturday 10 am to 4 pm
Sunday 11 am to 4 pm
Natural Food Store and Deli. Juice Bar. Limited organic produce.
Menu: Soups, salads and sandwiches. Fresh juices and smoothies.
Directions: This place is about a third-mile north of Malibu Lagoon State Beach. From Pacific Coast

Hwy, go north on S Cross Creek Rd and this place is a quarter-mile down.

Pacific Coast Greens
22601 West Pacific Coast Highway
310-456-0353
Hours: Daily 8 am to 9 pm
Natural Food Store and Deli. Organic produce. Has seating on the roof with a view of the ocean.
Directions: This place is a little east of Malibu on Pacific Coast Hwy.

MANHATTAN BEACH (Los Angeles County)

Trader Joe's
1821 Manhattan Beach; 310-338-9238

MARINA DEL REY

Rainbow Acres
Marina Waterside Shopping Center, 4756 Admiralty Way, Marina Del Rey; 310-823-5373
Hours: Monday to Friday 9 am to 9 pm; Sat & Sun 9 am to 7 pm; Deli Hours: 9 am to 6 pm.
Natural Food Store and Deli. Juice Bar. Organic produce.
Menu: Has a good selection of vegetarian dishes. Sandwiches, soups and a hot dishes.
Other Info: Counter service, take-out. Has seating. Accepts AMEX, MC, VISA.
Directions: From Hwy 90, go southeast on Lincoln Blvd (Rte 1) for a fifth-mile, at Bali Way turn right and go 1 block, at Admiralty Way turn left and this place is a quarter-mile down.

MAR VISTA

***Venus of Venice
12034 Venice Boulevard; 310-391-7674
Hours: Tuesday to Friday 11:30 am to 3 pm, 5 pm to 9 pm; Saturday & Sunday 11 am to 9 pm; closed Monday.
Fully Vegan. South United States and North Mexican.
Menu: Sweet and Sour Soy Chicken, Southern Soy Filet, veggie chicken burrito, honey lemonade and salads.
Comments: Food is freshly made. Has toys and music boxes on every table. The tablecloths are hand-painted by a Venice artist.
Other Info: Full service. Non-smoking. Reservations are recommended for six or more people. No credit cards. Price: $$.
Directions: This place is on Venice Boulevard

between Grandview Avenue and Inglewood Blvd. From I-405, take the Venice Blvd exit and go west on Venice Blvd and this place is ¾ mile down.

MEINERS OAKS

**The Farmer and the Cook
339 West El Roblar; 805-640-9608
Hours: Monday to Saturday 8 am to 7 pm
Natural Food Store and Fully Vegetarian All Organic Café. Vegan options, including baked goods. Salad Bar.
Menu: Has an all-organic salad bar and daily lunch and dinner specials.
Directions: Meiners Oaks is an hour and a half north of Los Angeles. From CA Hwy 33, go north on S La Luna Ave 1½ mile, at W El Roblar Dr turn right and this place is 4 blocks down.

MONTEREY PARK

**Happy Family
608 North Atlantic Blvd, a little south of I-10
626-282-8986
Hours: Mon to Thur 11:30 am to 2:45 pm, 5 pm to 8:45 pm; Fri 11:30 am to 2:45 pm, 5 pm to 9:15 pm; Sat 11:30 am to 8:15 pm; Sun 11:30 am to 8:45 pm
Vegetarian Authentic Chinese. Vegan options. Not pure vegetarian.
Menu: Has a large selection of vegetarian dishes. Has mock "meat" and "fish" dishes. Smoked Bean Curd Skin, Pork with Dry Bean Curd, Mock Chicken, Mustard Green with Bean Curd Sheet, Chinese Pancakes and tea. Food is not smothered in heavy sauces. Has an all-you-can-eat meal for dinner. Does not use MSG.
Comments: Gets high recommendations. All-you-can-eat dinners (around $10 per person) and brunch. Also has a branch in Rowland Heights. Very popular so you may have to wait for a table on the weekends. Dining room is very brightly lit. Play soft Chinese music.
Other Info: Full service, take-out. Accepts MC, VISA. Price: $$-$$$.
Directions: From I-10, take Atlantic Blvd exit towards Monterey Park, then go south on Atlantic Blvd and this place is a block down.
Directions: A few blocks south of Garvey, on the east side of the street.

Weidner's
127 East Garvey Avenue, at Garfield
626-288-4344
Hours: Monday to Thursday 9 am to 8 pm; Fri-

day 10 am to 4 pm; Sunday 9 am to 6 pm; closed Saturday.
Natural Food Store. One of the largest natural food stores in the valley. Big organic produce sections.
Directions: From I-10, take the New Ave exit, then go south on N New Ave a third-mile and this place is at the corner with Whitmore St.

NORTH HOLLYWOOD

**Leonor's
11403 Victory Boulevard; 818-980-9011
Hours: Monday to Friday 10 am to 9 pm; Saturday 10 am to 10 pm; Sunday 11 am to 9 pm
Vegetarian Mexican Restaurant. Mainly Vegan.
Menu: Mexican dishes such as enchilada, burritos, tostadas, quesadillas and tacos. Salads, sandwiches, pizza, Special Chicken Salad, quesadilla with soy chicken and soy cheese, lentil soup, whole-wheat flatbreads and Forever-Young Chicken Diner. Uses soy "meat," soy chicken and soy "cheese." Fresh juices. Flax Seed Iced Tea (flax seeds, prunes, cinnamon & honey) is recommended. Check for eggs.
Comments: Comes highly recommended. First class service. Casual, informal atmosphere. Darkly lit, intimate place. Reasonably priced. You should be careful in this neighborhood. Has another location in Studio City. Does not cook with salt, but can add your own. Sells their homemade soy cheese, which is excellent.
Other Info: Full service, take-out. Price: $-$$.
Directions: From Hwy 101, take CA Hwy 170 north towards Sacramento for ¾ mile, take Burbank Rd exit, then turn right at Burbank Rd and go a half-mile, at Tujunga Ave turn left and go 1 mile, at Victory Blvd turn left and this place is at the corner.

NORTHRIDGE

Café Graikos
19346 Rinaldi Street, Northridge; 818-831-1187
Hours: Sunday to Thursday 11 am to 9 pm
Friday & Saturday 11 am to 10 pm
Greek. Vegan friendly. Not pure vegetarian.
Menu: Has around 30 vegetarian dishes on the menu. Vegetarian Combo Platter, Stuffed Eggplant, Lentil Pilaf, Horiatiki salad, Stuffed Grape Leaves, Lentil Soup (very good), Greek Salad, vegetarian Greek Pizza, baba ghanouj, Spanikopita, Vegetarian Souvlaki Plate, hummus, Rice Pilaf, falafel and tahini.
Comments: Gets good ratings from the locals.

Marks vegan dishes with a red heart on the menu. May want to ask if eggs are added to any of the dishes.
Other Info: Accepts AMEX, MC, VISA. Price: $-$$.
Directions: In a shopping center on the southeast corner of Tampa and Rinaldi.

The Good Earth
19340 Nordhoff Street; 818-363-3933
Hours: Daily 8 am to 10 pm
Restaurant. Part of a national chain. About a third of the menu is vegetarian. Has a bakery.
Menu: Good salads, main dishes and desserts. Uses beans and soy foods.

Whole Foods Market (Mrs Gooch's)
19340 Rinaldi Street
818-363-3933; **fax:** 818-363-2940
On Reseda Blvd, half a block north of Prairie Street; **Web site:** www.wholefoodsmarket.com
Hours: Daily 9 am to 9 pm
Natural Food Store and Cafe. Deli, Bakery, Salad Bar and Juice Bar. Organic produce. Supermarket-type place. See Whole Foods Market information.
Comments: Prices are very reasonable. Does not sell anything containing refined sugar or MSG. Efficient, friendly place.
Directions: From CA Hwy 118, take Tampa Ave exit, then go north of Tampa Ave for a quarter-mile, at Rinaldi St turn right and this place is a quarter-mile down.

NORWALK

**Our Daily Bread Bakery
12201 Firestone Boulevard; 562-863-6897
Hours: Monday and Wednesday 10 am to 4 pm; Tuesday & Thursday 10 am to 7 pm; Friday 10 am to 2 pm; closed Saturday.
Vegetarian Deli and Bakery. Vegan options.
Menu: The menu changes regularly. Salads, several types of soups, Lasagna (recommended), stuffed peppers, quiche, veggie burgers, macaroni & cheese, enchiladas, breads and cookies. Has vegan desserts including vegan persimmon ice cream.
Comments: Run by the Seventh Day Adventists. The food gets really high recommendations. Has a section that sells vegetarian groceries and books. Rear patio seats around 30. Sugar and oil-free.
Other Info: Counter service, take-out. Price: $.
Directions: From I-5, take the San Antonio Dr/ Norwalk BL exit, then go southwest on San An-

tonio Drive 3 blocks, at Firestone Blvd turn left and this place is 2 blocks down at Funston Ave.

ORANGE

**Lotus Café
1515 West Chapman Avenue
714-385-1233; fax: 714-385-1040
Hours: Daily 11 am to 3 pm, 5 pm to 9 pm
Sunday Brunch NE
Fully Vegetarian Chinese. Mostly Vegan.
Menu: Has a large selection of vegetarian dishes and many mock "meat" dishes. Ginger Pesto Soy, Orange Flavor "Chicken," Hot Wok Special, Kong Pao Deluxe Won Ton Soup, Soy Meat Ball with Veggie Wrapped Soy Chicken and Lemon Chicken.
Comments: Friendly, cozy place. Service is good.
Other Info: Full service. Non-smoking. Price: $$-$$$. Reservations recommended. Accepts AMEX, DIS, MC, VISA.
Directions: It is in the middle of Orange, a mile east of Hwy 5, ten minutes from Disneyland. From I-5, take the City Drive exit towards State College Blvd, then go east on W Chapman Ave and this place is 1¼ mile down. This place is about 1 mile northeast of where I-5 and Hwy 22 meet.

99 Green Market
1388 South Fullerton Road; 626-965-7788
Hours: Sunday to Thursday 9 am to 9 pm
Friday & Saturday 9 am to 9:30 pm
Chinese Grocery Store and Chinese Deli. Vegan options. Not pure vegetarian.
Comments: Has a small area to sit and eat. Counter service, take-out.

Tandoor Cuisine of India
1132 East Katella Avenue; 714-538-2234
Hours: Daily 11 am to 2:30 pm, 5 pm to 10 pm
Indian. Vegan options. Not pure vegetarian.
Menu: Has vegetarian options such as salads, rice dishes, curried vegetables, samosas and main dishes.
Other Info: Full service, take-out. Price: $$.

PALM DESERT

Native Foods
73-890 El Paseo
760-836-9396; **Web site:** www.nativefoods.com
Hours: Monday to Saturday 11 am to 9 pm;
Deli Hours: Monday to Saturday 7 am to 4 pm
Closed Sunday.
Natural Food Store and Restaurant. Organic produce. Fully Vegan. Macrobiotic options.
Menu: Hollywood Bowl (steamed organic vegetables on top of brown rice with baked tofu and Thai peanut sauce), Yakisoba (stir-fry noodles), Jerk Burger (made from seitan), Indonesian Tempeh Chips, BBQ Love Burger (seitan with BBQ sauce), Reuben and hoagie sandwiches, mock "fish" dish and MadCowboy's Delight (soy chicken with BBQ sauce, corn & avocado). Cappuccino, espresso.
Comments: Specializing in homemade textured vegetable protein (TVP), tempeh and seitan. Has good service. Has two other locations in Westwood and Palm Springs. Local organic produce used when possible.
Other Info: Full service, counter, take-out, catering. Non-smoking. Does not take reservations. Accepts MC, VISA. Price: $$.
Directions: From Hwy 111, take the Portola Ave exit and go 1 block south, then turn right onto El Paseo.

Trader Joe's
Palm Desert Town Center
Fred Waring Drive at Town Center Drive.

Veggie & Tea House
72281 Hwy 111, at Fred Waring; 760-674-0350
Hours: Daily 11 am to 8 pm
Chinese. Juice Bar and Salad Bar. Vegan options. Not pure vegetarian.
Comments: Grows much of their own produce. Attractive décor. Tea rooms.
Other Info: Full service, counter service, take-out. Price: $$.

PASADENA

Clearwater Café
168 Colorado Boulevard; 818-356-959
Hours: Monday to Thursday 11:30 am to 10 pm; Saturday 11:30 am to 11 pm; Sunday 11:30 am to 9 pm; Saturday and Sunday Brunch
Natural Foods. Vegan options. Not pure vegetarian.
Menu: The menu changes daily. Good amount of salads. Tempura dishes, Chinese Vegetables, Organic Risotto, several salads, Grilled Vegetables and other dishes.
Other Info: Full service, take-out. Accepts AMEX, MC, VISA. Non-smoking. Price: $$$.
Directions: From CA Hwy 134, take the Colorado Blvd exit towards Orange Grove Blvd, then go east on Colorado Blvd and this place is a half-mile down.

Farmer's Market
Paloma & Sierra Madre
Saturday 8:30 am to 1 pm

Good Earth Restaurant
257 North Rosemead Boulevard
626-351-5488
Hours: Daily 8 am to 10 pm
International Natural Foods. 75% Vegetarian.
Not pure vegetarian.
Menu: Soups, salads, Eggplant Parmesan, Walnut Mushroom Casserole and other dishes. Fresh juices.
Other Info: Full service, take-out. Accepts AMEX, MC, VISA. Price: $$.
Directions: From I-210, take the Rosemead Blvd/Michillinda Ave exit, then go north on N Rosemead Blvd (Rte 19) and this place is a quarter-mile north of the exit.

Health Food City
3651 East Foothill Boulevard; 626-351-8616;
email: martin@healthfoodcity.com
Web site: www.healthfoodcity.com
Natural Food Store.

**Orean: The Health Express
817 North Lake Avenue, off I-210
626-794-0861
Hours: Daily 9:30 am to 9 pm
Pure Vegetarian Fast Food-style Restaurant.
Mainly Vegan.
Menu: Veggie burgers, tofu burgers, tacos, pizzas, salads, unfried French fries, Veggie hot dog, "Big-O" Chili Cheeseburger (soy cheese, beans, vegetables and grains), tacos, Oreanburger, Chicken-o-burger, chili dogs, burritos and Filet-o-soul. Breakfast burrito. French fries are cooked with hot air instead of oil. Fresh juices and good shakes. Vegan strawberry shakes.
Comments: Vegetarian fast food place. Has four outdoor tables. Soy cheese contains casein.
Other Info: Counter service, take-out. Non-smoking. Reservations not necessary. Price: $. Cash only; no credit cards.
Directions: From Freeway 210, take Lake Ave North exit. Then go north on Lake Ave and this place is five blocks down on the left, next to the McDonalds.

Pita! Pita! Restaurant
37 South Fair Oaks Ave; 626-356-0106
Hours: Sunday to Thursday 11 am to 10 pm
Friday & Saturday 11 am to 11 pm

Lebanese Mediterranean. Vegan-friendly. Not pure vegetarian.
Menu: Has several vegetarian options including falafel, hummus and the Royal Vegetarian Feast.
Other Info: Accepts AMEX, MC, VISA.

Trader Joe's (2 locations)
610 S Arroyo Parkway; 818-568-9254
1566 Colorado Boulevard, Eagle Rock
213-257-6422

Yujean Kang's
67 North Raymond Avenue, Pasadena
626-585-0855
Menu: Sunday to Friday 11:30 am to 2:30 pm, 5 pm to 9:30 pm
Saturday 11:30 am to 2:30 pm, 5 pm to 10 pm
Chinese. Not pure vegetarian.
Comments: Is rated as one of the top Chinese restaurants in the LA area.
Other Info: Accepts AMEX, MC, VISA.

Whole Foods Market
3751 East Foothill Boulevard, Pasadena
626-351-5994
Hours: Daily 8 am to 10 pm
Natural Food Store and Cafe. Deli, Bakery, Salad Bar and Juice Bar. Organic produce. Supermarket-type place. See Whole Foods Market information.
Directions: From I-210, take the Rosemead Blvd/Michillinda Ave exit, then go north on N Rosemead Blvd (Rte 19) a few blocks, then at Foothill Blvd turn right and this place is 100 yards down.

Wild Oats
603 South Lake Street, Pasadena
626-792-1778
Hours: Daily 8 am to 10 pm
Natural Food Store and Cafe. Deli, Bakery, Salad Bar and Juice Bar. Organic produce. Supermarket-type place. See Wild Oats Market information.
Directions: From I-210 (Hwy 134), take Lake Ave exit, then go south on Lake Ave and this place is 1 mile down.

RANCHO PALOS VERDES (Los Angeles County)

Trader Joe's
The Terraces; 28901 South Western Avenue
310-832-1241

REDLANDS

***Nature's Deli & Nutrition Center
202 East State Street; 909-792-6556
Hours: Monday to Friday 9 am to 7 pm (until 9 pm Thursday); Sun 11 am to 5 pm; closed Sat.
Vegan Natural Foods. Mainly everything is organic.
Menu: Has a whole-wheat vegan pizza, veggie pita, (tofu and spinach in a pita), tofu burger, avocado sandwich, veggie burgers, sandwiches, salads, wraps, Mediterranean wrap, a daily special, steamed vegetables, and desserts such as tofu cheesecake and pies. Smoothies.
Other Info: Counter service, take-out. Accepts AMEX, MC, VISA.
Directions: From I-10, take CA 38/Orange St exit towards downtown, then go south on Orange St and go a third-mile, at E Redland Blvd turn left and go 2 blocks, at N 6th St turn right and this place is 1 block down.

Trader Joe's
Orange Street Plaza; 552 Orange Street
909-798-2888

REDONDO BEACH

**Greens Temple
The Green Temple, A Veggie Place, 1700 South Catalina Avenue, at Ave I; 310-944-4525
Hours: Sunday, Tuesday to Thursday 11 am to 9 pm; Fri and Sat 11 am to 10 pm; closed Mon.
Vegetarian International, mainly Mexican. Very Vegan-friendly. Juice Bar.
Menu: House salad with tahini dressing, sandwiches, burritos, Savory Steamer (with their great Savory Sauce), Three Bean Soup and main dishes. The Savory Spuds are recommended. Fresh juices. Has a large selection of herbal teas. The Dragon Shot is a herbal tonic.
Comments: Has indoor and outdoor seating. Eclectic, funky décor. Friendly place. Local organic produce used when possible. Have herb garden.
Other Info: Full service, take-out. Price: $-$$.
Directions: This place is at the south end of the beach, a few blocks west of the ocean.

Trader Joe's
Hollywood Riviera; 1761 South Elena Avenue
310-316-1745

Whole Foods Market
405 North Pacific Coast Hwy; 310-376-6931
Hours: Daily 8 am to 9 pm

Natural Food Store and Cafe. Deli, Bakery, Salad Bar and Juice Bar. Organic produce. Supermarket-type place. See Whole Foods Market information.
Directions: This place is a half-mile due west of Seaside Lagoon and the ocean. From I-405, take the Artesia Blvd (Hwy 91) exit towards Redondo Beach, then go west on Artesia Blvd 1 mile, at Inglewood Ave turn left and go a third-mile, at Ripley Ave turn right and go 1¼ mile, turn left at Flagler and make an immediate right at 190th St/Anita St and go ¾ miles, then turn left at Pacific Coast Hwy (Hwy 1) and this place is a half-mile down.

RIVERSIDE

**Oasis Vegetarian Food
11550 Pierce Street; 909-688-5423
Hours: Monday to Thursday 9 am to 7 pm; Fri 9 am to 4 pm; Sun 10 am to 5 pm; closed Sat.
Vegetarian Latin and American. Vegan options. It is connected to a vegetable food market.
Menu: Has many vegetarian options including Pupusas (corn tortilla filled with vegetables), French fries, Garden Supreme Burger, tamales (stuffed cornhusks), Carnitas (mock "pork" burrito) and several vegetarian sandwiches. Smoothies
Other Info: Limited service, take-out. No credit cards; cash only.
Directions: From Hwy 91, take the Pierce Street exit, then go north on Pierce St and this place is 1.4 miles down.

ROWLAND HEIGHTS

Happy Family Vegetarian Restaurant
18425 East Colima Road; 626-965-9923
Hours: Monday to Friday 11:30 am to 2:45 pm, 5 pm to 9 pm; Sat & Sun 11:30 am to 9:15 pm
Vegetarian Authentic Chinese. Vegan options. Buffet Lunch.
Menu: Has a large selection of vegetarian dishes. Vegetarian fried "Chicken" with mushrooms.
Other Info: Full service, take-out. Non-smoking. Accepts MC, VISA. Price: $$.
Directions: From CA Hwy 60, take the Fullerton Rd exit, then go south a half-mile on Fullerton Rd, at Colima Rd turn left and this place is 2 blocks down.

Health Food City
18453 East Colima Road; 626-913-3188
Web site: www.healthfoodcity.com
Natural Food Store.

SAN GABRIEL

Health Food City
140 West Valley Boulevard #102; 626-288-3498
Web site: www.healthfoodcity.com
Natural Food Store.

**Tea Shaker and Vegetarian Food
7258 North Rosemead Boulevard
626-287-5850
Hours: Daily 11 am to 9 pm
Fully Vegetarian Asian. Mostly Vegan. The cooking style is from South East Asia, such as Hong Kong, Burmese and Thai Style.
Menu: Pad Thai, Vegetarian Chicken Steak, Tom Yum Vermicelli, Fried Noodles, Papaya Salad, Hot & Sour Soup, Beef Curry Rice Plate and vegetarian meat dishes. Bo-Bah-Tea is flavored ice tea that is recommended. The Vegetarian Chicken Steak is great. Tea Bar (30 special teas) with fruit flavored ice and hot teas, Iced Mango Green Tea and Passion Fruit Green Tea. The Tea Salad (shredded cabbage and carrot, mung beans, toasted sesame and peanuts, topped by fermented tea leaves) is recommended. The Coconut Ice Cream is great. Fresh juices. Soy milk.
Comments: Friendly staff.
Other Info: Full service, catering, take-out. Non-smoking. Accepts reservations but are not necessary. Accepts MC, VISA. Price: $-$$. Reservations recommended.
Directions: This store is at the intersection of Rosemead and Huntington Drive, next to Trader's Joe. From I-10, get off at the Rosemead exit and go north for about five minutes (three miles). From I-210, get off at the Rosemead South exit and go for about one mile. There is plenty of parking in front. It is in a strip mall just south of Huntington Drive. From Huntington Dr, go south on S Rosemead Blvd and this place is a half-block down.

Trader Joe's
7260 North Rosemead Boulevard, at Huntington Drive; 818-285-5862

SANTA BARBARA

Galanga Thai Restaurant
507 State Street; 805-899-3199
Hours: Thursday to Monday 11 am to 9:30 pm
Closed Wednesday.
Thai. Vegan options. Not pure vegetarian.
Menu: Has over twenty vegetarian dishes. Some dishes contain oyster sauce so you should ask about this before ordering. Non-alcoholic beer.
Other Info: Full service, take-out. Price $-$$. Accepts AMEX, MC, VISA.

Good Earth Restaurant
5955 Calle Real, in nearby Goleta
805-683-6101
Hours: Daily 7:30 am to 9:30 pm
Menu: Has some vegetarian dishes and healthy breakfasts.

Lazy Acres Market
302 Meigs Road; 805-564-4410
Hours: Daily 7 am to 10 pm
Juice Bar closes at 7 pm
Natural Food Store and Deli. Organic produce. Juice Bar, Salad Bar and Pizza Bar. Cappuccino, espresso. Has a large selection of international cheeses.
Menu: Has a large selection of vegetarian dishes. Soups, salads, sandwiches, veggie chili and tofu dishes.
Comments: Friendly place. Accepts AMEX, MC, VISA.
Directions: From US 101, take the Carrillo St exit, then go south on W Carrillo St and go 1 mile, W Carrillo St becomes Meigs and this place is a half-mile further down the road.

Main Squeeze Café
138 East Canon Perdido Street; 805-966-5365
Hours: Monday to Friday 11 am to 9 pm
Saturday & Sunday 9 am to 9 pm
Natural Food Café. Vegan options. Juice Bar. Not pure vegetarian.
Menu: Soups, salads, sandwiches, daily pasta specials, Mexican dishes and other dishes. Freshly baked desserts. Fresh juices, smoothies and shakes. Specializes in non-dairy smoothies. Espresso.
Other Info: Limited service, take-out. Price: $. Accepts AMEX, MC, VISA.
Directions: From Hwy 101, take the Laguna St/Garden St exit, then go northwest on Garden St 1 block, at E Gutierrez St turn left and go 1 block, at Santa Barbara St turn right and go a half-mile, at E Canon Perdido St turn left and this place is 1 block down.

Natural Café
508 State Street; 805-962-9494
Hours: Sunday to Thursday 11 am to 9 pm
Friday & Saturday 11 am to 9:30 pm
Natural Food Restaurant and Juice Bar. Vegan options. Not pure vegetarian.
Menu: Homemade soups, freshly made sand-

wiches, vegetarian chili, salads, veggie stir-fry, Chips and Guacamole, tacos and a few vegetarian main dishes. Fresh juices and wheatgrass.
Comments: Has a nice patio where you can watch what's happening on State Street. Also has a small store that sells herbs, vitamins and other things.
Other Info: Full service, take-out. Price: $-$$. Cash only or local checks; no credit cards. Has ATM in building.
Directions: This place is in downtown Santa Barbara, five blocks from the Pacific Ocean. From US 101, take the Laguna St/Garden St exit, then go northwest on Garden St for 1 block, at Gutierrez St turn left and go 3 blocks, at State St turn right and this place is 1 block down.

Sojourner Café

134 East Canon Perdido
805-965-7922; email: sojo@sojournercafe.com
Web site: www.sojournercafe.com
Hours: Monday to Saturday 11 am to 11 pm
Sunday 11 am to 10 pm
Natural Foods International Restaurant. Vegan options. Not pure vegetarian.
Menu: Has Mexican dishes and a Mediterranean Plate. Veggie burger, special salads, Avocado & Cheese sandwich, Tostada, Black Bean Stew, Veggie Burritos, Gazpacho (cold tomato soup), Linguini, Veggie Stir-fry, Tofu Egg Salad, Baked Potato with other vegetables, Rice & Vegetables, Dal and several other vegetarian dishes. Uses vegetarian (rennetless) cheddar and jack cheeses. Non-alcoholic special drinks including Carob Supreme and Mocha Frosted. Cappuccino, espresso.
Comments: Can have their daily special mailed to you daily by email. Display local artists' work.
Other Info: Full service, take-out. Non-smoking. Price: $$. Accepts MC, VISA.
Directions: From Hwy 101, go 1 block northwest on Garden St, at Gutierrez St turn left and go 1 block, at Santa Barbara St turn left and go a half-mile, at Canon Perdido St turn left and this place is 1 block down.

SANTA MONICA (Los Angeles County)

Anastasia's Asylum

1028 Wilshire Boulevard; 310-394-7113
Hours: Daily 6:30 am to 1 am
Mainly Vegetarian. Not pure vegetarian (serves chicken and fish).
Menu: Homemade Lasagna and Quesadilla Isabella (with avocado, mozzarella, artichoke hearts and mild chilis).

Comments: Artists and writers often come here. Accepts AMEX, MC, VISA.
Directions: From I-10, take Exit #1A towards Lincoln Bl/Rte 1, then go northwest on Lincoln Blvd (Rte 2) ¾ mile, at Wilshire Blvd turn right and this place is 2 blocks down.

Bistro of Santa Monica

2301 Santa Monica Boulevard; 310-453-5442
Hours: Monday to Friday 11 am to 10:30 pm
Saturday & Sunday 4 pm to 10:30 pm
Italian. European-style place. Vegan options. Not pure vegetarian. Northern Italian mainly.
Menu: There are over ten types of pasta. Has a variety of sauces including olive oil, tomato and cream. Fresh juices, cappuccino, espresso.
Comments: Everything is prepared on the premises. Dishes do not contain sugar, preservatives or salt.
Other Info: Full service, take-out. Accepts AMEX, DIS, MC, VISA. Price: $$-$$$.

**Chandni Vegetarian Cuisine of India

1909 Wilshire Boulevard, at 19th
310-828-7060
Hours: Daily 11:30 am to 2:30 pm, 5 pm to 10 pm
Pure Vegetarian North Indian. Vegan friendly. Daily inexpensive all-you-can-eat Lunch Buffet.
Menu: Has a large selection of vegetarian goods. Soups, breads, appetizers and other dishes.
Comments: Has a sister restaurant in Culver City. Gets good recommendations.
Other Info: Full service, take-out. Price: $-$$. Accepts MC, VISA.
Directions: From I-10, take Cloverfield Blvd exit, then go northwest on Cloverfield Blvd for a quarter-mile, at Olympic Blvd turn left and go a quarter-mile, at 20th St turn right and go ¾ mile, at Wilshire Blvd turn left and this place is 1 block down. This place is a few blocks west of St John's Hospital.

Co-opportunity Consumer Co-op: The Natural Food Grocer

1525 Broadway, at 16th; 310-451-8902
email: service@coopportunity.com
Web site: http://www.coopportunity.com
Hours: Daily 8 am to 10 pm
Deli Hours: 8 am to 8 pm
Natural Food Store and Deli. Organic produce.
Comments: Members get a 3% discount. Has around 3,000 members. Has the largest amount of organic foods in Southern California. Large Store. Cooking classes here. Recommended.
Directions: From I-10, take Cloverfield Blvd exit,

then go northwest on Cloverfield Blvd for a quarter-mile, at Olympic Blvd turn left and go a quarter-mile, at 20th St turn right and go 1 block, at Colorado Ave turn left and go 4 blocks, at 16th St turn right and go 1 block, at Broadway turn left and this place is 1 block down.

Farmer's Market
Second St & Arizona
Hours: Saturday 8:30 am to 12 noon (only organic); Wednesday 9:30 am to 2 pm.
Large farmer's market in the US.
Main & Ocean Park Boulevard
Hours: Sunday 9 am to 12 noon

Just in Case
2718 Main Street
310-399-3096, 800-326-4036, **fax:** 310-452-4427; **Web site:** http://socalnet.com/JustInCase
Hours: Daily 11 am to 7 pm
Mail Order Company. Sell cruelty free bags, gifts, wallets, briefcases, organizers, travel kits, luggage, etc. They have a catalog.

Lincoln Bay Mediterranean Cuisine
1928 Lincoln Boulevard; 310-396-4039
Hours: Tuesday to Sunday 5 pm to 10 pm
Greek, Middle Eastern and Italian. Vegan-friendly. Not pure vegetarian.
Menu: Soups (Lentil, Carrot), salads, Portabella Mushroom Salad, sandwiches, Stuffed Vegetables, Dolmathes, Fava Bean Spread, Grilled Japanese Eggplant, pastas, baba ghanoush, hummus & pita and falafel.
Comments: Good food. Plays Middle Eastern music. Belly dancers.

***Living Light House
1457 12th Street; 310-395-6337
Web site: www.livinglighthouse.com
Hours: Has nightly events. Best to call for weekly events.
Vegan Raw foods. Gourmet. Price: $$.
Menu: Raw meals.
Directions: From I-10, take Exit 1A towards Lincoln Bl/Rte 1, then go northwest on Lincoln Blvd 1 block, at Colorado Ave turn right and go 4 blocks, at 12 St turn left and this place is 1 block down.

Mani's Bakery
2507 Main Street; 310-396-7700
Hours: Daily 8 am to 10 pm
Vegetarian Bakery and Coffeehouse.
Menu: Sandwiches, fresh baked breads, desserts,

baked goods, cakes, pies, truffles, turnovers and breakfasts. You can get soy milk for your coffee.
Other Info: Counter service, take-out. Accepts AMEX, MC, VISA. Price: $.
Directions: From I-10, take the 4th St exit, then go northwest on 4th St ¾ mile, then go left at Ocean Park Blvd and go 3 block, at Main St turn right and this place is 50 yards down. This place is a few blocks from the beach.

Mrs Winston's Green Grocery
2901 Ocean Park Boulevard #107, Santa Monica
310-452-7770
Hours: Monday to Friday 8 am to 7 pm; Saturday 10 am to 5 pm; closed Sunday.
Natural Food Store.

Newsroom Café
530 Wilshire Blvd #102, Santa Monica
310-319-9100
Hours: Monday to Friday 8 am to 9:30; Saturday 9 am to 9:30 pm; Sunday 9 am to 3 pm
Natural Foods.
Menu: Has vegetarian dishes including soups, salads, veggie burger sandwiches and burritos. Usually has a vegan soup. Fresh juices, espresso, non-alcoholic beer.
Comments: There is a more upscale version of this restaurant in Hollywood.
Other Info: Limited service, take-out. Accepts MC, VISA. Price: $.
Directions: From I-10, take Exit #1A towards Lincoln Bl/Rte 1, then go northwest on 7th St for 0.65 mile, then turn left at Wilshire Blvd and this place is 2 blocks down.

One Life Natural Foods
3001 Main Street; 310-392-4501
Hours: Daily 7 am to 8 pm
Natural Food Store and Deli. Juice Bar. Organic produce.
Menu: Soups, salads, sandwiches, veggie Lasagna and more.
Other Info: Counter service, take-out. Has tables outside.
Directions: It is north on the coast, 2 blocks from the beach. From I-10, take the 4th St exit, then go northwest on 4th St ¾ mile, then go left at Ocean Park Blvd and go 3 blocks, at Main St turn left and this place is a third-mile down.

PF Chang's China Bistro
326 Wilshire Boulevard; 310-395-1912
Hours: Sunday to Thursday 11 am to 11 pm
Friday & Saturday 11 am to 12 pm

Chinese. Vegan options. Not pure vegetarian. Part of a national chain of Chinese restaurants.

**Real Food Daily

514 Santa Monica Boulevard
310-451-7544; Web site: www.realfood.com
Hours: Daily 11:30 am to 10 pm
Pure Vegetarian. Vegan and Macrobiotic options. Mainly organic.
Menu: They have daily special entrées, salads, vegetable dishes, beans, soup, Lasagna, tostadas, Seitan Fajitas, Reuben Sandwich, Roasted Vegetable Sandwich, Lentil Walnut Pate, Nori Maki, Caesar Salad, Salisbury Seitan Steak, Roasted Potato and Vegetable Pizza (with homemade tofu cheese), R&B Burrito, Black Bean Tostada, breads, Spanish Rice, Soba Noodles, Mashed Potatoes, hummus, tabbouleh, Sea Vegetables, Millet Croquettes, Thai specials and very good desserts such as Coconut Cream Pie, Chocolate Raspberry Cake, Carob Fudge Brownies and Banana Pudding with Cashew Cream. Macrobiotic Plate with homemade bread. Fresh juices and smoothies. Some recommended dishes are the Meatloaf and Mashed Potatoes with Gravy, the Lentil Walnut Pate and the No-cheez (blue and yellow corn chips with tofu sour cream guacamole, black bean and carrot salsa).
Comments: Has good versions of traditionally meat and dairy-based dishes. Great food. Great, relaxed atmosphere. Simple, attractive decor. Inexpensive. It has another branch in West Hollywood. Almost totally organic. Two floor dining area. Friendly, helpful staff.
Other Info: Full service, take-out, delivery. Nonsmoking. Reservations not necessary. Accepts AMEX, MC, VISA. Price: $$. Main courses range from about $7 to $13.
Directions: Between 5th and 6th Streets. Two blocks from 3rd Street Santa Monica Promenade and the Santa Monica Pier. From I-10, take exit 1A toward Lincoln Bl/Rte 1, then go northwest on 7th St for 3 blocks, at Santa Monica Blvd turn left and this place is 2 blocks down.

Toi On Wilshire

1120 Wilshire Boulevard; 310-394-7804
Hours: Daily 11 am to 3 am
Thai. Not pure vegetarian. Vegan-friendly.
Menu: Has some vegetarian options. The menu says that any dish can be made vegetarian. Vegetarian Curry, brown rice, Wonton Soup, Pad Ciw Tofu (ask to be made without egg) and Eggplant with Pumpkin and Tofu.
Comments: Formal place. It is one of the highest

rated Thai restaurants in the LA area. Played rock music. Toi means "young one." No MSG or preservatives.
Other Info: Accepts AMEX, MC, VISA.

Wild Oats Community Market

500 Wilshire Boulevard; 310-395-4510
Hours: 8 am to 10 pm
Natural Food Store and Cafe. Deli, Bakery, Salad Bar and Juice Bar. Organic produce. Supermarket-type place. See Wild Oats Market information.
Directions: From I-10, take exit #1A towards Lincoln Bl/Rte 1, then go northwest on 7th St for 0.65 mile, at Wilshire Blvd turn left and this place is 2 blocks down at 5th St.

Wild Oats Community Market

1425 Montana Avenue, Santa Monica
310-576-4707
Hours: 8 am to 10 pm
Natural Food Store and Cafe. Deli, Bakery, Salad Bar and Juice Bar. Organic produce. Supermarket-type place. See Wild Oats Market information.
Directions: From I-10, take the Cloverfield Blvd exit, then go northwest on Cloverfield Blvd, then turn left on Olympic Blvd for ¾ mile, at 14th St turn right and go 1¼ mile, at Montana Ave turn right and this place is 50 yards down.

SAUSALITO (Marin County)

Real Foods Co

200 Caledonia; 415-332-9640
Hours: Daily 8 am to 9 pm
Natural Food Store and take-out Deli. Organic produce.
Menu: Has a small selection of ready-made dishes.
Other Info: Counter service, take-out. Has some benches outside to sit at.
Directions: From Hwy 101, take the Alexander Ave exit, then go northeast ¾ mile on Sausalito Lateral Rd (becomes Alexander Ave) for 1 mile, at 2nd St turn right and go 2 blocks, at Richardson St turn right (road becomes Bridgeway after 1 block) and go 1 mile, at Turney turn left and this place is 1 block down.

SHERMAN OAKS

**Follow Your Heart

21825 Sherman Way, near Topanga Canyon Road
818-348-3240
Web site: www.followyourheart.com
Hours: Daily 8 am to 9 pm
Natural Food Store and Vegetarian Restaurant.

Vegan friendly.
Menu: Soups, salads, sandwiches and desserts. Quesadilla, Sautéed Mushrooms, Follow Your Heart Burger, Reuben Sandwich, Roasted Eggplant Sandwich, Falafel Plate, Vegetarian Barbeque, Stuffed Potatoes, Spinach Salad, Fresh Fruit Salad Plate, Wok Stir-fry, Spinach Lasagna, Organic Steamed Vegetable Plate, Angel Hair Pomadoro, pizzas, Scrambled Tofu, Two Bean Hash, French Toast (non-egg) Egg-free Buttermilk Pancakes and much more.
Comments: Good, reasonably priced place. Has their full menu on their web site. They are the creators of Vegenaise. Been open since 1970.
Other Info: Accepts AMEX, MC, VISA.

Genmai Sushi

4454 Van Nuys Boulevard, Sherman Oaks
818-986-7060
Hours: Monday to Thursday 12 noon to 2:30 pm, 5:30 pm to 10:15 pm; Fri & Sat 12 noon to 2:30 pm, 5:30 pm to 11 pm; Sun 5 pm to 10 pm
Asian and Japanese. Vegan options. Not pure vegetarian.
Menu: Has several vegan dishes. Really good vegetarian sushi and Reuben sandwich. Genmai means "brown rice," and the place serves a selection of it.
Other Info: Accepts AMEX, MC, VISA.

Healthy Discounts

14427½ Ventura Boulevard; 818-995-8461
Hours: Daily 9 am to 8 pm
Natural Food Store

Langano Restaurant

14838 Burbank Boulevard, at Burbank, Sherman Oaks; 818-786-2670
Hours: Tuesday to Sunday 11 am to 10 pm; Closed Monday.
Ethiopian. Vegan options. Not pure vegetarian.
Menu: Has a large amount of vegetarian dishes. Has two vegetarian combination platters that have African spiced vegetable stews, and lentil and yellow split pea dishes.
Comments: Basic atmosphere.

Trader Joe's

14119 Riverside Drive; 818-789-2771

Whole Foods Markets – West

4520 North Sepulveda Boulevard, Sherman Oaks
818-382-3700
Hours: Monday to Friday 7 am to 10 pm; Satur-

day & Sunday 8 am to 10 pm; Deli and Juice & Coffee Bar open Monday to Friday at 7 am.
Natural Food Store and Cafe. Deli, Bakery, Salad Bar and Juice Bar. Organic produce. Supermarket-type place. See Whole Foods Market information.
Directions: From I-405, take Ventura Blvd/Sherman Oaks exit and this place is a block from the exit.

Whole Foods – East

12905 Riverside Drive, Sherman Oaks
818-762-5548
Hours: Daily 8 am to 10 pm
Juice & Coffee Bar opens daily at 7 am
Natural Food Store and Cafe. Deli, Bakery, Salad Bar and Juice Bar. Organic produce. Supermarket-type place. See Whole Foods Market information.
Directions: From I-101, take the Coldwater Canyon Ave exit, then go north on Coldwater Canyon Ave 1 block, then turn left at Riverside Dr and this place is 25 yards down.

SOUTH EL MONTE

**Veggie-Life Restaurant

9324 East Garvey Avenue; 626 443-8687
email: info@veggieliferestaurant.com;
Web site: www.veggieliferestaurant.com
Hours: Tuesday to Sunday 8 am to 9 pm
Closed Monday.
Fully Vegetarian Vietnamese-French. Mainly Vegan.
Menu: Has a large amount of vegetarian dishes and a great selection of mock "meat" dishes. Rice dishes, Pho, drumsticks, Seaweed Soup, vegetable dishes and Crispy-Noodle. The Cabbage Lotus Salad is recommended if you like pungent flavors. The Clay Pot Fish with Pepper and Rice is good. Non-alcoholic beer. Soy milk.
Comments: Lots of vegetarian Vietnamese dishes. On the 1st and 15th of each month of the Chinese Lunar calendar it is extremely busy, so most likely it is a good idea to avoid those days. Is a pleasant, clean, informal café-style restaurant. Has a good atmosphere. No MSG.
Other Info: Full service, catering, counter, take-out. Non-smoking. Reservations not accepted. Accepts MC, VISA. Price: $-$$.
Directions: From I-10, take the Rosemead Blvd/Rte 19 exit, then go southeast on Rosemead Blvd for 0.65 mile, then at Garvey Ave turn right and this place is 1 block down, on the southwest corner of East Garvey and Rosemead Blvd.

South Pasadena (Los Angeles county)

Grassroots Natural Market
1119 Fair Oaks Avenue, South Pasadena
626-799-0156
Hours: Monday to Saturday 8 am to 7 pm
Sunday 9 am to 5 pm
Deli Hours: Monday to Friday 8 am to 5:30 pm
Saturday 9 am to 5 pm
Natural Foods Store and Deli.
Menu: Soups, salads, sandwiches and hot main dishes. Fresh juices.
Comments: The food is made freshly daily.
Other Info: Cafeteria style, take-out. Accepts AMEX, MC, VISA. Price: $.
Directions: From 1-10, take Fremont north exit to Monterray, at Monterray turn right and go two blocks, then turn left into shopping center where this place is located. From I-110, take the Fair Oaks Ave exit, then go south on Fair Oaks Ave and this place is a third-mile down.

Trader Joe's
613 Mission Street
818-441-6263

STUDIO CITY

Good Earth Restaurant
12345 Ventura Boulevard #12345C
818-506-7400
Hours: Sunday to Thursday 8:30 am to 10 pm
Friday & Saturday 8:30 am to 10:30 pm
Healthy Breakfast Place. Not pure vegetarian.
Tofu Scramble.

**Leonor's
12445 Moorpark Street, Unit C
818-762-0660
Hours: Daily 10 am to 10 pm
Vegetarian Mexican Restaurant. Mainly Vegan.
Menu: Mexican dishes such as enchilada, burritos, tostadas, quesadillas and tacos. Salads, sandwiches, pizza, Special Chicken Salad, quesadilla with soy chicken and soy cheese, lentil soup, whole-wheat flatbread and Forever-Young Chicken Diner. Uses soy "meat," soy chicken and soy "cheese." Fresh juices. "Flax seed iced tea" is recommended. Made of flax seeds, prunes, cinnamon and honey. Check for eggs.
Comments: Recommended. First class service. Casual, informal atmosphere. Darkly lit, intimate place. Reasonably priced. You should be careful in this neighborhood. Has another location in Studio City. Does not cook with salt, but can add your own. Sells their homemade soy cheese, which is excellent.
Other Info: Full service, take-out. Accepts AMEX, MC, VISA. Price: $-$$.
Directions: At the corner of Whitsett and Moorpark. From Hwy 101, take Laurel Canyon Blvd exit towards Studio City, go south on Laurel Canyon Blvd a third-mile, at Moorpark St turn right and this place is a half-mile down.

Thai Cottage
11266 Ventura Boulevard; 818-769-4653
Hours: Mon to Thur 11:30 am to 10 pm; Fri & Sat 11:30 am to 11 pm; Sun 12 noon to 10 pm
Thai. Not pure vegetarian.
Menu: Has several vegetarian dishes.
Comments: A romantic place to have dinner. Has candlelights and soft music. Has outdoor patio dinning.
Other Info: Full service, take-out. Accepts AMEX, MC, VISA. Price: $$.

THOUSAND OAKS (Ventura County)

Lassen's Health Foods
2857 East Thousand Oaks Boulevard
805-495-2609
Hours: Monday to Saturday 8 am to 9 pm
Closed Sunday.
Natural Food Store and Deli. Macrobiotic and Vegan options. Juice Bar.
Comments: Local organic produce used when possible.
Other Info: Full service, take-out. Price: $$.
Directions: From Hwy 101, take the Hampshire Rd exit, then go northeast on Hampshire Rd for 3 blocks, then turn left at E Thousand Oaks Blvd and this place is a quarter-mile down.

Whole Foods Market (Mrs Gooch's)
451 Avenida de los Arboles
805-492-5340
Hours: Daily 8 am to 9 pm
Natural Food Store and Cafe. Deli, Bakery, Salad Bar and Juice Bar. Organic produce. Supermarket-type place. See Whole Foods Market information.
Directions: From Hwy 101, take the Moorpark Rd exit, then go north on N Moorpark Rd 3 miles, at Avendida de los Arboles turn left and this place is 2 blocks down.

TOPANGA (CANYON)

Inn Of The Seventh Ray

128 Old Topanga Canyon Road; 310-455-1311
Hours: Monday to Friday 11 am to 3 pm, 5 pm
to 9:30 pm; Saturday 9 am to 3 pm, 5 pm to 11
pm; Sunday 9 am to 3 pm, 5 pm to 10 pm
Natural Food Restaurant. Vegan-friendly. Not
pure vegetarian.
Menu: Good selection of vegetarian and vegan
dishes. Gourmet vegetarian dishes. Acorn Squash
Stuffed with Curried Stuffing, Steamed Artichokes Stuffed with Tofu and Mushrooms. Non-
alcoholic beer and wine.
Comments: Romantic, upscale place. Outdoor
dining area next to a pleasant creek surrounded
by the Topanga Mountains. Plays classical music.
It is a good idea to call in advance to see if it is
open and to reserve a table. It is often closed for
weddings and banquets.
Other Info: Full service, take-out. Non-smoking.
Accepts MC, VISA. Price: $$$.
Directions: From Pacific Coast Hwy (Hwy 1),
go north on Topanga Canyon Blvd and go 4¼
miles, at Old Topanga Canyon Rd turn left and
this place is 1 block down.

TORRANCE (Los Angeles County)

Whole Foods Market

2655 Pacific Coast Highway; 310-257-8700
Hours: Daily 8 am to 10 pm
Natural Food Store and Cafe. Deli, Bakery, Salad
Bar and Juice Bar. Organic produce. Super-
market-type place. See Whole Foods Market
information.
Directions: From I-405, take the Hawthorne
Blvd/Rte 107 South exit towards Lawndale, then
go south on Hawthorne Blvd (Rte 107) for 5½
miles, at Pacific Coast Hwy turn left and this place
is 1½ mile down. From I-110, take the Pacific
Coast Hwy (Hwy 1) exit, then go west on Pacific
Coast Hwy and this place is 3 miles down.

TUSTIN

Juice Club

2930 El Camino Real; 714-505-2582
Hours: Daily 8 am to 9 pm
Vegetarian Juice Bar.
Menu: Has a large selection of juices.
Other Info: Counter service, take-out. Price: $.

Rutabegorz

158 West Main, at C Street; 714-731-9807
Hours: Monday to Thursday 11 am to 10 pm

Friday & Saturday 11 am to 11 pm
Sunday 4 pm to 9 pm
International Healthy Food. Vegan options. Not
pure vegetarian. See Fullerton, CA for details.
Menu: Has a good selection of vegetarian dishes.
Spinach Lasagna, sandwiches, stuffed mushrooms,
pastas and veggie burritos. A wide variety of cof-
fee. Fresh juices.
Comments: Bohemian-style coffeehouse.
Other Info: Full service, take-out. Price: $$.

Souplantation

13681 Newport Avenue #4; 714-730-5443
Hours: Sunday to Thursday 11 am to 9 pm
Friday & Sunday 11 am to 9:30
Soup Place. Not pure vegetarian.
Other Info: Accepts MC, VISA. Price: $.

Veggie Kitchen

13816 Red Hill Avenue
Vegetarian Restaurant.

Whole Foods Market

14945 Holt Avenue; 714-731-3400
Hours: Daily 9 am to 9 pm
Natural Food Store and Cafe. Deli, Bakery,
Salad Bar and Juice Bar. Organic produce. Supermarket-type place. See Whole Foods Market
information.
Directions: From I-5 going south, take the Fourth
St exit, then go west on E 4th St for 0.65, From
I-5, take Fourth St exit, then go east on 4th St for
0.65 mile, 4th becomes Irvine Blvd and go 1 mile,
then 4th St becomes Irvine Blvd and go another
1 mile, at Holt Ave turn right and this place is 1
block down. From I-5 going north, take Red Hill
Ave exit then go north on Red Hill for 0.65 mile,
at E 1st St turn left and go a half-mile, at Newport Ave turn right and go 1 block, then at Holt
Ave turn left and this place is 1 block down.

VENICE

Fig Tree Café

429 Ocean Front Walk, on Venice Boardwalk,
Venice Beach; 310-392-4937
Hours: Daily 9 am to 6 pm
American Natural Foods. Not pure vegetarian.
Menu: Has a good selection of vegetarian dishes.
Roasted Eggplant & Peppers, Stir-Fry Pizzete
(chapati pizza), Nutburger and Tostada.
Comments: Gets busy on the weekends in the
summer. Parking can be a bit rough to find, espe-
cially on a summer weekend.
Other Info: Full service, take-out. Accepts
AMEX, DIS, MC, VISA. Price: $$.

Venice Ocean Park Co-op
839 Lincoln Boulevard, at Brooks Avenue
310-399-5623
Natural Food Store. Organic produce.

Windward Farms
105 Windward Avenue, north along the coast
310-392-3566
Hours: Daily 8 am to 7 pm
Natural Food Store.

VENTURA (Ventura County)

Lassen's Health Foods
4071 East Main Street; 805-644-6990
Hours: Monday to Saturday 8 am to 9 pm
Closed Sunday.
Natural Food Store and Vegan-friendly Deli.
Organic produce.
Menu: Soups, hummus, Grilled Meat Balls,
couscous, Lasagna, brown rice, vegan Macaroni
Salads, Tofu Egg Sandwich, Carrot Roll,
tabbouleh, Veggie Chicken and Boca Burger. Ve-
gan cookies and desserts. Fresh juices and
smoothies. Power Shake.
Comments: Has supplement consultant.
Other Info: Accepts AMEX, MC, VISA.
Directions: Across from Target shopping center.
From US 101, take Telephone Road exit, then go
south on Telephone Road 1 block, go straight (or
turn right) onto Main St and this place is a third-
mile down. This place is a quarter-mile south of
where US 101 and Hwy 126 meet.

Tipps Thai Cuisine
512 East Main Street, at California
805-643-3040
Hours: Monday to Saturday 11:30 am to 3 pm,
5 pm to 10 pm; Sunday 2 pm to 10 pm
Thai. Vegan options. Not pure vegetarian.
Menu: Has a vegetarian menu with soups, salads, appetizers, mock meat dishes, noodles dishes
and rice dishes. Does not use MSG in the food.
Other Info: Full service, take-out. Accepts
AMEX, MC, VISA. Price: $$.

Trader Joe's
1751 South Victoria, next to K-mart
805-650-0478

WEST COVINA (Los Angeles County)

Trader Joe's
220 South Citrus
818-858-0408

WEST HOLLYWOOD

Flowering Tree
8253 Santa Monica Boulevard, West Hollywood
323-654-4332
Hours: Daily 10 am to 10 pm
Natural Food Café. Vegan options. Not pure
vegetarian.
Menu: Soups, salads, sandwiches, Zucchini Soup,
Sesame Tofu Sandwich, Baked Sesame Tofu and
veggie burgers. Non-alcoholic beer.
Comments: Casual, friendly place.
Other Info: Counter service, take-out. Accepts
AMEX, MC, VISA. Price: $.
Directions: From US 101, take the Rte 2/Santa
Monica Blvd exit towards Western Ave, then go
west on Santa Monica Blvd and this place is 3½
miles down.

***Real Food Daily
414 North La Cienega Boulevard
310-289-9910
Website: www.realfood.com
Hours: Daily 11:30 am to 11 pm
Fully Vegan Organic Gourmet Vegetarian.
Menu: Same menu as the Santa Monica location
with the addition of several different entrees and
a nightly Chef's Tasting Menu. Can call to find
out the daily special
Comments: Relaxed atmosphere. Has a jazzy
nightlife feel. There is also a branch in Santa
Monica. Very health conscious. Celebrities come
here. Trendy, popular place. One of LA's premier
organic vegetarian places.
Other Info: Full service, catering, counter ser-
vice, take-out, delivery. Non-smoking. Does not
take reservations. Accepts AMEX, MC and VISA.
Price: $$-$$$.
Directions: This place is between Beverly Blvd.
and Melrose Ave, two blocks north of the Beverly
Center. It located at where West Hollywood,
Beverly Hills and Los Angeles meet. Street park-
ing during the day, and street parking and valet
parking at night. From I-10, take the La Brea Ave
exit, then go north on La Brea Ave for 1 mile, at
San Vicente Blvd turn left and go 2½ miles, at La
Cienega Blvd turn slight right and this place is a
half-mile down.

Whole Foods Market
7871 West Santa Monica Boulevard
323-848-4200
Hours: Daily 8 am to 10 pm
Natural Food Store and Cafe. Deli, Bakery,
Salad Bar and Juice Bar. Organic produce. Su-
permarket-type place. See Whole Foods Market

information.
Directions: At Santa Monica and Fairfax. From US 101, take the Rte 2/Santa Moncia Blvd towards Western Ave, then go west on Santa Monica Blvd and this place is 3 miles down.

WESTMINSTER

**Vien Huong Vegetarian Restaurant
14092 Magnolia, #116-117
corner of Westminster Blvd, near Magnolia
714-373-1876
Hours: Daily 9 am to 10 pm
Vegetarian Vietnamese and Chinese Buddhists. Mainly Vegan.
Menu: Has a large vegetarian menu (over a hundred dishes) including soups, Crispy Chicken, Sweet & Sour Pork, Dim Sum, Beef with Peanut Butter Sauce, Shrimp Tempura, appetizers and main dishes.
Comments: The owners of the restaurant are Buddhist.
Other Info: Full service, take-out. Price: $-$$. Accepts MC, VISA.
Directions: From I-5, take the Rte 22 exit towards Long Beach, then go west on Rte 22 for 5 miles, exit towards Magnolia St, then at Trask Ave turn left and go 2 blocks, at Magnolia St turn left and this place is a half-mile down.

WHITTIER (Los Angeles County)

Trader Joe's
15025 E Whittier Boulevard
at Colima Road
310-698-1642

**Veggie Bistro
6557 Comstock Avenue, at Hadley
562-907-7898; Web site: www.veggiebistro.com
Hours: Tuesday to Sunday 11 am to 9 pm
Closed Monday.
Vegetarian International. Thai, Chinese, Italian.
Menu: Has many mock meat dishes.
Other Info: Price: $$.
Directions: From I-5, take Norwalk Blvd exit towards Norwalk, then go north on S Norwalk Blvd for 1½ mile, at Florence Ave turn right and go a half-mile, at Bloomfield Ave turn left (becomes Santa Fe Springs Rd after a half-mile, then after 2 miles becomes Pickering Ave) and go 2¾ mile, at Hadley St turn right and go 3 blocks, at Comstock Ave turn right and this place is a half-block down.

WOODLAND HILLS

Whole Foods Market
21347 Ventura Boulevard; 818-610-0000
Hours: Daily 8 am to 10 pm
Natural Food Store and Cafe. Deli, Bakery, Salad Bar and Juice Bar. Organic produce. Supermarket-type place. See Whole Foods Market information.
Directions: From US 101, take the Canoga Ave exit, then go south on Canoga Ave for 1 block, then at Ventura Blvd turn left and this place is 1 block down.

San Francisco Area

ALBANY

**Ambrosia Garden Vegetarian
843 San Pablo Avenue, at Solano
510-528-5388
Hours: Sunday, Monday, Wednesday, Thursday
11:30 am to 9:30 pm; Friday & Saturday 11:30
am to 10 pm; closed Tuesday.
Vegetarian Taiwanese. Has some Vegan dishes.
Menu: Soups, vegetarian mock "seafood," brown
rice and mock "meat." Non-alcoholic beer.
Comment: Food is good, the service is friendly
and the atmosphere is nice. Nice people. There is
a good chance that the fortune cookies contain
eggs. Use canola oil for cooking and does not use
hydrogenated oils for cooking.
Other Info: Full service, take-out. Accepts
AMEX, MC, VISA. Price: $-$$.
Directions: From I-580, take Buchanan St exit,
then go east on Buchanan St a half-mile, then
turn slight right at Marin Ave for 1 block, at
Buchanan St go slight right 1 block, at San Pablo
Ave (Hwy 123) turn left and this place is a quarter-mile down. This place is ¾ mile east of where
I-80 and I-580 meets.

BERKELEY

**Ashkenaz Community Center
1317 San Pablo Avenue, at Gilman Street
510-525-5054; **email:** ashkenaz@ashkenaz.com;
Web site: www.ashkenaz.com
Hours: Open during Music Hall events. Tuesday
to Sunday for late evening events only.
Fully Vegetarian.
Menu: Tofu sandwiches, vegetarian sandwiches,
bagels, vegetarian stew and chips & salsa. Non-
alcoholic beer.
Comments: This place has a good crowd of people
including UC Berkeley students. Wheelchair ac-
cessible. Free secure parking after 9 pm across the
street at REI.
Dancing: Is a nonprofit club and place where they
have dancing and international music. Dance to
Latin, African, Cajun, folk, Indian and other international beats. The founder of this place was
Mr Nolan who was an environmentalist and a
vegetarian. Celebrating 28 years of international
and ethnic music and dance. Every year they have
a dance marathon. Offers dance classes. The Web
site has information about dance events. Voted
"The Best Place To Dance" in the 1999 Best of
the East Bay poll by the East Bay Express.
Other Info: Non-smoking. Limited service. Price:
$$.
Directions: On San Pablo at Gilman Street, across
from the REI. Can park in the REI parking lot
for free.

Ay Caramba
1901 University, at Grove; 510-843-1298
Hours: Daily 11 am to 7:30 pm
Mexican. Not pure vegetarian.
Menu: Bean burritos. No lard. Fresh juices, in-
cluding carrot.

Bazaar of India
Ayurvedic Herbs, 1810 University Avenue
510-548-4110
Hours: Monday to Saturday 10 am to 6 pm
Sunday 12 noon to 6 pm
Indian Grocery Store. Has a good selection of
Ayurvedic medicine.
Other Info: Accepts AMEX, DIS, MC, VISA.

Berkeley Natural Grocery
1336 Gilman Street; 510-526-2456
Hours: Daily 9 am to 8 pm
Natural Food Store. Organic produce.
Menu: Ready-made sandwiches and salads.
Comments: Has some tables and chair outside
that can be used when the weather is good.
Friendly place.
Other Info: Accepts MC, VISA.
Directions: From I-80, take Gilman St exit and
this place is 1 mile down on the right.

Berkeley Bowl Market
2020 Oregon Street, between Shattuck and Mar-
tin Luther King Jr; 510-843-6929/28
Web site: http://bayarea.citysearch.com/
redirect?id=1028740
Hours: Monday to Saturday 9 am to 8 pm
Sunday 10 am to 6 pm

Natural Food Store and Deli. Organic produce and Juice Bar. Not pure vegetarian.
Menu: Has a large amount of vegetarian dishes. Roasted Red Potatoes, Roasted Vegetables, Vegetable Platter, fresh soups, salads and sandwiches.
Comments: One of the best natural food stores in the Bay Area. Has an excellent organic produce section that is the largest in Northern California. Has a large international items section. Friendly people.
Other Info: Accepts AMEX, DIS, MC, VISA.
Direction: From I-580, take the Ashby Ave exit, then go on Ashby for 1¾ mile, then at Adeline St turn left and this place is 1½ block down on the right, at the corner of Adeline and Oregon, across from a Walgreen.

Blue Nile

2525 Telegraph Avenue, at Blake Street
510-540-6777
Hours: Tuesday to Sunday 5 pm to 11 pm; closed Mondays and major holidays. May also be open in the future for lunch, but when I called these were the business hours.
Ethiopian, African. Vegan options. Not pure vegetarian.
Menu: Authentic Ethiopian cuisine. Vegetarian dishes are marked on the menu.
Comments: Pleasant atmosphere. Food is a good value. Plays traditional Ethiopian music. Romantic.
Other Info: Full service, take out. Accepts MC, VISA. Price: $-$$.

Bongo Burger

2154 Center Street; 510-548-7700
Hours: Sunday to Friday 8 am to 10 pm
Saturday 8 am to 5 pm
2505 Dwight Way, South Side 510-548-4100
1839 Euclid Way, North Side 510-548-3400
Hours: Daily 8 am to 10 pm
Mediterranean. Vegan options. Not pure vegetarian.
Menu: Has a good selection of vegetarian dishes. Veggie burgers and Mediterranean dishes.

Café Intermezzo

2442 Telegraph Avenue; 510-849-4592
Hours: Daily 8 am to 10 pm; Open at 8 am for coffee and bagels, but does not start serving meals until around 11 am.
Natural Food Restaurant. American Coffee Bar. Vegetarian-friendly. Not pure vegetarian.
Menu: Soups, salads, bagel and sandwiches. Sandwiches made with freshly baked bread. Grilled Eggplant Sandwich on artichoke-rosemary bread,

Marinated Tofu on focaccia, tofu salad, eggplant sandwich and veggie sandwiches. Havana is four shots of espresso in one cup. Adds white chocolate to coffees. Fresh juices.
Comments: Good value.
Other Info: Full service, take-out. No credit cards; cash only. Price: $.
Directions: This place is 3 blocks south of the University of California.

Capoeira Arts Café

2026 Addison Street; 510-666-1349
Hours: Monday to Friday 7 am to 8 pm; Saturday 9:30 am to 8 pm; closed Sunday.
Vegetarian-friendly Coffeeshop-type place. Not pure vegetarian.
Menu: Soups, salads and sandwiches. Veggie Lasagna. Hummus Sandwich, Tofu Sandwich, Marinated Mushroom Sandwich and more. Fresh juices and smoothies.
Comments: Offers an assortment of classes. Friendly place. No credit cards; cash or local checks.
Directions: This place is 2 blocks west of U of California, across the street from the Berkeley Repertory Theater.

***Cha-Ya

1686 Shattuck, between University and Cedar
510-981-1213
Hours: Tuesday to Sunday 5 pm to 9:30 pm
Closed Monday.
Fully Vegan Japanese.
Menu: Soups, Seaweed Salad, Miso Mushroom Soup, Tofu with Portobella Mushrooms, noodles dishes, Soba in Broth, veggie sushi, Tempura Vegetables and dishes with roots and tubers. Gomoku Sushi is sushi rice mixed with tofu, shiitake, yam, bamboo shoots, green beans, lotus root and pickled ginger. Vanilla "Ice Cream" with green tea.
Comments: Really small place that can comfortably accommodate only about 20 people. This place is especially busy on Saturday nights, and you may have to wait an hour for a seat. Good presentation and taste. There is a line on Saturday waiting to get in. Opened in January. Nice atmosphere.
Other Info: Reservation advised if more than four. Accepts AMEX, MC, VISA. Price: $$.
Directions: This place is one block west of the university.

Eat-a-Pita

2511 Durant Avenue, just east of Telegraph
510-841-6482
Hours: Daily 10:30 am to 10 pm

Middle Eastern. Vegan friendly. Not pure veg.
Menu: Good falafels. Hummus, stuffed grape leaves and baba ghanouj.
Comments: Popular with locals. Has a few tables and counter seating. Not much on the atmosphere.
Other Info: Fast food type place with counter service, take-out. Accepts MC, VISA.

Ethiopia Restaurant
2955 Telegraph Avenue, at Ashby
510-843-1992
Hours: Daily 11:30 am to 11 pm
Ethiopian. All-you-can-eat Lunch Buffet on the weekdays. Vegan-friendly. Not pure vegetarian.
Comments: Has indoor and outdoor patio seating. All-you-can-eat lunch special. Friendly, attentive service.
Menu: Red and Split Lentil, Collard Greens, Mushroom Stew, Atkilt We't (string beans, zucchini and carrots), Kinche (bulgur), Shro We't (garbanzo beans), Ye'dinch Genffo (potato porridge) and Teemateem (tomatoes, onions, green peppers). Has a Vegetarian Combination plate.
Comments: Plays soft exotic music. Open fireplace. Friendly service.
Other Info: Full service, take-out. Accepts DIS, MC, VISA. Price: $-$$.

Juice Bar Collective
2114 Vine, corner of Shattuck
510-548-8473
Hours: Monday to Saturday 10 am to 4:30 pm Closed Sundays.
Juice Bar and Cafe.
Menu: Great variety of freshly squeezed and pressed juices and smoothies. Black Bean Polenta (very good), vegetarian Split Pea Soup, Soy Bean Casserole, Lentil Loaf, hummus and vegetables in a spinach tortilla. Can add a shot of fresh ginger to vegetables juices.
Comments: Popular place. Uses only fresh organic produce. Healthy food. Cash only; no credit cards.
Directions: This place is northwest of the university. From I-580, take Buchanan St exit, then go east on Buchanan St a half-mile, turn slight right onto Marin Ave, then turn right at San Pablo Ave and go ¾ mile, at Cedar St turn left and go 1.35 mile, at Shattuck Ave turn left and go 1 block, at Vine St turn right and this place is halfway down the block.

Long Life Veggie House
2129 University Street, at Shattuck Avenue
510-845-6072

Hours: Sunday to Friday 11:30 am to 10 pm
Saturday 11:30 am to 10:30 pm
Chinese. Vegan options. Mainly vegetarian, but also serves seafood.
Menu: Has over 100 vegetarian dishes on the menu. Vegetable and Tofu soups, appetizers, Seaweed Salad, brown rice, Spring Roll and Sweet & Sour Pork. The Hunan Beef and Kung Pao Chicken are made from wheat-gluten and taste real good.
Comments: Plays classical Chinese music and has Chinese lanterns. Reasonably priced. No MSG. Small, busy place, so may have to share a table.
Other Info: Full service, take-out, catering. Accepts AMEX, ATM, DIS, MC, VISA. Price: $-$$.
Directions: This place is a block west of the university.

Lotus Vegetarian Restaurant
2272 Shattuck Avenue, at Bancroft, next to UA Theater; 510-841-7303
Hours: Monday to Saturday 11:30 am to 10 pm; Sunday 12 noon to 11 pm; closed Tuesday.
Chinese. Mainly vegetarian. Vegan friendly. Not pure vegetarian (serves fish).
Menu: Has many mock "meat" dishes and Chinese vegetable dishes.
Comments: People running the restaurant are Buddhist and are very friendly. The owner, David, is a good person. Discounts for San Francisco Vegetarian Society members.
Directions: Two blocks from the Bart downtown Berkeley station. Couple blocks from Hotel Shattuck. This place is 1 block west of the southwest corner of the University of California.

Maharani
1025 University Avenue, between 9th & 10th
510-848-7777
Hours: Monday to Thursday 11 am to 9:30 pm; Friday & Saturday 11 am to 10 pm; Sunday 11 am to 9 pm
Indian. Not pure vegetarian. Vegan options.
Menu: Has a large vegetarian menu.
Comments: Discount for San Francisco Vegetarian Society members.
Other Info: Full service, takeout. Accepts AMEX, DISC, MC, VISA. Price: $$.

Pasand Madras Cuisine
2286 Shattuck Avenue; 510-549-2559
Hours: Sunday to Friday 11 am to 10 pm
Saturday 11 am to 10 pm
South Indian. Vegetarian-friendly. Not pure vegetarian. Lunch buffet.

Other Info: Full service, take-out. Accepts MC, VISA. Price: $-$$.

**Raw Energy Organic Juice Café
2050 Addison Street
510-665-9464; Web site: www.rawenergy.net
Hours: Monday to Friday 8 am to 7 pm
Closed Saturday, Sunday & holidays.
Vegetarian Juice Bar.
Other Info: No credit cards. Smoking allowed outside only.
Directions: Between Shattuck and Milvia, one block north of the downtown Berkeley Bart station and 2 blocks west of the UC Berkeley.

Razan's Organic Kitchen
2119 Kittredge Street; 510-486-0449
Hours: Daily 10 am to 10 pm
100% Organic Restaurant. Not pure vegetarian.
Menu: Wraps, salads, burritos and other vegetarian dishes.
Comments: Has a small indoor seating area and outdoor seating. Healthy eating.
Directions: Across the street from the southwest corner of the UC Berkeley.

Smart Alec's Intelligent Fast Food
2355 Telegraph Avenue, at Durant Street
510-704-4000
Hours: Daily 11 am to 9 pm
Vegetarian-friendly Cafe. Vegan options. Fast Foods. Salad Bar & Juice Bar. Not pure vegetarian (serves chicken, eggs and tuna).
Menu: Gourmet large salads, low-fat air-cooked French fries (very good and recommended), sandwiches and veggie burgers (popular). Can add pesta, sun-dried tomato and chili to sandwiches. Fresh juices and smoothies. Cappuccino, espresso.
Comments: Fast-food type place. Popular with locals. Has combination meals where you can try more than one dish at one time.
Other Info: Limited service, take-out. Cash only. Price: $$.
Directions: This place is 1 block south of UC Berkeley.

Taste of Africa
3301 Adeline, at Ashby; 510-843-6316
Hours: Tuesday to Saturday 1 pm to 8 pm
Closed Sunday & Monday.
African Café. Vegan friendly. Not pure vegetarian.
Menu: A good selection of vegetarian dishes. Fried Plantains is a good side dish. Most meals come with rice. Has good tropical drinks, ginger beer

and herbal teas.
Comments: Has outdoor seating.
Other Info: Full service, take-out. Cash only.

U of C Berkeley Men's Faculty Club
On Campus
Open to public 12 noon to 1 pm
Great Salad Bar with brown rice with veggies, macaroni, vegetarian chow mien and vegetable dishes.

Urban Kitchen
1734 San Pablo Avenue, Berkeley, CA 94702
510-527-8970; email: urbankitchen@juno.com
Vegetarian Catering. Specializes in vegan pastries and wedding cakes.

***Vegi Food
2085 Vine Street, at Shattuck; 510-548-5244
Hours: Mon 5 pm to 9 pm; Tues to Fri 11:30 am to 3 pm, 5 pm to 9 pm; Sat & Sun 11:30 am to 9 pm
Fully Vegan Chinese.
Menu: The potstickers are good. No eggs, garlic or onions. Spicy Cabbage with Tofu. The Sweet & Sour Walnuts is a popular dish. Has brown rice and white rice.
Comments: Reasonably priced, basic place. Owners are Buddhist, therefore no egg or garlic in food. Family place. Friendly service. Quick service.
Other Info: Full service, take-out. No credit cards; cash only. Price: $-$$.
Directions: This place is about ¾ mile northwest of U C Berkeley.

Vik's Chaat Corner
726 Allston Way; 510-644-4412
Restaurant Hours: Tuesday to Sunday 11 am to 6 pm; Store Hours: Tuesday to Sunday 10:30 am to 6:30 pm; closed Monday.
Indian. Mainly Vegetarian fast food. Vegan-friendly. Not pure vegetarian.
Menu: Chaat Indian snacks, samosas, vegetable curries, mango lassi, spiced cashews, masala dosas and daily specials.
Comments: Gets good ratings from diners. Lacks in atmosphere. They say that they cook vegetarian and non-vegetarian dishes in separate parts of the kitchen. It is in a warehouse with a lossy décor. Serves food on plastic plates. Good food. Popular place with Indians. The place isn't so clean and the service is lacking. Weekends are very crowded.
Indian Grocery Store: There is an Indian grocery store next door where you can get spices and

Indian groceries.

Other Info: Counter service, take-out. Order at the counter and then wait for your name to be called. Accepts MC, VISA.

Directions: From I-580, take the University Ave exit, then go a few blocks east on University Ave, then turn right at 4th St and this place is 2 blocks down.

Westside Bakery & Café

2570 9th Street, corner of Parker
510-845-4852

Hours: Monday to Friday 7 am to 3 pm
Saturday & Sunday 8 am to 2 pm

Café. Not pure vegetarian.

Price: $.

Menu: Tofu Scramble, spinach salad, and hummus and eggplant sandwiches.

Whole Foods Market

3000 Telegraph Avenue, at corner of Ashby
510-649-1333

Hours: Daily 8 am to 10 pm

Natural Food Store and Cafe. Deli, Bakery, Salad Bar and Juice Bar. Organic produce. Supermarket-type place. See Whole Foods Market information.

Other Info: Cafeteria style, take-out. Accepts MC, VISA. Price $-$$.

Directions: This place is about 1 mile south of the UC Berkeley campus.

Wild Oats

1581 University Avenue
510-549-1714; **fax:** 510-549-9985

Hours: Monday to Sunday 8 am to 10 pm

Natural Food Store and Cafe. Deli, Bakery, Salad Bar and Juice Bar. Organic produce. Supermarket-type place. See Wild Oats Market information.

Directions: From I-580, take the University Ave exit, then go east on University and this place is 1 mile down.

BURLINGAME

Earthbeam Natural Foods

1399 Broadway Street, Burlingame
650-347-2058

Hours: Monday to Saturday 9 am to 7 pm
Sunday 10 am to 6 pm

Natural Food Store. Has ready-made sandwiches, but no deli. Organic produce.

Other Info: Accepts AMEX, DIS, MC, VISA.

Directions: From Hwy 101, take Broadway exit, then go west on Broadway and this place is a half-mile down, at Cappuccino. This place is 3 miles south of San Francisco International Airport.

CAMPBELL

Chez Soven

2425 South Bascom Avenue
between Dry Creek Road and Union
408-371-7711
Old Oakland Road, San Jose, near Hwy 101
408-287-7619

Hours: Monday to Thursday 11:30 am to 3 pm, 5 pm to 9 pm; Friday & Saturday 11 am to 3 pm, 5 pm to 10 pm; closed Sunday.

Cambodian. Vegan-friendly. Not pure vegetarian. See Santa Cruz for details.

Menu: Very good Spicy Tofu in Ginger Sauce and Noodles and Tofu with a Tamarind Sauce. Tropical Ice Tea is good.

Comments: Small place with interesting Cambodian artifacts and Cambodian dance show on Saturday nights. Friendly, knowledgeable staff.

Other Info: Full service, take-out. Accepts AMEX, DIS, MC, VISA. Price: $.

Fresh Choice

Hamilton Plaza
1654 South Bascom Avenue
408-559-1912

Hours: Daily 11 am to 9 pm

All-you-can-eat Salad Bar. Not pure vegetarian.

Menu: Nutritional information listed in pamphlets that mark the vegan dishes. Usually at least one soup each day is vegetarian. All the pastas contain eggs.

Other Info: Counter service, take-out. For take-out you get a container for salad and a separate container for soups. Accepts AMEX, DIS, MC, VISA.

Tasty Vegetarian Cuisine

2455 South Winchester Boulevard
408-374-9791

Hours: Tuesday to Sunday 11 am to 3 pm, 5 pm to 9 pm; closed Monday.

Vegetarian Chinese and Taiwanese. Mainly Vegan options. Does not use animal products.

Menu: Has a large selection of vegan and vegetarian Chinese dishes. Many mock "meat" dishes.

Comments: No MSG. Casual place. Friendly service.

Other Info: Full service, take-out. Accepts MC, VISA ($25 minimum). Price: $$.

Directions: From Hwy 17, take the San Tomas Expy/Camden Ave exit, then go northwest on San Tomas Exwy for a quarter-mile, then go northeast on S Winchester Blvd and this place is a quarter-mile down.

Whole Foods Market

1690 S Bascom Avenue
408-371-5000
email: mary.Michele.demay@wholefoods.com
Web site: www.wholefoodsmarket.com
Hours: Daily 8 am to 10 pm
Bakery, Juice & Deli opens at 7:30 am
Natural Food Store and Cafe. Deli, Bakery, Salad Bar and Juice Bar. Organic produce. Supermarket-type place. See Whole Foods Market information.
Menu: Has a salad bar with around 50 dishes, hot dishes, quiche, sushi and baked goods. A large cold salad bar, 20 sandwiches and many desserts.
Directions: From Hwy 17, take Hamilton Ave exit, then go east on Hamilton Ave a half-mile, at Bascon turn right and this place is 1 block down on the left.

CAPITOLA

**Dharma's Restaurant

4250 Capitola Road
831-462-1717; fax: 831-464-TOFU
Web site: www.dharmaland.com
Hours: Daily 8 am to 9 pm
Fully Vegetarian International. Mexican, Italian, American, Thai, Japanese and Chinese. Most of the food is organic. Mainly vegan. Has dairy, but no eggs.
Menu: Salads (can add tofu or cheese), American Sautéed Vegetables, Mexican Sauté, pastas, brown rice or basmati rice, French Fries (air-baked), Organic Yams, Steamed Veggies, Baked Potatoes, Portobello Mushroom & Artichoke Sub, Spaghetti A Florio, Pasta Con Pesto, daily soup, Chips and Salsa, Chili, Vegetable Turnover, Lasagna, Chow Mein, Macaroni & Cheese, Mexican dishes, Tofu Scramble, pancakes, Thai Tofu Scramble, Tofu Ranchero and dairy-free shakes. Fresh juices, espresso. The tahini dressing is recommended.
Comments: Has excellent food. Casual. Good size portions. Reasonably priced. Gets good recommendations. Their entire menu is on their Web site. Sometimes has entertainment in the evenings. Pleasant atmosphere.
Other Info: Cafeteria-style, limited service, take-out. Non-smoking. Reservations not accepted. Does not take credit cards. Price: $.
Directions: This place is a few blocks east of Capitola Mall. From Hwy 1, take the 41st Ave exit, then go south on 41st Ave a half-mile, turn right at Capitola Rd and this place is 1½ block down on the right. There is a parking lot in front.

Fresh Choice

Brown Ranch Marketplace
3555 Clares Street, off 41st Street, behind the Capitola Mall; 831-479-9873
Hours: Daily 11 am to 9 pm

Juice Club

Brown Ranch Mall; 831-475-2582
Hours: Sunday to Thursday 7:30 am to 8 pm
Friday & Saturday 7:30 am to 9 pm
Juice Bar. Price: $$.

**New Leaf Community Market and New Beet Café

1210 41st Avenue
831-479-7987; Web site: www.newleaf.com
Store Hours: Daily 8 am to 9 pm
Café Hours: Monday to Friday 7 am to 9 pm
Saturday & Sunday 8 am to 9 pm
Natural Food Store and Restaurant. Café is vegan and vegetarian. Deli. Organic produce.
Menu: The restaurant only has vegan and vegetarian dishes. The deli has vegetarian dishes, but also serves meat dishes. Fresh baked goods.
Comments: Has discount coupons on their web site.
Other Info: Full service, take-out. Accepts DIS, MC, VISA. Price: $.
Directions: This place is a few blocks east of Capitola Mall. From Hwy 1, take the 41st Ave exit, then go south on 41st Ave and this place is 1 mile down.

Trader Joe's

Brown Ranch Marketplace, 3555 Clares Streets
Off 41st Street behind Capitola Mall
831-464-0115
Hours: Daily 9 am to 9 pm

CASTRO VALLEY (Alameda County)

Health Unlimited Health Food

3446 Village Drive; 510-581-0220
Hours: Monday to Friday 9:30 am to 9 pm; Saturday 10 am to 6 pm; Sunday 12 noon to 5 pm
Natural Food Store.

CONCORD

Fresh Choice

Sunvalley Mall, 486 Sunvalley Mall Road
925-671-7222
Hours: Monday to Thursday 11 am to 9 pm; Friday & Saturday 11 am to 10 pm; Sunday 11 am to 9 pm

Harvest House
2395 Monument Boulevard; 925-676-2305
Hours: Monday to Friday 9 am to 8 pm; Saturday 9 am to 7 pm; Sunday 10 am to 7 pm
Natural Food Store.

Swagat Indian Cuisine
1901 Salvio Street; 925-685-2777
Hours: Daily 11 am to 3 pm, 5 pm to 10 pm
Indian. Not pure vegetarian.
Menu: Has a selection of vegetarian dishes.
Other Info: Full service, take-out. Accepts AMEX, DC, DIS, MC, VISA. Price: $$.

Trader Joe's
The Willows Shopping Center
1975 Diamond Boulevard, across from Hilton Hotel; 925-689-2990
Hours: Daily 9 am to 9 pm

CORTE MADERA (Marin County)

Super Natural Foods
Town Center Shopping Center, 147 Corte Madera, Downtown; 415-924-7777
Hours: Monday to Saturday 9 am to 8 pm
Sunday 10 am to 6 pm
Natural Food Store.
Directions: From 101 south take Paradise Dr exit. Turn left and go over the overpass. This place on right in Town Center Shopping Center, next to Safeway. From 101 north, take Madera Blvd exit and this place on right.

COTATI (Sonoma County)

Oliver's Market
546 East Cotati Avenue; 707-795-9501
Natural Food Store and Deli. Organic produce.
Menu: Has a selection of vegetarian dishes. Soups, salads and sandwiches.
Other Info: Counter service, take-out. Has seating. Accepts AMEX, MC, VISA.
Directions: From US 101, take Rte 116 W exit towards Rohnert Park/Sebastopol, at Gravenstein Hwy go east 1 block, at Old Redwood Hwy turn right and go a half-mile, at E Cotati Ave turn left and this place is a half-mile down.

CUPERTINO

Cupertino Natural Foods
10255 South De Anza Boulevard; 408-253-1277
Hours: Monday to Friday 10 am to 7 pm; Saturday 10 am to 5 pm; Sunday 12 noon to 5 pm
Natural Food Store.

Hobee's Restaurant
Oaks Shopping Center, 21267 Stevens Creek Blvd
408-255-6010
Hours: Monday to Thursday 6:30 am to 9 pm; Friday & Saturday 6:30 am to 10 pm; Sunday 7:30 to 9 pm
Mexican and International. Restaurant chain. Salad Bar. Not pure vegetarian.
Menu: Mexican dishes and black bean chili. Fresh juices.
Other Info: Full table service, take-out. Accepts MC, VISA. Price: $$.

**Kokila's Kitchen
20956 Homestead Road, at Stelling
408-777-8198
Hours: Tuesday to Sunday 11 am to 2 pm, 6:30 pm to 9:30 pm; closed Monday.
Vegetarian Indian. Lunch and Dinner Buffet. 80% vegan
Menu: Soups, dals, rice dishes, srikhand and Gujarati Thalis. Specializes in Gujarati cuisine.
Comments: Has an all-you-can-eat buffet. Food is good and reasonably priced. About 75% of the dishes are vegan. Won best vegetarian restaurant in the Bay area by Veg News Santa Cruz.
Other Info: Buffet, take-out, catering. Non-smoking. Reservations recommended. Accepts MC, VISA.
Directions: This place is a half-mile east of where Hwy 280 and Hwy 85 meet. From Hwy 85, take Homestead exit, then go east on Homestead 1 mile, at Stelling (third light) turn right, and this place is just past the McDonald's on the right a third-mile down, near D-Anza College.

Miyake
10650 South De Anza Boulevard; 408-253-2668
Hours: Daily 11:30 am to 10 pm
Japanese. Not pure vegetarian. See Palo Alto for details.
Menu: Has around ten types of vegetarian sushi.

Whole Foods Market
20830 Stevens Creek Boulevard, near Stelling
408-257-7000; **Web site:** www.wholefood.com
Hours: Daily 8 am to 10 pm
Natural Food Store and Cafe. Deli, Bakery, Salad Bar and Juice Bar. Organic produce. Supermarket-type place. See Whole Foods Market information.
Menu: Has a salad bar with around 50 dishes, hot dishes, quiche, sushi and baked goods. A large cold salad bar, 20 sandwiches and many desserts.
Directions: From Hwy 280, take N De Anza Blvd exit and go south 1 mile, at Stevens Creek Blvd

turn right and this place is a third-mile down, a few blocks east of the northeast corner of De Anza College. From Rte 85, take the Stevens Creek Blvd exit, then go east on Stevens Creek Blvd and this place is ¾ mile down.

EL CERRITO

El Cerrito Natural Grocery
10367 San Pablo Avenue; 510-526-1155
Hours: Daily 9 am to 8 pm
Natural Food Store. Organic produce. Has a good selection of bulk goods and breads.
Directions: From I-80, take Central Avenue exit. At San Pablo turn left, then at Stockton turn left and store near corner.

FAIRFAX

Good Earth Natural Foods
1966 Sir Francis Drake Boulevard, Fairfax
415-456-3418, 415-454-0123
Hours: Monday to Saturday 9 am to 8 pm
Sunday 10 am to 7 pm
Natural Food Store and Deli. Organic produce. Salad and Hot Bar. Juice Bar.
Menu: Has a good selection of vegetarian dishes. Soups, salads, sandwiches, veggie chili, veggie Lasagna, steamed vegetable, stir-fries and other dishes.
Other Info: Counter service, take-out. Accepts AMEX, MC, VISA. Has outdoor seating.
Directions: From Hwy 101, take Central San Rafael exit. Then go west on 4th St (or 3rd St) for about 2 miles through San Rafael (road becomes Red Hill Ave). Keep to the right when road merges onto Center Blvd and go 1½ mile, at Sir Francis Drake Blvd turn left and go 1 block and this place is at the corner with Claus Drive. This place is about 3½ mile wests of the exit.

FOSTER CITY

Jamba Juice
1000 Metro Center Boulevard, Suite B, Foster City; 650-571-6200
Juice Bar.
Hours: Monday to Saturday 6:30 am to 9 pm
Sunday 7:30 am to 7 pm

Joy Restaurant
1495 Beach Park Boulevard; 650-345-1762
Hours: Daily 11 am to 9:30 pm
Mandarin and Szechuan. Vegan options. Not pure vegetarian.

Menu: Has vegetarian soups, appetizers, sandwiches and entrees. Can make many of the dishes without meat or eggs. Meatless "chicken." The Singapore Curry Chow Mein is good.
Other Info: Full service, take-out. Accepts AMEX, MC, VISA. Price: $$.

FREMONT (Alameda County)

Fremont Natural Foods
5180 Mowry Avenue; 510-792-0163
Natural Food Store.

**Krishna Restaurant
Freemont Shopping Center, 40645 Fremont Blvd
510-656-2336
Hours: Tuesday to Sunday 11 am to 8 pm
Closed Monday.
Vegetarian Fast Food Indian. Vegan options.
Other Info: Full service, take-out. Accepts MC, VISA. Price: $.
Directions: From I-880, take the Auto Mall Parkway exit, then go east on Auto Mall Pkwy, then at Grimmer Blvd turn left (go north) for 2 miles, at Fremont Blvd turn right and this place is 1 block down.

Nature's Northwest (Wild Oats)
535 NE 15th; 503-288-3414
Hours: Daily 9 am to 10 pm
Natural Food Store and Cafe. Deli, Bakery, Salad Bar and Juice Bar. Organic produce. Supermarket-type place. See Wild Oats Market information.

Trader Joe's
Fremont, at intersection of Fremont and Mowry Blvds

GREENBRAE

Jamba Juice
301 Bon Air Shopping Center; 415-925-8470
Hours: Daily 7:30 am to 7 pm
Juice Bar and Café.

GUERNEVILLE

**Sparks
16248 Main Street; 707-869-8206;
Summer Hours: Wednesday to Monday 7:30 am to 11 am, 11:30 am to 2 pm; 5:30 pm to 9 pm
Closed Tuesday.
Winter Hours: Thursday & Friday 11 am to 3 pm, 5:30 to 9 pm; Saturday & Sunday 10 am to

3 pm, 5:30 pm to 9 pm; closed Mon to Wed.
Fully Vegetarian.
Menu: Biscuits and cashew gravy, soups, salads, sandwiches and desserts.
Other Info: Full service. Only accepts reservations for 5 or more
Directions: Across from West America Bank in downtown Guerneville.

HALF MOON BAY (San Mateo County)

Half Moon Bay Natural Foods
523 Main Street; 650-726-7881
Hours: Monday to Saturday 10 am to 6 pm
Sunday 11 am to 5 pm
Natural Food Store. Organic produce. Small well-stocked store.
Directions: From Hwy 1, go east on Kelley and this place on left at junction of Kelly and Main.

LOS GATOS

Whole Foods Market
15980 Los Gatos Boulevard; 408-358-4434
Hours: Daily 8:30 am to 9 pm
Bakery & Juice Bar opens at 7 am
Natural Food Store and Cafe. Deli, Bakery, Salad Bar and Juice Bar. Organic produce. Supermarket-type place. See Whole Foods Market information.
Directions: From CA Rte 17, take exit towards East Los Gatos, then go east on Los Gatos Saratoga Rd for a quarter-mile, at Los Gatos Blvd turn left and this place is 1 mile down.

MENLO PARK

St Bede's Church
2650 Sand Hill Road; 650-854-6555
Office Hours: Monday to Friday 8 am to 5 pm
Gourmet Macrobiotic Vegetarian Dinners every Monday (only) at 6:30 pm. Price: $$. Reservations required by Sunday at 9:30 pm.

Trader Joe's
720 Menlo Avenue, three blocks west of El Camino Real; 650-323-2134

MILL VALLEY

High Tech Burrito (over 15 locations)
Strawberry Village Shopping Center
Mill Valley; 415-388-7002
Web site: www.hightechburrito.com
Hours: Sunday to Wednesday 11 am to 9 pm

Thursday to Saturday 11 am to 10 pm
Mexican. Not pure vegetarian.
Menu: Has a good tasting vegan burrito. Black beans, nachos and other dishes.
Comments: Good place for a quick meal. Health-conscious Mexican food.
Other Info: Accepts MC, VISA.

Lucinda's Mexican Food To Go
930 Redwood Highway; 415-388-0754
Hours: Monday to Thursday 9:30 am to 9 pm; Friday 11 am to 10 pm; Saturday 9:30 am to 8 pm; closed Sunday.
Mexican. Not pure vegetarian.
Menu: Good veggie burritos.

Whole Foods Market
414 Miller Avenue; 415-381-1200
Hours: Daily 8 am to 8 pm
Natural Food Store and Cafe. Deli, Bakery, Salad Bar and Juice Bar. Organic produce. Supermarket-type place. See Whole Foods Market information.
Directions: From Hwy 101, take Tiburon Belvedere exit, then at East Blithedate go west, at Camino Alto turn left and at Miller Ave turn right and this place on left. From Hwy 101, take the Rte 1 exit towards Mill Valley/Stinson Beach, then go northwest ¾ mile on Rte 1, then keep going straight onto Atmonte Ave (take right road) for a half-mile, then keep going straight on to Miller Ave and this place is 1 mile down.

MILLBRAE

Jamba Juice
525 Broadway; 650-259-1595
Hours: Monday to Friday 6 am to 8:30 pm; Saturday 7 am to 9 pm; Sunday 7 am to 8 pm
Juice Bar.
Menu: Fresh juices and smoothies. Soups.

MILPITAS

Fresh Choice
Great Mall of the Bay Area; Great Mall Drive
408-934-9090
Hours: Sunday to Thursday 11 am to 10 pm
Friday & Saturday 11 am to 11 pm

China Garden
387 Jacklin Road; 408-262-9888
Hours: Tuesday to Sunday 11 am to 3 pm, 4 pm to 9:30 pm; closed Monday

Chinese. Vegetarian-friendly. Not pure veg.
Menu: Has a selection of vegetarian dishes.
Other Info: Full service, take-out. Accepts MC,
VISA. Price: $$.

**Lu Lai Garden
210 Barber Court; 408-526-9888
Hours: Monday to Friday 11 am to 2:30 pm, 5
pm to 9 pm; Saturday & Sunday 11 am to 9 pm
Vegetarian Chinese.
Directions: From I-880, take the Rte 237 (W
Caleveras Blvd) exit and this place is a quarter-
mile southwest of the exit.

**Milan Sweet Centre
296 South Abel Street, Milpitas; 408-946-2525
Hours: Monday 10 am to 2:30 pm; Tuesday to
Thursday 10 am to 8 pm; Friday & Saturday 10
am to 9 pm; Sunday 10 am to 8 pm
Fully Vegetarian Indian. Restaurant and Snacks.
Other Info: Full service, take-out. Accepts
AMEX, DC, DIS, MC, VISA.
Directions: From I-880, take the Rte 237 (W
Caleveras Blvd) exit, then go east on W Calaveras
Blvd a half-mile, at fork in road go right onto
Serra Way, then at Abel St turn left and this place
is near the corner.

Sugandh India Import
Abel Plaza, 188 South Abel Street, off Calaveras
Boulevard; 408-956-9509
Hours: Tuesday to Sunday 11 am to 9 am
Closed Monday.
Indian Food Store. Indian CDs. Good for In-
dian spices and groceries. Next to Swagat Indian
Cuisine.

Swagat Indian Cuisine
68 S Abel Street, at Calabasa 408-262-1128
613 Great Mall Drive 408-262-2536
Hours: Daily 11 am to 10 pm
Indian. Vegan options. Not pure vegetarian.
Menu: Has both South and North Indian dishes.
Dosas, uthappam, idly and sambar.
Comments: Good food, low on décor. Inexpen-
sive lunch buffet.
Other Info: Full service, take-out. Reservations
suggested for groups. Accepts AMEX, DC, DIS,
MC, VISA. Price: $-$$.

MONTEREY

Ama Rin Thai Cuisine
807 Cannery Row; 831-373-8811
Hours: Wednesday to Monday 11:30 am to 3:30
pm, 5:30 pm to 9:30 pm; closed Tuesday.

Thai. Not pure vegetarian.
Menu: Tofu can be substituted for meat in many
of the dishes.
Comments: Local organic produce used when
possible.
Other Info: Full service, take-out, delivery. Ac-
cepts AMEX, DIS, MC, VISA. Price: $$.

Great Wall
731 Munras Avenue; 831-372-3637
Hours: Sunday to Thursday 11 am to 9 pm
Friday & Saturday 11 am to 10 pm
Chinese. Vegan friendly.
Menu: Has a vegetarian menu that is mainly ve-
gan. Some of the dishes may have eggs in them,
so you may want to ask about this.
Comments: Has very reasonably priced lunch
specials.
Other Info: Full service, take-out. Accepts MC,
VISA. Price: $-$$.

India's Clay Oven
150 Del Monte Avenue; 831-373-2529
Hours: Daily 11 am to 2:30 pm, 5 pm to 10 pm
Saturday & Sunday Brunch 11 am to 4 pm
Indian. Not pure vegetarian. Vegan options.
Menu: Has a good amount of vegetarian dishes.
Other Info: Full service, take-out. Accepts
AMEX, DC, DIS, MC, VISA. Price: $$.

Whole Foods Market
800 Del Monte Center; 831-333-1600
Hours: Daily 8:30 am to 9 pm
Natural Food Store and Cafe. Deli, Bakery, Salad
Bar and Juice Bar. Organic produce. Supermarket-
type place. See Whole Foods Market information.
Directions: From Rte 1, take Soledad Drive exit
towards Munras Ave for a quarter-mile, then go
northwest on Soledad Drive 1 block, at Munras
Ave turn right and this place is 1 block down.

MOUNTAIN VIEW

Amarin Thai Cuisine
156 Castro Street, near Evelyn or Villa Street
650-988-9323
Hours: Monday to Thursday 11 am to 3 pm, 5
pm to 10 pm; Sat & Sun 12 noon to 10 pm
Thai. Vegan-friendly. Not pure vegetarian.
Menu: Has a separate vegetarian menu. Has sev-
eral mock "meat" wheat gluten dishes. Yellow
curry with potatoes and carrots, Tofu Salad (very
spicy) and Spicy Mushrooms with Basil. Veggies
Tempura, Taro Balls, Spicy Corn Cake, Thai
soups, Yellow Curry, Red Curry Stew, Tofu and
Mixed Vegetables, Tofu Sizzling with Peanut

Sauce, Spicy Eggplant, Hot & Sizzling Curry, Forrest Curry and Broccoli & Gravy.
Comments: Has really good vegetarian Thai food. Casual dress. Has indoor and outdoor dining. Very popular place. Amarin means "I shall live forever."
Other Branches: Bangkok Cuisine, 407 Lytton Ave, 650-322-6533; Bangkok Cuisine, 5235 Prospect Road, San Jose, 408-253-8424
Other Info: Full service, take-out. Accepts AMEX, DC, MC, VISA. Price: $-$$.

China Wok
2633 California; 650-941-4373
Hours: Daily 11 am to 12 midnight
Chinese. Vegetarian options. Not pure vegetarian.
Menu: Has a good selection of vegetarian dishes.
Other Info: Accepts AMEX, DIS, MC, VISA.

**Deedee's Indian Fast Food
2551 West Middlefield Road
650-967-9333; **email:** webmaster@deedees.com
Web site: www.mydeedees.com
Restaurant Hours: Monday to Saturday 11 am to 8:30 pm; closed Sunday.
India Store Hours: Tuesday to Sunday 9 am to 9 pm
Fully Vegetarian Indian Restaurant and Indian Store. Mainly Vegan. Lunch Buffet.
Menu: Aloo Chat (a snack), Idly, Dahi Vada, samosa, Pav-Bhaji, lassis, Gulabjamun, Aloo Mattar, puris, vegetable curry and rice. The lunch buffet is cheap.
Indian Store: Has an Indian store that has fresh Indian vegetables, paneer, frozen Indian curries, pickles and ghee.
Other Info: Counter, buffet. Non-smoking. Does not take reservations. Accepts AMEX, VISA.
Directions: From US 101, take Shoreline Blvd exit towards Middlefield Rd, then go west on Middlefield Rd and this place is 1 mile down.

**Garden Fresh Vegetarian Restaurant
1245 West El Camino Real (Rte 82), at Miramonte/Shoreline
650-961-7795; **Web site:** http://waiter.com/garden/
Hours: Sunday to Thursday 11 am to 9:30 pm Friday to Saturday 11 am to 10 pm
Fully Vegan Vegetarian. Buddhist Chinese-style and International.
Menu: Has a large selection of vegetarian dishes. Spring Rolls, several soups (Miso, Spinach Wonton, Vegetable Noodle, Hot & Sour Noodle), Scallion Pancakes, Stuffed Chinese Cabbage, Tofu

Delight (tofu stewed with fresh vegetables in brown sauce), vegetarian sushi, Fried Vegetable Dumplings, Veggie Wonton, House Veggie Steak, Vegetarian Fish, veggie ham, Brown Rice with Mixed Vegetables, steamed dumplings, Vegetarian Hunan-style Chicken (shredded soy bean gluten), Orange Vegetarian Beef (shitake mushroom gluten), Minced Vegetables Wrapped with Lettuce Cup and many more dishes. International dishes such as veggie burgers, veggie hot dogs, Spinach Linguine Salad and Basil with Vegetarian Kidney. Recommended are the steamed dumpling, Hot & Sour Soup, Sweet & Sour Pork and the Orange Beef.
Comments: Voted Best Vegetarian Restaurant in the San Francisco area for years. Reasonably priced and large portions. Friendly, clean. Excellent food, service and atmosphere. Very popular. Lunch specials on the weekdays, but not on the weekends. No MSG. Can order take-out food on their web site.
Other Info: Full service, cafeteria, counter, catering, take-out (can call or order on the Internet 15 minutes in advance). Non-smoking. Does not take reservations. Accepts MC, VISA. Price: $$.
Directions: From US-101 take Shoreline Blvd exit. Go 5 minutes to El Camino and this place is at the intersection of Miramonte and El Camino Real. Next to Baskin Robbins and close to the AAA office. From Hwy 85, take the El Camino Real (Rte82) exit, then go west on El Camino Real and this place is 1¼ mile down.

Hobee's Restaurant
2312 Central Expressway; 650-968-6050
Hours: Monday to Friday 6:30 am to 2:30 pm; Saturday & Sunday 8 am to 2:30 pm
Mexican and International. Salad Bar. Restaurant chain. Not pure vegetarian.
Menu: Veggie patties, Mexican dishes and black bean chili. Fresh juices.
Other Info: Full service, take-out. Accepts MC, VISA. Price: $-$$.

Kim's
368 Castro Street, between California & Dana
650-967-2707; **Web site:** http://www.themenupage.com/kimsm.html
Hours: Sunday to Thursday 11 am to 9:30 pm Friday & Saturday 11 am to 10 pm
Vietnamese. Vegan options. Not pure vegetarian.
Menu: Has a large separate vegetarian menu, which you have to ask for. Shredded Yam with Salad, Fried Tofu with Sauce, rice noodles, rice and Chinese vegetables. Vegetarian mock Chicken and Pork.

Comments: Seats around 120.
Other Info: Full service, take-out, delivery, catering. Accepts AMEX, MC, VISA.

Passage to India
1991 West El Camino Real between Reign
650-964-5532; **Web site:** www.passagetoindia.net
Hours: Daily 11:30 am to 2:30 pm; 5 pm to 10 pm
Vegetarian-friendly Indian. Not pure vegetarian.
Other Info: Accepts AMEX, DC, DIS, MC, VISA.
Directions: From Hwy 85, take El Camino Real (exit #82) exit towards Mountain View. This place is 1¼ mile west on El Camino Real on the left side. From Hwy 101, take the Rengstorrf exit and go south on Rengstorrf for 1¼ mile, then turn left at El Camino Real, and this place is two blocks down on the right.

Sue's Indian Cuisine
216 Castro; 950-969-1112; **Web site:** http://waiter.com/SUES/sues.mtnview.html
Hours: Mon to Wed 11 am to 2:30 pm, 5 pm to 9:30 pm; Thur to Sat 11 am to 2:30 pm, 5 pm to 10 pm; Sun 11:30 am to 2:30, 5 pm to 9:30 pm
Lunch Bunch: Daily 11 am to 2:30 pm
Indian. Vegan options. Not pure vegetarian.
Menu: Has a good amount of vegetarian dishes. Buffet lunch during the week.
Comments: Order take-out food on their Web site. Really good food. Excellent service.
Other Info: Accepts AMEX, DC, DIS, MC, VISA.

Swagat Indian Cuisine
2700 W El Camino Real, one block north of San Antonio Street; 650-948-7727
Hours: Daily 11 am to 2:30 pm, 5:30 pm to 10 pm
Indian. Vegan options. Not pure vegetarian.
Menu: Has both South and North Indian dishes. Dosas, uthappam, idly and sambar.
Comments: Good food, low on décor. Inexpensive lunch buffet.
Other Info: Accepts AMEX, DC, DIS, MC, VISA. Price: $-$$.

NAPA

Bistro Don Giovanni
4110 St Helena Highway; 707-224-3300
Hours: Sunday to Thursday 11:30 am to 10 pm Friday & Saturday 11:30 am to 11 pm
Italian and Mediterranean. Wood burning pizza oven. Not pure vegetarian.
Menu: Gourmet pizzas, pastas and appetizers.

Comments: Fireplace. Has outdoor seating.
Other Info: Full service, take-out. Reservations suggested. Accepts AMEX, DC, DIS, MC, VISA. Price: $$$.

Golden Carrot Natural Foods
River Park Shopping Center, 1621 West Imola Avenue; 707-224-3117
Hours: Monday to Friday 10 am to 6 pm; Saturday 10 am to 5 pm; Sunday 12 noon to 4 pm
Natural Food Store. Juice Bar. Organic produce.
Menu: Ready-made sandwiches, tofu sandwiches and salads.
Other Info: Accepts MC, VISA.
Directions: From Hwy 29, take Imola exit east. This place on right in River Park Shopping Center.

Optimum
633 Trancas; 707-224-1514
Hours: Monday to Friday 9 am to 6 pm Saturday & Sunday 10 am to 5 pm
Natural Food Store.

PJ's Café
1001 Second Street; 707-224-0607
Hours: Monday to Thursday 11:30 am to 8:30 pm; Friday to Saturday 8 am to 9 pm; Sunday 8 am to 2:30 pm
International Café. Vegan-friendly.
Menu: Many vegetarian dishes. Are flexible and will help to make dishes vegetarian.
Comments: Good food. Helpful, efficient service. Servers are willing to help adjust dishes.
Other Info: Full service, take-out. Reservations recommended on the weekends. Accepts AMEX, MC, VISA. Price: $-$$.

Novato (Marin County)

High Tech Burrito
Novato Fair Center, 942 Diablo Avenue
415-897-8083
Hours: Daily (late Thursday to Saturday)
Mexican. Health conscious.
Menu: Vegan burrito. Black Bean burrito.
Comments: A really good place for a quick meal.

OAKLAND

Café Eritrea d'Afrique
4069 Telegraph Avenue, at W Macarthur
510-547-4520
Hours: Monday to Friday 10 am to 11 pm; Saturday & Sunday 10 am to 12 pm; closed on major holidays.

Ethiopians, African. Not pure vegetarian.
Comments: Has outdoor dining. A good value.
Good place for a group.
Other Info: Full service, take-out. Accepts MC,
VISA.

Crepevine

5600 College Avenue; 510-658-2026
Hours: Sunday to Thursday 7:30 am to 11 pm
Friday & Saturday 7:30 am to 12 midnight
Middle Eastern, Crepes. Vegetarian dishes. Not
pure vegetarian.
Menu: Crepes with an option of fillings such as
grilled eggplants, cheddar cheese, spinach, peppers, pine nuts and peanut sauce.
Other Info: Cafeteria-style, take-out. Place order
at counter and food is brought to you. No credit
card; cash only. Price: $.

Food Mill

3033 MacArthur Boulevard; 510-482-3848
Hours: Monday to Saturday 8:30 am to 6 pm
Sunday 11 am to 4 pm
Natural Food Store.
Directions: From I-580, take the Coolidge Ave/
Fruitvale Ave, then go northeast on Coolidge Ave
2 blocks, then turn slight right onto MaCarthur
Blvd and this place is a quarter-mile down.

**Golden Lotus Vegetarian Restaurant

1301 Franklin Street, at 13th Street
510-893-0383
Hours: Monday to Thursday 10 am to 9 pm;
Friday to Saturday 10 am to 10 pm; Sunday 11
am to 9 pm
**Authentic Vegetarian Vegan Vietnamese and
Chinese Buddhist.** No eggs or meat products.
Menu: Has a buffet with several main dishes.
Lunch buffet with three sautéed vegetable or tofu
dishes for $5. There is a selection of Chinese
mock-meat dishes, several soups, Spring Rolls,
Noodle Soup, Pot Sticker, Sautéed Beef, fried
wonton, Curry "Chicken," spring rolls, vegan
desserts, vegan cupcakes and other dishes. The
"mock chicken" has a good texture and tastes good.
Cappuccino, espresso. Non-alcoholic beer and
wine.
Comments: Gets really high recommendations.
Other Info: Full service, take-out. Accepts DIS,
MC, VISA. Price: $-$$.
Directions: From I-880 N, take the Broadway
exit towards downtown, then go north on Broadway for a third-mile, at 13th St turn right and
go 1 block and this place is at the corner of
Franklin.

Great Wall

6247 College Avenue, between 63rd and
Claremont Streets; 510-658-8458
Hours: Sunday to Thursday 11:30 am to 9:30
pm; Friday & Saturday 11 am to 10 pm
Chinese. Mainly Vegetarian (serves fish and eggs).
Menu: Has a good selection of mock meat dishes.
Kung Pao Vegetables, Hot & Sour Soup, brown
rice, Eggplant with Garlic Sauce, Spring Rolls,
and Chinese soup,
Comments: Basic place. The service may not be
so good.
Other Info: Accepts AMEX, DIS, MC, VISA.
Price: $.

Holyland Kosher Foods

677 Rand Avenue; 510 272-0535
Hours: Sunday to Thursday 11:30 am to 9 pm;
Friday 11:30 am to 3 pm; closed Saturday.
Kosher. Not pure vegetarian.
Menu: Falafel, tabbouleh, stuff grape leave, hum-
mus and salads. Fresh juices.
Other Info: Comments: Has indoor and outdoor
seating. Full service, catering, take-out. Cash only.
Price: $.

Lakeshore Natural Foods

3331 Lakeshore Avenue; 510-452-1079
Hours: Monday to Friday 9:30 am to 7 pm; Sat-
urday 9:30 am to 6 pm; 12 noon to 6 pm
Natural Food Store.

Layonna Vegetarian Health Food Market

443 8th Street; 510-763-3168
Hours: Daily 9 am to 6 pm
Asian Vegetarian store. Everything is vegetarian.

***Layonna Kitchen

358 11th Street; 510-763-3168
Hours: Daily 11 am to 9 pm
Vegan Asian.
Menu: Has an all-you-can-eat lunch buffet. Veg-
etarian mock "meats."
Directions: It is in Oakland's Chinatown.

Nan Yang Rockridge

6048 College Avenue, near Claremont, North
Oakland; 510-655-3298
Hours: Tuesday to Friday 11:30 am to 3 pm, 5
pm to 10 pm; Saturday 11:30 to 10 pm;
Sunday 12 noon to 9:30 pm; closed Monday.
Burmese. Not pure vegetarian. Vegan options.
Menu: Has a good selection of vegetarian dishes
including Hot & Sour Soups, Cold Noodles,
Stir-fry, Curry Vegetables, Coconut Rice and

Stir-fried Vegetables.

Comments: Considered by many to be the best Burmese restaurant in the Bay Area. Good, friendly service.

Other Info: Full service, take-out. Accepts MC, VISA. Price: $$.

***New World Vegetarian House

464 8th Street, at Broadway
510-444-2891; fax: 510-835-7891
email: nwventerprise@mindspring.com
Web site: www.newworldvegetarian.com
Hours: Monday to Thursday 11 am to 9 pm; Friday & Saturday 11 am to 9:30 pm; Sunday 12 noon to 9 pm

Fully Vegan International Vegetarian. Italian, Thai, Mexican, Vietnamese, Brazilian, Chinese, Indian and Middle Eastern.Macrobiotic and Vegan options.

Menu: Has over 100 dishes on the menu. Mock Barbecue Pork, Vegetarian Eel, Veggie Patties and tofu dishes. The menu changes seasonally. Okra Red Bean, Chicken Cacciatore, Mushroom Basil, Indian Dharma, Tofu Stew, Teriyaki Beef, Tri Bean Stew, Spinach veggie Tuna Salad, Tabbouleh Masala, Brazilian Eggplant Salad, a variety of soups (Seaweed Tofu, Wonton, Vegetable Bean Mexicana), Black Pepper Steak, Chicken Parmigiana, Chicken Burrito and much more. The Eternal Life and Peace dishes are good. Claypot dishes are good. Vegan except for ice cream and milk for coffee.

Comments: The staff is very veg-educated and friendly. The entrées are mostly Vietnamese and Thai. New World was formerly named Bode Vegetarian Restaurant. Food gets high recommendations. Pleasant atmosphere. Reasonable prices. Their saying, "All vegetarian with respect for life." Got the 1999 Readers Choice Award of the Oakland Tribune for Best Vegetarian Restaurant. Makes mock meat dishes with soy products and wheat gluten. Food is well presented. Food prepared with homemade sauces that use sea salt, are free of MSG, and are low in oil.

Other Info: Full service, take-out, catering. Reservations recommended. Non-smoking. Accepts AMEX, DC, MC, VISA. Price: $-$$.

Directions: Located in downtown Oakland between Broadway and Washington, a few blocks north of I-880. From I-880 N, take the Broadway exit towards downtown, then go north on Broadway and this place 2 blocks down. Conveniently located parking lot next to restaurant. Can be easily reached by public transportation.

Organic Café and Macrobiotic Grocery

Macrobiotic Community Center
1050 40th Street, between Market & San Pablo
510-653-6510
Store Hours: Daily 9 am to 9 pm
Restaurant Hours: Monday to Friday 7 am to 10 am, 11:30 am to 2 pm, 5:30 to 8 pm
Saturday & Sunday 8 am to 8 pm
Macrobiotic Café, Deli and Bakery. Vegan and Macrobiotic options. Mainly Vegan. Buffet on the weekends. All Organic. Not pure vegetarian.

Menu: The food is simple, macrobiotic, and organic. The menu changes regularly. Greens salads, Braised Tofu, Mashed Potato & Gravy, Collard Greens, soups, breads, a tofu or bean dish, Cooked Greens, brown rice and spiced vegetable side dishes. Has gourmet macrobiotic food.

Comments: Casual, simple place. Has weekend brunches. Good size portions. Local organic produce used when possible. Meals can be excellent. Has a small produce section. Offers cooking classes. Been open for over 25 years. Desserts do not contain honey, dairy products, eggs or refined sugar.

Other Info: Full service, buffet (weekends), take-out, catering. Accepts AMEX, MC, VISA. Price: $$.

Directions: This place is two blocks north of MacArthur Blvd, between Adeline and Market. From I-80, take 27th St exit north, at Telegraph turn left, then at 40th turn left and this place on right. From coming from San Francisco on I-580 take San Pablo Ave west exit, then at San Pablo turn right. At 40th turn right and this place on corner of 40th and Linden. It a few blocks west of the MacArthur BART station.

Pizza Rustica

5422 College Avenue; 510-654-1601
Hours: Daily 11:30 am to 9 pm
Pizza. Not pure vegetarian.
Menu: Excellent pizza. Soy-cheese and no-cheese pizza. Pastas and salads. Excellent fresh-fruit drinks (pina-coladas).
Other Info: Full service, take-out. Accepts AMEX, MC, VISA.

Siddha Yoga Ashram

1107 Stanford Avenue, near San Pablo
510-655-8677
Hours: Monday to Thursday 8 am to 8:45 am, 12 noon to 1:30 pm, 6:30 pm to 7:45 pm; Saturday 6 pm to 7 pm; Sunday 9:30 am to 10:20 am & no lunch and dinner.

PACIFIC GROVE (Monterey County)

Harvest Natural Food
542 Lighthouse Avenue; 831-657-2800
Natural Food Deli.

Tillie Gort's Coffee House
111 Central Avenue, near the aquarium
831-373-0335
Hours: Daily 11 am to 10 pm
International. Mostly Vegetarian. Vegan-friendly.
Menu: Has a good selection of vegetarian dishes.
Comments: Friendly staff. Casual place. Price:
$.
Directions: From Hwy 1, take the Monterey exit,
then go west ¾ mile on Camino Aquajito, at
Abrego St turn right and go a half-mile, at Del
Monte Ave turn left and go a half-mile, then stay
straight onto Lighthouse Ave (road becomes Central) and this place is 1½ mile down.

PALO ALTO

Andale Taqueria
209 University Avenue; 650-323-2939
Hours: Monday to Friday 11 am to 10 pm; Saturday 11 am to 11 pm; Sunday 11 am to 9 pm
Mexican. A good selection of vegetarian dishes.
Not pure vegetarian.
Other Info: Full service, take-out. Accepts MC,
VISA.

Bangkok Cuisine
407 Lytton Avenue, at Waverley
650-322-6533
Hours: Monday to Thursday 11 am to 3 pm, 5:30
pm to 10 pm; Friday 11 am to 3 pm, 5 pm to 10
pm; Saturday 11 am to 3 pm, 5 pm to 10 pm;
Sunday 5 pm to 9:30 pm
Thai. Vegan-friendly. Not pure vegetarian.
Menu: Has a separate vegetarian menu that includes mock "meat" dishes. Good tasting curries,
Lab Tofu Salad (spicy), Spicy Mushrooms & Basil and Hot & Sour Mushroom Soup ("medium"
is fairly spicy). Pad Thai (they ask whether you
want egg or not), Fried Rice (with pineapple),
and various curry and peanut sauce dishes.
Comments: Food gets good ratings. The restaurant is quite small, and there can be a wait even
on a Tuesday evening.
Other Info: Full service, take-out. Accepts
AMEX, DC MC, VISA. Price: $$.

Benbo's
460 Ramona Avenue; 650-323-2555
Hours: Daily 5:30 pm to 9:30 pm

Mediterranean. Vegan-friendly. Not pure vege.
Menu: Hummus and pita bread, Lentil Soups,
Eggplant Pita, stuffed grape leaves, Stuffed Cabbage, Grilled Eggplant and Several Vegetarian
Plates.
Comments: Friendly waitresses. Small dining
area. Price: $$.

Country Sun
440 South California Avenue
650-324-9190; Web site: www.countrysun.com
Hours: Monday to Saturday 8 am to 9 pm; closed
Sunday; Deli Hours: Monday to Friday 8 am to
4 pm; Saturday 8 am to 3 pm; closed Sunday.
Natural Food Store and Deli. Juice Bar. Vegan
and Macrobiotic options. Not pure vegetarian.
Menu: Has salads, veggie burgers, sandwiches,
Tofu Salad, Avocado & Cheese and pizzas. Local
organic produce used when possible. Fresh juices
and smoothies.
Comments: The deli does not have much of a
selection.
Other Info: Limited seating, take-out. Has seating outside. Accepts MC, VISA. Price: $.
Directions: From Hwy 101, take Oregon Expressway west, then at El Camino Real turn right and
go 4 blocks, then at California turn right and this
place on left 1 block down.

Darbar Indian Cuisine
129 Lytton Street, near Alma; 650-321-6688
Web site: www.darbarindiancuisine.com
Hours: Monday 11 am to 2:30 pm, 5 pm to 9:30
pm; Tuesday to Friday 11 am to 2:30 pm, 5 pm
to 10 pm; Saturday & Sunday 5 pm to 10 pm
Indian. All-you-can-eat Buffet Lunch. Not pure
vegetarian.
Menu: Some good vegetarian Indian dishes.
Other Info: Full service, take-out. Accepts
AMEX, MC, VISA.

Fresh Choice
379 Stanford Shopping Center; 650-322-6995
Hours: Sunday to Thursday 11 am to 9 pm; Friday & Sat 11 am to 10 pm; Sun 10 am to 9 pm
Restaurant. See Menlo Park for details.

Homma's Brown Rice Sushi
2363 Birch, near California; 650-327-6118
Hours: Monday to Saturday 11:30 am to 2:30
pm, 5 pm to 9 pm. closed Sunday.
Japanese. Vegan options. Not pure vegetarian.
Menu: Good selection of vegetarian dishes.
Has a wide selection of sushi made with brown
rice.
Other Info: No credit cards; cash or check only.

**Juice Club

The Oaks Shopping Center, 69 Town and Country Village; 650-325-2582
Hours: Daily 6:30 am to 8:30 pm
Vegetarian Juice Bar.
Menu: Has a large selection of juices.
Other Info: Counter service, take-out.

Max's Opera Café

711 Stanford Shopping Center; 650-323-6297
Hours: Sunday to Thursday 11:30 am to 9:30 pm; Friday to Saturday 11 am to 11 pm
American. Not pure vegetarian.
Menu: Stuffed baked potato, polenta, vegetarian sub or club sandwich and Steamed Vegetables (with dipping sauce).
Comments: Good size portions.
Other Info: Accepts AMEX, MC, VISA. Reservations suggested for weekend dinners or may have to wait a half-hour for a table.

Molly Stone's Natural Food

164 South California Avenue; 650-323-8361
Natural Food Store and Deli. Bakery. Has an excellent selection of organic produce. A good Salad Bar.
Menu: Has a large amount of vegetarian dishes. Soups, salads, sandwiches and hot dishes.
Directions: From Hwy 101, take Oregon Expressway west, then at El Camino Real turn right and go 4 blocks, then at California turn right and this place is 4 blocks down.

Whole Foods Market

774 Emerson Street; 650-326-8676
Hours: Daily 8 am to 10 pm
Natural Food Store and Cafe. Deli, Bakery, Salad Bar and Juice Bar. Organic produce. Supermarket-type place. See Whole Foods Market information.
Comments: One of the best Whole Foods.
Other Info: Full service, take-out, catering. Accepts MC, VISA.
Directions: From Hwy 101, take University exit, then go southwest on University for 1¼ mile, at Emerson turn left and this place is on the right 3 blocks down.

PETALUMA

Food for Thought (Whole Foods Market)

621 East Washington Street; 707-762-9352
Hours: Daily 8 am to 9 pm
Natural Food Store and Cafe. Deli, Bakery, Salad Bar and Juice Bar. Organic produce. Supermarket-type place. See Whole Foods Market information.

Directions: From Hwy 101, take E Washington St exit, then head southwest a half mile and this place on right past Kenilworth Park.

Trader Joe's

4040 Pimlico, at Santa Rita Road & Fwy 580
707-734-3422

REDWOOD CITY (San Mateo County)

Bangkok Bay Thai Cuisine

825 El Camino Real
650-365-5369; **email:** neena@bangkokbay.com;
Web site: www.bangkokbay.com
Hours: Monday to Friday 11 am to 3 pm, 5 pm to 9:30 pm; Sat & Sun 5 pm to 9:30 pm
Thai. Vegan options. Not pure vegetarian.
Menu: Has a separate vegetarian menu. Hot & Sour Mushroom Soup, Sweet & Sour Tofu, Pan-fried Mixed Vegetables, Pad Spinach, Spicy Eggplant, Spicy Tofu, Curry Vegetable and Vegetarian Fried Rice.
Other Info: Full service, take-out. Accepts MC, VISA. Price: $-$$.
Directions: From north of Redwood City (for example, from the San Francisco Airport), proceed south on Highway 101, take the Whipple Avenue exit (in Redwood City), turn right at the first traffic light and proceed west, turn left on El Camino Real, and look for Bangkok Bay on your left at the corner of Broadway and El Camino Real.

Jamba Juice

1007 El Camino Real; 650-261-2130
220 Redwood Shores Parkway; 650-802-2900
Juice Bar.

Joy Meadow

701 El Camino Road; 650-780-9978
Hours: Daily 11:30 am to 9:30 pm
Asian, Indian, Pacific Rim, American. Not pure vegetarian.
Menu: Has a good selection of vegetarian dishes. Mashed potatoes with stuffing. Zen Banquet.
Comments: Indoor waterfalls, pool and plants. Nice atmosphere.
Other Info: Full service, take-out. Accepts AMEX, DC, DIS, MC, VISA. Price: $$.

SAN ANSELMO (Marin County)

Piccadilly Circus

222 Greenfield Avenue; 415-258-0660
Hours: Monday to Saturday 8 am to 10 pm

Sunday 9 am to 9 pm
Natural Food Store and Cafe. Deli, Bakery, Salad Bar and Juice Bar. Organic produce. Supermarket-type place. See Wild Oats Market information.
Comments: Has a Chinese herbalist.
Directions: From Hwy 101, take Central San Rafael exit. From south, turn left (go west) on 3rd St (becomes Red Hill Ave) and go about 2 miles, at Spring Grove Ave turn left, then make a quick left at Greenfield Ave and this place is 50 yards down. From north, take Central San Rafael exit and at 3rd St turn right. Same as above.

SAN BRUNO

**Green Valley Organic Vegetarian Rest.
422 San Mateo Avenue
at El Camino
650-873-6677
Hours: Tuesday to Thursday 11:30 am to 9:30 pm; Friday to Sunday 11:30 am to 10 pm; closed Monday.
Fully Vegetarian Oriental Buddhist and International. Mostly Vegan. Uses fresh organic vegetables.
Menu: Has a wide selection of vegetarian dishes. Menu changes frequently. Tofu Eggplant Lasagna, Organic Salad, Braised Tofu with Mixed Vegetables and Swiss Chard & Red Pepper in tomato sauce. Mock meat, seafood and chicken.
Comments: Purified water. All organic. Good tasting food. Friendly place.
Other Info: Full service, take-out. Non-smoking. Accepts AMEX, MC, VISA. Price: $$.
Directions: From I-380, take the El Camino Real/Rte 82 exit, then go south on El Camino Real for 1 mile. Then turn left at San Mateo Ave and this place is a half-block down at El Camino on the north side of street. Free parking in the back of the building.

SAN CARLOS (San Mateo County)

Fon Yong
1065 Holly Street, near El Comino Real
650-637-9238
Hours: Monday to Friday 11 am to 2:30 pm, 4:30 pm to 9:30 pm; Saturday 1 pm to 9:30 pm; Sunday 4:30 pm to 9:30 pm
Chinese. Mandarin Hunan style. Half of the menu is vegan. Not pure vegetarian.
Comments: Good place. Mock "meat" dishes are really good.
Other Info: Accepts MC, VISA.

SAN JOSE

Amarin Cuisine
156 Castro Street, at Saratoga Avenue, near Trader Joe's, Mountainview; 650-988-9323
Hours: Daily 11 am to 3 pm, 5:30 pm to 10 pm
Thai. Vegan-friendly. Not pure vegetarian.
Menu: Has a separate vegetarian menu that includes mock "meat" dishes. Curries, Lab Tofu Salad (spicy) and Spicy Mushrooms & Basil.
Other Info: Full service, take-out. Accepts AMEX, DC, DIS, MC, VISA. Price: $$.

Country Village Natural Foods
3982 South Bascom Avenue; 408-377-1431
Hours: Monday to Friday 9:30 to 7 pm; Saturday 10 am to 7 pm; Sunday 10:30 am to 5 pm
Natural Food Store.
Comments: Has ready-made sandwiches. Accepts MC, VISA.

***Di Da Vegetarian
2597 Senter Road; 408-998-8826
Hours: Daily 9 am to 9 pm
Vegan Vietnamese.
Other Info: Full service, take-out. Cash and check only; no credit cards.
Directions: From US 101, take Tully Road exit and go west on Tully Rd for 1 mile, at Senter Rd turn left and this place is a third-mile down.

**Di Lac Cuisine
1644 East Capitol Expressway (Silver Creek) 408-238-8686; **Web site:** www.dilac.com
Hours: Monday to Friday 9 am to 9 pm
Saturday to Sunday 10 am to 9 pm
Fully Vegetarian Chinese, Vietnamese and Thai. Mainly Vegan.
Menu: Has mock "meat" dishes. Roasted Vegetarian Chicken and Eggplant with Hot Bean Sauce.
Comments: Pleasant, relaxing atmosphere. Has a water fountain.
Other Info: Full service, take-out. Accepts AMEX, MC, VISA.
Directions: From Hwy 101, take the E Capitol Exwy exit, then go east on Capitol Exwy and this place is a quarter-mile down.

Fresh Choice
Westgate Shopping Center, 1600 Saratoga Avenue
408-866-1491
Almaden Plaza, 5353 Almaden Expressway #39A
408-723-7991
Restaurant. See Menlo Park.

**Fresh & Healthy Vegetarian Food To Go
388 East Santa Clara Street; 408-286-6335
Hours: Daily 9 am to 8 pm
Fully Vegetarian Vietnamese and International. Vegan options.
Menu: Fried Rice, Vegetable Deluxe and Chow Mien (noodles with vegetable). Mock meat dishes.
Other Info: Counter service, take-out. Non-smoking. Accepts reservations but are not necessary. Cash only.
Directions: From Santa Clara Street in downtown San Jose, turn onto 9th and it is in a big apartment at the corner. This place is 1 block north of the northeast corner of Cal State Univ–San Jose.

Gojo Ethiopian Restaurant
1261 West San Carlos Street; 408-295-9546
Hours: Tuesday to Sunday 11:30 am to 10 pm
Closed Monday.
Ethiopian. Not pure vegetarian. Vegetarian-friendly.

New Indian Market
2365 McKee Road; 408-923-5570
Indian Food Store.

**Saturn Café
145 Laurel Street; 831-429-8505
email: info@saturncafe.com
Web site: www.saturncafe.com
Hours: Sunday to Thursday 11:30 am to 3 am
Friday and Saturday 11:30 am to 4 am
Vegan and Vegetarian.
Menu: Vegan Nachos, veggie burgers, organic salad, homemade soups, French Fries, Chili Cheese Fries, Steamed Vegetables, Middle Eastern plate, Pasta Special, corn dogs, Soy Taquito Plate and other dishes. Has a wide assortment of desserts including baked goods and ice cream.
Other Info: Full service, take-out, downtown delivery. Accepts MC, VISA.

Sue's Indian Cuisine
895 Willow Street
408-993-8730; Web site: http://waiter.com/SUES/sues.sanjose.html
Hours: Tuesday to Thursday 11 am to 2:30 pm, 5 pm to 9:30 pm; Friday & Saturday 11 am to 2 pm, 5 pm to 10 pm; Sunday 5 pm to 9:30 pm; closed Monday.
Indian. Vegan options. Not pure vegetarian. Buffet lunch during the week.
Menu: Has many vegetarian options.
Other Info: Full service, take-out. Accepts AMEX, MC, VISA.

Trader Joe's (2 locations)
5985 Almaden Expressway, one mile south of Blossom Hill Road; 927-9091
5269 Prospect Road, between Lawrence Expressway & Saratoga Avenue; 446-5055

**Vegetarian House
520 East Santa Clara; 408 292-3798, 408-292-3832; email: smch99@hotmail.com; Web site: www.godsdirectcontact.com/vegetarian/
Hours: Monday to Friday 11 am to 2 pm, 5 pm to 9:30 pm
Saturday and Sunday 11 am to 9:30 pm
Fully Vegetarian Gourmet Asian, Chinese and International (no eggs or MSG). Mostly Vegan. Juice Bar.
Menu: Has a huge selection of vegetarian dishes. Has dishes from several Asian cuisines including Chinese, Vietnamese and Thai. Serves dishes from cuisine from all over the world including Italy, the Middle East, France and America. Chinese mock-meat dishes, Lasagna, Vegetable Quiche. Fettuccine Alfredo, Eggplant Parmigiana, Spring Rolls, Hummus with Pita Bread, Fried Tofu, Formosa Sushi, Vegetables Tempura, Mu Shu Vegetables, Kung Pao "Chicken," Szechuan "Chicken" Strips, Sizzling "Salmon," Vegetarian "Shrimps," Eggplant & Veggie "Beef," Eggplant Tofu, Tofu Rolls, Sweet & Sour Nuggets, Shish-Kebab, Crispy Mushroom Delight, Thai Curry Soup, Au-Lac Sweet & Sour Soup, Won Ton Noodle Soup and Gourmet Fried Rice. The Tofu Roll Deluxe served with fresh vegetables and special sauce is a very popular dish. A good selection of gourmet pizzas with toppings such as vegetarian Canadian bacon and sun-dried tomatoes. Non-alcohol mixed drinks, wine and beer.
Comments: Has a beautiful art gallery that contains the works of the well-known artist Ching Hai. Run by Ching Hai followers and the full name of this place is Suma Ching Hai International Association Vegetarian House. It is a religious place and also a restaurant. Good service and friendly. Often have loud videos of the spiritual leader giving her views of the world.
Other Info: Full service, take-out. Non-smoking. Accepts reservations but are not necessary. Accepts AMEX, DIS, MC, VISA. Price: $-$$.
Directions: This restaurant is a small green building between 11th St and 12th St. From Hwy 101 take Exit #130, then go west on Santa Clara St about 10 blocks, go to 12th St, then past the restaurant and turn left into parking lot. From Hwy 280, take exit #10 (11th St), then go north on 11th St about 1 mile, then turn right on Santa

Clara St, then immediately turn right into parking lot. Has their own parking lot.

**White Lotus Vegetarian Restaurant
80 North Market Street; 408-977-0540
Hours: Monday to Friday 11 am to 2:30 pm, 5:30 pm to 9 pm; Saturday 10:30 am to 10 pm; closed Sunday.
Vegetarian International (mainly Vietnamese and Chinese). Mainly Vegan.
Menu: Stuffed Braised Tofu and many mock meat dishes including vegetarian beef, fish, chicken and duck. Sweet & Sour Pork, Tofu & Asparagus, white & brown rice and Pumpkin Soup. Good vegan desserts.
Comments: The food is really good and the service is efficient. Pleasant atmosphere. This place has been around for a while. The food can be a bit greasy. Makes their own soy milk.
Warning: The "chicken" dishes are made from ingredients that contain egg white.
Other Info: Full service, take-out. Non-smoking. Accepts MC, VISA.
Directions: In downtown San Jose. From CA Hwy 87, take W Julian St exit, then go east on Julian St (becomes W St James St) 3 short blocks, at N Market St turn right and this place is 1 block down.

SAN LEANDRO (Alameda County)

Health Unlimited
182 Pelton Center Way	510-483-3630
340 Bay Fair Mall	510-483-3540
Natural Food Store.

Nature – Sunshine Health Store
1279 Cumberland, San Leandro
510-351-3003
Hours: Tuesday to Saturday 11 am to 11 pm
Sunday 11 am to 4 pm
Natural Food Store.

SAN MATEO (San Mateo County)

Fresh Choice
1952 South El Camino Real; 415-341-8498

Jamba Juice
44 East Fourth Avenue; 650-558-3918
1230 West Hillsdale Blvd # A; 650-357-0804
Hours: Monday to Saturday 6:30 am to 9:30 pm
Sunday 7 am to 9:30 pm
Juice Bar.

Trader Joe's
1820 South Grant Street; 650-570-6140

SAN RAFAEL

Bongkot Thai Express
857 Fourth Street; 415-453-3350
Hours: Monday to Saturday 11 am to 3:30 pm, 5 pm to 9:30 pm (until 10 pm Fri & Sat) Closed Sunday.
Thai. Vegan options. Not pure vegetarian.
Menu: Has over 15 dishes on its vegetarian menu. Noodles dishes, Thai vegetables, curried vegetables and others.
Comments: Reasonably priced.
Other Info: Full service, take-out. Accepts MC, VISA. Price: $.

Paradise Vegetarian Restaurant
1444 4th Street; 415-456-3572
Hours: Daily 11:30 am to 2:30 pm, 5 pm to 8:30 pm
Chinese and Vietnamese. Some American dishes. Vegetarian-friendly. Not pure vegetarian.
Menu: Has a large selection of vegetarian and vegan dishes.
Other Info: Accepts MC, VISA. Price: $.

Trader Joe's
Montecito Plaza, 337 Third Street
415-454-9530

Whole Foods Market
340 Third Street; 415-451-6333
email: anie.summerland@wholefoods.com
Web site: www.wholefoodsmarket.com
Hours: Daily 9 am to 9 pm
Bakery & Prepared Foods Hours: 8 am to 9 pm
Natural Food Store and Cafe. Deli, Bakery, Salad Bar and Juice Bar. Organic produce. Supermarket-type place. See Whole Foods Market information.
Directions: From Hwy 101 going south from SF, take Central San Rafael exit, then take first right, which is 2nd St (merges with 3rd St). This place one mile down on left.

Whole Foods Market
100 Sunset Drive
925-355-9000
Hours: Daily 8 am to 9 pm
Natural Food Store and Cafe. Deli, Bakery, Salad Bar and Juice Bar. Organic produce. Supermarket-type place. See Whole Foods Market information.

SAN FRANCISCO

Ace Hi Foods For Health
2863 Mission St, at 22nd
415-647-6999
Natural Food Store.

All You Knead
1466 Haight Street, at Masonic Avenue
415-552-4550
Hours: Wednesday to Monday 8 am to 11 pm;
Tuesday 8 am to 6 pm; Breakfast served until 4
pm
**American, Californian-style, Pizza, Natural
Food.** Not pure vegetarian.
Menu: Homemade soups, granola, pizzas, pastas, salads, veggie Lasagna, excellent quesadillas,
veg burritos, veggie burgers, Cheese Ravioli, sandwiches and scrambled tofu.
Comment: Offbeat, cheap place. Basic décor. The
food is not great, but the atmosphere is cool. A
good value.
Other Info: Does not accept reservations. Nonsmoking. Accepts AMEX, MC, VISA. Price: $-
$$.
Directions: Mini bus: #71 Haight–Fillmore, #7
Haight, #6 Parnassus, #22 Fillmore, #66
Quintara.

**Ananda Fuara Vegetarian Restaurant
1298 Market Street, at 9th and Larkin
415-621-1994;
Web site: http://anandafuara.citysearch.com/
Hours: Monday, Tuesday, Thursday to Saturday
8 am to 8 pm; Wednesday 8 am to 3 pm
closed Sunday. Open once a month for Sunday
Brunch 10 am to 2 pm (call for date)
Vegetarian Indian and Asian. Serves eggs. Vegan
and Macrobiotic options.
Menu: Salads, pizzas, sandwiches, samosas with
chutney, vegetarian burritos, Scrambled Tofu and
Curried Vegetables. Has two good veggie burgers
with homemade buns. The Vegan Veggie Burger
is made from grains and vegetables. The Vegan
BBQ Tofu Burger has a BBQ sauce. Infinite Bleu
Salad is sautéed cabbage, zucchini, broccoli,
mushrooms over brown rice with lettuce and
sprouts with blue cheese dressing. Chocolate
Cake. Has excellent breakfasts. Fresh juices, Indian lassi, herbal teas and smoothies. The Tofu
Ravioli and pizza are really good.
Comments: Gets really good recommendations,
but some people have told me they were not so
impressed. Run by disciples of Chinmoy and has
a meditation center. Women servers wear saris.
Casual. New age design with light blue walls.
Friendly, together service. Peaceful background
music. Limited seating. Discount for San Francisco Vegetarian Society members. Very busy during lunch. Good service. Rustic décor. Sometimes
has live music.
Note: The house specialty "Neatloaf" contains
eggs.
Warning: Street parking can be risky at night, as
break-ins are common. Best to park your car in a
lot at night.
Other Info: Full service, take-out, catering. Cash
only. Price: $-$$
Directions: In the Civic Center area. From I-80,
take Ninth St/Civic Center exit, then go southwest on Harrison St, at 9th St turn right and go a
half-mile, at Market St turn right and this place
is near the corner. For parking there are several
pay lots in the area.

**Bamboo Garden
832 Clement Street, at 9th Avenue
415-876-0832
Hours: Wednesday to Monday 11 am to 9:30
pm; closed Tuesday.
Fully Vegetarian Chinese. Mainly vegan.
Menu: Won Ton Soup, noodles, Veggie Roll,
Baked Pork Bun (gets good recommendations),
Moo Shu Pork and Chinese Hamburger. Mixed
Veg Deluxe, Curry Chicken, Sweet & Sour Pork,
and Steamed Tofu with Bok Choy all get high
recommendations. Veg Sausage is really good.
Good Dim Sum served during the day. One variety of Dim Sum may be made with eggs.
Comments: May be full on the weekends. Decent selection of vegan dishes. Really good place.
Other Info: Full service, take-out. Accepts MC,
VISA. Price: $-$$.
Direction: In the Clement shopping district,
about 1½ mile due south of the Golden Gate
Bridge. Richmond District neighborhood. From
I-80, merge onto US-101 N and go a half-mile,
then stay straight onto Central Skwy for a half-
mile, then exit and merge onto Fell St and go a
half-mile, at Divisadero St turn right and go 2/3
mile, then at Geary Blvd turn left and go 1½ mile,
at 9th Ave turn right and go 1 block, then at
Clements turn left and this place is near the corner. If you just crossed the Golden Gate Bridge,
go south on Hwy 1 and take it to the end, then
go 2 blocks south, then turn left at Clements St
and this place is 4½ blocks down.

Bangkok 900
900 Stanyan Street, at Frederick Street
415-665-5333
Hours: Monday to Saturday 11:30 am to 3 pm,

5 pm to 10 pm; Sunday 5 pm to 10 pm
Thai. Not pure vegetarian.
Menu: Has a selection of vegetarian dishes.
Comment: Good décor.
Other Info: Accepts MC, VISA. Price: $-$$.

Bay Area Organic Xpress
PO Box 460411; 415-695-9688
Hours: Monday to Friday 10 am to 4 pm
Delivers Organic Produce.

Bok Choy Garden
1820 Clement Street, at 19th Avenue
415-387-8111
Hours: Monday to Friday 11 am to 3 pm, 4:30
pm to 9:30 pm; Sat to Sun 11 am to 9:30 pm
Fully Vegan, Authentic Chinese Vegetarian. No
garlic, onion or egg served.
Menu: Stuffed Shitake Mushroom with Broccoli,
Kung Pao "Chicken," Vegetarian Chicken in
Hunan Sauce (hot spicy), Mongolian "Beef" (recommended), Toro Casserole (recommended),
Fried Walnuts with Sweet & Sour Sauce and
Stewed Soybean Sheet Rolls & Tofu. Very good
brown rice and seitan dishes. Fried "chicken" is
good.
Comments: Friendly service. Creative Chinese
vegetarian food. Gets high ratings. Reasonably
priced. Used to be called Vegi Food. Has Chinese
lanterns. Casual.
Other Info: Full service, take-out. Reservations
recommended. Accepts MC, VISA. Price: $-$$.
Directions: Located in the Richmond neighborhood, about 1½ mile due south of the Golden
Gate Bridge. If you just crossed the Golden
Gate Bridge, go south on Hwy 1 and take it
to the end, then go 2 blocks south, then turn
right at Clements St and this place is 6 blocks
down.

Buffalo Whole Foods (two locations)
598 Castro Street; 415-626-7038
Natural Food Store. Organic produce. Small place
with a bulk food section.

Buffalo Whole Food & Grain Co
598 Castro Street; 415-626-7038
Hours: Monday to Saturday 9 am to 8 pm
Sunday 10 am to 8 pm
Natural Food Store.
Menu: Has ready-made sandwiches and salads.
Other Info: Accepts MC, VISA.
Directions: From Hwy 101 south, follow signs
to Golden Gate Bridge, then take Fell St exit. At
Divisadero turn left and it becomes Castro and
this place on right. From north take Lombard St

exit to Van Ness, then at Fell turn right, then at
Divisadero turn left and this place on right.

Crepevine
624 Irving Street, at 7th and 8th Avenues
415-681-5858
Hours: Sunday to Thursday 7:30 am to 11 pm
Friday & Saturday 7:30 am to 12 midnight
Middle Eastern, Crepes. Vegetarian dishes. Not
pure vegetarian.
Menu: Crepes with an option of fillings such as
grilled eggplants, cheddar cheese, spinach, peppers, pine nuts and peanut sauce.
Comments: Popular with UCSF students. Has
sidewalk tables.
Other Info: Cafeteria-style, take-out. Place order
at counter and food is brought to you. No credit
cards; cash only.

Daily Health Natural Organic Foods
1235 9th Avenue, at Lincoln; 415-681-7675
Hours: Monday to Friday 10 am to 8pm
Saturday to Sunday 10 am to 5 pm
Vitamin Shop and small take-out **Vegetarian
Sandwich Shop.** Juice Bar.
Menu: Organic soups, salads, Garden Burgers and
sandwiches.

Feelmore Juice
254 Fillmore Street, Haight Asbury Area
415-255-6701
Hours: Monday to Friday 8 am to 6 pm
Saturday & Sunday 9 am to 6 pm
Juice Bar.
Menu: Fresh juices and smoothies. Fresh bagels,
breads and snacks.

Firefly
4288 24th Street, at Douglass Street
415-821-7652
Hours: Monday to Thursday 5:30 pm to 9:30
pm; Friday & Saturday 5:30 pm to 10 pm; Sunday 5:30 pm to 9 pm
Multi-ethnic. Asian, Mediterranean, Californian.
Not pure vegetarian
Menu: Has two vegetarian main dishes each day
that change daily. Mixed greens, tomato soup,
Tofu Thai Tofu Curry, Grilled Portobello Mushroom, Mixed Greens, Vegetarian Risotto (with
wild mushrooms, peppers and snap peas), Vegetable Stir-fry and Thai Tofu Curry.
Comments: Quiet, romantic place. Very popular place. Decorated by modern art. Contemporary, eclectic décor. Most people really like this
place, but some don't. One of the best restaurants in Noe Valley. Some people complain about

the service. Pleasant atmosphere. Good place for a special event.
Other Info: Reservations required. Full service. Accepts AMEX, MC, VISA. Price: $$-$$$.
Directions: In Noe Valley.

Fleur De Lys Restaurant

777 Sutter Street, between Taylor and Jones Streets; 415-673-7779; **fax:** 415-673-4619
Web site: www.fleurdelyssf.com
Hours: Monday to Thursday 6 pm to 9:30 pm; Friday & Saturday 5:30 pm to 10:30 pm; closed Sunday. Has two seatings.
French, American. Has emphasis on vegetarian meals. Salad Bar. Not pure vegetarian.
Menu: Separate vegetarian menu. Has a vegetarian feast for $60 per person. Cauliflower Mousseline, Ecuadrian Quinoa, Avocado & Asparagus Timbale, Cream of Petit Pea & Fresh Morels, Gratin of Fingerling Potatoes and Wild Mushroom in a Potato Shell.
Comments: Quiet, romantic, formal, upscale place. Excellent service. Considered to be one of the most romantic places in San Francisco. The vegetarian food gets great rating. Jacket and tie required. Open since 1970. Elegant décor. Has chandeliers and flowers on tables. Seats 65. Great place for an event. Rated as one of the top 25 Best Restaurants in America by Food and Wine. Good atmosphere. Chef Kellar is famous for his excellent vegetarian menu. Vegan meals can be arranged with advance notice.
Other Info: Full service. Has a private dining room for 12 people. Reservations required. Asks that you confirm reservations two days in advance. Accepts AMEX, DC, MC, VISA. Price: $$$$.
Directions: From Oakland take I-80, cross the Bay Bridge, take Fremont exit. Turn left on Howard, at 6th Street turn right (go north) and go 1 mile (crossing Market), then at Sutter Street turn left and this place is 1 block down. From Peninsula (101 N & 280), take 7th Street exit, stay left, turn onto 7th Street. Turn right at Folsom, then left at 6th Street, then left on Sutter Street.

**The Ganges

775 Frederick Street, at Arguello; 415-661-7290
Hours: Tuesday to Sunday 5:30 pm to 9:30 pm. Closed Monday.
Fully Vegetarian Indian. South Indian. Some American options. Mainly Vegan.
Menu: Appetizers such as samosas and pakoras with chutney. The Chili Pakoras and Green Chili Fritters are extremely hot (some may say unbearably hot). The potato dishes, Alu Gobi (potato

& cauliflower), Zucchini with Peanut Sauce, Rajma (kidney beans in a spicy sauce) and Dal soup are good. The samosas and vada are really good. A favorite is baked banana stuffed with coconut, rice, cilantro and spices. Special Thali Plate with Saffron Rice, dal, curries and Indian appetizers. The "Ganges Special Combinations" is a good choice for a full meal. Vegan desserts. Kulfi (Indian ice cream) and ladu are good desserts.
Comments: Gets high recommendations. One of the best vegetarian restaurants in San Francisco. Back section has low-level tables where you sit on the floor and take off your shoes. Live sitar and Indian classical music Thursday to Saturday. Relaxing music. Romantic (according to some) atmosphere. Food is a little expensive, but good. Good service, but may be a little slow. Casual place. Portions are a bit small for the price.
Other Info: Full service, take-out. Reservations highly advised for Friday and Saturday nights. Very popular. Accepts MC, VISA. Price: $$.
Directions: Between Stanyan and Arguello Street on the south side of Golden Gate Park. Just west of Haight-Asbury. Across from Kezar Stadium. It is a few blocks from UCSF. Can park on the street or in the nearby UCSF parking lot.

Gaylord's India Restaurant (two places)

1 Embarcadero Center, Promanade Level (at intersection of Sacramento and Battery, across from Park Hyatt Hotel); 415-397-7775
Hours: Monday to Friday 11:30 am to 2:30 pm, 5 pm to 10 pm; Sat & Sun 11:30 noon to 2:30 pm, 5 pm to 10:30 pm; Sun 5 pm to 10 pm
900 North Point Street; 415-771-8822
Hours: Monday to Saturday 11:45 am to 1:45 pm, 5 pm to 10 pm; Sunday Buffet Bunch 12 noon to 2:30 pm; Sun Dinner 5 pm to 10 pm
Indian. Vegan options. Not pure vegetarian.
Menu: Vegetarian appetizers and vegetarian main dishes. Bread baked fresh in clay oven. Fresh juices.
Comments: Formal. There is a Bay view from the Point Street branch. Comfortable, relaxed place. Elegant décor. Candle lit.
Other Info: Full service, take-out. Reservations suggested for groups. Non-smoking. Accepts AMEX, DC, DIS, MC, VISA. Price: $$-$$$.

**Golden Era Vegetarian Restaurant

572 O'Farrell Street, at Jones Street
415-673-3136; **fax:** 415-351-1682
Web site: www.goldeneravegetarian.com
Hours: Wednesday to Monday 11 am to 9:30 pm; closed Tuesday.
Fully Vegetarian Vietnamese and Chinese Bud-

dhist. Mostly Vegan.

Menu: Over 50 appetizers and entrées to choose from. Vietnamese Crepes, Wonton Soup (serves 4); Sautéed Garlic Beef, Fried Vegetable Fu Young, spring & summer rolls, Lemon Grass Tofu, Spicy Veg Prawns, Tamarind Beef (recommended), House Rice Claypot, Gourmet Chicken over Broken Rice, Grilled Tofu over Broken Rice, Vegetarian Lamb Claypot, Thousand Layers Tofu Eggplant, Curry Noodles, Eggplant Curry Claypot, Spicy Pineapple veg Salmon and mock "Chicken." Hong Kong Chow Mein is good. Buddha Buns (recommended) is bread filled with tofu, water chestnut and bean threads. Tay-ho Rolls, steamed crepes with tofu and veggies, is recommended. The Lemon Chicken tastes like the real thing. The Salted Plum Lemonade is interesting and recommended.

Comments: Gets great ratings for food and atmosphere. Award winning for vegetarian food. It has a peaceful, charming, casual atmosphere. Good food. Upscale Asian with a fancy décor. Plenty of seating available. Service is very good. Off-street parking is expensive. May want to take the BART train (Powell Street station is four blocks away). Run by followers of the Supreme Master Ching Hai.

Reviews: "You'll find some of the best Vietnamese fare in town here." BayInsider.com

"Proof that vegetarian food can be every bit as satisfying as meat-based fare." Bay Area Citysearch

Other Info: Full service. Non-smoking. Accepts reservations but are not necessary. Accepts MC, VISA. Price: $-$$.

Directions: Near Union Square in the Tenderloin area. From I-80 coming from Oakland, take Ninth St/Civic Center exit, keep right at fork in ramp, at Harrison St turn left and go 1 block, at 9th St turn right and go a half-mile, at Hayes St turn slight left and go 2 blocks, at Van Ness Ave (US 101) turn right and go a third-mile, at Turk St turn left and go a third-mile, at Laguna St turn right and go a quarter-mile, at Geary Blvd turn right and go 2 blocks, Geary Blvd become O'Farrell St and this place is 1 block down. This place is about 1 mile north of the exit in the center of San Francisco. Parking available two blocks from the restaurant between O'Farrell St and Taylor St.

Good Life Grocery

448 Cortland Avenue; 415-648-3221
Hours: Monday to Saturday 8 am to 8 pm
Sunday 9 am to 7 pm
Natural Food Store. Deli serving ready-made salads and main dishes. Not pure vegetarian.

Other Info: Accepts AMEX, DIS, MC, VISA.
Directions: From Hwy 101 north, take Army exit to Bayshore Blvd. At Cortland turn right and this place on left. From Hwy 101 south, take Silver Ave exit and at exit turn left, then at Cortland turn left and this place on left.

Good Life Grocery

1524 20th Street; 415-282-9204
Hours: Monday to Saturday 8 am to 8 pm
Sunday 9 am to 7 pm
Natural Food Store. Deli serving ready-made sandwiches, salads and main dishes. Not pure vegetarian.
Other Info: Accepts AMEX, DIS, MC, VISA.
Directions: From Hwy 101 south, take Vermont St exit. At Vermont turn right, then at 20th St turn left and this place on left. From Hwy 101 north go south on Van Ness, at 17th St turn left, at Connecticut St turn right, at 20th St turn left and this place on left.

**Greens Restaurant

204 Bay Street; Buchanan and Marina Blvd
Fort Mason Center, Bldg A, Marina District
415-771-6222; **fax:** 415-771-3472; **Web site:** http://greensrest.citysearch.com/
Hours: Tuesday to Friday 11.30 am to 2 pm, 5.30 pm to 9.30 pm; Saturday 11:30 am to 2:30 pm, 6 pm to 9 pm (4 course fix priced dinner on Saturday evening); Sunday Brunch 10 am to 2 pm
Take-out Deli Hours: Monday to Friday 8 am to 9:30 pm; Saturday 8 am to 4:30 pm; Sunday 9:30 am to 4:30 pm
Fully Vegetarian Gourmet. American. Organic food. Vegan options, but not very vegan friendly. Some of the dishes have eggs in them. Fixed Meal on Saturday nights.
Menu: The menu changes regularly. Cannelloni Pasta (provolone and ricotta cheese with spinach and mushrooms baked in a mushroom sauce). Pizza, Mesquite-grilled Polenta and Masa Harina (a thin pancake filled with potatoes, cheddar cheese, peppers and squash). Black Bean Chili, Risotto, Pita Sandwich, Tofu Sandwich, Baked Goat Cheese, Spring Vegetables & Aioli, Ravioli, Filo and Yellow Curry. Good stews, pasta dishes, pizza, Corn Griddle Cakes, soups and salads. Has a good selection of desserts. Fresh juices.
Comments: Gets great recommendations. World famous. Very expensive vegetarian restaurant with a great atmosphere. One of the first vegetarian restaurants in California. Open since 1979. Considered to be one of the best vegetarian restaurants in the country. It is on the water with a great view of the Golden Gate Bridge. Be sure to

ask for a table by the window for a great view of the San Francisco Bay and the Golden Gate Bridge. Excellent service. Comfortable seating and pleasing atmosphere. Great place to take a long walk before or after eating. High-class place with starched tablecloths. Much of the produce that they use comes for their own farm in Marin County. Sunday brunch is recommended. Some people feel the dinners are overpriced, the food is bland and the service in nothing spectacular. Cheese used may not be vegetarian. Food is well presented. Operated by Zen Buddhists. Owned and operated by the Zen Center. In a reconverted warehouse. Romantic. Great place for a special event.

Other Info: Full service, take-out (for take-out: 415-771-6330), catering (415-705-0806). Reservations recommended (accepted up to four weeks in advance, not accepted by email). Accepts DC, DIS, MC, VISA. Price: $$-$$$. $46 per person for fixed menu on Saturday nights (just for food).

Directions: Located at the Fort Mason Center on the San Francisco Bay, in a warehouse area. It is in the northeast corner of San Francisco, 3 blocks from the water.

Harvest Ranch Market

2285 Market Street, at Noe
415-626-0805
Hours: Daily 8:30 am to 11 pm, 364 days a year.
Natural Food Store and vegan-friendly Deli. Salad Bar. Not pure vegetarian.
Menu: Wide selection of vegetarian dishes. Ready-made sandwiches, vegan baked goods and desserts. Excellent salad bar with homemade soups (4 kinds daily), pasta salads, couscous, Black Bean Salad, Marinated Mushrooms and polenta.
Comments: Wide selection of seasonal organic fruits and vegetables. Some bulk foods and herbs, but not nearly as many or as cheap as The Rainbow. Great atmosphere, very friendly, good music. Has outdoor seating in front to check out the neighborhood. Does not carry vitamins, believes should eat food instead of pills.
Other Info: Accepts AMEX, MC, VISA.
Directions: From I-80 coming from Oakland, take the Duboce Ave/Mission St exit, keep left at fork in ramp, go straight onto Duboce Ave and go a third-mile, at Market St turn slight right and this place is a half-mile down. This place is in central San Francisco.

**Herbivore – The Earthly Grill

983 Valencia Street, at 20th and Mission
415-826-5657

Hours: Monday to Thursday 11 am to 10 pm
Friday to Saturday 11 am to 11 pm
Sunday 11 am to 10 pm
Fully Vegan American. Mainly Organic. International cuisine. No dairy used.
Menu: Sandwiches, salads and entrées. The Roasted Almonds is a good starter. The sandwiches come with fries and a large salad. Some favorite sandwiches are the Veggie Burger and Charbroiled Vegetables with Pesto. Shish Kebab (with tofu or seitan), Thai Salad, Ravioli (filled with seasonal vegetables, noodles, red curry, and either tomato or basil pesto) is recommended, Baked Falafel (gets great recommendations, can add potatoes and eggplant), Kung Pao (broiled vegetables, shitake mushrooms with peanuts sauce), Pad Thai (sautéed rice noodles & tofu), and brown and basmati rice. Lasagna is made of noodles, tofu ricotta, spinach, mushrooms, zucchini and tomato sauce. Has a large selection of noodle dishes. Grilled seitan sandwich and corn on the cob. Vegan desserts. Very good chocolate cake. The lemonade is recommended, as is the roasted almonds starter. Fresh juices, teas and smoothies. Organic coffees.
Comments: Highly recommended. By far one of the best places in San Francisco. Good vegan food that is reasonably priced. Has triangular tables. Has a busy location. Good quality ingredients are used. Food tastes good and is pleasant to look at. Gets really high recommendations. Good, friendly service (may be a bit slow which people complain about). Some dishes really hot, such as the Kung Pao and Pad Thai. Good, pleasant, casual, atmosphere. A bit upscale atmosphere. Outdoor patios in front and pleasant backyard seating. Generous portions. May be a line waiting for tables, especially on weekend evenings. Cakes and pies are made at the excellent Black China Bakery in Santa Cruz. Seat yourself style.
Other Info: Full service, self-service, take-out. Non-smoking. Reservations not necessary. Accepts AMEX, MC, VISA. Price: $$.
Directions: Located on a happening block in the Mission district. There is a parking garage on 21st, between Valencia and Mission Streets. From I-80 coming from Oakland, take Ninth St/Civic Center exit, keep right at fork in ramp, turn left at Harrison St and go a third-mile, at 13th St turn right and go a quarter-mile, at S Van Ness Ave turn left and go a half-mile, at 17th St turn right and go 1 block, at Mission St turn left and go a half-mile, at 21st St turn right and go 1 block, at Valencia St turn right and this place is near the turn. This place is about a mile south of the center of town.

Indian Oven

233 Fillmore Street, at Haight St, Haight Asbury area; 415-626-1628
Hours: Daily 5 pm to 11 pm
Indian. Not pure vegetarian.
Menu: Saag Aloo (spinach and potato), Channa Masala (chickpeas with spices), samosas, papadam and rice dishes. Good Indian food. The Vegetarian Thali is good.
Comments: One of the best Indian restaurants in San Francisco. Service can be slow. Excellent atmosphere. Upscale place with white tablecloths and fresh flowers on the table. Gets good recommendations (some people don't like it). The room in the back is romantic.
Other Info: Accepts AMEX, DC, DIS, MC, VISA. Price: $$.

Jamba Juice

1700 17th Street	415-865-1100
250 Montgomery Street	415-288-9980
70 Mission Street	415-227-3725
74 New Montgomery Street	415-597-5546
152 Kearny Street	415-616-9949
22 Battery Street	415-438-3321
2014 Market Street	415-703-6011
450 Sansome Street	415-434-7393
2223 Fillmore Street	415-447-1790
1300 Ninth Avenue	415-682-2200
2066 Chestnut Street	415-563-1875
1998 Union Street	415-674-0100

Web site: www.jambajuice.com
Juice Bar. Vegan friendly. Fresh juices, smoothies and wheat grass. Organic. Adds ice cream to some of the smoothies.

**Joubert's Restaurant

4115 Judah Street, at 46th Avenue
415-753-5448
email: joubertrestaurant@yahoo.com (reservations are only accepted by phone)
Website: www.jouberts.com
Hours: Wednesday to Saturday 6 pm to 10 pm; Sunday 5 pm to 9 pm; closed Monday & Tues.
Fully Vegetarian Authentic South African. A mixture of Indian, Malaysian, Dutch and Zulu. Some Asian. Mostly Vegan.
Menu: Everything is made fresh. Apple and banana chutneys (both sweet and spicy), Avocado Pate, homemade breads and desserts. South Africa food such as Malay Sosaties (vegetarian kabobs baked in peanut sauce), Cape French Huguenot, Mieliepap Tert (Vegetarian rissoles on mieliepap topped with tomato rougaille and cheddar cheese), Cape South African Bobotie (curried lentil, nut and fruit "meatloaf" with banana chutney), Inkowane (baked Portobello mushroom with almond and garlic) and Natal Indian curries. Meals often come with sides of bredie and potjiekos (South African style beans with a spicy masala). The Portobella Mushrooms and Baked Banana are good dishes. The Bananas in Crème is a good dessert.
Comments: Friendly, attentive, personal service. May want to reserve a table near the fireplace. Pleasant atmosphere. Good food and portions. Food is well presented and unique. Displays paintings done by local artists. Many South Africans live on a vegetarian diet. Their full menu is on their Web site. Patrick, the owner and chef from South Africa, uses his grandfather's favorite recipes. A unique dining experience. Recommended. Some people don't like the place, but the uniqueness of the food can possibly affect opinions. Good music. South African cuisine uses a lot of beans. Dishes are often spiced with lemon and cilantro.
Other Info: Full service. Non-smoking. Reservations are recommended for Friday and Saturday. Parties over 10 people should call in advance. Accepts AMEX, DIS, MC, VISA. Price: $$-$$$.
Directions: Judah at 46th Avenue. In the Sunset District, two blocks south of the southwest corner Golden Gate Park, two blocks west of Ocean Beach. The location is a bit out of the way.

Just Like Home

1851 Ceasar Shavez; 415-206-1739
Hours: Monday to Friday 6 am to 6 pm
Closed Saturday & Sunday.
Mediterranean, Lebanese. Deli. Not pure veg.
Menu: Hummus, tabbouleh, falafel and baba ghanouj.
Comments: One of the best falafels in San Francisco. Has a deli counter in the front. Good value.
Other Info: Full service, take-out. Accepts AMEX, DIS, MC, VISA. Price: $.

Kam's Vegetable Restaurant

2074 Mission Street, between 15th and 16th Streets; 415-252-9193
Hours: Daily 8 am to 8 pm
Mainly Vegetarian (90%) Japanese. Salad Bar.
Menu: Salads, vegetable & miso soups, Raw Green Soybean Shake (excellent), oatmeal, vegetarian sushi, seaweed salad and Marinated Shitake Mushrooms. Fresh juices and excellent smoothies. Vegan baked goods.
Comments: Friendly place. This place is inexpensive. Very reasonably priced. Sells some food by the pound. Price: $.
Warning: The "fake crab" may not be fake, so you may want to check it out.

Directions: It is next to the 16th Street BART stop. From I-80 coming from Oakland, keep right at fork in ramp, turn left at Harrison St and go a third-mile, at 13th St turn right and go a quarter-mile, turn left at S Van Ness Ave and go a half-mile, at 17th St turn right and go 1 block, at Mission St turn right and this place is right there.

**Legume

4042 24th Street, near Noe Street
415-401-7668
Hours: Monday to Saturday 11 am to 10 pm
Sunday 11 am to 9 pm
Fully Vegetarian International.
Other Info: Full service, take-out. Accepts MC, VISA.
Directions: At 24th and Castro in Noe Valley. From I-80 coming from Oakland, take Mission St/Fell St exit, merge onto US 101 and go a half-mile, then take the Duboce Ave/Mission St exit (keep left at fork in ramp), stay straight onto Duboce Ave and go a third-mile, at Market St turn slight right and go 1 block, at Dolores St turn left and go 1¼ mile, at 24th St turn right and this place is a third-mile down. This place is about 1 mile south of the main downtown area.

**Lucky Creation Vegetarian Restaurant

854 Washington Street, between Grant & Stockton in Chinatown
415-989-0818
Hours: Thursday to Tuesday 11 am to 9:30 pm
Closed Wednesday.
Vegetarian Chinese Buddhist. Mainly Vegan.
Menu: Over twenty main dishes. Rice plates, Chinese soups, appetizers, clay pot dishes, noodle soup and pan-fried noodles. Vegetarian Almond Chicken, Sweet and Sour Pork (very good), Black Mushrooms with Chinese Vegetables, deep-fried Taro Rolls, Vermicelli, Red Bean Clay Pot, Taro Root Fish, Eggplant & Tofu Casserole, Mushroom String Bean Lo Mein Noodles and Stuffed Tofu Sheet Rolls. Has good clay pot dishes (Chinese-style hearty stew). The Braised Eggplant with Bean Sauce is very good.
Comments: Authentic Chinese vegetarian food. Delicious and reasonably priced food. Casual atmosphere. As the place is small, you may have to wait for a table, or share a table. Basic décor. Fast, friendly, efficient service. Good portions. Popular with locals.
Other Info: Full service, take-out. Accepts MC, VISA. Price: $.
Directions: This place is in northeast San Francisco in Chinatown. It is hard to find a parking spot in Chinatown.

Maharani

1122 Post St, between Polk and Van Ness Streets
415-775-1988
Hours: Sunday to Thursday 11:30 am to 2:30 pm, 5 pm to 9:30 pm; Friday & Saturday 11:30 am to 2:15 pm, 5 pm to 10 pm; Lunch buffet only on Friday
North Indian. Not pure vegetarian.
Menu: Good selection of vegetarian dishes such as Chickpeas and Spinach & Cheese.
Comments: See Berkeley for other branch. Romantic atmosphere. Seats 120 people. Elegant décor. Has plants and flowers. Low-lit place. Discounts for San Francisco Vegetarian Society members. Good place for a special event.
Other Info: Full service, take out. Non-smoking. Accepts AMEX, DC, DIS, MC, VISA. Price: $$.

Main Squeeze

1515 Polk Street; 415-567-1515
Hours: Sunday to Friday 12 noon to 10 pm
Saturday 12 noon to 11 pm
Juice Bar and Café. Not pure vegetarian.
Menu: Fresh juices, coffee, bagels, frozen yogurts, soup of the day and baked potatoes with an assortment of toppings. Vegan and vegetarian sandwiches and salads such as domas, falafel and quinoa.
Other Info: Counter service, take-out. Accepts MC, VISA. Price: $.
Directions: This place is in northeast San Francisco. From I-80 coming from Oakland, take the Fremont St exit, then at Fremont St turn left and go a third-mile, at Pine St turn left and go 1¼ mile, at Polk St turn right and this place is 1 block down.

**Millennium

246 McAllister Street, between Hyde & Larkin
415-487-9800
email: mail@millienniumrestaurant.com
Website: www.millenniumrestaurant.com
Hours: Daily 5 pm to 9:30 pm; closed Monday.
Sunday Brunch
Fully Vegetarian Gourmet International. Mostly Vegan. Macrobiotic option. Often uses organic vegetables. It is a formal place, but you can dress casually.
Menu: Thai Curry Torte Quinoa Corn Cake (sautéed cake with avocado, pistachios over chili, with a pumpkin seed pesto), Plantain Torte, Asian Style Napoleon (recommended), Madras Tofu, Millennium Steak (mock "steak"), Turkish Tempeh, Latin Roulade, Asparagus Nori Roll Salad, Plantain Torte (creamy tofu in a whole-wheat tortilla

with salsa), Grilled Smoked Portobello Mushrooms (recommended), Mariana's Roulade (spicy seitan Portobello mushroom in a crisp pastry shell), tofu bread spread and grilled vegetables. Truffle Purse is recommended. The vegan Chocolate Almond Midnight is a rich dessert that gets high recommendations. Desserts are sugar and wheat-free. Cappuccino, espresso. Serves non-alcoholic beer and wine. Some people don't like the Herbal Elixer Martini.

Comments: Upscale, gourmet place. Very good place. Gets really high recommendations. Food is organic. Good service. Uses fresh ingredients. Excellent, peaceful, elegant atmosphere. Menu changes regularly. Expensive. Service is friendly and helpful. Colorful food. Get a table downstairs if possible. Special events include cooking demonstrations, Monthly Full Moon "Aphrodisiac nights" (four course dinner made of ingredients that are supposed to be aphrodisiacs) and a night in the Abigail hotel (in which the restaurant is in) for $125. Hotel and dinner packages available. The Millennium Cookbook has over 200 recipes that are made in the restaurant. Large parties welcome, private room seats 32. All produce is organic. Many dishes are oil-free and very low in fat. In the basement of the Abigail Hotel. Seats 100 people. Romantic atmosphere. Has outdoor seating. Great place for a special event.

Reviews: "San Francisco's Hippest Vegetarian Eatery" Bill Citara, SF Bay Guardian "Vegetarian and fine dining used to be mutually exclusive terms. That changed with the opening of Millennium, one of the Bay Area's finest restaurants." United Airline's Hemispheres Magazine

Other Info: Full Service, take-out, catering. Non-smoking. Reservations highly recommended. Best to call well in advance. You can also reserve a room online. For parties of five or more you should call or email them directly. You should call between 2 pm and 10 pm to make a reservation. You can leave a message and they will call you back to confirm the reservation. Accepts AMEX, DC, MC, VISA. Price: $$$.

Directions: Downtown San Francisco, in the historical Abigail Hotel, between Larkin and Hyde Streets. Near the San Francisco public library, City Hall and the Civic Center. Street parking or an underground parking garage at McAllister and Polk. Has valet service parking ($12 for three hours). Can get directions by calling their phone number. From I-80 coming from Oakland, take Ninth St/Civic Center exit, keep right at fork in ramp, turn left at Harrison St and go 1 block, at 9th St turn right and go a half-mile, at Larkin St turn slight right and go 3 blocks, at McAllister St turn right and this place is a half-block down.

Miss Millies

4123 24th Street; 415-285-5598

Hours: Tuesday to Sunday 6 pm to 10 pm Saturday & Sunday 9 am to 2 pm

American. Vegetarian-friendly. Not pure veg.

Menu: Tofu Scramble, Roasted Potatoes, Garlic Mashed Potatoes, Macaroni & Cheese, pizzas and much more. Minty Meyer lemonade.

Comments: Has outdoor dining in the pleasant back patio. The weekend brunch is very popular. Good service and food.

Other Info: Accepts MC, VISA. Price: $.

Directions: In Noe Valley. From I-80 coming from Oakland, take Mission St/Fell St and merge onto US 101, take the Duboce Ave/Mission St exit and keep left at fork in ramp, go straight onto Duboce Ave and go a third-mile, turn slight left onto Market St and go ¾ mile, at Castro St turn slight left and go ¾ mile, at 24th St turn right and this place is a little down the block.

Mother Melba's Home Cooked Delivery

415-705-0877

email: mother@mothermelba.com; **Web site:** http://www.geocities.com/mothermelba/

Food Delivery Hours: 12:30 pm to 2:30 pm. Orders must be placed before 5 pm the day before. Give name, delivery address and phone number by voicemail or email.

Vegan Delivery Service. International cuisine.

Menu: American Chop Suey (with macaroni in marinara sauce, garlic bread, sautéed peas and carrots, chocolate chip cookies), Pot Roast (with stewed vegetables, green beans, focaccia bread, apple crisp), Barbecued Mock Chicken, potato salad, macaroni salad, salad, corn bread, Chocolate Cream Pie and Tofu Veggie Kabobs. Daily specials are grilled mock "Chicken" Caesar Salad with bread and Chicken Noodle Soup with bread.

Comments: Local organic produce used when possible. Sunday brunch parties are available by request. Price: $$.

Note: $5 off first order.

The Nature Stop

1336 Grant Avenue, in North Beach 415-398-3810

Hours: Monday to Friday 9 am to 10 pm; Saturday & Sunday 10 am to 9 pm; Deli closes half an hour before the store.

Natural Food Store and take-out Deli. Salad Bar and Juice Bar. Not pure vegetarian. Medium size

place. Bulk foods.
Other Info: Accepts MC, VISA. Counter service, take-out. No seating.
Directions: This place is in the northeast San Francisco. From I-80 coming from Oakland, take Fremont Exit West and go right on 3rd (becomes Kerny, then Columbia), then at Grant turn right and this place on right. From Hwy 101 going north, take last San Francisco exit before Bay Bridge. At 3rd turn left. Same as above.

Other Avenue Natural Food Store

3930 Judah Street, between 44th & 45th Avenue
415-661-7475; fax: 415-661-0835
email: info@otheravenues.com
Web site: www.otheravenues.com
Hours: Daily 10 am to 8 pm
Natural Food Store. Organic produce.
Menu: Ready-made sandwiches and homemade salsa
Comments: Has a wide selection of groceries. Has a bulk section with over 500 items.
Other Info: Accepts DIS, MC, VISA.
Directions: In the Outer Sunset area between 44th and 45th Avenues. Near the Muni N–Judah line.

Rainbow Grocery

1745 Folsom Street, at 13th; 415-863-0620;
email: comments@raibowgrocery.org
Web site: www.rainbowgrocery.org
Hours: Daily 9 am to 9 pm.
Natural Food Store and take-out Deli. Organic produce. Most produce is high quality.
Menu: Vegetarian and vegan soups, sandwiches, salads, beans soups, brown rice and hot dishes.
Comments: Has a wide selection of bulk grains, sea vegetables, pasta, beans, nuts, dried fruits, cooking supplies and frozen goods.
Directions: From I-80 coming from Oakland, take Ninth St/Civic Center exit, keep right at fork in ramp, at Harrison St turn left and go a third-mile, at 12th St turn right and go 1 block, at Folson St turn left and this place is 1 block down, at corner of Folsom and 13th. Store parking lot is the first right after the restaurant. This place is a half-mile west of where I-80 and Hwy 101 split. Has a parking lot.

Real Food Company

2060 Fillmore Street; 415-567-6900
Hours: Daily 9 am to 9 pm
Natural Food Store and Deli. Organic produce.
Other Info: Counter service, take-out. Outdoor seating. Accepts AMEX, MC, VISA.
Directions: From I-80 coming from Oakland,

take Ninth Street/Civic Center exit and keep right at the fork in the ramp, at Harrison St turn left and go 1 block, at 9th St turn right and go a half-mile, at Hayes St turn slight left and go 2 blocks, at Van Ness Ave turn right and go 1 mile, at Pine St turn left and go 2/3 mile, at Fillmore St turn right and this place is a half-block down.

Real Food Company

1023 Stanyan, at Carl Street in Upper Haight
415-564-2800
Hours: Daily 9 am to 9 pm
Natural Food Store and Deli. Organic produce.
Other Info: Accepts AMEX, MC, VISA.
Directions: In Haight/Asbury area, up the hill from the southeast corner of Golden Gate Park.

Real Food Company

3939 24th Street, at Noe Valley; 415-282-9500
Hours: Daily 9 am to 8 pm
Natural Food Store and Deli. Organic produce.
Other Info: Accepts AMEX, MC, VISA.
Directions: This place in Noe Valley about 1½ mile southeast of the southeast corner of Golden Gate Park. From I-80 coming from Oakland, take Mission St/Fell St exit and merge onto US-101, take the Duboce Ave/Mission St exit, keep left at fork in ramp, then stay straight onto Duboce Ave and go a third-mile, at Market St turn slight left and go 1 block, at Dolores St turn left and go 1¼ mile, then at 24th St turn right and this place is 4½ blocks down.

Real Food Company

2140 Polk Street; 415-673-7420
Hours: Daily 9 am to 9 pm
Natural Food Store and Deli (mostly vegetarian). Large selection of organic produce.
Menu: Salads, baked good and hot dishes. Large selection of breads from local bakeries.
Comments: Large selections of goods.
Other Info: Accepts AMEX, MC, VISA.
Directions: Between Broadway and Vallejo in northeast San Francisco. From I-80 coming from Oakland, take the Fremont St exit, at Fremont St turn left and go a third-mile, at Pine St turn left and go 1 block, at Sansome St turn right and go a half-block, at Broadway St turn left and go a half-mile, turn left and go through the Broadway Tunnel and go a half-mile, at Polk St turn right and this place is near the corner.

**Shangri-La Chinese Vegetarian Rest.

2026 Irving Street, between 21st Avenue and 22nd Avenue; 415-731-2548
Hours: Daily 11:30 am to 9:30 pm

Fully Vegetarian North Chinese Buddhist. Has some American dishes. Vegan options. Does not use dairy. Kosher place. Eggs are used in some dishes.
Menu: Large menu with soups, appetizers and main dishes. The Hot and Sour Soup is good. Many specials.
Comments: Food gets good recommendations. Good peaceful atmosphere. Friendly, efficient service. Reasonably priced. No MSG. Discounts for San Francisco Vegetarian Society members.
Other Info: Full service, take-out. Non-smoking. Reservations are recommended. Accepts AMEX, MC, VISA. Price: $.
Directions: In Sunset district, between 21st and 22nd Avenues, one block south of Golden Gate Park (in the middle).

Soups
784 O'Farrell Street, at Larkin Street
415-775-6406
Hours: Monday to Friday 10 am to 6:30 pm Closed Saturday & Sunday.
Soup and Salads. Not pure vegetarian. Good amount of vegetarian options.
Menu: Good selection of soups. A bowl of soups with free refill, crackers and a choice of milk, coffee or tea. Pea, potato, vegetable and lentil soups.
Comments: Friendly staff. Price: $.

Tai Chi
2031 Polk Street
415-441-6758
Hours: Mon to Thur 11:30 am to 10 pm; Fri & Sat 11:30 am to 10 pm; Sun 4 pm to 10 pm
Chinese. Not pure vegetarian.
Menu: Chinese Pancakes, stir-fries, Hot & Sour Cabbage, curry vegetables and Spring Rolls.
Comments: No décor. Full service, take-out, delivery (fast). Reservations suggested.
Other Info: Accepts AMEX, MC, VISA. Price: $-$$.

Taiwan Restaurant
445 Clement Street, at 6th Avenue
415-387-1789
Hours: Sunday to Thursday 11 am to 9:30 pm Friday & Saturday 11 am to 10:30 pm
Chinese. Not pure vegetarian.
Menu: Mock "meat" dishes, Fried Rice, Steamed Dumplings and other vegetarian dishes.
Comments: Good atmosphere. Good value.
Other Info: Full service, take-out. Accepts AMEX, MC, VISA. Price: $-$$.

Thom's Health Food Store
5843 Geary Boulevard, between 22nd & 23rd Avenues; 415-387-6367
Web site: http://thomsfoods.citysearch.com/
Hours: Daily 9 am to 7 pm
Natural Food Store. Large organic produce section.
Comments: Has a large bunk food section. Has cosmetics and books.
Other Info: Accepts ATM, MC, VISA.
Direction: In the Richmond District, in northwest San Francisco. This place is about a half-mile north of Golden Gate Park (the middle). The #38 Geary bus comes here. After going over the Golden Gate Bridge, go south on Hwy 1 and take it until it ends, then go 3 blocks south, at Geary Blvd turn right and this place is ¾ mile down (about 10 blocks).

Ti Couz
3108 16th Street, at Valencia Street
415-252-7373
Hours: Monday to Wednesday 11 am to 11 pm; Thursday to Friday 11 am to 12 midnight; Saturday 10 am to 12 midnight; Sunday 10 am to 11 pm; closed on major holidays.
French Restaurant. Not pure vegetarian.
Menu: Has over a hundred kinds of crepes. Meals usually begin with savory buckwheat crepes and end with a sweet dessert crepe. The Gruyere Cheese and Mushroom Sauce Crepe, and the Nutelia Crepe with vanilla ice cream are good. Has crepes stuffed with ice cream and hot chocolate for dessert.
Comments: This place gets good reviews. Food gets mixed reviews, so I guess that how much you like crepes can really affect your judgment. The service doesn't get high recommendation by some (they say it is slow and rude), but other like the service, so I guess it depends on whom you get. I would suggest that you choice your server if possible (as least if there is a problem, you can blame it on yourself). Seating is a bit too close together when the place is busy. Popular place. Lively atmosphere. Reasonable prices.
Other Info: Accepts MC, VISA. Does not take reservations. Price: $$.
Directions: In the Mission Area.

Tortola
3251 205h Avenue	415-566-4336
3640 Sacramento Street, between Spruce and Locust Streets	415-929-8181
50 Post Street	415-986-8678
500 Parnassus Avenue	415-731-8670

1629 Beach Street   415-563-1500
Hours: Tues to Fri 11:30 am to 2:30 pm, 5 pm to 10 pm; Sat 11:30 am to 10 pm; Sun 5 pm to 9 pm 20th Avenue branch is open daily. Sacramento Street place is closed on Monday.
Tex-Mexican, Californian, American. Not pure vegetarian.
Menu: Burritos, tacos and tostadas.
Comments: Upscale. Pleasant atmosphere. Friendly service. Does not use lard in beans.
Other Info: Full service, take-out, delivery. Accepts MC, VISA. Price: $-$$.

Thep Phanom

400 Waller Street, at Fillmore, Haight Asbury area
415-431-2526
Hours: Daily 5:30 pm to 10:30 pm
Closed on major holidays.
Thai. Not pure vegetarian.
Menu: Has more than 10 main vegetarian dishes. Good Param Pak, Spinach & Tofu in a peanut sauce and Choo-Chee Tofu Curry.
Comments: Considered by many to be the top Thai restaurant in town. Some people do not like the place at all. Often full. Pleasant, casual, informal atmosphere. A bit upscale with tablecloths and fresh flowers. Exotic, comfortable place.
Other Info: Reservations recommended. Accepts AMEX, DC, DIS, MC, VISA. Price: $$.

Trader Joe's

555 9th Street, at Brannan   415-863-1292
3 Masonic Avenue   415-346-9964
299 Valencia Street   415-626-6363

Valencia Whole Foods

999 Valencia;   415-285-0231
Hours: Daily 9 am to 9 pm
Natural Food Store. Organic produce
Other Info: Accepts AMEX, MC, VISA.
Directions: From I-280 south, take San Jose exit (becomes Guerrero St), at 21st St turn right. This place at corner of 21st and Valencia. From I-101 north, take Lombard St exit and at Van Ness turn right, then at Mission turn right, at 21st turn right. Same as Above.

**Vegi Food

1820 Clement Street, near 19th Avenue
415-387-8111
Hours: Tuesday 11 am to 9 pm; Friday & Saturday 11 am to 9:30 pm; Sunday 11 am to 9 pm; closed Monday.
Vegetarian Chinese. Has some American dishes. Does not use eggs, MSG, onions or garlic.
Menu: Mock "meat" dishes, brown rice and veg-

etable dishes. Sweet & Sour Walnuts is popular.
Comments: Friendly service.
Other Info: Full service, take-out. Accepts MC, VISA. Price: $-$$.
Directions: In the Richmond District, in northwest San Francisco. This place is about a half-mile north of Golden Gate Park (the middle). After going over the Golden Gate Bridge, go south on Hwy 1 and take it until it ends, then go 2 blocks south, at Clements St turn right and this place is 6 blocks down.

Vicolo Pizzeria

201 Ivy Street, by Van Ness
415-863-2382; **Web site:** www.vicolopizza.com
Hours: Monday to Thursday 11:30 am to 2 pm, 5 pm to 9 pm; Friday: 11:30 am to 2 pm, 5 pm to 10 pm; Saturday 12 noon to 10:30 pm; Sun 12 noon to 9 pm; closed only on major holidays.
Pizza Place. Not pure vegetarian.
Menu: Good salads, vegetarian soups, and corn meal and wheat crust pizzas. Non-alcoholic beer. Sun-dried tomatoes, fresh basil and shitakes mushrooms.
Comments: Some of the best pizzas in San Francisco. Pizzas get really high recommendations.
Other Info: Counter service, take-out. Accepts MC, VISA. Price: $$.
Directions: Cross streets are Franklin and Gough.

Wheatgrass Grower's Farm and Depot

1785 5th Street; 415-864-3001
Menu: Serves wheatgrass juice with Rejuvalac chasers.
Comments: Has happy hour Wednesday and Friday 4 pm to 6 pm. Wheatgrass has a high amount of vitamins and high quality chlorophyll. Wheatgrass is healthy according to Ayurvedic medicine. The Rejuvalac contains enzymes that help break down chlorophyll.

Whole Foods Market

1765 California Street
415-674-0500
Hours: Daily 8 am to 10 pm
Natural Food Store and Cafe. Deli, Bakery, Salad Bar and Juice Bar. Organic produce. Supermarket-type place. See Whole Foods Market information.
Directions: This place is a mile north of the main downtown area. Go across Golden Gate Bridge taking Hwy 101 bearing first to the left and then bear to the right, at Divisadero St turn right and go 1 mile south, then at California turn left and this place is 1¼ mile down. Has parking right there on right.

Wu Kong Restaurant
101 Spear Street; 415-957-9300
Hours: Monday to Friday 11 am to 3 pm, 5:30
pm to 9:30 pm; Saturday & Sunday 10 am to 3
pm, 5:30 pm to 9:30 pm
Chinese. Not pure vegetarian.
Menu: Tofu and vegetable dishes. "Vegetable
Goose" is stuffed tofu and mushrooms.
Other Info: Full service, take-out. Accepts
AMEX, DC, MC, VISA. Price: $$.

SANTA ROSA

East West Restaurant
2323 Sonoma Avenue; 707-546-6142
Hours: Tuesday to Saturday 8 am to 9 pm
Sunday & Monday 8 am to 8 pm
Natural International Foods. Macrobiotic and
Vegan options. Not pure vegetarian.
Menu: Has International and Middle Eastern
foods, hummus, falafel, burrito, stir-fry and pas-
tas. Fresh juices, smoothies, non-dairy shakes and
desserts.
Other Info: Accepts DIS, MC, VISA. Price: $$.
Directions: In a shopping center. From US 101,
take the Rte12 exit towards Sonoma, then go 1
mile east on Rte 12, then at Farmers Lane (Rte
12) turn left and go 0.65 mile, then turn right at
Sonoma Ave and this place is at the corner.

Fresh Choice
277 Santa Rosa Plaza; 707-525-0912
Hours: Daily 11 am to 9 pm
American. Not pure vegetarian.
Menu: Has a large choice of salads. Has a veg-
etarian soup and vegetarian pasta. A set price in-
cludes a bread and dessert.
Other Info: Counter service, take-out. Accepts
MC, VISA. Price: $$.

Santa Rosa Community Market
1899 Mendocino Avenue; 707-546-1806
Hours: Monday to Saturday. 9 am to 9 pm
Sunday 10 am to 8 pm
Natural Food Store and take-out Deli. Has a large
selection of herbal medicines and spices. Good
amount of organic produce.
Menu: Has ready-made sandwiches and salads.
Other Info: Accepts MC, VISA.
Directions: From Hwy 101, take Steele Lane/
Guerneville Rd exit, then go east on Steele Lane
a half-mile, then at Mendocino Ave turn right
and this place on left a third-mile down. Behind
a Judo school.

Trader Joe's
3225 Cleveland Avenue, north of Piner Road
707-525-1406

Whole Foods Market
1181 Yulupa Avenue; 707-575-7915
Hours: Daily 8 am to 9 pm
Natural Food Store and Cafe. Deli, Bakery,
Salad Bar and Juice Bar. Organic produce. Su-
permarket-type place. See Whole Foods Market
information.
Directions: From Hwy 101, exit at Hwy 12 east.
Then go east on Hwy 12 for 1½ mile (becomes
Hoen), at Yulupa turn left and this place on left a
third-mile down.

SARATOGA

Natural Instincts
14435 Big Basin Way; 408-867-9670
Natural Food Store.
Hours: Monday to Friday 11 am to 6 pm; Satur-
day 11 am to 5 pm; closed Sunday.

SAUSALITO

Real Food Company
200 Calendonia Street; 415-332-9640
Hours: Daily 8 am to 9 pm
Natural Food Store. Organic produce.
Menu: Has ready-made sandwiches and salads.
Other Info: Accepts AMEX, MC, VISA.
Directions: From Hwy 101 south, take Sausalito
exit, and head south on Bridgeway. When it forks
go right onto Caledonia. This place on left at
Caledonia and Turney.

SEBASTOPOL

Andy's Produce & Natural Food Market
1691 Gravenstein Hwy N
707-823-8661
Hours: Daily 8:30 am to 7 pm
Natural Food Store. Organic produce.

East West Bakery and Café
128 North Main Street; 707-829-2822
Hours: Monday to Friday 7:30 to 9 pm; Satur-
day 8 am to 9 pm; Sunday 8 am to 8 pm
Café and Bakery. Mainly vegetarian. Homemade
non-dairy ice cream.
Menu: Has a wide selection of vegetarian dishes.
Soups, salads, sandwiches and hot dishes.
Other Info: Accepts AMEX, MC, VISA.

**Slice of Life

6970 McKinley Street, downtown next to Food for Thought; 707-829-6627

Hours: Tuesday to Thursday 11:30 am to 9 pm; Friday 11:30 am to 10 pm; Saturday 11 am to 10 pm; Sunday 11 am to 9 pm; closed Monday.

Fully Vegetarian International. Mostly Vegan. American, Italian and Mexican. Vegan and Macrobiotic options.

Menu: Has over sixty dishes on the menu. Soups, salads, sandwiches, veggie burgers, fat-free fries (air-baked), hot dogs, main dishes, smoothies, vegan muffin and good tasting vegan desserts. Daily specials are usually vegan. Vegan breakfasts served all day. Has organic wheat-crust pizzas that can be made with a choice of real or tofu cheese (or no cheese at all). Pizza can be ordered by the slice. Non-alcoholic beer and wine.

Comments: Opened in 1974. They have organic pastas that don't contain eggs or oil. Family run, friendly placed. Good service. Casual. Reasonably priced.

Other Info: Full service, catering, take-out. Non-smoking. No credit cards. Price: $-$$.

Directions: In downtown Sebastopol, across from the new downtown park. Right off Hwy 116. Parking lot next to the restaurant.

Whole Foods Market

6910 McKinley Street; 707-829-9801
email: Joe.Rogoff@wholefoods.com
Web site: www.wholefoodsmarket.com
Hours: Monday to Saturday 8 am to 9 pm
Sunday 9 am to 8 pm
Houseware Store Hours: Monday to Saturday 10 am to 7 pm; Sunday 11 am to 5 pm
Natural Food Store and Cafe. Deli, Bakery, Salad Bar and Juice Bar. Organic produce. Supermarket-type place. See Whole Foods Market information.
Directions: From Hwy 101, take Hwy 12 exit, then go west on Hwy 12 towards Sebastapol about 5 miles. In town, turn right at Petaluma Ave and go 1 block, at McKinley turn left and this place is a half-block down.

SONOMA

East West Restaurant

2323 Sonoma Avenue, Farmer Lane, in Montgomery Village; 707-546-6142
Hours: Daily 8 am to 9 pm
Natural Food Restaurant. Not pure vegetarian.
Menu: Soups, sandwiches and salads.
Other Info: Accepts DIS, MC, VISA. Full service, take-out. Casual place.

SUNNYVALE

**Bhavika's

1053 East El Camino Real, Suite 2, at Henderson
408-243-2118
Hours: Tuesday to Saturday 11 am to 9:30 pm; Sunday 9 am to 9 pm; closed Monday.
Vegetarian North Indian.
Menu: Has North Indian main dishes, samosa, snacks and Indian sweets.
Comments: Casual place. Has a few tables to sit at. Fast service.
Other Info: Counter service, take-out. Price: $.
Directions: It is located in shopping center behind a Carl's Jr. From I-280, take Lawrence Exwy and go north 2 miles, take the El Camino Real exit, then go west on El Camino Real (Rte 82) and this place is a half-mile down.

**Chaat House

839 East El Camino Real
408-733-9000
Hours: Daily 11:30 am to 9:30 pm
Vegetarian Indian.
Menu: Soups, dal, samosa, Indian breads, and lunch and dinner thalis.
Comments: Reasonably priced place. Has indoor and outdoor seating.
Other Info: Accepts AMEX, MC, VISA. Price: $. Counter service, take-out.

The Country Gourmet & Co

1314 South Mary Avenue
408-733-9446
Hours: Monday to Friday 7 am to 8:30 pm; Saturday 8 am to 9 pm; Sunday 8 am to 8:30 pm
Natural Foods. Vegan options. Not pure veg.
Menu: A large selection of salads, sandwiches, fresh baked goods, pastas, Mexican dishes and main dishes that change daily. Each night there are a couple of vegetarian specials. Kid's menu. Fresh juices. Some organic dishes.
Comments: Uses fresh ingredients that do not contain MSG or preservatives. Pleasant atmosphere. Popular with the locals.
Other Info: Limited service, take-out. Non-smoking. Accepts MC, VISA. Price: $$.
Directions: From Hwy 85, go east on W Fremont Ave ¾ mile, then at South Mary Ave turn right and this place is 50 yards down.

Fresh Choice (two locations)

Cala Center, 1105 West El Camino
408-732-7788
Moffett Park, 333 Moffet Park Drive
408-734-0661

**Great Veggie Land
562 South Murphy Avenue, at Hwy 82
408-735-8040
Hours: Monday to Saturday 11:30 am to 2:30
pm, 5 pm to 9 pm; Sunday 5 pm to 8:30 pm
Vegetarian Chinese.
Comments: Good food at reasonable prices. The
dumplings and veggie sushi are good.
Other Info: Accepts AMEX, DIS, MC, VISA.
Directions: From Hwy 85, take the El Camino
Real exit and go east on El Camino Real for 1¼
mile, at South Murphy Ave turn left and this place
is 50 yards down.

Hobee's Restaurant
800 Ahwanee Avenue; 408-524-3580
Web site: www.hobees.com.
Hours: Daily 8 am to 9 pm
Mexican and International restaurant chain.
Salad Bar. Not pure vegetarian.
Menu: Veggie patties, Mexican dishes and black
bean chili. Fresh juices.
Other Info: Full table service, take-out. Accepts
MC, VISA. Price: $$.

**Komala Vilas
1020 East El Camino Real; 408-733-7400; **fax:**
408-733-7880; **email:** sn@komalavilas.com
Web site: www.komalavilas.com
Hours: Wed to Mon 8:30 am to 11 am, 11:30
am to 2:30 pm, 5 pm to 10 pm; closed Tues.
Fully Vegetarian. Lunch for $8
Price: Has set meals for breakfast and lunch and
a la carte for dinner. Idly, dosas, Masala Dosa, vadai,
pongal, upma, sambhar, coconut chutney and
kichari.
Other Info: Counter service, take-out. Place or-
der at counter then pick it up. Accepts MC, VISA.
Directions: At the intersection of El Camino &
Henderson. From Hwy 101, take the N Lawrence
Exwy exit and go south on N Lawrence Exwy
2½ miles, then take the El Camino Real/Rte 82
exit, then go west on El Camino Real and this
place is a half-mile down.

**Panchavati Indian Vegetarian Rest.
460 Persian Drive; 408-734-9335
Hours: Monday to Friday 11:30 am to 2 pm, 5
pm to 8 pm; Saturday & Sunday 11 am to 8 pm
Fully Vegetarian Indian.
Other Info: Full service, take-out. Accepts MC,
VISA. Price: $.
Directions: From Hwy 237, take the Fair Oaks
Avenue exit and this place is a block west of the
exit.

Piccadilly Circus
1265 South Mary Street; 408-730-1310
Hours: Daily 9 am to 9 pm
Natural Food Store and Cafe. Deli, Bak-
ery, Salad Bar and Juice Bar. Organic produce.
Supermarket-type place.
Directions: From I-280, head north on Hwy 85,
then take the Freemont Rd ramp and go east on
(turn right) Fremont Ave a half-mile, then turn
left at South Mary St and this place on left corner,
1 block down.

Sneha Indian
1214 Apollo Way #404B; 408-736-2720
Hours: Daily 11 am to 3 pm, 5 pm to 10 pm
Indian. Vegetarian-friendly. Not pure vegetarian.
Menu: South and North Indian. Has all-you-can-
eat meal.
Comments: Good food. Very popular. Spacious
place. Good place for a private party and for
groups.
Other Info: Accepts MC, VISA. Price: $-$$.
Directions: Off Lawrence Expressway.

Taj India
889 East El Camino Real; 408-720-8396
Hours: Daily 11:30am to 2:30pm, 5:30pm to 10pm
India. Vegetarian-friendly. Not pure vegetarian.
Comments: Good food and service. Reasonably
priced. Gets good recommendations.
Other Info: Accepts AMEX, MC, VISA.

**Udupi Palace
976 East El Camino Real; 408-830-9600
Hours: Mon to Thur 11:30 am to 2:30 pm, 5:30
pm to 10 pm; Fri & Sat 11:30 am to 2:30 pm,
5:30 pm to 11 pm; Sun 11:30 am to 11 pm
Pure Vegetarian South Indian.
Menu: Dosa, Masala Dosa, idly, sambhar and rice.
Other Info: Accepts MC, VISA.
Directions: From I-280, head north on Hwy 85,
then take the Freemont Rd ramp and go east on
(turn right) Fremont Ave (becomes El Camino
Real) and this place is 1½ mile down.

**Udupi Palace
1146 East El Camino Real; 408-746-9583
Hours: Monday to Friday 11:30 am to 2 pm, 5
pm to 9:30 pm; Sat & Sun 11:30 am to 11 pm
Pure Vegetarian South Indian.
Menu: Dosa, Masala Dosa, idly, sambar and rice.
Other Info: Accepts MC, VISA.
Directions: From I-280, head north on Hwy 85,
then take the Freemont Rd ramp and go east on
(turn right) Fremont Ave and this place is 1½

mile down. From Hwy 101, take the N Lawrence Exwy exit and go south on N Lawrence Exwy 2½ miles, then take the El Camino Real/Rte 82 exit, then go west on El Camino Real and this place is a quarter-mile down.

WALNUT CREEK

Whole Foods Market

1333 East Newell, at Broadway; 925-274-9700

Hours: Daily 8 am to 10 pm

Natural Food Store and Cafe. Deli, Bakery, Salad Bar and Juice Bar. Organic produce. Supermarket-type place. See Wild Oats Market information.

Directions: Across from Macy's (Broadway Plaza). From I-680, take Mt Diablo Blvd exit, and go east on Mt Diablo Blvd for 0.65 mile, at S Main St turn right and go a third-mile, at Newell Ave turn left and go 2 blocks.

Colorado

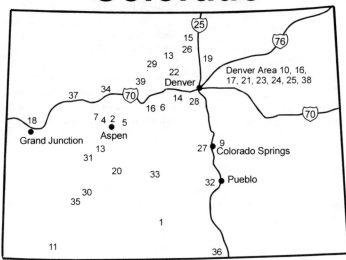

Vegetarian Society of Colorado – Denver, P.O. Box 6773, Denver, CO 80206; 303-777-4828, or 303-363-9581. Online vegetarian dining guide for Colorado, by city. Branches in Boulder, Denver, Durango, Evergreen, Ft. Collins Grand Junction and Pikes Peak.

ALAMOSA

Valley Food Co-op
7365 West Highway 160 #5; 719-589-5727
Hours: Monday to Saturday 9 am to 6 pm Closed Sunday.
Natural Food Store.
Directions: In Villa Mall, just west of Alamosa on Hwy 160.

ASPEN

**Explore Bookstore & Café
221 East Main Street; 970-925-5338
Hours: Daily 10 am to 9 pm (if it is slow may close at 7 pm)
Vegetarian Gourmet European-style Bistro. Has a high-end vegetarian cuisine. Vegan options.
Menu: Has a large selection of good vegetarian dishes. There is a daily international vegetarian special. Soups, salads, sandwiches, steamed vegetable, pastas, tofu burger and other dishes. Has a kid's menu.
Comments: In a contemporary bookstore in a Victorian house. Has good views of the mountains.

Other Info: Full service, take-out. Accepts AMEX, MC, VISA. Price: $$.
Directions: This place is in downtown Aspen on the main street in town.

Mountain Natural's
316B Aspen Airport Business Center
970-925-5502
Hours: Monday to Friday 8 am to 6 pm; Saturday 10 am to 5 pm; closed Sunday.
Natural Food Store and Deli. Bakery, Salad Bar and Juice Bar. Organic produce.
Menu: Three different soups, wraps, sandwiches, nori rolls, pizzas, salads and a daily special.
Other Info: Accepts MC, VISA. Counter service, take-out. Has counter seating (no tables).
Directions: This place is just off Hwy 82, next to the Amoco gas station, which you can see from the road. It is 2 miles northwest of the downtown, opposite the airport.

AURORA (Denver Suburb)

Maruti Gourmet Coffee and Café
12200 East Cornell Avenue; 303-745-4511
Hours: Daily 11 am to 3 pm, 5 pm to 10 pm
Indian. Vegan options. Not pure vegetarian.
Menu: Mainly South Indian. Everything is freshly cooked.
Comments: Food is very good. Cooks with oil, and not with ghee. Price: $.
Directions: From I-225, take Exit #4 and go west on S Parker Rd a quarter-mile, then at S Peoria St turn right and go a quarter-mile, then at E Cornell Ave turn right and this place is a block down.

Wild Oats Market
12131-F East Iliff Avenue; 303-695-8801
Hours: Daily 7 am to 11 pm
Natural Food Store and Cafe. Deli, Bakery, Salad Bar and Juice Bar. Organic produce. Supermarket-type place. See Wild Oats Market information.
Menu: Salads, baked goods and international specials. Fresh juices. Espresso.
Other Info: Counter service, take-out. Accepts DIS, MC, VISA. Price: $.
Directions: From I-225, take Iliff Ave exit (#5) and go west on Iliff 1¾ miles, then this place is on the corner of Peoria and Iliff.

BASALT

Bistro Basalt
202 Midland Avenue; 970-927-2682
Hours: Daily 11 am to 10 pm

New American Restaurant. Not pure vegetarian.
Menu: Emphasizes pastas. Sandwiches, some veggie soups (best to ask about) and salads.
Comments: Sometimes has live music.
Other Info: Full service, take-out. Reservations suggested. Accepts AMEX, MC, VISA. Price: $$.

BOULDER
Cjattaiqua Park and Settler's Park are good places for hiking.

Boulder Salad CO
2595 Canyon Boulevard; 303-447-8272
Hours: Monday to Saturday 10:30 to 9 pm
Sunday 11 am to 8 pm
American. Soup and Salad Bar.
Menu: Has over seventy dishes in the salad bar and sandwiches, baked potatoes, pasta dishes and freshly made soups.
Comments: Buffet is for a set price. Has several outdoor tables.
Other Info: Counter service, take-out. Accepts AMEX, DC, DIS, MC, VISA. Price: $$.

The Buff
1725 28th Street; 303-442-9150
Hours: Daily 6:30 am to 2 pm
Natural Foods. Not pure vegetarian.
Menu: This place has many vegetarian dishes. Fresh juices.
Comments: Often have to wait for 15 minutes for a table on the weekends.
Other Info: Full service, take-out. Accepts MC, VISA. Price: $-$$.
Directions: From US-36 going from Denver to Boulder US-36 becomes 28th St and this place is a few blocks down after entering town.

Chautauqua Dining Hall
900 Baseline Road, at 9th Street
303-440-3776; **fax:** 303-440-0926
Hours: Tuesday to Saturday 5:30 pm to 9 pm; Saturday 8 am to 2 pm; Sunday 8 am to 2 pm; closed Monday.
Menu: Has a limited vegetarian selection. Vegetarian Filet Mignon and Grilled Vegetables.
Comments: Children's menu. Has various classes such as Ashtanga Yoga classes and music classes. Has special banquet rooms. Busy during the summer, especially the weekend brunch. Buffet brunch on Saturday. Beautiful setting.
Other Info: Full service, take-out, catering. Has indoor and popular outdoor seating on the porch. Dinner reservations in the winter, but no reservations in the summer, first come, first served. Accepts AMEX, MC, VISA. Price: $$$.

Daddy's Boy

2100 Central Avenue; 303-443-8855
Hours: Monday to Friday 7 am to 2 pm
Closed Saturday and Sunday.
Cafeteria. Salad Bar. Not pure vegetarian.
Menu: Has vegetarian options including soups, salads, sandwiches, baked goods and specials. Fresh juices.
Comments: Upscale cafeteria.
Other Info: Accepts MC, VISA. Price: $$.

Dot's Diner

1333 Broadway Street, at University
303-447-9184
2716 28th Street; 303-449-1323
Hours: Monday 8 am to 2 pm; Tuesday to Friday 7 am to 2 pm; Saturday & Sunday 8 am to 2 pm
Natural Foods.
Menu: Homemade breakfasts, salads, sandwiches, grilled sandwiches, Mexican dishes and tofu and tempeh dishes. Fresh juices. Cappuccino, espresso.
Other Info: Full service, take-out. No credit cards accepted. Price: $.

Falafel King

1314 Pearl Street; 303-449-9321
Hours: Monday to Friday 10 am to 8 pm; Saturday 11 am to 9 pm; Sunday 11 am to 7 pm
Falafel Place. Middle Eastern. Not pure vegetarian.
Menu: Has falafel, tabbouleh and baba ghanouj. Fresh squeezed lemonade.
Other Info: Accepts MC, VISA.

Himalaya's

2010 14th Street, at Pearl, next to the Boulder Theater, one block from City Hall
303-442-3230
Hours: Sun to Thur 11 am to 2 pm, 5 pm to 9:30 pm; Fri & Sat 11 am to 2 pm, 5 pm to 10 pm
Nepali, Indian, Tibetan. Not pure vegetarian.
Menu: Has a good selection of Nepali, Tibetan and Indian food. Has a lunch buffet that includes several vegetarian dishes such as vegetable pakoras, dal, rice, Naan, Aloo Saag and Indian desserts. Bakes their breads in a Tandoori over.
Comments: The staff often doesn't speak much English.
Other Info: Full service, take-out. Non-smoking. Accepts AMEX, DIS, MC, VISA. Price: $$.

Ideal Market

1275 Alpine Avenue; 303-443-1354
Hours: Monday to Saturday 7 am to 10 pm
Sunday 8 am to 9 pm

Natural Food Store and Café. Deli, Bakery and Salad Bar.
Comments: Owned by Wild Oats.
Directions: From Denver take I-36 and it becomes 28th Street when you enter Boulder. At Canyon Blvd turn left and go about 15 blocks (1¼ mile), then at Broadway turn right and this place is ¾ mile (9 blocks) down in a plaza at the intersection of Alpine and Broadway.

Jalino's Pizza

1647 Arapahoe Avenue, at junction with 17th
303-443-6300
Hours: Sunday to Thursday 9 am to 1 am
Friday & Saturday 9 am to 2 am
Pizza Place. Not pure vegetarian. Has soy cheese pizzas.
Menu: Has many different toppings and a vegan pizza with soy cheese. Good sandwiches, Calzone, Veggie Lasagna and Pesto Pizza.
Comments: One of the best pizza places in Boulder.
Other Info: Full service, mainly take-out, catering. Has a few stools to seat on. Accepts AMEX, MC, VISA. Price: $.
Directions: Across from Bolder High School.

Jose Muldoon's

1600 38th Street
303-449-4543
Hours: Monday to Thursday 11 am to 10 pm; Friday & Saturday 11 am to 11 pm; Sunday Brunch 10 am to 10 pm
Mexican. Vegan options. Not pure vegetarian.
Menu: Authentic Mexican food. Has vegetarian dishes including soups, salads, burritos, sandwiches, tostada bar, veggie burgers and other dishes.
Other Info: Full service, take-out. Accepts AMEX, DC, MC, VISA. Price: $-$$.

Juices Wild

1433 Pearl Street; 303-541-0897
Hours: Monday to Friday 7:30 am to 5 pm; Saturday 10 am to 5 pm; Sunday 10 am to 4 pm
Juice Bar.
Menu: Has a good selection of vegetarian dishes. Has soups, sandwiches and salads. Fresh juices and smoothies.
Directions: From Denver take I-36 and it becomes 28th Street when you enter Boulder. At Canyon Blvd turn left and go about 14 blocks (1¼ miles), then turn right at 15th St and go 2 blocks, then turn right at Pearl St and this place is near the corner.

Mij Bani Indian Restaurant

2005 18th Street; 303-442-7000
Hours: Tuesday to Sunday 11 am to 2:30 pm,
5:30 pm to 10:30 pm; closed Monday.
Indian. South Indian, Gujarati & American.
Mainly Vegan. Buffet Lunch. Not pure veg.
Menu: Has excellent food. The dosas and idly
are recommended. Utappan, Pav Bhaji and Gajar
Halava (sweetened mashed carrots).
Comments: Good food. Service is a bit slow. The
buffet lunch is a good value. Has on the floor
seating on cushions.
Other Info: Full service, take-out. Accepts
AMEX, MC, VISA. Price: $-$$.

Moe's Broadway Bagel

2650 Broadway Street	303-444-3252
3075 Arapahoe Avenue	303-442-4427
1116 13th Street	303-448-9064

550 Grant Street, Unit D, Denver
303-733-7331
Hours: Daily 6 am to 6 pm
Bagel Place. Not pure vegetarian.
Menu: Has a cracked wheat bagel. Has cream
cheese, cheddar cheese, sun-dried tomato and
chilies to put on the bagels.
Comments: Popular places.

Mountain Sun Pub & Brewery

1535 Pearl Street, at 15th; 303-546-0886
Hours: Monday to Saturday 11:30 am to 1 am
Sunday 12 noon to 2 am
American. Not pure vegetarian. Mainly a bar but
also sells food.
Menu: Has a good selection of vegetarian dishes.
Veggie burgers, good French fries, hummus, salads and burritos.
Comments: Popular with hippies, mountain bikers and others. Plays plenty of Dead tunes. Has
free live music on Saturday or Sunday nights such
as acid jazz or bluegrass. A nice, relaxing place
with an excellent staff. No smoking or TVs. Price:
$$.
Directions: From Denver take I-36 and it be-
comes 28th Street when you enter Boulder. At
Canyon Blvd turn left and go about 14 blocks
(1¼ miles), then turn right at 15th St and go 2
blocks, then turn right at Pearl St and this place
is half-way down the block.

Mustard's Last Stand

1719 Broadway, Arapahoe Avenue
303-444-5841
American Fast Foods. Vegan options. Not pure
vegetarian. See Denver.

Pressto Sandwiches (two branches)

1035 Walnut, corner of 11th; 303-444-6786
Hours: Monday to Friday 8 am to 6 pm; Satur-
day 9 am to 5 pm; closed Sunday.
Italian Sandwich Place. Fast Foods. Not pure
vegetarian.
Menu: Has a selection of vegetarian sandwiches.
Has whole wheat and white focaccia bread.
Comments: Has quick service. Has outdoor seat-
ing.
Other Info: Non-smoking. Accepts AMEX, DIS,
MC, VISA.

Ras Kassa's Ethiopian

2111 30th Street, between Pearl & Walnut
303-447-2919; **Web site:** www.raskassas.com
Hours: Daily 5 pm to 10 pm
Ethiopian. Not pure vegetarian.
Menu: Has a good selection of vegetarian Ethio-
pian dishes such as Special Mushrooms, Grilled
Vegetable Stew, Spicy Sweet Potato Stew, Spicy
Organic Red Lentils, Butternut Squash Stew,
Beets & Potatoes, Yellow Split Peas, Farmer's
Cheese and a Combination Vegetable Plate.
Comments: One of the best Ethiopian restau-
rants in Colorado. Very popular and may have to
wait. Reasonably priced. No forks. Has live Afri-
can music. Accepts AMEX, MC, VISA.

Rocky Mountain Joe's Café

Second Floor, 1410 Pearl Street, at 15th Boulder
303-442-3969
Hours: Monday to Friday 7 am to 2 pm
Saturday & Sunday 7 am to 2:30 pm
Natural Foods. Not pure vegetarian.
Menu: Huevos Rancheros with a vegetarian chili.
Tofu Scramble, Garden Burgers, salads, tempeh
burgers and some breakfast dishes. Fresh juices,
cappuccino, espresso.
Comments: It is named after the 19th century
photographer who took thousands of pictures of
Boulder. There are photos of pioneers of Boulder
on the walls. Roses at each table.
Other Info: Full service, take-out. Non-smoking.
Accepts DIS, MC, VISA. Price: $.
Directions: From Denver take I-36 and it be-
comes 28th Street when you enter Boulder. At
Canyon Blvd turn left and go about 14 blocks
(1¼ mile), then turn right at 15th St and go 2
blocks, then turn right at Pearl St and this place
is at the corner.

Royal Peacock

5290 Arapahoe Avenue, at 55th Street
303-447-1409

Hours: Monday to Friday 11:30 am to 2:30 pm, 5:30 pm to 10:30; Saturday 5:30 pm to 10:30 pm; Sunday 5 pm to 10 pm
Indian. Not pure vegetarian.
Menu: Has many vegetarian options including Malai Koftas, rice dishes, paratha and Indian curries. Has fresh mint and pomegranate sauces.
Comments: Has outdoor dining.
Other Info: Full service, take-out, delivery. Non-smoking. Accepts AMEX, DC, DIS, MC, VISA.

Rudi's World Cuisine

4720 Table Mesa Drive; 303-494-5858
Hours: Tuesday to Sunday 11:30 am to 2:30 pm, 5 pm to 9 pm; Sunday 9 am to 2 pm, 5 pm to 9 pm; closed Monday. Saturday and Sunday Brunch.
International including Indian, Thai, Asian, American and Middle Eastern. Vegetarian-friendly. Bakery and Espresso Bar.
Menu: Thai Vegetable Curry in a coconut sauce. Saag Panir is spinach and fresh cheese. Spanalopita is filo stuffed with feta cheese & spinach. Desserts that are vegan are marked with a "V." All food is freshly made on the premises.
Comments: Gourmet dishes. Local organic produce used when possible. Healthy foods. Romantic, offbeat place. Good service. Has outdoor seating.
Other Info: Full service, take-out, catering. Non-smoking. Accepts DC, DIS, MC, VISA. Price: $$.
Directions: This place is in south Boulder. From Hwy 36, take Foothills Pkwy exit/CO Rte 157, keep right at fork in ramp, then go left onto S Boulder Rd (becomes Table Mesa Dr) and this place is a half-mile west of Hwy 36.

Rhumba

950 Pearl Street; 303-442-7771
Hours: Monday to Wednesday 4 pm to 10 pm; Thursday to Saturday 4 pm to 10 pm; Sunday 3 pm to 9 pm
Caribbean Island. African and South American influences. Not pure vegetarian.
Menu: Has three vegetarian special dishes each night. Yucca mashed potatoes and fried plantains. Yam fries are really good. Vegetable Curries.
Comments: Has live music on the weekends. Indoor and outdoor dining. One of the best restaurants in Boulder. Very popular on the weekends. Live music such as Reggae or jazz on Sunday 3 pm to 6 pm.
Other Info: Accepts AMEX, DC, DIS, MC, VISA. Price: $$$.

Siamese Plate & Sumida's Sushi Bar

1575 Folsom; 303-447-9718
Hours: Daily 11:30 am to 2:30 pm, 5 pm to 10 pm
Thai. Not pure vegetarian.
Menu: Has a good selection of vegetarian dishes including soups, appetizers and main dishes. Many of the dishes can be made vegetarian.
Comments: A really good place. Good atmosphere. Can be hard to find a parking spot.
Other Info: Full service, take-out. Non-smoking. Accepts AMEX, MC, VISA. Price: $$.

Sunflower

1701 Pearl Street; 303-440-0220
Hours: Mon to Fri 11 am to 2:30 pm, 5 pm to 10 pm; Sat & Sun 10 am to 2:30 pm, 5 pm to 10 pm
International Healthy Food. Macrobiotic options. Not pure vegetarian (serves seafood and chicken).
Menu: Has a good selection of vegetarian dishes. Tempeh Scalloppini, bread & yambutter and good vegan desserts.
Comments: Has a beautiful interior. Upscale place. Reasonably priced. Uses organic produce when possible. Does not use ingredients with preservatives. Has an all-you-can-eat Buffet. Romantic setting. Casual and happening atmosphere. Uses unrefined sea salt, filtered water, unrefined sugar and does not use aluminum pots. Good, friendly service.
Other Info: Accepts MC, VISA. Price: $$$-$$$$.
Directions: See directions for other Pearl Street restaurants.

Turley's

2350 Arapahoe Avenue, at 28th Street; 303-442-2800; Web site: http://turleys.citysearch.com/
Hours: Monday to Saturday 6:30 am to 9 pm Sunday 7 am to 9 pm
Natural Foods. Vegan options. Not pure vegetarian. Healthy foods.
Menu: Tofu Scramble, Tofu Salad, fresh salads, wraps, homemade granola, pasta, Vegetarian Lasagna, Thai Tofu & Vegetables, and Tempeh Cutlet with Mashed Potatoes. The Black Bean Chili is recommended. Fresh juices, wheatgrass and smoothies. Chai and cinnamon spice teas.
Comments: Comfortable place. Skylights. Good service. Breakfast all day. Has outdoor dining.
Other Info: Accepts AMEX, DC, DIS, MC, VISA. Price: $$.
Directions: This place is about a half-mile west of southwest corner of Crossroads Mall, at the north end of University of Colorado–Boulder.

Walnut Café
3073 Walnut Street
303-447-2315
Hours: Daily 7 am to 4 pm
Natural Foods. Vegan options. Not pure vegetarian
Menu: Huevos Rancheros, veggie burgers, quiche and soups. Daily specials. Homemade muffins. "Boulder Fare" is the vegetarian section. Soy cheese can be substituted for regular cheese. French Toast with maple syrup and honey margarine. Boulder Scramble (tofu, mushrooms, spinach, tomatoes and cheddar cheese). Dana's tempeh skillet is tempeh, mushrooms, onions and cheddar cheese with potatoes. Fresh juices. Espresso Bar.
Comments: There is an outdoor patio for dining in the summer.
Other Info: Full service, take-out. Accepts DIS, MC, VISA. Price: $-$$.
Directions: The place is a block west of the Crossroads Mall on Walnut St in south Boulder.

Whole Foods
Crossroads Common Shopping Center, 2905 Pearl Street; 303-545-6611
Hours: Daily 8 am to 10 pm
Natural Food Store and Cafe. Deli, Bakery, Salad Bar and Juice Bar. Organic produce. Supermarket-type place. See Whole Foods Market information.
Directions: This place is on Pearl St at the north end of Crossroads Mall in south Boulder.

Wild Oats
1651 Broadway, at Arapahoe
Store number: 303-442-0082
Café number: 303-442-0909
Hours: Daily 7 am to 11 pm
Natural Food Store and Cafe. Deli, Bakery, Salad Bar and Juice Bar. Organic produce. Supermarket-type place. See Wild Oats Market information.
Menu: Soups, salads, sandwiches and baked goods. Has a juice bar and organic salads. Four-cheese pie, Barbecue Tofu, Macaroni & Cheese, Spinach Salads, Lasagna, couscous, vegetarian burrito and grilled vegetables.
Comments: People tend to hang out here, like a community. Great natural food store with a little café in back. One of the best natural food stores in the country. Local organic produce used when possible. Very environmentally-friendly place.
Other Info: Counter service, take-out, catering. Accepts AMEX, DIS, MC, VISA. Price: $.

Directions: From Hwy 36 going north into town, just before Hwy 36 ends, take the Baseline Rd exit and go west onto Baseline Rd a quarter mile to Broadway, and go northwest on Broadway 2 miles, then at University make a U-turn and this place is a half-block down.

Wild Oats Market
2584 Baseline Road; 303-499-7636
Hours: Daily 7 am to 10 pm
Natural Food Store and Cafe. Deli, Bakery, Salad Bar and Juice Bar. Organic produce. Supermarket-type place. See Wild Oats Market information.
Directions: From Hwy 36, take Baseline Rd exit and go west on Baseline Rd and this place is a third-mile down in the Basemar Shopping Center on the left.

Zolo
2525 Arapahoe Avenue, at 26th; 303-449-0444; **Web site:** http://zologrill.citysearch.com/4.html
Hours: Monday to Saturday 11 am to 10 pm Sunday 4 pm to 9 pm
Southwestern/New World. Vegetarian-friendly restaurant.
Menu: The menu changes seasonally. The black beans and pinto beans are vegetarian. The food can be spicy. Chips and Salsa with Guacamole, soups, salads and Tortilla Soup. Mushroom Enchiladas and Black Bean Vegetable Cakes are good vegetarian dishes.
Comments: Great view of Flatiron Mountains. Good décor and service. Gets good reviews from the media. One of the most popular restaurants in Boulder. Hip place.
Other Info: Reservations not accepted. Price: $$. Accepts AMEX, MC, VISA.
Directions: From Foothills Pkwy, go west on Arapahoe Ave and this place is 1 mile down in a shopping center, just west of Crossroads Mall. Take Hwy 36 going north from Denver to where it ends, then go north on 28th St, then turn left at Arapahoe and this place is 1 block down.

BRECKENRIDGE SKI RESORT

Amazing Grace Natural Foods
213 Lincoln Avenue; 970-453-1445
Hours: Monday to Saturday 11 am to 8 pm Sunday 12 noon to 6 pm
Natural Food Store and Deli. The deli is mainly vegan and organic. Bakery and Juice Bar. Organic produce. Bulk foods.
Menu: Has chalkboard menu that changes regu-

larly. Includes soups, salads and sandwiches. Fresh juices and smoothies.
Comments: Located in a historical building.
Other Info: Deli service, take-out. Has one table. No credit cards; cash only. Price: $-$$.
Directions: From I-70, take Hwy 9 to Breckenridge. Make a left at the third light onto French St and this place is two blocks down on the corner of Lincoln and French.

Red Orchid
206 North Main Street; 970-453-1881
Hours: Daily 11:30 am to 9:30 pm
Chinese. Vegan options. Limited Vegetarian selection. Not pure vegetarian.
Menu: Szechuan, Mandarin and Hunan cuisines. Has several vegetarian options.
Other Info: Full service, take-out, deck dining. Accepts MC, VISA. Price: $$.

CARBONDALE

Clarks Market
1000 Hwy 133, at the light; 970-963-5991
Hours: Monday to Saturday 9 am to 8 pm
Sunday 10 am to 6 pm
Natural Food Store and Deli. Vegan-friendly deli. Organic produce. Excellent, friendly place. Homeopathic selections.
Menu: Soups, salads, sandwiches and hot dishes.
Other Info: Counter service, take-out. Has seating. Accepts MC, VISA.

CHERRY CREEK

Wild Oats
201 University; 303-442-0909
Hours: Daily 7 am to 11 pm
Natural Food Store and Cafe. Deli, Bakery, Salad Bar and Juice Bar. Organic produce. Supermarket-type place. See Wild Oats Market information.

COLORADO SPRINGS
The Garden of the Gods rock formation on the edge of Colorado Springs is worth seeing.

Dale Street Café
115 East Dale Street, near Mountain Valley Park
719-578-9898
Hours: Monday to Saturday 11 am to 3 pm, 4:30 pm to 9 pm; closed Sunday.
Italian and Mediterranean Natural Foods. Not pure vegetarian.
Menu: Soups, sandwiches, appetizers, Mediterranean dishes, hummus, Roasted Vegetables, Por-

tobello Sandwich, Pasta with Artichoke Hearts and good salads. Non-alcoholic beer.
Comments: Pleasant place. Prepares foods fresh.
Other Info: Full service, take-out. Accepts MC, VISA. Price: $$.
Directions: From I-25, take Uintah St exit (#143), then go east on W Uintah St for 0.65 mile, at N Nevada Ave (Rte 87) turn right and go a third-mile, at E Dale St turn right and this place is 1 block down.

Golden Dragon
903 South 8th Street; 719-632-3607
Hours: Thursday to Saturday 5 pm to 9 pm
Chinese and American. Vegan options. Not pure vegetarian.
Menu: Soups, salads, sandwiches, appetizers and main dishes.
Comments: One of the best Chinese places in town. Does not use MSG.
Other Info: Full service, take-out. Accepts AMEX, DIS, MC, VISA. Price: $$.

Jose Muldoon's
222 North Tejon Street; 719-636-2311
Hours: Monday to Saturday 11 am to 11 am
Sunday 9:30 am to 10 am
Mexican. Vegan options. See Boulder details.

Lettuce Head Restaurant
2917 Galley Road; 719-597-7476
Hours: Monday to Saturday 11 am to 4 pm
Closed Sunday.
California. Not pure vegetarian.
Menu: Has soups, salads and sandwiches.

Mountain Mama Natural Foods
1625-A West Uintah Street, Suite A
719-633-4139
Hours: Monday to Saturday 9 am to 7 pm
Sunday 11 am to 5 pm
Natural Food Store and take-out Deli. Organic produce. Bakery.
Menu: Daily soup, sandwiches, salads, pastas and hot dishes.
Comments: This is well-stocked place with a good selection of produce and other items. Family owned and operated.
Directions: From I-25, take West Uintah exit (#143) and go west one mile and this place is on the left.

Mountain Earth Whole Foods
405 4th Street; 970-349-5132
Hours: Daily 8 am to 8 pm
Natural Food Store and Vegetarian Deli (soups

and salads only). Small store with a limited selection. Small, but good selection of organic produce. Has a soy cheese pizza.
Other Info: Accepts MC, VISA.
Directions: From I-25, take Nevada Ave/I-25 Bus (#148A), then go south 1¾ mile on N Nevada Ave, at Winters Ave turn left and go 1 block, at Roberts Rd turn right and go a quarter-mile, at Nichols Blvd turn left and go 1 block, at N Stone Ave turn right and this place is a quarter-mile down, at 4th St.

Poor Richard's

324½ North Tejon; 719-632-7721
Hours: Daily 11 am to 10 pm
Pizza and Italian. Not pure vegetarian.
Menu: Has a good selection of vegetarian dishes. Has soups, salads, rice & beans, Tofu over Brown Rice, Vegetarian Lasagna, pastas and pizzas. Really good hand-tossed New York style pizzas by the slice or a whole pizza. Whole-wheat crusts and soy cheese topping are option. Topping includes artichoke hearts, zucchini, fresh basil, sundried tomatoes, spinach and pesto.
Comments: Friendly place.
Other Info: Accepts AMEX, DIS, MC, VISA.
Directions: From I-25, take Bijou St exit (#142), then go east on Bijou St for 2 blocks (road becomes W Kiowa St), at N Cascade Ave turn left and go 1 block, at E Platte Ave turn right and go 1 block, at N Tejon St turn left and this place is a half-block down.

The Vitamin Cottage

1780 East Woodmen Road; 719-536-9606
Hours: Monday to Friday 9 am to 8 pm; Saturday 9 am to 7 pm; Sunday 11 am to 6 pm
Natural Food Store. Organic produce.
Directions: From I-25, take Woodman Drive exit (#149) and then go east on Woodman for 1 mile. This store is behind Lenscrafters (cannot see it from the road) at the southeast corner of the intersection.

Wild Oats Market

5075 North Academy, near Canon
719-548-1667
Hours: Daily 8 am to 10 pm
Natural Food Store and Cafe. Deli, Bakery, Salad Bar and Juice Bar. Organic produce. Supermarket-type place. See Wild Oats Market information.
Comments: This is well-stocked place with a good selection of produce and other items.
Directions: From I-25, take Academy exit (#150), then go southeast on Academy and this place is about 3 miles down on the left in Union Square.

DENVER

Alexander's Healthy Mexican

4042 East Virginia Avenue; 303-320-0777
Hours: Daily 10 am to 12 midnight (until 10 pm on Monday)
Vegetarian-friendly Mexican. Not pure vegetarian.
Menu: Has over 50 vegetarian dishes.
Comments: Friendly place.
Other Info: Accepts AMEX, MC, VISA. Price: $$-$$$.
Directions: From I-25, take Colorado Blvd/Rte 2 (#204), then go north on S Colorado Blvd (Rte 2) for 1½ miles, then at Virginia Ave turn right and this place is 100 yards down.

Beau Jo's Pizza

2710 South Colorado Boulevard   303-758-1519
6045 W Alameda Avenue, Suite 201
303-234-0790
7805 Wadsworth, Arvada   303-420-8376
1517 Miner Street, at 1st Avenue, Idaho Springs (30m); 303-567-4376
2690 East County Line Road, Littleton; 303-694-9898
Hours: Sunday to Thursday 11 am to 9 pm
Friday & Saturday 11 am to 10 pm
Pizza Restaurant. Vegan options. Not pure vegetarian.
Menu: Has vegan pizzas with tofu topping. Has several good tasting vegetarian pizzas. Has a soup and salad bar. Has several different sauces and nine cheeses.
Other Info: Full service, take-out. Accepts AMEX, DIS, MC, VISA. Price: $.

Delhi Durbar

1514 Blake Street, in the Lower Downtown (LoDo) of Denver; 303-595-0680
Hours: Monday to Friday 11:30 am to 2:30 pm, 5:30 pm to 10 pm; Saturday 12 noon to 2:30 pm, 5:30 pm to 10 pm; Sunday 12 noon to 2:30 pm, 5:30 pm to 9:30 pm
Indian Tandoor. Not pure vegetarian. Inexpensive all-you-can-eat Lunch Buffet.
Menu: Many of the dishes are vegetarian such as Shahi Subji (vegetables and cream), which is very good. Buffet lunch. Has a vegetarian thali. Has freshly baked breads, good fruit lassis and chai. Has almond and pistachio kulfi Indian ice cream.
Comments: Food gets high recommendations. Has a branch in Boulder and Lakewood. Romantic atmosphere. In a historical building.
Other Info: Full service, take-out. Accepts AMEX, DC, DIS, MC, VISA. Price: $$-$$$.

Falafel King

Tabor Center, 303 16th Street 303-573-7203
Hours: Daily 11 am to 3 pm
1201 16th Street, Unit 308   303-629-6603
825 Colorado Boulevard   303-322-6077
Hours: Monday to Friday 11 am to 3 pm
Closed Saturday & Sunday.
Falafel Place. See Boulder. Not pure vegetarian.

Gemini

4300 Wadsworth Blvd, Wheat Ridge, western
suburbs of Denver; 303-421-4990
Hours: Daily 6:30 am to 10 pm
International. Mainly vegetarian. Not pure veg.
Menu: Has a wide selection of vegetarian dishes.
Spinach Lasagna, pastas, Mexican dishes, sand-
wiches, salads and stir-fried vegetables.
Other Info: Full service, take-out. Accepts MC,
VISA.

Goodfriends

3100 East Colfax Avenue; 303-399-1751
Hours: Monday to Thursday 11 am to 11 pm;
Friday 11 am to 12 midnight; Saturday 10 am to
12 midnight; Sunday 10 am to 11 pm
**Southwestern, Italian and Mexican Natural
Foods.** Not pure vegetarian.
Menu: Half the menu is vegetarian including stir-
fry vegetables, salads, Mexican dishes made with-
out lard, eggplant salad and other dishes. Nutty
Cheese Salad with avocado, sunflowers seed, nuts,
tomatoes, banana slices with a honey mustard
dressing. Eggplant Special with cheese, sour
creams and guacamole in a flour tortilla. Sizzling
fajita. Vegerito is a flour tortilla stuffed with vegetables, cheeses and salsa.
Comments: Reasonably priced dishes. Good
value. Casual, cozy place. Has artwork.
Other Info: Full service, take-out. Accepts
AMEX, DC, DIS, MC, VISA. Price: $-$$.
Directions: From I-25, take Colorado Blvd/Rte
2 (#204), then go north on S Colorado Blvd (Rte
2) for 4 miles, then at E Colfax Ave (US 287/US
40) turn left and go a half-mile.

**Govinda's Buffet

1400 Cherry Street, at 14th Avenue
303-333-5462; Web site: www.krishnadenver.com
Hours: Monday to Saturday 11:30 am to 2:30
pm, 5 pm to 8 pm; closed Sunday.
Fully Vegetarian Indian and International. West
stocked salad bar. Vegan options.
Menu: All-you-can-eat pure vegetarian buffet.
Menu changes daily and is mostly vegan. Does
not use eggs and uses vegetarian (rennetless)
cheese. Rich dishes, rolls, matar paneer, vegetable
curries, freshly made soups, pasta, tempeh and
seitan dishes, steamed vegetables and International
dishes. Menu changes daily.
Comments: This buffet-style restaurant is run by
a Hare Krishna temple and is attached to their
temple. The food is very good. Small, informal
place. Tuesdays and Thursdays are primarily vegan. Peaceful, spiritual atmosphere. There is a selection of several dishes, and sometime when the
favorites are finish, they are done. Highly recommended. Has indoor and outdoor patio seating. I really liked this place.
Other Info: Buffet, take-out. Accepts MC, VISA.
Price: $-$$.
Directions: From I-25, take Colorado Blvd/Rte
2 (#204), then go north on S Colorado Blvd (Rte
2) for 4 miles, then at E Colfax Ave (US 287/US
40) turn right and go a half-mile, then at Cherry
St turn right and this place is 1 block down.

Harvest Restaurant & Bakery

430 S Colorado Boulevard, at Virginia
303-399-6652
Hours: Daily 7 am to 9 pm
Restaurant. Not pure vegetarian. See Boulder for
details.
Menu: Has a good selection of vegetarian dishes.
Scrambled Tofu, sandwiches, salads and vegetable
dishes.

Jerusalem Restaurant

1890 East Evans Avenue; 303-777-8828
Hours: Sunday to Thursday 9 am to 4 am
Friday and Saturday for 24 hours
Middle Eastern. Vegan options. Not pure veg.
Menu: Has many vegetarian options including
hummus, falafel, baba ghanouj, stuffed grape
leaves and salads. There is a separate vegetarian
section on the menu. Good portions.
Comments: Has indoor and outdoor dining.
Considered to be one of the best restaurants in
Denver. Food, service and atmosphere all get good
ratings. Good value.
Other Info: Full service, take-out. Accepts
AMEX, DIS, MC, VISA. Price: $.

Josephina's

1433 Larimer Street; 303-623-0166
Hours: Daily 11 am to 10:30 pm
Italian. Vegan options. Not pure vegetarian.
Menu: Has several vegetarian options includ-
ing salads, pizza, pasta, Grilled Balsamic
Portobello, Fried Zucchini and Artichokes
& Provolone.

Comments: Has outdoor seating. Live jazz. Some of the pastas contain eggs.
Other Info: Full service, take-out. Reservations suggested. Accepts AMEX, DIS, MC, VISA. Price: $$.

Littleton Adventist Hospital
7700 South Broadway; 303-730-8900
Hospital Cafeteria. Not pure vegetarian.
Hours: Daily
Vegetarian Kosher. Vegan options. Not pure vegetarian.
Menu: Has a good selection of vegetarian dishes. The menu changes daily. Foods are freshly prepared on the premises. Fresh juices.
Comments: This is a Seventh Day Adventist hospital. The public is welcome.
Other Info: Counter service, take-out. No credit cards. Price: $.

Mataam FEZ Moroccan
4609 East Colfax Avenue; 303-399-9282
Hours: Monday to Thursday 5:30 pm to 9:30 pm; Friday & Saturday 5:30 pm to 10:30 pm; Sunday 5:30 pm to 9:30 pm
Moroccan. Not pure vegetarian.
Menu: Has several vegetarian options. Vegetarian Couscous, Artichoke dish and vegetables dishes.
Comments: Sit on the floor and eat with your hands. Has a branch in Boulder and Colorado Springs. Has belly dancing.
Other Info: Reservations suggested. Accepts AMEX, DC, DIS, MC, VISA. Price: $$-$$$.

Mediterranean Health Café
2817 East 3rd Avenue; 303-399-2940
Hours: Monday to Thursday 11 am to 8 pm; Friday 11 am to 2 pm; Sunday 12 noon to 7 pm; closed Saturday.
Kosher Mediterranean, Middle Eastern, American. Emphasis on vegetarian meals. Vegan options. Not pure vegetarian (only fish is served).
Menu: The menu is mainly vegetarian. Has many vegetarian options including hummus, sandwiches, falafel, Vegetarian Chili and veggie burgers.
Comments: Gets high recommendations. Has outdoor seating.
Other Info: Full service, take-out. No smoking. Accepts AM, DC, DIS, MC, VISA. Price: $.

Mercury Café
2199 California Street, central Denver
303-294-9281
Hours: Tuesday to Friday 5:30 pm to 11 pm; Saturday & Sunday 9 am to 3 pm, 5:30 pm to 2 am; closed Monday.
Mainly Vegetarian. Vegan-friendly. Not pure veg.
Menu: Tempeh and tofu dishes.
Comments: There is nightly live music: jazz, exotic music, samba, Celtic, salsa, belly dancing, and other music. Has private dining rooms. Poetry reading and theater. Sunday is popular. Often uses organic produce. Has dance lessons.
Other Info: No credit cards; cash only. Price: $$$.
Directions: From I-25, take Colfax Ave/US 49 exit (#210), then go east 0.65 mile on W Colfax Ave, then at Stout St turn left and go 1 mile, at 22nd St turn right and go 1 block, at California St turn right and this place is right at the corner.

Moe's Broadway Bagel
550 Grant Street; 303-733-7331
Hours: Daily 5 am to 4 pm
Bagel Shop. New York style bagel. Good Coffee. Not pure vegetarian.

Mount Everest Restaurant
1533 Champa St, at 15th, in the Lower Downtown (LoDo) of Denver; 303-620-9306
Hours: Monday to Saturday 11 am to 9:30 pm Closed Sunday.
Nepalese. Also Tibetan and Indian dishes. Many of the vegetarian dishes are vegan. Not pure vegetarian. All-you-can-eat lunch buffet on weekdays.
Menu: Has a separate vegetarian menu. Samosa Chaat is spiced potatoes with a sweet and sour sauce with yogurt. Popular is the Sherpa trek food, which is vegetable momos, chapatti, fried noodles, vegetables, lentil soup and an acha sauce. Meals often end with rice pudding.
Comments: Nepalese food is like Indian food, but is often not cooked as spicy hot. Nepalese food is often a good selection of small portion dishes. There is a shop in front of the restaurant that sells Nepalese goods and crafts. Friendly service. There are several theaters near this restaurant. Free parking for customers.
Other Info: Full service, take-out. Non-smoking. Accepts AMEX, DC, DIS, MC, VISA. Price $$-$$$.

Mustard's Last Stand II
2081 South University Boulevard, Denver
303-722-7936
Hours: Monday to Friday 10:30 am to 9 pm Saturday & Sunday 11 am to 9 pm
American Fast Foods. Vegan options. Not pure vegetarian.

Menu: Has tempeh burgers, veggie chili, veggie dogs and very good freshly made French fries.

Organic Orbit

1700 Broadway; 303-832-2677
Hours: Monday to Friday 8:30 am to 3:30 pm
Closed Saturday & Sunday.
Organic Restaurant. Healthy food. Not pure veg.
Menu: Soups, sandwiches, salads and hot dishes.

Paul's Place

Cherry Creek Shopping Center, 3000 E 1st Avenue, Suite 115, at Cherrycreek; 303-321-5801
Hours: Monday to Friday 10 am to 9 pm; Saturday 10 am to 8 pm; Sunday 11 am to 6 pm

Gourmet Fast Food. Salad Bar. Vegan options. Not pure vegetarian.
Menu: Has many vegetarian options including sandwiches, various salads, veggie hot dogs, chili, tacos, tamales, Paul's Veggie, large baked potatoes, burritos, Portobello Sandwich, Sauté Bean Burger and Garden Burgers.
Other Info: Counter service, take-out, catering. No smoking. Accepts AM, DIS, MC, VISA. Price: $.
Directions: This place is in southeast Denver. From I-25, take Colorado Blvd/Rte 2 (#204), then go north on Colorado Blvd for 1½ mile, at Cherry Creek North Dr turn left (becomes S Steele St) and go 1 mile, go straight onto E 1st Ave and this place is 2 blocks down.

Pressto Sandwiches

555 17th Street, Suite 180; 303-294-0449
Hours: Monday to Friday 6:30 am to 3 pm; closed Saturday & Sunday.
Italian Sandwich Place. Fast Food. Not pure vegetarian.
Menu: Has a selection of vegetarian sandwiches. Has whole wheat and white focaccia bread.
Comments: Has quick service. Has outdoor seating.
Other Info: Non-smoking. Accepts AMEX, DIS, MC, VISA.

Rosewood Café

Porter Memorial Hospital,
2525 South Downing Street; 303-778-1955
Hours: Daily
Vegetarian-friendly Kosher. Vegan options. Not pure vegetarian.
Menu: The menu changes daily. Foods are freshly prepared on the premises. Fresh juices.
Comments: This is a Seventh Day Adventist hospital. The public is welcome.

Other Info: Counter service, take-out. No credit cards. Price: $.
Directions: From I-25, take University Blvd South exit (#205B), then go south a half mile on University Blvd, at Evans Ave turn right and go ¾ mile, at S Downing St turn left and this place is a half-mile down. This place is in south Denver near Englewood.

Seoul Food

701 East 6th Avenue, at Washington Street
303-837-1460
Hours: Monday to Saturday 11 am to 3 pm, 5 pm to 10 pm; closed Sunday.
Korean. Not pure vegetarian.
Menu: Has a separate vegetarian section on the menu.
Comments: Has outdoor dining.
Other Info: Full service, take-out. Non-smoking. Accepts AMEX, DIS, MC, VISA. Price: $.

Twin Dragon

3021 South Broadway Street, Englewood
303 781-8068
Web site: www.twindragonrestaurant.com
Hours: Monday to Friday 11 am to 10 pm; Saturday 12 noon to 10 pm; Sun 4:30 pm to 10 pm
Chinese. Specializes in Szechuan and Mandarin. Not pure vegetarian.
Menu: Has a separate vegetarian menu with Sesame Bean Curd, Rainbow Bean Sprouts, Moo Shu Vegetable Pancakes, noodle dishes and Shredded Potato in Peking Sauce. Rice comes with most dishes.
Comments: Gets good recommendations. No MSG. Food freshly prepared.
Other Info: Full service, take-out, delivery. Accepts AMEX, MC, VISA.

T-WA Inn

555 South Federal Boulevard; 303-922-4584
Hours: Daily 11 am to 11 pm
Vietnamese and Chinese. Vegan options. Not pure vegetarian.
Menu: Has a separate vegetarian section on the menu that including 15 main vegetarian dishes that include eggplant dishes, curried vegetables, rice noodles and rice dishes.
Comments: Casual.
Other Info: Full service, take-out. Accepts AMEX, DIS, MC, VISA. Price: $$.

Walnut Café

338 East Colfax Avenue, at Logan; 303-832-5108
Hours: Monday to Friday 6 am to 2 pm

Saturday & Sunday 7 am to 2 pm
Natural Foods. Not pure vegetarian.
Menu: Tofu can be substituted for meat and eggs in many of the dishes.
Comments: Breakfast and lunch place.
Other Info: Full service, take-out. No smoking. Accepts MC, VISA. Price: $.

**WaterCourse Foods Restaurant
206 East 13th Avenue, at Sherman
303-832-7313
Hours: Tuesday to Sunday 8 am to 10 pm
Closed Monday.
Vegetarian Restaurant. Vegan options.
Menu: Has Scrambled Tofu, Breakfast Burrito, sandwiches, very good tempeh burger, mashed potatoes, veggie wraps, Tempeh Scaloppini, banana bread, Sesame Seitan (good), Macrobiotic Plate, Biscuits & Gravy and tempeh dishes. Has a good selection of vegetarian options.
Comments: Voted as the best vegetarian restaurant in Denver. Reasonable prices. Food gets high ratings (some people don't like the food). Has a children menu. Has a community table. Some people think the service is good and friendly and other think it is a bit weak. Service is usually slow. One of the best vegetarian restaurants in Denver.
Other Info: Accepts MC, VISA. Price: $.
Directions: In the downtown Denver area, a block south of the capital building. From I-25, take the Lincoln St exit (#207A) towards Broadway, then go north 2¼ miles on S Lincoln St, at E 12th Ave turn right and go 1 block, at Sherman St turn left and this place is 1 block down.

Wild Oats
900 East 11th Avenue, Capitol Hill
303-832-7701
Directions: From I-25, take #213 towards W 38th Ave/Park Ave, then go southeast on Park Ave (becomes 22nd St and go 1 mile, at 23rd St turn right and go ¾ mile, turn sight right onto Ogden St and go a third-mile, turn left at E Colfax Ave, then make a quick right onto Corona St and go a half-mile, at 11th Ave turn right and this place is 1 block down at the corner of Emerson St. This place is about 2 miles southwest of Exit #213.
201 University Boulevard, Denver; 303 442-0909
Directions: This place is a block north of the Cherry Creek Shopping Center and the Denver Country Club, a few miles southeast of the downtown. This place is in southeast Denver. From I-25, take Colorado Blvd/Rte 2 (#204), then go north on Colorado Blvd for 2 miles, then turn left at Second Avenue and this place is ¾ mile

down in a strip mall.
1111 South Washington, Denver 303-733-6201
Comments: Has a good amount of seating.
Directions: From I-25, take Washington St exit (#206B). And this place is at the corner of Buchtel Road and S Washington, a block east of the exit.
Hours: Daily 7 am to 10 pm
Natural Food Store and Cafe. Deli, Bakery, Salad Bar and Juice Bar. Organic produce. Supermarket-type place. See Wild Oats Market information.
Menu: Rice, Black Bean Salad, BBQ Tofu, Sautéed Vegetables and some vegan cakes. Large amount of salad items.

Wolfe's BBQ
333 East Colfax Avenue, at Grant
303-831-1500
Hours: Monday to Friday 11:30 am to 3 pm, 5 pm to 8 pm; closed Saturday & Sunday
American. Emphasize on barbecue and vegetarian dishes. Not pure vegetarian.
Menu: Has several vegetarian options such as BBQ Tofu, vegan cole slaw and yogurt carrot salad. Good vegetarian baked beans. Has great barbeque sauce.
Comments: Friendly place. The BBQ Tofu gets high recommendations. Has a children menu. The place is really low on the atmosphere. Traditional hole-in-the-wall place.
Other Info: Limited service, take-out. Non-smoking. Accepts MC, VISA. Price: $.
Directions: In Capitol Hill, a block from the capitol building in downtown Denver.

DURANGO

Buzz House
1019 Main Avenue; 970-385-5831
Hours: Monday to Friday 7 am to 4 pm; Saturday 8 am to 4 pm; Sunday 8 am to 2 pm
Vegetarian-friendly Restaurant. Not pure veg.
Menu: Sandwiches, burrito, wraps and salads.
Other Info: No credit cards; cash only. Counter service, take-out.

Carver's Restaurant and Bakery
1022 Main Avenue; 970-259-2545
Hours: Monday to Saturday 6:30 am to 11 pm
Sunday 6:30 am to 1 pm
American. Vegetarian-friendly Restaurant. Not pure vegetarian.
Menu: Has a good selection of vegetarian dishes. Soups, salads, sandwiches, veggie Lasagna, Garden Burger and more.

Other Info: Full service, take-out. Accepts AMEX, DIS, MC, VISA. Price: $$.

Cyprus Café
725 East Second Avenue; 970-385-6884
Hours: Tuesday to Saturday 11:30 am to 2:30 pm, 5 pm to 9 pm; closed Sunday and Monday
Mediterranean. Vegetarian-friendly Restaurant. Not pure vegetarian.
Menu: Has a good selection of vegetarian dishes including hummus, Butternut Squash and Spanikopita.
Other Info: Accepts AMEX, MC, VISA. Full service, take-out.

Durango Natural Foods
575 East 8th Avenue, at East College
970-247-8129
Hours: Monday to Saturday 8 am to 8 pm
Sunday 9 am to 7 pm
Natural Food Store and Deli. Salad Bar. Organic produce.
Menu: Has a good selection of vegetarian dishes. Mushroom Rice, Nori Roll, Tofu Sandwich, Spring Roll, basmati rice, sandwiches and more.
Other Info: Accepts AMEX, MC, VISA. Counter service, take-out. One table inside and some outside seating.
Directions: From Hwy 160 coming from the southeast, turn north at Rte 3 and it becomes 8th Ave, this place is on the left at the first light. From Hwy 160 coming from the west, go north on Camino Del Rio, then at 6th St turn right. This place is at the corner of 8th and 6th (also called College Drive) Streets on the right.

Gazpacho New Mexican Restaurant
431 East Second Avenue; 970-259-9494
Vegetarian-friendly New Mexican. Not pure vegetarian.
Menu: Has a good selection of vegetarian dishes. New Mexican cuisine uses a lot of hot chilies.

Nature's Oasis Deli
1123 Camino Del Rio Road
970-247-1988
Hours: Monday to Saturday 8 am to 8 pm
Sunday 9 am to 7 pm
Natural Food Store and Deli. Juice Bar. Organic produce. Not pure vegetarian.
Menu: Homemade soups, salads and vegetarian specials. Fresh organic juices.
Other Info: Accepts AMEX, MC, VISA. Counter service, take-out. Has seating.
Directions: This place is on Hwy 160, a half-mile south of the downtown.

ENGLEWOOD (Denver Suburb)

Twin Dragon Restaurant
3021 South Broadway; 303-781-8068
Hours: Monday to Friday 11 am to 9 pm; Saturday 12 noon to 10 pm; Sunday 4 pm to 9:30 pm
Mandarin and Szechuan Chinese. Vegan option. Not pure vegetarian.
Menu: Has over 15 vegetarian dishes on the menu.
Other Info: Full service, take-out. Accepts AMEX, DIS, MC, VISA. Price: $$.

ESTES PARK
Estes Park is the eastern gateway to Rocky Mountain National Park. People come through here on the way to camping, trekking, rafting tours and to visit the park.

Buckwheat's Natural Foods
870 Moraine Avenue; 970-586-5658
Natural Food Store.

Molly B's
200 Moraine Avenue; 970-586-2766
Hours: Thursday to Tuesday 6 am to 3 pm
Closed Wednesday.
Natural Foods. Vegan options. Not pure veg.
Menu: Has Lasagna, stir-fry dishes, pastas and salads. Has daily vegetarian specials. Homemade pies and other baked goods. Fresh juices.
Other Info: Full service, take-out. Accepts AMEX, MC, VISA. Price: $$.

Notchtop Bakery & Café
459 East Wonderview Avenue, Upper Stanley Village; 970-586-0272
Hours: Sunday & Monday 7 am to 9 pm; Tuesday to Thur 7 am to 6 pm; Fri 7 am to 11 pm
Natural Foods. Vegan options. Not pure veg.
Menu: Pasta dishes, salads, Stir-fries, sandwiches, Black Bean Burger and other dishes. Has a tofu scramble for breakfast.
Comments: It is a happening place. Sometimes there is live entertainment.
Other Info: Full service, take-out. Price: $$.
Directions: This place is at the junction of Hwy 34 and Hwy 36.

EVERGREEN

Wildflower
28035 Main Street; 303-674-3323
Hours: Daily 7:30 am to 2 pm
Vegetarian-friendly Restaurant. Not pure veg.
Menu: Salads, Black Bean Burger and sandwiches.

FORT COLLINS

Avogadro's Number

605 South Mason Street; 970-493-5555
Hours: Sunday to Friday 7 am to 10 pm
Saturday 7 am to 11 pm
Sandwich Shop. Vegetarian-friendly. Not pure vegetarian.
Menu: Veggie chili, Big Tofu Sandwich, Tempeh Burger, salads, soups and several other vegetarian dishes.
Comments: Gets good recommendations.
Other Info: Counter service, take-out. Accepts MC, VISA.
Directions: From I-25, take the CO-14 Exit (#269B) towards Ft Collins, then go west on Mulberry St/Co 14 for 4 miles, at College Ave turn left and go 1 block, at W Myrtle St turn right and go 1 block, at S Mason St turn left and this place is a 100 yards down. This place is a few blocks north of the northeast corner of Colorado State University.

Big City Burrito

510 South College; 970-482-3303
Hours: Daily 10 am to 10 pm
Mexican. Not pure vegetarian.
Menu: Has a veggie burrito and potato burrito.

Cozzola's Pizza

241 Linden Street   970-482-3557
111 Oakridge Drive   970-229-5771
Hours: Tuesday to Friday 11 am to 9 pm; Saturday 11:30 am to 9 pm; Sunday 4 pm to 8 pm; closed Monday.
Pizza Place. Gourmet Pizzas. Vegan options. Not pure vegetarian.
Menu: Has topping such as artichoke hearts, roasted red peppers and fresh herbs. Soy cheese can be used instead of regular cheese. Has wholewheat, herb or white crusts. Some of the sauces contain cheese.
Other Info: Full service, take-out. No credit cards accepted. Price: $.

Fort Collins Co-op

250 East Mountain Avenue
970-484-7448; **Web site:** www.ftcfoodcoop.com
Hours: Monday to Friday 8:30 am to 7:30 pm; Saturday 8:30 am to 7 pm; Sun 11 am to 6 pm
Natural Food Store and take-out Deli. Organic produce.
Menu: Has ready-made sandwiches. Fresh juices.
Comments: Organic produce, bulk items. Has a reading room and a place for classes.
Other Info: Deli service, take-out. No credit cards

accepted. Price: $.
Directions: Walking distance from Colorado State University and downtown. From I-25, take Mulberry exit west. At College Ave turn right and go 4 blocks, at Mountain turn right and this store is 1 block down on the left.

Rainbow Restaurant

212 West Laurel Avenue; 970-221-2664
Hours: Monday 6 am to 2 pm; Tuesday to Sunday 6 am to 8 pm (until 9 pm on Fri & Sat)
Natural Foods, American. Emphasis on vegetarian dishes. Not pure vegetarian.
Menu: Has several vegetarian options including salads, soups, pastas, Mexican dishes and sandwiches.
Comments: Voted as having the best vegetarian food in Fort Collins. Has outdoor seating.
Other Info: Full service, take-out. No smoking. Accepts DC, DIS, MC, VISA. Price: $$.
Directions: Opposite the northeast corner of Colorado State University. From I-25 take Mulberry exit and go west for 4 miles to downtown Fort Collins. At S Mason St turn left and go 2 blocks, then at W Laurel Ave turn right and this place is a half-block down.

Tontevecchio

130 South Mason Street, in the middle of the Old Town; 970-221-0399
Hours: Tuesday to Sunday 11 am to 2 pm, 5 pm to 9 pm; closed Monday.
Italian. Vegan options. Not pure vegetarian.
Menu: Has several vegetarian options. Has international dishes such as Asian, French, Pacific Northwest, Southwestern, Cajun and Italian.
Comments: Upscale, formal place. Gourmet food. Has a chalkboard menu that changes daily. Has good food and service.
Other Info: Full service, take-out. Reservations required for dinner. Accepts AMEX, MC, VISA. Price: $$$.

Wild Oats

200 West Foothills Parkway; 970-225-1400
Hours: Daily 7:30 am to 10 pm
Natural Food Store and Cafe. Deli, Bakery, Salad Bar and Juice Bar. Organic produce. Supermarket-type place. See Wild Oats Market information.
Directions: This place is a half-block west of Foothills Fashion Mall. From I-25, take Harmony Rd exit and go west towards the downtown for 4½ miles, then turn right at College Ave and go 1½ mile, at Foothills Pkwy turn left and this place is 1 block down.

FRISCO

Alpine Market
320 Main Street, at 3rd (at the four-way stop)
970-668-5535
Hours: Monday to Saturday 8 am to 8 pm
Sunday 9 am to 7 pm
Natural Food Store and Vegan-friendly Deli.
Organic produce.
Menu: Soups, salads, veggie burgers, sandwiches
and hot dishes.
Comments: Friendly place.
Other Info: Counter service, take-out. Has some
seating.
Directions: From I-70, take Exit #201, then go
east on Main St and this place is a half-mile down.

GLENDALE

Whole Oats
870 South Colorado Boulevard; 303-691-0101
Hours: Daily 7 am to 10 pm
Natural Food Store and Cafe. Deli, Bakery, Salad
Bar and Juice Bar. Organic produce. Supermarket-type place. See Wild Oats Market
information.
Other Info: Accepts AMEX, DC, MC, VISA.
Directions: From I-25, take the Colorado/Rte 2
(#204), then go north on Colorado Blvd and this
place is 1¼ mile down.

Good Health Grocery
730 Cooper Avenue; 970-945-0235
Hours: Monday to Friday 9 am to 7 pm; Satur-
day 10 am to 6 pm; Sunday 12 noon to 5 pm
Natural Food Store and Deli. Organic produce.
Hours: Soups and sandwiches.
Other Info: Accepts MC, VISA.
Directions: From I-70, take Glenwood Springs
exit, at 8th Avenue turn left. This place is then
on the right at the corner of 8th and Cooper.

GRAND JUNCTION (in Western Colorado)

Appleseed
East Gate Shopping Center, 2830 North Avenue;
970-243-5541
Hours: Monday to Saturday 9 am to 6 pm
Closed Sunday.
Natural Food Store.
Directions: From I-70, take Exit #37 for the I-
70 business loop, then go southeast on the I-70
Business Loop for 3 miles, then continue straight
onto Hwy 6/North Ave and this place is 2 miles
down in the East Gate Shopping Center.

Sundrop Grocery
321 Rood Avenue
1 street north of Main (downtown)
970-243-1175
Hours: Monday to Saturday 9 am to 7 pm
Closed Sunday.
Natural Food Store and mainly Vegetarian Deli.
Bakery. Organic produce. Vegan options. Not
pure vegetarian.
Menu: Salads, nori roils, pre-made sandwiches,
bagels, pasta salad, Spanish rice salad, veggie pie,
baked goods and soy dishes. Sandwiches include
hummus, veggie pita, tempeh salad, guacamole
and tofuna.
Comments: Local organic produce used when
possible.
Other Info: Counter service, take-out. Has a few
tables. Accepts MC, VISA. Price: $.
Directions: From I-70, take Horizon Drive exit
(#31) and go southwest on Horizon Drive for 1
mile, at Rte 27 turn left (becomes 12th St/Rte
27) and go 1¾ mile, at North Ave (US 6) turn
right and go 0.65 mile, at 5th St turn left and go
0.65 mile, then at Rood Ave turn right and this
place is 2 blocks down on the left between 3rd
and 4th Streets.

GUNNISON

Firebrand Deli
108 North Main Street
970-641-6266
Hours: Daily 7 am to 3 pm
Deli. Not pure vegetarian. Vegetarian friendly.
Menu: Several vegetarian sandwiches, a daily veg-
etarian soup, salads, gourmet sandwiches and
other dishes. Cappuccino, espresso.
Other Info: Limited service, take-out, catering.
Price: $.

IDAHO SPRINGS

Beau Jo's Pizza
1517 Miner Street
303-567-4376
Hours: Sunday to Thursday 11 am to 9 pm
Friday & Saturday 11 am to 9:30 pm
Pizza Restaurant chain. Soup and Salad Bar. Ve-
gan options. Not pure vegetarian.
Menu: Has pizza with over 15 toppings and a
vegan tofu pizza.
Comments: Has 20 years of napkin art displayed
in the restaurant.
Other Info: Full service, take-out. Accepts
AMEX, DIS, MC, VISA. Price: $$.

LAFAYETTE

Efrain's Mexican Restaurante & Cantina
101 East Cleveland; 303-666-7544
Hours: Monday to Saturday 11 am to 9 pm
Sunday 11 am to 8 pm
Mexican. Vegan options. Not pure vegetarian.
Menu: Freshly prepared dishes. Vegetarian dishes
are marked on the menu. Nachos, burritos and
tacos.
Other Info: Full service, take-out. Accepts MC,
VISA. Price: $.

LAKEWOOD (west Denver suburb)

Wild Oats
14357 West Colfax Avenue; 303-277-1339
Hours: Daily 7 am to 10 pm
Natural Food Store and Cafe. Deli, Bakery,
Salad Bar and Juice Bar. Organic produce. Supermarket-type place. See Wild Oats Market
information\.
Directions: From I-70, take Denver West Blvd
exit (#263), then go southeast on Denver West
Blvd for a quarter-mile, at Colfax Ave turn right
and this place is a quarter-mile down.

Vitamin Cottage
Mission Trace Shopping Center, 3333 South
Wadsworth Boulevard; 303-989-4866
Hours: Monday to Friday 9 am to 8 pm; Satur-
day 9 am to 7 pm; Sunday 11 am to 6 pm
Natural Food Store. Organic produce.
Menu: Has ready-made sandwiches.
Comments: Has a holistic dietitian who gives
nutritional advice for free.
Directions: From I-285, take Wadsworth Blvd
exit. This place is in the Mission Trace Shopping
Center on the west side of the road, two blocks
north of I-285.

LITTLETON (Denver suburb)

Vitamin Cottage
11550 West Meadows Drive, a little off of Ken
Karyl St; 303-948-9944
Natural Food Store. Organic produce. Has a wide
selection of vitamins.

Wild Oats
5910 South University Boulevard; 303-798-9699
Hours: Daily 8 am to 9 pm
Natural Food Store and Cafe. Deli, Bakery, Salad
Bar and Juice Bar. Organic produce. Supermarket-
type place. See Wild Oats Market information.

Other Info: Counter service, take-out. Accepts
DIS, MC, VISA. Price: $$.
Directions: From I-25, take Orchard Rd exit
(#205B), then go south on Orchard Rd for 5 miles
and this place is at the corner of University Av-
enue and Orchard.

LOUISVILLE

Karen's Kitchen
700 Main Street; 303-666-8020
Hours: Tuesday to Friday 6:30 am to 2 pm, 4 pm
to 8 pm; Saturday & Sunday Brunch 7:30 am to
2 pm; closed Monday.
Natural Foods. American. Vegan options. Not
pure vegetarian.
Menu: Lasagna, salads, burritos, Eggplant
Parmesan and other dishes.
Other Info: Full service, take-out, catering. No
smoking. Accepts AMEX, DC, DIS, MC, VISA.
Price: $$.

LOVELAND

Cabin Country Natural Foods
248 East 4th Street; 970-669-9280
Hours: Monday to Friday 9 am to 6 pm; Saturday 9 am to 5 pm; closed Sunday
Natural Food Store.

MANITOU SPRINGS

Adam's Mountain Café
110 Canon Avenue; 719-685-1430
Hours: Daily 7:30 am to 9 pm
Winter Hours: Tuesday to Thursday 11 am to 3
pm, 5 pm to 9 pm; Fri & Sat 8 am to 3 pm, 5 pm
to 9 pm; Sun 8 am to 3 pm; closed Mon.
Natural Foods. Vegan options. Not pure veg.
Menu: Has Small Planet Burgers, burritos and
Southwestern cuisine.
Comments: Gets really high recommendations.
Has some good views of the local scenery.
Other Info: Full service, take-out. Non-smoking.
Accepts MC, VISA. Price: $$.

MORRISON

Dream Café
119 Bear Creek Avenue; 303-697-1280
Hours: Wednesday & Thursday 11 am to 2 pm;
Friday 11 am to 2 pm, 5 pm to 9 pm; Saturday 9
am to 2 pm, 5 pm to 9 pm; Sun 9 am to 12 noon
International. Vegan options. Not pure veg.
Menu: Vegetarian Stir-fry, Vegetarian Panini

Sandwich (grilled eggplants, red peppers, mozzarella, and yellow squash), hummus and other dishes. Cappuccino, espresso.
Other Info: Full service, take-out. Accepts MC, VISA. Price: $$.

Red Rock Amphitheater Café
There is a café at the top of the hill next to the amphitheater. It has a veggie burger, vegetarian nacho, French Fries and a few other vegetarian snacks.

NEDERLAND

Mountain Peoples Co-op
26 East First Street; 303-258-7500; **Web site:** http://csf.colorado.edu/co-op/mountain.html
Summer Hours: Daily 9 am to 8 pm
Winter Hours: Daily 9 am to 7 pm
Natural Food Store and take-out Deli. Bakery.
Menu: Has a good selection of sandwiches and soups.
Other Info: Counter service, take-out. No seating.
Directions: Coming from Boulder on Canyon Blvd (Rte 119) after entering Nederland make a left at the traffic circle. Then at First St turn left and this place is a half-block down on the right.

OURAY

Ground Keeper Coffeehouse
524 Main Street; 970-325-0550
Hours: Wednesday to Monday 8 am to 6 pm Closed Tuesday.
Natural Foods Restaurant. Vegan options. Not pure vegetarian.
Menu: Has several vegetarian options including Bagel Sandwich, Tempeh & Tofu Breakfast Burrito, Black Bean Chili and baked potatoes. Cappuccino, espresso.
Other Info: Accepts DIS, MC, VISA. Price: $. Limited service, take-out.

PAONIA

**Sunnyside Coop Café
101 Main Street; 970-527-3737
Hours: Monday to Saturday 10 am to 7 pm; café closes at 6 pm; closed Sunday.
Natural Food Store and Vegetarian Cafe. Deli, Bakery and Juice Bar. Organic produce.
Menu: Has a wide selection of vegetarian dishes.
Comments: Local organic produce used when possible. Grinds own flour. Has a good selection of bulk items.

Other Info: Cash or local checks; no credit cards.
Directions: Taking Hwy 133 into Paonia, go right at the first right and go into Paonia and this place is at Main St.

PUEBLO

Ambrosia Natural Foods Co-op
112 Colorado Avenue; 719-545-2958
Hours: Monday to Saturday 8 am to 8 pm Sunday 9 am to 5 pm
Natural Food Store. Organic produce.
Comments: Funky place.
Directions: From I-25, take Abriendo Ave exit (#97B), then go northwest on E Abriendo Ave for ¾ mile, then turn left at Colorado Ave and this place is on the left a half-block down.

Gaetano's
910 West US Highway 50 West; 719-546-0949
Hours: Monday to Friday 11 am to 10 pm; Saturday 4 pm to 10 pm; closed Sunday.
Italian, Vegetarian-friendly Restaurant.
Comments: Pleasant décor. Paintings by local artists. Has flowers and plants. Tablecloths on tables. Has live music on Friday and Saturday. Has outdoor dining on the patio. Has a children menu.
Other Info: Full service, take-out. Accepts AMEX, DC, DIS, MC, VISA. Price: $$.

SALIDA
Known as a base for white-water rafting. You also may come through here on the way to the Monarch ski area twenty minutes away.

First Street Café
137 East 1st Street; 719-539-4759
Hours: Monday to Thursday 11 am to 8 pm; Friday & Sunday 11 am to 9 pm; closed Sunday.
American. Not pure vegetarian.
Menu: Has several vegetarian options including Mexican dishes, salads and veggie burgers. Smoothies.
Comments: It is located in a building built in 1882, one block from the Arkansas River in the historical area of Salida.
Other Info: Full service, take-out. Accepts AMEX, DIS, MC, VISA. Price: $-$$.

SILVERTHORNE

Sunshine Café
Summit Place Shopping Center; 970-468-6663
Hours: Daily 7 am to 3 pm
Vegetarian-friendly Restaurant. Not pure veg.

Menu: Breakfast burrito made of refried beans, avocado, tomatoes and onions with spicy green chili. Sandwiches, vegetarian soups, salads, tofu dishes and more.

SPRINGS

Beau Jo's Pizza

1517 Miner; 303-567-4376
Hours: Daily 11 am to 9:30 pm
Pizza Place. Not pure vegetarian.

TRINIDAD

The Natural Food Store

316 Prospect Street; 719-846-7577
Hours: Monday to Friday 10 am to 5:30 pm; Saturday 10 am to 5 pm; closed Sunday.
Natural Food Store. Organic produce.
Comments: Well-stocked small store.
Directions: From I-25, take exit #12B and then go west on Hwy 12, which becomes Prospect Street. Then this place is on left (1.5 blocks down).

WESTMINSTER

Wild Oats

9229 North Sheridan Boulevard; 303-650-2333
Hours: Monday to Saturday 7:30 am to 9 pm
Sunday 8 am to 9 pm
Natural Food Store and Cafe. Deli, Bakery, Salad Bar and Juice Bar. Organic produce. Supermarket-type place. See Wild Oats Market information.
Directions: From US 36, take the Hwy 95/ Sheridan Blvd exit, then go north on Sheridan Blvd and this place is a quarter-mile down on the left.

Wheatridge (Denver suburb)

Gemini Restaurant

4300 Wadsworth Boulevard, Loehmann's Plaza
303-421-4990
Hours: Daily 6:30 am to 10 pm
Weekend brunch
International, American Natural Foods. Vegan options. Not pure vegetarian.
Menu: Has a large menu that includes vegetarian soups, salads, sandwiches, Mexican dishes and pastas. Has a kid's menu. Fresh juices.
Other Info: Full service, take-out. Reservations suggested for groups. Accepts MC, VISA. Price: $$.

WINTER PARK

Carvers Bakery Café

93 Cooper Creek Way, downtown Winter Park
970-726-8202
Hours: Daily 7 am to 3 pm
Bakery, American. Not pure vegetarian.
Menu: Has several vegetarian options including Grilled Vegetables Sandwich, Tempeh Burgers, salads, veggie chili, veggie burgers and burritos. Fresh juices, cappuccino, espresso.
Other Info: Full service, take-out, catering. Accepts AMEX, DC, DIS, MC, VISA. Price: $$.

Great Mother Market

540 Highway 40, Freser; 970-726-4704
Natural Food Store. Organic produce.

Connecticut

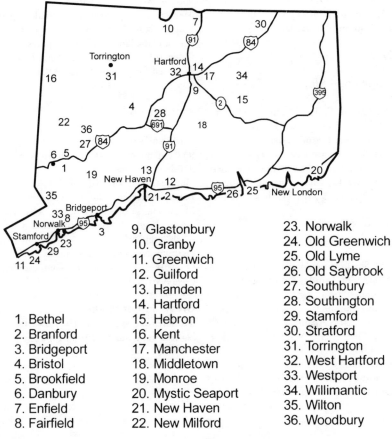

9. Glastonbury
10. Granby
11. Greenwich
12. Guilford
13. Hamden
14. Hartford
15. Hebron
16. Kent
17. Manchester
18. Middletown
19. Monroe
20. Mystic Seaport
21. New Haven
22. New Milford

23. Norwalk
24. Old Greenwich
25. Old Lyme
26. Old Saybrook
27. Southbury
28. Southington
29. Stamford
30. Stratford
31. Torrington
32. West Hartford
33. Westport
34. Willimantic
35. Wilton
36. Woodbury

1. Bethel
2. Branford
3. Bridgeport
4. Bristol
5. Brookfield
6. Danbury
7. Enfield
8. Fairfield

BETHEL

Body and Soul
25 Grassy Plain Road; 203-792-4555
Hours: Monday to Saturday 10 am to 7 pm
Closed Sunday.
Natural Food Store and Deli. Limited organic produce.
Directions: This place is about a half-mile west of the downtown. From I-84, take Rte 39 (#5) exit towards downtown Danbury/Bethel. Turn right onto N Main St (Rte 39) and go 1¾ mile. At South St (Rte 53) turn left and go 1¾ mile (becomes Grassy Plain St). At Grassy Plain Ter turn right and this place is 50 yards down next to the Dunkin' Donuts.

**Sage Café
153 Greenwood Avenue; 203-794-9394
Hours: Tuesday to Sunday 11 am to 7 pm
Closed Monday; closed Sundays during winter.
Vegetarian Café and Juice Bar. Not pure veg.
Comments: Creative dishes. Good food. Relaxed place. Nice people.
Other Info: Full service, take-out. Price: $$.

BRIDGEPORT

**Bloodroot
85 Ferris Street
203-576-9168
Web site: http://bloodroot.com/
Hours: Tuesday, Thursday 11:30 am to 2:30 pm,

6 pm to 9 pm; Wednesday 6 pm to 9 pm; Friday, Saturday 11:30 am to 2:30 pm, 6 pm to 10 pm; Sunday Brunch 11:30 am to 2:30 pm; closed Monday and Wednesday.
Fully Vegetarian International and American. Vegan options.
Menu: The menu changes basically every month. Portuguese Kale & Potato, Cream of Cauliflower, Quinoa Potato, Grilled Cheese Platter, a variety of salads, Bloodroot Burger and more. Homemade breads. Vegan desserts such as Tofu Mousse and Chocolate Devastation Cake.
Comments: Comfortable atmosphere. Local organic produce used when possible. Outside seating. Has a good atmosphere. Located next to the water at an inlet on Long Island Sound. Has own cookbook. Open for 25 years. Has cooking classes. Feminist bookstore in restaurant.
Other Info: Counter service, take-out. Has seating. Non-smoking. Reservations recommended for groups of 5 or more. Accepts personal checks. No credit cards. Price: $$.
Directions: It is on dead-end street right next to Long Island Sound. Coming from New York on I-95, take exit #24, then go straight through intersection, and turn right onto Black Rock Turnpike/Brewster Street. Turn left on Fairfield Avenue (fourth traffic light). Then turn right on Ellsworth Street (next traffic light). Turn left onto Thurston Street (second street). Turn right on Harbor Avenue. Turn left on Ferris Street (third street). Coming from New Haven on I-95 take exit #25. Turn left on Fairfield Avenue. Turn left on Ellsworth Street (third traffic light). Turn left on Thurston Street (second street). Turn right on Harbor Avenue. Turn left on Ferris Street (third street).

BRISTOL

Super Natural Market & Deli
430 North Main Street
860-582-1663
Hours: Monday to Friday 8 am to 7 pm; Saturday 9 am to 5 pm; closed Sunday.
Natural Food Store and Deli.
Menu: Soups, salads, pasta, tabbouleh, rice dishes, veggie chili and sandwiches.
Other Info: Counter service, take-out. Has seating.
Directions: From I-84, take Rte 72 W exit and go 5½ miles and it becomes Riverside Ave when it enters town. At N Main St turn right and this place is 0.60 miles down.

BROOKFIELD

Pancho's & Gringo's Mexican Restaurant
77 Federal Road, Brookfield; 203-775-0096
Hours: Daily 11 am to 10:30 pm
Mexican. Not pure vegetarian. See Southbury.
Other Info: Full service, take-out. Reservations not accepted. Accepts AMEX, DC, DIS, MC, VISA. Price: $$.

DANBURY

Chamomile Natural Foods
58-60 Newtown Road (Route 6); 203-792-8952
Hours: Monday to Friday 9 am to 7 pm (Thursday closes at 8 pm); Saturday 9:30 am to 6 pm; closed Sunday.
Natural Food Store. Organic produce. Has a nutritionist.
Directions: From I-84, take exit #8 and take Newtown Road south/west a half-mile. This place is in the Rte 6 Plaza one mile down on the right.

Sesame Seed
68 West Wooster Street, Danbury; 203-743-9850
Hours: Monday to Thursday 11:30 to 3 pm, 5 pm to 9:30 pm; Friday & Saturday 11:30 am to 3 pm, 5 pm to 9:30 pm; closed Sunday.
Middle Eastern Natural Foods. Not pure vegetarian.
Menu: Vegetable Pie, Vegetarian Combination Plate, hummus, falafel and Middle Eastern dishes. Non-alcoholic beer.
Other Info: Full service, take-out. Reservations suggested for groups. Non-smoking. Accepts MC, VISA. Price: $$.
Directions: From I-84, take US-7 S Exit (#3) on left towards Norwalk and then after a half-mile take Park Avenue exit. Merge onto Backus Ave (becomes Park Ave) and go ¾ mile. At Wooster St turn right and this place is a half-block down.

ENFIELD

Health Matters Natural Foods
640 Enfield Street; 860-745-1617
Hours: Monday to Friday 9:30 am to 6 pm Saturday 9:30 am to 5 pm
Natural Food Store.
Other Info: Accepts MC, VISA.
Directions: From I-91, take Exit #48, then go west on Elm St a half-mile. At Enfield St turn right and this place is ¾ mile down.

FAIRFIELD

Bombay Indian Kitchen

222 Post Road #C (also called Fairfield Avenue)
203-255-1970
Hours: Mon to Thur 11 am to 10 pm; Fri & Sat 11 am to 11 am; Sun 12 noon to 10 pm
Indian. Vegan friendly. Not pure vegetarian.
Menu: Has a wide selection of vegetarian dishes.
Comments: Supposed to use separate utensils for cooking meat and non-meat dishes.
Other Info: Full service, take-out, delivery. Accepts AMEX, MC, VISA. Price: $-$$.
Directions: From I-95, take Fairfield Exit (#25), towards Rte 130, then at Fairfield Ave turn left and this place is 1½ mile down.

Fairfield Diner

90 Kings Highway, Cut Off; 203-335-4090
Hours: Daily 6 am to 12 midnight
American. Vegan options. Not pure vegetarian.
Menu: Has a separate vegetarian section on the menu with a good selection of vegetarian dishes. Middle Eastern dishes, Grilled Tofu, Portobello Mushroom Sandwich, Tempeh Reuben Sandwich, vegetarian chili, pastas and salads. Chocolate Vegan Cake.
Comments: Typical old-type diner. Full service, take-out. Reservations not accepted.
Other Info: Accepts AMEX, DIS, DC, MC, VISA. Price: $-$$.
Directions: From I-95, take Exit #24 towards Black Rock Turnpike, At Chambers St turn right (if going south on I-95, if going north on I-95 turn left), then at Kings Hwy E (Hwy 1) turn right and go northeast and this place is ¾ mile down. This place is north of I-95.

Mrs Green's

1916 Post Road; 203-255-4333
Hours: Monday to Saturday 9 am to 7 pm Sunday 9 am to 5 pm
Natural Food Store and take-out Deli. Salad Bar and Juice Bar.
Other Info: Counter service, take-out. Accepts AMEX, MC, VISA.
Directions: From I-95, take exit #21 and go southeast on Mill Plain Rd a quarter-mile. At Post Rd (Rte 1), turn right and this place is less than a fourth-mile down on right.

Sprouts For Better Living

2250 Black Rock Turnpike; 203-333-3455
Hours: Monday to Friday 8:30 am to 8 pm; Saturday 8:30 am to 6 pm; Sunday 8:30 am to 5 pm
Natural Food Store and Restaurant. Vegan options. Gourmet Organic. Organic produce. Not pure vegetarian.
Menu: Soups, sandwiches, vegetarian Lasagna, veggie chili, salads and more.
Comments: Has a big restaurant and deli inside this store.
Other Info: Accepts AMEX, DIS, MC, VISA. Price: $$.
Directions: From I-95, take Exit #24 towards Black Rock Turnpike. At Chambers St turn right (if going south on I-95, if going north on I-95 turn left), then at Kings Hwy E (US 1) turn right and go northeast ¾ mile. Take a slight left onto Villa Ave and go two blocks. At Tunxis Hill Rd (Rte 58) turn left and go a third-mile. Go straight onto Tunxis Hill Cut Off (becomes Black Rock Turnpike, Rte 58) and go one mile. This place is about a mile northeast of Exit #24.

GLASTONBURY

Garden of Light Natural Foods Market

2836 Main Street, at Griswold
860-657-9131; **Web site:** www.gardenoflight.net
Hours: Monday to Friday 9:30 am to 8 pm; Saturday 9:30 am to 7 pm; Sunday 11 am to 5 pm
Natural Food Store and Deli. Salad Bar and Juice Bar. Organic produce.
Menu: Has an excellent deli with a good selection of vegetarian dishes. Soups, salads, sandwiches, hot dishes and freshly baked goods. Has good daily specials.
Comments: Award-winning vegan chef Ken Bergeton. Uses organic ingredients when possible. Food is mainly sold by the pound. One of the best natural food stores in the Hartford area. Has a good catering service.
Directions: From I-91, take Putnam Bridge exit (exit #25-26) and go east on Rte 3 across the bridge, then take Main St Glastonbury exit. At Griswold turn left, then at Main St turn right. This place is a half-mile down on the left in a shopping center, at the next traffic light.

GRANBY (north of Hartford)

Granby Village Health Inc

10 Hartford Avenue; 860-844-8608
Hours: Monday to Thursday 10 am to 6 pm; Friday 10 am to 7 pm; Saturday 9 am to 5 pm; Sunday 11 am to 5 pm
Natural Food Store. Organic produce.
Comments: Has vitamins, herbs, skincare items and books.

Other Info: Accepts AMEX, DIS, MC, VISA.
Directions: From I-91, take Rte 20 west 10 miles. When you enter town at Rte 202 turn left (go south) and go 150 yards, then at Hartford Ave turn left and this place is 100 yards down.

GREENWICH

Fresh Fields (Whole Foods Market)
90 East Putnam Avenue
203-661-0631; **fax:** 203-661-9375
Hours: Daily 8 am to 9 pm
Natural Food Store and Cafe. Deli, Bakery, Salad Bar and Juice Bar. Organic produce.
Comments: Has no indoor seating, but has three tables outside.
Directions: This place is a mile east of the downtown. From I-95, take exit #4, then go north on Indian Field Rd about 1 mile. At Putnam Ave turn right and this place is a half-mile down on left.

GUILFORD

Foodworks
1055 Boston Post Road; 203-458-9778
Hours: Monday, Thursday 9:30 am to 7:30 pm; Tuesday, Wednesday, Friday 9:30 am to 7 pm; Saturday 10 am to 7 pm; Sunday 11 am to 6 pm
Natural Food Store and Deli. Café and Juice Bar. Fully Vegetarian (except serves tuna). Organic produce.
Comments: Has three or four tables. Often uses organic produce.
Directions: From I-95, take exit #58. Follow signs to Guilford (downtown) and at Rte 77 go south for a half-mile. This place is at intersection of Rte 77 and Rte 1. From I-95, take Exit #57, then go southwest on Boston Post Rd and this place is 1 mile down. This place is 2 miles northwest of downtown.

Shoreline Dinner & Vegetarian Enclave
345 Boston Post Road (Route 1); 203-458-7380
Hours: Daily 7 am to 12 midnight
American Diner. Not pure vegetarian.
Menu: Has a wide selection of vegetarian dishes. Wild Rice and Mushrooms, Vegetable Pie, Grilled Tofu, Polenta, pastas, veggie burgers, veggie Lasagna, Stuffed Green Pepper, veggie chili, Tempeh Kebabs and more.
Comments: Good service. Food is well-presented. Food gets good ratings. Has non-dairy cheese and eggless mayonnaise.
Other Info: Accepts AMEX, DC, DIS, MC,

VISA. Price: $.
Directions: From I-95, take Exit #59, then go south on Soundview Rd 150 yards, then at Boston Post Rd turn left and this place is a half-mile down.

HAMDEN

Thyme & Season
3040 Whitney Avenue; 203-407-8128
Hours: Monday to Friday 9 am to 7:30 pm; Saturday 9 am to 7 pm; Sunday 11 am to 5 pm
Natural Food Store and take-out Deli. Organic produce.
Menu: Sandwiches, salads and three or four hot vegetarian dishes daily.
Other Info: Accepts AMEX, DC, DIS, MC, VISA.
Directions: From I-91, take exit #10 and take Hwy 40 north until it ends. Then at Whitney Ave turn right (go north) and this place is a half-mile down.

HARTFORD

Congress Rotisserie
333 North Main Street; 860-231-7454
24 Fenn Road, Newington; 860-231-1446
691 Silas Deane Hwy, Wethersfield
860-563-4300
Hours: Monday to Wednesday 11 am to 8 pm; Thursday & Friday 11 am to 9 pm
Saturday 11 am to 8 pm; Sunday 11 am to 5 pm
American. Not pure vegetarian.
Menu: Good choice of soups and vegetarian sandwiches. Vegetarian pasta dish and stir-fries.
Other Info: Accepts AMEX, VISA, MC.

**Lion's Den Vegetarian Restaurant
403 1/2 Woodland Street; 860-241-0512
Vegetarian Caribbean. Vegan options.
Comments: Basic place with just a few tables.
Other Info: Counter service, take-out. Price: $.
Directions: The neighborhood is a little strange.

Timothy's Restaurant
243 Zion Street, Hartford; 860-728-9822
Hours: Monday to Wednesday 8 am to 8 pm
Thursday to Sunday 8 am to 9 pm
Eclectic American, Tex-Mex. Not pure veg.
Menu: Good quesadillas with avocado. Good selection of salads. Freshly cooked daily soups, vegetable soup, fresh baked homemade bread, Cold Gazpacho and homemade jams. Quiches (ask about eggs) come in different varieties such as broccoli and cheese. Portobello Mushroom Sand-

wich with goat cheese and roasted red pepper. Mushroom Enchilada with black beans and feta cheese with fruit salsa. Has good selection of desserts. The key lime pie is good.

Comments: Very vegetarian friendly. Simple place in laid-back atmosphere. During the summer ingredients are gotten from local farmers. Service not that fast. Fresh flowers on tables. Grows fresh herbs in own garden.

Other Info: Full service, take-out. Cash only; no credit cards. Price: $-$$.

Directions: Located near Trinity University (on west side). From I-91, take US-6 west 1¼ mile, then take Sigourney St exit. At Sigourney St turn left and go a quarter-mile. Then take a slight right onto Park Terrace and go 4/10 miles. At Summit St take a slight left and go a block. Then take a slight right onto Zion St and this place is a half-mile down.

HEBRON

Hebron Health & Harvest
32 Main; 860-228-4101
Hours: Monday, Tuesday, Wednesday, Saturday 9:30 am to 6 pm; Thursday & Friday 9:30 am to 7 pm; closed Sunday.
Natural Food Store.
Directions: From Rte 2, take exit #13, then turn left onto Rte 66. This store is at second light, across from Mobil station, 150 yards past Rte 85.

MANCHESTER

Bombay Raj Mahal
836-840 Main Street, Manchester; 860-646-5330
Hours: Daily 11:30 am to 10 pm
Indian. Vegan options. Not pure vegetarian.
Menu: Has a selection of vegetarian dishes including Aloo Matar, samosas, Vegetable Curry and rice dishes.
Other Info: Full service, take-out. Accepts AMEX, MC, VISA. Price: $$.

Natural Rhythms
964 Main Street; 860-645-9898
Hours: 9:30 am to 5 pm; Saturday 9:30 am to 3 pm; closed Sunday.
Healthy California. Vegan and Vegetarian friendly. Not pure vegetarian.
Menu: Has a selection of vegan and vegetarian dishes. Homemade soups, breads, frozen yogurt, sandwiches and salads. Organic coffee.
Comments: Can call ahead and meal will be ready to go.

Other Info: Full service, take-out, catering. Has limited seating and some outdoor seating.
Directions: From I-84 east, go east on I-384 three miles, then take Exit #3 and go north on Rte 83 (Main St). This place is a half-mile down on the left. Ten minutes east of Hartford.

Parkade Health Shoppe
Manchester Parkade Shopping Center.
378 Middle Turnpike W; 860-646-8178
Natural Food Store.
Menu: Has ready-made sandwiches. Eggplant Parmigiana, hummus, etc.
Comments: Has a registered pharmacist, clinical nutritionist. Has herbs, homeopathic medicines, books, natural cosmetics and macrobiotic items.
Directions: This place is a mile northeast of the downtown.

MIDDLETOWN

It's Only Natural Restaurant
Main Street Market (in rear); 386 Main Street
860-346-9210; **Web site:** www.ionrestaurant.com
Hours: Monday to Thursday 11:30 am to 9 pm
Friday & Saturday 11:30 am to 10 pm
Sunday Bunch 11 am to 3 pm
International Gourmet Restaurant. Juice Bar. Vegetarian and vegan friendly (serves fish). Macrobiotic options.
Menu: Vegan Crab Cakes, Mediterranean Pasta, soups, Pierogis (potato spinach dumpling with brown rice). Spring Rolls, Indian Samosas, Fried Rice, Sweet Potato Fries, freshly baked breads, dairy specials and desserts. Cappuccino, espresso.
Comment: Has an outdoor patio. A bit upscale. Located next to a good health food store. Desserts contain organic flours and natural sweeteners. Friendly, good service. Relaxed place. Often has live entertainment. Regularly wins the award given by Connecticut Magazine for best Natural Food Restaurant. Has a children's menu. Gets high ratings. Has an art gallery. Has tofu sour cream.
Other Info: Accepts AMEX, MC, VISA. Full service, take-out, catering. Price: $$.
Directions: This place is in the rear of the Main Street Market.

Main Street Market
386 Main Street; 860-346-1786
Store Hours: Monday to Saturday 9 am to 8 pm
Sunday 11 am to 4 pm
Natural Food Store. Organic produce.
Comments: Has a good selection of books. Only Natural Restaurant (below) is in the back of the

store.

Directions: From Rte 9, take exit #15. Go a half-block towards Main Street, take a left into Columbus Place. Large municipal parking lot on the left. The entrance of the restaurant is on the right. From I-91, get on Rte 9 and then take exit #15, take second left into Melilli Plaza (if reach Main St, just missed it). The restaurant is in the back of Main St Market.

MONROE

Sunwheel Health Foods

444 Main Street; 203-268-2688
Hours: Monday to Friday 10 am to 6 pm; Saturday 10 am to 5 pm; closed Sunday.
Natural Food Store.
Directions: This place on Rte 25 (Main St), at the junction of Rte 59. It is in the back of a big yellow house.

MYSTIC SEAPORT

Wokery In Mystic

6 Greenmanville Avenue; 860-572-7964
Hours: Monday to Thursday 11 am to 10 pm; Friday & Saturday 11 am to 11 pm; Sunday 12 pm to 10
Chinese. Not pure vegetarian
Menu: Has Chinese food and a health food section on the menu.
Other Info: Accepts MC, VISA.

NEW HAVEN

Avanti's

45 Grove Street; 203-777-3234
Hours: Monday to Saturday 11:30 am to 4 pm
Closed Sundays.
Italian, Pizzas. Vegan options. Not pure veg.
Menu: Pizza, vegetarian soup and some vegan dishes. Cappuccino, espresso.
Other Info: Full service, take-out. Accepts VISA, MC. Price: $$.

**Claire's Corner Copia

1000 Chapel Street, at College Street; 203-562-3888; **Web** site: www.clairescornercopia.com
Hours: Daily 8 am to 9 pm
Vegetarian Vegan International Restaurant. Italian, Mexican, Asian, Middle Eastern, French and Jewish. Vegan friendly. Kosher. Not totally vegetarian (serves tuna)
Menu: Soy and tempeh dishes. Has daily specials. Soups, salads, veggie burgers, stir fry, sand-wiches, veggie Lasagna, bean burritos, breads and pastas. Has many baked dishes. Fresh juices.
Comments: Open over 25 years. Has won many awards. Has several of their own vegetarian cookbooks.
Other Info: Cafeteria style, counter service, takeout, catering. Reservations not accepted. No credit cards; cash only. Price: $-$$.
Directions: Across from Yale University. From I-91 coming south, take Trumbull St exit (#3) and go a block on Trumbull St, at Orange St turn left and go a block, at Audubon St turn left and go a block, at State St turn right and go 0.4 mile, then at Chapel St turn right and this place is a third-mile down. From I-95 going east take Rte 34 (#47) and merge left onto Rte 34 and after a half-mile take Exit 1 towards downtown New Haven/Coliseum. Stay straight onto N Frontage Rd and go a block. At Church St turn right and go a quarter-mile. At Chapel St turn left and this place is 2 blocks down.

**Edge of the Woods

Market Square Shopping Center, 379 Whalley Avenue, near Edgewood Park and Norton 203-787-1055
Hours: Monday to Friday 8:30 am to 7:30 pm; Saturday 8:30 am to 6:30 pm; Sun 9 am to 6 pm
Natural Food Store and Vegetarian Deli. Bakery, Salad Bar and Juice Bar. Large organic produce section. Supermarket-type place.
Menu: Has a good take-out deli. Has vegan dishes, soups, sandwiches, main dishes and baked goods. Bagels, Tofu Lasagna, pastas, Lasagna, Un-Chicken Cutlets (really good), Black-eyed Peas, Lemon Curry Rice, Roasted Tofu, Cajun Rice and much more. Fresh juices.
Comments: Best natural food store in town. Does not sell any meat products. Has a nice seating area upstairs for 50.
Other Info: Cafeteria style, take-out. Has indoor seating area.
Directions: This place is about a mile west of Yale University and the downtown. From I-91, take Downtown Exit #3 (Trumbull St) and go a block. At Orange St turn left and go a block. At Audubon St turn left and go 1 block. At State St (US 5 S) turn right and go a half-mile, then at Chapel St turn right and this place is a third-mile down on left in Market Square Shopping Center.

House of Chao

898 Whalley Avenue; 203-389-6624
Hours: Tuesday to Sunday 12 noon to 9:30 pm
Closed Monday.

Chinese. Vegan options. Not pure vegetarian.
Comments: Has a good selection of vegetarian
dishes.
Other Info: Full service, take-out. Price: $$.

India Palace
65 Howe Street; 203-776-9010
Hours: Sunday to Thursday 11:30 am to 10:30
pm; Friday & Saturday 11:30 am to 11 pm
Indian. Daily Lunch Buffet. Vegan options. Not
pure vegetarian.
Menu: Samosas, vegetable pakoras, Indian breads,
soups, main dishes and desserts.
Other Info: Full service, take-out. Reservations
suggested on weekends. Accepts AMEX, DIS,
MC, VISA. Price: $$.

Mamoun's Falafel Restaurant
85 Howe Street; 203-562-8444
Hours: Daily 11 am to 3 am
Middle Eastern. Vegan options. Not pure veg.
Menu: Falafel, hummus, salads, baba ghanouj and
other dishes.
Other Info: Limited service, take-out. Non-smok-
ing. No credit cards. Price: $.
Directions: This place is a few blocks from Yale
University, a little away from the downtown.

Pad Thai Restaurant
1170 Chapel Street; 203-562-0322
Hours: Monday to Thursday 11:30 am to 3 pm,
5 pm to 10 pm; Friday 11:30 am to 3 pm, 5 pm
to 10:30 pm; Saturday 11:30 am to 10:30 pm;
Sunday 11:30 am to 10 pm
Thai. Not pure vegetarian.
Comments: One of the best Thai restaurants in
town.
Other Info: Full service, take-out. Reservations
not accepted. Accepts AMEX, DIS, MC, VISA.
Price: $-$$.

Rainbow Café
1022 Chapel Street, New Haven; 203-777-2390
Hours: Monday to Thursday 11 am to 8 pm; Fri
& Sat 10 am to 9 pm; Sun 10 am to 8 pm
American, Natural Foods. Salad Bar. Has many
vegan options. Not pure vegetarian.
Menu: Menu changes daily. Has about 15 veg-
etarian dishes. Has salads, several vegetarian sand-
wiches, pastas, soups, Tofu Stir-fry and daily spe-
cials. No alcohol.
Comments: Laid-back place.
Other Info: Self service, take-out. Non-smoking.
Accepts AMEX, DIS, MC, VISA. Price: $.
Directions: See above directions for Claire's Cor-

ner Copia and this place is on the next block
down.

NEW MILFORD

Bank Street Natural Foods
10 Bank Street; 860-355-1515
Hours: Monday to Friday 9:30 am to 6 pm; Sat-
urday 9:30 am to 5 pm; closed Sunday.
Natural Food Store and Juice Bar.
Other Info: Accepts AMEX, MC, VISA.
Directions: From the town green, at Bank St turn
right and this place second store on right.

NORWALK

Food for Thought
596 Westport Avenue; 203-847-5233
Hours: Monday to Saturday 8 am to 9 pm
Sunday 9 am to 6 pm
Natural Food Store and Deli. Bakery, Juice Bar
and Salad Bar. Good selection of organic produce.
Not pure vegetarian.
Other Info: Counter service, take-out. Has three
tables for sitting.
Directions: From I-95 going west/south, take exit
17 (Rte 33) towards Westport/Saugatuck. This
place is a mile north of Exit #17 on Hwy 1. From
I-95 going north/east take Exit #17, then turn
left onto Saugatuck Ave (go north) and go about
a mile. At Sylvan Rd turn left and go a half-mile.
At Westport (US1, next light) turn left and this
place is on the left about a mile down.

The Lime Restaurant
168 Main Avenue; 203-846-9240
email: cenzo1@aol.com
Hours: Monday to Saturday 11 am to 4 pm, 5
pm to 10 pm; Sunday 4 pm to 9:30 pm
American Natural Foods. Not pure vegetarian.
Menu: Vegetable Phyllo (vegetables, sunflower
seeds and cheese in a pastry dough), good Black
Bean Chili, Zucchini Loaf, Veggie Nut-Burger,
burritos, Soy-Carrot Loaf and Tofu Salad Pita.
Comments: Has outdoor seating. Everything
made fresh on the premises. Casual, popular place.
Good service and food. Gets high ratings.
Other Info: Full service, take-out, catering. Res-
ervations recommended. Non-smoking. Accepts
AMEX, DC, MC, VISA. Price: $$.
Directions: From I-95, take Exit #14 and go 3
miles north on Hwy 7, then go east (north) a
third-mile on Hwy 15, then take Exit #40A and
go north on Main Ave and this place is a quarter-
mile down.

OLD LYME

The Grist Mill
Old Lyme Shopping Center, 19 Halls Road, PO Box 6741; 860-434-2990
Hours: Monday to Saturday 9 am to 6 pm Sunday 11 am to 5 pm
Natural Food Store.
Directions: From I-95, take exit #70 (going north turn left and go under I-95). Then take an immediate left at Halls Rd and this place is a quarter-mile down at Old Lyme Shopping Center. From I-95 going south, at exit go straight to Halls Rd, and this place is a quarter-mile down on right in Shopping Center.

OLD SAYBROOK

Foodwork II
17 Main Street; 860-395-0770
Hours: Monday to Friday 9:30 am to 6 pm; Saturday 10 am to 6 pm; Sunday 11 am to 5 pm
Natural Food Store. Organic produce.
Menu: Has prepared dishes such as salads, sandwiches, hummus, pasta salad, couscous and more.
Directions: From I-95 south, take Old Saybrook exit (#67), then take Middlesex Turnpike (Rte 154) south for 0.40 miles (becomes Boston Post Rd, Hwy 1), then take a slight left onto Main St and this place is first building on right. From I-95 north, take Old Saybrook exit and bear right at the exit fork. At Main St (third light) turn left and this place first building on right.

SOUTHBURY

Senior Pancho's Mexican Restaurant
Union Square Mall; 203-262-6988
Hours: Sunday to Thursday 11 am to 10 pm Friday & Saturday 11 am to 11 pm
Mexican. Not pure vegetarian.
Menu: Has a selection of vegetarian Mexican dishes. Smoothies, cappuccino, espresso.
Comments: Cook says no lard in beans.
Other Info: Full service, take-out, catering. Reservations requested for groups. Smoking at bar. Accepts AMEX, DC, MC, VISA. Price: $-$$.

SOUTHINGTON

El Sombrero
Oak Hill Mall, 151 Queen Street; 860-621-9474
Hours: Sunday to Thursday 11 am to 10 pm Friday & Saturday 11 am to 11 pm

Mexican. Not pure vegetarian.
Menu: Has several vegetarian options including Black Bean Soup, burritos, Vegetable Fajitas and others. Smoothies, cappuccino, espresso.
Comments: Good Mexican food and good service.
Other Info: Full service, take-out, catering, delivery. Accepts AMEX, MC, VISA. Price: $$.

STAMFORD

Natural Nutrition
1055 High Ridge Road; 203-329-7400
Hours: Monday to Friday 9 am to 7 pm; Saturday 9 am to 6 pm; Sunday 11 am to 5 pm
Natural Food Store. Has a small amount of organic produce.
Comments: Little place.
Directions: From Merritt Parkway (Rte 15), take exit #35 and bear right onto High Ridge Rd (go south). This place on left a half-mile down.

STRATFORD

Nature's Way Natural Foods
922 Barnum Avenue Cutoff; 203-377-3652
Hours: Monday to Saturday 9 am to 9 pm Sunday 9 am to 5 pm
Natural Food Store. Has a large selection of organic produce.
Directions: From I-95 going west (south), take West Broad/Stratford exit (#32). Then turn right onto Linden Ave and go a quarter-mile, then turn left onto Main St (go north) and go a third-mile, then at Barnum turn right and this place on left. From I-95 north (east), take Exit #32 and go on W Broad St a few blocks, then at Main St turn left and go 2/3 mile.

TORRINGTON

Natural Life – Gabriella's Market
634 Migeon Avenue; 860-482-9199
Hours: Monday to Saturday 9 am to 9 pm Closed Sunday.
Natural Food Store and Deli. Organic produce.
Comments: Both Gabriella's Market and Natural Life are in same building. Natural Life has organic produce, and Gabriella's has groceries.
Other Info: Counter service, take-out. Has some seating at the counter.
Directions: This place on Rte 4, west of Rte 8 and town. From Rte 8, take Exit #44, then go west on Rte 4 and this place is 1 mile down.

WEST HARTFORD

Lemon Grass Restaurant

7 South Main Street; 860-233-4405
Hours: Monday to Friday 11:30 am to 10 pm
Saturday & Sunday 4 pm to 10 pm
Thai. Not pure vegetarian.
Comments: It is a good Thai place.
Other Info: Accepts AMEX, DC, DIS, MC, VISA.

Tapas

1150 New Britain Avenue; 203-521-4609
Hours: Monday to Thursday 11 am to 9 pm; Fri & Sat 11 am to 10 pm; Sun 12 noon to 9 pm
Mediterranean. Not pure vegetarian. Vegan options.
Menu: Pizza, salads and daily specials.
Comments: Patio dining.
Other Info: Accepts AMEX, DC, DIS, MC, VISA. Price: $$.

Wild Oats Market

340 North Main Street
860-523-7174; **fax:** 860-523-7606
Hours: Monday to Saturday 9 am to 9 pm
Sunday 8 am to 8 pm
Natural Food Store and Deli. Bakery, Juice Bar and large Salad Bar. Organic produce. Supermarket size place.
Menu: Has a large selection of vegetarian dishes in its deli such as Curried Tofu with Broccoli, Basmati and Wild Rice, Stuffed Grape Leaves, Roasted Potatoes and Peas, Veggie Rice Burgers, quesadillas, burritos, Organic Whole-wheat Pizza, pastas, Lasagna, Un-chicken Salad, Tofu Salad and Potato Pancakes.
Comments: Has plenty of seating. Has a good selection of take-out sandwiches in its coolers.
Directions: This place is about 4 miles northwest of downtown Hartford. From Hartford take US 44 (Albany Ave) west for 4 miles, then at N Main St turn left and this place is in a shopping center a quarter-mile down. Also from I-84, take West Hartford exit and go through downtown West Hartford and this place is about two miles north of the downtown on the right in a shopping center. It is next to Bertucci's, which is a good Italian and pizza restaurant.

WESTPORT

The Chef's Table

44 Church Lane; 203-226-3663
Hours: Monday to Friday 8 am to 8 pm; Saturday & Sunday 8 am to 7 pm; closed Sunday.
Natural Food Store and Vegetarian-friendly Deli. Not pure vegetarian.
Menu: Grilled Vegetable Sandwich, Sesame Noodles & Wild Mushrooms, hummus and salads.
Comments: Has a pleasant outdoor patio for sitting.
Other Info: Counter service, take-out. Seating only for summer at outdoors patio. Accepts AMEX, DIS, MC, VISA.
Directions: From I-95, take Exit #17 and go north on Saugatuck Ave 1½ miles to Westport. Cross the Saugatuck River to the right into town and go two blocks, then turn left on Church Lane and this place is 1 block down.

**Fountain of Youth

1789 Post Road, East; 203-259-9378
Hours: Monday to Saturday 9 am to 7 pm
Sunday 10 am to 5 pm
Natural Food Store and fully Vegetarian Deli. Juice Bar and Salad Bar. Organic produce.
Menu: Has salads, soups, hot vegetarian meals and daily specials.
Comments: Gives out free hot tea in the winter. Does not sell any meat products.
Directions: From I-95, take exit #19. Coming from the north, go straight past stop sign. At first light turn right and this place is on the right after ¾ mile. Coming from south, turn left, then at Post Rd turn left and this place half-mile down on right.

**Organic Market

285 Post Road E; 203-227-9007
Hours: Monday to Saturday 9 am to 7 pm
Sunday 11 am to 5 pm
Natural Food Store and Vegetarian Café. Juice Bar and Deli. Has organic lunch bar.
Menu: Soups, sandwiches, salads and fresh juices.
Directions: From I-95, take exit #18 and go north (left off ramp coming from north, right coming from south). At Post Rd (third light) turn left and this place ¾ mile down on right.

Westport Wild Oats Natural Marketplace

399 Post Road West
203-227-6858; **fax:** 203-227-5605
Hours: Monday to Saturday 8 am to 9 pm
Sunday 8 am to 8 pm
Natural Food Store and Deli. Bakery, Juice Bar and large Salad Bar. Organic produce. Supermarket-size place.
Menu: Has a large selection of vegetarian dishes

in its deli such as Curried Tofu with Broccoli, Basmati and Wild Rice, Stuffed Grape Leaves, Veggie Rice Burgers, quesadillas, burritos, Organic Pizza, Un-chicken Salad, Tofu Salad and Potato Pancakes.

Comments: This place has plenty of seating. Has a good selection of take-out sandwiches in its coolers.

Directions: From I-95, take exit #18 and go north (left off ramp coming from north, right coming from south). At Post Rd (third light) turn left and this place ¾ mile down on right.

WILLIMANTIC

Willimantic Food Co-op
27 Meadow Street; 860-456-3611
Web site: http://users.neca.com/foodcoop/
Hours: Monday to Friday 9am to 8 pm; Saturday 9 am to 6 pm; Sunday 10 am to 5 pm (closed Sunday in July & August)
Natural Food Store.
Menu: Has prepared foods such as salads and sandwiches.
Other Info: Counter service, take-out. Has no seating.
Directions: Near the Everyday Café. From Rte 44, head south on Rte 32 (becomes Rte 66 and then Main St in Willimantic). At Walnut St turn left and go a block, at Meadow turn right and this place is a half-block down on left.

WILTON (near Norwalk)

Wilton Organic Gourmet
33 Danbury Road, Wilton; 203-762-9711
Hours: Monday to Friday 9:30 am to 6:30 pm; Saturday 8 am to 6 pm; Sunday 11 am to 4 pm
Natural Food Store and Deli. Juice Bar. Not pure vegetarian. Organic produce.

Other Info: Counter service, take-out only.
Directions: From I-95, take Rte 7 Connector north for 4 miles to Rte 7 north (Danbury Rd), then this place is on the left after three-fourth mile.

WOODBURY

Good News Café
694 Main Street South; 203-266-4663
Hours: Wed to Mon 11:30 am to 10 pm
Natural Food Restaurant. Mainly Organic. Not pure vegetarian.
Menu: Has a good selection of vegetarian dishes. Soups of the days (always vegetarian), several excellent salads, Thai Spice Noodles and Rice, Vegetable Casserole, Pasta with Vegetables, Portobello Mushrooms and more.
Comments: Very good food. Friendly place.
Other Info: Mainly only uses organic vegetables. Accepts AMEX, MC, VISA.

New Morning Country Store
Main Street South, PO Box 429; 203-263-4868
Hours: Monday to Wednesday 8 am to 6 pm; Thursday & Friday 8 am to 8 pm; Saturday 8 am to 6 pm; Sunday 11 am to 5 pm
Natural Food Store and Café. Deli, Juice Bar and Bakery. Mostly vegetarian and organic. Not pure vegetarian.
Other Info: Counter service, take-out. Has two tables. Accepts AMEX, DIS, MC, VISA.
Directions: From I-84 east, take exit #15 (Southbury), and at Rte 67 turn left and it becomes Rte 6 in Woodbury. This place on left in strip mall. From I-84 west, take exit #17 and go straight. Take Rte 64 into Woodbury and at Rte 6 turn left. This place on the right in a strip mall a fourth-mile down.

Delaware

1. Bethany Beach
2. Dover
3. Hockessin
4. Lewis
5. New Castle
6. Newark
7. Rehoboth Beach
8. Wilmington

BETHANY BEACH

If you are going to Bethany Beach you may want to stop at Wholesome Habits (302-537-0567) on Route 1 on the way.

Wholesome Habits

Route 1 Beach Plaza; 302-537-0567
Hours: Daily 9 am to 6 pm
Natural Food Store. No produce except organic carrots.
Comments: The Stress Management Center next door has massages, hypnosis and others things.
Directions: Opposite Sea Colony.

HOCKESSIN

Capriotti's

300 Lantana Square Shopping Center
Route 7 & Valley Road; 302-234-2322
Hours: Daily for lunch and dinner
Deli with vegan options. Not pure vegetarian.
Menu: Has vegetarian options. Has veggie burgers, veggie hot dogs and veggie tuna, ham, and turkey. Makes both subs and sandwiches.
Warning: Regrettable the hot dogs and veggie burgers most likely are cooked on the same grill as meat (this is what I was told). So I would ask about this.
Other Info: Counter service, take-out only. Price: $.

Harvest Market

1252 Old Lancaster Pike
302-234-6779
Hours: Monday to Saturday 10 am to 7 pm
Closed Sunday.
Natural Food Store. Organic produce.
Comments: Has vegetarian sandwiches in the cooler.
Directions: Take Rte 41 (coming southeast) into Hockessin; at light (only one in town) turn left. After a block the road ends and this place is right there.

LEWIS

Gertie's Green Grocer

119 2nd Street
302-645-8052
Hours: Monday to Saturday 10 am to 5:30 pm
Sunday 12 noon to 4 pm
Natural Food Store. Organic produce.
Directions: This place is in the downtown historical area of Lewis. Coming from Rte 1 turn left at 2nd St (one way) and this place on right.

NEW CASTLE

Cellar Gourmet

208 Delaware Street
302-323-0999

Hours: Monday 11 am to 2 pm
Tuesday to Sunday 9 am to 4 pm
Café. Vegan options. Not pure vegetarian.
Menu: Has a "Vegetarian Low-Cholesterol" page
on the menu. Has veggie burgers, salads, soy club
sandwich, mock BLT, Tofu Chili, non-dairy waffle
and several other dishes. Three vegetarian soups
during the week and a couple during the weekends.
No credit, cash only.
Directions: In the middle of the downtown. From
I-295, take Rte 9 (New Castle Ave) and go south
on Rte 9, when enter town go straight on Rte 9
(also E 6th St), turn left onto Delaware St and
this place is four blocks down at corner of E 2nd
St.

Capriotti's
708 West Basin Road
302-322-6797
Hours: Daily for lunch and dinner
Deli with vegan options. Not pure vegetarian.
See Hockessin.
Directions: From I-95, take exit #5A-B towards
New Castle/Newport, then go south on Rte 202
(Rte 141) and this place is 1½ mile down, near J
Dr.

NEWARK

Capriotti's
614 Newark Shopping Center; 302-454-0200
Hours: Monday to Saturday 10 am to 8 pm
Sunday 11 am to 6 pm
Deli with vegan options. Not pure vegetarian.
See Hockessin.
Menu: Has vegetarian options. Has veggie
burgers, veggie dogs, and veggie tuna, ham and
turkey hoagies & sandwiches.
Other Info: Take-out. Price: $.
Directions: From I-95, take Rte 896 exit and go
north. At Delaware Ave turn right, then at S
Chapel St turn left and go a quarter-mile, then at
Main St turn right and this place on left a quarter
mile down.

King's Chinese Restaurant
Meadowood Shopping Center
2671 Kirkwood Highway
302-731-8022
Hours: Daily 11 am to 10 pm
Chinese. Vegan options. Not Pure Vegetarian.
Menu: Has a large selection of vegetarian dishes.
Soups, mock meat dishes and mushrooms dishes.
Comments: Are willing to prepare food the way

you like.
Other Info: Full service, take-out. Accepts
AMEX, DIS, MC, VISA. Price: $$.
Directions: This place is on the side of a shop-
ping center and can be hard to see from the road.
From Rte 141, take Kirkwood Hwy exit towards
Newark/Elsemre/Rte 41 and this place is 4 mile
down.

Newark Natural Foods Co-op
280 East Main Street
302-368-5894; **email:** nnfoods@delanet.com;
Web site: http://newarknaturalfoods.com
Hours: Monday to Saturday 9 am to 8 pm
Sunday 9 am to 3 pm
Natural Food Store with a small Deli. Organic
produce. Vegan options.
Menu: Salads, and vegan and vegetarian sand-
wiches in the deli.
Other Info: Counter service, take-out. Has seat-
ing. Price: $.
Directions: From I-95, take Rte 896 exit and go
north. At Delaware Ave turn right, then at S
Chapel St turn left and go a quarter-mile, then at
Main St turn right and this place on left a quar-
ter-mile down.

REHOBOTH BEACH
Many of the places in town are only open from
April to October.

Chez Le Mar
210 2nd Street, at Wilmington Avenue
302-227-6494
Hours: April to October 5:30 pm to 10 pm
French. Not pure vegetarian.
Menu: Has some good vegetarian selections. Has
a separate vegetarian menu with vegetarian soups,
appetizers and main dishes. Wild Mushroom Loaf
(tofu and mushroom baked into a loaf). Sautéed
Seitan Medallions.
Comments: A bit upscale. Has a rooftop deck
and enclosed sun porch for dining. Very nice
owner. Said if call in advance they would make
sure that they would have something very special
for you. Price: $$$.
Directions: This place is a mile west of beach.
From Rte 1, turn left at Church St, turn slight
right onto Rehoboth Ave and go 6/10 mile, turn
slight right at Christian St, then at 2nd turn left
and this place at corner.

Planet X Café
35 Wilmington Avenue
Rehoboth Beach

302-226-1928
Hours: Easter to Halloween Daily 5:30 pm to 11:30 pm
Vegetarian-friendly Coffeehouse. Not pure vegetarian.
Menu: Has 2 or 3 vegetarian appetizers and 4 or 5 main dishes nightly.
Comments: Laid-back, friendly place,.
Other Info: Accepts AMEX, MC, VISA. Catering.

Rainbow Earth Natural Foods
220 Rehoboth Avenue
302-227-3177
Hours: Monday to Saturday 9:30 am to 6 pm
Sunday 10 am to 5:30 pm
Natural Food Store. Organic produce.
Menu: Has hummus and sandwiches in the cooler.
Directions: This place is opposite the fire station, 1½ mile from beach. From Hwy 1 get on bypass 1A, go east on Church St a quarter-mile, turn slight right onto Rehoboth and this place is ¾ mile down.

WILMINGTON
Wilmington and Newark are located right next to each other.

Capriotti's (two locations)
510 North Union Street, Wilmington
302-479-9818
Directions: From I-95, take exit #7B towards Rte 52 N/Delaware Ave, then get on N Jackson St, at Delaware Ave turn right, take a slight right onto Pennsylvania Ave (Rte 52) and go 6/10 of a mile. Then at N Union St turn left and this place is a half-mile down.
2124 Silverside Road, Barba Plaza
302-454-0200
Directions: From I-95, take Marsh Rd (#9) exit, then go north on Marsh Rd 1.4 miles, at Veale Rd turn right, at Silverside Rd turn left.
Web site: www.capriottis.com
Hours: Monday to Saturday 11 am to 7 pm
Sunday 11 am to 6 pm
Deli with vegan options. Not pure vegetarian.
See Hockessin for details.

Country Health Food Store
2199 Kirkwood Highway, Elsmere
302-995-6620
Hours: Monday to Saturday 9:30 am to 9:30 pm
Sunday 10 am to 7 pm
Natural Food Store. Organic produce.
Comments: Has a good section of health related books.
Directions: Right next door to Value City.

Indian Paradise
1710 Newport Gap Pike A, Wilmington
302-999-0855
Hours: Tuesday to Sunday 11 am to 2:30 pm, 5 pm to 10 pm; closed Monday.
Indian. Vegan options. Not Pure Vegetarian.
Menu: Has a good selection of vegetarian dishes. Spinach and Chickpeas, samosas, Potatoes & Cauliflower, rice dishes and others.
Other Info: Full service, take-out, catering. Accepts DC, DIS, MC, VISA.
Directions: It is in the Prices Corner Shopping Complex. From I-95, take exit #5A-B towards New Castle/Newport (US13), stay right at fork in ramp and merge onto Rte 141 N and go 2 miles. Take Kirkwood Hwy (Rte 2) exit towards Elsemere/Newark (Rte 41) and get on Robert W Kirkwood Hwy (Rte 2 W) and go ¾ mile. At Newport Gap Pike turn left and this place is a third-mile down.

Mikasa
3602 Kirkwood Highway
302-995-8905
Hours: Monday to Thursday 11 am to 2:45 pm, 4:30 pm to 10 pm
Friday 11 am to 2:45 pm, 4:30 pm to 10:30 pm
Saturday 11:30 am to 2:45 pm, 4:30 pm to 10:30 pm
Sunday 5 pm to 9 pm
Japanese. Not pure vegetarian.
Other Info: Accepts AMEX, MC, VISA.

Florida

1. Alachua
2. Altamonte Springs
3. Atlantic Beach
4. Aventura
5. Big Pine
6. Boca Raton
7. Bonita Springs
8. Brandon
9. Brooksville
10. Cape Canaveral
11. Cape Coral
12. Casselberry
13. Celebration
14. Cocoa
15. Coral Springs
16. Daytona Beach
17. Dunedin
18. Fort Lauderdale
19. Fort Myers
20. Gainesville
21. Gulf Breeze
22. Hallandale
23. Holiday
24. Hollywood
25. Indian Rocks Beach
26. Jacksonville
27. Jupiter
28. Key West
29. Kissimmee
30. Lake Buena Vista
31. Largo
32. Madeira Beach
33. Margate
34. Melbourne
35. Merritt Island
36. Miami

37. Miami Beach
38. Naples
39. North Miami
40. Ocala
41. Orange Park
42. Orlando
43. Oviedo
44. Palm Beach
45. Pensacola
46. Pinecrest
47. Plantation
48. Sarasota
49. St Augustine
50. South Miami
51. Tallahassee
52. Tampa
53. Tequesta
54. West Palm Beach
55. Winter Park
56. Ybor City

ALACHUA

Joseph Selvester, is an Ayurvedic Practitioner and Master Herbalist. His radio show "Healing With Herbs" is on WSKY 97.3 FM every Sunday at 12 noon.

**Govinda's Restaurant

14603 Main Street
386-462-4500; catering: 386-418-0234 email: www.govindas.net
Web site: www.govindas.net
Hours: Tuesday to Friday 11 am to 2 pm, 5 pm to 9 pm; Saturday 11 am to 9 pm, Sunday Brunch 11 am to 3 pm; closed Monday.
Pure Vegetarian Natural Food Restaurant. International. Juice Bar and Salad Bar (good selection). All-you-can-eat Buffet. Vegan options. Often uses organic produce.
Menu: One of the main highlights of this place is the all-you-can-eat hot buffet and salad bar. Featured dishes are rice, vegetables main dishes, pastas, two soups, breads, tempeh or tofu dishes and a good selection of salad items. An assortment of pizzas. Fresh juices, smoothies and organic coffee.
Lunch: Pakoras, samosas, BBQ Burger, French fries, Govinda's Cole Slaw, Herbed Tofu Lasagna, Garden Burger and Eggplant Parmigiana.
Dinner: Lasagna, Eggplant Parmigiana with spinach, Dinner Burger Plate, Big Baked Potato, Soba Noodle Salad, Garden Salad, Tempe Salad and more. The Eggplant Parmigiana is recommended and it will definitely satisfy you.
Sunday Brunch Buffet: Home-fried potatoes, several types of pancakes, scrambled tofu, potato pancakes, soup, mock "sausage," vegetable dishes and more.
Comments: The all-you-can-eat hot buffet and salad bar tastes good and is reasonably priced and is a very good value. The place is a pleasant surprise. One of the better pure vegetarian restaurants in the country. The food is good and the atmosphere is first-class. It has a beautiful garden. The lunches are a real bargain and the dinner meals are a bit higher priced. Don't miss this place if you are in the Gainesville Area. Sometimes has live music during dinner (on Fridays). The Sunday brunch is highly recommended. This place has a pleasant, relaxed atmosphere.
Special Events: Has special dinners on Valentine's Day, Halloween, Thanksgiving, Christmas and New Years. Menu such as Vegettabel En Croutes, Herbed Tempe Samosa, Lasagna, Sapanakopita, Tofu Marsala and Strawberry Shortcake.
History of Building: It is located in the large,

former old home of Williams-LeRoy, one the first families of Alachua and has been beautifully restored to look just like it is new. Furman E William, the builder of this house, and his brothers are credited with establishing the town of Alachua.
Other Info: Full service, take-out, catering. Accepts AMEX, MC, VISA. Price: $-$$.
Directions: This place is on the main street of town, a block from the downtown. It is minutes off I-75. From I-75, take Alachua/High Springs exit (Hwy 441 south) #78, and go towards Alachua (turn right if coming from Gainesville) for 1 mile, turn right on Main Street (a block before the traffic light) and this restaurant is about four blocks down on the left in a large white house.

**Hare Krishna (ISKCON) Temple

2½ miles from 441 on Route 235, Alachua
386-462-1372
Hours: Sunday Feast program from 4:15 pm to 7 pm.
Indian Vegetarian Feast. Menu changes weekly.
Comments: There is a vegetarian feast on Sunday at 5:30 pm. Besides the feast there is kirtana (public chanting of Hare Krishna) and a Bhagavad Gita class.
Directions: From I-75, take Alachua/High Springs exit (Hwy 441 south) #78, and go towards Alachua (turn right if coming from Gainesville) for 1 mile to the light. Then turn left onto Rte 235. This place is 2½ miles down on the left. There is a sign outside that says Hare Krishna Farm.

Healthy, Wealthy, & Wise Natural Foods Market

14862 North Main Street, Alachua
386-462-4090
fax: 386-462-4375
Hours: Monday to Saturday 10 am to 7 pm; Sunday 11 am to 3 pm
Natural Food Store. Organic produce.
Comments: This place has a decent selection of items and some organic produce. It has a good selection of natural nutritional aids.
Other Info: Accepts AMEX, MC, VISA. Price: $-$$.
Directions: This place is on the main street of town. It is a few minutes off I-75. From I-75, take Alachua/High Springs exit (Hwy 441 south) #78, and go towards Alachua (turn right if coming from Gainesville) for 1 mile to Main St. Then turn right onto Main St and this place is 3 blocks down on the right, in the middle of the downtwon.

Southcare Home Delivered Meals
14603 Main Street, Alachua
386-418-8000, 904-418-3524
Hours: Monday to Friday for lunch.
Home delivered vegetarian meals. Natural food meals for the elderly or persons who have physical problems. This is a non-profit organization that home delivers freshly cooked vegetarian meals. The meals change daily. Meals are around $5.
Menu: Sample meals are: spaghetti, salad, bread, walnut cookies, juice and milk. Baked Bean, Baked Potato, Broccoli & Carrots and Apple Crisp.
Comments: Meals are prepared at Govinda's Restaurant in Alachua. Whenever possible organically grown local produce is used. Call them to have the meals delivered. Very reasonably priced. Recommended.
Directions: Their office building is next to Govinda's Restaurant.

ALTAMONTE SPRINGS (Orlando suburb)

Bangkok Restaurant
260 Douglas Avenue
407-788-2685
Hours: Monday to Saturday 11:30 to 3 pm, 5 pm to 10 pm; Sunday 5 pm to 10 pm
Thai. Vegan options. Not pure vegetarian.
Menu: Has several vegetarian dishes on the menu. Has a lunch buffet Monday to Friday.
Other Info: Full service, take-out. Accepts AMEX, DIS, MC, VISA. Price: $$.

Chamberlin's Market and Café
Gooding's Plaza, 1086 Montgomery Road
407-774-8866
Web site: www.chamberlins.com
Store Hours: Mon to Sat 9 am to 8:30 pm (Friday to 9 pm); Sunday 11 am to 5:30 pm
Café Hours: Monday to Saturday 9 am to 7:30 pm; Sunday 11 am to 4:30 pm
Natural Food Store and Café. Deli, Bakery, Salad Bar and Juice Bar. Vegan options. Organic produce. See Winter Park for details.
Menu: Homemade soups, salads, sandwiches, vegetarian chili, fresh fruit smoothies, organic juices and vegetarian main dishes.
Comments: This is a large place that has a good selection of items.
Directions: From I-4, take exit #49 and go west on Hwy 434 for 1 mile. Make a left at Montgomery Rd and this store is a quarter-mile down on the right in Goodings Plaza.

Economy Health Foods
1035 Academy Drive
407-869-0000;
Web site: www.economyhealth.com
Hours: Sunday to Thursday 8 am to 8 pm Friday 8 am to 5 pm; closed Saturday.
Natural Food Store. Organic produce. No Deli.

Kohinoor
The Village Shoppes
249 West Highway 436 #1093
407-788-6004
Hours: Tuesday to Friday 11:30 am to 2:30 pm, 5 pm to 10 pm; Sat & Sun 12 noon to 2:30 pm, 5 pm to 10 pm
Closed Monday.
Indian. Lunch Buffet. Vegan options. Not pure vegetarian.
Menu: Has a good selection of vegetarian dishes. Lentil soup, rice, Indian breads, samosas, several chutneys and several entrees.
Other Info: Full service, take-out. Accepts AMEX, DC, DIS, MC, VISA. **Price:** $$.

AVENTURA

Whole Foods Market
21105 Biscayne Boulevard; 305-933-1543 **Web site:** www.wholefoodsmarket.com
Hours: Daily 8 am to 11 pm
Natural Food Store and Deli. Bakery and Juice Bar. Organic produce. Supermarket-type place. See Whole Foods information.
Directions: Next to the Aventura Hospital–Medical Center. From I-95, take NE 203 St/Ives Dairy Rd exit (#20). Go east on Ives Dairy for 1¼ mile, then at Biscayne Blvd (US 1) turn left and this place is a half-mile down. From US 1, go on 207th St and this store is on the right, just east of Biscayne (US 1). Right after horse race track.

BIG PINE (on the way to Key West)

Good Food Conspiracy
US Route 1, Mile Marker 30; 305-872-3945
Hours: Monday to Saturday 9:30 am to 7 pm; Sunday 11 am to 5 pm
Natural Foods Store and Café. Deli and Juice Bar. Organic produce. Not pure vegetarian.
Menu: Vegetarian soups, salads, sandwiches and more. Fresh juices and smoothies.
Other Info: Full service, take-out. Sit-down Café. Accepts MC, VISA. Price: $$.

BOCA RATON

All American Nutrition, Inc.
652 Glades Road; 561-395-9599
Hours: Monday to Friday 9 am to 8:30 pm
Sat 9 am to 6:30 pm; Sun 11 am to 6 pm
Natural Food Store. No organic produce.
Other Info: Accepts DIS, MC, VISA.
Directions: From I-95, take Rte 808/Glades Rd
exit (#39) and go east on Glades Rd 1¼ mile and
this place is in Oaks Plaza.

**Bombay Café
628 Glades Road; 561-750-5299
Hours: Monday to Saturday 11:30 am to 3 pm, 5
pm to 8 pm; closed Sunday.
Fully Vegetarian Indian. Vegan options.
Menu: Has a wide selection of vegetarian dishes
including curry vegetables, dal, rotis (flat wheat
bread) and rice dishes. Fixed menu, no buffet.
Other Info: Counter service, self service, take-
out. Have tables to sit at. Accepts AMEX, MC,
VISA. Price: $.
Directions: From I-95, take Rte 808/Glades Rd
exit (#39) and go east on Glades Rd 1½ mile.

Organically Fresh
21338 St Andrews Blvd; 561-362-0770
Hours: Monday to Friday 8:30 am to 7 pm
Saturday 10 am to 5 pm; closed Sunday.
Natural Food Store and Café. 100% Organic
Deli and Juice Bar. Organic produce. Has a nu-
tritionist.
Directions: From I-95, take the Glades Rd exit.
Head west and make a left at St Andrews. The
store is in the Town Square Plaza on the right.

Pine Garden
1668 North Federal Highway, north of Glades
Road; 561-395-7534
Hours: Monday to Saturday 11:30 am to 10 pm;
Sunday 3 pm to 10 pm
International and Chinese. Not pure veg.
Menu: Has a good-size separate vegetarian menu.
No MSG. Uses only vegetable oil in cooking.
Uses fresh produce.
Comment: Efficient service.

BONITA SPRINGS

Martha's Natural Food Market
9118 Bonita Beach Road; 941-992-5838
Hours: Monday to Friday 9 am to 6 pm
Saturday 9 am to 5:30 pm; closed Sunday.
Natural Food Store, Café and Juice Bar.

Directions: From I-75, take Exit #18 and get on
Bonita Beach Road going west. The store is in
the Sunshine Plaza on the right 3 miles down,
just before the intersection of US 41 (S Tamiami).

BRANDON (near Tampa)

Chuck's Natural Food Marketplace and Purple Plate Cafe
114 North Kings Avenue; 813-657-2555
Hours: Monday to Friday 9 am to 8 pm
Sat 9 am to 6 pm; Sun 12 noon to 6 pm
Café Hours: Monday to Friday 9 am to 5 pm; Sat
9 am to 3 pm; Sun 9 am to 3 pm
Natural Food Store and Café. Deli and Juice Bar.
A large 100% organic produce section. Super-
market-size store.
Menu: Soups, salads, sandwiches and other dishes.
Comments: Has a good selection of natural prod-
ucts such as food, vitamins, herbs, cosmetics, body
products and organic shampoo. Don't sell things
that have been tested on animals. The café is very
popular. Has specials just like a normal supermarket. Offers a 10% discount on most items
when you join the VIP Membership club.
Other Info: Counter service, take-out. Has tables.
Accepts AMEX, DIS, MC, VISA.
Directions: From I-75 exit, take Rte 60 exit (#51)
towards Brandon, go east on Adamo Dr (becomes
Brandon Blvd) for 2¼ miles, at N Kings Ave turn
left and this place is 1 block down.

Discount Herbs
10065 East Adamo Drive; 813-653-9500
Hours: Monday to Friday 10 am to 5 pm
Closed Saturday & Sunday
Natural Food Store. Organic produce.

BROOKSVILLE

Go To Health
13007 Cortex Boulevard (State Road 50 & Mariner Blvd); 352-592-0717
Hours: Monday to Saturday 10 am to 7 pm
Sunday 12 noon to 5 pm
Natural Food Store. Juice Bar. Organic produce,
bulk foods, herbs and vitamins.
Menu: Juice bar serves juices and smoothies, but
nothing else.
Directions: This place is on the main highway
going through town.

CAPE CANAVERAL

Living Greens

205 Merrit Island; 321-454-2268
Store Hours: Monday to Friday 10 am to 4 pm;
Saturday 11 am to 3 pm; closed Sun.
Deli & Juice Bar Hours: Monday to Saturday 11
am to 3 pm; Kitchen closed Mon also.
Natural Food Store & Deli. Organic produce.
Menu: Sandwiches, wraps and salads. Fresh juices,
smoothies and wheatgrass juice.
Other Info: Counter service, take-out. Has tables
to sit at. No credit cards: cash only.

Sunseed Food Co-op

6615 North Atlantic Avenue (A1A)
321-784-0930
Hours: Monday to Saturday 10 am to 6 pm
Closed Sunday.
Natural Food Store.
Other Info: Accepts DIS, MC, VISA.
Directions: From Hwy 528, turn right onto North
Atlantic Ave (A1A). Turn left onto A1A and drive
about 1½ mile.

CAPE CORAL

Back To Nature

1217 SE 47th Terrace; 941-549-7667
Hours: Monday to Friday 9 am to 6 pm
Saturday 9 am to 5 pm; closed Sunday.
Natural Food Store. Small selection of organic
produce. Has a nutritionist.
Menu: Has small selection of ready-made sandwiches.
Directions: Go over the bridge on College Parkway. After crossing the bridge go ¾ mile, then
turn right onto Vincennes and go 1 block, then
make a right on 47th Terrace and store immediately on the right.

Mother Earth Natural Foods

1721 Del Prado Boulevard; 941-574-6333
Hours: Monday, Wednesday, Friday 9 am to 6
pm; Tuesday, Thursday 9 am to 6:30 pm
Saturday 9 am to 5:30 pm; closed Sunday.
Natural Food Store.
Comments: Does not have organic produce or a
deli.
Other Info: Accepts AMEX, MC, VISA.
Directions: From I-75, take Exit #26 (Pine Is-
land Rd, State Rd 78). Go west to Cape Coral.
At Del Prado turn left and go south. It is on the
left in the Coral Point Shopping Center. Or from
I-75, take Colony Blvd exit and head west to

Cape Coral, after going over the Midpoint Bridge
take first exit Del Proto and then make right and
this place is about 1 mile north.

CASSELBERRY (Orlando suburb)

Chamberlin's Natural Foods

Lake Howell Square,1271 Semoran Boulevard
(Highway 436); 407-678-3100
Web site: www.chamberlins.com
Hours: Monday to Saturday 9 am to 8:30 pm
(Friday to 9 pm); Sun 11 am to 5:30 pm
Natural Food Store and Café. Deli, Bakery, Salad
Bar and Juice Bar. Organic produce. Vegan op-
tions. Supermarket-type place. See Winter Park
for details.
Menu: Homemade soups, salads, sandwiches,
vegetarian chili, fresh fruit smoothies, organic
juices and vegetarian entrees.
Comments: This is a large place that has a good
selection of items.
Directions: One mile north of Howell Branch
Road. From Central Florida Greeneway, take Rte
426 (#38) towards Aloma Ave, go on Rte 426 for
1½ mile, at Semoran Blvd (Fl-436) turn right (go
north) and this place is 1½ mile down.

CELEBRATION

Cafe D' Antonio

691 Front Street, Suite 110
407-566-CAFE (2233)
Web site: http://www.antoniosonline.com/
cafe.htm
Hours: Monday to Friday: 11:30 am to 3 pm; 5
pm to 10 pm; Saturday 11:30 am to 10 pm; Sunday 11:30 am to 9 pm
Italian. Not pure vegetarian.
Menu: Has homemade bread, Penne Pomodora
Pasta, calzones, pizzas and sorbetti (imported
sorbets from Italy) for dessert.
Comments: Overlooks the lake and the downtown. Make it clear that no meat stock is put
into any of he pastas. Romantic place with candlelight dining.
Other Info: Accept AMEX, DIS, MC, VISA.
Price: $$-$$$.

Seasons Restaurant

Florida Hospital Celebration, 400 Celebration
Place; 407-303-4000
Mainly Vegetarian Cafeteria. Price: $.
Directions: From I-4, take exit #25 and this place
is a half-mile southeast of the exit.

Max's Cafe

701 Front Street, Suite 160; 407-566-1144
Hours: Daily 8 am to 10 pm
American. Vegetarian friendly. Not pure veg.
Menu: Has a good homemade veggie burger, pastas and a good selection of salads.

CLEARWATER

Nature's Food Patch and Bunny Hop Café

1225 Cleveland Street, in Clearwater a little out of the downtown; 727-443-6703
email: nfp@livingnaturally.com;
Web site: www.naturesfoodpatch.com
Hours: Monday to Saturday 9 am to 9 pm
Sunday 10 am to 7 pm; **Deli Hours:** Monday to Saturday 10 am to 8 pm; Sunday 10 am to 7 pm;
Café Hours: 11 am to 3 pm
Natural Food Store and Café. Deli, Juice Bar, Bakery and large Salad Bar. Very large organic produce selection (over 100 items). International and Macrobiotic. Mainly Vegetarian (serves fish). Uses organic produce. Vegan options.
Menu: Salads, sandwiches, four homemade soups daily and a daily special. Salad bar includes avocado, BBQ Seitan, Nut Loaf (very good), veggie burgers, Tofu Lasagna (very good), vegetables, Tofu "Egg" Salad, wraps, stir-fry, Blackened Tofu and hummus. Has good desserts, some of which are vegan. Soy mozzarella. Fresh juices and smoothies. Has a great salad bar with around 50 items. The Sesame Tahini is good.
Restaurant Comments: Bunny Hop Café is in the back of the store. Casual coffee-shop type atmosphere. Happening on Friday and Saturday nights. Popular with the locals. Has around 15 tables. At the salad bar you pay by the pound or $6.95 for all-you-can-eat. Low-fat, high-fiber foods. Use frozen bananas to thicken smoothies.
Store Comments: Big place with a large organic produce section. Bulk foods, organic dairy, organic baby food, aromatherapy items, books, vitamins, minerals, homeopathic items and herbs. Has cooking classes. Helpful and efficient staff. Will go out of their way to help you.
Other Info: Counter service, take-out. Accepts MC, VISA. Price: $-$$.
Directions: From US Highway 19, drive west on Gulf to Bay Boulevard. As you approach the light at Highland, take the right fork in the road. The sign will say Downtown/Beaches. After several blocks the road will turn into Cleveland Street. The store is located at the corner of Cleveland Street and Missouri Avenue in Cleveland Shopping Plaza on the left.

Lonni's Sandwiches, Etc.

33 North Garden Avenue, 727-441-8044
Hours: Monday to Friday 8 am to 4 pm
Closed Saturday & Sunday.
Natural Foods. Not pure vegetarian.
Menu: Several vegetarian options including a vegetarian soup, bagels, Crispy Vegetable Platter (raw vegetables and baby corn, needs advance notice), Wild Rice Soup, pasta, Fruit & Cheese Plate, Garden Salad and vegetarian sandwiches. Cappuccino.
Comments: Friendly service.
Other Info: Counter service, take-out, catering, delivery (11 am to 2:30 pm to businesses only). Accepts AMEX, DIS, MC, VISA. Price: $$.

COCOA

Gardener's Cottage Natural Kitchen

902 Florida Avenue; 321-631-2030; fax: 321-631-2402; email: garpatch@aol.com; **Web site:** www.gardeners-cottage.org
Store Hours: Monday to Friday 8:30 am to 6 pm; Saturday 9 am to 1 pm; closed Sun.
Café Hours: Breakfast 8:30 am to 10:30 am Saturday 9 am to 12 noon; Lunch 11 am to 2:30 pm; closed Sunday.
Natural Food Store and Café. Vegetarian friendly (serves fish). Bakery. Organic produce. Vegan options.
Menu: Tofu Scramblers, Garden Burrito, granola, waffles, Boca Sausage Patties, Giant Cinnamon Rolls and muffins for breakfast. Village Rueben, Mock "Chicken" Sandwich, veggie burgers, vegetarian soups (White Bean & Tomato, Cream of Broccoli, Spring Vegetables) and salads for lunch. Fresh juices and smoothies.
Other Info: Counter service, take-out. Reservations not necessary. Non-smoking. Price: $.
Directions: From Hwy A1A, take US 1 exit towards Cocoa Titusville, and go south on US 1 for 4 miles, at Poinsett Drive turn left and this place is a quarter-mile down.

The New Habit

3 North Atlantic Avenue, near Minute Man Causeway & Hwy A1A; 321-784-6646
Hours: Daily 11 am to 6 pm
Yogurt Shop with some vegetarian dishes. Vegan options. Not pure vegetarian.
Menu: A variety of yogurts. Sandwiches and ready-made dishes. Tofu burgers, Black Bean Burritos, Vegetable Pies, and Gardenburgers. Smoothies.
Comments: Located right on the beach.
Other Info: Counter service, take-out. No credit cards; cash only. Price: $.

CORAL SPRINGS

The New Habit
33 Garden Avenue
Hours: Daily for lunch and dinner
Natural Foods. Vegan options. Not pure veg.
Menu: Tofu burgers, Black Bean Enchiladas, Oriental Vegetable Pies and Gardenburgers. Smoothies.
Comments: Located right on the beach. Other Info: Limited services, take-out. Price: $.

Whole Foods Market
810 University Drive; 954-753-8000
Hours: Daily 8 am to 9 pm
Natural Food Store and Deli. Bakery and Juice Bar. Organic produce. Supermarket type place. See Whole Foods Market information.
Directions: This place is near the Coral Square Mall. From Hwy 869, take SR-814/Atlantic Blvd exit (#6), then go west on Atlantic Blvd and this place is 2½ miles down.

DAVIE

Heres To Your Health
2541 South University Drive; 954-370-1966
Hours: Monday to Friday 10 am to 6 pm; Saturday 10 am to 5 pm; closed Sunday.
Natural Food Store. Mostly discount vitamins.

DAYTONA BEACH

Harvest House Natural Foods
4032 South Ridgewood Ave; Port Orange 386-756-3800
Natural Food Store and Coffee Shop. See Port Orange for details.
Directions: Port Orange is just south of Daytona Beach.

DEERFIELD BEACH

Smoothie King
2032 NE Second Street; 954-574-0699
Hours: Monday to Saturday 9 am to 8 pm
Sunday 10 am to 6 pm
Smoothie Bar. See Miami Beach.

DOVER

Discount Herbs
14650 MLK Boulevard; 813-659-0349
Hours: Monday to Friday 10 am to 5 pm
Closed Saturday & Sunday.

Natural Food Store. Organic produce.

DUNEDIN (near Clearwater)

Casa Tina Gourmet Mexican & Vegetarian Restaurant
369 Main Street, downtown Dunedin
727-734-9226
Hours: Sunday to Thursday 11 am to 10 pm
Friday & Saturday 11 am to 11 pm
Vegan-friendly Mexican. Not pure vegetarian.
Menu: Has very good burritos. Salads, quesadillas and enchiladas.
Comments: Very good food and atmosphere. Gets good reviews by food critics. Pleasant décor. Does not use any meat in their base sauces or beans. So basically anything can be made vegetarian.
Other Info: Accepts DIS, MC, VISA. Price: $.

Lonni's Sandwiches, Etc.
1153 Main Street, Dunedin
813-734-0121; email: lonnisandw@aol.com; Web site: www.lonnissandwiches.com
Hours: Monday to Friday 8 am to 4 pm; Saturday 10 am to 2 pm; closed Sunday.
Delivery Hours: 11 am to 2:30 pm
Natural Foods. Not pure vegetarian. See Clearwater.

FORT LAUDERDALE

Berry's Café & Juice Bar
4822 North Federal Highway
954-489-1122
Hours: Monday to Saturday 7 am to 8 pm; closed Sunday.
Restaurant and Juice Bar. Not pure veg.
Menu: Has some vegetarian sandwiches. Fresh juices and smoothies.
Other Info: Counter service, take-out. Accepts AMEX, MC, VISA.
Directions: From I-95, take Commercial Blvd exit (#32) and go east on Commercial Blvd for 2¼ miles, at Federal Hwy (US 1) turn right and this place is a quarter-mile down.

East Coast Burrito Factory
261 East Commercial Blvd; 954-772-8007
Hours: Monday 11 am to 10 pm; Tuesday to Sat 11 am to 4 am; Sun 11 am to 7 pm
Mexican Restaurant. Not pure vegetarian.
Menu: Everything is supposed to be vegetarian unless meat is added to it. No meat in the beans and rice. Good big burritos, veggie taco, veggie

quesadilla, super veggie burritos, grilled zucchini, guacamole and other dishes.
Comments: Makes an effort to be vegetarian friendly. Friendly, efficient service.
Other Info: Accepts AMEX, DIS, MC, VISA. Price: $-$$.
Directions: From I-95, take Commercial Blvd exit and this place is three blocks east, in a couple little houses.

Healthy Bites Grill
1538 East Commercial Boulevard
954-776-9985
Hours: Monday to Saturday 11 am to 7 pm Closed Sunday.
Vegetarian-friendly Restaurant. Healthy American.
Menu: Has a large selection of vegetarian dishes. Hummus, veggie burgers, Portobello Sandwiches and much more. No alcohol.
Comments: Outdoor seating. Contemporary décor with moderate lighting. Seats 40 people. Quick service. Comfortable, relaxed place.
Other Info: Smoking allowed outside. Price: $$.

Nature Boy Health Foods
220 East Commercial Boulevard, near the beach;
954-776-4696
Hours: Monday to Saturday 10 am to 5 pm Sunday 11 am to 4 pm
Natural Food Store and Deli. Vegan options.
Menu: Soups, salads, sandwiches, veggie burgers, fruit salads and other main dishes. Fresh juices and smoothies.
Other Info: Full service, take-out. Accepts MC, VISA. Price: $.

Royal India
3801 North Griffin Road; 954-964-0071
Hours: Mon to Fri 5 pm to 10:30 pm; Sat & Sun 12 noon to 3 pm, 5 pm to 10:30 pm
Indian. Not pure vegetarian. Lunch buffet only on weekends.
Menu: Has over 10 vegetarian dishes.
Comments: Good food and atmosphere. Excellent service.
Other Info: Full service, take-out. Accepts AMEX, DC, DIS, MC, VISA. **Price:** $$.

Smoothie King
1303 SE 17th Street   954-
525-0258
2941 SE Fifth Street   954-
832-9200
1755 East Commercial Blvd 954-928-0700

2350 North Federal Hwy   954-630-8315
See Miami Beach.

Herbal Garden (two locations)
1166 North State Road 7; 954-584-6601
Natural Food Store. Good selection of herbs.
Hours: Monday to Thursday 8 pm to 8 pm; Friday 8 am to 6 pm (sunset); Sunday 11 am to 6 pm; closed Saturday.
20717 North State Road 7
Just south of Country Line and State Road 7 (Hwy 441); 305-651-1473
Hours: Mon to Thur 9 am to 8 pm; Fri 8 am to 6 pm (sunset); Sun 11 am to 6 pm; closed Sat.
Natural Food Store and Juice Bar.
Comments: The branch at 20717 N State Road has a juice bar and the other branch doesn't. Neither place has organic produce. These two places have a good selection of herbs. Friendly, helpful people.
Other Info: Accepts AMEX, DIS, MC, VISA.

Wild Oats Community Market
2501 East Sunrise Boulevard
954-566-9333; **Web site:** www.wildoats.com
Hours: Daily 8 am to 10 pm
Natural Food Store and Deli. Salad Bar and Juice Bar. Organic produce. Supermarket-type place. See Wild Oats information.
Directions: From I-95, take the W Sunrise Blvd/ Rte 838 (#30A) exit (becomes N Federal Hwy then E Sunrise Blvd), and this place is 3 miles east on Sunrise Blvd (¾ mile west of the ocean).

Whole Food Market
2000 North Federal Hwy; 954-565-7423
Hours: Daily 8 am to 10 pm.
Natural Food Store and Deli. Juice Bar and Bakery. Organic produce. Vegan options. Supermarket type place. See Whole Foods information.
Comments: This is a good place. Art-deco design. The Wild Oats Community Market is even bigger.
Other Info: Counter service, take-out. Plenty of seating.
Directions: From I-95 coming south, take Oakland Park exit (#31) and go east on Oakland Park for 2 miles. Turn right on US 1 and go 1 mile then the store is on the left. Right across from Barnes and Noble. From I-95 coming north, take the W Sunrise Blvd/Rte 838 (#30A) exit (becomes N Federal Hwy) and go east on W Sunrise Blvd, turn left onto US 1 and this place is 1 mile down.

FORT MYERS

Ada's Natural Food Market
11705 South Cleveland Ave; 941-939-9600
Hours: Monday to Saturday 9 am to 7 pm
Sunday 10 am to 5 pm
Natural Food Store and Deli. Juice Bar. Organic produce.
Menu: Has a large selection of vegetarian dishes.
Other Info: Accepts AMEX, DC, DIS, MC, VISA.
Directions: From I-75, take exit #22 (Colonial). Go west on Colonial and turn right on Fowler. The store is then on the left.

Healthy Habits
11763 South Cleveland Avenue, Ft Myers
800-262-5379
Hours: Monday to Friday 9 am to 7 pm; Saturday 10 am to 6 pm; closed Sunday.
Natural Food Store. Organic produce.
Other Info: Accepts DIS, MC, VISA.
Directions: From I-75, take SR-884 exit (#22) towards Ft Meyers, go west on Colonial Blvd for 4 miles, at Fowler St turn left (go northwest) and go 1¼ mile, at S Cleveland Ave (Hwy 41) turn left and this place is 1 mile down.

Mother Earth Natural Foods
15271 McGregor Boulevard
941-489-3377
Hours: Monday, Wednesday, Friday 9 am to 6 pm; Tuesday & Thursday 9 am to 6:30 pm Saturday 9 am to 5:30 pm; closed Sunday.
Natural Food Store. Organic produce. Fairly big place (3000 sq ft).
Other Info: Accepts AMEX, DIS, MC, VISA.
Directions: From I-75, take SR-884 exit (#22) towards Ft Meyers, go west on Colonial Blvd for 4 miles, at Fowler St turn left (go northwest) and go 1¼ mile, stay straight onto Boy Scout Dr for a half-mile, at Summerlin Rd turn slight left and go 2½ miles, at Cypress Lake Dr turn right and go 1¾ miles, at McGregor Blvd (FL-867) turn left and this place is 2½ miles down.

Thai Gardens
7091 #15 College Parkway; 941-275-0999
Hours: Monday to Saturday 11:30 pm to 3 pm, 5 pm to 10 pm
Sunday 11:30 to 3 pm, 5 pm to 9:30 pm
Thai. Vegan options. Not pure vegetarian.
Menu: Several vegetarian dishes including Sautéed Vegetables with Tofu, Vegetable Fried Rice, Vegetable Curry and more.

Other Info: Full service, take-out. Accepts AMEX, DIS, MC, VISA. Price: $$.

GAINESVILLE

Bahn Thai Restaurant
1902 SW 13th Street; 352-335-1204
Lunch Buffet Hours: Monday to Friday 11 am to 2:30 pm; **Dinner Hours:** Monday to Saturday 5 pm to 10 pm; closed Sunday.
Thai. Vegetarian friendly. Not pure veg.
Menu: The lunch buffet has two types of rice, Thai noodles, salad, vegetarian spring roll (no eggs) and several types of vegetable dishes. Baked Tofu with Broccoli, Asparagus with Tofu, Bahn Thai Tofu, Sweet'n Sour Tofu with Sizzling Rice, Stir-fried Vegetables and Baked Tofu with Baby Corn. Has a vegetarian section on the dinner menu.
Comments: Friendly, efficient service. The lunch buffet has two sections, 2/3 is vegetarian and the other section is non-vegetarian. The lunch buffet is a good value. This place gets good ratings and is reasonably priced. You may want to ask if there are eggs in any of the vegetarian dishes.
Other Info: Accepts MC, VISA. Full service, take-out. Price: $-$$.
Directions: This place is in south Gainesville. From the center of town go south on 13th Street (Hwy 441) a few mile and this place is on the right in the Motel 8.

**Book Lover's Café (in Books Inc)
505 NW 13th Street; 352-374-4717
Hours: Daily 10 am to 10 pm
Small Pure Vegetarian Natural Food Café. Vegan options.
Menu: African Lentils, French coleslaw, hummus, sweet pea guacamole, pasta, garden salad, Greek Salad, soups, Tofu Burger, T.L.T. (tempeh, lettuce and tomato), quiche, Lasagna, cookies, vegan carrot cake, and fresh baked goods. Fresh juices, smoothies, cappuccino, espresso.
Comments: It is located in Books Inc, a used bookstore. It is a good place and is reasonably priced. Theme nights: Tuesday: Vegetarian Sushi, Wednesday: Greek food, Thursday: Ethiopian food, Friday: Acoustic music.
Other Info: Counter service, take-out. Both indoor and outdoor seating. Accepts AMEX, DC, DIS, MC, VISA. Price: $.
Directions: Located next to Mother Earth natural food store.

Falafel King Sandwiches

3252 SW 35th Boulevard; 352-375-6342
Hours: Monday to Saturday 11 am to 9 pm
Sunday 12 noon to 6 pm
Middle Eastern. Vegan options. Not pure vegetarian.
Menu: Falafels (vegan), tabbouleh, gyros and other sandwiches.
Other Info: Counter service, take-out. Deli- like place. Price: $.

Chop Stix Cafe

3500 SW 13th Street
352-367-0003
fax: 352-372-7333
Hours: Monday to Thursday 11 am to 10 pm; Friday & Saturday; closed Sunday.
Vegetarian-friendly Chinese. Has a separate vegetarian kitchen. Not pure vegetarian.
Menu: Has a separate vegetarian menu with an excellent selection of vegetarian dishes. Vegetarian Spring Rolls, Vegetable Fried Rice, tofu dishes, Sesame Eggplant, Vegetable Tempura, Vegetarian Steamed Dumplings, soups and noodle dishes.
Comments: Has really good food. Good value. Has an excellent location next to a lake with a view of sunbathing alligators. Service can be slow when they are busy. Recommended.
Other Info: Full service, take-out. Price: $-$$.

**Hare Krishna (ISKCON) Temple

214 NW 14th Street, 352-336-4183
Web site: www.iskcon.net/gainesville
Hours: Wednesday and Friday 6 pm to 8 pm (when U of Florida is in session).
Vegetarian Indian Feast.
Comments: There is a vegetarian feast on Sunday at 6 pm. Besides the feast there is kirtana (public chanting of Hare Krishna) and a *Bhagavad Gita* class.
Direction: It is on 14th St, between University Avenue and NW 3rd Avenue.

Health Addiction

501 NW 23rd Avenue; 352-335-5132; fax: 352-335-5132; **Web site:** www.healthyes.net
Hours: Monday to Friday 3 am to 7 pm
Saturdays 11 am to 5 pm; closed Sunday.
Natural Food Store and Deli. Juice Bar. Pure vegetarian. Organic produce.
Menu: Vegan cheese-less pizza. Greek Pizza with seitan, Hummus Pizza with seitan, Untraditional Pizza with tempeh, Green Salad, Tempeh Sandwich, Seitan Sandwich, and Tofu Sandwich. Non-diary smoothies with apple juice, soy milk or rice milk. Homemade cookies.
Comments: The tempeh sandwiches are really good. The Deli is in a health food store, which is small and does not have a very good selection. Sells really good fresh tempeh. Can make special orders of grocery items.
Directions: This place is about a mile west of Hwy 441 on 23rd St, next to Ward's supermarket, in a small shopping center.

Mother Earth Market (two locations)

521 NW 13 Street; 352-378-5224
1237 NW 76th Boulevard, Newberry Crossing; 352-351-5224
Hours: Monday to Saturday 9 am to 9 pm
Sunday 11 am to 7 pm
Natural Food Store. Organic produce. Juice Bar.
Comments: Has a large selection of organic produce. It is basically the size of a supermarket and has a great selection of vegetarian "mock" meats, frozen meals, juices, and health supplements. Highly recommended. One of the best natural food restaurants in the country. The 13th Street branch has a better selection.
Directions: To get to the Newberry Crossing store from I-75, take Newberry Rd exit (#76), then go west on FL-26 a third-mile, then at NW 76th Blvd turn right and this place is in a small shopping center a half-mile down. The 13th Street store is on Rte 441, which becomes 13th Street when coming from the north.

Nature's Table Café (two location)

Gator Plaza, 106 NW 13th Street
352-372-9972
Oakes Malls
Natural Food Restaurant. Juice Bar. Not pure vegetarian.
Menu: Bagels, salads, Avocado & Cucumber Sandwich, vegetarian sandwich, hummus and veggie pita, cheese sandwich, Garden Burger, veggie chili and pasta salad. Fresh juices and smoothies.
Other Info: Counter service, take-out.

Sunflower Health Foods

87 SW 34th Street; 352-372-7482
Natural Food Store.

**Vegetarian Palace

2106 SW 34th Street; 352-377-8344
Hours: Monday to Thursday 11 am to 3 pm, 5 pm to 9 pm; Fri & Sat 11 am to 3 pm, 5 pm to 9:30 pm; Sun Brunch 9 am to 1 pm
Fully Vegetarian Indian and International. Vegan options. All-you-can-eat Buffet.

Menu: Indian dishes, Mexican dishes, Chinese dishes, Italian dishes and more.

Comments: Run by Hare Krishna devotees. The food is reasonably priced.

Other Info: Counter service, take-out, delivery (within five miles).

Directions: From I-75, take Gainesville/Archer Rd exit (#75) and go east on Archer Rd (Rte 24) for 1 mile, then turn left onto 34th St and go a half-mile. This place is on the left in a shopping center.

Ward's

523 NW 6th Street, at NW 23rd Avenue

Super Market with organic produce and a good selection of natural food items. Has an excellent produce section. It is a really good place to do one-stop shopping. Recommended.

Directions: From Hwy 441 (13th St), at 23rd St go west and this place is 1 mile down on the right.

GRAND PLANTATION

Smoothie King

700 S Pine Island Drive; 945-423-4087

HIALEAH (near Miami)

Hale's Health Foods

16427 NW 67th Avenue
305-821-5331

Hours: Monday to Friday 9:30 am to 6:30 pm; Saturday 10 am to 6 pm; closed Sun.

Natural Food Store. Just has carrots, but no other produce.

Other Info: Accepts AMEX, MC, VISA.

HOLIDAY (near Tampa)

Judy's Natural Foods

1922 US Highway 19 North
727-943-0020

Store Hours: Mon to Fri 7 am to 6 pm; Saturday 9 am to 5 pm; Sunday 10 am to 4 pm

Café Hours: Monday to Friday 11 am to 3 pm; closed Saturday & Sunday.

Natural Food Store. Organic produce.

Menu: Sandwiches, salads, soups, Garden Burger, Vegetarian Chili and Portobello Sandwiches. Always has a vegetarian soup.

Other Info: Counter service with seating, take-out. Order at counter and then food is brought to you. Accepts DIS, MC, VISA.

Directions: This place is on the main highway

going north–south through town.

HOLLYWOOD

Natural Foods Restaurant

4907 Sheridan Street; 954-981-0555

Hours: Monday to Friday 11 am to 3 pm Closed Saturday & Sunday.

Natural Foods Restaurant. Vegetarian friendly Salad Bar and Juice Bar. Vegan options. Not pure vegetarian.

Menu: Soups, pizzas, pita sandwiches, a salad bar and more. Fresh juices.

Comments: Beautifully designed and painted by a Venezuelan artist. Looks like a garden.

Other Info: Cafeteria style, take-out. Non-smoking. Accepts AMEX, MC, VISA. Price: $$.

Directions: From I-95, take Hwy 822/Sheridan St exit (#24) and then go west on Sheridan St and this place is 1¾ mile down.

Sara's

3944 North 46th Avenue; 954-986-1770

Hours: Sunday to Thursday 9 am to 10 pm Friday 8 to 3 pm; Saturday 7 pm to 2 am

Kosher Natural Food. Mainly vegetarian, but serves fish. Vegan options.

Menu: Has a good selection of vegetarian dishes. Salads, sandwiches, quiche, Middle Eastern dishes, pizzas and other dishes. Has a good selection of mock "meat" dishes including Soy Chicken, Soy Steak and Soy Bacon.

Comments: Friendly, efficient service.

Other Info: Full service, take-out. Accepts AMEX, DIS, MC, VISA. Price: $-$$.

Directions: From I-95, take exit #25 (Sterling Rd), then go west on Sterling Rd for 1¾ mile. At 46th Avenue turn left and this place is in a plaza on the right. Southwest corner of junction of Sterling and 46th.

Smoothie King

360 North Park Road; 954-893-6934

See Miami Beach.

JACKSONVILLE

Good Earth Market

10950 San Jose Boulevard; 904-260-9547

Hours: Monday to Saturday 9 am to 7 pm Sunday 12 noon to 5 pm

Natural Food Store. Has a small amount of organic produce. No deli. Not such a big place.

Other Info: Accepts AMEX, MC, VISA.

Directions: From I-295, take exit #2A and go

south a quarter-mile on San Jose Blvd and this place is on the right in a shopping center. This place is about 5 miles south of the downtown.

**Heartworks Café

820 Lomax Street; 904-355-6210
Hours: Mon to Wed 11 am to 3 pm; Thur & Fri 11 am to 3 pm, 6 pm to 9:30 pm; Sat 12 noon to 4 pm; Sun 10 am to 2 pm
Vegetarian Café. Vegan friendly.
Menu: Tofu and Vegetable Sandwich, salads, Vegetable Stir-fries, veggie burritos, Tofu Cheesecake and daily specials.
Comments: The restaurant is attached to an art gallery. Casual, relaxed place.
Other Info: Accepts only cash; no credit cards.
Directions: It is located in the happening Five Points District. From I-95, take exit #109, go south on College St 2 blocks, turn left at Margaret St and go 1 block, at Park St turn left, then make a quick right onto Lomax St and this place is 1 block down.

Native Sun Natural Foods

10000 San Jose Boulevard; 904-260-6950
Hours: Tue, Thur 10 am to 8 pm; Mon, Wed, Fri, Sat 10 am to 7 pm; closed Sun.
Natural Food Store. Organic produce. Size of a small grocery store.
Comments: Does not have a deli.
Other Info: Accepts AMEX, DIS, MC, VISA.
Directions: From I-295, take SR-13/San Jose Blvd exit (#2A), then go north on San Jose and this place is 1¼ mile down.

Pattaya Thai Restaurant

10916 Atlantic Boulevard, Suite 12
904-646-9506
Hours: Tue to Fri 11 am to 2 pm, 5 pm to 9:45 pm; Sat & Sun 5 pm to 9:45 pm; closed Mon.
Thai. Not pure vegetarian.
Menu: Has a good selection of vegetarian dishes. Spring Rolls, Vegetables with Tofu, Sweet & Sour, Fried Rice, various curried vegetables, Tofu Soup and other dishes.
Comment: Has good food and atmosphere, personal service, and is a good value. Food gets excellent ratings. Has lunch specials. Popular with business people during lunch. Good size portions.
Other Info: Full service, take-out. Accepts AMEX, DIS, MC, VISA. Price: $-$$.

JUPITER

Nature's Way Café

US 1, at Indiantown Road; 561-743-0401
Hours: Monday to Friday 8 am to 4 pm
Saturday 11 am to 3 pm; closed Sunday.
Sandwich Shop. Vegetarian friendly. Not pure vegetarian.
Menu: Cheese Melt, hummus sandwiches, Garden Burger, salads, protein shake and fresh juices.
Other Info: Accepts AMEX, MC, VISA.

JUNO BEACH

Healthy Heart Natural Food Market & Juice Bar

Plaza LaMer, 835 Donald Ross Road, at US 1; 561-622-4104
Hours: Monday to Saturday 10 am to 6 pm
Closed Sunday.
Natural Food Store. Juice Bar.
Menu: Salads, sandwiches, veggie burger, hummus sandwich and veggie sandwiches.
Other Info: Counter service, take-out. No sit-down area, just take-out. Accepts AMEX, DIS, MC, VISA. Price: $.
Direction: It is on US 1, north of Palm Beach.

KEYSTONE HEIGHTS (30 miles east of Gainesville)

Healthy Living – Health Food Shoppe

165 East Nightingale Street
352-473-3663; 888-830-3663; **Web site:** www.iam4healthyliving.com/hlweb001.htm
Hours: Monday to Saturday 10 am to 6 pm (Thursday 7 pm); closed Sunday.
Natural Food Store. Organic produce.
Comments: Friendly place.
Other Info: Accepts MC, VISA.

KEY WEST

Good Food Conspiracy

US 1, Mile Marker 30.2, Big Pine Key, on the Overseas Highways; 305-872-3945
Hours: Monday to Saturday 9:30 am to 7 pm (juice bar closes around 5 pm)
Sunday 11 am to 5 pm (juice bar closed around 4 pm)
Natural Food Store and Deli. Juice Bar and small organic produce section. Vegetarian friendly. Not pure vegetarian.
Menu: Sandwiches, salads, Avocado Cashew Pesto, Spinach Salads and Vegetable Melt. Soy

cheese, vegan pesto and vegan potato salad. Sandwiches can be made with brown bread or chapatti. Vegan Chocolate Chip Cookies.
Comments: Friendly, efficient service. The owner is a really nice person. Bulk herbs and other goods.
Other Info: Accepts AMEX, DIS, MC, VISA. Counter service, take-out. Has seating for 8 people at the counter. Big backyard with seating.
Direction: Coming into Big Pine Key, after going over Five-Mile Bridge, this place is a quarter-mile down on left side.

Island Wellness Café
530 Simonton Street, at Southard Street
305-296-7353
email: lsaZoe711@aol.com;
Web site: www.keywestislandwellness.com
International. Macrobiotic and Vegan options. Juice Bar. Not pure vegetarian.
Menu: Hummus Platter, Tortilla Pie, Organic Black Beans & Brown rice with tofu sour cream, Cold Sesame Udon Noodles, soups, salads, sandwiches and other dishes.
Comments: Has licensed massage therapist. Full service, take-out. Price: $$.
Directions: This place is a half-mile west of the sea. From Hwy 1, go north on Simonton St and this place is 5½ blocks down.

Lotsa Pasta
609 Duval Street; 305-294-7874
Hours: Thursday to Monday 6 pm to 10 pm
Closed Tuesday & Wednesday.
Italian. Not pure vegetarian.
Menu: Eggplant Parmesan, Cheese Ravioli, pastas and other vegetarian dishes. Cappuccino, espresso.
Other Info: Full service. Accepts AMEX, DC, DIS, MC, VISA. Price: $$$.

Mangoes
700 Duval Street, at Angela Street
305-292-4606
Hours: Daily 11 am to 2:30 pm, 5:30 pm to 12 midnight
Flor-abbean Caribbean, International. Not pure vegetarian.
Menu: Pastas, wood-oven pizzas, salads and vegetable dishes.
Comments: Has outdoor patio with umbrellas. Enjoyable, happening, popular, in-place to eat. If you see something on the menu they are more than willing to make it vegetarian if possible.
Other Info: Accepts AMEX, DC, DIS, MC, VISA. Price: $$-$$$.

Natural Food Market
107 Simonton Street; 305-296-3800;
Web site: www.naturalfoodmarkets.com
Hours: Daily 9 pm to 9 pm
Natural Food Store and Deli. All-organic produce. See Miami Beach.
Comments: The store manager is a nutrition specialist.
Other Info: Counter service, take-out. Has plenty of seating. Accepts AMEX, DIS, MC, VISA.
Directions: Located in the middle of Key West, at the corner of Front and Simonton Streets, one block north of Duvall Street.

**Sugar Apple Veggie Deli
917 Simonton Street; 305-292-0043
Store Hours: Monday to Saturday 10 am to 6 pm; **Café Hours:** 11 am to 4 pm
Closed Sunday.
Natural Food Store and Vegetarian Café. Deli, Juice Bar and organic produce. Mainly Vegan (no eggs).
Menu: Veggie burgers, barbecued tofu, Tofu Eggless Sandwich (recommended), Italian Veggie "Sausage," baked tofu, vegetarian chili, salads and many other dishes including homemade daily specials. Fresh juices.
Comments: Has a good selection. Reasonably priced, good, friendly place.
Other Info: Counter service, take-out. Non-smoking. Reservations not necessary. Accepts AMEX, DIS, MC, VISA. Price: $-$$.
Directions: This place is a half-block north of Hwy 1.

Thai Cuisine
513 Greene Street; 305-294-9424
Hours: Monday to Friday 11:30 am to 3 pm, 5 pm to 10 pm; Saturday & Sunday 5 pm to 10 pm (not open for lunch)
Thai. Not pure vegetarian.
Menu: Over ten vegetarian dishes including Spring Rolls, soups, noodle dishes, Pad Thai, fried tofu and vegetable curry dishes.
Other Info: Full service, take-out. Accepts AMEX, DIS, MC, VISA.

KISSIMMEE

Kissimmee Co-op
830 Lake Cecile Drive; 407-870-9839 **email:** kissimmeeorganic@yahoo.com;
Web site: http://members.tripod.com/kissimmeeorganiccoop/
Natural Food Store.

Punjab Indian Restaurant

3404 West Vine Street; 407-931-2449
Hours: Tues to Sat 11:30 am to 11 pm; Sun &
Mon 5 pm to 11 pm (for dinner only)
Indian. Not pure vegetarian.
Menu: Has a good selection of vegetarian dishes.
Other Info: Accepts AMEX, DC, DIS, MC,
VISA.

LAKE BUENA VISTA (Orlando suburb)

California Grill

Walt Disney World Contemporary Resort
Hours: Daily 5:30 pm to 10 pm
Restaurant. Not pure vegetarian.
Menu: Has an assortment of vegetarian dishes.
Comments: One of the best Disney restaurants.
Live entertainment. Romantic place. Theme Res-
taurant. Has a children's menu. Notable Chief.
Located on the 15th floor of Disney's Contem-
porary Resort and has a great view of the nightly
fireworks at Disney World's Magic Kingdom.
Other Info: Cannot make an actual reservation
at any of Disney's restaurants except Albert's and
Victoria. But you can call ahead for priority seat-
ing. Accepts AMEX, MC, VISA. Price: $$$$.

Jungle Jim's

Crossroads Plaza, 12501 State Road 535
407-827-1257
Hours: Daily 11 am to 10:30
American. Not Pure Vegetarian.
Menu: Has a really good selection of vegetarian
dishes. Has over 23 versions of the original Garden Burger including the "Teiyaki Pineapple" or
the "Philly Dilly." Salads, baked potatoes and
pastas.
Comments: The original Garden Burger does not
contain eggs but contains cheese.
Directions: This place is located at the entrance
to the Walt Disney Land property.

LARGO

Pioneer Natural Foods

12788 Indian Rocks Road; 727-596-6600
Hours: Monday to Friday 9 am to 7 pm
Saturday & Sunday 9:30 am to 6 pm
Natural Food Store, Deli and Juice Bar.
Menu: Sandwiches, salads and hot dishes. Good
hummus sandwiches.
Other Info: Accepts AMEX, MC, VISA. Counter
service, take-out. Has seating.
Direction: From US-19, take Rte 688 west. Make
a right turn on Indian Rocks Rd and the store is
on the left.

Sweet Tomatoes

Largo Mall, in front of Target, 13101 Seminole
Boulevard, Largo; 727-584-9100
Hours: Sunday to Thursday 11 am to 9 pm
Friday & Saturday 11 am to 10 pm
Salad and Soup Place. Salad and Soup Bar.
Menu: Has a good selection of vegetarian items
in the salad bar. Many varieties of salads. Three of
the prepared salads are vegetarian. Says pastas
don't contain eggs.
Other Info: Accepts DC, DIS, MC, VISA.

MELBOURNE

Community Harvest Café

1405 Highland Avenue, off US 1
321-242-2398
Store Hours: Monday to Friday 9 am to 8 pm;
Saturday 9 am to 6 pm
Café Hours: Monday to Friday 9 am to 7 pm,
Saturday 9 am to 4 pm, closed Sunday.
Natural Food Store and Restaurant. Vegan and
Macrobiotic options. Mainly Vegetarian (but
serves tuna). Organic produce.
Menu: Pancakes, veggie burgers, hummus, tofu
salad, hummus, sandwiches, tempeh salad and
more. Fresh juices and smoothies.
Comments: Non-profit place. Good people.
Friendly place. Recommended.
Other Info: Full service, take-out. Store accepts
MC, VISA, but café accepts only cash. Price: $.
Directions: From I-95, take Rte 518/Eau Gallie
Blvd exit (#72) towards Melbourne, then get on
Rte 518 and this place is 5 miles down. This
place is a block before the bridge.

Nature's Market

461 North Harbor City Boulevard (US 1)
321-254-8688
Hours: Monday to Thursday 9 am to 8 pm, Friday & Saturday 9 am to 7 pm, closed Sun.
Natural Food Store and Juice Bar. Large selection of organic produce.
Menu: Soups, vegetarian chili, wraps, fresh juices
and smoothies
Comments: Very friendly and efficient place. Has
a nutritionist, supplement expert and certified
herbalist. Marks up products less than 20% and
never sells products at suggested retails. Has a
large selection of books. There is a Vietnamese
Thai Gourmet restaurant next door with vegetarian options (321-255-6471)
Other Info: Limited service, take-out. Accepts
AMEX, DIS, MC, VISA. Price: $.
Directions: This place is on US 1, about 1 mile
northeast of the airport.

Wild Oats Market
1135 West New Haven Avenue, at Route 192
407-674-5002
Hours: Monday to Saturday 9 am to 8 pm
Sunday 10 am to 6 pm
Natural Food Store and Deli. Salad Bar. Organic
produce. Supermarket-type place. See Wild Oats
information.
Directions: From I-95, take US-192 exit (#71)
towards Melbourne, then go east on US-192 and
this place is 4¼ miles down on the left.

MERRITT ISLAND

***Living Greens, Sprout Garden
205 McLeod Street; 407-454-2268
Café Hours: Monday to Saturday 11 am to 3
pm; Organic produce and really made dishes 10
am to 4 pm; closed Sunday.
Fully Vegan Restaurant. Mostly raw, strictly organic vegan. Also sells organic produce and prepared items.
Menu: Ginger Cashew Pesto, Veggie Sushi, Parsley Walnut Pesto and other dishes.
Comments: The produce market is open 10 am
to 4 pm. Totally vegan. Everything here is really
good. Very friendly people.
Other Info: Full service, counter, take-out. Non-
smoking. Accepts reservations, but are not necessary. No credit cards.
Directions: This place is two blocks north of Rte
520, and one block west of Courtenay (Rte 3) &
Merritt Island Shopping Center. From I-95, take
Rte 520 exit (#75) towards Cocoa, go east on
Rte 520 for 6 miles, then at McLeod St turn left
and this place is 2 blocks down.

MIAMI
Miami Beach, Coconut Grove.

Granny Feelgood's Restaurant & Market Place
25 West Flagler Street; 305-377-9600
Hours: Monday to Friday 7 am to 4 pm
Closed Saturday & Sunday
Natural Food Restaurant and limited Natural
Food Store. Macrobiotic and Vegan options. Fast
food. Not pure vegetarian.
Menu: Has some vegetarian options for breakfast and lunch. Soups, salads, sandwiches, veggie
burgers, international entrees and desserts. Fresh
juices.
Comments: Low-cholesterol, low-sodium and
low-fat options. Mainly a restaurant with some
vitamins and other products.

Other Info: Full service, take-out. Accepts AMEX,
MC, VISA. Price: $-$$.
Directions: From I-95, take exit #3A and this
place is 2 blocks east of the exit.

Jackies Vegetarian Restaurant
15044 Northeast 6 Avenue
305-947-3996
Hours: Monday to Saturday 10 am to 10 pm
Closed Sunday.
Vegetarian-friendly Jamaican Restaurant. Not
pure vegetarian (also serves fish).
Other Info: Counter service, take-out. Has a few
table. Cash only.

Hale's Health Foods
109 W Plaza, Northside Shopping Center
305-696-2115
Hours: Monday to Saturday 10 am to 6 pm
Closed Sunday.
Natural Food Store. Organic produce.
Other Info: Accepts AMEX, MC, VISA.

**The Honey Tree
5138 Biscayne Boulevard, at 51st Street
305-759-1696;
email: thehoneytreemiami@hotmail.com
Hours: Mon to Thur 8 am to 8 pm; Fri 8 am to 7
pm; Sat 9 am to 6 pm; closed Sunday.
Natural Food Store and Fully Vegetarian Deli.
Juice Bar and organic produce. 95% Vegan. Everything juiced is organic. Mainly vegan baked
goods.
Menu: Soups, salads, sandwiches, macaroni &
cheese, tofu and seitan dishes, pastas, rice dishes
and vegetables dishes. Organic juices and
smoothies.
Comments: The food in the deli gets good recommendations. Has books, music, supplements,
vitamins, body care items and much more. Casual, relaxed atmosphere. Friendly people.
Other Info: Buffet, counter service, take-out,
lunch delivery, catering. There is a place to eat in
the store. Accepts AMEX, DIS, MC, VISA.
Directions: This place is near downtown Miami,
2 blocks west of Morningside Park. From I-95,
take Exit #7 and get on I-195 going east for 1
mile, take exit towards US 1/Biscayne Blvd, and
then go right (north) onto Biscayne Blvd/US 1
and this place is 1 mile down.

Natural Food Market
9455 S Dixie Highway, Kendall
305-666-3514; **fax:** 305-666-5526
Hours: Monday to Saturday 8:30 am to 9:30

pm; Sunday 10 am to 7 pm
Natural Food Store and Deli. Organic Juice Bar. All organic produce. See Miami Beach.
Other Info: Counter service, take-out. Has seating outside. Accepts AMEX, DIS, MC, VISA.
Directions: At the junction of Kendall Drive and US 1 in Pinecrest. Follow I-95 south until it ends, then take a slight right onto S Dixie Hwy (US 1) and this place is 8 miles down.

Smoothie King
6637 South Dixie, Miami; 305-661-5465
See Miami Beach.

Wild Oats Market
1020 Alton Road; 305-532-1707
Hours: Daily 7 am to 11 pm
Natural Food Store and Cafe. Deli, Bakery, Salad Bar and Juice Bar. Organic produce. Supermarket-type place. See Wild Oats Market information.

Wild Oats Market
11701 South Dixie Highway, Kendall
305-971-0900
Hours: Daily 7 am to 10 pm
Natural Food Store and Cafe. Deli, Bakery, Salad Bar and Juice Bar. Organic produce. Supermarket-type place. See Wild Oats Market information.
Directions: Follow I-95 south until it ends, then take a slight right onto S Dixie Hwy (US 1) and this place is 9 miles down.

MIAMI BEACH

Apple A Day Natural Food Market
1534 Alton Road; 305-538-4569
Hours: Monday to Saturday 8 am to 11 pm
Sunday 8 am to 9 pm
Natural Food Store and Deli. Organic produce. Fairly big place.
Menu: Has a selection of vegetarian dishes.
Other Info: Counter service, take-out. Has some tables. Accepts AMEX, MC, VISA.
Directions: At 15th Terrace.

Athens Juice Bar
1214 Washington Avenue, South Beach
305-672-4648
Hours: Monday to Saturday 8 am to 7 pm
Sunday 9 am to 3 pm
6976 Collins Avenue, between 69th & 70th Streets; 305-672-4648
Hours: Monday to Saturday 8 am to 7 pm

Sunday 11 am to 5 pm
Juice Bar.
Menu: Fresh squeezed juices and fresh fruit salads.
Other Info: Accepts MC, VISA. Price: $.

Natural Food Market
1011 5th Street, Miami Beach
305-535-9050
Hours: Monday to Saturday 9 am to 9 pm
Sunday 11 am to 8 pm
Natural Food Store and Deli. Bakery and Juice Bar. Has large organic produce section.
Menu: Veggie burgers, Tofu Eggless Salad, falafel, BBQ Seitan, Grilled Tofu, hummus, couscous salad, vegan cakes and cookies, Guacamole, Fresh Grilled Portobello Mushrooms, Stuffed Grape Leaves, Steamed Curry Vegetables, Chick Peas, Stuffed Cabbage & Artichoke and Vegetable Rice.
Comments: This is a large natural food store the size of a supermarket that has an excellent selection of items including organic cereals, breads, teas, juices, natural cosmetics and much more. This place has a well-stocked deli and salad bar. Price: $.
Directions: Take I-395 from downtown Miami to South Beach, take Rte 41 and when it reaches South Beach this place is on the left on the northwest corner of Michigan Streets and Fifth. It is a big place with a big sign.

News Café
800 Ocean Drive, Miami Beach
305-538-6397
Hours: Daily 24 hours. Breakfast all day.
Menu: Has really good salads and a good vinaigrette. Greek Salad with tofu. Spinach Salad with goat cheese. Good Spinach-Artichoke Dip. Pasta with Mushrooms, Spinach and Artichokes. Middle Eastern Platter with tabbouleh, grape leaves, hummus and tahini.
Comments: Good place for a late night. Has outdoor seating and is a good place for people watching. Interesting place to sit and check out the scene.
Other Info: Accepts AMEX, MC, VISA. Price: $-$$.
Directions: On the main strip in Miami's South Beach.

Oasis Café
976 41st Street; 305-674-7676
Hours: Monday to Saturday 11 am to 10 pm; Sunday 5 to 10 pm.
Mediterranean. Vegan options. Not pure vegetarian.

Menu: The most popular thing on the menu is the Coriander Cumin Fries. Good selection of sandwiches and salads. Often has a vegan daily special. Penne with feta cheese, walnuts, olives and spinach. Brown rice with raisins. Grilled Sesame-Tofu as a main course or on a sandwich. The sandwiches come with carrots and vegetables.
Comments: Good service. Good place to take a date.
Other Info: Full service, take-out. Accepts AMEX, MC, VISA.

Pacific Time

915 Lincoln Road, a few blocks from the beach; 305-534-5979
Hours: Sunday to Thursday 6 pm to 11 pm
Friday & Saturday 6 pm to 12 midnight
Upscale Asian, Pacific Rim, Eclectic American. Vegan options. Not pure vegetarian.
Menu: Has a good selection of vegetarian dishes. Sautéed Japanese Eggplant, Steamed Asparagus with a Special Sauce, Noodles with Artichokes & Mushrooms, Sautéed Vegetables and rice. Fresh juices, cappuccino, espresso and non-alcoholic beer & wine.
Comments: Has outdoor dining. Very popular place and gets high ratings in various publications. Nice décor. Upscale, a bit formal.
Other Info: Full service. Reservations recommended. Accepts AMEX, DC, MC, VISA. Price: $$$-$$$$

Smoothie King

1525 Alton Road, at 15th Street, South Beach; 305-672-6595
Hours: Monday to Saturday 8 am to 8 pm
Sunday 9 am to 6 pm
6637 South Dixie Highway, Coral Gables
305-661-5464
Hours: Daily 9 am to 9 pm
Juice and Smoothie Bar.
Other Info: Accepts AMEX, MC, VISA.
Directions: Bus F, M, S.

South Beach Smoothie

1229 Washington Avenue, between 12th & 13th Streets, South Beach   305-531-5633
7222 SW 57th Avenue   305-666-2153
8855 SW 107th Avenue   305-271-4114
1549 Sunday Drive,   305-666-2153
Hours: Monday to Thursday 10 am to 10 pm; Friday & Saturday 10 am to 11 pm; Sunday 11 am to 9 pm
Juice and Smoothie Bar.
Comments: All fruit with no-preservative shakes, with or without pure vitamin supplements.
Other Info: No credit cards.
Directions: Bus C, H, K, W.

MIAMI: COCONUT GROVE

**Govinda's Dining Club

3220 Virginia Street; 305-442-7218
Hours: 12 noon to 8 pm.
Pure Vegetarian Restaurant.
Menu: Brown and basmati rice, two vegetable curries, several vegetable dishes, soups, an excellent dal, a few salads and bread are included in the buffet. Pizza and the sweets are not included in the buffet price. New menu daily. Multi-ethnic and vegan dishes. Natural juices and salad bar.
Comments: This place is one of the best values in the country. The food is really good. The atmosphere is laid back. This place is a dining club in the Hare Krishna (ISKCON) temple. To eat here you need to get a membership card, which is free. Highly recommended. Everything prepared fresh on premises. All natural ingredients and no preservatives. Peaceful, laid-back place. Price: $. $5 for all you-can-eat-buffet. "Best kept secret in the Grove" Miami Herald.
Directions: This place is located a few blocks from the main downtown area of Coconut Grove. Follow I-95 south until it ends, take a slight right onto S Dixie Hwy (US 1) and go south 2 miles, at Virginia St turn left and this place is a half-mile down.

Greenstreet Café

311 Commodore Plaza (3468 Main Highway); 305-444-0244
Hours: Sunday to Thursday 7.30 am to 11 pm; Fri & Sat 7:30 am to 12 midnight
Italian, Greek Café. Not pure vegetarian.
Comments: A good place.
Other Info: Full service, take-out. Does not accept reservations. Accepts AMEX, DC, MC, VISA. Price: $$-$$$.
Directions: At the corner of Commodore Plaza and Main Highway.

The Last Carrot

3133 Grand Avenue; 305-445-0805
Hours: Monday to Saturday 10 am to 7 pm
Sunday 10 am to 6 pm
Natural Food Café and Deli. Juice Bar. Vegetarian friendly. Vegan options.
Menu: Soups, good salads, sandwiches, hummus pita, spinach pies, tofu sandwich, veggie burger,

veggie pita and vegan desserts. Soups are vegan. Fresh juices and smoothies. The banana smoothie is good.

Comments: This is a really small place.

Other Info: Counter service, take-out. Counter seats and 2 tables. Cash only.

Directions: Follow I-95 south until it ends, take a slight right onto S Dixie Hwy (US 1) and go south 2½ miles, turn left at 32nd Ave (become McDonald) and go a half-mile, at Grand Ave turn left and this place is 1 block down.

Oak Feed Natural Foods Market

283 Oak Avenue; 305-448-7595

Hours: Daily

Natural Food Store and Deli. Bakery. Vegan and Macrobiotic options. Not pure veg.

Menu: Has a good selection of vegetarian and vegan dishes in its deli. Fresh juices.

Comments: Has herbal supplements, cruelty free cosmetics, natural cosmetics, aromatherapy and ear-wax cleaning kits.

Other Info: Full service, take-out. Accepts AMEX, MC, VISA. Price: $$.

MIRAMAR

***Things Vegetarian

6060 Miramar Parkway; 954-965-3672

Hours: Monday to Saturday 12 noon to 8 pm; closed Sunday.

Fully Vegan Caribbean and Rasta.

Menu: Different menu every day. Veggie burgers, stews, vegetable dishes, salads, smoothies and fresh juices.

Other Info: No credit cards; cash only.

Directions: From Florida's Turnpike, take exit #49 towards Hollywood, go east on Hollywood Blvd (Rte 820) for a quarter-mile, at US-441/Rte 7 turn right and go 1¾ mile south, at Miramar Pkwy turn right and this place is 1 block down. From I-95, take exit #21, then go west on SW 30th St (becomes Miramar Pkwy) and this place is 3 miles down.

NAPLES

Sunsplash Market & Café

850 Neapolitan Way; 941-434-7221

Hours: Monday to Saturday 11 am to 7 pm Sunday 10 am to 6 pm

Natural Food Store and Salad Bar. Juice Bar with sandwiches and salads. Vegan options. Organic produce.

Menu: "Eggless" Tofu Salad, Thai Tempeh Salad,

Curried Red Lentil Salad and other main dishes. The salad bar has over thirty items. Fresh juices and smoothies.

Comments: Has organic and vegan dishes in salad bar. This is a big place with a large selection of items. Only uses organic produce. No refined sugar or artificial sweeteners.

Other Info: Cafeteria style, catering. Accepts DIS, MC, VISA. Price: $$.

Directions: From I-75, take the Pine Ridge Rd exit (#16) and go west on Pine Ridge Rd for 3 miles. At 9th St turn left and go a half-mile, then make a right on Neapolitan Way and this store is in the Neapolitan Way Shopping Center on the right.

NORTH MIAMI BEACH

Artichoke's

3055 NE 163rd Street (Rte 826), North Miami Beach

305-945-7576

Hours: Mon to Thu 5:30 pm to 10 pm; Fri & Sat 5:30 pm to 10: 30 pm; Sun 5 pm to 9:30 pm

International Natural Foods Restaurant. Vegan and Macrobiotic options. Not pure vegetarian.

Menu: Appetizers, salads, entrees and desserts. The main house dish is Steamed Artichoke stuffed with peas, spinach and breadcrumbs. Has three daily vegetarian specials. You can call and ask what they are. Served with a really good honey Dijon mustard. Broccoli Ziti is a pasta dish with an olive oil and garlic sauce. Tofu or Tempeh Delight is a macrobiotic dish that comes with vegetables.

Comments: Relaxed place. New-age atmosphere. Has quotes on the tables and model airplanes hanging from the ceiling.

Other Info: Full service, take-out. Accepts AMEX, MC, VISA. Price: $$.

Directions: From I-95, take Rte 826 exit #18, then go east on Rte 826 (become NE 163rd St) and this place is 4 miles down.

Hong Kong Harbour

17053 West Dixie Highway, North Miami

305-949-8617

Hours: Monday to Thursday 11:30 am to 10 pm; Saturday 11:30 am to 11 pm; Sunday 3 pm to 10 pm

Chinese. Vegan options. Not pure veg.

Menu: Has a good-size separate vegetarian menu. Corn Soup, Tofu Casserole, Buddha Roll (Tofu skin with vegetables), Vegetable Curry and many mock "meat" dishes.

Comments: Gets good recommendations.
Other Info: Full service, take-out, catering. Accepts AMEX, MC, VISA. Price: $$.

Kebab Indian Restaurant
514 NE 167th Street, North Miami
305-940-6309
Hours: Tuesday to Sunday 10 am to 10 pm
Closed Monday.
North Indian. Vegan options. Not pure vegetarian. Monday to Thursday Lunch Buffet.
Menu: Has a good-sized vegetarian dinner thali. The meal starts with lassi and soup. The thali has samosas, matar paneer (cheese and spinach), rice, mixed curry vegetable, chapati, raita, papadam and a gulabjamun for dessert.
Comments: Gets really good recommendations. Use a lot of onions in their food, so be prepared for this.
Other Info: Full service, take-out. Accepts: AMEX, DIS, MC, VISA.

Life Natural Foods
12501 NE 8th Avenue; 305-891-5808
Hours: Monday to Friday 9 am to 6 pm
Saturday 9 am to 4 pm; closed Sunday.
Natural Food Store. Has fresh juices.

Miami Juice
16210 Collins Avenue, North Miami Beach
305-945-0444
Hours: Monday to Saturday 8 am to 8 pm
Closed Sunday.
Juice Bar and Café. Mostly vegetarian.
Menu: Sandwiches, salads and hot dishes. Fresh juices and smoothies.
Comments: Has indoor and outdoor seating.

Sara's Natural Food & Pizza
2214 NE 23rd Street, North Miami
305-891-3312
email: simchatamir@yahoo.com
Web site: www.saraskosherfood.com
Hours: Sun to Thur 6:30 am to 10 pm; Fri 6:30 am to 3 pm; Sat 6 pm (sunset) to 2 am
Kosher, Mainly Vegetarian International with Middle Eastern & Italian. Vegan options. Not pure vegetarian.
Menu: Falafel, pita sandwiches, bagels, pizzas, knishes and other dishes. Fresh juices, cappuccino, espresso.
Comments: Uses a lot of soy bean and tofu products. Has whole-wheat pizza crust. The toppings are mainly vegetarian and include vegetarian lamb,

shredded lettuce, fresh pesto, corn, spinach and broccoli. Friendly, efficient service.
Other Info: Full service, take-out, pizza delivery, catering. Accepts AMEX, DIS, MC, VISA. Price: $$.

MIAMI LAKES

Hale's Health Foods
16427 NW 67 Avenue, Miami Lakes
305-821-5331
Hours: Monday to Friday 9:30 am to 6 pm
Saturday 10 am to 6 pm
Natural Food Store.
Directions: From I-95, take the 67th exit and this place is 1 block south of the exit.

OCALA

B-Healthy
2202 East Silver Spring Boulevard
352-867-8727
Hours: Monday to Friday 9 am to 7 pm
Saturday 9 am to 6 pm
Sandwiches prepared in Deli until 4 pm
Natural Food Store and Deli. Juice Bar. Organic produce.
Menu: Fresh salads, tabbouleh, hummus, Veggie Lasagna, Veggie Chili, Vegetable Stir-fry, sandwiches and fresh homemade soups. Fresh juices and smoothies.
Other Info: Accepts DIS, MC, VISA. Counter service, take-out. Has seating.
Directions: From I-75, take SR-40 exit (#69) towards Ocala/Silver Springs, then go east on Hwy 40 and this place is 4½ miles down.

B-Healthy
8447 SW Highway 200; 352-854-4577
Hours: Monday to Friday 9 am to 7 pm; Saturday 9 am to 6 pm; closed Sunday.
Natural Food Store. No deli in this branch.
Other Info: Accepts DIS, MC, VISA.

Mother Earth Market
Ocala Shopping Center
1917 East Silver Springs Boulevard (FL State Road 40); 352-351-5224
Hours: Monday to Saturday 9 am to 8 pm
Sunday 11 am to 6 pm
Natural Food Store and Juice Bar. Organic produce.
Comments: Has a great selection of organic produce. It is basically the size of a supermarket and has a great selection of vegetarian "mock" meats,

frozen meals, juices and health supplements. Highly recommended. Price: $$.
Directions: From I-75, take US 27 exit (#70) towards Ocala/Silver Springs and go southeast on US 27 for 4 miles, then at FL State Road 40E turn left (go east) and this place is 1¾ mile down.

ORANGE PARK (suburb of Jacksonville)

The Granary Whole Foods
1738 Kingsley Avenue
904-269-7222
Hours: Monday to Saturday 9 am to 6 pm Closed Sunday.
Natural Food Store and Deli. Bakery, Juice Bar and organic produce. Vegan and Macrobiotic options. Not pure vegetarian.
Menu: The deli is mainly vegetarian. Soups, salads, sandwiches and other dishes. Uses organic produce when possible. Fresh juices.
Comments: This place has a great selection of items.
Other Info: Limited service, take-out. Price: $.
Directions: From I-295, take US 17 exit (#3). Go south on US 17 for two miles and then make a right on Kingsley and go 1½ mile west. The store is on the left after the railway tracks in a yellow house, a quarter-mile east of Columbia–Orange Park Medical Center.

ORLANDO

Baja Burrito Kitchen
4642 Kirkman Road   407-299-5001
2716 East Colonial Drive   407-895-6112
Hours: Monday to Saturday 11 am to 10 pm Sunday 11:30 am to 9 pm
Cal-Mex. Not pure vegetarian.
Menu: Has free chips with 6 different salsas. Vegetable tacos and veggie burritos.
Comments: Has no lard in the beans or chicken stock in the rice.
Directions: A little north of Universal Orlando on Route 435.

Bee Line Diner
9801 International Drive, Peabody Hotel
407-352-4000
Hours: Daily 24 hours
International with Vegetarian section on menu. Not pure vegetarian.
Menu: Garden burgers, salads, Lasagna, vegetarian chili and falafel. Non-alcoholic beer.
Other Info: Full service, take-out. Accepts AMEX,

DC, DIS, MC, VISA. Price: $$.
Directions: From I-4, take Kirkman Rd exit (#30A) and go south on S Kirkman Rd (FL-435) for 1 mile, take (SR-482) Sand Lake Rd ramp and go a quarter-mile west, at Universal Blvd turn left and go 1½ mile south, then take a slight left onto International Dr and this place is a quarter-mile down.

Cafe Tu Tu Tango
8625 International Drive
407-248-2222
International. Not pure vegetarian.
Menu: Has salads, sandwiches, Wild Mushroom Soup, couscous, and other dishes.
Comments: Has painted tiles and art. Has a tarot card reader and a strolling minstrel.
Other Info: Accepts AMEX, MC, VISA. Price: $$-$$$.

Dux
9801 International Drive; 407-352-4000
International. Not pure vegetarian.
Menu: Has a three-course Vegetarian Meal. The meal changes regularly. With 24 hours advance notice, can have a three-course vegan meal. Has vegan desserts such as orange sorbet.
Comments: The food is beautifully presented. Good atmosphere. Food gets high ratings.
Other Info: Accepts AMEX, MC, VISA. Price: $$$$.

Chamberlin's Market & Café
4960 East Colonial Drive, Herndon Village Shoppes, east Orlando; 407-894-8452
Hours: Monday to Saturday 9 am to 8:30 pm (Friday to 9 pm); Sunday 11 am to 5:30
Natural Food Store and Café. Deli, Bakery, Salad Bar and Juice Bar. Organic produce. Supermarket-type place. See Winter Park for details.
Menu: Homemade soups, salads, sandwiches, vegetarian chili, fresh fruit smoothies, organic juices, frozen yogurts and vegetarian entrees.
Comments: This is a large place that has a good selection of items.
Directions: From I-4, take US-17/Colonial Dr (#42) exit, and go 4 mile east on Colonial Dr and this place is on the left. This place is a half-mile east of Fashion Square.

Chamberlin's Market and Café
The Market Place Shopping Center
7600 Dr Phillips Blvd, southwest Orlando
407-352-2130;
Web site: www.chamberlines.com

Hours: Monday to Saturday 9 am to 8:30 pm (Friday to 9 pm); Sun 11 am to 5:30 pm
Natural Food Store and Café. Deli, Bakery, Salad Bar and Juice Bar. Organic produce. Supermarket-type place. See Winter Park for details.
Menu: Has a large selection of hot and cold vegetarian dishes. Homemade soups, salads, sandwiches, vegan Lasagna, vegetarian chili, fresh fruit smoothies and organic juice. Has a large salad bar.
Comments: This is a large place that has a good selection of items.
Direction: From I-4, take Sand Lake Rd and go west one mile, then turn left at Dr Phillips Blvd and this place is 1 block down. Minutes from major attractions. It is the closest Chamberlin's to Walt Disney World and Universal Orlando.

Florida Hospital Cafeteria

601 East Rollins Street, Orlando
407-897-1793 (number for Nutritional Service of hospital)
American Cafeteria. Good Salad Bar. Not pure vegetarian, but very vegetarian friendly.
Menu: There is a good selection of vegetarian items. Vegetarian Corn Dog, Cheeseless Macaroni & Cheese, homemade bread, Mock "Chicken" Soup, meatless "sausage" & "chicken" gravy, corn-on-the-cob, Steamed Vegetables, mock "Turkey" Lentil Stew, salads, taco bar and rice.
Comments: This place is in the Florida Hospital managed by the Seventh-Day Adventist. This place serves over 5,000 vegetarian meals each day. It has a pleasant atmosphere and is very well run.
Other Info: Counter service, take-out. Price: $.
Directions: From I-4, take Princeton St exit (#43), then go east on Princeton St a third-mile, then turn left at Bedford Rd and this place is a quarter-mile down. From Colonial Drive go north on N Orange Ave for 1½ mile, then turn left on E Rollin St and this place is a quarter-mile down. This place is in northeast Orlando. There is free parking across the street in a parking deck.

**Garden Café

810 West Colonial Drive, near the downtown; 407-999-9799; **fax:** 407-999-9796; **Web site:** www.orlando.com
Hours: Tuesday to Friday 11 am to 10 pm Saturday & Sunday 12 noon to 10 pm
Fully Vegetarian Chinese. Also has International cuisine. Vegan options.
Menu: This place has a large vegetarian menu. Several types of Chinese soups, tofu dishes, Chi-

nese vegetables and mushroom dishes. Rice, noodles, Harvest Burger, Portabella Sandwich, Sauté Pasta and Pasta Garbanzo Bean Salad. Meal begins with Chinese crackers and homemade sweet and sour sauce. Mock lamb, seafood, pork, beef, chicken, duck, tempeh squid, duck, goose and frog legs. The satay lamb is made from mushrooms stems and has vegetables (water chestnut, snap peas, mushrooms, ginger and celery) and a nice sauce. Stuffed Bell Pepper, Satay Lamb, Salt & Pepper Ribs, Sesame Eel and Squid.
Comments: Their mission statement: "Forgo the meat without giving up the taste." This is a friendly, laid-back place. The food is really good and reasonably priced. Good, friendly service. Gets good recommendations from several people that I know, plus from me. Most likely the best vegetarian place to eat at in Orlando. Fresh flowers in the windows and brightly painted. Has cheaply priced lunch specials. There is 10% off any order over $10.
Other Info: Full service, take-out. Non-smoking. Reservations are suggested on weekend nights. Accepts DC, DIS, MC, VISA. Price: $$.
Directions: This place is west of the Orlando Arena. From I-4, take the Colonial Drive Exit (#41), then go west on Colonial Drive and this place is a half-mile down. Has a parking lot. This place is in northwest Orlando.

Green Earth Health Foods

2336 West Oakridge Road, in the Oakridge Plaza; 407-859-8045
Hours: Monday, Wednesday, 9:30 am to 8 pm; Tuesday, Thursday, Friday 9:30 am to 7 pm; Saturday 10 am to 6 pm; closed Sun.
Natural Food Restaurant. Vegan options.
Menu: Salads, homemade soups, sandwiches, chili and other dishes. Fresh juices and smoothies.
Comments: Uses organic produce when possible. Uses foods that are low-fat and low-salt. Does not use foods containing preservatives or chemicals. All dishes are made on the premises.
Other Info: Limited service. Accepts MC, VISA. Price: $.
Directions: From Florida's Turnpike, take US-17/US-441 exit (#254) towards Orlando South, then go north on US-17/S Orange Blossom Trail for 2¾ miles, at W Oak Ridge Rd turn left (go west) and this place is 2/3 miles down. From I-4, take Exit #30, then go east on W Oak Ridge Rd and this place is 2 miles down.

Passage to India Restaurant

5532 International Drive; 407-351-3456
Hours: Daily 11 am 11 pm
Indian. Not Pure Vegetarian.
Menu: Has around 20 vegetarian dishes. Soups, vegetarian appetizers, good samosas, vegetable korma and entrees.
Comments: They say that the vegetarian and meat dishes are cooked using separate pots and utensils. "Passage To India is worth the trip!" Scott Joseph, Orlando Sentinel. "Passage To India is a gem!" Susan Shumaker and Than Saffel, Vegetarian Times Magazine. Consistently rated best Indian food restaurant in town. Orlando Magazine Reader's Choice.
Other Info: Full service, take-out, delivery. Accepts AMEX, DIS, MC, VISA
Directions: From Disney World, take I-4 East to Exit #30A, to International Drive. Take a left, go three lights and it is on the right, opposite the Burger King.

Power House

111 East Lyman Avenue, Winter Park
407-645-3616
Hours: Monday to Saturday 8 am to 7 pm
Saturday 8 am to 5 pm; closed Sunday.
Juice Bar. Natural Foods. Vegan options. Not pure vegetarian.
Menu: Makes good fresh juices, shakes and smoothies. Some vegetarian sandwiches, soups. vegetarian chili and salads.
Comments: The manager is vegetarian.
Other Info: Counter service, take-out. Accepts MC, VISA.
Directions: From I-4, take Fairbanks Ave exit (#45) and go east on Fairbank Ave for 2 miles, at S Park Ave turn left and go 2 blocks and this place is at the corner of Park and Lyman.

New Punjab Indian Restaurant

7451 International Drive; 407-352-7887
Hours: Tuesday to Saturday 11 am to 11 pm
Lunch Buffet Tuesday to Saturday 11 am to 2:30 pm; Sunday & Monday 5 pm to 11 pm (open only for dinner)
Indian, mainly east Indian. Vegan options. Not pure vegetarian.
Menu: Several appetizers and vegetable curries. Fresh juices.
Comment: Authentic décor.
Other Info: Full service, take-out, catering. Reservations required. Accepts AMEX, DC, DIS, MC, VISA. Price: $$.

**Rasoi

852 Lancaster Road; 407-859-0111
Hours: Wednesday to Monday 11:30 am to 8:30 pm; closed Tuesday.
Fully Vegetarian Indian. Vegan options.
Price: $. Has an all-you-can-eat lunch buffet Monday to Friday for $5.99 and Weekends and holidays for $7.99.
Menu: All-you-can-eat lunch buffet. Samosa, pakoras, vegetable burger, kachori, vada, bhel puri, idly, several varieties of dosas, naan, roti, basmati rice, special vegetarian biryani rice, lassi and masala tea. Gujarati Thali for $9.99 and Punjabi Thali for $10.99.
Other Info: Catering, take-out.
Directions: It is located just off Orange Blossom Trail on Lancaster Road. From I-4, take exit #33 and then go towards Beeline Expressway Rte 528, turn left on Lancaster Rd and this place is on the right. From Florida's Turnpike, take US-17/US-441 exit #254 towards Orlando South/Kissimmee, then go north on Orange Blossom (US-17/US-441) for 2¼ miles, then turn right at W Lancaster Rd and this place is a quarter-mile down.

**Taste of India

Bib Plaza, 9251 South Orange Blossom Trail
407-855-4622; **fax:** 407-251-5532
Web site: www.tasteofindia.net
Hours: Tuesday to Sunday 11 am to 9 pm
Closed Monday.
Buffet Hours: 11 am to 2 pm, 6 pm to 8:30 pm. All day buffet on Saturday and Sunday.
Fully Vegetarian Indian.
Menu: Rice, curried vegetables, soups, breads, dal, chutney, papadam and salad. Samosas, kachori, dhokla, French fries, idly, vada, puri, bhel puri, dosa, sambar, uthappam, gulabjamun, shrikhand and ice cream. Drinks include lassi, Indian tea and coffee.
Comments: This place is fairly good. One of my friends didn't like the buffet at all while the other did. The all-you-can-eat buffet is a good value.
Other Info: Counter service, take-out, catering. Accepts credit cards. Price: $.
Direction: This place is in a small shopping center 5 miles south of downtown Orlando on Orange Blossom Trail (Rte 441). From the Florida Turnpike, take US-17/US-441 Exit #254 towards Orlando South/Kissimmee. It is near the Florida Mall, a half-mile south of the exit on Orange Blossom Trail.

White Wolf Cafe

1829 N Orange Avenue; 407-895-9911
American. Not pure vegetarian.
Menu: For lunch has a selection of vegetarian sandwiches such as Cool Cuke (cream cheese, cucumber & tomatoes on whole-wheat bread), hummus and black bean hummus sandwiches. For dinners there is a wide selection of vegetarian dishes including Greek Salad, pizzas, Spinach & Eggplant Rolatini and more.
Comments: Casual, friendly place.
Other Info: Full service, take-out. Accepts MC, VISA.

ORMOND BEACH

LOVE WHOLE FOODS

Williamson Road
Natural Food Store. Juice Bar. Organic Bar.

OVIEDO

Chamberlin's Market and Café

Oviedo Marketplace Super Store
407-359-7028
Hours: Monday to Saturday 9 am to 9 pm; Sunday 11 am to 5:30
Natural Food Store and Café. Deli, Bakery, Salad Bar and Juice Bar. Organic produce. Supermarket-type place. See Winter Park for details.
Menu: Homemade soups, salads, sandwiches, vegetarian chili, fresh fruit smoothies and organic juice.
Comments: This is a large place that has a good selection of items.
Other Info: Counter service, take-out. Has seating.
Directions: New Oviedo Mall, Red Bug Rd & The Greenway at Hwy 417. The entrance is outside next to Bed, Bath & Beyond.

PALM BEACH

Nutrition World

2568 PGA Blvd, Palm Beach Gardens
561-626-4377
Hours: Daily 9 am to 9 pm
Natural Food Store and Juice & Smoothie Bar. Organic produce.
Other Info: Accepts AMEX, DIS, MC, VISA.

Sunrise Health Food Store

233 Royal Ponnisiana Way
561-655-3557
Hours: Monday to Friday 8:30 am to 6 pm

Saturday 8:30 am to 5 pm; closed Sunday.
Deli and Juice Bar Hours: Monday to Saturday 11 am to 4 pm
Natural Food Store and Deli. Macrobiotic. Not pure vegetarian.
Menu: Soups, pastas, Spinach Pie, sandwiches, salads and other vegetarian dishes. Non-alcoholic beer and wine.
Other Info: Counter service, take-out only. Accepts AMEX, MC, VISA. Price: $.
Directions: From I-95, take Okeechobee Blvd (SR-704) exit #52A, then go east on Okeechobee Blvd for 1½ mile towards ocean, cross bridge and then turn left at 2nd light after bridge (go north) and go about a half-mile. This place is a half-block past the Breaker's Hotel (a huge hotel on the ocean).

Palm Harbor Natural Foods

Seabreeze Shopping Center, 30555 US Highway 19 North, Palm Harbor; 727-786-1231
Natural Food Store and Deli. Juice Bar. Organic produce
Hours: Monday to Saturday 8:30 am to 8 pm; Sunday 10 am to 7 pm
Menu: Has a wide selection of vegetarian dishes. Most of dishes in the deli are vegetarian. Seitan dishes, veggie burgers, sandwiches, salads, pastas, tabbouleh, Veggie Lasagna and much more.
Other Info: Accepts AMEX, DIS, MC, VISA.

PENSACOLA (Florida Panhandle)

EverMan's Natural Foods

315 West Garden Street, downtown
850-438-0402; fax: 850-438-0402;
email: info@everman.org;
Web site: www.everman.org
Hours: Monday to Saturday 7 am to 7 pm
Deli closes at 6 pm; closed Sunday.
Natural Food Store and Deli. Organic produce.
Menu: Eggplant & Zucchini Sandwich, soups, Avocado & Tomato Sandwich, red bean & rice wraps, hummus sandwich, Eggless Tofu Salad, bagels and salads. Daily specials include pizza, enchiladas and Lasagna. Fresh juices and smoothies.
Comments: It a good size co-op with over 8,000 members. Has a seating area. Membership is $12 per year. Non-members have to pay a 15% surcharge. There is no surcharge for first time customers. Arranges special events such as yoga classes and classes on herbs and health.
Other Info: Counter service, take-out, ca-

tering.
Directions: From I-10, take I-110 exit (#4) towards Pensacola and go south 6 miles, then take the Garden St/US-98 exit (#1C) towards Historical District. At US 98 (W Garden St) turn right and this place is a half-mile down.

Hip Pocket Deli
4130 Barrancas Avenue
850-455-9319
Hours: Monday to Saturday 10 am to 3 pm
Closed Sunday.
Deli. Not pure vegetarian.
Menu: Vegetarian subs and sandwiches, and a vegetable calzone (cheese & spinach).
Other Info: Take-out, catering. No credit cards; cash only. Price: $.

PLANTATION (near Ft Lauderdale)

Smoothie King
700 S Pine Island Road; 954-423-4087
See Miami Beach.

Whole Foods Market
7720 Peters Road; 954-236-0600
Hours: Daily 8 am to 10 pm
Natural Food Store and Cafe. Deli, Bakery, Salad Bar and Juice Bar. Organic produce. Supermarket-type place. See Whole Foods information.
Directions: From I-595, take SR-817 exit #6 towards University Dr, then go north on S University Dr (Rte 817) a half-mile, at Peters Rd turn left and this place is 1 block down.

PORT ORANGE

Harvest House Natural Foods
4032 South Ridgewood Avenue
386-756-3800
Hours: Monday to Friday 7 am to 7 pm
Saturday 7 am to 6 pm; closed Sunday.
Natural Food Store and Coffee Shop. Not pure vegetarian. Organic produce.
Menu: Vegetarian wraps, salads and soups and a few fresh juices.
Other Info: Accepts MC, VISA.
Directions: Port Orange is just south of Daytona Beach.

SARASOTA

Bulk-n-Natural
3737 Bahia Vista Street; 941-957-0595
Hours: Monday to Saturday 8 am to 5 pm (until

6 pm on Friday); closed Sunday.
Natural Food Store. Offers discounts on bulk products.

Dynamic Health
4141 South Tamiami Trail (near Chili's)
941-923-4525
Hours: Monday to Saturday 9 am to 5:30 pm
Natural Food Store. No produce or deli.
Other Info: Accepts AMEX, MC, VISA.

The Granary Natural Foods
1279 Beneva Road South; 941-365-3700
Directions: The Beneva Road store is located a ten-minute drive south of downtown Sarasota in a small shopping center just off US 41.
1930 Stickney Point Road; 941-924-4754
Directions: To get to the Stickney Point Road branch from I-75 take exit #37 (Clark Rd, SR-72) west for 5 miles. After passing US 41, the road becomes Stickney Rd. Store is on the left. This place is a quarter-mile west of Gulf Gate Mall.
email: granaryinc@aol.com
Hours: Monday to Saturday 9 am to 8 pm
Sunday 10 am to 6 pm
Natural Food Store and Deli. Salad Bar and Juice Bar. Organic produce.
Menu: This place has a large deli and salad bar ($5.99 per pound) with a good selection of dishes. It has tofu, steamed vegetables, Eggless Salad, Artichoke Hearts, Lasagna, hummus, falafel, tabbouleh, Eggplant Parmesan and BBQ Seitan.
Comments: This place is the size of a supermarket and has an excellent selection of organic produce and other items. 10% off everything in the stores on the first Thursday of every month.
Other Info: Counter service, take-out. Has seating outside in front of both stores.

Lonni's Sandwiches, Etc
1535 Main Street; 941-363-9222
Hours: Monday to Friday 10 am to 4 pm
Closed Saturday & Sunday
Sandwich Place. Not pure vegetarian. See Clearwater.

Nature's Way Cafe
1572 Main Street; 941-954-3131
Hours: Monday to Friday 7:30 am to 4 pm
Saturday 7:30 am to 3 pm; closed Sunday.
Natural Food Cafe. Not pure vegetarian.
Menu: Has a good selection of vegetarian dishes. Has good salads and a good selection of homemade vegetarian soups. Hummus, Garden Burger,

Vegetable wraps, fruit salads and other dishes. Fresh juices.
Other Info: Full service, take-out. Accepts AMEX, MC, VISA.
Directions: From I-75, take SR-780 exit (#39) towards Sarasota, then go west on Fruitville Rd for 6 miles, at N Orange Ave turn left and go 3 blocks, at Main St turn right and this place is a half-block down.

The Front
3800 South Tamiami Trail #3; 941-954-1330
Hours: Monday to Friday 7 am to 3 pm
Sunday 8 am to 2 pm
American and International. Mainly vegetarian. Has over 20 vegan options.
Menu: Mainly a vegetarian menu with soups, salads, sandwiches and main dishes. Scrambled Tofu and veggie sausages for breakfast.
Comments: Casual. Cooks meat and vegetarian items in a separate area.
Other Info: Full service, take-out. Reservations not necessary. Non-smoking. Accepts AMEX, MC, VISA. Price: $$.
Directions: From I-75, take SR-780 exit #39 towards Sarasota/Gulf Beaches, go west on Fruitville Rd for 3 miles, at S Beneva Rd turn left and go 2 miles, at Webber St turn right and go 1 mile, at S Tuttle Ave turn left and go 2 blocks and go around circle and take 1st exit onto Siesta Dr and go 1 mile, at S Tamiami Trail turn left and this place is a quarter mile down in Paradise Plaza.

ST AUGUSTINE

Diane's Natural Food Market
240 SR 312, St Augustine
904-808-9978
Hours: Monday to Saturday 9:30 am to 6 pm; Sunday 12 noon to 5 pm
Natural Food Store and Juice Bar. No organic produce.
Menu: Has some ready-made sandwiches and a counter where they make fresh sandwiches and juices.
Comments: Vitamins, herbs, natural cosmetics, spices, bulk nuts and grains, homeopathic remedies, books and pet products. This is a small place and doesn't have many options for freshly made foods.
Directions: Next to Albertson's in Portman Plaza shopping center. From US 1 you go east on Rte 312, then turn right onto State Rd 3. Then turn right into the Portman Plaza.

**Manatee Café
179 San Marco Avenue; 904-826-0210;
Web site: www.manateecafe.com
Hours: Sunday to Thursday for breakfast 8 am to 3 pm; Friday & Sat 8 am to 3 pm
Fully Vegetarian Natural Food Restaurant. Vegan options.
Menu: Soups, salads, sandwiches, Middles Eastern dishes, Tofu Reuben Sandwich and veggie burgers. Fresh juices. Cappuccino, espresso.
Comments: Uses organic produce when possible. Friendly service. Casual, relaxed place. Gets good recommendations. They supply ready-made sandwiches to the local health food stores. Donates some of its profits to save the endangered manatee. Full menu is on their web site.
Possible Warning: When I called they only served breakfast and lunch. When they served dinner in the past they also served chicken and fish. So if they also serve dinner (which may be done in the future) they may serve meat, but when this book was published they were full vegetarian (with eggs).
Other Info: Full service, take-out. Accepts DIS, MC, VISA.
Directions: From I-95, take Rte 207 exit (#94) towards St Augustine Beach. Go east on Rte 207 for 5 miles, at S Ponce De Leon Blvd turn left and go 2 miles, at W San Carlos Ave turn right and this place is 2 blocks down (becomes San Marco).

ST PETERSBURG

Ambrosia's
201 7th Avenue; 727-898-5194
Hours: Mon to Thurs 11 am to 3 pm, 5 pm to 10 pm; Fri & Sat 11 am to 3 pm, 5 pm to 11 pm; Sun 11 am to 3 pm, 5 pm to 9 pm
New American. Vegetarian friendly. Not pure vegetarian.
Menu: Has salads, a good selection of vegetarian appetizers and two main dishes nightly are vegetarian.
Comments: Upscale. Good place for a romantic dinner. High priced. Won awards for best vegetarian food in Tampa area.
Other Info: Accepts AMEX, DC, DIS, MC, VISA.

Ben Thanh Restaurant
2880 34th Street; 813-522-6623
Hours: Monday, Tuesday, Thursday, Friday 11 am to 8:45 pm; Saturday & Sunday 10 to 8:45; closed Wednesday.
Vietnamese. Not pure vegetarian. Vegan op-

tions.
Menu: Has a good selection of vegetarian dishes. Curry Tofu, Spring Rolls, curried vegetables, Rice and Tofu, and soups.
Comments: Friendly people.
Other Info: Full service. Accepts MC, VISA.
Price: $.

Lonni's Sandwiches
133 1st Street NE; 727-894-1944
Hours: Monday to Friday 8 am to 4 pm
Closed Saturday & Sunday
Natural Foods. Not pure vegetarian. See Clearwater.
Menu: Several vegetarian options including soups, salads and sandwiches. Cappuccino.
Other Info: Counter service, take-out, catering. Accepts AMEX, DIS, MC, VISA. **Price:** $$.

Nature's Finest Foods
6651 Central Avenue; 727-347-568
Natural Food Store and Deli. Large Salad Bar. Macrobiotic and Vegan options. Organic produce. Supermarket-type place.
Menu: The food gets good recommendations. Organic vegetable pizza, soups, salads, sandwiches, Vegan Lasagna and Bean Stew.
Directions: From I-275, take Rte 595/5th Ave N exit (#11), go west on 5th Ave for 3¼ miles, at Tyrone Blvd turn right and go 1¼ mile, at 22nd Ave turn left and go 1 block, at 66th St N (US 19A) turn left and go 1¼ mile, at Pasadena Ave turn slight right and go a quarter-mile, at Pinellas Way turn left and go 1 block, at Central Ave turn left and go a half-block.

Nature's Table
6901 22nd Avenue N, Suite VCO3, St Petersburg; 727-347-2275
Natural Foods. Not pure vegetarian. See Gainesville.

Rollin' Oats Market & Café
2842 9th Street N (Dr ML King Street), at 27th Avenue; 727-821-6825
Café Number: 727-895-4910
Store Hours: Mon to Fri 7:30 am to 7 pm; Sat 9:30 am to 6 pm; Sun 10 am to 4 pm
Café Hours: Monday to Saturday 11 am to 5 pm; Sunday Brunch 10 am to 3 pm
Natural Food Store and Vegetarian-friendly Restaurant & Deli. Vegan options.
Menu: Sandwiches, pasta dishes, Seitan Fajitas, hummus salad, Penne Pasta with Three Cheeses (very good), Middle Eastern dishes, salads with

homemade dressings, veggie burgers, Tempeh Burger, Smoked Tofu and many other dishes. Fresh juices.
Comments: Lists the daily specials on the blackboard.
Other Info: Full service, take-out. Accepts DIS, MC, VISA. **Price:** $-$$.
Directions: From I-275, take 22nd Ave N exit (#12), then go a half-mile west on 22nd Ave, at 14th St turn left and go 1 block, at Woodlawn Circle turn right and go a quarter-mile, go straight onto Greenwood Ave and go 1 block, at 26th Ave turn slight right and go 1 block, at 11th St turn left and go 1 block, go around circle and take 2nd exit onto 28th Ave for block, at Dr ML King St (9th St) turn left and this place is 1 block down.

Saffron's
1700 Park Street N; 727-345-6400
Web site: www.saffroncuisine.com
Hours: Mon to Thur 11 am to 9 pm; Fri & Sat 11 am to 10 pm; Sun 3 pm to 8:30 pm
Jamaican. Not pure vegetarian.
Menu: Caribbean Iced Tea is made from boiled ginger root, cinnamon, lemon juice, cloves and sugar. Vegetables can be prepared in different ways: jerked, sweet and sour, sautéed, stir-fried or Creole. The special jerk sauce is made of peppers, onion, garlic, cilantro and "island spices." The stir-fried vegetables are sautéed in ginger-soy sauce. Main courses come with Jamaican rice (rice with pinto beans), plantains and johnnycakes (fried corn and sugar balls). Cappuccino, espresso.
Comments: In a historical building in a residential area, next to the water. Has live music daily. Has tropical plants and is candle-lit. Not cheap. Often grows their own vegetables. Has a coupon on their Web site to buy five meals and get the sixth one free. Friendly service.
Other Info: Full service, catering. Accepts AMEX, DC, DIS, MC, VISA. **Price:** $$.

Thai-Am Restaurant
6040 4th Street N; 727-522-7813
Hours: Mon to Thur 11 am to 9 pm; Fri & Sat 5 pm to 10 pm; Sun 5 pm to 9 pm
Thai. Vegan options. Not pure vegetarian. Has separate vegetarian menu.
Menu: Large number of vegetarian dishes. Spring Rolls, Cashew Nut Salad, Tofu Coconut Milk Soup, curry dishes, rice and other dishes.
Other Info: Full service, take-out. Accepts MC, VISA. **Price:** $$.

TALLAHASSEE

***Higher Taste
411 St Francis Street, near J St
850-894-4296
Hours: Mon, Tues, Fri 11 am to 3 pm; Wed & Thur 11 am to 3 pm, 5:30 pm to 9 pm; Closed Saturday & Sunday.
Pure Vegetarian Indian and International Restaurant. Salad Bar. Vegan options.
Menu: Has a lunch buffet with around 12 dishes daily. Has a lunch special meal with rice, a vegetable dish, breads and soup for $9. Quiche, salads, pita pizza, Spanikopita, Veggie Kibbie, Focaccia, Palaka's Veggie Burger, Tofu Cutlet, Avocado & Vegetables Sandwich, Banana Bread, Cinnamon Rolls, Apricot Cake, German Carob Cake and Stromboli. Freeze squeezed lemonade, iced tea and herbal teas.
Comments: Run by Hare Krishna devotees. Good food. Recommended.
Other Info: Full service, take-out. Accepts MC, VISA and local checks. Price: $-$$.
Directions: Next to Education Building. From I-10, take Rte 61 exit (#30) towards Tallahassee, then go south on Rte 61 for 5 miles, at E Gainses St turn right and go 5 blocks (1/3 mile), at S Boulevard St turn left and go 1 block, at St Francis St turn right and this place is half-way down the block.

Honeytree Natural Food
1660 North Monroe Street
850-681-2000
Store Hours: Mon to Fri 9 am to 7 pm; Sat 9 am to 6 pm; Sun 12 noon to 6 pm
Juice Bar Hours: 11 am to 2:30 pm
Natural Food Store and Juice Bar. Macrobiotic and Vegan options.
Menu: At the juice bar they serve fresh juices, smoothies, sandwiches, and daily hot specials such as Tofu Pizza or Veggie Chili.
Other Info: Counter service, take-out. Has some seating. Accepts AMEX, DIS, MC, VISA.
Directions: From I-275, take Pinellas Point Dr exit (#3) towards 34th St, at Pinellas Point Dr go east for ¾ mile, at 66th Ave stay straight to go onto 66th Ave and go a half-mile, at 20th St turn right and go a quarter-mile, at Pinellas Point Dr turn left and go 1 block, at Bethel Way turn right and go 1 block, at Serpentine Dr turn left and go a quarter-mile, at Manor Way turn right and this place is 1 block down.

New Leaf Co-op and Café
Parkway Shopping Center, 1235 Apalachee Parkway
850-942-2557; fax: 850-877-9384;
Web site: www.newleafcoop.com
Hours: Monday to Saturday 9 am to 9 pm
Sunday 12 noon to 7 pm
Deli Hours: Monday to Saturday 11 am to 3 pm (prepared foods for take-out after 3 pm)
Natural Food Store and Café. Salad Bar. Bakery and Juice Bar. Organic produce. Vegan options. Not pure vegetarian. Specializes in vegan and vegetarian foods.
Menu: Menu changes daily. Has a good selection of vegetarian dishes. Has a large selection of salads and sandwiches. Szechuan Noodles, hummus, rice salad and fruit salads. Soups, beans, rice, Deli Salads (sold by the pound), Miso, Shezuan Noodle, Masidonian, tempeh, couscous, tabbouleh, Rosemary Rice, Greek Tofu and baked goods. Prepared sandwiches such as Baked Tofu, Miso Tofu and Tomato & Cheese. Fresh juices and smoothies.
Comments: Deli salads sold by the pound. Has the special New Leaf Friday night gourmet dinners during which there is a featured seitan, tempeh or tofu entrée. Their Web site has links to many other Co-ops across the country. Can call and find out what are the Deli Specials of the day.
Other Info: Counter service, take-out, catering. Has seating during the day. Accepts MC, VISA.
Directions: From I-10, take Apalachee Parkway (US27) south towards the capital. At intersection of Apalachee Pkwy and Magnolia. Border Books across the street. In a small shopping center.

Samrat Indian Restaurant
2529 Apalachee Parkway
850-942-1993
Hours: Monday to Saturday 11 am to 2:30 pm, 5 pm to 10 pm
Sunday 5 pm to 10 pm
Indian. All-you-can-eat Saturday buffet 11:30 am to 2:30 pm. Vegan options. Not pure vegetarian. On Saturdays the buffet is fully vegetarian.
Menu: Has a large selection of vegetarian dishes.
Other Info: Accepts AMEX, DC, MC, VISA. Price: $.

TAMPA

Ansley's Natural Marketplace
3936 West Kennedy; 813-879-6625
Hours: Mon to Fri 9 am to 7 pm; Sat 9 am to 5

pm; Sun 11 am to 5 pm
Natural Food Store. No deli or organic produce. About a third of the size of their other branch.
Directions: From I-275, take US 92/Dale Mabry Northbound exit (#23A), then go south on N Dale Mabry Hwy (US 92) for ¾ mile, at John F Kennedy Blvd turn right and this place is 1½ block down on the left.

Ansley's Natural Marketplace
402 East Sligh Avenue
813-239-2700
Hours: Mon to Fri 9 am to 7 pm; Sat 9 am to 6 pm; Sun 11 am to 5 pm
Deli Hours: Daily 10 am to 2 pm (prepared dishes for take-out all day)
Natural Food Store and Deli with Prepared food section. Bakery. Supermarket-type place. Organic produce.
Other Info: Accepts AMEX, DIS, MC, VISA. Counter service, take-out. Has plenty of seating.
Directions: From I-275, take Sligh Ave exit (#31), then go west on Sligh Ave and this place is 2 blocks down.

Bertha's All Natural Café
3802 West Neptune Way, at South Dale Mabry Highway; 813-251-3547
Hours: Monday to Thursday 9 am to 7 pm Friday 9 am to 6:30 pm; Saturday 9 am to 6 pm; Sunday 12 noon to 5 pm
Natural Food Store and Café. Vegan friendly. Not pure vegetarian. Organic produce.
Menu: Homemade soups, salads, sandwiches and a daily special.
Other Info: Counter service, take-out. Order at counter and then sit down at tables. Accepts AMEX, DIS, MC, VISA.
Directions: From I-275, take Dale Mabry Northbound exit (#23A), then go south on N Dale Mabry Hwy (US 92) and this place is 1¾ mile down.

Chuck's Natural Food Marketplace
11301 North 56th, at Fowler Avenue
813-980-2005
Hours: Mon to Fri 9 am to 8 pm; Sat 12 am to 8 pm; Sun 12 noon to 6 pm
Natural Food Store and Deli. Organic Salad Bar and Juice Bar. A large 100% organic produce section. Supermarket-size store.
Menu: A large selection of vegetarian dishes. Soups, salads, sandwiches and other dishes.
Comments: Has a good selection of natural products such as foods, vitamins, herbs, cosmetics,

body products and organic shampoo. Does not sell things that have been tested on animals. The café is very popular. Has specials just like a normal supermarket. Offer a 10% discount on most items when you join the VIP Membership club.
Other Info: Full service, take-out. Accepts AMEX, DIS, MC, VISA.
Directions: From I-75, take Fowler Ave/SR-582 exit (#54) towards Temple Terrace, then go west on E Fowler Ave (SR-382) for 2 miles, at 56th St N turn left and go a quarter-mile and this place is on the left.

Chuck's Ultimate Vitamin Shop
10414 North Dale Mabry Highway
813-968-5422

EVOS' (two branches)
609 South Howard Avenue, at Swann Avenue; 813-258-EVOS (3867)
Directions: From 1-275, take exit #24 towards Howard Ave/Armenia Ave and go south on N Armenia Ave ¾ mile, at W John F Kennedy Blvd turn left and go 1 block, at S Moody Ave turn right and go a quarter-mile, at W Azeele St turn left and go 1 block, at S Howard turn right and go 2 blocks.
10410 North Bruce B Down Boulevard
813-226-EVOS (3867)
Hours: Daily 11 am to 10 pm
Vegetarian-friendly Healthy Fast-food Restaurant. Caters to Vegetarian. Not pure vegetarian (serves fish). Vegan friendly.
Menu: Great Potato "Air Fries," BBQ Veggie Burgers, Soy Burgers, Garden Burgers, cayenne catsup and desserts. Fresh juices and smoothies.
Comments: Some of the best vegetarian food in the Tampa area. Food gets excellent ratings. Friendly, efficient place. Reasonable prices. Has a children's menu. Casual place. Young people and a hip place. Modern décor. A good selection of low-fat, low-calorie fast-foods. Helpful, friendly owners.
Other Info: Full service, take-out, counter service. Accepts AMEX, DC, DIS, MC, VISA. Price: $$.

Jasmine Thai Restaurant
13248 North Dale Mabry, just off I-275
813-968-1501
Hours: Monday to Thursday 11:30 am to 10 pm; Friday & Saturday 11:30 am to 11 pm; Sunday 11:30 am to 9 pm
Thai. Macrobiotic and Vegan options. Not pure vegetarian.

Menu: Has a good selection of vegetarian dishes. Jasmine and Lemon grass. Non-alcoholic beer and wine.
Comments: Good atmosphere and food. Seats are a bit close together. Food gets good ratings from customers. Friendly management.
Other Info: Full service, take-out, catering. Accepts AMEX, DC, DIS, MC, VISA. Price: $$.

Lonni's Sandwiches, Etc
513 Jackson Street; 813-223-2333
Sandwich place. Not pure vegetarian. See Clearwater.

Nature's Harvest Market & Deli
1021 North MacDill Avenue
813-873-7428; **fax:** 813-876-0742
Hours: Monday to Friday 9 am to 9 pm; Saturday 9 am to 8 pm; Sun 11 am to 7 pm
Café usually closes down a couple hours before store.
Natural Food Store and Café. Deli, Bakery and Juice Bar. Organic produce. Not pure vegetarian. Supermarket-type place. Biggest natural food store in area.
Menu: Sandwiches, salads, soups, Tofu Meatloaf, grilled vegetables, Macrobiotic plate and daily vegan specials. Poppy seed muffins are good.
Comments: Free vegetarian cooking classes on Wednesday and Thursday. During lunch, service from a counter only. Has around 10 tables. Fairly big store with a good selection.
Other Info: Counter service, take-out. Has plenty of seating. Accepts AMEX, DIS, MC, VISA. Price: $.
Direction: From I-275, take Howard/Armenia exit (#24). Go south on Armenia, turn right at Cypress and go 6 blocks, then turn right on MacDill and this store is on the right a half-block down.

The NK Café (The Natural Kitchen)
3218 West Kennedy Boulevard
813-874-2233
Hours: Lunch: Monday to Friday 11 am to 2:30 pm; Dinner: Tuesday to Friday 6 pm to 9 pm; Ccosed Sunday.
Natural Food Restaurant. Uses organic produce. Limited Vegan options. Not pure vegetarian (serves chicken and fish).
Menu: Non-dairy Lasagna, salads, sandwiches, main dishes, veggie fruits, granola, fresh fruits and desserts. The Greek Salad is good. Vegetable Cashew Sauté is shitake mushrooms, cashews, crispy broccoli, snow peas and bean sprouts.

Couscous with Vegetables. Sprout and Veggie Sandwich. One of the highlights of this place are its smoothies made from organic fruits and vegetables. Fresh juices, protein shakes and smoothies.
Comments: NK stands for Natural Kitchen. Does not use processed foods or foods that contain chemicals or preservatives. Good healthy food.
Other Info: Full service, take-out. Accepts AMEX, DIS, MC, VISA. Price: $$.

Trang Viet Cuisine
1524 East Fowler Avenue; 813-979-1464
8502 North Armenia Avenue, Suite 1A
813-931-5119
Hours: Monday to Thursday 11 am to 9:30 pm; Friday 11 am to 11 pm; Saturday 11 am to 10:30 pm. closed Sunday.
Vietnamese. Vegetarian friendly. Not pure vegetarian.
Menu: Has a wide selection of vegetarian dishes including several tofu dishes, vegetarian soups, salads and main dishes. Vegan Curry Stew is good. Vegetarian Hot and Sour Soup, Veggie Steamed Buns and Tofu Loaf with Tomato Sauce.
Comments: Grows their own herbs. Food gets very good ratings.
Other Info: Accepts AMEX, MC, VISA. **Price:** $-$$.

WEST PALM BEACH

Wild Oats Market
7735 South Dixie Highway; 561-585-8800
Hours: Monday to Saturday 8 am to 8 pm
Sunday 10 am to 6 pm
Natural Food Store and Eat-In Café. Bakery, Deli and Juice Bar. Has a nutritionist. Vegan and Macrobiotic options. Organic produce. Supermarket-type place. See Wild Oats information.
Directions: From I-95, take Forest Hill Blvd exit (#49), and go east on Forest Hill Blvd (Rte 882) for 1 mile, at S Dixie Hwy (US 1) turn right (go south) and this place is a half-mile down.

WINTER PARK (Orlando Suburbs)

Chamberlin's Market and Café
Winter Park Mall, 430 North Orlando Avenue, at Canton Avenue; 407-647-6661 **email:** cmcinfo@chamberlins.com
Web site: www.chamberlins.com
Hours: Monday to Saturday 9 am to 9:30 pm (Friday to 9 pm); Sunday 10 am to 7 pm
Natural Food Store and Café. Deli, Bakery, Salad Bar and Juice Bar. Organic produce. Supermar-

ket-type Store. See Winter Park for details.

Menu: Has a rotating menu of over 500 dishes. Has a variety of vegan, vegetarian, organic and macrobiotic dishes. Homemade soups, salads, sandwiches, vegetarian Lasagna, Butternut Squash with Tofu, brown rice, steamed vegetables, vegetarian chili, Vegan "Chicken" Salad and fresh fruit. Pizza can have rice cheese or organic mozzarella on sourdough wheat or sun-dried tomato crusts. Bakes their own bread. Organic juices and smoothies with the options of added healthy ingredients such as flax oil, ginkgo, aloe juice and nutritional yeast. Coffee bar with organic coffee, cappuccino, espresso and hot chocolate. Soy or rice milk can be added to coffee.

Comments: This is a large place that has a good selection of items. One of the best places for vegetarian food in the Orlando area. Organizes cooking classes and various natural health classes.

Other Info: Accepts AMEX, DIS, MC, VISA. Price: $.

Comments: From I-4, take Lee Rd/Hwy 423 exit (#46) and then go west on Lee Rd (Hwy 4230 for 1¼ mile, at US-17/92 (N Orlando Ave) turn right and this place is a third-mile down.

Whole Foods Market

1989 Aloma Avenue

407-673-8788

Hours: Daily 8 am to 10 pm

Natural Food Store and Cafe. Deli, Bakery, Salad Bar and Juice Bar. Organic produce. Supermarket-type place. See Whole Foods Market information.

Directions: From I-4, take Fairbanks Ave exit (#45), and go east on W Fairbanks Ave (Rte 426) for 4 miles (becomes Brewer than Aloma Ave) and then this place is on the left.

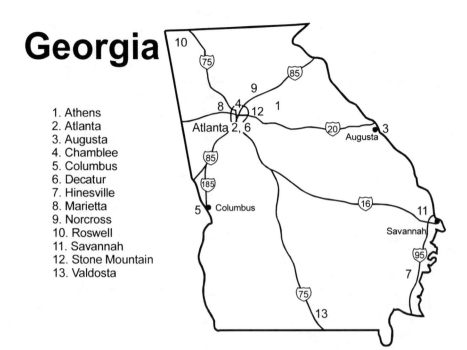

Georgia

1. Athens
2. Atlanta
3. Augusta
4. Chamblee
5. Columbus
6. Decatur
7. Hinesville
8. Marietta
9. Norcross
10. Roswell
11. Savannah
12. Stone Mountain
13. Valdosta

ATHENS

Broad Street is the happening street in town.

**Bluebird Café

493 East Clayton Street
706-549-3663
Hours: Daily 8 am to 3 pm.
Vegetarian and Vegan International, American, Indian and Mexican.
Menu: Salads, enchiladas, quiche, burritos, sandwiches and desserts. Basil Walnut Pesto (linguine with homemade pesto, tomatoes, Parmesan cheese and black olives). Some vegan options are Spinach Cilantro Quesadilla (with brown rice, tomato and onion) and Bindi Masala (okra, onion, tomatoes).
Comments: Very popular place. Has wooden tables and red brick walls. Has a good atmosphere. Vegan dishes have a "V" next to them.
Other Info: Full service, take-out. No credit cards.
Price: $.
Directions: From US-29 going east (south) into town, take the US-78 (Rte 10) exit towards downtown Athens, take US-78 (Rte 10) going west a quarter-mile and stay straight onto US-78 Bus (Rte 10) and go 1 mile northwest, at N Jackson St turn left, then at E Clayton turn right and this place is 1 block down at the corner with N Thomas St.

Daily Groceries Food Co-op

523 Prince Avenue, corner of Pope and Prince next to The Grit; 706-548-1732; **Web site:** http://www.members.tripod.com/eatdaily/
Hours: Monday to Friday 8 am to 10 pm
Saturday & Sunday 9 am to 10 pm
Natural Food Store and Deli. Organic produce.
Menu: Has a selection of vegetarian dishes in the deli. Sandwiches, tofu dishes, salads items and more.
Comments: Gives a 5% discount to other coop member besides their own.
Other Info: Counter service, take-out. Has a table outside.
Directions: From I-85, take the Commerce and 441 south exit. Take 441 South to the loop that goes around Athens. Go south (or west) on Route 10. Exit at Chase St and turn left (go south) and go 1 mile, then turn left onto Prince Ave (Rte Alt 15) and the store is a half-mile down on the right.

Earth Fare

1689 South Lumpkin Street, Five Points
706-227-1717
Hours: Monday to Saturday 8 am to 9 pm
Sunday 9 am to 8 pm
Natural Food Store and Café. Deli, Juice Bar, Bakery and Salad Bar. Organic produce.

Macrobiotic and Vegan options. Supermarket-type place. Not pure vegetarian.
Menu: Has a wide selection of vegetarian dishes. Has a hot and cold buffet.
Comments: This is a large natural food store with a massive selection. Recommended. Cooking classes and lectures. Books and magazines.
Other Info: Counter service, take-out. Accepts AMEX, DIS, MC, VISA. Price: $$.
Directions: This place is 1½ mile south of the downtown. From Hwy 78, take Alt Hwy 15/S Milledge Ave and go north on Alt Hwy 15 for 2 miles, then at Lumpkin St turn left and this place is a quarter-mile down.

**The Grit

199 Prince Avenue
706-543-6592
Hours: Monday to Thursday 11 am to 10 pm; Friday 11 am to 10:30 pm; Saturday and Sunday Brunch 10 am to 3 pm; Saturday Dinner 5 pm to 10:30 pm; Sunday Dinner 5 pm to 10 pm.
Full Vegetarian International. American, Italian, Indian, Chinese, Middle Eastern, Southern and Mexican. Good selection of vegan options.
Menu: Burritos, black bean chili, tomato soup, Middle Eastern Platter (falafel, hummus), New Potatoes, veggie burgers and daily specials. The Indian Special is brown rice, Indian samosa, dal (split pea soup), curry sauce and a daily special. The "Golden Bowl" gets good recommendations. Has several vegan desserts. Cappuccino, espresso.
Comments: Laid-back, funky atmosphere. Reasonably priced. Popular with University of Georgia students. Mosaic tile floor. The rock band R.E.M. used to come here when they lived in Athens. Most meals are under seven dollars.
Other Info: Full service, take-out. Accepts MC, VISA. Price: $-$$.
Directions: Located in the middle of "Normaltown." From I-85, take the Commerce and Hwy 441 south exit. Take Hwy 441 South to the loop that goes around Athens. Go south (or west) on Route 10. Exit at Chase St and turn left (go south) and go 1 mile, then turn left onto Prince Ave (Rte Alt 15) and this place is a mile down.

The Grill

171 College Avenue
706-543-4770
Hours: Daily 24 hours
American. Not pure vegetarian.
Menu: Vegetarian dishes include veggie burgers,

tofu dogs, Sun Burger, Mock Turkey Sandwich, Veggie Melt, mashed potatoes and more.
Comments: I was told that the vegetarian and meat items are prepared in different areas, but you may want to ask about this.

Khun Al Thai Restaurant

149 North Lumpkin Street; 706-548-9222
Hours: Monday to Saturday 5 pm to 10 pm
Closed Sunday.
Thai. Not Pure Vegetarian.
Other Info: Full service, take-out. Accepts AMEX, DC, DIS, MC, VISA. Price: $-$$.

Mellow Mushroom

235 East Broad Street; 706-613-0892
1661 South Lumpkin Street; 706-613-0555
Hours: Sunday to Thursday 11 am to 11 pm
Friday & Saturday 11 am to 12 midnight
Pizza. Not Pure Vegetarian.
Menu: Has some really good vegetarian pizzas.

Phoenix Natural Food Market

296 West Broad Street, corner of Broad & Pulaski, downtown
706-548-1780
Hours: Monday to Saturday 9:30 am to 7 pm
Closed Sundays.
Natural Food Store and Deli. Decent organic produce section.
Menu: Has some ready-made sandwiches and salads.
Directions: From the loop that goes around Athens (Hwy 29, Hwy 8), take the Downtown Athens exit. From north, turn right onto Broadway (Hwy Bus 78), and from south, turn left. The store is about a mile down on the corner of Pulaski and Broad. It is across the street from University of Georgia. Also can go from I-85, take the Commerce and 441 south exit. Take 441 South to the loop that goes around Athens. Go south (or west) on Route 10. Exit at Chase St and turn left (go south) and go 1 mile, then turn left onto Prince Ave (Rte Alt 15) and go about ¾ mile, then at Pulaski St turn right and this place is 4 blocks down on Broadway.

Planet Smoothie

184 College Avenue
706-353-8181
Hours: Monday to Saturday 9 am to 7 pm
Sunday 12 noon to 5 pm
Directions: This place is downtown on College Ave, a block north of Broadway (Hwy Bus 78).

ATLANTA

The Little Five Points area (where Sevananda Natural Food Store is located), is a happening place with used bookstores, plenty of interesting shops and an assortment of restaurants.

Abbay Ethiopian Restaurant

3375 Buford Highway; 404-321-5808
Hours: Daily 11 am to 11 pm
Ethiopian. Vegan options. Not pure vegetarian.
Menu: Vegetarian Sampler Meal. Injera, an Ethiopian flatbread.
Comments: Friendly staff. Open since 1985. Comfortable atmosphere. Often has live music.
Other Info: Full service, take-out. Accepts AMEX, MC, VISA. Price: $-$$.
Directions: In northeast Atlanta next to the Northeast Plaza Fashion Square. From I-85, take the N Druid Hills Rd (Rte 42) exit (#89), then turn left (if going north), and go a third-mile on N Druid Hills Rd, then at Buford Hwy NE (Rte 13) turn right and this place is 1 mile down.

Arden's Garden

985 Monroe Drive
404-817-0707; **Web site:** www.ardensgarden.com
Juice Bar. Central Office.
Directions: This place is 2 miles northeast of where I-75 & I-85 split. From I-75 (also I-85) take Spring St (Rte19) exit (#249) towards W Peachtree St (Rte 29) going north into Atlanta keeping left at fork in ramp, then merge onto Linden Ave and go 1 block, at W Peachtree St turn left and go 1 block, at North Ave (Rte 29) turn right and go a third-mile, at Piedmont Ave turn left and go 1 block, then at Ponce De Leon Ave (Rte 29) turn right (go east) and go 2/3 mile, then at Monroe Dr turn left (go north) and go a half-mile, then at Virginia Ave turn right and this place is 1 block down. Basically go a quarter-mile east on Ponce De Leon Ave, then a half-mile north on Monroe Dr.

Broadway Café

2168 Briarcliff Road, at La Vista Road
404-329-0888
Hours: Sunday to Thursday 11 am to 9 pm; Friday 11 am to 3 pm; closed Saturday.
Mainly Vegetarian International. Italian, Chinese, Mexican and Middle Eastern. Kosher. Vegan options. Not pure vegetarian (serves fish)
Menu: Specializes in mock meat dishes. Has pizzas, pastas, salads and soups. "Lo mein Noodles" is noodles, mock "beef" and "chicken," and stir-fried vegetables in a spicy soy sauce. "The Tem-

pest" is a cheeseless pizza with eggplant, sun-dried tomatoes and olives. Jambalaya is mock "sausage" with tomatoes and green and red peppers. Fresh juices, cappuccino, espresso.
Comments: Voted as the number one kosher restaurant in Atlanta. The Broadway (NY) has vaudeville masks, musical scores and theater posters. Plays Broadway music. Has outdoor patio dining. Has live country music. Has outdoor seating.
Other Info: Full service, take-out, catering. Reservations not necessary. Smoking only on the patio. Accepts AMEX, DIS, MC, VISA. Price: $-$$.
Directions: In northeast Atlanta in a strip mall.

**Café Sunflower

2140 Peachtree Road, Buckhead
404-352-8859; **Website:** www.cafesunflower.com
Hours: Monday to Thursday 11:30 am to 2:30 pm, 5 pm to 9 pm; Friday 11:30 am to 2:30 pm, 5 pm to 10 pm; Saturday 12 noon to 2:30 pm, 5 pm to 10 pm; closed Sunday.
Fully Vegetarian International. Asian, Southwestern, Italian. Mostly Vegan. Gourmet vegetarian.
Starters and Salads: Spring Rolls, Chips & Salsa, Steamed Dumplings, Stuffed Mushrooms, Hummus, Sunflower Sampler, Tossed Salad, Soup of the Day, Garden Steak Salad, Greek Salad and Sesame Noodles Salads.
Lunch Menu: Stir-fried Vegetables with Tofu, Black Bean Quesadilla, Vegetable Quesadilla, burritos, Portobello Mushrooms Wrap, Moo Shu Vegetables, chili, veggie burgers, Sweet & Sour Soy Chicken, Macro Stir-Fry, Spicy Pad Thai Noodles, Pasta a la Pesto and Risotto of the Day.
Dinner Menu: Stir Fried Vegetables with Tofu, Macro Stir Fry, Stuffed Acorn Squash, Baked Samosas, Mediterranean Platter, Stuffed Mushrooms, Wild Mushroom Fettuccine and some of the same dishes that are served for lunch. The veggie Meatloaf & Potatoes and the Sweet & Sour Chicken are very good.
Desserts and Drinks: Vegan Carrot Cake with tofu cream cheese, vegan Chocolate Cake, soy ice cream and regular ice cream. Fresh juices, herbal teas.
Commons: Tasteful, contemporary décor. Comfortable, upscale, but casual place. Friendly, efficient service. Voted Atlanta's best vegetarian restaurant. The food is really good and the place is recommended. One of the better places that I have been too. On Saturday night they have buffet night for $14. The place is definitely not cheap. Has friendly, efficient service. Has a children meal.

They give cooking classes and have their own cookbook.

Awards and Reviews: Creative Loafing Magazine awarded Sunflower "Best Vegetarian" restaurant in Atlanta in 1998. The Atlanta Magazine awarded Sunflower "Best Place to Take a Vegetarian Meal." They got good reviews in Atlanta Homes & Lifestyles, Southern Comfort, Heart Wise, and Meatless in Atlanta. The reviews can be seen on their Web site.

Other Info: Full service, catering, take-out. Non-smoking. Reservations recommended. Accepts AMEX, DIS, MC, VISA. Price: $-$$.

Directions: This place is about three miles south of Lenox Mall and a half-mile north of Piedmont Hospital. Located in the Brookwood Square Center, north of Bennett Street on Peachtree Road. Free parking in the shopping center. From I-85, take Exit #85 and go north on Peachtree and this place is 1½ mile down.

**Café Sunflower
5975 Roswell Road, Suite 353, Sandy Springs
404-256-1675
Web site: www.cafesunflower.com
Hours: Monday to Thursday 11:30 am to 2:30 pm, 5 pm to 9 pm; Friday 11:30 am to 2:30 pm, 5 pm to 9:30 pm; Saturday 12 noon to 2:30 pm, 5 pm to 9:30 pm; closed Sunday.
Fully Vegetarian International. Mostly Vegan.
Menu: Black Bean Quesadilla, Moo Shu Vegetables, veggie burgers, Wild Mushroom Fettuccine, Carrot Cake and Spring Rolls. Fresh juices. No alcohol. See above for more details.
Comments: Very friendly service. Relaxed atmosphere. Beautiful outdoor seating with cypress trees. Has a cookbook. Small place with an intimate atmosphere. The food is well-presented. A good place for a special event. The place is definitely not cheap.
Other Info: Full service, catering. Non-smoking. Reservations recommended. Accepts AMEX, DIS, MC, VISA. Price: $$-$$$.
Directions: This place is in due north Atlanta a little outside the beltway. From I-285, take Roswell Rd (#25) exit and go north on Roswell Rd a half-mile, at the second traffic light, turn right on Hammond Drive (Amoco gas station). Turn right into the shopping center, and the restaurant is on the corner.

California Pizza Kitchen
Lexon Square; 404-262-9221
4600 Ashford Dunwoody Road NE, Atlanta
770-393-0390

6301 North Point Parkway, Alpharetta
770-664-8246
3393 Peachtree Road NE, Atlanta; 404-262-9221
Hours: Sunday to Thursday 11 am to 10 pm
Friday & Saturday 11 am to 10:30 pm
Pizza. Not pure vegetarian.
Menu: Has an excellent cheeseless pizza (non-vegan). The pizza crusts are not vegan. Toppings such as sun-dried tomatoes, roasted eggplant and fresh spinach. Has whole-wheat crusts. Tuscan Bean Soup is vegetarian. Salads and pasta.
Other Info: Non-smoking.

**Chinese Buddha Vegetarian Restaurant
144 14th Street, near I-85; 404-874-5158
Hours: Monday to Friday 11:30 am to 10 pm; Saturday 11:30 am to 11 pm; Sun 4 pm to 10 pm
Vegetarian Chinese. Vegan friendly. Owned by the same people that owns Sam's.
Menu: Has around 30 vegan Chinese dishes.
Other Info: Full service, counter service, take-out, delivery. Price: $$.
Directions: In central Atlanta a half-mile east of I-75/I-85. From I-85, take Techwood Dr exit (#84) towards Fourteenth St/Tenth St and go southeast on Peachtree St NE 1½ mile, then at 14th St turn left.

Eat's
600 Ponce de Leon Avenue, between Glen Iris Drive & Lakeview Avenue; 404-888-9149
Hours: Daily 11 am to 11 pm
Italian & Southern. Not pure vegetarian, but has a good selection of vegetarian dishes.
Menu: Rice & Cornbread, pastas, Spinach Tortellini with marinara sauce and vegetable dishes.
Comments: 60s Greenwich Village type atmosphere. Casual, hip place. Has an ATM machine. Good, cheap food. No frills place. Interesting atmosphere. Gets high ratings for both the food and atmosphere.
Other Info: Full service, take-out. Non-smoking. No credit cards. Price: $.
Directions: In the Ponce area of East Atlanta, between downtown and Virginia Highlands area. Right across the street from City Hall East.

El Myr
Little Five Points, 1091 Euclid Avenue, at Moreland Avenue; 404-588-0250
Hours: Sunday to Thursday 12 noon to 2 am
Friday & Saturday 12 noon to 4 am

Tex Mex. Not pure vegetarian.
Menu: Has a good selection of vegetarian dishes.
Comments: Indoors and outside dining. Offers valet parking. Accept MC, VISA.

Euclid Avenue Yacht Club
1136 Euclid Avenue, Little 5 Points
404-688-2582
Hours: Daily 3 pm to 2 am
Restaurant. Mainly a bar. Vegan options. Not pure vegetarian.
Menu: Veggie burgers, black bean burritos, chips and salsa, mashed potatoes and Red Beans & Rice.
Comments: Bikers dine on Sunday during the day. Preppies, punk and hippie.
Other Info: No credit cards. Price: $.

The Flying Biscuit Café (two locations)
1655 McLendon Avenue, Midtown in Candler Park NE; 404-687-8888
Directions: This place is a few blocks east on the southeast corner of Candler Park. In Little 5 Points (east of downtown), which is a hip area and a center of the alternative scene in Atlanta. From I-75/85 coming south, take the North Avenue exit (#249) and go east on North Ave about 2 miles, then at Oakdale Rd turn right and go ¾ mile, then turn left onto McLendon and this place is ¾ mile down. From I-75 coming north, take I-20 going east about 1½ mile, then take Moreland Ave N exit (#60) and then go north on Moreland Ave about 1 mile. Turn right at McLendon Ave (Zesto's on corner) and this place is about 1 mile down on right.
1001 Piedmont Avenue
404-874-8887
Directions: This place is about 2 miles north of the junction of I-20 & I-75. From I-75/85 coming south into Atlanta, take 10th St/14th St exit (#250), turn left onto 10th St and go east about ¾ mile. This place is on the left, at corner of 10th St and Piedmont Ave. From I-75 coming north into Atlanta, take the 10th St/14th St exit (#250), stay straight on Williams St NW, turn right on 10th Street. Same as above.
Web site: www.flyingbiscuit.com
Hours: Sunday to Thursday 7 am to 10 pm; Friday & Saturday 7 am to 10:30 pm; Take-out counter opens at 7:30 am
Southern and Soul. Not pure vegetarian.
Menu: Has a good selection of vegetarian dishes. Tofu Wrap, Veggie Scramble Tofu, veggie burgers, Black Bean Quesadilla and Mashed Potatoes with sun-dried tomatoes and olive oil. "Love Cakes" is cornmeal and black-bean cakes with feta cheese, sour cream and salsa. Has good baked good. Homemade cranberry apple butter by the jar. Has good biscuits.
Comments: Popular place and you may have to wait for a while on the weekends. Efficient service. Good place for people watching. Comfortable place.
Other Info: Full service, take-out, delivery. Non-smoking. Accepts AMEX, MC, VISA. Price: $-$$.

***Fung's Vegetarian Chinese Rest.
Green's Corner Shopping Center, 4975 Jimmy Carter Boulevard, Norcross; 770-925-8322
Hours: Tuesday to Friday 11 pm to 2:30 pm, 5 pm to 9:30 pm
Saturday & Sunday 12 noon to 9:30 pm
Closed Monday.
Pure Vegetarian Vegan Chinese. Fully Vegan.
Menu: Has many mock "meat" dishes. Over 100 dishes on menu. Soups, rice, Veggie Spareribs (made of walnuts), Tofu with Cashew Nuts, Chinese appetizers, noodle dishes and main dishes. The vegetarian chicken is really good. Inexpensive lunch specials. Curry Spring Rolls (filled with vegetables and mock "chicken"), Tofu with Broccoli Won Ton Soup, chicken nuggets and Chinese vegetable dishes.
Comments: The food get really good recommendations. Very reasonably priced. Friendly, efficient service. Has several newspaper articles on the wall written about this restaurant. Friendly, helpful people. Often the service can be a bit slow. Recommended.
Other Info: Full service, take-out. Accepts AMEX, MC, VISA. Price: $-$$.
Directions: Located in Green's Corner Shopping Center outside the I-285 beltway. From I-85, take Hwy 140/Jimmy Carter Boulevard exit (#99) and get on Jimmy Carter Blvd NW going southeast at, at the fork in the road take the right fork on Jimmy Carter Blvd and this place is on the left 1¼ mile down in a small shopping center.

**The Good Earth and Veggieland Restaurant
211 Pharr Road NE, Buckhead area
404-266-2919
Store Hours: Monday to Friday 9 am to 6 pm
Saturday 9 am to 5:30 pm
Restaurant Hours: Monday to Friday 11:30 to 3 pm, 5 pm to 9 pm; Saturday 11:30 am to 8 pm; closed Sunday.
Natural Food Store and Vegetarian Natural Food Restaurant. Mainly vegan. International, Asian,

Mexican, Southern and Mexican.
Menu: Has a large selection of vegetarian dishes including soups, salads, appetizers, stir-fries, South-fried mock "Steak" with Gravy, pastas, sandwiches, BLT Sandwich, chili (very good), veggie dogs, Sweet Potato Fries, Lasagna, Coleslaw, desserts and specials. Fresh juices.
Comments: Friendly, quick service. Uses filtered water. Popular on the weekends. Small place with not much atmosphere.
Other Info: Full service, take-out. Accepts AMEX, MC, VISA. Price: $$.
Directions: This place is in North Atlanta. From I-85, take Exit #27 and go north about 1½ mile on Piedmont Rd NE, then at Pharr Rd turn left and this place is ¾ mile down. Can also from I-84, take exit #84 and go north on Peachtree Rd for about 3 miles, then turn right onto Pharr Rd and this place is a block down.

Harry's Farmers Market
696 Cleburne Terrace; 404-724-0951

Haveli Indian Cuisine
490 Franklin Rood (Rte 120); 770-955-4525
Hours: Monday to Friday 11:30 am to 2:30 pm, 5:30 pm to 10:30 pm; Saturday & Sunday, 12 noon to 2:30 pm 5:30 pm to 10:30 pm
Indian. Buffet. Vegan options. Not pure veg.
Menu: Has a large selection of vegetarian Indian dishes. Has one of the best buffets in town.
Comments: Food gets high ratings. Tandoori cooking. Sometime the service may not be up to standard.
Other Info: Full service, take-out, catering. Accepts AMEX, DC, DIS, MC, VISA. Price: $$.

**Healthful Essence
2329 Cascade Road, at Beecher Road, SW
404-753-0130
Hours: Monday to Friday 11 am to 8 pm; Saturday 12 noon to 9 pm; Sunday 12 noon to 6 pm
Vegetarian Caribbean. Vegan options. Not pure vegetarian.
Comments: Local organic produce used when possible.
Other Info: Buffet, take-out. Accepts MC, VISA. Price: $.
Directions: This place is in southwest Atlanta in the Cascade Height area, about 1½ mile north of Lakewood Fwy. From I-20, take the Langhorn St exit (#54) towards Cascade Rd, then go on Langhorn St for a half-mile, then turn right at RD Abernathy Blvd and go 1 block, then stay straight onto Cascade Ave and go southwest and this place is about 2¼ mile down. From I-85/I-

75, take Lakewood Fwy and go 2 miles west, then take the Stanton Rd/Delowe Dr SW exit and this place is about 1½ mile northwest of the exit.

Imperial Fez
2285 Peachtree Road, south Buckhead
404-351-0870
Hours: Sunday to Thursday 6 pm to 11 pm Friday & Saturday 6 pm to 12 noon
Moroccan. Vegan options. Not pure vegetarian.
Menu: Has a good amount of vegan dishes. A five-course dinner that starts with very good lentil soup, then cold salad sampler, spicy eggplant & tomatoes, vegetarian b'stella, Moroccan vegetable & pastry dish, vegetable couscous and Moroccan desserts.
Comments: Has belly dancers. Remove your shoes when entering the restaurant and sit on decorated pillows. Wash hands in rosewater. Popular place for the food and entertainment. Romantic, luxurious, exotic place. No utensils. Place gets great rating for food and especially atmosphere. Good service. Good place for a special event. Has a palm reader and photographer. Has seating on the half hour during belly dancing performances. Food is eaten Arab style, with right hand. Good place for a special occasion.
Other Info: Accepts AMEX, DC, DIS, MC, VISA. Price: $$$.

Lettuce Souprise You
Loehmann's Plaza, 2470-47 Briarcliff Road
404-636-8549
1784 Peachtree Street; 404-874-4998
Hours: Monday to Friday 11 am to 9 pm Saturday & Sunday 12 noon to 8 pm
Soup and Salad Bar Place. Not pure vegetarian.
Menu: All-you-can-eat salad bar. Baked potatoes, soups, a large amount of salad dishes, fresh fruit, and breads.
Other Info: Non-smoking. Buffet style, take-out. Price: $-$$

**Madras Restaurant
North Dekalb Square shopping center
2179 Lawrenceville Highway, just opposite North DeKalb
404-636-4400
Hours: Monday to Friday 11:30 am to 3 pm, 5 pm to 9:30 pm
Saturday & Sunday 12 noon to 9:30 pm
Vegetarian South Indian. Has some American dishes. Buffet Lunch.
Menu: Dosas, sambar (lentil soup), Peshawari Chole Puri, masala dosa, rice dishes, Idly and more. The Dal Makhani and Chatt Samosa are

good.

Comments: Pretty good casual place. Food gets good ratings. The décor is not so nice. Serves food on paper plates. Good place for a quick meal but low on atmosphere. Good value. Popular with Indians.

Other Info: Full service, take-out, delivery. Accepts AMEX, DIS, MC, VISA. Price: $-$$.

Directions: In northeast Atlanta.

Nuts & Berries

4274 Peachtree Road, NE, in Brookhaven
404-237-6829; **fax:** 404-237-4305; **Web site:** www.nutsnberries.com

Hours: Monday to Friday 9 am to 8 pm; Saturday 9 am to 7 pm; Sunday 10 am to 6 pm

Natural Food Store. Vegan options. Not pure vegetarian.

Menu: Soups, salads, sandwiches, chili, homemade baked goods and hot dishes. Fresh juices.

Comments: One of the best-stocked natural food stores in the Atlanta area. A big place.

Other Info: Limited service, take-out. Accepts MC, VISA. Price: $.

Raging Burrito (two locations)

1529 B Piedmont Avenue, downtown on the Square; 404-885-9922
141 Sycamore Street, at Church Street
404-377-3311

Hours: Sunday to Thursday 11 am to 10 pm
Friday & Saturday 11 am to 10:30 pm

Californian Mexican. Not pure vegetarian.

Menu: Has a good selection of vegetarian options. Has vegetarian chili and California-style burritos.

Comments: Has very good size portions. Friendly service. Has a nice patio for outdoor dining. There are veggie options that you can add to the burritos.

Other Info: Non-smoking. Accepts MC, VISA. Price: $.

Raja Indian Restaurant

2955 Peachtree Road NE, Buckhead
404-237-2661

Hours: Monday to Thursday 11:30 am to 2:30 pm, 5 pm to 10:30 pm; Friday & Saturday 11:30 am to 11 pm; Sunday 5:30 am to 10:30 pm

Indian. Not pure vegetarian.

Menu: Has inexpensive three course lunches. Good soups, raita, samosas, fresh salads and daily specials. Lunch special (rice, curry and a soup) are served from 11:30 am to 2:30 pm.

Comments: Small, friendly place. Authentic cooking. Food gets good ratings. Good service.

Other Info: Full service, take-out. Non-smoking. Does not accept reservations. Accepts AMEX, MC, VISA. Price: $-$$.

Directions: Located on the main street in Buckhead.

Return to Eden

Cheshire Square Shopping Center, 2335 Cheshire Bridge Road; 404-320-3336 (EDEN)
email: customerservice@return2eden.com
Web site: www.returntoeden.com

Hours: Monday to Friday 9 am to 8 pm; Saturday 10 am to 8 pm; Sunday 10 am to 6 pm

Natural Food Store and Deli. All vegetarian Supermarket-type store. Produce section only sells organic goods.

Comments: Can order on line through their web site. Gets much of its organic produce from local Georgia farmers.

Directions: From I-75/I-85 coming north towards downtown Atlanta. Take I-85 North, then take first Exit #88 towards Cheshire Bridge Rd/GA-400, then go on Lenox Rd (becomes Cheshire Bridge Rd NE) and this place is a third-mile down. From I-85 coming southeast into Atlanta, take Cheshire Bridge Rd/Lennox exit. Turn left onto Cheshire Bridge Rd and go past three lights and this place is in Cheshire Square shopping center. Take the train north to the Lindbergh station (N-5). Take any of the following buses: #6, #27, #30, #33, and get off at the first stop past Cheshire Bridge.

R Thomas Deluxe Grill

1812 Peachtree Street, Buckhead area, Midtown
404-881-0246

Hours: Monday to Thursday 9 am to 6 am
Friday to Sunday: Daily 24 hours

Healthy Southern, American. Creative gourmet food. Emphasis on healthy food. Macrobiotic meal. Not pure vegetarian.

Menu: Has around 20 vegetarian dishes on its menu. Has mashed red potatoes and onions with gravy, Smashed Butternut Squash, Tempeh Burgers, quesadillas, Stuffed Potatoes and Millet Corn Casserole. Main meals come with cabbage, lemon juice and dill weed. Fresh juices and smoothies.

Comments: Has very good food. Gets really happening after 11 pm. Has an outstanding outside patio. Organic grains and sprouts. Has dozens of parakeets and running water. Has a painting of the route of the Olympic torch to Atlanta in 1996 painted on the tarp covering the patio.

Other Info: Reservations not necessary or accepted. Accepts AMEX, DC, DIS, MC, VISA. Price: $$.

**Sam's Gourmet
5750 Roswell Road; 404-252-8878
Hours: Daily 11:30 am to 11 pm
Vegetarian Chinese. Vegan-friendly. No eggs, onions or garlic used.
Menu: Has some great vegetarian mock "meat" dishes. Has a large selection of vegetarian dishes. Roast Duck, Pan Fried Fish, Prawn in Chile Sauce, Bird's Nest, Asparagus with Shrimp and Meatball in Abalone Mushroom.
Comments: Good service.
Directions: Connected to a Day's Inn. Full service, take-out. Free delivery within 3 miles with minimum of $12.

Sevananda Natural Foods Market
457 Moreland Avenue NE
404-681-2831; **email:** sev@mindspring.com
Web site: www.sevananda.com
Hours: Daily 9 am to 10 pm
Natural Food Store. Organic produce.
Menu: Has a wide selection of ready-made sandwiches and deli items. Salads, hummus and soups.
Comments: This is one of the better health food stores in the country. It is the size of a supermarket. Offers cooking, health and nutrition classes. Has a great selection of take-out sandwiches, salads and baked goods. Many of the sandwiches are made by Soul Vegetarian Restaurant. Recommended.
Directions: In the middle of Little 5 Points, in eastern Atlanta. Coming on I-75/I-85 north into Atlanta, take I-20 going east for 1½ mile, then take Moreland Avenue (#60A) and go north on Moreland and this place is about 1 mile down on the right. From coming south on I-75 or I-85 into Atlanta, take North Avenue exit. At North Avenue turn left (go east) and go 2 miles, then at Moreland turn right and this place is a third-mile down.

Shipfeifer on Peachtree
1814 Peachtree Street; 404-875-1106
Hours: Sunday to Thursday 11 am to 10 pm
Friday & Saturday 11 am to 10:30 pm
Mediterranean and American. Vegetarian-friendly. Vegan options. Not pure vegetarian.
Menu: Salads, Mediterranean Platter, wraps, desserts and main dishes. Foods are freshly prepared. Has a Sampler Plate with hummus, falafel, tabbouleh and baba ghanoush. Iced tea.
Comments: Has outdoor patio dinning. Good food. Service gets mixed opinions.
Other Info: Non-smoking. Accepts AMEX, DIS, MC, VISA. Price: $-$$.

***Soul Vegetarian South Restaurant
652 North Highland Avenue NE
404-875-0145; 404-875-1106
See below for other branch.
Hours: Tuesday to Saturday 11 am to 10 pm; Sunday 10 am to 2 pm, 5 pm to 10 pm; closed Monday.
Fully Vegan Soul, Ethiopian and International. See below for details.
Other Info: Full service, cafeteria style, catering. Non-smoking. Accepts reservations but are not necessary. Accepts AMEX, DC, DIS, MC, VISA. Price: $-$$.
Directions: From I-85/I-75 North, you take the Rte 10E/Freedom Parkway exit (#248C) towards International Blvd and follow signs to Jimmy Carter Center taking Freedom Pkwy NE northeast for 1½ mile, take Rte 42 E ramp towards Carter Center and go a half-mile, at North Highland Avenue turn left, and this restaurant is one block down on the right, behind a church. This place is about 2 miles northeast of the junction of I-20 and I-75.

***Soul Vegetarian South Restaurant
879-A Ralph David Abernathy Boulevard SW
404-752-5194
Hours: Monday to Saturday 11 am to 10 pm
Sunday 10 am to 2 pm, 5 pm to 10 pm
Fully Vegan Soul, Ethiopian and International.
Menu: Serves live salads such as Tofu Salad, Carrot Supreme or Garden Salad. Soups of the day such as Marak Afunah (split-pea soup with garlic), cornbread, side vegetables, BBQ Wheat-Gluten, Sweet Potato Fries, Kale Greens, Garvey Burgers (with mushrooms and onions), Tofu Filet (tofu patty), Barbeque Kalebone and Macaroni & Cheese. There are several types of sandwiches such as Tofu Sandwich, Veggie Gyros, veggie burgers, and Carrot Salad in a Pita Pocket. The Saleem Basket is a choice of mushroom, tofu, cauliflower or kalebone. There is also a Fried Platter, which some people may consider to be a bit undercooked, so you might want to request in advance that it is well-done. The mixture of organic greens is red chard, kale, turnips and mustard. For dessert there is Soy Ice Cream and Shake Bars. You can add a creamy soy cheese sauce to any sandwich. During the Sunday brunch (popular) there are multi-grain pancakes, veggie sausage, scrambled tofu, potatoes and biscuits. The special dinners are around $10, and lunch special around $8. Has Soy Cream Cones.
Comments: Holistic, friendly, casual, family atmosphere. Spiritually based place. Dinners are

candle-lit and there is a new menu every night. The food gets high recommendations from many people. Some people may not like the place; at least one reason might be because they use a lot of garlic in the food. The garlic sauce was really too much for me, but many people love it. It is a cool place with really excellent service. Servers are dressed in white. Serves all natural, freshly cooked food, using fresh vegetables. Does not use ingredients that contain preservatives. Has a children's menu. There are two locations in metro-Atlanta. Kalebone is their own wheat gluten protein that they use to make veggie "steaks" and "burgers." Serves mainly fat-free food.
Other Info: Full service, cafeteria, catering, take-out. Non-smoking. Accepts reservations but not necessary. Accepts AMEX, DIS, MC, VISA. Price: $-$$.
Directions: From I-20, take the Ashby Street exit (#55), then go south on Ashby St 2 blocks, then turn left on Ralph David Abernathy, and this restaurant is 1 block down on the left. Parking directly across the street. It is in the West End, near Morehouse College.

Tortilla's
774 Ponce De Leon Avenue Northeast
404-892-0193
Hours: Daily 11 am to 10 pm
Mexican. Vegan-friendly. Not pure vegetarian.
Menu: Has a very good veggie burrito with beans, potatoes and tomatoes. Has a selection of topping such as broccoli, chilies, spinach and jalapenos. The chips and salsa is good.
Comments: Happening, hip place with a young crowd. Cool atmosphere. Has outdoor dining. Does not use lard in their beans. Price: $.
Directions: Across the street from the Clairemont Hotel

***Unicorn Place Vegetarian Restaurant
220 Sandy Springs Circle NE, #209
404-252-1165
Hours: Monday to Friday 11 am to 2:30 pm, 5 pm to 9 pm; Saturday 12 noon to 3 pm, 5 pm to 9 pm; closed Sunday.
Fully Vegan Chinese.
Menu: Has a wide selection of vegetarian dishes including Vegetarian Shrimp in Coconut Sauce, Stuffed Tofu and Tempeh with vegetables, Okra with Cumin, Vegetarian Fish with Vegetables, Sweet & Sour Pork, Thai Spicy Wonton, Curry Tempeh, dim sum, brown rice and Green Bean Pastries. Fresh juices.
Comments: Very good vegetarian Chinese food. Use fresh vegetables. Does not use MSG. Gets

really good recommendations. Friendly, good service. Has outdoor seating.
Other Info: Full service, take-out. Non-smoking. Accepts reservations but are not necessary. Accepts AMEX, DC, DIS, MC, VISA. Price: $$.
Directions: From I-285, take exit #25 and go north on Roswell Rd for 1½ mile, turn left on Johnson Ferry Road and go a quarter-mile, then turn right at the first light, and this place is on the right in the Springs Landing Shopping Center. This place is about 1½ mile north of the Atlanta Beltway (I-285), due north of the center of town.

Unity Natural Foods
2955 Peachtree Road North; 404-261-8776
Hours: Monday to Saturday 10 am to 7 pm
Sunday 12 noon to 6 pm
Natural Food Store. Organic produce. Deli and Juice Bar.
Comments: Has a nutritionist.
Directions: From I-85, take GA Rte 400 north for 1½ mile, then take the Lenox/Piedmont Rd exit (#2), keep left at fork in ramp and merge onto GA Rte 141 Lenox Rd (going southwest) towards Buckhead and go a third-mile, at Piedmont Rd turn left and go a third-mile, then turn right onto Peachtree Rd and this place is 1 mile down. This place is in northeast Atlanta.

**Veggieland
211 Pharr Rd, NE, at Peachtree in the middle of Buckhead; 404-231-3111
Hours: Monday to Friday 11:30 am to 3 pm, 5 pm to 9 pm; Saturday 11:30 am to 8 pm; closed Sundays.
Vegetarian Restaurant. Vegan options. Healthy low-salt, sugar-free, and low-calorie foods.
Menu: Soups, salads, sandwiches, veggie burgers and appetizers. Macrobiotic lunches and dinners. Excellent sweet potato fries. Good Spinach Salad.
Comments: Has delicious food. Friendly service. Food is good. Reasonably priced. Fast service.
Other Info: Full service, take-out. Non-smoking. Accepts credit cards. Price: $$.
Directions: From I-85, take GA Rte 400 (Piedmont & Bufford Hwy) north for 1½ mile, then take the Lenox/Piedmont Rd exit (#2), keep left at fork in ramp and merge onto GA Rte 141 Lenox Rd (going southwest) towards Buckhead and go a third-mile, at Piedmont Rd turn left and go ¾ mile, then at Pharr Rd turn right and this place is about ¾ mile down, just before the third-light (just after big fish), in a little shopping center called Buckhead Walk on the left. This place is in northeast Atlanta.

Whole Foods Market

2111 Briarcliff Road; 404-634-7800
Web site: www.wholefoodsmarket.com
Hours: Monday to Saturday 8 am to 10 pm; Sunday 8 am to 9 pm; Coffee Bar opens at 7 am Monday to Friday
Natural Food Store and Cafe. Deli, Bakery, Salad Bar and Juice Bar. Organic produce. Supermarket-type place. See Whole Foods Market information.
Directions: This place is in northeast Atlanta. From I-85, take Exit #89 towards Druid Rd (GA Rte 42) and go southeast on N Druid Hills Rd a half-mile, then take a slight right onto Briarcliff Rd and this place is 1 mile down.

Whole Foods Market

5930 Roswell Road, Sandy Springs; 404-236-0810; email: Omar.Gaye@wholefoods.com
Web site: www.wholefoodsmarket.com
Hours: Daily 8 am to 9 pm
Natural Food Store and Cafe. Deli, Bakery, Salad Bar and Juice Bar. Organic produce. Supermarket-type place. See Whole Foods Market information.
Directions: The place is in northeast Atlanta, about 3 miles north of the I-285 beltway. From I-285, take GA Rte 141 N/Peachtree Industrial Blvd exit and go northeast on Peachtree Ind Blvd for 3 miles, take exit towards Jimmy Carter Blvd (GA Rte 140), turn left onto Jimmy Carter Blvd and go 2 miles north, then at Spalding Dr NW turn left and this place is ¾ mile down.

AUGUSTA

Foods For Better Living

2606 McDowell Street; 706-738-3215
Hours: Monday to Friday 9 am to 6 pm (Thursday until 5pm)
Closed Saturday & Sunday.
Natural Food Store. No organic produce.
Directions: From I-20, take Bobby Jones Expressway (I-520, exit #196A) and go 1½ mile, at Wrightsboro Rd (#2) turn left towards Daniel Field and go 3½ miles east. At Highland Avenue turn left and go 4 blocks north, at McDowell turn right and this place on right 2 blocks down.

CHAMBLEE (northeast Atlanta suburb)

Farmers' Market

5593 Peachtree Industrial Boulevard,
Corner of Peachtree Industrial, at Chamblee-Tucker Road; 770-455-1777

Hours: Monday to Friday 10 am to 9 pm; Saturday 9 am to 9 pm; Sunday 10 am to 10 pm
Excellent Farmer's Market with a great selection of produce and also spices.
Directions: From 285, take Peachtree Industrial Exit and this place is 2 miles down on left. From I-85, take Chamblee-Tucker Rd exit and this place is 2 miles down on right.

***Harmony Vegetarian Chinese

4987 Buford Highway, Suite 109, at Chamblee Tucker Road; 770-457-7288
Hours: Sunday, Monday, Tuesday, & Thursday 11 am to 10:30 pm
Friday & Saturday 11 am to 11 pm
Lunch Special Hours: Monday to Friday 11 am to 3 pm
Fully Vegan Vegetarian Chinese. Juice Bar. Mainly Vegan.
Menu: Has over 100 vegetarian dishes including a large selection of mock meat dishes. Spinach and Tofu Soup, a good selection of dumpling dishes, hot pots, noodles dishes, Pot Stickers, Sweet & Sour Spareribs, Hunan Lamb, Szechuan String Beans, Lemon Chicken, Fish Fillet with Black Bean Sauce, Mongolian Beef, Stir-fried Mixed Vegetables, Vegetable Lo Mein, Shredded Pork & Pepper, Pan-fried Leek Dumpling, Cold Sesame Noodles, Sesame Chicken, Bean Curd with Mushrooms, Vegetarian Shrimp, Vegetable Roast Duck and Hot & Sour Soup. The General Tao's Chicken is their most popular dish.
Comments: Gets really high ratings from my friends who love Chinese. It is one of their main places to eat in Atlanta. Recommended. Food gets good recommendations. Friendly service. Reasonable prices. Has a boring décor. Casual place. Buddhist-style cooking. The place can be quite busy and you may have to wait on weekend nights. One of the best vegetarian places in town. Has inexpensive weekday lunch specials.
Other Info: Full service. Non-smoking. Does not take reservations unless 8 or more persons. Accepts AMEX, MC, VISA. Price: $-$$.
Direction: From I-285, take exit #32 (Buford Highway) and go northeast on Buford Highway away from Atlanta and this places is about a half-mile down on the left in the Orient Center, opposite Kelley Toyota on Buford Highway. It is in a strip mall.

COLUMBUS

**Country Life

1217 Eberhart Avenue

706-323-9194; fax: 706-323-9144; email: countrylife@ucheepines.org; Web site: http://www.ucheepines.com/country_life.htm
Hours: Monday to Friday 11:30 am to 2 pm
Fully Vegetarian American. Mostly Vegan. Lunch Buffet.
Menu: Has a large menu of vegetarian dishes that changes daily. Soup and Salad Bar.
Comments: Run by the Seventh Day Adventist church. Reasonably priced. The restaurant is self-serve and there is a health food store in front. It is in a large Victorian house, off a main street. It is vegan, except for honey.
Other Info: Accepts AMEX, DIS, MC, VISA. Price: $. Counter service, take-out. Does not take reservations unless over 8 people. Non-smoking.
Directions: From I-185, take exit #6 for Macon Road (Rte 22), then go southwest on Macon Road (Spur Rte 22) about 1¾ mile, then at Eberhart turn right (just past the Shell station) and this place is 1 block down.

DECATUR (north east Atlanta suburb, within beltway)

Bombay Bazaar
1082 Oaktree Road, off N Druid Hill Road
404-321-0116; fax: 404-321-0040
Indian Grocery Store.
Directions: Next to Market Square Mall. From I-285, take exit #29 and go west on Lawrenceville Hwy, then turn left at N Druid Hill Road, then make a quick left on Oak Tree Rd and this place on right.

Cherians
751 Dekalb Industrial Way
404-299-0842; fax: 404-299-8789
Hours: Monday 10:30 am to 6 pm; Tuesday to Saturday 10:30 am to 9 pm; Sun 1 pm to 9 pm
Indian Grocery Store.
Directions: From I-285, take exit #30A towards Decatur. Move to left lane and turn left at 2nd traffic light onto Dekalb Ind Way and then this place is 5th building on left.

Dekalb Farmers Market
3000 East Ponce De Leon Avenue; 404-377-6400
Hours: Monday to Friday 9 am to 9 pm
Organic produce. Deli and Juice Bar.
Directions: Two miles from downtown Decatur.

**Indian Delights
1707 Church Street, Suite C-5A (Lawrenceville Hwy); 404-296-2965

Hours: Tuesday to Thursday 11:30 am to 8:30 pm; Friday 11:30 am to 9 pm; Saturday 12 noon to 9 pm; Sunday 12 noon to 8:30 pm; closed Monday.
Fully Vegetarian Indian. Mostly Vegan. Specializes in Gujarati, North and South Indian dishes.
Menu: Has vegan and lacto entrées, appetizers, soups, drinks, side orders and desserts. Has a good variety of snacks and main dishes. Bhel Puri, Dahi Puri, Pani Puri, samosas, Curried Chick Peas, Coconut Chutney, Saag Panir (spinach and cheese), Vegetable Pakora, Aloo Tikki with Chole, Pani Chole, Thalis, Masala Dosa and Mango Lassi.
Comments: Voted as Atlanta's best Indian restaurant. Friendly service. Popular place. Open for over ten years and has been steadily good. Gets consistently good reviews in the local papers. Gets great recommendations. Lacks a bit in atmosphere with paper plates.
Other Info: Cafeteria style, counter service, take-out, catering. Non-smoking. Accepts DIS, MC, VISA (usually minimum $20). Price: $.
Directions: From Hwy 285, take Exit #30A (Hwy 78W) and go about 1½ mile, at Church St turn left, then take an immediate left into the Scott Village Shopping Center. From downtown can go east on Ponce de Leon and after a few miles, go left onto Rte 78 (also Rte 29), stay left on Scott Blvd and go 2½ miles north, then at North Decatur turn right, then Church St turn left and this place is half-mile down on right in Scott Village Shopping Center.

Patel Brothers
763 Delkalb Industrial Way; 404-292-8235
Indian Grocery Store.

Rainbow Natural Foods
2118 North Decatur Road NE, at Clairmont Road; 404-636-5553
Hours: Monday to Saturday 10 am to 8 pm; Sunday 11 am to 5 pm; Sunday Brunch.
Natural Food Store and Vegetarian-friendly Restaurant. Salad Bar and Deli. Organic produce. Not pure vegetarian (serves tuna).
Menu: Soups, salads and daily specials. Daily special such as Mushroom Stroganoff, Lentil Loaf with Orange Sesame Sauce, Vegetable Chili, Thai Asian Noodles with Tofu, Baked Ziti Siciliana, Creole Beans & Rice and Spinach & Mushroom Manicotti. Has sandwiches, Scrambled Tofu Burrito, Nachos Supreme, ABLT Sandwich, Sunburger, veggie dogs, veggie tortilla, Guacamole, bean burrito, veggie burgers, nachos, veg-

etarian chili and Vegetables & Rice. Desserts such as Pumpkin Pie, cakes, muffins and Pecan Pie. Fresh juices and smoothies.
Comments: Popular, friendly place. If you get a sandwich here you should request egg-less mayonnaise. Fairly good place. Specials are reasonably priced. Excellent service. Popular, small place. The store is a fairly small place with a good selection of items. Marks dairy-free and egg-free dishes. Can substitute soy cheese for regular cheese.
Other Info: Full service, take-out, delivery. Nonsmoking. Reservations not necessary. Price: $.
Directions: From downtown Atlanta head north on I-85. Take the Clairemont Rd exit (#91) and bear right and take an immediate right. Then drive about 4½ miles southeast (about 10 minutes), and this store at the junction of North Decatur and Clairemont, off the road in the North Decatur Plaza on the left. This place can be gotten to by using the Indian Delight directions (change it when reach N Decatur).

**Udipi Café
1850 Lawrenceville Highway, Suite 700, at Woodridge Drive; 404-325-1933
Hours: Monday to Thursday 11:30 am to 9:30 pm; Friday to Sunday 11:30 am to 10 pm
Vegetarian Indian. Mostly vegan. Mainly South Indian.
Menu: Has a large menu that includes dosas, Ravi Masala Dosa, rice dishes, sambar soup and tomato soup. The Eggplant Curry is very good. The Mysore Royal Thali is recommended.
Comments: Gets good recommendations. Inexpensive. Good service. Pleasant atmosphere. Low on décor. Not well located. The food can be quite spicy. Casual place.
Other Info: Limited service, take-out, catering. Non-smoking. Reservations not necessary. Accepts AMEX, DIS, MC, VISA. Price: $$.
Directions: From I-285, take exit #39A and go northwest on Hwy 78, which runs into Lawrenceville Hwy (bears left onto it). This place is then on the right just past the North Dekalb Mall about 1½ mile down. From I-285, take exit #29 and go west on Lawrenceville Hwy and this place is on the right.

**Woodland Vegetarian Restaurant
1080 Oaktree Road; 404-321-6005
Hours: Sunday to Thursday 12 noon to 8:30 pm Friday & Saturday 12 noon to 9:30 pm
Lunch Buffet Hours: Tuesday to Sunday 12 pm to 3 pm

Full Vegetarian Indian.
Menu: A great selection of South Indian and North Indian dishes. Basmati rice, Chat Puri, Bhel Puris, samosas, dal, dosas, idly, uthappam, Naan, curried vegetables and lassi.
Comments: Most likely this is the best Indian vegetarian food in the Atlanta area. The food is good and this place is recommended. Good for buffet lunch. The place doesn't have much atmosphere. Lunch buffet is served on paper plates and cups. Casual place. Quick service. Price: $-$$; Lunch Buffet is 5.95 on weekdays, $6.95 on weekends.
Directions: From I-285, take US-78 W exit (#39A) towards Decatur/Atlanta and merge onto Stone Mountain Pkwy going west and go 1 mile, then at N Druid Hills Rd/Valley Brook Rd) exit, keep right at fork in ramp and merge onto N Druid Hills Rd (going northwest) for a third-mile, then at Oak Tree Rd turn left and this place is a block down in a small mall.

HINESVILLE

Farmer's Natural Foods
754 EG Miles Parkway; 912-368-7803
Hours: Monday to Friday 9 am to 7 pm; Saturday 9 am to 6 pm; closed Sunday.
Natural Food Store. Some organic produce.
Directions: From I-95, take Midway/Hinesville exit. This place is near the downtown on Rte 119.

MARIETTA (Atlanta suburb)

Dana Bazaar
East Marietta Shopping Center, 1482 Roswell Road; 770-578-8666
Hours: Tuesday to Friday 12 noon to 8 pm; Saturday 12 noon to 7 pm; Sunday 12 noon to 6 pm; closed Monday (except for the cooking class)
Indian Grocery Store and Vegetarian Deli. Organic produce. Has Indian vegetarian cooking class on most Monday evenings.
Menu: Meals are mainly lunchtime Indian snacks.
Comments: Has some seating.
Directions: This place is down the road from Life Grocery.

Harry's Farmers Market
70 Powers Ferry Road SE, Marietta
770-578-4400
Hours: Daily 9 am to 8 pm
Natural Food Store and take-out Deli. International food and a good selection of produce.

**Life Grocery

1453 Roswell Road NE, near the Big Chicken Hwy 41; 770-977-9583

Hours: Monday to Saturday 9 am to 8 pm Sunday 11 am to 6 pm

Natural Food Store and Vegetarian Café. Deli. Organic produce. Bookstore and bulk herbs.

Menu: Has raw food dishes.

Comments: A good place to get organic foods. Helpful management.

Directions: From I-75 going north, take exit #263 for Hwy 120 W toward Marietta/Southern Tech. Turn right onto S Marietta Pkwy going northeast and go 2 mile, then exit right to Hwy 120 (Roswell Rd). Make a left at the light onto Roswell Rd and go one mile, then this place is on the right.

ROSWELL

Harry's Farmers Market

1180 Upper Hembree Road
770-664-6300

Hours: Daily 9 am to 8 pm

Natural Food Market and take-out Deli. International food and a good selection of produce.

Comments: Gets good ratings.

SAVANNAH

Savannah has an interesting historical district with some outstanding old houses.

Brighter Day Natural foods

1102 Bull Street
912-236-4703

Store Hours: Monday to Saturday 10 am to 6 pm; Sunday 12:30 pm to 5:30 pm

Deli Hours: Monday to Saturday lunch 11 am to 2 pm

Natural Food Store and Deli. Juice Bar. International. Macrobiotic and Vegan options. Not pure vegetarian.

Menu: Sandwiches, salads and ready-made dishes. Fresh juices.

Comments: After 2 pm can still get some salad dishes that are left from lunch, but cannot get any sandwiches. Has a view of Forsyth Park. Is in a building built in 1911. Is a pleasant place. It is a fairly big store with a good selection of items

Other Info: Limited service, take-out. Accepts MC, VISA. Price: $-$$.

Directions: From I-95, take the I-16 exit to Savannah, take the Gwinnett (GA Hwy 404) exit (#166), turn right off Gwinnett exit and go a half-mile. At Whitaker St turn right and go 3 blocks,

then at Park Ave turn left and go one block and this store is on the right. It has a mural of organic tomatoes wearing sunglasses.

Elizabeth's On 37th

105 East 37th
912-236-5547

Hours: Daily 6 pm to 9:30 pm

Southern style American, . Not pure vegetarian.

Menu: Has a separate vegetarian menu. Roasted Eggplant. Cappuccino, espresso. Non-alcoholic beer and wine.

Comments: Upscale, formal place. In a historic mansion. Jacket and tie are required. Elegant décor. Has antiques. Has four dining rooms. Seats 80 people. Good place for an event or a romantic evening.

Other Info: Full service. Reservations suggested. Accepts AMEX, DC, DISC, MC, VISA. Price: $$$.

Nature's Pantry

Varsity Plaza; 11410 Abercorn, at Largo
912-925-8952

fax: 912-920-8022

email: muscle2flex@msn.com;

Web site: www.natures-pantry.com

Natural Food Store and Juice Bar. Mainly supplements.

Comments: Can microwave frozen dishes. Small place. Mainly has supplements. Cheese and tofu sandwiches. Doesn't have much of a selection for eating.

Directions: This place is a little outside of town in Varsity Plaza.

STONE MOUNTAIN

Basket Bakery and Garden Café

6655 Memorial Drive
770-498-0329

Hours: Tuesday to Saturday for 8 am to 10 am; Sunday 10 am to 9 pm; closed Sunday.

German Café. Not pure vegetarian.

Menu: Salads, sandwiches, veggie burger and other dishes. Fresh breads.

Comments: Has good size portions.

Other Info: Full service. Accepts AMEX, DC, DIS, MC, VISA. Price: $$.

In My Nature

Rockmore Shopping Center
4859 Memorial Drive
770-413-0450

Hours: Monday to Friday 11 am to 7 pm; Satur-

day 12 noon to 6 pm; closed Sunday.
Natural Food Store.
Directions: This place is east of Atlanta, about three miles east of the I-285 beltway. From I-285, take GA Hwy 19/Memorial Drive exit (#41) towards Avondale Estates, then go east on Memorial Dr and this place is about 3½ miles down.

VALDOSTA

Atlanta Bread Company
1531 Baytree Road; 912-259-8469; **fax:** 912-253-8499
Hours: Monday to Thursday 7 am to 9 pm; Friday & Sat 7 am to 10 pm; Sun 8 am to 10 pm
Bakery and Sandwich Place. Not pure veg.
Menu: Good sandwiches and some vegetarian soups.
Comments: They have a book that list all the dishes that they sell and a detailed ingredient list. According to their menu the following soups are vegetarian: Tomato with Fennel & Dill, Spicy Black Bean with Rice, Szechuan Hot & Sour and Garden Vegetable. Good place. Has many places in Georgia and other states.

Ma Perkins Natural
2110 North Ashley Street; 229-244-5440
Hours: Monday to Saturday 9:30 am to 6 pm
Closed Sunday.
Natural Food Store. No organic produce.
Directions: Downtown on North Ashley, across the street from Checkers.

Hawaii

Hawaii
1. Hilo
2. Kailua Kona
3. Keaau
4. Ocean View
5. Pahoa
6. Papaikou

Kauai Island
7. Hanalei
8. Kapaa
9. Kilauea
10. Koloa
11. Lihue

Oahu Island
12. Aiea
13. Haleiwa
14. Honolulu
15. Kailua

Maui Island
16. Haiku
17. Kahului
18. Kihei
19. Lahaina
20. Makawao
21. Paia
22. Wailuku

Molokai Island
23. Kuanakalai

Lanai Island
24. Lanai City

Fruit trees that grow on public land are considered to be public property and anyone can pick them. There are many guava trees.
The Web site of the **Vegetarian Society of Hawaii** (http://vsh.org/welcome) has a list of about 70 vegetarian restaurants and natural food stores in Hawaii.

OAHU
Honolulu is on this island.

HALEIWA (on the north shore)

Celestial and Paradise Found Café
66-443 Kamehameha Highway, North Shore Oahu; 808-637-6729
Hours: Monday to Saturday 9 am to 6:30 pm
Sunday 10 am to 6 pm
Natural Food Store and Vegetarian Restaurant. Chinese, Thai, Indian, International, Gourmet. Juice Bar. Vegan-friendly. Organic produce.
Menu: Has vegetarian soups, sandwiches and specials. Tempeh Mushroom Walnut Melt. Waimea Shorebreak Smoothie. Fresh juices and wheatgrass (grows their own).

Comments: Small, casual place. Friendly staff. Good food and music. Pleasant atmosphere. Good dining experience. Best natural food store in area.
Other Info: Full service, take-out, counter service, catering. Price: $.
Directions: From Hwy 99 going northwest into the city, turn right at Hwy 83 and this place is a half-mile down just past Helemano Stream.

The Coffee Gallery
66-250 Kam Highway
808-637-5355; **Web site:** www.roastmaster.com
Hours: Daily 7 am to 8 pm
Coffee Shop. Not pure vegetarian
Menu: Has a decent selection of vegetarian dishes. Soups, veggie chili, salads and sandwiches. Has decaf coffees.
Comments: Can order coffee on their web site.
Other Info: Accepts AMEX, MC, VISA.

HONOLULU

Aloha Health Foods
1050 Ala Moana Boulevard (Rte 92)
808-591-8803

Hours: Monday to Saturday 10 am to 9 pm Sunday 10 am to 5 pm
Natural Food Store.
Other Info: Accepts AMEX, MC, VISA.
Directions: This place is on Rte 92, near to the ocean.

**Buddhist Vegetarian Restaurant

100 North Beretania Street, Suite 109, In the Cultural Plaza in China Town; 808-532-8218
Hours: Thursday to Tuesday 10:30 am to 2 pm, 5:30 pm to 9 pm; closed Wednesday.
Fully Vegetarian Chinese. Vegan options.
Menu: Has a good selection of mock meat dishes. Sweet and Sour Pork is very good. Rare mushroom dishes. Stir-fries and vegan Dum Sum.
Comments: Clean place. Clothe tablecloths and crystals. Well-presented dishes.
Other Info: Full service, take-out, catering. Accepts MC, VISA. Price: $-$$.
Directions: This place is 1 mile northwest of the downtown. From H-1, take Exit #21A, then go northwest on Nuuana Ave a half-mile, then at N Beretania St turn right and this place is 2 blocks down.

California Pizza Kitchen

Kahala Mall, 4211 Waialae Avenue
808-737-9446
1450 Ala Moana Boulevard (in Ala Moana Shopping Center); 808-941-7715
98-1005 Moanalua Road, Suite 554, Alea
808-487-7741
Hours: Sunday to Thursday 11 am to 10:30 pm
Friday & Saturday 11 am to 11 pm
Pizza Restaurant. Not pure vegetarian.
Menu: Pizzas, pastas, salads and cheese pizza. Tuscan Bean Soup does not have meat stock.
Comments: Has excellent pizzas. Fresh spinach, sun-dried tomatoes and roasted eggplant on whole-wheat crust. Pizza crust contains dairy. Only has individual size pizza.
Other Info: Non-smoking. Price: $-$$.

Chiang Mai Thai Cuisine

2239 South King Street, midtown, Moilili neighborhood; 808-941-1151
Hours: 11 am to 1:30 pm, 5:30 pm to 10 pm
Saturday & Sunday 5:30 pm to 10 pm
Northern Thai. Vegetarian-friendly. Vegan options. Not pure vegetarian.
Menu: Has a large selection of vegetarian dishes. Soups, appetizers, tofu dishes, noodle and brown rice dishes, and main dishes.
Comments: Reasonable prices. Popular place.
Other Info: Full service, take-out. Accepts

AMEX, DC, DIS, MC, VISA. Price: $-$$.
Directions: Parking arranged for customers.

**Down to Earth Natural Food Store

2525 South King Street, Moilili neighborhood
808-947-7678; **email:** info@healthys.net
Web site: www.downtoearth.org
Hours: Daily 7:30 am to 10 pm
Natural Food Store and Fully Vegetarian Deli.
Mostly Vegan. Salad Bar, self-serve Hot Bar and Bakery
Menu: Wide variety of vegetarian dishes. Summer Rolls, Eggplant Parmigiana, mock Chicken Tofu, salads, sandwiches, Teriyaki Tofu, Herb Potatoes, enchiladas, Lasagna and tapioca pudding. Avocado, tofu and cheese sandwiches. Fresh juices.
Comments: About 90% of the ingredients are organic. The natural food store has a large selection of organic produce and other items. 5% discounts for VSH members. Has an excellent lunch buffet, deli items and baked goods. They sell nothing in the entire store that has eggs, though there are dairy products. Many vegan items
Other Info: Cafeteria-style, take-out. Non-smoking. Accepts AMEX, MC, VISA.
Directions: Located a half-block from intersection of University Avenue and King Street, a little off H-1 Freeway, a few blocks from University of Hawaii and 1 mile from Waikiki. Coming from airport, take Bingham Street exit to Isenberg St, then turn right, go to the second traffic light (King St) and turn left. This place is 2 blocks down on the right. From H-1, take Exit #24B for University Ave, then go a quarter-mile south on University, then at S King St turn right and this place is 2 blocks down.

The Fresh Garden Deli

212 Merchant Street #9; 808-524-8242
Web site: www.freshgardendeli.com
Hours: Monday to Friday 11 am to 3 pm
Closed Saturday & Sunday.
California Sandwich Place. Vegan friendly.
Menu: Veggie Delight (artichoke hearts, avocado, cucumber slices), salads, pastas, Vegetarian Black Bean Chili, Vegetarian Curry and Black Bean Burrito.
Comments: Good place for lunch. There is a daily vegetarian special that changes each day. You can check their web site for what the special is each day.
Directions: From H-1, take Exit #21A, then go south on Rte 61 (Pali Hwy) and go southwest on Pali Hwy towards the water ¾ mile, then turn left at Merchant St and this place is a block down.

**Gauranga's Pure Vegetarian

51 Coelho Way, Nuuanu area, located in the Nuuana Hills above Honolulu, opposite the Philippines Embassy; 808-595-3947
Hours: Monday to Friday 11 am to 2 pm Closed Saturday & Sunday.
Fully Vegetarian. No eggs, but dairy. Vegan options. All-you-can-eat-buffet. Full Salad Bar.
Menu: Homemade whole-grain bread, dal, brown and basmati rice, vegetable dishes and Lasagna. Desserts such as fresh baked cookies (no eggs). Has a different International main dish nightly. Fresh juices.
Comments: Part of the Hare Krishna vegetarian restaurants. Quiet, peaceful atmosphere. Has a variety of tropical foliage. Located on beautiful three-acre piece of land. Has the largest banyan tree on the island.
Other Info: Buffet-style, take-out. No credit cards. Price: $-$$.
Directions: This place is in the hills north of Honolulu. From H-1 take Exit #21A and then go 1 mile northeast on Hwy 61. Then at Coelho Way turn left and this place is 1 block down.

**Huckleberry Farms

Nuuanu Shopping Plaza
1613 Nuuanu Avenue, at School
808-599-1876; **Deli number:** 808-524-7960
Hours: Monday to Saturday 9 am to 8 pm Sunday 9 am to 6 pm
Natural Food Store and Vegetarian Deli. Large, well-stocked store. 10% off vitamin prices only for VSH members.
Menu: Soups, salads, sandwiches, vegetarian Lasagna and hot dishes.
Other Info: Accepts AMEX, MC, VISA.
Directions: From H-1, take Exit 21, and this place is near the exit. This place is a quarter-mile northwest of the junction of H-1 and Hwy 61.

India Bazaar Madras Café

2320 South King Street, #4, Moiliili area
808-949-4840
Hours: Daily 11 am to 7 pm
Indian. Mainly Vegetarian. Not pure vegetarian.
Menu: Has South Indian dishes and other Indian cuisine.
Comments: Good food. Does not use ghee for cooking; use vegetable oil.
Other Info: Cafeteria style, take-out. Cash only; no credit cards. Price: $.

Jamba Juice (two locations)

130 Merchant Street, downtown 808-585-8359
4211 Waialee Avenue   808-734-7988

Hours: Monday to Friday 5:30 am to 6 pm; Saturday 7 am to 1 pm; closed Sunday.
Juice Bar.
Menu: Fresh juices and smoothies. Pretzels and some baked goods.

Keo's Thai Cuisine

Ambassador Hotel, 2028 Kuhio Avenue
808-943-1444
1200 Ala Moana Boulevard; 808-596-0020
Hours: Sun to Thur 7 am to 2 pm, 5 pm to 10 pm; Fri & Sat 7 am to 2 pm, 5 pm to 10 pm
Gourmet Thai. Vegan options. Not pure veg.
Menu: Vegetarian appetizers, soups, salads, curry dishes and rice. Most dishes can be made vegetarian.
Comments: The Thai food at these places is good. Casual place. The place at Ala Moana Boulevard has a pleasant tropical design with a tropical garden. Elegant décor. Has won awards.
Other Info: Full service, take-out. Accepts AMEX, DC, DIS, MC, VISA. Price: $$.

Kokua Co-op

2643 South King Street, Moiliili area
808-941-1922
Hours: Daily 8:30 am to 8:30 pm
Natural Food Store and Vegetarian Deli. Organic produce.
Menu: Sandwich, soups, veggie chili, curry dishes and salads.
Other Info: Counter service, take-out. Patio seating outside. Accepts AMEX, DIS, MC, VISA.
Directions: From H-1, take exit #24B, then go a third-mile south on University towards the water, then at S King St turn left and this place is 2 blocks down.

***Legend Vegetarian Restaurant

100 North Beretania Street, Suite 109
808-532-8218
Hours: Thursday to Tuesday 10:30 am to 2 pm, 5:30 pm to 9 pm; closed Wednesday.
Fully Vegan Chinese. Hong Kong style vegetarian food.
Menu: Vegetarian Dim Sum (lunch only), Vegetarian Butterfish, Vegetarian Chicken/Duck/Pork, Braised Elm Fungus, noodle dishes, Sweet & Sour Pork, Tofu Cashew Stir-fry and Bamboo Pith in Coconut Milk.
Comments: Seats 90 people. Validated parking.
Other Info: Full service, take-out. Private room available. Non-smoking. Reservations recommended. Accepts MC, VISA.
Directions: In Chinatown, 15 minutes from Waikiki, 15 minutes from Airport. Parking lot of

Chinatown Cultural Plaza, entrance at Maunakea St. From H1, take Exit #21A and go southwest on Nuuanu Ave a half-mile, then turn right onto Beretania St and this place is 2 blocks down.

Lifestream Natural Foods

702 Kapahulu Avenue; 808-732-6253
Hours: Monday to Friday 9 am to 6 pm; Saturday 9 am to 4 pm; closed Sunday.
Natural Food Store. Not very big.

Little Bit of Saigon

1160 Maunakea Avenue, in Chinatown
808-528-3663
Hours: Daily 9 am to 10 pm
Vietnamese. Not pure vegetarian.
Menu: Stir-fried vegetables with tofu, roll-ups made of rice paper, Peanut sauce dishes and many tofu dishes.
Other Info: Accepts AMEX, MC, VISA.

Mekong Thai

1295 South Beretania Street, Makiki area
808-591-8842
1726 South King Street, Makiki area
808-941-6184
Hours: 11 am to 2 pm, 5 pm to 9:30 pm
Saturday & Sunday 5 pm to 9:30 pm
Thai. Not pure vegetarian.
Menu: Has a variety of vegetarian dishes on the menu.
Comment: Food gets good recommendations. Oldest Thai restaurant in Hawaii. Good atmosphere and service. Run by same people who own Keo's.
Other Info: Full service, take-out. Non-smoking. Accepts AMEX, DC, DIS, MC, VISA. Price: $-$$.
Directions: Parking arranged for customers.

Mocha Java Café

Ward Centre, 1200 Ala Moana Boulevard
808-591-9023
Hours: Monday to Thursday 8 am to 9 pm; Fri & Sat 8 am to 10 pm; Sun 8 am to 6 pm
Natural Foods Restaurant. Vegan options.
Menu: Dinner dishes are mainly vegetarian, with a good selection of vegan dishes. Garden Burgers, Tofu Burgers, Curry Burgers and daily specials such as Veggie Lasagna. Daily soups. Fresh juices, cappuccino, espresso.
Other Info: Limited service, take-out. Accepts AMEX, MC, VISA. Price: $-$$.
Directions: This place is located on Rte 92 in south Honolulu near the water. It is a third-mile west of Piikoi St.

Pineland Chinese Restaurant

1236 Keeaumoku Street, Makiki area
808-955-2918
Hours: Daily 10:30 am to 2 pm, 4:30 pm to 9 pm
Chinese. Vegan options. Not pure vegetarian.
Menu: Has a separate vegetarian menu (need to ask for it). Hot & Sour Noodle Soup, Eggplant with Sauce and tofu dishes.
Comments: Does not use chicken stock in dishes.
Other Info: Full service, take-out. Price: $.

Ruffage Natural Foods

2442 Kuhio Street, Waikiki area; 808-922-2042
Hours: Monday to Saturday 9 am to 7 pm
Closed Sunday.
Natural Food Store and Deli.
Menu: Has a selection of sandwiches and salads.
Directions: This place is about 3 miles southeast of downtown Honolulu. From H-1, take Exit #26A, then go north on 10th Ave for 2½ miles, then at Waiomao Rd turn right and go a quarter-mile, then turn right on Kuahee St and this place is 3 blocks down.

VIM & Vigor Foods

Ala Moana Shopping Center, 1450 Ala Moana Boulevard, Suite 1014; 808-955-3600
Comments: This branch has ready-made foods, but the other branches don't.
Directions: This place is on Rte 92, right on the water a third-mile southeast of Pikoi St.
98-199 Kamehameha Highway, Suite E88 0 8 - 488-5160
Directions: This place is 2 miles southwest of downtown Honolulu.
345 Hahani Street, Kailua   808-261-4036
Office and Mailorder number: 808-943-0600
Hours: Monday to Saturday 9 am to 9 pm
Sunday 10 am to 7 pm
Web site: www.vimandvigor.com
Natural Food Store and Deli. Juice Bar. Bakery.
Comments: Uses eggs in some of the dishes. Small, fairly limited place.

Yen King

4211 Waialee Avenue, in the Kahala Mall
808-732-5505
Hours: Daily 10 am to 9:30 pm
Chinese. Shanghai, Mandarin, Szechuan. Vegan options. Not pure vegetarian.
Menu: Has a good selection of vegetarian dishes. Over thirty vegetarian dishes on menu. Soups, mock meat dishes, noodle dishes, gluten dishes and vegetable dishes.
Comments: No MSG. Full service, take-out. Accepts AMEX, MC, VISA. Price: $$.

KAILUA (a little north of Honolulu)

Down to Earth
201 Hamakua Drive, Kailua; 808-262-3838
Hours: Daily 8 am to 8 pm
Natural Food Store and Vegetarian Deli. See Honolulu.

Pali Garden
Castle Medical Center, Cafeteria, 640 Ulukahiki Street, Kailua; 808-263-5500, 808-262-5604
Hours: Daily 8 am to 10 pm, 12 noon to 2 pm, 4:30 pm to 6:30 pm
Hospital Cafeteria. Vegetarian-friendly.
Menu: Has a large selection of vegetarian dishes.
Comments: Quick service. Inexpensive. Seventh Day Adventist hospital.
Directions: This place is a mile east of the downtown. From H-1, take Exit #23 and go northeast on Punahou St and go ¾ mile, then turn left at Nehoa St and go a block, then turn onto Ulukahiki St.

The Source Natural Foods and Juice Bar
32 Kainehe Street; 808-262-5604
Hours: Monday to Friday 9 am to 9 pm; Saturday 9 am to 6 pm; Sunday 10 am to 5 pm
Natural Food Store. Organic produce.
Other Info: Limited service, take-out. No credit cards. Accepts MC, VISA. Price: $.

NORTH SHORE

**Celestial National Foods
66-443 Kamehameha Highway; 808-637-6729
Hours: Monday to Saturday 9 am to 6:30 pm
Sunday 10 am to 6 pm
Natural Food Store and Fully Vegetarian Deli.
Menu: Pita pockets, nachos, couscous and many other dishes.

**Down to Earth—Pearlridge
98-131 Kaonohi Street; 808-488-1375
Natural Food Store and Vegetarian Deli. Organic produce. See Honolulu.
Menu: Soups, salads, sandwiches, veggie Lasagna and hot dishes.
Other Info: Counter service, take-out. Seating.

MAUI ISLAND

Cheeseburger In Paradise
811 Front Street, Lahaina; 808-661-4855
Hours: Daily 8 am to 10:30 pm
American. Not pure vegetarian.
Menu: Has veggie burgers, Gardenburgers, Tofu Burgers and Grilled Cheese. Smoothies.
Comments: Live music in the evening. Located on the beach. Be careful of the Tuna Melt on the vegetarian menu.
Other Info: Full service, take-out. Accepts AMEX, MC, VISA. Price: $.
Directions: This place is in Lahaina on the southwest shore of Maui Island, just off Rte 30.

**Down to Earth
305 Dairy Road, Kahului
808-877-2661; **Web site:** www.downtoearth.org
Hours: Monday to Saturday 7 am to 9 pm
Sunday 8 am to 8 pm
Natural Food Store and Fully Vegetarian Deli.
Buffet, Bakery, Salad Bar and self-serve Hot Bar. Mostly Vegan. It is a large natural food store. Organic produce. See Honolulu.
Menu: Has a wide variety of dishes. Summer Rolls, mock Chicken Tofu, Teriyaki Tofu, good tofu dishes, Chinese Tofu Dish, Sweet & Sour Seitan, Szechuan Broccoli, herb potatoes, enchilada, Lasagna and Tapioca Pudding. Menu changes regularly.
Comments: About 90% of the ingredients they use are organic. Quaint place. Good food.
Other Info: Buffet, counter service, take-out. Has seating upstairs. Non-smoking. Does not take reservations. Accepts AMEX, MC, VISA. Pay-by-the-pound.
Directions: This place is on the northwest shore, 2 miles east of Wailuku. This place is one mile from the airport on Dairy Road. From coming from airport heading in the direction of Lahaina, after passing the first traffic light, you will see Costco and K-Mart on your left, then go to second light, Alamaha St, then turn right and this place is 100 yards down. Starbucks Coffee is across the street. Plenty of parking in front.

**Down to Earth
1169 Makawao Avenue, Makawao; 808-572-1488
Hours: Daily 8 am to 8 pm; Saturday 8 am to 6 pm; Sunday 10 am to 5 pm
Natural Food Store and Vegetarian take-out Deli.
Vegan-friendly. See Honolulu.
Comments: Labels vegan dishes in deli. Vegetarian-friendly store.
Other Info: Accepts AMEX, MC, VISA.
Directions: This place is in the middle of the island a few miles northeast of Pukalani (which is on Rte 37) on Makawao.

**Down to Earth
193 Lahainaluna Road, Lahaina; 808-667-2855
Hours: Monday to Saturday 7:30 am to 9 pm

Sunday 8:30 am to 8 pm
Natural Food Store and Deli. Buffet and Salad Bar. Organic.
Menu: Lentil Paté Sandwich, Tofu Chicken, sandwiches and salads. Fresh juices and smoothies.
Comments: Has several tables to eat at.
Other Info: Accepts AMEX, MC, VISA.
Directions: This place is on the west shore of the island in the northwest part of the island.

Lahaina Coolers
180 Dickenson Street, #107, Lahaina
808-661-7082
Hours: Daily 8 am to 12 midnight
International, American, Mexican, Italian Restaurant. Not pure vegetarian.
Menu: Gourmet place that has several vegetarian dishes. Soba Salad with Grilled Tofu, Zaru Soba with green noodles, pizzas, pastas, Boca Burger and Mango Sorbet.
Other Info: Full service, take-out. Accepts AMEX, DC, DIS, MC, VISA. Price: $$.
Directions: This place is on the west shore, in the northwest part of the island. From Rte 30 coming into town, turn left at Dickenson St and this place is 1½ block down.

Loving Foods Raw Experience
42 Baldwin Avenue, Paia, north shore Maui
808-573-4207; **Web site:** www.lovingfoods.com

Mana Natural Foods
49 Baldwin Avenue, Paia, Maui; 808-579-8078
Hours: Daily 8:30 am to 8:30 pm
Natural Food Store. Salad Bar and Bakery. Organic produce.
Menu: Has salad items and a small selection of hot dishes. The bakery makes vegan breads, pies and carob brownies. Has a good salad Bar.
Directions: From Rte 36 coming from Wailuku, at Baldwin Ave turn right and this place is right near the turn.

Margarita's Beach Cantina
101 North Kihai Road, Kihei, Maui
808-879-5275
Hours: Sunday to Thursday 11:30 am to 9 pm Friday & Saturday 11:30 am to 10 pm
Mexican. Not pure vegetarian.
Menu: Tofu Tacos, Gardenburgers and Tofu Enchiladas.
Comments: Has a large balcony with a great beach view. Refried beans have lard in them, but the black beans don't.
Other Info: Full service, take-out. Accepts AMEX, MC, VISA. Price: $-$$.

Picnic's
30 Baldwin Road, Paia
808-579-8021; **email:** picnics@aloha.net
Web site: http://www.aloha.net/~picnics/
Hours: Daily 7 am to 3 pm (maybe open 7 am to 7 pm in future)
Restaurant. Not pure vegetarian.
Menu: Tofu burgers, fruit salad, Spinach Nut Burger (very good), salads and fresh baked breads.
Comments: Can stop here on the way to Hana. They make take-out lunches. Uses freshly grown produce.
Directions: On north shore. From Rte 36 coming from Wailuku, at Baldwin Ave turn right and this place is a third-mile down.

Polli's Mexican Restaurant
1202 Makawao Road, Makawao; 808-572-7808
Hours: Daily 9 am to 10 pm
Mexican. Vegan options. Not pure vegetarian.
Menu: Burritos with veggie taco mix. Vegan chimichanga. Salsa is good.
Comments: Are willing to make any dishes vegetarian by substituting tofu or vegetarian taco mix. Very good burritos.
Other Info: Accepts AMEX, MC, VISA.

Royal Thai Cuisine
Azeka Shopping Center, 55 Aliialana Place, Kihai, Maui; 808-874-0813
Hours: Monday to Friday 11 am to 3 pm, 4:30 pm to 9:30 pm
Saturday & Sunday 4:30 pm to 9:30 pm
Thai. Not pure vegetarian.
Menu: Has a large selection of vegetarian dishes.
Comments: Reasonably priced.
Other Info: Full service, take-out. Accepts AMEX, MC, VISA. Price: $-$$.

Saeng's Thai Cuisine
2119 Vineyard Street, in Wailuku next to Kahului
808-244-1567
Hours: Daily 11 am to 2:30 pm, 5 pm to 9:30 pm
Thai. Not pure vegetarian.
Menu: Has around 15 vegetarian dishes. Tofu dishes.
Comments: Has a pleasant garden to eat at with a small waterfall.
Other Info: Full service, take-out. Accepts AMEX, MC, VISA. Price: $$.

Siam Thai
123 North Market Street; 808-244-3817
Hours: Monday to Friday 11 am to 2 pm, 5 pm

to 9 pm; Saturday & Sunday 5 pm to 9 pm
Thai. Not pure vegetarian.
Menu: Has good vegetarian dishes.

Stella Blues Café
1215 South Kihei Road (in Long's Center)
Kihei, Maui; 808-874-3779
Hours: Daily 8 am to 9 pm
Restaurant. Vegan options. Not pure vegetarian.
Menu: Vegetarian sandwiches, veggie Lasagna, veggie chili, pastas, salads, soups and other dishes.
Other Info: Accepts DIS, MC, VISA.

Thai Chef Restaurant
Lahaina Shopping Center, Lahaina; 808-667-2814
Hours: Monday to Friday 11 am to 2 pm, 5 pm to 9 pm; Saturday & Sunday 5 pm to 9 pm
Thai. Vegan options. Not pure vegetarian.
Menu: Has a separate vegetarian menu with around 15 vegetarian dishes. Vegetable curry and tofu dishes.
Comments: Authentic Thai cuisine. Relaxed, cozy place. Can make most of the dishes meat-free.
Other Info: Full service, take-out. Accepts DIS, MC, VISA. Price: $$.

***The Vegan Restaurant
115 Baldwin Avenue, Paia (north shore Maui)
808-579-9144; **Web** site: http://www.future-link.com/vegan.html
Hours: September to March, Tuesday to Sunday 2 pm to 9 pm; Closed Monday. April to September, Tuesday to Sunday 4 pm to 9 pm
Fully Vegan International, Asian.
Menu: Large selection of dishes. Lasagna, Pad Thai, Noodles with Coconut, burritos, tortillas, mashed potatoes & gravy, Tofu Loaf, Tofu Wrap, soups, Grilled Polenta, hummus and salad. Potato Knish, Hummus Wrap, Veggie Pate Wrap, Avocado Delight Wrap, Tofu Salad, Tofu Soft Taco, Vegan Burger, Grilled Tempeh Ruben (very good), Tempeh Burger, Carrot Salad, Potato Knish and Organic Salad Greens. Fresh juices. Non-alcoholic beer.
Comments: A small café with only several tables. Relaxed, laid-back place. Reasonably priced. Has vegan cheeses and vegan meats. Good size portions. Their menu is on their web site. Home-made dishes. The food gets high rating. Good size portions. Sometimes has live music. Friendly, pleasant atmosphere. Run by people from Gentle World, a vegan community in Paia, who have published several books.
Other Info: Counter service, take-out. Non-smoking. Accepts MC, VISA. Price: $-$$.

Directions: On north shore. From Rte 36 coming from Wailuku, at Baldwin Ave turn right and this place is a third-mile down. Baldwin Ave is the main street in town.

**Veg-Out
810 Kokomo Road, Haiku
808-575-5320
Hours: Monday to Friday 10:30 am to 7:30; Saturday 10:30 am to 6 pm; closed Sunday.
Vegetarian Café. Mainly vegan.
Menu: Has a large selection of vegetarian dishes. Has sandwiches, salads, Baked Lasagna, Oriental Stir-fry, homemade chili, veggie burgers, Boca Burger, homemade bread and burritos. Has a good selection of Mexican dishes.
Comments: Good, friendly place.
Other Info: Accepts AMEX, MC, VISA.
Directions: Haiku is on the north-central part of the island. Haiku is 5 miles south of the sea. From Hwy 36, this place is 1½ south of the town of Haiku.

MOLOKAI ISLAND
Has sea cliffs as high as 3,300 feet high.

Outpost Natural Foods
70 Makaena, in Kuanakalai (Central Molokai)
808-553-3377
Hours: Monday to Friday 9 am to 6 pm; Saturday 9 am to 4 pm; closed Sunday.
Natural Food Store and Deli.
Menu: Salads, sandwiches, veggie burgers, burritos, tempeh burgers and fresh juices.
Other Info: Counter service, take-out. Has a picnic table out back

HAWAII (The Big Island)

Abundant Life Natural Foods
292 Kamehameha Avenue, downtown Hilo
808-935-7411
Hours: Monday to Saturday 8:30 am to 7 pm
Sunday 10 am to 5 pm
Natural Food Store and Deli. Organic produce.
Menu: Soups, salads and sandwiches.
Comments: It is the largest natural food store on the island. Sells locally grown fruits and vegetables.
Other Info: Accepts AMEX, MC, VISA.
Directions: This place is a third-mile southwest of the junction of Rte 20 & Rte 19, a block from the water. Coming northeast into town on Rte 20, a half-block from the sea, turn right onto Kamehamha Ave.

Café Ohia

525 Lotus Blossom Lane, Ocean View, Kau District; 808-929-8086
Hours: Tuesday to Friday 11 am to 8 pm; Saturday 8 am to 8 pm; closed Sunday & Monday.
Mexican. Vegan friendly
Menu: Salads, sandwiches, burritos and more.

Farmers' Market

Kamehameha Avenue
Wednesday and Saturday

Island Natural's Market & Deli

303 Makaala, Hilo; 808-935-5533
Natural Food Store and Deli. Salad Bar. Organic produce.
Menu: Salads, sandwiches, soups, vegan split pea soup and hot dishes.
Other Info: Counter service, take-out. Has seating. Accepts AMEX, MC, VISA.
Directions: This place is about 2 miles south of downtown Hilo and the sea just off Rte 11. Go south on Rte 11 from the downtown, then turn right at Makaala St and this place is a half block down.

Kalani Honua

RR2, Box 4500, Pahoa, Hawaii 96778; 808-965-7828; fax: 965-9613; email: kh@ILHawaii.net
Restaurant open to the public: Breakfast 7:30 am to 8:30 am, Lunch 12 noon to 1 pm, Dinner 6 pm to 7:30 pm
Retreat Center and institute for cultural studies. Buffet Vegetarian food. Vegan options.
Comments: Outdoor sheltered patio dining. Beautiful grounds.

Keaau Natural Foods

Keaau, Hawaii Island
808-966-8877
Hours: Monday to Friday 8:30 am to 8 pm; Saturday 8:30 am to 7 pm; Sunday 9:30 am to 5 pm
Natural Food Store. Has ready-made sandwiches.

Kona Natural Foods

75-1027 Henry Street, Kailua-Kona, North Kona District; 808-329-2296
Natural Food Store and Deli. Organic produce.
Menu: Soups, salads, sandwiches and hot dishes.
Other Info: Counter service, take-out. Has indoor and outdoor seating.

Low's International Food

222 Kilauea Avenue, Hilo; 808-969-6652
Restaurant and Bakery. Has some vegetarian dishes such as Garden Burgers and salads. Bakery with exotic breads made from coconuts and fruits. They ship them all over the world.

Pahoa Natural Groceries

Pahoa; 808-965-8322
Hours: Daily 7:30 am to 8 pm
Natural Food Store and Deli. International. Salad Bar. Large selection of organic produce.
Menu: Has a good selection of vegetarian dishes. Has a daily international cuisine, such as Chinese.
Other Info: Counter service, take-out. Has some tables outside. Accepts AMEX, MC, VISA.
Directions: Coming from Hilo, when get on main street in town this place is a big yellow store on left side.

What's Shakin

27-999 Old Mamalahoa Highway, Papaikou, Hilo District; 808-964-3080
Hours: Daily 10 am to 5 pm
Fast Food Place. Not pure vegetarian.
Menu: Salads, Garden Burger, Ginger Tempeh and pizza. Fresh juices and smoothies. Makes juices from fruit they grow on their farm.
Directions: About 15 minutes north of Hilo on the Scenic Route.

KAUAI ISLAND

Hawaiin Farmers' Market

In Waipa on the road to Haena, a half-mile west of Hanalei.

Hanalei Health & Natural Foods

Ching Young Village, Kuhio Highway, Route 56, North Shore, West shore, Hanalei
808-826-6990
Hours: Daily 8 am to 8 pm
Natural Food Store and Deli. Organic produce.
Menu: Soup, sandwiches, salads and more. Hummus, tabbouleh and other dishes.
Other Info: Accepts AMEX, MC, VISA. Counter service, take-out. Has seating outside
Directions: Right in the downtown with a huge red awning,

**Hanapepe Café

3830 Hanapepe Road (West Side) Hanapepe; 808-335-5011
Web site: www.hanapepecafe.com
Hours: Tuesday to Thursday, Saturday 9 am to 2 pm; Friday 9 am to 2 pm, 6 pm to 9 pm; closed Sunday & Monday.
Vegetarian Café. Vegan-friendly. Gourmet.

Menu: Soups, salads, Garden Burgers, sandwiches and pasta.
Comments: Food gets high ratings. Friendly, efficient service. Nice people.
Other Info: Non-smoking. Reservations highly suggested for dinner. Accepts MC, VISA. Price: $$.

King & I
4-901 Kuhio Hwy, Kapaa, Kauai Island
808-822-1642
Hours: Daily 4:30 pm to 9:15 pm
Thai. Not pure vegetarian.
Menu: Has a good selection of vegetarian dishes. Noodles & tofu dishes, Sweet & Sour Soup, eggplant dishes and Mixed Vegetable Curry.
Comments: The food can be quite spicy.
Other Info: Accepts AMEX, MC, VISA. Price: $$.
Directions: It is located in the center of Waipouli, seven miles north of Lihue.

Mango Mamas Café
4460 Hookui Street, Kilauea (North Shore)
808-828-1020
Hours: Monday to Saturday 7 am to 6 pm Closed Sunday.
Menu: Soups, salads, sandwiches, Hummus Sandwich, Tempeh Sandwich and Boca Burgers.

Norberto's El Café
4-1373 Kuhio Highway (Route 56), Kapaa
808-822-3362
Hours: Tuesday to Sunday 5 pm to 9 pm Closed Monday.
Mexican. Not pure vegetarian.
Menu: Burritos, Taro Enchilada and other Mexican dishes. Beans and rice are vegetarian. Has an eggplant dish.
Comments: Does not cook with animal fats.
Directions: Right in the middle of town.

Papaya's Natural Food Café
4-831 Kuhio Highway (Route 56), Kapaa (East Side); 808-823-0190
Hours: Monday to Saturday 9 am to 8 pm Closed Sunday.
Natural Food Store and Deli. Organic produce.
Menu: Main dishes and salads sold by the pound. Homemade breads, soups, sandwiches and salads.
Comments: It is the largest natural food store on Kanai Island. The deli is really good. Has hot dishes. Often uses organic produce in cooking.
Other Info: Counter service, take-out. Has tables outside.

Directions: This place is on the main Hwy coming through town. A mile south of the downtown. Kapaa is on the east shore, in the center part of the island.

Postcard Café
5-5075 Kuhio Highway, Hanalei, Kauai
808-826-1191; **Web site:** www.postcardscafe.com
Hours: Daily 8 am to 11 am, 6 pm to 9 pm
Natural Foods. International, Asian, Japanese, Mexican, Italian. Vegan friendly. Not pure vegetarian. Vegan dishes.
Menu: Has a wide variety of vegetarian dishes. Veggie burgers, Spring Rolls, soups, salads, Grilled Vegetables, quesadillas, enchiladas and other dishes. Fresh juices, cappuccino and espresso. Freshly made baked goods.
Comments: Local organic produce used when possible. Healthy food. Many of the dishes are vegan. Romantic. Patio has beautiful mountain views. Has old Kauai photographs that used to be in a now closed museum.
Other Info: Full service, take-out. Accepts AMEX, DC, MC, VISA. Price: $$-$$$.
Directions: This place is at the end of Rte 56 on the north shore of the island.

Sunshine Farmers' Market
808-245-3212.
It is held in a different place each day and you have to call for information.

Vim & Vigor
Rice Shopping Center, Lihue, Kauai
808-245-9053
Hours: Monday to Friday 8 am to 5 pm; Saturday 8 am to 2 pm; closed Sunday.
Natural Food Store.
Menu: Has ready-made sandwiches and salads.

Zababaz One World Café (Surf Café)
Ching Young Village, 5300 Ka Haku Road, Kuhio Highway, Hanalei (Route 56) (North Shore)
808-826-1999
Hours: Daily 7 am to 9 pm
Vegan-friendly International, Italian. Mainly vegan except the ice cream.
Menu: Salads, wraps, Tofu dishes, Stir-fry dishes, Mexican dishes, quesadillas, Falafel Plate and daily specials.
Comments: Good value.
Directions: This place is at the end of Rte 56 on the north shore of the island.

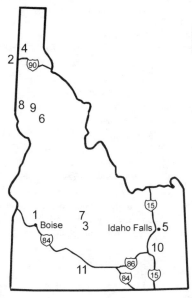

Idaho

1. Boise
2. Coeur D'Alene
3. Hailey
4. Hayden Lake
5. Idaho Falls
6. Kamiah
7. Ketchum
8. Moscow
9. Orofinio
10. Pocatello
11. Twin Falls

BOISE

Aladdin Traditional Egyptian
111 Broadway Street, Suite. 115
208-368-0880
Hours: 11 am to 3 pm, 5 pm to 11 pm; Friday 11 am to 11 pm; Sunday 5 pm to 10 pm
Egyptian and Middle Eastern cuisine. Not pure vegetarian.
Menu: Mah Shi (Stuffed vegetables in a tomato sauce), baba ghanouj, falafel and hummus. For dessert there is baklava.
Comments: Belly dancers perform Thursday to Saturday nights. Price: $$.
Other Info: Accepts AMEX, DIS, MC, VISA.

Boise Co-op
888 West Fort Street
208-342-6652; **fax:** 208-342-0587
email: info@boisecoop.com
Web site: http://www.users.qwest.net/~bccoop;
http://csf.colorado.edu/co-op/boise.html
Hours: Monday to Saturday 9 am to 9 pm
Sunday 9 am to 8 pm
Natural Food Store and Vegan-friendly Café. Deli and Bakery. Organic and local produce. Not pure vegetarian.
Comment: Has the best selection of organic produce in Boise. The café has 20 seats.
Directions: From I-84 east, take City Center exit

and go towards downtown. At Capital turn left, at 8th turn right. From I-84 west, take Broadway exit, go north on Broadway, at Fort St turn left (near hospital). This place on right one mile down.

Dong Khanh
Broadway 111 Shopping Center
111 Broadway Avenue, Suite 139
208-345-0980
Hours: Monday to Saturday 11 am to 3 pm, 4 pm to 10 pm
Closed Sunday.
Vietnamese. Not pure vegetarian.

Flying Pie
6508 Fairview Avenue
208 376-3454
4320 West State Street
208 345-8585
Hours: Daily 11 am to 10:30 am (until 11:30 pm Friday & Saturday)
Popular Pizza Place. Not pure vegetarian.
Other Info: Counter service, take-out, delivery. Has seating. Accepts AMEX, DIS, MC, VISA.

***Kulture Klatsch
409 South 8th Street, in the 8th Street Marketplace shopping center
208-345-0452
Hours: Monday 8 am to 3 pm; Tuesday to Thurs-

day 8 am to 10 pm; Friday & Saturday 8 am to 11 pm; Sunday 8 am to 3 pm
Vegetarian-friendly (at least 90% vegetarian). About half the menu is vegan. Excellent Juice Bar. Not pure vegetarian (Only serves deli Turkey meat on sandwiches). Nothing cooked is non-vegetarian.
Menu: Has an excellent selection of vegetarian dishes. Cran-Tempeh-Avocado Sandwich, sandwiches, veggie chili, Spuds, Pesto Pizza, veggie burgers, Wasabi Soba Noodles, Gnocchi and salads. Has some organic dishes for breakfast. Fresh juices, milkshakes and smoothies
Comments: Reasonable prices. Has art displayed by local artists on the walls. Has live music Monday to Saturday night and on Sunday afternoon. Has live plants hanging from the ceiling. Gets good recommendations. Used to be called Koffee Klatsch for 20 years. Coffeeshop type place.
Other Info: Non-smoking. Accepts DIS, MC, VISA. Price: $$.
Directions: In the downtown area of the 8th Street market district. From I-84 coming west into Boise, take Exit #54 (Rte 20/Broadway Ave/Rte 26) and go towards City Center, at S Broadway Ave turn right and go 3 miles. At E Front St turn left and go half a mile (becomes W Front St), then at 8th St turn left and this place is one block down.

Lucky 13 Pizza
1602 North 13th Street
208-344-6967
Hours: Friday to Saturday 11 am to 9 pm
Sunday to Thursday 11 am to 8 pm
Pizza Place. Not pure vegetarian.
Menu: Has several vegetarian pizzas including the "Zucchini Meanie."
Directions: In downtown Boise.

Mrs Beesley's Healthy Foods
10370 Overland Avenue
208-376-8484
Hours: Monday to Friday 9:30 am to 8 pm
Saturday 10 am to 6 pm
Natural Food Store and Deli. Juice Bar.
Menu: Veggie Sandwiches, a daily salad and a daily soup. A small place.
Other Info: Counter service, take-out. Has seating. Accepts MC, VISA.
Directions: From I-84 coming west into Boise, take Cole Rd (#50 A) exit and go towards Overland Rd, stay right at fork in the ramp. Merge onto S Cole Rd, and make a slight right onto W Overland Rd and this place is about 2 miles down.

Twin Dragon
2200 Fairview Avenue
208-344-2141
Hours: Monday to Saturday 11:30 am to 2 am
Sunday 11:30 am to 12 midnight
Chinese. Not pure vegetarian.
Menu: Has a decent selection of vegetarian dishes.

Yen Ching
305 North 9th Street   208-284-0384
7609 West Overland Road 120   208-378-5888
132 North Milwaukee Street   208-375-7557
Hours: Monday to Thursday 11 am to 9 pm; Friday & Saturday 12 noon to 10:30 pm; Sunday 12 noon to 8 pm
Chinese. Not pure vegetarian.
Comments: Can cook food really spicy hot.
Other Info: Accepts AMEX, MC, VISA.

COEUR D'ALENE

A Trip to Bountiful
1316 North 4th Street
208-676-9730
Hours: Monday to Saturday 9 am to 7 pm
Sunday 12 noon to 5 pm
Natural Food Store and Deli. Organic produce.
Menu: Has freshly made sandwiches, soups and salads. Fresh juices, smoothies, espresso.
Comments: Friendly staff.
Other Info: Accepts MC, VISA. Counter service, take-out. Has some seating.
Directions: From I-90, take 4th St (#13) exit and go south 8 blocks. At E Walnut Ave turn left and this place at corner.

HAILEY

Atkinson's
Alturas Plaza
208-788-2294
Hours: Daily 7:30 am to 9 pm
Natural Food Store and Café. Deli, Bakery and Juice Bar. Organic produce.
Other Info: Accepts AMEX, DIS, MC, VISA.
Directions: From Hwy 75, turn east onto Croy St and drive to Alturas Plaza.

HAYDEN LAKE

Flour Mill Natural Foods
88 West Commerce Drive
208-772-2911
Hours: Monday to Friday 9 am to 5:30 pm; Saturday 10 am to 5 pm; closed Sunday.

Natural Food Store.
Comments: Mills own flour.
Other Info: Accepts AMEX, MC, VISA.
Directions: From I-95, exit at Hwy 95, drive north about 6 miles to Hayden Lake. At Honeysuckle Ave turn right, then make a quick left onto Commerce and follow the road around to the right and this place is a half-mile down on the right.

IDAHO FALLS (north on I-15)

Wealth of Health
489 Park Avenue
208-523-7600
Hours: Monday to Friday 9 am to 6 pm; Saturday 9 am to 6:30 pm; closed Sunday.
Natural Food Store. No produce.
Directions: From I-15, take Bus US-20/Broadway (Exit #118) and go east on Broadway (Bus-20). After crossing the river take the first left onto Memorial Dr, and go 2 blocks. At B St turn right and go two blocks and this place is on right.

KETCHUM

Atkinson's
Giacobbi Square
208-726-5668
Hours: Daily 7:30 am to 9 pm
Regular Supermarket that has organic produce and other natural foods.
Directions: From Hwy 75, at 4th Ave turn east and go one block to Giacobbi Square.

MOSCOW

The Moscow Food Cooperative
221 East 3rd Street, Moscow
208-882-8537
Web site: www.moscowfoodcoop.com
Hours: Daily 9 am to 8 pm
Natural Food Store and Vegan friendly Deli. Juice Bar and Bakery. Not pure vegetarian. Has a good selection of organic produce.
Menu: Soups, salads, sandwiches, vegan muffins, baked breads and baked desserts. Saturday morning breakfasts have scrambled tofu and potatoes.
Comments: Friendly people. Has plenty of bulk items. Has very good whole-grain "Upper Crust Bakery," connected to this place. Seating for 30.
Directions: Near the University of Idaho and

downtown. From Rte 95, at Third St (Hwy 8) turn west and this place is a half-block down on the right.

OROFINIO

Clearwater Valley Natural Food
300 Michigan Avenue
208-476-4091
Hours: Monday to Friday 10 am to 5:30 pm
Saturday 10 am to 2 pm
Natural Food Store. No produce.
Directions: This place is in the Viesta View building. It is close to the post office, just across bridge. From Rte 12, go east on Rte 7 and it becomes Michigan Ave and this place is a mile down.

POCATELLO (junction of 1-15 and 1-86)

Oliver's Quality Restaurant
130 South 5th Street
208-234-0672
Hours: Monday to Saturday 6:30 am to 10 pm
Sunday 6:30 am to 9 pm
American. Not pure vegetarian.
Menu: Has a good selection of vegetarian dishes. Eggplant Parmigiana, veggie Lasagna, veggie Ravioli, Garden Burger Platter and several more dishes.
Comments: Uses organic grown potatoes. Friendly place.
Other Info: Full service, take-out. Accepts MC, VISA. Price: $-$$.

TWIN FALLS

The Health Food Place
Centennial Square
657 Blue Lakes Boulevard North
208-733-1411
Hours: Monday to Friday 9:30 am to 6:30 pm; Saturday 10 am to 5:30 pm; Sunday 12 noon to 4 pm
Natural Food Store. Organic produce sometimes in the summer.
Directions: From I-84, take Rte 93 Twin Falls/Wells, Nevada exit (#173). Stay right at fork in ramp and get on Rte 93 S to Twin Falls. Drive 5½ miles into Twin Falls crossing Snake River and road becomes Blue Lakes Blvd. This place on the right in Centennial Square.

Illinois

Chicago Area 1, 2, 3, 4, 6, 10, 12, 15, 16, 18, 19, 20, 22, 24, 25, 27, 29, 32, 36, 37

1. Arlington Heights
2. Aurora
3. Barrington
4. Berwyn
5. Bloomington
6. Buffalo Grove
7. Carbondale
8. Champaign
9. Chicago
10. Deerfield
11. De Kalb
12. Downers Grove
13. Edwardsville
14. Elgin
15. Elmhurst
16. Evanston
17. Geneva
18. Highland Park
19. Hinsdale
20. Matteson
21. Moline
22. Mount Prospect
23. Mount Vernon
24. Naperville
25. New Lenox

26. Normal
27. Oak Park
28. Peoria
29. River Forest
30. Rockford
31. Roscoe
32. Schaumburg
33. Springfield
34. Urbana
35. Vandalia
36. Westmont
37. Wheaton

ARLINGTON HEIGHTS (Chicago suburb)

**Chowpatti Vegetarian Restaurant

1035 South Arlington Heights Road (Chicago suburb); 847-640-9554

Hours: Tuesday to Thursday, Sunday 11:30 am to 3 pm, 5 pm to 9 pm; Friday to Saturday 11:30 am to 3 pm, 5 pm to 10 pm; closed Monday.

Fully Vegetarian North and South Indian. Also International vegetarian cuisine including: American, Italian, French, Mexican, Indian and Middle Eastern. Has many vegan dishes. Gourmet.

Menu: Has over 300 items on the menu. Menu is over 20 pages. Specializes in Indian cuisine. Has good "Indian Nachos." Vegan ice cream called a Softie. Has a large selection of fresh juices and teas. Non-alcoholic beer and wine.

Comments: Family owned and operated since 1982. Gourmet food. Very friendly and helpful. Food is freshly prepared so may take a while to prepare. Knowledgeable staff.

Other Info: Full service, take-out, catering. Non-smoking. Reservations recommended for groups of 5 or more. Accepts AMEX, DIS, MC, VISA.

Directions: Twenty minutes from O'Hare Airport and 5 to 10 minutes from Arlington Race Track. From I-90, take Arlington Hts Rd Exit, then go north on S Arlington Heights and this place is 1½ mile down.

Sweetgrass Market

1742 West Golf Road, Mt Prospect
847-956-1939

Hours: Monday to Friday 9 am to 9 pm; Saturday 9 am to 6 pm; Sunday 10 am to 5:30 pm

Natural Food Store. Organic produce.

AURORA (Chicago suburbs)

Fruitful Yield

902 North Lake Street; 630-897-3490; **Web site:** www.the-naturalway.com

Natural Food Store.

Fruitful Yield

4334 Fox Valley Center Drive #E, Aurora; 630-585-9200; **Web site:** www.the-naturalway.com

Hours: Monday to Friday 9:30 am to 8:30 pm; Saturday 10 am to 6 pm; Sunday 11 am to 5 pm

Natural Food Store.

BARRINGTON

Here's Health
704 South Northwest Highway; 847-381-4210
Hours: Mon to Thur 9 am to 8 pm; Fri 9 am to
6 pm; Sat 9:30 am to 6 pm; Sun 12 noon to 5 pm
Natural Food Store.

BERWYN (Chicago suburbs)

Fruitful Yield
7003 Cermak Road, Berwyn; 708-788-9103
Web site: www.the-naturalway.com
Hours: Monday to Friday 9 am to 8 pm; Satur-
day 9 am to 6 pm; Sunday 11 am to 5 pm
Natural Food Store.

BLOOMINGDALE (Chicago suburbs)

Fruitful Yield
154 South Bloomingdale Road; 630-894-2553
Web site: www.the-naturalway.com
Hours: Monday to Friday 9 am to 8 pm; Satur-
day 9 am to 6 pm; Sunday 11 am to 5 pm
Natural Food Store.

BLOOMINGTON
Illinois State University is here.

Common Ground Grocery
516 North Main Street; 309-829-2621
Hours: Monday to Saturday 9:30 am to 5:30 pm
Closed Sunday.
Natural Food Store. Organic produce.
Directions: From I-55, take the Market St/Hwy
150 exit and go east on Market St for 2 miles, at
Main St turn left and this place near the corner.

BUFFALO GROVE (Chicago suburbs)

Blue Sky Market
39 Hungtington Lane, actual in Wheeling (one
block in); 847-541-8118
Hours: Monday to Friday 9:30 am to 7 pm; Saturday 10 am to 7 pm; Sunday 11 am to 4 pm
Natural Food Store.

CARBONDALE

Neighborhood Co-op
104 East Jackson Street
618-529-3533; email: fmurphy7@juno.com;
Web site: http://www.neighborhoodco-op.com/
Hours: Monday to Friday 9 am to 8 pm; Saturday 9 am to 6 pm; Sunday 12 noon to 6 pm
Natural Food Store and carry-out Deli. Bakery.

Organic produce.
Other Info: Counter service, take-out. No seating, take-out only. Accepts AMEX, MC, VISA.
Directions: From Rte 13, going west into town,
at Washington St turn right (go north) and go 1
block, then at Jackson turn right and this place is
1 block down on the right.

CHAMPAIGN

Common Ground Food Co-op
610 East Springfield Avenue; 217-352-3347
Hours: Monday to Friday 3 pm to 8 pm; Saturday 11 am to 4 pm; Sunday 11 am to 7 pm
Natural Food Store. Organic produce. No deli.
Menu: Breads is baked twice a week. Breads are
both vegan and non-vegan. Have ready-made
dishes such as hummus, granola, desserts, tempeh and other things.
Comments: Friendly place. Volunteer-run co-op.
Sells locally grown produce.
Directions: From I-74, take Neil St exit (#182),
then go south on Neil St for 1½ mile, then at
US-45/US 150 turn left and this place is ¾ mile
down.

Fiesta Café
216 South First Street; 217-352-5902
Hours: Daily 11 am to 12 m
Mexican. Not pure vegetarian.
Menu: Has many vegetarian dishes. No lard in
the beans.
Other Info: Accepts AMEX, DC, DIS, MC,
VISA. Full service, take-out. Reservations not
accepted on weekends. Price: $-$$.
Directions: Parking arranged for customers.

Natural Gourmet
2215 South Neil Street, 217-355-6365
Hours: Monday to Saturday 9 am to 6 pm
Closed Sunday.
Natural Food Store.

CHICAGO
Arlington Heights, Downers Grove, Evanston,
Glen Ellyn, Highland Park, Oak Park, Palatine,
Rolling Meadows, Skokie, St Charles, Villa Park,
West Dundee and Westmont.

Addis Abeba
3521 North Clark Street, at Cornelia Avenue
312-929-9383
Hours: Monday to Thursday 5 pm to 10 pm; Fri
& Sat 5 pm to 11 pm; Sun 4 pm to 10 pm
Ethiopian, African Restaurant. Vegan options.
Not pure vegetarian.

Menu: Has a selection of traditional Ethiopian dishes. European-style Kinche is wheat pilaf with kibbeh. Gomen is spinach and onion. Has a vegetarian combo plate. Non-alcoholic beer.
Comments: Has African art on the walls and woven-basket tables. Good size portions. Good, pleasant, helpful service. Good place for a group.
Other Info: Full service, take-out. Accepts AMEX, DC, DIS, MC, VISA. Price: $$.
Directions: Located in the Lakeview district of Chicago, a few minutes walk from the L train Belmont or Addison stations (Red Line). Bus #22 to Cornelia Avenue or #152 to Clark Street.

Amitabul

3418 North Southport Avenue
773-472-4060
Hours: Daily 11 am to 9:30 pm
Korean. Macrobiotic options. Not pure veg.
Menu: Maki Rolls, soups, Vegan Tofu Young, noodles dishes, vegan pancakes, vegan egg rolls, Kimchee Du Be Do (vegetables and noodles in a broth), stews, Bok Choy (with walnuts, almonds, oriental vegetables), Sweet Potato Noodles with Mushrooms & Vegetables, Wheat Noodles with Plum Sauce. Oceans of Health dish is seaweed and vegetables. Wolfmans Dreamed Treats is vegetables, nuts and miso sauce. Tempeh Vegetable Stir-fry is good. Chef Dave's Super Surprise Special can be different every time. Fresh juices. Special drinks are Green Heaven and Awakening Energy. Has spicy miso and spicy sweet plum sauce in squeeze bottles.
Comments: Amitabul means "awakening" in Sanskrit. This restaurant gets high ratings. Food is creatively presented. Good size portions. Dave Special is whatever the owner and head chef choice to cook at the moment. Casual, friendly place. Reasonable prices. Food is often spicy and unique. The hot dishes are extremely hot, and the medium level is really hot for most people. Teaches cooking classes
Other Info: Full service, take-out. Non-smoking. Accepts AMEX, MC, VISA. Price: $-$$.
Directions: Located in the Lakeview district of Chicago, a few minutes walk from the L train (Belmont or Addison stations). From the Kennedy Exwy, take the Armitage Ave/2000 N exit (#48A), then go east on N Ashland Ave for 1½ mile, at Belmont Ave turn right and go a quarter-mile, at N Southport Ave turn left and this place is a quarter-mile down.

A Natural Harvest

7122 South Jeffrey Boulevard; 773-363-3939
Hours: Monday to Friday 10 am to 7 pm; Saturday 10 am to 6:30 pm; closed Sunday.
Natural Food Store.
Other Info: Accepts AMEX, DIS, MC, VISA.

Andie's Restaurant

5253 North Clark Street, Farragut Avenue, Andersonville;
773-784-8616
1467 West Montrose Avenue; 312-348-0654
Hours: Sunday to Thursday 11 am to 11 pm; Friday & Saturday 10 am to 12 midnight; Sunday 10 am to 3 pm
Mediterranean, Lebanese, Greek. Vegan options.
Menu: Has a good selection of vegetarian dishes. Falafel, several vegetarian pitas, pizza, moussaka, Stuffed Artichokes, hummus, couscous, Moroccan Eggplant and salad with yogurt sauce. Has a Vegetarian Combo Plate.
Comments: Popular, friendly place. Reasonable prices. Live jazz during the weekend brunch.
Other Info: Full service, take-out, catering, delivery. Reservations suggested on weekends. Accepts AMEX, DC, MC, VISA. Price: $-$$.
Directions: Bus #22 to Berwyn Avenue; #50 to Berwyn Avenue; #82 to Clark Street. Parking arranged for customers.

**Arya Bhavan

2508 West Devon Avenue
773-274-5800; **fax:** 773-262-4465
email: Aryabhavan@Aol.com
Web site: www.aryabhavan.com
Hours: Monday to Thursday 11:30 am to 10 pm
Friday to Sunday 11:30 am to 10:30 pm
Fully Vegetarian South & North Indian. Buffet.
Menu: Has a large selection of vegetarian dishes. Soups, samosas, Tandoori dishes, Vankai Koora, Mirch Bengan Ka Salam, Paneer Tikka Masala, Pakoda Korma, Shahi Paneer Korma, Paneer Bhurji, uttappams, dosas, parathas, Malai Kofta, Indian breads, Vegetable Pulao, Matar Paneer, Aloo Gobi and Palak Paneer. Gulabjamun, Shrikhand and a selection of ice creams. Mango lassi, Pista Shake and juices.
Comments: Friendly, helpful service. Has a lunch and weekend buffet. Has a dinner buffet with a good selection of dishes. Some people think that Woodlands is better
Other Info: Full service, take-out, catering. Accepts AMEX, DIS, MC, VISA. Price: $$.
Directions: In the middle of India town in north Chicago. From the Kennedy Expy, take the Fullerton Ave/2400 N exit (#47A) and take the Western Ave ramp, then go north on N Western Ave for 5 miles, then at W Devon Ave turn left and go 2 blocks.

Bonne Sante
1512 East 53rd Street; 773-667-5700
Hours: Monday to Friday 9:30 am to 7 pm; Saturday 9:30 am to 6 pm; Sunday 11 am to 5 pm
Natural Food Store. Juice Bar.
Other Info: Accepts AMEX, MC, VISA.

Bukhara
2 East Ontario Street, in north Chicago
312-943-0188
Hours: Daily 11:30 am to 2:30 pm, 5:30 pm to 9 pm
Indian. Lunch Buffet. Vegan options. Not pure vegetarian.
Menu: Rice dishes, dal, Indian breads and vegtable dishes.
Comments: Uses traditional Tandoor clay oven for cooking. Candlelight dinners. Reasonably priced for lunch and more expensive during dinner.
Other Info: Full service, take-out, catering. Reservations suggested on weekends. Accepts AMEX, DC, DIS, MC, VISA. Price: $-$$.

Café Selmarie
4729 North Lincoln Avenue; 773-989-5595
Hours: Tuesday to Thursday 8 am to 10 pm; Friday & Saturday 8 am to 11 pm; Sunday 10 am to 10 pm; closed Monday.
Café. Not pure vegetarian.
Menu: It is fairly vegetarian friendly. Soups, vegetarian chili, Penne Pasta, Spinach Pie, granola and pizza. Cappuccino, espresso.
Comments: Casual atmosphere. Has local artists' works (for sale) hanging on the walls. Has a nice outdoor dining area.
Other Info: Accepts MC, VISA. Price: $$. Full service, take-out.

**Café Voltaire
3441 N Halsted Street; 773-281-9320
Hours: Sunday to Thursday 11 am to 11 pm; Friday 5 pm to 1 am; Saturday 5 pm to 3 am
Vegetarian. Vegan-friendly.
Menu: Pastas, veggie burger, salads and some vegetarian soups. Fresh mango frappes. Fresh juices. Cappuccino, espresso. Non-alcoholic beer.
Comments: Hip, artsy place. Has shows downstairs in the performance theater with a rotating schedule of over 50 events. Upstairs art gallery. Mostly organic food. Local organic produce used. Small place.
Other Info: Full service, take-out, delivery. Accepts MC, VISA. Price: $$.
Directions: From Lake Shore Drive take the W Belmont Ave ramp and go west on W Belmont Ave for ¾ mile, then turn right and this place is a half-mile down, just past W Newport Ave. This place is a few miles north of downtown Chicago.

Charlie Trotter's
Wyndham Chicago Hotel; 816 West Armitage Avenue, at North Halsted Street, Old Town, Lincoln park area; 773-248-6228
Web site: www.charlietrotters.com
Hours: Tues to Thur 6 pm to 9:30 pm; Friday & Saturday 5:30 pm to 9:30 pm; closed Sat & Mon.
American, International, Eclectic Restaurant. Not pure vegetarian.
Menu: Has a separate section on the menu for vegetarian dishes. Has two tasting menus daily, one of them is vegetarian. Dishes can be made vegan by requesting such when you make your reservation.
Comments: One of the best restaurants in Chicago. Elegant. Must wear a jacket and tie. Famous Notable Chef: Charlie Trotter. In a renovated 1908 townhouse. Excellent dinning experience. Romantic. Elegant décor.
Other Info: Reservations required usually a few weeks in advance for weekdays and months in advance for weekends. Non-smoking. Accepts AMEX, DC, DIS, MC, VISA. Price: $$$$. Around $100 for a meal.
Directions: Between Armitage and Halsted in north Chicago. From Kennedy Exwy, take the North Ave/IL-64 exit (#48B), then go east on W North Ave for 1 mile, at N Halsted St turn left and go a half-mile, then at W Armitage Ave turn left and this place is 1 block down. Brown line El train to Armitage.

**Chicago Diner
3411 North Halsted; 773-935-6696
Hours: Monday to Friday 11 am to 10 pm
Saturday and Sunday 10 am to 10 pm
Fully Vegetarian Eclectic, International. Vegan Bakery. Mostly Vegan. Most dishes can be made vegan if requested. Macrobiotic options.
Menu: Has several pages of vegetarian dishes on their menu. Vegan soups, salads, sandwiches, Grilled Portobello Sandwich, Scrambled Tofu, Potato Hash, Tofu hot dogs, Lentil Loaf, Sloppy Joe's, tempeh burgers, tofu burgers, Cabbage Rolls with artichoke sauce, macrobiotic meals, pastas, Tofu Roulades, Paella and vegetarian chili. Breakfast menu with eggless French Toast, scrambled tofu and fakin bacon. Has a good selection of vegan desserts. Vegan Chocolate Cake. Tofu Chocolate Chip Cheesecake, vegan Carrot Cake, vegan German Chocolate Cake, and Lemon Coconut Cake. Fresh juices and smoothies. Non-alcoholic beer. Good soy shakes.

Comments: Non-vegan dishes are marked. No preservatives or artificial ingredients. Local organic produce used when possible. Owners active in the animal rights movement in the Midwest. Has outdoor patio dining. Has kid's menu. Food gets good rating. Good, friendly atmosphere. Relaxed, casual place. Regular cheese can be replaced with soy cheese.
Other Info: Full service, take-out, catering. Non-smoking. Accepts AMEX, DC, DIS, MC, VISA. Price: $$.
Directions: From Lake Shore Drive, take the W Belmont Ave ramp and go west on W Belmont Ave for ¾ mile, then turn right and this place is a half-mile down. This place is a few miles north of downtown Chicago. Free parking evenings after 6 pm (in adjacent alley) and all day on Saturday and Sunday. Street parking on weekdays. Near the Addison station. El Train to Belmont. Bus #36.

Clark Street Bistro
2600 North Clark Street, at corner of Wrightwood Avenue; 773-525-9992
Hours: Monday to Thursday 4:30 pm to 10 pm; Friday 12 noon to 11 pm; Saturday 4 pm to 11 pm; Sunday 10 am to 10 pm
Mediterranean, French. Vegan options. Not pure vegetarian.
Menu: Salad Penache is good. Pastas, pizzas and salads.
Comments: Owned by people from Morocco. Has outdoor dining. Sidewalk café. Romantic place. Candlelit and white tablecloths. Good service.
Other Info: Reservations highly suggested on weekends. Non-smoking. Accepts AMEX, DC, DIS, MC, VISA. Price: $$.
Directions: Bus #76 to Broadway St/Clark St; #22, #36 to Wrightwood Avenue. Parking at 2515 N Clark Street for free. In Lincoln Park area.

Earwax Café
1564 West Milwaukee Avenue; 773-772-4019
Hours: Monday to Friday 8 am to 12 midnight Saturday & Sunday 10 am to 12 midnight
Eclectic International. Mainly Vegetarian. Vegan options. Not pure vegetarian.
Menu: Mostly vegetarian menu. For breakfast there is granola, oatmeal, bagels and yogurt. For lunch there is falafel sandwiches, Spinach Pie, veggie burgers, a selection of salads, vegetable burritos, tempeh burgers, sun-dried tomato pesto, quesadillas and a daily specials. Chocolate-coconut shake. Cappuccino, espresso and an unlimited cup of coffee for $1.90. Non-alcoholic beer

and wine.
Comments: Friendly, funky place. Has Eastern European circus motif. Friendly, slow service.
Other Info: Full service, take-out. Accepts MC, VISA. Price: $-$$.
Directions: From Kennedy Exwy, take the Division St/1200 North exit (#49A), then go west on W Division St a third-mile, then take a slight right onto N Milwaukee Ave and this place is ¾ mile down.

Far Eastern Barbecue
3418 North Southport Street, at Roscoe, Chinatown; 773-472-4060
Hours: Daily 11:30 am to 9:30 pm
Korean. Vegan and Vegetarian-friendly.
Comments: At the former location of Amitabul (which has moved) and is run by the same family. Friendly people.
Other Info: Accepts AMEX, DC, DIS, MC, VISA. Non-smoking. Price: $.
Directions: El Brown Line to Southport.

Feast
1616 North Damen; 773-772-7100
Hours: Monday to Friday for lunch and dinner 11:30 am to 3 pm, 5:30 pm to 10 pm
Multi-ethnic. Not pure vegetarian.
Menu: Soups, veggie burger, Black Bean Ravioli, salads, burritos, Black Bean Soup, pastas and Pumpkin Ravioli.
Other Info: Accepts AMEX, MC, VISA. Price: $$$.

Foodlife
Water Tower Place (mezzanine level), 835 North Michigan Avenue, in north Chicago
312-335-3663
Hours: Monday to Thursday 11 am to 9 pm; Friday & Saturday 11 am to 10 pm; Sunday 11 am to 9 pm
International. There are several counters here in an upscale food court. This place has 10 different kitchen areas. Juice Bar. Vegan options. Not pure vegetarian.
Menu: Has Tuscan Veggies, Portobello Mushrooms, Stir-Fry Heaven, Mediterranean dishes and soy burgers. Fresh juices, cappuccino, espresso.
Comments: Unique place.
Other Info: Accepts AMEX, DIS, MC, VISA. Price: $-$$.

Gaylord India Restaurant
678 North Clark Street; 312-664-1700
Hours: Monday to Friday 11:30 am to 2:30 pm,

5:30 pm to 10 pm; Saturday & Sunday 12 noon to 3 pm, 5:30 pm to 10 pm
Indian. Lunch Buffet is $8.99. Vegan options. Not pure vegetarian.
Menu: Has a wide selection of vegetarian dishes. Saag Panir, Saffron Rice, puris, Indian breads and curry dishes.
Comments: Reasonable prices. Tuxedoes waiters. Food can be quite spicy hot, so you may want to ask for them to cool it down. May add gratuity charge with bill, so you may want to check it before tipping.
Other Info: Full service, take-out, delivery. Accepts AMEX, DC, MC, VISA. Price: $$-$$$.
Directions: Near the Rainforest Café and Hard Rock Café, north of the downtown (Clark Street) and the Chicago River, to the west of the Magnificent Mile. Red Line El train to Grand. Bus #22. Corner of Clark and Huron.

Heartland Café
7000 North Glenwood Avenue; 773-465-8005
Web site: www.heartland-café.com
Hours: Monday to Friday 7 am to 10 pm
Saturday and Sunday 8 am to 12 midnight
American, International and Mexican. Health (Natural) Foods. Vegan options. Not pure vegetarian.
Menu: Soups, salads, sandwiches, main dishes, granola, scrambled tofu, cornbreads and vegetarian specials. Fresh juices, flavored iced tea.
Comments: Comfortable, laid-back place. Wholesome foods. Has outdoor terrace dining. Live music and dancing on the weekends (Thursday to Sunday). Connected to general gift shop that has holistic magazines and merchandise. Has spider plants and wood beams.
Other Info: Full service, take-out. Accepts AMEX, MC, VISA. Price: $-$$.
Directions: Located in Rodgers Park, near Loyola University. At the north end of Chicago about 6 miles north of the downtown, a few blocks from the lake. From Lake Shore Dr, take Bryn Mawr Ave/US 14 ramp, then go north on N Sheridan Rd for 2 miles, then at Lunt Ave turn left and this place is 2 blocks down. Close to the Morse train stop. Red Line train to Morse.

Here's Health
22 West Maple, Chicago; 312-397-1501
Hours: Monday to Friday 7:30 am to 7:30 pm (closes 6:30 pm Friday); Saturday 8 am to 5:30 pm; Sunday 10 am to 5:30 pm
Natural Food Store and Deli. Juice Bar. Organic produce.
Menu: Sandwiches, soups, veggie chili, mock

chicken and salad dishes.
Other Info: Counter service, take-out. Has seating. Accepts DIS, MC, VISA.
Directions: From Kennedy Exwy, take the East Ohio St exit (#50B), then go 1½ mile east on W Chicago Ave, at N L La Salle Blvd turn left and go 0.65 mile, at W Maple St turn right and this place is 2 blocks down.

Hyde Park Coop and Café
1526 East 55th Street, at Lake Park Avenue
773-667-1444; **Web site:** www.hpcoop.org/hpcoop/, http://www.igc.org/hpcoop/
Hours: Daily 7 am to 11 pm
Natural Food Store and Café. Bakery and Coffee Bar. Organic produce.
Menu: Soups, salads, sandwiches, Spinach Pies and veggie pizza.
Comments: The Museum of Science and Industry is a little down the road.
Directions: This place is in the South side of Chicago. From Lakeshore Dr, take 53rd St exit and go 4 blocks west. At Lake Park Ave, turn left (go south) and this place is 3 blocks down in Hyde Park Shopping Center, at corner of 55th and Lake Park Ave.

Irazu
1865 North Milwaukee Avenue, at Moffat Street
773-252-5687
Hours: Monday to Saturday 10 am to 9 pm
Closed Sunday.
Costa Rican. Not pure vegetarian.
Menu: Good veggie burrito. Black Bean & Avocado Burrito. Tortillas, Gallo Pinto with white rice and Black Beans & Plantains. Fruit shakes and milkshakes.
Comments: Has outdoors patio dining. Has a wall mural of a village house. Popular for take-out. Gets good recommendations. Voted to have some of the best vegetarian food in the city.
Other Info: Non-smoking. Cash only.
Directions: Blue Line to El train to Damen. Bus #50 to Cortland Street; #73 to Damen Avenue.

It's Natural
324 North Michigan Avenue; 312-269-0618
Vitamin Store and Juice Bar.
Menu: Has some pre-made sandwiches in their cooler.

Jamba Juice
2800 North Clark Street; 773-755-8472
Hours: Monday to Friday 7 am to 9 pm; Saturday 8 am to 9 pm; Sunday 8 am to 8 pm
Juice Bar. Not pure vegetarian.

Menu: Has 16 types of smoothies. Uses real fruits and has supplements such as ginseng and bee pollen. Breads, veggie chili and vegetarian soups.
Comments: Friendly place. Counter service, take-out.
Directions: Lakeview, Wrigley area. From downtown go north about 5 miles on Lake Shore Dr (becomes US 41), take Fullerton Pkwy ramp and go 1 block west on Fullerton, at N Cannon Dr turn right and go a half-mile, then take a slight left at Diversey Pkwy and this place is a third-mile (4 blocks) down at Clark Street.

Jane's

1655 West Cortland Street; 773-862-5263
Hours: Monday to Friday 5 pm to 10 pm
Saturday & Sunday 11 am to 2:30 pm, 5 pm to 10 pm
American. Vegetarian-friendly. Not pure veg.
Menu: Artichoke-stuffed Spinach Ravioli, burritos with tofu or goat cheese, Garden Burger, salads and other dishes. Cappuccino, espresso.
Comments: Has outdoor dining. Has flowers on table.
Other Info: Reservations suggested. Accepts MC, VISA.
Directions: El train 8 to Corland Street. Bus #73 to Paulina Street.

John's Place

1202 West Webster Avenue, in the Lincoln Park area; 773-525-6670
Hours: Tuesday to Thursday 11 am to 10 pm; Friday 11 am to 11 pm; Saturday 8 am to 11 pm; Sunday 8 am to 9 pm; Saturday and Sunday Brunch; closed Monday.
American, International, Eclectic. Vegetarian friendly.
Menu: Veggie burrito, tofu dishes, hummus, quesadillas, Noodles, Vegetarian Chili and other vegetarian dishes. Fresh juices, cappuccino, espresso.
Comments: Uses organic produce when possible. Has a fireplace. Popular place.
Other Info: Full service, take-out. Accepts AMEX, DC, DIS, MC, VISA. Price: $$.

***Karyn's Fresh Corner

3351 North Lincoln Avenue, in Lakeview area
773-296-6990; **fax:** 773-296-0583
Hours: Daily 11:30 am to 9 pm
Fully Vegan Gourmet Raw Cuisine. All-you-can-eat Salad Bar. Juice Bar.
Menu: Raw Carob Cake, uncooked raw pizzas, Broccoli Soup, sushi, Energy Soup, Seaweed Salad, Karyn's Cashew Supreme and other dishes. Raw Apple Pie made with tofu.

Comments: Special Herbal Elixirs made with fresh special herbs. Has an Oxygen Bar, where you can get shots of pure oxygen. Friend said it was the best salad ever had. I though the food was a bit unusual. $12.95 for all-you-can-eat or $5.99 a pound for salad bar.
Other Info: Full service, counter-service, take-out, catering. Non-smoking. Accepts AMEX, DC, DIS, MC, VISA and personal cheques.
Directions: Lake Shore Drive to Belmont Exit, then go west on Belmont Ave, then at Lincoln turn right and this place is 3 blocks down. From Kennedy Exwy, take Armitage Ave/2000 N exit (#48A), go west 1¼ mile on N Ashland, at Nelson St turn right and go 1 block, at N Greenview Ave turn left and go 1 block, at N Lincoln Ave turn slight left and this place is a third-mile down.

Kopi, A Traveler's Café

5317 North Clark Street; 773-989-KOPI (5674)
Hours: Monday to Thursday 8 am to 11 pm; Friday 8 am to 12 noon; Saturday 8 am to 12 midnight; Sunday 10 am to 11 pm
International Café. Full Espresso Bar. Mainly vegetarian place. Vegan options. Not pure veg.
Menu: Salads, hummus pita, tortilla chips and sandwiches. Fresh juices, cappuccino, espresso and special teas.
Comments: Has various clocks showing the different time zones around the world. Has an area where you sit on the floor on pillows with low tables, and you take off your shoes. Has masks on one of the walls. Kopi means "coffee" in Indonesian. Has a bookshelf with literature about international destinations. Has an international shop with clothing, jewelry, books and arts & crafts from around the world.
Other Info: Accepts MC, VISA. Price: $-$$.

Life Spring Health Food & Juice Bar

3178 North Clark; 773 327-1023
1463 West Webster Avenue; 773-832-0000
Web site: www.mylifespring.com
Hours: Monday to Friday 9:30 am to 7:30 pm; Saturday 9:30 am to 6 pm; Sunday 12 noon to 5 pm
Natural Food Store.

Lo-Cal Zone

912 North Rush Street; 312-943-9060
Hours: Monday to Saturday 11 am to 8 pm
Sunday 11 am to 5 pm
Natural Foods. Vegan options.
Menu: This place is mainly vegetarian. Tofu Burgers, BBZ Lo-calzone with tofu, hummus burrito and veggie burgers. Smoothies, cappuccino,

espresso.
Other Info: Limited service, take-out. No credit cards. Price: $.
Directions: This place is in north Chicago. From Kennedy Exwy, take the East Ohio St exit (#50B), then go 1½ mile east on W Chicago Ave, at N Rush St turn left and this place is 3 blocks down.

Local Grind

1585 North Milwaukee Avenue, at North Avenue
773-489-3490; **Web site:** www.localgrind.com
Hours: Monday to Thursday 6 am to 1 am; Friday 6 am to 3 am; Saturday 7 am to 3 am
Sunday 7 am to 12 midnight.
American Coffeeshop. All-you-can-eat Sunday Brunch Buffet. Not pure vegetarian.
Menu: Has a good selection of vegetarian dishes. Veggie Pita Pizza, fried potatoes, Thai Cucumber Salad with peanuts, Hummus Plate, Potato Pancakes and smoothies.
Comments: Friendly, comfortable place. Popular for Sunday brunch. Has couches and easy chairs.
Other Info: Smoking at bar after 4 pm. Accepts AMEX, DC, DIS, MC, VISA. Price: $.

Mama Desta's Red Sea

3216 North Clark Street, at Belmont
773-935-7561
Hours: Monday to Friday 4 pm to 10:30 pm
Saturday & Sunday 4 pm to 12 midnight
Ethiopian. Not pure vegetarian.
Menu: Has many vegetarian dishes. Lentil and spinach sandwich.
Comments: Has an African décor with African paintings, crafts, and bamboo & reed-covered walls. Reasonable prices. Food gets good ratings. Pleasant, cool atmosphere. Service is often slow.
Other Info: Full service, take-out. Accepts AMEX, DC, MC, VISA.
Directions: Can be gotten to from the Addison or Belmont L train stations. Near the corner of Belmont and Clark.

Moti Mahal

1031 West Belmont Avenue, at Kenmore
773-348-4392
Hours: Monday to Thursday 12 noon to 9:30 pm; Friday & Saturday 12 noon to 10:30 pm; Sunday 12 noon to 9:30 pm
Lunch Buffet Hours: Daily 12 noon to 3:30 pm
Indian. Lunch Buffet. Not pure vegetarian.
Menu: Has a selection of vegetarian dishes. Aloo Mattar, Saag Paneer, rice dishes and much more
Comments: The lunch buffet is popular.

Other Info: Full service, take-out, catering. Accepts AMEX, DIS, MC, VISA. Price: $.
Directions: Near Kenmore train stop. In the Indian area.

Mr G Co-op

Kimbark Plaza; 1226 East 53rd Street; 773-363-2175; **Web site:** http://www.hpcoop.org/hpcoop/pages/mrgcoop.html
Hours: Daily 7 am to 11 pm
Natural Food Store and Deli.
Menu: Has a limited menu with only salads and spinach pies.
Directions: From I-94, take 55th St exit and go east. At Woodlawn turn left and go two blocks and drive into Kimbark Plaza, where this place is located.

**Mysore Woodlands

2548 West Devon Avenue
773-338-8160
Hours: Daily 11:30 am-3:30 pm, 5 pm-9:30 pm
Fully Vegetarian South Indian. Kosher. Lunch Buffet. Vegan friendly.
Menu: Dosa, Idly and Mysore Coffee (authentic south Indian-style brewed coffee). Rava Dosa and Medhu Vada are good. The lunch buffet has over 20 dishes.
Comments: Recommended. Really good South Indian food. Popular place and there is often a half hour waiting time on weekends.
Other Info: Full service, take-out. Non-smoking. Reservation recommended. Accepts AMEX, DIS, MC, VISA. Price: $$.
Directions: This place is in north Chicago. From I-90W, take Nagel Ave pass Milwaukee Ave. From I-94E, take Peterson Ave, then turn left on California Ave, then turn right on Devon Avenue. From Kennedy Exwy, take Fullerton Ave/2400 N (#47A), then go north on N Western Ave for 5 miles, then turn left at W Devon Ave and this place is 2 blocks down.

The Mitchell's Original Restaurant

101 West North Avenue   312-642-5246
1953 North Clybourn Avenue   773-883-1157
Hours: Sunday to Thursday 6 am to 1 am
Friday & Saturday 24 hours
Natural Foods Restaurant. Not pure vegetarian.
Menu: Vegetarian sausages, homemade muffins, Oatmeal Walnut Burgers, veggie chili and daily vegetarian specials. Fresh juices.
Comments: Known for good breakfasts.
Other Info: Accepts DC, MC, VISA. Full service, take-out. Price: $.

Nature's Way Health Store
8504 South Stony Island Avenue; 773-721-6611
Hours: Monday to Saturday 9:30 am to 7:30
Closed Sunday.
Natural Food Store.

Pattie's Heart-Healthy
700 North Michigan Avenue; 312-751-7777
Hours: Daily
Sandwich Place. Not pure vegetarian.
Menu: Has sandwiches, soups, pizzas, muffins,
vegetarian focaccia sandwiches, calzones and
sweets. Fresh juices, cappuccino, espresso. Has a
breakfast menu.
Other Info: Counter service, take-out. No credit
cards.
Directions: Located at The Magnificent Mile on
North Michigan Avenue, a little north of the
Chicago River.

Pegasus Restaurant
130 South Halsted Street, at West Adams Street,
West Side Greektown; 312-226-3377
Web site: www.pegasuschicago.com
Hours: Monday to Thursday 11 am to 12 midnight; Friday 11 am to 1 pm; Saturday 12 noon
to 1 am; Sunday 12 noon to 12 midnight
Middle Eastern, Greek. Not pure vegetarian.
Menu: Has a good selection of vegetarian and
vegan dishes.
Comments: Nice atmosphere. Live music on the
rooftop patio during the summer. Has an excellent view of the city's skyline. Good service. Au-
thentic Greek. Nice experience.
Other Info: Full service. Reservations recommended on the weekends. Accepts AMEX, DC,
DIS, MC, VISA. Price: $$.
Directions: West of The Loop, on the other side
of the South Branch of the Chicago River.

Planet Smoothie
852 West Belmont Avenue; 773-929-3850
Hours: Monday to Thursday 7 am to 9 pm; Fri-
day 7 am to 10 pm; Saturday 9 am to 10 pm;
Sunday 10 am to 9 pm
Smoothie Place. Not pure vegetarian.
Menu: Smoothies, soups and sandwiches.
Other Info: Accepts AMEX, DIS, MC, VISA.

Reza's Restaurant
432 West Ontario   312-664-4500
5255 North Clark   773-561-1898
Hours: Monday to Saturday 10 am to 12 am
Closed Sunday.
Middle Eastern and Persian. Vegan options.

Menu: Has over 20 vegetarian dishes on the
menu. Roasted Zucchini, falafel, bean soup, Egg-
plant Steak, hummus and a Vegetarian Platter.
Has several vegetarian combination lunches.
Comments: Good food and service. Elegant
1920's décor. Has a DJ playing music. Roman-
tic. Good place for a special event. Has outdoor
seating. Has valet parking. Can be hard to find
parking.
Other Info: Reservations required. Valet parking.
Accepts AMEX, DC, DIS, MC, VISA. Full ser-
vice, take-out, catering, delivery. Price: $-$$.

Rose Angelis
1314 West Wrightwood Avenue, at Lakewood
Avenue; 773-296-0081
Hours: Tuesday to Thursday 5 pm to 10 pm;
Friday & Saturday 5 pm to 11 pm; Sunday 4:30
pm to 9 pm; closed Monday.
Vegetarian-friendly Italian. Not pure vegetarian
(no red meat).
Menu: Has a good selection of vegetarian dishes.
Lasagna, pasta and salads.
Comments: Friendly service. Casual place. The
wait can be quite long on weekend nights. Good
food and service. Has good outdoor seating area.
Other Info: Accepts DIS, MC, VISA.

Russian Tea Time
77 East Adams Street, between Michigan &
Walbash, Downtown Loop neighborhood
312-360-0000
Web site: www.russianteatime.com
Hours: Sunday & Monday 11 am to 9 pm; Friday & Saturday 11 am to 12 midnight
Russian. Also has Polish and American. Vegan
options. Not pure vegetarian.
Menu: Good selection of vegetarian and vegan
dishes. Vegetarian and vegan items are marked
on the menu. Potato Pancakes, Spinach Salad,
Baked Eggplant stuffed with Sautéed Vegetables,
Vegetable & Mung Stew, Stuffed Green Bell Pep-
pers, Carrot Salad (very good) and Grilled Portobello Mushrooms. Cappuccino, espresso.
Comments: Very fast, excellent service. Russian
folk songs on speakers. Pleasant, fun, elegant,
upscale place. European décor. Seating for 110.
Romantic. Good place for a special event. Has
got some excellent reviews by the media.
Other Info: Full service, take-out, catering, delivery. Reservations recommended. Accepts
AMEX, DC, DIS, MC, VISA. Price: $$-$$$.
Directions: Near Chicago Symphony Orchestra
and Art Institute. Within The Loop. CTA trains
to Adams/Wabash. Parking arranged.

Sherwyn's
645 West Diversey Parkway, at North Clark Street
773-477-1934
Hours: Monday to Friday 9 am to 8 pm; Saturday 9 am to 6 pm; Sunday 11 am to 7 pm
Natural Food Store and Deli. Organic produce
Menu: Has salads and sandwiches.
Comments: Has an outlet store that sells overstock & discontinued products. Have large amounts of vitamins and herbs. Also sells appliances. Has a certified herbologists and a herb pharmacy.
Other Info: Accepts DIS, MC, VISA.
Directions: In Lincoln Park in Lakeview area. From I-90/94 (be in local lanes), take California exit (#46A), and go east on Diversey 3 miles to junction of Diversey, Clark and Broadway, where this place is located. From Kennedy Exwy, take Armitage Ave (#48A), then go on N Ashland Ave a half-mile, at W Fullerton turn right and go a half-mile, at N Racine Ave turn left and go a half-mile, at Diversey Pkwy turn right and this place is ¾ mile down. Brown Line El stop to Diversey. Bus line #22, #36, #76. CTA train to Diversey.

***Soul Vegetarian East
205 East 75th Street, at Indiana Avenue
773-224-0104; **Web site:** http:/www.kingdomofyah.com/SV.htm
Hours: Monday to Thursday 11 am to 10 pm; Friday 11 am to 11 pm; Saturday 9 am to 11 pm; Sunday 9 am to 9 pm
Fully Vegan African and International. Middle Eastern, Italian, Greek, South American and American. All food is completely vegan and 100% natural. They use some honey
Menu: BBQ Roast made from wheat gluten, Vegetarian Ribs, soups, salads, Sunflower-seed Burger, Chickenless Noodle Soup, Gyros, BBQ Roast, lentil soup, Gravy Burger, Spaghetti & Tofu, Greens and Cornbread, Chicken-less Noodle Soup, Veggie Gyro, Tofu Fish, and BBQ Twist Sandwich. Barbeque sauce. Homemade dairy-free soft-serve ice cream.
Comments: Food gets high ratings from most people, but everyone may not like this place. Friendly, helpful service. Casual place. Good people. Popular place, so may be hard to get a table on weekend nights. Has small vegan grocery store next door.
Other Info: Full service, take-out, catering. Non-smoking. Accepts AMEX, MC, VISA.
Directions: This place is in south Chicago, about 5 miles south of the downtown. From Dan Ryan Expressway, take the 75th Street exit (#60), then go east on 75th St for 3 blocks and this place is at the corner of Indiana Avenue. Bus #3 to 75th Street, #75 to Prairie Avenue.

Smooth: A Juice Bar
6 West Ohio Street, at State Street; 312-440-0100
Hours: Monday to Saturday 8 am to 6 pm Closed Sunday.
Juice Bar. Not pure vegetarian.
Menu: 20 types of smoothies. Skin milk, vanilla yogurt, granola, blueberries, bananas and supplements such as Echinacea and ginseng. Fresh juices. Soups, salads and sandwiches.
Comments: Good place to hangout. Has comfortable couches.
Other Info: Non-smoking. Accepts MC, VISA.
Directions: In River North area. Red line El train to Grand. On the south side of the State Street Embassy Suites hotel.

Star of Siam
11 East Illinois Street
at North State Street, in north Chicago
312-670-0100
Hours: Sunday to Thursday 11 am to 9:30 pm Friday & Saturday 11 am to 10:30 pm
Thai. Vegan options. Not pure vegetarian.
Menu: Most dishes can be made without meat. Can add tofu to dishes instead. Thai ice coffee.
Comments: Reasonably priced. It is very popular and sometimes there is a wait for a table. Friendly, attentive service.
Other Info: Full service, take-out, delivery. Accepts AMEX, DC, DIS, MC, VISA. Price: $.
Directions: Near North/ Magnificent Mile. CTA train to Grand. Red Line El train to Grand.

Stone Soup Cooperative
4637 North Ashland; 773-561-5131
Natural Food Store.

**Udupi Palace
2543 West Devon Avenue, at Western Avenue, Rodgers Park area; 773-338-2152; **fax:** 773-338-2155; **Web site:** http://www.udupipalace.com/
Hours: Daily 12 noon to 9:30 pm
Fully Vegetarian South Indian. Mainly vegan.
Menu: South Indian Royal Thali, Madras Lunch, idly, Rava Masala Dosa, Sambar, breads, rice dishes, samosas, vegetable curries, Panir Pakoras, Palak Panir, batura (puffed up fried breads), soups and main dishes. Dinner Specials. Badam halava is a sweet made of ground almonds, butter and honey. Rose ice cream. Fresh juices, mango lassi. No alcohol.

Comments: Good service. Very good food. Gets high ratings from people. Good size portions. Popular, so may have to wait on Friday and Saturday night for a table. Has menu on their web site. Popular place.
Other Info: Full service, take-out, catering, delivery. Non-smoking. Reservations recommended, especially on weekend nights. Accepts AMEX, DIS, MC, VISA. Price: $-$$.
Direction: This place is in north Chicago. From downtown Chicago take Lakeshore Dr going north, then take Sheridan Rd north for 1 mile, then turn left at Devon Ave and this place is 1½ mile down. Bus #49 to Devon Avenue or #155 to Campbell Avenue.

Uncommon Ground

1214 West Grace Street, at Clark Street.
773-929-3680
Hours: Saturday to Wednesday 9 am to 11 pm
Thursday & Friday 9 am to 12 midnight
Coffeehouse. Not pure vegetarian.
Menu: Salads and sandwiches. For breakfast has homemade granola, organic vanilla yogurt and fresh fruit. Has a variety of premium coffee.
Comments: Comfortable happening place. Outdoors dining area. Has live entertainment on Tuesdays, Wednesdays and on the weekend. Hardwood floors. Recycled art on the walls. Friendly staff.
Other Info: Accepts AMEX, DC, DIS, MC, VISA. Price: $-$$.
Directions: Red Line El train to Sheridan. Bus #22 to Grace Street.

***Vegetarian Express Gourmet

3031 West 111th Street, at Whipple
773-238-2599
Hours: Tuesday to Saturday 12 am to 9 pm; Sunday 12 noon to 8 pm; closed Monday.
Vegan. Vegetarian Weekend Buffet
Menu: Jerk Tofu, Steak Wrap (made from seitan is recommended), sandwiches, fresh salads, cornbread, steamed greens, pastas, Raw Plate and a daily special. They have a great salad dressing called the Prince.
Comments: Has an excellent vegetarian weekend buffet.
Other Info: Full service, take-out. Non-smoking. Reservations not necessary. Accepts AMEX, MC, VISA. Price: $-$$.
Directions: From I-57, take exit #355 towards Monterey Ave, then take 112th Place west (becomes W Monterey Ave) for a half-mile, W Monterey becomes 111th St and keep going 1¼

miles, then at S Whipple St turn left and this place is at the corner.

***Vegetarian Fun Foods Supreme

1702 East 87th Street
773-734-6321
Hours: Monday to Saturday 10 am to 9 pm
Closed Sunday and holidays.
Vegan Fast Food. Natural Foods.
Menu: Sandwiches, salads, and whole-wheat crust pizza with soy meats.
Other Info: Counter service, take-out. Accepts AMEX, MC, VISA. Price: $$.
Directions: A block east of Stoney Island. This place is in south Chicago, about 5 miles south of downtown Chicago. From I-57N, take the I-94E/Bishop Ford Freeway towards Indiana, merge onto Bishop Ford Exwy going east for 1 mile, then take Stony Island Ave exit (#65), keep left at fork on ramp and merge onto S Stony Island Ave and go 1 mile north, at E 87th St turn right and go a quarter-mile, at S Cregier Ave turn left and go 1 block, at E 86th Place turn left and go 1 block, then at S East End Ave turn left and this place is 1 block down.

**Victory's Banner

2100 West Roscoe
773-665-0227
Hours: Wednesday to Monday 8 am to 3 pm
Closed Tuesday
Vegetarian. Vegan-friendly.
Menu: Erin's Eggless Wonder is a tofu scramble (contains goat cheese). Soups, salads, sandwiches, Spinach Salad (tell them no eggs), Bliss Burger, brown rice, mashed potatoes with gravy, Grilled Potatoes and multi-grain bread.
Comments: Good, peaceful atmosphere.
Other Info: Full service, take-out. Accepts AMEX, MC, VISA.
Directions: This place is in north Chicago. From Kennedy Exwy, take Damen Ave/2000 W exit (#47B), then go north on N Damen Ave for 1½ mile, at Roscoe St turn left and this place is 2 blocks down.

Whole Food Market and Quixotic Café

1000 West North Avenue, Lincoln Park area
312-587-0648; **fax:** 312-587-0606
Hours: Daily 8 am to 10 pm.
Natural Food Store and Cafe. Deli, Bakery, Salad Bar and Juice Bar. Organic produce.
Menu: Had a wide selection of vegetarian dishes. Quesadillas, Tofu Salad, Artichoke Pesto Pizza and other dishes. Has a large selection of fresh juices

and smoothies. Cappuccino, espresso.
Comments: Has a restaurant upstairs with seats.
Directions: From Kennedy Exwy, take North Ave exit (#48B), then go east on North Ave and this place is a half-mile down at corner of Sheffield and North (turn left at Sheffield). This place is north of I-290. There is also a North Ave exit off I-55.

Whole Food Market
3300 North Ashland, Lakeview
773-244-4200; **fax:** 773-244-4074
Hours: Daily 8 am to 10 pm
Natural Food Store and Cafe. Deli, Bakery, Salad Bar and Juice Bar. Organic produce. Supermarket-type place. See Whole Foods Market information.
Directions: From Lakeshore Drive, exit at Belmont (also 3200 North), then go west one mile, then at Ashland (at a 6 way intersection) turn right and this place on west side of road 2 block down. From Kennedy Exwy, take Armitage Ave exit #48, then go north on Ashland Ave for 1½ mile, then turn left at W School Rd and this place is at the corner. At Ashland turn right and this place is 3 blocks down on west side of road.

Whole Foods Market
30 West Huron Street, Gold Coast
312-932-9600; **fax:** 312-932-9700
Hours: Daily 8 am to 10 pm
Natural Food Store and Cafe. Deli, Bakery, Salad Bar and Juice Bar. Organic produce. Supermarket-type place. See Whole Foods Market.
Other Info: Limited service, take-out, delivery. Has a $5 delivery fee.
Directions: From Kennedy Exwy, take E Ohio St (#50B), then go east on W Ohio St 1¼ mile, then at N State St turn left and go 3 blocks, at W Huron St turn left and this place is 1 block down. Red Line El train to Chicago.

Zoom Kitchen
923 North Rush Street
312-440-3500
Hours: Monday to Saturday 11 am to 10 pm; Sun 2 pm to 8 pm; Sun Brunch 10 am to 2 pm
Deli and Salad Bar. Not pure vegetarian.
Menu: Salads items such as corn off the cob, chickpeas and pumpkin seeds. Mashed potatoes, Stir-fry vegetables, vegetarian soups, sandwiches and breads.
Other Info: Comments: Friendly, quick service. Counter service, take-out, delivery. Accepts AMEX, MC, VISA. Price: $.

DEERFIELD

Here's Health Stores
178 South Waukegan Road, Deerfield
847-564-8870
Hours: Monday to Friday 10 am 8 pm; Saturday 10 am to 6 pm; Sunday 10 am to 5 pm
Natural Food Store.

Whole Foods Market
760 Waukegan Road; 847-444-1900
Hours: Daily 8 am to 10 pm
Natural Food Store and Cafe. Deli, Bakery, Salad Bar and Juice Bar. Organic produce. Supermarket-type place. See Whole Foods Market infomation.
Directions: From I-94, take Deerfield Rd exit, then merge onto Deerfield Rd and go east 1¼ mile, then at Waukegan Rd (IL-43) turn left and this place is 1 block down.

DE KALB

Duck Soup Co-op
129 East Hillcrest Drive
815-756-7044
email: Baddogs@nib.com
Hours: Monday to Friday 9 am to 8 pm Saturday & Sunday 9 am to 5 pm
Natural Food Store. Organic produce.
Directions: From I-88, take Annie Glidden exit and go 2 miles north. At Hillcrest turn right and this place one mile down on left.

DOWNERS GROVE (Chicago suburbs)

Fruitful Yield
2129 63rd Street, Downer Grove
630-969-7614
Hours: Monday to Friday 9 to 8:30; Saturday 9 am to 5:30 pm; Sunday 12 noon to 5 pm
Natural Food Store.

EDWARDSVILLE (10 miles northeast of St Louis)

Green Earth
441 South Buchanan (Route 159)
618-656-3375
Hours: Monday to Friday 9 am to 7 pm; Saturday 9 am to 5 pm; Sunday 12 noon to 5 pm
Natural Food Store and Deli. Organic produce.
Menu: Has sandwich, soups, marinated tofu, wraps, veggie burgers and pasta.
Comments: Small, friendly place. Has 8 seats and

also counter seats.
Other Info: Accepts MC, VISA. Counter service, take-out.
Directions: This place is a little south of downtown Edwardsville, at junction of N Kansas and Hillsboro.

ELGIN

Al's Café & Creamery
43 DuPage Court; 847-742-1180
Hours: Monday 11 am to 3 pm; Tuesday 11 am to 9 pm; closed Sunday.
Café. Not pure vegetarian.
Menu: Soups, sandwich and salads. Shakes and sundaes.
Comments: In a historical building. Pleasant atmosphere. Has some creative dishes.
Other Info: Full service, take-out. Accepts AMEX, MC, VISA. Price: $$.

Jalapenos
7 Clock Tower Plaza; 847-468-9445
Hours: Daily 9 am to 10 pm
Mexican. Vegan options. Not pure vegetarian.
Menu: Has a good selection of vegetarian dishes. Limited vegan dishes. Authentic Mexican dishes.
Other Info: Full service, take-out. Price: $$.

Elmhurst (Chicago suburbs)

Fruitful Yield
214 North York Street
630-530-1445
Hours: Monday to Friday 9 am to 8:30 pm; Saturday 9 am to 5:30 pm; closed Sunday.
Natural Food Store.

EVANSTON (north Chicago suburb)

**Blind Faith Café
525 Dempster Street
847-328-6875
Web site: http://www.blindfaithcafe.com/
Hours: Monday to Saturday 9 am to 9 pm
Sunday 8 pm to 9 pm
Vegetarian International. Mexican, American, Middle Eastern, Chinese. Has own bakery. Macrobiotic and Vegan options.
Menu: Extensive menu. Garden Salad, poppyseed dressing, Indian Platter, Tostadas, Jasmine Rice, guacamole, pastas, sandwiches, pizzas, chili, brown rice and BBQ Seitan Sandwich. Caribbean Fricassee is stewed seitan and potatoes with plantain over rice. Mu-shu Tempeh with vegetable and

Mandarin Pancakes. Tofu Cornmeal Cakes, Seitan Fajita, Potstickers, Mongolian Stir-fry, Nobu Yaki. Corn and Potato Enchiladas. Guacamole is a really good. Brazilian Salad is very good. Daily macrobiotic plate. Has a great selection of freshly-made vegan desserts. Cranberry bar is good. Vegan Chocolate Cake. Whole-wheat apple cake with caramel sauce. Fresh juices and smoothies. Nondairy smoothies.
Comments: Reasonably prices. Good size portions. Food gets really high ratings. Beautiful décor. Casual place. Popular place. Friendly service. Has outdoor dining.
Other Info: Full service, counter service, take-out. Divided into two sections, one is sit down and at the other you order at a counter. Non-smoking. Accepts AMEX, MC, VISA. Price: $$-$$$.
Directions: From Edens Exwy, take Exit #39B towards E Touhy Ave, then take Cicero Ave north for a half-mile (becomes IL-50), then it becomes Skokie Blvd for another half-mile, at Oakton St turn right and go 2 miles, at McCormick Blvd turn left and go 1 mile, at Dempster St (IL 58) turn right and this place is 1½ mile down. Purple Line train to Dempster. Evanston is just north of Chicago. This place is about a half-mile west of the lake.

Dave's Italian Kitchen
1635 Chicago Avenue; 847-864-6000
Hours: Monday to Thursday 4 pm to 10pm
Friday 4 pm to 11:30 pm
Saturday 4 pm to 11:30 pm
Sunday 4 pm to 10:30 pm
Italian, Pizza. Not pure vegetarian. Vegan options.
Menu: Has sandwiches, homemade pastas, salads, breads, calzones and pizzas.
Other Info: Full service, take-out, delivery. Accepts MC, VISA. Price: $-$$.
Directions: Close to Northwestern University, across from Whole Foods

J D Mills Food Company Inc
635 Chicago Avenue, Suite 4
847-491-0940
Hours: Monday to Friday 8 am to 8 pm; Saturday 8 am to 6:30 pm; Sunday 11 am to 5 pm
Natural Food Store.
Comments: Has a large amount of bulk foods and spices.
Directions: From Chicago, go north on Lakeshore Drive, then take Sheridan Blvd into Evanston. At Chicago Ave turn right and this place on right.

Lulu's

626 Davis Street, at Orrignton, downtown
847-869-4343
Hours: Monday to Thursday 11:30 am to 10 pm;
Friday & Saturday 11:30 am to 11 pm; Sunday
11:30 am to 9 pm
Asian, Chinese, Thailand, Japanese. Not pure
vegetarian.
Menu: Half the menu is vegetarian.
Other Info: Accepts AMEX, MC, VISA.

The Lucky Platter

514 Main Street, just east of Chicago Avenue
847-869-4064
Hours: Monday to Saturday 7 am to 9:30 pm
Sunday 7 am to 9 pm
American Coffee Shop. Not pure vegetarian.
Menu: Has several vegetarian dishes. Mexican
Polenta. Fresh squeezed orange juice. Homemade
cream soda.
Comments: Has valet parking.
Other Info: Non-smoking. Accepts DIS, MC,
VISA. Price: $-$$.

Whole Foods Market

1640 Chicago Avenue
847-733-1600; **fax:** 847-733-1670
Hours: Monday to Saturday 8 am to 10 pm
Sunday 8 am to 9 pm
Natural Food Store and Deli. Juice Bar and Bakery. Organic produce.
Directions: This place is 3 blocks from Lake
Michigan. From I-94, take Dempster St exit east.
Go about 8 miles and at Chicago Ave turn left
and this place on the left 4 blocks down.

Wild Oats People's Market

1111 Chicago Avenue
847-475-9492
fax: 847-475-9497
Hours: Daily 8 am to 10 pm
Natural Food Store and Cafe. Deli, Bakery,
Salad Bar and Juice Bar. Organic produce. Supermarket-type place. See Wild Oats Market
information.
Directions: From Edens Exwy, take Exit #39B
towards E Touhy Ave, then take Cicero Ave north
for a half-mile (becomes IL-50), then it becomes
Skokie Blvd for another half-mile, at Oakton St
turn right and go 2 miles, at McCormick Blvd
turn left and go a half-mile, at Main St turn right
and go 1½ mile down, at Chicago Ave turn left
and this place is a quarter-mile down. This place
is about a half-mile west of the lake. Evanston is
just north of Chicago.

GENEVA

Soup to Nuts

716 West State Street; 630-232-6646
Natural Food Store.

HIGHLAND PARK

**Chicago Diner

581 Elm Place, at 2nd; 847-433-1228
Hours: Monday to Friday 10 am to 9 pm
Saturday & Sunday 11 am to 8:30 pm
Vegetarian International. Mostly Vegan. See
Chicago branch for details.
Menu: Mock Philly 'Steak' sandwich (made with
seitan and soy cheese), fajitas, Sloppy Joes and
much more.
Other Info: Accepts AMEX, DIS, MC, VISA.
Price: $$. Full service, take-out.
Directions: From I-294, take I-94 W for a half-
mile, then take Deerfield Rd exit, then go 2 miles
east on Deerfield Rd, then go 1¼ mile northeast
on Deerfield, then keep going straight onto Cen-
tral Ave and go another mile, at Green Bay Rd
turn left and go 1 block, at Elm Place turn right
and this place is 1½ block down. This place is
about 20 miles north of downtown Chicago and
is about 1 mile west of the lake.

HINSDALE

Wild Oats Market

500 East Ogden Avenue
630-986-8500; **fax:** 630-986-8588
Hours: Daily 7 am to 10 pm
Natural Food Store and Cafe. Deli, Bakery,
Salad Bar and Juice Bar. Organic produce. Su-
permarket-type place. See Wild Oats Market
information.
Directions: From I-294, take Ogden Ave (US 34)
exit, then go west on E Ogden Ave and this place
is right next to the exit.

MATTESON

South Suburban Food Co-op

21750 Main Street; 708-747-2256;
email: lidbury@spideyweb.net; **Web site:**
http://www.spideyweb.net/Co-op/
Hours: Monday, Tuesday 11 am to 8 pm; Thurs-
day 2 pm to 8 pm; Friday 11 am to 8 pm
Saturday 9:30 pm to 3:30 pm; closed Sunday.
Natural Food Store. Organic produce.
Comments: This is a very good store. Only serves
members and once-only people who are travel-

ing through.
Directions: From I-57, take Rte 30 East exit and go 5 miles into Matteson where the road turns into Main St. After the road turn right, this place is two miles south on the right in Stawicki Industrial Park (hard to see from road).

MOLINE

Jalapeno's
3939 16th Street; 309-736-1011
Hours: Sunday to Thursday 11 am to 9 pm
Friday & Saturday 11 am to 10 pm
Mexican. Not pure vegetarian.
Menu: Has a good selection of vegetarian dishes including good vegetarian enchiladas and chili rellenos.
Other Info: Accepts AMEX, MC, VISA.

Le Mekong Restaurant
1606 Fifth Avenue; 309-797-3709
Hours: Daily 5 pm to 9 pm
Tuesday & Friday lunch only 11 am to 2 pm
Southeast Asian, French. Vegan options. Not pure vegetarian.
Menu: Has a separate vegetarian section. Tofu and mock meat dishes.
Other Info: Full service, take-out. Accepts AMEX, MC, VISA. Price: $$.

MOUNT CARROLL

Straddle Creek Food Co-op
112 West Market Street; 815-244-2667
Hours: Thursday & Friday 12 noon to 4 pm
Saturday 10 am to 4 pm
Natural Food Store. Only has organic carrots, but no other produce.
Directions: From I-80, take Rte 88 toward Mount Carroll to Hwy 78 north (in town). At Market St go west and this place is on left a few blocks down.

MOUNT PROSPECT

Sweetgrass Vitamin & Health Market
1742 West Gold Road; 847-956-1939
Hours: Monday to Friday 9 am to 9 pm; Saturday 9 am to 6 pm; Sunday 10 am to 5:30 pm
Natural Food Store.
Directions: From Kennedy Expressway, go west on Northwest Tollway leaving Chicago. Take Elmhurst Rd exit and at Gold Rd go north. At Gold turn left and this place at corner of Busse and Gold.

MOUNT VERNON

Nature's Way Food Center
102 South 4th Street; 618-244-2327
Hours: Monday to Friday 9:30 to 5 pm; Saturday 9:30 am to 1 pm; closed Sunday.
Natural Food Store. No organic produce.
Directions: From Hwy 15, go east and at Fourth St turn north and then this place is on the right.

NAPERVILLE

Gateway of India
417 East Odgen Avenue; 630-717-7600
Hours: Monday to Friday 11 am to 2 pm, 4:30 pm to 9 pm; Saturday 11 am to 9 pm; Sunday 2 pm to 8 pm
Indian. Not pure vegetarian.
Menu: Aloo Gobi, Kofta, Aloo Mattar, dal, rice dishes, Bindi Chana and more.
Comments: Good food. Small place.

NEW LENOX

Natural Choices Health Food Store
1340 North Cedar Road; 815-485-5572
Hours: Monday to Friday 10 am to 6 pm; Saturday 10 am to 4 pm; closed Sunday.
Natural Food Store. No organic produce.
Directions: From I-80, take Maple St (Rte 30) exit and go east on Rte 30. At Cedar Rd (third light) turn left (go north) and then this place is on the right a mile down in a beige building.

NORMAL

**Coffeehouse & Deli
114 East Beaufort Street
309-452-6774
Hours: Monday to Saturday 7 am to 10 pm
Sunday 8 am to 9 pm
Vegetarian Coffeehouse.
Menu: Soups, salads, veggie chili, wraps, quesadillas, Falafel on a pita, Grilled Tofu, veggie burgers and Lasagna. Has a good selection of coffees. Cappuccino, espresso.
Other Info: Accepts MC, VISA. Counter service, take-out. Order at counter then dishes are brought to table. Non-smoking. Price: $. Reservations requested for large groups.
Directions: From I-74, take US 51 Bus/Main St exit (#135) towards Bloomington, then go north on Bus US 51 for 5 miles, at W Beaufort St turn right and this place is 1 mile down.

OAK PARK

Khyber Pass
1031 Lake Street, to Forest Lake; 708-445-9032
Hours: Daily 11:30 am to 3:30 pm, 5 pm to 10 pm
Indian. All-you-can-eat Buffet. Vegan options. Not pure vegetarian.
Menu: Has a large selection of vegetarian dishes. Rice dishes, vegetable curries, Channa Masala and Aloo Saag. For dessert there are Mango Kulfi and Almond Badami Kheer (rice pudding).
Comments: Plays classical Indian music. Good place for a special event. Oriental rugs, candles and fancy wallpaper. Popular place. Casual.
Other Info: Full service, take-out. Non-smoking. Accepts AMEX, MC, VISA. Price: $$.
Directions: Green Line El train to Harlem/Lake. Opposite the Classic Cinemas Lake Theatre.

PALATINE (Chicago suburb next to Oak Park)

Park Place Shopping Center
1331 North Rand Road
847-776-8080; **fax:** 847-776-8083
Hours: Monday to Saturday 8 am to 10 pm
Sunday 8 am to 9 pm
Natural Food Store and Cafe. Deli, Bakery, Salad Bar and Juice Bar. Organic produce. Supermarket-type place. See Whole Foods Market information.
Comments: Has about 10 tables.
Directions: From Hwy 53, take US 12/Rand exit west, then go northwest on Rand Rd for ¾ mile, then turn right into Park Place Shopping Center.

PEORIA

Cyd's Sendsationals, Ltd.
4607 North Prospect
309-685-1100
Hours: Monday to Friday 10 am to 6 pm; Saturday 10 am to 5 pm; closed Sunday.
American, International. Not pure vegetarian.
Menu: Gourmet vegetarian dishes. Sandwiches and veggie Lasagna.
Other Info: Take-out only. Price: $-$$.

El Sombrerito
323 Main Street   309-673-9119
1112 West Pioneer Parkway   309-691-9119
Hours: Monday to Friday 10:30 am to 3 pm
Closed Sunday & Monday
Mexican. Vegan options. Not pure vegetarian.

Menu: Salads, appetizers and vegetarian main dishes. Non-alcoholic beer and wine.
Comments: Vegetarian dishes are marked on the menu with a carrot.
Other Info: Full service, take-out. Accepts AMEX, DIS, MC, VISA. Price: $-$$.
Directions: Parking arranged for customer.

Main Street Nutrition and Café
537 Main Street
309-676-1485
Hours: Monday to Friday 9 am to 5 pm
Saturday 10 am to 4 pm; closed Sunday.
Natural Food Store, Café and Deli. Vegan options. Not pure vegetarian.
Menu: Has several vegetarian dishes. Fresh juices.
Comments: Friendly café. Good natural food store.
Other Info: Limited service, take-out. Accepts DIS, MC, VISA. Price: $.
Directions: From I-74, take the Jefferson St exit (#93A), then go west on US 24 for 2 blocks, then at Main St turn right and this place is 2 blocks down at Main St.

Naturally Yours Grocery
Metro Shopping Center, 4700 North University Street; 309-692-4448
Hours: Monday to Saturday 10 am to 9 pm
Closed Sunday.
Natural Food Store and Café. Limited produce. Not pure vegetarian.
Comments: Has around 25 seats.
Directions: From I-474, take University exit north, then go north on University and this place is on the right two miles down in Metro Shopping Center.

One World Coffee and Cargo
1245 West Main Street, at University
309-672-1522
Hours: Monday to Saturday 7 am to 10 pm
Sunday 7 am to 8 pm
Coffeehouse. Eclectic menu. Vegan options. Not pure vegetarian.
Menu: Soups, salads, veggie chili, sandwiches and hot dishes. Any dish that is not vegetarian can be made vegetarian. Cappuccino, espresso.
Comments: Vegetarian dishes are marked with an Earth symbol, and vegan dishes are marked with two Earths. Has live entertainment including live music, theater and poetry. Has an international gift shop. Food is good.
Other Info: Full service, take-out. Accepts MC, VISA. Price: $-$$.

Directions: From I-74, take University St Exit (#91), then go south on University St for ¾ mile, then at Main St turn left and this place is a half-block down.

Taste of Thai
1301 West Pioneer Parkway; 309-692-8837
Hours: Monday to Friday 11 am to 9 pm; Saturday 12 am to 9 pm; closed Sunday.
Thai. Vegan options. Not pure vegetarian.
Menu: Has around 15 vegetarian dishes. The Bean Curd with mushrooms is good.

RIVER FOREST (Chicago suburb next to Oak Park)

Whole Foods Market
7245 Lake Street
708-366-1045
fax: 708-366-1044
Hours: Monday to Saturday 8 am to 10 pm
Sunday 8 am to 9 pm
Natural Food Store and Cafe. Deli, Bakery, Salad Bar and Juice Bar. Organic produce. Supermarket-type place. See Whole Foods Market information.
Comments: Has around 10 tables.
Directions: From I-290, take Harlem exit north (#21B). Then go north 2 miles on Harlem to River Forest Town Center, at Harlem and Lake.

ROCKFORD

Keedi's
3231 North Main Street
815-877-5715; **fax:** 815-877-5730
Hours: Daily 6 am to 12 midnight
American Restaurant and Bakery. Not pure vegetarian.
Menu: Falafel Sandwich, veggie burgers, Vegetarian Chili, Calzones, Vegetarian Lasagna, pita sandwiches, Rice & Lentil Burger, Potato Vegetable Casserole, Broccoli Pie, Tofu Stir-fry, vegetarian quiche and Cabbage Rolls.
Other Info: Full service, take-out. Accepts AMEX, DC, DIS, MC, VISA. Price: $-$$.
Directions: Parking arranged for customers.

ROSCOE

Mary's Market
4431 East State Street   815-397-7291
1654 North Alpine Street   815-394-0765
Hours: Daily

American Cafe. Vegan options. Not pure veg.
Menu: Has a good selection of vegetarian dishes. Roasted Portobello Mushrooms, Roasted Vegetables, grilled vegetables, Minestrone, salads, several pasta dishes, Vegetable Stack, veggie burgers (very good), fresh breads and other dishes. Vegetarian dishes are marked on the menu.
Other Info: Full service, take-out. Accepts AMEX, DIS, MC, VISA. Price: $-$$.

SCHAUMBURG (Chicago northwest suburbs)

Jamba Juice
601 Martingale Road; 847-995-1445
Hours: Monday to Friday 7:30 am to 9 pm; Saturday 10 am to 10 pm; Sunday 9 am to 8 pm
Juice and Smoothie Bar.
Menu: Has 16 types of smoothies. Uses real fruits and has nutritional supplements such as ginseng and bee pollen. Healthy breads and soups.
Comments: Friendly place.
Other Info: Counter service, take-out.

Fruitful Yield
5005 Oakton Street, Skokie; 847 679-8882; **Web site:** http://www.the-naturalway.com/
Natural Food Store.

Slice of Life
4120 West Dempster Street; 708-674-2021
Hours: Monday to Thursday 11:30 am to 9 pm; Friday 11:30 am to 2 pm; Sunday 10:30 am to 9 pm; Saturday 6:30 pm to 12:30 am
Kosher Natural Foods. Italian. Mainly Vegetarian. Not pure vegetarian (serves fish).
Menu: Has a large selection of vegetarian dishes. Soups, salads, sandwiches, pastas, veggie burgers and main dishes. Has a children's menu. Fresh juices, cappuccino, espresso.
Comments: Monday is Mexican night during which there are several vegetarian dishes.
Other Info: Full service, take-out. Price: $$.

SPRINGFIELD

Food Fantasies
1512 West Wabash Avenue
217-793-8009
Web site: http://www.livingnaturally.com/retailer/store/
Hours: Monday to Friday 9 am to 8 pm; Saturday 9 am to 6 pm; Sunday 12 noon to 4 pm
Natural Food Store. Bakery. Organic produce.
Menu: Has some vegan baked goods.

Comments: Has discount coupons on their web site.
Directions: From I-55, take the Rte 4 (#93) exit towards Springfield, then go north on IL Rte 4 for 1¼ mile, at Wabash Ave turn right and this place is 1½ mile down.

Holy Land Diner
Old State Capital Place, downtown
518 East Adams, between 5th and 6th
217-544-5786
Hours: Monday to Thursday 11 am to 7 pm; Friday & Saturday 11 am to 9 pm; closed Sunday; Lunch Buffet Daily 11 am to 2:30 pm; Dinner Buffet Friday & Saturday 5 pm to 9 pm; Vegan Saturday Buffet 5 pm to 9 pm.
Middle Eastern, Lebanese, Greek. Vegan options. Not pure vegetarian.
Menu: Falafel, hummus, stuffed grape leaves, baba ghanouj, Middle Eastern salads, spinach pies and other dishes. Fresh juices, cappuccino, espresso.
Comment: Plays Lebanese music.
Other Info: Full service, take-out, catering. Accepts DIS, MC, VISA. Price: $$.

URBANA

Jerry's IGA
Southgate Shopping Center
2010 South Philo Road
217-367-1166
Hours: Daily for 24 hours
Regular Supermarket with a Natural Food Section. Has a limited selection of organic produce.
Directions: From I-74, take Cunningham exit south. Cunningham becomes Vine. At Florida turn left, then at Philo turn right. This place on left in Southgate Shopping Center.

Red Herring Vegetarian Restaurant
1209 West Oregon Street
University of Illinois Campus
217-367-2340
Hours: Monday to Friday 11 am to 3 pm; Friday 5 pm to 8 pm; closed Saturday & Sunday. May not be open in summer.
Vegan International. Italian, Mexican, Caribbean, African, Chinese, Korean, Thai, American.
Menu: Menu changes daily. Wide selection of soups, sandwiches, entrées and freshly baked desserts. West African Ground-Nut Stew, Tofu-Spinach Lasagna, Jab Chai, Mushroom Sesame Tofu Soup, Pakistani Rice and Thai Garlic Soup. On Friday's evening has all-you-can-eat pasta.

Comments: RHVR is a not-profit, cooperatively-run business open since 1977. Uses local organic and natural foods when possible. Supports local farmers and cooperatives. All food freshly made.
Other Info: Cafeteria style, counter service, take-out. Accepts reservations but not necessary. No credit cards accepted.
Directions: From I-74, take Lincoln Ave South exit, then go south on S Lincoln Ave for 1½ mile, then turn right (go west) on Oregon St and go to it dead ends and this place is the last building on left, at corner of Oregon and Matthews. Parking available in lots nearby.

Strawberry Fields
Old Main Square Plaza
306 West Springfield Avenue
217-328-1655
fax: 217-328-1574
email: sfields@pdnt.com
Web site: www.strawberry-fields.com
Hours: Monday to Saturday 7 am to 8 pm; Sunday 10 am to 6 pm; Café opens at 7:30 am
Natural Food Store and Deli. Organic produce. Fresh baked breads. Large selection of products in store.
Menu: Has salads and vegetarian dishes. Hummus Sandwich, Cheese Sandwich, Barbeque Tofu Sandwich, Avocado & Cheese Sandwich, Vegetable Sandwich, Israeli Sandwich, Tabbouleh, Spinach Calzones, Stir-fried Vegetables, Sweet & Sour Seitan, Cumin Cauliflower and more.
Comments: Has 50 seats.
Directions: From I-74, take Lincoln Ave South exit, then go south on Lincoln Ave for 1 mile, then at Main St turn left and this place is ¾ mile down on the left in Old Main Square Plaza, a block west of Race St.

VANDALIA

Sunshine House Health Food Store
420 West Gallatin Street
618-283-0888
Hours: Tuesday to Saturday 9 am to 5 pm
Closed Sunday & Monday.
Natural Food Store.

WESTMONT

**Shree Vegetarian Restaurant
655 North Cass Avenue
630-655-1021
Hours: Sunday, Tuesday to Thursday 11:30 am to

2:30 pm, 5:30 pm to 9:30 pm; Friday & Saturday 11:30 am to 2:30 pm, 5:30 pm to 10:30 pm Closed Monday.

Vegetarian Indian. Buffet

Menu: Has a large selection of vegetarian dishes. Lunch buffet has around 20 dishes. Fresh juices.

Comments: Friendly places. Plays Indian music. Nice atmosphere. Great food.

Other Info: Full service, take-out. Reservations required Friday to Sunday. Accepts AMEX, MC, VISA. Price: $$.

Directions: From I-294, take the Ogden Ave/US-34 exit, then go west on Ogden Ave (US 34) for about 3½ miles, then at N Cass Ave turn right and this place is 1 block down. Parking arranged for customers. This place is about 10 miles due west of downtown Chicago.

WHEATON

Whole Foods Market

151 Rice Lake Square, Butterfield Road
630-588-1500; **fax:** 650-588-0292

Hours: Monday to Saturday 8 am to 10 pm Sunday 8 am to 9 pm

Natural Food Store and Cafe. Deli, Bakery, Salad Bar and Juice Bar. Organic produce. Supermarket-type place. See Whole Foods Market information. Seats 30.

Directions: From I-88 (E West Tollway), take Highland Ave exit, then go north on Highland Ave 1 block, then go west on Butterfield Rd and this place is 4 miles down on the right (north side), next to Borders Bookstore. This place is about 15 miles west of downtown Chicago.

Indiana

1. Anderson
2. Berne
3. Bloomington
4. Crown Point
5. Fort Wayne
6. Goshen
7. Greenfield
8. Indianapolis
9. Kokomo
10. Mishawaka
11. New Albany
12. Richmond
13. West Lafayette

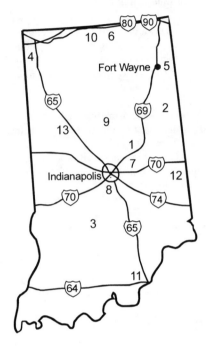

ANDERSON

First Health Food Center
1203 East 53rd Street; 765-642-8992
Hours: Mon to Wed 9 am to 6 pm; Thur 9 am to 7 pm; Fri 9 am to 5 pm; Sun 1 pm to 5 pm
Natural Food Store. Bakery.
Directions: From I-26, take Rte 9 (#26) north and go a half-mile, then at 53rd turn right and this place is a half-mile down on right.

BERNE

Eathern Treasure's Natural Food Market
906 North US Highway 27; 219-589-3675
Natural Food Store and Café. Organic produce.
Comments: Seats 50.
Directions: From I-69, take State Rd 218 exit and go west about 35 miles into Berne, then turn left (go north) on US 27 and this place is 1 mile down the road on the west side of street.

BLOOMINGTON

Beijing
220 Williamsburg Drive #1, across from Barnes & Noble; 812-332-5867
Hours: Sunday to Thursday 11 am to 9 pm
Friday & Saturday 11 am to 9:30 pm
Chinese. Vegan friendly.
Menu: Has a wide selection of vegetarian dishes. There is a Vegetarian Buffet on Wednesday. Has a vegetarian buffet bar.
Comments: Good value. Good food.
Other Info: Accepts AMEX, MC, VISA. Price: $-$$.

Bloomingfoods Coop Market & Deli (two locations)
3220 East 3rd Street; 812-336-5400
Web site: www.bloomingfoods.org
Hours: Monday to Saturday 8 am to 10 pm
Sunday 9 am to 7 pm
Directions: From Hwy 37, take 45 Bypass east about 3½ miles, then at Third St (Rte 46) turn left and this place on right a half-mile down.
419 East Kirkwood Avenue
812-336-5300
Hours: Monday to Saturday 8 am to 10 pm
Sunday 9 am to 7 pm
Directions: From Hwy 37, take 45-Bypass east, then at College Ave turn right and go 1½ mile. At Kirkwood Ave turn left and this place is 4 blocks east, down an alley on the left.

Email: bfoods@bloomingfoods.org; Web site: www.bloomingfoods.org
Natural Food Store and Deli. Café buffet style. Bakery and Juice Bar. Organic produce.
Comments: The staff is usually helpful in reference to a vegan and vegetarian diet. The Third Street place is bigger and has about 20 seats inside and patio seating outside. The Kirkwood Avenue place has seating outside on the porch.

Dragon
Whitehall Plaza; 812-332-6610
Hours: Daily 11 am to 11 pm
Chinese. Not pure vegetarian.
Menu: Has a wide selection of vegetarian dishes.
Comments: Quick service. Has good food.
Other Info: Full service, take-out. No credit cards. Price: $.

Ekimae
825 North Walnut, by the railroad viaduct 812-334-1661
Hours: Monday, Wednesday to Saturday 5 pm to 10 pm; Sunday 4 pm to 9 pm; closed Tuesday.
Japanese and some Korean. Not pure veg.
Menu: Has a good selection of vegetarian and vegan dishes. Soups, salad, Makisushi, Tofu Vegetable Yakisoba, Wakame Salad and Goma-ae.

Encore Café
316 West 6th Street; 812-333-7312
Hours: Sunday to Thursday 11 am to 10 pm Friday & Saturday 11 am to 12 midnight
Restaurant. Vegetarian-friendly. Not pure vegetarian.
Menu: Has a wide variety of vegetarian sandwiches, veggie chili, soups (usually vegetarian), salads, Oven Roasted Potatoes and main dishes.
Comments: Friendly place.
Other Info: Accepts AMEX, MC, VISA.

La Bamba
502 East Kirkwood Avenue; 812-332-5970
Mexican. Not pure vegetarian.
Menu: Large burritos. Good hot sauce.
Comments: Has a sign that say there is no animal fat in the beans. Quick service. Good food.
Other Info: Reservations not accepted. Accepts MC, VISA. Price: $-$$.

Laughing Planet Café
322 East Kirkwood Avenue, at Grant, downtown 812-323-2233
Hours: Daily 11 am to 9 pm
International Café. Vegan friendly. Not pure veg.

Menu: Black Bean Burritos, Hummus, Steamed Vegetables with Beans, Chips & homemade Salsa, homemade veggie burgers, vegan soups, vegan quesadillas, rice and steamed vegetables.
Comments: In a hundred year old building with character. Nice place. Large reasonably priced Mexican burritos. Local organic produce used when possible. Gets good recommendations. Can substitute soy cheese.
Other Info: Counter service, take-out. Accepts AMEX, DIS, MC, VISA. Price: $.
Directions: From Hwy 37, take 45-Bypass east and go one mile, then at College Ave turn right and go 1½ mile. At College Ave turn left and this place is 4 blocks down. This place is close to Bloomingfoods Co-op Market.

Lennie's
1795 East Tenth Street; 812-323-2112
Hours: Sunday to Thursday 11 am to 12 midnight; Friday & Saturday 11 am to 1 am
Pizza Place. Not pure vegetarian.
Menu: Has some of the best pizzas in town. Roasted Portobello and good salads.
Warning: The Portobello Mushroom may be marinated with Worcestershire Sauce, which usually contains anchovies (fish).
Other Info: Non-smoking. Accepts AMEX, MC, VISA.

Peterson's
Crosstown Shopping Center, 1811 East 10th Street; 812-336-5450
Hours: Daily 11 am to 9 pm
American. Vegan friendly. Good fast food place. Not pure vegetarian.
Menu: Has a wide selection of vegetarian dishes. Large vegetarian burritos, veggie Sloppy Joe, soups, good selection of salads, sandwiches and vegan chili. Fresh juices and smoothies.
Comments: Good food. Clean place. Quick service.
Other Info: Counter service, take-out. Accepts AMEX, DIS, MC, VISA. Price: $.
Directions: From Hwy 37, take Hwy 45-Bypass east and go 3 miles, then at E 10th St turn left and this place is ¾ mile down, between E University Rd and Sunrise Dr.

The Red Sea
404 East 4th Street; 812-331-8366
Hours: Daily 11:30 am to 2 pm, 5 pm to 9 pm
Ethiopian. Some American dishes. Not pure veg.
Menu: Has Vegetarian Combination Platter, lentil spinach soup, injera bread and more.

Comments: Good size servings. Reasonable prices. Traditional décor. Tropical plants, candles, white tablecloths and traditional artifacts. Small, relaxed place. Has outdoor seating. Plays authentic music. Good place for a special event. Romantic place.
Other Info: Full service, take-out, catering. Nonsmoking. Accepts MC, VISA. Price: $-$$.

Rockit's Famous Pizza
222 North Walnut Street
812-336-ROCK/336-ROLL
Hours: Sunday to Thursday 5 pm to 3:30 am
Friday & Saturday 4 pm to 11 pm
Pizza Place. Vegan friendly. Caters to vegetarians. Not pure vegetarian.
Comments: Voted to have the best pizza in town. Soy cheese contains casein. Friendly, helpful service. Has vegan cheese.
Other Info: Counter service, take-out, delivery.

Sahara Deli
106 East 2nd Street; 812-333-0502
Gourmet International Grocery Store and take-out Deli.
Menu: Has falafel, hummus and baba ghanouj.
Comments: Has a wide selection of bulk goods.
Other Info: Counter service, take-out. No seating.

Soma
East Kirkwood, below the Laughing Planet (under same management); 812-331-2770
Hours: Sunday to Thursday 7 am to 11 pm
Friday & Saturday 11 am to 12 midnight
Juice Bar.
Menu: Has organic fresh juices, smoothies and baked goods. PB & J (peanut butter and jelly) smoothie. Has vegan baked goods.
Comments: Has table seating and couches to sit on. Has reading material. Bulletin board.
Other Info: Accepts AMEX, DIS, MC, VISA.

CROWN POINT

Twin Happiness Restaurant
1188 North Main Street
219-663-4433
Hours: Monday to Thursday 11 am to 9 pm; Friday & Saturday 11 am to 10 pm; Sunday 12 noon to 9 pm
Chinese. Not pure vegetarian.
Menu: Has a wide variety of vegetarian dishes. Vegetable and tofu dishes.
Comments: Uses corn oil for cooking. Willing to make special requests.
Other Info: Full service, take-out. Accepts AMEX, MC, VISA. Price: $$.

FORT WAYNE

Health Food Shoppe
3515 North Anthony Boulevard; 219-483-5211
Hours: Monday to Saturday 9 am to 7 pm
Closed Sunday.
Natural Food Store and take-out Deli. Organic produce.
Menu: Ready-made dishes and sandwiches. Salad Bar Tuesday to Friday with fresh soups and salad items.
Other Info: Counter service, take-out. Does not have seating inside and is take-out only. Has seating outside in the summer. Accepts AMEX, MC, VISA.
Directions: From I-69 N, take US-27 S exit (#111A) towards Ft Wayne. Then go south ¾ mile on US-27, at Rte 24/Rte 30/Rte 33 turn left (becomes Rte 14) and go 2½ miles, then at N Anthony Blvd turn right and this place is about 6/10 mile down.

Three Rivers Co-op Natural Foods & Deli
1126 Broadway Street; 219-424-8812
Hours: Monday to Friday 9 am to 9 pm; Saturday 9 am to 6 pm; Sunday 12 noon to 6 pm
Natural Food Store and Deli. American. Vegan friendly. Not pure vegetarian.
Menu: Menu changes weekly. Homemade soups. The chili is a special dish.
Comments: Pay by weight. Has about 10 seats.
Directions: Store is west of the downtown. From I-69, take US-14 east (Illinois Rd) (becomes Jefferson Blvd) about 4 miles. At Broadway turn right and this place on the right several blocks down.

GOSHEN

Centre-In Co-op
314 South Main Street; 219-534-2355
Web site: http://centre-in.hypermart.net/
Hours: Monday to Friday 9:30 am to 6:30 pm; Saturday 9:30 am to 5:30 pm; closed Sunday.
Natural Food Store and Deli.
Menu: Has ready-made foods, fresh salads, tabbouleh, sandwiches and other dishes.
Directions: From I-20 Bypass /going south/east/, take US 33 (Goshen) exit and go southeast about 5 miles to downtown Goshen. This place on east side of road on US 33.

GREENFIELD

The Good Things Naturally
610 West Main Street; 317-462-2004
Hours: Monday to Friday 10 am to 6 pm; Saturday 10 am to 1 pm; closed Sunday.
Natural Food Store. No produce.
Directions: From I-70, take Greenfield (#104) exit (Hwy 9 south) 2½ miles. At Hwy 40 (Main St) turn right and this place on right several blocks from the downtown.

INDIANAPOLIS

Aesop's Tables
600 Massachusetts Avenue; 317-631-0055
Hours: Monday to Thursday 11 am to 9 pm; Friday & Saturday 11 am to 10 pm; closed Sun.
Mediterranean and Greek. Not pure vegetarian.
Menu: About 25% of the menu is vegetarian. Vegetarian Pita Grill, falafel, pastas, Wild Bill's Spinach Supreme, hummus and tabbouleh.
Comments: Has good Greek food. Has outdoor seating. Authentic décor. Has live music on Friday and Saturday. Good place for a group. Friendly, relaxed place.
Other Info: Accepts AMEX, DIS, MC, VISA. Full service, take-out. Price: $$.

Bazbeaux Pizza
344 Massachusetts Avenue   317- 636-7662
832 East Westfield Boulevard 317-255-5711
Hours: Sunday to Thursday 11 am to 10 pm
Friday & Saturday 11 am to 11 pm
Italian, Pizza. Vegan options. Not pure veg.
Menu: Has a good selection of vegetarian pizzas. Gourmet pizza. Has artichoke hearts and sun-dried tomatoes for toppings. Sandwiches and salad
Comments: Makes some of the best pizzas in town. Has outdoor seating. Has won awards for best pizza in Indianapolis. Good service.
Other Info: Limited service, take-out, delivery. Accepts DIS, MC, VISA. Price: $$.

Café Patachou
4911 North Pennsylvania Street, at 49th Street
317-925-2823
8691 River Crossing Boulevard; 317-815-0765
4733 East 126th Street, Carmel (at Gray)
317-569-2965
Hours: Monday to Saturday 7 am to 3 pm
Sunday 8 am to 2 pm
Natural Food Café. Mostly Vegetarian. Vegan friendly.

Menu: Soups, salads, sandwiches and desserts. Cinnamon toast, fruit & yogurt and granola.
Comments: Known for breakfasts and coffee. Gets really crowded on the weekends.
Other Info: Accepts AMEX, DIS, MC, VISA.
Directions: This place is 4 miles north of the downtown, just east of Rte 31. From the downtown go north on Rte 37 (N Meridean St) about 4 miles. Then at 49th St turn right and this place is one block down at N Pennsylvania.

**Georgetown Market
4375 Georgetown Road; 317-293-9525; **fax:** 317-216-7479; **email:** info@georgetownmarket.com
Web site: www.georgetownmarket.com
Hours: Monday to Saturday 9 am to 8 pm
Sunday 11 am to 5 pm
Natural Food Store and Vegetarian Deli. Juice Bar, Salad Bar and Bakery. Vegan friendly. Organic produce. Supermarket-size place.
Menu: Soups, salads, sandwiches, baked sweet potatoes, Black Beans, Brown Rice, wraps, Lasagna, and a deli with a good selection of dishes. Soy milk and soy cheese. Healthy shakes. Fresh juices and smoothies.
Comments: Good food. Been open over 20 years. Everything is homemade. Has ready-made dishes in their cold case.
Other Info: Counter service, take-out. Has a nice seating area.
Directions: From I-65, take Exit #121 and take Lafayette Rd southeast one mile, then at Georgetown Rd turn left and this place is 100 yards down.

Good Earth Natural Food Stores
6350 North Guilford Avenue; 317-253-3709;
fax: 317-251-9258; **email:** info@good-earth.com;
Web site: www.good-earth.com
Hours: Monday to Saturday 9 am to 7 pm
Sunday 12 noon am to 5 pm
Natural Food Store. Organic produce and bulk goods.
Comments: Has 10 tables. In a historic house in Broad Ripple area. One of the best health food stores in Central Indiana. Arranges cooking classes.
Other Info: Accepts MC, VISA.
Directions: From north side of I-465 beltway, head south on US 31 (Meridian St). At 71st turn left and go 7 blocks, then at College Ave turn right and go 5 blocks, then at 64th St turn left. At Guilford (the third right) turn right and this place is a block down on the right.

India Palace

4213 Lafayette Road; 317-298-0773
Web site: http://www.indyshopperonline.com/
indiapalace.html
Hours: Mon to Fri 11:30 am to 2:30 pm, 5 pm
to 10 pm; Sat & Sun 11:30 am to 10:30 pm
Indian. Lunch Buffet. Not pure vegetarian.
Menu: Has many vegetarian dishes. Indian breads,
Biryani, paneer dishes and curry dishes.
Comments: Good service.
Other Info: Full service, take-out, catering. Accepts MC, VISA. Price: $$.

Some Guys Pizza

6235 North Allisonville Road; 317-257-1364
Hours: Tues to Thur 11:30 am to 2 pm, 4 pm to
10 pm; Fri 11:30 am to 2 pm, 4 pm to 11 pm; Sat
4 pm to 11 pm; Sun 4 pm to 11 pm; closed Mon.
International Café and Pizza. Vegan friendly. Not
pure vegetarian.
Comments: Good vegetarian pizzas and pasta.
The pizza gets great ratings. Often has live entertainment at night. Gets very busy on the weekends. Good, quick service.
Other Info: Limited service, take-out, delivery.
Accepts MC, VISA.

Three Sisters Café & Bakery

6360 Guilford Avenue, at 64th Street
317-257-5556
Hours: Tues to Thur 8 am to 9 pm; Fri & Sat 8
am to 10 pm; Sunday 8 am to 3 pm; closed Mon.
American. Not pure vegetarian.
Menu: Has a good selection of vegetarian dishes.
Has sandwiches and vegetarian dishes. Multigrain
oatmeal, granola, Calico Potatoes, soups, veggie
chili, pastas, salads, Hummus Pizza, Potatoes &
Tofu, Grilled Veggie Sandwich and more.
Comments: Has an interesting décor. Laid back,
nice atmosphere.
Other Info: Smoking allowed outside. Accepts
AMEX, DC, DIS, MC, VISA. Price: $-$$.

**Udupi Café

4225 Lafayette Road
317-299-2127; Web site: www.saibazaar.com
Hours: Tues to Thur 11:30 to 3 pm, 5:30 pm to
9:30 pm; Fri & Sat 11:30 am to 3 pm, 5:30 pm
to 10 pm; closed Mon.
Fully Vegetarian South Indian. Buffet. Vegan
friendly.
Menu: Has full menu and buffet. A variety of
dosas, uthappam, Channa Batura, Uppama, Vegetable Palao, Lemon Rice, Indians breads, Aloo

Gobi, Aloo Jeera, Vegetable Korma, Palak Paneer,
Mater Paneer, sambar, raita and full Indian Thalis. Desserts such as Gulabjamun, Carrot Halava,
Kheer and mango ice cream.
Comments: Good food.
Other Info: Full service, take-out, catering. Reservations suggested for groups of 6 or more. Accepts MC, VISA. Price: $$.
Directions: From I-65, take Exit #121 and take
Lafayette Rd southeast one mile and this place is
a little northwest of Lafayette Square Shopping
Center.

Vintage Whole Foods

Shadeland Station Shopping Center, 7391 North
Shadeland Avenue; 317-842-1032
Hours: Monday, Wednesday, Friday 9 am to 7
pm; Tuesday, Thursday 9 am to 8 pm; Saturday 9
am to 6 pm; Sunday 12 noon to 5:30 pm
Natural Food Store. Has a large produce section.
Directions: This place is in northeast Indianapolis, just outside of the Beltway. From I-465 south,
take Shadeland Ave exit north (#40). This place
is then 1½ miles north on Shadeland in the
Shadeland Station Shopping Center. From I-465
north, take Rte 37B south, then at 75th go east a
quarter-mile, then at N Shadeland Ave turn right
and this place is about a half-mile south.

Wild Oats

1300 East 86th Street; 317-706-0900
Hours: Monday to Saturday 8 am to 9 pm
Sunday 9 am to 8 pm
Natural Food Store and Cafe. Deli, Bakery, Salad
Bar and Juice Bar. Organic produce.
Directions: This place is north of the downtown,
just inside I-465 north beltway. From I-465, take
Rte 31 (N Meridian St, Exit #31) exit and go
south on Meridian St, then at 86th St turn left
and this place is one mile down.

Winding Way Farm Health Foods Store & Taste of the World Deli

5888 East 82nd Street
317-849-3362
Hours: Monday to Saturday 10 am to 9 pm
Closed Sunday.
Natural Food Store. Limited organic produce.
Directions: This place is in northeast Indianapolis, a little outside of the beltway, a mile northwest of the junction of I-69 & I-465. From I-465, take I-69 northeast for two miles and take
the E 82nd St (#1) exit and then go west on E
82nd St and this place is 2 miles down.

KOKOMO

Sunspot Natural Foods
314 East Markland Avenue
765-459-4717
Hours: Monday to Saturday 9 am to 6 pm
Closed Sunday.
Natural Food Store.
Directions: Going north on Rte 31, at Markland Ave (Hwy 22/35) go west and this place is 1½ mile down on the north side of the road at the 4th traffic light. It has a dark green awning.

MISHAWAKA (South Bend suburb)

Garden Patch Market
228 West Edison Road, between Grape Road and Main Street
219-255-3151
Hours: Monday to Saturday 10 am to 7 pm
Closed Sunday.
Natural Food Store. Just has organic carrots and apples. No deli.
Comments: Has a good selection of bulk foods.
Directions: From I-80/90 (Indiana Toll Road), take Mishawaka exit (#83) and go a half-mile northwest of Capital Ave. At Rte 23 go west 1½ mile, then at Main St turn left (south) and go 2 miles south, then at Edison turn right and this place is 2 blocks down on the right.

NEW ALBANY

Lady Hawk's Café
614 Hausfeldt Lane, inside Creekside Outpost
812-948-9118
Hours: Tuesday to Saturday 10 am to 7 pm
Closed Sunday & Monday.
Native American Natural Foods Café. Not pure vegetarian.

Menu: Has a good selection of vegetarian dishes. Sandwiches, salads and main dishes. Yellow-eye Bean Chili is good. Good sarsaparilla tea. Has diabetic desserts.
Comments: Interesting atmosphere.

RICHMOND

Clear Creek Food Co-op
Box E290, Earlham College in Physical Plant building, 701 West National Road
765-983-1547
Hours: Monday to Friday 11 am to 6 pm
Saturday & Sunday 11 am to 5 pm
Natural Food Store and Café. Deli.
Menu: Has a selection of vegetarian and vegan dishes. Has ready-made sandwiches.
Comments: Deli is only open during the school year.
Other Info: Accepts MC, VISA.
Directions: From I-70, take Rte 35 south (exit #149) in the direction of Earlham College. At Hwy 40 turn right and this place is a quarter-mile down. On the road before the main entrance turn left at College Ave. On Earlham College campus.

WEST LAFAYETTE

SAS Health Foods
Osco Shopping Plaza
951 Sagamore Parkway West
765-463-4827
Hours: Monday to Saturday 9:30 am to 7 pm
Closed Sunday.
Natural Food Store. No produce.
Directions: From I-65, take exit #178 and take Hwy 43 southwest towards Lafayette about 3 miles. At US 52 turn right and this place is one mile down on the left in Osco Shopping Plaza.

Iowa

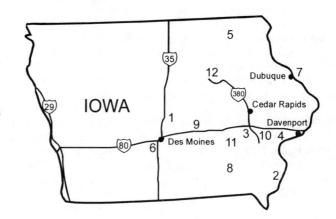

1. Ames
2. Burlington
3. Coralville
4. Davenport
5. Decorah
6. Des Moines
7. Dubuque
8. Fairfield
9. Grinnell
10. Iowa City
11. Kalona
12. Waterloo

AMES

Café Beaudelaire
2504 Lincoln Way; 515-292-7429
Hours: Sunday to Thursday 10 am to 12 pm
Friday & Saturday 10 am to 2 pm
Brazilian and Mediterranean. Not pure vegetarian.
Menu: The Iron Vegetarian is good. Salads, Vegetarian Fettuccine and Veggie Pita.
Other Info: Full service, take-out. Accepts AMEX, DIS, MC, VISA.

Café Lovish
2512 Lincoln Way; 515-292-9900
Hours: Daily for lunch and dinner
International Natural Foods. Not pure veg.
Menu: Has a wide variety of vegetarian dishes. Veggie burgers, stir-fry, Mexican dishes and veggie burritos.
Other Info: Full service, take-out. Price: $-$$.
Directions: It is located near Iowa State University. From I-35 N, take Exit #111B (Ames/Iowa State U) and get on Rte 30 going west for 3½ miles. Take Elwood Dr (#146) exit, stay right at fork and get on Elwood Dr and go 1½ mile. At Lincoln Way turn left and go ¾ mile.

Pizza Kitchens
120 Hayward Avenue; 515-292-171
Hours: Monday to Thursday 11:30 am to 10 pm
Friday & Saturday 11:30 am to 12 midnight
Sunday 11:30 am to 9 pm
Gourmet Pizza. Not pure vegetarian.

Menu: Has Italian pastas and pizzas. Cappuccino, espresso.
Other Info: Full service, take-out. Accepts AMEX, MC, VISA. Price: $$.
Directions: Located near Iowa State University.

Wheatfield Grocery Coop
413 Douglas Avenue
515-232-4094; **email:** wheatsfield@uswest.net
Hours: Monday to Saturday 9 am to 9 pm
Closed Sunday.
Natural Food Store. Organic produce. No deli.
Comments: Small store with a fairly good selection of dishes. Reasonable priced.
Directions: From I-35 coming north from Des Moines, take Exit #111B (Ames/Iowa State U) and go west two mile on Rte 30, then take Duff Avenue exit (#148) towards Huxley and go north on Rte 69 (Duff Ave) 1½ mile, at Main St turn left and go one block and at Douglas Ave turn right and this place near corner on left.

BURLINGTON

Nature's Corner
423 Jefferson Street
319-754-8653
Hours: Monday to Friday 9:30 am to 5:30 pm; Saturday 9:30 am to 5 pm; closed Sunday.
Natural Food Store.
Directions: From Hwy 34, take downtown exit near bridge. Go three blocks south on Main, at Jefferson turn right and go 3 blocks. This place at bottom of hill at Jefferson and 5th.

CORALVILLE (NEAR IOWA CITY)

Mekong

222 1st Avenue; 319-337-9910
Hours: Monday to Saturday 4:30 pm to 9:30 pm
Closed Sunday.
Vietnamese and Chinese. Not pure vegetarian.
Other Info: Full service, take-out. Price: $.

New Pioneer Co-op

City Center Square; 1101 2nd Street, Coralville;
319-358-5513; fax: 319-358-5514; email:
jmasada@newpi.com, newpi@newpi.com
Web site: www.newpi.com
Hours: Daily 7 am to 10 pm
Natural Food Store and Deli. Organic Coffee
Bar and Bakery. Locally grown produce and bulk
items.
Menu: Has a large selection of vegetarian and
vegan dishes.
Comments: Knowledgeable staff. On web site has
a list of breads and baked goods they make and
their ingredients. Has a wide selection of bulk
and other items. One of the better natural foods
stores in the country.
Other Info: Counter service, take-out only. There
is no seating.
Directions: From I-80 take the Rte 965 exit
(#240) towards Coralville/North Liberty (Rte 6),
at fork in ramp stay left, then turn left onto Rte
965 and go a half-mile. Then turn left onto Rte 6
and this place is about 2 miles down.

DAVENPORT

The Greatest Grains On Earth

1600 Harrison Street; 563-323-7521
Hours: Mon to Fri 11 am to 8:30 pm; Sat 11 am
to 7:30 pm; Sun 12 noon to 6:30 pm
Natural Foods Store and Deli. Bakery and Juice
Bar. Vegan options. Not pure vegetarian. Super-
market-type place. Organic produce.
Menu: Freshly made soups, salads, sandwiches,
Zucchini Feta Casserole, Artichoke Squares,
burritos, quesadillas, veggie burgers, Steamed
Vegetables, Tabbouleh Salad, Bean & Grain Salad,
Vegetarian Lasagna, Fruit Salad, BBQ Tempeh,
Spinach Potato Pie, AuGratin Potatoes, enchila-
das, pizzas and desserts. Apple Pie and Tofu Pud-
ding Pie. Fresh juices and smoothies.
Comments: Food is sold by the pound and by
the piece.
Other Info: Counter service, take-out. Price: $.
Directions: From I-74, take Middle Rd exit (#3)
toward Locust Rd. Go west 3 miles on Middle
Rd into Davenport (road becomes Locust). At

Harrison (US 61) turn left and this place two
blocks down on right corner of 16th St.

India House

220 North Harrison Street; 563-322-3755
Hours: Daily 11:30 am to 2:30 pm, 5 pm to 10
pm; Lunch Buffet: Daily 11:30 am to 2 pm
Indian. Vegan friendly. Not pure vegetarian.
Comments: One of best Indian places in town.
Other Info: Full service, take-out. Accepts MC,
VISA. Price: $-$$.

DECORAH

Oneota Community Co-op

415 West Water Street
563-382-4666; email: foodcoop@oneota.net;
Web site: www.oneota.net/~foodcoop
Hours: Monday to Thursday 9 am to 8 pm; Fri
& Sat 9 am to 5 pm; Sun 12 noon to 4 pm
Natural Food Store and Deli. Organic produce
and locally grown produce. Not pure vegetarian.
Comments: Has a wide selection of bulk goods.
Open since 1985. Seats 12.
Directions: From Hwy 52 north, turn onto Rte
9 and go half a mile, at Division St turn left and
go a quarter-mile, at Short St turn right (north,
becomes Mechanic) and this place is ¾ mile down
at corner of W Water and Mechanic. Coming
south on Hwy 52 turn off onto College Dr and
go southeast into town, then turn slight left onto
W Water St and this place is two blocks down.

DES MOINES

A Taste of Thailand

215 East Walnut Street; 515-282-0044
Hours: Monday to Friday 11 am to 2 pm, 5 pm
to 9 pm; Saturday 5 pm to 9 pm; closed Sunday.
Thai. Vegan options. Not pure vegetarian.
Menu: Has a large selection of vegetarian dishes.
Soups, Thai Salad, Spring Rolls, and rice and
noodles dishes. Tom Kha Soup is good. Has wheat
gluten and tofu mock meat dishes. Fresh juices.
Comments: Got reviews in the New York Times
and USA Today.
Other Info: Full service, take-out. Accepts
AMEX, MC, VISA. Price: $$.

Campbell's Nutrition Center

4040 University Avenue, Suite D; 515-277-6351
Hours: Mon to Thur 9 am to 7 pm; Fri 9 am to
6 pm; Sat 9 am to 5 pm; closed Sun.
Natural Food Store and Deli. Organic produce.
Menu: Has a selection of vegetarian sandwiches,
soups and salads. Vegetarian pita sandwiches.

Comments: Store sells herbs and aromatherapy products.
Other Info: Counter service, take-out. Has 12 seats. Price: $
Directions: From I-235 east, take 42nd St exit and go north three blocks, then at University turn right and this place on right 1½ block down between 40th and 41st.

Drake Diner
1111 25th Street; 515-277-1111
Hours: Monday to Saturday 7 am to 11 pm
Sunday 7 am to 10 pm
American Diner. Vegan friendly. Not pure veg.
Menu: Has good selection of vegetarian dishes. Two types of veggie burgers, steamed vegetables and pasta dishes.
Comments: Good food. Reasonable prices.
Directions: From I-235 E, take ML King Jr Pkwy/Airport exit, and then go northwest on Cottage Grove Ave a third-mile (bear right coming from east and turn left coming from west), at 25th turn right and this place is a block down.

El Patio Mexican Restaurant
6111 37th Street; 515-274-2303
Hours: Tuesday to Sunday 5 pm to 9:30 pm
Closed Monday.
Mexican. Not pure vegetarian.
Other Info: Full service. Accepts MC, VISA. Price: $$.

India Café
3729 86th Street, Urbandale; 515-278-2929
Hours: Daily 11:30 am to 2:30 pm, 5 pm to 9:30 pm (closed 9 pm on Sunday)
Indian. Vegan options. Not pure vegetarian.
Menu: Good Northern Indian dishes. Has a good selection of vegetarian dishes. Good variety of Indian breads.
Comments: Pleasant atmosphere.
Other Info: Accepts AMEX, DC, DIS, MC, VISA.

New City Market Natural Grocery
4721 University Avenue
515-255-7380
Hours: Monday, Friday 9 am to 6:30 pm; Tuesday to Thursday 9 am to 8 pm; Saturday 9 am to 6 pm; Sunday 11 am to 5 pm
Natural Food Store. Organic produce. Small place.
Directions: From I-235 east, take 42nd St exit and go north three blocks, then at University turn left. This place on right 5½ blocks down between 47th and 48th.

North End Dinner
5055 Merle Hay Road; 515-276-5151
Hours: Sunday to Thursday 6 am to 10 pm
Friday & Saturday 6 am to 11 pm
American Diner. Same as Drake Dinner above. Used to be under same ownership.

Sheffield's Restaurant
10201 University, near Valley West Mall
515-224-6774
Hours: Monday to Saturday 10 am to 8 pm
Sunday 10 am to 5 pm
Natural Foods. Not pure vegetarian.
Menu: Soups, salads, sandwiches, pizzas and other dishes. Everything is made on premises including the salad dressings. Fresh juices.
Other Info: Full service, take-out. Accepts AMEX, DIS, MC, VISA. Price: $.

Timbuktuu Coffee Bar
821 42nd Street; 515-255-8681
Hours: Monday to Saturday 6 am to 9 pm
Sunday 7 am to 8 pm
Vegan friendly Coffee Shop. Eclectic.
Menu: Eggplant Lasagna, Grilled Sandwich, a daily vegetarian soup and Veggie Wrap. Has a Veggie Quiche that contains eggs.
Other Info: Accepts AMEX, DIS, MC, VISA.

West End Dinner
3535 West Town Parkway; 515-222-3131
Hours: Sunday to Thursday 6 am to 10 pm
Friday & Saturday 6 am to 11 pm
American Diner. Same as Drake Dinner above. Used to be under same ownership.

DUBUQUE

Breitbach's Farmers' Market Food Store
1109 Iowa Street; 319-557-1777
Hours: Monday to Friday 10 am to 5:30 pm
Saturday 8 am to 5 pm
Natural Food Store. Organic produce.
Directions: In the downtown, near City Hall. From Hwy 61, get on Rte 52 and go a mile, at 11th St turn left and this is place is on the next block.

FAIRFIELD

Everybody's Market and Backstage at Everybody's
501 North 2nd St (Highway 1); 641-472-5199
Store Hours: Monday to Friday 8:30 am to 9 pm
Saturday & Sunday 8:30 am to 4 pm
Café Hours: Monday to Friday 11:30 am to 2

pm, 6 pm to 8 pm. Closed Saturday & Sunday. **Natural Food Store and International Café.** All-you-can-eat Buffet. Juice Bar. Vegan friendly. Not pure vegetarian. Good selection of organic produce. **Menu:** Organic veggie buffet food. Pizza. **Comments:** Good food at reasonable prices. This place is an excellent health food store with an extensive amount of vegetarian products. Uses organic produce. Good, friendly store. **Other Info:** Buffet style, take-out. Non-smoking. Accepts AMEX, DIS, MC, VISA. **Directions:** This place is on Rte 1, at the junction of Lowe Ave.

**Mohan Delights
101 West Broadway; 641-469-6900
Hours: Mon to Sat 11:30 am to 1:30 pm
Vegetarian Indian.
Comments: Authentic Indian food. Uses Ayurvedic methods. Has a set menu. Uses Styrofoam dishes and plastic utensils. Only open during lunch.
Directions: From junction of Rte 1 and Hwy-34 go north on Rte 1 one block, then turn left onto W Broadway Ave and this place is one block down.

**The Raj
Ayurvedic Health Center; 1734 Jasmine Avenue 641-472-9580, 800-248-9050; **email:** theraj@lisco.com; **Web site:** www.theraj.com
Hours: 12 noon to 2 pm
Serves dinner but is not open to the public.
Fully Indian Vegetarian. Some International. Organic produce used. Buffet and Salad Bar.
Menu: Has a good lunch buffet with several vegetarian dishes. Has a different ethnic cuisine each day. Salads, fresh baked rolls, homemade pizzas, dal, rice and dessert.
Comments: Upscale in Maharishi Ayurvedic Health Center. Food is excellent and restaurant is peaceful. A good place. Use organic and non-GMO foods as often as possible as it is important with them. Has information about Ayurvedic medicine on their web site. Has Raj Recipe Book available on web site.
Other Info: Reservations recommended for weekend brunch. Price: $-$$.
Directions: This place is outside of town, northwest of Fairfield, near the municipal airport.

GRINNELL

Juli's Health & More Food Store
931 West Street, at Highway 146 & 4th
641-236-7376; **Web site:** http://www.julishealth

food.homestead.com/health.html
Hours: Monday to Friday 8 am to 6 pm; Saturday 8 am to 12 pm; closed Sunday.
Natural Food Store and Cafe. Organic produce.
Menu: Has a selection of vegetarian dishes.
Comments: Has a good bulk food section.
Other Info: Full service. Accepts MC, VISA.
Directions: From I-80, take Rte 146 (#182) exit towards Grinnell/New Sharon, at Rte 146 go north and go 3½ miles (becomes West St).

IOWA CITY

Cottage Bakery
14 South Linn Street, corner Iowa Avenue 319-351-0052
Hours: Monday to Saturday 6:30 am to 7 pm Sunday 8 am to 4 pm
American. Not pure vegetarian.
Menu: Veggie sandwiches, usually a vegetarian soup and fresh baked breads.
Other Info: Accepts AMEX, MC, VISA.

Givanni's
109 East College Street; 319-338-5967
Hours: Monday to Thursday 11 am to 10 pm; Fri & Sat 11 am to 11 pm; Sun 4 noon to 10 pm
Italian. Not pure vegetarian.
Menu: About half of the dishes on the menu are vegetarian. Veggie Lasagna, Cheese Ravioli, salads, sandwiches, gourmet pizzas, pasta dishes, breads and Pasta Florentine.
Other Info: Full service, take-out. Accepts AMEX, DC, DIS, MC, VISA. Price: $-$$.

Hamburg Inn
214 North Linn Street; 319-337-5512
Hours: Daily 6 am to 11 pm
American. Vegan friendly.
Menu: Homemade veggie burgers and veggie breakfast meats (order at any time), French fries, and vegan Pasta Salad.
Comments: Small, relaxed place. Price: $$.
Warning: According to my conversation the veggie burgers are cooked on the same grill as meat (didn't get a totally straight answer), so you should definitely request that it is cooked separately.
Directions: In an historical area, near the University of Iowa.

**Masala Indian Vegetarian Cuisine
9 South Dubuque Street; 319-338-6199
Hours: Daily 11 am to 2:30 pm, 5 pm to 10 pm
Fully Vegetarian authentic Indian. Daily Lunch buffet has over 20 items. Mostly Vegan.
Menu: Has a wide selection of vegetarian dishes.

Menu changes daily and there are nightly specials. Fresh homemade breads from the clay oven. Masala Dosa with coconut sauce and sambar, Malai Kofta, Bengan Bartha (roasted eggplant with tomatoes), Sag Paneer (fresh spinach & cheese) and rice dishes. Special Dinner Thali. Cappuccino, espresso.

Comments: Uses fresh vegetables and fruit. Grinds own spices for freshness. Can choice spice levels. Monday dinner is $3.99. Tuesday is Chat (snacks) Night with traditional Indian snacks like Channa Chat, Aloo Tikkia, and Bhel Poori,

Other Info: Full service, catering, buffet, take-out. Non-smoking. Accepts reservations but not necessary. Accepts DIS, MC, VISA and Personal Cheques. Price: $-$$

Directions: Located Downtown. From I-80 take exit #244 (Dubuque St.). Then go south on Dubuque two miles. This place on the right after Iowa Avenue in downtown Iowa City. Parking in front of the restaurant on Dubuque St and on the north side on Iowa Ave.

New Pioneer Co-op
22 South Van Buren Street, at Washington
319-338-9441; **fax:** 319-338-0635; **email:** jmasada@newpi.com, newpi@newpi.com
Web site: www.newpi.com
Hours: Daily 8 am to 10 pm
Natural Food Store and Deli. Bakery. Locally grown produce. Organic Coffee Bar.
Menu: Has a large selection of vegetarian dishes.
Comments: Knowledgeable staff. On web site has a list of breads and baked goods they make and their ingredients. Has a wide selection of bulk and other items. One of the better natural food stores in the country.
Other Info: Counter service, take-out. Seating.
Directions: This place four blocks east of Old Capital. From I-80 it is 12 blocks. From I-80, take University of Iowa exit (#244, Dubuque St). Go south on Dubuque about two miles. At Washington St (a block after Iowa City) turn left, then at S Van Buren (third block) turn left and this place is at end of block on left.

Panchero's Mexican Grill
32 South Clinton Street
319-338-6311
Hours: Sunday to Thursday 11 am to 2 am
Thursday to Saturday 11 am to 3 am
Mexican. Not pure vegetarian.
Menu: Has no-lard beans and rice (uses vegetable shortening), homemade tortillas, grilled vegetable burritos (grilled on same grill as meat but is

cleaned in between) and fresh salsas.
Other Info: Accepts AMEX, DIS, MC, VISA.

**The Red Avocado
521 East Washington Street #3
319-351-6088; **Web site:** www.theredavocado.com
Hours: Tuesday to Friday 11 am to 2:30 pm, 5:30 pm to 10 pm; Saturday 11 am to 2:30 pm, 5:30 pm to 9 pm; Sun 12 noon to 9 pm; closed Mon.
Fully Vegetarian. Mostly Vegan. 98% of ingredients used are organic.
Menu: Coconut Corn Soup, baba ghanouj, Salad Organica, Cashew Coconut Pasta, Sesame Potatoes, Hummus & Pita, Tempeh Reuben Sandwich, veggie burgers, Caribbean Chili, Grilled Seasonal Vegetables, Jerked Tempeh, Emerald Stew & Rice, burritos, Vegetable & Tempeh Stir-fry with Rice, Raw Vegetable Plate and desserts. All organic fresh squeezed juices and spritzers.
Comments: Mainly uses organic ingredients. Very friendly place.
Other Info: Full service, take-out. Smoking allowed only outside. Reservations recommended. No credit cards. Price: $$.
Directions: From I-80, take Dubuque St exit (#244), go south on Dubuque about 2 miles to downtown Iowa City. At Jefferson turn right and go 3 blocks to Van Buren. Turn right at Van Buren, go 2 blocks to Washington. Turn left and this place is half way down this block.

KALONA

Foods Naturally
603 B Avenue
319-656-3437; **Web site:** http://www.netins.net/showcase/balancedlife/foodsnat.htm
Hours: Monday to Friday 10 am to 6 pm; Saturday 9 am to 5 pm; closed Sunday.
Natural Food Store. Only sells vegetarian items. Has local homemade food products.
Other Info: Accepts AMEX, MC, VISA.
Directions: In downtown area of Kalona. From Rte 22, go south on 7th St three blocks.

WATERLOO

Green Fields Health Food Center
2920 Falls Avenue; 319-235-9990
Hours: Monday to Friday 9:30 am to 5:30 pm
Saturday 9:30 am to 5 pm
Natural Food Store.
Directions: From I-20, go north on Green Hill Rd. At University turn left, then at Falls Ave turn left. This place on left.

Kansas

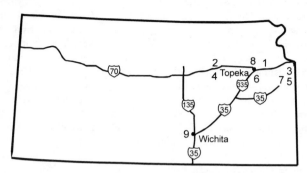

1. Lawrence
2. Manhattan
3. Mission
4. Overland Park
5. Prairie Village
6. Shawnee
7. Shawnee Mission
8. Topeka
9. Wichita

LAWRENCE

***Community Mercantile Co-op
901 Iowa Street (Rte 59), at West 9th Street
785-843-8544; **fax:** 785-843-7572; **email:**
themerc@communitymercantile.com
Store Hours: Daily 7 am to 10 pm
Hot Deli Case Hours: Monday to Friday 11 am
to 1:30 pm, 4:30 pm to 7 pm
Saturday 8 am to 2 pm
Salad Bar Hours: Monday to Friday 9 am to 8
pm; Saturday & Sunday 9 am to 6 pm
Natural Food Store and Deli. Large Salad Bar
and Hot Bar. Juice Bar. Organic produce. Not
pure vegetarian.
Menu: Has a great salad bar and vegan friendly
carryout deli. Vegetable of the Day, Mash Potatoes, Macaroni & Cheese, rice, Gravy Beat Loaf,
bagels and sourdough bread.
Comments: Has fresh baked goods and large bulk
department. Has a good selection of dishes and is
a friendly place.
Directions: From I-70, take Exit #202 toward
Rte 59 S/West Lawrence. Go south on McDonald
Dr for 1¼ mile (McDonald merge into Rte 59),
and this place on Rte 59 on the right about 1½
mile south of I-70. This place is in a large yellow building at Mississippi and 9th. From I-70,
take East Lawrence exit. At N 2nd St (at stop
sign) turn left. After crossing bridge 2nd St become Vermont. At 9th turn right.

Paradise Café
728 Massachusetts Street; 785-842-5199
Hours: Monday to Saturday 6:30 am to 2:30 pm;
Wednesday to Saturday 5 pm to 10 pm; Sunday
8 am to 2:30 pm
International Natural Foods. Vegan options. Not
pure vegetarian.
Menu: Italian, Mexican and other international
cuisines. There are some vegan dishes for break-
fast. Homemade breads and desserts. Garden
Burger, Spinach Enchilada and pastas
Other Info: Full service, take-out. Accepts DIS,
MC, VISA. Price: $$.
Directions: From I-70, take Exit #204 toward
Rte 24/ East Lawrence/Rte 59. Go south on Rte
40 and go about a mile crossing a bridge. After
crossing the bridge get on Massachusetts St (40
turns right & Mass goes straight). This place is
1½ block down, a little past E 7th St.

Yello Sub (2 locations)
624 West 12th   785-841-3268
1814 West 23rd   785-843-6000
Hours: Sunday to Thursday 10 am to 11 pm
Friday & Saturday 10 am to 12 midnight
Sandwich Place. Not pure vegetarian.
Menu: Hot and cold subs and salads. Has good
vegetarian subs (10 different kinds) including tem-
peh and tofu sandwiches.

MANHATTAN

People's Grocery Cooperative Exchange
517 S 17th St, at Yuma; 785-539-4811
email: organic@flinthills.com; **Web site:**
http://www.flinthills.com/~organic
Hours: Monday to Friday 10 am to 7 pm; Satur-
day 9 am to 6 pm; closed Sunday
Natural Food Store. Organic produce.
Directions: From I-70, take the Manhattan Exit

and take Hwy 177 north eight miles. Hwy 177 bears left and becomes Pillsbury Dr (then also becomes Rte 18). After crossing the river entering town make a slight left onto Pierre after 1½ block and go straight about 5 blocks, then at Juliette turn left and go one block, then at Colorado turn right. This place on left after a block.

MISSION (7 miles southwest of Kansas City)

Wild Oats Market

5101 Johnson Drive, at Roseland Drive
913-722-4069
Hours: Daily 8 am to 10 pm
Natural Food Store and Cafe. Deli, Bakery, Salad Bar and Juice Bar. Organic produce. Supermarket-size place.
Directions: This place is next to the Mission Center Mall (northwest of it). From I-35, take S 18th St Expressway south (becomes W Roe Blvd) for 1½ mile. Take Johnson Dr ramp and this place is just past the mall.

OVERLAND PARK (about 15 mile southwest of Kansas City)

Kashmir Restaurant

9036 Metcalf Avenue
913-341-0415
Hours: Daily 11 am to 2 pm (Lunch Buffet), 5 pm to 9:30 pm
Indian. Not pure vegetarian.
Menu: Samosas, pakoras, rice, Aloo Chole and other vegetarian dishes. Set vegetarian dinner.
Other Info: Full service. Accepts AMEX, DC, DIS, MC, VISA. Price: $$.

Wild Oats Marketplace

6621 West 119th Street, at Metcalf
913-663-2951
Hours: Daily 7 am to 10 pm
Natural Food Store and Cafe. Deli, Bakery, Salad Bar and Juice Bar. Organic produce. Supermarket-size place.
Directions: From I-435 S, take Metcalf Ave (Rte 169, #79) exit. Go south on Rte 169 for 1½ mile. Then at W 119 St turn left and this place is 4/10 mile down.

PRAIRIE VILLAGE

Manna Nutrition Store

5235 West 95th
913-381-6604
Natural Food Store.

SHAWNEE

Food Bin

12268 Shawnee Mission Parkway
913-268-4103
Hours: Monday to Wednesday, Friday 10 am to 7 pm; Thursday 10 am to 8 pm; Saturday 10 am to 6 pm; Sunday 12 noon to 5 pm
Natural Food Store. Coffee shop.
Directions: From I-35, take Shawnee Mission Parkway exit (#228B) and go two miles west on Shawnee Mission Park. This store is 1½ block west of junction of Quivira Rd and Shawnee.

SHAWNEE MISSION

Shawnee Mission Medical Center

9100 West 74th Street, Box 2923
913-676-2496
Hours: Daily 6 am to 9:30 pm, 11 am to 2:30 pm, 4 pm to 7 pm
Hospital Cafeteria. Not pure vegetarian.
Menu: Has many vegetarian dishes.
Comments: Seventh Day Adventist hospital.
Other Info: Cafeteria style, take-out. Price: $.
Directions: Right off I-35, at 74th Street.

TOPEKA

Akin's

Brookwood Shopping Center
2913 SW 29th Street; 785-228-9131
Hours: Daily 9 am to 9 pm
Natural Food Store. Organic produce. Supermarket-size place.
Directions: From I-470, take Exit #4, then go north on SW Gage Blvd a third-mile, then at SW 29th St turn right and this place is a half-mile down.

Tallgrass Bakery & Café

2701 SW 17th Street; 785-357-1003
Hours: Daily 7 am to 3 pm
Vegetarian Restaurant. Vegan options.
Menu: Potato Leek Soup, homemade breads, salad and sandwiches.
Comments: Local organic produce used when possible. Good food.
Directions: From I-70 take exit #362A toward 4th Street, then go west on SE 3rd St a half mile, then turn left onto Rte 75 Alt. At Huntoon St turn right (go west) and go about 1½ mile, then turn left onto SW Medford Ave (go south) and go ¾ mile, at 17th turn right and this place is a block down.

Topeka Food Co-op
1195 Southwest Buchanan Street
785-235-2309
Hours: Monday to Friday 4 pm to 7 pm; Saturday 11 am to 5 pm; Sunday 12 noon to 2 pm
Natural Food Store.
Directions: From I-70, take either #362B or #362C exit and then go south and get on 12th St. Turn right (go west). This place is about 1½ mile west of the exit. Go past Buchanan a half-block and turn right into an alley. Then follow signs to Topeka Food Co-op. This place at backside of the Buchanan school (center).

WICHITA

Food For Thought, Inc
2929 East Central Avenue, at Hillside
316-683-6078; **email:** store@fft.net; **fax:** 316-683-4141; **Web site:** www.fft.net
Hours: Monday to Friday 9 am to 6 pm; Saturday 9:30 am to 5:30 pm; closed Sunday.
Natural Food Store and take-out Deli. Vegan options. Not pure vegetarian. Organic produce, vitamins, cosmetics and books.
Menu: Vegan Tex-Mex Lasagna, vegetarian chili, Tempeh-tation, enchiladas, California Dreamin' and soups. Fresh juices.
Other Info: Accepts AMEX, DIS, MC, VISA. Price: $.
Directions: From I-135 north, take Central Ave exit and go east around 12 blocks (0.6 mile). This store is on the right between Grove and Hillside. From I-135 south, take 1st St exit and then go east. At Grove St, turn left, then turn right on Central, and this store is 6 blocks down on the right.

Nature's Mercantile Ltd.
2900 East Central Avenue
316-685-3888
Hours: Monday to Friday 9:30 am to 6 pm; Saturday 9:30 am to 5:30 pm; closed Sunday.
Natural Food Store.
Directions: From I-135 north, take Central Ave (7A) exit and go east around 9 blocks (half-mile). This store is at the corner of Erie and Central. Grove and Hillside. From I-135 south, take 1st St exit and then go east. At Grove St, turn left, then turn right on Central, and this store is 3 blocks down.

Kentucky

1. Bowling Green
2. Danville
3. Lexington
4. Louisville

Louisville
Lexington
Bowling Green

DANVILLE

Two Roads Café
132 Church Street
859-236-9847
Hours: Monday to Friday 11 am to 3 pm; Friday 6 am to 8:30 pm; closed Saturday & Sunday
Restaurant. Not pure vegetarian.
Menu: Has a selection of vegetarian dishes. Spinach Quiche, pastas, Roasted Vegetarian Pita, Olive Nut Sandwich and a good selection of salads.
Other Info: Accepts AMEX, DIS, MC, VISA.

LEXINGTON

Alfalfa Restaurant
557 South Limestone Street
859-253-0014
Hours: Monday 11 am to 2 pm; Tuesday to Saturday 11 am to 2 pm, 5:30 pm to 9 pm (until 10 pm on Friday & Saturday); Saturday & Sunday Brunch 10 am to 2 pm
International and Regional. Vegetarian friendly. Vegan options. Not pure vegetarian.
Menu: Has four vegetarian specials along with their regular vegetarian dishes. Salads, homemade whole-grain breads, desserts and main dishes. Garden Burger, pastas, vegan burritos, salads, rice dishes, steamed vegetables and more.
Comments: Causal place. Specializes in vegetarian dishes. Food gets good ratings. Sometimes has live music on the weekends. Wednesday is international night, when food from around the world is served.
Other Info: Full service, take-out. Accepts MC,

VISA. Price: $-$$
Directions: From US-60, take Rte 4 S (New Circle Rd) exit, and go southeast 2 miles on Rte 4 S. Then take Harrodsburg Rd (Rte 68) exit (#2) towards Lexington/Harrodsburg. Turn left onto Rte 68 E and go about 3 miles. At Rte 27 (S Limestone St) turn right and this place is about a half-mile down.

Everybody's Natural Foods & Deli
371 South Limestone
859-255-4162
Hours: Monday to Friday 9 am to 6 pm; Saturday & Sunday 10 am to 6 pm; Saturday & Sunday Brunch 10 am to 3 pm
Natural Food Restaurant. 95% Vegetarian. Good selection of vegan options. Organic produce.
Menu: For breakfast has tofu scramble, soy-sausage and vegan pancakes with maple syrup. Deli serves sandwiches (30 different ones), soups, vegetable Lasagna, calzones, Vegetable Pot Pie and salads. Also serves vegetarian and vegan main dishes. Homemade vegan desserts. Fresh juices and smoothies.
Comments: Open since 1978. Creative dishes. Pleasant, happening place. Food is good.
Other Info: Limited service, take-out. Accepts DIS, MC, VISA. Price: $.
Direction: Near the University of Kentucky.

Good Foods Co-op
439 Southland Drive, Suite D
859-278-1813
Hours: Monday to Saturday 9 am to 9 pm
Sunday 11 am to 7 pm

Natural Food Store and Deli. Organic produce. Menu: Has ready-made sandwiches and salads. Comments: Largest natural food store in Kentucky. Large selection of bulk foods, organic produce, cruelty-free body care items, herbs, frozen goods and more. Gives 5% discount to members of other co-ops.

Directions: From I-64, take 922 south exit and then turn right onto Nicholasville Rd. Go in the direction of the downtown and pass through center of town. At Southland turn right. This place on right. Or from US-60, take Rte 4 S/New Circle Rd ramp and go south on Rte 4 two miles. Take Rte 66 (Harrodsburg Rd) exit #2 towards Lexington/Harrodsburg. Turn left onto Rte 68 E, then turn right at Lane Allen Rd (becomes Rosemont Garden) and go a half-mile, turn slight right onto Southland Dr and this place is 0.40 down the road.

Rainbow Blossom Natural Foods

4101 Tates Creek Center (on Man-O-War Blvd)
859-273-0579
Hours: Monday to Saturday 9 am to 8 pm
Sunday 12 noon to 6 pm
Natural Food Store. No produce.
Directions: This place is south of the Rte 4 beltway directly south of downtown. From I-75, take Man-O-War Blvd exit (#108) go southwest about 6 miles on Man-O-War Blvd (it is a fast moving local road). Then this place is a quarter-mile past Tates Creek Rd on the right. You can also take Tates Creeks Rd exit from Rte 4 beltway and, then turn left at Man-O-War Blvd and this place is a quarter-mile down on right in Tate's Creek Centre.

LOUISVILLE

**Amazing Grace Whole Foods & Nutrition Center

1133 Bardstown Road; 502-485-1122; Web site: http://www.amazinggracewholefoods.com/
Hours: Monday to Saturday 9 am to 9 pm
Sunday 11 am to 6 pm
Natural Food Store and Vegetarian & Vegan Deli. Bakery. Sometimes has organic produce.
Menu: Serves organic vegan food. Soups, salads, wraps and mock meat sandwiches.
Comments: Food gets good ratings.
Other Info: Counter service, take-out. Has sitdown area. Non-smoking. Accepts AMEX, DIS, MC, VISA.

Directions: This place is in southeast Louisville. From I-64, take Grinstead Dr (#8) exit and go west on Grinstead Dr 2 miles. Then at Bardstown Rd turn left. This place on left one block down.

Grape Leaf Restaurant

2217 Frankfort Avenue
502-897-1774
Hours: Monday to Thursday 11:30 am to 8:30 pm; Friday & Saturday 11:30 am to 9:30 pm; Sunday 11:30 am to 7:30 pm
Middle Eastern. Vegan friendly. Not pure veg.
Menu: Grilled vegetables with beans and brown rice. Falafel, hummus and more.
Other Info: Full service, take-out. Smoking allowed outside. Accepts AMEX, DIS, MC, VISA. Price: $-$$.

Rainbow Blossom Natural Foods & Deli

3738 Lexington Road,
502-896-0189, 502-893-3627
Web site: www.rainbowblossom.com
Hours: Monday to Saturday 9 am to 10 pm
Sunday 11 noon to 7 pm
Natural Food Store and Vegetarian Deli. Organic produce.
Menu: Has a wide selection of vegan and vegetarian dishes. Gourmet foods. Fresh juices and smoothies.
Comments: Organic produce used when possible. Has 20 seats. Another branch in Middle Town and one in Summit.
Other Info: Counter service, take-out only. Accepts MC, VISA. Price: $.
Directions: From I-264, take exit #20A and take Shelbyville Rd 2.5 miles, then at Fairfax turn left. This place is a half-block down on right. Located by the Vogue Theater.

Rainbow Blossom

12401 Shelbyville Road (Middletown)
502-244-2022
Hours: Monday to Saturday 9 am to 9 pm
Sunday 12 am to 6 pm
Natural Food Store and Deli. Vegan friendly. Organic.
Comments: Good food and atmosphere. Next to Great Harvest, which is a natural bakery.
Other Info: Counter service, take-out. There is no seating. Accepts MC, VISA. Price: $$.
Directions: From I-265, take Shelbyville Rd/Hwy 60 (#27) exit and go towards town (west) one mile. This place on right.

Health & Harvest Natural Food Market and Café

3030 Bardstown Road
502-451-6772
Store Hours: Monday to Saturday 9 am to 9 pm
Sunday 11 am to 7 pm
Café Hours: Monday to Friday 7 am to 8 pm;
Saturday 8 am to 7 pm; Sunday 10 am to 6 pm
Natural Food Store and Deli. Organic produce.
Menu: Soups, salads, veggie sandwich, veggie chili, pastas and wraps. They use organic produce.
Other Info: Accepts AMEX, DC, DIS, MC, VISA.
Directions: From I-264, take Exit #16 (Bardstown Rd), then this place is a quarter-mile northwest on Bardstown Rd in a shopping center.

Shariat's

2901 Brownsboro Road
502-899-7878
Web site: www.shariats.com
Hours: Monday to Saturday 5 pm to 11
Closed Sunday.
American, Southwestern, European, Middle Eastern. Gourmet. Vegan friendly. Not pure veg.
Menu: Four-course vegetarian meal for $40.

About half the menu is vegetarian. Grilled Eggplant, salads, vegetarian soups and more.
Comments: This place is a bit upscale, elegant. Owned by a vegetarian. Local organic produce used when possible. Very good food. Got several good reviews in the local media.
Other Info: Full service, take-out, catering. Reservations suggested. Accepts AMEX, DIS, MC, VISA. Price: $$.
Directions: From I-71, take Zorn Ave (#2) exit, then go southeast on Zorn Rd 1 mile, then at Rebel Rd turn right, then at Brownsboro Rd (Rte 42) turn right and this place is one block down. Parking arranged for customers.

**Zen Garden

2240 Frankfort Avenue; 502-895-9114
Hours: Monday to Wednesday 11 am to 10 pm; Thursday to Saturday 11 am to 11 pm; Sunday 12 noon to 5 pm
Vegetarian Asian. Chinese, Thai, Japanese, Vietnamese. Vegan options.
Menu: Has a wide selection of vegetarian dishes.
Comments: Food gets good recommendations. New restaurant. Pleasant atmosphere.
Other Info: Accepts AMEX, MC, VISA.

Louisiana

1. Baton Rouge
2. Lafayette
3. Lake Charles
4. La Place
5. Metairie
6. New Orleans
7. Shreveport

BATON ROUGE

**Fortune Kitchen

254 West Chimes Street, at Highland Road
225-383-5206; **Web site:** http://www.che.lsu.edu/
veg/Fortune.htm
Hours: Monday to Thursday 11 am to 5 pm
Closed Saturday & Sunday.
Fully Vegetarian Chinese & Indian. Also American.
Menu: Fried Rice Combo, Stir-fried Vegetables
Lo Mien, Veggie Burger, Veggie Steak, Fries,
Veggie Delight, Stir Fried Vegetables, Indian
Chickpeas Curry, Hash Browns, samosas,
tempuras and much more.
Comments: Low on ambiance. Good food. Reasonably priced.
Other Info: Full service, take-out. Accepts MC,
VISA. Price: $.
Directions: On the Louisiana State University
campus. From I-10, take Dalrymple Dr Exit
(#156) towards LSU. Go south on Dalrymple and
go ¾ mile. Then at E State St turn right and go a
half-mile. State St becomes Lake St, at W Chimes
St turn left and this place is a block down.

India's

5230 Essen Lane (next to Lady of Lake Hospital)
225-769-0600
Hours: Daily 11 am to 2:30 pm, 5 pm to 9:30 pm
Indian, International. All-you-can-eat daily

Lunch Buffet. Vegan friendly. Not pure vegetarian.
Menu: Has a good selection of vegetarian dishes.
Comments: Buffet for lunch and a la carte in
evening.
Other Info: Full service, take-out, catering. Accepts AMEX, DC, DIS, MC, VISA. Price: $-$$.

Living Foods

3033 Perkins Road; 225-346-1886
Hours: Monday to Saturday 9 am to 6 pm
Sunday 12 noon to 6 pm
Natural Food Store. Ready-made sandwiches.
Organic produce.
Other Info: Accepts AMEX, DIS, MC, VISA.
Directions: From I-10, take Perkins Rd exit
(#157A). Go northwest 3 blocks and this place
on right.

Living Foods

Laurel Lea, 8875A Highland Rd; 225-767-8222
Hours: Monday to Friday 9 am to 7 pm; Saturday 9 am to 6 pm; Sunday 12 noon to 5 pm
Natural Food Store. Organic produce.
Directions: From I-10 coming west from New
Orleans, take Bluebonnet Rd (#162) exit. Then
turn left onto Bluebonnet Blvd and go 3 miles,
then at Highland Rd turn right and this place is a
mile down in a shopping center. This place on
corner of Staring and Highland.

Our Daily Bread

9414 Florida Boulevard; 225-924-9910
Hours: Monday to Friday 8 am to 6 pm; Saturday 9 am to 6 pm; Sunday 12 noon to 6 pm
Deli Hours: Monday to Saturday 11 am to 3 pm
Natural Food Store. Bakery, Juice Bar and Deli. Organic produce.
Menu: Fresh breads, salads, sandwiches and hot lunches. Has a daily vegetarian soups and specials (such as veggie Lasagna).
Other Info: Accepts AMEX, DIS, MC, VISA.
Directions: From I-12, take Airline Hwy (#2) exit for Hwy 61 (Airline Hwy) east, then go about 3 miles northeast. At Florida turn right and this place is 1 mile down, two blocks east of Cortana Mall on the right.

LAFAYETTE

Oil Center Health Foods

326 Travis; 337-232-7774
Hours: Mon to Fri 9 am to 5:30 pm; Sat 9 am to 3 pm; Kitchen 9 am to 3 pm; closed Sun.
Natural Food Store and Deli. Juice Bar and Bakery. Often has organic produce.
Menu: Has a selection of vegetarian dishes. Has salads, sandwiches, a daily soup and specials (such as veggie Lasagna or veggie chili).
Other Info: Accepts AMEX, DIS, MC, VISA.
Directions: From I-49 south, take Hwy 167 two miles to Rte 90, then go one mile southeast on Rte 90. Then at Pinhoook, turn right and go about 2 miles. At Travis turn right and this place is two blocks down on the right.

LAKE CHARLES

LaTruffe Sauvage

815 Bayou Pines West; 337-439-8364; **fax:** 337-436-5954; **email:** info@latruffesauvage.com
Web site: www.latruffesauvage
Hours: Tuesday to Friday 11 am to 2 pm, 6 pm to 10 pm; Saturday 6 pm to 10 pm; Sunday Brunch 11 am to 2 pm
International. Mediterranean, French, Italian, Greek, Spanish, North African and southwest Louisiana.
Menu: Has some vegetarian dishes such as Marinated Vegetables, Linguini Primavera, organic salads, Fresh Beet & Asparagus Salad and homemade breads.
Comments: Upscale. Has cloth tablecloths and a high ceilings. Good place for a special event.
Other Info: Full service, take-out. Reservations are recommended. Non-smoking. Accepts AMEX, DC, DIS, MC, VISA. Price: $$-$$$.

Directions: A little off Lake Street, 1 block south of West Sallier. From Loop 210 West, take Lake Street exit. Turn right (north) and pass two traffic lights. Then at Bayou Pines West turn left (there are four mailboxes at this point) and then this place is on the left.

LA PLACE

Naturally Yours Health Foods

421 West Airline Highway; 985-652-2975
Hours: Monday to Friday 10 am to 6 pm; Saturday 10 am to 2 pm; closed Sunday.
Natural Food Store.
Other Info: Accepts MC, VISA.
Directions: From I-10 west, take second La Place exit (#209) and get on Rte 51 going southwest into La Place for about 4 miles. At Airline Hwy (where 51 ends), turn right and go a quarter-mile. This place is at the intersections of Airline Hwy and Rte 51, in a group of pink buildings.

METAIRIE (northwest New Orleans)

India Palace Restaurant

3322 North Turnbull Drive, one block from Veterans Boulevard; 504-889-2436; **Web site:** http://www.indiapalacerestaurant.com/
Hours: Wednesday to Monday 11:30 am to 2:30 pm, 5:30 pm to 10 pm; closed Tuesday.
Indian. Lunch Buffet. Not pure vegetarian.
Menu: Has a selection of vegetarian dishes. Good eggplant dish.
Other Info: Non-smoking. Accepts AMEX, DC, DIS, MC, VISA. Price: $$.
Directions: Visible from Veterans Memorial Blvd, the closest main road. From I-10, take Bonnabel Blvd exit (#229), then go a third-mile on Bonnabel Blvd, then at Veterans Blvd turn right and go 1¾ mile, at N Turnbull Dr turn right and this place is near the corner.

Nature Lovers

Cleary Village Shopping Center
3014 Cleary Avenue, between Veteran and I-10
504-887-4929
Hours: Monday to Friday 9 am to 6:30 pm; Saturday 9 am to 6 pm; closed Sunday.
Natural Food Store.
Other Info: Accepts AMEX, MC, VISA.
Directions: From I-10, take Clearview Pkwy (#226) exit and go south on Clearview Pkwy toward Huey Long Br, keep right at fork in ramp and get immediately onto the S Service Rd for a half-mile, then go east on W Napoleon Ave (turn left) a mile, then at Madison Ave turn right and

go a long block, then at Alberta St turn left and go one block, then at Cleary Ave turn right and this place is a quarter-block down.

Smoothie King

2725 Mississippi Avenue	504-885-1000
2222 Clearview Parkway	504-454-8002
5928 West Metairie Avenue	504-733-8956

Hours: Daily
Smoothie and Juice Bar.
Menu: Fresh juice and smoothies. Wraps.
Other Info: Counter service, take-out. Accepts AMEX, MC, VISA. Price: $.

Taj Mahal

923 C Metairie Rd, at Rosa Ave; 504-836-6859
Hours: Tuesday to Sunday 11:30 am to 2:30 pm, 5:30 pm to 10:30 pm; closed Monday.
Indian. Not pure vegetarian.
Menu: Fresh Indian bread, dal, rice dishes, Saag Dish, Aloo Gobi and other dishes. Salad with mango dressing. Potato in Red Curry.
Comments: Has got the annual "People Choice" award for best Indian restaurant in the New Orleans area several times. Uses oil for cooking. Seats 35. Silver tableware. Good, helpful service. Some people really like this place. Upscale. Food gets high ratings.
Other Info: Full service, take-out. Accepts AMEX, DC, MC, VISA. Price: $$.
Directions: Bus 27 Louisiana, 48 Esplanade, then E4 Metairie Road, 40, 41 or 44 to Canal.

Vegetarian Shoppe

4201 West Esplanade Avenue; 504-454-2306
Hours: Tuesday to Thursday 10 am to 6 pm Friday 10 am to 4 pm; closed Sat to Mon.
Natural Food Store. Organic groceries.
Directions: Located a half-mile south of the water on Esplanade Ave, just north of East Jefferson Hospital.

NEW ORLEANS

All Natural Foods

5517 Magazine Street, at Octavia Street
504-891-2651
Hours: Monday to Thursday 9 am to 8 pm; Friday & Saturday 9 am to 7 pm; Sun 9 am to 6 pm
Natural Food Store and Deli. Organic produce. Macrobiotic and Vegan options. Not pure vegetarian (serves tuna fish).
Menu: Falafel, TLT (tempeh bacon, lettuce, tomato), hummus, Tofu Burgers, tabbouleh, Greek Salad, Tempeh Spread, Tempeh Gumbo, Stir-fry

on Organic Brown Rice, soups, Cheddar Melt (on an English muffin with sprouts), vegetarian sushi, Tempeh Burgers and daily hot specials. Has good sandwiches. Fresh juices, smoothies and herbal teas.
Comments: Friendly staff. Very popular during lunchtime. Has a Lunch Club Card where after ninth lunches, the tenth one is free. Has 45 seats.
Other Info: Counter service, take-out. Smoking is only allowed outside. Accepts AMEX, MC, VISA. Price: $.
Directions: From I-10, take Carrollton Ave/Airline Hwy (Rte 61, Exit #232) exit and go south/west towards river (towards Tulane Ave). Go south on Carrollton Ave and go one mile, at S Claiborne Ave turn left and go a half-mile, then at Broadway St turn right and go one mile, then at St Charles Ave turn left and go one mile, then at Octavia St turn right and go a half-mile, then turn right at Magazine St and this place is near the corner.

Apple Seed Shoppe

336 Camp Street, Suite 100
504-529-3442; **Web site:** www.nola.com
Hours: Monday to Friday 10:30 am to 3 pm
Closed Saturday & Sunday
Natural Foods Café. Not pure vegetarian.
Menu: Has good salads, sandwiches and soups. Good avocado dishes. Fresh juices and smoothies. Does not do any cooking on premises.
Comments: You can call in advance for take-out orders.
Other Info: Counter service, take-out, free delivery. Accept cash or local checks; no credit cards. Price: $.
Directions: In the CBD (Central Business District), next to the Queen and Crescent hotel. Coming west on I-10 into New Orleans, take Exit #234B on the left towards Poydras St/Superdome. Then go southeast on Poydras St for one mile, then at Camp St turn left and this place is two blocks down.

Back to the Garden

833 Howard Avenue; 504-299-8792
Hours: Monday to Friday 7 am to 4 pm; Saturday 9 am to 3 pm; closed Sunday.
Vegetarian-friendly Restaurant. Vegan options. Not pure vegetarian.
Menu: Has a vegetarian section on the menu. Brown Rice, salads, vegetarian tacos, Veggie Stir-fry, hummus pita sandwich, bean chili and much more. Fresh juices and smoothies.
Comments: Simple place, but good food. Rea-

sonably priced.
Other Info: Counter service, take-out. Price: $-$$.
Directions: In the CBD (Central Business District) area, across from WDSU TV (Channel 6).

Bennachin Restaurant
133 North Carrollton Avenue, at Iberville Street
504-486-1313
Hours: Monday to Thursday 11 am to 9 pm; Friday 11 am to 10 pm; Saturday 5 pm to 10 pm; closed Sunday.
African. Not pure vegetarian.
Menu: Many dishes can be made vegetarian.
Other Info: Full service, take-out. Non-smoking. Accepts AMEX, DIS, MC, VISA. Price: $$.

East African Harvest
1643 Gentilly Boulevard; 504-943-0787
Hours: Monday to Saturday 11 am to 10 pm
Closed Sunday.
Vegetarian International and East African Catering Service.
Menu: Green Bananas with Peanut Sauce, Black-eyed Peas Fritters, Okra Stew and more.
Comments: Good food. Price: $$.

End of The Rainbow Natural Foods
215 Dauphine Street, French Quarter
504-529-3429
Hours: Monday to Friday 9:30 am to 5:30 pm
Closed Saturday & Sunday
Natural Food Store.
Comments: It is a bit small.
Directions: Coming west on I-10 into New Orleans, take Orleans Ave exit #235A towards Vieux Carre and merge onto Orleans Ave (becomes Basin St) and bear right a third-mile. At Conti St turn left and go three blocks, then at Dauphine St turn right and this place is 2 blocks down.

Eve's Market
7700 Cohn Street, at Adams Street
504-861-4015
Hours: Monday to Saturday 9 am to 6:30 pm
Closed Sunday.
Natural Food Store and Deli. Juice Bar. Supermarket-type size.
Menu: Soups, salads, sandwiches, hummus and other dishes. Has pre-made sandwiches.
Other Info: Accepts MC, VISA.
Directions: This place is a block northeast of Carrollton Cemetery. Bus 22 to Broadway. From I-10 going west into New Orleans, take Carrollton Ave (Rte 61/Airline Hwy) exit (#232) and go

south on S Carrollton Ave 1½ mile passing Hwy 90. Then at Coln turn left and this place is a quarter-mile down on right.

Five Happiness Chinese Restaurant
3605 South Carrolton Avenue, Midtown
504-482-3935
Hours: Monday to Thursday 11:30 am to 10:30 pm; Friday & Saturday 11:30 am to 11:30 pm; Sunday 12 noon to 10:30 pm
Chinese. Not pure vegetarian.
Menu: Has a good selection of vegetarian dishes.
Comments: Popular place. Won awards for best Chinese food.
Other Info: Accepts AMEX, DC, DIS, MC, VISA.

Juan's Flying Burrito
2018 Magazine Street, at St Andrew Street
504-569-0000
Web site: www.juansflyingburrito.com
Hours: Monday to Saturday 11 am to 11 pm
Sunday 12 noon to 10 pm
Mexican. Not pure vegetarian.
Menu: Good veggie burritos.
Comments: Has outdoor dining. Says beans and rice are all ready for vegetarians. No lard in the beans or meat products in the rice.
Other Info: Accepts AMEX, DIS, MC, VISA. Price: $.

Kokopelli's
3150 Calhoun Street, between Claiborne Avenue and Tonti Street; 504-861-3922
Hours: Daily 11 am to 10 pm
International, Eclectic, Southwestern. Not pure vegetarian.
Menu: Brown and white rice, tortillas, burritos, taco and other dishes.
Comments: Has outdoor dining.
Other Info: Non-smoking. Accepts AMEX, MC, VISA. Price: $-$$.
Directions: A few blocks from Tulane University.

Old Dog—New Trick
517 Frenchmen Street, in the Faubourg Marigny
504-522-4569; **email:** old-dog@travelbase.com;
Web site: www.olddognewtrick.com
Hours: Monday to Thursday 11:30 am to 9 pm
Friday to Sunday 11 am to 10 pm
Gourmet Natural Food. Mainly Vegetarian (serves seafood). International, American, Korean, Buddhist. Mainly Vegan. Macrobiotic options.
Menu: Soups, salads, homemade veggie burgers,

tempeh burgers, sandwiches, pizzas and desserts. Tofu Rancheros, Potato Frittata, organic yogurt, bagels, Grilled Vegetables, Tempeh Brauten, Tofurama Sandwich, Grilled Polenta, Vegetarian Black Beans & Rice, Teriyaki Tempeh over Brown Rice, Spinach Salad, wraps, Udon Noodle Bowl, bean and rice tortillas, Tofu with Peanut Ginger Sauce and Polenta stuffed with feta cheese & black beans. Vegan desserts. Organic Ben-burger are good. Hibiscus ice tea (sweetened with organic maple syrup) is recommended. No alcohol.
Comments: Small, casual café-type place. Uses fresh ingredients. Creative dishes. Food gets good ratings. Outdoor seating. Sidewalk café. Friendly, helpful staff. Pleasant atmosphere. May use mayonnaise made from eggs, so best to ask for Nayonaise. Got several awards for its vegetarian food.
Other Info: Full service, take-out. Non-smoking. Reservations not accepted. Accepts AMEX, MC, VISA. Price: $-$$.

Sara's

724 Dublin Street, at Maple Street & Hampton Street; 504-861-0565
Web site: www.sarasrestaturant.com
Hours: Tuesday to Saturday 11:30 am to 2:30 pm, 5:30 pm to 10 pm; closed Sun & Mon.
International, Indian. Not pure vegetarian.
Menu: Has a selection of vegetarian dishes. Hummus on pita bread, Saag Paneer (spinach and soft cheese) and more. Some vegan dishes.
Comments: Relaxed place. Accepts AMEX, DC, DIS, MC, VISA. Price: $$.
Directions: St Charles Streetcar.

Whole Foods Market

3135 Esplanade Avenue, at Mystery Street
504-943-1626
Hours: Daily 8:30 am to 9:30 pm
Natural Food Store and Deli. Juice Bar and Bakery. Organic produce. Supermarket-type place.
Comments: Has no seating inside, but has tables outside. Is relatively small size compared to other Whole Foods Markets.
Other Info: Accepts AMEX, DIS, MC, VISA.
Directions: The place is a few blocks south of the Fair Grounds. From I-10 west, follow signs to the business district in New Orleans. Take I-610 exit (#230) on the left towards Slidell and go 2½ miles east on I-610. Then take St Bernard Ave (#2A) and take right fork and merge onto St Bernard Ave and go ¾ mile. At N Broad Ave (Hwy 90 W) turn right and go 6/10 miles. Then at Esplanade Ave turn right and this place is about a half-mile down. From I-10 east go west on I-610. Take Paris Ave exit, and at the end of exit turn left onto Paris Ave and go 2 blocks. At Gentilly Blvd turn right and go 1½ mile. At Ponce De Leon turn right and this place at end of road on left 4 long blocks down, at corner of Esplanade Ave.

SHREVEPORT

Eartheral Restaurant & Bakery

3309 Line Avenue, Shreveport
318-865-8947
Hours: Monday to Saturday 9:30 am to 3:30 pm (Bakery until 4 pm); closed Saturday & Sunday.
American. Macrobiotic options on Wednesday. Not pure vegetarian.
Menu: Salads, sandwiches, vegetarian soups, tacos with avocado or mock "meats" and daily specials. Fresh juices.
Comment: Laid-back place.
Other Info: Counter service, take-out. Cash only; no credit cards.

Good Life Health Foods & Deli

6132 Hearne Avenue; 318-635-4753
Hours: Monday to Friday 9 am to 5 pm; Saturday 10 am to 5 pm; closed Sunday.
Natural Food Store and Deli. Juice Bar. Organic produce.
Menu: Veggie burgers, salads and sandwiches.
Comments: Has around 25 seats.
Directions: From I-20, take Hearne Avenue (#16A) exit and go south 1½ mile and this place is on the right at the corner, between Hollywood and 70th. Within a group of store.

Sunshine

5751 Youree Drive; 318-219-4080
Hours: Monday to Saturday 9 am to 6 pm Closed Sunday.
Natural Food Store and Deli. Juice Bar and Salad Bar. Large selection of organic produce.
Menu: Has a good selection of vegetarian dishes.
Comment: Friendly place.
Other Info: Counter service, take-out. Has seating.
Directions: From I-20, take Line Ave exit (#1) and go south on Line Ave. Store on the right ¾ mile down.

Maine

1. Auburn
2. Augusta
3. Bangor
4. Bar Harbor
5. Belfast
6. Bethel
7. Biddeford
8. Blue Hill
9. Brewer
10. Bridgton
11. Brunswich
12. Cape Elizabeth
13. Cape Neddick
14. Castine
15. Damariscotta
16. Ellsworth
17. Farmington
18. Freeport
19. Gardiner
20. Gorham
21. Hallowell
22. Hulls Cove
23. Kennebunk
24. Kittery
25. Lewiston

26. Norway
27. Orono
28. Portland
29. Rockland
30. Rumford
31. Scarborough
32. Unity
33. Waterville
34. Wiscasset

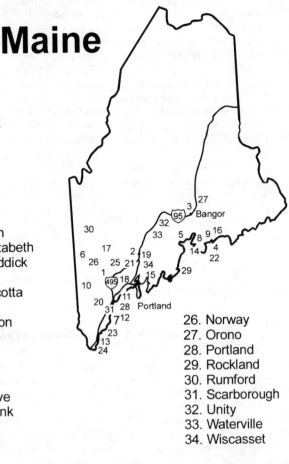

AUBURN (across river from Lewiston)

Axis Natural Foods Limited
250 Center Street; 207-782-3348
Hours: Monday to Friday 9:30 am to 8 pm
Saturday 9:30 am to 6 pm; closed Sunday.
Natural Food Store. Organic produce.
Directions: From Maine Turnpike, take US-202 exit number 12 towards Farmington/Rumford, stay left at fork, then turn left onto US-202 going northeast towards Auburn and after 5 miles it becomes Rte 4 (Union St BYP) for a half-mile, keep straight and go to Center St and this store is in a strip mall on the left, opposite Dexter Shoes.

AUGUSTA

Harvest Time Natural Foods
Capital Shopping Center, 110 Western Avenue
207-623-8700
Hours: Monday & Tuesday 9 am to 6 pm; Wednesday to Friday 9 am to 8 pm; Saturday 9 am to 6 pm; Sunday 10 am to 4 pm
Natural Food Store. Organic produce.
Directions: From I-95, take exit #30 (Augusta exit). Then go east on Rte 202 (Western Ave) towards Augusta. This store is in the second strip mall on the right.

BANGOR

Bahaar Pakistani Restaurant
23 Hammond Street, downtown
207-945-5979
Hours: Sunday to Thursday 11 am to 3 pm, 5 pm to 9 pm; Friday & Saturday 11 am to 3 pm, 5 pm to 10 pm
Pakistani. Not pure vegetarian.
Menu: Has over 15 vegetarian options including special rices and curries.

Comments: Food gets high ratings. The vegetarian dishes are prepared separately from the meat dishes. Friendly place.

Natural Living Center
570 Stillwater Avenue; 207-990-2646
Hours: Monday to Saturday 9:30 am to 7 pm
Sunday 12 noon to 5 pm
Natural Food Store and Café. Not pure veg.
Menu: Has a good selection of vegetarian dishes.
Comments: Has around 20 seats.
Directions: From I-95, take exit #49, then go north on Hogan Rd (turn left if going north on I-95) one mile, then at Stillwater Ave turn left and this place is 1½ mile down. This place is behind the Bangor Mall at the entrance of the cinema.

BAR HARBOR

Café Bluefish
122 Cottage Street; 207-288-3696
Hours: Daily during the summer 5:30 pm to 10 pm; During winter, hours vary but usually open for dinner
American. Not pure vegetarian.
Menu: Has some gourmet dishes such as Cajun Tempeh and Hungarian Mushroom Strudel. Salads and desserts.
Comments: Upscale.
Other Info: Non-smoking. Reservations suggested. Non-smoking. Accepts AMEX, MC, VISA. Price: $$.

Nakorn Thai
58 Cottage Street; 207-288-4060
Seasonal Hours May to October: Monday to Saturday 11 am to 9 pm; Sunday 4 pm to 9 pm. During winter open Thursday to Saturday.
Thai. Vegan options. Not pure vegetarian.
Menu: Has a selection of vegetarian dishes. Substitutes tofu for meat.
Comments: Has exotic, oriental décor. Has white tablecloths on the tables. Seats 100. Comfortable, casual, relaxed place.
Other Info: Reservations not accepted. Non-smoking. Accepts AMEX, MC, VISA. Price: $-$$.
Directions: Opposite the Post Office.

BELFAST

Belfast Co-Op Deli
123 High Street
207-338-2532; **email:** info@belfastcoop.com

Web site: www.belfastcoop.com
Hours: Monday to Saturday 9 am to 8 pm
Sunday 10 am to 5 pm
Natural Food Store, Café and Deli. Juice Bar. Organic produce. Vegan friendly. Not pure vegetarian.
Menu: Has soups, salads, bagels, baked goods, cheeses, sandwiches, pasta salad, breads and main vegetarian dishes. Fresh juices.
Comments: Has both indoor and outdoor seating for 30. Local organic produce used when possible. Non-members can shop.
Other Info: Limited service, take out. Price: $.
Directions: From I-95, take Augusta exit and take Rte 3 towards downtown Belfast. It becomes Belmont Ave for 1 mile, then it becomes Main St. At High St turn right and this place on left 100 yards down. From Rte 1 north, take Belfast Business District exit onto Northport Ave (becomes High St). This place is on the right about 2 miles down on right.

Darby's
155 High Street; 207-338-2339
Hours: Daily 11:30 am to 3:30 pm, 5 pm to 9 pm (closed 9:30 pm on Friday & Saturday)
Natural Foods. Macrobiotic and Vegan options. Not pure vegetarian.
Menu: Has three or fours vegetarian main dishes daily and a daily macrobiotic special. Soups, Fiesta Salad and will substitute tofu for meat in many of the dishes.
Comments: Has live guitar music Wednesday, Thursday and Sunday. The building that the restaurant is in dates to 1845 and has an antique bar.
Other Info: Accepts AMEX, DIS, MC, VISA. Full service, take-out. Price: $-$$.
Directions: From I-95, take Augusta exit onto Rte 3, and take Rte 3 towards downtown Belfast. It becomes Belmont Ave for 1 mile, then it becomes Main St. At High St turn right and this place is 4 blocks down. From Rte 1 north, take Belfast Business District exit onto Northport Ave (becomes High St). This place is on the right after about 1¾ mile down.

BETHEL

**Café DiCocoa
125 Main Street
207-824-JAVA; **email:** dicocoa@megalink.net;
Web site: www.cafedicocoa.com
Hours: Friday & Saturday for dinner
Saturday & Sunday Brunch

Vegetarian International Restaurant. Special International Dinner on Friday (Italian, Middle Eastern, Sicilian). Vegan options.
Menu: Menu changes daily. Soups, sandwiches, homemade bread, pastas and hot dishes.
Comments: Relaxed, friendly place with good service. Grows own organic produce. Kathy DiCocco, the owner, is a really nice lady who gives classes. Does catering and cooking classes. Has a store next door where they serve soups by the pint, cappuccino, espresso and other dishes.
Other Info: Reservations are suggested for the special dinners.
Directions: This place is at the junction of Rte 26 and Rte 35 in the center of town on the main street.

BIDDEFORD

New Morning Natural Food Market & Café
230 Main Street; 207-282-1434
Store Hours: Monday to Saturday 9 am to 5:30 pm (Thursday until 7 pm)
Café Hours: Monday to Friday 11 am to 2 pm Closed Sunday.
Natural Food Store and Café. Has a good selection of organic produce.
Menu: Organic salads, homemade soups, a good selection of sandwiches, vegetarian chili and a daily vegetarian special. Fresh juices.
Comments: Has good, reasonably priced food.
Other Info: Counter service, take-out. Counter service, take-out. Price: $.
Directions: From I-95 coming from south, take Biddeford exit (#4), at Rte 111 (Alfred Rd) turn left and go 2½ miles into town towards the "Five Points" area. At Elm St (Rte 1) turn left and go 1½ mile, then at Main turn right and this place on left 3 blocks down. From I-95 coming from north, take Saco exit (#5), then go southeast on North St 1½ mile, then at Rte 1 turn right and go across the river into Biddeford, then at Main St turn left and this place on right 3 blocks down.

BLUE HILL

Blue Hill Co-op
Greene's Hill Place, Route 172; 207-374-2165
Hours: Monday to Friday 8 am to 7 pm; Saturday 8 am to 6 pm; Sunday 10 am to 4 pm
Natural Food Store and Café. Bakery. Organic produce.
Menu: Has a large selection of vegan and vegetarian dishes. Soups, salads, sandwiches and breakfast dishes.
Directions: Take Rte 172 into town and this place on left. Or take Rte 15 south into Blue Hill, then at Rte 172 turn left and this place a fourth-mile down on left.

BREWER

Natural Living Center
Brewer Shopping Center, 421 Wilson Street
207-989-7996
Hours: Monday to Thursday & Saturday 9 am to 6 pm; Friday 9 am to 6:30 pm; Sunday 12 noon to 2 pm
Natural Food Store. Also sells wood and coal stoves.
Directions: From I-95, take exit for I-395, then take Exit #45A towards Hwy 1A Brewer and go 2 miles, then take North Main St exit (#4) and go northeast on Rte 15 N for a mile. At Main (Hwy 1A) turn right and this place is 1¼ mile down on the left in Brewer Shopping Center.

Morning Dew
24 Portland Street (Route 302); 207-647-4003
Hours: Monday to Friday 9:30 am to 6:30 pm; Sat 9:30 am to 5:30 pm; Sun 10 am to 5 pm
Natural Foods and a small Country Store. Café and Deli. Not pure vegetarian.
Menu: Has a selection of vegetarian dishes.
Comments: Seats 10.
Directions: This place on Rte 302, south of light.

BRUNSWICK

Rosita's
212 Maine Street; 207-729-7118
Hours: Sunday to Thursday 11 am to 8:30 pm Friday & Saturday 11 am to 9 pm
Mexican. Not pure vegetarian.
Menu: Has a wide variety of vegetarian dishes. Has whole-wheat tortillas. Vegetarian Combo Plate. Pinto and Black Beans are vegetarian. Several types of vegetarian quesadillas.
Comments: The owner is a vegetarian. Friendly place.
Other Info: Counter service, take-out. Order at counter and the food is brought to you.

CAPE NEDDICK

Frankie & Johnny's Natural Foods
1594 Route 1; 207-363-1909
Spring & Fall Hours: Thursday to Sunday 5 pm to 9 pm; **Summer Hours:** Wednesday to Mon-

day 5 pm to 9 pm
International. Juice Bar. Vegan options. Not pure
vegetarian.
Menu: Salads, pastas and other vegetarian dishes.
Fresh juices, cappuccino, espresso.
Directions: This place is in the middle of town.
From I-95, take Exit #4 towards Hwy 1/Yorks/
The Berwicks and get on I-95 Spur E for ¾ mile,
then turn left onto US-1 and this place is 3½
miles down.

DAMARISCOTTA

Rising Tide Co-op
Business Route 1, Box 38; 207-563-5556
Hours: Monday to Saturday 8 am to 7 pm
Sunday 10 am to 4 pm
Natural Food Store and Café.
Menu: Soups, salads, sandwiches and breads.
Comments: Seats 20.
Directions: Go on Rte 1 to Business Rte 1. This
place is on the west side of street about 2 miles
south of Rte 1.

ELLSWORTH

John Edward's Whole Foods Market
158 Main Street (Rte 1); 207-667-9377
Hours: Mon to Thur 9 am to 5:30 pm; Fri 9 am
to 6 pm; Sat 9 am to 5 pm; Sun 1 pm to 5 pm
Natural Food Store.
Directions: On main street of town.

FARMINGTON

Basics Natural Food Market & Café
181 Front Street; 207-778-6018
Hours: Monday to Thursday 7:30 am to 6 pm;
Friday 7:30 am to 3 pm; Sunday 12 noon to 5
pm; closed Saturday.
Natural Food Store and Deli. Organic produce.
Menu: Mainly only makes sandwiches in deli.
Fresh juices.
Other Info: Accepts MC, VISA.

FREEPORT

Corsican Restaurant
9 Mechanic Street; 207-865-9421
Hours: Daily 11 am to 8 pm
Italian, Pizza. Healthy Food. Not pure veg.
Menu: Has a wide selection of vegetarian dishes.
Homemade soups, Greek Pizza, Pesto Pizza, pas-
tas, salads, sandwiches, baked breads, calzones,
whole-wheat pizzas, cakes and pies.

Other Info: Non-smoking. Full service, take-out.
Accepts DC, MC, VISA. Price: $$.
Directions: Form I-95, take Exit #20 for Freeport,
then take Mallett Dr a half-mile towards town.
Then at Hwy 1, turn right and go a quarter-mile,
then at Justins Way turn left and this place is 1
block down.

Royal River Natural Foods
443 US Route 1; **Web site:** www.rrnf.com
207-865-0046
Hours: Monday to Saturday 8 am to 8 pm
Sunday 10 am to 6 pm
Natural Food Store and Café. Deli.
Directions: From I-95 coming from south, take
exit #16, off exit go right onto Hwy 1 going north
and this place is 2½ miles north on Hwy 1. This
place in second shopping on left. From I-95 com-
ing from the north, take exit #17 (Rte 1 south)
and this place on right ¾ mile down.

GARDINER

A-1 Diner
Bridge Street; 207-582-4804
Hours: Monday to Thursday 7 am to 8 pm; Fri-
day & Saturday 7 am to 9 pm; Sunday Brunch 8
am to 1 pm
Railway Diner type place. Vegan options. Not
pure vegetarian.
Menu: Soups, salads, sandwiches, veggie burger,
veggie hot dogs, Asian noodle dishes and other
vegetarian options.
Other Info: Full service, take-out. Non-smoking.
Reservations not accepted. Accepts DIS, MC,
VISA. Price: $-$$.

GORHAM

The Natural Grocer
104 Main Street; 207-839-6223
Hours: Monday to Friday 9 am to 7 pm; Satur-
day 9 am to 6 pm; Sunday 11 am to 4 pm
Natural Food Store and take-out Deli. Has a
good selection.
Menu: Soups, salads, sandwiches and hot dishes.
Directions: From Maine Turnpike, take exit #8.
Go toward Westbrook and street turns into Rte
25. In Gorham store on right (6 miles down).

HALLOWELL

Slate's
167 Water Street; 207-622-9575
Hours: Monday to Saturday 7:30 am to 9:30 pm

Sunday 9 am to 2 pm
International. Vegetarian-friendly. Not pure veg.
Menu: Has several vegetarian dishes including pasta, vegetarian soups, veggie burgers (sometimes), vegetable bean burrito and other dishes.
Comments: Has folk music on Friday and Saturday nights and for the Sunday brunch. Displays artwork. Casual, friendly place.
Other Info: Reservations suggested for groups. Smoking allowed in bar. Accepts DIS, MC, VISA. Price: $-$$.

HANCOCK

Sweet Onion Inn
Route 100, PO Box 66
802-767-3734; **Web site:** www.soi.com
Menu: Has an entire vegan breakfast. Sunrise Burritos (with veggie sausage), Scrambled Tofu, etc. Also has Mountain Burgers, Shepherd's Pie (made with tempeh) and other dishes.
Comments: There is skiing, canoeing, local historical sites and hiking in the area.
Directions: In the Green Mountains.

KENNEBUNK

New Morning Natural Foods
1 York Street (Hwy 1); 207-985-6774
Hours: Monday to Saturday 9:30 am to 6 pm
Closed Sunday.
Natural Food Store.
Directions: From I-95, take exit #3 and go west on Rte 35 for 1½ mile toward Kennebunk. At Hwy 1 turn right and go south and this place is 4/10 miles down. Go across a small bridge and this place is on the right in a brick building at the top of the street.

KITTERY

Enchanted Nights Bed & Breakfast
Scenic Route 103, 29 Wentworth Street
207-439-1489
email: info@enchanted-nights-bandb.com
Web site: www.enchanted-nights-bandb.com
Bed & Breakfast with Vegetarian friendly breakfasts.
Comments: Has an assortment of rooms for two plus breakfast for $60 to $160.
Directions: They have detailed directions on their Web site. From Boston, take I-95 north to Maine, then take Exit #2 and take Rte 236 south and go 1 mile, then turn right onto Route 103, then turn left at stop sign and this place is on the right.

From Portland and points north, take 95 South or Route 1 South, and exit at Route 236 South towards Kittery and go 1 mile. Same as above.

Rising Tide
165 State Road; 207-439-8898
Hours: Monday to Saturday 9 am to 7 pm
Sunday 11 am to 4:30 pm
Natural Food Store and Deli.
Menu: Has prepared vegan and vegetarian dishes.
Other Info: Counter service, take-out. Does not have seating.
Directions: From I-95, take exit #2 and follow signs to 236, then go east on Rte 236 a half mile, then get on Hwy 1 going south and this place is a half-mile down. This place is the first building past the circle on Rte 1 south.

LEWISTON
Home of Bates College.

Nothing But The Blues Café
81 College Street; 207-784-6493
Web site: www.nothingbutthebluescafe.com
Hours: Monday to Saturday 11:30 am to 2:30 pm, 5 pm to 8:30 pm; closed Sunday.
Eclectic American. Emphasis on vegetarian meals. Vegan options. Not pure vegetarian.
Comments: Has vegetarian lunches and dinners. Pastas and two or three vegetarian dishes. Soups are usually vegetarian. Lasagna and other dishes.
Comments: Has menu on their web site. Gets good recommendations. Friendly place.
Other Info: Non-smoking. No credit cards; cash only. Price: $-$$.
Directions: From I-495, take exit US-202/Rte 100 exit (#12) towards Farmington/Rumford. Then turn left and go north/east on US-202 for 5½ miles, then when you get into the downtown at Sabattus St (Rte 126) turn right and go 2 blocks (bearing left), at College St turn left and this place is 1 block down.

NORWAY

Fair Share Co-op
443 Main Street; 207-743-9044
Hours: Monday to Friday 9 am to 5 pm
Saturday 10 am to 4 pm; closed Sunday.
Natural Food Store. Prepared food in cooler.
Menu: Soups, salads, sandwiches, wraps and muffins.
Other Info: Counter service, take-out. Does not have seating.
Directions: From coming into town on Rte 26,

at Rte 117 go west towards Norway on Main St (if coming from south) and go ¾ mile, then at Tannery St (near the radio station) turn right and this place is near the corner.

ORONO

The Store & Ampersand
22 Mill Street; 207-866-4110
Hours: Monday to Saturday 7 am to 7 pm Sunday 9 am to 4 pm
Natural Food Store and Deli & Café. No organic produce.
Menu: Has a large selection of vegetarian dishes.
Comments: Seats around 20.
Directions: From I-95, take exit #50. This place is in the middle of town (2 miles down).

PORTLAND
Portland Restaurant site (www.foodinportland.com)

Bagel Works
15 Temple Street; 207-879-2425
Hours: Monday to Saturday 6:30 am to 5 pm Sunday 6:30 am to 4 pm
Bagel Deli. Vegan options. Not pure vegetarian.
Menu: Sixteen types of bagels. Has toppings such as tofutti spreads, cream cheeses, salads and other vegetarian toppings. Fresh juices.
Comments: Uses only natural ingredients.
Other Info: Counter service, take-out. Price: $.

Café Uffa
190 State Street, at Congress, In Longfellow Square; 207-775-3380
Hours: Wednesday to Saturday for breakfast and dinner 5:30 pm to 10 pm (closed for lunch); Saturday 8 am to 12 noon; Sunday Brunch 9 am to 2 pm; closed Monday & Tuesday.
Vegetarian-friendly Restaurant. Eclectic American. Not pure vegetarian.
Menu: Has several vegetarian dishes. Organic salads. Pasta with Grilled Eggplant, Asiago Cheese and sauce.
Comments: Comfortable, casual place with antique furniture, high ceiling, candles on the tables and artwork on the wall. Has a live band every other Sunday. Outdoor dining. One of the better restaurants in Portland. Good value. Plays world beat music.
Other Info: Full service, take-out. Does not accept reservations. Can be busy so it may be a good idea to arrive early. Non-smoking. Accepts MC, VISA. Price: $-$$.
Directions: From I-295, take US 1/Forest Ave exit (#6A), merge onto US-1/Rte 302 and go ¼

mile, then at State St (US-1) turn right and this place is a half-mile down, at junction with Rte 22.

The Great Lost Bear
540 Forest Avenue; 207-772-0300; **email:** bear@ime.net; **Web site:** www.greatlostbear.com http://www.foodinportland.com/link7.html
Hours: Daily 11:30 am to 11:30 pm
International Natural Foods. Vegan options. Not pure vegetarian.
Menu: Has a good selection of vegetarian dishes and a large amount of salads. Garden Burger, vegan chili and daily vegetable soups.
Comments: This place is mainly a bar with a large selection of beers on tap. Got a good review in USA Today.
Other Info: Accepts AMEX, DIS, MC, VISA.
Directions: From 295, take exit #6B. Head northwest on Forest Avenue about 2/3 miles and this place is on the left.

**Little Lads Bakery
58 Exchange Street; 207-871-1636
Hours: Sunday to Thursday 11 am to 7 pm; Friday 11 am to 3 pm; closed Saturday.
Vegetarian. Mainly Vegan. All-you-can-eat Buffet.
Menu: Soups, salads, sandwiches, homemade breads, baked goods, vegan Macaroni & Cheese and vegan desserts. Black Bean Soup, French Onion, Navy Bean & Vegetable Soup, veggie Shepherd Pie, veggie Salisbury "Steak", wheat bread, Chop Suey, Mashed Potatoes, popcorn, organic Tortilla Wrap, veggie Chicken Salad, Veggie "BLT", "Meet-n-Loaf" Sandwich and Veggie and Cheese sandwich. Has vegan baked goods.
Comments: Very reasonably priced. Friendly, efficient service. Pleasant, relaxing atmosphere. Has all-you-can-eat meals. Has take-out meals in their take-out counter. Good food. This place gets good ratings.
Other Info: Cash or checks; no credit cards. Price: $$.
Directions: From I-295 going into town, take Hwy 1A/Franklin St exit (#7) and merge onto Franklin St Arterial/Hwy 1A S and go a half-mile, at Congress St turn right and go a few block, then at Exchange turn left and this place is a couple block down on right.

Katahdin
106 High Street; 207-774-1740; **Web site:** http://www.foodinportland.com/link28.html
Hours: Tuesday to Thursday 5 pm to 10 pm; Fri & Sat 5 pm to 11 pm; closed Sunday Mon.

International, New American. Vegan options. Not pure vegetarian.

Menu: Has several vegetarian dishes and salads. The Mushroom Ravioli is a good vegan dish. Good salads.

Comments: Eclectic décor. Plants, flowers and artwork. Comfortable, relaxed place.

Other Info: Full service, take-out. Does not accept reservations. Accepts MC, VISA. Price: $$-$$$.

Mesa Verde

618 Congress Street; 207-774-6089
Hours: Wednesday to Sunday 11:30 am to 9 pm
Closed Monday & Tuesday.

Baja Mexican (Californian-style). Vegetarian-friendly. Juice Bar. Vegan options. Not pure veg.

Menu: Has a large selection of vegetarian dishes. Burritos, quesadillas and tacos. Can put tofu, beans or vegetables on burritos. Hummus and Veggie Plate. Organic rice. Vegan soups. Fresh juices and smoothies.

Comments: Food gets a really good rating. Friendly place.

Other Info: Accepts MC, VISA. Price: $$.

Directions: From I-295 going into town, take Hwy 1A/Franklin St exit (#7) and merge onto Franklin St Arterial/Hwy 1A S and go a half-mile, at Congress St turn left. A good place to park is around the corner on Park St.

Pepperclub

78 Middle Street
207-772-0531
Hours: Daily 5 pm to 9 pm
Mediterranean. Emphasize on vegetarian meals. Not pure vegetarian.

Menu: Has a wide selection of vegetarian and vegan selections. Hummus, Sun-dried Tomato Pesto, Mashed Potatoes, Roast Portobello Mushrooms and dairy-free desserts. Two vegetarian soups, 5 vegetarian main dishes and 5 vegetarian appetizers daily.

Comments: It is a seafood place (about 50% vegetarian), so you may want to take that into consideration. The food gets good ratings. Friendly, family restaurant.

Other Info: Full service, take-out. Non-smoking. Reservations are necessary for parties of 6. Accepts AMEX, DIS, MC, VISA. Price: $$.

Directions: From I-295 going into town, take Hwy 1A/Franklin St exit (#7) and merge onto Franklin St Arterial/Hwy 1A S and this place is ¾ mile down.

Silly's Pizza

40 Washington Avenue; 207-772-0117
Winter Hours: Monday to Saturday 9 am to 9 pm; closed Sunday. May be open on Sundays during summer.

Middle Eastern, Pizza. Not pure vegetarian.

Menu: Has a good selection of vegetarian dishes. Pizzas, falafel, Jamaican Beans & Rice, hummus, sandwiches and other dishes.

Comments: It is a reasonably priced, popular, small place. Laid-back place. Popular with young people. Has patio outdoor dining. Has live music on Tuesdays.

Other Info: Full service, take-out. Accepts AMEX, MC, VISA. Price: $.

Walter's Café

15 Exchange Street, Old Port; 207-871-9258; **Web site:** http://www.foodinportland.com/link18.html
Hours: Monday to Saturday 11 am to 3 pm, 5 pm to 9:30 pm; Sunday 5 pm to 9 pm
American and International. Not pure veg.

Menu: Soups, sandwiches, pasta, Veggie Lasagna and some gourmet dishes.

Comments: Casual and popular lunch place. First-class service.

Other Info: Full service, take-out. Reservations required for groups. Non-smoking. Accepts AMEX, MC, VISA. Price: $$.

Directions: From I-295, take exit #7 (Franklin Arterial), stay on Franklin Arterial and go ¾ mile, turn right at Congress St and go 4 blocks, make a left at Exchange St (across from City Hall a little after Market St), go over the hill past Middle St. This place on the left, 1½ block down just after Milk St. Can park at Fore Street Parking Garage (go to the end of Exchange Street, turn right at Fore St, garage is half a block down on the right).

The Whole Grocer

127 Marginal Way; 207-774-7711
Hours: Monday to Friday 9 am to 8 pm; Saturday 9 am to 7 pm; Sunday 11 am to 6 pm
Natural Food Store and Deli. Organic produce. Vegan options. Not pure vegetarian.

Menu: Soups, salads, sandwiches and baked goods.

Comments: Has a good selection of international specialties.

Other Info: Self service, take-out. Price: $.

Directions: It is off the Forest Avenue exit off I-295. Has plenty of parking. From I-295, take Franklin Arterial exit and go ¾ miles into town, at Marginal Way turn right. This place on left 2 blocks down.

Wok Inn
1209 Forest Avenue
207-797-9052
Hours: Sunday & Monday 11:30 am to 9:30 pm;
Tuesday to Thursday 11 am to 11 pm; Friday &
Saturday 11 am to 2 am
Chinese. Not pure vegetarian.
Comments: Uses vegetable oil for cooking and
does not use MSG. Low on ambiance.
Other Info: Full service, take-out, delivery. Does
not take reservations. Non-smoking. Accepts DIS,
MC, VISA. Price: $$.

ROCKLAND

Good Tern Co-op
216 South Main Street
207-594-9286
Hours: Monday to Friday 9:30 am to 6 pm; Sat-
urday 9:30 am to 5 pm; closed Sunday.
Natural Food Store.
Directions: If driving into Rockland on Rte 1,
when the road ends turn right at S Main St and
go 1 block and this place on the right, at junction
with Rte 73.

RUMFORD

Red Hill Natural Foods
29 Hartford Street
207-369-9141
Hours: Monday to Saturday 9 am to 6 pm (Thurs-
day until 7 pm); closed Sunday.
Natural Food Store. Some organic produce.
Directions: If taking Rte 2 west into Rumford.
In downtown turn right at Canal St. The road
ends at this place at Hartford St.

SCARBOROUGH (5 miles south of Portland)

Lois' Natural Marketplace
152 Route 1
207-885-0602

Hours: Monday to Friday 9:30 am to 7:30 pm;
Saturday 9 am to 6:30 pm; Sunday 11 am to 5
pm; Deli closed on weekend.
Natural Food Store and Deli. Vegan friendly.
Fresh breads.
Comments: Friendly place.
Directions: From I-95, take exit #6A and go to-
wards Portland. After tollbooth take first exit to
South Portland. Take 2nd exit to Scarborough and
get on Hwy 1. This place a half-mile down on
the left on Hwy 1.

WATERVILLE

New Moon Rising Natural Foods
110 Pleasant Street
207-873-6244
Hours: Monday to Saturday 9 am to 6 pm (Fri-
day until 7 pm); Sunday 10 am to 5 pm
Natural Food Store. Some organic produce. Has
a large selection of bulk items.
Menu: Has spinach pies.
Directions: From I-95, take Main St exit (#34)
and go southeast on Main St 1¼ miles. Follow
signs to Waterville. This place on right.

WISCASSET

Sarah's Pizza & Café
Route 1, Main Street
207-882-7504
Hours: Monday to Thursday 11 am to 8 pm;
Friday 11 am to 9 pm; Saturday 7 am to 9 pm;
Sunday 7 am to 8 pm
Italian and Pizza. Not pure vegetarian.
Menu: Has vegetarian specials. Cheese Ravioli,
veggie burrito, a selection of salads, Greek Sal-
ads, Greek Sandwich and pita sandwiches.
Comments: Has outside sitting with a good view
of the Wiscasset waterfront.
Other Info: Full service, take-out. Reservations
not accepted. Non-smoking. Accepts AMEX,
MC, VISA. Price: $$.

Maryland

1. Adelphi
2. Annapolis
3. Baltimore
4. Bel Air
5. Beltsville
6. Bethesda
7. Cabin John
8. Capital Heights
9. Cantonsville
10. Catonsville
11. Chevy Chase
12. Clarksville
13. Cockeysville
14. College Park
15. Columbia
16. Easton
17. Ellicott City
18. Frederick
19. Frostburg
20. Gaithersburg
21. Germantown
22. Greenbelt
23. Knoxville
24. Langley Park
25. Largo
26. Laurel
27. Leonardtown
28. Mt Rainier
29. Ocean City
30. Olney
31. Pikesville
32. Randallstown
33. Rockville
34. Silver Springs
35. Spencerville
36. Takoma Park
37. Timonium
38. Towson
39. Waldorf
40. Westminster
41. Wheaton

ANNAPOLIS

Bertucci's Brick Oven Pizza
Hechinger Shopping Center, 2207 Forest Drive
410-266-5800
Hours: Monday to Thursday 11 am to 12 midnight; Friday to Saturday 11 am to 1 am; Sunday 12 noon to 11 pm
Pizza and Italian. Not pure vegetarian.
Menu: Several vegetarian specialty pizzas. Pasta and salad.

Fresh Fields
Harbor Place Shopping Center, 2504 Solomon's Island Road; 410-573-1800
email: Pul.Barnett@wholefoods.com
Web site: www.wholefoodsmarket.com
Hours: Monday to Saturday 8 am to 9 pm
Sunday 9 am to 8 pm

Natural Food Store and Cafe. Deli, Bakery, Salad Bar and Juice Bar. Organic produce. Supermarket-type place. See Whole Foods Market information Seats 20.
Directions: From heading east on Hwy 50, take exit #22 and get on Aris T Allen Blvd going southeast. Follow signs to Solomon Island Rd (Rte 2). After 1½ mile turn left at Solomon Island Rd. This place a half-mile down on left in the Harbor Place Shopping Center.

Good Life Natural Foods
570 Benfield Village Shopping Center, Severna Park; 410-647-6602
Natural Food Store.

India's
257 West Street; 410-263-7900
Hours: Sunday to Thursday 11:30 am to 2:30

pm, 5 pm to 9 pm; Friday & Saturday 11:30 am to 2:30 pm, 5 pm to 10 pm
Indian. Not pure vegetarian.
Menu: Has a wide selection of vegetarian dishes.
Comments: Pleasant atmosphere. Plays classical Indian music.
Other Info: Full service, take-out, catering. Accepts AMEX, MC, VISA. Price: $$$.

Mexican Café
975 Bay Ridge Road
410-626-1520; Web site: www.mexicancafe.com
Hours: Sunday to Thursday 11 am to 9:30 pm
Friday & Saturday 11 am to 10:30
Mexican. Vegan options. Not pure vegetarian
Comments: Has several vegetarian dishes. Their beans don't contain lard.
Other Info: Full service, take-out. Accepts MC, VISA. Price: $-$$.

The New Moon Café
137 Prince George Street; 410-280-1956
Hours: Monday to Friday 8 am to 8 pm
Saturday & Sunday 8 am to 10 pm
Mediterranean, Middle Eastern, Greek. Vegan options. Not pure vegetarian.
Menu: Has many vegetarian dishes. The veggie burger gets a great rating. Excellent desserts.
Other Info: Full service, catering, take-out. Accepts AMEX, MC, VISA. Price: $$.

Potato Valley Café
47 State Circle, Suite 100; 410-267-0902
Hours: Monday to Saturday 10 am to 6 pm
Café. Vegan options. Not pure vegetarian.
Menu: Has gourmet potatoes with different toppings, salads and sandwiches. Some toppings are sour cream, corn, beans, garlic butter, peppers, beans and cilantro. Cappuccino, espresso. Salads and sandwich. Soy milk.
Other Info: Limited service, take-out. Accepts DIS, MC, VISA. Price: $-$$.
Directions: This place is a few blocks southwest of the Naval Academy. From Hwy 50, take Rowe Blvd and go 1½ mile, when the road forks go straight (road becomes Bladen St) 3 blocks and go past College Ave and after a block follow the circle around and this place is on the other side of the circle, just before East St.

Sun & Earth Foods
1933 West Street; 410-266-6862
Hours: Monday to Saturday 9:30 am to 6:30 pm
Sunday 12 noon to 4 pm
Natural Food Store. Some organic produce. Has

ready-made sandwiches.
Directions: Take Rte 50 to exit #28 to Chinquapin Round Rd. At West St turn left and go about 1 mile, and this place is at junction of West and Lee, a mile west of the downtown.

BALTIMORE

Acropolis
Light Street Pavilion, 2nd Floor, Harborplace
4718 Eastern Avenue, 5 minutes from Inner Harbor; 410-727-0804
Hours: Daily 9 am to 9 pm
Greek. Not pure vegetarian.
Menu: Has several vegetarian dishes including salad, falafel, hummus, vegetable sandwiches and spinach pies. Open daily.
Comments: Authentic décor. Comfortable place.
Other Info: Counter service, take-out. Has tables. Has a banquet room. Price: $$.

Akbar
823 North Charles, Charles Street Corridor
410-539-0944
Web site: www.akbar-restaurant.com
Hours: Monday to Friday 11:30 am to 2:30 pm, 5 pm to 11:30 pm; Saturday & Sunday 12 noon to 3 pm, 5 pm to 11 pm
Indian and some Middle Eastern. Vegan options. Not pure vegetarian.
Menu: Has a large variety of vegetarian dishes.
Comments: Excellent, quick service. A bargain buffet. Relaxing place.
Other Info: Full service, take-out, catering. Accepts AMEX, DIS, MC, VISA. Price: $$.
Directions: Just off St Charles Street in the Mount Vernon area. Between Madison and Read St.

Ambassador Dining Room
3811 Canterbury Road, at University Parkway, north of Mount Vernon, Charles Street Corridor
410-366-1484
Hours: Daily 11:30 am to 2:30 pm, 5pm to 10pm
Indian. Not pure vegetarian.
Menu: Has a large variety of vegetarian dishes. The food is usually spicy hot, so you might want to ask to have the food more mild.
Comments: Formal, white-glove dining. Has an outdoor patio next to a garden. Has terrace dining in a beautiful garden with a fountain. Very good food. Buffet service. Good atmosphere and service.
Other Info: Full service, take-out, catering. Accepts MC, VISA. Price: $$$.
Directions: It is near Johns Hopkins University.

Azebs Ethiopian Restaurant
322 North Charles Street, Mount Vernon area
410-625-9787
Hours: Tuesday to Sunday 4:30 pm to 9 pm
Closed Monday.
East African, Ethiopian. Vegan options. Not pure vegetarian.
Menu: Has several Ethiopian dishes including Lentil Stew, Cabbage, Potato & Carrot Stew, collard greens and Yellow Pea Stew.
Other Info: Full service, take-out. Accepts AMEX, MC, VISA. Price: $$.

Ban Thai
340 North Charles Street; 410-727- 7971
Hours: Monday to Saturday 11 am to 10 pm
Closed Sunday.
Thai. Not pure vegetarian.
Menu: Has several vegetarian dishes.
Other Info: Full service, take-out. Accepts AMEX, MC, VISA. Price: $$.

Banjara
1017 South Charles Street, at Hamburg Streets, Federal Hill area; 410-962-1554
Hours: Sunday to Thursday 11:30 am to 2:30 pm, 5 pm to 10:30 pm
Friday & Saturday 12 noon to 3 pm, 5 pm to 11:30 pm
Indian. Vegan options. Not pure vegetarian.
Menu: Has many vegetarian options.
Comments: Curry in a hurry type place. Reasonable prices. Buffet service.
Other Info: Full service, takeout. Accepts AMEX, DIS, MC, VISA. Price: $$.
Directions: In south Baltimore.

Bombay Grill
2 East Madison Street
410-837-2973; **Web site:** www.bombaygrill.com
Hours: Daily 11:30 to 10 pm
Indian. Lunch Buffet at a good price. Vegan options. Not pure vegetarian.
Menu: Has many vegetarian options including Eggplant Stir-fry, Vegetable Kofta, Okra subji, Grilled Vegetable Kebab, rice dishes and Indian snacks.
Comments: Has a pleasant atmosphere. Foods are fried in vegetable oil. Has live music on the weekends. Friendly manager.
Other Info: Full service, take-out, catering. Accepts AMEX, DC, DIS, MC, VISA. Price: $$.

Bombay Grill Restaurant
114 East Lombard Street, Harborplace
410-539-2233
Hours: Monday to Friday 11:30 am to 9:30 pm
Saturday & Sunday 11:30 am to 10 pm
North and South Indian. Vegan options. Not pure vegetarian.
Menu: Has many vegetarian options including samosas, masala dosas, rice dishes, uthappam, main vegetable dishes, Indian breads and desserts.
Comments: Authentic décor. Comfortable place.
Other Info: Full service, take-out. Accepts AMEX, DIS, MC, VISA. Price: $$.

Brick Oven Pizza
800 South Broadway; 410-563-1600
Hours: Sunday to Thursday 11 am to 12 midnight; Friday & Saturday 11 am to 3 am
Pizza. Vegan options. Not pure vegetarian.
Menu: Can put soy cheese on pizzas. Whole-wheat crusts.
Comments: Rated by many to have the best pizzas in Baltimore. Has wood oven.
Other Info: Full service, takeout. Price: $$.

Cafe Zen
438 East Belvedere Avenue, at York Rd
410-532-0022; **Web site:** www.cafezen.com
Hours: Monday to Thursday 11:30 am to 9:30 pm; Fri & Sat 11:30 am to 11 pm; Sun 11 am to 9:30 pm; Special Lunches 11:30 am to 3 pm
Chinese and Japanese. Not pure vegetarian.
Menu: Has several vegetarian options including Spring Rolls, Eggplant in Garlic Sauce, tofu dishes Moo Shu Vegetables, veggie dumplings, string beans and noodle dishes.
Other Info: Full service, take-out. Accepts credit cards. Price: $$.
Directions: Near the Senator movie theater.

California Pizza Kitchen
1st Floor, 201 Pratt Street, Harborplace
410-783-9339
Hours: Monday to Thursday 11 am to 10pm; Friday & Sat 11 am to 11; Sun 11 am to 9 pm
Italian. Vegan options. Not pure vegetarian.
Menu: Has several varieties of pizza (which can be ordered without cheese) and pasta dishes.
Other Info: Full service, take-out. Price: $$.

China City
2nd Floor, Light Street Pavilion, Harborplace
200 East Pratt Street; 410-539-0711
Hours: Daily 10 am to 9 pm
Chinese. Vegan options. Not pure vegetarian.
Menu: Has several vegetarian options including rice, stir-fried bean curd, noodle dishes and Chinese vegetables.
Other Info: Counter service, take-out. Price: $.

City Café

1001 Cathedral Street; 410-539-4252
Hours: Sun 9 am to 11 pm; Mon to Thur 8 am to 11 pm; Fri 8 am to 12 mid; Sat 9 am to 12 mid
Natural Foods. Vegan options.
Menu: Has several vegetarian options including salads and several vegetarian sandwiches including veggie burgers, Hummus Sandwich, Roasted Eggplant Sandwich and Black Bean Burger. Fresh juices, cappuccino, espresso.
Other Info: Counter service, take-out. Accepts DC, DIS, MC, VISA. Price: $-$$.
Directions: From I-95, take I-395 north and take the Martin Luther King Jr Blvd exit to the left and go north on MLK Jr for 2 miles, then at Read St take a slight right and go 1 block, then at W Chase St take a slight left and go 1 block, then at Brexton St turn right and go 1 block, then at Tyson St turn left and go 1 block, then at Cathedral St turn right and this place is 1 block down. From I-83, take Exit #3 and this place is a half-mile west of the exit. This place is a few blocks east of Maryland General Hospital.

The Daily Grind Coffee House

501 West Cold Spring Lane, Charles Street Corridor; 410-235-8118
1720 Thames Street; 410-558-0399
Hours: Daily 7 am to 6:30 pm
Coffee Shop and Deli. Vegan options. Not pure vegetarian.
Menu: Has several vegetarian options including fresh salads and soups, hummus and other sandwiches, Powerhouse Sandwich and hummus sandwich. Hot flavored soy milk. Fresh coffee, espresso, cappuccino
Comments: Friendly, efficient service. Casual place.
Other Info: Counter service, with tables and booths available. Price: $.

Ding How

631 South Broadway, Fell Point area
410-327-8888
Hours: Daily 11 am to 10 pm
Chinese. Not pure vegetarian.
Menu: Has many Chinese vegetarian options including soup, tofu dishes, rice dishes and vegetables.
Other Info: Full service, take-out. Accepts AMEX, DC, DISC, MC, VISA. Price: $-$$.
Directions: In the Fells Points area.

Donna's Coffee Bar

2 West Madison Street, at Charles Street
410-385-0180

1819 Reisterstown Road, Bibelot Books
410-653-6939
Coffeeshop Place. Not pure vegetarian. See description under Baltimore.
Hours: Daily 7:30 am to 10 pm (until 11 pm on Friday & Saturday)
Italian. Vegan options. Not pure vegetarian
Menu: Soup, freshly baked breads, salads, pasta, salads and several vegetarian Italian dishes. Cappuccino, espresso. About half the menu is vegetarian.
Comments: Popular hangout. Has several locations in Baltimore.
Other Info: Full service, take-out, catering. Accepts AMEX, MC, VISA. Price: $

EgyptianPizza

811 South Broadway, Fell Point area;
410-327-0005
542 East Belvedere Avenue; 410-323-7060
Hours: Sunday to Thursday 11 am to 10 pm
Friday & Saturday 11 am to 12 midnight
Middle Eastern, Pizza. Not pure vegetarian.
Menu: Pizzas and Middle Eastern dishes,
Other Info: Accepts AMEX, DC, DIS, MC, VISA. Price: $$.

Fells Point Coffee and Cheese Co.

1641 Aliceanna Street; 410-522-0612
Hours: Monday to Saturday 6 am to 6 pm.
Coffeehouse Place. Natural Foods. Not pure veg.
Menu: Has healthy sandwiches.
Directions: In the Broadway Market.

Fresh Fields

1330 Smith Avenue, Mount Washington
410-532-6700
Web site: www.wholefoodsmarket.com
Hours: Monday to Saturday 8 am to 9 pm
Sunday 8 am to 8 pm
Natural Food Store and Cafe. Deli, Bakery, Salad Bar and Juice Bar. Organic produce. Supermarket-type place. See Whole Foods Market information.
Directions: From the Baltimore Beltway (I-695), go south on I-83 for 3 miles, then take Northern Parkway exit (#10) and then go east on W Northern Pkwy a quarter-mile. At Falls Rd turn left and to go a half-mile past two traffic lights, then at Smith turn left and this place is 1 block down on the right.

Funk's Democratic Coffee Spot

1818 Eastern Avenue, Fell Point Area, east of Harborplace; 410-276-3865

Hours: Monday to Friday 4 pm to 11 pm Saturday & Sunday 10 am to 12 midnight **Coffeehouse.** International. Vegan options. Not pure vegetarian.
Menu: The menu changes daily. Has many vegetarian options including soups, sandwiches, hummus sandwiches, falafel and salads. Has daily vegan specials.
Comments: Casual place. Has a happening atmosphere and an interesting décor. Sometimes has live music.
Other Info: Counter service, take-out. Price: $.

Golden West Café

842 West 36th Street, between Chestnut & Elm Avenues, in the Hampton area
410-889-8891
Hours: Monday 8 am to 3 pm; Wednesday to Friday 8 am to 9 pm; Saturday 8 am to 10 pm; Sunday 9 am to 2 pm; closed Tuesday.
International & Southwestern. Vegetarian options. Not pure vegetarian.
Menu: Breakfast burritos and other dishes.
Comments: Indoor and outdoor seating.
Other Info: Accepts AMEX, MC, VISA.

Green Earth Natural Food Market

823 North Charles Street, Suite A
410-752-1422
Hours: Monday to Saturday 10 am to 8 pm Sunday 11 am to 5 pm
Natural Food Store and Deli. Organic produce. Juice Bar. Macrobiotic and Vegan options.
Menu: Has a good selection of vegetarian dishes. Fresh juices.
Comments: Local organic produce used when possible.
Other Info: Take-out only. Accepts MC, VISA. Price: $.
Directions: Take I-695 towards Harbor, take Russell St exit, go on Russell (curvy road) and get in far right lane. At Pratt turn right, bear left and at Charles turn left. This place is then on right. This place is a quarter-mile west of exit #3 on I-83.

Green Earth Natural Food Market

823 North Charles Street; 410-752-1422
Natural Food Store.

The Helmand

806 North Charles Street; 410-752-0311
email: helmand@erols.com
Web site: www.helmand.com
Hours: Sunday to Thursday 5 pm to 10 pm Friday & Saturday 5 pm to 11 pm

Afghan. Not pure vegetarian.
Menu: Has several vegetarian specials. The vegetarian Korma Stew is very good.
Comments: One of the best restaurants in Baltimore. Listed by Zagat as one of the top 100 restaurants in the nation. Comfortable atmosphere. Food gets good ratings. Good service. Traditional Afghani design. Has white tablecloth. Authentic Afghani cuisine. Good service.
Other Info: Full service, take-out, catering. Reservations highly suggested, especially on weekends. Non-smoking. Accepts AMEX, DIS, MC, VISA. Price: $$.

Hollywood Diner

400 East Saratoga, at Holliday; 410-962-5379
Hours: Monday to Friday 7 am to 2:30 pm Closed Saturday & Sunday.
American. Not pure vegetarian.
Menu: Has a large selection of vegetarian sandwiches. The Paul McCartney (hummus and sprouts), Bob Dylan (veggie burger), Vegetable Stir-fry, veggie Lasagna and a good selection of salads.
Other Info: Full service, counter service. Accepts MC, VISA. Price: $.

Holy Frijoles

908 West 36th Street, between Rolands & Elm Aves, Hampden area; 410-235-2326
Hours: Tuesday to Saturday 11 am to 11 pm; Sunday 12 noon to 10 pm; closed Monday.
Mexican. Vegan options. Not pure vegetarian.
Menu: Has a large variety of vegetarian and vegan options including salads, burritos, enchiladas, fajitas and tacos. No alcohol.
Comments: Casual place. Service can be a bit slow. Eclectic décor. Mismatched furniture and funky paintings. Dishes are vegetarian, unless you ask for meat.
Other Info: Full service, take-out. Accepts DIS, MC, VISA. Price: $-$$.

Home Harvest Garden Supply

3712 Eastern Avenue, Baltimore
800-348-4769; Web site: www.homeharvest.com
Hours: Monday to Friday 10 am to 7 pm; Saturday 10 am to 6 pm; closed Sunday.
Gardening Shop. Sells items for organic farming such as non-chemical fertilizers and natural pest control. They have biodegradable or recyclable materials.

Johnny Rockets

301 Light Street, Light Street Pavilion, Harborplace; 410-347-5757

Hours: Daily 9 am to 9 pm
American. Vegan options.
Menu: Has several vegetarian options including vegan Boca Burger and salads.
Comments: Casual. 1950s style décor.
Other Info: Counter service with tables nearby. Non-smoking. Price: $-$$

Liquid Earth

1626 Aliceanna Street, Fells Point area
410-276-6606
Hours: Monday to Friday 7 am to 7 pm; Saturday 9 am to 7 pm; Sunday 9 am to 3 pm
Fully Vegetarian. Juice Bar and Coffee Bar. Vegan options.
Menu: Vegetarian sandwiches, vegan soups, freshly made salads, Lentil Spinach soup, baked goods, Vegetarian Reuben, "The Picnic" is melted Brie, pears, Granny Smith apples, bitter greens and organic walnuts. Submarine sandwich is baked tofu, provolone, tomato and mushrooms. Organic salads. Cactus soup. Daily dinner specials. Fresh juices and smoothies. Wheatgrass juice. Cappuccino, espresso.
Comments: Really casual place. In a building built in the 1890's. Beautifully large juice bar. Displays local artists' work. Well-presented food. Food gets good recommendations.
Other Info: Full service, take-out. Non-smoking. Accepts reservations but are not necessary. Does not take credit cards. Price: $-$$.
Directions: Located in the Fells Point area, one block off Broadway. From I-895, take Moravia Rd exit (#14) towards US-40/Pulaski Hwy, then go west on US 40 (Pulaski Hwy) for 2 miles, keep going straight onto Orlean St (US 40) for 1 mile, at N Broadway turn left and go ¾ mile, then at Aliceanna St turn right and go 1 block and this place is at the corner with Bethel St.

Minato Japanese Restaurant

800 Charles Street; 410-332-0332
Hours: Monday to Friday 11:30 am to 2:30 pm; Sunday to Thursday 5 pm to 10 pm; Friday to Saturday 5 pm to 11 pm
Japanese and Vietnamese. Not pure vegetarian.
Menu: Has many vegetarian options including Miso Soup, vegetarian Tempura Teriyaki, sushi, vegetable Garden Rolls and main dishes.
Other Info: Full service, take-out. Price: $$-$$$.

Mt Washington Pizza & Subs

1620 Kelly Avenue; 410-664-1111
Hours: Daily 11 am to 11 pm
Italian/Indian. Vegan options.
Menu: Has vegetarian pizza subs and several veg-

etarian Indian dishes.
Other Info: Full service, takeout. Price: $-$$

Mughal Garden Restaurant

920 North Charles Street, between Eager & Read Streets, downtown; 410-547-0001; **Web site:** http://mammen.clark.net/mughal.htm
Hours: Sunday to Thursday 11:30 am to 2:30 pm, 5 pm to 11 pm
Friday & Saturday 11:30 am to 2:30 pm, 5 pm to 11:30 pm
Indian. Vegan options. Not pure vegetarian.
Menu: Has several vegetarian options including vegetable curries, freshly baked Tandoori bread, dal and rice dishes.
Comments: High class, attentive service. Buffet served.
Other Info: Full service, take-out. Accepts AMEX, DC, DIS, MC, VISA. Price: $$-$$$.

Nile Café

811 South Broadway; 410-327-0005
900 Cathedral Street, Charles Street Corridor
410-962-8859
6080 Falls Road, Mt Pleasant; 410-377-3132
1809 Reistertown Road at Woodholme, Pikesville
410-653-6868
542 East Belvedere Avenue, in the Belvedere Market; 410-323-7060
Web site: www.nilecafe.com
Hours: Sunday to Thursday 11 am to 11 pm
Friday & Saturday 11 am to 12 midnight
Middle Eastern, Italian and Pizza. Vegan options. Not Full Vegetarian.
Menu: Has Middle Eastern food and pizza. Hummus, falafel, pita bread and other dishes. Has an India pizza served with curry and an Egyptian Pizza. Pizza can be served with soy cheese or without cheese.
Comments: Popular bustling café. Can substitute soy cheese for milk cheese. Pizza cooked in wood burning oven.
Other Info: Full service, take-out. Accepts MC, VISA. Price: $$.

OK Natural Food Store

11 West Preston Street; 410-837-3911
Hours: Monday to Friday 9:30 am to 8:30 pm; Sat 10 am to 8:30 pm; Sun 10:30 am to 5 pm
Natural Food Store. Organic produce. Macrobiotic and Vegan options.
Other Info: Counter service, take-out. Accepts MC, VISA.
Directions: Located one block west of Charles Street. Take I-83, then take St Paul St exit. At Preston turn right and this place is 2 blocks down.

One World Café (two locations)
904 South Charles Street, Federal Hill
410-234-0235
100 West University Parkway, at North Charles
Street, across from Johns Hopkins campus
410-235-5777
Hours: Monday 8 am to 10 pm; Tuesday to Friday 8 am to 11 pm; Saturday 8 am to 12 midnight; Sunday 8:30 am to 5 pm
Mainly Vegetarian Café. Vegan options. Uses organic produce. Coffeehouse type place
Menu: Has granola for breakfast. Soups, salads, breads, sandwiches, falafel, chili, fresh baked goods, Eggplant Gyro with feta cheese and Roasted Eggplant. Spinach and Black Olive on a Pita, served with blue corn chips and cucumber raita is a favorite. Black Bean Burger with avocados, tomatoes, sprouts and lettuce. Cappuccino, espresso and a good amount of other coffees. Smoothies.
Comments: Casual and relaxed. Dark-wood setting. Lists organic selections on a blackboard. The restaurant is in a beautifully renovated house. Both locations have pool tables. Has indoor and outdoor seating.
Other Info: Upstairs table service, counter service, take-out. Reservations not allowed. Accepts AMEX, MC, VISA. Price: $.
Directions: It is a few blocks south of Inner Harbor, in the Federal Hill area.

Paper Moon Diner
227 West 29th Street, north of the Mount Vernon area; 410-889-4444
Hours: 24 Hours
American. Not pure vegetarian.
Menu: Has some vegetarian dishes including Sautéed Greens, salads and Grilled Eggplant with avocado and sprouts sandwich.
Other Info: Full service, take-out. Price: $.

Sam's Bagels
915 Light Street; 410-837-5447
Hours: Monday to Saturday 6 am to 3 pm
Sunday 7 am to 2 pm
Bagel Shop. Vegan options.
Menu: Has a large variety of bagels, sandwiches, Reuben Sandwich and other vegetarian dishes. Fresh juices, cappuccino, espresso.
Other Info: Limited service, take-out. Price: $.

Sam's Bagels
500 West Cold Spring Lane	410-467-1809
3121 St Paul Street	410-467-1809
325 South Dukeland Street	410-945-6980
728 Frederick Road, Catonsville	410-719-6668

| 915 Light Street | 410-837-5447 |

Bagel Shop.

Tamber's
3327 St Paul Street, Charles Street area
410-243-0383
Hours: Monday to Thursday 10 am to 10 pm; Friday & Saturday 9 am to 11 pm; Sunday 9 am to 10 pm
American, Indian and International. Vegan options.
Menu: Has pizzas, salads and a good amount of Indian dishes.
Comments: 1950s style décor. Parking arranged for customers.
Other Info: Full service, takeout, delivery. Non-smoking. Accepts AMEX, DC, DIS, MC, VISA. Price: $$

Sunsplash
Colonial Village Shopping Center, 7006 Reisterstown Road, Pikesville; 410-486-0979
Hours: Monday to Friday 9:30 am to 8 pm; Saturday 9 am to 6 pm; Sunday 9 am to 5 pm
Natural Food Store and Cafe. Deli, Juice Bar, Salad Bar and Bakery.
Directions: From I-695, take Reisterstown Rd exit (#21). Then go southeast on Reisterstown Rd (Rte 140) two miles and this place is on the right.

The Zodiac
1726 North Charles Street, Attached to Club Charles; 410-727-8815
Hours: Wednesday, Thursday 5:30 pm to 10 pm; Friday, Saturday 5:30 pm to 11 pm; Sun 11:30 am to 10 pm; closed Mon to Tues.
Electic American. Vegan options. Not pure vegetarian.
Menu: Has several vegetarian dishes, including veggie burgers, Red Beans & Rice, Curried Tofu Sandwich and Lasagna. Espresso, cappuccino, non-alcoholic beer.
Other Info: Full service, take-out. Accepts MC, VISA. Price: $.

BEL AIR

David's Natural Market
3 Red Pump Road; 410-803-0784
Hours: Monday to Saturday 10 am to 8 pm; Saturday 10 am to 6 pm; Sunday 12 noon to 5 pm
Natural Food Store. Juice and Sandwich Bar.
Menu: Has sandwiches and salads. Fresh juices and smoothies.
Comments: Friendly, helpful place.
Directions: From I-95, take MD Hwy 24 exit

(#77A) towards Edgewood, then go northwest on Hwy 24 for 8 miles, then take Forest Hill/Rocks Spring Rd exit, then go northwest on Rock Spring Rd and this place is a quarter-mile down.

BELTSVILLE

El Mexicano
10413 Baltimore Avenue
301-572-4000
Hours: Monday to Friday 7 am to 9 pm
Saturday & Sunday 10 am to 9 pm
Mexican. Vegan options. Not pure vegetarian
Menu: Has a separate vegetarian menu with a good amount of dishes such as quesadillas, burritos, enchiladas, tacos and a tamale platter. No lard in the beans.
Other Info: Full service, take-out. Price: $.

BETHESDA (northwest DC suburb)

Bacchus
7945 Norfolk Avenue; 301-657-1722
Hours: Monday to Friday 12 noon to 2 pm, 6 pm to 10 pm
Saturday & Sunday 6 pm to 10:30 pm
Lebanese, Mediterranean, Middle Eastern. Vegan options. Not pure vegetarian
Menu: Has several vegetarian options including Eggplant Salad, Stuffed Grape Leaves, falafel, hummus, tahini, baba ghanouj and salads.
Comments: Has outdoor dining.
Other Info: Full service, take-out, catering. Reservations suggested. Accepts AMEX, DIS, MC, VISA. Price: $$-$$$.
Directions: From I-495 (Capital Beltway), take the Rte 185 (Connecticut Ave) exit and then go south towards DC on Connecticut. Go about a mile and turn right onto Jones Bridge Rd, then take a quick left onto Rockville Pike (Rte 355), which becomes Wisconsin Ave. After about a third-mile turn right onto Cordell Ave, then turn right at Norfolk Ave and this place is right there on the right. Parking arranged for customers.

Faryab
4917 Cordell Avenue; 301-951-3484
Hours: Tuesday to Thursday 11:30 am to 2 pm, 5 pm to 9:30 pm; Friday 11:30 am to 2 pm, 5 pm to 10:30 pm; Saturday 5 pm to 10:30 pm; Sunday 5 pm to 9:30 pm; closed Monday
Afghan. Not pure vegetarian.
Menu: Has several vegetarian options.
Other Info: Full service, take-out. Non-smoking. Reservations recommended. Accepts AMEX, MC, VISA. Price: $$.

Directions: From I-495 (Capital Beltway), take the Rte 185 (Connecticut Ave) exit and then go south towards DC on Connecticut. Go about a mile and turn right onto Jones Bridge Rd, then take a quick left onto Rockville Pike (Rte 355), which becomes Wisconsin Ave. After about a third-mile turn right onto Cordell Ave. This place a third-mile down on left.

Fresh Fields (Whole Foods)
Kenwood Station Shopping Center, 5269 River Road; 301-984-4860
Hours: Monday to Saturday 8 am to 9 pm
Sunday 8 am to 8 pm
Natural Food Store and Cafe. Deli, Bakery, Salad Bar and Juice Bar. Organic produce. Supermarket-type place. See Whole Foods Market information.
Other Info: Counter service, take-out. No seating.
Directions: From I-495, take River Rd (MD-190) south exit and go toward Washington DC. This place is about 3 miles down on the left in the Kenwood Station Shopping Center.

Garden Café
7825 Woodmont Avenue; 301-654-6800
Hours: Monday to Friday 8 am to 2 pm; Saturday 9 am to 2 pm; closed Sunday.
Deli and Juice Bar. American. Vegetarian-friendly. Not pure vegetarian.
Menu: Freshly made juices, smoothies, espresso, organic coffees. Vegetable Energizer (carrot, celery, beet, cucumber, ginger, parsley). Has vegetarian and vegan sandwiches, vegetarian chili and Pinzimonio Panini (mozzarella & raw vegetables).
Comments: Pleasant, cheery atmosphere.
Other Info: Limited service, take out. Accepts MC, VISA. Price: $-$$.
Directions: From I-495 (Capital Beltway), take the Rte 185 (Connecticut Ave) exit and then go south towards DC on Connecticut. Go about 1 mile and turn right onto Jones Bridge Rd, then take a quick left onto Rockville Pike (Rte 355), which becomes Wisconsin Ave. Turn right onto Fairmont Ave. Turn left onto Woodmont Ave.

Oodles Noodles
4907 Cordell Avenue; 301-986-8833
Hours: Monday to Thursday 11:30 am to 3 pm, 5 pm to 10 pm; Friday 11:30 am to 3 pm, 5 pm to 10:30 pm; Saturday 11:30 am to 10:30 pm; Sunday 5 pm to 10 pm
Asian. Including Chinese, Japanese, Thai, Vietnamese and Indonesian. Not pure vegetarian.
Menu: Has a good selection of Asian noodle

dishes.
Other Info: Accepts AMEX, DC, DIS, MC, VISA. Price: $$.
Directions: From I-495 (Capital Beltway), take the Rte 185 (Connecticut Ave) exit and then go south towards DC on Connecticut. Go about a mile and turn right onto Jones Bridge Rd, then take a quick left onto Rockville Pike (Rte 355), which becomes Wisconsin Ave. After about a third-mile turn right onto Cordell Ave and this place is a third-mile down on left.

Tako Grill

7756 Wisconsin Avenue; 301-652-7030
Hours: Mon to Thur 11:30 to 2 pm, 5:30 am to 10 pm; Fri 11:30 am to 2 pm, 5:30 pm to 10:30 pm; Sat 5:30 pm to 10:30 pm; Sun 5 pm to 9:30 pm
Japanese. Not pure vegetarian.
Menu: Has many vegetarian options including soups, salads, sandwiches, Mediterranean Platter, Vegetable Pot Stickers, pasta dishes, grilled vegetables and Roasted Tomatoes with Polenta.
Comments: Has gotten good reviews in Washingtonion Magazine.
Other Info: Full service, take-out. Reservations suggested. Accepts AMEX, MC, VISA. Price: $$-$$$.
Directions: From I-495 (Capital Beltway), take the Rte 185 (Connecticut Ave) exit and then go south towards DC on Connecticut. Go about a mile and turn right onto Jones Bridge Rd, then take a quick left onto Rockville Pike (Rte 355), which becomes Wisconsin Ave. This place on Wisconsin just past Cheltenham Dr.

Thyme Square

4735 Bethesda Avenue, at Woodmont
301-657-9077; **fax:** 301-657-4505
Hours: Sunday to Thursday 11:30 am to 9:30 pm; Friday & Saturday 11 am to 10 pm
Natural Foods International and New American Restaurant. Mainly vegetarian. Not pure vegetarian (serves fish).
Menu: Has many vegetarian options including pasta, pizza, excellent salads, quesadillas, Roasted Vegetables and noodle dishes. Vegetarian and vegan dishes are marked on the menu. Fresh juices, cappuccino, espresso.
Comments: Fashionable atmosphere. Food gets good ratings.
Other Info: Full service, take-out. Reservations suggested. Accepts AMEX, DIS, MC, VISA. Price: $$-$$$.
Directions: From I-495 (Capital Beltway), take the Rte 185 (Connecticut Ave) exit and then go south towards DC on Connecticut. Go about a

mile and turn right onto Jones Bridge Rd, then take a quick left onto Rockville Pike (Rte 355), which becomes Wisconsin Ave. Turn left at Bethesda Ave (a block past Elm St) and this place on right after 150 yards.

CABIN JOHN (northwest DC suburb)

Bethesda Co-op

6500 Seven Locks Road, Cabin John
301-320-2530; **email:** bethesdacoop@erols.com
Web site: http://members.tripod.com/~co_op
Hours: Monday to Saturday 9 am to 9 pm
Sunday 9 am to 8 pm
Natural Food Store. Fresh breads. The deli is vegan friendly. Organic produce.
Menu: Has ready-made sandwiches and salads. Take-out only. The hummus and black bean dip are good.
Directions: From I-495, take River Road (Rte 190) exit going west toward Potomac. At Seven Locks Rd turn left. Go 1½ mile and this place on right at corner of MacArthur Blvd and Seven Locks Road in MacArthur Shopping Center.

CLARKSVILLE (Baltimore suburb)

Roots Market

5805 Clarksville Square Drive
443-535-9321; **Web site:** www.rootsmkt.com
Hours: Monday to Friday 9 am to 8 pm; Saturday 9 am to 7 pm; Sunday 10 am to 7 pm
Natural Food Store and take-out Deli. Organic produce. Fresh Baked Breads.
Comments: Plans to open deli in fall, 2002.
Directions: On Route 108, at Route 32.

COCKEYSVILLE (Baltimore Suburbs)

The Natural

Cranbrook Shopping Center, 560 Cranbrook Road; 410-628-1262
Hours: Monday to Friday 9 am to 8 pm; Saturday 10 am to 6 pm; Sunday 11 am to 6 pm; Café closed on weekends.
Natural Food Store and Deli.
Menu: Has some sandwiches and salads. Not much of a selection.
Comments: Has 15 seats.
Other Info: Accepts AMEX, MC, VISA. Counter service, take-out.
Directions: From I-83, take Padonia Rd exit and go east on Padonia Rd a half-mile. At York turn left and go 1½ mile, then at Cranbrook turn right and this place is about ¾ mile down on the left in Cranbrook Shopping Center.

COLLEGE PARK

Bagel Place
7423 Baltimore Boulevard, next to the Maryland Book Exchange
301-779-3900; fax: 301-779-5730
Bagel Place. Not pure vegetarian.
Menu: Has bagels, bagels sandwiches and salads. Cappuccino, espresso.

Berwyn Café
5010 Berwyn Road; 301-345-9898
Hours: Tuesday to Saturday 11 am to 8 pm; Sunday Brunch 10 am to 3 pm; closed Monday.
Vegetarian Café. Juice Bar. Macrobiotic and Vegan options. Mainly organic food.
Menu: Has many vegetarian and vegan dishes. Veggie burgers, Steamed Vegetables, Tempeh Burger (excellent), Tofu Gyro, organic French Fries, organic steamed vegetables, Veggie Lasagna (sometimes), Corn Tamales, bean and rice dishes, pita sandwiches, veggie dogs and salads. Baked desserts. Really good fresh vegan cookies. Fresh juices.
Comments: This place is very good and is recommended. Popular with locals and college professors from U of Maryland. Often has live music or poetry recitals on Friday evening. The couple that runs this place is really nice. Nice, pleasant, casual atmosphere. Very reasonably priced. Conveniently located 1 block from the Smile Herb Shop (the people here are very knowledgeable about the herbs).
Other Info: Counter service, take-out. Price: $.
Directions: From I-495, take Rte 1/Baltimore Ave exit (#25), and go towards College Park (south). Go about 1.5 miles, then at Berwyn turn left and this place is two blocks down on the left. It is in a residential area by no other stores.

Maryland Food Co-op
B-0203 Student Union Building, University of Maryland; 301-314-8089
Hours: Tuesday to Thursday 7:30 am to 7:30 pm; Friday 7:30 am to 5 pm; Saturday 12 noon to 5 pm; Sunday 12 noon to 3 pm
Natural Food Store and Deli. Organic produce.
Menu: Freshly made sandwiches, juices, organic coffee, bagels and trail mixes. Makes various sandwiches with mock "meat."
Direction: Located on the University of Maryland campus, in the basement of the Student Union Building, which everyone knows how to get to. From I-95, take College Park exit and go south toward College Park. After about 2 miles make a right at the main entrance of Maryland State University. Go straight for about a half-mile and at the third traffic lift turn right and park in the parking garage. You have to park in the guest parking garage right night to the Union Building and pay a fee for parking.

My Organic Market
9827 Rhode Island Avenue; 301-220-1100
Hours: Monday to Friday 10 am to 9 pm; Saturday 10 am to 8 pm; Sunday 10 am to 7 pm
Natural Food Store. Organic produce.
Menu: Has ready-made sandwiches in the cooler.
Other Info: Accepts AMEX, MC, VISA.
Directions: From the Capital Beltway (I-495), take US 1/Balitmore Ave exit and go south towards College Park a third-mile, at Edgewood Rd turn left and go a third-mile, then at Rhode Island Ave turn right and this place is a block down.

Smoothie King
7403 Baltimore Avenue; 301-277-2771
Smoothie Place. Has a large selection.
Menu: Has malts, shakes, Peanut Power, Yogurt D-lite, Coconut Surprise, high-protein smoothies, and various fruit smoothies. They make their smoothies with natural ingredients, fruits, fruit juices, natural proteins and vitamins.
Directions: On the main street in downtown College Park (Rte 1), across from the entrance of University of Maryland.

COLUMBIA

Akbar
9400 Snowden River Parkway (Rte 175), Columbia; 410-381-3600
Hours: Monday to Friday 11:30 am to 2:30 pm, 5 pm to 10 pm (until 11 pm Friday); Saturday 12 noon to 3 pm, 5 pm to 11 pm; Sunday 12 noon to 3 pm, 5 pm to 10 pm
Indian. Not pure vegetarian. See description under Baltimore.

Bombay Peacock Grill
10005 Old Columbia Road; 410-381-7111
Hours: Sunday to Thursday 11:30 am to 2:30 pm, 5 pm to 10 pm
Friday & Saturday 11:30 am to 11 pm
Indian. Vegan options. Not pure vegetarian.
Menu: Has many vegetarian options including Vegetable Kebab, vegetable curries, Vegetable Kofta, rice dishes, samosa, Indian breads and Indian desserts.
Comments: Pleasant place to eat at. Good atmo-

sphere. Cooks with vegetable or olive oil.
Other Info: Full service, take-out, catering. Accepts AMEX, DC, DISC, MC, VISA. Price: $$.
Parking arranged for customers.

David's Natural Market
Wild Lake Shopping Center, 5430-C Lynx Lane
410-730-2304
Hours: Monday to Friday 9 am to 7 pm; Saturday 9 am to 6 pm; Sunday 11 am to 5 pm
Natural Food Store and Café. Deli and Juice Bar.
Directions: From Hwy 29, take Columbia Town Center exit west (Rte 175). When road forks take Governor Warfield Parkway to the right. Then at Twin Rivers, turn right and go about 1 mile, then at Lynx turn left and this place is 1 mile down on the right in Wild Lake Shopping Center.

Hunan Manor
7091 Deepage Drive; 410-381-1134
Hours: Monday to Thursday 11 am to 10 pm; Friday & Saturday 11 am to 11 pm; Sunday 12 noon to 10 pm
Chinese. Vegan options. Not pure vegetarian
Menu: Has many vegetarian options including many mock "meat" dishes, rice, Szechuan String Beans, Tofu & Vegetables, Sautéed Broccoli & Garlic Sauce and Chinese vegetables.
Other Info: Full service, take-out. Accepts AMEX, MC, VISA. Price: $$-$$$.

**The Mango Grove
6365B Dobbin Road
410-884-3426; **email:** info@mangogrove.com;
Web site: www.mangogrove.com
Hours: Wednesday to Monday 11:30 am to 3 pm, 5 pm to 9:30 pm
Friday & Saturday 11 am to 10 pm
Vegetarian South Indian. Vegan options.
Menu: Has South Indian dishes, vegetable curries and rice. The Mango-filled Dosa is good. Has a good lunch buffet. Mango lassi.
Comments: Friendly, efficient service. Good atmosphere. Excellent place. The restaurant is vegetarian, but the catering service offers meat dishes. Good food.
Other Info: Full service, take-out, catering. Accepts AMEX, DC, DISC, MC, VISA. Price: $-$$
Directions: Located near Friendly's Restaurant in a shopping center. From I-95 take Exit #41B (175 West towards Columbia). At Dobbin Road turn left. Then turn left at first light into Dobbin Center, then take immediate left towards Wendy's. This place is just behind Wendy's.

EASTON

Railway Market
Marlboro Shopping Center
108 Marlboro Road, Suite 1
410-822-4852
Hours: Monday to Friday 9 am to 7 pm; Saturday 9 am to 6 pm; Sunday 10 am to 7 pm
Natural Food Store and Café. Deli, Juice Bar, Salad Bar and Bakery.
Directions: Get on Rte 50 going towards Ocean City. Take bypass (Rte 322) going around Easton and go about 1½ mile, then turn left at Marlboro Rd and this place is in the second strip mall down called Marlboro Shopping Center.

ELLICOTT CITY

***Sarah and Desmond Concepts
8198 Main Street; 410-465-9700
Hours: Tuesday to Sunday 9 am to 6 pm
Closed Monday
Vegetarian Coffeehouse. Vegan options.
Menu: Has several vegetarian options including baked pita sandwiches, salads, veggie chili, Veggie Lasagna, a selection of sandwiches and breakfast all day. Cappuccino, espresso. Good selection of baked good. Smoothies, soy milk.
Comments: Friendly, helpful people. Causal, relaxed place. Recommended.
Other Info: Counter service, take-out, catering. Order at counter and food is brought to you. Accepts AMEX, DC, MC, VISA. Price: $-$$.
Directions: This place is on the main street of town.

FREDERICK

Bombay Grill
137 North Market Street; 301-668-0077
Hours: Daily 11:30 am to 10 pm
Indian. Not pure vegetarian.
Menu: Indian breads, vegetable kofta, potato dishes and grilled vegetable kabob. Dishes are prepared with vegetable or olive oil.
Other Info: Full service, take-out, catering. Accepts AMEX, DC, MC, VISA. Price: $$.

Common Market Co-op
5813 Buckeystown Pike (Rt 85), in the middle of the downtown; 301-663-3416
email: host@commonmarket.com
Web site: www.commonmarket.com
Hours: Monday to Saturday 9 am to 9 pm; Sunday 11 am to 5 pm; closed on major holiday.

Natural Food Store and mainly Vegetarian Deli. Organic produce. Vegan options. Not pure vegetarian.

Menu: Has salads, wraps, burritos, baked goods, soups and sandwiches. Fresh juices.

Comments: Local organic produce used when possible. Large selection of organic herbs. One of the best natural food stores in the Baltimore area. Has a good selection of bulk goods, teas, herbs, etc. Has a bulletin board to exchange information.

Other Info: Counter service, take-out only. Has no seating. Price: $. Accepts AMEX, MC, VISA.

Directions: From I-270, take Market Street exit (#31) and go north on Route 85 and this place is 1 mile down on the right in the Point Plaza shopping center. This place is located on the left end of the shopping plaza. From Rte 70, take South Market Street exit (#54) and go south onto Rte 85 and when you get to fork in road, stay right and go a half-mile, then turn left at the first traffic light into Point Plaza shopping Center.

Health Express Food Market

1450 West Patrick Street; 301-662-2293

Hours: Monday to Saturday 10 am to 7 pm
Sunday 12 noon to 5 pm

Natural Food Store and Deli. Not pure vegetarian. Vegan-friendly. Organic produce. Lunch Buffet.

Menu: Homemade soups, salads, sandwiches and main dishes. Fresh juices.

Other Info: Limited service, take-out. Has a couple of tables. Price: $.

Directions: This place is a half-mile west of the Frederick Towne Mall on US 40, about 3 miles west of the downtown.

The Orchard

45 North Market Street, at Church
301-663-4912

Hours: Tuesday to Saturday 11:30 am to 2:30 pm, 5 pm to 10 pm
Closed Sunday and Monday

Natural Gourmet Food Restaurant. International, Chinese, Thai and Indian. Vegan options. Not pure vegetarian.

Menu: Has a large amount of vegetarian dishes.

Comments: Everything is homemade.

Other Info: Full service, take-out. Non-smoking. Accepts AMEX, DC, MC, VISA. Price: $$.

Directions: Located in downtown Frederick.

Wildflowers Café

10 North Market Street; 301-695-9533

Hours: Monday to Saturday 11 am to 4 pm
Closed Sunday.

Vegetarian International. Organic produce.

Menu: Sells organic breads. Sandwich, soups and wraps.

Comments: All the produce they use is organic. Also sells some produce.

Other Info: Full service, take-out. Limited seating. Non-smoking. Reservation suggested. Accepts MC, VISA.

Directions: Located in downtown Frederick.

FROSTBURG

Gandalf's Restaurant

24 West Main Street
301-689-2010

Hours: Monday to Saturday 5 pm to 12 pm
Closed Sunday.

International African, Mediterranean, and Thai. Vegan options. Not pure vegetarian.

Menu: Soy Reuben Sandwich, falafel, Grilled Tofu Squares, kitfo (veg meatballs) and several specialty salads, Has several vegetarian sandwiches.

Comments: Local organic produce used when possible.

Other Info: Full service, take-out. Price: $-$$.

Directions: This place is right downtown.

GAITHERSBURG

El Mexicano

12150 Darnestown Road; 301-330-5620

Hours: Monday to Thursday 11 am to 9 pm; Friday & Saturday 11 am to 9:30 pm; Sunday 12 noon to 8:30 pm

Mexican. Vegan options. See description under Beltsville.

Menu: Has a separate vegetarian menu including enchiladas, tacos, yuca fries, burritos, tamale platter and more.

**Madras Vegetarian Indian Cuisine

74 Bureau Drive, at Qunice Orchard Road
301-977-1600

Hours: Monday to Thursday 11:30 am to 2:30 pm, 5:30 pm to 9:30 pm; Fri 11:30 am to 2:30 pm, 5:30 pm to 10 pm; Sat & Sun 11:30 am to 4 pm, 5:30 pm to 10 pm

Vegetarian Indian. Lunch Buffet.

Menu: Serves North and South Indian food. Samosas, dosas, curries, Indian breads, uthappam, rice, Saag Paneer, Malai Kofta, raita, papadam and dal. No alcohol.

Comments: It is a big place with around 200 seats. Good food. The lunch buffet is a very good value. Cooks with vegetable oil.

Other Info: Accepts MC, VISA. Price: $-$$.
Directions: From I-270 north, take exit #10 (Rte 117). Turn right at end of ramp and go a half-mile west on Rte 117. At Bureau Dr, turn right and this place is a third-mile down.

Roy's Place

2 East Diamond Avenue; 301-948-5548
Hours: Monday to Thursday 11 am to 11 pm; Friday to Saturday 11 am to 12 midnight; Sunday 11:30 am to 11 pm
American. Tavern. Not pure vegetarian.
Menu: Has four vegetarian sandwiches including the George Bernard Shaw, Mahatma Gandhi, or Susan B Anthony.
Comments: Sandwiches are not cheap here. Service can be a bit slow, so best to plan for it.
Other Info: Full service, take-out. Accepts AMEX, DIS, MC, VISA. Price: $$. Parking arranged for customers.
Directions: From I-495, take I-270 Local north, then take Shady Grove Road/Redland Road exit, stay left at fork in ramp, then keep right at fork in ramp and merge onto Shady Grove Rd, At Frederick Rd (Rte 355) turn left and it becomes Frederick Ave. Go 1½ mile, then turn slightly right onto S Summit Ave, then at E Diamond Ave turn left.

Thai Sa-Mai Restaurant

8369 Snouffer School Road; 301-963-1800
Hours: Tuesday to Thursday 11 am to 2:30 pm, 5 pm to 9:30 pm; Friday 11:30 am to 3 pm, 5 pm to 10 pm; Saturday 5 pm to 10; Sunday 5 pm to 9 pm; closed Monday.
Thai. Vegan options. Not pure vegetarian
Menu: Has over 25 dishes on their menu. Has good curry dishes.
Comments: No MSG used. Washingtonian Magazine gave them a good review. Make sure you request that fish sauce is not put in food. Parking arranged for customers.
Other Info: Full service, take-out. Reservations necessary for groups. Accepts DIS, MC, VISA. Price: $$.

GERMANTOWN

El Mexicano

12922 Middlebrook Road;
301-972-0500
Hours: Monday to Saturday 8:30 am to 10 pm
Sunday 9:30 am to 9 pm
Mexican. Not pure vegetarian. See description under Beltsville.

GREENBELT (DC suburb)

Greenbelt Consumer Cooperative

121 Centerway
301-474-0522; **email:** radcoop@aol.com
Hours: Monday to Saturday 9 am to 9 pm
Sunday 10 am to 6 pm
Natural Food Store and Deli. Organic produce.
Menu: Soups, a good amount of salads, sandwiches and hot dishes.
Other Info: Accepts MC, VISA.
Directions: From MD-295, take exit towards Greenbelt/MD-193, then go north (then east) on Southway (becomes Centerway) and this place is a third-mile down.

Maharajah

8825 Greenbelt Road; 301-552-1600
Hours: Daily 11 am to 2:30 pm, 5pm to 9:30pm
Indian. Vegan options. Not pure vegetarian
Menu: Has many vegetarian options including vegetable stir-fry, curried vegetables, rice dishes and samosas.
Comments: Casual place. Parking arranged for customers. Owner is a vegetarian.
Other Info: Full service, take-out. Reservations suggested. Accepts AMEX, DIS, MC, VISA. Price: $$.

KNOXVILLE

Blue Ridge Organic Catering

301-834-7520; **fax:** 301-834-5070; **email:** BlueRidgeCooking@aol.com
Organic catering service. Organic Juice Bar.
Menu: Organic breads, pastas, cakes and cookies. Organic lunches.

LANGLEY PARK (Northeast Washington DC suburb)

Udupi Palace

1329 University Boulevard East, near New Hampshire Avenue
301-434-1531; **email:** manager@udupipalace.com; **Web site:** www.udupipalace.com
Hours: Daily 11:30 am to 9:30 pm
Fully Vegetarian South Indian.
Menu: Has over a hundred dishes on the menu. Has a good size menu. Masala Dosa, Idly, Vegetable Uthappam, Indian breads, vegetable curries, special rice dishes, Mixed Vegetable Pakoras, Paneer Pakoras, Vegetable Cutlet, Mattar Paneer, Aloo Gobhi, Channa Masala, Vegetable Korma,

Palak Paneer and Indian desserts such as Gulab jamun. Has special Thali with over 15 dishes. The "Udupi Special" is sambar, vada, dosa or uthappam. You can ask for vegan dishes. Fresh juices.

Comments: Original and authentic South Indian food. Popular place. Has full menu on their Web site. Got good reviews in The Washington Post, Washingtonian, the Takoma Voice and the Vegetarian Society of DC. Because food is cooked freshly will have to wait for 20 to 30 minutes for the food to be prepared. Good value. Very good service. Food gets high ratings.

Other Info: Full Service, catering. Non-smoking. Does not take reservations. Accepts AMEX, DC, MC, VISA. Price: $-$$

Directions: This place is near the intersection of New Hampshire and University Boulevard. From the I-495 Beltway, take #29B exit (Rte 193E to Langley Park). Go about two miles southwest and you will pass New Hampshire Ave (Rte 650, a major street with two shopping centers on left). This place is then a block down in a strip mall on the left.

****Woodland Indian Vegetarian**

8046 New Hampshire Avenue, at University Boulevard; 301-434-4202

email: woodlands@pocketmail.com

Web site: www.woodlandsrestaurant.com

Hours: Sunday to Thursday 11:30 am to 9:30 pm

Friday & Saturday 11:30 am to 10 pm

12 Course Daily Lunch Buffet 11:30 am to 3 pm

Pure Vegetarian Indian. Weekday Lunch Buffet. Vegan-friendly.

Menu: Has a good selection of vegetarian dishes including dosas, uthappam, rice dishes, samosas, curries and Indian desserts. The mango lassis are really good. Has an excellent lunch buffet. A dinner thali includes cutlet, samosa, roti, special rice, sambar, channa curry, kootu, yogurt, pickle, papad and dessert.

Comments: Reasonable prices. Popular, welcoming place. Next door to a sari shop and near an Indian Grocery. Got a good review in The Washington Post Magazine.

Other Info: Full service, take-out, catering. Non-smoking. Reservations not necessary. Accepts AMEX, MC, VISA. Price: $$-$$$.

Directions: From the I-495 Beltway, take the Rte 650 exit (#28), and then go south towards DC on Rte 650 (New Hampshire Ave) for about two miles. This place is at the intersection of University (Rte 193, a major road) and New Hampshire.

LARGO

Everlasting Life

Hampton Mall

9185 Central Avenue, Largo

301-324-6900 **Web site:** www.everlastinglife.net

Hours: Monday to Saturday 9 am to 9 pm

Sunday 11 am to 9 pm

Natural Food Store and Deli. Organic produce.

Menu: Salads, sandwiches and soups.

Other Info: Full service, take-out. Has a banquet hall. Accepts AMEX, MC, VISA.

Directions: From Capital Beltway (I-495), take exit #15B, proceed to Hampton Mall, which is right off the beltway.

LAUREL

Laurel Health Food

131 Bowie Road; 301-498-7191

Hours: Monday to Friday 10 am to 8 pm

Saturday 10 am to 6 pm

Natural Food Store. Sandwich Bar. Organic produce.

Menu: Has sandwiches and salads. Hummus, tabbouleh and others.

Comments: Has a sandwich counter. Accepts MC, VISA.

Directions: This place on US 1, near the junction of Bowie Rd and Rte 198 East, near the Office Depot.

Mr Wang Hunan

675 Main Street; 301-317-8888

Hours: Sunday to Thursday 11:30 am to 10 pm

Friday & Saturday 11:30 am to 11 pm

Chinese. Vegan options. Not pure vegetarian

Menu: Has a separate vegetarian menu with a large selection of vegetarian dishes. Crispy Sesame Chicken. Some of the dishes have eggs in them.

Other Info: Full service, take-out, catering. Price: $$. Accepts AMEX, MC, VISA.

LEONARDTOWN

The Good Earth Natural Foods Co.

22750 Washington Street; 301-475-1630

Hours: Tuesday to Sunday 10 am to 6 pm; Sunday 10 am to 4 pm; closed Monday.

Natural Food Store. Organic produce.

MT RAINIER (northeast DC suburb)

Glut Food Co-op

4005 34th Street; 301-779-1978

Hours: Tuesday to Friday 10 am to 8 pm

Saturday to Monday 10 am to 7 pm
Natural Food Store. Organic produce.
Other Info: Accepts AMEX, MC, VISA.
Directions: From Rte 1, go west on 34th Street
and this place on left.

OCEAN CITY

Café Iguana
12701 Coastal Highway; **410-250-8700**
Hours: Daily for three meals; hours change during winter months
American Natural Foods. Not pure vegetarian
Menu: Menu changes weekly. Has several vegetarian options. Some dishes they may have are various salads, hummus, Spinach Ravioli, veggie burgers, Vegetable Pita Pocket, stuffed grape leaves and quesadillas. Cappuccino, espresso.
Other Info: Full service, take-out. Price: $.

OLNEY

Olney Ale House
2000 Olney Sandy Spring Road; 301-774-6708
Hours: Sunday to Thursday 11:30 am to 9:45 pm; Friday & Sunday 11 am to 10:45 pm; closed Monday.
Natural Foods Restaurant. Vegan options. Not pure vegetarian.
Menu: Has a good selection of vegetarian dishes. Salads, veggie burgers, chili, homemade breads, Tofu Sandwich, Veggie burger, Eggplant Wrap, Baco Burger, Veggie BLT Sandwich and Portobello Mushrooms.
Comments: Friendly, relaxed place. Popular place so you may have to wait on the weekend. Cozy place with a fireplace in the winter.
Other Info: Full service, take-out. Accepts DISC, MC, VISA. Price: $$.
Directions: From the Capital Beltway (I-495), take Georgia Ave/MD-97 exit (#31) and go north on Georgia Ave (merges into Rte 97, then become Baltimore Rd) for 10 miles, then at Olney Sandy Spring Rd (MD-108) turn right and this place is a half-mile down.

PIKESVILLE

Panera Bread
1852 Reisterstown Road; 410-602-5125
Hours: Monday to Saturday 6 am to 9 pm
Sunday 8 am to 7 pm
Deli and Bakery. Not pure vegetarian.
Menu: Bagels, veggie sandwiches and a vegetarian soup (varies daily). They also have an extensive coffee and espresso selection.

Other Info: Accepts AMEX, DIS, MC, VISA.
Price: $$.

Mr Chan's Szechuan Restaurant
1000 Reisterstown Road; 410-484-1100
Hours: Monday to Thursday 10:30 am to 10 pm;
Friday 10:30 am to 11 pm; Saturday 11 am to 11 pm; Sunday 12 noon to 10 pm
Chinese. Macrobiotic and Vegan options. Not pure vegetarian.
Menu: Has many vegetarian options including Spring Rolls, Hot and Sour Soup, Orange Spicy Tofu, Chinese vegetables, non-fried dumpling, and tempeh and tofu dishes.
Comments: Has a buffet on Friday nights.
Other Info: Full service, take-out, catering. Accepts AMEX, DIS, MC, VISA. Price: $$.

Village Market Natural Grocer and Simply Delicious
Colonial Village Shopping Center, 7006 Reisterstown Road; 410-486-0979
Store Hours: Monday to Friday 9 am to 8 pm;
Saturday 9 am to 6 pm; Sunday 10 am to 5 pm
Natural Food Store. Organic produce.
Menu: Has some ready-made sandwiches.
Other Info: Accepts MC, VISA. Price: $.
Directions: From I-695, take Hwy 140 (Reisterstown Rd) exit (#20) south. Then go southeast on Hwy 140 for about 1½ mile and this place is on the right in the Colonial Village Shopping Center.

RANDALLSTOWN (Baltimore suburb)

Akbar Restaurant
3541 Brenbrook Drive, at Liberty Road
410-655-1600
Hours: Sunday, Tuesday to Thursday 11:30 am to 2 pm, 5 pm to 10 pm; Friday & Saturday 12 noon to 2 pm, 5 pm to 11 pm; closed Monday.
Indian. Not pure vegetarian. See description under Baltimore.
Other Info: Accepts AMEX, DC, DIS, MC, VISA. Price: $$.

Szechuan Best
8625 Liberty Road; 410-521-0020
Hours: Sunday to Thursday 11:30 am to 10 pm
Friday & Saturday 11:30 am to 11 pm
Chinese. Not pure vegetarian
Menu: Has a large vegetarian menu.
Comments: Parking arranged for customer.
Other Info: Full service, take-out. Accepts MC, VISA. Price: $$.

ROCKVILLE (DC suburb)

Bombay Bistro
98 West Montgomery Avenue; 301-762-8798
Hours: Monday to Thursday 11 am to 2:30 pm, 5 pm to 9:30 pm; Friday 11 am to 2:30 pm, 5 pm to 10:30 pm; Saturday 12 noon to 3 pm, 5 pm to 10:30 pm; Sunday 12 noon to 3 pm, 5 pm to 9:30 pm
Indian. North and South Indian. Vegan options. Not pure vegetarian
Menu: Samosas, Uthappam, Vegetable Biryani, Vegetable dishes and rice dishes. Cappuccino, espresso.
Comments: Good service. Good place for a private party. Food is not too spicy. Parking arranged for customers.
Other Info: Full service, take-out. Does not accept reservations. Accepts AMEX, DC, DIS, MC, VISA. Price: $-$$.
Directions: From I-495, get on I-270 Local going north. Take the W Montgomery Ave East (Rte 28 W) exit. Go straight onto Montgomery Ave and this place is down about a mile.

The Dairy Nosh
10048 Darnestown Road; 301-838-8522
Hours: Monday to Friday 7 am to 8 pm; Saturday 8 am to 6 pm; Sunday 8 am to 5 pm
Deli. Not pure vegetarian.
Menu: Has salads, Cheese Lasagna, Potato Latkas, Vegetable Kugel, Spinach Bagels and Cheese Blintzes.
Other Info: Counter service, take out. Price: $-$$.

Fresh Fields (Whole Foods)
Congressional Plaza; 1649 Rockville Pike; 301-984-4880; **email:** Rockville@wholefoods.com; **Web site:** www.wholefoodsmarket.com
Hours: Monday to Saturday 8 am to 9 pm Sunday 8 am to 8 pm
Natural Food Store and Cafe. Deli, Bakery, Salad Bar and Juice Bar. Organic produce. Supermarket-type place. See Whole Foods Market information.
Directions: From I-495, take North Rockville Pike exit (Rte 355, Wisconsin Ave exit). Go northwest on Rockville Pike about 2½ miles and this place on left in Congressional Plaza.

Hard Times Café
1117 Nelson Street; 301-294-9720
Hours: Monday to Thursday 11 am to 10 pm; Friday & Saturday 11:30 am to 11 pm; Sunday 12 pm to 12 midnight

International, American. Not pure vegetarian
Menu: Has several types of good vegetarian chilis, veggie burgers and salads.
Comments: Has live country music. Parking arranged for customers.
Other Info: Full service, take-out. Accepts AMEX, MC, VISA. Price: $.

Metro Dhaba Inc
8941 North Westland Drive; 301-590-9225
Hours: Daily 11 am to 10 pm
Indian. Not pure vegetarian.
Menu: Has many vegetarian dishes including samosas, kachori, gulabjamun, Shahi paneer, Malai kofta, curries and chat pappri. Smoothies, lassi.
Other Info: Full service, take-out. Price: $.
Directions: Just past the Food Lion.

My Organic Market (MOM'S)
11711 Parklawn Drive; 301-816-4944
Hours: Monday to Friday 10 am to 9 pm; Saturday 9 am to 7 pm; Sunday 11 am to 6 pm
Natural Food Store and take-out Deli. Has one of the best selections of organic produce in the area. Not pure vegetarian.
Menu: Soups, salads and sandwiches.
Other Info: Accepts AMEX, MC, VISA.
Directions: From I-495, take Rte 355 (Wisconsin Ave) exit and head north on Rte 355 two miles, then turn right at Nicholson Lane (turns into Parklawn after a half-mile) and this place is on the right a half-mile down.   o

Pangea
2381 Lewis Avenue
301-816-9300; **Web site:** www.veganstore.com
Hours: Monday to Friday 11 am to 6 pm for phone and web orders. Storefront closed. Saturday & Sunday Store is open 11 am to 6 pm
Vegan Product Store.
Comments: Has vegan products such as food items, belts, clothing, books, videos, wallets, bags, gifts, candles, and dog & cat products. They have a large mail order business.
Directions: Behind the Twinbrook Metro near Rockville Pike. From I-495, take Rte 355 (Wisconsin Ave) exit and head north on Rte 355 for 3 miles. At Twinbrook Parkway turn right, at Ardennes Ave turn left, then at Halpine Rd turn left, at Lewis Ave turn right and this place is near the intersection.

***The Vegetable Garden
11618 Rockville Pike; 301-468-9301
Web site: www.thevegetablegarden.com

Hours: Sunday to Thursday 11:30 am to 10 pm
Friday & Saturday 11:30 am to 10 pm
Fully Vegetarian Chinese. Mostly Vegan. Organic and Macrobiotic cuisine.
Menu: Has a great menu with a large selection of dishes. Mock "meat" dishes made with wheat gluten and seitan. Several soups such as Wanton, Hot & Sour, Asparagus & Corn Soup, Miso & House Vegetable soup. Veggie-Orange Beef, Eight Treasure Eggplant, Curled & Carved Shiitake Mushrooms with Asparagus, Eggplant with Black Bean Sauce, Sweet & Sour Delight, Veggie Chicken, Soba Noodles with Vegetable, Veggie Gyro Sandwich, Black Pea Rolls, Penne Primavera, homebaked breads and good brown rice. Macrobiotic Garden Pan is seitan, shitake mushroom, tempeh, lotus root and tofu skins. Eight Treasure Eggplant is eggplant, tofu, pinenuts, cashews, cranberries and zucchini in a sweet brown sauce. Organic shitake mushrooms and string beans in a sauce. Very good organic desserts such as Pumpkin Pie, Rhubarb Pie and organic Sweet Potato Pie. The authentic Key Lime Pie (made with tofu) is recommended. Fresh juices
Comments: Highly recommended, popular place. One of the best vegetarian Chinese restaurants in the country. Mostly organic, low sodium, wheat-free tamari soy sauce, no MSG. Offers regular cooking classes by the head chef. Menu marks macrobiotic, spicy dishes and the ones that use organic vegetables. Efficient service. Nice atmosphere.
Other Info: Full service, take-out. Non-smoking. Reservations required for groups of five or more. Accepts AMEX, DIS, MC, VISA. Price: $$.
Directions: This place is a few blocks from Nicholson, opposite the White Flint Metro station on the red line. From I-495 going west, take Exit #34 (Rte 355/Wisconsin Ave) and get on Rockville Pike and go three miles northwest on Rockville Pike and this place is on the left side in a small shopping center (to get here make a U-turn at Marinelli Rd and this place is a 100 yards down on right). From I-270 take Exit #4 (Montrose Road East) and this place is 2½ miles down the road.

Yuan Fu Vegetarian
798 Rockville Pike; 301-762-5937
Hours: Sunday to Thursday 11 am to 9:30 pm; Friday & Saturday 11 am to 10:30 pm; Lunch buffet 11 am to 2 pm; closed Sunday.
Vegetarian Chinese. Mainly Vegan options.
Menu: Serves mock "beef" and "chicken" dishes and a good selection of vegan entrées. Mock duck, Green Beans & Chicken, Sesame Chicken, Chinese soups, mock "beef," rice dishes, noodles

dishes, Kung-pao Chicken, Fried Eggplant and Springs Rolls. Good tofutti dishes. The Lunch Box buffet has a choice of three main dishes and white or brown rice.
Comments: Service is friendly and efficient. Food is really good. Gets really good recommendations. The lunch buffet is inexpensive.
Other Info: Full service, take-out and counter service for Lunch Box. Non-smoking. Reservations suggested for over five persons. Accepts AMEX, MC, VISA ($10 minimum). Price: $-$$.
Directions: From I-465 (the Beltway), go northwest on Rockville Pike for 5 miles, and then this place is in a small strip mall on the right, just after passing First Street.

SILVER SPRING (DC suburb)

Fresh Fields (Whole Foods Market)
833 Wayne Avenue; 301-608-9373
email: asksilverspring@wholefoods.com
Web site: www.wholefoodsmarket.com
Hours: Monday to Friday 9 am to 10 pm; Saturday 8 am to 10 pm; Sunday 8 am to 8 pm
Natural Food Store and Cafe. Deli, Bakery, Salad Bar and Juice Bar. Organic produce. Supermarket-type place. See Whole Foods Market information.
Directions: This place is in downtown Silver Spring. From Capital Beltway (I-495), take the US 29S (Colesville Rd) exit and go south on Colesville Rd one mile. At Woodside Parkway turn left, then make a quick right onto Ellsworth Dr, at Cedar St turn left, then at Wayne Ave turn right. From I-495, take New Hampshire Ave exit and go south toward DC. At Rte 410 turn right, and this place is on the left a quarter-mile down.

SILVER SPRING (DC suburb)

Thai Derm Restaurant
939 Bonifant Street; 301-589-5341
Hours: Monday to Saturday 11 am to 3 pm, 5 pm to 9:30 pm; closed Sunday.
Thai. Not pure vegetarian.
Menu: Has many vegetarian options including noodles dishes and curried vegetables.
Comments: Can make food without MSG if asked.
Other Info: Full service, take-out. Accepts MC, VISA. Price: $$.

Takoma Park (Silver Springs) Co-op
201 Ethan Allan Avenue, Silver Spring
301-891-2667

Hours: Daily 9 am to 9 pm
Closed on Thanksgiving and Christmas
Natural Food Store and small Vegetarian Deli.
Half the dishes in the deli are vegan. Organic produce.
Menu: Has many vegetarian options including soups, appetizers, dosa, salads, uthappam, curried vegetables and dinner specials.
Other Info: Accepts MC, VISA. Price: $-$$.
Directions: From I-495, take the Rte 650 S (New Hampshire Ave) exit, and go south on New Hampshire towards DC for 3½ miles. At Ethan Allen Ave turn right and this place is a little more than a half-mile down.

SPENCERVILLE

Edgewood Inn
16101 Oak Hill Road, at Route 198
301-421-9247
Hours: Saturday & Sunday 1:30 pm to 9 pm (best to call in advance)
Closed Monday to Friday (may be open more in the future).
American. All-you-can-eat Buffet.
Menu: Has a vegetarian buffet that includes Nut Loaf, salads, homemade breads, tofu dishes, Eggplant Parmesan, Spinach Pie, Lasagna and desserts.
Comments: In a historic house. If you contact them in advance they will bake some cakes and pies without eggs. Seventh-Day Adventist. Run by a really nice lady (very spiritual).
Other Info: Buffet, catering. Reservations recommended. Price: $$$.

TAKOMA PARK (north DC suburb)

Mark's Kitchen
7006 Carrol Avenue; 301-270-1884
Hours: Monday to Saturday 9 am to 9 pm
Sunday 9 am to 8 pm
American and Korean. Vegetarian-friendly. Not pure vegetarian.
Menu: Grilled tofu, sesame noodles, noodles with vegetables, spaghetti, Garden Burgers and sandwiches on Focaccia. Fresh juice and smoothies. Cappuccino, espresso.
Comments: Casual place.
Other Info: Full service. Price: $-$$.
Directions: From I-495, take Rte 650 S (New Hampshire Ave) exit and go south on New Hampshire Ave almost 4 miles. At Poplar Ave turn right, then at Elm Ave turn left, then make a slight right

onto Westmoreland Ave, then at Carroll Ave (Rte 105) turn left and this place is right there at the corner.

Savory
7071 Carroll Avenue, near Columbia Avenue
301-270-2233
Hours: Monday to Thursday 7 am to 9 pm; Friday 7 am to 12 midnight; Saturday 8 am to 12 midnight; Sunday 9 am to 4 pm
Coffeehouse type place. American. Vegan-friendly. Not pure vegetarian.
Menu: Has some vegetarian options. Menu changes often. Gourmet sandwiches.
Comments: Has outdoor seating. Sometimes has live entertainment. Casual place.
Other Info: Accepts MC, VISA.

Washington Adventist Hospital
7600 Carroll Avenue
301-891-5012
Hours: Monday to Friday 6:30 am to 10:30 am, 11 am to 2 pm, 5 pm to 7 pm
Saturday & Sunday 6:30 am to 9:30 am, 11:30 am to 2 pm, 5 pm to 6:30 pm
Vegetarian Cafeteria. Seventh Day Adventist place.

TIMONIUM (Baltimore suburb)

Cafe Isis
12240 Tullamore Road; 410-666-4888
Hours: Daily 11 am to 10 pm
Middle Eastern and Pizza. Vegan options. Not pure vegetarian.
Menu: Creative pizzas and good Middle Eastern dishes.
Other Info: Full service, take-out. Accepts MC, VISA. Price: $-$$$.

Donna's Coffee Bar
2080 York Road, Bibelot; 410-308-2041
Hours: Monday to Thursday 8 am to 10 pm; Friday & Saturday 8 am to 10 pm; Sunday 8 am to 9 pm
Italian. Not pure vegetarian. See description under Charles St. Corridor, Baltimore.

TOWSON (Baltimore suburb)

Frisco Burritos
3 West Chesapeake Avenue; 410-296-4004
Hours: Monday to Wednesday 11:30 am to 8 pm; Thursday to Saturday 11:30 am to 9 pm;

Sunday 12 noon to 8 pm
Mexican. Vegan options. Not pure vegetarian.
Comments: All food is made fresh daily. Beans, rice, salsa and sauces do not contain lard or animal products. They make a huge tofu burrito, as well as bean, pepper & onion tacos and bean quesadillas. Can put tofu and spinach on burritos.
Other Info: Limited service. Accepts MC, VISA.
Price: $.

The Health Concern
28 West Susquehanna Avenue; 410-828-4015
Hours: Monday to Friday 9:30 am to 8 pm; Saturday 9:30 am to 6 pm; Sunday 12 noon to 5 pm; Salad Bar closed on weekend, but has premade salad bar dishes in cooler.
Natural Foods Store and Salad Bar. Organic produce.
Menu: Has a salad bar with a selection of salad items and fresh soups. Ready-made sandwiches. Hummus, tabbouleh and pasta salads.
Other Info: Counter service only. Accepts MC, VISA. Price: $.
Directions: From I-695, take exit #26 south and go south on Rte 45 for 1 mile. At Washington turn right and go about a half-mile (three blocks) down a hill. At Susquehanna turn left and then this place is 1 block down on the left. This place is a little south of the downtown.

Waldorf

Country Nutrition
950 Old Line Centre; 301-645-1525
Natural Food Store.

WESTMINSTER (Baltimore suburb)

Sam's Bagels
1 East Main Street; 410-876-2593
Hours: Monday to Saturday 6 am to 3 pm
Sunday 6 am to 2 pm
Bagel Shop. Not pure vegetarian. See at Federal Hill, Baltimore.

Westminster Consumers Co-op
28 Westminster Shopping Center; 410-848-3200
Hours: Monday to Saturday 8 am to 9 pm
Sunday 9 am to 5 pm
Natural Food Store and Deli. Salad Bar. Organic produce.
Menu: Soups, salads, sandwiches and hot dishes.
Directions: This place is on Rte 97 (Rte 140) near the Town Mall of Westminster.

WHEATON

Nut House Pizzeria
11419 Georgia Avenue; 301-942-5900
Hours: Sunday to Thursday 11 am to 9 pm; Friday until one hour before sundown; Saturday one hour after sundown to 1:30 am
Mainly Vegetarian Kosher and Pizza Place. Italian and Israeli. Not pure vegetarian. Not pure vegetarian (serves tuna)
Menu: Has many vegetarian options including pizza, knishes, soy meatball subs made with vegetarian meats, falafel, veggie burgers and Israeli salads. Pizza can be served with soy cheese.
Comments: Casual place.
Other Info: Limited service, take-out, catering. Has several tables. Cash or local checks; no credit cards. Price: $.
Directions: From the Capital Beltway (I-495), take the Georgia Ave (MD Hwy 97) (Exit #31) towards Wheaton, then go north on Georgia Ave (Hwy 97) and this place is 2 miles down.

Sabang Indonesian Restaurant
2504 Ennall's Avenue
301-942-7859
Hours: Sunday to Thursday 12 noon to 10 pm
Friday & Saturday 12 noon to 11 pm
Indonesian. Vegan options. Not pure vegetarian
Menu: Has many vegetarian options including soups, several main dishes and desserts.
Other Info: Full service, take-out. Accepts AMEX, MC, VISA. Price: $$-$$$.

SAIGONese
11232 Grandview Avenue
301-946-8002
Hours: Monday to Saturday 11 am to 10 pm
Sunday 12 noon to 9 pm
Vietnamese. Vegan options. Not pure vegetarian.
Menu: Has many vegetarian options including soups, mock "meat" dishes, Tofu with Lemon Grass, Vegetarian Pot (curried stew with vegetables and gluten) and vegetable dishes.
Other Info: Full service. Accepts AMEX, MC, VISA. Price: $$.

Wooden Shoe Bakery
11301 Georgia Avenue; 301-942-9330
Hours: Tuesday to Friday 10 am to 7 pm; Saturday 11 am to 6 pm; Sunday 7 am to 3 pm
Bakery. Vegan options. Not pure vegetarian.
Menu: Has some vegan cakes and breads.

Massachusetts

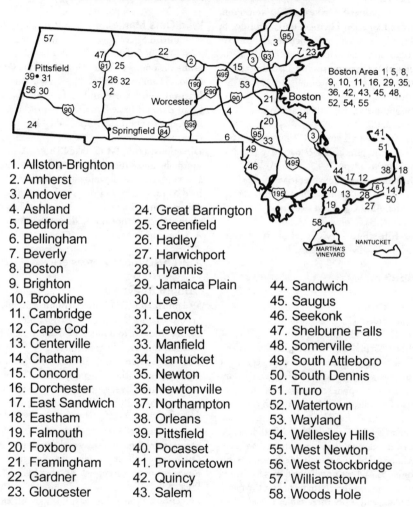

```
57
47    22                          3  (95)
Pittsfield  (91) 25          (2)      3 (93)  7  23
39 • 31           26 32     (495)  15
56  30     37  2            (190)       53      Boston Area 1, 5, 8,
                                   (290)  (90)  9, 10, 11, 16, 29, 35,
       (90)        Worcester •           21  Boston  36, 42, 43, 45, 48,
                                   4              52, 54, 55
24                  (395)          (20)   34
        Springfield (84)      6  (95) 33    (3)        41
                              49                       51
                              46   (495)      44    38  18
                                          17 12
                                   (195)  40  13  (6) 14
                                        19  28   50
                              58                27
                                        NANTUCKET
                              MARTHA'S
                              VINEYARD
```

1. Allston-Brighton
2. Amherst
3. Andover
4. Ashland
5. Bedford
6. Bellingham
7. Beverly
8. Boston
9. Brighton
10. Brookline
11. Cambridge
12. Cape Cod
13. Centerville
14. Chatham
15. Concord
16. Dorchester
17. East Sandwich
18. Eastham
19. Falmouth
20. Foxboro
21. Framingham
22. Gardner
23. Gloucester
24. Great Barrington
25. Greenfield
26. Hadley
27. Harwichport
28. Hyannis
29. Jamaica Plain
30. Lee
31. Lenox
32. Leverett
33. Manfield
34. Nantucket
35. Newton
36. Newtonville
37. Northampton
38. Orleans
39. Pittsfield
40. Pocasset
41. Provincetown
42. Quincy
43. Salem
44. Sandwich
45. Saugus
46. Seekonk
47. Shelburne Falls
48. Somerville
49. South Attleboro
50. South Dennis
51. Truro
52. Watertown
53. Wayland
54. Wellesley Hills
55. West Newton
56. West Stockbridge
57. Williamstown
58. Woods Hole

ALLSTON-BRIGHTON (southwest Boston suburb)

**Grasshopper Vegetarian Restaurant
1 North Beacon Street; 617-254-8883
Hours: Monday to Thursday 11 am to 10 pm; Friday to Saturday 11 am to 11 pm; Sunday 12 noon to 10 pm
Fully Vegan Vietnamese, Chinese and New American.
Menu: Has over 100 items on the menu. Has monthly specials. Has a large selection of mock "meat" dishes. Sizzling platters, hot pots, Wheat Gluten Sausage, Bok Choy, Asparagus & Carrots, Lemon Grass Soup, Garlic & Pepper Seitan, Coconut Curries, Vegetarian Dumpling, Seaweed Salad Seitan, Spicy Tofu Hot Pots, Spicy Lemongrass Gluten, Grilled Chicken and Chicken Fingers (nuggets). The Appetizer Platter is good. Garlic & Pepper Seitan (#69) and the Grilled Chicken are good.
Comments: Modern design with bonsai plants and green walls. Place gets high ratings from customers. Reservations recommended. Creative

dishes. Reasonably priced and good size portions. Comfortable setting. Nice, pleasant atmosphere. Friendly, attentive service. Uses MSG.
Other Info: Full service, take-out. Non-smoking. Reservations recommended. Accepts DIS, MC, VISA. Price: $$.
Directions: From I-93, take exit #20 west. From I-90, take Exit #18. Then get on Cambridge St going southwest a half-mile, then at Brighton Ave turn right and this place is immediately at the corner. Can be difficult to find a parking spot.

Rangoli
129 Brighton Avenue, at Harvard Avenue
617-562-0200
Hours: Sunday to Thursday 11:30 am to 3 pm, 5 pm to 10:30 pm; Friday & Saturday 11 am to 3 pm, 5 pm to 11 pm
South Indian. Not pure vegetarian.
Menu: Dosa, idly, sambar, Bhel Samosa, uthappam, raita, Aloo Gobi and rice dishes.
Comments: Basic place.
Other Info: Full service, take-out. Accepts AMEX, DC, DIS, MC, VISA. Price: $-$$.

AMHERST

Amber Waves
63 Main Street; 413-253-9200
Hours: Daily 11:30 am to 10 pm
Southeast Asian. Vietnamese, Cambodian, Thai and Indian. Vegan options. Not pure vegetarian.
Menu: Has a large selection of vegetarian and vegan dishes. Japanese soups, Thai noodles, variety of noodle dishes, South Indian dosas and Vietnamese food. Exotic noodle dishes.
Comments: Popular with U of M students because of its reasonable prices and good size servings. Some of the dishes include egg noodles, but rice or eggless wheat noodles can be substituted. An asterisk marks the vegan dishes on the menu. Small place with only three tables outside. Fast, friendly service.
Other Info: Limited service, take-out. Accepts AMEX, MC, VISA. Price: $.
Directions: On Boltwood Walk. In a parking lot behind Main Street

Amherst Chinese
62 Main Street; 413-253-7835
Hours: Daily 11:30 am to 3 pm, 4:30 pm to 10 pm
Chinese. Not pure vegetarian.
Comments: During the summer many of the vegetables are fresh from the owner's farm.
Other Info: Non-smoking. Price: $-$$. Accepts AMEX, DIS, MC, VISA.

Mixed Nuts
Hampshire College, 893 West Street
413-549-4600, ext 2223
Natural Food Store.

ANDOVER

Wild Oats Market
40 Railroad Street
978-749-6664; **fax:** 978-749-0621
Hours: Monday to Saturday 7:30 am to 10 pm
Sunday 8 am to 9 pm
Natural Food Store and Cafe. Deli, Bakery, Salad Bar and Juice Bar. Organic produce. Supermarket-type place. See Wild Oats Market information.
Directions: From I-495, take Exit #41A and go south on Rte 28 (becomes N Main St) four miles and you come to downtown Andover. At Railroad St turn right and this place is a third-mile down. From I-95, take Rte 125 north, when you reach Rte 28 go north into downtown Andover. At Chestnut St turn left.

ASHLAND (near Worcester)

**Udupi Bhavan
59 Pond Plaza, Pond Street (Route 126 South, next to Market Basket); 508-820-0230
Hours: Tuesday to Sunday 12 noon to 9:30 pm
Closed Monday.
Fully Vegetarian South Indian. Also has some North Indian dishes. Vegan options.
Menu: Dosas (very good), Thali, vada and sambar. Rava Idly and Kancheepuram Idly. No Alcohol.
Comments: Well prepared Indian cuisine. Often has a waiting line on Friday and Saturday nights.
Other Info: Full service, take-out. Non-smoking. Reservations not accepted. Accepts MC, VISA. Price: $$.
Directions: From I-90 Mass Pike, get on either Rte 9 or Rte 30, then take Rte 126 South 4½ miles to Ashland and junction with Walcott Rd. Rte 126 becomes Pond St. Parking in front of the restaurant.

BEDFORD

Bread & Circus (Whole Foods Market)
170 Great Road, Bedford
781-275-8264; **fax:** 781-275-1571
Hours: Daily 8 am to 9 pm
Natural Food Store and Cafe. Deli, Bakery, Salad Bar and Juice Bar. Organic produce. Supermarket-type place. See Whole Foods Market information.

Menu: Has a large selection in deli.
Directions: From I-95, take Exit #31B and go northwest on Bedford St (becomes Great Rd) towards downtown Bedford and this place is about 2 miles down.

BELLINGHAM

Bread & Circus (Whole Foods)
255 Hartford Avenue
508-966-3331; fax: 508-966-0994
Hours: Daily 8:30 am to 9 pm
Natural Food Store and Café. Juice Bar, Salad Bar, Deli and Bakery. Organic produce. Supermarket-size place.
Menu: Has a large selection in deli.
Directions: From I-495, take Exit #18 and this place is just off the exit on the east side of the road, by The Gap and the movie theaters.

BEVERLY (30 miles NE of Boston)

**Organic Garden
294 Cabot Street
978-922-0004; Web site: www.vegorganic.com
Hours: Sunday to Thursday 11 am to 9 pm; Friday to Saturday 11 am to 10 pm; Sunday Brunch
Fully Vegan International. Features Living Foods. 100% Organic, about 95% raw vegan restaurant. Juice Bar.
Menu: Has daily special main dishes and dessert specials. Juliano's falafel, raw pizza, Miso Soup, Arabian Nights (falafel on wild rice and raw vegetables), Vietnamese Dream (vegetables in cabbage leaves with two dipping sauces) Mongolian (marinated shitake mushrooms and sun-dried tomatoes on wild rice and greens) and Organic Garden Live (sampler plate). Fresh juices and wheatgrass.
Comments: Elegant atmosphere. Candlelit dining. One of the better raw foods restaurants. Friendly service. Exotic dishes. Nice décor with murals on walls. Has regular events such as music and free lectures.
Other Info: Full service, take-out, catering. Nonsmoking. Reservation recommended. Accepts AMEX, DIS, MC, VISA. Price: $$.
Directions: On the north side of Boston. Take Rte 128 North to Exit #22E (Beverly Rte 62), then take Rte 62 about five minutes, then at Cabot St turn right and this place is next to the Cabot Cinema. From Salem, go over the bridge from Salem to Beverly on Rte 1A, just after the bridge bear right onto Cabot St and go 1½ mile and this place is on the left. The Commuter Rail T from

North Station comes here. From Beverly Stop go up the hill from Rantoul St to Cabot St, turn left and the place is a third-mile down on the left. Plenty of parking behind restaurant and on adjacent lot.

Tapas
284 Cabot Street, Route 62, off of Route 128
978-927-9983
Hours: Monday to Saturday 11 am to 9 pm Closed Sunday.
Comments: Gourmet foods. Interesting atmosphere. Has outdoor seating.
Other Info: Full service, take-out. Price: $.

BOSTON
Arlington, Braintree, Brookline, Burlington, Cambridge, Concord, Jamaica Plain, Somerville and Waltham.

Addis Red Sea Ethiopian Restaurant
544 Tremont Street, at Clarendon Street, in the Back Bay; 617-426-8727
Hours: Monday to Friday 5 pm to 10:30 pm Saturday & Sunday 12 noon to 10:30 pm
Ethiopian. Vegan options. Not pure vegetarian.
Menu: Has a good selection of vegetarian dishes. Tomato salad, Red Pepper Cottage Cheese and Butecha (chickpeas & green pepper). Cappuccino, espresso.
Comments: Common to eat off the same plate. Exotic place. Has low wooden stools with woven grass tables. Friendly, helpful staff. Very good service. Food gets high ratings. Good place for a group.
Other Info: Full service, take-out. Accepts AMEX, DC, MC, VISA. Price: $-$$.
Directions: Across from the Cyclorama.

Arirang House
162 Massachusetts Avenue, near the Berklee College of Music; 617-536-1277
Hours: Daily 11:30 am to 10 pm
Asian, Chinese, Japanese. All-you-can-eat Buffet. Not pure vegetarian.
Menu: Has a good selection of vegetarian dishes. Seaweed Plate and miso soup. Good lunch buffets.
Other Info: Accepts MC, VISA. Price: $-$$.
Directions: In Back Bay west of the Boston Common.

Bread & Circus (Whole Foods Market)
15 Westland Avenue, Symphony
617-375-1010; fax: 617-375-0169
Hours: Daily 9 am to 10 pm

Natural Food Store and Café. Juice Bar, Salad Bar, Deli and Bakery. Organic produce. Supermarket-size place.

Menu: Has a large selection in deli.

Directions: From I-90, take the Prudential Center/Copley Sq exit, stay left at fork in ramp, merge on Avenue of the Arts/Huntington Ave and go a third-mile, at Massachusetts turn right and go 1 block, at Westland Ave turn slight left and this place is half-way down the block. From I-93, take Massachusetts Ave exit (#18), then go west about 2 miles and this place is in the middle of Boston, across from Symphony Hall in the Fenway area.

Bruegger's Bagel Bakery

64 Broad Street, in Financial District 261-7115
636 Beacon Street, near Boston University 262-7939
659 VFW Parkway, West Roxbury   327-6465
32 Bromfield Street, downtown   327-5577

Bagel Place. Not pure vegetarian.

Menu: Good bagel sandwiches and some vegetarian soups.

Comments: Very reasonably priced.

**Buddha's Delight

3 Beach Street, upstairs, Chinatown
617-451-2395; Web site: http://aq.org/~js/places/boston/buddhas/bd4.gif

Hours: Sunday to Thursday 11 am to 10 pm
Friday & Saturday 11 am to 11 pm

Fully Vegetarian Chinese Buddhist. Also serves some Vietnamese. Mainly Vegan.

Menu: Has over 125 dishes with a large selection of mock meat and fish dishes made of gluten and tofu. Various soups including Hot & Sour Soup, Noodle Soup and salads. Stir-fried Tofu with Mushrooms, BBQ Gluten, Tofu Stir-fried Rice, Stir-fry Noodles, Vegetarian Lo-Main, rice noodle dishes, BBQ Pork, Spring Rolls, steamed rice, Tofu Stir-fry, Gluten chicken, Tofu-ki (Chinese Sweet-and-Sour Pork), and mock beef, lobster and chicken. Has an assortment of unique drinks. Jasmine Tea. Vietnamese juices are made of lynches, jackfruit and rabutans.

Comments: Traditional Chinese cuisine. Large dinning room on the second floor, which has large windows with a good view of the downtown. Very good vegan restaurant. Efficient, friendly service. Food gets good ratings. Reasonable prices.

Other Info: Full service, take-out. Accepts MC, VISA. Price: $-$$.

Directions: Located in Chinatown. Orange line to Chinatown. From I-93 (Rte 3), take exit Essex St (#21) and this place is a third-mile west of the

exit. The streets are all one way, so your may have to work your way to this place. This place is about a half-mile south of the center of Boston.

Buteco Restaurant

130 Jersey Street; 617-247-9508

Hours: Monday to Thursday 12 noon to 10 pm; Friday 12 noon to 11 pm; Saturday 3 pm to 11 pm; Sunday 3 pm to 10 pm

Brazilian, Portuguese, Latin American. Not pure vegetarian.

Menu: Has a vegetarian soup and appetizers. Has one vegetarian main dish daily.

Comments: Friendly place. Has live guitar music. Good place for a special event.

Other Info: Full service, take-out. Reservations suggested. Accepts AMEX, DIS, MC, VISA. Price: $$.

Directions: Parking arranged for customers.

***Country Life Vegetarian Restaurant

200 High Street, Boston Common area
617-951-2534; Menu: 617-951-2462; Web site: http://www.countrylifeboston.home-page.org/

Hours: Monday 11:30 am to 3 pm; Tuesday to Thursday 11:30 am to 3 pm, 5 pm to 8 pm
Fri 11:30 am to 3 pm; Sun Brunch 10 am to 3 pm, 5 pm to 8 pm; closed Sat (Biblical Sabbath).

Businessman's Lunch: Monday to Friday 11:30 am to 2:30 pm

Fully Vegan. Fast foods. American and some International such as Mexican, Italian, Thai and Indian. Big Soup and Salad Bar. All-you-can-eat self-service Buffet.

Menu: The menu changes daily. Has over 50 dishes on the menu. Brunch has tofu scramble, blueberry and corn muffins, French toast, and whole-wheat waffles. Breads, soups, Tofu Tacos, BBQ mock Chicken Nuggets, Minestrone Soup, pasta dishes, Eggplant Parmesan, Pasta Alfredo, spaghetti, Thai Stir-fry, Pizza with soy cheese, Cuban Black Bean Soup, salads, Lasagna, enchiladas, rice dishes, Black-eyed Pea, Spaghetti & Wheat Balls, Tofu Spinach, Vegetable Pot Pie, Thai Stir-fried Noodles with spicy peanut sauce, Hawaiian BBQ, Sun Burgers and Thai Sweet Potatoes. Chocolate tofu pudding and fruit, soy ice cream, cookies, cakes and pies. Fresh juices.

Comments: Can hit their Web site to view the daily menus. Friendly staff. Has a cookbook. Good value. The Pizza and Taco Night, every other Wednesdays, is excellent. Food sold by weight or by the plate. Casual place. Food gets high recommendations. The vegan Sunday brunch gets really high ratings. Thanksgiving feast is very good. Run by the Seventh Day Adventist Church. Has several other branches in the US and around the world.

Other Info: Buffet service, take-out, catering. Non-smoking. Accepts AMEX, DC, MC, VISA. Price: $-$$.

Directions: In Boston's Financial District (right downtown), where High Street and Broad Street come together at Surface Artery, near Route 93 (raised highway). Next to "O! Deli". The entrance is on Surface Artery. Opposite Rowe's Wharf. From south, take I-93 north, as enter city, there is a tunnel. Before tunnel ends, take Exit #22 on the right. Follow signs to High Street. Street metered parking and local parking garages. All street parking is free on Sundays. Red Line train to South Station. Orange Line to State. Red or Orange lines to Downtown Crossing, Blue Line to Aquarium, Green Line to Government.

India Quality

484 Commonwealth Avenue, Kenmore Square, near Fenway Park; 617-267-4499
Hours: Monday to Friday 11:30 am to 3 pm, 5 pm to 11 pm; Sat & Sun 11:30 am to 11 pm
Indian. Vegan options. Not pure vegetarian.
Menu: Has a large selection of vegetarian dishes. Bakes breads in Tandoor clay oven.
Comments: Food gets good ratings. Good size portions.
Other Info: Full service, take-out. Accepts AMEX, DIS, MC, VISA. Price: $$.

Kashmir

279 Newbury Street, at Gloucester Street
617-536-1695; email: planet3s@bellatlantic.net;
Web site: http://kashmir.citysearch.com/
Hours: Monday to Friday 11:30 am to 11:30 pm
Saturday & Sunday 11:30 am to 12 midnight
Indian. Vegan options. Not pure vegetarian.
Menu: Has a selection of vegetarian dishes. Aloo Palak, basmati rice, salads, chutneys, soups, samosas, curry dishes, Tandoor dishes and desserts. Has a good buffet.
Comments: One of the best Indian restaurants in Boston. Upscale. Nice elegant décor. Has been judged to be one of the best Indian restaurants in Boston by various publications including the Boston Magazine. Authentic Indian food. Romantic. Good place for special events. Has outside patio dining.
Other Info: Full service, take-out, catering. Reservations suggested. Non-smoking. Accepts AMEX, DC, MC, VISA. Price: $$-$$$.
Directions: Parking arranged for customers.

Kebab-N-Kurry

30 Massachusetts Avenue, near Newberry Street
617-536-9835
Hours: Monday to Saturday 12 noon to 3 pm, 5 pm to 11 pm; Sunday 5 pm to 11 pm
Indian. Vegan options. Not pure vegetarian.
Menu: Has a selection of vegetarian dishes. Has a vegetarian thali.
Other Info: Full service, take-out, delivery. Non-smoking. Accepts AMEX, DC, MC, VISA. Price: $$.

King & I

145 Charles Street, at Cambridge; 617-227-3320
Hours: Sunday to Thursday 11:30 am to 9:30 pm; Saturday 12 noon to 10:30 pm; Sunday 12 noon to 9:30 pm
Thai, Vietnamese. Vegan options. Not pure veg.
Menu: Will substitute tofu for meat in many dishes. Ice cream.
Comments: Good size portions. Quick, efficient service. Comfortable place with chandeliers.
Other Info: Full service, take-out. Reservations suggested. Non-smoking. Accepts AMEX, DIS, MC, VISA. Price: $-$$.

Milk Street Café

50 Milk Street; 617-542-3663
Hours: Monday to Friday 7 am to 3 pm
Closed Saturday & Sunday.
Post Office Square; 617-350-PARK (7275)
Hours: Monday to Saturday 7 am to 5 pm
Closed Sunday.
Kosher Dairy Sandwich Restaurant. Mainly vegetarian. Not pure veg (just serves fish).
Menu: Has a large selection of vegetarian dishes. Veggie melts, soups, salads, hummus, sandwiches, pizza, quiche, fresh fruits and daily specials. Wrap with wild mushrooms, sun-dried tomatoes and greens.
Comments: The Post Office Square place has indoor and outdoor seating. Gives a 20% discount from 11 am to noon and 2 pm to 3 pm.
Other Info: Cafeteria style, take-out. Price: $. Accepts AMEX, MC, VISA.

Other Side Café

407 Newbury Street, on the corner of Newbury and Massachusetts; 617-536-9477
Hours: Daily 11 am to 1 am
American Coffeehouse. Not pure vegetarian.
Menu: Has a large selection of vegetarian dishes. Has a full page on the menu dedicated to wheatgrass and juices. Has good unique salads, hummus, tabbouleh, whole-wheat bread & Cheese,

Bread & Fruit Plate. Fresh juices, teas, cappuccino, espresso.
Comments: Has outdoor deck seating. Has couches and booth seating.
Other Info: Cash only; no credit cards. Price: $.
Directions: This place is a quarter-mile east of Fenway Park. From I-90, take exit #18 towards Allston/Cambridge, then go east on Soldiers Field Rd (becomes Storrow Dr) for 1½ mile, take ramp towards Kenmore Sq, merge onto Charlesgate and go 1 block, at Commonwealth Ave (US 20) turn left and go a quarter-mile, at Massachusetts Ave turn right and go 1 block, at Newbury St turn right and go 1 block.

Phoenicia

240 Cambridge Street; 617-523-4606
Hours: Daily 11 am to 10 pm
Middle Eastern, Lebanese. Vegan options. Not pure vegetarian.
Menu: Falafel, hummus, salads, Broccoli-noodle Casserole, homemade yogurt and Pumpkin Kibby.
Comments: Good food.
Other Info: Full service, take-out. Non-smoking. Accepts AMEX, DIS, MC, VISA. Price: $-$$.
Directions: At the bottom of Beacon Hill.

Souper Salad

102 Water Street	617-367-2582

Hours: Monday to Friday 6:30 am to 4 pm
Closed Saturday & Sunday.

82 Summer Street	617-426-6834
119 Newbury Street	617-247-4982
103 State Street	617-227-9151
3 Center Piz	617-367-6067
125 High Street	617-542-3157

Salad and Soup Place. Restaurant Chain. Salad Bar. Vegan options. Not pure vegetarian.
Menu: Soups, salads, sandwiches, Mexican dishes and main dishes. Fresh juices.
Comments: Everything is freshly made.
Other Info: Full service, take-out. Accepts AMEX, MC, VISA. Price: $.

Steve's Restaurant

316 Newbury Street; 617-267-1817
Hours: Monday to Saturday 7:30 am to 11 pm
Sunday 10 am to 10 pm
Greek. Vegan options. Not pure vegetarian.
Menu: Has a good variety of vegetarian dishes. Falafel, hummus, grape leaves, baba ghanoush (can be spicy hot), Greek salad, tabbouleh and other dishes. Has a sampler plate.
Comments: Good value.

Other Info: Full service, take-out. Reservations not accepted. Non-smoking. Price: $-$$. Accepts DIS, MC, VISA.

Sultan's Kitchen

Bullfinch Building, 72 Broad Street, at Route 1, downtown; 617-728-2828
Hours: Monday to Friday 11 am to 8 pm; Saturday 11 am to 3 pm; closed Sunday.
Turkish, Middle Eastern, Mediterranean. Vegan options. Not pure vegetarian.
Menu: Mixed vegetables cooked in olive oil, hummus, tabbouleh, baba ghanoush, stuffed grape leaves and other dishes.
Comments: Good chance that the baklava contains eggs. Gets mixed ratings.
Other Info: Full service, take-out. Non-smoking. Accepts AMEX, DC, MC, VISA. Price: $.
Directions: Parking arranged for customer.

White Star Tavern

565 Boylston Street, Back Bay area, west of the Boston Common
Copley Square; 617-536-4477
Hours: Monday 5 pm to 12 midnight; Tuesday to Sunday Saturday 11:30 am to 12 midnight
Vegetarian-friendly International, Indian, Asian. Not pure vegetarian.
Menu: Has a good selection of vegetarian dishes. Portobello Mushroom Sandwich, Biryani, Asian Stir-fry Noodles, Roasted Sweet Potatoes with Tomato Chutney and Maza Plate with hummus and tabbouleh.
Comments: Has outdoor sidewalk seating. Ceiling cloud mural. Romantic place.
Other Info: Full service, take-out, catering. Reservations necessary for groups. Accepts AMEX, DC, DIS, MC, VISA. Price: $-$$.

BRIGHTON (southwest Boston suburb)

Bread & Circus (Whole Foods)

15 Washington Street
617-738-8187; **fax:** 617-566-8268
Hours: Daily 9 am to 9 pm
Natural Food Store and Deli. Café, Salad Bar and Juice Bar.
Comments: Has seating outside.
Directions: From I-90, take Brighton/Allston exit (#18) and get on Cambridge going southwest for 2 miles, then turn right at Washington St and this place is ¾ mile down. Also from I-90, take Exit #17 towards Newton/Watertown, then go southeast on Tremont St ¾ mile, at Washington St turn right and this place is 1½ mile down.

BROOKLINE (southwest Boston suburb)

Bruegger's Bagel
375 Longwood Avenue
731-8993
Bagel Shop. Not pure vegetarian.
Menu: Has a good selection of bagels and bagel sandwiches. Has some vegetarian and vegan soups.
Comments: Very reasonably priced. Good food and atmosphere.
Directions: In the Harvard Medical School Area.

**Buddha's Delight 2
404 Harvard Street, Brookline
617-739-8830
Hours: Sunday to Thursday 11 am to 9 pm
Friday & Saturday 11 am to 10:30 pm
Fully Vegetarian Asian. Mainly Vietnamese. Cambodian, Thai, American. See Boston for more details.
Menu: Has a large selection of vegetarian dishes. Stir-fried tofu with mushrooms, mock Chicken Fingers, Gluten Chicken, baby corn, lemon grass and steamed rice. Tofu-ki is Chinese sweet-and-sour veggie pork. Vietnamese juices are made of leeches, jackfruit and rabutans.
Comments: Popular place. Food gets good ratings.
Other Info: Full service, take-out. Reservations suggested for groups. Non-smoking. Accepts MC, VISA. Price: $-$$.
Directions: This place is about 1 mile south of Exit #20 on I-90.

Souper Salad
Burlington Mall, 100 Middlesex Turnpike
781-270-4133
Soup and Salad Place. See Boston, MA.

CAMBRIDGE (west-central Boston suburb)

Asmara
739 Massachusetts Avenue
617-864-7447
Hours: Sunday to Thursday 11:30 am to 10:30 pm; Friday & Saturday 11:30 am to 11:30 pm
Ethiopian. Vegan options. Not pure vegetarian.
Menu: Has several vegan dishes on the menu.
Comments: Reasonable prices. Large wicker chairs and small wicker tables and glass-topped tables. Doesn't get high ratings. Has outdoor seating.
Other Info: Full service, take-out, catering, delivery. Non-smoking. Accepts MC, VISA. Price: $-$$.
Directions: T-stop: Red line to Central Square.

Bombay Club
57 JFK Street, at Winthrop Street, in Harvard Square; 617-661-8100
Hours: Daily 11:30 am to 11 pm
Indian. Vegan options. Not pure vegetarian.
Menu: Has a vegetarian menu. Curry dishes, Tandoor dishes, dal, samosas and vegetable dishes. Mango lassi.
Comments: Has a view of Harvard Square. Has outdoor dining. Friendly, quick service. Good food. Award-winning restaurant. This place gets really high ratings.
Other Info: Accepts AMEX, DC, MC, VISA. Price: $-$$.

The Border Café
32 Church Street, at Brattle Street, in Harvard Square; 617-864-6100
Hours: Monday to Thursday 11 am to 11 pm; Friday & Saturday 11 am to 12 midnight; Sunday 12 noon to 11 pm
Mexican, Creole, Cajun. Vegan options. Not pure vegetarian.
Menu: Has a separate vegetarian menu. Chili Relleno is good.
Comments: Happening, loud place. May have to wait a while for your dishes. Order at counter and they give you a beeper. Popular place and may have to wait for a table on the weekends. Nice décor. One of the best Mexican places in Boston. Gets good reviews from customers.
Other Info: Full service, take-out. Reservations accepted. Accepts AMEX, DIS, MC, VISA. Price: $.
Directions: Parking arranged for customers.

Bread & Circus (Whole Foods Market)
Fresh Pond Shopping Center, 200 Alewife Brook Parkway 617-491-0040; **fax:** 617-497-9469
Hours: Daily 9 am to 9 pm
Natural Food Store and Café. Organic produce. Juice Bar, Salad Bar, Deli and Bakery. Supermarket-size place.
Menu: Has a large selection in deli.
Directions: Take Rte 2 east until it ends, then go south on Alewife Brook Parkway and this place is ¾ mile down in the Fresh Pond Shopping Center.

Bread & Circus (Whole Foods Market)
115 Prospect Street (Central Square T Sop)
617-492-0070; 617-492-9045
Hours: Monday to Saturday 9 am to 10 pm
Sunday 9 am to 9 pm
Natural Food Store and Deli. Bakery.

Macrobiotic and Vegan options. Organic produce.
Menu: Has a large variety of vegan and vegetarian dishes. Excellent produce section.
Other Info: Counter service, take-out. Accepts MC, VISA. Price: $.
Directions: From I-90, take Cambridge exit (#18, this place is 1 mile northeast of this exit) and get on Cambridge and go over bridge (road becomes River St) and go ¾ mile. River St becomes Prospect St. After passing Massachusetts Ave this store is on left.

Bread & Circus (Whole Foods) and Putnam Café

Cambridgeport Marketplace, 340 River Street; 617-876-6990; 617-876-6694
Hours: Daily 9 am to 9:30 pm
Putnam Café Hours: 8 am to 3 pm
Natural Food Store and Cafe. Deli, Bakery, Salad Bar and Juice Bar. Organic produce.
Directions: From I-90, take Cambridge exit (#18), this place is 1 mile northeast of this exit) and get on Cambridge and go over bridge (road becomes River St) and this place is immediately on the other side of the river.

Bruegger's Bagel Bakery (2 locations)

82 Mt Auburn Street, Harvard Square
661-4664
1876 Massachusetts Avenue (Porter Square)
576-6163
Bagel Place. Not pure vegetarian.
Menu: Bagel sandwiches. Some soups are vegetarian or vegan.
Comments: Good, reasonable prices.

Christopher's Restaurant

1920 Massachusetts Avenue, at Porter Square, Cambridge; 617-876-9180, 876-5405
Hours: Monday to Friday 4 pm to 12 midnight; Saturday & Sunday 12 noon to 12 midnight; Sunday Brunch 10:30 am to 3 pm
Natural Foods. International, American, Mexican. Vegan options. Not pure vegetarian.
Menu: Has a good selection of vegetarian and vegan dishes. Pastas, Spinach Chimichangas (goat cheeses, cheddar, jack, spinach and sesame seeds), stir-fries, Portobello Mushroom Burger, Veggie Fajitas, Tofu Fajitas, Roasted Eggplant & Hummus Sandwich, Sesame Spinach, Tofu Pad, Tofu Stir-fry over Rice, veggie burritos and vegetarian chili. Church's veggie BelloBurger is popular. Often has a daily vegan special.
Comments: Is a happening place. Has a fireplace in the winter. Healthy food. Owner has been a

vegetarian for a long time. Does not use ingredients that contain preservatives, or artificial flavors or colors. Sauces and dressings are all homemade. Is politically correct. Service can be a bit slow. Friendly staff. Place gets good ratings. Has rotating exhibits by local artist. Wood finished décor. Has a fireplace. Has live music. Romantic place. First floor is a pub and the second floor is more formal.
Other Info: Full service, take-out. Reservations suggested for groups. Accepts AMEX, DC, DIS, MC, VISA. Price: $-$$.
Directions: T-stop: Red line to Porter Square.

Gandhi Restaurant

704 Massachusetts Avenue; 617-491-1104
Hours: Daily 12 noon to 11 pm
Indian. Vegan options. Not pure vegetarian.
Menu: Has a selection of vegetarian dishes. Soups, appetizers and South Indian dishes.
Other Info: Full service, take-out. Non-smoking. Accepts AMEX, DC, MC, VISA. Price: $$.

Grendel's Den Restaurant

89 Winthrop Street, at John F Kennedy Street; 617-491-1160
Hours: Monday to Saturday 12 noon to 1 am
Sunday 4 pm to 1 am
International, Eclectic. Bar, Club. Large Salad Bar. Vegan friendly. Not pure vegetarian.
Menu: Quesadillas, Eggplant Parmesan, Moussaka, tabbouleh, Aloo Choe (chickpea, potatoes and tomato curry), fruit salads, veggie Lasagna and pasta salad. Smoothies, cappuccino, espresso.
Comments: In an old fraternity house. Casual. Hippie hangout. Service gets low ratings.
Other Info: Full service. Accepts AMEX, DC, DIS, MC, VISA. Price: $-$$.
Directions: T stop to Harvard Square.

Harvest Coop and Café At The Harvest

581 Massachusetts Avenue, near Prospect
617-661-1580; email: cdurkin@harvestcoop.com
Web site: www.harvestcoop.com
Store Hours: Daily 9 am to 9 pm
Café Hours: Monday to Friday 7 am to 9 pm; Saturday 8 am to 9 pm; Sunday 7 am to 9 pm
Natural Food Store and Café. Excellent Deli. Salad Bar and Juice Bar. Supermarket-type place. Organic produce.
Menu: Has a wide selection of vegetarian and vegan dishes. Vegan baked goods. Smoothies and salads. Apple Chai.
Comments: The store has a good selection. It is

an excellent place. Reasonably priced place. Gives discounts on case purchases.
Other Info: Counter service, take-out. Good seating area. Accepts MC, VISA.
Directions: Central Square red line stop. Buses #1, #64, #83, #91. From I-90, take Cambridge exit (#18), then go across bridge (road become River St) and go ¾ mile. Then River St becomes Prospect. After passing Massachusetts Ave (store 1½ block to right), at Bishop Allen Drive turn right to find a parking place.

The Helmand
143 First Street, between Lechmere and Kendall
617-492-4646
Hours: Sunday to Thursday 5 pm to 10 pm
Friday & Saturday 5 pm to 11 pm
Afghan. Not pure vegetarian.
Menu: Has a vegetarian section on the menu with appetizers and main dishes.
Comments: Elegant, popular place. Food is good. Good atmosphere. Food gets high ratings. Has a fireplace.
Other Info: Full service, take-out. Reservations suggested on weekends. Non-smoking. Accepts AMEX, MC, VISA. Price: $$.

Indian Club
1755 Massachusetts Avenue; 617-491-7750
Hours: Daily 11 am to 3 pm, 5 pm to 10:30 pm
Indian. Daily Lunch Buffet. Not pure veg.
Menu: The food can be really spicy hot. Dosa, uthappam, pakoras, dal, Channa Masala and yogurt lassi.
Comments: Gets really high recommendations. High ceiling, chandeliers and large windows. Elegant place.
Other Info: Non-smoking. Accepts AMEX, DIS, MC, VISA. Price: $$.
Directions: This place is between Harvard and Porter Squares.

Marino's Ristorante and Market
2465 Massachusetts Avenue
617-868-5454
Hours: Daily 11:30 am to 10 pm
Italian Restaurant. Not pure vegetarian.
Menu: Has a good selection of vegetarian dishes. Homemade Gelati (Italian ice) is very good.
Comments: Much of the produce comes from their own farms. Helpful with vegetarian requests. Good atmosphere and service. Reasonable prices. Accepts AMEX, DIS, MC, VISA.
Directions: Near Alewife MBTA Red Line station

Moody's Falafel Palace
25 Central Square; 617-864-0827
Hours: Daily 11 am to 12 midnight
Middle Eastern. Not pure vegetarian.
Menu: Falafel, hummus, tabbouleh and other dishes.
Comments: Popular lunch place. Cash only; no credit cards.
Directions: Near the police station.

Passage To India
1900 Massachusetts Avenue; 617-497-6113
Hours: Monday to Saturday 11 am to 3 pm, 5 pm to 10:30 pm; Sunday 5 pm to 10:30 pm
Indian. Not pure vegetarian.
Menu: Has a separate vegetarian menu with a wide variety of dishes. Soups, appetizers, pakoras, breads, rice dishes and main dishes.
Comments: Does not use eggs. Uses vegetable oil for cooking. Friendly, helpful staff.
Other Info: Limited service, take-out. Reservations suggested. Non-smoking. Accepts AMEX, DC, DIS, MC, VISA. Price: $$.
Directions: Parking arranged for customers.

Picante
735 Massachusetts Avenue, Central Square
617-576-6394
Hours: Monday to Thursday 10 am to 10:30 pm; Friday 11 am to 11 pm; Saturday 10 am to 11 pm; Sunday 10 am to 10 pm
Mexican, Tex-Mex. Fast food style. Not pure veg.
Menu: Has a good selection of vegetarian dishes. Black beans are meat-free. Good burritos, cheese nachos, tacos, enchiladas and salsa bar,
Comments: Reasonable prices. Good food. Interesting place to eat. Good value. People like this place. Has outdoor seating.
Other Info: Counter service, take-out, catering. Reservations not accepted. Non-smoking. Cash only. Price: $.

CAPE COD
Buzzards Bay, Centerville, East Sandwich, Nantucket, Provincetown, Sandwich, Wood Hole.

CENTERVILLE (near Hyannis, Cape Cod)

Cape Cod Natural Foods
Bell Tower Mall, 1600 Falmouth Road (Route 28), Centerville; 508-771-8394
Hours: Monday to Saturday 9 am to 7 pm
Sunday 12 noon to 5 pm
Natural Food Store. Organic produce. Vegan options. Not pure vegetarian. Supermarket-size

place.

Menu: Has ready-made salads and sandwiches.

Other Info: Counter service, take-out. Accepts DIS, MC, VISA. Price: $.

Directions: From Rte 3, at roundabout take 2nd exit onto US 6/Mid Cape Hwy and go 13 miles, at Shootflying Hill Rd turn right and go 2¼ miles, at Old Stage Rd turn left and go a quarter-mile, then at Falmouth Rd (MA 28) turn left and this place is a quarter-mile down.

CHATHAM

Chatham Natural Foods

1291 Main Street; 508-945-4139

Hours: Monday to Saturday 9 am to 5:30 pm Sunday 10 am to 5 pm

Natural Food Store. Organic produce.

Directions: From Rte 6, take exit #11. Turn left onto Ret 128 and this place is 3.5 miles down on left.

DORCHESTER (Boston suburb)

Dorchester Avenue

2243 Dorchester Avenue; 617-298-1020

Hours: Monday to Thursday 10 am to 3 pm; Friday 10 am to 3 pm; Store open Sunday 10 am to 3 pm, but café is closed Sunday; Both Store & Café closed Saturday.

Natural Food Store and International Cafe. Vegetarian friendly. Not pure vegetarian.

Menu: Has a good selection of vegetarian dishes. Nachos with salsa, homemade wheat bread, bean burrito, soups and more. No alcohol.

Comments: Unique design. Live Irish and folk music on Wednesday nights. Friendly, pleasant atmosphere. Has an attached store, Common Sense, that sells Vermont pine furniture and unique products.

Other Info: Full service, take-out. Accepts MC, VISA.

Directions: From Rte 3 going north, take a slight left onto Willard St and go 1 block, keep going straight onto Granite Ave and go a half-mile, at Adam St turn slight right and go 1¾ mile, stay straight and go onto Dorchester Avenue (Pierce Sq) and this place is at the corner. This place is about ¾ mile due west of Rte 3.

EAST SANDWICH

The Beehive Tavern

406 Route 6A; 508-833-1184

Hours Seasonal: Mon to Fri 11:30 am to 3 pm,

5 pm to 9 pm; Sat & Sun 8 am to 11:30 pm

American. Not pure vegetarian.

Menu: Salads, sandwiches, pastas, Hummus–Tabbouleh Platter, Middle Eastern foods and main dinner dishes.

Comments: Colonial style décor. Good place for special event.

Other Info: Full service. Reservations not accepted. Non-smoking. Accepts MC, VISA. Price: $$.

Directions: Parking arranged for customers.

EASTHAM

Box Lunch

Route 6A; 508-255-0799

Hours: Friday to Wednesday 10 am to 4 pm Closed Thursday

Sandwich Place. Vegan-friendly. Not pure veg.

Menu: Has a good selection of roll-up sandwiches with a good selection of vegetarian items.

FALMOUTH (Cape Cod area)

Amber Waves Natural Foods

445 Main Street (Route 28); 508-540-3538

Hours: Monday to Saturday 10 am to 6 pm Sunday 12 noon to 5 pm

Natural Food Store. Organic produce.

Directions: This place is in the middle of Falmouth.

FOXBORO

Bangkok Café

369 Central Street; 508-543-8424

Hours: Monday to Thursday 11:30 am to 9 pm; Fri & Sat 11:30 am to 10 pm; Sun 4 pm to 9 pm

Thai. Vegan options. Not pure vegetarian.

Menu: Has a large selection of vegetarian dishes. Soups, salads, appetizers, tofu dishes and main dishes.

Other Info: Full service, take-out, delivery. Reservations not accepted. Non-smoking. Accepts AMEX, DC, DIS, MC, VISA. Price: $$.

FRAMINGHAM

Rasoi Gourmet Indian Kitchen

855 Worcester Road, Trolley Square (Rear) 508-872-4060

Hours: Daily 11:30 am to 10 pm

North Indian. Vegetarian-friendly. Vegan options. Not pure vegetarian.

Menu: Has good South Indian dishes on the

weekends.
Other Info: Non-smoking. Accepts AMEX, DIS, MC, VISA. Price: $-$$.

Bread & Circus (Whole Foods)
575 Worcester Road (Route 9)
508-628-9525; fax: 508-628-3573
Hours: Monday to Saturday 9 am to 9 pm
Sunday 8 am to 9 pm
Natural Food Store and Cafe. Deli, Bakery, Salad Bar and Juice Bar. Organic produce. Supermarket-type place. See Whole Foods Market information.
Directions: From I-95, take Rte 9E exit (#20A) towards Brookline/Boston and go east on Rte 9 and this place is 10 miles down. This place is about 10 miles west of downtown Boston.

GARDNER

Happy Trails
24 Main Street; 978-632-4076
Hours: Monday to Wednesday, Friday 9:30 am to 5:30 pm; Thursday 9 am to 7 pm; Saturday 9 am to 5 pm; closed Sunday.
Natural Food Store.
Directions: From Rte 2, take Rte 68 exit and go north. Rte 68 becomes Main Street. This place on right.

GLOUCESTER

Cape Ann Food Co-op
26 Emerson Avenue; 978 281-0592; email: cafcoop1@tiac.net: **Web site:** www.cafc.org
Hours: Daily 8 am to 8 pm
Natural Food Store. Organic produce. Bakery and whole grains. Homeopathic remedies.
Menu: Has ready-made sandwiches and salads.
Directions: Coming into Gloucester going north on Rte 128, when you reach rotary take first exit on Washington St and go a quarter-mile. At Centennial Ave turn right and go 1 short block, then at Emerson Ave turn right and this place is 1 block down on left.

GREAT BARRINGTON

Berkshire Co-op Market
37 Rosseter Street; 413-528-9697
Hours: Monday to Friday 9 am to 7:30 pm; Saturday 9 am to 6 pm; Sunday 11 noon to 5 pm
Natural Food Store and take-out Deli. Organic produce.
Menu: Soups, salads, sandwiches, hot dishes and

desserts.
Other Info: Counter service, take-out. No seating.
Directions: This place is in the middle of Great Barrington. From Rte 7, go west on Rosseter and this place is 1 block down on the left.

Guido's Fresh Marketplace
760 South Main Street; 413-528-9255
Hours: Monday to Saturday 9 am to 6 pm (Friday until 7 pm); Sunday 10 am to 5 pm
Natural Food Store and Deli. Bakery.
Directions: This place is on the right on Main St (Rt 7) about a mile south of the downtown area.

Locke, Stock and Barrel
265 Stockbridge Road; 413-528-0800
Hours: Monday to Saturday 9 am to 5:30 pm
Closed Sunday.
Natural Food Store.
Directions: From I-90, take Lee exit (#2) to Rte 7. On Rte 7 go south towards Great Barrington. This place is on the right diagonally opposite the McDonalds on Rte 7.

Martin's
49 Railroad Street; 413-528-5455
Hours: Daily 6 am to 3 pm
American. Vegan options. Not pure vegetarian.
Menu: Has a vegetarian section on the menu. Scrambled tofu.

GREENFIELD

Green Field Market
144 Main Street; 413-773-9567
email: coop@greenfieldsmarket.com
Web site: www.greenfieldsmarket.com
Hours: Monday to Friday 8 am to 8 pm; Saturday 9 am to 6 pm; Sunday 10 am to 5 pm
Natural Food Store and Café. Deli, Bakery and Salad Bar. Organic produce.
Directions: From I-91, take Greenfield exit south and drive on Main St into town and this place is on the left. Has large green awning.

HADLEY (Amherst suburb)

Bread & Circus Café (Whole Foods)
Mt Farms Mall, Russell Street (Route 9), Hadley
413-586-9932; fax: 413-584-4588
Hours: Daily 9 am to 9 pm
Natural Food Store and Deli. Bakery, Juice Bar and Salad Bar. See Cambridge.
Comments: Excellent health food store. Has a good area for seating. Has prepared dishes that

are heated up.
Directions: From I-91 south, take exit #19, then make a right turn off the ramp going east on Rte 9. Drive over bridge and go 4 miles and this place is on right. From I-91 north, take exit #20 and follow signs for Rte 9 east. Coming on the ramp at the light turn left, then at next light turn left onto Rte 9. This place is on the right 4 miles down.

HARWICHPORT (middle of Cape Cod)

Wild Oats Natural Foods
509 Route 28; 508-430-2507
Hours: Monday to Saturday 9 am to 6 pm
Sunday 12 noon to 6 pm
Natural Food Store and Cafe. Deli, Bakery, Salad Bar and Juice Bar. Organic produce. Supermarket-type place. See Wild Oats Market information.
Directions: From US 6, take Rte 124 exit (#10), then make a right (end of ramp) and merge onto Pleasant Lake Ave (Rte 124) and go 1¼ mile. In Harwich, turn right at Main St, then turn left at Sisson Rd (Rte 124) and a go 1.35 mile, then take a slight left at Main St (Rte 28) and this place is about 1 mile down on the left.

HYANNIS

Pavilion Indian Cuisine
511 Main Street; 508-790-0985
Hours: Daily 11am to 2:30pm, 4:30pm to 10pm
Indian. Not pure vegetarian.
Menu: Has a selection of vegetarian dishes. Vegetable curry, dal, rice dishes and samosas.
Other Info: Full service, take-out, catering. Accepts AMEX, MC, VISA. Price: $$.

JAMAICA PLAIN (southwest Boston suburb)

Center Street Café
669A Centre Street; 617-524-9217
Hours: Mon to Fri 11:30 am to 3 pm, 5 pm to 10 pm; Sun 9 am to 3 pm, 5 pm to 9:30 pm
American, International, Indian, Thai, Mexican. Weekend Brunch. Vegan options. Not pure veg.
Menu: Has a good selection of vegetarian dishes. Veggie Stir-fry and fresh juices.
Comments: Small, funky place. Does not serve red meat but serves chicken and fish. Dishes are all freshly prepared. Good food. Often uses organic and locally grown produce. Has 30 seats. The weekend brunch is very popular.

Other Info: Full service, take-out. Reservations not necessary. Non-smoking. Accepts MC, VISA. Price: $$.
Directions: From Southeast Exwy, take Southampton St (#16) towards Andrew Sq, then go west on Southampton St for a half-mile, at Melnea Cass Blvd turn left and this place is 1 mile down, at Tremont St (Rte 28) turn left and go a half-mile, keep going straight onto Columbus Ave and go 2/3 mile, at Centre St turn right and this place is 1¼ mile down. Parking arranged for customer.

Harvest Co-op Markets
57 South Street, Jamaica Plain; 617-524-1667
email: cdurkin@harvestcoop.com
Web site: www.harvestcoop.com
Hours: Daily 9 am to 9 pm
Natural Food Store and take-out Deli. Organic produce. Owned by members. Good nutritional supplement section.
Other Info: Counter service, take-out. no seating. Accepts MC, VISA.
Directions: From Rte 3, take Southampton St exit (#16) towards Andrew Sq, go west on Southampton St for ¾ mile, at Melnea Cass Blvd turn left and go 1 mile, at Tremont St (Rte 28) turn left at Tremont and go a half-mile, then road becomes Columbus Ave and go 2/3 mile, at Centre St turn right and go 1½ mile, at South St turn slight left and this place is 2 blocks down.

LEE

Cactus Café
54 Main Street; 413-243-4300
Hours: Daily 11:30 am to 2:30 pm, 5 pm to 9 pm
Mexican. Not pure vegetarian.
Menu: Salads, burritos, quesadillas, enchiladas and nachos. Fresh juices, cappuccino, espresso. Non-alcoholic beer and wine.
Other Info: Full service, take-out, catering. Accepts MC, VISA. Price: $$.

Sunflower Natural Foods
42 Park Street
413-243-1775
Hours: Monday to Saturday 9:30 am to 6 pm (Friday until 7 pm)
Sunday 12 noon to 5:30 pm
Natural Food Store. Organic produce.
Menu: Has some ready-made sandwiches.
Directions: From I-90, take exit #2 and go west on Rte 20 one mile. This place on north side of road.

LENOX

Clearwater Natural Foods
11 Housatonic Street; 413-637-2721
Hours: Monday to Saturday 9:15 am to 6 pm
Sunday 11 am to 3 pm
Natural Food Store. Organic produce.
Menu: Has some prepared sandwiches and wraps.

LEVERETT

Village Co-op
180 Rattlesnake Gutter Road; 413-367-9794
Hours: Daily 7 am to 7 pm
Natural Food Store and Deli. Bakery and organic
produce.
Menu: Sandwiches, salads, soups and other dishes.
Friday is pizza night.
Comments: Pleasant staff.
Other Info: Cash and checks; no credit cards.
Directions: From I-91, take Deerfield exit onto
Rte 116 south. Go about a mile and turn left
onto Rte 47, then follow the road as it weaves for
miles. Rte 47 after it goes past Rte 63 becomes N
Leverett, then at Rattlesnake Gutter Rd turn right
and this store is about 1 mile down.

MANSFIELD

Green Earth Grocery
310 Main Street, Common Market Place
508-261-1400
email: onatural@greenearthgrocery.com
Web site: www.greenearthgrocery.com
Hours: Monday to Thursday 10 am to 6 pm;
Friday & Saturday 10 am to 9 pm; closed Sun.
Natural Food Store.
Other Info: Accepts MC, VISA.
Directions: Near Rte 105, I-495, I-95 and Rte
140.

MEDFORD

Wild Oats Market
2151 Mystic Valley Parkway
781-395-4998; **fax:** 781-393-0784
Hours: Monday to Saturday 7 am to 10 pm
Sunday 8 am to 9 pm
Natural Food Store and Cafe. Deli, Bakery,
Salad Bar and Juice Bar. Organic produce. Supermarket-type place. See Wild Oats Market
information.
Directions: From I-95, take Rte 2 exit (#29A)
toward Arlington/Cambridge, turn onto Rte 2
and go 6 miles, then take road to Medford and

get on Alewife Brook Pkwy (Rte 16) and go 1½
mile, at traffic circle take 2nd exit onto Mystic
Valley Pkwy (Rte 16) and this place is a quarter-
mile down.

MELROSE (northwest Boston suburb)

Green Street Natural Foods
164 Green Street; 781-662-7741
Hours: Monday to Friday 9 am to 6 pm (Thursday until 7 pm); Saturday 9 am to 5 pm; Sunday
12 noon to 5 pm
Natural Food Store. Organic produce. Has some
vegetarian ready-made sandwiches.
Other Info: Accepts AMEX, MC, VISA.
Directions: From I-93, take exit #34 and this
place is in downtown Melrose about 2 miles east
of the exit.

NANTUCKET

Something Natural
50 Cliff Road
508-228-0504
Hours: Open May to October:
Bakery and Sandwiches. Not pure vegetarian.
Menu: Bakes over 20 types of breads daily. Sal-
ads and sandwiches.
Comments: Has outdoor garden seating.
Other Info: Counter service, take-out. Price: $.

NEWTON (southwest Boston suburb)

Bread & Circus (Whole Foods)
916 Walnut Street
617-969-1141; **fax:** 617-964-5773
Hours: Daily 8 am to 9 pm
Natural Food Store and Cafe. Deli, Bakery, Salad
Bar and Juice Bar. Organic produce.
Directions: From I-90, take I-95/Rte 128 south.
Then take Rte 9 (#20) and go 1 mile east on Rte
9, then take the Center St exit (a little past Dunkin
Donuts) and bear right at the exit, then at Wal-
nut turn left (go north) and this place is 1 mile
down on the right.

Sabra Restaurant
45 Union Street (also 57 Langley Road)
617-964-9275
Hours: Monday to Saturday 11:30 am to 10:30
pm; Sunday 12 noon to 10:30 pm
Middle Eastern. Daily Lunch Buffet. Vegan options. Not pure vegetarian.
Menu: Has a good selection of vegetarian and
vegan dishes. Falafel, hummus, grape leaves, baba

ghanouj and salads.
Other Info: Full service, take-out. Reservations not accepted. Accepts AMEX, DC, DIS, MC, VISA. Price: $-$$.

NEWTONVILLE (southwest Boston suburb)

Bread & Circus (Whole Foods Market)
647 Washington Street
617-965-2070
fax: 617-956-9104
Hours: Daily 8 am to 9 pm
Natural Food Store and Cafe. Deli, Bakery, Salad Bar and Juice Bar. Organic produce. See Whole Foods Market information.
Comments: This place is larger than the Walnut Street branch.
Directions: From I-90, take exit #17 towards Watertown/Newton, then go to the north side of the highway to Washington St, then turn left and this place is a half-mile down. This place is a half-mile west of the exit, right next to the north side of I-90.

NORTHAMPTON (AMHERST SUBURB)
One of the cooler towns in the US. Known for art and culture.

**Bela
68 Masonic Street
413-586-8011
Hours: Tuesday to Saturday 12 noon to 9 pm Closed Sunday & Monday.
Pure Vegetarian International Natural Foods. Vegan options.
Menu: Eclectic vegetarian dishes. The Veggie Cutlet with mashed potatoes gravy is recommended (just like home cooking). Pasta dishes and brown rice dishes. Seitan, tempeh and tofu dishes. Four specials a day that change daily.
Comments: Main dishes and desserts are often dairy free. Displays local women's artwork. Has outdoor seating. Small place with 7 tables. Really nice women running the place. Highly recommended.
Other Info: Full service, take-out. Non-smoking. Price: $. Cash only.
Directions: Downtown, a quarter-mile east of Smith College, on same street as Packard, which is a popular bar. From I-91 coming from Springfield, take US 5 exit (#18) towards Northampton, keep left at fork in ramp, turn left at Mt Tom Rd/Pleasant St (US 5) and go 1 mile, at Main St turn left and go 3 blocks, at Masonic St turn right and this place is 1 block down.

Cornucopia
Thornes Marketplace, 150 Main Street #8
413-586-3800
Hours: Monday to Wednesday 9:30 am to 7 pm; Thursday & Friday 9:30 am to 9 pm; Saturday 9:30 am to 9 pm; Sunday 12 noon to 6 pm
Natural Food Store. Organic produce.
Menu: Has some ready-made sandwiches and lunches.
Comments: Small place but has a good selection of products.
Other Info: Accepts AMEX, MC, VISA.
Directions: From I-91, take exit #18 (Northampton), then go north onto Rte 5. At Main St (Rte 9) turn left. This place is in the basement of Thornes Market (green awning) on the left.

Fire & Water
5 Old South Street, at Main Street, 1 block from Thorns Market; 413-586-8336
Hours: Daily 11 am to 11 pm
Natural Foods. Gourmet. Vegetarian-friendly (90% vegetarian, serves tuna). Vegan options. Quick service.
Menu: Most of the dishes served here are vegetarian. Sunshine Burger, Curried Tofu (recommended), falafel, hummus, baba ghanouj, curried rice, baked tofu and Peanut Noodle. Avocado Sandwich is good. Fresh juices, smoothies, cappuccino, espresso. Vegan chocolate chip cookies and vegan chocolate cake.
Comments: Often have live performances such as music, poetry or acting. Food is good. Good place to hang out. Sometimes has good music. Seating for 35 and performance stage in back.
Other Info: Counter service, take-out. Order, call out name and pick up or bring to table. Non-smoking. Price: $-$$.
Directions: Across from Paul and Elizabeth's. Right downtown.

**Haymarket Café
185 Main Street (Amber Lane) (Cracker Barrel Alley); 413-586-9969
Hours: Monday to Thursday 7 am to 10 pm; Friday & Saturday 7 am to 11 pm; Sunday 8 am to 10 pm
Fully Vegetarian International. Italian, Chinese, Korean, Indian, Japanese. Mainly vegan dishes.
Menu: Tempeh Burger is very good. A lot of rice dishes. South Indian Dal and Idlys with Sambar. Has all kinds of juices with funny name. A good one is Whiplash.
Comments: Has two floors; mainly coffee and desserts upstairs. Has comfortable couches and

chairs. Serves food downstairs. Relaxed, casual.
Other Info: Counter service, take-out.
Directions: On main street of downtown. Entrance is easy to miss on Main Street.

India House

45 State Street; 413-586-6344
Hours: Sunday to Thursday 5 pm to 9:30 pm
Friday & Saturday 5 pm to 10 pm
Indian. Not pure vegetarian.
Menu: The Saag Paneer is recommended. No alcohol.
Other Info: Full service, take-out. Reservations suggested for groups. Non-smoking.
Directions: Parking arranged for customers.

La Cazuela

7 Old South Street; 413-586-0400
Hours: Daily 5 pm to 10 pm
Mexican and Southwestern. Not pure veg.
Menu: The vegetarian dishes on the menu are marked.
Comments: Reasonably priced.
Other Info: Reservations suggested for groups. Non-smoking. Accepts AMEX, DIS, MC, VISA. Price: $-$$.

Paul and Elizabeth's

150 Main Street, in the middle of the downtown (Thornes Marketplace); 413-584-4832
Hours: Daily 11:30 am to 9:30 pm
Natural Food Restaurant. Macrobiotic (sells fish). Vegan friendly.
Menu: Soups, salads, pastas and Fried Rice. Vegetables with Tofu and Japanese Tempura are good. Non-alcoholic beer and wine.
Comments: Macrobiotic dishes, vegan dishes and dishes that contain dairy are marked on the menu. Good size portions. Reasonably priced. Nice atmosphere. Place is a bit loud. Helpful staff.
Other Info: Full service, take-out. Accepts AMEX, MC, VISA. Non-smoking. Price: $$.
Directions: In the downtown. Parking arranged for customers.

Pizzeria Paradiso

12 Crafts Avenue; 413-586-1468
Hours: Daily 5 pm to 10 pm (sometime later)
Italian, Pizza. Not pure vegetarian.
Menu: Has really good pizza. Pizza Primavera is nice. Some of the best pizzas in town. Soy cheese can be replaced for real cheese.
Other Info: Counter service, take-out, delivery. Reservations suggested for groups. Non-smoking. Accepts AMEX, MC, VISA. Price: $-$$.

Sylvester's Restaurant

111 Pleasant Street; 413-586-5343
Hours: Daily 7 am to 2:30 pm
American. Vegan options. Not pure vegetarian.
Menu: Has several vegetarian dishes including salads, sandwiches, veggie burgers and main dishes. Sylvester's Home-fries with potatoes, broccoli, cheese and sourcream is a good dish for breakfast. Cappuccino, espresso.
Comments: In the historic Victorian house of Dr Sylvester Graham.
Other Info: Full service, take-out, catering. Accepts MC, VISA. Price: $-$$.

Thai Kitchen

2 Bridge Street; 413-587-0683
Hours: Monday 5 pm to 10 pm
Tuesday to Sunday 11:30 am to 2:30 pm, 5 pm to 10 pm
Thai. Not pure vegetarian.
Menu: Vegetarian Rolls with a great dipping sauce. The Buddha Delight is tofu skins, vegetables (an elegant dish) and rice (can substitute noodles for rice).
Comments: Really good. Very nice atmosphere.
Directions: Near the railway bridge.

ORLEANS (Cape Cod)

Lo Cicero's Restaurant

Orleans Marketplace, Rt. 6A, Orleans Off Route 6A at Orleans Marketplace; 508-255-7100
Hours: Sunday to Thursday 4:30 pm to 9 pm
Friday & Saturday 4:30 pm to 10 pm
Italian, American. Macrobiotic and Vegan options. Not pure vegetarian.
Menu: Has a selection of vegetarian dishes. Non-alcoholic beer and wine.
Other Info: Full service, take-out, catering. Reservations not accepted. Non-smoking. Accepts AMEX, MC, VISA. Price: $$.

Orleans Whole Food Store

46 Main Street; 508-255-6540
Winter Hours: Monday to Saturday 8:30 am to 6 pm; Sunday 9 am to 6 pm
Summer Hours: Monday to Saturday 8:30 am to 9 pm; Sunday 9 am to 9 pm
Natural Food Store and take-out Deli. Organic produce.
Menu: Has sandwiches, salads and soups.
Other Info: Accepts MC, VISA.
Directions: From Rte 6 going west, take Rte 6A exit at roundabout (circle), then go southwest on 6A for 1 mile, then at Main St turn left and this

store is 1 block down. From Rte 6 going north-east, take Rte 6A exit, then go northeast on 6A for 1 mile, then turn right onto Main St and this place is 1 block down.

PITTSFIELD

Guido's
1020 South Street, on Route 7; 413-442-9912
Hours: Monday to Saturday 9 am to 6 pm
Sunday 10 am to 5 pm
Natural Food Store and Deli. Bakery.
Directions: Take Route 7 south into Pittsfield and this place on right. From I-90, take exit #2 and go north on Route 7.

Pittsfield Health Food Center
407 North Main Street; 413-442-5662
Hours: Monday to Saturday 9:30 am to 5:30 pm
Closed Sunday.
Natural Food Store. No produce.
Other Info: Accepts AMEX, MC, VISA.
Directions: From I-91, take Lee exit and then go north on Rte 7. Go through rotary and at North St bear right. Drive past two traffic lights and this place is on the left, opposite a large church.

POCASSET

Stir Crazy
626 MacArthur Boulevard; 508-564-6464
Hours: Tuesday to Thursday, Saturday & Sun 4 pm to 9 pm; Fri 11 am to 9 pm; closed Mon.
Southeast Asian. Thai, Cambodian, Chinese, Vietnamese. Vegetarian friendly. Vegan options. Not pure vegetarian.
Comments: No MSG or artificial color. Uses olive oil for cooking.
Other Info: Full service, take-out. Reservations suggested for groups. Non-smoking. Accepts MC, VISA. Price: $$.
Directions: Parking arranged for customers.

PROVINCETOWN (at end of Cape Cod)
It is a popular party town. Has an active gay scene. Whale watching, and some museums and art galleries.

**Café Crudite
336 Commercial Street, #6
508-487-6237; Web site: www.cafecrudite.com
Hours: Daily during the summer 9 am to 2 pm
Spring and Fall Hours: Thursday to Monday
Closed in the winter.
Vegetarian International, American, Indian.

Macrobiotic and Vegan options.
Menu: Vegetarian soups, salads, sandwiches and desserts. Indonesian Tofu and Vegetables, bean burritos, Stir-fries, Spicy Seitan Vegetables, a macrobiotic plate, Pacific Rim Sautéed Tempeh, Miso Soup, Brown Rice with Vegetables, Gazpacho Soup, Saag Tofu, veggie burgers, Tempeh Reuben, Jamaica Jerk Seitan, Tofu Burrito, Eggless Salad Sandwich, Steamed Vegetables, Spicy Sesame Indian Saag Tofu, Noodles, Grill Tofu in Peanut Sauce, organic brown rice and steamed broccoli. Very good homemade veggie burgers. Vegan desserts. Fresh juices, cappuccino, espresso. Non-alcoholic beer and wine.
Comments: Has seating on the rooftop outdoor deck with a view overlooking the harbor and street. Casual place. Place gets good ratings.
Other Info: Counter service, take-out. Order at counter and then call you when food is ready. Price: $$.
Directions: In the Pilgrim House Complex. This place is a block from the water, a few blocks southwest of the main pier.

Healthy Appetites Natural Foods
44 Long Pond Road; 508-747-8100
Hours: Monday to Friday 9 am to 7 pm; Saturday 9 am to 5 pm; closed Sunday.
Natural Food Store. Organic produce.

The Martin House
157 Commercial Street; 508-487-1327
Summer Hours: Daily 5:30 pm to 9 pm
Winter Hours: Thursday to Monday 5:30 pm to 9 pm
American, Continental. Vegan options. Not pure vegetarian.
Menu: Has at least three vegetarian main dishes. Wild Mushroom Ravioli and Spring Vegetable Paella. Cappuccino, espresso.
Comments: In the second oldest house in Provincetown (1750). Has a view of Provincetown Harbor.
Other Info: Full service, take-out, catering. Accepts AMEX, DC, DIS, MC, VISA. Price: $$$.

Napi's Restaurant
7 Freeman Street; 508-487-1145
Hours: Daily 11:30 am to 3 pm, 5 pm to 10 pm
International. Chinese, Brazilian, Greek and Thai. Vegan options. Not pure vegetarian.
Menu: Falafel, soups, Japanese soups, veggie burgers, hummus, veggie sandwiches and Curry Stir-fry.
Comments: Stained glass, artwork, carousel

horses. One of the best restaurants in town.
Other Info: Full service, take-out. Reservations recommended. Non-smoking. Accepts MC, VISA. Price: $$$.
Directions: Reservations arranged for customers.

QUINCY

Good Health Natural Foods
1627 Hancock Street; 617-773-4925
Hours: Monday to Saturday 9 am to 9 pm; Saturday 9 am to 6 pm; Sunday 11 noon to 5 pm
Natural Food Store. Organic produce.
Menu: Has a small selection of ready-made sandwiches.
Directions: From I-93, take Furnace Brook Parkway exit. Take Furnace Brook to Hancock St and make a right. Store on left.

SALEM

The Grapevine
26 Congress Street; 978 745-9335
Hours: Daily 5:30 pm to 10 pm
New American. Not pure vegetarian.
Menu: Has a good selection of vegetarian dishes. Baked Eggplant & Cheese, Tofu & Mushroom and pasta dishes.

SANDWICH (Cape Cod)

Marshland Restaurant
109 Route 6A, Sandwich; 508 888-9824
Seasonal Hours: Monday 6 am to 2 pm Tuesday to Sunday 6 am to 8 pm
American. Not pure vegetarian.
Menu: Middle Eastern dishes, salads, Veggie stir-fry, pastas and sandwiches. Non-alcoholic beer.
Comments: A popular place. Part of a Citgo gas station.
Other Info: Full service. Price: $$.
Directions: Parking arranged for customers.

SAUGUS (northeast of Boston)

Wild Oats Market
357 Broadway
781-233-5341; **fax:** 781-233-0821
Hours: Monday to Saturday 8 am to 10 pm Sunday 8 am to 9 pm
Natural Food Store and Cafe. Deli, Bakery, Salad Bar and Juice Bar. Organic produce. Supermarket-type place. See Wild Oats Market information.
Directions: This place is on Newburyport Turn-

pike, at the southeast corner of Breakheart Reservation. From I-95, take exit # 44, then go south on Broadway (Newburyport Turnpike) and this place is 2 miles southwest.

SEEKONK

The Good Seed
138 Central Avenue; 508-399-7333
Hours: Monday, Tuesday, Friday, Saturday 10 am to 6 pm; Wednesday & Thursday 10 am to 8 pm; Sunday 12 noon to 5 pm
Natural Food Store.
Directions: From I-195, take Neort Ave (Rte 1A) exit towards Pawtucket. At Benefit St turn left. Benefit becomes Central. This place on left at intersection of Rte 152 and Central.

SHELBURNE FALLS

Copper Angel Café
2 State Street; 413-625-2727
Hours: May to October.
Closed during the winter.
American Natural Foods. Vegan options. Not pure vegetarian.
Menu: Has a good selection of vegetarian dishes. Cappuccino, espresso. Non-alcoholic beer and wine.
Other Info: Full service, take-out. Non-smoking. Accepts MC, VISA. Price: $-$$.

Mccusker's Market
3 State Street, at the Bridge of Flowers
413-625-2548
Hours: Monday to Saturday 7 am to 7 pm Sunday 7 am to 6 pm
Natural Food Store and Café. Deli and Bakery.
Comments: There is a nice place to swim here.
Other Info: Counter service, take-out. Has seating.
Directions: From I-91 north, take exit #26 (Rte 2) west and go about 7 miles. At 2A turn left near the blinking light (at Sweetheart Restaurant). Enter town and this place is across the iron bridge.

SOMERVILLE (Boston suburb)

India Palace
23 Union Square; 617-666-9770
Hours: Monday to Saturday 11 am to 3 pm, 5 pm to 11 pm; closed Sunday.
Indian. Vegan options. Not pure vegetarian.
Menu: Has a wide selection of vegetarian and vegan dishes. Soups, vegetable samosas, Indian

breads, Aloo Gobi, Matar Paneer and other dishes. Kheer.

Comments: Has indoor and outdoor dining. Good service.

Other Info: Full service, take-out. Price: $$.

Johnny D's Uptown Restaurant

17 Holland Street; 617-776-2004
email: jdoffice@world.com
Web site: www.johnnyds.com
Hours: Monday to Friday 4:30 am to 1 am
Sat & Sun 9 am to 2:30 pm, 4:30 pm to 1 am
American. Blues Bar, Club. Vegetarian-friendly. Vegan options. Not pure vegetarian.
Menu: Has several vegetarian dishes. Bean and vegetable burritos, sandwiches, tofu dishes, vegetarian soups, salads, pastas, Asian Stir-fry, veggie burger, pizzas and more. Has a separate brunch menu during the weekends with dishes such as Grilled Marinated Tofu with Goat Cheese, granola, yogurt & fruit and bagels. Smoothies.
Comments: Has a wide selection of live music such as blues, folk and Cajun. Dancing. Friendly, relaxed atmosphere. Place gets good ratings. Got good reviews in the Boston Globe and Boston Magazine. Has schedule of events on web site.
Other Info: Full service, take-out. Accepts AMEX, DIS, MC, VISA. Price: $-$$.
Directions: In Davis Square, opposite the Davis Square T station. Redline T to Davis Square.

Picante

217 Elm Street, at Cutter Avenue; 617-628-6394
Hours: Sunday to Thursday 11 am to 10 pm; Friday 11 am to 11 pm; Sat 10 am to 11 pm
Mexican, Tex-Mex. Not pure vegetarian. See Cambridge for detail.
Menu: Has a wide selection of vegetarian dishes. Quesadillas, salads, nachos, tacos, enchiladas and burritos.
Comments: Reasonably priced. Good food. Nice atmosphere. Casual. Black beans are vegetarian.
Other Info: No credit cards.

SOUTH ATTLEBORO

Fuller Memorial Hospital

231 Washington Street; 508-761-8500
Hours: Daily
Vegetarian-friendly Cafeteria. Vegan options. Not pure vegetarian.
Comments: Non-profit hospital operated by the Seventh-Day Adventist.
Other Info: No credit cards. Price: $. Cafeteria style.

SOUTH DENNIS (Cape Cod)

Shady Hollow Inn

370 Main Street; 508-394-7474
Vegetarian Bed and Breakfast.
Other Info: Reservations required. Non-smoking. Accepts MC, VISA.

TRURO (Cape Cod)

***Masao's Kitchen

581 Moody Street; 781-647-7977
Hours: Monday to Thursday 12 noon to 8 pm; Friday & Saturday 12 noon to 9 pm; closed Sun.
Fully Vegan International. Macrobiotic options. Buffet.
Menu: Tempeh, tofu and seitan dishes. Fried Tempeh Spiral is very good. Dairy-free Strawberry Shortcake. Fresh juices
Comments: Good food. Has good macrobiotic dishes. Local organic produce used when possible. No MSG, chemical, refined sugars, preservations, or genetically engineered foods. Local organic produce used when possible. Very good food. Friendly, quick service. Extra for take-out.
Other Info: Counter service, buffet-style, take-out. Reservations not accepted. Non-smoking. Accepts AMEX, MC, VISA. Price: $-$$.
Directions: This place is right off Rte 6 in Truro.

WATERTOWN

Sepal's

17 Nichols Street; 617-924-5753
Hours: Monday to Saturday 11 am to 8 pm
Sunday 1 pm to 8 pm
Middle Eastern. Not pure vegetarian. Vegan options.
Menu: Baked and fried falafel, baba ghanouj, veggie burgers and hummus.
Comments: Gets really high recommendations.
Other Info: Full service, take-out. Non-smoking. Accepts AMEX, MC, VISA. Price: $$.

WAYLAND

Bread & Circus (Whole Foods Market)

317 Boston Post Road (Route 20)
508-358-7700; **fax:** 508-358-7515
Hours: Daily 8 am to 9 pm
Natural Food Store and Café. Organic produce. Juice Bar, Salad Bar, Deli and Bakery. Supermarket-size place.
Menu: Has a large selection in deli.
Directions: From I-95, take US Rte 20 exit (#26)

towards Waltham/Weston, then go on Weston/ Rte 20 a half-mile, road becomes Boston Post Rd and this place is 5 miles down.

WELLESLEY HILLS (southwest Boston suburb)

Bread & Circus (Whole Foods Market)
278 Washington Street
781-235-7262; **fax:** 781-431-9730
Hours: Daily 8 am to 9 pm
Natural Food Store and Café. Deli, Juice Bar, Salad Bar and Bakery. Organic produce.
Directions: From I-95, take Rte 9 exit (#20), then go west on Rte 9 and this place is 1½ mile down, at the junction of Rte 9 and Washington on the left.

WEST NEWTON (southwest Boston sub)

**Life & Light Vegetarian Restaurant
115 Elm Street, at Route 16; 617-630-8101
Hours: Tuesday to Thursday 11 am to 9 pm; Friday 11 am to 10 pm; Saturday 11 am to 9 pm; Sunday 11:30 am to 9 pm; closed Monday.
Vegetarian Chinese Restaurant and food store. Vegan-friendly. Not pure vegetarian.
Menu: Has a wide variety of vegetarian dishes. Has a large selection of mock meat dishes. Recommended are H29 Veggie Sesame Beef and H11 Sautéed Mushroom. Spaghetti & mock "meat balls."
Comments: Run by Asian family who are associated with the International Supreme Master Ching Hai Meditation Association. Most of the dishes are vegan except the desserts. One of the better vegetarian places in the Boston area. Food gets good ratings. Friendly, helpful service. Good size portions and reasonable prices. Has frozen mock meat products that you can take home.
Other Info: Limited service, take-out. Accepts AMEX, DC, DIS, MC, VISA. Price: $-$$.
Directions: From the Massachusetts Turnpike (I-90), take Rte 16 exit (#16) towards West Newton/Wellesley and this place is a quarter-mile northeast of the exit.

WEST STOCKBRIDGE

Truc Orient Express
2 Harris Street; 413-232-4204
Hours: Wednesday to Monday 5 pm to 9 pm
Closed Tuesday.
Vietnamese. Not pure vegetarian.
Menu: Has a separate vegetarian menu. Fried

Rice, salads, soups, Tofu & Rice Noodles and curry vegetables.
Other Info: Full service, take-out, catering. Accepts AMEX, DIS, MC, VISA. Price: $$-$$$.

WILLIAMSTOWN

Wild Oats Food Co-op
Colonial Shopping Center, 248 Main Street, Route 2; 413-458-8060
Hours: Monday to Saturday 8:30 am to 7 pm
Sunday 9 am to 6 pm
Natural Food Store and Cafe. Deli, Bakery, Salad Bar and Juice Bar. Organic produce. Supermarket-type place. See Wild Oats Market information.
Directions: A little east of the center of Williamstown on the north side of Rte 2. A little west of North Adams.

WOODS HOLE

Fishmonger's Café
56 Water Street; 508-548-9148
Hours: Monday 11 am to 3 pm; Thursday 11 am to 3 pm, 5:30 pm to 9 pm; Friday to Sunday 7 am to 9:30 pm; closed Tuesday. Closed December 7 to February 28.
Natural Foods. American and Italian. Not pure vegetarian.
Menu: Has a wide selection of vegetarian dishes. Often have a vegetarian special. Pumpkin Sage Ravioli. Homebaked breads and pies.
Comments: Is located right next to the water. Has natural products. Sometimes has live music.
Other Info: Full service, take-out. Reservations not accepted. Non-smoking. Accepts AMEX, MC, VISA. Price: $$-$$$.

El Basha
424 Belmont Street; 508-797-0884
Hours: Monday to Saturday 11:30 am to 3 pm, 4:30 pm to 10 pm; closed Sunday.
Middle Eastern. Not pure vegetarian.
Other Info: Accepts MC, VISA. Price: $.
Directions: Parking arranged for customers.

**Lily Pad
755 Grafton Street; 508-890-8899
Hours: Tuesday to Friday 4 am to 10 pm; Saturday 12 noon to 10 pm; Sunday 12 noon to 9 pm
Fully Vegetarian Asian. Chinese, Vietnamese, Japanese. Mostly Vegan.
Menu: General Chicken, House Lo Mein, Sesame Beef, Fried Rice, Beef Teriyaki, Sesame Beef and

much more.

Comments: Family owned and operated. Casual, comfortable atmosphere. Place gets good ratings. **Other Info:** Full service, take-out. Non-smoking. No credit cards.

Living Earth

232 Chandler Street, at Park; 508-753-1896, 617-451-2395

Hours: Monday to Friday 9 am to 9 pm; Saturday 9 am to 6 pm; Sunday 11 am to 6 pm

Café Hours: 11 am to 4 pm

Natural Food Store and Garden Café. Deli, Juice Bar and Bakery. Vegan friendly.

Menu: Has many vegetarian and vegan dishes.

Comments: Helpful staff. Good selection of books. Accepts AMEX, MC, VISA.

Directions: On the west side of Rte 122 (Chandler St). At the intersection of Chandler and Park Ave, a little south of Rte 9.

***Quan Yin

56 Hamilton Street

508-831-1322

Hours: Monday to Thursday 11 am to 9 pm; Friday to Saturday 11 am to 10 pm; closed Sun.

Fully Vegan Vietnamese, Chinese, American, Thai and Indian.

Menu: Mock meat dishes, daily lunch specials, noodle dishes, vegetables dishes and a large selection of mock meat dishes.

Comments: Gets some very good recommendations. No eggs or MSG is used. Dishes are freshly prepared. Small place with several tables. Mainly take-out. In a nice neighborhood. Some of the desserts are not vegan. Reasonable prices. Friendly place.

Other Info: Full service, take-out. Non-smoking. No credit cards. Accepts personal checks. Price: $.

Michigan

1. Ann Arbor
2. Battle Creek
3. Berkley
4. Berrien Springs
5. Birmingham
6. Canton
7. Dearborn Heights
8. Detroit
9. East Lansing
10. Farmington Hills
11. Ferndale
12. Grand Rapids
13. Grosse Pointe
14. Harper Woods
15. Hillsdale
16. Houghton & Hancock
17. Kalamazoo
18. Lansing
19. Livonia
20. Madison Heights
21. Marquette
22. Petoskey
23. Plymouth
24. Port Huron
25. Richmond
26. Rochester
27. Royal Oak

28. Saginaw
29. Southfield
30. Suttons Bay
31. Traverse City
32. Troy
33. West Bloomfield
34. Woodland
35. Ypsilanti

ANN ARBOR

Arbor Farms

2215 West Stadium Boulevard; 734-996-8111
Hours: Monday to Saturday 9 am to 9 pm
Sunday 10 am to 6 pm
Natural Food Store and take-out Deli. Organic produce.
Menu: Soups, sandwiches, pastas, salads and hot dishes.
Other Info: Accepts AMEX, MC, VISA.
Directions: From I-95, take Jackson Ave exit (#172), then go 1 block east on Jackson, At W Stadium Blvd turn right and this place is a half-mile down.

Chia Shiang Restaurant

2016 Packard Road, Pittsfield Township
734-741-0778
Hours: Sunday to Thursday 10:30 am to 10 pm
Friday & Saturday 10:30 am to 11 pm
Chinese. Vegan options. Not pure vegetarian.
Menu: Spring Rolls, rice dishes, curry dishes, Vegetarian Dim Sum and other dishes.
Other Info: Full service, take-out. Accepts AMEX, MC, VISA. Price: $$.

Del Rio

122 West Washington; 734-761-2530
Hours: Monday to Friday 4:30 pm to 1:35 am;
Sat 1:30 pm to 1:35 am; Sun 5:30 pm to 2 am

Mexican, American and Italian. Mainly Vegetarian. Not pure vegetarian.
Menu: Salads, nachos, wheat crust pizzas, tempeh burgers and quesadillas.
Comments: Hip and popular.
Other Info: Cash only; no credit cards. Price: $-$$.

**Earthen Jar
311 South Fifth Avenue; 313-327-9464
Hours: Monday to Thursday 11 am to 8 pm; Friday 11 am to 9 pm; closed Saturday & Sun.
Fully Vegetarian Indian. Vegan options. Buffet-style.
Menu: Has a large selection of vegetarian dishes.
Comments: Indian food buffet-style where you pay by the pound. Several vegan options are available. Communal seating. Reasonably priced.
Other Info: Limited service, take-out. Non-smoking. Reservations not necessary. No credit cards; cash or checks only. Price: $-$$.
Directions: It is near the Ann Arbor District Library. From I-275 (Rte 14), take the Ann Arbor/Toledo exit, then take the Rte 14 exit (#45) on left towards Ann Arbor, then get on Rte 14 going west for 1 mile, then take US-23 Br exit (#3) towards downtown Ann Arbor, merge onto N Main St (bear right) and go 1.4 miles south, at E Liberty St turn left and go 2 blocks, at S 5th Ave turn right and this place is right there.

Merchant of Vino Marketplace (owned by Whole Foods)
2789 Plymouth Road, Ann Arbor; 313-769-0900
Hours: Monday to Saturday 9 am to 10 pm Sunday 9 am to 9 pm
Natural Food Store and Cafe. Deli, Bakery, Salad Bar and Juice Bar. Organic produce. Supermarket-type place. See Whole Foods Market information.
Directions: This place is about 2 miles northeast of downtown Ann Arbor. From I-275 (Rte 14), take Hwy 23 S exit (#8) towards Toledo and merge onto Hwy 23 going south for ¾ mile, then take Plymouth Rd exit (#41), at Plymouth Rd turn right and this place is ¾ mile down.

People's Food Co-op and Café Verde
216 North 4th Avenue, Ann Arbor
734-994-9174; **email:** pfc@izzy.net
Web site: http://www.izzy.net/~pfc/
Store Hours: Monday to Saturday 9 am to 10 pm; Sunday 8 am to 10 pm
Hot Bar Hours: Monday to Friday 11 am to 3 pm, 5 pm to 8 pm; Saturday 11 am to 2 pm; Sunday 4 pm to 7 pm

Natural Food Store. Good Salad Bar. Organic produce.
Menu: Vegetarian sandwiches, salads, Tempeh Reuben sandwich and soups are available all day. The Hot Bar has Rice & Beans, main dishes, beans, kale, steamed vegetable and other dishes.
Comments: Friendly, helpful people. The items in the cold deli and soups are available all days. The hot dishes in the Hot Bar are available for lunch and dinner and is closed part of the time.
Other Info: Accepts AMEX, DC, DIS, MC, VISA. Counter service, take-out.
Directions: This place is in the middle of town. From I-94, take Jackson Ave exit (#172), then go east on Jackson Ave (becomes W Hurron St) for 2¼ miles, then at N 4th Ave turn left and this place is 1½ block down.

**Seva
314 East Liberty Street; 734-662-1111
Hours: Monday to Thursday 10:30 am to 9 pm; Friday 10:30 am to 10 pm; Saturday 10 am to 10 pm; Sunday 10 am to 9 pm; Sunday Brunch.
Vegetarian Mexican, American and International. Mostly vegan. Organic produce is used whenever possible. Juice Bar. Serves eggs.
Menu: Has a large selection of interesting vegetarian meals. Soups, salads, whole-wheat bread, a good selection of tofu dishes, sandwiches, nachos, Sesame Noodle Salad, Wild Mushroom Salad, Chinese dishes, Italian pastas, couscous, veggie burgers, Curry with Brown Rice & Lentils, Tempeh Wrap in Baked Tortilla (recommended), Caribbean Quesadilla (recommended), brown rice, Portabella Burger, BBQ Eggplant Sandwich, Walnut Mushroom Pasta, pizzas, Yam Fries (excellent), Salsa & Guacamole, Stir-fried Vegetables, Spicy Tofu Jerk with Rice & Red Beans and desserts including Tofutti vegan "ice cream" and vegan Chocolate Cake. The Sunday brunch is good. Scrambled Tofu Platter is recommended. Fresh juices and smoothies.
Comments: Their Mexican dishes get very high recommendations. Very poplar. Vegan dishes are marked on the menu. Has health conscious foods. Has a pleasant location and a relaxed, romantic atmosphere. Has an outdoor patio area for dining. Friendly, efficient service. Local organic produce is often used. Plants, stained glass windows. Happening, in place. Got an award for best vegetarian restaurant in Michigan. Main Street Comedy Showcase is downstairs.
Other Info: Full service, take-out, catering. Non-smoking. Reservations suggested for weekends. Accepts AMEX, DC, DISC, MC, VISA. Price: $-$$.

Directions: This place is in the middle of town. From I-94, take Jackson Ave exit (#172), then go east on Jackson Ave (becomes W Hurron St) 2¼ miles, then at N 5th Ave turn right and go 2 blocks, then at E Liberty St turn left and this place is near the corner.

Sunflower Café

211 East Washington, between 4th & 5th Avenue; 734-302-7701
Hours: Tuesday to Thursday 11 am to 9 pm; Friday & Saturday 11 am to 10 pm; Sunday Brunch.
International. Very Vegetarian friendly. Not pure vegetarian (serves fish). Macrobiotic and Vegan options.
Menu: Sunrise Burrito, large selection of salads, Nori Rolls, pizzas, Scrambled Tofu, tortilla, Roasted Potatoes, Brown Rice, Portabella Burger, Tempeh Burger, Sunflower Burger, Open Face Sandwich, soups, Chips & Salsa, Vegetable Stir-fry, Enchiladas, Taos Burrito, spaghetti, Shanghai Noodle Factory and vegan desserts. On the pizzas can have either cheese or soy cheese (is not vegan). Organic coffee.
Comments: Food freshly prepared. Has Sunday Brunch. Local organic produce used when possible.
Directions: This place is in downtown Ann Arbor. From I-94, take Jackson Ave exit (#172), then go east on Jackson Ave (becomes W Hurron St) for 2¼ miles, then at N 5th Ave turn right and go 1 block, then at E Washington St turn right and this place is 1 block down near S 4th Ave.

Whole Foods Market

2398 East Stadium Blvd, east of the university
734-971-3366
Hours: Daily 9 am to 10 pm
Natural Food Store and Cafe. Deli, Bakery, Salad Bar and Juice Bar. Organic produce. Supermarket-type place. See Whole Foods Market information.
Directions: Located in the Lamp Post Plaza, just west of the East Stadium Blvd and Washtenaw Avenue junction. From US 23, take exit #37B and you are on Washtenaw Avenue heading west toward Ann Arbor. Go about 1½ mile and at the fork in the road stay left and you will be on East Stadium Blvd. Lamp Post Plaza is immediately on the left. Whole Foods Market is at the back of the plaza.

BATTLE CREEK

Apple Valley Natural Foods

5275 Beckley Road; 616-979-2257
Hours: Monday to Friday 9 am to 7 pm; Sunday

11 am to 4 pm; closed Saturday.
Natural Food Store.
Directions: This place is about 4 miles south of downtown Battle Creek. From I-94, take Exit #97, and this place is a quarter-mile west of Capital Ave SW. If you are coming west on I-94, turn left at exit and go a quarter-mile, then turn left at Beckley Rd and this place is a quarter-mile down. If going east on I-94, after coming off the ramp this place is a quarter-mile straight.

BERKLEY

Amici's Pizza

3249 West 12 Mile Road; 248-544-4100
Hours: Sunday to Thursday 4 pm to 10 pm
Friday & Saturday 4 pm to 12 midnight
Italian, Pizza. See Royal Oak.
Other Info: No credit cards; cash only.
Directions: Downtown Berkley, between Coolidge and Greenfield on the south side of the road.

BERRIEN SPRINGS

**Andrews University

US 31 North; 616-471-3161
Hours: Daily during school year
Summer call for hours
Vegetarian Cafeteria Café. Large Salad Bar.
Menu: Menu changes often. Soups, salads, sandwiches, main dishes, mock "meat" dishes and desserts.
Other Info: Cafeteria style, take-out. Price: $.

Apple Valley

9067 US Highway 31; 616-471-3234
Hours: Monday to Thursday 7 am to 11 am; Friday 7 am to 5 pm; Sunday 8 am to 11 pm
Deli Hours: 11 am to 2 pm, 5 pm to 7 pm; closed Saturday.
Natural Food Store and Deli. Supermarket-type place. Bakery. Does not sell meat.
Other Info: Counter service, take-out. Has some seating. Accepts AMEX, DC, DIS, MC, VISA.
Directions: Near Andrews University.

CANTON (Detroit Suburb)

Good Food Company

Canton Corners Shopping Center, 42615 Ford Road; 734-981-8100
Hours: Monday to Saturday 8 am to 9 pm; Sunday 10 noon to 6 pm; Deli closes an hour or two before the store.
Natural Food Store and small Café. Deli, Juice

Bar and Bakery. Organic produce. Macrobiotic and Vegan options. Not pure vegetarian.
Menu: Has over 40 dishes in the deli. Homemade soups, salads and vegan baked goods. Fresh juices and smoothies.
Comments: Sit-down restaurant. Also has a good bookstore. Has a second branch in Troy.
Other Info: Cafeteria style, take-out. Has seating. Accepts MC, VISA.
Directions: West of I-275. From I-275, take Ford Rd exit (#25) and go west 2 miles. This place on the left in the Canton Corners Shopping Center.

DEARBORN HEIGHTS (Detroit suburb)

La Pita
22435 Michigan Avenue; 313-565-7482
Hours: Sunday to Thursday 10 am to 10 pm
Friday & Saturday 11 am to 10 pm
Middle Eastern. Vegan-friendly. Good food and service.
Menu: Has several vegetarian options including hummus, tabbouleh, baba ghanoush and falafel.
Comments: Parking arranged for customers.
Other Info: Full service, take-out. Reservations suggested for groups. Accepts AMEX, DC, DIS, MC, VISA. Price: $$-$$$.

La Shish
12918 Michigan Avenue, East
313-584-4477; **Web site:** www.lashish.com
22039 Michigan Avenue, near Monroe
313-562-7200
Hours: Daily 10 am to 12 midnight
Lebanese, Middle Eastern. Vegan options.
Menu: Has several vegan dishes. Lentil Soup, Stuffed Grape Leaves, hummus, Potato Kibbee (steamed potato, cracked wheat, olive oil), Bulgar (cracked wheat with tomato, green peppers and mushrooms) and falafel.
Comments: One of the best Middle Eastern restaurants in town. Has many traditional Lebanese objects in the restaurant, giving the design an authentic touch.
Other Info: Full service, take-out. Does not accept reservations. Accepts AMEX, DC, DIS, MC, VISA. Price: $$.

Thai Place
22433 Michigan Avenue;   313-278-5252
13919 Michigan Avenue   313-584-2048
Hours: Daily 11 am to 10 pm
Thai. Not pure vegetarian.
Menu: Good vegetarian options.
Other Info: Full service, take-out. Accepts DC, DIS, MC, VISA. Price: $-$$.

DETROIT

Blue Nile
508 Monroe Street, downtown; 313-964-6699
Hours: Monday to Tuesday 5 pm to 10 pm; Fri & Sat 5 pm to 11 pm; Sun 3 pm to 9 pm
Ethiopian. Not pure vegetarian. See description under Ann Arbor.
Menu: Has an all-you-can-eat Vegetarian Meal with cabbage, red lentil, green lentil, yellow lentils and collard greens.
Other Info: Reservations not necessary. Accepts AMEX, DC, MC, VISA. Price: $$.
Directions: From I-75, take I-375 and then exit towards Lafayette Ave and go 2 blocks, then at Macomb St turn right and go 2 blocks, then at Beaubien St turn left and this place is 1 block down.

Cass Corridor Food Co-op
456 Charlotte Avenue; 313-831-7452
Hours: Monday to Friday 9 am to 7 pm; Saturday 9 am to 6 pm; Sunday 11 am to 5 pm
Natural Food Store.
Other Info: Accepts MC, VISA.
Directions: From I-10 (John C Lodge Fwy), take Forest/Warren St exit and go east on Forest 3 blocks. At Cass turn right (go south) and this place on right 3 blocks down.

Detroit Pizza Factory
1250 Griswold Street
313-963-2149
Hours: Monday to Thursday 11 am to 10 pm; Friday 11 am to 11 pm; Saturday 1 pm to 11 pm; Sunday 3 pm to 9 pm
Pizza, American Fast Food. Not pure vegetarian.
Menu: Mainly good pizzas, subs, bread sticks and salads. No alcohol.
Comments: Really good pizzas. Basic design. Has inexpensive slices of pizza. Mainly carryout and delivery. Has several tables.
Other Info: Full service, take-out, delivery. No credit cards.

Don Pedros
24366 Grand River
313-537-1450
Hours: Sunday to Thursday 10 am to 10 pm
Friday & Saturday 10 am to 11 pm
Mexican. Not pure vegetarian.
Comments: Has no lard in the beans or chicken broth in the rice. Pleasant atmosphere.
Other Info: Full service, take-out. Reservations recommended for groups. Accepts AMEX, DIS, DC, MC, VISA. Price: $$.

***Govinda's in the Fisher Mansion

383 Lenox Street; 313-331-6740
Hours: Friday to Sunday
Pure Vegetarian Indian and International.
Vegan options.
Menu: Has Indian Dinner with rice, vegetable subji, chapatis, papadam, Spinach Lasagna, bread, salads and desserts. The desserts are excellent. Fresh juices. Decaf coffee and herbal tea.
Comments: Managed by Hare Krishna devotees. Everything is homemade prepared with fresh ingredients. This place is recommended. The neighborhood where the restaurant is located is not considered very safe, but there is a secured fenced in parking lot.
Building: The restaurant is in the beautiful 1927 mansion of Lawrence Fisher of Fisher Body (later Fisher Cadillac), one of the great Detroit industrialists. Has tours Friday to Sunday May to October 12:30 pm, 2 pm, 3:30 pm for $6. The restaurant is located in the formal dinning room of the mansion. The mansion was purchased for the Hare Krishnas with donations from Alfred Ford (grandson of Henry Ford) and Elisabeth Reuther (daughter of former union president Walter Reuther). It is now a temple, museum and restaurant. You can take a tour of the mansion, which is definitely worth a visit. It has French Villa, Italian Renaissance and Moorish designs. Has French fireplaces, carved walnut doors, Tiffany lamps, and gold leaf and silver leaf overlaid in various places in the building. Has an indoor fancy tiled boatwell. It is one of the most beautiful buildings you will every see. The grounds are nice to.
Other Info: Full service, take-out. Accepts AMEX, MC, VISA. Price: $-$$.
Directions: In Gross Point directly next to the canal, in Eastern Detroit. From I-94, take the Conner Ave exit (#220B) towards City Airport and keep right at fork in ramp and go straight onto Conner St for 2¼ miles, then at Jefferson Ave turn left and go a quarter-mile, then at Dickerson St turn right (becomes Lenox St) and this place is ¾ mile down.

Harmone Garden Café IV

87 West Palmer Street; 313-831-4420
Hours: Monday to Friday 7 am to 9 pm; Saturday 9 am to 9 pm; Sunday 10 am to 7 pm
Mainly Syrian and some American. Not pure vegetarian.
Comments: Has a good selection of vegetarian dishes including falafel, baba ghanoush and hummus.
Other Info: Accepts AMEX, DIS, MC, VISA.

H2O, Essence of Life

15800 West McNichols; 313-272-2000
Hours: Tuesday to Friday 11 am to 7 pm; Saturday 12 noon to 7 pm; closed Sunday & Monday.
Mainly Vegetarian. Not pure vegetarian.
Menu: Soups, sandwiches, wraps and vegetable dishes.
Comments: Nice people.
Other Info: Counter service, take-out only. No credit cards; cash only.
Directions: From Hwy 39, take exit #13 towards McNichols Rd and get on Outer Dr W going west and go 1 mile, then at Winthrop St turn right and go a quarter-mile, then at NcNichols Rd turn right and this place is at the corner, 1½ block west of Greenfield.

Sprout House

15233 Kercheval Street, near Grosse Point Park on Lake St Clair; 313-331-3200
Hours: Monday to Saturday 10 am to 6 pm
Closed Sunday.
Natural Food Store. Organic produce. Has a good selection of macrobiotic items.
Directions: From I-94, take Conner Ave exit (#220B) towards City Airport then go southeast on Conner St for 2¼ miles, then at Jefferson Ave turn left and go 1¼ mile, then at Lakepointe St turn left and go 4/10 mile, then at Kercheval St turn right and this place is a little down the block.

Traffic Jam & Snug

511 West Canfield Street; 313-831-9470
Web site: www.trafficjam-snug.com
Hours: Monday to Thursday 11 am to 10:30 pm; Friday 11 am to 12 midnight; Saturday 12 noon to 12 midnight; closed Sunday.
General Cuisine. Bakery. Not pure vegetarian.
Menu: Has a wide selection of vegetarian dishes. Homemade breads (has own bakery). Macaroni and Cheese, Mashed Potatoes & Pumpkin, Goat Cheese on Greens and Pecan & Dried Cherry Salad. Fresh juices.
Comments: Friendly service. Good atmosphere. Good place for a before or after theater meal.
Other Info: Full service, take-out. Reservations not accepted. Accepts AMEX, DIS, MC, VISA. Price: $$.

EAST LANSING

Beggar's Banquet

218 Abbott Road; 517-351-4540
email: banquets@beggarsbanquet.com
Web site: www.beggarsbanquet.com

Hours: Monday to Thursday 11 am to 11:30 pm; Friday 11 am to 12 midnight; Saturday 10 am to 12 midnight; Sunday 10 am to 10:30 pm
American. Not pure vegetarian.
Menu: The menu changes every six months. Has a selection of vegetarian dishes. "Vegomatic" Sandwich, Three Bean Vegetarian Chili, Chili Nachos, Artichoke Dip, hummus, Vegetarian Manicotti Pasta, Wild Mushroom Napoleon and an assortment of salads
Comments: Has paintings and sculptures done by local artists. The Black Bean Burger has eggs in it.
Other Info: Accepts AMEX, MC, VISA.
Directions: Near the Michigan State U campus. This place is on the north side of the Michigan State U campus. From Hwy 127, take Michigan Ave/Kalamazoo exit. Head east on Michigan Ave for 1½ mile. The road then bends to the right and becomes E Grand River Ave. A block later turn left at Abbott and this place is at the corner.

East Lansing Food Co-op
4960 Northwind Drive; 517-337-1266
Hours: Monday to Saturday 9 am to 8 pm Sunday 11 noon to 7 pm
Natural Food Store. Local and organic produce.
Menu: Has some ready-made dishes and salads.
Comments: Largest natural food store in the area.
Other Info: Accepts AMEX, MC, VISA.
Directions: This place is about 1 mile from Michigan State University. From Hwy 127, take Michigan Ave/Kalamazoo exit. Head east on Michigan Ave (becomes Grand River) for 2½ miles, at Northwind Dr turn right and this store is a block down on right.

Foods For Living
2655 East Grand River; 517-325-9010
Hours: Monday to Friday 9 am to 8 pm; Saturday 9 am to 7 pm; Sunday 11 am to 6 pm
Natural Food Store and take-out Deli. A good selection of organic produce.
Menu: Wraps, pizzas, sandwiches and Mediterranean dishes.
Other Info: Counter service, take-out only.

Gourmet Village
Hannah Plaza, near Michigan State University, 4790 South Hagadorn Road, Suite 102
517-333-6666
Hours: Monday to Thursday 11 am to 10 pm; Friday & Saturday 11 am to 11 pm; Sunday 12 noon to 10 pm
Vegan-friendly Chinese. Not pure vegetarian.

Menu: Has some good vegetarian dishes.
Comments: Popular place.
Other Info: Accepts MC, VISA.
Directions: From Hwy 127, take Michigan Ave/Kalamazoo exit. Head east on Michigan Ave (becomes Grand River) for 2 miles, then at S Hagadorn Rd turn right and this place is a half-mile down.

Sultan's
Hannah Plaza, 4790 South Hagadorn Road
517-333-4444
Hours: Monday to Friday 11 am to 9 pm; Saturday 3 pm to 10 pm; Sunday 12 noon to 8 pm
Middle Eastern and Mediterranean. Vegan friendly.
Menu: Has around 20 vegetarian options. Vegetarian dishes are marked on the menu. Stuffed grape leaves, hummus, baba ghanouj, falafel and others. Good variety of fresh juices.
Comments: The food gets good recommendations.
Other Info: Accepts AMEX, MC, VISA.
Directions: From Hwy 127, take Michigan Ave/Kalamazoo exit. Head east on Michigan Ave (becomes Grand River) for 2 miles, then at S Hagadorn Rd turn right and this place is a half-mile down.

Woody's Oasis
970 Trowbridge Road
517-351-2280; **Web site:** www.woodoasis.com
Hours: Monday to Friday 10 am to 10 pm; Saturday 10 am to 9 pm; Sunday 11 am to 8 pm
Mediterranean Café and Grocery. Vegan friendly.
Menu: Has many vegetarian options including falafels, hummus, lentil soup, tabbouleh, samosas, Eggplant dish and other dishes.
Other Info: Counter service, take-out, catering. Accepts AMEX, MC, VISA.
Directions: From the North: take 127 South to Exit #9 towards Trowbridge Road. This place is on the left in Trowbridge Plaza. From the West: I-496 East to 127 South, then same as above.

FARMINGTON HILLS (Detroit suburb, 15 miles northwest of Detroit)

Anita's Kitchen
31005 Orchard Lake Road, south of 14th, Farmington Hills; 248-855-4150
Hours: Daily 10 am to 9 pm
Middle Eastern, Lebanese. Not pure vegetarian.
Menu: Black Bean Soup, hummus, salads, vegetarian chili, sandwiches, falafel and other dishes.

Other Info: Full service, take-out. Accepts AMEX, DISC, MC, VISA. Price: $-$$.

House of India
28841 Orchard Lake Road, Farmington Hills
248-553-7391
Hours: Monday to Friday 11:30 am to 10 pm; Sat 12 noon to 11 pm; Sun 12 noon to 10 pm
Indian and small Nepali Café. Vegan options. Not pure vegetarian.
Menu: Has many vegetarian options including an inexpensive vegetarian lunch platter. Has good Indian breads, chutneys, papadam, Spinach & Cheese, Aloo Gobhi, Rasamalai and Mango Lassi. Salad, Naan and raita are included with main dishes.
Comments: Basic place in a strip mall. Popular with Indians. Very reasonably priced. Good food and polite, quick service. The owner is Nepali and many of the dishes are Nepali cuisine.
Other Info: Accepts AMEX, DIS, MC, VISA. Price: $.
Directions: On Orchard Lake Road, at mile 12.5 in North Oakland County

**Udipi
29210 Orchard Lake Road; 248-626-6021
Hours: Monday to Thursday 11:30 am to 2:30 pm, 5 pm to 9 pm; Friday 11:30 am to 2:30 pm, 5 pm to 10 pm; Saturday 11:30 am to 10 pm; Sunday 12 noon to 9:30 pm
Vegetarian Indian. Vegan options.
Menu: Serves South Indian dishes including dosas, Masala Dosa, sambar (lentil soup), coconut chutney and Indian breads.
Other Info: Accepts MC, VISA. Full service, take-out.
Directions: From I-696, take Orchard Lake Rd exit (#5), then go north on Orchard Lake Rd for 1 block, then turn right onto W 12 Mile Rd and go a quarter-mile east, then at Orchard Lake Rd turn left and this place is 1 mile down.

FERNDALE (Detroit suburbs)

Om Café
23136 North Woodward Road; 248-548-1941
Hours: Monday to Saturday 11 am to 2 pm, 4 pm to 9 pm; Sunday Brunch: Second & Fourth Sundays of each month 11 am to 2 pm
Sunday Dinner: Fourth Sunday 5 pm to 7 pm Closed First & Third Sundays.
Mainly Vegetarian and Vegan (serves fish). Macrobiotic food.
Menu: Has a good selection of macrobiotic veg-

etarian foods. Stir-fries, Tempeh Patties with Basmati Rice, Seitan Pepper Steak with brown rice & kale, Steamed Vegetables, Mexican Plate (very good), Tofu Sauté and Nori Rolls. The Macrobiotic plate has adzuki bean, steamed vegetables, organic brown rice and arame sea vegetables. The OM Burger is recommended. Special comes with a choice of soups or salads. Has vegan desserts. No alcohol.
Comments: Casual, relaxed place with local artwork on the wall.
Other Info: Non-smoking. Full service, take-out. Does not accept reservations. Accepts DC, DIS, MC, VISA. Price: $.
Directions: Ferndale is 10 miles north of downtown Detroit. From I-696, take Woodward Ave Exit #16 and go southeast on Woodward and this place is 1 mile down on the left. It is a third-mile northwest of 9 Mile Rd.

GRAND RAPIDS

Gaia Coffeehouse
209 Diamond Avenue SE; 616-454-6233
Hours: Tuesday to Friday 8 am to 8 am; Saturday 8 am to 3 pm closed Sunday.
Vegetarian. Vegan options.
Menu: Has a Macrobiotic Plate, soups, sandwiches, Portobello Sandwiches, veggie burger, Caesar Salads, Stir-fries, pizza (as a special) vegetarian hash and a special of the day. Fresh juices, smoothies, cappuccino, espresso.
Other Info: Full service, take-out. Price: $.

Harvest Health Foods
1944 Eastern SE; 616-245-6268
Hours: Monday & Friday 9 am to 8 pm; Tuesday, Wednesday, Thursday, Saturday 9 am to 6 pm; closed Sunday.
Directions: From I-96, take 28th St West Exit (#43A) towards Rte 11/Kent Co Airport and get on 28th St SE going west for 5½ miles, at Eastern Ave SE turn right and go 1 mile, then at Ardmore St SE turn left and this place is near the corner. From Hwy 131, take Exit #82, and then go east on Burton St for about 2 miles, at Eastern Ave SE turn left and go 1 block, then at Ardmore St SE turn left and this place is near the corner.
6807 Cascade Road, SE
616-975-7555
Hours: Monday to Saturday 9 am to 8 pm Closed Sunday.
Web site: http://www.harvesthealthfoods.com/index.htm
Natural Food Store. Organic produce.

GROSSE POINTE

**Atoms's Juice Café
345 Fisher Road; 313-885-0095
Hours: Monday to Friday 10 am to 7 pm; Saturday 11 am to 6 pm; Sunday 12 noon to 4 pm
Vegetarian Café and Juice Bar. Vegan.
Menu: Soups, salads, sandwiches, snacks and desserts. Fresh juices, herbal teas and smoothies.
Other Info: Counter service, take-out. Accepts AMEX, MC, VISA.

HARPER WOODS

Steve's Back Room
19870 Kelly Road; 313-527-5047
Hours: Monday to Saturday 9 am to 9 pm
Closed Sunday.
Middle Eastern, Lebanese. Not pure vegetarian.
Menu: Has a good selection of vegetarian dishes. Hummus, Veggie Cabbage Rolls, soups, baba ghanoush, Shankleesh (a sharp cheese), tabbouleh, Mediterranean Stew (eggplant, peppers, chick peas, grape leaves & tomato served over rice), couscous, wheat pita, stuffed grape leaves, stuffed eggplant and mujadara.
Comments: Has Impressionist paintings on the wall and fresh flowers on the tables. Popular on the weekends.
Other Info: Full service, take-out. Reservations suggested for groups. Accepts AMEX, DC, DIS, MC, VISA. Price: $-$$.

HILLSDALE

Hillsdale Natural Grocery
31 North Broad; 517-439-1397; **Web site:** http://members.tripod.com/~foodcoop/
Hours: Monday to Thursday 9 am to 6 pm; Friday 9 am to 6:30 pm; Saturday 9 am to 5 pm; closed Sunday.
Natural Food Store.
Directions: Broad St is also Rte 34/99, the main street in town. On east side of street.

HOUGHTON AND HANCOCK

Keweenaw Co-op
1035 Ethel Avenue, Hancock; 906-482-2030
Hours: Monday to Saturday 10 am to 8 pm
Sunday 12 noon to 5 pm
National Food Store and take-out Deli. Organic produce. Not pure vegetarian.
Other Info: Counter service, take-out only. No seating. Accepts MC, VISA.

Directions: Coming south on US 41, at Ethel (where US 41 turn a sharp left) turn right and this place is on the right two blocks down.

Marie's Deli & Restaurant
518 Shelden Avenue; 906-482-6811
Hours: Monday to Friday 7 am to 6 pm; Saturday 7 am to 5 pm; closed Sunday.
Mediterranean. Not pure vegetarian
Menu: Salads, sandwiches, falafel, Broccoli & Feta Cheese Sandwich, Spinach Pie, tofu sandwiches, Bean Pita and main dishes. Fresh juices, smoothies.
Comments: Has authentic Lebanese food.
Other Info: Full service, take-out, catering. Accepts DISC, MC, VISA. Price: $-$$.

KALAMAZOO

Apple Valley Natural Foods
6749 South Westnedge Street; 616-329-1611
Hours: Monday to Thursday 9 am to 8 pm; Friday 9 am to 4 pm; Sun 11 to 5 pm; closed Sat.
Natural Food Store.

Food Dance Café
161 East Michigan Avenue; 616-382-4901
Hours: Tuesday to Saturday 7 am to 10 pm; Sunday 8 am to 3 pm; closed Monday.
International Natural Food Café. Not pure vegetarian.
Menu: Soups, salads with homemade dressings, sandwiches and hot dishes.
Comments: In a historical building.

Hunan Gardens
5057 West Main Street; 616-373-1188
Hours: Monday to Thursday 10 am to 10 pm; Friday 11 am to 11 pm; Saturday 12 noon to 11 pm; Sunday 12 noon to 10 pm
Vegan-friendly Chinese. Not pure vegetarian.
Menu: Has many vegetarian options.
Other Info: Price: $.

Just Good Food Deli and Market
Rose Street Market (downstairs), 303 North Rose Street; 616-383-1033
Hours: Monday to Friday 9 am to 6 pm; Saturday 10 am to 4 pm; closed Sunday.
Natural Food Store and Deli. Organic produce.
Menu: Salads, freshly made sandwiches, soups and veggie pesto pastas.
Comments: Friendly place.
Other Info: Accepts AMEX, MC, VISA. Counter service, take-out. Order at counter and called

when food is prepared. Has seatings.
Directions: From Hwy 131, take exit #36 and go northeast on Bus Hwy 94 for 2½ miles, then at N Rose St turn left and this place is 2 blocks down.

Kalamazoo People's Food Co-op
436 South Burdick South; 616-342-5686
Hours: Monday to Saturday 9 am to 8 pm Sunday 12 noon to 6 pm
Natural Food Store.
Directions: From I-94, take Westnedge exit (#76) and go north a few miles. At Cedar, turn right and this place is 6 blocks down at intersection of Cedar and Burdick on the left.

Panda Forest
5216 South Westnedge Avenue; 616-382-1128
Hours: Monday to Thursday 11 am to 10 pm; Friday 11 am to 11 pm; Saturday 12 noon to 11 pm; Sunday 12 noon to 10 pm
Chinese. Vegan options. Not pure vegetarian.
Menu: Has over 10 vegetarian dishes on the menu.
Other Info: Accepts AMEX, MC, VISA.

Sawall Health Foods
2965 Oakland Drive; 616-343-3619
Hours: Monday to Saturday 9 am to 8 pm Sunday 12 noon to 5 pm
Natural Food Store. Organic produce.
Menu: Has homemade natural foods.
Other Info: Accepts AMEX, MC, VISA.
Directions: From I-94, take Oakland Drive exit (#75) and go one mile north on Oakland and this place on right, just past Whites Rd.

LANSING

Apple Jade
300 N Clippert Street, Suite 9; 517-332-1111
Hours: Monday to Thursday 11:30 am to 9 pm; Friday & Saturday 11:30 am to 10 pm; Sunday 11:30 am to 8 pm
Chinese. Not pure vegetarian.
Menu: Has a good selection of vegetarian options including Pot Stickers, rice dishes and curry vegetables.
Other Info: Full service, take-out. Accepts MC, VISA. Price: $$.

LIVONIA

Sweet Lorraine's
17100 North Laurel Park Drive; 734-953-7480
Hours: Mon to Thur 6:30 am to 11 pm; Fri &

Sat 7 am to 12 midnight; Sun 7 am to 11 pm
Restaurant. See Southfield.

MADISON HEIGHTS

Sweet Lorraine's
1451 West 14 Mile Road; 248-585-0627
Restaurant. See Southfield.

MARQUETTE

Marquette Food Co-op
325 West Washington Street; 906-225-0671
Hours: Monday to Friday 10 am to 7 pm; Saturday 10 am to 5 pm; closed Sunday.
Natural Food Store. Organic produce.
Directions: From Rte 41 going north, turn right at N 4th St and go north a half-mile, then turn left onto Washington (Bus Hwy 41) and this place is a half-block down. This place is between 4th and 5th.

Sweet Water Café
517 North 3rd Street; 906-226-7009
Web site: www.sweetwatercafe.org
Hours: Wednesday to Sunday 7 am to 9 pm Monday & Tuesday 7 am to 3 pm
Vegetarian-friendly Restaurant. Many Vegan options. Not pure vegetarian.
Menu: Has a good selection of vegetarian dishes. Vegetarian sandwiches, pastas, salads, soups and more.
Other Info: Accepts DIS, MC, VISA.

PETOSKEY

Grain Train Co-op
421 Howard Street; 231-347-2381
email: graintrn@freeway.net
Hours: Monday to Friday 8 am to 8 pm; Saturday 10 am to 6 pm; Sunday 11 am to 5 pm
Natural Food Store and Deli. Bakery. Organic produce.
Menu: Soups, pre-made salad & sandwiches and other dishes.
Other Info: Accepts AMEX, MC, VISA.
Directions: Coming into town from the west on Rte 131 (becomes Hwy 31 North, then become W Mitchell), in town bear right onto E Mitchell and go 2 blocks, then at Howard turn right and store is a half-block down on left.

Bistro 550
Westchester Square Mall, 550 Forrest Avenue
734-455-4141

Fast Foods. Not pure vegetarian.

Menu: Tempeh Burgers, Tofu Chicago Dogs and other vegetarian dishes. Vegetarian soups and salads.

Directions: From Hwy 14, take Sheldon Rd exit (#20) toward Plymouth and go a half-mile, then at N Sheldon Rd turn left and go a quarter-mile, then at Penniman Ave turn left and go a half-mile, then at S Harvey St turn right and go 1 block, at W Ann Arbor Trail turn left and go 1 block, then at Forest Ave turn right and go 1 block.

PORT HURON

Honeycomb Natural Foods

3900 Pine Grove Road, Suite 11; 810-984-1773

Hours: Monday to Friday 9 am to 7 pm; Saturday 9 am to 6 pm; Sunday 12 noon to 4 pm

Natural Food Store.

Directions: This place is about 3 miles northwest of the downtown. From I-69, get on Hwy 25 going northwest, this place is about 1½ mile northeast of I-69, a quarter-mile west of Hwy 25 on Pine Grove Rd.

RICHMOND

Rainbow Health Food Store

Lenox Square Shopping Mall, 66783 Gratiot Avenue; 810-727-5475

Hours: Monday to Friday 10 am to 4:30 pm (until 6 pm on Friday); Saturday 10 am to 3 pm; closed Sunday.

Natural Food Store.

Directions: From I-94, take Rte 19 exit (#247) toward Richmond/New Haven, then at Rte 19 (Washington St) go north (becomes New Haven Rd/Rte 19) and this place is about 7 miles north on Gratiot Ave in Lenox Square Shopping Mall on left.

ROCHESTER HILLS (Detroit suburbs)

Whole Foods Market

1404 Walton Boulevard, Detroit suburbs
248-652-2100

Hours: Daily 9 am to 9 pm

Natural Food Store and Cafe. Deli, Bakery, Salad Bar and Juice Bar. Organic produce. Supermarket-type place. See Whole Foods Market information.

Directions: This place is about 15 miles north of downtown Detroit, near Pontiac. From I-75, take University Dr exit (#79) towards Rochester, then at University Dr go 1¼ mile east, at N Squirrel

Rd turn left and go a half-mile, at E Walton Dr turn right (becomes Walton Blvd) and this place is 3 miles down the road.

ROYAL OAK (Detroit suburbs, 7 miles northwest of Detroit)

Amici's Pizza

Holiday Market Shopping Center, 1201 South Main; 248-547-7117

Web site: www.amicispizza.com

Hours: Sunday to Thursday 4 pm to 10 pm
Friday & Saturday 4 pm to 11 pm

Pizza Place. Vegan options. Not pure vegetarian.

Menu: Has three vegan pizzas with a whole-wheat crust. Can put soy cheese on pizzas. Toppings include artichokes, fresh spinach, walnuts, smoked corn, pesto, roasted garlic, broccoli, eggplant and cilantro. Good salads.

Directions: East of Woodward and just north of 696.

***Inn Season Natural Food Cafe

500 East Fourth Street, at Troy Street just off Main Street; 248-547-7916

Web site: http://oeonline.com/~innseasn/

Hours: Tuesday to Thursday 4 pm to 9 pm; Friday & Sat 4 am to 9:30 pm; closed Sun & Mon.

International, American, Mexican, Middle Eastern, Japanese. Macrobiotic and Vegan options. Mainly Vegetarian, but has some seafood items.

Menu: Soups, salads, sandwiches, hummus, large burritos, veggie burgers (tempeh, mushroom or grain), pizzas, wraps, stir-fry, Black Bean Avocado Quesadilla (recommended), vegetarian Lasagna and daily specials. Sugar-free desserts. Fresh juices, non-alcoholic beer, organic coffee. No alcohol.

Comments: Gets really high recommendations. Pleasant, relaxing atmosphere. Friendly, efficient service. Usually gets voted as the best vegetarian restaurant in the Detroit area. Local organic produce used when possible. Good place for a special occasion. Romantic, comfortable, intimate, happening place. Antique tables, dimly lit chandeliers, hardwood floors and lace curtains. Uses only fresh ingredients and does not use a microwave. Rated by some non-vegetarians as the best restaurant in Michigan.

Other Info: Full service, take-out. Non-smoking. Reservations for 6 or more only. Accepts AMEX, DC, DIS, MC, VISA. Price: $$.

Directions: It is off the main strip in Royal Oak, east of Main St and south of 11 Mile. From I-696, take Exit #16 towards Woodward Ave/Main St/Detroit Zoo (Rte 1) and go on Woodward Ave

(Rte 1) a third-mile northwest, then at S Lafayette Ave turn right and go a third-mile, at W Lincoln Ave turn right and go 3 blocks, then at S Main St turn left and go 2 blocks, then at 6th St turn right and go 1 block, then at S Troy St turn left and go 2 blocks, then at E 4th St turn right and this place is 2 blocks down.

Nutri-Foods

120 South Main Street; 248-541-6820
Hours: Monday 9 am to 6 pm; Tuesday, Wednesday, Thursday 9 am to 7 pm; Friday & Saturday 9 am to 9 pm; Sunday 11 am to 3 pm
Natural Food Store. Organic produce. Macrobiotic products.
Menu: Has some ready-made sandwiches and salads in their cooler.
Comments: It is a good-size place.
Directions: It is on the main strip in Royal Oak, at the main junction in town. From I-696, take Exit #16 towards Woodward Ave/Main St/Detroit Zoo (Rte 1) and go on Woodward Ave (Rte 1) a third-mile northwest, then at S Lafayette Ave turn right and go a third-mile, at W Lincoln Ave turn right and go 3 blocks, then at S Main St turn left and this place is 7 blocks (2/3 mile) down at the junction with E 11 Mile Rd.

Pronto

608 South Washington Avenue, downtown
248-544-7900
Hours: Monday to Thursday 11 am to 10 pm; Friday 11 am to 12 midnight; Saturday 9 am to 12 midnight; Sunday 9 am to 10 pm
Restaurant. Vegan options. Not pure vegetarian.
Menu: Has a good selection of vegetarian dishes. Gourmet sandwiches, soups, salads, calzones, pizzas (very good) and pastas. The hummus and avocado sandwich is very good.
Comments: Has indoor and outdoor patio seating. Has good food. This place is divided into two sides; one is a bar and the other a full service restaurant. Has good, friendly service. Younger crowd. Can be a long wait during lunch.
Other Info: Full service, take-out, catering. Non-smoking dining room. Smoking in the bar. Accepts AMEX, MC, VISA. Price: $.

SAGINAW

Grains & Greens

3641 Bay Road; 989-799-8171
Hours: Monday to Friday 9 am to 8 pm; Saturday 9 am to 6 pm; Sunday 12 noon to 5 pm
Natural Food Store. No produce.

Directions: From Hwy 675, take Tittabawsee exit and go 1 mile to Bay Rd. At Bay Rd, turn left and the store is on left.

Heritage Natural Foods

717 Gratiot Avenue; 989-793-5805
Hours: Monday to Saturday 9:30 am to 5:30 pm Closed Sunday.
Natural Food Store.
Directions: From I-75, take Holland Ave (Rte 46) exit west. Rte 46 runs into Gratiot. This place is two blocks past Michigan on right.

SOUTHFIELD (Detroit suburb, about 7 mile northwest of Detroit)

Better Health Foods

21750 Lahser Road, at 11th; 248-356-0223
Natural Food Store, Deli and Juice Bar. Organic produce. Macrobiotic products.
Menu: Soups, salads, pasta salad, veggie chili and more.
Other Info: Counter service, take-out. Has seating.
Directions: From I-696, take Lahser Rd exit (#10) and this place is a half-mile south of the exit on Lahser Rd. This place is a half-mile south of the intersection of I-696 and John C Lodge Fwy (can also take Lahser Rd exit for this highway).

Jerusalem Pizza

26025 Greenfield Road; 248-552-0088
Hours: Sunday to Thursday 11 am to 9 pm; Friday 11 am to 2 pm; Sun 8:30 am to 10:45 pm
Pizza Place. Kosher.
Menu: Pizzas, sandwiches and salads. Can put mock "meats" on pizzas. About 50% of the menu is vegan.

Sweet Lorraine's Café

29101 Greenfield Road, at 12 Mile Road
Southfield; 248-559-5985
Web site: www.sweetlorraines.com
Hours: Monday to Thursday 11 am to 10 pm; Friday 11 am to 11 pm; Saturday 10 am to 11 pm; Sunday 10 am to 9:30 pm
International Café and Deli. Not pure vegetarian.
Menu: Has dishes from around the world: Asian, Italian, Greek, Asian, Creole and more. Soups, salads, pizzas, Brie with dried cranberries, pastas, veggie burgers and excellent desserts. Lorraine's special salad is blue cheese, hazelnuts, pears and dried cranberries with a vinaigrette sauce.
Comments: Has a far out design with French

theater posters. Romantic place. This place gets great ratings. The Lite Lunch with half a sandwich, salad and soup is a bargain. Food gets great ratings. Friendly, efficient service. Also has a branch in Livonia and Madison Heights. Often has live jazz music.

Other Info: Full service, take-out. Reservations recommended (especially for groups). Accepts AMEX, DC, DIS, MC, VISA. Price: $$.

Directions: From Woodward Ave (Rte 1), go west on W Mile Rd 1 mile, then at Greenfield turn left and this place is a half-block down.

SUTTONS BAY

Café Bliss

Highway M-22

231-271-5000

Hours: Open in the summer for lunch

Open on weekends during the fall. Closed for winter (opens on Memorial Weekend).

International Natural Food Café. Vegan friendly. About half the dishes on the menu are vegetarian. Southeast Asian, Mexican and American.

Menu: Tofu Gahn (Marinated and baked stuffed tofu). Seitan and tempeh dishes. Homemade desserts that are naturally sweetened.

Comments: Located in an old Victorian home. Good atmosphere. Local organic produce used when possible.

Other Info: Reservations are recommended on summer weekends. Price: $$-$$$.

Directions: On the main street of town.

TRAVERSE CITY

Oryana Food Co-op

260 East 10th Street, at Lake

231-947-0191; email: oryana@traverse.com

Web site: http://www.oryana.com

Hours: Monday to Saturday 8 am to 8 pm (Winter 8 am to 7 pm); Sunday 12 noon to 5 pm

Natural Food Store and Deli. Organic produce.

Other Info: Counter service, take-out. Has a few seats at counter. Accepts AMEX, MC, VISA.

Directions: From Rte 31/37, at 10th St go east 1 mile until it dead-ends. This place at corner of Lake and 10th on south side of road.

Poppycocks

128 East Front Street

231-941-7632

Hours: Monday to Thursday 11 am to 9 pm Friday & Saturday 11 am to 10 pm

Closed Sunday during winter.

American and Italian. Not pure vegetarian.

Menu: Has a vegetarian daily special and other vegetarian dishes. Soups, salads, sandwiches and pastas. Has good food.

Other Info: Full service, take-out. Does not accept reservations. Accepts MC, VISA. Price: $$.

TROY (Detroit suburb, 12 miles north of Detroit)

Anita's Kitchen

110 West Maple Road, Troy, Southwest Oakland County, Detroit suburbs

248-362-0680

Hours: Daily 6 am to 9 pm

Middle Eastern, Lebanese, American. Not pure vegetarian.

Menu: Has many vegetarian options. Good vegetarian soups.

Other Info: Full service, take-out, delivery. Accepts AMEX, DIS, MC, VISA. Price: $$.

Good Food Company

74 West Maple Road, Troy

248-362-0886

Hours: Monday to Saturday 8 am to 9 pm

Sunday 10 am to 6 pm

Natural Food Store and small Café. Deli and Juice Bar. Macrobiotic and Vegan options. Organic produce.

Menu: Has a good selection of vegetarian dishes. Has baked goods.

Comments: Also has a good bookstore with magazines, CDs and videos on natural health related subjects. One of the largest health food stores in the Detroit area. Has a small area for seating. Has a second branch in Canton.

Other Info: Cafeteria style, take-out.

Directions: Located a half-block west of junction of Maple Rd and Livernois. From I-75, take Livernois Rd exit (#69) and go south on Livernois 1 mile. At Main St turn right. This place at intersection of Maple and Livernois on left.

Whole Foods Market

2880 West Maple, Detroit suburbs

248-649-9600

email: aaron.mckee@wholefoods.com

Web site: www.wholefoodsmarket.com

Hours: Daily 8 am to 9 pm

Natural Food Store and Cafe. Deli, Bakery, Salad Bar and Juice Bar. Organic produce. Supermarket-type place. See Whole Foods Market information.

Directions: From I-75, take Livernois Rd exit

(#69) and go south on Livernois 1 mile. At Main St turn right and this place is 2 miles down, on the northeast corner of Coolidge & Maple Rd, near the Somerset Collection Mall.

WEST BLOOMFIELD (Detroit suburb, 15 miles northwest of Detroit)

Whole Foods Market

7350 Orchard Lake Road; West Bloomfield
248-538-4600
fax: 248-538-4601
Web site: www.wholefoodsmarket.com
Hours: Monday to Saturday 9 am to 10 pm Sunday 9 am to 9 pm
Natural Food Store and Cafe. Deli, Bakery, Salad Bar and Juice Bar. Organic produce. Supermarket-type place. See Whole Foods Market information. Has special events such as cooking classes and classes on other subjects.
Directions: Near the junction of Northwestern Hwy and Orchard Lake Rd. From I-696, take Orchard Lake Rd exit (#5) and go north on Orchard Lake Rd and this place is 2½ miles down.

WOODLAND

Woodland Co-op

116 North Main Street
616-367-4188
Hours: Monday, Wednesday, Friday 12 noon to 5 pm; Saturday 9 am to 12 noon
Natural Food Store.
Directions: This place is a block south of Rte 43.

YPSILANTI

Ypsilanti Food Co-op

312 North River Street
734-483-1520
Hours: Monday to Friday 10 am to 8 pm (Wednesday until 9 pm); Saturday 9 am to 8 pm; Sunday 12 noon to 5 pm
Natural Food Store. Organic produce.
Directions: From I-94, take Huron St exit (#183) and go north on Huron 1¼ mile, then at Michigan Ave turn right and go a third-mile, then at River St go north (turn left) a half-mile and this place is on east side of road.

Minnesota

11. Edina
12. Ely
13. Grand Marais
14. Grand Rapids
15. Hasting
16. Litchfield
17. Long Prairie
18. Maple Grove
19. Minneapolis
20. Monnetonka
21. Morris
22. Oak Center
23. Owatonna
24. Plymouth
25. Preston
26. Rochester
27. Roseville
28. Saint Cloud
29. St Paul
30. St Peter
31. Stillwater
32. Virginia
33. Willmar
34. Windom
35. Winona
36. Woodbury

1. Albert Lea
2. Anoka
3. Austin
4. Baxter
5. Bemidji
6. Blue Earth
7. Brainerd
8. Cambridge
9. Columbia Heights
10. Duluth

ALBERT LEA

Wintergreen Natural Foods
1442 West Main Street; 507-373-0386
Hours: Monday to Friday 10 am to 5:30 pm; Saturday 9 am to 5 pm; closed Sunday.
Natural Food Store. Organic produce.
Directions: This place is north of Skyline Mall, one mile west of the downtown on Main St. Take Hwy 69 north until it ends, then turn right onto Main St going east and this place is a couple blocks down.

ANOKA

Anoka Co-op Grocery & Café
1917 2nd Avenue South; 763-427-4340

Store Hours: Monday to Friday 8 am to 8 pm; Saturday 8 am to 6 pm; Sunday 12 noon to 4 pm
Café Hours: Monday to Friday 11 am to 2 pm; closed Saturday and Sunday.
Natural Foods Café. Deli. International cuisine. Vegan options. Not pure vegetarian.
Menu: Soups, salads, sandwiches, quiche, veggie burgers, Spanakopia, Wild Rice Stir-fry, cakes, pies and other desserts. Fresh juices.
Comments: Things left over at the café can be purchased after café closing time.
Other Info: Full service, take-out. Price: $.
Directions: From I-94, take Hwy 169 north about 6 miles to Anoka. Cross bridge and go 4 blocks, then at Main St turn right and go 2 blocks, then at 2nd Avenue turn right and this place is 1 block down.

AUSTIN

Good Earth Natural Foods
120 3rd Avenue Northwest; 507-433-8463
Natural Food Store.
Directions: This place is in the middle of town near Main St.

BAXTER

Life Preserver
875 Edgewood Drive
218-829-7925
Hours: Monday to Friday 9 am to 6 pm; Saturday 9 am to 5 pm; closed Sunday.
Natural Food Store. Organic produce.
Directions: This place is a mile north of Paul Bunyan Amusement Center on Hwy 371 (parallel to 371N), on west side of street. It is about 3 miles northeast of downtown Baxter.

BEMIDJI

Harmony Food Co-op
117 3rd Street NW; 218-751-2009
Hours: Monday to Friday 9 am to 7 pm; Saturday 9 am to 6 pm; Sunday 12 noon to 5 pm
Natural Food Store, Café and Deli. Good selection of organic produce. Baked goods. One of the best natural food stores in the area.
Menu: Soups, sandwiches and salads.
Comments: Friendly place.
Directions: This place is west of Bemidji Ave (Hwy 197), on the Bemidji waterfront.

Sunrise Natural Foods
802 Paul Bunyan Drive SW; 218-751-9005
Hours: Monday to Friday 9 am to 6 pm; Saturday 10 am to 5 pm; closed Sunday.
Natural Food Store.
Directions: On side of Lake Bemidji. It is about a mile south of Paul and Babe.

BLUE EARTH

Rainbow Food Co-op
103 South Main Street
507-526-3603
Hours: Monday to Friday 10 am to 5:30 pm; Saturday 10 am to 3 pm; closed Sunday.
Natural Food Store.
Directions: From I-90, take Rte 169 exit (#119) south about 1 mile. At 7th turn right and go about 10 blocks, then at Main Street turn right and this place on right 1 block down.

BRAINERD

Crow Wing Food Co-op
823 Washington Street; 218-828-4600
Hours: Monday to Friday 9:30 am to 6 pm; Saturday 10 am to 4 pm; closed Sunday.
Natural Food Store. Organic produce.
Directions: This place is 3 blocks east of the "water tower," at intersection of Hwy 210 (also Hwy 371) and Washington St, on left. Washington St is Hwy 210 in the middle of town.

CAMBRIDGE

Minnesota Org Merchant (MOM) Natural Foods Co-op & Garden Fresh Deli
1709 East Highway; 763-689-3424
Hours: Monday to Saturday 9 am to 8 pm
Saturday 9 am to 6 pm; closed Sunday.
Natural Food Store and Deli. Vegan only.
Menu: A selections of vegetarian and vegan dishes in the deli. Dishes usually made with local produce when possible.
Other Info: Take-out only, catering. Price: $.
Directions: A fourth-mile east of where Hwy 95 and country road 65 meet. This is about 3 miles west of downtown Cambridge on Hwy 95.

COLUMBIA HEIGHTS (Minneapolis suburb)

**Udupi Café
4920 Central Ave NE, Columbia Heights
763-574-1113
Hours: Daily 11 am to 9:30 pm
Pure Vegetarian South Indian. Mainly Vegan.
Menu: Idly, Vada, Masala Dosa, Uthappam, South Indian Thali and South Indian-style curries. Lunch buffet includes three curried vegetables, variety of rice, soup, dessert and dosa.
Comments: The food is good, but a little expensive. The atmosphere is comfortable. Saturday buffet lunch. One of the best Indian restaurants in the Twin City area. Authentic South Indian food.
Other Info: Full service, take-out. Non-smoking. Accepts MC, VISA. Price: $$.
Directions: From I-694, take Central Avenue exit (#38), then go south on Central Ave NE and this place is a half-mile down at Central Avenue and 50th. In the north Minneapolis suburb.

DULUTH

**Amazing Grace Bakery and Café
394 Lake Avenue, South;

Lower lever of the De Witt-Seitz Marketplace in Canal Park; 218-723-1399
Hours: Daily 7 am to 11 pm
Fully Vegetarian Bakery and Café.
Menu: Soups, salads, sandwiches, pizza and baked good.
Comments: Has live folk music. Friendly, good place.
Directions: From I-35, take the 5th Ave W exit (#256B) towards Lake Ave, then go south on Lake Ave and this place is a quarter-mile down.

India Palace
319 W Superior Street; 218-727-8767
Hours: Sunday to Thursday 5 pm to 9 pm
Friday & Saturday 5 pm to 10 pm
Indian. Vegan options. Not pure vegetarian.
Menu: Has several vegetarian main dishes. Has an all-you-can-eat buffet.

Scenic Café
5461 North Shore Drive; 218-525-6274
Hours: Tuesday to Thursday 11 am to 8 pm; Friday 11 am to 9 pm; Saturday 8 am to 9 pm; Sunday 8 am to 8 pm; closed Monday.
Natural Foods. Raw and low-fat foods.
Menu: Has a really good selection of vegetarian dishes.
Comments: Friendly place.
Other Info: Full service, take-out. Reservations are suggested. Accepts MC, VISA. Price: $$.
Directions: This place is on the north shore of Lake Douglas about 8 miles northeast of Duluth. From town take the scenic route north.

Taste of Saigon
DEWitt-Seitz Marketplace, 394 S Lake Ave; 218-727-1598
Hours: Daily 11 am to 9 pm
Thai. Vegan options. Not pure vegetarian.
Menu: Has a selection of vegetarian dishes. Tofu and mock "meat" dishes.
Other Info: Full service, take-out. Price: $-$$.
Directions: In the Canal Park district, in sight of the Aerial Lift Bridge, which goes to Superior, Wisconsin.

**Whole Food Co-op
1332 East 4th Street
218-728-0884; **email:** cvonrabe@wfco-op.com;
Web site: www.wfco-op.com
Hours: Daily 7 am to 9 pm
Natural Food Store with Vegetarian Deli. Organic produce. Natural product.
Menu: Soups, salads, sandwiches and hot dishes

for take-out.
Other Info: Counter service, take-out. Accepts DIS, MC, VISA.
Directions: From I-35 N, take 5th Ave W exit (#256) towards Lake Ave and go a half-mile, then at Lake Ave turn left and go a quarter-mile, then at MN-23 E turn right and go a half-mile, turn left onto MN-185 and go 1 block, then at E 4th St turn right and this place is ¾ mile down. From I-35, take Mesaba Ave exit. At 2nd St turn right, at 14th Ave turn left. This place on left at corner of 4th St and 14th Ave.

EDINA

Good Earth
Galleria Mall, 3460 Galleria; 952-925-1001
Hours: Monday to Saturday 8 am to 10 pm
Sunday 8 am to 9 pm
Restaurant. Not pure vegetarian. See Roseville.
Comments: Known for cinnamon-orange tea. Fruit breakfasts. Branch of California chain. Has outdoor dining.
Directions: Edina is south of the airport between Minneapolis and St. Paul. Cross streets are France Avenue and 69th Street.

ELY

Northwoods Whole Food Co-op
125 North Central Street; 218-365-4039
Hours: Tuesday to Friday 11 am to 5:30; Saturday 10 am to 5:30 pm; closed Sunday & Monday.
Natural Food Store. Produce only in summer.
Comments: Small store.
Directions: This place is just off the main intersection in town, several stores down from Moose Restaurant.

GRAND MARAIS

Cook Country Whole Foods Co-op
20 1st Avenue West; 218-387-2503
Hours: Monday to Friday 10 am to 6:30 pm; Saturday 10 am to 5 pm; closed Sunday.
Natural Food Store. Organic produce.
Directions: From Hwy 61, follow signs to downtown Grand Marais. This place is on left, opposite the Blue Water Café.

GRAND RAPIDS

Brewed Awakening
105 NW 4th Street; 218-327-1088

Hours: Mon to Thur 7 am to 8 pm; Fri 7 am to 9 pm; Sat 8 to 9; Sun 10 am to 4 pm
Café. Not pure vegetarian.
Menu: Only serves soups and bagel sandwiches. All the soups are vegetarian and many of the sandwiches are.

Circle Whole Foods
204 Northwest 1st Avenue; 218-326-3663
Hours: Monday to Friday 9 am to 6 pm; Saturday 9 am to 4 pm; closed Sunday.
Natural Food Store. Organic produce.

HASTINGS

Spiral Food Co-op
307 East 2nd Street; 651-437-2667
Hours: Monday to Thursday 10 am to 7 pm; Friday & Sat 9 am to 5 pm; Sun 11 am to 5 pm
Natural Food Store and Deli. Has local produce in the summer. Has frozen yogurt.
Menu: Soups, sandwiches and salads.
Directions: From Hwy 61 north, make the first right after bridge onto 3rd Street. Make two quick rights and get on 2nd Street, and this place on left. From Rte 61 south, at 3rd St turn south (before bridge), at Ramsey turn left, then at 2nd St turn right. This place on left.

LITCHFIELD

Natural Foods Co-op
230 North Sibley Street; 320-693-7539
Hours: Monday to Friday 10 am to 6 pm; Saturday 10 am to 5 pm; closed Sunday.
Natural Food Store. Organic produce.
Directions: West of Minneapolis on Hwy 12. This place is on Main St in middle of town.

LONG PRAIRIE

Everybody's Market Food Co-op
11 1st Street North; 320 -732-3900
Hours: Monday to Friday 9 am to 5:30 pm; Saturday 9 am to 1 pm; closed Sunday.
Natural Food Store.
Directions: From Rte 71, go east on Central St a block and this place is on the left at junction of Central and 1st Streets.

MAPLE GROVE (Minneapolis northwest suburb)

Noodles & Company – Maple Grove
7840 Maple Grove, at Elm Creek Drive, in Ar-

bor Lakes; 763-416-1404
Hours: Daily 11 am to 9 pm
Asian, Japanese, International and Health foods. Not pure vegetarian.
Menu: Most of the dishes on the menu are vegetarian. Pesto linguine, spicy peanut salad and Japanese Pan Noodles. Indonesian Peanut Sauté is spicy hot. Tofu can be added to any dish.
Comments: Busy place. Good food and efficient service. Pleasant atmosphere. Reasonably priced.
Other Info: Full service, take-out. Price: $. Accepts MC, VISA.
Directions: On the main street in town.

MINNEAPOLIS

Asase Yaa
2929 Bryant Ave, at Lake
612-821-6484
Hours: Monday to Saturday 9 am to 9 pm
Sunday 10 am to 6 pm
Juice Bar.
Menu: Large amount of juices and smoothies. Sandwiches, soups, rice, Beans & Plantains and other vegetarian options.
Comments: Named after Ghanian mythology's Asase Yaa, Mother Earth. Has a gift shop in back selling art, bags and other items.

Birchwood Café
3311 East 25 Street, at 33rd Avenue, Seward
612-722-4474
Web site: www.birchwoodcafe.com
Hours: Tuesday to Friday 7 am to 9 pm; Sat 8 am to 8 pm; Sun 9 am to 2 pm; closed Mon.
Natural Food Café. Coffee house type place. Vegan and Organic options. Not pure vegetarian.
Menu: Salads, sandwiches, pizza, homemade breads, Mexican dishes such as enchiladas, curries and other dishes. Has good desserts. Cappuccino, espresso.
Comments: Gets good recommendations. Custom-made dishes are brought to you and you get salads, beverages and desserts at the counter. Quick, efficient service.
Other Info: Semi-cafeteria style. Non-smoking. Accepts DIS, MC, VISA. Price: $-$$.
Directions: Four blocks from the Mississippi and a few blocks from Riverside Park in the Steward area. From I-94, take Exit #235A (this place is about ¾ mile southeast of this exit) towards 25th Ave/Riverside Ave, then go south on 27th Ave (or any other street) 3 blocks and at 25th St turn left and this place is 6 blocks down.

Blooming Prairie Natural Foods
510 Kasota Ave SE; 612-378-9774
Natural Food Store.

Café Brenda
300 1st Avenue, N, at Third Street, downtown
Warehouse District; 612-342-9230
Hours: Monday to Thursday 11:30 am to 2 pm,
5:30 pm to 9 pm; Friday 11:30 am to 2 pm, 5:30
pm to 10 pm; Saturday 5:30 pm to 10 pm
Natural Food American Restaurant. Macrobiotic
and Vegan options. Organic produce. Not pure
vegetarian.
Menu: Has a good selection of vegetarian appetizers, sandwiches, pasta, Sautéed Tofu and Pickled Cabbage, brown rice and a daily special. An
appetizer is Caspian (pita bread, raw vegetables,
olives with a hummus dip and a walnut, pome-
granates and peppers dip) and Wild Mushroom
Pistachio Pate. The Sazoi dish is the macrobiotic
plate of organic brown rice, arame (seaweed), organic broccoli, marinated tofu and natto miso.
Has a kid's menu. Fresh juices. Non-alcoholic
beer. Cappuccino, espresso.
Comments: One of the best natural food restaurants in the country. A bit upscale and elegant,
but casual with high ceilings and floral carpeting.
It is in a restored warehouse in the historic dis-
trict of the downtown. The quiche has eggs in it.
One of the in places to go in town. Whole-grains.
Other Info: Full service, take-out. Non-smoking.
Reservations suggested. Accepts AMEX, DC,
DIS, MC, VISA. Price: $$.
Directions: From I-35, take the Washington Ave
exit (#17C), then go west on S Washington Ave
for 1 mile, at 1st Ave turn left and this place is 1
block down. From I-94, take the Hwy 55 exit,
then go east on Hwy 1 mile until it ends, then go
straight for 2 blocks, then turn right at 3rd St
and this place is 1 block down.

Cayol Natural Foods
811 La Salle Avenue; 612-339-2828
Hours: Monday to Friday 8:30 am to 6:30 pm;
Saturday 9:30 am to 4:30 pm; closed Sunday.
Natural Food Store. No produce.
Directions: Take Hwy 394 downtown, then take
11th St exit (#9B), then go south on 11th St a
few blocks, at La Salle turn right and this place
on right 1½ block down, opposite Dayton's.

Nataraj India Kitchen
1123 West Lake Street; 612-823-2866
Hours: Monday to Saturday 11:30 to 3 pm, 5
pm to 10 pm; Sunday 12 noon to 9:30 pm

Indian. Also Middle Eastern and American. Ve-
gan options. Not pure vegetarian.
Menu: Has many vegetarian dishes such as cur-
ried vegetables, hummus and chili.

***Ecopolitan Restaurant
2409 Lyndale Avenue
612-874-7336; **Web site:** www.ecopolitan.com
Hours: Sunday to Thursday 9 am to 10 pm
Friday & Saturday 9 am to 11 pm
Vegan Health Foods. Raw and Organic ingredi-
ents.
Menu: Organic Guacamole with Flax Crackers
& Fresh Vegetable Chips, homemade soups, sal-
ads with homemade dressings, burritos, Hummus
Plate, pizzas and desserts. Fresh juices, smoothies
and herbal teas.
Comments: Friendly, good place. Has an oxygen
bar. Has their menu on their web site.
Other Info: Non-smoking.
Directions: From I-94, take the Lyndale Ave/
Hennepin Ave exit (#231B), then go south on
Lyndale Ave and this place is a third-mile down.

Falafel King
701 West Lake Street (Lake & Lyndale)
612-824-7887
121 S 8th Street, TCF Tower Skyway
612-339-5560
Web site: www.falafelking.com
Hours: Daily 9 am to 11 pm
Middle Eastern, Mediterranean. Fast food. Ve-
gan-friendly. Not pure vegetarian.
Menu: Has a wide selection of vegetarian dishes.
Baba ghanouj (eggplant), dolmades (rice, herbs,
tomatoes, etc), Skoradalea, Saganaki (Sautéed feta
cheese with vegetables and herbs), Foule
Muddammas, falafel, hummus and various sal-
ads. Really good tahini sauce.
Comments: Vegetarian dishes are marked on the
menu and do not contain any dairy. Has outdoor
seating. King Potatoes are good and are fried in
vegetable oil. Basic décor. Good food and service.
The Lake Street place has outdoor dining.

Farmers Market
312 East Lyndale Avenue N, between Glenwood
Avenue & Hwy 55
333-1737, 222-1718
Hours: Daily 6 am to 1 pm

French Meadow Bakery & Café
2610 Lyndale Ave S, at 26th Street
612-870-7855; **email:** info@frenchmeadow.com;
Web site: www.frenchmeadowbakery.com

Hours: Sunday to Thursday 6:30 am to 9 pm Friday & Saturday 6:30 am to 10 pm
Bakery and Café. Vegan and Vegetarian friendly. Not pure vegetarian.
Menu: Has a wide variety of vegetarian dishes including soups, salads, sandwiches, breads and desserts. Cheese, spinach and mushroom quesadilla (really good), Roasted Vegetable Sandwich, Organic Veggie Burger, Barbeque Seitan, tempeh wraps, Asian Wrap, Vegan Black Bean Chili, organic oatmeal and good baked goods. Good coffees and chai.
Comments: Gets really high recommendations. Food is really good. Has outdoor dining. Often uses organic ingredients. Happening atmosphere. Uses fresh ingredients. Service is friendly, but can be a bit slow. Has yeast-free bread. Breads do not contain dairy.
Other Info: Full service, take-out, delivery. Can smoke on the patio, but not inside. Accepts AMEX, MC, VISA. Price: $-$$.
Directions: From I-94, take the Lyndale Ave exit (#231B), then go south on Lyndale Ave and this place is a half-mile south.

Fresco Juice Company

1426 West Lake Street, at junction with Hennepin Avenue
612-825-6556
Hours: Monday to Friday 10:30 am to 7 pm; Saturday to 11 am to 7 pm; Sun 11 am to 4 pm
Juice Bar.
Menu: Fresh squeezed fruit and vegetable juices. Juices can be blended with milk, soy milk, yogurt or fruit. Makes really good juices and smoothies. Just serves juices and energy bars.

Jerusalem's

1518 Nicollet Avenue
612-871-8883
Hours: Monday to Thursday 11 am to 10 pm; Friday 11 am to 11 pm; Saturday 12 noon to 11 pm; Sunday 12 noon to 10 pm
Middle Eastern. Not pure vegetarian.
Menu: Good falafel, hummus, tabbouleh, veggie sandwiches, spinach pie, Lentil soup and a vegetarian platter.
Comments: Reasonable prices. Interesting decor. Has a red cloth hanging from the ceiling and colorful tapestries on the walls to give the feel of a tent in the Middle East. Has belly dancer performances on Friday and Saturday
Other Info: Reservations suggested for groups. Accepts DC, DIS, MC, VISA. Price: $-$$.
Directions: Conveniently located downtown.

Joe's Garage

1610 Harmon Place, at Hennepin Avenue
612-904-1163
Hours: Monday to Wednesday 11 am to 10 pm; Thursday to Saturday 11 am to 11 pm; Sunday 10 am to 2 pm, 5 pm to 10 pm
American. Vegetarian options. Not pure vegetarian.
Comments: Has outdoor dining on the patio. Has a good view of the downtown skyline and Loring Park from the rooftop dinning.
Other Info: Full service, take-out. Accepts AMEX, DC, DIS, MC, VISA. Price: $$.

Lakewinds Natural Foods

17523 Minnetonka Boulevard
952-473-7875
Web site: www.lakewinds.com
Hours: Monday to Saturday 8 am to 9 pm Sunday 9 am to 8 pm
Free coffee from 8 am to 9 am
Natural Food Store and Deli. Organic produce. Juice Bar.
Menu: A wide variety of salads, soups, sandwiches and desserts. Fresh juices and smoothies.
Comments: Has an excellent selection of items in the store. Arranges classes (for info call 952-473-7875) on natural food cooking, health and wellness, gardening and aromatherapy. Helpful and knowledgeable staff.
Directions: From I-494, exit at Minnetonka Blvd, then go west on Minnetonka Blvd and this place is about 2 miles down at the corner of Highway 101 and Minnetonka Blvd.

Linden Hills Food Co-op

2813 West 43rd Street
612-922-1159
email: info@lindenhillscoop
Web site: www.lindenhillscoop.com
Hours: Daily 9 am to 9 pm
Natural Food Store and Deli. Organic produce. Juice Bar, Bakery and Salad Bar.
Menu: Has a good selection of vegetarian dishes. Soups, salads, sandwiches and hot dishes.
Directions: Located just west of Upton Avenue South on West 43rd Street, just west of Lake Harriet and south of Lake Calhoun, between Vincent and Upton Avenues. From I-35 going north into the city, take 35W north to the Diamond Lake Road exit, then at Diamond Lake Road turn left (becomes 54th Street), then at Xerxes Avenue turn right (go north), then at W 43rd Street turn right, then this place is the cream-colored building. Parking lot just past the co-op.

Loring Café

1624 Harmon Place; 612-332-1617
Hours: Monday to Saturday 5:30 am to 11 pm
Closed Sunday.
Café. Not pure vegetarian.
Menu: Appetizers, salads, sandwiches and vegetarian main dishes.
Comments: Romantic place.
Other Info: Full service, take-out. Accepts MC, VISA. Price: $$-$$$.

Lotus Vietnamese

113 Grant Street, Grant Mall	612-870-1218
313 SE Oak Street, Campus	612-825-1781
3037 Hennepin Avenue, Victoria Crossing, Uptown	612-825-2263
1917 Cliff Road, East Burnsville	612-890-5573
867 Grand Avenue, St. Paul	651-870-1218

Hours: Daily 11 am to 9:30 pm
Vietnamese. Vegan options. Not pure vegetarian.
Menu: Has a good selection of gluten, tofu mock "meat," and vegetable dishes. Has a vegetarian section on the menu. Does not use eggs.
Other Info: Full service, take-out. Does not accept credit cards. Price: $.

Mud Pie Vegetarian Restaurant

2549 Lyndale Avenue S, at 26th Street
612-872-9435; **Web site:** www.mudpiefoods.com
Summer Hours: Monday to Thursday 11 am to 10 pm; Friday 11 am to 11:30 pm; Saturday 10 am to 11:30 pm; Sunday 10 am to 10 pm; **Winter Hours:** Monday to Thursday 11 am to 9:30 pm; Friday 11 am to 10:30 pm; Saturday 10 am to 10:30 pm; Sunday 10 am to 9:30 pm; Vegan Breakfast Saturday and Sunday 10 am to 2 pm
Pure Vegetarian Restaurant. International cuisine including Mexican, Italian, Middle Eastern. Mainly vegan.
Menu: There is a large selection of vegetarian dishes (over 100) including soup, salads, pizza, sandwiches, spaghetti, breads and great desserts. Middle Eastern Plate (falafel, hummus, tahini & tabbouleh), Mexican Veggie Burger and Avocado Dip with Pita Bread. Mexican dishes are tacos, burritos, nachos and enchiladas. Tofu Stroganoff is baked tofu and mushrooms over pasta or rice. Makes their own Mudpie veggie burger. The Pesto and Pasta is good. Has good split pea soup, vegetarian chili, veggie burgers and dhal dip. Has a good size children's menu with peanut-butter-and-jelly sandwiches, tofu dogs and grilled cheese sandwiches. Has some very good desserts such as Oatscream, non-dairy sundaes, carrot cake and carob mouse. Fresh juices.

Comments: Highly recommended. It is one of the best places to eat in Minneapolis. Relaxed, friendly place. Has wooden booths, plants and abstract art. You can get soy mozzarella instead of real cheese. Dishes that cannot be prepared without dairy are marked on the menu. Totally vegan breakfasts on Saturday and Sunday. Great atmosphere.
Other Info: Full service, take-out. Reservations necessary for groups. Non-smoking. Accepts AMEX, DIS, MC, VISA. Price: $$.
Directions: Located in the Lyndale community in southwest Minneapolis, just out of the downtown. From I-94 coming from Wisconsin, drive about a mile past the main downtown and then take Hennepin Ave/Lyndale Ave (#231B) exit. Head south on Lyndale Ave and this place is half a mile down the road on the left.

Noodles & Company – Calhoun

3040 Excelsior Blvd; 612-915-6440
Hours: Monday to Saturday 11 am to 9 pm
Sunday 11 am to 10 pm
Asian, Japanese, International and Health foods.
Not pure vegetarian. See Maple Grove for details.
Directions: Across the street from Calhoun Lake.

North Country Food Co-op

1929 South 5th Street; 612-338-3110
Web site: www.northcountrycoop.com
Hours: Daily 8 am to 9 pm
Natural Food Store and Deli. Good organic produce section. This is a big place.
Menu: Soups, salads, sandwiches and baked goods.
Comments: Friendly, helpful staff. Has. Gift items and houseware items. Has a few tables in front for seating.
Directions: Corner of Riverside and 20th Avenue S, near the intersection of Cedar and Riverside on the West Bank. Near the KFAI public radio station. From I-94 west, take 25th Street exit. Riverside go west and this place is a half-mile down on corner of 20th and Riverside. From I-94 east, take River exit west and this place on left at junction of 20th and River. Has a parking lot on the west side of the store.

Café Organica

400 Central Avenue, SE, at 4th Avenue
612-378-7413
Hours: Tuesday to Saturday 10:30 am to 3 pm
Closed Sunday & Monday.
Organic Natural Food Deli. Vegan options.
Menu: Organic bean burritos, salads, baked goods

(such as muffins and cookies), sandwiches and main dishes. Fresh juices.
Comments: In the same building with the Aveda Institute. Environmentally friendly, natural products. Healthy food.
Other Info: Counter service, take-out. Non-smoking. Price: $. No credit cards; cash or checks only.
Directions: From I-94, take the Huron Blvd exit (#235B), then go northwest on Huron Blvd (road becomes 4th St after a half-mile) and go 2 miles, this place is at Central Ave.

People's Company Bakery Co-op
1534 Lake Street E; 612-721-7205
Hours: Monday to Friday 8 am to 1 pm; Saturday 9 am to 2 pm; closed Sunday.
Natural Food Bakery.
Menu: Sells baked goods at good prices.
Directions: From I-94, take Cedar Ave Exit (#234C), then go south on Cedar Ave 1 block, at Minnehaha Ave turn slight left and go 2 blocks (go south), at Cedar Ave S turn right and go 1 mile, at E Lake St turn right and this place is 4 blocks down.

Ping's Szechuan Bar & Grill
1401 Nicollet Avenue, at East 14th Street
612-874-9404
Hours: Monday to Thursday 11 am to 10 pm; Friday 11 am to 12 midnight; Saturday 12 noon to 12 midnight; Sunday 12 noon to 9 pm
Chinese. Vegan options. Not pure vegetarian.
Menu: Emphasis on Szechuan cuisine. Also serves foods from other Chinese cuisines. Has several vegetarian dishes on the menu. Has mock "duck," and good fried rices. Can substitute tofu in some meat dishes. Fruit-filled drinks.
Comments: Inexpensive lunch buffet. Sunday dinner buffet.
Other Info: Full service, take-out, delivery. Accepts AMEX, DIS, MC, VISA. Price: $$.
Directions: Near the Convention Center.

Pizza Luce
119 North 4th Street, Second Avenue North
612-333-7359; **Web site:** www.pizzaluce.com
Hours: Sunday to Thursday 11 am to 2 am
Friday & Saturday 11 am to 3 am
Italian and Pizza. Not pure vegetarian.
Menu: Vegan specials are hoagies (ask for bread without eggs), fresh focaccia bread with olive oil, Garden Salad, whole-wheat pizza and pasta. Toppings are fresh spinach, tomatoes, artichoke hearts, olives, feta, broccoli, sun-dried tomatoes, jalapeno

peppers, black beans, salsa and mushrooms.
Comments: Has gotten many good reviews in various newspapers. Won awards for best pizza in Minneapolis and for late night dining.
Other Info: Reservations not necessary. Smoking allowed. Full service, take-out, catering, delivery. Accepts AMEX, DIS, MC, VISA. Price: $-$$.

Pizza Luce'll
3200 Lyndale Avenue S
612-827-5978; **Web site:** www.pizzaluce.com
Hours: Daily 11 am to 12 midnight
Italian and Pizza. Not pure vegetarian. See above.

Rainbow Foods
over 20 locations
Has a fairly good health food section.

Sawatdee
118 North 4th Street
612-373-0840
Has outdoor seating.
Hours: Monday to Saturday 11:45 am to 11:45 pm; Sunday 5 pm to 10 pm
607 Washington Ave, S; 612-338-6451
Hours: Sunday to Thursday 11 am to 9:30 pm
Friday & Saturday 11 am to 10:30 pm
2650 Hennepin Avenue; 612-377-4418
Hours: Monday to Saturday 11:30 am to 11 pm
Sunday 12 noon to 10 pm
Web site: www.sawatdee.com
Pan-Asian, Thai. Not pure vegetarian.
Menu: Many of the items on the menu are vegan or vegetarian. Spicy Noodles, Tofu with Cashews, Vegetarian Spring Roll and some other vegetarian dishes. Tofu can be substituted for meat in many of the dishes.
Comments: Hip, friendly place. Has nine branches.
Other Info: Full service, take-out delivery. Reservations accepted for parties of 6 or more. Accepts AMEX, DIS, MC, VISA. Price: $-$$.

Seward Community Co-op &
2111 East Franklin Avenue, Steward
612-338-2465
Hours: Daily 9 am to 9 pm
Natural Food Store. Locally grown produce at good prices.
Directions: It is located on a commercial strip south of I-94. From I-94, take Riverside exit (#235A) south, then go south on 25th Ave 1 block, at Franklin turn right and this place is a third-mile down on left.

Seward Café
2129 East Franklin Avenue, Steward
612-332-1011
Café Hours: Monday to Friday 6:30 am to 3 pm
Saturday & Sunday 8 am to 4 pm
Natural Food Restaurant. All Organic, mostly
vegetarian café. Deli, Salad Bar and Juice Bar.
Vegan options. Not pure vegetarian.
Menu: Has a good selection of vegetarian dishes.
Soups, salads, sandwiches and desserts. Outdoor
terrace dining in the back. Has good vegetarian
breakfasts.
Other Info: Cafeteria style, take-out. Cash or
check only; no credit cards. Price: $$.
Directions: It is located on a commercial strip
south of I-94. The Seward Community Café is
located on the corner, opposite Seward Co-op.

**St Martin's Table
2001 Riverside Avenue, West Bank near the Ce-
dar Avenue strip; 612-339-3920
Hours: Mon to Sat 9:30 am to 5 pm; 10 am to 4
pm; Lunch Hours: 11 am to 2:30 pm; closed Sun.
Vegetarian International Natural Foods. Non-
profit restaurant and bookstore run by a Chris-
tian group.
Menu: Menu changes daily. Soups, sandwiches
and homemade whole-grains breads. Has special
salads, two soups daily and three sandwiches. Has
freshly baked goods.
Comments: St. Martin's is a nonprofit restaurant
and bookstore run by the Community of St Mar-
tin. Chalkboard menu. Bring your own container
for take-outs. Often uses organic produce.
Other Info: Full service, take-out (you bring own
container). No credit cards. Price: $.
Directions: From I-94, take Exit #235A towards
25th Ave/Riverside Ave, then go northwest on
Riverside Ave and this place is a half-mile down.

Tao Natural Foods
2200 Hennepin Avenue South; 612-377-4630
Store Hours: Monday to Thursday 9 am to 8 pm;
Fri & Sat 9 am to 6 pm; Sun 11 am to 6 pm
Café Hours: Monday to Friday 9 am to 5 pm;
Saturday 9 am to 4 pm; Sunday 11 am to 3 pm
Natural Food Store and Deli. Small Juice Bar.
Book store. No produce.
Menu: Soups, sandwiches and specials. Fresh
juices.
Comments: Tao is next to an eco-store. There is
a good selection of health products, herbs, vita-
mins, books and bulk goods.
Other Info: Limited service, take-out. Price: $.
Directions: In the uptown area, a block south of
Hennepin and Franklin. From I-94, take the Lyn-

dale Ave/Hennepin Ave exit (#231), then go
southwest on Hennepin Ave S and this place is a
quarter-mile down.

Triple Rock Social Club
629 Cedar Street, at 7th Street South
612-333-7399
Hours: Sunday to Friday 4 noon to 1 am
Saturday 10 am to 1 am
Club. Not pure vegetarian.
Menu: Has a good selection of vegetarian and
vegan dishes. Meatless loaf is a vegan soy loaf
served with mashed potatoes and gravy. The Irish
dish has mashed potatoes and other vegetables
with either tofu or veggie sausage. Nacho, mashed
potatoes and hummus. Soy cheese can be substi-
tuted for milk cheese.
Comments: It is inside a punk rock and alterna-
tive rock club with some booths for dining. Has
billiards tables. Outdoors dinning. It is a 19-and-
over club until 8 pm and 21-and-over club there-
after. Has a young crowd.
Other Info: Accepts AMEX, MC, VISA. Price:
$-$$.
Directions: West Bank on the Mississippi near
the University of Minnesota. From I-94, take
Cedar Ave exit (#234C), then go north on Cedar
Ave and this place is 1 block down.

Wedge Community Co-op and Deli
2105 Lyndale Avenue, South   Minneapolis
612-871-3993; **email:** wedge@wedgecoop.com;
Web site: www.wedgecoop.com
Hours: Monday to Friday 9 am to 10 pm
Saturday & Sunday 9 am to 9 pm
Natural Food Store and Deli. Juice Bar and Bakery. Supermarket-size place. Vegan options. Not
pure vegetarian.
Menu: The Deli counter in the back of the Co-
op has a large selection of vegetarian and vegan
dishes. Soups, salads, sandwiches, read-made
dishes and hot dishes. Pizza, Steamed Vegetables,
Cajun Tofu Steak, Lentil Yogurt Hummus, Eggless
Tofu Salads, Asparagus Antipasto, Pad Thai,
Veggie Mushroom Gravy, Macaroni & Cheese
with Tofu Franks and much more. Has a large
selection of vegan cakes and cookies. Vegan
Chocolate Cake. Fresh juices and smoothies.
Comments: This large natural food store has a
deli counter in the back. Gives classes on cooking, diet, Indian cooking and more. Excellent
place with a huge selection of items. Price: $.
Directions: From I-94, take Lyndale exit (231B),
then go south and this place is 1½ block down
on the left. This place is in southwest Minneapolis, not far from the downtown.

Whole Foods Market

3060 Excelsior Boulevard; 612-927-8141
Hours: Daily 8 am to 10 pm
Natural Food Store and Cafe. Deli, Bakery, Salad Bar and Juice Bar. Organic produce. Supermarket-type place. See Whole Foods Market information.
Directions: This place is next to Lake Calhoun. From Hwy 100, take CR-25 exit, then go east on CR-25 for 1 mile, then road becomes W Lakes and go another 0.40 mile, at Market turn right and go 1 block, at Excelsior Blvd turn right and this place is 1 block down.

Zumbro Café

2803 West 43rd Street, in Linden Hills
612-920-3606
Hours: Tuesday to Friday 7 am to 2:30 pm
Saturday & Sunday 7:30 am to 2:30 pm
American. Vegan-friendly. Not pure vegetarian.
Menu: About half the menu is vegetarian. Marinated Eggplant with Goat Cheese.
Comments: Seats about 40 in the winter times and 60 in the summer (the extra 20 in the screened in patio). Busy place. Price: $.

MINNETONKA

Lakewinds Natural Foods

17523 Minnetonka Blvd, at Minnetonka Blvd & Hwy 101; 952-473-0292; **To reserve a class:** 952-473-7875 extension 2-248;
email: lakewinds@lakewinds.com
Web site: www.lakewinds.com
Hours: Monday to Saturday 8 am to 9 pm
Sunday 9 am to 8 pm
Natural Food Store and Deli. Salad Bar. Organic produce.
Menu: Soups, salads, sandwiches and freshly made juices.
Comments: A good store. Natural food cooking, health and wellness, aromatherapy and gardening classes. Has a take-out deli with no seating.
Directions: From Hwy 494, exit at Minnetonka Boulevard and this place is about 2 miles down. At the corner of Hwy 101 and Minnetonka Blvd.

The Marsh Restaurant

15000 Minnetonka Boulevard, at Williston Road
952-935-2202; **email:** info@themarsh.com
Web site: www.themarsh.com
Hours: Monday to Friday 7 am to 8:30 pm
Saturday & Sunday 8 am to 2 pm
Health Club Restaurant.
Menu: Has some vegetarian dishes. Fresh juices.

Comments: Inside Marsh Gym and Spa.
Other Info: Cafeteria style, take-out. Accepts MC, VISA. Price: $$.

MORRIS

Pomme De Terre Food Co-op

613 Altantic Avenue; 320-589-4332
Hours: Monday to Saturday 10 am to 6 pm (Thursday until 8 pm); closed Sunday.
Natural Food Store.
Directions: From Rte 28, go south into town on Atlantic. At 7th turn left. This place on left 2 blocks down.

OAK CENTER

Oak Center General Store Food Co-op

Route 1 Box 52BB, Highway 63; 507-753-2080
Hours: Monday to Saturday 8 am to 6 pm
Sunday 12 noon to 5 pm
Natural Food Store. Organic produce from store's farm. Limited produce in the winter.
Comments: Often has live music from November to April.
Directions: On Hwy 63, 10 miles south of Lake City.

OWATONNA

Harvest Food Co-op

137 East Front Street; 507-451-0340
Hours: Monday to Friday 9:30 am to 5:30 pm; Saturday 9 am to 1 pm; closed Sunday.
Natural Food Store.
Directions: On the north side of town, near a big grain elevator.

PLYMOUTH (Minneapolis west suburb)

Noodles & Company – Plymouth

3425 Vicksburg Ln N, Plymouth; 763-559-4336
Asian, Japanese, International and Health foods.
Not pure vegetarian. See Maple Grove for details.

ROCHESTER

The Good Food Store Co-op

1001 6th Street NW; 507-289-9061
Hours: Monday to Friday 9 am to 9 pm; Saturday 9 am to 8 pm; Sunday 9 am to 6 pm
Natural Food Store. Local and organic produce.
Comments: Has a large bulk food section.
Directions: From Hwy 52, exit at Civic Center Drive, then go east on Civic Center Drive and go

a half-mile, at 11th Ave turn left and go 1 block, at 6th St turn right and this place is the first building on left.

ROSEVILLE (near St Paul)

Good Earth
1901 Highway 36 W
651-636-0956
Hours: Monday to Saturday 7 am to 10 pm Sunday 7 am to 9 pm
American Natural Foods. Not pure vegetarian.
Menu: Has a good selection of vegetarian dishes. Quesadilla, bean burrito, Spinach Salad, pita pizzas, wraps and baked goods. Fresh juices and smoothies. Has excellent iced tea.
Comments: Known for cinnamon-orange tea. Fruit breakfasts. Branch of California chain. Has outdoor patio dining. Good food. Has a children's menu.
Other Info: Non-smoking. Accepts AMEX, DC, DIS, MC, VISA. Price: $.

SAINT CLOUD

Good Earth Food Co-op
Centennial Plaza, 2010 8th Street North
320-253-9290
Hours: Monday to Friday 8:30 am to 9 pm; Saturday 8:30 am to 8 pm; Sunday 11 am to 6 pm
Natural Food Store and Deli. Salad Bar. Good selection of organic produce.
Menu: Soups, pasta salads, grain salads and a salad bar. A few wrap sandwiches.
Comments: Has limited seating. Friendly place.
Directions: From I-94, take the Hwy 15 N exit towards St Cloud and go north on Hwy 15 for about 4 miles, then at 8th St turn right and this place is 1 mile down on the left, opposite Northwest Fabrics.

Inez Natureway Foods
3715 3rd Street North
320-259-0514
Hours: Monday to Friday 9 am to 7 pm; Saturday 9 am to 3 pm; closed Sunday.
Natural Food Store. No produce.

Sawatdee Thai Restaurant
800 St Germain; 320-240-1135
Hours: Sunday to Thursday 11 am to 10 pm Friday & Saturday 11 am to 11 pm
Thai. Vegan options. Not pure vegetarian. See Minneapolis.

ST PAUL

Caravan Serai
2175 Ford Parkway; 651-690-1935
Hours: Tuesday to Thursday 5 pm to 10 pm; Fri & Sat 5 pm to 11 pm; Sun 5 pm to 9 pm
Middle Eastern and Indian. Not pure veg.
Menu: Has several vegetarian dishes such as hummus, Naan.
Comments: Has belly dancers. Separate restaurant and cafe have the same food, but different atmosphere. In restaurant sit on pillows on the floor in a dimly lit room with tapestries. The cafe (Café Madone) has a basic look with tables and chairs. It is mainly a deli for take-out. Restaurant menu, and a deli case. Some of the Tandoori dishes take a half hour to prepare.
Other Info: Full service, take-out. Price: $$. Reservations recommended on the weekend. Accepts AMEX, MC, VISA.

Hampden Park Food Co-op
928 Raymond Avenue; 651-646-6686; **Web site:** http://www.freenet.msp.mn.us/org/hampden/
Hours: Monday to Friday 9 am to 9 pm; Saturday 9 am to 7 pm; Sunday 10 am to 7 pm
Natural Food Store and Deli. Organic produce.
Menu: Has a good selection of vegetarian dishes. Soups, salads, sandwiches, hot dishes and daily specials.
Directions: This place is on Raymond, 4 blocks north of University Ave. From I-94, take the Hwy 280 exit (#236), then go north on Cromwell Ave for a third-mile, at Bayless Place turn right and go 1 block, then turn left at Raymond Ave and this place is 1 block down.

Khyber Pass Café
1571 Grand Avenue; 651-690-0505
Hours: Tuesday to Saturday 5 pm to 9 pm Closed Monday.
Afghan. Not pure vegetarian.
Menu: Has several vegetarian dishes. Traditional Afghan dishes are served including Aush (chickpea, mung beans, green peas and kidney beans), Shrowa (vegetable soups), Kachaloo (potatoes and green peas), Bouranee Baunjaun (eggplant in tomato sauce), Rice with Chutney on top and other dishes. The eggplant dish is really good.
Comments: Pleasant, casual, cozy place with plants. Often has a sitar player on Friday and Saturday nights. Candlelite. Plays Afghan music.
Other Info: Full service. Non-smoking. Price: $$.

La Cucaracha

36 Dale, at the corner of Grand Avenue
651-221-9682
Hours: Monday to Thursday 11 am to 10 pm; Friday & Saturday 11 am to 11 pm; Sunday 11 am to 10 pm
Mexican. Not vegan-friendly.
Menu: Has several vegetarian options including enchiladas. The food is a bit spicy.
Comments: Food is good. The refried beans are lard-free. Has good size portions. Very good service. Very popular place and will most likely have to wait a while on a summer weekend night. Nearby you can take an interesting walk along Summit Avenue. F Scott Fitzgerald house is at 599 Summit. Nice décor with paintings. Comfortable place. Price: $$.

Lotus Victoria Crossing

867 Grand Ave, at South Victoria Street
651-228-9156
Hours: Monday to Thursday 11 am to 9 pm; Friday & Saturday 11 am to 10 pm; Sunday 11 am to 9 pm
Vietnamese. Vegan options. Not pure vegetarian.
Menu: Has a good selection of gluten, tofu mock "meat," and vegetable dishes. It has a vegetarian section on the menu. Does not use eggs.
Comments: Has simple, tasteful décor. Has flower on the tables. One of the best Vietnamese restaurants in the state. Has outdoor dining.
Other Info: Full service, take-out. Non-smoking. Accepts AMEX, DIS, MC, VISA. Price: $.

Mississippi Market

1810 Randolph Ave; 651-690-0507
Directions: This place is next to the northeast corner of College of St Catherine–St Paul. From I-94, take the Snelling Avenue exit (#238), then go south on Snelling and go 1¾ mile, at Randolph Avenue turn right (go west) and this place is four blocks down on the southeast corner of Fairview and Randolph Avenues.
622 Selby Ave; 651-224-1300, 651-310-9499
Directions: From I-94, take the Dale Avenue exit (#240), then go south on Dale a third-mile, at Selby Avenue turn right and this place is on the southwest corner of this intersection. Parking is behind the store, off Dale. Has a parking lot next door and also across the street.
Web site: www.msmarket.org
Hours: Daily 8:30 am to 9 pm
Natural Food Store and Deli. Juice Bar and Bakery. Good selection of organic produce. Vegetarian-friendly. Vegan options.

Menu: Has a vegetarian menu. Soups, salads, sandwiches, main dishes and desserts. Fresh juices and smoothies.
Comments: Arranges various classes (call 651-310-9462 or see Web site). Has over 150 varieties of cheese. Has dishes free of wheat, dairy, gluten and refined sugar. Local organic produce used when possible. Has seating by the juice bar.
Other Info: Take-out. Accepts MC, VISA. Price: $.

Sawatdee

289 East 5th Street
651-222-5859; **Web site:** www.sawatdee.com
Hours: Monday to Thursday 11 am to 10 pm; Friday & Saturday 11 am to 10 pm; Sunday 5 pm to 10 pm
Thai. Vegan options. Not pure vegetarian. See Minneapolis.

White Lily

758 Grand Avenue; 651-293-9124
Hours: Monday to Thursday 11 am to 9:30 pm; Friday & Saturday 11 am to 10:30 pm; closed Sunday (may be open for dinner in summer).
Vietnamese. Vegan-friendly.
Menu: Has over 10 vegan entrees such as mock dock, bean curd, and a variety of vegetables.
Comments: Spring rolls usually contain animal-based ingredients, but you can ask them to make them from scratch.
Other Info: Full service, take-out, delivery. Accepts MC, VISA. Price: $-$$.

Whole Foods Market

30 South Fairview Avenue; 651-690-0197
Hours: Daily 9 am to 10 pm
Natural Food Store and Cafe. Deli, Bakery, Salad Bar and Juice Bar. Organic produce. Supermarket-type place. See Whole Foods Market information.
Directions: From I-94 going east, take Exit #238 towards Rte 51/Snelling Ave, then go south on Snelling Ave (Rte 51) ¾ mile, at Grand Ave turn right and go a half-mile, at Fairview Ave S turn right and this place is a half-block down.

SAINT PETER

Saint Peter Food Co-op and Deli

119 West Broadway; 507-934-4880
Hours: Monday to Saturday 8 am to 8 pm Sunday 9 am to 7 pm
Natural Food Store and Deli. Café and Bakery. Large organic produce section. Vegan options.

Menu: The deli has soups and hot dishes. There are pre-made sandwiches and salads in the cooler. Fresh baked goods.
Comments: Casual place. Has a large bulk food section.
Other Info: Cafeteria style, take-out. Price: $.
Directions: This place at the junction of Broadway (Hwy 99) and Hwy 169.

STILLWATER

River Market Community Co-op
221 North Main Street
651-439-0366
email: rivermarket@qwest.net
Hours: Monday to Friday 8 am to 9 pm; Saturday 8 am to 8 pm; Sunday 10 am to 7 pm
Natural Food Store and Deli.
Menu: Soups, salads, sandwiches and a vegetarian special of the day.
Comments: Friendly place. Has seating.

VIRGINIA

Natural Harvest Food Co-op
505 3rd Street North
218-741-4663
email: natharv@spacestar.net
Web site: www.naturalharvestco-op.com
Hours: Monday to Friday 8 am to 8 pm; Saturday 8 am to 6 pm; Sunday 11 am to 5 pm
Natural Food Store, Café and Deli. Organic produce.
Menu: Has a decent selection of vegetarian dishes. Daily specials.
Comments: Has seating.
Directions: On Bailey's Lake. From Hwy 169, go north on Hwy 53, then at Hwy 135 turn right and go 1 mile, at 6th Ave turn right (go south) and go a half-mile. At 2nd St turn left and go 1 block, then turn left at 5th Ave and go 1 block, then at 3rd St turn left and this place is near the corner.

WILLMAR

Kandi Cupboard Food Co-op
412 Litchfield Avenue SW; 320-235-9477
Hours: Monday to Friday 9 am to 6 pm; Saturday 10 am to 5 pm; closed Sunday.
Natural Food Store. Organic produce.
Directions: This place is a few blocks west of where Hwy 12 and Hwy 71 meet.

WINDOM

Plum Creek Food Co-op
4th Avenue, between 9th St and 10th
507-831-1882
Hours: Monday 9:30 am to 8 pm; Tuesday to Friday 9:30 am to 5 pm; Saturday 9:30 am to 3 pm; closed Sunday.
Natural Food Store. No produce.
Directions: Next to the library.

WINONA

Bluff Country Food Co-op
114 East 2nd Street; 507-452-1815
Hours: Monday to Wednesday 8:30 am to 6 pm; Thursday & Friday 8:30 am to 8 pm; Saturday 8:30 am to 6 pm; Sunday 10:30 am to 5 pm
Natural Food Store and Deli. Organic produce.
Menu: Has a good selection of vegetarian dishes.
Comments: Has seating. Friendly place.
Directions: This place is in the middle of town, a block from the river and a half-mile east of where the Hwy 43 bridge crosses the river.

WOODBURY

La Cucaracha – Woodbury
1750 Weir Drive; 651-264-1948
Hours: Monday to Thursday 11 am to 10 pm
Friday & Saturday 11 am to 11 pm
Mexican. Not pure vegetarian. See St Paul for details.

Mississippi

1, Biloxi
2. Gulfport
3. Jackson
4. Pass Christian

BILOXI

Five Springs
601 Washington Avenue
228-875-8882
Natural Food Store.
Comments: Macrobiotic foods, bulk grains, and other goods.
Other Info: Accepts MC, VISA.
Directions: From I-10, take Exit (#46B) for Hwy 110 and go south towards Biloxi and it deadends, at Rte 90 go east for a mile, then turn left at Main St and go a quarter mile north. Then at Howard Ave turn right and this place is 2½ blocks down at Nixon St.

GULFPORT

Renaissance Natural Foods
1702 West Pass Road
228-864-4898
Hours: Monday to Friday 10 am to 5 pm; Saturday 10 am to 4 pm; closed Sunday.
Natural Food Store.
Directions: From I-10, take exit #34B and take Rte 49 south 5 miles to Gulfport, at W Pass Rd turn left (go east) and this place is 8 blocks down in an old white house with green trim in a small shopping center.

JACKSON

For Health's Sake
235 Highland Village, 4500 I-55, North Jackson
601-981-2838
Hours: Monday to Friday 10 am to 6 pm; Saturday 10 am to 5:30 pm; closed Sunday.
Natural Food Store and small Deli. Bakery.
Menu: Sandwich and yogurt.
Comments: Largest natural food store in Mississippi.
Other Info: Accepts AMEX, MC, VISA (not under $10)
Directions: From I-55 coming from north, take Northside Drive exit (#100). From I-55 coming from south, take Exit #99. Store is under the highway facing I-55 (at exit #100). Go a quarter mile east on E Northside and turn right at first intersection. And this place is about a quarter-mile down in Highland Village.

**Rainbow Whole Foods Coop and High Noon Café
2807 Old Canton Road, at Lakeland Drive.
Store number: 601-366-1602; **Café number:** 601-366-1513;
email: sendinfo@rainbowcoop.org; **Web site:** http://www.rainbowcoop.org/menu.htm
Store Hours: Monday to Saturday 9 am to 6:30

pm; **Restaurant Hours:** 11 am to 2:15 pm
Bakery, Deli & Juice Bar Hours: Monday to Saturday 9 am to 6:30 pm; closed Sunday.
Natural Food Store and Vegetarian Restaurant. Vegan except honey. Juice Bar, Salad Bar, Bakery and Deli. Macrobiotic options.
Menu: The menu changes daily. Soups, salads, sandwiches, organic whole-wheat pizzas and a daily special. Harmony (steamed vegetables with special sauce), Nori Rolls, Fiesta Bowl (black beans with organic brown rice), Rainbow Burrito, Chili Dog, Boca Burger, Tempeh Burger, mock Chicken Salad Sandwich, High Noon Ruben sandwich, Hummus Plate, organic mashed potatoes, Baked Tofu and other dishes. Whole-grain organic bread. Fresh juices and smoothies.
Comment: One of the best vegetarian places in Mississippi. A bit upscale. Good food. Vegan every day but Saturday, when this place is vegetarian. Has soy cheese for pizzas.
Other Info: Counter service, take-out. Nonsmoking inside. Reservations not necessary. Accepts AMEX, DIS, MC, VISA. Price: $-$$.
Directions: The store is at the intersection of Lakeland Drive and Old Canton Road, just north of the University Medical Center. From I-55, take Lakeland Dr exit and go west on Lakeland Dr about 1 mile, and this store is where Lakeland Dr dead-ends, at Old Canton Rd.

PASS CHRISTIAN

Morning Market
101 East Market Street
228-452-7593
Hours: Monday to Saturday 9:30 am to 5:30 pm
Natural Food Store. Organic produce.

Missouri

1. Columbia
2. Creve Coeur
3. Fenton
4. Kansas City
5. St Louis
6. St Peters
7. Springfield
8. Webster Groves

CHESTERFIELD

First Watch
120 Hilltown Village Center, at Olive Boulevard
636-530-1401
Hours: Daily 7 am to 2:30 pm
American Health Foods. Vegetarian friendly. Not pure vegetarian.
Menu: Granola, oatmeal, salads and sandwiches. Fresh fruits such as kiwi, bananas, strawberries, etc.
Comments: Popular breakfast place and you may have to wait for a table. Gets excellent ratings. Has a children's menu. Excellent, friendly, helpful service. Recommended family restaurant.
Other Info: Non-smoking. Accepts AMEX, DC, DIS, MC, VISA.
Directions: From I-64, take Rte 340/Olive Blvd exit (#19B) towards Clarkson Rd, go north on Olive Blvd (Rte 340 E) and go a half-mile, then at Hilltown Village Center St turn left and this place is a half-block down.

Lettuce Leaf Restaurants
444 Chesterfield Centre #130; 636-537-1808
Hours: Monday to Thursday 11 am to 8 pm; Friday & Saturday 11 am to 9 pm; closed Sun.
Natural Foods. Not pure vegetarian.
Menu: Mainly serves salads. Pizza, sandwiches and homemade soups. Fresh ingredients used when possible.
Other Info: Full service, take-out. Accepts AMEX, DIS, MC, VISA. Price: $$.

COLUMBIA

Clover's Natural Market
802 Business Loop 70 E; 573-449-1650
Directions: From I-70, take Rangeline St (#127) exit and go south a half-mile, then at Business Loop 70, turn right and this place is one block down.
2100 Chapel Plaza Ct; 573-445-0990
Hours: Monday to Saturday 9 am to 7 pm
Sunday 12 noon to 5 pm
Natural Food Store. Organic produce.

International Café
209 Hitt Street; 573-449-4560
Hours: Monday to Saturday 11 am to 9 pm
Closed Sunday.
Middle Eastern and International. Not pure vegetarian.
Menu: Has veggie burgers. Appetizer Combo is good.
Comments: Has patio dinning.
Other Info: Counter service, take-out. Accepts MC, VISA. Price: $.

**Main Squeeze Natural Foods Café & Juice Bar
28 South Ninth Street; 573-817-5616
Hours: Monday to Saturday 10 am to 3 pm
Closed Sunday.
Fully Vegetarian. Features locally grown organic produce
Menu: Peasant Plate (organic brown rice, daily

steamed vegetable, and spiced organic beans with creamy tahini sauce), QUYNBI (grilled organic tempeh, Colby cheese, spinach, tomato, red onion and tofu dressing on sourdough bread).
Comments: Creative menu. Emphasizes low-fat, soy and grain-based dishes. Pleasant design. The tables and chairs are made of old school desks and doors. The "Hand Wall" is a plaster wall that has the hand- and footprints of the people that built this place.
Other Info: Counter service, catering. Non-smoking. Reservations not accepted. Accepts AMEX, MC, VISA. Price: $.
Directions: From I-70 W, take Rangeline St (Rte 763) exit (#127), at Rangeline go south a third-mile, then at Business Loop 70, turn left and go 3 blocks, then at Rte 763 (N College Ave), turn right (go south) and go 1 mile, at E Broadway turn right and go 5 blocks. Then at S 9th St turn left and this place is half way down the block.

CREVE COEUR

Natural Way
12345 Olive Boulevard
314-878-3001
Web site: www.thenatway.com
Hours: Monday to Friday 9:30 am to 8 pm; Saturday 9:30 am to 6:30 pm; Sunday 9 am to 5 pm
Natural Food Store and small Deli. Juice Bar. All produce is 100% organic.
Menu: Salads, pizzas and sandwiches. Fresh juices and smoothies.
Comments: Has a good selection of natural food products. Has a selection of books on cooking, aromatherapy, homeopathy and magazines.
Other Info: Accepts AMEX, MC, VISA. Counter service, take-out. Has 1 table to sit at.
Directions: From Hwy 270, take Olive Blvd exit, then go west on Olive ¼ mile and this place is on right in Woodcrest Center.

FENTON

Natural Way
468 Old Smizer Mill Road
636-343-4343
Web site: www.thenatway.com
Hours: Monday to Friday 9 am to 9 pm; Saturday 9 am to 6 pm; Sunday 10 am to 6 pm
Natural Food Store. No deli or produce.
Comments: Has a good selection of natural food products. Has a selection of books on cooking, aromatherapy, homeopathy and magazines.
Directions: From Highway 270 South, take Exit

#3 for Hwy 30 and go west on Hwy 30 for 2 miles, then exit on Hwy 141 going northwest and this place is located in the Dierbergs Crossing Center 1 block down.

KANSAS CITY

Blue Bird Bistro
1700 Summit Street; 816-221-7559
Hours: Monday & Tuesday 11 am to 2 pm; Wednesday to Saturday 10 am to 2 pm, 5 pm to 10 pm; closed Sunday.
Restaurant and Bakery. Vegetarian-friendly. Not pure vegetarian.
Menu: Has several vegetarian dishes (a decent selection). Hummus, Smoked Gouda Sandwich, Veggie & Rice Plate, Vegetarian Green Curry with Rice, Roasted Eggplant & Red Pepper Sandwich, pasta, soups and salads.
Comments: Uses organic vegetables, fruits and grains. Fresh seasonal ingredients. Casual, but just a bit formal. Friendly place. It used to be in a health food store, but is now only a restaurant. Sometimes has live music at night.
Other Info: Full service, take-out, catering. Non-smoking. Accepts DC, DIS, MC, VISA Price: $.
Directions: From I-70, take Broadway exit (#2R), at Broadway go south 3 blocks, then at 17th St turn right (go west) and then this place is 4 blocks down on the southwest corner. From I-35 north, take Broadway exit, at Broadway go south. Then follow above.

**Eden Alley
707 West 47th Street
at Jefferson, (basement of Unity Temple), on the Plaza
816-561-5415
Hours: Monday to Friday 11 am to 9 pm
Closed Saturday & Sunday
Vegetarian American. Vegan friendly. Not pure vegetarian.
Menu: The menu changes regularly. Soups, salads, specials and entrées. Mushroom Dil Soups, Tomato Soups, an assortment of salads including Apple Cranberry Salad & Organic Greens, hummus, vegan Spinach & Mushroom Loaf, veggie burgers, tacos, basmati rice, falafels, mash potatoes and pastas.
Comments: Good vegetarian menu. Live music on Wednesday evenings by Minarets of the West.
Other Info: Full service, take-out, catering. Reservations required for groups. Non-smoking. Accepts cash and local checks only; no credit cards. Price: $-$$.

Directions: This place is about 3 miles southwest of the downtown. Eden Alley is located in the basement of the Unity Church in the Plaza of Kansas City. From I-670 (I-70) go south on I-35 for 1 mile, then take Southwest Trafficway exit (#1A) on left and merge onto Southwest Tfwy going south and after 2 miles it become Belleview Ave and go another third-mile, then at Roanoke Pkwy take a slight left and go 1 block, at W 47th St (Rte 56) turn left and this place is 2 blocks down.

Red Dragon

312 West 8th Street; 816-221-1388
Hours: Monday to Friday 11 am to 11 pm; Sat 11:30 am to 11 pm; Sun 11:30 am to 9 pm
Chinese. Not Pure Vegetarian.
Comments: Considered to be one of the best Chinese restaurants in town.
Other Info: Accepts AMEX, MC, VISA.

Wild Oats Community Market

4301 Main Street
816-931-1873; fax: 816-931-7734
Hours: Monday to Friday 8 am to 9 pm
Saturday & Sunday 9 am to 8 pm
Natural Food Store and Cafe. Deli, Bakery, Salad Bar and Juice Bar. Organic produce. Supermarket-type place. See Wild Oats Market on page WO.
Directions: This place is about 3 miles south of downtown Kansas City. From I-670 (I-70) go south on I-35 for 1 mile, then take Southwest Trafficway exit (#1A) on left and merge onto Southwest Tfwy going south and after 2 miles it becomes Belleview Ave, then at 43rd turn left and go ¾ mile (west). This place on left at intersection of 43rd and Main.

ST LOUIS

Café Natasha

6623 Delmar Boulevard, at Leland Avenue
314-727-0419
Hours: Sunday, Tuesday to Thursday 5 pm to 10 pm; Fri & Sat 5 pm to 11 am; closed Mon.
Middle Eastern and Persian. Not pure vegetarian.
Menu: Has a good selection of vegetarian dishes.
Comments: Family run. Sidewalk tables on a happening street. Small, pleasant dining room. Service is helpful and efficient. Fresh food.
Other Info: Full service, take-out, delivery. Reservation highly suggested on weekends. Accepts AMEX, DC, MC, VISA. Price: $$.

California Pizza Kitchen

St Louis Galleria, 1493 Street; 314-863-4500
Hours: Monday to Thursday 11 am to 10 pm; Friday to Saturday 11 am to 11 pm; Sunday 11 am to 9 pm
Italian, Pizza. Not pure vegetarian.
Menu: Pastas, pizzas and salads. Excellent cheeseless pizza (non-vegan). Roasted eggplant, fresh spinach and sun-dried tomatoes on a whole-wheat crust, with a honey-mustard dressing. None of their pizza crusts are vegan, as they all contain dairy products. The Tuscan Bean Soup is made without meat stock.
Comments: In the Galleria, which is a large up-scale shopping center. The pizzas get great ratings. Has a honey-wheat crust. Only one size pizza: Individual.
Other Info: Non-smoking. Full service, take-out. Price: $$.

Cardwell's

94 Plaza Frontenac; 314-997-8885
Hours: Monday to Thursday 11 am to 3:30 pm, 5 pm to 10 pm; Friday & Saturday 11 am to 3:30 pm, 5:30 pm to 11 pm; Sunday 11:30 am to 3:30 pm, 5:30 pm to 9 pm
American and International. Vegan options. Not pure vegetarian.
Menu: Large menu with several vegetarian and vegan options. Vegan dishes are marked on menu. Salads, sandwiches, pastas, Mediterranean dishes and pizzas made in a wood-burning oven. Cappuccino, espresso, non-alcoholic beer.
Comments: Up beat atmosphere. Wood burning oven. Spacious dinning room.
Other Info: Full service, take-out, catering. Reservations suggested. Accepts AMEX, DC, DIS, MC, VISA. Price: $$.

Cardwell's

8100 Maryland Avenue;
314-726-5055
Web site: www.cardwellsinclayton.com
Lunch Hours: Monday to Saturday 11:30 am to 3 pm; Dinner Hours: Monday to Thursday 5:45 pm to 10 pm; Friday & Saturday 5:45 pm to 11 pm; Sunday 5 pm to 9 pm
Comments: The chef is a vegetarian, so the vegetarian dishes are good. Is considered to be one of the best restaurants in St Louis.
Other Info: Accepts AMEX, MC, VISA.
Directions: Take Hwy 40 to Brentwood Blvd, go north on Brentwood Blvd 1.5 miles and this place is at the northwest corner of Brentwood and Maryland.

Duff's Restaurant

392 North Euclid Avenue, at McPherson Avenue
314-361-0522
Hours: Tuesday to Thursday 11 am to 10 pm;
Friday 11 am to 10:30 pm; Saturday 10 am to 11
pm; Sunday 10 am to 10 pm
International, American. Vegetarian options. Not
pure vegetarian.
Menu: Mediterranean platter with baba ghanouj,
tabbouleh and pita. Boca Burgers.
Comments: Excellent outdoor patio. Popular
place, so may have to wait. Fresh foods. Roman-
tic place.
Other Info: Full service, take-out, counter ser-
vice. Reservations suggested on weekends. Accepts
AMEX, DC, DIS, MC, VISA. Price: $$-$$$.
Directions: In Central West End St Louis.

Fitz's Soda Bar & Grill

6605 Delmar Boulevard; 314-726-9555
Hours: Sunday, Monday to Thursday 11 am to
10 pm; Friday & Saturday 11 am to 12 pm
American Restaurant. Not pure vegetarian.
Menu: Has a good selection of vegetarian salads
and pastas. Grilled veggie sandwiches, Vegan
Black Beans & Rice, Pasta (with tomato sauce,
artichokes & mushrooms), vegetable burritos and
Couscous Burgers. Cappuccino, espresso. Has a
special root beer made from roots, bark, herbs
and cane sugar.
Comments: Has outdoor dining. The service may
be a bit weak. Has a good children menu.
Other Info: Full service. Accepts AMEX, DISC,
MC, VISA. Price: $-$$.

Golden Grocer and Juhari's Café

335 North Euclid Avenue, between Pershing and
Maryland Avenues
314-367-0405; **Café number:** 314-361-0915
Hours: Monday to Saturday 10 am to 7 pm
Sunday 12 noon to 5 pm
Natural Food Store and Vegetarian Deli. Salad
Bar. Vegan options. Sold by weight. Organic pro-
duce.
Menu: Mostly organic produce is used. Hummus,
pizzas, vegan burritos and tofu dishes. Most of
the baked items are pure vegetarian. Four entrees
daily, sold by weight. Some eggless baked goods.
Scrambled tofu, multigrain bread, potato roll,
mock tuna, mock chicken, vegan and vegetarian
quiches, veggie burgers, Barbecued Tofu Pork.
Vegan Sweet Potato Pie. Fresh juices.
Comments: Casual, friendly place. Counter service, take-out. Has several tables to sit at.
Other Info: Accepts AMEX, DIS, MC, VISA.

Price: $.
Directions: Central West End area. From I-40,
take King Hwy north. At Maryland turn right,
then at Euclid turn left. This place on left a bit
off road.

**Govinda's Vegetarian Restaurant

3926 Lindell Boulevard; 314-535-8085
Hours: Mon to Fri 11:30 am to 2:30, 5:30 pm to
8 pm; Sun 6:30 pm to 8:30 pm; closed Sat.
Pure Vegetarian Indian and International. Hare
Krishna Vegetarian Restaurant. Vegan options.
All-you-can Buffet.
Menu: Brown and basmati rice, bread or chapati,
pakoras or steamed vegetarian, Eggplant
Parmigiana, pastas, Halava. Pappadam, hot teas,
salads, dal and soups. Fresh juices.
Comments: Spiritual, friendly place. Has good
food. Seating for 80. In a Hare Krishna temple.
If Maha Muni is still the president when you go,
he is definite worth meeting and is a really nice
person (good for a genuine spiritual discussion).
Recommended for the spiritual atmosphere.
Other Info: The buffet is a great deal. Buffet,
take-out. Price: $. $6 for all-you-can-eat buffet.
$4 student discount.
Directions: Between the park and the downtown.

Hacienda Mexican Restaurant

9748 Manchester Road, at McKnight Road,
Overland; 314 962-7100
Hours: Monday to Thursday 11 am to 10 pm;
Fri & Sat 11 am to 11 pm; Sun 12 noon to 9 pm
Mexican. Not pure vegetarian. Vegan options.
Menu: Separate vegetarian menu. Black Bean
Soup, chili, quesadillas, pizza, tacos, fajitas and
salads. Everything is homemade. Non-alcoholic
beer and wine.
Comments: Has a pleasant outdoor patio dining
area. Is one of the best Mexican restaurants in St
Louis. Has a children's menu. Gets good recom-
mendations from diners. Excellent atmosphere.
Singles place.
Other Info: Full service, take-out, catering. Ac-
cepts AMEX, DC, DIS, MC, VISA. Price: $$.

House of India

8501 Delmar, at Interstate I-170; 314-567-6850
Hours: Mon to Sat 11:30 am to 2:30 pm, 5 pm to
10 pm; Sun 11:30 am to 2:30 pm, 5 pm to 9 pm
Indian. Vegan-friendly. Not pure vegetarian. All-
you-can-eat Buffet
Menu: Has several vegetarian options. Tandoori
food.
Comments: All-you-can-eat buffet. Food can be

very spicy hot. Good lunch buffet that is mainly vegetarian dishes (many are vegan). Gets rated by many as the best Indian restaurant in St Louis. Service usually gets rated high, but some people complain about the service. The naans contain eggs.
Other Info: Full service, take-out. Accepts AMEX, DC, DIS, MC, VISA. Price: $$.
Directions: Near the University City loop.

International Natural Food & Bakery
3586 Adie Road, St Louis; 314-298-8586
Hours: Monday to Saturday 10 am to 8 pm
Sunday 11 am to 6 pm
Middle Eastern. Vegan-friendly. Bakery & food store. Small lunch bar.
Menu: Vegan falafel, spinach pie, fava bean salad and tabbouleh. Fresh baked pita breads.
Other Info: Accepts MC, VISA.

La Patisserie
6269 Delmar Blvd; 314-725-4902
Hours: Daily 7 am to 7 pm
Ethnic. Not pure vegetarian.
Menu: Vegetarian sausage for breakfast. Soups, sandwiches and Barbecued Tofu.

Mai Lee
8440 Delmar Boulevard, at I-70; 314-993-3754
Hours: Tuesday to Thursday, Sunday 11 am to 9 pm; Fri & Sat 11 am to 10 pm; closed Mon.
Vietnamese, Chinese. Vegetarian friendly. Not pure vegetarian.
Menu: Has a good variety of vegetarian dishes.
Comments: The food and service gets great ratings. The décor is a bit basic. Large portions. Very popular place. Good quality at a low price. Quick, efficient service. The most popular Vietnamese restaurant in St Louis for years.
Other Info: Full service, take-out. Reservations recommended. Accepts AMEX, DIS, MC, VISA. Price: $.

The Natural Way
12345 Olive Boulevard; 314-878-3001
Hours: 9:30 am to 8 pm; Saturday 9:30 am to 6:30 pm; Sunday 12 noon to 5 pm
Natural Food Store and Juice Bar.
Menu: Garden Burger and veggie wraps only. Fresh juices and smoothies.
Other Info: Counter service, take-out. A few seats. Accepts AMEX, MC, VISA.
Directions: From I-270, take Olive St exit west. This place is two blocks down at junction of Woodcrest Center and Olive.

Nik's Wine Bar
307 Belt Avenue, at Pershing Avenue
314-454-0403
Hours: Tuesday to Saturday 4 pm to 1:30 am
Closed Monday & Sunday.
International, Greek. Vegetarian options. Not pure vegetarian.
Menu: Has a selection of vegetarian dishes such as salads, pastas, sandwiches and Mediterranean dishes.
Comments: Good place for late-night dining. Has funky artwork. Casual, happening, good coffee-house atmosphere. Has outdoor seating. Eclectic music. Fun place.
Other Info: Accepts AMEX, DIS, MC, VISA. Price: $$.

Obie's of Soulard
728 Lafayette Avenue; 314-231-2401
Hours: Tuesday to Sunday 11 am to 10 pm; Sat & Sun Brunch 9 am to 2 pm; closed Mon.
American. Vegetarian-friendly. Vegan options.
Menu: Good selection of vegetarian dishes including soup, sandwiches and main dishes. Portobello Mushroom Sandwich, large burritos, pastas, veggie burgers and Black Bean Chili.
Comments: In the historic Soulard area, opposite the Soulard Market.
Other Info: Full service, take-out. Accepts AMEX, DC, DIS, MC, VISA. Price: $-$$.

Saleem's
6501 Delmar Boulevard, at West Gate
314-721-7947
Hours: Monday to Thursday 5 pm to 10 pm; Friday & Saturday 5 pm to 11 pm; closed Sun.
Middle Eastern, Greek, Lebanese. Not pure vegetarian.
Menu: Eggplant dish and Vegetarian Plate. Vegetarian Plate contains falafel, hummus and sautéed eggplant. Serves dishes on a bed of long-grain rice.
Other Info: Full service, take-out. Accepts DIS, MC, VISA. Price: $$.
Directions: University City area.

Sen Thai Cuisine
224 North 7th Street, between Pine and Olive Streets; 314-436-3456; **fax:** 314-436-8849
Hours: Monday to Thursday 11 am to 2:30 pm, 5 pm to 9 pm; Friday 11 am to 2:30 pm, 5 pm to 10 pm; Saturday 5 pm to 10 pm; closed Sun.
Thai Restaurant. Not pure vegetarian.
Menu: Has a good selection of vegetarian dishes.
Comments: In a basement in a building in downtown St Louis. Many people believe this is the

best Thai restaurant in St Louis. Reasonably priced. Gets great ratings. Some diner really compliment the vegetarian dishes served here.
Other Info: Reservations suggested for weekday lunches. Can fax in an order. Accepts AMEX, MC, VISA. Price: $. Full service, take-out, catering.

Sunflour Café
5513 Pershing Avenue, at Belt Avenue
314-367-6800
Hours: Mon 5 pm to 9 pm; Tues to Thur 5 pm to 10 pm; Fri & Sat 5 pm to 11 pm; closed Sun.
Pizza. Not pure vegetarian.
Menu: Has a variety of good vegetarian pizza. Mashed sweet potatoes and cheddar cheese pizza. Blue cheese and caramelized apples and pears pizza. Has some unique vegetarian toppings such as rum-soaked raisins, Romano or ricotta cheese, smoked tomato and pine nuts.
Comments: Outdoor seating on the sidewalk. Happening place. Laid-back scene.
Other Info: Accepts AMEX, DC, DIS, MC, VISA. Price: $.
Directions: Near St Louis University.

Tangerine
1405 Washington Avenue
314-621-7335; **Web site:** www.saucecafe.com
Hours: Tuesday to Saturday 5:30 pm to 10 pm
Mainly Vegetarian American (except for a few seafood dishes). Vegan options.
Menu: Menu changes weekly. Mashed Potatoes and Herbed Gravy, BBQ Tofu, pastas, salads and sandwiches.
Comments: Got awards for best vegetarian food in St Louis. Dancing. Popular place on the weekends. Uses seasonal produce. Food gets high ratings. Bar scene (full bar). Good, funky music (no techno or house music). Good, polite service.
Other Info: Accepts MC, VISA. Price: $-$$.
Directions: Downtown near the Riverfront. St Louis near Washington University in a historic neighborhood.

Thai Country Café
6223 Delmar Boulevard; 314-862-0787
Hours: Wednesday 5 pm to 9:30 pm; Monday, Thursday, Sunday 11:30 am to 3 pm, 5 pm to 9:30 pm; Friday & Saturday 11:30 am to 3 pm, 5 pm to 10 pm; closed Tuesday.
Thai. Vegetarian appetizers.
Menu: Will substitute tofu for meat in most entrees. Reasonable prices. Ask to not use fish or non-vegetarian ingredients in the dishes.
Other Info: Accepts AMEX, MC, VISA. Price:

$-$$.
Comments: One of the best Thai restaurants in St Louis. Popular with locals and students. Good size portions and reasonable prices. Service is usually friendly and quick.

Wild Oats Market
8823 Ladue Road, at 170th Street, St Louis
314-721-8004; **fax:** 314-721-8011
Hours: Daily 7 am to 10 pm
Natural Food Store and Cafe. Deli, Bakery, Salad Bar and Juice Bar. Organic produce. Supermarket-type place. See Wild Oats Market on page WO.
Menu: Has a good variety of vegetarian dishes in the deli. Raw foods.
Comments: Excellent food. Largest natural food store in St Louis. On-site masseuse. Health related magazines. Cooking and natural subject classes.
Other Info: Accepts AMEX, DIS, MC, VISA.
Directions: This place is a half-mile east of I-70, on east side of road.

ST PETERS

Nutrition Stop
4101 Mexico Road; 314-928-7550
Hours: Monday to Friday 9 am to 8 pm; Saturday 9 am to 5 pm; closed Sunday.
Natural Food Store. Organic produce.

SPRINGFIELD

Akin's Natural Foods
Fremont Shopping Center, 1330 East Battlefield Road; 417-887-5985
Hours: Monday to Saturday 9 am to 8 pm Sunday 12 noon to 5 pm
Natural Food Store.
Other Info: Accepts AMEX, MC, VISA.
Directions: From I-65, take Battlefield Rd exit, and then go west on Battlefield. This place at the corner of Battlefield and Fremont in Fremont Shopping Center.

Spring Valley
1738 South Glenstone Avenue; 417-882-1033
Hours: Monday to Saturday 10 am to 10 pm; Saturday 10 am to 6 pm; Sun 12 noon to 4 pm
Natural Food Store. No produce.
Directions: From I-44, head south on Business 65, then take Sunshine exit west (becomes Glenstone). This place is on the right, next to Park Inn.

**Wellspring Café
300 West McDaniel; 417-865-1818
Hours: Tuesday to Saturday 10 am to 6 pm; Sunday 10 am to 2 pm; closed Monday.
Fully Vegetarian Tex-Mexican. Mostly Vegan.
Menu: Good selection of vegetarian dishes. Salads, soups, hot and cold sandwiches, stir-fry vegetables, falafel wrap, quiche and special of the day. The Tortilla Soup, Vegetarian Chili and Grilled Reuben Sandwich are popular. Homemade whole-wheat pitas and breads. A daily special.
Comments: Mostly everything is homemade, even the salad dressings.
Other Info: Counter service, take-out catering. Non-smoking. Accepts reservations but not necessary. Accepts MC, VISA.
Directions: From I-44, take Exit #77 for Hwy 13 S and go south on Hwy 13 for 3 miles, at W College St turn left and go 1 mile, at W Central Square Park Loop turn right and go 1 block and it becomes McDaniel St and this place is a half-block down. Free parking on McDaniel St opposite the café. This place is 1 block northwest of Park Central Sq. Take the Glenstone Bus (#44) to Cherry. Then go west on Cherry, north on Kimbrough, and west on McDaniel.

UNIVERSITY CITY

Brandt's Market and Café
6525 Delmar, at Leland Avenue
314-727-3663; **Web site:** www.brandtscafe.com
Hours: Tuesday to Thursday 11 am to 11 pm; Friday & Saturday 11 am to 12 midnight (until 1 am in summer); Sunday 10 am to 11 pm; Sunday Brunch 10 am to 2 pm.
Natural Food Store and Café. Eclectic, International. Vegan options. Not pure vegetarian.
Menu: Has a very good selection of vegetarian dishes. Veggie burger, pastas, Pesto Pasta, nachos, sandwiches, quesadillas, Spinach Salad, hummus & pita, Portobello Burger, mixed greens, eggplant Parmigiana, spring rolls, black bean chili, and pizza. Fresh juices.
Comments: Has specialty gourmet foods. Has indoor and outdoor sidewalk seating. Has live music nightly and all day Sunday including folk, classical music, blues and jazz. See their Web site for schedule of events. Place gets good ratings. Friendly, helpful staff. Service may be a bit slow.
Other Info: Full service. Accepts AMEX, DIS, MC, VISA. Price: $$.

The Red Sea
6511 Delmar Boulevard, between Westgate and Leland Avenues; 314-863-0099
Hours: Monday to Saturday 5 pm to 1 am
Sunday 5 pm to 12 midnight
Ethiopian. Not pure vegetarian. Vegan options.
Menu: Good selection of vegetarian dishes. Vegan options. Traditional style with injera bread. Typical East African stews. Has vegetarian pasta.
Comments: Sidewalk Café.
Other Info: Full service, take-out, catering. Accepts AMEX, DIS, MC, VISA. Price: $-$$.

WEBSTER GROVES

The Natural Fact
7919 Big Bend Boulevard, Suite A, Webster Groves; 314-961-2442
Hours: Monday to Thursday 11 am to 6:30 pm; Friday 11 am to 7:30 pm; Saturday 11 am to 5 pm; closed Sundays.
Natural Foods and Deli. Vegan options. Not pure vegetarian.
Menu: About half the menu is vegetarian. Pastas, Three-rice Salad (brown rice, wild rice, basmati rice, red peppers, celery, scallions), burritos, hummus, stir-fry, veggie burgers, burritos and salads. Can add avocado, sprouts or cheese to any sandwich.
Comments: Casual.
Other Info: Counter service, take-out. Order at counter and food is brought to the table when done. Accepts AMEX, MC, VISA. Price: $-$$.
Directions: From I-270, take I-44 exit east and take La Clede Station Rd/Murdock exit (this place is near the exit). At Laclede Station turn right, then at Murdock turn right, then at Big Bend turn left and store on left.

The Natural Way
8110 Big Bend
314-961-3541 **Web site:** www.thenatway.com
Hours: Monday to Friday 9 am to 9 pm; Saturday 9 am to 7 pm; Sunday 10 am to 6 pm
Natural Food Store. All produce is 100% organic.
Comments: Has a good selection of natural food products. Has a selection of books on cooking, aromatherapy, homeopathy and magazines.
Other Info: Accepts AMEX, MC, VISA.
Directions: From Highway 44, take Murdoch-Laclede Station Rd exit. At the stop sign, turn left onto Big Bend.

Montana

BIG SKY (near Gardiner)

By Word of Mouth
2815 Aspen Drive #3, Big Sky
406-995-2992
Hours: Monday to Saturday 11 am to 10 pm
Sunday 4 pm to 10 pm
Restaurant. Not pure vegetarian.
Menu: Has vegetarian pastas, vegetarian stew and
good salads.
Other Info: Accepts AMEX, DIS, MC, VISA.

BILLINGS

Good Earth Market
3115 10th Avenue N
406-259-2622
Hours: Monday to Saturday 8 am to 8 pm
Sunday 10 noon to 5 pm
Deli Hours: 8 am to 2 pm
Natural Food Store and Deli. Organic produce.
Menu: Sandwiches, salad items and soups. Deli
is open from 8 am to 2 pm and has ready-made
sandwiches and salads in the cooler after 2 pm.
Other Info: Accepts MC, VISA.
Directions: From I-90/94, take 27th St (Rte 3)
exit and then go north. At 10th Ave turn left and
this place is 4 blocks down at the corner of 10th
and 31st.

Great Wall of China
1309 Grand Avenue
406-245-8601
Hours: Sunday to Thursday 11 am to 9:30 pm

Friday & Saturday 11 am to 10 pm
Chinese. Not pure vegetarian.
Menu: Has a good selection of vegetarian dishes.
Other Info: Accepts MC, VISA.

Thai Orchid
2926 2nd Avenue
406-256-2206
Hours: Monday to Friday 11 am to 2 pm, 5 pm
to 9 pm; Saturday 5 pm to 9 pm; closed Sunday.
Thai. Not pure vegetarian.
Menu: Has tofu and other vegetarian dishes.
Comments: Has high standard Thai food. Has
lunch buffet on weekdays.

BOZEMAN

Community Food Co-op
908 West Main Street
406-587-4039; **fax:** 406-587-7955; **email:**
bozocoop@imt.net; Web site: http://csf.colorado.
edu/co-op/bozeman.html
Hours: Daily 9 am to 8 pm (in winter closes one
hour earlier); **Deli Hours:** 9 am to 7 pm
Natural Food Store and Deli. Bakery, Salad Bar
and Espresso & Juice Bar. Macrobiotic and Vegan options. Not pure vegetarian.
Menu: The menu changes with the seasons. Sandwiches, soups and salad items. Good casseroles
cooked with fresh vegetables during the season.
Fresh juices. Organic coffee and tea.
Comments: There is outdoor seating on the
large lawn with an excellent view of Bridger
Mountain.

Other Info: Counter service, take-out. Has seating. Non-smoking. Accepts DIS, MC, VISA. Price: $.

Direction: The town of Bozeman is close to US 89, the road that lead to Yellowstone. This place is in the middle of town. From I-90 take Bozeman MSU exit (#308). Follow signs to Bozeman going west on Rte 191 and this place is about two miles down. Across from the Safeway.

BUTTE

Dancing Rainbow Natural Grocery
9 South Montana Street
406-723-8811
Hours: Monday to Friday 10 am to 5:30 pm; Saturday 10 am to 5 pm; closed Sunday.
Natural Food Store. Organic produce. Has frozen food that can be microwaved.
Directions: From I-90, take Montana exit (#126) and go north on Montana (uphill) for about 1¼ mile. This store is on the left, at W Park St, next to Butte Hill Bakery.

Natural Healing
1875 Harrison Avenue
406-782-8314
Hours: Monday to Saturday 9 am to 6:30 pm Closed Sunday.
Natural Food Store and Deli. Organic produce.
Other Info: Counter service, take-out. Has some seating. Accepts AMEX, DIS, MC, VISA.
Directions: From I-90, take Harrison Ave (#127) exit. Go north on Harrison Ave (Bus Hwy 15) and this place is about a mile down the road.

CORWIN SPRINGS

**The Four Winds
Highway 89
406-848-7891; **Web site:** www.the4winds.com
Hours: Monday to Friday 11 am to 7 pm Saturday & Sunday 11 am to 5 pm
Full Vegetarian American Natural Foods. Weekend buffet.
Menu: Huevos Rancheros Sandwich, veggie burgers, Macrobiotic specials, Vegetable Stir-fry, Oriental Noodles seitan dishes, miso soup, salads and many other dishes.
Comments: Owned by the Church Universal and Triumphant. During the summer there are theater performances by the The Paradise Players. Has fruit sweetened desserts. Non-alcoholic beer and wine. Really nice people.
Other Info: Full service, take-out. Accepts AMEX, DIS, MC, VISA. Price: $$-$$$.
Directions: This place is located eight miles north of the town of Gardiner on US 89, not far from the entrance of Yellow Stone National Park.

GREAT FALLS

2J's Produce
105 Smelter Avenue NE
406-761-0134
Hours: Monday to Saturday 9 am to 7 pm Closed Sunday.
Natural Food Store. Organic produce.
Comments: Has a good selection of organic produce and other goods. Free coffee during shopping.
Directions: From I-15, take Center Ave W (#280) towards Rte 87 N. At Central Ave W (Rte I-15 Br S) turn right and go 1¼ mile, at 3rd St NW (Rte 87 Bypass N) and go 1.35 miles, 3rd St NW (Rte 87 BYP N) become Smelter Ave (Rte 87 Bypass N). At Smelter turn left and this place is a third-mile down.

HELENA

**Real Food Market
501 Fuller Avenue; 406-443-5150
email: management@realfoodstore.com
Web site: www.realfoodstore.com
Hours: Monday to Friday 8 am to 8 pm Saturday & Sunday 9 am to 6 pm
Natural Food Store and Vegetarian Café. Deli, Bakery, Salad Bar and Juice bar. Supermarket-size place. Organic produce.
Comments: Biggest natural food store in Montana.
Directions: In downtown Helena. From I-15 take Capital Area exit (US-12/US-287 S) and take Prospect Ave (Rte 120, W/I-15 Br N) and go west about a mile, at Montana turn right and go a half-mile (becomes SW Lyndale Ave/Rte 12 W) and go another mile. At Benton Ave (Rte 12 BYP) turn left and go a quarter-mile, At N Park Ave go straight, then at W Lawrence St turn right and go 1 block, then at Fuller Avenue turn left and this place is one block down on right.

KALISPELL

Mountain Valley Foods
404 1st Avenue East
406-756-1422
Hours: Monday to Saturday 9 am to 5:30 pm Closed Sunday.

Natural Food Store. Organic produce.
Comments: Good, helpful service. Family owned and operated. Reasonable prices. Good selection of items.
Other Info: Accepts MC, VISA.
Directions: From Rte 93, take 4th St E one block, at 1st Ave E turn right and this place is immediately on the right.

Wild Rose Health Foods
2121 Hwy 2 East
406-257-8806
Hours: Monday to Friday 9 am to 6 pm; Saturday 10 am to 5 pm; closed Sunday.
Natural Food Store.
Other Info: Accepts AMEX, MC, VISA.
Comments: Has a good bulk and herb products section. Good selection.
Directions: A quarter-mile south of the True Value hardware store.

MISSOULA
This place is located halfway between Yellowstone National Park and Glacier National Monument.

**Bernice's Bakery
190 South 3rd Street W
406-728-1358
Hours: Sunday to Thursday 6 am to 10 pm Friday & Saturday 6 am to 11 pm
Vegetarian Café and Bakery. Vegan options.
Menu: Baked goods, hard rolls, Bean Rolls, Italian sandwiches and coffee.
Comments: Good atmosphere.
Other Info: Accepts MC, VISA.
Directions: From I-90 take Exit #105 (Van Buren exit) and go west on Bus-Hwy 90 (Broadway) about one mile, then at N Higgins Ave turn left (go south) and go a half-mile. Then at 3rd St turn right and this place is one block down.

The Black Dog
138 West Broadway Street
406-542-1138
Hours: Monday to Tuesday 11 am to 2 pm; Wednesday to Saturday 11 am to 9 pm; closed Sunday.
Vegetarian-friendly Restaurant. Good selection of vegan dishes. Not pure vegetarian.
Menu: The menu changes daily. Has a few vegetarian soups, sandwiches, Tempeh Burger, Lentil Burger, daily specials and desserts. Has several vegetarian dishes.
Comments: Mostly uses organic produce. Has a good selection of vegan dishes. Non-vegan dishes

marked on menu.
Other Info: Full service, take-out, catering. No credit cards; cash only. Price: $$
Directions: From I-90, take Exit #105 (Van Buren exit) and then go west on Bus-Hwy 90 (Broadway) one mile and this place is a half-block past Higgins Ave.

Butterfly Herbs
232 North Higgins Street
406-728-8780
Hours: Monday to Friday 8:30 am to 6 pm; Saturday 9 am to 5:30 pm; Sunday 9 am to 5 pm
Vegetarian-friendly Restaurant. Not pure vegetarian.
Menu: Has a good selection of vegetarian dishes. Has good sandwiches. Hummus, veggie sandwiches, organic vegetables, vegetarian soups and more.
Comments: Makes an effort to be vegetarian friendly.
Other Info: Accepts MC, VISA.

China Garden
2100 Stephens Avenue
406-721-1795
Hours: Monday to Friday 11 am to 2:30 pm, 4:30 pm to 9:30 pm; Saturday 12 noon to 9:30 pm; closed Sunday.
Chinese. Not pure vegetarian.
Menu: Has vegetarian soups, noodle dishes, curried dishes, Vegetable Fried Rice and more.
Comments: No MSG.
Other Info: Full service, take-out. Accepts AMEX, MC, VISA. Price: $$.

Food For Thought
504 Daly Road
406-721-6033
Hours: Monday to Thursday 7 am to 9 pm; Friday & Saturday 7 am to 4 pm; Sun 8 am to 9 pm
Coffee-type place. Not pure vegetarian.
Menu: Has a healthy type menu. Some vegetarian soups, veggie chili, sandwiches, salads, pastas, burritos and more.
Other Info: Accepts AMEX, MC, VISA.

The Good Food Store
720 Kensington Avenue
just off Stephens Avenue
406-728-5823
Hours: Monday to Sunday 8 am to 9 pm
Natural Food Store and small Deli. Salad Bar. Organic produce.
Other Info: Counter service, take-out. Has seat-

ing outside, but not inside. Accepts MC, VISA.
Directions: From I-90, take Orange St exit south.
Orange becomes Stephens. This place is at the
junction of Kensinton and Stephens on the left.

Mustard Seed

Southgate Mall
406-542-7333
Hours: Sunday to Thursday 11 am to 9 pm
Friday & Saturday 11 am to 10 pm
Asian and International. Not pure vegetarian.
Menu: Separate vegetarian menu. Sushi, Spring
Rolls, tofu dishes, vegetables dishes and much
more. Non-alcoholic beer and wine.
Other Info: Full service, take-out. Non-smoking.
Accepts AMEX, DIS, MC, VISA. Price: $.

**Tipu's

115½ South 4th West, behind The Independent
406-542-0622
Web site: www.tipustiger.com
Hours: Daily 11:30 am to 9 pm
Lunch Buffet Hours: Daily 11:30 am to 5 pm
Fully Vegetarian Indian. Mostly Vegan. Daily
Lunch Buffet.
Menu: Samosas, pakoras, stuffed chapatis, chut-
neys, Currito (burrito type wrap) with curry, ap-
petizers, soups, corn muffins, raita, dal, basmati
rice, several curries, Indian breads, salads, and
Aloo Brinjal Eggplant. Desserts such as Kheer,
Gulab Jamun, ice cream and Mango Sorbet (non-
dairy). Chai, lassi, hot Ginger Brew and Turkish
Coffee.
Comments: Place run by Buddhist. Often uses
organic ingredients. Everything freshly made.
Other Info: Full service, counter service, buffet,
take-out, catering. Non-smoking. No reservations.
Accepts AMEX, DIS, MC, VISA. Price: $.
Directions: From downtown, go across the
Higgins St Bridge, then take 2nd right and this
place is in alley beside Holiday Station. From I-
93, take Orange St exit, then go across bridge,
then turn left at the light and go to the end of
road, then at Higgins turn right, then at 1st right
turn into alley by Holiday Station.

Tipu's Tiger

531 South Higgins Avenue
406-542-0622; **Web site:** www.tipustiger.com
Hours: Daily 8 am to 6 pm
Breakfast Hours: Daily 8 am to 11 am
Mainly Vegetarian International. Indian, Mexi-
can, Greek, Southeast Asian, Italian, Middle East-
ern. Vegan options. Serves eggs.
Menu: For breakfast there is breakfast burritos,
granola, bagels, yogurt and fruit salad. Organic
Black Beans, Vegetarian Sausages, Mexican Rice,
Tofu "eggless" Salad, Greek Salad, Pasta Salad,
hummus, feta cheese, tabbouleh, Garden Salad
Platter, wraps, soups, stews, Lasagna, Spanakopita,
Quiche and fresh breads. Organic coffee and soy
chai.
Other Info: Counter service, take-out. Take-out
cooler. Non-smoking. Price: $.
Directions: From I-90 take Exit #105 (Van Buren
exit) and go west on Bus-Hwy 90 (Broadway)
and go about one mile, then at N Higgins Ave
turn left (go south) and go a half-mile, and this
place is on Higgins Ave at S 3rd St.

RED LODGE

Genesis Natural Food & Deli

123 South Broadway Street
406-446-3202
Natural Food Store.
Menu: Sandwiches, trail mix.
Directions: This place is on the main street in
the middle of Red Lodge.

WHITEFISH

Third Street Market

244 Spokane Avenue
406-862-5054
Hours: Monday to Saturday 9 am to 6 pm
Closed Sunday.
Natural Food Store. Organic produce.
Directions: Take Hwy 93 to Whitefish. This store
at intersection of Hwy 93 and 2nd St E, where
Rte 93 turns, across from the Exxon gas stations.

Nebraska

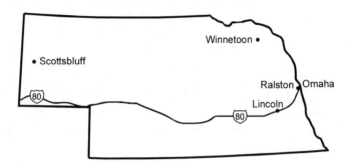

LINCOLN
www.lincoln.org/cvb is a Web site for the city.

Akin's Natural Foods Market
Meridian Park Shopping Center, 6900 "O" Street,
at 69th; 402-466-5713
Hours: Monday to Saturday 9 am to 9 pm
Sunday 12 noon to 6:30 pm
Natural Food Store. Organic produce.
Directions: From I-80, take exit #409 (Waverly/
East Lincoln), and then go west on Cornhusker
Hwy (Hwy 6) about 2¾ miles. At 84th go south
(turn left) and go about 4 miles, then at "O" Street
turn right. This place is then on right about a
mile down in Meridian Park Shopping Center.

Crane River Café
Eleventh and "P" Street; 402-476-7766
Hours: Monday to Saturday 11 am to 1 am
Sunday 12 noon to 11 pm
American. Not pure vegetarian.
Menu: Garbanzo Burger (very good), Tomato
Dill, Macaroni & Cheese, Eggplant Sandwich,
Veggie Melt, lots of salads, Veggie Burrito, Veggie
Chili and Red Beans & Rice. Brews own root beer.
Comments: The vegetarian dishes are marked on
the menu. Price: $$.
Directions: Just across the street from Embassy
Suites Hotel.

***Dining by Design
6941 Forest Lake Boulevard; 402-327-8880
Web site: www.diningbydesign.com
Hours: Sunday to Thursday 8 am to 9 pm
Fully Vegan On-line Delivery Service. Eclectic,
Chinese, Thai, International. Juice Bar and Salad
Bar. Fast food.
Menu: Has a large selection of mock meat dishes.

Has sugar-free and preservative free desserts.
Comments: Mostly uses organic produce. This
restaurant ships complete vegetarian meals coast-
to-coast, available via their web site. Will ship
next-day or 2-day air.
Other Info: Catering, take-out, delivery. Accepts
reservations but not necessary. Accepts AMEX,
DIS, MC, VISA. Price: $$.

Green Gateau Café & Patisserie
330 South 10th Street #110; 402-477-0330
Hours: Monday to Saturday 6:30 pm to 9 pm
Sunday 7:30 am to 3 pm
Restaurant. Not pure vegetarian
Menu: Portobello Mushroom Sandwich, some
veggie soups, homemade breads and Fiesta
Vegetables.
Comments: Candlelit at night.
Other Info: Accepts DC, DIS, MC, VISA. Price:
$$-$$$.
Directions: Parking arranged for customers.

**Maggie's
311 North 8th Street, Suite 101; 402-477-3959
Hours: Monday to Friday 8 am to 3 pm
Closed Saturday & Sunday.
Vegetarian Wraps and Café. Vegan friendly.
Menu: Daily soups and daily special such as veg-
gie chili or veggie Lasagna. Tofu and Tempeh
wrap. Three vegetarian and three vegan wraps.
Other Info: Counter service, take-out. Has some
tables.
Directions: Just north of Q and 8th Streets in
the Haymarket area.

Open Harvest
1618 South Street; 402-475-9069; **Web site:**
http://www.openharvest.com/

Hours: Daily 9 am to 9 pm
Natural Food Store and Deli. Bakery. Organic produce. Mainly Vegetarian (serves seafood). Vegan-friendly deli.
Menu: Has a good selection of vegetarian dishes. Whole-grain bakery.
Comments: It is a co-op that gives discounts to its members. Has limited seating.
Other Info: Counter service, take-out. Price: $.
Directions: At 17th and South, next to Blockbuster Video, a little north of Bryan Light Medical Center. From I-80, take I-180/Rte 34 E exit (#401B) on left towards 9th St (downtown). Keep right at fork in ramp and merge onto Rte 34 E and go 3.5 miles. Stay straight onto S 9th St and go 1.5 miles. At South St turn left and this place is a half-mile down.

The Oven

201 North 8th Street, Suite 117
402-475-6118
Hours: Monday to Thursday 11:30 am to 2 pm, 5:30 pm to 9:30 pm; Friday & Saturday 5:30 pm to 10:30 pm; Sunday 5:30 pm to 9:30 pm
North Indian. Vegan options. Not pure veg.
Menu: Has a wide selection of vegetarian dishes. Rice dishes, curry dishes, pakoras, samosas and more.
Comments: Pleasant place. A bit formal. Live music on Thursday and Sunday.
Other Info: Full service, take-out. Reservations suggested on weekends. Accepts AMEX, DC, DIS, MC, VISA. Price: $$.

Taj Mahal

5500 Old Cheney, Suite 4
402-420-1133
Indian. Not pure vegetarian.
Menu: Has a separate vegetarian menu with a large variety of dishes.
Comments: Generous portions. The mulligatawny contains chicken broth.

Thai Garden

245 North 13th Street
402-477-0811
Hours: Monday to Friday 11 am to 8:30 pm; Friday & Saturday 11 am to 9:30 pm; Sunday 12 noon to 8 pm
Thai. Not pure vegetarian.
Menu: Has over 25 vegetarian dishes. Soups have an authentic taste. Basil Tofu is really good. Good noodle dishes.
Other Info: Non-smoking. Reservations not necessary. Accepts AMEX, MC, VISA.

NORTH PLATTE

Happy Heart Specialty Foods

301 South Jeffers; 308-532-1505
Hours: Monday to Friday 9 am to 5:30 pm; Saturday 9 am to 5 pm; closed Sunday.
Natural Food Store. Organic produce.
Other Info: Accepts AMEX, MC, VISA.
Directions: From I-80, take North Platte US-83 exit (#177) towards McCook/North. Turn right onto Rte 83 and this place is 1.5 miles down. This place is at intersection of "C" and Jeffers.

Natural Nutrition House

203 West 6th Street; 308-532-9433
Hours: Monday to Saturday 9 am to 5:30 pm
Closed Sunday.
Natural Food Store. No produce.
Directions: From I-80, take Rte 83 (#177) exit north, at 5th St turn left, then at Vine turn right. This place is at corner of 6th and Vine, in a large white house.

OMAHA

Ahmad's

1006 Howard Street; 402 341-9616
Persian. Not Pure Vegetarian.

Broadmoor Market

8722 Pacific Avenue
402-391-0312
Hours: Monday to Friday 8 am to 7 pm; Saturday 8 am to 6 pm; Sunday 12 noon to 4 pm
Natural Food Store and Deli. Organic products and bulk foods.
Menu: Has a good selection of vegetarian dishes.
Other Info: Counter service, take-out. Has no seating. Accepts AMEX, DIS, MC, VISA.

Community National Foods Co-op

3928 Blondo Street; 402-431-8494
Hours: Monday to Friday 9:30 am to 8 pm; Saturday 10 am to 6 pm; Sunday 12 noon to 5 pm
Natural Food Store and Deli. Locally grown organic produce.
Menu: Most of the dishes are vegetarian. Hummus, Greek Salad, sandwiches, Angel Hair Pasta, sometimes has soups and other dishes.
Other Info: Counter service, take-out. Has seating.
Directions: From I-680, take Maple St (#4) exit. Go west on Maple St about half a mile, then at 108th go south (turn left). This place is one mile south at corner of Blondo and 108th.

Grainery Whole Food Market

7409 Main Street, at 74th, Ralston
402-593-7186
Hours: Monday to Friday 10 am to 6:30 pm; Saturday 10 am to 6 pm; Sun 1 pm to 4:30 pm
Vegetarian Lunch Hours: Monday to Saturday 11 am to 2 pm (usually serves lunch until closes)
Natural Food Stores and Café. Deli. Organic produce.
Comments: Has a good selection of vegetarian cookbooks. Has bulk items.
Other Info: Accepts AMEX, MC, VISA. Price: $-$$.
Directions: From I-89, take 72nd Street exit (#449), then go south on S 72nd St 1½ miles, then at Main St turn right and this place is a quarter-mile down.

Indian Oven

1010 Howard Street, downtown
402-342-4856
Hours: Monday to Thursday 11:30 am to 2 pm, 5:30 pm to 10 pm; Friday & Saturday 11:30 am to 2 pm, 5:30 pm to 10:30 pm; closed Sunday.
Indian. Not pure vegetarian.
Menu: Has a selection of vegetarian dishes. Tandoori dishes, pakoras, samosas, curry vegetables, rice dishes and Indian breads. Fresh juices.
Comments: Has a good selection of vegetarian dishes. Cooks Naans in their clay oven. Popular place.
Other Info: Full service, take-out. Accepts AMEX, DC, DIS, MC, VISA. Price: $$.
Directions: In the middle of Old Market.

Jane's Benson Health Market

6103 Maple Street, at North 61st
402-558-8911
Hours: Monday to Thursday 9 am to 7 pm; Friday 9 am to 6 pm; Saturday 9 am to 5 pm; Sunday 12 noon to 5 pm
Natural Food Stores and Deli. Juice Bar. Organic produce. Limited produce section.
Menu: Has ready-made dishes in the deli. Also has sandwiches.
Other Info: Counter service, take-out. Has seating. Accepts AMEX, DIS, MC, VISA.
Directions: From I-80, take I-680 N (#446) north and go about 6.5 miles, then take Rte 133 exit (#6) toward Irvington/Blair. At Blair High Rd turn right (becomes Military Ave) and go about 4 miles. At Maple St (Rte 64) turn left. This place is a half-block down at the corner of N 61st St and Maple.

McFoster's Natural Kind Café

302 South 38th Street (38th and Farnam)
402-345-7477
Hours: Monday to Thursday 11 am to 10 pm; Friday & Saturday 11 am to 11 pm; Sunday Brunch 10 am to 3 pm
Vegetarian friendly Natural Foods. Eclectic American. Juice Bar. Macrobiotic and Vegan options. Not pure vegetarian.
Menu: Excellent selection of vegetarian dishes. Tempeh Artichoke Mornay, falafel, soups, Grilled Eggplant and Avocado Sandwiches. Sunday Brunch has Scrambled Tofu and pancakes (most likely with eggs). Homemade Tofu Cheesecake and frozen Rice Dream Bars. Fresh juices, cappuccino, espresso.
Comments: A happening place. Has live jazz music. Live bands upstairs on weekends. Has outdoor patio dining. Acoustic music. Casual, friendly atmosphere. Freshly prepared food. Full bar.
Other Info: Full service, take-out. Reservations necessary for groups. Non-smoking. Accepts AMEX, DIS, MC, VISA. Price: $-$$.
Directions: From I-80, take I-480 N/US-75 (#452) exit toward Downtown/Epplyey Airfield via Kennedy Freeway. Merge onto US-75 N and go 1½ mile, then take Exit #2A towards Harney St/Dodge St. Go straight onto S 28th St, then at Farnam St turn left and go ¾ mile down and this place is at the junction of 38th and Farnam.

No Name Nutrition

14469 West Center Road	402-333-1300
2032 North 72nd Street	402-393-5812

Natural Food Store. Has a little produce.

Tamam

1009 Farnam Street
402-344-2722
Hours: Tuesday to Saturday 11 am to 9 pm; Sunday 5 pm to 9 pm; closed Monday.
Middle Eastern. Not pure vegetarian.
Menu: Has a good selection of vegetarian dishes.
Comments: Classic décor. Candlelit and white tablecloths. Good place for a special event. Seats 110. Friendly management.
Other Info: Full service, take-out. Accepts MC, VISA.

Thai Pepper

12775 Q Street
402-895-7788
Hours: Monday to Saturday 11 am to 9 pm

Closed Sunday
Thai. Not pure vegetarian.
Comments: Gets good recommendations.
Other Info: Full service, take-out. Reservations suggested for groups. Accepts MC, VISA. Price: $-$$
Directions: Parking arranged for customers.

Wild Oats Market
7801 Dodge Street, at 78th
402-397-5047
Hours: Monday to Saturday 8 am to 10 pm
Sunday 8 am to 9 pm
Natural Food Store and Cafe. Deli, Bakery, Salad Bar and Juice Bar. Organic produce. Supermarket-type place. See Wild Oats Market information. Has a good book section.
Directions: From I-80, take Exit #446 and get on I-680, stay left at fork in ramp and go 2 miles on I-680. Take Dodge Rd (Rte 6) exit (#3) towards Boys Town, keep right at fork in ramp and merge onto W Dodge Rd (becomes Dodge St/Rte 6) and this place is 2 miles down at Beverly Dr.

RALSTON

**Grainery Whole Foods Market & Restaurant
7409 Main Street; 402-593-7186
Hours: Monday to Friday 10 am to 6:30 pm;

Saturday 10 am to 6 pm; Sun 1 pm to 4:30 pm
Natural Food Store and Vegetarian Restaurant. Deli and Bakery.
Comments: Restaurant seats 25.
Directions: From I-80, take 72nd St (#449) exit and go south on 72nd St about a mile. At Main St (second light south of L St) turn right and this place on left a quarter-mile down.

SCOTTSBLUFF

Tamarak's Foods of the Earth
1914 Broadway
308-635-1514
Hours: Monday to Saturday 9 am to 5:30 pm (until 6 pm on Thursday)
Closed Sunday.
Natural Food Store and small Café.
Directions: From Rte 26, take 20th St west about a mile. At Broadway turn left. This place on right a half-block down.

WINNETOON

Winnetoon Mini mall Co-op
Main Street
402-847-3368
Hours: Monday to Thursday 8 am to 4 pm
Friday 8 am to 9 pm
Natural Food Store. No produce.
Directions: This place is in the center of town.

Nevada

1. Boulder City
2. Henderson
3. Las Vegas
4. Reno

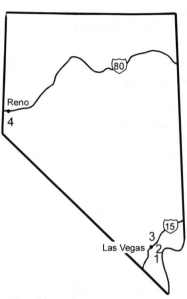

BOULDER CITY

Health Nuts
1311½ Nevada Highway; 702-293-1844
Hours: Monday to Friday 9:30 am to 6 pm; Saturday 10 am to 5 pm; closed Sunday.
Natural Food Store. No organic produce.

HENDERSON

Bangkok 9
633 North Stephanie Street, at Sunset
702-898-6881
Hours: Daily 11 am to 9 pm
Vietnamese and Chinese. Not pure vegetarian.
Menu: Has a good selection of vegetarian dishes.
Comments: Has outdoor dining.
Other Info: Full service, take-out, delivery. Accepts AMEX, MC, VISA. Price: $.

Café Sensations
4350 East Sunset Road, Suite 110; 702-456-7803
Hours: Monday to Friday 7 am to 4 pm; Saturday 8 am to 6 pm; closed Sunday. Longer hours in the summer.
Coffeehouse. Not pure vegetarian.
Menu: Homemade granola and fresh baked goods. Salads, Hummus Pita Sandwich, Vegetarian Sandwich (eggplant, cucumber, squash and pesto), smoothies and Raspberry Iced Tea.
Comments: Has indoor and outdoor dining. Area for kids to play. Has local artists' works on the walls. Friendly, helpful service.
Other Info: Accepts AMEX, DIS, MC, VISA.

Trader Joe's
2716 North Green Valley Pkwy
702-433-6773
Hours: Daily 9 am to 9 pm
Natural Food Store. Limited organic produce.
Directions: At Green Valley and Sunset Road.

Wild Oats Market
517 North Stephanie Street
702-458-9427
fax: 702-458-9431
Hours: Daily 7 am to 10 pm
Natural Food Store and Cafe. Deli, Bakery, Salad Bar and Juice Bar. Organic produce.

LAS VEGAS
Many of the hotels have inexpensive buffets with many vegetarian options.

Capriotti's Sandwich Shop
3981 East Sunset Road	702-898-4904
324 West Sahara Avenue	702-474-0229
7440 West Cheyenne Avenue, Suite 101	
702-648-336	
450 South Buffalo Drive, Suite 103	
702-838-8659	

Hours: Monday to Saturday 10 am to 7 pm
Closed Sunday.
Sandwich Shop. Not pure vegetarian. Price: $.
Menu: Has good sandwiches. Has a good selection of veggie meats. Veggie burgers and veggie hot dogs.
Warning: Usually cook the veggie burgers on the same grill as the meat burgers.

Gandhi India's Cuisine

4080 Paradise Road, Unit 9, at East Flamingo Road, East of Strip; 702-734-0094
Hours: Daily 11am to 2:30pm, 5pm to 10:30pm
Indian. Vegan-friendly. Not pure vegetarian. All-you-can-eat Lunch Buffet.
Menu: Has South Indian and North Indian cuisines. Basmati rice, pakoras, naan, Peas & Paneer, and more.
Comments: Friendly service. Nice décor. Food is good. Reasonably priced. Most likely the best Indian restaurant in Las Vegas. Some customers give this place bad reviews. Large place.
Other Info: Accepts AMEX, DC, DIS, MC, VISA. Price: $$.
Directions: Bus #108, #202. Located in a shopping center near the Strip.

Indian Oven

Enchant Village Shopping Center; 226 West Sahara Avenue, at Las Vegas Blvd; 702-366-0222
Hours: Daily 11:30am to 2:30pm, 5pm to 10pm
Indian. Not pure vegetarian.
Menu: Has a wide selection of vegetarian dishes. Curry dishes, rice, pakoras, eggplant dish, Vegetable Korma and much more.
Other Info: Accepts AMEX, DIS, MC, VISA. Price: $$.

Kokmol Restaurant

953 East Sahara Avenue, in the Commercial Center, Maryland Parkway/Paradise; 702-731-6542
Hours: Monday to Saturday 11 am to 10 pm
Sunday 12 noon to 10 pm
Thai. Vegan friendly. Not pure vegetarian.
Menu: Has a large selection of vegetarian dishes (over 70 dishes). Has tofu and seitan dishes.
Other Info: Full service, take-out. Reservations not necessary. Accepts AMEX, DIS, MC, VISA. Price: $-$$.

Mediterranean Café & Market

4147 South Maryland Parkway
702-731-6030; **fax:** 702-731-2220
Hours: Monday to Thursday 11 am to 9 pm; Friday & Saturday 11 am to 3 pm; Sunday 11 am to 5 pm
Mediterranean, Greek and Moroccan. Not pure vegetarian.
Menu: Falafel, hummus and others.
Comments: Is both a Mediterranean market and a restaurant. Exotic décor. Has a nice outdoor patio for dining.
Other Info: Accepts AMEX, MC, VISA. Price: $-$$.
Directions: Parking arranged for customers.

**Rainbow's End Natural Foods

1100 East Sahara Avenue; 702-737-7282
Store Hours: Monday to Saturday 9 am to 8 pm
Sunday 11 am to 6 pm
Restaurant Hours: 10 am to 4:30 pm
Natural Food Store and Vegetarian Deli. Good Salad Bar.
Menu: Soups, salads, sandwiches and desserts. Has wheat-less and eggless main dishes.
Comments: Helpful chef. Has 50 seats.
Directions: Six blocks east of the strip.

The Raw Truth Café

3620 East Flamingo Road, at Pecos
702-450-9007
Web site: www.rawfoodists.com/rawtruth/
Hours: Monday to Friday 9 am to 10 pm; Saturday 9 am to 9 pm; Sunday 12 noon to 6:30 pm
Kitchen closed an hour before closing time. Still has take-out dishes in the cooler.
Natural Food Store and Raw Food Cafe. Juice Bar. Mainly vegan. Gourmet. Organic dishes.
Menu: Has a good selection of vegetarian dishes. Raw organic dishes, pizzas, salads and desserts. Organic juices.
Comments: Healthy food. Casual. Usually quick service. Has a healing center and health oriented book store. Friendly place.
Other Info: Counter service, take-out. Accepts AMEX, DIS, MC, VISA.

Souper Salad

Albertson's Shopping Center; 4022 South Maryland Parkway, at Flamingo; 702-792-8555
2051 North Rainbow Boulevard
702-631-2604
Web site: www.soupersalad.com
Hours: Monday to Saturday 10:30 am to 9:30 pm; Sunday 11 am to 8:30 pm
Buffet Restaurant. Not pure vegetarian.
Menu: Has a large selection of salad items, baked potatoes, soups and more.
Other Info: Full service, take-out, catering. Accepts AMEX, DIS, MC, VISA. Price: $.

Stay Healthy!

840 South Rancho Drive #14
702-877-2494
Web site: www.lvstayhealthy.com
Hours: Monday to Friday 9 am to 7 pm; Saturday 9 am to 6 pm; closed Sunday.
Natural Food Store. Small store with a good selection.
Comments: Has aromatherapy products and incense. Friendly place. Has discount coupons on web site.

Sweet Tomatoes

2080 North Rainbow; 702-648-1957
Hours: Sunday to Thursday 11 am to 9 pm
Friday & Saturday 11 am to 10 pm
Buffet Restaurant. All-you-can-eat Buffet.
Menu: Wide selection of salad items, breads, soups, pastas, fresh fruits, pizzas and yogurt.
Comments: Has a good selection of vegetarian dishes. Health orientated food.
Other Info: Accepts AMEX, DIS, MC, VISA. Price: $.

Trader Joe's

2101 South Decatur Boulevard   702-367-0227
2716 Green Valley Parkway   702-433-6773
Food Store.

Viva Mercado's Mexican Restaurant

Raleys Shopping Center, 6182 West Flamingo Road, at Jones; 702-871-8826
Hours: Mon to Wed 11 am to 10 pm; Thur to Sat 11 am to 11 pm; Sun 11 am to 10 pm
Mexican. Not pure vegetarian.
Menu: Has a page of vegetarian dishes.
Comments: Happening place. Friendly, helpful service. Use Canola oil instead of lard for cooking. Food gets good ratings.
Other Info: Reservations suggested for groups. Accepts AMEX, DIS, MC, VISA. Price: $-$$.
Directions: Parking arranged for customers.

Wild Oats Market

7250 West Lake Mead Boulevard (Summerlin)
702-942-1500; **fax:** 702-458-9431
Hours: Daily 7 am to 10 pm
517 N Stephanie (Henderson)
702-942-1500, 702-434-8115
Directions: From I-15, take West Sahara exit and go 3½ miles and store on right.
Hours: Daily 7 am to 10 pm
Natural Food Store and Cafe. Deli, Bakery, Salad Bar and Juice Bar. Organic produce. Supermarket-type place. See Wild Oats Market information.
Menu: Has a large selection of vegetarian dishes. Boca Burgers, organic coffee and tea.

RENO

Many of the hotels have inexpensive buffets with many vegetarian options. Some of the better hotel buffets are at the Ascuaga's Nugget, Atlantis, and the Reno Hilton.

Deux Gros Nez

249 California Street
775-786-9400

Hours: Daily 7 am to 12 midnight
Mainly Vegetarian Natural Foods. Not pure vegetarian, but everything cooked is vegetarian. Vegan options.
Menu: Has a large selection of vegetarian dishes. Soups, salads, quiches, focaccias & rice and noodle dishes. Fresh juices, cappuccino, espresso.
Comments: On the second floor of a building. Has a large amount of cycling jerseys on the walls.
Other Info: Counter service, take-out. Accepts MC, VISA. Price: $-$$.

The Garden Restaurant

2999 South Virginia, at Brinkby Avenue
775-826-9711
Hours: Monday to Friday 9 am to 9 pm; Saturday 11 am to 8 pm; closed Sunday.
Restaurant. Vegan-friendly. Not pure vegetarian.
Menu: Veggie Burgers, Portobello Mushroom Sandwich, salads, veggie wraps and more dishes.
Other Info: Accepts AMEX, MC, VISA. Price: $$.

Pneumatic Diner

501 West 1st Street, at Ralston Street
775-786-8888 Ext 106
Hours: Monday to Friday 11 am to 11 pm; Saturday 9 am to 11 pm; Sunday 7 am to 11 pm
International Natural Foods. Mostly Vegetarian (90%). Mexican, Middle Eastern. Vegan options. Not pure vegetarian.
Menu: Has a wide selection of vegetarian dishes. Hummus, vegetarian soups, pastas, veggie burgers, fruit salads, salads with good dressing, hot dishes and much more. Fresh juices, cappuccino, espresso.
Comments: Small, friendly, happening place. Eclectic atmosphere. Good food and atmosphere.
Other Info: Full service, take-out. Non-smoking. Accepts DIS, MC, VISA. Price: $-$$.
Directions: Located upstairs in the Truckee River Lodging House. Couple blocks west of the downtown.

Wild Oats Market, at Meadowood

5695 South Virginia Street
775-829-8666
fax: 775-829-8114
Hours: Daily 7 am to 10 pm
Natural Food Store and Cafe. Deli, Bakery, Salad Bar and Juice Bar. Organic produce. Supermarket-type place. See Wild Oats Market information.
Directions: This place is next to Best Buy and across the street from the Meadowood Mall.

New Hampshire

1. Concord
2. Dover
3. Durahm
4. Exeter
5. Hampton Beach
6. Hanover
7. Keene
8. Lebanon
9. Manchester
10. Milford
11. Nashua
12. New London
13. New Market
14. Northwood
15. Peterborough
16. Plaistow
17. Portsmouth
18. Plymouth
19. Salem
20. Tilton
21. Wolfeboro

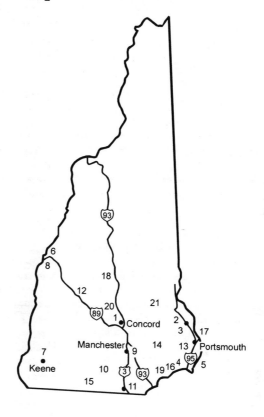

CONCORD

Bagel Works Inc.
42 North Main Street; 603-226-1827
Hours: Daily 6 am to 6 pm
Bagel Deli. Vegan options. Not pure vegetarian.
Menu: 16 varieties of bagels and vegetarian toppings available. Toppings include tofutti, cream cheeses, salad and hummus. Veggie burgers. Fresh juices.
Comments: Uses all natural ingredients with no preservatives.
Other Info: Counter service, take-out. Cash only; no credit cards. Price: $.

Concord Food Co-op
24½ South Main Street; 603-225-6840
Hours: Monday to Friday 9 am to 7 pm; Saturday 9 am to 6 pm; Sunday 11 am to 5 pm
Natural Food Store. Organic produce.

Menu: Has all vegetarian and vegan ready-made sandwiches and salads.
Comments: Has a good selection of macrobiotic products and frozen foods.
Directions: From I-93, take Exit #13 (Concord exit) and go north toward downtown on Rte 3A about 1¼ mile. This place is at the junctions of Pleasant St (Rte 202), behind Mailboxes Etc.

The Sandwich Depot
49 Hall Street; 603-228-3393
Hours: Monday to Friday 7:30 am to 7:30 pm; Saturday 8 am to 3 pm; closed Sunday.
Sandwich Place. Not pure vegetarian.
Menu: Has homemade veggie burgers (may have eggs in it, so may want to check it), Veggie Subs, burritos, salsa, brown rice, oatmeal and other vegetarian options.
Comments: Casual place.
Other Info: No credit cards; cash only.

Tea Garden Restaurant
184 North Main Street; 603-228-4420
Hours: Daily 11:30 am to 9:30 pm
Chinese. Not pure vegetarian.
Comments: Has vegetarian selections.
Other Info: Accepts AMEX, DC, MC, VISA.
Price: $-$$.

DOVER

**Dover Natural Food & Café
24 Chestnut Street; 603-749-9999
Hours: Monday to Saturday 9 am to 9 pm
Sunday 11 pm to 5 pm
Café Hours: 11:30 am to 2 pm
Natural Food Store and Vegetarian Café. Mostly
vegan. Deli, Bakery and Salad Bar. Organic produce.
Menu: Soups, salads, sandwiches and hot dishes.
Comments: On a riverside and it is a good area
to take a walk.
Other Info: Accepts AMEX, MC, VISA. Counter
service, take-out. Has seating.
Directions: Close to downtown Dover. From I-
95 get on Spaulding Turnpike (Rte 16) north
going toward Dover. Take exit #8A (Silver St) and
go on Rte 9 towards town (northeast), then at
Locust (second light) turn left and go a mile. After Police station, when road forks take left road,
which becomes Chestnut St. Go over bridge and
this place on right 4 blocks down.

DURAHM

The Bagelry
45 Mill Road Plaza; 603-868-1424
Hours: Monday to Friday 6 am to 7 pm
Saturday & Sunday 6 am to 6 pm
American. Not pure vegetarian. Vegan options.
Menu: A variety of bagels, sandwiches and sal-
ads.
Other Info: Counter service, take-out. Accepts
MC, VISA. Price: $.

Great Bay Food Cooperative
12 Pedibrook Lane
603-868-3166; Web site: http://www.unh.edu/
gbfc/coop/coopfaqs.htm#w
Hours: Monday & Wednesday 4 pm to 7 pm
Thursday to Saturday 11 am to 2 pm
Natural Food Store. Organic produce, often locally grown.
Comments: Student-run natural food store.

EXETER

The Blue Moon Market
8 Clifford Street; 603-778-6850
Hours: Monday to Friday 9 am to 6 pm; Saturday 9 am to 4 pm; Sunday 12 noon to 4 pm
Natural Food Store and Deli. Mainly vegetarian
(only serves tuna). Organic produce.
Menu: Four different soups, salads, wraps, sandwiches, bean and rice salads, tofu dishes and more.
Other Info: Counter service, take-out. Has seating. Accepts AMEX, MC, VISA.
Directions: From Rte 101, take Rte 108 exit towards Stratham/Portsmouth. Then go southwest
on Rte 108 (Portsmouth Ave) 1¼ mile. At light
go right onto High St and go three blocks. When
the road splits after going over the bridge, go left
onto Clifford and this place on left after 100 yards.

HAMPTON BEACH

Hampton Natural Foods
321 Lafayette Road (Route 1), Hampton Beach
603-926-5950
Hours: Monday to Saturday 9am to 6 pm
Sunday 12 noon to 4 pm
Natural Food Store. Good Soup and Salad Bar.
Organic produce.
Menu: One soup and salad items only. On Tuesday and Thursday makes ready-made sandwiches.
Other Info: Counter service, take-out. No seating. Accepts AMEX, DIS, MC, VISA.
Directions: From I-95, take Rte 101 for 2 miles
southeast, then take Rte 1 (Lafayette Rd) exit and
this place is right at the exit. This place in same
building as Hampton Cinemas.

HANOVER

Hanover Consumer Cooperative
45 South Park Street; 603-643-2667; email:
rosemary@coopfoodstore.com; Web site:
http://www.consumercoop.com
Hours: Daily 8 am to 8 pm
Natural Food Store and Deli.
Menu: Veggie Burger, Bean Salad, Tabbouleh,
Chickpea Salad, Baby Carrots, steamed vegetables
and more.
Other Info: Accepts AMEX, DIS, MC, VISA.
Directions: From I-89, take exit 18 (Hanover).
Take Rte 120 for 2 miles into Hanover. This place
is on right when you enter town. At S Park St
turn right and this place is a quarter-mile down.

KEENE

Bagel Works Inc.

120 Main Street   603-357-7751
30 Production Avenue   603-358-6360
Hours: Daily 6 am to 6 pm
Bagel Deli. Vegan options. Not pure vegetarian.
Menu: 16 varieties of bagels and vegetarian toppings available. Toppings include tofutti, cream cheeses, salad and hummus. Veggie burgers. Fresh juices.
Comments: Uses all natural ingredients with no preservatives.
Other Info: Counter service, take-out. No credit cards; cash only. Price: $.

Blueberry Fields Market

48 Emerald Street; 603-358-5207
Hours: Monday to Friday 9 am to 7 pm; Saturday 9 am to 6 pm; Sunday 11 am to 5 pm
Juice Bar Hours: 9 am to 2 pm
Natural Food Store and Juice Bar.
Menu: Sandwiches, salads and a daily soup. Fresh juices and smoothies.
Other Info: Accepts AMEX, DIS, MC, VISA.
Directions: From I-91, take Rte 9 north, then go east on Rte 12 (Rte 101) and go 2 miles. In Keene at Main St turn left (at third light). Go about 1 mile and at Emerald St turn left (opposite the Bagelry). This place on left a block down.

***Country Life Natural Foods Store and Restaurant

15 Roxbury Street; 603-357-3975
email: clkeene@tagnet.org
Web site: www.tagnet.org/clkeene/
Store Hours: Sunday to Thursday 9 am to 5 pm; Friday 9 am to 3 pm; closed Saturday.
Restaurant Hours: Monday to Friday Lunch 11:30 am to 2:30 pm; Sunday Brunch 10 am to 3 pm (first and third Sun only); closed Saturday.
Natural Food Store with Fully Vegan Café and Bakery. Salad Bar. Seventh Day Adventist place.
Menu: Many of the dishes change each day. Homemade mock meat dishes, Hawaiian BBQ, Sweet N' Sour "Chick" Meat, Sea Cakes, Chicken Enchiladas, Zucchini Corn, Green Beans Cauliflower, Potato Knish, chili, Cream of Spinach Soup, falafels, pizza, Wheat Meat Stroganoff, Tofu Spinach, Vegetable Crepes, Salisbury "Steaks", Stuffed Shells and Vegetable Pot Pie. Some dishes served during the Sunday Brunch are scrambled tofu, home fries, rice, fruit salad, French toast, waffles and more.
Comments: Small health food store, café and

vegan bakery. Casual, buffet style. Everything cooked on the premises. Makes own dressings and condiments. Reasonable prices. Homemade soups are the specialty of this place. Makes own mock "meats" from scratch. The food is sold by the pound, but during the Sunday brunch is all-you-can-eat. Casual, relaxing place. All natural, home cooking. Dressings and condiments are homemade. Reasonable prices. The dishes are made to order. Their menu is on their Web site. Local organic produce used when possible.
Other Info: Cafeteria, self serve buffet, take-out, catering, buffet. Non-smoking. Price: $$. Accepts personal cheques.
Directions: From Main street in Keene you go north to Center Circle, then take right road (Washington St), then a block down make a right at the light onto Roxbury St and then the store is about a half-block down.

Vitality Shop

116 Main Street; 603-357-3639
Hours: Mon to Thur 9 am to 6 pm; Fri 9 am to 7 pm; Sat 9 am to 5 pm; Sun 11 am to 4 pm
Natural Food Store. Small organic produce section.
Other Info: Accepts MC, VISA.
Directions: From I-91, take Rte 9 north, then go east on Rte 12 (Rte 101) for 2 miles. In Keene, at Main St turn left (at third light) and this place is a quarter-mile down on right.

LEBANON

Lebanon Co-op Foodstore

12 Centerra Parkway, Suite 75; 603-643-2667; email: rosemary@coopfoodstore.com
Web site: http://consumercoop.com
Hours: Daily 7 am to 9 pm
Natural Food Store and Cafe. Deli and Coffee Bar.
Menu: Has a good selection of vegetarian dishes.
Comments: Friendly place.
Directions: From I-89, take exit #18 (Hanover) and take Rte 120 (Lebanon St) northwest into Hanover. Go about two miles from I-89, then at Centerra Pkwy turn right and this place a block down on right in Centerra Marketplace.

Healthy Rhino

106 Main Street; 603-444-2177
Hours: Monday to Saturday 9 am to 6 pm (until 8 pm on Friday); Sunday 11 am to 5 pm
Natural Food Store.
Other Info: Accepts AMEX, MC, VISA.

Directions: From I-93, take Exit #11 (Hospital/ Littleton). At Cottage St go east. At Main (at first traffic light) turn left. This place is 2 blocks down on right in Parker's Marketplace.

MANCHESTER

A Market
125 Loring Street; 603-668-8445
Web site: www.amarketnaturalfoods.com
Hours: Monday to Saturday 9 am to 7 pm
Sunday 10 am to 6 pm
Natural Food Store. Organic produce. Salad Bar. Good variety of items.
Menu: Has an assortment of ready-made salads and sandwiches for take-out in their cooler.
Other Info: Accepts DIS, MC, VISA.
Directions: From I-293, take exit for Rte 101 (#3) and go east on Rte 101 two miles, then take Exit #1 and go north on Rte 28 (S Willow St) for one mile. At Loring turn left and this place on left a half-block down.

Bagel Works Inc.
581 Second Street; 603-647-6560
Hours: Monday to Friday 5:30 am to 5 pm
Saturday & Sunday 7 am to 4 pm
Bagel Deli. Not pure vegetarian. Vegan options.
Menu: 16 varieties of bagels and vegetarian toppings available. Toppings include tofutti, cream cheeses, salads and hummus. Veggie burgers. Uses all natural ingredients with no preservatives. Fresh juices.
Other Info: Counter service, take-out. Price: $.

Lakorn Thai
470 South Main Street; 603-626-4545
Hours: Monday to Thursday 11:30 am to 3 pm, 5 pm to 9 pm; Friday 11:30 am to 3 pm, 5 pm to 10 pm; Saturday 5 pm to 10 pm; Sunday 4 pm to 8:30 pm
Thai. Not pure vegetarian.
Menu: Can get most dishes without meat.
Comments: Reasonably priced.
Other Info: Accepts AMEX, DIS, MC, VISA.

MILFORD

Earthward
Route 101A; 603-673-4322
Hours: Monday to Saturday 9 am to 6 pm
Sunday 9 am to 5 pm
Natural Food Store. Organic produce. Efficient place.

Other Info: Accepts AMEX, MC, VISA.
Directions: This place is on Amherst St, near the middle of town.

NASHUA

Earth Energies
295 Daniel Webster Highway; 603-888-2900
Hours: Monday to Friday 10 am to 9 pm; Saturday 10 am to 7 pm; Sunday 12 noon to 6 pm
Natural Food Store. Books. Has therapeutic massages.
Other Info: Accepts MC, VISA.
Directions: From Rte 3, take Exit #1 and go east a quarter-mile to Middlesex Rd, turn left and this place is quarter-mile down, opposite the Pheasant Lane Mall.

Giant of Siam
5 East Hollis Street; 603-595-2222
Hours: Monday to Thursday 11:30 am to 3 pm, 5 pm to 9 pm; Friday 11:30 am to 3 pm, 5 pm to 10 pm; Saturday 5 pm to 10 pm; Sunday 4 pm to 8:30 pm
Thai. Not pure vegetarian.
Comments: Good atmosphere. Can add tofu to any of the dishes.
Other Info: Full service, take-out. Reservations suggested for groups. Accepts AMEX, DIS, MC, VISA. Price: $$.

Michael Timothy's
212 Main Street; 603-595-9334
Hours: Sunday to Thursday 11:30 am to 2 pm, 5:30 pm to 9 pm; Friday 11:30 am to 2 pm, 5:30 pm to 9:30 pm; Saturday 5 pm to 9:30 pm; Sunday Brunch 11:30 am to 2 pm
New American. Not pure vegetarian.
Menu: Has a daily vegetarian main dish and various vegetarian appetizers.
Comments: One of the best places in town. Friendly, pleasant, romantic atmosphere. Decently priced. Often uses local produce. Has some good views. European style décor. Flowers on tables and contemporary artwork. Live jazz Thursday to Sunday. Good place for a special event.
Other Info: Reservations suggested. Non-smoking. Accepts AMEX, MC, VISA. Price: $$$.

NEW LONDON

Flying Goose Brew Pub
Routes 11 & 14; 603-526-6899
Hours: Monday to Saturday 11:30 am to 9 pm

Sunday 12 noon to 9 pm
American. Not pure vegetarian.
Menu: The feta cheese, tomato, grilled eggplant, onions sprout sandwich on an onion roll is good. Salads. Garden Ravioli and Garden Quesadilla.
Comments: Has some vegetarian dishes.
Other Info: Accepts AMEX, DIS, MC, VISA.
Directions: From I-89 north, take exit #11. This place is about 5 minutes west on Route 11.

Fourteen Carrots Natural Foods Market

New London Shopping Center; 603-526-2323
Hours: Mon to Wed, Sat 9 am to 5:30 pm; Thur & Fri 9 am to 6 pm; Sun 11 am to 3 pm
Natural Food Store and Café. Bakery, Salad Bar and Juice Bar.
Directions: From I-89 north, take exit #11. At end of ramp turn right and go a mile up hill. At Main St turn left. Go a mile and bear left when road bends and this place on the left a few blocks down in New London Shopping Center. From I-89 south take exit #12 and turn left at end of ramp. Go a few miles into New London and this place on right behind a bank in New London Shopping Center.

Millstone Restaurant

Newport Road; 603-526-4201
Hours: Monday to Thursday 11:30 am to 2:30 pm, 5:30 pm to 8:30 pm; Friday & Saturday 11:30 am to 2:30 pm, 5:30 am to 8:30 pm; Sunday 11 am to 8 pm
American. Not pure vegetarian.
Menu: Has a selection of vegetarian main dishes. The Vegetarian Paella (grilled Portobello mushroom with basmati rice, vegetables and lentil) is good.
Other Info: Accepts AMEX, DIS, MC, VISA.
Price: $$.

NEW MARKET

***Corner Café

170 Main Street, New Market; 603-659-0433
Hours: Sunday to Thursday 11 am to 3 pm
Friday & Saturday 11 am to 9 pm
Vegan Natural Foods Café. Deli. No produce. See Susty's below.
Menu: Same menu as Susty's in Northwood as both places are owned by same person.
Directions: Take Rte 85 north (becomes Exeter St) into New Market. The store is on the main street in town, on the left at the blinking light.

NORTHWOOD

Susty's & Radical Vegan Foods

159 1st New Hampshire Turnpike
603-942-5862
Hours: Sunday to Thursday 11 am to 3 pm
Friday & Saturday 11 am to 9 pm
Vegan Restaurant. 98% Organic.
Menu: Has a wide selection of vegan dishes. Fried Tofu Sandwiches, salads, soups and hot dishes. Vegan cakes and cookies.
Comments: Sells their dishes to various shops in the area.
Other Info: Cash and personal checks; no credit cards.

PETERBOROUGH

Maggies Market Place

14 Main Street; 603-924-7671
Hours: Monday to Friday 8 am to 6 pm (until 7 pm on Thursday); Saturday 9 am to 5 pm; Sunday 11 am to 3 pm
Natural Food Store. Excellent organic produce section. Fresh baked goods. Good selection of items.
Directions: From Rte 101, go north on Grove St one mile. At Main St turn right. This place on right a block down just past Summer St.

PLAISTOW

Bread and Honey

Plaza 125 Shopping Center, 18 Plaistow Road
603-382-6432
Hours: Monday to Friday 9 am to 5:30 pm
Saturday 9 am to 5 pm; closed Sunday.
Natural Food Store.
Other Info: Accepts MC, VISA.
Directions: From Rte 495 going north, take exit #51B (still in Massachusetts), go northwest on Main St and go 1½ mile and at fork in the road, go right onto Plaistow Rd. This place is then about ¾ mile down on left.

PORTSMOUTH

Bagel Works Inc.

9-11 Congress Street; 603-431-4434
Hours: Daily 6 am to 5 pm
Bagel Deli. Not pure vegetarian. Vegan options.
Menu: 16 varieties of bagels and vegetarian toppings available. Toppings include tofutti, cream

cheeses, salad, and hummus. Veggie burgers. Fresh juices. Uses all natural ingredients with no preservatives.
Other Info: Counter service, take-out. Price: $.

Ceres Street Bakery
51 Penhallow Street
603-436-6518
Hours: Monday to Saturday 7 am to 5 pm
Closed Sunday.
Menu: Has a good selection of vegetarian dishes. Has some vegetarian soups, breads, salads, chili, vegan Lasagna, vegan pizza and vegetarian specials.
Comments: Good place. Serves breakfasts. Informal place. Also has frozen meal (that they make themselves) that can be brought home.

Portsmouth Health Food
151 Congress Street, Portsmouth
603-436-1722
Hours: Monday to Friday 9 am to 7 pm; Saturday 9 am to 4 pm; Sunday 12 noon to 4 pm
Natural Food Store. Organic produce. Medium size place.
Comments: Has a bulletin board with listings of local events. Has ready-made sandwiches and drinks.
Directions: From 1-95, take Market St exit (#7). From north take a left onto Market and from south turn right onto Market St. Go one mile to downtown. At blinking yellow light bear right. At Deer St (at stop sign) turn right and go 3 blocks, then at Maplewood Ave turn left and go 2 blocks. Go past light and turn left at parking lot. This place at corner of Maplewood Ave and Congress.

Portsmouth Farmer's Market
Saturday from 8 am to mid-afternoon.

Shalimar Restaurant
80 Hanover Street
603-427-2959
Hours: Monday to Saturday 11 am to 2:30 pm, 5 pm to 9:30 pm
Sunday 5 pm to 9:30 pm
Indian. Vegan options. Not pure vegetarian.
Other Info: Non-smoking. Accepts DIS, MC, VISA. Price: $$.

SALEM

Chao Praya River
322 South Broadway; 603-898-3222
Hours: Tuesday to Thursday 11:30 am to 3 pm, 5 pm to 9 pm; Friday to Saturday 11:30 am to 3 pm, 5 pm to 10 pm; Sunday 4:30 pm to 8:30 pm; closed Monday.
Thai. Vegan-friendly. Not pure vegetarian.
Menu: Has a selection of vegetarian dishes Will substitute tofu in any dish.
Other Info: Accepts AMEX, DIS, MC, VISA.

Natural Marketplace
419 South Broadway; 603-893-2893
Hours: Monday to Wednesday 10 am to 6 pm
Thursday & Friday 10 am to 8 pm
Saturday 10 am to 5:30 pm; closed Sunday.
Natural Food Store.
Other Info: Accepts DIS, MC, VISA.
Directions: From Rte 93, take exit #1 and go southeast on Kelly Rd 1½ miles, then take South Broad 1 mile and this place is on the left.

TILTON

Swan Lake Natural Foods
266 Main Street; 603-286-4405
Hours: Monday to Thursday 9 am to 6 pm
Friday 9 am to 8 pm
Saturday 9 am to 6 pm; closed Sunday.
Natural Food Store. Organic produce (comes in on Wednesday).
Comments: The person who runs this place is ready friendly and helpful.
Other Info: Accepts DIS, MC, VISA.
Directions: From 93, take exit #20 and go southwest on Rte 3 towards the downtown. This place is on left 1½ mile down.

WOLFEBORO

Evergrain
45 North Main Street; 603-569-4002
Hours: Monday to Saturday 9:30 am to 5:30 pm
Closed Sunday.
Natural Food Store. Organic produce (comes on Wed).
Directions: Going northwest on Rte 28 into town, this store is on left on the main street in town.

New Jersey

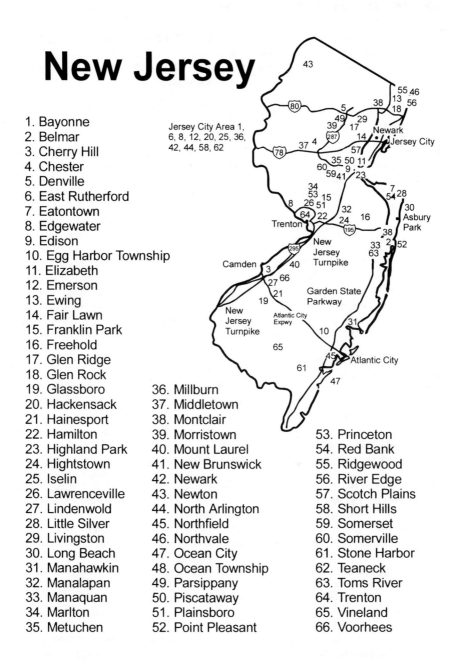

1. Bayonne
2. Belmar
3. Cherry Hill
4. Chester
5. Denville
6. East Rutherford
7. Eatontown
8. Edgewater
9. Edison
10. Egg Harbor Township
11. Elizabeth
12. Emerson
13. Ewing
14. Fair Lawn
15. Franklin Park
16. Freehold
17. Glen Ridge
18. Glen Rock
19. Glassboro
20. Hackensack
21. Hainesport
22. Hamilton
23. Highland Park
24. Hightstown
25. Iselin
26. Lawrenceville
27. Lindenwold
28. Little Silver
29. Livingston
30. Long Beach
31. Manahawkin
32. Manalapan
33. Manaquan
34. Marlton
35. Metuchen
36. Millburn
37. Middletown
38. Montclair
39. Morristown
40. Mount Laurel
41. New Brunswick
42. Newark
43. Newton
44. North Arlington
45. Northfield
46. Northvale
47. Ocean City
48. Ocean Township
49. Parsippany
50. Piscataway
51. Plainsboro
52. Point Pleasant
53. Princeton
54. Red Bank
55. Ridgewood
56. River Edge
57. Scotch Plains
58. Short Hills
59. Somerset
60. Somerville
61. Stone Harbor
62. Teaneck
63. Toms River
64. Trenton
65. Vineland
66. Voorhees

BAYONNE

John's Natural Foods

486 Broadway
201-858-0088
Hours: Monday, Thursday 9:30 am to 8 pm;
Tuesday, Wednesday, Friday, Saturday 9:30 am
to 6 pm; Sunday 10 am to 5 pm
Natural Food Store. Organic produce.
Directions: From NJ Turnpike, take exit #14A,
and go south on Avenue E for 1½ mile. At 22nd
turn right and go 2 blocks, then at Broadway turn
right and this place on right in middle of block.

BELMAR

Veggie Works

817 Belmar Plaza, Belmar; 732-280-1141
Web site: www.veggieworksworld.com
Hours: Tuesday to Friday 12:30 pm to 4 pm, 5
pm to 10 pm; Saturday 5 pm to 10 pm; Sunday
10 am to 1 pm, 5 pm to 9 pm; Sunday Brunch

10 am to 1 pm; closed Monday.

Mostly Vegetarian and Vegan. International, Italian, Mexican, American. All-you-eat Salad Bar. About 95% vegan. Serves tuna.

Menu: Has a large organic salad bar with over 100 dishes including vegan desserts. Has a vegan Sunday brunch that includes Tofu Eggs, French toast, pancakes, mock sausage and bacon, fresh fruits and waffles. Has a good selection of mock vegetarian meat dishes. All-you-can-eat salad bar is included with the meal for dinner. Home-made soups, a wide selection of sandwiches, Miso Soup, Gluten Diablo, Jamaican Jerk Tofu, stuffed grape leaves, Tempeh Parmigiana (soy cheese), Tempeh Steak, Shepherd's Pie, Chili, hummus, mashed potatoes with very good brown vegan tofu gravy, Grilled Portobello Mushroom, falafels, Tofu Tacos, Garlic Sesame Tofu, Buffalo Wings, Veggie "Meat" Loaf and tahini dressings. Singing Cowboy is a fried gluten steak with cornbread, mashed potatoes and vegan gravy. Hungarian-style Pierogis is sautéed strips of seitan in vegan gravy. Thanksgiving dinner with tofu turkey, mashed potatoes, stuffing, Tofu Lasagna, yams and vegan gravy. Good vegan desserts such as Tofu Cheesecake. Fresh juices and smoothies.

Comments: Gets really high recommendations. Mostly organic. Live music (a guitarist) on Friday and Saturday nights. Complimentary salad bar with any entrée. Pleasant atmosphere. Reasonably priced. The Web site has the entire menu. The Sunday brunch is really good. Definitely worth checking this place out.

Reviews: Veggie Works Vegetarian Restaurant was nominated for the 1996 Vegetarian Times Reader's Choice Award. "Acknowledged by Vegetarian Times Magazine as one of the best restaurants of its kind in the Nation."

The New York Times Restaurant Critic Joe Brescia says about Veggie Works, "Vegetables work their magic on a meat lover. A dieter's or vegetarian's delight. The food was delicious. Veggie Works homemade wheat bread served with each meal, is delicious."

"This isn't your ordinary Shore restaurant. The best kept secret in Monmouth County!"
Asbury Park Press

Other Info: Full service, take-out. Non-smoking. Accepts AMEX, DIS, MC, VISA. Price: $$.

Directions: From Garden State Parkway, take Exit #98. Take Rte 138 east for 5 miles into Belmar (bearing left in town), then turn right at the traffic light after the 7-11, Go to Main Street and make a left and this place is on the left in a plaza set back from the road (hard to see from road) with the Acme Supermarket.

CHERRY HILL

***Evergreen Gourmet Vegetarian Cuisine
Clover Shopping Center
2087 East Marlton Pike (Route 70)
856-751-8599
Hours: Tuesday to Thursday 11:30 am to 9:30 pm; Friday 11:30 am; 10:30 pm; Saturday 12 noon to 10:30 pm; Sunday 3 pm to 8:30 pm; Lunch Special until 3 pm; closed Monday.
Fully Vegan Chinese. Mexican, Middle Eastern, Italian and some American.
Menu: Has a large selection of vegetarian dishes. Mostly Chinese meat-substitute vegan dishes, with a few Mexican, Italian and Middle Eastern choices. Steamed dumplings, Spring Rolls, Hummus and Pita Bread, veggie burgers, Veggie Duck, Veggie Chicken Nuggets, Cold Noodles with Sesame Sauce, salads, soups, Mongolian Beef, Crispy Stuffed Tofu, Steamed Japanese Eggplant, Crispy Sliced Fish, Tempeh Delight, Seitan Savory, Pan Fried Noodles, Ravioli Primavera, Curry Chicken, falafel and much more. Vegan Cheeseless Cheese Cake and Chocolate Mousse.
Comments: On Friday nights there is a live pianist. Quiet atmosphere, peaceful music. Gets good ratings. Has good size portions. Got some good reviews in newspapers and magazines. On Friday and Saturday there is Karaoke from 8 pm until closing.
Other Info: Full service, take-out. Non-smoking. Reservations recommended. Accepts AMEX, DIS, MC, VISA and Personal Cheques.
Directions: From I-295 North, take exit #34A, then go east on Route 70 for a few miles and this place is on the right in the Clover Shopping Center. This place is 1 mile west of where Rte 70 and Rte 73 meet. From New Jersey Tpke take Exit #4, then go east on Rte 73 for 2 miles, then at Rte 70 turn right and go 1 mile and this place is in a small shopping center on the left.

**Singapore Kosher Vegetarian Rest.
The Centrum Shoppes, 219-H Berlin Road
609-795-0188
Hours: Monday to Thursday 11:30 am to 10 pm; Friday & Saturday 11:30 am to 10:30 pm; Sunday 11:30 am to 9:30 pm
Fully Vegetarian Southeast Asian. Mostly Vegan. Malaysia, China, Singapore and India. Certified Kosher. Buddhist.
Menu: General Tsao's Chicken, Vegetable Lo Mein, Golden Shrimp, Golden Lion's Head (blend of broccoli and mock meat noodles), Sesame Herbal Duck, Shrimp with Szechuan

Sauce, Orange Beef, Vegetarian Roast Duck, Seafood Combo, Hot & Sour Soup and Veggie Fried Rice with bits of vegetarian "pork." "Lovely Couple in Taro Nest" is vegetables and mock pork & chicken (made with seitan) served in a "bird's nest" made from taro root.
Comments: Peaceful and romantic atmosphere. Plays classical Chinese music. Karaoke room. Ambiance and service is first class. Reasonably priced. Has main branch at 1006 Race Street in Philadelphia.
Other Info: Full service, take-out. Non-smoking. Reservations are recommended. Accepts AMEX, DIS, MC, VISA. Price: $$.
Directions: From I-295, take exit #32 and then go northwest and this place is 1 mile down on Berlin Rd 1. From Hwy 70 (coming east from Philly), turn right onto Grove St and go 2½ miles, when the road forks take the right road onto Berlin Rd and this place is a half-mile down.

CHESTER

Health Shoppe
Chester Spring Shopping Center
Route 206, Chester; 908-879-7555
Hours: Monday to Friday 9 am to 9 pm; Saturday 9 am to 6 pm; Sunday 9 am to 6 pm
Natural Food Store and Deli. Juice Bar, Bakery and Salad Bar. Some vegan dishes. Good selection of organic produce and other items.
Menu: Has good selection of sandwiches, hot dishes and a good salad bar. Fresh juices.
Other Info: Accepts MC, VISA, DC. Price: $.
Directions: North side of Route 206 in Chester Springs Shopping Center.

DENVILLE

Café Metro
60 Diamond Spring Road
973-625-1055; **Web site:** www.thecafemetro.com
Hours: Monday 11:30 am to 3 pm, 5 pm to 9 pm; Tuesday to Friday 11:30 am to 3 pm, 5 pm to 10 pm; Sat 5 pm to 10 pm; Sun 4 pm to 9 pm
International. Not pure vegetarian. Vegan options.
Menu: Soups, salads, sandwiches, Garden Burger, Hummus Veggie Wrap, Veggie Sandwich (zucchini, sautéed mushrooms, tomato), Vegetable Stir-fry with tofu, Steamed or Stir-fried Organic Vegetables, pastas, pizzas and desserts.
Comments: Casual place.
Other Info: Reservations requested for parties of 5. Non-smoking. Accepts AMEX, MC, VISA.
Directions: From I-80, take Denville exit (#37),

get on Rte 46 east and go a quarter-mile. Make a left and then a quick right onto Broadway and go 1 block, then at Diamond Spring Rd take a slight right and this place is 2 blocks down. You can also get to Denville from Rte 46.

Mrs Erb's Good Food
20 First Avenue
973-627-5440
Hours: Monday to Friday 9 am to 8 pm; Saturday 9 am to 7 pm; Sunday 10 am to 5 pm
Natural Food Store and Deli. Bakery and Juice Bar. Vegan-friendly. Has a nutritionist. Organic produce.
Menu: Soups, sandwiches, salads, tempeh and tofu dishes and pastas.
Other Info: Accepts AMEX, MC, VISA. Counter service, take-out. Has seating.
Directions: From I-80, take Denville exit (#37), get on Rte 46 east and go a quarter-mile. Make a left and a quick right onto Broadway. Make first left onto First Ave and store is on the right.

EAST RUTHERFORD

Park and Orchard Restaurant
240 Hackensack Street
201-939-9292; **fax:** 201-939-1743
Hours: Monday to Friday 12 noon to 10 pm Saturday & Sunday 2 pm to 9 pm
Eclectic American and International. Good vegetarian menu. Not pure vegetarian.
Menu: Has a large vegetarian gourmet menu. Fresh juices.
Comments: Upscale. Mainly meats dishes, but has good stir-fries. Voted best restaurant in north Jersey by readers of the New Jersey Magazine. Gets high recommendations. Has a fireplace.
Other Info: Full service, take-out. No reservations. Accepts AMEX, DC, DIS, MC, VISA. Price: $$-$$$.
Directions: From Rte 17, exit onto Paterson Ave and go west on Paterson a half-mile and then at Hackensack St turn left and this place is ¾ mile down.

Third Day Fresh Food Market
220 Park Avenue, East Rutherford
201-935-4045
Hours: Wednesday to Friday 10 am to 8 pm; Monday, Tuesday and Saturday 10 am to 6 pm; closed Sunday.
Natural Food Store and take-out Deli. Juice Bar, Salad Bar and Bakery. Organic produce. Macrobiotic foods.
Menu: The hot dish menu changes daily. Salads,

sandwiches, soups, stew of day, rice dishes, bean dishes, brown basmati rice, tomato rice, lentil soups, vegetable dishes and more.
Other Info: Counter service, take-out.
Directions: From NJ Turnpike, take Exit 16W and then go west on Rte 3. Get off at Ridge Rd and go northeast for 1 mile, then turn right onto Park Ave and this place is a half-mile down on the right. Drive through Rutherford and go around the traffic circle, past the railway tracks and this place is 1½ mile from Rte 3.

EATONTOWN

Tokyo Japanese Restaurant
26 State Route 35; 732-389-1673
Hours: Monday to Thursday 11 am to 2:30 pm, 5 pm to 10 pm; Friday & Saturday 11 am to 2:30 pm, 5 pm to 11 pm; Sunday 4 pm to 10 pm
Japanese. Vegan options. Not pure vegetarian.
Menu: Has a good variety of veggie sushi and Avocado Rolls.
Other Info: Full service, take-out. Accepts AMEX, DC, DIS, MC, VISA. Price: $$-$$$.

EDGEWATER

Whole Foods Market
905 River Road; 201-941-4000
Hours: Daily 8 am to 9 pm
Natural Food Store and Cafe. Deli, Bakery, Salad Bar and Juice Bar. Organic produce. Supermarket-type place. See Whole Foods Market information.
Directions: This place is about a mile west of the Hudson River and 2½ miles north of the Lincoln Tunnel. From NJ Turnpike take Lincoln Tunnel side, then take the Rte 3 exit (#16E) towards Lincoln Tunnel and merge onto I-495 E and go a third-mile, then take Kennedy Blvd exit (get on Rte 1/9 going north). At Columbia Ave turn right and go 1 block, at Paterson Plank Rd turn right and go 1 block, at 29th St turn left and go 1 block, then at Tonnelle Ave (US 1/9) turn right and go 2½ miles, at 79th St turn right and go 1 mile east, (enter circle and take 2nd exit), then turn left and go a third-mile north on JFK Blvd E, then turn right onto Bulls Ferry Rd and go a quarter-mile, then take a slight left onto River Rd and this place is right there.

EDISON

**Rangoli
825 Route 1, in a strip mall
732-855-1177; fax: 732-283-9350
Hours: Daily 11:30 am to 10:30 pm

Vegetarian Indian.
Comments: Friendly place. Pleasant atmosphere. Good food at a reasonable price.
Other Info: Accepts AMEX, DIS, MC, VISA. Price: $$.
Directions: From NJ Turnpike, take Rte 18 exit (#9) towards New Brunswick (Rte 1), keep right at fork in ramp and merge onto Rte 18 going north toward New Brunswick and go a quarter-mile, then go north on Rte 1 towards Newark, and this place is 3 miles down on Rte 1.

EGG HARBOR TOWNSHIP

Banterra Market
3112 Fire Road; 609-484-1550
Hours: Monday to Friday 9 am to 7:30 pm; Saturday 9 am to 5 pm; Sunday 11 am to 4 pm
Natural Food Store and take-out Deli. Bakery. Large selection of organic produce. Supermarket-size place.
Other Info: Counter service, take-out. Accepts AMEX, DC, DIS, MC, VISA.
Directions: From Garden State Pkwy, take exit #36 (Road 563) towards Northfield/Margate and go southeast on Tilton Rd a quarter-mile, then at Fire Rd turn right and this place is a quarter-mile down.

ELIZABETH

Jerusalem Restaurant
150 Elmora Avenue; 908-289-0291
Hours: Sunday to Thursday 11 am to 8:30 pm Friday 11 am to 2:30 pm; Sat 6 pm to 9 pm
Kosher Middle Eastern. Vegan options. Not pure vegetarian.
Menu: Middle Eastern food, pizzas, salads, sandwiches and other dishes.
Other Info: Limited service, take-out, catering. Accepts AMEX, MC, VISA. Price: $.

EMERSON

Old Hook Farm
650 Old Hook Road (Route 502); 201-265-4835
Hours: Tuesday to Saturday 9 am to 5 pm; Sunday 9 am to 4 pm; closed Monday.
Natural Food Store and Farm. Organic produce.
Directions: From Garden State Parkway, take exit #168 towards Westwood/Washington and get on Washington Ave going east (Rte 502) (turn right if going north on GSP) for 2 miles, then take a slight right onto Broadway (Rte 502) and after a quarter-mile the road becomes Old Hook Rd (Rte 502) and this place is 2 miles down.

EWING (north of Trenton)

Big Bear Natural Foods
1870 Olden Avenue, Ewing
609-771-4002
Hours: Monday to Friday 9 am to 6 pm; Saturday 9 am to 5 pm; Sunday 12 noon to 4 pm
Natural Food Store.
Directions: From I-295, take Arena Drive West exit (#61B) towards Olden Ave, go northwest on Arena Dr and go a quarter-mile, at Reeves Ave turn right and go a third-mile, at Olden Ave turn right and this place is a quarter-mile down just past I-295.

Simply Natural
1505 Parkway Avenue, Ewing
609-406-0818
Hours: Monday to Friday 10 am to 7 pm; Saturday 9 am to 5 pm; closed Sunday.
Natural Food Store.
Comments: Vegetarian frozen goods and herbal teas.
Directions: This place is just south of the airport. From I-95, take exit #2 and go southeast on Bear Tavern Rd for 1 mile, then turn right at Parkway Ave (W Upper Ferry Rd) and this place is a half-mile down.

FAIR LAWN

Back to Nature
22-18 Broadway; 201-791-8122
Hours: Sunday to Friday 11 am to 5:30 pm
Saturday 10 am to 4 pm
Natural Food Store.
Directions: From Garden State Parkway, take US-46 exit (#156) towards Rte 20/River Drive, then take an immediately slight left onto Rte 20 (River Dr) and go north 1¾ mile, then take a slight left onto the ramp towards Rte 4 E and merge onto Broadway going east and this place is 1 mile down. Can also from I-80, take exit #61 and go north on Rte 20 (River Dr) a mile then same as above. This place is a mile west of GSP Exit #160.

FRANKLIN PARK

**Udipi Café
3029 Route 27 S; 732-422-8301
Hours: Daily 11 am to 10 pm
Vegetarian South Indian.
Menu: Has a good selection of vegetarian dishes.
Other Info: Counter service, take-out, catering. Non-smoking. Accepts reservations but not necessary. Accepts AMEX, DIS, MC, VISA.

Directions: From Rte 1, go west on Henderson Rd for 1¼ mile, then turn right at Lincoln Hwy (1st light) and this place is ¾ mile down inside Dunkin Donuts complex on right.

FREEHOLD

Pauline's Health Foods
3585 Route 9 North, Freehold
732-303-0854
Hours: Monday to Friday 9:30 am to 8 pm; Saturday 9:30 am to 6 pm; Sun 11:30 am to 5 pm
Natural Food Store.
Directions: From NJ Turnpike, take Exit #8 towards Hightstown/Freehold and go east on Rte 33 (Franklin St, keep right at fork in ramp) for 9 miles, then go north on Rte 9 and this store is about 1 mile north, near the railway tracks.

GLEN RIDGE

Purple Dragon Co-op
289 Washington Street, Glen Ridge; 973-429-0391; email: membership@purpledragon.com
Web site: www.purpledragon.com
Hours: 9 am to 8 pm
Organic produce Co-op Delivery Service. Delivered in New York and north New Jersey area. FedExs local produce nationally.

GLEN ROCK

Better Health
912 Prospect Street; 201-445-5853
Hours: Monday to Friday 10 am to 8 pm; Saturday 10 am to 6 pm; Sunday 11 am to 4 pm
Natural Food Store. The owner is a knowledgeable person.
Directions: From Garden State Pkwy, take Exit #160 towards Rte 208/Hackensack/Fair Lawn and get on S Paramus Rd going northwest a third-mile, then take Rte 4 W ramp towards Rte 208/Paterson and go a quarter-mile west on Rte 4, then take Saddle River Rd ramp (keep right at fork in ramp) and go 2 miles north on Saddle River Rd, then at Prospect St turn slight right and this place is right there.

GLASSBORO (Gloucester County)

Don's Bagels
Doubletree Shopping Center, 800 North Delsea Drive; 856-582-4455
Hours: Monday to Friday 6:30 am to 3 pm
Saturday & Sunday 6:30 am to 2 pm
Bagel Place. Has veggie burgers.

HACKENSACK

Aywards Natural Food Center
342 Main Street; 201-342-1932
Natural Food Store.

HAINESPORT

Hainsport Health Haven
Route 38, at Lumberton Road; 609-267-7744
Hours: Monday to Saturday 10 am to 6 pm
Sunday 10 am to 5 pm
Natural Food Store with Hot Bar and Salad Bar.
Menu: Many vegetarian dishes including rice
dishes, Garden Burger and salads.
Other Info: Limited service, take-out. Accepts
MC, VISA. Price: $.

HAMILTON

Black Forest
1001 Route 33
609 586-6187
Hours: Monday to Friday 9:30 am to 7:30 pm;
Saturday 9:30 am to 6 pm; Sunday 11 am to 4
pm; Deli closed Sunday; Hot food out until
around 2:30 pm.
Natural Food Store and Deli. Organic produce.
Menu: Has a good selection of vegetarian dishes.
Soups, veggie chili, sandwiches and salads. Hot
food until 2:30 pm.
Other Info: Counter service, take-out. Seating.

**Golden Teapot
1750 Whitehorse Mercerville Rd
609-890-4881
Hours: Monday to Thursday 11 am to 9:30 pm;
Friday & Saturday 11 am to 10:30 pm; Sunday
12 noon to 9 pm
Vegetarian Asian. Specializes in Vegan dishes.
Menu: Has a wide selection of vegetarian and
mock "meat" dishes.
Other Info: Accepts AMEX, DIS, MC, VISA.
Price: $$.

HIGHLAND PARK

**Jerusalem Restaurant & Kosher Pizza
231 Raritan Avenue; 732-249-0070
Hours: Monday to Thursday 11 am to 9 pm;
Friday 11 am to 2 pm; Saturday 7:30 am to 9
pm; Sunday 11 am to 9 pm
Vegetarian Pizza and Middle Eastern. Kosher.
Not pure vegetarian.
Menu: Has good salads, falafel and sandwiches.
Comments: Casual, relaxed place.

HIGHTSTOWN

Black Forest II
549 US Highway 130; 609-448-4885
Hours: Monday to Friday 9:30 am to 7:30 pm;
Saturday 9 am to 6 pm; Sunday 12 noon to 4 pm
Natural Food Store. Organic produce.
Menu: Ready-made sandwiches, salads and hot
dishes.
Directions: From I-295, get on I-195 going east
(Exit #60) and go 4½ miles, then take US 130
exit (#5B) towards New Brunswick and go north
on US 130, then this place is 6½ miles down.
From New Jersey Turnpike, take exit #8 and go
west on Franklin St ¾ miles, then turn left onto
Main St and go 1 block, then turn right at Stock-
ton Ave and go 1 mile, then turn left and go south
on US 130 and this place is ¾ mile down.

ISELIN

Udupi Indian
1380 Oak Tree Road, Iselin
732-283-0303
Hours: Sunday to Thursday 11:30 am to 3:30
pm, 5 pm to 10 pm; Fri & Sat 12 noon to 10 pm
South Indian. Not pure vegetarian.
Menu: Has a large selection of vegetarian Indian
dishes. North and South Indian dishes in good
buffet. Dosa, Idly, uthappam and rice dishes.
Other Info: Full service, take-out. Accepts DIS,
MC, VISA. Price: $-$$.

LAWRENCEVILLE

Palace of Asia
400 Mercer Mall; 609-987-0606
Hours: Daily 11:30 am to 10 pm
Indian. Vegan options. Not pure vegetarian.
Menu: Good selection of vegetarian dishes in-
cluding samosas, curried vegetables, Vegetable
Biryani, pakoras, rice dishes and other Indian
dishes. Fresh juices.
Other Info: Full service, take-out. Accepts
AMEX, DC, DIS, MC, VISA. Price: $$.

Simply Radishing
Lawrenceville Shopping Center
2495 Brunswick Pike (Route 1); 609-882-3760
Hours: Daily 11:30 am to 3 pm, 5 pm to 9 pm
Fresh Food Restaurant and Juice Bar.
Menu: Has a good selection of vegetarian dishes.
Soups, pastas, veggie burger, Bean Veggie Burger
and more. Dishes are cooked fresh, so most things
can be made vegetarian.
Other Info: Accepts AMEX, MC, VISA.

LINDENWOLD

Natural Health

Blackwood-Clementon & Laurel Roads
856-784-1021
Hours: Monday 9 am to 8 pm; Saturday 10 am
to 5 pm; Sunday 12 noon to 5 pm
Natural Food Store.
Directions: From NJ Turnpike, take exit #3 (Rte
168, Black Horse Pike) and go south. At Rte 42
turn right towards Atlantic City. Take Clementon
exit and on Clementon turn right. This place on
right three miles down.

LITTLE SILVER

Healthfair

625 Branch Avenue; 732-747-3140
Hours: Monday to Friday 9 am to 8 pm; Saturday 9 am to 6 pm; Sunday 10 am to 5 pm
Hot Bar and Salad Bar closed on Sunday
Natural Food Store and Salad Bar & Hot Bar.
Juice Bar. Vegan and Macrobiotic options.
Menu: Salads, sandwiches, soups, vegan desserts
and many other dishes. Fresh baked breads and
bagels. Fresh juices.
Other Info: Limited service, take-out. Accepts
AMEX, MC, VISA. Price: $$.
Directions: From Garden State Parkway, take
Redbank/Newman Springs Rd exit (#109). Get
on Rte 520 (Rte 50) going east (becomes Newman
Springs Rd) for 1 mile, at Broad St (Rte 35) turn
right and go 2 blocks, at White Rd turn left and
go 1 mile, then at Branch turn right (go south)
and this place on right 1 mile down. Basically
from Exit #109 go east for 2 miles and then south
on Branch.

LONG BEACH

Jessie's Café

West End, just south of Long Beach
139 Brighton Avenue; 732-229-6999
Hours: Monday to Friday 9:30 am to 5:30 pm;
Saturday 9:30 am to 5 pm; Sun 11 am to 4 pm
Vegetarian-friendly Café. Not pure vegetarian.
Menu: Vegan soups, Tofu Burgers, veggie burgers, veggie chili, pastas, salads, vegetables dishes
and more.
Other Info: Cash only; no credit cards.

MANAHAWKIN

Earth Goods Natural Food Market

777 East Bay Avenue
609-597-7744

Hours: Monday to Friday 10 am to 7 pm; Saturday 10 am to 6 pm; Sunday 11 am to 4 pm
Natural Food Store. Organic produce.
Comments: Has a good selection of vegetarian
dishes. Makes fresh juices daily.
Directions: From Garden State Parkway, take
Manahawkin exit (#63), then go east on Rte 72
for 1¼ mile. When Rte 72 reaches Rte 9, take
Bay Ave to the left and this place on right after
1¼ mile.

MANALAPAN

Pauline's Health Foods

299 Route 9 South; 732-308-0449
Hours: Monday to Friday 9:30 am to 8:30 pm;
Saturday 9:30 am to 6 pm; Sun 11 am to 5 pm
Natural Food Store. Organic produce.
Directions: From Garden State Parkway, take exit
#123 (Sayreville) and get on Rte 9 going south.
This place is then on Rte 9 about 11 miles down.

MANAQUAN

Monmouth Health Foods

181 Main Street
732-223-4900
Hours: Monday to Saturday 9 am to 6 pm (until
8 pm Friday); Sunday 11 am to 5 pm
Natural Food Store.
Menu: Has some ready-made sandwiches.
Directions: On the main street in town.

MARLTON

Fresh Fields Whole Foods Market

940 Route 73N
856-797-1115
Hours: Monday to Saturday 8 am to 10 pm
Sunday 9 am to 9 pm
Natural Food Store and Cafe. Deli, Bakery,
Salad Bar and Juice Bar. Organic produce. Supermarket-type place. See Whole Foods Market
information.
Directions: From New Jersey Turnpike, take exit
#4 and go southeast on Rte 73 and this place is
1½ mile down on the left in a small shopping
center. From I-295, take exit #36A and then go
southeast on Rte 73 for 2 miles.

Good Nature Health Food Store

952 State Highway 34
732-583-3800
Hours: Monday to Friday 10 am to 6 pm
Saturday 9:30 am to 5 pm
Natural Food Store.

Mexican Food Factory
State Highway 70 and Cropwell Road
856-983-9222
Hours: Sunday to Thursday 11:30 am to 10 pm
Friday & Saturday 11:30 am to 11 pm
Mexican. Vegan options. Not pure vegetarian.
Menu: There is no lard in the refried beans.
Comments: Has outdoor dinning on the patio.
Other Info: Full service, take-out. Accepts
AMEX, MC, VISA. Price: $$

Zagara's
501 Route 73 S; 856-983-5700
Hours: Monday to Friday 9 am to 8 pm; Saturday 8 am to 8 pm; Sunday 8 am to 7 pm
Natural Food Store and Deli. Hot Bar. Vegan options.
Menu: Much of the menu changes daily. Some dishes served are Rice Tempeh, sandwiches, Seitan & Broccoli, soups and salads. Fresh juices and smoothies.
Other Info: Counter service, take-out, catering. Accepts AMEX, MC, VISA. Price: $$.
Directions: From New Jersey Turnpike, take Exit #4 and go southeast on Rte 73 and this place is 3½ miles down. From I-295, take exit #36A and then go southeast on Rte 73 for 4 miles.

METUCHEN

Radhana's Thai Kitchen
10 Pearl Street; 732-548-9747
Hours: Tuesday to Friday 11:30 am to 2 pm, 5:30 pm to 9 pm; Saturday 5:30 pm to 10 pm, Sunday 5:30 pm to 9 pm; closed Monday.
Thai. Vegan options. Not pure vegetarian.
Menu: Has a separate vegetarian menu. Soups, salads, appetizers, Gluten Curry, Tofu Coconut Milk Soups, Thai Tempura and other dishes.
Comments: Friendly, reasonably priced place.
Other Info: Full service, take-out. Accepts MC, VISA. Price: $-$$.

MILLBURN

Fresh Fields Whole Foods Market
187 Millburn Ave; 973-376-4668
Web site: www.wholefoodsmarket.com
Hours: Monday to Saturday 7:30 am to 9 pm
Sunday 7:30 am to 8 pm
Natural Food Store and Cafe. Deli, Bakery, Salad Bar and Juice Bar. Organic produce. Supermarket-type place. See Whole Foods Market information.
Menu: Starts serving breakfast at 7:30 am that

has granola, yogurt, oatmeal, potatoes and muffins. Has large selection of dishes for lunch and dinner.
Directions: On the other side from CVS and the Motion Fitness Gym, in downtown Milburn. From Rte 78 going west, take exit #50B (Millburn) and go west on Vauxhall Road. At Milburn Ave turn left. This place on right two blocks down.

MIDDLETOWN

Harmony Natural Foods
1521 State Highway 35, at Harmony Road
732-671-7939
Hours: Monday to Friday 10 am to 7 pm; Saturday 10 am to 6 pm; Sunday 11 am to 4 pm
Natural Food Store and Juice Bar. Organic produce.
Menu: Has sandwiches and salads. Fresh juices.
Other Info: Accepts MC, VISA.
Directions: From Garden State Parkway, take Rte 36 Exit (#117) towards Keyport/Hazlet/Rte 35, then take Rte 36 northeast a quarter-mile to Rte 35, then go southeast on Rte 35 towards Matawan/Middletown and this place is 4½ miles down.

MONTCLAIR

Fresh Fields Whole Foods Market
701 Bloomfield Avenue
973-746-5110
Hours: Daily 7:30 am to 10 pm
Starts serving breakfast at 7:30 am
Natural Food Store and Cafe. Deli, Bakery, Salad Bar and Juice Bar. Organic produce. Supermarket-type place. See Whole Foods Market information.
Directions: On the other side of Starbucks. From Garden State Parkway, take exit #148 (Bloomfield Ave) and go northwest on Bloomfield Ave for 2½ miles into Montclair. This place on right a block after Valley Rd.

The Health Shoppe
539 Bloomfield Avenue (Louis Harris Building)
973-746-3555
Hours: Monday to Friday 9 am to 9 pm; Saturday 9 am to 6 pm; Sunday 11 am to 5 pm
Natural Food Store.
Directions: From Garden State Parkway, take exit #148 (Bloomfield Ave) and go northwest on Bloomfield Ave for 2 miles into Montclair. This place is a block after N Fullerton Ave.

MORRISTOWN

Café India
79 Washington Street (Rte 24W)
973-539-7433
Hours: Daily 11 am to 9 pm
Indian. Vegan options. Not pure vegetarian.
Menu: Has a good selection of vegetarian dishes including rice dishes, vegetable curries, Indian breads, samosas and other dishes.
Comments: Good Indian vegetarian food. Buffet is good. Gets great recommendations. Affiliated catering operation does serve non-veg food. Good service and atmosphere. Does not use eggs in food.
Other Info: Full service, take-out. Accepts AMEX, DC, DIS, MC, VISA. Price: $$
Directions: From I-287, take exit #35 and go northwest on Madison Ave (becomes South St then Washington St) and this place is 2 miles down.

The Health Shoppe
Midtown Shopping Center, 66 Morris Street
973-538-9131
Hours: Monday to Friday 9 am to 9 pm; Saturday 9 am to 7 pm; Sunday 9 am to 6 pm
Natural Food Store and take-out only Deli. Organic Salad Bar, Bakery and Juice Bar. The largest natural food store in New Jersey. Has an excellent organic produce department.
Comments: Has a first-class deli, bakery and a good selection of other items. One of the best health food stores in country. Environmentally friendly place. Friendly, efficient staff.
Other Info: Counter service, take-out. No seating. Accepts AMEX, MC, VISA.
Directions: From I-287 north, take Lafayette exit (#36) and stay on service road (bear right) for a third-mile. At Morris St (at 2nd traffic light) turn right just after Giant Bag & Shop and this store is a block down in Midtown Shopping Center, on right. From I-287, take exit #36 and go straight to second light, where you turn right. This place then on right.

NEW BRUNSWICK

Evelyn's Restaurant
45 Easton Avenue; 732-246-8792
Hours: Daily 11 am to 2:30 pm
Lebanese and American. Vegan friendly. Not pure vegetarian.
Comments: Plays authentic music.
Other Info: Reservations suggested for groups. Accepts AMEX, DIS, MC, VISA. Price: $$-$$$.

George Street Co-op Natural Foods
89 Morris Street, at Livingston Avenue; 732-247-8280; **email:** gscoop@georgestreetcoop.com
Web site: www.georgestreetcoop.com
Hours: Monday to Friday 10 am to 8 pm; Saturday 10 am to 6 pm; Sunday 11 am to 6 pm
Natural Food Store. Organic produce.
Comments: Open to the public and members get discounts. There are detailed directions to this store on their Web site. This is a large store with a good selection of organic produce and other goods.
Other Info: Accepts DIS, MC, VISA.
Directions: From NJ Turnpike, take Exit #9. Go north (right) on Rte 18 for 2 miles going past 2 lights and exit at New Street. Stay straight onto New St for 3 blocks, then at Livingston Ave turn left and go 1 block, then turn left at Morris St (which is one-way) and this place is first building on left.

Makeda Ethiopian Restaurant
338 George Street; 732-545-5115
Hours: Monday to Thursday 11:30 am to 10:30 pm; Friday & Saturday 12 noon to 12 midnight; Sunday 12 noon to 10 pm
Ethiopian. Not pure vegetarian.
Comments: Has live music Thursday to Sunday.
Other Info: Accepts AMEX, DC, MC, VISA. Price: $$-$$$.

***Zafra Vegetarian Restaurant
46 Paterson Street, at George Street
732-214-1005
Hours: Monday to Friday 11 am to 10 pm; Saturday 5 pm to 10 pm; closed Sunday.
Vegan Restaurant. Vegetarian. Vegan options.
Menu: Soups, sandwiches, pastas, veggie chili, chicken Finger, Black Bean Soup, Macaroni & Cheese, corn, veggie burgers, Pan-Fried Tofu, French Toast and Chicken Meat Loaf.
Comments: Extremely friendly and helpful.
Other Info: Accepts AMEX, MC, VISA. Price: $.

NEWTON

Sussex County Foods
30 Morran Street
973-579-1882
Hours: Monday to Thursday, Saturday 9:30 am to 5:30 pm; Fri 9 am to 9 pm; Sun 1 pm to 5 pm
Natural Food Store. Has seasonal organic produce.
Directions: This place is in the center of Newton.

NORTH ARLINGTON

Surrey International Natural Foods

33 Ridge Road, North Arlington
201-991-1905
Hours: Monday to Saturday 9 am to 7:30 pm
Sunday 10 am to 3 pm
Natural Food Store and Café. Deli, Salad Bar
and Juice Bar.
Menu: Salads, baked goods, pre-made sandwiches
and more.
Directions: From New Jersey Turnpike, take
exit #15W toward Newark/The Oranges and
go west on I-280 for 3 miles, then take Rte 21
exit (#15) towards Newark/Belleville (keep
right at fork in ramp) and merge onto
McCarter Hwy (Rte 21) and go north 3 miles,
then take the Rte 7 exit (#6) towards Belleville/
N Arlington, then turn right onto Rutgers St
(Rte 7) which becomes Belleville Turnpike (Rte
7) and go a half-mile, then at Ridge St (Rte 7)
turn left and this place is 1 block down. Has a
green awning.

NORTHFIELD (NEAR ATLANTIC CITY)

Bonterra Market

3112 Fire Road, Northfield
609-484-1550
Hours: Monday to Friday 9 am to 7:30 pm; Sat-
urday 10 am to 5 pm; Sunday 11 am to 4 pm
Natural Food Store and Deli. Organic produce.
Menu: Soups, sandwiches, salads, veggie chili,
mock chicken salads and other dishes.
Comments: Friendly place.
Other Info: Counter service, take-out. Has a few
tables for seating.
Directions: From Garden State Parkway, take
Road 563 exit (#36) towards Northfield and get
on Tilton Rd going southeast and this place is
1.35 miles down on right, at Burton Ave.

NORTHVALE

Organica Natural Foods

246 Livingston Street
201-767-8182
Hours: Monday to Friday 9 am to 7 pm; Saturday 10 am to 6 pm; Sunday 10:30 am to 5 pm
Natural Food Store.
Directions: This place is about a half-mile south
of the border with New York State. From 9W,
take Exit #5 and then go south on Rte 303 (becomes Livingston St) and this place is 1½ mile
down.

OCEAN CITY

Bashful Banana Café & Bakery

944 Ocean City Boardwalk—Colonial Walk
609-398-9677
Hours: Memorial Day to Labor Day Daily
Saturday and Sunday in April, May, September
and October
Natural Foods Restaurant and Bakery. Mainly
Vegetarian. Vegan options.
Menu: Has a large vegetarian menu. Fresh juices.
Comments: Has outdoor seating and an ocean
view. Low-fat, low-calorie, some dairy-free and
sugar-free dishes. Grams of fat, cholesterol and
calories are listed on the menu for each dish.
Other Info: Full service, take-out, catering. Ac-
cepts MC, VISA. Price: $.

OCEAN TOWNSHIP

Dean's Natural Food Market

1119 State Highway 35, Ocean Township
732-517-1515
Hours: Monday to Friday 9 am to 8 pm; Saturday 9 am to 6 pm; Sunday 10 am to 6 pm
Natural Food Store. Organic produce. Is a large
place with a great selection.
Menu: Has ready-made sandwiches in their
cooler.
Other Info: Accepts AMEX, MC, VISA.

PARSIPPANY

Chand Palace

257 Littleton Road
973-334-5444; **fax:** 973-402-8403
email: bajaj@chandpalace.com
Web site: www.chandpalace.com
Hours: Monday to Thursday 11:30 am to 2:30
pm, 5 pm to 10 pm; Friday 11:30 am to 2:30
pm, 5 pm to 10:30 pm; Saturday 12 noon to 3
pm, 5 pm to 10:30 pm; Sunday 12 noon to 3
pm, 5 pm to 10 pm; closed Tuesday. Has Tuesday night buffet at the Banquet facility (next to
the restaurant) for $12.95 but it is not vegetarian
Mainly Vegetarian North and South Indian. Not
pure vegetarian, but is mostly. Vegan options.
Menu: Has a good selection of vegetarian dishes
including rice dishes, vegetable curries, Indian
breads, pakoras, Vegetable Cutlet, Idly, Dosa,
Vegetable Curries, Indian Breads, Aloo Tikki,
Aloo Channa, Panir Tikka, samosas and many
other dishes. Has a twelve-course dinner buffet.
Comments: Good Indian vegetarian food. Buffet is good. Affiliated catering operation does serve

non-veg food, but restaurant is fully vegetarian. Has a catering facility that seats 250 people, which is a new facility with crystal chandeliers, a sculptured ceiling and black granite dance floor. Does not use eggs in food.
Other Info: Full service, take-out, catering. Price: $$.
Directions: It is at the intersection of Routes 80, 46, 287 and 202. It is a half-mile northwest of the intersection of I-80 and I-287. From I-80, take exit #41B and go west on Littleton Rd and this place is a half-mile down.

Health Shoppe
Troy Shopping Center, 1123 Route 46 East
973-263-8348
Hours: Monday to Friday 9 am to 9 pm; Saturday 9 am to 6 pm; Sunday 11 am to 6 pm
Natural Food Store.
Directions: From I-80, take Lake Hiawatha exit west (#47), then go west on Rte 46 and this place is a half-mile down in the Shopping Center.

Hong Kong Delight
48 North Beverwyck Road
973-402-8883
Hours: Daily 11 am to 10 pm
Chinese. Vegan-friendly. Not pure vegetarian.
Comments: Was totally vegetarian, but now serves meat.
Other Info: Accepts AMEX, MC, VISA.

**Veggie Heaven
1119 Route 46 East, #8A
973-335-9876
Hours: Monday to Thursday 11:30 am to 10 pm; Friday to Saturday 11:30 am to 10:30 pm; Sunday 11:30 am to 9:30 pm
Fully Vegetarian Chinese. Vegan options.
Menu: Large menu. Spring roll, soups, daily specials, Fresh Garden Walnut, noodle dishes, scallion pancakes, Steamed Spinach Dumplings (really good), Paper Wrapped Vegetarian Lamb, Sesame Chicken, Crispy Chicken, BBQ Spare Ribs, Veggie Beef Chow Fun, Spinach Rolls, Vegan German Chocolate cake and many other dishes. The mock meats and seafood are very good. Has some Americanized dishes.
Comments: Gets high recommendations. Attentive and helpful service. Warm and comfortable atmosphere. Mock "meat" or "seafood" is made from soybean or wheat gluten.
Other Info: Non-smoking. Reservations recommended. Full service, take-out. Accepts AMEX, MC, VISA. Price: $$-$$$.
Directions: From I-80, take Lake Hiawatha exit

west (#47), then go west on Rte 46 and this place is a half-mile down.

PISCATAWAY

**Bombay Hut
1347 Stelton Road; 732-777-9595
Hours: Monday to Friday 12 noon to 3 pm, 5:30 pm to 9 pm; Saturday 12 noon to 9:30 pm; Sunday 12 noon to 9 pm
Vegetarian India. South India and Bombay cuisine.
Menu: Has South Indian and Mumbai type dishes such as Bhel Puri.
Other Info: Counter service, take-out. Order at counter then dishes are brought to table. Accepts AMEX, MC, VISA.

**Malabar House
1665 Stelton Road; 732-819-0400
Hours: Tuesday to Sunday 12 noon to 3 pm (lunch buffet), 5 pm to 10 pm; closed Monday.
Vegetarian Indian. Vegan options. All-you-can-eat Lunch Buffet with North and South India dishes.
Menu: Authentic South Indian. Masala dosas, Indian breads, rice dishes, uttama, curried vegetables and more. Has North Indian dishes such as Matar & Palak Paneer and Malai Kofta.
Other Info: Full service, take-out, catering. Accepts MC, VISA. Price: $$.
Directions: From I-287, take Exit #6 and go north on Washington Ave for a half-mile, then turn right at S Road 529 (Stelton Rd) and this place is a half-mile down.

PLAINSBORO

Crown of India
Prince Meadows Shopping Center
660 Plainsboro Road; 609-275-5707
Hours: Sunday to Thursday 11:30 am to 2:30 pm, 4:30 pm to 10 pm; Friday & Saturday 11:30 am to 2:30 pm, 4:30 pm to 11 pm
Indian. Vegan-friendly. Not pure vegetarian.
Menu: Has a good lunch buffet with vegetarian soups, rice, curried vegetables and naan.
Other Info: Full service, take-out. Accepts AMEX, MC, VISA. Price: $$.

Lee's Castle I
Prince Meadows Shopping Center
660 Plainsboro Road; 609-799-1008
Hours: Sunday to Thursday 11:30 am to 9:30 pm; Friday & Saturday 11:30 am to 10 pm
Chinese. Vegan options. Not pure vegetarian.

Menu: Large selection of vegetarian dishes includes soups, rice, appetizers and main dishes. **Other Info:** Full service, take-out, catering. Accepts AMEX, MC, VISA. Price: $$.

PRINCETON

King's Castle I
Princeton Shopping Center, North Harrison Street; 609-924-8001
Hours: Daily 11:30 am to 9:30 pm
Chinese. Vegan options. Not pure vegetarian.
Menu: Large selection of vegetarian dishes including soups, rice, appetizers and main dishes.
Other Info: Full service, take-out, catering. Accepts AMEX, MC, VISA. Price: $$.

**Whole Earth Center
360 Nassau Street
609-924-7429; **Deli:** 609-924-7421
Store Hours: Monday to Friday 10 am to 7 pm; Saturday 9 am to 6 pm; Sunday 10 am to 5 pm
Deli Hours: Monday to Saturday 10 am to 6 pm Closed Sunday.
Natural Food Store and Vegetarian Deli. Bakery and Juice Bar. Large selection of organic produce.
Menu: Soups, salads, sandwiches and hot dishes.
Comments: Friendly place.
Other Info: Counter service, take-out. Seating.
Directions: From Rte 1, go northwest on Harrison for 1 mile. Then at Nassau St (Rte 27) turn right and then turn left at first driveway, and this place is hidden behind another store.

Wild Oats Community Market
255 Nassau Street; 609-924-4993
Hours: Monday to Saturday 7:30 am to 9:30 pm Sunday 8 am to 9 pm
Natural Food Store and Cafe. Deli, Bakery, Salad Bar and Juice Bar. Organic produce. Supermarket-type place. See Wild Oats Market information.
Directions: From Rte 1, go northwest on Harrison for 1 mile. Then at Nassau St (Rte 27) turn left and this place is a half-mile down.

RED BANK

***Down to Earth
7 Broad Street; 732-747-4542; **fax:** 732-747-4518
email: cheflacey@home.com
Web site: www.downtoearthnj.com
Hours: Monday to Saturday 11 am to 3 pm, 5 pm to 10 pm; Sunday 5 pm to 9 pm; closed Tuesday. Lunch 11 am to 3 pm.

Fully Vegan International. 95% organic.
Menu: The menu features a wide variety of vegan dish, both raw (appetizers and salads) and cooked. Chickpea Socca with White Bean Purée, Seitan Satay, Tempeh Delight, Apricot Glazed Tofu, Raw Maki Roll with Brazil Nut Paté, nachos, Lasagna, Vietnamese Spring Rolls with peanut ginger sauce, Samosa Wrap (potatoes, peas and onions baked in a chili shell, on top of coconut cashew pilaf) and "Cruelty-Free Caesar Salad" (greens, sun-dried tomatoes, olives, lemon caper dressing). Vegan "milk" shakes and smoothies, Baked goods, such as Tropical Cake with mango, kiwi, berries & pineapple and Chocolate & Peanut-Butter Mousse.
Comments: It is a good, recommended place. Generous portions. Fresh deli case. Weekend specials. Downstairs, below street level seating. Has around 45 seats. Fresh flowers and plants. Community table. Wheat-free dishes are labeled. Has its full menu on its Web site. This place is at least 90% organic.
Other Info: Full service, counter service, take-out, catering. Non-smoking. Does not take reservations. Accepts AMEX, MC, VISA.
Directions: From Garden State Parkway take Rte 520 Exit #109, toward downtown Red Bank, then go east on Rte 50 (become Rte 520 after a half-mile) for 2 miles, then at Broad St (Route 35) turn left and this place is ¾ mile down on right side, just before the road ends at Front St. Parking can be hard to find. There is a parking garage on Front St, around the corner. This place is at the north end of the main downtown area.

Eurasian Eatery
110 Monmouth Street; 732-741-7071
Hours: Tuesday to Thursday 11:30 to 8:30 pm; Friday & Saturday 11:30 am to 9:30 pm; Sunday 4 pm to 8:30 pm; closed Monday.
Asian, European & International Restaurant. Vegetarian friendly. Vegan options.
Menu: Has a good selection of vegetarian dishes.
Other Info: Full service, take-out. Accepts AMEX, MC, VISA. Price: $-$$.

Second Nature
65 Broad Street
732-747-6448
Hours: Monday to Friday 10 am to 8 pm; Saturday 10 am to 6 pm; Sunday 10 am to 5 pm
Natural Food Store and Juice Bar. Salad Bar. Good selection of organic produce.
Menu: Has organic vegan soup and ready-made sandwiches.

Directions: Take Garden State Parkway to exit #109 (Red Bank). Get on Rte 520 and go east until it ends at the railway tracks, at Broad St (Rte) turn left and go 3 lights (half-mile) and this place is on the right just past the light.

RIDGEWOOD

Nature's Market Place and Deli Café
1 West Ridgewood Avenue, Ridgewood
201-445-9210
Hours: Monday to Saturday 10 am to 6 pm (until 8 pm on Thursday); closed Sunday.
Natural Food Store.
Other Info: Counter service, take-out. Accepts AMEX, MC, VISA.
Directions: From Hwy 17, take Ridgewood/Oradell exit and follow signs to Ridgewood going west to where road ends after 2 miles, then at N Maple (CR 507) turn right and go 1 block. Then at the light, Franklin Ave, turn left and go a half-mile. Go under railroad tracks, then at next left turn right and this place is at the corner.

Whole Foods Market
Ridgewood Plaza, 44 Godwin Avenue
201-670-0383
Hours: Daily 8 am to 9 pm
Natural Food Store and Cafe. Deli, Bakery, Salad Bar and Juice Bar. Organic produce. Supermarket-type place. See Whole Foods Market information.
Directions: From Hwy 17, take Ridgewood/Oradell exit and follow signs to Ridgewood going west to where road ends after 2 miles, then at N Maple (CR 507) turn right and go 1 block. Then at the light, Franklin Ave, turn left and go ¾ mile. After going past the railway tracks the road bear sharply to the left. Franklin Ave become Garber Sq, then Wilsey Sq then Godwin Ave.

RIVER EDGE

Happy Carrot
636 Kinderkamack Road; 201-986-0818
Hours: Monday to Friday 9:30 am to 7:30 pm; Saturday 9:30 am to 6 pm; Sun 11 am to 4 pm
Natural Food Store and Gourmet Deli. Juice Bar and organic produce. Vegan-friendly.
Menu: Soups, salads, ready-made sandwiches, main dishes and desserts. Local organic produce used when possible.
Other Info: Accepts AMEX, DIS, MC, VISA.
Directions: From Garden State Pkwy, take Rte 4 exit (#161) towards Paramus, and go east 1½ mile on Rte 4, then turn left onto Forest Ave going north for a half-mile, then at Howland Ave turn right and go a third-mile east, then at 5th Ave turn right and go 2 blocks, then at Wayne Ave turn right and go a quarter-mile, then at Elm Ave turn left and go a half-mile, then at Monroe Ave turn right and go a quarter-mile, then at Kinderkamack Rd (CR 503) turn left and then this place is 1 block down.

SCOTCH PLAINS

Autumn Harvest Health Foods
1625 2nd Street; 908-322-2130
Hours: Monday to Friday 9:30 am to 7 pm; Saturday 9:30 am to 5:30 pm; Sunday 10:30 am to 3:30 pm
Natural Food Store. Organic produce. No deli.
Menu: Has ready-made sandwiches in cooler.
Other Info: Accepts MC, VISA.
Directions: From Rte 22, at Terrill Rd head southeast a half-mile, then at 2nd St turn left and then this place is a half-mile down on the left.

SOMERSET

Nature's Weight Health Food Store
1075 Easton Avenue; 732 247-0070
Hours: Monday to Friday 10 am to 8 pm; Saturday 10 am to 5:30 pm; Sunday 11 am to 5 pm
Natural Food Store.
Menu: Has ready-made sandwiches and salads.
Other Info: Accepts DIS, MC, VISA.

SOMERVILLE

Nature's Holaday
194 West Main Street; 908-725-7716
Natural Food Store and Deli. Organic produce.
Menu: Has sandwiches, soups, salads and hot dishes.
Comments: Has a food bar where you seat down and eat.

STONE HARBOR

**Green Cuisine
302 96th Street
609-368-1616; fax: 609-638-6486
Hours: Seasonal, May to September Daily 11 am to 8:30 pm
Vegetarian Natural Foods.
Menu: Unique salads, gourmet sandwiches, hummus and pita, veggie burgers, tabbouleh salad and

much more. The Brie, Avocado and Green Grape Sandwich and the California Pita are good. Fresh fruit salads. Fresh juices.
Other Info: Full service, take-out. No credit cards.
Price: $$.
Directions: This place is on the main street coming into Stone Harbor.

TEANECK

Aquarius
408 Cedar Lane, Teaneck; 201-836-0601
Hours: Monday to Friday 10 am to 7 pm; Saturday 10 am to 6 pm; Sunday 10 am to 2 pm
Natural Food Store and Juice Bar.
Menu: Soups, Rice & Beans, pre-made sandwich and salads.
Directions: From New Jersey Turnpike, take Washington Br/Meadowlands side, take Exit #70 towards Rte 93/Teaneck (keep left at fork in ramp, then right at second fork) and merge onto E Degraw Ave and go ¾ mile west, then at Teaneck Rd turn right (go north) and go 1 mile, then at Cedar Lane turn left (go east) and this place is ¾ mile down.

Chopstix
172 West Englewood Ave; 201-833-0200
Hours: Sunday to Thursday 11:30 am to 10 pm; Friday 11:30 am to 2:30 pm; Closed Saturday.
Kosher Chinese. Not pure vegetarian. Take-out only.
Menu: Has a large selection of vegetarian dishes. Several soups, dumplings, tofu dishes, rice dishes, noodles dishes and many other vegetarian dishes. Fresh juices.
Other Info: Take-out only, catering. Accepts DC, DIS, AMEX, MC, VISA. Price: $$.

**Veggie Heaven
473 Cedar Lane; 201-836-0887
Hours: Sunday to Thursday 11 am to 10 pm Friday & Saturday 11 am to 11 pm
Fully Vegetarian Chinese. 100% natural. Mostly Vegan. Some of the desserts contain eggs. Kosher.
Menu: Has over 100 vegetarian dishes including soups, noodles dishes, sizzling platters, dumplings, tofu dishes and clay hot pot dishes. Daily specials and lunch specials. Wonton Soup, veggie shrimp (in the shape of a shrimp), Chicken Hot Pot, Miso Soup, Mock Shrimp, General Tso's Chicken, vegetarian chicken and steak (with black mushrooms, broccoli, water chestnuts, peas, and carrots in a spicy brown sauce), mock "beef," seitan and taro

root, Scallion Pancake, Crispy Tofu, Noodle Soup, Boneless BBQ Ribs, Beef with Broccoli and vegan tofu vanilla ice cream with chocolate-covered almonds.
Comments: Gets really high recommendations. Service is first class. Lunch specials.
Other Info: Full service, take-out, delivers. Accepts AMEX, MC, VISA. Price: $$-$$$.
Directions: From New Jersey Turnpike, take Washington Br/Meadowlands side, take Exit #70 towards Rte 93/Teaneck (keep left at fork in ramp, then right at second fork) and merge onto E Degraw Ave and go ¾ mile west, then at Teaneck Rd turn right (go north) and go 1 mile, then at Cedar Lane turn left (go east) and this place is 1 mile down.

TOMS RIVER

General Store & Natural Foods Vegetarian Café
675 Batchelor Street, Highway 37
908-240-0024
Store Hours: Monday to Saturday 10 am to 6 pm; **Café Hours:** Monday to Friday 10 am to 2 pm; closed Sunday.
Natural Foods Store and Cafe. Deli. Mainly Vegetarian. Vegan options.
Menu: Veggie Loaf Platter, Tempeh, Tofu Scramble, Falafel, Un-chicken Salad, veggie burgers, Chickpea Curry and Vegan German Platter. Fresh juices and smoothies.
Comments: Small place with a few tables.
Other Info: DIS, MC, VISA. Price: $. Limited service, take-out. Accepts AMEX,
Directions: From the Garden State Parkway, take Exit #82 for Seaside Heights/Island Heights and then go east on Rte 37 for 2 miles, then turn right at Peter Ave and go 1 block, then at Batchelor St turn right and this place is a block down.

TRENTON (Mercer County)

**Adventist Book & Food Center
2160 Brunswick Avenue
609-392-8010
Hours: Mon to Thur 8 am to 5 pm; Second and fourth Sun of each month; Closed Fri & Sat.
Fully Vegetarian Café.
Menu: Vegan burgers, salads, soups and many other things.
Directions: This place is 3 miles north of the downtown area. From Rte 1, go northwest on Whitehead Rd a half-mile, then at Brunswick Ave turn right and this place is a block down.

Black Forest Acres

1100 Route 33, at Paxson Avenue

609-586-6187

Hours: Monday to Friday 9:30 am to 7:30 pm; Saturday 9:30 am to 6 pm; Sunday 11:30 am to 4 pm; Deli closes 7 pm weekdays and 4 pm on Saturday.

Natural Food Store and Deli. Organic produce.

Menu: Soups, salads, sandwiches and hot dishes.

Other Info: Non-smoking. Counter service, takeout. Has a seating area.

Directions: From I-295, take Exit #63 and then go west on Nottingham Way a half-mile, then take a slight right onto Rte 33 and this place is 1½ mile down. This place is 3 miles east of the downtown area.

UPPER MONCLAIR

Evergreen Restaurant

594 Valley Road; 973-744-4120

Hours: Monday to Saturday 11:30 noon to 2:30 pm, 5 pm to 9:30 pm; Sunday 5 am to 9:30 pm

American and International. Not pure veg.

Menu: Has some good vegetarian dishes. Vegetable Stir-fry, Black Bean Enchiladas, Stuffed Eggplant and Eggplant Rollatine.

Comments: Has outdoor courtyard dining. Good service. Romantic atmosphere.

Directions: From the Garden State Pkwy, take Watchung Ave Exit (#151) towards Montclair, turn left onto Watchung Ave and go 1½ miles west, at Waterbury Rd turn right and go a quarter-mile, at Gordonhurst Ave turn left and go a third-mile, then at Valley Rd turn right and this place is a half-mile down.

VINELAND

Health Now

1301 North Delsea Drive (Rte 47)

856-794-4856

Natural Food Store.

Hours: Tuesday, Wednesday Saturday 10 am to 5 pm; Thursday & Friday 10 am to 7 pm; closed Sunday & Monday.

Directions: From Hwy 55, take exit #32 and go east on W Landis Ave for 1½ mile. Then at N Delsea Drive (Rte 47) turn left and this place is 1½ mile down.

New Mexico

1. Albuquerque
2. Farmington
3. Las Cruces
4. Las Vegas
5. Santa Fe
6. Silver City
7. Taos

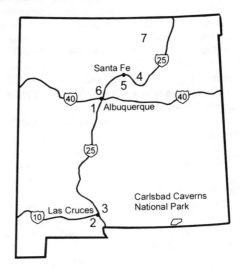

ALBUQUERQUE

Artichoke Café
424 Central Avenue SE, near Route 66
505-243-0200; Web site: www.artichokecafe.com
Hours: Mon to Fri 11 am to 2:30 pm, 5:30 pm
to 10 pm; Sat 5:30 pm to 10 pm; closed Sun.
International, Italian, French, American. Not
pure vegetarian.
Menu: Has some interesting vegetarian dishes.
Sea Bean Salad, sun-dried cherries & cranberries,
Grilled Eggplant & Mozzarella Sandwich, Roasted
Portobello Mushroom & Avocado Wrap, pasta,
Ravioli, Steamed Artichoke, salads including an
organic one and soups. Fresh juices.
Comments: It is a bit upscale and is not cheap.
Elegant décor. Has an excellent changing art ex-
hibit. Romantic. Good service and food. One of
the most popular places in town.
Other Info: Full service, take-out, catering. Non-
smoking. Accepts AMEX, MC, VISA. Price: $$$.
Directions: From I-25, take Central Ave/Dr ML
King Jr Ave (#224), and go west on Central Ave
and this place is 5 blocks (third-mile) down.

Bangkok Café
5901 Central NE; 505-255-5036
Hours: Monday to Thursday 11 am to 2 pm, 5
pm to 9 pm; Friday 11 am to 2 pm, 5 pm to 9:30
pm; Saturday & Sunday 5 pm to 9:30 pm

Thai. Vegan options. Not pure vegetarian.
Menu: Has a vegetarian section on the menu in-
cluding rice, soups, appetizers, noodle dishes,
curry dishes and desserts. Food can either be made
mild or hot.
Comments: Authentic Thai. This place is often
voted as the best Thai restaurant in Albuquerque
and is considered to be one of the better restau-
rants in town.
Other Info: Full service, take-out. Accepts
AMEX, DIS, MC, VISA. Price: $$.

Barry's Oasis Restaurant
5400 San Mateo Boulevard, NE; 505-884-2324
Hours: Tue to Thur 11 am to 2 pm, 5 pm to 9
pm; Fri 11 am to 2 pm, 5 pm to 10 pm; Sat 12
noon to 3 pm, 5 pm to 10 pm; Sun 5 pm to 9 pm
Mediterranean. Deli. Vegan options. Not pure
vegetarian.
Menu: Has a vegetarian menu with dishes from
various places such as Italy, Spain, France, Greek
and the Middle East. Vegetarian dishes include
pasta, moussaka, hummus, Lasagna, tabbouleh,
falafel and homemade desserts.
Comments: Live entertainment in the evening
Wednesday to Saturday.
Other Info: Full service, take-out. Reservations
recommended. Accepts DC, MC, VISA. Price:
$$-$$$.
Directions: From I-25, take Exit #229 for

Jefferson St NE and go a half-mile south on Jefferson St NE, then at McLeod Rd NE turn left and go a half-mile, then at San Mateo Blvd NE turn left (north) and this place is a half-mile down.

Chef Du Jour

119 San Pasquale SW; 505-247-8998
Hours: Monday to Friday 11 am to 2 pm
Weekends for lunch and dinner
New World. Not pure vegetarian.
Menu: Has some vegetarian main dishes.
Comments: Upscale place.
Other Info: Full service, take-out. Non-smoking. Accepts MC, VISA. Price: $$-$$$.

El Patio Restaurant

142 Harvard Drive SE; 505-268-4245
Hours: Monday to Saturday 11 am to 9 pm
Sunday 12 noon to 9 pm
Mexican and American. Vegan options. Not pure vegetarian.
Menu: Vegetarian Red Chili and Greens. Vegetarian burritos with beans, avocado and tomato. Usually has a daily vegetarian special.
Comments: Has more vegetarian dishes than meat dishes. Has outdoor patio dining. Friendly, little, popular place. Has live Spanish guitar music. Says everything is vegetarian unless you order meat in a dish.
Other Info: Full service, take-out. No smoking inside, but smoking is allowed on the patio. Reservations not accepted. Accepts MC, VISA. Price: $$.
Directions: Located near the university.

El Pinto, Authentic New Mexican Restaurant

10500 4th Street NW; 505-898-1771
Hours: Sunday to Thursday 11 am to 9 pm
Friday & Saturday 11 am to 10 pm
Mexican. Not pure vegetarian.
Menu: Has a selection of vegetarian dishes.
Comments: Elegant décor. Romantic atmosphere. Good place for a special event. Outdoor patio dining. Big place. Gets good recommendations. Sometimes has live music.
Other Info: Reservations necessary for groups. Accepts AMEX, DC, DIS, MC, VISA. Price: $$-$$$.

India Kitchen Restaurant

6910 Montgomery Boulevard NE, at Louisiana
505-884-2333
Hours: Sunday, Tuesday to Thursday 5 pm to 9

pm; Friday & Saturday 5 pm to 9:30 pm; closed Monday.
Indian. Vegan options. Not pure vegetarian.
Menu: Has several vegetarian dishes such as vegetarian soups, salads and several main dishes. All dishes are freshly made.
Comments: Has authentic décor with Indian statues, artifacts and tapestries. One of the best places in town for vegetarian Indian food. Popular place on weekend nights. There is a good Indian grocery store next to the restaurant.
Other Info: Full service, take-out. Reservations suggested for weekend nights. Accepts AMEX, MC, VISA. Price: $.

India Palace

4410 Wyoming Boulevard NE; 505-271-5009
Hours: Daily 11:30 am to 2.30 pm, 5 pm to 10 pm.
Indian. Not pure vegetarian. Good lunch buffet and a small salad bar.
Menu: The vegetarian dishes are marked on the menu. The lunch buffet has around five vegetarian dishes. There is a full vegetarian dinner, which consists of rice, dal (lentil soup), Vegetable Korma, Navartan Korma (mixed vegetable curry), Sag Paneer (spinach and cheese), vegetarian Mulligatawny and raita (yogurt and cucumber).
Comments: Formal, pleasant place. Nice atmosphere. There are daily specials. Sells wine. Good Indian grocery store next to the restaurant.
Other Info: Accepts AMEX, DIS, MC, VISA. Price: $$-$$$.
Directions: It is in a shopping center at the corner of Montgomery and Wyoming.

Kanome: An Asian Diner

3128 Central Avenue SE
at Bryn Mar Avenue
505-265-7773
Hours: Sunday, Tuesday to Thursday 5 pm to 10 pm; Fri and Sat 5 pm to 11 pm; closed Mon.
Asian. Chinese, Thai, Japanese, Vietnamese, Korean. Not pure vegetarian.
Menu: Tempura tofu and vegetable sticks with black beans served on top of rice. Asian Spinach Soup with tofu and taro crackers. There is a Noodle Bowl with mushrooms, ginseng and ramen.
Comments: The place is interestingly designed. Has gotten some really good reviews. Modern dining room. Sometime has a Saturday Asian cooking class. Friendly, helpful service.
Other Info: Accepts AMEX, DIS, MC, VISA. Price $$-$$$.

La Montanita Co-op Supermarket
Nob Hill Shopping Center, 3500 Central Avenue, SE; 505-265-4631
Web site: www.lamontanita.com
Hours: Monday to Saturday 7 am to 9 pm
Sunday 8 am to 8 pm
Directions: From I-40, take Carlisle exit (#160) south and go about 2 miles. This place is in the Nob Hill Shopping Center. From I-25, take Exit 224 for Central Ave and go 1½ mile and this place at junction with Girard.
2400 Rio Grande Boulevard, NW; 505-242-8800
Hours: Monday to Saturday 8 am to 8 pm
Sunday 8 am to 8 pm
Directions: This place is in northwest Albuquerque. From I-40, take exit #157A and go north on Rio Grande Blvd for 1 mile north and this place is near junction with Matthew Ave NW.
Natural Food Store and Deli. Juice Bar. Organic produce. Vegan options. Not pure vegetarian.
Menu: The menu changes regularly. Has salads, soups, sandwiches and main dishes. Has vegan desserts such as pies, pastries and cookies. Fresh juices.
Other Info: Counter deli service, take-out. Has outdoor seating. Non-smoking. Accepts AMEX, DC, DIS, MC, VISA. Price: $.

May Café
111 Louisiana Boulevard SE; 505-265-4448
Hours: Monday to Saturday 10 am to 9 pm
Closed Sunday.
Vietnamese. Vegan friendly. Not pure veg.
Comments: Some of the vegetarian dishes have eggs in them, so you should ask about this.
Other Info: Accepts MC, VISA.

Richard's Mexican Restaurant
3301 Menaul Boulevard NE; 505-881-1039
Hours: Daily 8 am to 3:30 pm
Mexican. Not pure vegetarian.
Menu: Does not use meat stock in its posole or green chili. Vegetarian Tamale Plate with brown rice and lentils. The Santa Fe Enchilada is two bean enchiladas with cheese, tomato and lettuce. It comes with a wheat tortilla or sopaipilla.
Comments: It is a relaxed place with friendly service. The Fidelio noodles contain chicken stock.
Other Info: Accepts AMEX, DIS, MC, VISA. Price: $.

Thai Ginger
834 San Mateo Boulevard, SE; 505-255-5930
Hours: Monday to Thursday 11 am to 2 pm, 5 pm to 9 pm; Friday 11 am to 2:30 pm, 5 pm to 9:30 pm; Sat 5 pm to 9:30 pm; closed Sun.
Thai. Not pure vegetarian. Buffet.
Menu: Has a separate vegetarian menu. Sir-fried Rice Noodles and Fried Tofu with peanut sauce. No Alcohol.
Comments: Really basic décor.
Other Info: Accepts MC, VISA.

Twenty Carrots Café
2110 Central Ave SE, near Yale, across the street from the University of Mexico; 505-242-1320
Hours: Monday to Saturday 10 am to 5 pm
Sunday 10 am to 4 pm
Southwestern Restaurant. Vegan and Macrobiotic options. Not pure vegetarian.
Menu: Soups, salads, Japanese Nori Roll (nori wrapped around brown rice, sprouts & avocado with plum sauce), tamales, Vegan burrito (whole-wheat tortilla with veggie burger, vegetables and salsa), veggie burgers and other dishes. Fresh juices and good smoothies. "Wild Thing" is 20 ounces of orange, apple and lemon with an ounce of wheatgrass.
Comments: Outdoor seating. The price is not exactly cheap. The meat dishes are cooked on a separate grill than the vegetarian dishes.
Other Info: Limited service, take-out. Non-smoking. Accepts MC, VISA. Price $-$$.
Directions: Next to southwest corner of the University of New Mexico. From I-25, take Exit #224 and this place is ¾ mile east on Central Ave, 4 blocks east of University Blvd.

Wild Oats
Far North Shopping Center, 6300-A San Mateo NE; 505-823-1933
Hours: Daily 7:30 am to 10 pm
Directions: From I-25, take San Mateo Blvd (#230) exit. Go south on San Mateo. Store is in Far North Shopping Center a quarter-mile down.
11015 Menaul Boulevard NE; 505-275-6660
Hours: Daily 7:30 am to 9 pm
Directions: From I-40, take Exit #164 towards Kirtland AFB, then go north onto Wyoming Blvd NE and go 1¼ mile, then at Menaul Blvd NE turn right (go east) and this place is 2 miles down.
2103 Carlisle Boulevard NE (Indian School Plaza) 505-260-1366
Hours: Daily 7:30 am to 10 pm
Directions: From I-40, take Carlisle Blvd exit (#160) and go south on Carlisle Blvd and this place is a quarter-mile down.
Natural Food Store and Cafe. Deli, Bakery, Salad Bar and Juice Bar. Organic produce. Supermarket-type place. See Wild Oats Market information.

FARMINGTON

Wildly Natural Foods

Hutton Plaza, 2501 East 20th Street, Suite 1
505-326-6243
Hours: Monday to Friday 9 am to 6:30 pm; Saturday 9 am to 6 pm; Sunday 11 am to 5 pm; Juice bar closed on Sunday.
Natural Food Store. Juice Bar. Organic produce.
Menu: Has a good selection of vegetarian dishes. Fresh juices and smoothies.
Directions: Taking Main St going east from the downtown, then at Hutton turn left (north). At 20th St turn left and this place on left after one long block. This place is about 1 mile northeast of the downtown.

LAS CRUCES

Organ Mountain Food Co-op

1300 El Paseo Road, Suite M, Las Cruces
505-523-0436
Hours: Monday to Saturday 8 am to 8 pm
Sunday 11 am to 5 pm
Natural Food Store. Organic produce.
Comments: Has soups during the week and not much else.
Other Info: Accepts AMEX, MC, VISA.
Directions: From I-25, take University Ave exit (#1), and go west on E University for 1 mile, turn right (go north) onto El Paseo Rd and this place is 1 mile down. Store on the left in Idaho Crossing Shopping Center. From I-10, take exit #140 and go east on Rte 28 for 1 mile, when road forks go right onto E Idaho Ave and this place is a half-mile down at junction with El Paseo.

LAS VEGAS

Semilla Natural Foods

510 University Avenue; 505-425-8139
Hours: Monday to Friday 10 am to 6 pm; Saturday 10 am to 5 pm; closed Sunday.
Natural Food Store.
Directions: From I-25, take University Ave exit (2nd Las Vegas exit #345) and go west on University and this place on right a half-mile down.

SANTA FE

Baja Tacos

2621 Cerrillos Road; 505-471-8762
Hours: Monday to Saturday 7 am to 9 pm
Sunday 8 am to 8 pm
Mexican. Vegan options. Not pure vegetarian.

Menu: Has a separate vegetarian menu. Fresh food with no additives or preservatives.
Other Info: Counter service, take-out. Accepts AMEX, DC, DIS, MC, VISA. Price: $.

Blue Corn Café

133 Water Street, Sante Fe   505-984-1800
4056 Cerrillos Road   505-438-1800
Hours: Saturday to Thursday 11 am to 9 pm
Friday 11 am to 10 pm
Southwestern. Vegan options. Not pure veg.
Menu: Marks the vegetarian dishes with a blue spiral. Grilled Corn, creamy Chipotle Soup, Portobello Veggie Fajitas, Tortilla Burger, black-bean pasta salad and Jalapeno-stuffed Pretzels.
Comments: Has an outdoor patio with a good view of the street. Full service, take-out.
Other Info: Reservations suggested for groups. Accepts AMEX, DC, DIS, MC, VISA. Price: $$.
Directions: It has a central location near the plaza. Has an adobe interior.

Café Oasis

526 Galisteo Street, Santa Fe; 505-983-9599
Hours: Sunday 10 am to 12 midnight
Saturday and Sunday 9:30 am to 2:30 pm.
It is best to call in advance to see what time the place is open.
Southwestern American. Not pure vegetarian.
Menu: Vegan dishes. Layered granola comes with fresh fruit and yogurt in a tall glass. Greek Salad with feta cheese, Mediterranean dish, Tempeh dish, Black-bean Burger, Basmati Rice, pinto beans and corn tortillas
Comments: Uses organic produce as much as possible. Has an assortment of theme rooms and you choose the one you want to sit in. There is an outdoor patio, a mystic room where you take your shoes off, a romantic room with low tables, and a smoking room. Has a far out looking front entrance.
Other Info: Full service, take-out. Accepts DC, DIS, MC, VISA. Price: $$.
Directions: From I-25, take St Frances (Hwy 84) exit number #282 and go north about 2¾ miles. At Cerrillos Rd (Rte 14) turn right and go a half-mile northeast, then at Paseo Dr Peralta (Rte 589) turn right and go 2 blocks, then at Galisteo St turn left and this place is a block down.

Café Pasqual's

121 Don Gaspar; 505-983-9340
Hours: Monday to Thursday 7 am to 3 pm, 5:30 pm to 9:30 pm; Friday & Saturday 7 am to 3 pm, 5:30 pm to 10:30 pm; Sunday 8 am to 2

pm, 5:30 pm to 9 pm

Southwestern, Eclectic Mexican Natural Foods. Local traditional dishes. Not pure vegetarian.
Menu: Has a fair selection of vegetarian dishes. Has two vegetarian main dishes. Thai Curry Vegetable with Rice, Spinach Jack Cheese Enchiladas, quesadillas, Chili, vegetarian tamales and other dishes. Fresh juices.
Comment: One of the most popular restaurants in Santa Fe.
Other Info: Full service, take-out. Reservations suggested on weekend nights and for Sunday brunch. Good idea to arrive a half-hour before you want to eat to put your name on a reservation list. Accepts AMEX, MC, VISA. Price: $$-$$$.

Carlos' Gosp'l Café
125 Lincoln Avenue; 505-983-1841
Hours: Monday to Saturday 8 am to 3 am Closed Sunday.
Restaurant. Not pure vegetarian.
Menu: Large sandwiches and salads. Carlos Hangover Stew is made of corn, potatoes and Monterey Jack cheese with green chili.

Cherry Valley Market
1708 Llano Street, at St Michael
505-473-4943
Hours: Monday to Friday 8 am to 9 pm
Saturday & Sunday 9 am to 8 pm
Natural Food Store and Deli. Juice Bar. Organic produce.
Menu: Has a good selection of vegetarian dishes. Soups, salads, sandwiches, Tempeh dishes and much more.
Other Info: Accepts AMEX, DIS, MC, VISA.
Directions: This place is right next to the College of Santa Fe. From I-25, take Cerrillos Rd exit (one direction). At St Michael's turn right. This place on the right at corner of St Michael's and Llano. From I-25, take St Frances (Hwy 84) exit number 282 and go north about 1 mile, then take St Michael's Drive ramp (keep left at fork in ramp) and merge onto St Michael's Dr and go 1 mile west, then at Llano St turn left and this place is a block down.

Cloud Cliff Bakery & Restaurant
1805 Second Street; 505-983-6254
Lunch Counter Hours: Monday 7 am to 5 pm
Saturday & Sunday 8 am to 3:30 pm
Restaurant Hours: Monday to Friday 7 am to 2:30 pm; Saturday & Sunday 8 am to 2:30
Natural Food. Vegetarian-friendly. Not pure veg-

etarian.
Menu: Baked breads and baked goods. Uses organic grains. Fresh juices.
Other Info: Full service, take-out. Accepts MC, VISA. Price: $$.

Hunan Chinese Restaurant
2440 Cerrillos Road; 505-471-6688
Hours: Monday to Friday 11 am to 9 pm
Saturday & Sunday 11:30 am to 10 pm
Chinese. Vegan options. Not pure vegetarian.
Menu: Has a good variety of vegetarian dishes including soups, appetizers and over 15 main dishes.
Other Info: Full service, take-out. Accepts AMEX, DIS, MC, VISA. Price: $$.

India House
2501 Cerrillos Road; 505-471-2651
Hours: Daily 11:30 am to 2:30 pm, 5 pm to 10 pm
Menu: Has a good selection of vegetarian dishes such as pakoras, samosas, rice dishes and curry dishes.
Other Info: Full service. Accepts AMEX, DIS, MC, VISA. Price: $$.

The Marketplace
627 West Alameda Street; 505-984-2852
Hours: Monday to Saturday 7:30 am to 9 pm
Sunday 9 am to 8 pm
Natural Food Store and take-out Deli. Juice Bar (mainly carrot juice). Very good selection of organic produce.
Menu: Has a good selection of vegetarian dishes. Salads, sandwiches, soups and daily specials.
Other Info: Accepts AMEX, MC, VISA.
Directions: From I-25, take St Francis exit north and go about 3 miles, then at Alameda St turn right and this place is ¾ mile down on the left.

Tecolote Café
1203 Cerrillos Road, Sante Fe; 505-988-1362
Hours: Tuesday to Sunday 7 am to 2 pm
Closed Monday.
Southwestern. Not pure vegetarian.
Menu: Does not use meat products in the beans or chilis. Fresh baked goods. Pinon Hot Cakes. There is a breakfast burrito with vegetarian sausage. Fresh juices.
Comments: Bean and chili sauces contain pure soy oil and do not contain lard.
Other Info: Full service, take-out. Accepts AMEX, DC, MC, VISA. Price: $-$$.
Directions: This place is located about a mile northwest of the main tourist area. From I-25,

take St Francis exit and go about 2 miles north on St Francis, then at Cerrillos Rd turn left and this place is a half-mile down.

Tomasita's Santa Fe Station
500 South Guadalupe; 505-983-5721
Hours: Monday to Saturday 11 am to 10 pm Closed Sunday
New Mexican. Vegan options. Not pure veg.
Menu: Vegetarian dishes are marked on the menu. Green Chili with no meat is vegetarian (best to confirm).
Comments: Located in a historic red-brick house. The red chili contains beef.
Other Info: Full service, take-out. Accepts DIS, MC, VISA. Price: $$.

Whistling Moon Café
402 North Guadelupe Street; 505-983-3093
Hours: Monday to Thursday 11:30 am to 2:30 pm, 5 pm to 9 pm; Friday 11:30 am to 2:30 pm, 5 pm to 9:30 pm; Saturday 5 pm to 9:30 pm; Sunday 5 pm to 9 pm
Mediterranean. Not pure vegetarian.
Menu: Middle Eastern dishes such as Spicy Coriander-cumin Fries, hummus, tabbouleh and Ghanouj Plate. Also pizzas, salads and other dishes. Cappuccino, espresso. Non-alcoholic beer and wine.
Other Info: Full service, take-out, catering. Reservations suggested for groups. Accepts MC, VISA. Price: $-$$

Whole Foods Market (two places)
753 Cerrillos Road; 505-992-1700
Hours: Daily 8 am to 10 pm
Directions: This place is located about a mile northwest of the main tourist area. From I-25, take St Francis exit and go about 2 miles north on St Francis, then at Cerrillos Rd turn right and this place is a third-mile down.
1090 St Francis Drive; 505-983-5333
Hours: Daily 7 am to 11 pm
Directions: From I-25, take St Francis Drive exit (#282), then go north on St Francis Dr and this place is 2½ miles down on the left.
Natural Food Store and Cafe. Deli, Bakery, Salad Bar and Juice Bar. Organic produce. Supermarket-type place. See Whole Foods Market information.
Menu: This is a large natural food store that has a good selection in its deli. Baked goods. Fresh juices.
Other Info: Counter service, take-out. Accepts MC, VISA. Price: $.

SILVER CITY

Silver City Food Co-op
520 North Bullard Street; 505-388-2343
Hours: Monday to Friday 9 am to 6 pm; Saturday 9 am to 5 pm; closed Sunday.
Natural Food Store. Organic produce.
Menu: Has ready-made sandwiches.
Directions: From Hwy 180, go south on Hwy 90 for 1 mile, then at College turn right and go 2 blocks, then at Bullard St turn left and this place is 2½ blocks down on left. This place is basically in the center of town.

TAOS

Apple Tree Restaurant
123 Bent Street; 505-758-1900
Hours: Monday to Saturday 11:30 am to 3 pm, 5 pm to 9 pm
Sunday 11 am to 3 pm (Brunch), 5 pm to 9 pm
Eclectic American and Mexican Natural Foods. Emphasis on vegetarian meals. Vegan options. Not pure vegetarian.
Menu: Some soups, salads, appetizers and entrees are vegetarian. The beans, and the red and green chilis are vegetarian. Cappuccino, espresso.
Other Info: Full service, take-out. Accepts AMEX, DC, DIS, MC, VISA. Price: $$-$$$.
Directions: This place is in the center of town. From Hwy 64 (Paseo Del Puebho Norte) go west on Bent St and this place is a half-block down.

The Caffe Tazza
122 Kit Carson Road; 505-758-8706
Hours: Daily 6:30 am to 7 pm (closes at 9 pm if there is an event)
Café. Not pure vegetarian.
Menu: Pesto Roasted Vegetable Sandwich, veggie tamale, veggie chili, pizza, veggie burritos, soups (sometimes), salads and other dishes. Cappuccino, espresso.
Comments: Courtyard seating. Good selection of magazines to read. Has music, poetry and other events.
Other Info: Limited service, take-out. No credit cards. Price: $.

Mainstreet Bakery & Café
112 Dona Luz Plaza; 505-758-9610
Hours: Monday to Friday 7:30 am to 2 pm Saturday & Sunday 7:30 to 12 noon
Southwestern. Vegan options. Not pure veg.
Menu: Has Scrambled Tofu with Tortilla Chips, Black Beans, freshly baked Corn Bread, Garden

Burger, Idaho Volcano (a potato with chili mushroom sauce and cheese), Orange Date-nut and Carrot Poppy Seed Bread. Has organic mixed vegetables with seeds. Has a variety of dressing including pesto vinaigrette, lemon, Dijon, jalapeno honey and tahini.

Comments: Often uses organic produce. Cheap prices. Has an outdoor patio in front.

Other Info: Cash only; no credit cards.

Directions: From Hwy 64 or Rte 68 (Paseo del Pueblo Sur) in center of town, go west on Ranchitos Rd a quarter-mile, then turn right at Dona Luz Plaza and this place is near the corner.

The Outback

712 Paseo del Pueblo Norte
505-758-3112

Hours: Sunday to Thursday 11 am to 9 pm
Friday & Saturday 11 am to 10 pm

Pizza. Not pure vegetarian.

Menu: Salads, pastas and gourmet pizzas. Some toppings are artichoke, spinach and sun-dried tomatoes.

Other Info: Full service, take-out. Accepts MC, VISA. Price: $$.

New York

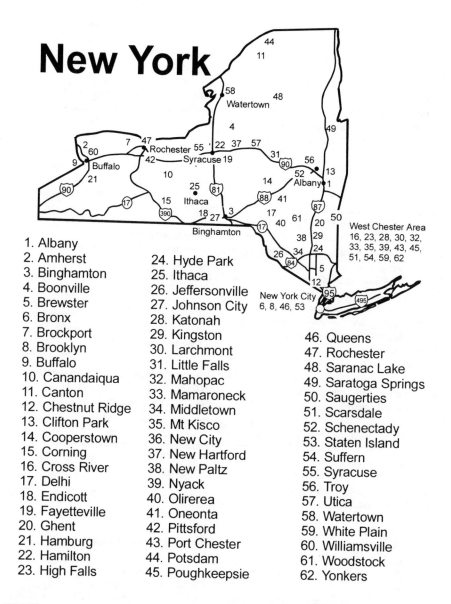

44
11

58
Watertown
48

4

49

47
2
60
7
Rochester 55
22 37 57
31
42 — Syracuse 19
90
56
9
Buffalo
52 13
21
90
10
14
Albany 1
25
81
88 41
15 Ithaca
390
18 27
3
17
40 61
20 50
Binghamton
17
38 29
34
26
84
24
5
12

9
Buffalo

West Chester Area
16, 23, 28, 30, 32,
33, 35, 39, 43, 45,
51, 54, 59, 62

New York City
6, 8, 46, 53
95
495

1. Albany
2. Amherst
3. Binghamton
4. Boonville
5. Brewster
6. Bronx
7. Brockport
8. Brooklyn
9. Buffalo
10. Canandaiqua
11. Canton
12. Chestnut Ridge
13. Clifton Park
14. Cooperstown
15. Corning
16. Cross River
17. Delhi
18. Endicott
19. Fayetteville
20. Ghent
21. Hamburg
22. Hamilton
23. High Falls

24. Hyde Park
25. Ithaca
26. Jeffersonville
27. Johnson City
28. Katonah
29. Kingston
30. Larchmont
31. Little Falls
32. Mahopac
33. Mamaroneck
34. Middletown
35. Mt Kisco
36. New City
37. New Hartford
38. New Paltz
39. Nyack
40. Olirerea
41. Oneonta
42. Pittsford
43. Port Chester
44. Potsdam
45. Poughkeepsie

46. Queens
47. Rochester
48. Saranac Lake
49. Saratoga Springs
50. Saugerties
51. Scarsdale
52. Schenectady
53. Staten Island
54. Suffern
55. Syracuse
56. Troy
57. Utica
58. Watertown
59. White Plain
60. Williamsville
61. Woodstock
62. Yonkers

ALBANY

BFS Catering Restaurant

1736 Western Avenue, #2, in the west suburbs
518-452-6342
Hours: Monday to Saturday 10 am to 8:30
Closed Sunday.
Mediterranean. Vegan options. Not pure veg.
Menu: Soups, salads, hummus, sandwiches, grape leaves, falafel and tabbouleh. Cappuccino, espresso.

Comments: Does catering and weddings.
Other Info: Full service, take-out, catering. Accepts AMEX, MC, VISA. Price: $.

El Loco Mexican Café

465 Madison Avenue, at Lark Street
518-436-1855
Hours: Tuesday to Thursday 11:30 am to 10 pm; Friday 11:30 am to 11 pm; Saturday 12 noon to 11 pm; Sunday 4:30 pm to 9 pm
Mexican. Not pure vegetarian.

Menu: Soups, Mexican rice, blue cornbread, veggie chili, vegetarian Black Bean Soup, veggie burritos and quesadillas. There is no lard in the refried beans. Most dishes can be made vegetarian. Can substitute soy cheese.
Comments: Outdoor patio seating. Relaxed place. Tribal masks and blankets on the walls. Authentic food. Voted the best Mexican restaurant in the Albany area.
Other Info: Full service, take-out, catering. Reservations for groups. Accepts AMEX, MC, VISA. Price: $$.
Directions: This place is at the junction of Rte 20 and Rte 9, a little west of the downtown. Can find parking on Madison or in Washington Park.

Honest Weight Food Co-op
484 Central Avenue; 518-482-2667; email: email@hwfc.com; Web site: www.hwfc.com
Hours: Monday to Friday 9 am to 8 pm; Saturday 9 to 6 pm; Sunday 12 noon to 6 pm
Natural Food Store and Café. Deli, Bakery, Salad Bar and Juice Bar. Organic produce.
Menu: Soups, salads, sandwiches and baked goods. Veggie Cheese Sandwich, Hummus Sandwich, Grilled Portabella Sandwich, Fakin BLT, Tofu Supreme (Sautéed tofu, vegetables over brown rice), Tofu Jambalaya (New Orleans style tofu dish on brown rice), Sesame Noodles, Moroccan Carrots and Rosemary Potatoes.
Other Info: Accepts AMEX, DIS, MC, VISA. Price: $.
Directions. Centrally located in the Capitol District. From I-90, take Everett Rd exit (exit #5) and go south a half-mile, then at Central Ave (Rte 5) turn left and this place is about 1 mile down. Can also take Exit #4 from I-90 and go east on Central Ave 1½ miles.

Mamoun's Falafel
206 Washington Avenue; 518-434-3901
Hours: Daily 11:30 am to 10 pm
Middle Eastern and Greek. Vegan options. Not pure vegetarian.
Menu: Stuffed grape leaves, vegetarian sandwiches, salad, falafel, couscous and Tahini over Rice & Eggplant. Fresh juices. Turkish coffee
Comments: Well priced. Has nice music.
Other Info: Full service, take-out. Accepts AMEX, MC, VISA. Price: $-$$.
Directions: Next to Washington Park, near the capitol.

Shades of Green
187 Lark, near the capitol; 518-434-1830

Hours: Monday to Thursday 11 am to 9 pm; Friday & Saturday 11 am to 10 pm; closed Sunday.
Natural Food Restaurant and Juice Bar. Vegan options. Mainly vegetarian.
Menu: Soups, salads, sandwiches, vegetarian chili, veggie burgers, Tofu Burrito with black beans and organic brown rice, Grilled Tempeh (with black beans, sweet potato puree, apple-corn salsa), burritos, Tempeh Reuben, quesadillas on whole-wheat tortillas, Portobello Delights (mushrooms, grilled potatoes, black beans with spicy pineapple sauce), Sunshine Burger (recommended), Tofu Russian Dressing, Mexican dishes, ginger cookies and hot entrees. Has a good selection of fresh juices, smoothies and wheatgrass.
Comments: Casual. Good size servings. Good food. Local organic produce used when possible. Can get quite busy.
Other Info: Full service, counter service, take-out. Cash only; no credit cards.
Directions: From the main downtown area go west on Washington Ave for several blocks, then at Lark (Rte 9) turn left and this place is a half-block down on the left.

ALBERTSON

Vincent's Restaurant & Pizzeria
1004 Willis Avenue; 516-621-7530
Hours: Daily 11 am to 11 pm
Italian. Not pure vegetarian.
Menu: Has several vegetarian dishes. Pizza, pasta and Cheeseless Potato Pizza.
Other Info: Full service, take-out. Reservations are suggested. Accepts AMEX, DC, MC, VISA. Price: $$.

AMHERST (near Buffalo)

Feel-Rite Fresh Market
3912 Maple Road; 716-834-3385
Hours: Monday to Saturday 9 am to 9 pm Sunday 11 am to 7 pm
Deli Hours: Monday to Friday 9 am to 6 pm Sunday 11 am to 5 pm
Natural Food Store and Café. Deli, Bakery and Juice Bar. Organic produce.
Menu: Has a good selection of vegetarian dishes.
Comments: This is a large place that has a good selection.
Other Info: Accepts AMEX, MC, VISA.
Directions: From I-290, take Niagara Falls Blvd (#3) exit and go south 1 mile. At Maple Rd turn left and this place is on the left a third-mile down.

Pizza Plant

8020 Transit Road 716-632-0800
5110 Main Street 716-626-5566
Hours: Monday to Thursday 11 am to 10 pm;
Fri & Sat 11 am to 12 noon; Sun 11 am to 9 pm
American with Natural Food. Not pure vegetarian. Vegan options.
Menu: Pizzas (some with soy cheese), pastas, homemade soups, salads, vegan veggie burgers, Vegetable Stew (in winter), burritos and vegetarian chili.
Other Info: Full service, take-out, catering. Accepts AMEX, DIS, MC, VISA. Price: $$.
Directions: From I-290, take Exit #2 and go south on Colvin Blvd 1 mile, then at Sheridan Drive turn left and this place is 1 block down.

BINGHAMTON

Lost Dog Cafe and Coffeehouse

222 Water Street; 607-771-6063
Hours: Monday to Thursday 10 am to 10 pm;
Friday & Saturday 10 am to 11 pm; closed Sun.
Menu: Has veggie burgers, Veggie Melt and tofu sandwiches.
Comments: Can substitute tofu for meat in most dishes. Has rice milk. Funky atmosphere. Outdoor seating in the summer.

Sunrise Health Foods

219 Main Street; 607-798-6231
Hours: Monday to Friday 9 am to 8 pm; Saturday 10 am to 6 pm; closed Sunday.
Natural Food Store.
Directions: In downtown Binghamton, near Foundry Plaza.

SUNY Binghamton Co-op

Student Union SUNY Binghamton
607-777-4258
Hours: Monday to Friday 11 am to 5 pm (closed in the summer); closed Saturday & Sunday.
Natural Food Store.
Directions: On second floor of Student Union. From Rte 17, take exit #208, and then follow signs to SUNY Binghamton.

Whole In The Wall

43 South Washington Street; 607-722-0006
Hours: Tuesday to Saturday 11:30 am to 9 pm
Closed Sunday & Monday.
Natural Foods Restaurant and Bakery. Vegan and Macrobiotic options. Not pure vegetarian.
Menu: Has Middle Eastern dishes, brown rice and tempeh & tofu dishes. Bagel, pies and breads

are baked daily. Fresh juices.
Comments: Vegetarian dishes are cooked separately from the non-veg dishes. Has live music on Saturday nights.
Other Info: Full service. Reservations not necessary. Non-smoking. Accepts DIS, MC, VISA. Price: $$.
Directions: Form I-81, take Exit #4 and go south on Hwy 7 (becomes Hwy 363) for 1½ mile, then turn left onto Colleir St and go across the bridge and go 1 block and then turn right onto Rte 434 (Vestal Pkwy) and go 2 blocks, then turn left and this place is a half-block down.

BOONVILLE

There are cross-country ski trails in the area.

For Goodness Sake

17 Schuyler; 315-942-4585
Hours: Tuesday to Friday 10 am to 5 pm; Saturday 10 am to 3 pm; closed Sunday.
Natural Food Store. Seasonal produce.
Directions: By the park in downtown Boonville.

BREWSTER

Jaipore

Route 22; 845-277-3549
Hours: Daily 12 noon to 3 pm, 5 pm to 10 pm
Indian. Vegan options. Not pure vegetarian.
Menu: Has an assortment of vegetarian main dishes. Freshly baked breads, rice dishes, vegetable curry dishes and more.
Comments: It is in a historical Victorian manor.
Other Info: Full service, take-out, catering. Accepts AMEX, MC, VISA. Price: $$.

BUFFALO

Amy's Place

3234 Main Street; 716-832-6666
Hours: Daily 6 am to 9 pm
American and Middle Eastern Natural Foods. Not pure vegetarian.
Menu: About half of their large menu is vegetarian. Sandwiches, home-fries, lentils, soups and falafels.
Comments: Has very reasonable prices. Good size portions. Good, relaxing atmosphere.
Other Info: Full service, take-out. Cash only; no credit cards. Price: $.

Feel-Rite Fresh Market

5425 Transit Road
716-636-1000

Hours: Monday to Saturday 10 am to 9 pm
Sunday 11 am to 7 pm
Natural Food Store and Café. Deli and Juice Bar.
Large selection of organic produce.
Menu: Has a wide selection of vegetarian dishes.
Other Info: Counter service, take-out. Has seating. Accepts AMEX, MC, VISA.
Directions: From I-90 take exit #49 and then go north on Transit Ave (Rte 78) and this place is a half-mile north of the exit. It is near the Eastern Hills Mall.

Feel-Rite Natural Food

720 Elmwood Avenue; 716-885-7889
Hours: Monday to Saturday 9 am to 9 pm
Sunday 12 noon to 6 pm
Natural Food Store and take-out Deli. Juice Bar.
Large selection of organic produce.
Menu: Salads, sandwiches, four vegan salads, vegetarian hummus wraps, vegan chocolate chip cookies and more.
Other Info: Counter service, take-out. No seating.
Directions: From Main St go west on W Ferry St ¾ mile, then turn right at Elmwood and this place is one block down. One block north of the junction of Elmwood and Westberry.

Feel-Rite Natural Food

247 Cayuga Road   716-633-5472
1451 Hertel Avenue   716-837-7661
4018 Seneca Street   716-675-6620
1694 Sheridan Drive   716-877-6095
Main Place Mall   716-842-1120
Natural Food Store. These places have limited or no produce.

Golden Parachute

5735 Main Street; 716-632-1666
Hours: Monday to Friday 9 am to 3 pm
Vegan-friendly Restaurant. Not pure vegetarian.
Menu: Good soups, salads and vegetarian chili.
Will adjust ingredients to suit. The Spinach Bread (can minus the cheese) is good.

Lexington Real Food Community Co-op

230 Lexington Ave, one block off Elmwood
716-884-8828; email: lexcoop@juno.com; Web
site: http://members.aol.com/LexTalk/; http://
users.aol.com/lextalk/
Hours: Daily 9 am to 9 pm
Natural Food Store. Organic produce. Baked goods.
Directions: Near Elmwood, the cool street in Buffalo. From I-90, take the exit for Rte 33 west.

Get off on East Ferry and then head west. Turn right on Elmwood and right on Lexington. The store is on the left.

CAMBRIDGE

Village Store Co-op

25 East Main Street; 518-677-2765
Hours: Monday to Saturday 10 am to 5 pm (until 8 pm on Thursday); closed Sunday.
Natural Food Store. Organic produce.
Directions: Next to Hubbard Hall in the middle of Cambridge, on the main street in town.

CANANDAIQUA

Catskill Bagel & Deli

103 South Main Street; 716-394-5830
Bagels Place. Has bagels sandwiches and salads.
Not pure vegetarian.
Directions: On the main street in the middle of the downtown.

Root Cellar

94 South Main Street; 716-394-8210
Hours: Monday to Friday 10 am to 6 pm; Saturday 9 am to 5 pm; Sunday 12 noon to 4 pm
Natural Food Store. Has supplements, Homeopathic medicines, natural cosmetic and foods.
Small place with a decent selection.
Comments: Plans to open a café in the future.
Directions: On the main street in the middle of the downtown.

CANTON

Nature's Storehouse

21 Main Street (Route 11); 315-386-3740
Hours: Monday to Thursday 9 am to 5 pm; Friday 9 am to 6 pm; Sat 9 am to 5 pm; closed Sun.
Natural Food Store and Deli. Whole foods and bulk grains.
Menu: Only has a few take-out sandwiches, a soup and a few salad items.
Directions: On the main street in town.

CHESTNUT RIDGE

Hungry Hollow Co-op

841 Chester Ridge Road; 845-356-3319
Hours: Monday to Thursday 10 am to 7 pm;
Friday & Saturday 10 am to 6 pm; closed Sun.
Natural Food Store and Deli.
Menu: Soups, salads, sandwiches and hot dishes.
Directions: From Garden State Parkway, take exit

#172 (last exit in New Jersey). Then turn right, then at Chestnut Ridge Rd turn left. Drive five miles to New York State (this road becomes Rte 45). This place is on the left.

CLIFTON PARK

The Green Grocer
Half Moon Plaza, 1505 Route 9; 518-383-1613
Hours: Monday to Friday 10 am to 8 pm; Saturday 10 am to 6 pm; Sunday 12 am to 5 pm
Natural Food Store. Has a large selection of organic produce.
Directions: From I-87, take Grooms Rd (exit #8A). Go two miles east on Drive Grooms Rd to Rte 9. At Rte 9 turn left and go 1 mile, then turn right onto the Half Moon Plaza.

COOPERSTOWN

Clare's Cornucopia Co-op
4959 State Highway 28, Cooperstown
607-547-2612; **email:** clare@telenet.net
Web site: www.clarescornucopia.com
Natural Food Store.
Directions: This place is 1½ mile northwest of downtown Cooperstown on Hwy 28.

CORNING

Medley's Café
88 West Market Street; 607-936-1685
Hours: Monday to Thursday 10 am to 5 pm; Friday & Saturday 10 am to 8 pm; closed Sun.
Mostly Vegetarian International. Vegan options. Uses organic grains, rice and herbs.
Menu: Soups, salads, sandwiches, pastas and more. Non-alcoholic beer and wine.
Comments: Laid-back place. Eclectic design. Has live music and poetry on Thursday through Saturday evenings. Good size portions. Friendly service. Reasonably priced.
Other Info: Full service for dinner. Counter service for lunch. Accepts AMEX, DIS, MC, VISA. Price: $-$$.
Directions: From Hwy 17, take Exit #45 and then go southeast 1½ mile on Denison Pkwy, then at Slate St turn left and this place is a block down at corner with Market.

CROSS RIVER

Nature's Temptations
Route 35, near the the D'agostino Shopping Center; 914-763-5643

Hours: Monday to Friday 9:30 am to 7 pm; Saturday 9 am to 5 pm; Sunday 10 am to 3 pm
Natural Food Store and Deli. Organic produce.
Menu: Soups, salads, sandwiches and hot dishes.
Comments: Often uses organic produce.
Other Info: Counter service, take-out. Has two tables up front.
Directions: From Rte 684, take Rte 35 and go east to Rte 121. In a shopping center at intersection of Rte 121 and Rte 35.

DELHI

Good Cheap Food Co-op & Quarter Moon Café
53 Main Street
607-746-6562; **Café number:** 607-746-8886
Store Hours: Monday to Saturday 10 am to 5 pm (until 6 pm Friday); closed Sunday.
Café Hours: Tuesday to Saturday 11:30 am to 3 pm; Friday & Saturday 6 pm to 9 pm; Sunday 12 noon to 7 pm; closed Monday
Natural Food Store and Café. Vegan options.
Menu: Most of the dishes are vegetarian. Soups, salads, sandwiches, daily specials and hot dishes.
Comments: Has a bookstore. Sells clothing. Has a licensed acupuncturist.
Other Info: Full service, take-out. Price: $.
Directions: From Oneonta, take Rte 28 north, then at Rte 10 in Delhi turn left. Go to second traffic light (a half-mile) and this place is on the left just past the light.

ENDICOTT

Down to Earth Whole Foods
305 Grant Avenue; 607-785-2338
Hours: Monday to Friday 9 am to 9 pm; Saturday 10 am to 6 pm; Sunday 12 noon to 6 pm
Natural Food Store and Deli. Juice Bar and Bakery. Vegan-friendly deli. Largest natural food store in the Binghamton area.
Directions: From Hwy 17, take the Endicott exit and go north on Rte 26 a half-mile. Get off when you see the sign for Owego. Then go west on Grant Ave (Rte 17C) and this place is 1 block down on the left.

FAYETTEVILLE

Wegmans Market Café
6789 East Genesse Street; 315-446-2950
Store Hours: Daily 7 am to 10 pm
Natural Food Store and American Restaurant.
Juice Bar. Vegan options. Not pure vegetarian.

Menu: Soups, salads, pizza, Chinese dishes and much more. Fresh juices.
Other Info: Counter service, take-out, catering. Accepts AMEX, DIS, MC, VISA. Price: $-$$.
Directions: From I-481, take Exit #3 and go east on Dewey Ave and this place is a half-mile down.

GHENT

Hawthorne Valley Farm Store
327 Route 21C;
518-672-7500; email: HVFS@taconic.net
Web site: www.hawthornevalleyfarm.org
Natural Food Store and Deli. Bakery. Organic produce.

HAMBURG (Buffalo suburb)

Feel-Rite Natural Food
6000 South Park Avenue; 716-649-6694
Natural Food Store.

HAMILTON

Hamilton Whole Foods
28 Broad Street; 315-824-2930
Hours: Monday to Saturday 10 am to 5:30 pm; closed Sunday. Deli Hours: 11 am to 4:30.
Natural Food Store and Café. Bakery and Deli. Vegan options.
Menu: Makes sandwiches at the deli. Salads, soups, tabbouleh, Baked Tofu and more.
Comments: Has a good selection of bulk goods, environmentally friendly clothing, books and alternative magazines.
Other Info: Counter service, take-out. Has seating. Accepts MC, VISA.
Directions: This place is the middle of town, opposite the Village Green.

HIGH FALLS

High Falls Co-op
1398 State Road 213, at Lucas Avenue
845-687-7262
Hours: Monday to Saturday 9 am to 7 pm
Sunday 10 am to 6 pm
Natural Food Store and Deli. Organic produce. Has seasonal produce.
Menu: Has soups, sandwiches and salads.

HYDE PARK

Mother Earth's Storehouse
Jamesway Shopping Plaza, Route 9

845-229-8593
Hours: Monday to Saturday 9 am to 8 pm
Sunday 12 noon to 5 pm
Natural Food Store. Organic produce. Has a good selection of items.
Menu: Has ready-made sandwiches.
Directions: In the back of a plaza across from Shoprite.

ITHACA
Cornell Plantations has beautiful flower gardens. Has some nice parks.
See http://astrosun.tn.cornell.edu/students/wilson/food.html for ratings of vegan dishes at Ithaca restaurants. (Listings maintained by Cornell Students For The Ethical Treatment Of Animals.)

**ABC Café (Apple Blossom Café)
308 Stewart Avenue, at Buffalo Street
617-277-4770
Web site: http://www.publiccom.com/web/abc/
Hours: Tuesday to Friday 11 am to 12 midnight; Sat & Sun 9:30 am to 12 midnight; closed Mon. Closed between Christmas and New Year's
Vegetarian International. Vegan and Macrobiotic options. Sometimes the special is real shrimp.
Menu: A large selection of vegan items. Wide selection of vegetarian entrées, including soups, salads, sandwiches and stir-fries. Homemade pastries. Has regular specials. Broccoli-Cashew Stir-fry with tempeh, ABC Burger and Tempeh Reuben. ABC burgers are tofu, sunflower seeds, sesame seeds and vegetables on a pita bread. Has good vegan desserts. Smoothies, cappuccino.
Comments: Very casual place. Different international dinner specials nightly. Tuesday is pasta night, Sunday macrobiotic dinner. Traditional breakfast fare for Saturday and Sunday brunch. Tuesday live music. Sunday brunch. Monthly art show. Food gets high recommendation.
Other Info: Table service at dinner and brunch only. Counter service at other times. Take-out. Non-smoking. Does not take reservations. Not necessary. Accepts AMEX, DIS, MC, VISA. Price: $-$$.
Directions: Located in lower "Collegetown", within easy walking distance of both Cornell University and downtown Ithaca. From Hwy 13, go east on W Buffalo St, at corner with Steward.

Aladdin's Natural Eatery
100 Dryden Road; 607-273-5000
Hours: Daily 11:30 am to 11 pm
Middle Eastern and International. Vegan op-

tions. Not pure vegetarian.
Menu: Soups, salads, sandwiches, pasta and Middle Eastern dishes. Falafel, stuffed grape leaves and tabbouleh. Non-alcoholic beer.
Other Info: Full service, take-out. Accepts AMEX, MC, VISA. Price: $$.

Collegetown Bagels
415 College Avenue; 607-273-9655
400 North Meadow Street; 607-273-4975
Hours: Daily 6:30 am to 1 am
Bagel Shop. Not pure vegetarian.
Menu: Has a good salad bar, usually at least one vegetarian hot entree.
Comments: Another location at 203 N Aurora only has bagels and bagel sandwiches.

Greenstar Cooperative Market

701 West Buffalo Street, corner of Seneca & Fulton; 607-273-9392
Web site: www.greenstarcoop.com
Hours: Daily 7 am to 11 pm
Natural Food Store and mainly Vegetarian Deli. Bakery. Organic produce.
Comments: Non-members can shop here, but pay slightly more. Has good prices and a good selection.
Other Info: Counter service, take-out. Has seating. Accepts AMEX, MC, VISA.
Directions: This store is about a half-mile west of the downtown, opposite the bus station. This place is a quarter-mile west of Hwy 13.

**Harvest Deli
171 East State Street, Box 133, The Commons at Center Ithaca; 607-272-1961
email: harvestjuna @hotmail.com
Web site: www.harvestdeli.com
Hours: Monday to Wednesday 7:30 am to 6 pm; Thursday to Friday 7:30 am to 8 pm; Saturday 9 am to 6 pm; Sunday 11 am to 5 pm
Fully Vegetarian Restaurant. Mostly Vegan. Juice Bar and Smoothie Bar.
Menu: Homemade soups, salads, subs, grilled sandwiches, breakfast, desserts and daily entrée. Pesto Veggie Cheese Melt, Eggplant Sub, Spicy Seitan Cuban Sub, Marinated Portabella Sub, Artichoke & Roasted Red Pepper Sub, Cheezy Macaroni and Potato Leek Soup. Good tasting scrambled tofu for breakfast plus muffins, Tofu Burrito, Tofu Rancheros, home fries, fresh fruit and vegetable juices. Fresh juices, smoothies, gourmet coffees.
Comments: Fresh foods. Indoor courtyard. Got

a good review in Ithaca Times.
Other Info: Counter service, catering (good at it). Has seating in the food court. Takes call-in orders. Non-smoking. Accepts reservations, but are not necessary. Price: $. Accepts MC, VISA.
Directions: Follow signs to "Ithaca Commons" and this place is located in Center Ithaca Atrium in the middle of the Commons, in the middle of downtown Ithaca's pedestrian mall. Has plenty of seating. From Hwy 13, go east on State St ¾ mile.

Ithaca Farmers' Market
Steamboat Landing
Hours: Saturday 9 am to 2 pm; Sunday 10 am to 2 pm; Open only spring, summer and fall.
Comments: Open air market that has local organic produce. The Vegan Epicure stand sells seitan.

**Juna's Café
145 The Commons
607-256-4292; **email:** harvestjuna@hotmail.com;
Web site: www.harvestdeli.com
Hours: Monday to Thursday 7:30 am to 9 pm; Friday 7:30 am to 11 pm; Saturday 9 am to 11 pm; Sunday 10 am to 7 pm
Vegetarian. Many Vegan options. Not pure vegetarian (serves poultry).
Menu: Sandwiches, Pita Platter (hummus and salad), Italian Wrap, Asian Wrap (baked tempeh, brown rice, muffins, vegetable and peanut miso dressing), Mediterranean Wrap, Greek Salads, turnovers, homemade soups, salads and bagels. Cappuccino, espresso.
Comments: Owned by the same people who owe the Harvest Café. Often has live music on Friday and Saturday. Displays artwork from local artists that changes monthly.
Other Info: Counter service, call-in take-out. Has seating upstairs. Price: $.
Directions: From Hwy 13, take State St west for about ¾ mile and this place is a half-block east of S Cayuga St.

Ludgate Produce Farm
1552 Hanshaw Road; 607-257-1765
Hours: Daily 9 am to 9 pm
Natural Food Store. Has a large selection of organic produce. Also has locally grown regular produce. Has a wide selection of goods.
Comments: Family owned and operated. Has fresh flowers. Accepts AMEX, MC, VISA.
Directions: This place is 3 miles northeast of downtown. This place is off Rte 13, between Hwy

366 and Warren Rd. From Hwy 13, take Hanshaw in the direction of Ithaca (west) and this place is about 1 mile down on the right.

Moosewood

Dewitt Mall, 215 North Cayuga Street, near Buffalo Street; 607-273-9610/5327
Web site: www.moosewoodrestaurant.com
Summer Lunch Hours: Monday to Saturday 11:30 am to 2 pm; Café Menu 2 pm to 4 pm
Summer Dinner Hours: Sunday to Thursday 5:30 pm to 9 pm; Friday and Saturday 6 pm to 9:30 pm
Winter Café Hours: 11 am to 11 pm; Friday & Saturday 11 am to 12 midnight
Winter Dinner Hours: Sunday to Thursday 5:30 pm to 8.30 pm; Friday and Saturday 5:30 pm to 9 pm
Café and Gift Shop Hours: Sunday to Thursday 11 am to 11 pm; Friday and Saturday 11 am to 12 midnight
American Gourmet and Natural Foods. Vegan options. Organic produce.
Menu: One main dish and a few desserts are vegan. The menu changes daily rotating between the hundreds of recipes in the Moosewood Cookbooks. The daily special changes each day. Some dishes that they serve are Enchilada, Avocado Tomatillo Soup, Orzo & Pesto Stuffed Tomatoes, Grilled Portabello Mushrooms, moussakea, Stuffed Red and Yellow Peppers, muffin of the day, fresh salads, good breads, several soups, homemade dressings, homemade desserts such as Chocolate Vegan Cake. Has four main dishes daily. Savannah Banana Pudding is a famous Moosewood dessert. Has a bar that sells many interesting non-alcoholic drinks, fresh juices, smoothies and coffees.
Comments: Cooperatively owned and managed restaurant. This place is known to be one of the best vegetarian-friendly restaurants in the US. It has a gift shop also. They have published several Moosewood Vegetarian Cookbooks, which are some of the most popular vegetarian books sold. Friendly place. Outdoor seating in season. Also sells clothing, t-shirts, books, hats, their own salad dressing and other things. Has outside patio seating. Peaceful, relaxed, friendly place. Sunday night is ethnic, when specialties of places all over the world are served. Fish is served Thursday to Sunday. Can call 607-273-9610 to get the menu of the day. Does cooking classes.
Other Info: Full service, take-out, catering. Accepts MC, VISA. Price: $$-$$$.
Directions: This place at corner of Cayuga and

Seneca Streets. The shopping mall where the restaurant is located used to be DeWitt High School. From Hwy 13 go west on Hwy 79 a half-mile, then at Cayuga turn right and this place is near the corner.

New Alexandrian Bookstore

Clinton Hall; 607-272-1663
This bookstore has many vegetarian resources and spiritual books.

Oasis Natural Grocery

DeWitt Mall, 215 North Cayuga
607-273-8213
Hours: Monday to Friday 9:30 am to 7 pm; Saturday 9:30 am to 6 pm; Sunday 12 noon to 5 pm
Natural Food Store and Café. Deli and Bakery. Organic produce.
Menu: Soups, sandwiches, salads and usually two hot dishes daily.
Comments: Bakes fresh bread and makes granola. Sells books. Open over 20 years.
Other Info: Counter service, take-out. Has seating in back of store. Accepts AMEX, MC, VISA.
Directions: From Rte 13, get on Buffalo St going east. It is in the DeWitt Mall next to Moosewood Restaurant on the right at the corner of Cayuga and Buffalo. Has a maroon awning.

Sangam Indian Cuisine

424 Eddy Street; 607-273-1006
Hours: Daily 11:30 am to 2:30 pm, 5 pm to 10 pm
Northern Indian. Several of the vegetable dishes are vegan. Not pure vegetarian.
Menu: The dishes containing dairy are clearly marked as such. Lunch buffet with at least two vegetarian main dishes.
Comments: Good food. Everything is cooked with vegetable oil.
Other Info: Full service, take-out. Accepts AMEX, DIS, MC, VISA. Price: $-$$.

Thai Cuisine

501 South Meadow Street (Route 13)
607-273-2031
Hours: Monday, Tuesday to Friday 5 pm to 9:30 pm (until 10 pm on Friday); Saturday 11:30 am to 2:30 pm, 5 pm to 10 pm; Sunday 11 pm to 2:30 pm, 5 pm to 9:30 pm; closed Tuesday.
Thai. Vegan-friendly. Not pure vegetarian.
Menu: Has a good selection of vegetarian dishes. Soups, salads, noodle dishes, sweet and sour dishes, curry dishes and more. The food can be really spicy hot. Medium is really hot for many people.

Comment: A bit formal. Food gets good ratings.
Other Info: Reservations recommended. **Price:** $$.

Viva Taqueria
101 North Aurora Streets, at State; 607-277-1752
Hours: Daily 11 am to 10 pm
California-style Mexican. Vegan-friendly. Not pure vegetarian.
Comments: Everything made fresh daily. Good food. Good size portions. Casual. Can be hard to get a seat during lunch. No lard in the beans. **Price:** $$.

JEFFERSONVILLE

The Good Earth
Main Street, across from the video store
914-482-3131
Hours: Monday to Saturday 10 am to 6 pm Closed Sunday.
Natural Food Store. Organic produce.
Directions: This place is in the middle of town, opposite the post office.

JOHNSON CITY

Health Beat Natural Foods and Deli
214 Main Street; 607-797-1001
email: info@healthbeatfoods.com
Web site: www.healthbeatfoods.com
Hours: Monday to Friday 9 am to 8 pm; Saturday 9 am to 6 pm; Sunday 9 am to 5 pm
Natural Food Store and Café. Deli and Juice Bar. Mostly Vegan. Not pure vegetarian. Organic produce.
Menu: Has both hot and cold dishes.
Comments: Offers cooking classes. Has eat-in and take-out deli. Has mailorder. Large selection of items.
Other Info: Counter service, take-out. Has seating. Accepts MC, VISA. **Price:** $.
Directions: This place is on the main street in town.

KATONAH

Mrs Greens
202 Katonah Avenue
914-232-7574; Web site: www.mrsgreens.com
Hours: Monday to Friday 8:30 am to 6:30 pm (until 7 pm Thursday); Saturday 8:30 am to 6 pm; Sunday 11 am to 5 pm
Natural Food Store and a good Deli. Has large selection of organic produce. Bakery and a cater-ing service.
Directions: From Saw Mill Pkwy, take the Katanoh exit. Coming from the north, turn right on Bedford (Rte 117), bear right onto Katonah Ave. Store is on the right. Coming from south, get on Harris Rd, turn left onto Harris, then turn right onto Bedford Rd. Same as above.

KINGSTON

Mother Earth's Storehouse
King's Mall, Route 9W North, 1200 Ulster Avenue; 845-336-5541
Hours: Monday to Friday 9 am to 9 pm; Saturday 10 am to 6 pm; Sunday 12 noon to 5 pm
Natural Food Store. Juice Bar and Salad Bar. Some organic produce.
Menu: Soups, salads, sandwiches and hot dishes. Fresh juices and smoothies.
Other Info: Counter service, take-out. Has seating.
Directions: On Ulster Avenue (Rte 9), a mile south of Rte 209.

LARCHMONT

Mrs Green's Natural Market
2460 Boston Post Road
914-834-6667; Web site: www.mrsgreens.com
Hours: Monday to Friday 9 am to 8 pm; Saturday 9 am to 7 pm; Sunday 10 noon to 6 pm
Natural Food Store and a good Deli. Bakery and Juice Bar. Large selection of organic produce.
Comments: The web site has a map to their locations. Counter service, take-out, catering.
Directions: Boston Post Road is the main street in town (called Main St a little south).

LITTLE FALLS
Scenic town on the Old Erie Canal and the Mohawk River.

Community Co-op
589 East Albany Street; 315-823-0686
Hours: Tuesday to Friday 9:30 am to 5 pm (until 8 pm Thursday); Saturday 9:30 am to 1 pm; closed Sunday.
Natural Food Store. Organic produce (best to come on Tuesday).
Directions: If coming from the east take Rte 5 into town, turn right onto Main St, then turn left at Albany St and this place is a block down. If coming from west take Rte 5 into town, turn left onto Main St, then at William St turn right and this place is a block down.

MAHOPAC (north New York city suburb)

Mrs Greens
Lake Plaza Shopping Center, Route 6
845-628-0533; Web site: www.mrsgreens.com
Hours: Monday to Saturday 9 am to 7 pm; Sunday 12 noon to 5 pm
Natural Food Store and good Deli. Juice Bar, Bakery and a catering service. Has a large selection of organic produce. The web site has a map to their locations.
Directions: From I-84, take Exit #19, turn right onto Rte 312 going towards Carmel. Turn right at the first light, then turn left on Rte 6 and then this store is on the left five miles down in the Lake Plaza Shopping Center.

MIDDLETOWN

The Rose Garden
19 West Main Street
845-342-4007; Web site: www.rosehealth.com
Hours: Wednesday to Saturday 10:30 am to 5:30 pm; closed Sunday, Monday, Tuesday
Natural Food Store.
Comments: Has nutritional counseling on Monday and Tuesday by appointment.
Directions: This place is in downtown Middletown. From Rte 17 take exit #120 and then go west on Rte 211. The road goes from a four-lane road to two lanes. In town turn left at North St (third light), then take the first left into the city parking lot.

MT KISCO

**Good Earth Health Foods
13 Main Street; 914-241-3500
Hours: Monday to Friday 9:30 am to 6:30 pm; Saturday 10 am to 5:30 pm; Sun 11 am to 5 pm
Natural Food Store and Vegetarian Café. Deli and Juice Bar. Organic produce.
Menu: Soups, sandwiches, steamed vegetables, Thai dishes (specials) and salads.
Other Info: Counter service, take-out. Has three tables.
Directions: From Saw Mill River Parkway, take Kisco Ave (Rte #133) exit. At Kisco Ave turn left and go 2/3 mile, at Crow Hill Rd turn right and go a third-mile, at Main St turn slight right and this place is 1 block down on the left.

Mrs Greens
666 Lexington Avenue
914-242-9292; Web site: www.mrsgreens.com

Hours: Monday to Friday 9 am to 8 pm Saturday & Sunday 10 am to 7 pm
Natural Food Store and good Deli. Bakery and a catering service. Large selection of organic produce.
Comments: Reservations recommended.
Directions: Their web site has a map to their locations. From Saw Mill River Parkway, take Reader's Digest exit towards Roaring Brook Rd, then go on Reader's Digest (become Roaring Brook Rd) for a half-mile, go pass tracks and at light bear right. At the next light turn left onto Rte 117 (N Bedford Rd) and go 1 mile, road becomes Main St and go a third-mile. At Lexington Ave turn right and go 1 block, then turn right into shopping center.

NEW CITY

Back to the Earth Natural Foods
306A South Main Street; 845-634-3511
Hours: Monday to Friday 9 am to 7:30 pm; Saturday 9 am to 6 pm; Sunday 10 am to 6 pm
Natural Food Store and take-out Deli. Bakery, Salad Bar and Juice Bar.
Menu: Has a large selection of vegetarian dishes.
Directions: From I-87, take Palisade Parkway north exit (#13N) and go 2 miles. From Palisade Parkway take exit #10 towards New City/Middletown, merge onto Germonds Rd and go 1 block. At Little Tor Rd turn right and go 1¼ mile. At Collyer turn right and go a half-mile, then turn left at Main and this place is on right halfway down block. Between A&P and the Bank of New York.

NEW HARTFORD

Peter's Cornucopia
52 Genesee Street; 315-724-4998
Hours: Monday to Friday 9:30 am to 8 pm; Saturday 9:30 am to 6 pm; Sunday 12 noon to 5 pm (closed Sunday in July & Aug)
Natural Food Store. Juice Bar. Organic produce.
Directions: From I-90, take Genesee exit and take Genesee Street three miles and this place on right.

NEW PALTZ (Catskill Mountains)

The Bakery
13-A North Front Street
845-255-8840
email: david@ilovethebakery.com
Web site: www.ilovethebakery.com
Hours: Daily 7 am to 6 pm

Natural Food Restaurant. Vegetarian-friendly.
Menu: Baked goods. Bagels, Grilled Marinated Tempeh, Garden Burgers, Vegetarian main dishes, soups, salads, vegetarian chili, Ratatouilli, Gazpacho, Mushroom Soup, Tomato-Basil Soup, Brown Rice & Red Beans with Tofu & Vegetables, Fresh Fruit Salad and Stuffed Cabbage with Mashed Potatoes.
Comments: Has outdoor seating and a beautiful garden.
Other Info: Reservations not necessary. Non-smoking. Accepts AMEX, DIS, MC, VISA.
Directions: From New York Thruway (I-87), take Rte 299 exit (#18) towards New Paltz, keep left at fork in ramp, then turn left at Rte 299 and go 1½ mile, at N Chestnut St turn right and this place a block down.

Earthgoods Natural Foods, Inc
71 Main Street, Route 299 &Thruway
845-255-5858
Hours: Monday to Saturday 10 am to 9 pm
Sunday 10 am to 7 pm
Natural Food Store. Organic produce. Has some ready-made sandwiches.
Directions: From I-87, take New Paltz exit, then turn towards town and this place is on the left in the middle of town.

***Vagabond
72 Main Street; 845-255-0816; **Web site:** http://vagabondcafe.freehomepage.com
Hours: Monday to Friday 11 am to 7 pm
Saturday & Sunday 10 am to 7 pm
Fully Vegan.
Comments: Really nice people and good food.
Directions: Across the street from Earthgoods Natural Food, downtown.

NYACK

Born of Earth
1 South Broadway; 914-353-3311
Hours: Monday to Saturday 10 am to 7 pm (until 7:30 pm Thursday); Saturday 11 am to 6 pm; Sunday 11 am to 5 pm
Natural Food Store and take-out Deli. Bakery and Juice Bar.
Menu: Has a good selection of vegetarian dishes.
Other Info: Counter service, take-out only. No seating.
Directions: From New York Thruway (I-287) going south, take exit #11 and past a stop sign. At next light (9W) turn right, at Rte 59 turn left (going east) and it becomes Main St. Store is at

corner of Broadway and Main St. From I-287 south, take exit #11, at the traffic light (Rte 59) turn left and go a third-mile, road becomes Main St and then this place is 0.65 mile down.

OLIREREA

Mountain Gate Indian Restaurant
212 McKinky Hollow Road, on Route 47 three miles off Route 28; 914-254-6000
Hours: Daily 8:30 am to 10 pm
Vegetarian Indian and Ethnic. Vegan options. Juice Bar. Buffet.
Menu: Has a vegetarian buffet. Naan, Malai Kofta, Saag Paneer, Kashmiri Pulao, rice dishes, puri, paratha and samosa.
Comments: This place is in the Catskill mountain in the Mountain Gate Lodge (has around 20 rooms). Outdoor seating. The lodge has a swimming pool and hiking in the area.
Other Info: Full service, take-out, buffet, catering. Accepts AMEX, DC, DIS, MC, VISA, personal checks. Price: $$.
Directions: From the New York Throughway (Rte 87), take exit #19 for Kingston. Then take Rte 28 west to Rte 47 going towards Oliverea and go around three miles, at McKinley Hollow Road turn right and this place is on the right 1 mile down.

ONEONTA

**Autumn Café
244 Main Street, Oneonta; 607-432-6845
Hours: Tuesday to Saturday 11:30 to 9 pm; Sunday Brunch 10:30 am to 2:30 pm; closed Mon.
Natural Food Restaurant. Uses organic produce. Not pure vegetarian.
Menu: Has vegetarian specials.
Comments: Everything is prepared on the premises. Uses whole foods.
Other Info: Full service, take-out, catering. Accepts AMEX, MC, VISA. Price: Lunch: $; Dinner: $$.
Directions: On the main street in town.

The Green Earth
7 Elm Street; 607-432-7160
Hours: Monday to Friday 10 am to 6 pm (until 8 pm Thursday); Sat 10 am to 5 pm; closed Sun.
Natural Food Store. Large selection of organic produce.
Directions: From I-88, take exit #15, and drive into town. Turn right on Main and at Elm turn right and this place is at the corner.

PITTSFORD (near Rochester)

Aladdin's Natural Eatery
8 Schoen Place, Pittsford
716-264-9000
Hours: Sunday to Thursday 11 am to 10 pm
Friday & Saturday 11 am to 11 pm
Middle Eastern, Greek and International. Vegan options. Not pure vegetarian.
Menu: Soups, salads, sandwiches, pasta and Middle Eastern dishes.
Comments: Has outdoor patio seating overlooking the Erie Canal in the summer. Good value. The food and service is good.
Other Info: Full service, take-out. Reservations recommended for groups. Accepts AMEX, DC, MC, VISA. Price: $$.

Mangia Pizza and Pasta
496 Cornelia Street
518-562-5555
Hours: Monday to Friday 11:30 am to 9 pm; Sat 12 noon to 10 pm; Sun 12 noon to 8 pm
Pizza. Not pure vegetarian.
Menu: Wood fire oven pizzas with a good choice of toppings. Soups, salads and good pasta dishes. Has some vegan options and low-fat dishes. Grilled vegetable and eggplant sandwiches.
Comments: Good pizzas.
Other Info: Accepts AMEX, MC, VISA.

North Country Co-op
25 Bridge Street
518-561-5904
Hours: Monday to Saturday 10 am to 7 pm; Saturday 10 am to 4 pm; Sunday 12 noon to 5 pm
Natural Food Store and take-out Deli. Limited produce. Small place.
Menu: Soups, sandwiches and salads.
Directions: This place is in downtown Plattsburgh opposite the city parking lot. From I-87, take Plattsburgh exit (#38S) toward Plattsburgh, merge onto Rte 22 going south and go ¾ mile, at Rte 3 turn left and go a quarter-mile, then at US 9 turn right and this place is 2 blocks down. Head east following signs to Rte 9 and for Plattsburgh.

SunFoods
Hours: Daily 24 hours
Supermarket with a natural food section. Has veggie mock meats and Worthington Foods products.

PORT CHESTER (in a suburb of Westchester)

***Green Symphony
Kohl's Shopping Center
427 Boston Post Road
914-937-6537
Hours: Sunday to Thursday 11:30 am to 10 pm
Friday to Saturday 11:30 am to 11 pm
Fully Vegan Vegetarian Chinese. Kosher.
Menu: This place has many mock "meat" dishes. Sliced Golden Chips (fried seaweed sticks and sesame seeds), Veggie Sesame "Chicken," Veggie "Beef" Mongolian, Veggie Squid, Veggie Chicken, Barbecued Veggie "Duck," General Tao's Chicken, Veggie Shrimp, Celery Pancakes, Orange Beef, Moo Shu Basil Roll, Triple Delight Hot Pot, Wontons, Veggie Spare Ribs, Orange Sensation, and Triple Mushrooms with Bean Curd. Have black mushrooms, snow peas, Chinese cabbage, carrot and bean thread noodle. Has tofu ice cream.
Comments: The food gets good recommendations. Modern design. No MSG in food. Got a good review in the New York Times. Is designed according to Feng Shui.
Other Info: Full service, take-out. Non-smoking. Accepts reservations but are not necessary. Accepts AMEX, MC, VISA.
Directions: This restaurant is in the Kohl Shopping Center. From I-287 (Cross Westchester Expressway), take Exit #11. If you are going east turn left at end of ramp, if coming from the west, turn right. Then go a quarter-mile to the Kohls Shopping Center on the right and this place is on left side of Kohl department store.

POTSDAM

Potsdam Consumer Co-op
24 Elm Street
315-265-4630
email: coopmail@northnet.org
Web site: http://www.northnet.orgpotsdamcoop/index.html
Hours: Monday to Friday 9 am to 7 pm; Saturday 9 am to 6 pm; Sunday 12 noon to 4 pm
Natural Food Store. Has an excellent organic produce section.
Directions: Across from the Big M Market next the Village Offices. From Rte 81, take Rte 11 into Potsdam. At Union St turn left, at Elm turn right and then this place is on the right.

POUGHKEEPSIE

Mother Earth's Storehouse
804 South Road Square; 845-296-1069
Hours: Monday to Saturday 9 am to 9 pm; Saturday 10 am to 8 pm; Sunday 12 noon to 6 pm
Natural Food Store and Deli. Organic produce.
Directions: On Rte 9 next to the Galleria Mall.

RED HOOK

**Luna 61
61 East Market Street
845-758-0061
Hours: Wednesday to Sunday 5 pm to 9 pm
Closed Monday & Tuesday
Fully Vegetarian Restaurant. Organic meals.
Comments: It is in the Catskills, near some skiing slope. Has non-sugar and non-wheat desserts.
Other Info: No credit cards. Accepts major credit cards.

ROCHESTER

**Abundance Cooperative Market
62 Marshall Street, Rochester
716-454-COOP; email: missive@hotmail.com;
Web site: http://www.wab.org/co-op/
Hours: Monday to Friday 8 am to 8 pm; Saturday 9 am to 6 pm; Sunday 11 pm to 6 pm
Natural Food Store and Vegetarian Deli. Organic produce.
Menu: Has a good selection of vegetarian dishes. Soups, sandwiches, wraps, noodle dishes and veggie Lasagna.
Other Info: Accepts MC, VISA. Counter service, take-out. Has seating.
Directions: From I-490, take Monroe Ave/Rte 31 exit (#18), turn right at Monroe Ave (Rte 31) turn right and go 1 mile, at Marshall St turn slight left and this place is 1 block down. This place is where the Inner Loop meets I-490, a quarter-mile south of Manhattan Square Park, just south of downtown Rochester.

Aladdin's Natural Eatery
646 Monroe Avenue
716-442-5000
Hours: Sunday to Thursday 11 am to 10 pm
Friday & Saturday 11 am to 10 pm
Middle Eastern and International. Vegan options. Not pure vegetarian.
Menu: Soups, salads, sandwiches, pasta and Middle Eastern dishes.
Other Info: Full service, take-out. Price: $$.

Bangkok
155 State Street; 716-325-3517
Hours: Monday to Thursday 11 am to 9 pm; Friday & Saturday 11 am to 10 pm; closed Sun.
Thai. Vegan-friendly.
Menu: Has a good vegetarian selection with vegetarian springs rolls, Sesame Tofu and good vegan dishes.
Comments: In many dishes they will substitute tofu for meat.
Other Info: Accepts MC, VISA.

Basha
798 South Clinton Avenue; 716-256-1370
Hours: Sunday to Thursday 10:30 am to 9 pm
Friday & Saturday 11 am to 10 pm
Middle Eastern. Not pure vegetarian.
Menu: Has good falafel, hummus, baba ghanoush and other dishes.
Comments: Comfortable atmosphere. Live guitar music on Thursday. Has outdoor seating on the patio. Food gets good recommendations.
Other Info: Full service, take-out. Reservations necessary for groups. Accepts AMEX, DIS, MC, VISA. Price: $-$$.

**Indian House Vegetarian Café
1009 South Clinton Avenue; 716-271-0242
Hours: Tuesday to Sunday 11:30 am to 2:30 pm, 5 pm to 9:30 pm; closed Monday.
Pure Vegetarian Indian. Daily lunch buffet.
Comments: Casual place. The lunch buffet is good and well priced. The Indian House is two different restaurants, one that serves South Indian cuisine and the other serves meat and North Indian food. There is an Indian store next door that sells spices and other Indian goods.
Other Info: Full service, take-out, catering. Non-smoking. Reservations not necessary. Accepts AMEX, DC, MC, VISA. Price: $-$$.
Directions: From I-490, take exit #17 towards Inner Loop, at S Goodman St go south 3 blocks, at S Clinton Ave turn left and go 1 block, at Caroline St turn right and this place is near the corner.

King & I
1475 East Henrietta Road; 716-427-8090
Hours: Monday to Thursday 11 am to 9:30 pm; Friday & Saturday 12 noon to 11 pm; Sunday 12 noon to 9:30 pm
Asian, mainly Thai. Vegan-friendly. Not pure vegetarian.
Menu: Has a vegetarian menu including soups, appetizers and main dishes. Uses tofu in mock

meat dishes. The Phat Thai and the Spring Rolls are really good. Has vegan ice cream made with coconut milk.
Comments: Have their own garden. Said to be the best Thai restaurant in Rochester.
Other Info: Good service. Accepts AMEX, MC, VISA.

**Leena's Garden
716-388-2128
Vegan Bakery. No retail, just catering and wholesale.
Menu: Cakes, brownies, cookies and breads.
Comments: Supplies Savory Thyme and Genesee Co-op. Does special orders for events. Really nice people. Very helpful. Recommended.

Lori's Natural Foods
Genesee Valley Regional Market, Building Number 1; 900 Jefferson Road
716-424-2323; **email:** lorisnatural@earthlink.net;
Web site: www.lorisnatural.com
Hours: Monday to Saturday 8 am to 8 pm
Sunday 12 noon to 6 pm
Natural Food Store. Organic produce.
Comments: This place is the largest natural food store in Rochester. Has a nutritionist.
Directions: From I-390, take Jefferson Rd (#14) exit and go west on Jefferson Rd and this place is a half-mile down. This place is behind the Road House Grill, between East Henrietta Rd and Clay Rd.

Mamasan's Restaurant
309 University Avenue; 716-262-4580
Hours: Monday to Saturday 11 am to 9 pm; Friday & Saturday 11 am to 10 pm; closed Sunday.
Thai, Vietnamese and Chinese. Not pure veg.
Menu: Curries, salads, noodle dishes and other vegetarian dishes.
Comments: Popular place.
Other Info: Full service, take-out. Accepts AMEX, MC, VISA. Price: $$.

Savory Thyme
105 East Avenue; 716-423-0750
Hours: Monday to Saturday 11 am to 9 pm
Closed Sunday.
Vegetarian-friendly Restaurant. Not pure veg.
Menu: Serves mock "meat" dishes that contain seitan, tempeh and tofu. Also serves fish and chicken. The Jerked Tempeh Sandwich is really good (cooked separately from any meat).
Comments: Local organic produce used when possible. Sells Lena's Garden baked goods.

Other Info: Full service, take-out, catering. Accepts AMEX, MC, VISA.
Directions: From I-490, take Clinton Ave exit (#16) towards downtown, then go south on S Clinton Ave, at Woodbury Blvd turn right and go 1 block, at Chestnut St turn left and go 2 blocks, at East Ave turn right and this place is 1 block down.

Slice of Life Café
742 South Avenue; 716-271-8010
Hours: Tuesday to Saturday 11:30 am to 8 pm; Sunday Brunch 10 am to 2 pm; closed Monday.
Mainly Vegetarian International. Vegan options. Not pure vegetarian.
Menu: Assortment of sandwiches (both hot and cold), Scrambled Tofu, Primavera Sub, Tempeh Reuben, veggie burgers, lentil club-sandwich, salads, wraps, bean burritos, enchiladas and noodle salads. The Buffalo Tempeh Sandwich is good.
Comments: Feminist vegetarian café. Friendly, clean atmosphere with good service and good people. Sunday brunch.
Other Info: Full service, take-out. Price: $-$$.
Directions: It is located a half-mile from the University of Rochester, a half-mile west of Exit #17. From I-490, take Goodman St exit (#17) towards Inner Loop, then go south on Goodman St a block, at Uhlen Place turn right and go 1 block, at S Clinton Ave turn right and go a quarter-mile, at Gregory St turn left and go a quarter-mile, at South Ave turn left and this place is 1 block down.

ROSENDALE

The Rosendale Café
434 Main Street; 845-658-9048
Hours: Monday 5 am to 10 pm
Wednesday to Sunday 11 am to 10 pm
Very Vegetarian-friendly American Natural Foods. Everything cooked is vegetarian. Vegan options. Not pure vegetarian (serves tuna and turkey sandwiches).
Menu: Soups, salads, sandwiches, pasta dishes, vegetarian chili and other entrees. Menu changes daily. Cappuccino, espresso.
Comments: Has special events including storytelling, poetry readings, music and more. Often has live music on the weekends. The dishes are labeled whether they are vegan or vegetarian.
Other Info: Full service, take-out. Non-smoking. Accepts MC, VISA. Price: $$.
Directions: This place is on the main street in town.

SARANAC LAKE

Nori's Whole Foods

65 Main Street; 518-891-6079
Hours: Monday to Friday 9 am to 8 pm; Saturday 10 am to 7 pm; Sunday 10 am to 4 pm
Natural Food Store and Café. Deli.
Menu: Has soups, sandwiches, salads and hot dishes.
Other Info: Counter service, take-out. Has three tables.
Directions: On the main street of town, next to the post office.

SARATOGA SPRINGS

Four Seasons Natural Foods and Café

33 Phila Street; 518-584-4670
Hours: Monday to Thursday 9 am to 8 pm; Friday & Saturday 10 am to 8 pm; Sunday 9:30 am to 5 pm
Natural Food Restaurant and Food Store. Pure Vegetarian Buffet, Bakery and Juice Bar.
Menu: Usually has around twenty vegetarian dishes in the buffet. Has salads, brown rice, steamed vegetables, noodles, soups, sandwiches, fresh breads, salads and baked deserts. New menu daily. Fresh juices.
Comments: Sit down or take out. Food is sold by the pound. Pay by weight. It is a good and healthy place. It is in a natural food store with organic vegetables. It is a small, casual place with around 15 seats.
Other Info: Counter service, take-out, catering. Non-smoking. Reservations not necessary. Accepts DIS, MC, VISA. Price: $-$$. Set price per pound.
Directions: This place is located down a side street in the middle of town. If you are coming north on Rte 9 you drive into the middle of town and then make a right on Phila St and this place is 1 block down at the corner on the left. If you turn right at the corner you will see a parking lot on the left where you can park.

SAUGERTIES (Catskill Mountains, on the Hudson River)

Mother Earth's Storehouse

249 Main Street; 845-246-9614
Hours: Monday to Thursday 9 am to 6 pm; Friday 9 am to 8 pm; Saturday 10 am to 6 pm; Sunday 12 noon to 5 pm
Natural Food Store.
Directions: From I-87, take exit #20, get on Ulster Ave and stay on it until it ends, turn left at the light and this store is on the left.

SCARSDALE

Mrs Green's Natural Market

365 Central Park Avenue
914-472-9675; **email:** harold@mrsgreens.com; **Web site:** www.mrsgreens.com
Hours: Monday to Saturday 9 am to 7 pm
Sunday 11 am to 6 pm
Natural Food Store and a good Deli. Bakery and Juice Bar. Has a large selection of organic produce. Vegan options.
Menu: A large selection of vegetarian, vegan and fat-free dishes. Sandwiches. Fresh juices.
Comments: The web site has a map to their locations.
Other Info: Limited service, take-out, catering. Accepts AMEX, DIS, MC, VISA.
Directions: From I-287, take Exit #5. Coming from the west go right (southeast) on Rte 119. Then make a right on Central Park Ave (100S) and the store is on the right 2 miles down. Coming from the east, take Exit #5 and then make a left on Tarrytown Rd (Rte 119). Same as above.

Mrs Green's Natural Market

780 White Plains Road
914-472-0111; **Web site:** www.mrsgreens.com
Hours: Monday to Friday 8:30 am to 8 pm (until 9 pm Thursday); Saturday 9 am to 7 pm; Sunday 10 am to 7 pm
Natural Food Store and a good Deli. Bakery and Juice Bar. Has a large selection of organic produce. Vegan options.
Comments: Has a catering service. The web site has a map to their locations.
Directions: From Major Degan going north, take exit #4 to Bronx River Parkway and go north. Take Harvey Rd exit (#10) and go right to White Plain Rd and this place is on the left 1.5 miles down.

SCHENECTADY

Earthly Delights Natural Food

162 Jay Street; 518-372-7580
Hours: Monday to Saturday 9 am to 6 pm (Thursday until 8 pm)
Closed Sunday.
Natural Food Store and Deli. Juice Bar.
Menu: Has fresh ready-made sandwiches, daily soups and a grain salad.
Other Info: Accepts AMEX, MC, VISA.

Directions: From I-90, take Exit #25 towards Schenectady and then merge on I-890 going towards Schenectady, then take Michigan Ave exit (#6), then turn right at S Brandywine Ave and go 3 blocks, at State St (Rte 5) turn left and go 1 mile, at Clinton St turn right and go 1 block, at Franklin St turn left and go 1 block, then at Jay St turn right and this place is 50 yards down on the left (no cars on Jay St). This place is ¾ mile due east of exit 4C of I-890.

SUFFERN (just north of New York city)

Mrs Green's Natural Market
26 Indian Rock Shopping Center
845-369-6699; Web site: www.mrsgreens.com
Hours: Monday to Saturday 9 am to 7 pm
Sunday 10 am to 6 pm
Natural Food Store and a good Deli. Has a large selection of organic produce. Bakery and a catering service.

SYRACUSE

Aladdin's Natural Eatery
163 Marshall Street; 315-471-4000
Hours: Monday to Saturday 11 am to 9 pm
Sunday 11 am to 10 pm
Middle Eastern and International. Vegan options. Not pure vegetarian.
Menu: Soups, salads, hummus, falafel, sandwiches, pasta and Middle Eastern dishes.
Other Info: Full scale restaurant. Full service, take-out. Accepts AMEX, MC, VISA. Price: $$.
Directions: Located right downtown at the strip of restaurants right night to Syracuse University (north of the main campus area).

King David's Restaurant
129 Marshall Street; 315-471-5000
Hours: Monday to Saturday 11 am to 9 pm
Closed Sunday.
Middle Eastern Food. Not pure vegetarian.
Menu: Good hummus and falafel.
Comments: Reasonable prices. Good size portions. Sometimes has belly dancing.
Other Info: Full service, take-out. Reservations suggested for groups. Accepts AMEX, DC, DIS, MC, VISA. Price: $$.
Directions: Located right downtown at the strip of restaurants right next to Syracuse University (north of the main campus area).

Nature-Tyme Discount Vitamin &
527 Charles Avenue, #12A; 315-488-6300

Hours: Monday to Friday 9 am to 7 pm; Saturday 9 am to 6 pm; Sunday 10 am to 5 pm
Natural Foods Restaurant. Not pure vegetarian.
Menu: Burritos, veggie burgers, salads, stir-fries, soups, vegetarian Lasagna, pastas, tofu dishes and more dishes.
Other Info: Limited service, take-out, catering. Accepts AMEX, MC, VISA. Price: $-$$.
Directions: It is located in Geddes Plaza. From I-690, take N Geddes St exit (#10), then go south on Geddes St for 2 blocks, at Genesee St turn right and go 1½ mile, at Charles Ave turn right and this place is a quarter-mile down.

Syracuse Real Food Coop
618 Kensington Road
315-472-1385; email: aspeno@mindspring.com;
Web site: http://www.foodcoop.org.srfc/
Hours: Daily 9 am to 9 pm
Natural Food Store and take-out Deli. Organic produce.
Other Info: Accepts AMEX, DIS, MC, VISA.
Directions: From I-81, take exit #17 towards Salina St/Brighton Ave, then go north on S Salina St (US 11) 2/3 mile, at E Colvin St turn right and go 1¼ mile, at Buckingham Ave turn left and go a quarter-mile, at Meadowbrook Dr turn slight right and go 2 blocks, at Westcott St turn left and go a third-mile, at Kensington Rd turn right and this place is 1 block down on the right.

TROY

Uncle Sam's Good Natural Products
77 4th Street; 518-271-7299
Hours: Monday to Friday 10 am to 6:30 pm; Saturday 10 am to 5 pm; closed Sunday.
Natural Food Store and Deli. Organic produce.
Directions: From I-87 take Rte 7 exit and go east. Then take Downtown Troy exit and you will be on 6th St going south. At Congress turn right, then turn right at 4th and this place on left.

UTICA

The Phoenician Restaurant
623 French Road
315-733-2709
Hours: Monday to Thursday 11:30 am to 10 pm; Fri & Sat 11:30 am to 11 pm; closed Sun.
Middle Eastern. Not pure vegetarian.
Menu: Falafel, hummus, tabbouleh, fattoush and other Middle Eastern dishes.
Other Info: Full service, take-out. Accepts MC, VISA. Price: $.

WATERTOWN

The Mustard Seed
1304 Washington
315-788-2463
Hours: Monday to Friday 9 am to 7 pm; Saturday 9 am to 5 pm; Sunday 10 am to 2 pm
Natural Food Store. Organic produce.
Directions: From I-81, go to downtown Watertown. At Washington turn left. This place is behind Pizza Hut across from the high school.

WHITE PLAINS

Manna Foods
171 Mamaroneck Avenue, between Maple and Post Road; 914-946-2233
Hours: Monday to Friday 9 am to 6 pm; Saturday 9 am to 5 pm; closed Sunday.
Restaurant Hours: Monday to Friday 11:30 am to 2:30 pm.
Natural Food Store and Café. Deli, Salad Bar and Juice Bar. Organic produce.
Menu: Vegetable dishes, soups, Chicken Parmesan, veggie Meatball Loaf, sandwiches, tofu dishes and other dishes. Organic salads.
Comments: Often uses organic produce. The food store has a good selection of organic items.
Other Info: Counter service, take-out. Has seating. Price: $-$$. Accepts AMEX, MC, VISA.
Directions: From Hutchinson Parkway, take the Mamaroneck Exit (#23) towards Mamaroneck. Then go northwest on Mamaroneck Ave and this place is on the right 3½ miles down the road. Has municipal parking by the rear entrance.

WILLIAMSVILLE (Buffalo suburb)

Earth Spirit Natures Market
5353 Main Street
716-634-5510
Hours: Monday to Friday 10 am to 6 pm
Closed Sunday.
Natural Food Store.
Comments: Has a large selection of herbs.
Other Info: Accepts MC, VISA.

Pizza Plant
8020 Transit Road   716-632-0800
5110 Main Street   716-626-5566
Hours: Daily 11 am to 11 pm
Pizza and International. Not pure vegetarian.
Menu: A large selection of pizzas, vegetarian chili, vegetarian stew and nachos. Vegetarian dishes are marked with a carrot. There are various crusts

including spinach, garlic, whole-wheat and sesame.
Other Info: Accepts AMEX, DIS, MC, VISA. Price: $$.

WOODSTOCK

**Bluestone County Foods
54-C Tinker Street, off the road
845-679-5656
Hours: Wednesday to Monday 11 am to 7 pm
Closed Tuesday.
Vegetarian Restaurant. Mainly Vegan. Organic produce. Macrobiotic options.
Menu: Has many vegetarian and vegan dishes. Soups, salads, sandwiches and main dishes. Fresh juices.
Comments: There are a few tables to dine at.
Other Info: Limited service, take-out, catering. Price: $-$$.
Directions: After entering town from highway this place is a little past the creek.

Sunflower Natural Foods
Bradley Meadows Shopping Center
845-679-5361
Hours: Monday to Saturday 9 am to 9 pm
Sunday 10 am to 7 pm
Natural Food Store. Organic produce.
Directions: From I-87, coming from the north, take Exit #20 (the Saugerties), and then go west on Rte 212 eight miles. The store is on the right. From the south, take Exit #19 and go west on Rte 28 around five miles. Turn right on Rte 375, and then left onto Rte 212. This store is on the right.

YORKTOWN HEIGHTS

Mrs Green
12 Triangle Shopping Center
914-962-4462
Web site: www.mrsgreens.com
Hours: Monday to Saturday 9 am to 7 pm
Sunday 10 am to 5 pm
Natural Food Store and a good Deli. Bakery and a catering service. Has a large selection of organic produce.
Comments: The web site has a map to their locations.
Directions: From the Taconic State Pkwy, take the Underhill Ave exit towards Yorktown Heights, then go northeast on Underhill Ave for 1½ mile, at Rte 118 turn left and this place is a half-mile down, near the junction with Hanover St.

NEW YORK CITY

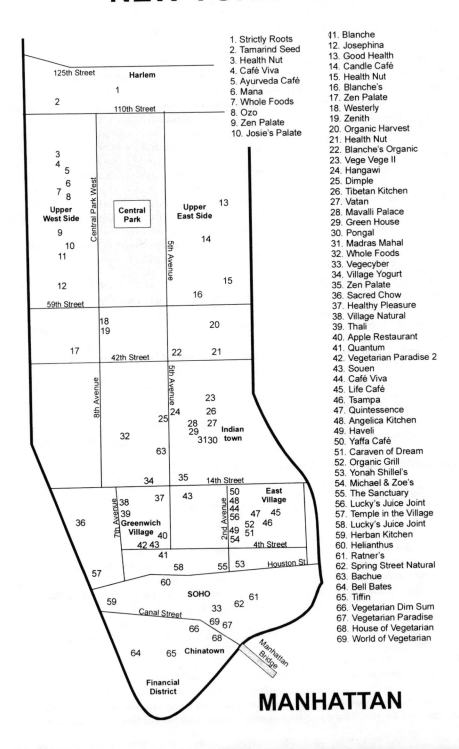

1. Strictly Roots
2. Tamarind Seed
3. Health Nut
4. Café Viva
5. Ayurveda Café
6. Mana
7. Whole Foods
8. Ozo
9. Zen Palate
10. Josie's Palate

11. Blanche
12. Josephina
13. Good Health
14. Candle Café
15. Health Nut
16. Blanche's
17. Zen Palate
18. Westerly
19. Zenith
20. Organic Harvest
21. Health Nut
22. Blanche's Organic
23. Vege Vege II
24. Hangawi
25. Dimple
26. Tibetan Kitchen
27. Vatan
28. Mavalli Palace
29. Green House
30. Pongal
31. Madras Mahal
32. Whole Foods
33. Vegecyber
34. Village Yogurt
35. Zen Palate
36. Sacred Chow
37. Healthy Pleasure
38. Village Natural
39. Thali
40. Apple Restaurant
41. Quantum
42. Vegetarian Paradise 2
43. Souen
44. Café Viva
45. Life Café
46. Tsampa
47. Quintessence
48. Angelica Kitchen
49. Haveli
50. Yaffa Café
51. Caraven of Dream
52. Organic Grill
53. Yonah Shillel's
54. Michael & Zoe's
55. The Sanctuary
56. Lucky's Juice Joint
57. Temple in the Village
58. Lucky's Juice Joint
59. Herban Kitchen
60. Helianthus
61. Ratner's
62. Spring Street Natural
63. Bachue
64. Bell Bates
65. Tiffin
66. Vegetarian Dim Sum
67. Vegetarian Paradise
68. House of Vegetarian
69. World of Vegetarian

MANHATTAN

BRONX

**Everything Natural
3810 White Plain Road, between 219th and 220th Streets; 718-652-9070
Hours: Monday to Saturday 8 am to 12 midnight; Sunday 8 am to 9 pm
Vegetarian West Indian take-out Place. No eggs or dairy.
Menu: Good selection of items sold by the plate. Vegetarian "Duck," Coconut Rice & Peas, Spiced Potatoes, okra and white beans.
Comment: Has a natural food store. Friendly people.
Other Info: Counter service, take-out. No credit card; cash only. Price $-$$.
Directions: From Bronx River Pkwy, take Gun Hill Rd exit (#9), then go east on E Gun Hill Rd a few blocks, then turn left at White Plains Rd and this place is a half-mile down.

BROOKLYN

Appletree Natural Foods
7911 3rd Avenue, between 79th & 80th; 718-745-5776
Hours: Monday to Friday 9:30 am to 6:30 pm (until 7:30 pm Thursday); Saturday 9:30 am to 6 pm; closed Sunday.
Natural Food Store. Organic Juice Bar. Organic produce (delivers on Thursdays)
Menu: Good ready-made sandwiches. Fresh juices and smoothies.
Other Info: Accepts AMEX, MC, VISA.
Directions: In Bay Ridge area. This place is about a mile north of the Verrazano Narrows Bridge. From I-278 (Brooklyn-Queens Exwy), take 6th Ave exit, then go south on 6th Ave 1 block, at 66th St turn right and go 2 blocks, at Leif Ericson Sq turn slight left and go 1 block, at 4th Ave turn left and go south 0.65 mile (about 10 blocks), at 78th St turn right and go 2 blocks, and at 3rd Ave turn left and this place is 1 block down. Or take Ft Hamilton exit (from I-278) and get on 4th Avenue going north. At Shore 79th turn left and this place is 1 block down at 3rd.

**Back to Eden Vegetarian Castle
2242 Church Avenue, near Prospect Park 718-703-1275
Hours: Daily 10 am to 11 pm
Vegetarian Caribbean. Juice Bar.
Other Info: Full service, take-out. Non-smoking. Accepts AMEX, MC, VISA. Price: $.
Directions: This place is about a quarter-mile

southeast of Prospect Park. From downtown Brooklyn, go south on Flatbush about 3 miles, then at Church Avenue turn left and this place is near the corner.

Back to Nature
535 Kings Highway, between 4th and 5th 718-339-0273
Hours: Sunday to Friday 12 noon to 10 pm Saturday 7 pm to 12 midnight
Kosher Natural Foods. American, Middle Eastern, International. Macrobiotic and Vegan options. Not pure vegetarian (some fish dishes).
Menu: The menu is mainly vegetarian. Fresh juices. Cappuccino, espresso.
Other Info: Full service, take-out. Accepts AMEX, MC, VISA. Price: $$.
Directions: From the Belt Pkwy (POW/MIA Memorial Hwy), take exit #7N towards Ocean Pkwy North, merge onto Shore Pkwy for a few blocks, then go north on Ocean Pkwy 1½ mile, then at Kings Hwy turn left and this place is 2½ blocks down.

Back To The Land
142 7th Ave, Park Slope neighborhood 718-768-5654
Hours: Daily 9 am to 9 pm
Natural Food Store. It is a big place with organic produce. Has ready-made sandwiches and macrobiotic goods. Accepts AMEX, DC, DIS, MC, VISA.
Directions: Near Garfield Place, about two blocks west of Prospect Park

**Bliss Café
191 Bedford Avenue, between 6th & 7th Streets 718-599-2547
Hours: Monday to Friday 8 am to 11 pm; Saturday & Sunday 10 am to 11 pm; Sunday Brunch 10 am to 4 pm
Fully Vegetarian International. Mostly Vegan except has egg omlettes. Organic Juice Bar. No eggs in baked goods.
Menu: Orange Citrus Sensation with homemade seitan, vegetarian BLT, Tofu sandwiches, veggie burgers, Seaweed & Yam with carrot ginger sauce, Mixed Vegetables and brown rice with orange sauce. The Bliss Bowl (brown rice, beans, tofu, broccoli, kale, cauliflower & tahini) is a popular dish. Has excellent daily specials. Vegan cookies. Has good fresh organic juices.
Comments: Good food and service. Pleasant atmosphere.
Other Info: Full service, take-out. Non-smoking.

Does not accept reservations. No credit cards. Price: $$.
Directions: Between North 6th and North 7th Streets in North Williamsburg area. From Brooklyn Queens Exwy (I-278) going southeast, take Exit #32B towards Metropolitan Ave, then go southwest on Meeker Ave for 2 blocks, at N 6th St turn right and go 4 blocks, at Bedford Ave turn right and this place is near the corner. This place is about a third-mile due west of Exit #32B. Take L train to Bedford Avenue stop (first stop in Brooklyn). Five shops from the subway stop.

Café Melange
444 Atlantic Avenue, between Bond and Nevins Streets; 718-935-1220
Hours: Daily 10 am to 9 pm
International, Electic, French, Italian. Not pure vegetarian.
Comments: Has a good selection of vegetarian dishes. Also sells cheese, breads, olives, etc. Has a pleasant outdoor patio in the back for dining.
Other Info: Accepts AMEX, DC, DIS, MC, VISA. Price: $$$.

California Taqueria (two locations)
72 Seventh Avenue, between Berkeley and Lincoln Place, Park Slope, Brooklyn; 718-398-4300
341 Seventh Avenue, between 9th and 10th Streets, Park Slope, Brooklyn 718-965-0006
Web site: http://caltaqueria.citysearch.com/
Hours: Monday to Thursday 11 am to 11 pm Friday & Saturday 11 am to 12 midnight Sunday 12 noon to 11 pm
Los Angeles Mexican Food. Not pure veg.
Menu: Vegetarian burrito, Vegetable Platter, vegetarian taco, rice and beans. Uses sour cream and cheese in many dishes. Can ask to have no dairy.
Comments: Good quality food. Gets really high recommendations. Good size portions.
Other Info: Full service, take-out, delivery. No credit cards; cash only. Price: $$.

Divine Health Food Emporium
559 Nostrand Avenue, Brooklyn; 718-774-8772
Hours: Daily 8:30 to 9 pm
Natural Food Store.

Everything Vital
300 Troy Avenue, Crown Heights; 718-953-9433
Hours: Daily 9 am to 9 pm
Natural Food Store and Restaurant. Deli, Salad Bar and Juice Bar.
Menu: Vegetarian "Duck" (tofu skins, lima beans and sweet red peppers), Bulgur and fresh juices

(including carrot and apple mix). Fresh sugar cane pieces and Sweet Potato Pudding.
Comments: Branch of Everything Natural in the Bronx.
Other Info: Full service, take-out. No credit cards; cash only. Price: $-$$.
Directions: This place is 1 block south of Eastern Parkway, in the middle of Brooklyn about 1½ west of Prospect Park. From downtown Brooklyn go south on Flatbush Ave for about 2 miles, then turn left at Eastern Pkwy and go east 1¼ mile, at Dr W McDonald Holder Ave/ Schenectady Ave turn left and go 1 block, at President St turn right and go 2 blocks, then turn right at Troy Ave and this place is 1 block down.

**Fall Café
307 Smith Street, between Union and Presidents Streets, Brooklyn; 718-403-0230
Hours: Monday to Friday 7:30 am to 9 pm; Saturday 8 am to 9 pm; Sunday 9 am to 8 pm
Vegetarian Café. Vegan options. Serves eggs.
Comments: Sunday Poetry readings.
Other Info: No credit cards; cash only. Price: $$.
Directions: This place is 1 mile southeast of the Brooklyn Battery Tunnel. From Brooklyn Queens Exwy (I-278) southwest, take exit #27 towards Atlantic Ave, then turn right at Atlantic Ave and go 2 blocks, at Henry St turn right (go south) and go a half-mile, at Union St turn left and go 2 blocks, at Court St turn right and go 1 block, Carroll St turn left and go 1 block, then at Smith Street turn left and this place is a half-block down. F train to Carroll Street.

Flatbush Food Co-op
1318 Cortelyou Road, near Prospect Park 718-284-9717; **email:** co-op@dorsai.org
Web site: www.dorsai.org/~coop/
Hours: Daily 7 am to 10 pm
Natural Food Store. Organic produce. Kosher foods. Whole foods grocery store.
Menu: Does not have a deli. Has veggie subs and sandwiches, tabbouleh, baba ghanoush, hummus and other ready-made items.
Other Info: Accepts AMEX, DIS, MC, VISA.
Directions: From Ocean Pkwy, go east on Cortelyou. Store is about two blocks from the Cortelyou stop of the D train.

Fresh Health Food Emporium
1276 Fulton Street, Brooklyn; 718-230-5091
Hours: Daily 9 am to 8 pm
Natural Food Store and Deli. Salad Bar. Organic produce. Counter service, take-out. No seating.

Directions: This place is a few blocks southwest of the Bedford-Stuyvesant area, 2 blocks north of Atlantic Ave.

The Garden

921 Manhattan Avenue, Greenpoint area
718-389-6448
Hours: Monday to Saturday 8 am to 8 pm
Sunday 9 am to 7 pm
Natural Food Store and limited Juice Bar. Has a good selection of organic produce.
Comments: Has ready-made salads and sandwiches, but not a full deli. Also has non-organic produce.
Other Info: Accepts AMEX, DC, DIS, MC, VISA.

**The Greens

128 Montaque Street, 1st Floor (near Borough Hall Station); 718-246-1288
Hours: Monday to Thursday 11 am to 10:30 pm; Fri and Sat 11 am to 11 pm; Sun 1 pm to 10 pm
Vegetarian Kosher Chinese. Vegan options. Monday to Saturday lunch specials.
Menu: Wheat gluten dishes, several soups, vegetables and soy protein, noodle soup and stuffed cabbage. Peking Style Vegetarian Cutlet is a tofu loaf with pancakes, brown rice and vegetables. Vegetarian Boat is a boat shaped platter appetizer. "Mock meat" made with soy gluten. Serves Jasmine Tea while ordering. Large Greens's Salad is raw and steamed salad vegetables with soy protein and pineapple cubes. Fresh juices.
Comment: Good Chinese vegan restaurant with reasonable prices. Huge menu with colorful pictures of many of the dishes. Delicious food. Attractive dining room. No music. Great place to eat. Monatque Street is a nice area to walk around. No desserts. Friendly service.
Other Info: Full service, take-out. Non-smoking. Accepts reservations, but are not necessary. Accepts MC, VISA. Price: $-$$.
Directions: The place is about a half-mile northeast of exit #27 of the BQE. From Brooklyn Queens Exwy (I-278) going west, take Tillary St exit (#29) towards Manhattan Bridge, then go a half-mile west on Tillary, at Cadman Plaza turn right and go 1 block, at Clarks St turn left and go 1 block, then at Henry St turn left and this place is 3 blocks down. From Brooklyn Queens Exwy (I-278) going northeast, take exit #27, turn right onto Atlantic Ave, then take an immediate left turn at Hicks St and go 4 blocks north, at Pierrepont St turn right and go 1 block, then at Henry St turn right and this place is 1 block down.

Kar

5908 Avenue N, between Ralph Avenue & 59th Street, Mill Basin, Brooklyn; 718-531-8811
Hours: Monday to Thursday 12 noon to 10 pm; Friday 12 noon to 11 pm; Saturday 1 pm to 11 pm; Sunday 1 pm to 10 pm
Chinese. Not pure vegetarian.
Menu: Brown Rice, Sautéed Spinach, Baby Eggplant with garlic sauce, Sautéed String Beans, Spicy Tofu and whole-wheat vegetable dumplings. Tofu pot is good.
Comments: Does not use MSG. Low-salt, low-fat and fresh food. Good place. Good service.
Other Info: Full service, take-out. Accepts AMEX, MC, VISA. Price: $$.

Kar Luk

437 Fifth Avenue, near 9th Street, Park Slope, Brooklyn; 718-832-4500
Hours: Monday to Thursday 11:30 am to 10:30 pm; Friday & Saturday 11:30 am to 11:30 pm; Sunday 12:30 pm to 10:30 pm
Chinese. Not pure vegetarian.
Menu: Good selection of vegetarian items. Vegetarian Hot and Sour Soup. Vegetarian "chicken." Soups may be too salty, so you may want to ask for less salt.
Comments: A few tables, mainly a take-out place. Health oriented place.
Other Info: Take-out only. No credit cards; cash only. Price: $.

King Falafel

7408 3rd Avenue
718-745-4188
Hours: Daily 12 noon to 12 midnight
Middle Eastern. Vegan options. Not pure veg.
Menu: Has a good amount of vegetarian options. Vegetarian sandwiches, hummus, stuffed grape leaves and falafel. Fresh juices, cappuccino, espresso.
Other Info: Full service, take-out, catering. Accepts AMEX, DIS, MC, VISA. Price: $-$$.

Mr Falafel

226 7th Avenue
718-768-4961
Hours: Daily 10:30 am to 11 pm
Egyptian. Not pure vegetarian.
Menu: Has a good selection of vegetarian dishes. Caters to vegetarians. Falafel, hummus, fresh juices, cappuccino and Turkish coffee.
Comments: Friendly, helpful people.
Other Info: Full service, take-out. Accepts AMEX only. Price: $.

Moustache Middle Eastern Pitza

405 Atlantic Avenue, between Hoyt and Bond Streets, downtown Brooklyn
718-852-5555
Hours: Daily 11 am to 11 pm
Middle Eastern. Not pure vegetarian.
Menu: Mediterranean dishes including hummus, falafel and lentil-bulghar salad. Eggplant Pizzas and pizza on pita bread, which can be made without cheese. Can get artichoke topping. Fresh baked bread. Mideastern citrus drink. No alcohol.
Comments: Has garden seating with tables and umbrellas in the back.
Other Info: Full service, counter service, take-out, delivery. No credit cards; cash only. Price: $.

New Prospect Café

393 Flatbush Avenue, between Plaza Street and Sterling Place, Park Slope
718-638-2148
Hours: Mon 5 pm to 10 pm; Tue to Thursday 11 am to 3:30 pm, 5 pm to 10 pm; Fri 11 am to 3:30 pm, 5 pm to 11 pm; Sat for Brunch 11 am to 3:30 pm, 5 pm to 11 pm; Sun for Brunch 11 am to 4 pm, 5 pm to 10 pm
American and Ethnic. Vegan and Macrobiotic options. Not pure vegetarian.
Menu: Grilled vegetables, tempeh and watercress. Cappuccino, espresso. Non-alcoholic beer and wine.
Comments: A bit high-end. Often uses organic ingredients.
Other Info: Full service, take-out, catering. Accepts AMEX, DIS, MC, VISA. Price: $$-$$$.
Directions: 2, 3 trains to Grand Army Pl; Q train to 7th Avenue.

Park Slope Food Co-op

782 Union Street
718-622-0560; **Web site:** www.foodcoop.com
Hours: Monday, Tuesday, Wednesday, Thursday 10:30 am to 10 pm; Fri 8:05 am to 10 pm; Sat 8:05 am to 7:30 pm; Sun 8:05 am to 7:30 pm
Hours to Get Membership Cards: Monday & Thursday 9:30 am to 10 pm
Tuesday, Wednesday, Friday 9:30 am to 5 pm
Natural Food Store. Large selection of organic produce. Only open to working members.
Menu: Has ready-made products such as subs, veggie sandwiches, hummus, baba ghanoush, tabbouleh and other dishes.
Comments: Does not have a deli.
Directions: Located on Union Street between 6th and 7th Avenues. IRT 2 or 3 trains to Grand Army Plaza. D train to 7th Avenue.

Perelandia

175 Remsen Street; 718-855-6068
Hours: Monday to Friday 8:30 am to 8:30 pm; Sat 8:30 am to 7:30 pm; Sun 11 am to 7 pm
Natural Food Store and Deli. Has a good selection of macrobiotic foods and organic items. Organic produce.
Menu: Soups, casseroles, rice dishes, cold salads, vegan cakes and more.
Directions: In Brooklyn Heights, across from St Francis College. The place is about ¾ mile northeast of exit #27 of the BQE. From Brooklyn Queens Exwy (I-278), take exit #27, then go east on Atlantic Ave and go 2 blocks, then turn left at Clinton St and go 5 blocks, at Remsen St turn right and this place is a half-block down.

Red Hot Szechuan Restaurant

347 Seventh Avenue, at 10th Street, Park Slope, Brooklyn; 718-369-0700/0702
Hours: Monday to Thursday 11:30 am to 10:30 pm; Friday & Saturday 11:30 am to 11:30 pm; Sunday 1 pm to 10:30 pm
Chinese. Vegan friendly. Not pure vegetarian.
Menu: Snow peas, Veggie "Pork" with barbecue sauce, Hot & Sour Soup, cold Sesame Noodles, Bean Curd with hot pepper and peanut sauce (good) and Sweet & Sour "Rib." Can substitute regular white rice for brown rice. No MSG.
Other Info: Full service, take-out. Accepts AMEX, DC, DIS, MC, VISA. Price: $$-$$$.

2nd Street Café

189 7th Avenue, Park Slope; 718-369-6928
Hours: Sunday to Thursday 8:30 am to 10:30 pm; Friday & Saturday 8:30 am to 12 midnight; closed between 4 pm and 4:45 pm on Sat & Sun.
International. Vegetarian-friendly. Not pure vegetarian.
Menu: Garden Burgers, Focaccia Sandwiches, Black Bean Chili and vegetarian pastas.
Comments: Popular place.
Other Info: Full service, take-out. Accepts AMEX, MC, VISA. Price: $$.

Steve & Sons Bakery and Restaurant

9305 Church Avenue, near East 93rd Street, Brownsville, Brooklyn
718-498-6800; **fax:** 718-345-7216; **Web site:** www.steveandsonsbakery.com
Hours: Sunday to Thursday 7 am to 12 midnight; Friday 7 am to 6 pm (sunset); Saturday 6 pm (sunset) to 12 midnight; Sun 7:30 am to 12 noon
West Indian, American & Ethnic Restaurant and Bakery. About 60% vegetarian.

Menu: Vegetarian patties made with soy protein and a whole-wheat crust. Vegetarian stews, salads, Vegetarian Cutlet Parmigiana, Vegetarian Steak, Baked Ziti Parmigiana and Barbecue Ribs (very good). Main dishes are served with rice and peas. Fresh baked breads. Good desserts. Fresh juices.
Comments: Good place. Owner is a Seventh Day Adventist. Makes many dishes with wheat gluten.
Other Info: Full service, take-out. Accepts AMEX, DC, DIS, MC, VISA. Price: $$.

Tofu On 7th
226 7th Avenue; 718-768-5273
Hours: Monday to Saturday 11:30 am to 10:30 pm; Sunday 1 pm to 10:30 pm
Chinese. Not pure vegetarian.
Menu: Mock meat dishes made with soybean, tofu, beans, wheat gluten, yams and mushrooms. Moo Goo Gai Pan and vegetarian Orange Beef.

Urban Organic
230A 7th Street; 718-499-4321; **toll-free:** 888-487-2260; **email:** Urorganic@aol.com
Web site: www.urbanorganic.net
Delivers Organic Produce and grocery items. Weekly delivery of organic produce and groceries. Boxes of 16 to 20 items. Has organic vegetables, fruits, beans, pasta, nuts, juices, tofu products and coffee. 50% discount off the first box. Deliveries to Queens and the Bronx cost $3 extra.

Vegetarian Garden
37 East 29th Street, between Park and Madison Avenues; 212-686-9691
Hours: Daily 11 am to 11 pm
Chinese. Vegetarian-friendly. Buddhist. Not pure vegetarian.
Menu: Has a good selection of vegetarian dishes. Has meat substitutes such as vegetarian "Pork Chops," Sweet & Sour "Rib," "Beef" with Broccoli, Snow Cabbage and Fresh Mushrooms Casserole.
Comments: Lunch specials from 11 am to 3:30 pm are a good value.
Other Info: Full service, take-out. Accepts AMEX, DC, DIS, MC, VISA. Price: $-$$.

Veggie Castle
2242 Church Avenue, between Flatbush & Bedford Avenues; 718-703-1275
Hours: Daily 10 am to 11 pm
International. Mainly Caribbean. Vegan Fast Foods and Juice Bar.
Menu: Soups, salads, sandwiches, Caribbean dishes, vegan Macaroni & Cheese, veggie burgers and other dishes.
Comments: It is located in a former White Castle building. Their slogan is "Home of the Veggie Castle Burger." Cheap daily lunch specials.
Other Info: Counter service, take-out. Accepts AMEX, MC, VISA. Price: $.
Directions: Between Flatbush and Bedford Ave, about a third-mile southeast of Prospect Park. From downtown Brooklyn go south on Flatbush Ave about 3 miles, then turn left at Church Ave and this place is about 50 yards down. Can be reached by taking the D or 2 trains.

MANHATTAN

A Matter of Health
1478 1st Avenue, at 77th Street; 212-288-8280
Hours: Monday to Friday 9 am to 9 pm
Saturday & Sunday 10 am to 7:30 pm
Natural Food Store.
Directions: Near Lexington Avenue and 77th Street subway station.

American Café
160 Broadway, Basement; 212-732-1426
Hours: Monday to Thursday 7:30 am to 4:30 pm; Fri 7:30 am to 2 pm; closed Sat & Sun.
American. Not pure vegetarian. Kosher.
Menu: Veggie burgers (vegetables and beans on seven-grain bread), Israeli dishes, hummus, falafel, baba ghanoush, Vegetable Chili and brown rice.
Comments: Little place. Price: $.
Directions: In middle of the financial district. Near Maiden Lane. 4, 5 trains to Wall Street.

***Angelica Kitchen
300 East 12th Street, between First and Second Avenues, East Village; 212-228-2909
Hours: Daily 11.30 am to 10.30 pm
Vegetarian Vegan Natural Food Restaurant. 98% organic. Many macrobiotic options.
Menu: Has a good selection of items. Beverages, appetizers, soups, salads, entrées, side dishes and desserts. Sea Caesar Salad, Mashed Potatoes (with pesto or vegetarian gravy), Seven Grain Croquettes (with butternut squash) and Dasahi & Noodles in traditional Japanese broth. Roasted and steamed vegetables. Tofu sandwiches, barbecued tempeh and Soba Noodles with sesame sauce. Brown Rice and Pickled Carrots wrapped in seaweed. Shitake-kombu Dashi with soba noodles. Three-bean Chili Soup (kidney, black bean and

lentils) is good. Rice, steamed vegetables, simple salad, sea vegetables or beans for $3. Has a salad special for $10. Dragon Bowls are made up of grains, beans, assorted vegetables, seaweed, greens, and salad. Half Dragon Bowl is a good meal. Fresh cooked cornbread with carrot butter or tahini sauce is very popular. Homemade sauerkraut. Mu Tea (macrobiotic tea) at end of meal. Maple whip on desserts. Good coolers (a variety of cold teas). Good freshly made desserts such as peanut butter cookies, apple kanten (no wheat), muffins, and Mixed Fruit Crisp with maple tofu whip (no wheat). Fresh juices and smoothies.

Comment: Highly recommended. Considered to be one of the best vegetarian restaurants in the country. Very popular, so may have to wait for a table for dinner (maybe a long time on Saturday nights). Laid-back, friendly, pleasant, casual, cozy atmosphere. Cool people. Good place for meeting people. Sociable, informal, hip place. Has community table. Has about 70 seats. Recycled napkins. No salt and pepper on the table, but a bottle of soy sauce. Good, friendly service. Community oriented. Cozy and warm décor. A good percentage of produce is harvested less than 48 hours before use. No refined sugars, no preservatives, no animal products including dairy and eggs. Reasonable, moderate prices. Healthy cooking style. No cell phones allowed in restaurant. Established in early 1970s. Guarantees that 95% of produce is organic.

Other Info: Does not take credit cards or reservations. Full service, take-out, delivery. Price: $$. A main meal is around $12 to $15. The Daily Special is $12 and $15 with two basic extras.

Directions: Located in the East Village. 4, 5, 6, N, R to the 14 Street – Union Square stop; L to First Avenue stop

Apple Restaurant

17 Waverly Place, between Greene and Mercer Streets, East Village; 212-473-8888; **Web site:** www.applerestaruant.citysearch.com

Hours: Monday to Thursday 12 noon to 11 pm; Friday & Saturday 12 noon to 12 midnight; Sunday 12 noon to 10 pm

Vietnamese Restaurant mainly. International cuisine includes Mexican, Japanese and Middle Eastern. Has two separate kitchens, one that cooks vegetarian food and the other non-vegetarian.

Menu: Wonton Soup, Vegetarian mock "meat" dishes, Tempeh Burger, Yam Tempura, Soba Noodles, Watercress Salad, BBQ Seitan, Stir-fried Cabbage, Garden Vegetables with Tempeh, Steamed Vegetable Dumpling, Portobello Mushroom Sushi Rolls, Vegetable Spring Rolls, Organic Mashed Potatoes, Udon Noodles and Shitake Mushrooms. Seitan and Pecans over Spinach Noodles. Has some international dishes such as Mexican Enchilada, Vegetarian Quesadilla, Vegetable Fajita, BBQ Tempeh, Seitan Parmigiana, Spinach Lasagna Rolls and Pita Platter. Has good desserts that do not contain either dairy or honey.

Comments: Serves meat dishes, but uses separate cooking facilities for making vegetarian foods. Upscale. Features Karaoke sing-a-long. Has a fancy interior with white tablecloths, chandeliers and high ceilings. Beautifully designed big place. Plays good jazz music and old movies on a screen. Live jazz music on the weekends. Got some good reviews in the newspapers.

Warning: Ask whether the oyster sauce is vegetarian.

Other Info: Full service, take-out, catering. Accepts AMEX, MC, VISA. Price: $$-$$$.

Directions: N, R trains to 8th Street stop. 6 train to Astor Place.

Ayurveda Café

706 Amsterdam Avenue, between 94th & 95th Streets; 212-932-2400

Hours: Daily 11:30 am to 10:30 pm

Vegetarian Indian. Vegan friendly. Not pure veg.

Menu: Appetizers, salads, dal, rice dishes, raita, Indian breads, chutney and Indian desserts.

Comments: Has set daily Ayurvedic based meals. Good food. Décor is a bit simple. Price: $-$$.

Review: "This vegetarian place is just wonderful…The food runs into the cooking of all parts of India and is subtle, light and refreshing." The Underground Gourmet Joseph O'Neil, New York Magazine 4/12/99.

Directions: 1, 2, 3, 9 trains to 96th Street and Amsterdam Avenue.

Ayurveda Center

204 West 96th Street, between Amsterdam & Broadway; 212 280-1000; **fax:** 212 280-5300; **email:** ayurvedacenter@email.msn.com

Web site: www.ayurvedacenter.com

Ayurvedic products and Ayurvedic consultations. Ayurvedic massages and gift items.

B & H Dairy

127 Second Avenue, near 8th Street
212-505-8065

Hours: Daily 7 am to 10 pm

Mainly Kosher Dairy Restaurant. Coffeehouse. Vegan options. Not pure vegetarian. No meat, but serves fish.

Menu: Sandwiches, salads, vegetarian soups, baked goods and desserts. Freshly baked Challah Bread, Vegetable Lasagna, Mushroom Barley Soup, Cheese Blintzes, Vegetarian Chili and Stuffed Cabbage. Daily specials (changes daily) and sandwich specials. Fresh juices.
Comments: Good place. Reasonable prices. Really small place.
Other Info: Limited service, take-out. No credit cards. Price: $-$$.
Directions: 6 train to Astor Place. From here it is about a three-minute walk. R train to Broadway and 8th Street. F train to 7th and 8th Street stop.

***Bachue

36 West 21st Street, between Fifth and Sixth Avenues; 212-229-0870
Hours: Monday to Friday 8 am to 10 pm; Saturday 10 am to 10 pm; Sunday 11 am to 7 pm; Breakfast served until 3 pm; Lunch served 11:30 am to 4:30 pm; Dinner served after 5 pm
Fully Vegan South America and International. Mainly organic.
Menu: Good vegan breakfasts of scrambled tofu, pancakes, French toast and waffles. Burritos, enchiladas, chickpea crepes, Miso Soup, whole-grain Mexican Tacos, Lentil Veggie Burger, Cheese Ravioli, Japanese Brown Rice Nori Rolls, Organic Vegetable of the Day, Sea Vegetable of the Day, brown rice, grilled tempeh, Sensational Seitan, Spanish Rice, Sweet Plantains, Spiced Pinto Beans (with choice of seitan, tofu or grilled tempeh), and Stuffed Cabbage with Grilled Tofu. Beans, seitan and grilled vegetables. The Mediterranean Pasta has a white sauce with mushrooms, capers and sun-dried tomatoes. Tempeh and grilled tofu sandwiches. Pastas can be topped by seitan, mushrooms, tofu or grilled tempeh. Ravioli filled with wild mushroom. Has a variety of desserts. Carob Almond Cake and Fig Tart with Vanilla Ice Cream. Fresh juices and shakes.
Comments: Bachue is named after Chibcha, a fertility goddess of Colombia. The name is pronounced "bah-chu-way." Has good vegan food. Good-size portions. They usually use organic grains, fresh vegetables and fruits as much as possible. They cook on cast iron and use stainless steel cookware. Flour is ground on premises. Desserts are sweetened with maple syrup, rice syrup or barley mart and do not contain refined sugar or honey. Cream soups and dressings are made with nuts and oats instead of dairy. The staff is helpful and will be glad to answer questions about ingredients. Bohemian setting. Often do cooking classes. Cooks with filtered water.

On the same block as the Natural Gourmet Cooking School. Got a good review in Zagat Survey. Wholesome organic food. Low on décor. Service is often slow.
Other Info: Full service, take-out, home delivery, catering. Accepts AMEX, DC, DIS, MC, VISA. Price: $-$$.
Directions: In the Flatiron District and Union Square area. Midtown East and Gramercy Park, just south of Madison Square Park. Down a side street in Chelsea. F, N, R trains to 23rd Street.

Bamiyan

157 East 26th Street, at 3rd Avenue
212-481-3232
Hours: Monday to Friday 12 noon to 11 pm
Saturday & Sunday 12 noon to 12 midnight
Afghan, Middle Eastern. Some American dishes. Emphasis on vegetarian meals. Not pure veg.
Menu: Has good pilafs, dal, rice dishes, eggplant dishes, salads, noodle dishes and steamed vegetables. Turkish coffee is really good.
Comments: Elegant décor.
Other Info: Full service, take-out, delivery. Accepts AMEX, DC, DIS, MC, VISA. Price: $$.
Directions: 6 train to 26th Street and 3rd Avenue.

Bell Bates Natural Foods

97 Reade Street, Tribeca area; 212-267-4300;
Web site: http://www.bellbates.citysearch.com/
Hours: Monday to Friday 9 am to 8 pm
Saturday 10 am to 6 pm; closed Sundays.
Natural Food Store and Deli. Juice Bar. Organic produce.
Menu: Has a wide selection of vegetarian dishes. Homemade vegetarian soups, salads and sandwiches. Fresh brewed ice-tea. Organic juices and smoothies.
Comments: Has a coupon on their Web site that you can download to get a 5% discount on a minimum $50 order. Relaxed, casual place. Has a good selection of items in store and good prices.
Other Info: Accepts AMEX, DC, DIS, MC, VISA.
Directions: Between Hudson and Greenwich. Cross streets are Broadway and Church Streets. 1, 9; 2, 3 trains to Chambers St station.

Benny's Burritos

113 Greenwich Avenue, between Jane Street and West 12th Street, West Village; 212-727-0584
Directions: Between Red and Blue line. A, C, E, 1, 2, 3, 9 to 14th Street.
Hours: Sunday to Thursday 11:30 am to 11 pm

Friday & Saturday 11 am to 12 midnight
93 Avenue A, near 6th Street, East Village
212-254-2054
Hours: 11 am to 12 midnight
Directions: F train to 2nd Avenue.
Mexican. California-style burritos. Vegetarian-friendly and hip. Vegan options. Not pure veg.
Menu: Has a vegetarian and vegan menu. Really large burritos. The veg of the day burrito is good. Enchiladas, tacos and quesadillas. Has whole-wheat, non-dairy burritos.
Comment: Reasonable prices and good authentic Mexican food. Often have to wait in line to enter. No lard or MSG in food. East Village place has a take-out place next door. West Village place has a take-out place across the street. Good place for a quick, good tasting meal. Pleasant place. The Greenwich Street place has outdoor dining and sidewalk café. Red salsa is vegan. The mole and green sauce have chicken stock in them. Uses whole-wheat tortillas, brown rice and non-dairy sour cream. Can ask for soy cheese (with casein) and tofu sour cream instead of regular cheese.
Other Info: Full service, take-out, catering. Price: $$-$$$.

Blanche's Organic Café (four branches)
22 East 44th Street, near Grand Central Station, between 5th Avenue and Madison; 212-599-3445
Hours: Monday to Friday 7 am to 7:30 pm
Closed Saturday & Sunday.
Directions: Take 4, 5, 6, 7 or S trains to 42nd St–Grand Central.
Upstairs in DKNY Department Store, 60th Street & Madison Avenue; 212-223-3569 (call DKNY phone number and then transferred to Blanche's)
Hours: Monday to Friday 10 am to 7 pm; Saturday 11 am to 8 pm; Sunday 11 am to 7 pm
Directions: N, R, W trains to 5th Avenue; 4, 5 6 trains to 59th and Lexington.
Upper West Side, 274 Columbus Avenue, at 73rd Street; 212-579-3179
Hours: Monday to Saturday 8:30 am to 7:30 pm
Sunday 9 am to 6 pm
Directions: B, C trains to 72nd Street. 1, 2, 3, 9 trains to 72nd Street and Broadway stop.
In DKNY Department Store
74 Thomson Street, between Price and Spring Streets
Hours: Daily 12 noon to 8 pm
Directions: Closest subway stops are 6th and Spring, or Spring and Lafayette.
Web site: www.blanches.net (has menu on site)
Organic, Gourmet. Juice Bar. Vegan and Macrobiotic options. Not pure vegetarian (serves

eggs, fish and chicken).
Menu: Sandwiches (white bean, sun-dried tomato on whole-wheat bread, hummus with roasted vegetables), salads (Blanche's Mesclun Salad, wheat bean salad, couscous salad), Roasted Vegetables and Goat Cheese Roll Up, Blanche's Vegetable Burger, soups (Wild Mushrooms, Miso Sea Vegetable), Vegetable Nori Rolls and desserts (cookies, kantens, tarts). Daily specials. Fresh juices. No alcohol.
Comments: Good tasting food. A good place. The menu has nutritional information about the dishes. Healthy food. Has menu on web site.
Other Info: Counter service, take-out, catering, delivery. Accepts all major credit cards. Price: $$.

Burritoville
451 Amsterdam Avenue, between 81st and 82nd Streets 212-787-8181 (1, 9 to 79th St)
166 W 72nd, near Broadway 212-580-7700
1606 Third Avenue, between 90th and 91st Streets 212-410-2255 (4, 5, 6 to 86th St stop)
866 Third Avenue, near 52nd Street 212-980-4111
625 Ninth Ave, at 44th Street 212-333-5352 (A, C, E to 42nd St)
1489 First Avenue between 77th and 78th Streets 212-472-8800 (6 to 77th St stop)
352 West 39th Street, at Ninth Ave 212-563-9088 (A, C, E to 42nd St)
264 West 23rd Street, between 7th and 8th Streets 212-367-9844 (C, E to 23rd St stop)
141 Second Avenue, between 8th and 9th Streets, East Village 212-260-3300 (6 to Astor Place stop)
298 Becker Street, near 7th Ave 212-633-9249 (1, 9 to Christopher St–Sheridan Square, outdoor dinning)
20 John Street, between Broadway & Nassau Streets 212-766-2020 (A, C; J, M, Z to Fulton St–Broadway–Nassau)
36 Water Street, just north of Broad Street, below Canal Street 212-747-1100 (N, R to Whitehall St)
144 Chambers Street, near Hudson Street, below Canal Street 212-964-5048 (A, C; 1, 2, 3 to Chambers St)
Web site: www.burritoville.com (has an online delivery service and menu on their web site)
Hours: Sunday to Thursday 11 am to 1 am
Friday & Saturday 11 am to 2 pm
Mexican and American. Vegetarian and vegan options. Has some macrobiotic choices. Also serves meat, fish and chicken.
Menu: Vegetarian burritos. Austin Burrito (mush-

rooms, fresh spinach, cheese, beans, brown rice and sour cream). Santa Fe Burrito is vegan with grilled vegetables, rice, black beans and tofu sour cream. Nachos, vegetarian chili, soups, Mega-Soy, guacamole, tacos, fajitas and Tempeh Burger Wrap. No alcohol.
Comments: Good places with large cheap burritos. Can get soy cheese (contains casein) and tofu sour cream instead of cow milk ones. Marks fully vegetarian items with carrots on menu. You have to ask for a whole-wheat tortilla to get one, instead of a white flour one. Tortillas are home-made. Everything is freshly made. Loud music. Has brown rice. Regrettably it is not totally veg-etarian. No décor. Reasonably priced. No lard, MSG or canned goods are used. If you get a burrito, you also get all-you-can-eat tortilla chips and salsa. Children's menu. The Water Street place serves breakfasts.
Other Info: Counter service, take-out, free de-livery (minimum $10). Reservations not neces-sary. Non-smoking. Accepts AMEX, DC, DIS, MC, VISA. Price: $-$$.

**Café Viva Herbal Pizzeria
2578 Broadway, between 97th and 98th Streets, Upper West side of Central Park
212-663-8482 (VIVA)
Web site: www.healthmap.com/CAFEVIVA
Hours: Sunday to Thursday 11 am to 12 pm Friday & Saturday 11 am to 11:30 pm
Vegetarian Italian Pizzeria. Juice Bar. Organic, kosher and vegan options.
Menu: Great selection of pizzas. Soy cheese pizza, whole-wheat pizza, spelt crust (wheat free) piz-zas, spaghetti, cornmeal pizza, sandwiches, Veg-etarian Lasagna, calzones and Ravioli. Selection of salads. Fresh juices. Has pasta with soy sau-sage, seitan meat sauce, grilled eggplant, roast red peppers and pesto sauce. Some toppings such as seitan pepperoni, soy sausage, broccoli, zucchini, homemade mozzarella and tofu.
Comments: Has casein-free soy cheese for vegans. Uses unbleached flour, sea salt, filter water and natural sweeteners. No preservatives, emulsifiers or chemicals.
Other Info: Full service, take-out, delivery in the Columbia University area. Accepts AMEX, DC, MC, VISA. Price: $.
Direction: 1, 2, 3, 9 trains to 96th Street. Near Columbia University.

**Café Viva
179 Second Avenue, between 11th and 12th Street, East Village; 212-420-8801

Vegetarian and Vegan Pizzeria. Italian restaurant. Juice Bar. Kosher
Hours: Sunday to Friday 11:30 am to 11:30 mid-night; Saturday 11:30 am to 12 midnight
Menu: Great selection of pizzas. Soy cheese pizza, whole-wheat pizza, cornmeal pizza, spelt crust (wheat-free), hemp crust (wheat-free), Vegetar-ian Lasagna, calzones and Ravioli. Selection of salads and soups. Soy Sausage Stromboli. Vegan soups and desserts. The green-tea crust pizza is good. Has special teas including: green sea anemone, kava, astragulus, yohimbe, Chinese ginseng and green teas. Super anti-oxidant pizza (on hemp crust) with maitake and shitake mushrooms. Fresh juices.
Comments: You can have either soy or regular cheese on a pizza.
Other Info: Counter service, take-out, delivery. Accepts AMEX, MC, VISA. Price: $-$$.
Direction: 4, 5 6 trains to 14th Street stop, then walk 2 blocks east. 6 train to Astor Street stop, then walk three blocks north.

**Candle Café
1307 3rd Avenue, at 75th Street, Upper East Side of Central Park; 212-472-0970; fax: 212-472-7169; Web site: www.candlecafe.com
Hours: Monday to Saturday 11:30 am to 10:30 pm; Sunday 11:30 am to 9:30 pm
Delivery Hours: Monday to Saturday 11:30 am to 9 pm; Sunday 11:30 am to 9 pm
Pure Vegetarian International. Juice Bar. Mostly vegan. Some macrobiotic dishes. Raw items. Mainly organic produce used.
Menu: Appetizers, salads, soups, sandwiches, macrobiotic entrées, desserts, and daily special grain salad. Sesame Crusted Seitan over Soba Noodles with Wilted Asian Greens and Wasabi. Crystal Roll appetizers (grilled tofu and vegetables in rice paper with spicy peanut sauce). New York Seitan Steak with soy mozzarella is recommended. Quesadilla, steamed dumplings, Lasagna, Portobello Sandwich, goods salads (five kinds), Tofu Club, Stir-Fry and Grilled Soy Burger. Mexi-can Burrito is whole-wheat with grilled tempeh, chili, steamed greens, and is served with brown rice, salsa and tofu sour cream. Very good soups. Grilled Tempeh Portobello burger. Steamed and roasted vegetables and baked potatoes. Good spe-cial of millet, black beans and sweet potato on steamed kale. Paradise Casserole is toasted millet with black beans, with a layer of mashed sweet potatoes, roasted root veggies and mushroom gravy. Vegan pies and cakes. Banana Cream Pie with Fudge Sauce, Chocolate Cake, Banana Cake

with tofu frosting, Lemon Tofu Cheesecake and Chocolate Mousse Pie with chocolate chips. Wheatgrass juice, fresh lemonade, protein shakes, Candle Colada, smoothies, cappuccino and espresso.
Comment: Casual, relaxed place. Good, friendly service. Considered to be one of the best vegetarian restaurants in New York. Busy, little place. Freshly made dishes with organic products. Reasonable prices. Pleasant, laid-back atmosphere. A totally happening place. Good selection on menu. Been open for around 50 years. Can ask for ingredients of any dishes. The Tofu Club sandwich made of grilled tofu, tempeh bacon, lettuce and tomato is recommended. If you are in the area, it is the place to go to.
Celebrities often visit here. My friend who used to cook here (she makes great vegan cakes) told me that several times Woody Harrelson asked her for recipes. She also said he was an extremely nice, down-to-earth person. A newspaper article on the front window says which tables celebrities like to sit at. In their brochure they write: "We at the Candle Café are dedicated to your health through our commitment to excellent vegetarian cuisine." Judged to be the best vegan, organic restaurant in the city by Times Out magazine.
Other Info: Full Service, take-out, catering, delivery (free delivery within 15 blocks. Minimum order lunch $10, dinner $15). Non-smoking. Reservations recommended for groups of 4 or more for weekend dinners. Seats around 50. Price: $$-$$$. Sandwiches are $8 to $12. Main meals range from $11 to $17. Accepts DIS, MC, VISA.
Directions: Uptown, Upper East Side, four blocks east of Central Park. 6 train to 77th St and Lexington Ave, then walk one block over to 3rd Avenue. 3rd Avenue bus. Street parking in the area after 7 pm. Otherwise metered parking.

Caravan of Dreams

405 East 6th Street, between 1st Ave and Avenue A, East Village; 212-254-1613; **fax:** 212-254-9229; **email:** Angel@caravanofdreams.net
Web site: www.caravanofdreams.net
Hours: Monday 5 pm to 11 pm; Tuesday to Thursday 11 am to 11 pm; Friday & Saturday 11 am to 12 midnight; Sunday 11 am to 11 pm
Fully Vegetarian Vegan. Organic. Live Raw Gourmet Food. International, American, Mediterranean, Kosher (under Rabbinical supervision). Macrobiotic friendly. Most items are dairy and wheat free. Serves eggs.
Menu: Black Bean Chili, Polenta, Vegetable Medley, Caravan Pizza, Tempeh Reuben Sandwich,

Grilled Polenta, burritos, sandwiches and salads. Nachos with black or pinto beans, guacamole, sour cream (vegan) and homemade salsa. Live (raw) specials, soups and desserts. Grilled Tempeh cooked in miso with a mustard sauce, served on lettuce and sprouts. Special soups such as corn-avocado or vegetable. Seven-grain bread, flatbreads, hummus and polenta. Salads with ginger-tamari-lemon or tahini-lemon dressing. Spanish Rice with beans and fried plantains. The "Angel's Caravan" is a veggie burger and vegetables with a sweet potato sauce. Carbo Platter (polenta with squash sauce and grain of the day). Excellent smoothies. Banana and Carob Shake with almond milk. Cookies, pies and brownies, apple pie, carob shake (made with almond milk) and banana splits. Raw food pies and raw brownies. Organic fresh-squeezed juices. Grain moccachino with soymilk. Filtered water. No alcohol.
Comments: Very good place. Gets good recommendations. Laid-back, relaxed, down-to- earth place. Uses mainly organic ingredients. At night it is a romantic dimly lit place. Unique décor with beaded lamps, paintings, Seashell mosaic tables, colorful walls and tablecloths with half-moon mirrors and lanterns. Colorful paintings. Angel, the owner, is a Sufi devotee. Most food is dairy-free and many dishes are wheat-free. Often has live music. Educational programs in the back. Has gotten awards for being the best restaurant in New York. Friendly, efficient service. Some people believe that this place is overpriced.
Classes and Programs: Live acoustic music most nights after 8 pm (bluegrass, folk, banjo, etc). Yoga classes in back room. Lectures, conferences in nutrition, and cooking classes. Tarot card readings on Thursday.
Other Info: Full service, take-out, delivery, cafeteria style. Non-smoking. Reservation are not usually necessary, but may be needed on weekends. Accepts AMEX, DIS, MC, VISA. Prices: $$.
Directions: In the lower East Village near Little India. Between 1st Ave and Ave A. F train (subway) to 2nd Ave & 6 train to Astor Place. N train to 8th St & Bus 13 to 9th St. Parking available at Lafayette and 4th St and 3rd Ave (Bowery) and 4th St. Meters on First Ave.

Commodities East

165 1st Avenue, at 10th Street; 212-260-2600
Hours: Monday to Saturday 9 am to 9 pm
Sunday 10 am to 9 pm
Natural Food Store. This is a large place. Has ready-made sandwiches.
Accepts AMEX, DIS, MC, VISA.

Commodities Natural
117 Hudson, at Northmore; 212-334-8330
Hours: Monday to Friday 9 am to 8 pm
Saturday & Sunday 10 am to 8 pm
Natural Food Store. Juice Bar.
Directions: 1, 9 trains to Franklin.

Curry In A Hurry
119 Lexington Avenue, 28th Street
212-683-0900
Hours: Daily 11 am to 12 noon
Indian. Not pure vegetarian.
Menu: Does not use ghee (butter) for cooking,
but oil instead. No alcohol.
Comments: Painted a strange color blue. Good
food with reasonable prices. On the second floor
they play Indian music videos. Some people think
the food is good, and some don't have such a high
opinion of the food. Not much on the decor.
Other Info: Cafeteria style, take-out. Accepts
AMEX, MC, VISA. Price: $.
Directions: 6 train to 28th Street.

Diamond Dairy
4 West 47th Street (2nd floor, in back)
212-719-2694
Hours: Monday to Thursday 8 am to 5 pm; Fri-
day 8 am to 2 pm; Closed Saturday & Sunday.
Dairy Restaurant. Not pure vegetarian.
Price: $.
Menu: Has dairy dishes. Vegetable Cutlet is good.
Potatoes and baked pudding.
Directions: In the middle of the Diamond dis-
trict on 47th Street.

**Dimple (two branches)
11 West 30th Street
212-643-9464; **fax:** 212-643-9468
Hours: Monday to Friday 9:30 am to 8 pm; Saturday 10 am to 8 pm; Sunday 10 am to 7 pm
723 37th Avenue, at 73rd Street, Queens
718-458-8144
Hours: Daily 11 am to 9 pm
Directions: F, E, R, 7 trains to 74th Street and
Roosevelt Avenue
Vegetarian Indian. Buffet lunch that changes
daily.
Menu: Has several vegetarian options including
dosas, Sev Puris and curry dishes. Has coconut
water to drink.
Comments: According to some people the atmosphere is not so good. Good food. There are several Indian groceries stores in the area. Fresh ingredients and spices.
Other Info: Full service, mainly take-out. No
credit cards. Price: $.

Dojo Restaurant
24 St Mark's, near Second Avenue, East Village
212-674-9821
14 West 4th Street, near Mercer Street (between
Broadway & Mercer), Greenwich Village near
NYU; 212-505-8934
Hours: Daily 11 am to 1 am (sometimes closes
at 12 noon)
General and Japanese. Has a vegetarian emphasis. Not pure vegetarian.
Two places: One hip, happening place in the east
Village at St Mark's Place. The other is near New
York University.
Menu: Japanese brunch served until 5 pm. Has
salads, home-fries, vegan soups, miso, brown rice
with tofu sauce and steamed broccoli. Soy Burger
Platter (really good), Tofu Salad (gets good recommendations), Cold Sesame Noodles, brown
rice and Stir-fried Vegetables. The Soy Burger is
cheap and good. The carrot dressing is good.
Comment: Some say the Soy Burger is the best
veggie burger in New York. Plays rock & roll
music. Ask for the food hot, as sometimes because this place is so popular it may come out
cold. Some people really talk bad of the place
(liked it in the past but not now). The West 4th
Street place has outdoor seating. A good value.
Other Info: Cash only. Price: $.
Directions: To get to St Mark Place restaurant, 6
train to Astor Place. To get to the West 4th St
place take the F train to Broadway-Lafayette; A,
C, E; D, F, Z to W 4th St–Washington Square;
N, R to 8th St; 6 to Astor Place.

**18 Arhans Vegetarian Home Cooking
Eighteen Arhans Corp, 227 Centre Street, be-
tween Broome and Grand; 212-941-8986
Vegetarian Asian.
Hours: Monday to Saturday 12 noon to 7 pm
Sunday and Holiday 1 pm to 6 pm
Menu: Crepes and dumplings.
Comments: Got reviews in NY Times and The
Village Voice. Doesn't use MSG.
Other Info: Limited seating, take-out. Cash only.

Eva's
11 West 8th Street, between Fifth and Sixth Avenues; 212-677-3496
Hours: Monday to Saturday 11 am to 11 pm
Sunday 11 am to 10 pm
Middle Eastern Fast Food. Not pure vegetarian
(also serves meat and fish).
Menu: Serves meat, but the menu is mainly vegetarian. Has a good selection of vegetarian dishes.
Veggie burger (brown rice, sunflower seeds), salads, brown rice, broiled vegetables, falafel, baked

tofu and veggie nuggets. No alcohol.
Comment: If you purchase the Special of the Day, you get the second one at a discount price. Friendly, efficient service. There is a natural food store in the back.
Other Info: Counter service, take-out. Accepts AMEX, DC, DIS, MC, VISA.
Directions: 6 train to Astor stop. N, R trains to A Street.1, 9 trains to West 4th Street.

Fez Under Time Café
380 Lafayette Street, at Great Jones Street
212-533-7000; **For Reservations:** 212-533-2680; email: info@feznyc.com
Web site: www.feznyc.com
Hours: Monday to Friday Breakfast: 8 am to 12 noon; Lunch: 11:30 am to 4 pm; Light menu: 4 pm to 6 pm; Dinner 6 pm to 12 midnight (Friday and Saturday until 1 pm); Saturday and Sunday Brunch: 10 am to 4 pm.
American. Vegetarian-friendly. Tends to use organic items. Not pure vegetarian.
Menu: Salads, Tofu Burger, veggie burger and pasta.
Comments: Has live music performances at night. Comedy, Cabaret. By hitting their web site you can get a list of scheduled entertainment.
Directions: B, D, F, Q trains to Broadway–Lafayette; From Upper East Side take the 6 train to Astor Place. From downtown take the 6 train to Bleecker Street. N, R trains to 8th Street. Located where the N, R, 6, B, D, F, Q trains cross.

Flying Burritos
165 West 4th Street, a little west of 6th Avenue
212-691-3663
Hours: Sunday to Thursday 11:30 am to 12:30 am; Friday & Saturday 11:30 am to 2 am
Mexican. Not pure vegetarian.
Menu: Quesadilla, burritos and nachos. Tofu sour cream.
Comments: Loud music. Antique lamps. Friendly, efficient service.
Other Info: Full service, take-out. Reservations suggested for groups. Cash only. Price: $$.
Directions: West 4th Street.

4th Street Food Co-op
58 E 4th Street, between Bowery & 2nd Avenue
212-674-3623; **email:** danielc@panix.com
Web site: www.4thstreetfoodcoop.org
Hours: Sunday to Friday 3 pm to 9 pm Saturday 1 pm to 9 pm
Natural Food Store.
Comments: Anyone can shop here. Member dis-

counts of 25%.
Other Info: No credit cards. Accepts checks from members.
Direction: On Manhattan's Lower East Side. 6 train to Astor Place or Bleecker St; N, R trains to 8 Street–NYU. B, D, Q trains to Broadway–Lafayette Street; F train to 2nd Avenue; L train to 3 Avenue.

Fresh Fields (Whole Foods)
24th St & 7th Avenue
National 512-477-4455
Natural Food Store.

The Friday Night Dinner Club
48 West 21st Street, Second Floor; 212-645-5170; Web site: www.naturalgourmetschool.com
Hours: Open only on Friday nights. Closed on major holidays.
Menu: Four-course vegetarian meals. The menu changes weekly.
Comments: Sugar and dairy free.
Other Info: Full service, take-out, catering. Reservations are required. Accepts MC, VISA. $27.50 for the dinner.

Ghion Ethiopian Restaurant
686 Amsterdam Avenue, between 92nd and 93rd Streets; 212-875-8722
Hours: Wednesday to Monday 2 pm to 11 pm Closed Tuesday.
Ethiopian and American. Vegetarian friendly.
Menu: Has a good selection of vegetarian meals.
Comments: Live music on Saturday. Very friendly, relaxed place. Impressed by friendliness.
Other Info: Full service, take-out. Non-smoking. Accepts AMEX, DC, DIS, MC, VISA. Price: $$. $14 for buffet.
Directions: 1, 2, 3 trains to 96th and Broadway.

Good Earth Foods
1330 1st Avenue, between 71st & 72nd Streets
212-496-1616
Hours: Monday to Friday 9 am to 7:30 pm; Saturday 9:30 am to 6 pm; Sunday 12 noon to 6 pm
Natural Food Store and Deli. Juice Bar. Organic produce.
Other Info: Counter service, take-out. Has seating. Accepts AMEX, MC, VISA.
Directions: 6 train to 68th St–Hunter College.

Good Health Café
324 East 86th Street, between First and Second Avenues, Upper East Side; 212-439-9680
Hours: Monday to Thursday 11:30 am to 10 pm;

Friday 11:30 am to 11 pm; Saturday 10 am to 11 pm; Sunday 10 am to 10 pm
Natural Food Restaurant. Japanese, Italian, Middle Easter and Macrobiotic. Juice Bar. Most dishes are vegan. Not pure vegetarian (serves fish). Some dishes have eggs in them.
Menu: Features Italian, Mexican, Middle Eastern and Japanese dishes. Daily specials and casserole of the day. Whole-wheat dumplings with steamed vegetables and tamari ginger sauce. Macro Plate with hijiki, brown rice, black-eyed peas and steamed vegetables. Millet Croquette is a fried millet vegetable patty with soba noodles and vegetables with a burdock sauce. Chinese Vegetables and Tofu in a spicy peanut sauce. Blueberry-Peach Pie and other desserts. Fresh juices, non-alcoholic beer.
Comments: Natural food store inside. Some foods are made with eggs. Most dishes are dairy free.
Other Info: Full service, take-out, delivery. Accepts AMEX, DC, DIS, MC, VISA. Price: $$. Main dishes are around $10.
Direction: Upper East Side. 4, 5, 6 trains to 86th Street.

**Great American Health Bar

35 West 57th Street, between Fifth and Sixth Avenues; 212-355-5177
Hours: Daily 8:30 am to 10 pm
Vegetarian American and Kosher. Vegan options. Not pure vegetarian.
Menu: Large selection of vegetarian dishes. Avocado Salad, Eggplant Parmesan, brown rice, falafel, pizza and pasta of the day, curried vegetables, homemade soups, Garden Patch and hummus. Not many choices for vegan because much of the food contains cheese. Has a good selection of fresh juices. Frozen yogurts. No alcohol.
Other Info: Full service, catering, take-out. Price: $.

**Green House

37 East 29th Street, between Madison & Park Avenues; 212-686-9692
Hours: Daily 11 am to 11 pm
Vegetarian, Chinese Buddhist.
Menu: Good dishes include: Orange Beef (made from Portobello mushrooms), Crispy Stuffed Bean Curd Roll, Peking Duck (made from tofu), and Pork with Spicy Sauce (tofu and potatoes). The soups are good.
Comments: Good, inexpensive food.
Other Info: Accepts AMEX, DC, DIS, MC, VISA. Price: $.
Directions: 6 train to 28th Street and Park.

Hale and Hearty Soups

849 Lexington Avenue, between 64th & 65th Streets; 212-517-7600
75 Ninth Avenue (Chesea Market), between 14th and 15th Streets
Hours: Monday to Friday 9:30 am to 8 pm; Saturday 10:30 am to 6 pm; Sunday 11 am to 5 pm
Soup and Salad Place. Not pure vegetarian.
Menu: Soups, salads and sandwiches. Specializes in healthy soups. Soups come in three different sizes and are marked if they are vegetarian, contain dairy, or are low-fat. Lentil and Spinach, Tomato Lentil, pastas and Cheddar Mashed Potato.
Comments: Pleasant staff.
Other Info: Free delivery within 10 blocks. Price: $.
Directions: To Lexington St place take 6 train to 68th St. To Ninth Avenue place take A, C, E, L trains to 14th St.

Hana Restaurant

675 Ninth Avenue, between 14th and 58th Streets
212-582-9742
Hours: Monday to Saturday 11 am to 11 pm
Sunday 4 pm to 10 pm
Korean and Japanese. Serves meat, but has separate vegetarian menu. Vegan options.
Menu: Woo Dong Soup (noodles and vegetables), Vegetarian Sushi, stir-fired noodles and rice noodles dishes. Carrot juice.
Comments: Efficient service.
Other Info: Full service, take-out, catering. Accepts AMEX, MC, VISA. Price: $$.
Directions: 1, 9 trains to Time Square and 42nd Street.

***Hangawi

12 East 32nd Street, between 5th and Madison Avenues; 212-213-0077; **fax:** 212-689-0780
email: hangawi@aol.com
Web site: www.hangawirestaurant.com
Hours: Mon to Thur 11 am to 3 pm, 5 pm to 10:30 pm; Fri 12 noon to 3 pm, 5 pm to 11 pm; Sat 11 am to 11 pm; Sun 12 noon to 10 pm
Fully Vegan Vegetarian Korean.
Menu: Tofu patties, vegetarian dumplings, soup of the week, bean paste soup, vegetarian dumpling soup, combination pancakes (leek, kimchi, mushroom and mung bean), HanGawi Salad (in sesame soy sauce), Avocado Lettuce Salad, Ginseng Salad, Seaweed Salad, Acorn Noodles Salad, several rice dishes, Vegetarian Rice Bowl, Tofu Sandwich with Lemon Delight, Tofu with Mixed Vegetables in brown sauce, bean curd and Vegetable Stew. Choice of porridges includes: pump-

kin, Sweet Corn & Spinach and Black Sesame & Pine nut. "Supreme Meal" is bean soup, eight side dishes, seven types of greens, mini-pancakes, deep fried vegetables & mushroom dish and dessert. "Hangawi Stone Bowl" (ginko nuts, pine nuts, green beans, mushrooms, chestnuts over rice). Pumpkin Porridge, Mountain Roots & Greens, tofu & rice dishes and Stuffed Button Mushrooms. Emperor's Meal has pumpkin or sweet corn spinach porridge, kimchee, mountain root, pancakes, sweet & sour mushrooms, tofu sandwich and rice. Tofu Pudding (lemon or chocolate). Several full course meals (cannot be shared). **Comments:** Peaceful, Zen atmosphere. High-class place. The place is very unique. You remove your shoes and sit on low cushions at low tables. There is space below the table to extend your legs. Soft candlelight during dinner. Sound system plays running water and traditional folklore music. Authentic décor. Very clean place. Excellent service and experience. Has bargain box lunches. Won Zagat's Best Vegetarian Restaurant of the Year 98. Korean food often contains greens and mountain roots. Regularly wins awards for being one of the best restaurants in New York. **Author's Comment:** Unless you like exotic Oriental food, especially considering the price, you may not like this place. Opinions go both ways about this place (mostly very good). The food can be really heavy on the garlic, so if you don't like garlic you may want to ask them to leave it out. **Other Info:** Full service, take-out, delivery within 10 blocks (Monday to Friday 12 noon to 5 pm). Non-smoking. Reservations are recommended. Accepts AMEX, DC, MC, VISA. Price: $$$. **Directions:** In Little Korea area, about 10 shops east of 5th Avenue. Nearest garage on 32nd Street, at the corner of Broadway. Street parking available on right side after 6 pm and on left side after 7 pm. 6 train to 33rd St; N, R trains to 28th Street.

Haveli

100 Second Avenue, at 6th Street; 212-982-0533
Web site: http://haveli.citysearch.com/
Hours: Daily 12 noon to 12 midnight
Indian. East Indian. Vegan options. Not pure vegetarian.
Menu: Plain Mushroom Curry, Mixed Vegetable Curry, Saag Curry and rice dishes.
Comments: Popular, elegant, romantic place. Got good reviews from Zagat and the Daily News. Excellent atmosphere. Good place for a special event. Got awards for best Indian restaurant in New York. Upscale place. Carpeted. Has art and Indian artifacts.
Other Info: Full service, take-out. Does private parties and weddings upstairs. Accepts AMEX, DC, DIS, MC, VISA. Price: $$.
Directions: F train to 2nd Avenue. 6 train to Astor Place.

The Health Nuts

1208 Second Avenue, between 63rd and 64th Streets; 212-593-0116
Hours: Monday to Friday 9:30 am to 8:30 pm; Saturday 10 am to 8 pm; Sunday 11 am to 8 pm
835 Second Avenue, between 44th and 45th Streets; 212-490-2979
Hours: Monday to Friday 8:30 am to 8:30 pm; Saturday 10 am to 7 pm; closed Sunday.
2611 Broadway, between 98th and 99th Streets 212-678-0054
Hours: Monday to Saturday 9 am to 9 pm; Sunday 11 am to 7 pm
Natural Food Store and Cafe. Vegan Deli, Salad Bar and Juice Bar.
Menu: Fancy salads, pastas, pizzas, soups and snacks. Cakes, pastries and sometimes vegan cheese cake. Fresh juices.
Comments: A large health food store. Vitamins, frozen foods, cosmetics, books and dietary products. 2611 Broadway place has a nutritionist.
Other Info: Counter service, take-out. Deli with seats. Accepts AMEX, MC, VISA. Price: $.

The Health Nuts

2141 Broadway, between 75th and 76th Streets 212-724-1972
Hours: Monday to Saturday 9 am to 9 pm Sunday 11 am to 7 pm
Natural Food Store.

Healthy Pleasures

93 University Place, between 11th & 12th Streets, Greenwich Village
212-353-3663; fax: 212-353-3224; **Web site:** www.healthypleasures.com
Hours: Daily 7:30 am to 11:30 pm
Natural Food Store and large hot and cold Salad Bar. Organic produce.
Comments: One of the largest natural food stores in New York City.
Other Info: Accepts AMEX, MC, VISA.
Directions: 4, 5, 6, N, R, Q trains to 14th Street-Union Square.

Healthy Pleasures Market

489 Broome Street, SoHo, corner West Broadway; 212-431-7434

Web site: www.healtypleasures.com
Hours: Daily 7 am to 10 pm
Natural Food Store with a large hot and cold Salad Bar. Organic produce.
Directions: E, W, N, R trains to Canal Street.

Healthy Chelsea
248 West 23rd Street, near Eighth Avenue
212-691-0286
Hours: Monday to Saturday 10 am to 10 pm Sunday 12 noon to 8 pm
Natural Food Store. Salad Bar and Juice Bar.
Menu: Has vegetarian steam table. Sandwiches, hummus sandwiches, tempeh burgers, avocado sandwiches, juices and shakes.
Other Info: Take-out. Counter to sit at with around 15 seats. **Price:** $
Directions: C, E trains to 8th Avenue and 23rd Street. 1, 9 trains to 23rd Street and 7th Avenue.

Healthy Pleasures
489 Broome Street, SOHO
212-431-7434
Hours: Daily 8 am to 10:30 pm
Natural Food Store. Same as below.

Healthy Pleasures
93 University Place, near 11th Street, Greenwich Village; 212-353-FOOD (212-353-3663)
Hours: Daily 7:30 am to 11:30 pm
Natural Food Store, Bakery and Juice Bar. Large hot and cold Salad Bar.
Menu: Curried tempeh, sautéed seitan, salads items, baked goods and fresh juices.
Comment: One of the largest natural food stores in Manhattan. Has a large salad bar with a good selection of both hot and cold vegetarian dishes.
Other Info: Counter service, take-out. No seating. **Price:** $$-$$$. Accepts AMEX, DIS, MC, VISA.
Directions: Between 11th St and 12th St. 4,5 6, N, R, W, Q trains to 14th Street-Union Square.

Health Pleasure
2493 Broadway, between 92nd & 93rd Streets
212 787-6465
Hours: Daily 7 am to 12 midnight
Natural Food Store. Same as above.

Heartbeat
W Hotel, 149 East 49th Street, between Lexington and 3rd Avenues, Midtown; 212-407-2900
Hours: Mon to Fri 7 am to 11 am (breakfast), 12 noon to 2:30 pm (lunch), 6 pm to 10 pm (dinner); Sat 8 am to 12 noon (breakfast), 6 pm to 10 pm.; closed for lunch on Sat; closed Sun.

Progressive American with Asian influence. Macrobiotic and Vegan options. Not pure veg.
Menu: Chinese food, mushroom Ravioli and other dishes.
Comments: Outstanding décor. Plays new age music. Good place for a business dinner. Can call in advance to have an entire vegetarian meal. No butter, cream or saturated fats used in cooking.
Other Info: Accepts AMEX, DC, DIS, MC, VISA. **Price:** $$$.
Directions: 4, 5, 6 trains to 51st Street and Lexington Avenue. 6 train is best. In the W Hotel near Union Square.

**Helianthus
48 MacDougal Street, near King Street, between Houston and Prince Streets, Greenwich Village
212-598-0387
Hours: Monday to Friday 11:30 am to 10:30 pm; Sunday 1 pm to 10 pm; closed Saturday.
Vegetarian Chinese and Japanese. Juice Bar. Vegan and Macrobiotic options. Has eggs in some of the dishes.
Menu: Good appetizers are Mock Sesame "Eel" and Country Blanket. Lily Bulb & Spinach soup and Japanese-style Lily Flower soup. Veggie "Lamb." Sunflower Casserole, Lamb of Happiness, Curry Supreme (soy protein, potato, broccoli, peas in special sauce), Helianthus Forest (fried bean, shitake mushrooms, baby corn, water chestnuts wrapped in lettuce) and Shojin Land (steamed Japanese vegetables with seaweed). Veggie "Pork" with Vegetables (green peppers, carrots and pineapple) in sweet and sour sauce. Good Veggie "Chicken." Orange Flavor Sensation is orange-flavored soy protein and wheat gluten with kung-pao sauce.
Comments: Helianthus is Latin for "sunflower," and there are sunflowers all over the walls, menu and the waiter's clothes. Has pictures of sunflowers. The walls are painted bright yellow. It is a small restaurant in the Soho area. Gets good recommendations. Good service. Opened in 1994. Menu changes seasonally. Everything is made fresh. Has reasonable prices. The Chinese herbs and vegetables used are supposed to be healthy. Open on Christmas and some other major holidays when other restaurants are closed. Nice people.
Other Info: Full service, take-out, delivery. No smoking. Reservations are recommended. Accepts AMEX, DIS, MC, VISA. **Price:** $-$$ ($5 to $11).
Directions: A, B, D, C, E to West 4th Street. C, E to Prince Street. It is in the SoHo area, one block east of 6th Avenue, between Houston & Prince in the Soho Area.

Herban Kitchen

290 Hudson Street, at Spring Street, between Spring and Dominick Streets, below Houston 212-627-2257; fax: 212-627-2513 Web site: www.herbankitchen.com
Hours: Monday to Thursday 11 am to 4 pm, 5 pm to 10:30 pm; Friday 11 am to 4 pm, 5 pm to 11 pm (sometimes until 11:30 pm); Saturday 5 pm to 11 pm; closed Sunday.
International & American. Mainly uses organic vegetables. Vegan and Macrobiotic options. Vegan friendly. Not pure vegetarian.
Menu: Several daily specials. Mexican, Asian, South American and North American. Tofu Club Sandwich, Tempeh Scaloppini, veggie burgers, Quinoa Bean Loaf and more.
Comments: Won the 1998 New York Naturally's Restaurant of the Year. Very good food. The oils they use are cold-pressed. Uses extra virgin olive oil. Uses filtered water. Sweeteners and herbs are unrefined. Uses local produce whenever possible. Has outdoor dining. Good delivery program.
Other Info: Reservations recommended. It is a small place so reservations are recommended on Friday and Saturday. Full service, take-out, delivery, catering. Non-smoking. Credit cards accepted. Price: $$-$$$.
Directions: 1, 9 trains to Houston St; C, E trains to Spring St. SoHo, Little Italy area.

**House of Vegetarian

68 Mott Street, at Canal Street; 212-226-6572
Hours: Daily 11 am to 10:30 pm
Vegetarian Chinese. Vegan and Macrobiotic options. Has Cantonese and Szechuan Chinese food from Hong Kong.
Menu: Has over 200 items on menu. Features meat substitutes. Macrobiotic cuisine. Lemon "chicken," Veggie Steak (made from white yams), vegetarian roast duck, Sesame Chicken (made from soy beans), braised chicken, Sweet & Sour Chicken, Steak (made with yams), Orange Beef, Seaweed Fish with black bean sauce, Veggie Ham, vegetarian egg rolls, veg "fish" and mock "steak." Good appetizers are Spring Rolls, Carrot or Spinach Dumplings and Gluten "Duck." Brown and white rice.
Comments: Gets very good reviews. Prices reasonable for what you get. Popular place. Open for 15 years. Has wheel chair access. No atmosphere. Plastic tablecloths. Does not use MSG.
Other Info: Full service, take-out. Cash only; no credit cards. Price: $$.
Directions: On main street of Chinatown. J, M, Z; N, R, 6 trains to Canal St.

**Integral Yoga

229 West 13th Street, between 7th and 8th Avenues, West Greenwich Village
212-243-2642; email: iyf@aol.com; Web site: http://www.integralyogany.org/YogaNF/
Hours: Monday to Friday 9 am to 9:30 pm Saturday & Sunday 9 am to 8:30 pm
Natural Food Store and Vegetarian Deli. Salad Bar and Juice Bar. Organic produce. Macrobiotic products.
Menu: Mock "tuna," Tofu Ravioli, Bok Choy & Tofu, Lemon Tempeh and "Foloney" Sandwich.
Comments: Really good place. Has vegetarian cooking classes. Has book store next door. Excellent natural food store. Many items are dairy free. Uses canola oil for cooking. One of the best natural food stores in Manhattan. Has a vitamin store across the street. There are yoga classes next door.
Other Info: Take-out salad and steam table. Accepts AMEX, DIS, MC, VISA. Price: $-$$.

Joe's Shanghai

9 Pell Street, Chinatown, between Mott Street and Mott Street (6, Q, W trains to Canal Street, and then this place is about 5 blocks away)
212-233-8888
24 West 56th Street, between 5th and 6th Avenue 212-333-3868
Hours: Daily 11 am to 11 pm
Chinese. Vegan options. Not pure vegetarian.
Comments: Very popular place. Some people think it is the best Chinese restaurant in New York, and other people think the place stinks. Basic décor. May have to wait for a table, and also may have to share a table if you are by yourself.
Other Info: Full service, take-out. Cash only for Chinatown branch. Uptown 56th Street branch accepts credit cards. Price: $$.

Josephina

1900 Broadway, between 63rd & 64th Streets, across from Lincoln Center; 212-799-1000
Hours: Monday to Friday 12 noon to 12 midnight; Saturday 11:30 am to 12 midnight; Sunday 11:30 am to 11 pm; Wed, Sat & Sun Brunch.
Natural Food Restaurant (serves meat). Not pure vegetarian.
Menu: Good selection for vegans and vegetarians. Wheat tortillas, soups, mashed potatoes, Veggie Burgers and Grilled Vegetable Plate with brown rice & three-grain cake.
Comments: High class place. Often uses organic food, and many items are dairy-free. Has good food. Can dress casually. Has indoor and outdoor

seating. Good food and décor.
Other Info: Full service, take-out. Reservations are suggested for dinner. Accepts AMEX, DC, MC, VISA. Price: $$$. **Directions:** 1, 9 trains to 66th Street stop. It is across from Lincoln Center.

Josie's Restaurant
300 Amsterdam Avenue, near 74th Street
212-769-1212
Hours: Monday 12 noon to 11 pm; Tuesday to Friday 12 noon to 12 midnight; Saturday 11:30 am to 12 midnight; Sunday 11 am to 11 pm
Natural Food Restaurant and Juice Bar. Vegan options. Dairy free, so vegetarian dishes are vegan.
Menu: Several vegetarian dishes on the menu. Soups, Grilled Vegetables, Portobello Mushroom, baked sweet potato, Vegetable Meatloaf, brown rice, mashed potatoes, mock "meat" dishes and Mexican dishes. Whole-wheat tortilla. Non-alcoholic beer and wine. Fresh juices.
Comments: Uses recycled napkins. Good food. Uses organic produce when possible.
Other Info: Full service, take-out, catering. Reservations are advised, or you may have to wait an hour for a table. Accepts AMEX, DC, MC, VISA. Price $$-$$$.
Direction: 1, 2, 3, 9 trains to 72nd Street.

Juice Generation
644 9th Avenue; 212-541-5600
Hours: Monday to Friday 8 am to 8 pm; Saturday 9 am to 8 pm; Sunday 9 am to 8 pm
Juice Bar.

Karen's on Astor
1 Astor Place, at Broadway; 212-979-8000
Hours: Monday to Saturday 7:30 am to 9 pm; Sunday 11 am to 7 pm
Natural Food Store and Deli.
Other Info: Counter service, take-out. Has seating. Accepts AMEX, MC, VISA.
Directions: 6 train to Astor place

**Kate's Joint
56-58 Avenue B, between 4th and 5th St (corner of Avenue B and 4th Street); 212-777-7059
Hours: Sunday to Thursday 9 am to 12 midnight Friday & Saturday 9 am to 1 am
Fully Vegetarian Chinese, French, Continental and Southern (serves eggs). Mostly vegan. Fresh juices.
Menu: Burgers, pastas, burritos, Southern Fried Tofu Cutlets, Vegan Mashed Potatoes & gravy, and Pasta with Red Sauce. Wheat-free Angel Hair

Pasta with Artichokes, organic greens and tomatoes. Un-Turkey Club, French fries and un-Buffalo Wings with vegan dip. Southern-fried veg-chicken cutlets with mash potatoes and vegetables with homemade gravy. The soup of the day comes by the cup and bowl. Inexpensive breakfasts with a choice of scrambled tofu, focaccia toast, granola; or organic oatmeal with pecans, apples and raisins. The breakfast includes coffee or tea.
Comments: Popular with local musicians, artists and celebrities. Relaxed, friendly, cozy, hip atmosphere. Has a bar that serves wheatgrass during the day and real alcohol at night. Has velvet couch seating in front. Hip East Village place. Has a bar.
Other Info: Full service, free delivery. Reservations recommended for groups of 8 or more. Accepts AMEX, DIS, MC, VISA. Price: $-$$.
Directions: F train to 2nd Avenue and Houston. Walk to Ave B and 4th St.

Le Poeme
14 Prince Street, at the corner of Elizabeth Street & Prince Street, SoHo; 212-941-1106
Hours: Tuesday to Sunday 12 noon to 12 pm Closed Monday.
French, Mediterranean. Not pure vegetarian.
Menu: Salad and sandwiches. Three Dip Du Jour, which is eggplant, hummus and tapenade (black olives and garlic). Vegetable Lasagna (said to be vegan) and good homemade whole-wheat bread. Not many options for vegans.
Comments: Laid-back, friendly, reasonably priced place. Food is fresh. Good place for an afternoon tea.
Other Info: Full service, take-out. Accepts AMEX, MC, VISA. Price: $$.
Directions: N, R trains to Prince St; 6 train to Bleecker St or Spring St. B, G, R Q trains to Lafayette St. Near Little Italy and the Lower East Side.

Lexington Market
859 Lexington Avenue; 212-861-8051
Hours: Daily 10:30 am to 9 pm
Natural Food Store and take-out Deli.
Other Info: No credit cards; cash only.

Life Café
343 East 10th Street, near Avenue B, East Village; 212-477-9001, 212-477-8791
Web site: www.lifecafenyc.com
Hours: Sunday to Thursday 11 am to 12 midnight (1 am in summer); Friday & Saturday 11 am to 2 am (3 am in summer); **Breakfast and**

Lunch: Monday to Friday 11 am to 5 pm; **Brunch:** Saturday and Sunday 11 am to 5 pm **Dinner:** Sunday to Thursday 5 pm to 12 midnight; Friday and Saturday 5 pm to 2 am **Mainly Vegetarian American and Mexican.** Has a good selection of Vegetarian and Vegan options. Not totally vegetarian.
Menu: Has many vegan and vegetarian selections. A starter is vegetable fritters with corn, zucchini and soy ginger dip. Seitan Burrito, quesadillas, veggie burger, Peanut Stir-fry, Grilled Seitan, Eggplant & Squash Linguini, soy drinks, Garden Burgers and Seitan Steak Sandwich. Vegan nachos (oven-baked) with soy cheese (contains casein). Thai stir-fried vegetables with ginger. Vegetables over rice with fried seitan. Has many real meat items on its menu. Fresh juices, soya cappuccino.
Comment: Good place to hang out. Hip place. It is a small place and is often full. It has a full bar. Spray-painted walls. Loud music. Outdoor seating. You can get either milk or soy cheese.
Other Info: Full service, take-out, delivers to parts of the Lower East Side after 6 pm. Accepts DC, DIS, MC, VISA. Price: $$.
Directions: Take any train to 14th Street. Transfer to the "L" train going towards Canarsie (Brooklyn) to First Avenue exit. Walk south (downtown) on First Avenue four blocks to E 10th Street. Walk east (turn left) two blocks to the Northwest corner of Avenue B and 10th Street. Across from Tompkins Square Park. 6 train to Astor Place stop. N, R trains to 8th Street. Walk east to Tompkins Square Park.

Lifethyme Natural Market
410 6th Avenue, between 8th & 9th Streets
212-420-9099
Hours: Monday to Saturday 8 am to 10 pm
Sunday 9 am to 10 pm
Natural Food Store & Salad Bar. Organic produce.
Menu: Has a selection of vegetarian dishes.
Other Info: Accepts AMEX, MC, VISA. Counter service, take-out. Has a seating area.
Comments: One of the best natural food stores in New York. Has another branch at 82nd St & Broadway.

Lucky's Juice Joint
75 West Houston Street, near West Broadway
212-388-0300
Hours: Monday to Saturday 9 am to 8:30 pm; Sunday 10 am to 8:30 pm; Stops serving juices at 7:30 pm, stops serving smoothies at 8:30 pm. Closes an hour earlier in the winter.
Juice Bar. Vegan options.

Menu: Good selection of fresh fruit and vegetable juices, smoothies, salads, Hemp Burger, Nori Rolls, Tofu hot-dogs, Vegetable Avocado Sandwich, Vegan Lentil Soup, Potato Leek Soup, veggie burgers, un-chicken sandwiches, hummus sandwiches and desserts. Vegan Carob Chips Cookies. Organic carrot juice.
Comments: Friendly, relaxed place. Counter service, take-out. Has outdoors seating. Price: $.
Directions: 6 train to Bleecker Street. N train to Prince Street. A, C, E trains to West 4th Street.

Lucky's Juice Joint
170 Second Avenue, corner of 11th Street
212-358-0300
Summer Hours: (May to Sept): 8 am to 12 midnight; **Winter Hours:** 8 am to 10 pm
Juice Bar and Café. Same information as its downtown counterpart (see above).
Comments: Has counter seating, but no tables.
Directions: 4, 5 6, N, R, L trains to 14th Street–Union Square.

**Madras Café
79 Second Avenue, between 4th and 5th Streets, East Village; 212-254-8002
Hours: Monday to Friday 1 pm to 11 pm; Saturday 12 noon to 11 pm; Sun 12 noon to 10 pm
Vegetarian Indian. Vegan friendly.
Menu: Has a good selection of vegetarian Indian dishes.
Comments: Basic décor and low on atmosphere. Very good Indian food. Price: $-$$.
Directions: In the Lower East Side. 6 train to Astor Place. F train to 2nd Street. About a 10-minute walk from the closest subway stop.

**Madras Mahal Restaurant
104 Lexington Avenue, between 27th and 28th Streets; 212-684-4010
Hours: Monday to Friday 11:30 am to 3 pm, 5 pm to 10 pm; Sat and Sun 12 noon to 10 pm
Fully Vegetarian South Indian, North Indian and Gujarati. Kosher. Vegan options. Items are clearly marked if they are spicy or contain dairy.
Menu: Masala Dosa, idly (not so good), Alu (potato) Paratha and Chole-Batura (chick peas). Has excellent Vegetable Fried Rice for $6.99 for a good size plate (some of the best I ever tasted). Mixed vegetable uthappam is very good. Good coconut chutney. Soups and salads. A selection of about 15 North Indian curried vegetables and Kala Channa (black chickpea curry). Chapati, samosa, puri, pakora and papadam. Has set thali meals for $15. Lassi, raita, mango chutney and French

fries. Desserts such as gulabjumun, shrikhand, halava, ice cream and kulfi.
Comments. Recommended place. Fairly conservative place, but not fancy. Friendly service. Owner is a first class gentleman. Really liked the place. Seating for around 50. Mahal means "palace." Uses dairy products, but definitely no eggs or meat. One of main cooks is an ISKCON devotee. Brahmin cooks.
Awards: Awarded best Dosa in Manhattan by the Village Voice. Won Best Vegetarian Restaurant in USA award.
Other Info: Full service, take-out, delivers up to 10 blocks away ($15 minimum order). Non-smoking. Reservations recommended for dinner on weekends. Accepts AMEX, DIS, MC, VISA. Price: $$.
Directions: 6 train to 28th St stop. Located in the "Little India" area. Little India is the area on 3rd Avenue and Lexington Avenue between 21st and 29th Streets. There are several places with similar names on the same street, such as the New Mahal Place (which is also vegetarian) directly across the street.

Mana
646 Amsterdam Ave, between 91st and 92nd Streets, Upper West Side; 212-787-1110
Hours: Monday to Saturday 11:30 am to 11 pm
Sunday 11 am to 10 pm
Japanese-style Macrobiotic. Also some International dishes. Vegan options. Not pure vegetarian (serves fish).
Menu: Seitan Sukiyaki is good. Sushi rolls with tempeh, cucumber, burdock and pickle. Teriyaki, Japanese whole wheat and buckwheat noodles, tempura, Seitan Stroganoff, Norimaki (sushi style brown rice and vegetables that are wrapped in nori) and Seitan Cutlet. Has some good international dishes including Lasagna, pasta, Ravioli, Stuffed Mushroom, tofu dishes and noodles dishes. Curried Seitan is good. Vegan Mocha Pie for dessert.
Comments: No dairy products, preservatives, chemicals or sugar. Uses organic ingredients. Fairly reasonable prices. Uses filtered water.
Other Info: Full service, take-out. Accepts MC, VISA. Price: $$.
Directions: 1, 2, 3 trains to 96th Street. Leave the station at the Broadway and 94th Street exit.

Mary Ann's (two or three branches)
116 8th Avenue; 212-633-0877
(A, C, E trains to 14th Street)
2452 Broadway, at 91st Street; 212-877-0132 (1, 2, 3, 9 trains to 96th Street stop)
1503 2nd Avenue, between 78th and 79th Streets
212-249-6165 (6 train to 77th Street stop)
http://maryannsmexicanny.citysearch.com/
Hours: Monday to Thursday 12 noon to 11 pm
Friday & Saturday 12 noon to 11:30 pm
Sunday 12 noon to 10:30 pm
Mexican. Not pure vegetarian.
Menu: Good selection of vegetarian dishes. Avocado Burritos, quesadilla, nachos, avocado tostadas, Black Bean Burritos, tacos and brown rice. Whole-wheat tortillas or rice can come with each meal.
Comments: Has tofu jack cheese. Foods are fried in 100% canola oil.
Other Info: Full service, catering, take-out, delivery. Accepts AMEX, MC, VISA. Accepts only cash at the 8th Ave restaurant. Price: $$.

**Mavalli Palace
46 East 29th Street
between Park and Madison Avenues
212-679-5535
Hours: Daily 12 noon to 3 pm, 5 pm to 10 pm
Closed Monday.
South Indian Vegetarian. Vegan friendly.
Menu: Good size menu. Masala dosa, idly, rasa vada and samosas. Channa Masala (chick pea curry), Dhringri Gobhi (broccoli, mushrooms, cauliflower and coconut) and Eggplant Curry are very good. Appetizer platter.
Comments: One of the best South Indian restaurants in the US. Good service and food. Has pleasant Indian design. White tablecloths and flowers on tables. Good, friendly service. Good place for a special event. Serves dairy products, but can remove if you want. Food not greasy. Most things are made with ghee, but can be prepared without it, if you ask.
Other Info: Full service, take-out. Accepts AMEX, DC, MC, VISA. Price: $$.
Directions: 6 train to 28th Street and Park Avenue.

**Mei-Ju Vege Gourmet
154 Mott Street
646-613-0643
Hours: Daily 8 am to 8 pm
Vegetarian Chinese. Vegan options.
Menu: Has a Chinese Buffet with a good selection of dishes. Dumplings, Veggie Rolls, Chinese vegetables and rice dishes.
Other Info: Cash only. Price: $.
Direction: 6, B, Q trains to Canal. S train to Grand Street.

Michael & Zoe's (formerly Brownie Points)
101 Second Avenue, between 5th and 6th Streets,
at Avenue B, East Village; 212-254-5004
Hours: Sunday to Thursday 7 am to 12 midnight
Friday & Saturday 7 am to 1 am
American Snack food. Vegetarian friendly. Not
pure vegetarian (has meat sandwiches). Vegan
options.
Menu: Good selection of items. Vegetarian sandwiches (many are not vegan), soups, veggie
burgers, Tempeh Burger, Vegetarian "Chicken"
Salad, Sunshine Burger, "Tofurky" Sandwiches,
Tofu Burger, brown rice, Vegetarian Chili. Vegan
desserts. Baked goods and ice cream. Tofutti Sun-
dae with carob, Hydrox Cookies and homemade
brownies (many are vegan). Hot chai tea with soy
or regular milk (gets good recommendations).
Fresh juices, smoothies, cappuccino, espresso.
Good selection of fruit shakes.
Comments: Outdoor seating. Has eggs in many
things. Has some baked goods without dairy or
honey.
Other Info: Full service, take-out, delivery. No
credit cards; cash only. Price: $$.
Directions: 6 train to Astor Place; F train to
Second Avenue.

Natural Green Market
162 3rd Avenue; 212-780-0263
Hours: Sunday to Friday 9 am to 11 pm
Saturday 9 am to 10 30 pm
Natural Food Store with Deli and Salad Bar.
Organic produce.
Other Info: Accepts AMEX, MC, VISA.

Natural Frontier Market
266 Third Avenue, between 21st & 22nd Street
212-228-9133; **fax:** 212-228-9711
(6 train to 23rd Street and Park Avenue)
Hours: Monday to Friday 8 am to 10 pm
Saturday & Sunday 9 am to 10 pm
Counter service, take-out only. Has no seating.
1424 Third Avenue, at 81st Street
212-794-0922; **fax:** 212-794-0814
Hours: Daily 9 am to 10 pm
Website: www.natfrontiermarket.com
http://naturalfront1.citysearch.com/
Natural Food Store and take-out Deli. Juice Bar.
Organic produce.
Other Info: Accepts AMEX, MC, VISA, ATM.
Free delivery within 10 blocks.

**Natural Gourmet Cookery School
Friday Night Dinning Club, 48 West 21st Street,
between Fifth and Sixth Avenues
212-645-5170 (ext 10)
Web site: www.naturalgourmetschool.com
Hours: Friday only. Seating at 6:30 pm.
Closed on major holidays.
Vegetarian.
Menu: Serves a five-course vegetarian dinner made
by a chef instructor and students. New menu each
week. Appetizer, soups, salads, entrées and des-
serts. A sample menu is Butternut Squash & Sweet
Potato Fritter, Baby Greens with Toasted Spicy
Walnuts, Cranberry Bean Soup, Wild Rice Pilaf,
Thai Mushroom Sauté, Bok Choy and Raspberry
Sorbet. A Southwestern menu is Yellow Corn
Grits with Grilled Okra, Roasted Chili Pepper
Soup, Refried Black & White Bean with Cilantro
Salsa and salad.
Comments: Food is cholesterol-free, low-fat,
natural, fresh and high in fiber. No dairy or re-
fined sugar. Communal seating. Uses fresh, sea-
sonal produce. Uses organic grains and beans. In
candlelit, comfortable dining rooms.
Cooking Classes: Famous cooking teacher and
cookbook author Annemarie Colbin has been
teaching classes since 1977. Teaches a variety of
cuisines emphasizing vegan and vegetarian tech-
niques. Teaches professional and home cooks.
Other Info: Full service, catering. Reservations
required. Accepts AMEX, MC, VISA. Price: $$$.
Directions: F; N, R trains to 23rd Street.

New Nutrisserie Natural Food Market
142 West 72 Street, between Columbus and
Broadway; 212-799-2454; **fax:** 212-799-5806
email: nutrisserie@msn.com
Hours: Monday to Saturday 9 am to 8 pm
Sunday 10 am to 7 pm
Natural Food Store and Deli. Organic Juice Bar.
Organic produce.
Menu: Large selection of vegetarian dishes. Veggie
Burgers in pita bread, salads, soups and hot main
dishes. Vegan cakes and muffins.
Other Info: Cafeteria, counter service, take-out,
catering. Food bar in back of natural food store.
Has a small area in the back for seating. Accepts
AMEX, MC, VISA. Price: $.
Direction: 1, 2, 3, 9 trains to 72nd Street and
Broadway.

Nha Trang
87 Baxter, Chinatown, between Canal and Bayard
Streets, near Mott Street; 212-233-5948
Hours: Daily 10 am to 9:30 pm
Vietnamese. Also Chinese. Not pure vegetarian.
Menu: Has a good selection of vegetarian dishes.
Comments: Food is authentic and reasonably

priced. A bit higher-end than other places in Chinatown. In-crowd of the Asian American Community come here. Sometimes can see famous actors and models. Happening place, but casual for dressing. Good value.

Other Info: No credit cards; cash only. Price: $$.
Directions: N, R; J, M, Z trains; 6 train to Canal Street.

Nirvana

30 Central Park South, between Fifth and Sixth Avenues; 212-486-5700
Hours: Daily 12 noon to 12:30 am
India. Not pure vegetarian.
Menu: Vegetarian plate, Tandoori bread, curries and rice dishes.
Comments: It is fifteen floors up and has a great view of the Central Park. Live sitar music and a fortune teller. Romantic setting. Many people love the food and others don't like it. Everyone loves the view, but many people don't feel the food was worth the price.
Other Info: Reservations suggested. Accepts AMEX, DC, DIS, MC, VISA. Price: $$$$.
Direction: Near the 57th Street stop of the B, Q and N, R trains at Fifth Ave.

Organic Grill

123 First Avenue, at 7th Street; 212-477-7177
Web site: www.theorganicgrill.com
Hours: Monday to Thursday 11 am to 10 pm; Friday 11 am to 11 pm; Saturday 10 am to 11 pm; Sunday 10 am to 10 pm
International Organic Food. Over 90% Vegetarian (serves fish). Vegan options. Not pure vegetarian. During the Sunday brunch they don't use the menu.
Menu: Vegan pancakes and waffles, soy sausage, Home Fries, Tofu Scramble and Tempeh Bacon. Tofu Rancheros, Hummus with Pita Bread, Grilled Eggplant, TLT, homemade Veggie Burger, Macro Plate Meal, Broccoli & Cheddar Sauté, soups of the day, salads, Tostada Salad, Quesadillas, brown rice, Bean of the Day, Mashed Sweet Potatoes, Miso Soup, Eggplant Caponata, good cornbread, Marinated Tempeh (very good), Grilled Tofu Sandwich, BBQ Seitan Sandwich, Grilled Portobello Sandwich, Macro Plate Special and daily specials. Fresh juices, good vegan soymilk shake and great smoothies. Cappuccino, espresso. Wide selection of herbal teas.
Comments: Gets really high recommendations for good food. Sunday brunch can be really busy and you may have to wait a half-hour for a table. Relaxing, pleasant atmosphere.

Reviews: "The Organic Grill… GOOD CLEAN FOOD! Local and artisanal ingredients in clean, fresh and seasonal preparations." NEW YORK MAGAZINE, Oct 2000.
"Located in the heart of the East Village, this inviting cafe offers vegan, vegetarian & macrobiotic dishes that are sure to please your body without depleting your wallet." NEW YORK NATURALLY, Spring 2001
"Wake up and Smell the Tofu! Flavorful scrambled tofu lures East Villagers out of bed for brunch at The Organic Grill!" TimeOut New York June 2001
"The Organic Grill" still manages to shine. Their motto is "Good Clean Food" and they prove it by putting forth delicious food made to order!" SATYA July/August 2001
Other Info: Full service, take-out, catering. Accepts AMEX, MC, VISA. Price: $-$$.
Direction: In the East Village between St Marks Place and 7th Street on First Avenue.

Organic Harvest Café

53rd Street, between 2nd & 3rd Avenues
212-421-6444
Hours: Monday to Friday 11 am to 10 pm; Saturday 11 am to 8 pm; Sunday 11 am to 9 pm
Completely Organic Restaurant. Many Vegetarian dishes. Vegan options. Price: $$.
Directions: E, F trains to 53rd Street and Lexington Avenue.

Health For You Market

432 Park Avenue South, between 29th & 30th Streets; 212-532-2644
Hours: Monday to Friday 8 am to 8 pm; Saturday 10 am to 7 pm; closed Sunday.
Natural Food Store and ready-made sandwich Deli. Salad Bar (on weekdays only). Organic produce. Vegan-friendly.
Directions: 6 train to 33rd Street stop or 28th Street stop.

Organic Market

275 7th Avenue, between 23rd and 24th Street
212-243-9927
Hours: Monday to Friday 9 am to 9 pm; Saturday 10 am to 7 pm; Sunday 12 noon to 7 pm
Natural Food Store. Juice Bar. Organic produce
Directions: 1, 9 trains to 28th Street.

Other Foods Organic Café

47 East 12th Street, between Broadway and University Place (Central Village/SoHo)
212-358-0103

Hours: Daily 11 am to 10 pm
Mostly Vegetarian. Organic Café. Not pure vegetarian.
Menu: Has a good selection of vegetarian dishes.
Comments: Gets good recommendations.
Other Info: Full service, take-out. Price: $$.

Our Kitchen

520 East 14th Street; 212-677-8018
Hours: Monday, Wednesday to Sat 11:30 am to 11 pm; Sun 3:30 pm to 10:30 pm; closed Tue.
Asian. Chinese, Thai, Japanese (a little of everything). Not pure vegetarian.
Menu: Has a large selection of vegan and vegetarian dishes. Has really good mock "meat" dishes. The Sesame Chicken is really good.
Comments: Friendly, helpful people
Directions: L train to 1st Avenue stop.

Ozo

566 Amsterdam Avenue, at 87th Street
Upper West side
212-787-8316
Hours: Daily 11:30 am to 10:30 pm
Macrobiotic Japanese. Vegan options. Not pure vegetarian. Serves fish.
Menu: Mainly a Japanese menu. Has soups, salads, breads, tofu, seitan, noodles, rice, vegetables, tempura, lotus root sandwich and desserts. Soba Mariko (sautéed noodles & vegetables with deep-fried seitan), Ozu Roll (tofu, beans and eggplant wrapped in a flour tortilla with tahini sauce) and Nimono Stew (turnip, daikon and tofu in a sweet soup). Large option of tofu dishes. Has many non-dairy and sugar free desserts including Tofu Pie and Almond Crème Caramel. Cashew Crème for dessert is recommended. Serves unlimited free grain-tea.
Comments: High-end menu. Vegan options. Friendly place. One of the best macrobiotic places in town.
Other Info: Full service, take-out. Accepts MC, VISA. Price $$-$$$$.
Directions: In Upper West Side. 1, 9 trains to 86th Street stop.

Papaya King Inc

179 East 86th Street, at 3rd Avenue
212-369-0648
Hours: Sunday to Friday 8 am to 11 pm
Saturday 8 am to 2 am
Juice Bar. Tropical drinks. No vegetarian food items.
Directions: 5, 6 trains to 86th Street and Lexington Avenue. Can take any east town train.

Plum Tree

1501 First Avenue, between 78th and 79th Streets
212-734-1412
Hours: Tuesday to Sunday 12 noon to 10 pm
Closed Monday.
Macrobiotic Asian and Chinese. Vegan options. Not pure vegetarian.
Menu: Soy corn bread, dairy-free buckwheat pancakes and scrambled tofu. Woman Warrior Stew (tofu & vegetables), Chili, Azuki, cornbread, seitan, seaweed, brown rice, tofu dishes and Black Bean Soup. The veggie burger on pita bread is good. Has several daily lunch specials, which includes a main dish, salad and soup. Fresh-baked desserts. Recommended is the brown rice and sautéed vegetables in a wheat and soy crepe. Fresh juices.
Comment: Has brunch from noon to 4 pm on Saturday and Sundays. Healthy food. Relaxed place. Open since 1981. It is a small place. The service is a little slow.
Other Info: Full service, take-out. Non-smoking. Reservations not necessary. No credit cards. Price: $$.
Direction: 6 train to 77th Street and Lexington Avenue.

**Pongal

110 Lexington Avenue, between 27th & 28th Streets; 212-696-9458; **fax:** 212-545-8092
email: pongal@worldnet.att.net
Web site: www.pongal.org
Hours: Monday to Friday 12 noon to 3 pm, 5 pm to 10 pm
Business Lunch Hours: Monday to Friday 11:30 am to 3 pm
Saturday to Sunday 12 noon to 10 pm
Fully Vegetarian South Indian, Punjabi and Gujarati. Kosher. Vegan options.
Menu: Has a large selection of vegetarian choices including rice, vegetable subjis from Gujarat, Indian breads, Punjabi subjis and Indian desserts. South Indian dishes include idly, dosas, Masala Dosa, uthappam, Rava Dosa and vada. Has set lunch and dinner specials.
Comments: Friendly atmosphere. Fresh cooked food. Beautiful authentic Indian decor. Since the food is freshly prepared it takes about 20 to 30 minutes to prepare a meal. Some people complain badly about the service (Indian servers can be a bit curt and unresponsive, so it definitely pays to take your time).
Other Info: Full service, take-out. Non-smoking. Does not take reservations. Accepts DIS, MC, VISA. Price: $-$$.

Directions: East side of Lexington between 27th and 28th Streets. 6 train to 28th Street and Park Avenue stop. One block from stop. By bus take local buses M101, M102 or M103, or express buses X2, X5 or X31.

Prana Natural Foods
125 1st Avenue, between 7th Street and St Marks
212-982-7306
Hours: Monday to Saturday 9 am to 9 pm
Sunday 10 am to 7 pm
Natural Food Store.

Quantum Leap
88 W 3rd Street, between Thompson and Sullivan Street, Greenwich Village; 212-677-8050
Hours: Monday to Saturday 11 am to 11 pm
Sunday 11 am to 10 pm
Natural Food Restaurant. Japanese, Middle Eastern, Mexican, Italian. Vegan and Macrobiotic options. Not pure vegetarian (fish).
Menu: Many vegan and macrobiotic dishes. Natural pies, casseroles, salads, house dressing, soups, Sweet Potato Tempura, seitan, falafel, pastas, tofu dishes, hummus, Mexican dishes and miso soup with vegetables. The spaghetti and meatballs are good. Weekend brunch includes waffles and pancakes. Has daily specials such as Seitan Parmigiana and Mexican Fiesta. Good salad dressings. Tofu Pie dessert. Has some vegan desserts made with maple syrup and with no dairy. No alcohol.
Comments: Relaxed, friendly, laid-back, peaceful place. The original branch is in Queens. Good place. The grocery section has organic vegetables. Some of the dishes can come with either tofu cheese or fried or steamed ingredients.
Other Info: Full service, take-out, delivery. Does not accept reservations. Accepts AMEX, MC, VISA. Price: $$.
Directions: B, D, F, Q, A, C, E trains to West 4th Street. Take the West 3rd Street exit at the station.

Quintessence
263 East 10th Street, between 1st Ave & Avenue A, East Village; 646-654-1823
Web site: www.quintessencerestaurant.com
Hours: Daily 11:30 am to 11:30 pm
Vegan Raw Food Restaurant. Mainly Organic Gourmet. Lunch combos for $10 from 11:30 am to 3 pm.
Menu: Guacamole & Chips, Black Olive & Cream Dim Sum, Sun Burger, Nut Loaf, Wild Rice Salad, Middle Eastern Platter, Italian Pasta, soups, Sesame Sea Salad, Nori Roll and a special

of the day. Asian Paté is fresh vegetables, herbs, and mushrooms stuffed in tomato halves on greens. A Lunch Special may include special of the day, side dish of the day and mixed greens. Juliano's Livioli is a stuffed turnip with nut and basil filling with an Italian marinara or pesto sauce. The nut loaf with mushroom gravy is recommended. "Peter's Pot" (tomato, cucumber and yellow pepper). Desserts such as fruit bowl, berry carob, mousse pie & fruit fondue, Pecan Pie made with raw pecans & fresh vanilla bean and Coconut Cream Pie. Electrolyte Lemonade.
Comments: Has good variety. This place is a small, friendly, relaxed place. The food is really good. The décor is a bit lacking. Service is excellent and attentive. Desserts are vegan and do not contain sugar.
Other Info: Full service, take-out, catering. Accepts AMEX, MC, VISA. Price: $$.
Directions: L train to 1st Avenue.

Ratner's Restaurant
138 Delancy Street
between Norfolk and Suffolk Streets
212-677-5588
Hours: Monday to Thursday 6 am to 11 pm; Friday 6 am to 3 pm; Sunday 8 am to 8 pm
Kosher Dairy Restaurant. Not pure vegetarian; has many fish dishes.
Menu: Has a large, good menu. Potato pancakes, blintzes and desserts.
Other Info: Full service, take-out, delivery. Non-smoking. Reservations requested for groups. Accepts AMEX, DC, MC, VISA. Price: $$-$$$.
Directions: F train to Delancy Street. J, M trains to Essex Street.

***Sacred Chow
522 Hudson Street, 10th and Charles
212-337-0863
Hours: Monday to Friday 8 am to 9:30 pm
Saturday & Sunday 9 am to 9 pm
Fully Vegan International. Mainly organic. Kosher. Healthy food.
Menu: Roasted Black Olive Seitan, Grilled Marinated Tofu, Baked Ginger-miso Tempeh, Vanilla Rice Custard, Toasted Walnut Brownies and Sinner Bars. The pizza and truffles are good. Seitan Robai, Grilled Vegetables and Soysage with Roasted Tomatoes. Soups, stews, sandwiches and entrées. Desserts, biscuits, breads, home-brewed teas, orange blossom almond milk, and blended fruit drinks with herbs. Fresh juices.
Comment: Gourmet cooking. Cozy, friendly place. Street parking near the restaurant. Plays

pleasant music. Has grain-free dishes made with no refined sweeteners. No refined, artificial or hydrogenated products. Serves food free of preservative, white flours, chemicals and cholesterol. Some dishes sold by the pound such as Seitan Roulade and Chestnut Pesto.

Other Info: Counter service, delivery, take-out, catering. Non-smoking. Accepts reservations, but are not necessary. Accepts AMEX, MC, VISA. Price: $$.

Directions: In northwest Greenwich Village. In the Chelsea and Garment District. 1 train to Christopher Street. Walk south on Christopher Street to Hudson Street; turn right on Hudson, then go two blocks to West 10th Street. This place is second shop on east side of W 10th Street.

**The Sanctuary

25 First Avenue (just above Houston St between 1st & 2nd St), Lower East Village
212-780-9786
Hours: Tuesday & Wednesday 11:30 am to 9:30 pm; Thursday to Saturday 11:30 am to 10 pm; Sunday 11:30 am to 9 pm; closed Monday.
Pure Vegetarian Indian, Chinese and International Restaurant. Juice Bar. Vegan options.
Menu: Very good sandwiches, salads (the dressing are really good) and main courses. Daily specials. Indian dishes. Buddha's Delight, Malaysian Bi-Hun noodles, Japanese noodles, Indian curries, French fries, a great veg BLT sandwich, Aloo Gobhi, and vegan Tofu Cheesecake. Fresh juices.
Comments: Run by the Interfaith League of Devotees (mainly Hare Krishna devotees). One of the best places in New York. Reasonably priced. Food is first offered to God before serving it. Relaxed, friendly place. Good atmosphere. It also has a bed and breakfast, which cost $65 a night for one person and $95 a night for a double, which includes breakfast. Offers hatha yoga classes. Recommended. Price: $-$$.
Directions: F train to 2nd Avenue.

Simply Pasta

120 West 41st Street
between 6th Avenue and Broadway
212-391-0805
Hours: Monday to Friday 11:30 am to 9 pm; Saturday 4 pm to 9 pm; closed Sunday.
Italian. Not pure vegetarian.
Menu: Has a good selection of vegetarian dishes. Most of the hard pastas are eggless. The soft pastas usually have eggs in them.
Other Info: Accepts AMEX, DC, MC, VISA. Price: $$.

Souen

28 East 13th Street, between University Place and Fifth Avenue, East Village 212-627-7150
210 Sixth Avenue, at the corner of Prince Street, SoHo; 212-807-7421; **fax:** 212-627-4309
Web site: www.souen.net
Hours: Monday to Saturday 11 am to 11 pm; Sunday 11 am to 10 pm; Delivery until 10 pm.
Macrobiotic Japanese (serves fish). Natural Foods. Vegan options.
Menu: Appetizers, soups, noodle dishes and salads. Noodles with Kuzu Sauce (carrot and burdock), Seitan Cutlets, Tempeh Dumplings, Vegan Sushi, Seitan Sushi, Tempeh Croquettes and tofu entrees. One of the best miso soups in New York. Good breakfasts including fakin' bacon, and mochi waffles. Vegan desserts. Fresh juices. Organic soy-coffee. No Alcohol.
Comments: Indoor seating and seating in the outdoor garden. A real good macrobiotic place. Often uses organic produce. Vegan and macrobiotic dishes. Quiet, relaxing place. No sugar, chemicals, preservatives, meat or dairy.
Other Info: Full service, take-out, catering. Accepts AMEX, DC, DIS, MC, VISA. Price: $$-$$$.
Directions: For 6th Ave place take C, E trains to Spring Street; 1, 9 trains to Houston Street, N, R trains to Prince Street. For E 13th St place take L; N, R, 4, 5, 6 trains to University Place; 1, 2, 3, 9, L trains to 14th Street–Union Square.

Spring Street Natural

62 Spring Street (entrance on Lafayette Street), SoHo; 212-966-0290; **email:** springRS@aol.com; **Web site:** www.springstreetnatural.com
Hours: Sunday to Thursday 11:30 am to 11:30 midnight; Friday & Saturday 11:30 am to 12:30 am; Saturday & Sunday Brunch Hours: 11:30 am to 4 pm
Natural Organic foods. Vegetarian-friendly. Serve non-vegetarian dishes such as chicken and seafood.
Menu: Vegetarian soups and salads. Broiled Tofu with Peanut Sauce. Corn-fried Seitan with Sauce is good. Tempeh Burger, Spinach Pie, Shiitake Mushrooms, Pumpkin Ravioli, Stir-fry with Organic Brown Rice and Semolina Fettuccine. Some options for vegans are Rice-seaweed and Vegetable Dish, Fettuccine Primavera without cream or cheese, Stir-fry with Organic Brown Rice, Black Bean Hummus and Tofu & Seitan Stir-fry. Has some sugar-free and dairy-free desserts. Fresh juices. Soymilk cappuccino.
Comments: Often uses organic produce. Reason-

ably priced. Offers good portions. Is a big, popular place. Plays jazz music. Has potted trees. **Other Info:** Full service, take-out, catering. Reservations requested for large groups. Accepts AMEX, MC, VISA. Price: $$. **Directions:** It is in the SoHo area. SoHo is south of Houston Street. 6 train to Prince Street.

***Strictly Roots
2058 Adam Clayton Powell Boulevard (7th Ave), between 122nd and 123rd Streets in Harlem 212-864-8699; email: deecee@strictlyroots.net; Web site: www.strictlyroots.net **Hours:** Daily 12 noon to 10 pm **West Indian Vegan food.** Rastafarian Restaurant. Juice Bar. **Menu:** The menu changes daily. Tofu and Broccoli, lima beans, salads, falafel, Chickpea Stew, Tofu-vegetable Curry, Tofu Croquettes, Tofu Tempura, fried plantain, Seitan Stew, collard greens, Macaroni and Soy Cheese (soy cheese may contain casein, a milk product), Root Mash (yam, potatoes, etc.), mixed vegetables, rice and peas, Veggie "Duck," Jamaican Veggie Patty and sandwiches. Non-dairy desserts, smoothies, ginger beer, soy milk and fresh juices. Very good Pineapple Upside-down Cake. No alcohol. The veggie burgers are good. **Comments:** Neighborhood restaurant. They state "We don't serve anything that walks, flies, crawls, or swims." Some dishes are only $2 per serving. Three dishes for $6 is a good size meal. You can order small, medium or large portions of each dish. Has seating for around 20 people. Uses fresh produce and filtered water. Sandwiches feature whole-grain breads. Casual, relaxed place. **Other Info:** Seating, counter service, take-out. Non-smoking. Reservations not necessary. Accepts AMEX, MC, VISA. Price: $. **Directions:** In Harlem. A, B, C, D trains to 125th Street.

Super Natural
728 Ninth Avenue, between 49th & 50th Streets 212-399-9200 **Hours:** Monday to Friday 9 am to 8:30 pm; Saturday 9 am to 7 pm; Sunday 10 am to 5:30 pm **Natural Food Store.** Juice Bar. Homeopathic & Nutritional Consulting and Remedies. **Direction:** E, C trains to 50th Street.

Tamarind Seed
2935 Broadway, at 115th Street, Upper Westside 212-864-3360 **Hours:** Monday to Saturday 8 am to 10 pm

Sunday 10 am to 9 pm **Mostly Vegetarian Salad Bar.** **Other Info:** Counter service, take-out.

**Temple in the Village
74 West 3rd Street, between LaGuardia Place & Thompson Streets, Greenwich Village 212-475-5670 **Hours:** Monday to Saturday 11 am to 10 pm Closed Sunday. **Pure Vegetarian Health Food Restaurant.** Macrobiotic options. Vegetarian Salad Bar. **Menu:** Rice, hot & cold noodles, fried tofu and curried & steamed vegetables. Teas. Most things are made without eggs, dairy and honey. **Comments:** Macrobiotic items. Food cooked on premises. Food sold by weight. Food gets high recommendations. **Other Info:** Cafeteria style, buffet-style, take-out, catering. Limited seating; has a few tables. Can eat in nearby Washington Square Park (one block away). Price: $. **Directions:** Near NYU. A, C, D, E, F, Q trains to West 4th Street.

**Thali
28 Greenwich Avenue, at corner of West 10th Streets, between 6th & 7th Avenues; 212-367-7411; **Web** site: http://thalinyc.citysearch.com **Hours:** Daily 12 noon to 3:30 pm, 6 pm to 9:30 pm Saturday Brunch 12 noon to 4 pm **Fully Vegetarian Indian.** Vegan friendly. **Menu:** Thalis are $10 for a full meal. Vegetarian thali have vegetable subji, dal, basmati pilaf, roti, chutney and a dessert. **Comment:** It is a really small place. **Other Info:** Full service, take-out, catering. No credit cards; cash only. Price: $$. **Directions:** A, C, E, F, S trains to West 4th Street.

Tibetan Kitchen
444 Third Avenue, at 31st Street; 212-679-6286 **Hours:** Monday to Friday 12 noon to 3 pm, 5 pm to 11 pm; Sat & Sun 5 pm to 11 pm **Tibetan.** Vegan options. Not pure vegetarian. **Menu:** Traditional Tibetan style cooking. Salad, momos and other dishes. **Comments:** Has outdoor seating. **Other Info:** Full service, take-out, delivery. May be a good idea to reserve a table for dinner, as it is always busy. Non-smoking. Accepts AMEX, DC, MC, VISA. Price: $$. **Directions:** In the Murray Hill area. 6 train to 28th Street.

**Tiffin

18 Murray Street, between Charles and West 10th Streets; 212-791-3510

Hours: Monday to Friday 11 am to 3:30 pm, 5:30 pm to 10 pm; closed Sunday.

Pure Vegetarian Indian. Vegan options.

Menu: Has different fixed lunches from different areas of India for $10. Monday, Rajasthan: poori, vegetable dish, dal baati, Kaju Chawal (cashew rice); Tuesday, South India: Vada, Nilgiri Korma, sambar, Limbu Chawal (lemon rice); Wednesday, Mumbai; Thursday, Gujarati: Dhokla, Undhiya, Moong Dal, Gobhi Pulao (cauliflower rice), roti, chutney; Friday, North India; and Saturday, Goa. The fixed dinner includes an appetizer, main dishes, and dessert for $20. All meals come with roti and chutney. Has desserts. Good tasting fried bananas and mango ice cream. Some dishes are dosas, Banrsi Samosas filled with feta cheese (excellent), potato and pomegranate seeds. The Bhara Khumb (roasted Portobello with cottage cheese) is worth trying. Good Aloo Tikka. Some drinks are masala chai and lassi.

Comments: It has a friendly majestic atmosphere. It is a pleasant place to have a meal. Food is very good. Reasonably priced. They have 2½ hours cooking classes for $75 and four classes are $200. Has got some great reviews in locate newspapers and magazines. Has dark wooden tables, hanging lights, and silver benches. Quick service.

Other Info: Full service, take-out, free deliveries ($15 minimum). Accepts AMEX, VISA. Price: $$.

Directions: It is in the Tribeca area. In the City Hall area. A, C, 1, 2, 3 trains to the Chambers Street Station.

Tsampa

212 E 9th Street, between 2nd and 3rd Avenues 212-614-3226

Hours: Daily 5 pm to 11:30 pm

Tibetan. Vegan friendly. Not pure vegetarian.

Menu: Has many vegetarian options including momos (dumplings) and desserts. The Barley Tea is good.

Comments: Relaxing, comfortable place. Dimly lit, candle lit. Friendly staff. Plays pleasant Tibetan music. Excellent Tibetan décor with Tibetan art, prayer flags and statues. One of the top Tibetan restaurants in New York. Excellent atmosphere. Often used organic ingredients. Popular place.

Other Info: Full service, take-out, catering. Price: $$$.

Directions: N, R trains to 8th Street; 6 train to Astor Place.

**Uptown Juice Bar Tribeca

116 Chambers Street   212-964-4316
54 West 125 Street   212-987-2660

Hours: Daily 8 am to 9 pm

Vegetarian Caribbean Restaurant and Juice Bar.

Menu: Has a good selection of vegetarian dishes. Has smoothies and desserts.

Comments: Has good size portions. Reasonably priced. Accepts MC, VISA.

Uptown Whole Foods

2421 Broadway, at 89th Street
212-874-4000

Hours: Daily 8 am to 11 pm

Natural Food Store and Cafe. Deli, Bakery, Salad Bar and Juice Bar. Organic produce. Supermarket-type place. Owned by While Oats.

Comments: One of the best natural food stores around.

Directions: 1, 9, 2, 3 trains to 89th Street.

Vatan Indian

409 3rd Avenue (at 29th Street)
in Little Indian
212-689-5666

Web site: www.vatanny.com

Hours: For dinner only Tuesday to Saturday 5:30 pm to 10 pm; closed Monday.

Vegetarian Indian, Gujarati Restaurant.

Menu: Has all-you-can-eat meals for a set price. Does not use ghee in cooking. Has a set meal for $21.95 per person (meal is large). Channa Masala, Sev Puri, samosa, Batatavada, dal, Cauliflower & Pea Subji, kheer, puri, papadam, khitdri (rice and lentil mixture), Pulao (rice and peas) and chilled mango soup. Mango Ice Cream, Masala Chai and Pistachio-sprinkled Kheer.

Comments: The prices charged are reasonable for what you get. Good, efficient service. Friendly staff. Casual. No windows. Excellent décor. A beautifully reconstructed mock-up of an Indian village, with stucco walls and a well in the center. Has table seating upstairs or you can sit on cushions on the floor. One of the best vegetarian restaurants in the US. Spacey place with high ceilings. Can remove your shoes and sit on the floor traditional Indian style. Got a good review in The New York Times. Good service, but can be a little slow.

Other Info: Reservation suggested, especially on the weekends. Accepts AMEX, MC, VISA. Price: $$-$$$.

Directions: In the Union Square and Murray Hill neighborhood. 6 train to 28th Street.

**Veg City Diner

55 West 14th, between Fifth and Sixth Avenues
212-490-6266
Hours: Daily 6 am to 4 am (closes just two hours a day)
Fully Vegetarian. Many Vegan options.
Menu: Has mock "meat" dishes including Philly Cheese Steak (recommended), "Chicken" Parmesan, marinated beans, Barbecued Tempeh, burritos, mock "chicken and much more.
Comments: Owned by the same people who own the Burritoville chain of restaurants. Well-managed, friendly place.
Other Info: Accepts AMEX, DC, DIS, MC, VISA. Non-smoking. Price: $$.
Directions: In the East Village. 6 train to 14th Street.

**Vegecyber

210 Center Street, between Canal & Grand Streets, in Chinatown
212-625-3980
Web site: www.vegecyber.com
Hours: Daily 9:30 am to 7 pm
Natural Food Store and Internet Mail Order. Chinese and International. Vegetarian Lunch Box. Veggie meats, rice and vegetable dishes.
Comments: Has a wide selection of vegetarian and vegan frozen dishes. Many of the dishes are organic. Can order many items by mail-order from their Web site. Price: $-$$.
Directions: 6, N, R, J trains to Canal or Broadway stops.

***Vege Vege II

544 Third Avenue
between 36th and 37th Streets
212-679-4710/4702
Hours: Daily 11:30 am to 11 pm
Vegan Chinese. Certified kosher.
Menu: Large selections of items. A good appetizer is Moo Shu Basil Rolls (nut filled and wrapped in basil). Vegetarian "chicken," orange "beef," "Chicken" a la King and Veggie "lamb" (made from Formosan mushrooms). Has brown rice and vegetable side dishes. Fresh orange juice.
Comments: Gets high recommendations as a really good place. Has high-class food in a relaxed atmosphere. Good, attentive service. The food is well presented. Elegant place.
Other Info: Full service, take-out, delivery, catering. Does not accept reservations. Accepts AMEX, DC, DISC, MC, VISA. Price: $$-$$$.
Directions: S; 4, 6, 7 trains to 43rd St–Grand Central stop.

**Vegetarian Dim Sum House

24 Pell Street, between Bowery & Mott, Chinatown; 212-577-7176
Hours: Daily 10:30 am to 10:30 pm
Pure Vegetarian Chinese. Fully Vegan.
Menu: Has a large menu. Dim Sum, Chinese soups, mock shrimp, Spring Rolls, Rice Flour Rolls, Chinese pastries, vegan dumplings, steamed buns and sweet cakes. Fresh juices.
Comments: Good size portions. Reasonably priced. Owned by the same people as House of Vegetarian.
Other Info: Full service, take-out, catering. Price: $-$$.
Directions: N, R, W, 6 trains to Canal Street. Walk about three blocks towards the Bowery and Mott Street.

***Vegetarian's Paradise 2

144 West 4th Street, between Sixth Avenue and MacDougal Street, Greenwich Village
212-260-7130/7141
Hours: Sunday to Thursday 12 noon to 11 pm Friday & Saturday 12 noon to 12 midnight
Fully Vegan Chinese. Macrobiotic options.
Menu: Large menu. Large selection of vegan dumplings both steamed and fried. Cold and hot appetizers, soups, salads and desserts. Noodle soup with vegetables, mock meats, bean curd, mushrooms, wheat gluten and rice. Popular dishes are Peking Spare Ribs, Mongolian Pepper Steak, Squid in Black Bean Sauce, Nobu Soy Chicken Teriyaki and Pungent Pork. Soy dishes are Edamame, tofu steak and soy ice cream. Chicken Nuggets, Crispy Soul Chicken, Salisbury Steak, and Taro Vegetarian Whole Fish. Stuffed Lotus Leaf, Spinach Dumpling and Pumpkin Pie a la Mode. Vegan ice cream is very good. Delicious spring rolls. Fresh juices.
Comments: Highly recommended. Service is fairly fast and efficient. Reasonably priced. Waiters can be a bit dry with children. The owner's son served me great and gave some good suggestion for what to serve children. Quite a good place. Receives excellent recommendations. Warm, cozy, and unpretentious restaurant. The food is authentic. Makes their own soy milk daily. They use wheat, soy and arrowroot to make the meat substitute.
Other Info: Full service, take-out, catering (caters weddings). Non-smoking. Accepts reservations, but are not necessary. Accepts AMEX, DIS, MC, VISA. Price: $-$$$.
Directions: Two blocks west off Washington Square Park in the Village. Near the west 4th street

station in the Village. Between 6th Ave and McDougal. A, B, C, D, E, F, Q trains to West 4th Street.

***VP 2 Go
140 West 4th Street; 212-260-7049
Hours: Sunday to Thursday 12 noon to 11 pm Friday & Saturday 12 noon to 12 midnight
Fully Vegan Chinese take-out.
Menu: Large selection of vegan dumplings both steamed and fried. Noodle soup with vegetables. Popular are Peking Spare Ribs, Mongolian Pepper Steak and Nobu Soy Chicken Teriyaki. Makes own soy milk daily. Edamame, Tofu Steak and Soy Ice Cream.
Comments: This place is next to Vegetarian Paradise 2. Can also get dishes wholesale.
Other Info: Take-out only. Non-smoking. Accepts AMEX, MC, VISA.
Directions: Between 6th Avenue and McDougal. A few blocks from Washington Square Park. A, B, C, D, E, F, Q trains to West 4th Street.

**Vegetarian Paradise 3
33-35 Mott Street, between Chatham Square and Pell Street, lower Manhattan; 212-406-6988; email: atang@mindspring.com; Web site: http:/ /vegetarianparadise3.citysearch.com/
Hours: Sunday to Thursday 11 am to 10 pm Friday & Saturday 11 am to 11 pm
Pure Vegetarian Authentic Chinese.
Menu: Chinese vegetarian (same at VP2 above). Vegetarian Fish, vegetarian Roast Duck and Kam Wak Chicken.
Comments: Same as Vegetarian Paradise 2. Clean, well-designed place. Has special lunches between 11 am and 4 pm. Good service.
Other Info: Full service, take-out. Delivers within ten blocks. Accepts AMEX, MC, VISA. Price: $-$$
Directions: In the middle of Chinatown. Two blocks south of Canal Street. J, M, Z, N, R trains; 6 train to Canal Street.

Village Natural Food Corp
46 Greenwich Avenue, between 6th and 7th Avenues, Greenwich Village; 212-727-0968
Hours: Monday to Friday 11 am to 11 pm; Saturday 10 am to 11 pm; Sunday 10 am to 10 pm; Saturday & Sunday Bunch 10 am to 4:30 pm
Natural Food Restaurant. Macrobiotic and Vegan options. Not pure vegetarian (serves fish).
Menu: Daily specials. Whole grains, beans, cheese, sour cream and guacamole. Millet Croquettes with brown rice, steamed vegetables,

adzuki beans and tamari ginger sauce. Tofu Pies with maple syrup. Seitan Parmigiana. Middle Eastern dishes. Fresh juices, smoothies, organic coffee.
Comments: Large, friendly, nice, non-pretentious place. Good service. Items marked with a star can be made without dairy. Dining in basement
Other Info: Full service, take-out. Accepts AMEX, DC, DIS, MC, VISA. Non-smoking. Price: $$.
Directions: In the West Village. 1, 9 trains to Christopher St–Sheridan Square; 1, 2, 3, 9 trains to 14th Street.

**Village Yogurt & Health Foods Café
547 6th Avenue, at 15th Street, second shop from corner; 212-929-3752
Hours: Monday to Friday 10:30 am to 8 pm; Saturday 11 am to 6 pm; closed Sunday.
Vegetarian International. Nothing fried. Healthy food.
Comments: Friendly place. Price: $-$$.
Directions: F train to 14th Street. One block away.

Westerly Natural Market
911 8th Avenue, at 54th Street
212-586-5262; fax: 212-315-5412
email: westerlyfoods@livingnatural.com
Web site: www.westerlynaturalmarket.com
Hours: Monday to Friday 8 am to 9:30 pm Saturday & Sunday 9 am to 9:30 pm
Natural Food Store and Juice Bar. Organic produce. Large place.
Menu: Ready-made salads and sandwiches. Fresh juices and smoothies.
Comments: Has a large selection and is reasonably priced. Friendly place.
Directions: Near the southwest corner of Central Park. A, C trains to 59th Street. Then walk five blocks south.

***Whole Earth Bakery & Kitchen
130 St Mark's Place, between 1st and A Avenues
212-677-7597; fax: 212-677-7597; email: Info@W-Earth.com; Web site: www.w-earth.com
Hours: Monday to Friday 9 am to 12 midnight Saturday & Sunday 10 am to 12 midnight
Vegan Bakery (no eggs in anything).
Menu: Makes vegan cakes including carrot cake, strawberry cake, chocolate cake, blueberry cake and carob cake. Tofu chocolate cupcakes, chocolate chip cookies, pies, muffins, brownies, whole-grain cookies, tofu chocolate cupcakes, vegan turnovers, vegan cheeseless pizza, vegan cake, rai-

sin bun, key lime pie and fruit. Vegan wedding cakes to order. Whole-grain baked goods can be a bit dry. Sandwiches and soups. Usually no sugar, honey or dairy products are used. Veggie Rolls, Black Bean Turnovers, Tofu Vegetable Turnovers, whole-wheat poppy-seed crackers and cheese biscuits. Fresh Juices.

Comment: Prices range from $1 to $5. Small place. Uses only the freshest natural ingredients. Reasonable prices. Over 35 take-out items. It is also a grocery with a good selection of vegetarian goods. Has a good selection of Indian spices. Has a blue storefront.

Other Info: Cafeteria style, no seating, take-out, catering. Price: $.

Directions: F train to 2nd Avenue. Exit at 1st Avenue exit.

Whole Foods Market
250 7th Avenue, at 24th Street; 212-924-5969
email: Otto.Leuschel@wholefoods.com
Web site: www.wholefoodsmarket.com
Hours: Daily 8 am to 10 pm
Natural Food Store and Cafe. Deli, Bakery, Salad Bar and Juice Bar. Organic produce. Supermarket-type place. See Whole Foods Market information.

Directions: Whole Body at Whole Foods Market is located at the opposite end of the block at the intersection of Seventh Avenue and 25th Street. 1, 9, A, C, E trains to 23rd Street. Has a garage on 25th Street between 7th and 8th Avenues. Parking is free for 2 hours with a fifty-dollar purchase.

Whole Body at Whole Foods
260 7th Avenue, at 25th Street
212-924-9972
Web site: www.wholefoodsmarket.com
Hours: Daily 9 am to 9 pm
Comments: Carries health, wellness and skin care products. Has a huge selection of these products. Has vitamins, natural food supplements, energy bars, medicines, homeopathic remedies, books and cookbooks, scented candles, and yoga gear. Located next to their main branch, above.
Directions: 1, 9 trains to 23rd Street.

**World of Vegetarian
24 Pell Street; 212-577-7176
Hours: Daily 10:30 am to 10:30 pm
Vegetarian Chinese.
Menu: Dim Sum, mock Shrimp Dumplings, sandwiches, mock Roast Pork Buns and more.
Comments: There are parking arrangements for

customer. No atmosphere. Good food. Efficient service.
Other Info: No credit cards; cash only. Price: $$.
Directions: In Chinatown. W, N, R trains to Canal Street.

Yaffa Café
97 Saint Mark's Place, between 1st & 2nd Avenues; 212-674-9302
Hours: Daily for 24 hours. Never closes.
Natural Food Café. American and Mediterranean. Mostly Vegetarian. Vegan options. Not pure vegetarian.
Menu: Salads, baba ghanouj, hummus, stir-fry, pastas, tofu and crepes. Fresh juices. Some of the better dishes are the Veggie Burger, Pesto Spinach Fettuccine, and Curry Vegetables & Rice. Carrot dressing is really good.
Comments: Seating in the back garden during summer. Sidewalk café with dining in the front. Hip place with an eclectic décor. Good place for really late dining. It is a happening place with an excellent atmosphere. Some people think the food has something to be desired.
Other Info: Full service, take-out, delivery. Reservations not necessary. Smoking allowed outside. Accepts AMEX, MC, VISA. Price: $$.
Directions: 6 train to Astor Place.

Yonah Shimmel's
137 East Houston Street, between 1st and 2nd Avenue; 212-477-2858
Hours: Sunday to Friday 9 am to 6 pm
Saturday 9 am to 7 pm
Kosher Cafe. Not pure vegetarian.
Menu: Homemade knishes. Cheese, potato, kasha and other kind of knishes. Uses natural ingredients. Has bagels, yogurts and muffins.
Comments: Celebrities often come here such as Barbara Streisand and Eleanor Roosevelt. Good atmosphere. Good bargain.
Other Info: Limited service, take-out. Price $.
Directions: F train to Second Avenue.

**Zen Palate
There are three Zen Palate restaurants in Manhattan. Web site: www.zenpalate.com
663 Ninth Avenue, at 46th Street
212-582-1669
34 Union Square East, near E 16th Street, East Village; 212-614-9345
Hours: Daily 11:30 am to 1 am for take-out
Dinning room closed Monday to Saturday 3 pm to 5:30 pm.
Dinning room open Sunday 5 pm to 1 pm.

2170 Broadway, between 76th & 77th Streets 212-501-7768; **Reservations:** 212-582-1276 **Hours:** Monday to Friday 11:30 am to 10:30 pm; Saturday 11 am to 11 pm; Sunday 12 noon to 10:30 pm
Vegetarian Chinese. Mostly Vegan. Serves eggs during breakfast.
Menu: Delicious appetizers including scallion pancakes, Zen Veggie-burger (sunflower seeds, kale, brown rice), Vegetable Dumplings, Stir-fried Brown Rice with minced vegetables and Spinach Wonton Soup. Sweet and Sour Delight is puffed pecans, soy protein and pineapple in a sweet & sour sauce. Tofu-chestnut Mini Loaves, Kale & Seaweed Salad, Vegetarian Squid, Spinach Wonton Soup, Sautéed Artichoke, Eggplant in Garlic Sauce and Stuffed Chinese Cabbage. Good hot and sour vegetable soup. Batter-fried Potatoes on top of steamed broccoli. The Sesame Medallions in Barbecue Sauce made of wheat gluten tastes like beef. Most main preparations come with brown rice, moo shu roll or spring roll. Special teas and fresh juices. Some good dairy and vegan desserts. Fresh juices.
Comments: Features gourmet dishes. Conservative. Good food and good quick service. A bit impersonal. Delicious food, relaxed atmosphere. Lots of variety. Good selection of dishes. Clean bathrooms. Friendly staff. There are three Zen Palate restaurants in Manhattan. The one at 663 Ninth Avenue is a small informal place with about 20 seats. The one in Union Square is the original one. It is like two restaurants in one. The one upstairs is formal and upscale with tuxedoed waiters and is expensive. It has a view of Union square. The downstairs one is informal where you sit on cushions cross-legged and the prices are cheaper. Upstairs in the Union Square branch is conservative and downstairs is cheaper and friendlier.
Vegan Warning: I read on the Internet some things written by a Zen employee about egg in various products, so you may want to ask about these dishes. The Yam Fries, Orange Sensation (eggs in the batter), Zen Rolls (eggs in the veggie ham), Spinach Linguini Salad (eggs in the noodles), Jewel of Happiness (eggs in tempura batter), Sheppard's Pie Croquets, and the Veggie Ham contain eggs. The soy dairy in the Zen Ravioli contains casein. The Veggie Burger with Yam Fries contains eggs, but the Zen Veggie Burger is completely vegan.
Other Info: Full service and take-out counter (has items found in the dining room plus others, such as veggie-burgers). Delivers. Accepts AMEX, MC, VISA (minimum $15). Price: $$-$$$.

Directions: L, N, R, 4, 5, 6 trains stop near the Union Square branch. To the 2127 Broadway place take 1, 9 trains to 79 Street.

Zenith

888 8th Avenue, between 52nd and 53rd Street 212-262-8080
Web site: http://www.nydelivery.com/zenith/html
Hours: Daily 11:45 am to 11 pm
Assorted Asian (Chinese, Japanese, Thai, Indian). Vegetarian-friendly. Vegan options. Not pure vegetarian.
Menu: Thai Soup, Veggie Duck, Steamed Chinese Eggplant, Black Bean Soup, brown rice, spring rolls, burritos, Sautéed Artichokes, vegetarian cold cuts, pastas, soups, noodles dishes, and Rice & Broccoli in garlic sauce. Organic Salad with Miso-mustard Dressing, Steamed Eggplant with Spicy Black Bean Sauce, Marinated Seaweed, Soybean Gluten with vegetables in a curry sauce and Mushroom Steak. Fresh juices, teas, cappuccino, espresso.
Comment: High class place. The food is first-class. Caters to business people during lunch. Good quick service for lunch. The service can be slow for dinner. Spring rolls can be very small and I did not think they were so good. Reasonably priced lunch specials for NYC. Servings for lunch specials can be small, but will be enough for some people. Service during lunch can be very quick (it took me less than five minutes to get my food). Got a high recommendation in the Zagat Survey in 1998. I had set meal of veg chicken and beef sauté with brown rice and some very small spring roils for $7.95. It was really good, but if you are really hungry it will not be enough. Recommended.
Warning: This place used to be fully vegan, but recently they started serving real meat products and fish. So you definitely should ask about this, as they may not tell you.
Other Info: Full service, take-out, delivery, catering. Accepts: AMEX, DC, DIS, MC, VISA. Price: $$-$$$$.
Direction: Near Columbus Circle.

QUEENS

**Anand Bhavan

3566 73rd Street, near Roosevelt Avenue, Jackson Heights, Queens; 718-507-1600
Hours: Daily 12 noon to 9:30 pm
Pure Vegetarian Indian.
Menu: Medhu Vada (fried lentil donut), Gobi

Masala Curry (cauliflower and spices), Kanchipurum Idly (lentil patties with cashews), and Coconut Uthappam. Has full thali (rice, vegetables, papadam, soup and raita). Masala Dosa is large crepe with potatoes and onions. Badam Halava is ground almonds and honey cooked in butter. Coconut and cilantro sauce is good.
Comments: Good, inexpensive Indian food. Lunch special is a good deal. Full dinners from $12 to $17. Most dishes under $7. One of the better vegetarian Indian restaurants in New York City. Price: $$.
Directions: From Long Island Exwy, take Queens Blvd exit (#19) towards Grand Ave/Rte 25, then go west on Queens Blvd ¾ mile, at Broadway turn right and go 1 mile (northwest), at 74th St turn right and go 3 blocks, at 35th Ave turn left and go 1 block, at 73rd St turn left and this place is 1 block down. In the "Little India" area of Jackson Heights.

**Annam Brahma
8443 164th Street, by 85th Avenue, Jamaica, Queens; 718-523-2600
Hours: Monday, Tuesday & Thursday to Saturday 11 am to 10 pm; Wednesday 11 am to 4 pm; Sunday 12 noon to 10 pm
Vegetarian East Indian. Vegan options. Not pure vegetarian (serves eggs, but no meat or fish).
Menu: Good size menu that changes daily. On special days Italian and Chinese preparations are served. Does special Thanksgiving (unturkey, chestnut stuffing, sweet potatoes and dessert), Christmas and New Years feasts. Vegetable kebabs, rice, curry vegetables, samosas and pakoras. Fresh juices.
Comments: Good place. Good atmosphere. Run by disciples of Sri Chinmoy. Have free meditation classes in the evening and on weekends. Got an award as the best vegetarian restaurant in Queens.
Other Info: Full service, take-out, catering. Non-smoking. Reservations requested for large groups. No credit cards. Price: $-$$.
Directions: From Grand Central Pkwy going east (from LI), take Exit #17 towards 168th St, then stay on the connector road for a half-mile, then turn left at 164th St and this place is 2 blocks down.

**Buddha Bodai Vegetarian Restaurant
42-96 Main Street, Flushing
718-939-1188; fax: 718-939-2100
Hours: Daily 10:30 am to 10:30 pm
Fully Vegetarian Chinese Restaurant. Kosher and vegan option.
Menu: Mock meat is really good and is made of soy and wheat gluten. Dim Sum, Sweet & Sour Vegetarian Ribs, veg steak, veg "Lemon Chicken" and veg lamb stew.
Comments: Friendly service. Valet parking. Seats around 100.
Other Info: Full service, take-out, delivery. Accepts MC, VISA. Price: $$.
Directions: In Flushing area of Queens. From Long Island Exwy coming from Long Island, take exit #23 towards Main St, then merge onto Harace Harding Exwy for a quarter-mile, then turn right (go north) at Main St and this place is about 1 mile down.

Guru's Health Food
86-18 Parson's Boulevard; 718-291-7406
Hours: Monday to Friday 10:30 am to 7 pm; Sat 10:30 am to 6 pm; Sun 12:30 am to 5 pm
Natural Food Store. Organic produce.
Directions: Between Grand Central Parkway and Hillside Avenue, 2 blocks from Hillside Avenue.

**Happy Buddha Vegetarian Restaurant
13537 37th Avenue; 718-358-0079
Hours: Daily 11 am to 10 pm
Vegetarian Chinese.
Menu: Salads, mock "meat" dishes, rice dishes, Shredded Buddha Delight (taro), Bamboo Garden Soup and veggie eel. The Veggie Fried Shrimp is good. Free hot tea and free re-fills.
Comments: Friendly service. Good food. Have own parking.
Other Info: Full service, take-out. Non-smoking. Accepts AMEX, MC, VISA (minimum $20). Price: $-$$.

Health Nut
212-03 26th Avenue; 718-225-8164
Hours: Monday 9:30 am to 7 pm; Tuesday to Friday 9:30 am to 8 pm; Saturday 9 am to 7 pm; Sunday 10 am to 5 pm; Juice Bar and Deli closes at least an hour before the store closes.
Natural Food Store and Deli. Salad Bar and Juice Bar.
Comments: Friendly, efficient place. Accepts AMEX, DIS, MC, VISA.

Knish Nosh
10102 Queens Boulevard, near 67th Road, Forest Hills, Queens; 718-897-5554
Hours: Mon & Sat 9 am to 7 pm; Tuesday to Friday 9 am to 7:30 pm; Sun 9 am to 6 pm
Kosher place. Not pure vegetarian.

Menu: Fresh broccoli, spinach, potato and carrot knishes. Kasha.
Comments: Everything made on premises. The food and service gets really good ratings. Price: $.

Kosher Corner

73-01 Main Street, near 73rd Avenue, Kew Garden Hills, Queens; 718-263-1177
Hours: Sunday to Thursday 9 am to 10 pm; Friday 7:30 am to 2 pm; Saturday 6 pm to 10 pm
Kosher place. Not pure vegetarian.
Menu: Vegetable Cutlet and Mushroom Sauce is good. French onion soup, sandwiches and salads.
Comments: In orthodox Jewish community.
Other Info: Counter service, take-out. Price: $$.
Directions: Near Main Street and Jewel Avenue.

Linda's Natural Kitchen & Market

8122 Leffers Boulevard A, Kew Gardens, Jamaica
718-847-2233
Hours: Monday, Tuesday, Thursday & Friday 10 am to 7 pm; Wednesday 10 am to 8 pm, Saturday 10 am to 6 pm, Sunday 11 am to 5:30 pm
Vegetarian International. Italian, Mexican and Asian. Juice Bar. Mostly Vegan. Macrobiotic options.
Menu: Features raw foods. Homemade soups, organic sprout salad, organic casseroles and pasta. Tofu cheesecake. Fresh juices, smoothies and wheat grass. Wheat-free vegan baked goods are made without refined sugars.
Comments: A friendly place.
Other Info: Counter top seating, mainly take-out, delivery. Accepts AMEX, DIS, MC, VISA. Price: $.
Directions: This place is a half-block from the Kew Garden train station.

**Oneness-Fountain-Heart

15719 72nd Avenue, Flushing
718-591-3663 (591-FOOD)
Hours: Thursday to Tuesday 11:30 am to 9 pm; Sunday 11 am to 9 pm; Sunday Brunch 11 am to 3 pm; closed Wednesday.
Full Vegetarian International. Gourmet cooking. Macrobiotic options. Vegan-friendly.
Menu: Bliss Burger, mock "Duck" Surprise (sautéed veg duck and broccoli with a spicy pineapple sauce over rice) and Portobello Mellow (grilled Portobello mushrooms, spinach, melted mozzarella, red peppers in a wrap).
Comments: Beautifully designed. Has a Japanese garden and two indoor fountains.
Other Info: Full service, take-out, delivery. Accepts AMEX, DIS, MC, VISA. Price: $.

Directions: This place is about 1 mile northwest of St John's U. From Long Island Exwy coming from Long Island, take exit #25 towards Utopia Pkwy/164 St, turn left onto Utopia Pkwy and go a half-mile, at Jewel Ave turn right and go a half-mile, at 164th St turn left and go a quarter-mile, at 72nd Ave turn right and this place is a third-mile down.

Quantum Leap

65-64 Fresh Meadow Lane, Fresh Meadows, Flushing
Restaurant: 718-461-1307; **Store:** 718-762-3572; **email:** neil@quantumleapnatural.com;
Web site: www.quantumleapnatural.com
Hours: Sunday to Thursday 11:30 am to 10 pm; Friday 11:30 am to 11 pm; Saturday 10 am to 11 pm; Sunday 10 am to 10 pm; Saturday Brunch 11 am to 4:30 pm; Sun Brunch 10 am to 4 pm
Natural Food Store and Restaurant. Organic produce. Not pure vegetarian.
Menu: Many vegan and macrobiotic dishes. Natural pies, casseroles, salads, house dressing, soups, tempura, Sweet Potato Tempura and miso soup with vegetables. Weekend brunch includes waffles and pancakes. Have daily specials such as Seitan Parmigiana and Mexican Fiesta. Tofu pie dessert.
Comments: Relaxed, friendly place. The original branch is in Queens and has a large natural food store. Good place. It has a big selection of organic produce.
Other Info: Full service, take-out. Non-smoking. Accepts AMEX, MC, VISA. Price: $$.
Directions: From LIE, take Exit #25, then go south two blocks. Turn right on 67th Avenue and this store is on the right at the corner of Fresh Meadow Lane and 67th Ave. Near the Long Island Expressway and Utopia Parkway.

Queens Health Emporium

15901 Horace Harding Expressway
718-358-6500
Hours: Monday to Saturday 9:30 am to 8 pm Sunday 10 am to 6 pm
Natural Food Store and Café. Juice Bar, Deli and a Bookstore. Has a large selection of organic produce.
Menu: Has a good selection of hot and cold vegetarian dishes. Often uses organic produce. The menu is mainly vegetarian except for the tuna salad and eggs. Fresh juices.
Comments: There is seating upstairs.
Other Info: Limited service, take-out. Accepts AMEX, MC, DIS, VISA. Price: $-$$.
Directions: From Long Island Expressway going

west, take Exit #24. Head towards 164th Street and this place is on the corner of Horace Harding Exit and 159th Street. From LIE going east, take Exit #24 and this store is on the right.

Smile Of The Beyond

8614 Parsons Boulevard #A, near Hillside Avenue, Jamaica; 718-739-7453

Natural Food Restaurant. Basically a breakfast and lunch place. Not pure vegetarian.

Hours: Monday to Friday 7 am to 4 pm; Saturday 7 am to 3 pm; closed Sunday.

Menu: Soy "Steak" Burgers, salads, brown rice, salads, vegetarian "B.L.T" and "Turkey" Club Sandwich. Chocolate Cake with vanilla icing. Fresh juices.

Other Info: Counter service, take-out. Price: $.

Comments: Good place. Some items have eggs. Affiliated with the Annam Brahma (Sri Chinmoy) Restaurant. Waiters are Sri Chinmoy disciples. Pleasant place.

Directions: From Grand Central Pkwy, take exit #17 towards 168 St, then go south on 164th St a quarter-mile, then at 85th Ave turn right and go a quarter-mile, at 159th St turn left and go 2 blocks, at Parsons Blvd turn left and this place is 1 block down at Main St.

STATEN ISLAND

**Dairy Palace

2210 Victory Boulevard, near Bradley Avenue, Staten Island; 718-761-5200

Hours: Sunday to Thursday 10:30 am to 8:30 pm; Friday 11 am to 2 pm; Saturday sundown to 12 midnight

Vegetarian International, Kosher, Dairy Restaurant. Vegan options.

Menu: Chinese food, vegetarian "Chicken," Pep-

per "Steak," fries, pizza, sushi and ice cream.

Comments: Laid-back place. Food can be greasy. Service may not be so good.

Other Info: Cafeteria style, take-out. Accepts MC, VISA (for orders over $30). Price: $$.

Directions: From I-278, take exit #11 towards Bradley Ave, then at Bradley Ave (or any other street) go north 2 blocks, at Victory Blvd turn left and this place is 5 blocks down.

Tastebuds Natural Food

1807 Hylan Boulevard; 718-351-8693

Hours: Monday to Saturday 9 am to 8 pm Sunday 10:30 am to 7 pm

Natural Food Store and Deli. Salad Bar and Juice Bar. Organic produce.

Menu: Soups, salads, sandwiches and hot dishes.

Directions: This place is a third-mile west of Staten Island U Hospital. From I-278, coming from Brooklyn, take Hylan Blvd exit, keep left at fork in ramp and then go left onto Fingerboard Rd south and go a third-mile, then turn slight left onto Hylan (go southwest) and this store is on the right 2 miles down.

Taste of India Restaurant

287 New Dorp Lane, Staten Island
718-987-4700

Hours: Sunday to Thursday 12 noon to 10:30 pm; Friday & Saturday 12 noon to 11 pm

Indian. Not pure vegetarian.

Menu: There are ten vegetarian dishes on the menu. Has a Saturday and Sunday buffets with some vegetarian dishes. Coconut Soup.

Other Info: Full service, take-out. Accepts AMEX, MC, VISA. Price: $$.

Directions: From I-278, take Hylan Blvd/South Beach exit and then go south on Hyland Blvd for 3¼ miles, then at New Dorp Lane turn right.

Long Island

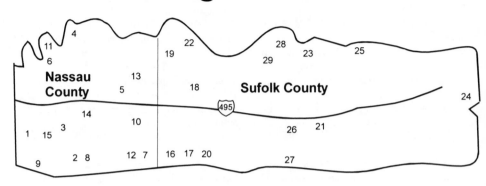

Nassau County
1. Floral Park
2. Freeport
3. Garden City
4. Glen Gove
5. Jericho
6. Manhasset
7. Massapequa
8. Merrick
9. Oceanside
10. Plainview
11. Port Washingiton
12. Seaford
13. Syosset
14. Westbury
15. West Hempstead

Sufolk County
16. Amityville
17. Babylon
18. Commack
19. Huntington
20. Islip
21. Medford
22. Northport
23. Port Jefferson
24. Riverhead
25. Rocky Point
26. Ronkonkoma
27. Sayville
28. Setauket
29. St James

AMITYVILLE

**Santosha Vegetarian Dining
40 Merrick Road, Amityville; 631-598-1787
Hours: Tuesday to Thursday, Sunday 5 pm to 9 pm; Friday & Saturday 5 pm to 10 pm
Fully Vegetarian Continental and African. Bakery. Macrobiotic and Vegan options.
Menu: Vegan soups, hummus, Ragin' Cajun Tempeh, Quesadillas (wheat tortillas with various fillings), Tofu Scallop Platter and Africana couscous. All entrees come with a hummus appetizer and choice of vegan soup of the day or salad. Veggie burgers are good (and vegan). Good soups and salads with excellent dressings. Vegan Chocolate Raspberry Cake. A variety of coffees, fresh juices, cappuccino, non-alcoholic beer.
Comments: Good atmosphere. Simple place. Oldest vegetarian restaurant in Long Island. Some dairy. Efficient service. Santosha is Sanskrit for contentment. Food prepared fresh.
Other Info: Full service, catering, take-out. Non-smoking. Accept reservations, but not necessary. Accepts DIS, MC, VISA. Price: $$-$$$.
Directions: From Southern State Parkway, take Exit #32 south (Rte 110). Go south on Rte 110 about 3 miles, Then at Merrick Road (Rte 27A) turn right. Go two traffic lights and this place is at the right. It has a green awning. Parking in rear.

BABYLON VILLAGE

Sherry's—The Healthy Gourmet
89 Deer Park Avenue; 631-661-5552
Hours: Monday to Friday 9 am to 7 pm
Saturday & Sunday 9 am to 5 pm
Natural Food Store. Organic produce. Large health food store

Comments: Vitamins, supplements, salt free food, macrobiotic & oriental foods, cosmetics & beauty products, bulk grains, herbs, nuts and organic baby food. Reasonably priced. Accepts AMEX, MC, VISA.
Directions: From Sunrise Hwy, take Exit #38, then go south on Little East Neck Rd N (may have to go south first on Belmont Ave) for 2 miles, then at Montauk Hwy (Rte 27A) turn left and go about 1 mile, at Deer Park Ave go north and this place is a block down.

COMMACK

The Mung Bean Natural Foods
Commack Corners Shopping Center
6522 Jericho Turnpike; 631-499-2362
Hours: Monday to Friday 9 am to 7 pm; Saturday 9 am to 6 pm; Sunday 11 am to 5 pm
Natural Food Store and Juice Bar. Organic produce.
Menu: Fresh juices and ready-made sandwiches.
Other Info: Counter service, take-out, delivery.
Directions: From LI Expressway, take exit #52 and go north on Commack Rd to Jericho Turnpike (about 2 mile) and it is in the Commack Corners Shopping Center at the intersection. From Northern State Pkwy, take Sagtikos Pkwy and go 2 miles, then take Exit Sm1W, then go west on Jericho Turnpike and this place is 1 mile down at Commack Rd.

Trader Joe's (East Inc.)
5010 Jericho Turnpike, Commack
631-493-9210; **Web site:** www.traderjoes.com
Natural Food Store.

EAST HAMPTON

Babette's
66 Newtown Lane, between Main Street & Osborne, East Hampton; 631-329-5377
Summer Hours: Daily 8 am to 11 pm
Winter Hours: Friday to Sunday 9 am to 10 pm
Closed Monday to Thursday
International Restaurant. Juice Bar. Vegan and Macrobiotic options. Not pure vegetarian.
Menu: Soups, exotic salads, pastas, BBQ Tofu, falafel, Wasabi Tofu Teriyaki, Waldorf Salad and Asian Burritos with Thai Peanut Sauce. Good desserts, some vegan ones. Breakfast served all day.
Comments: Plays jazz music. Dimly lit. Have plants and trees. A bit upscale. Has a selection of creative dishes. Reasonable prices. Sidewalk café with outdoor seating. Good place for people watching.
Other Info: Full service, take-out, catering. Non-smoking. Accepts AMEX, MC, VISA. Price: $$.
Directions: From Montauk Hwy (Main St, Rte 27), go east on Newtown Lane and this place is a quarter-mile down.

FLORAL PARK

Nature's Pantry Health Foods
324 Jericho Turnpike; 516-437-0633
Hours: Monday to Saturday 9:30 am to 6 pm
Closed Sunday.
Natural Food Store.

FREEPORT

Living Natural
177A West Merrick Road; 516-771-9230
Natural Food Store and Juice Bar. Organic produce.
Menu: Has a juice bar with fresh carrot juice. The protein shakes are excellent. Has some ready-made sandwiches and salads, but not much of a selection.
Comments: Has a fairly decent selection of grocery items.
Directions: This place is a block west of the post office and Library on the opposite side of the street in a small shopping center that has a McDonald's in front.

Sunrise Health Store
129 West Sunrise Highway, Freeport
Natural Food Store. Organic produce. Their branch, Living Natural (above) has a better selection of items.
Directions: This place is on Hwy 27 in a small shopping center on the south side of the road.

GARDEN CITY

Akbar Restaurant
1 Ring Road, West, at Roosevelt Field
516-248-5700
Hours: Sunday to Thursday 12 noon to 3 pm, 5:30 pm to 10 pm; Friday & Saturday 12 noon to 3 pm, 5:30 pm to 11 pm
Indian. Vegan options. Not pure vegetarian.
Menu: Has a good selection of vegetarian dishes. Usually has several vegetarian main dishes. Can ask to have food either spicy hot or not. Has an inexpensive lunch buffet.
Other Info: Full service, take-out. Accepts AMEX, DIS, MC, VISA. Price: $$.

GLEN COVE

Rising Tide Natural Market
42 Forest Avenue, Glen Cove
516-676-7895
Hours: Monday to Friday 9 am to 8 pm; Saturday 9 am to 7 pm; Sunday 10 am to 6 pm
Natural Food Store and Deli. Bakery and Juice Bar. Vegan and Macrobiotic options. Organic produce. Good mid-size natural food store.
Menu: Offers around 30 homemade dishes. Vegetarian wraps, Tofu Teriyaki, seitan dishes, vegan salads, sandwiches, vegetarian chili and Sesame Ginger Tofu. Non-dairy pudding and organic muffins. Fresh juices.
Comments: Uses only organic produce. Outdoor seating. Macrobiotic supplies, homeopathic items and herbs.
Other Info: Counter service, take-out, catering, delivery. Accepts AMEX, MC, VISA. Price: $.
Directions: From LIE, take exit #39N (Glen Cove Road), then go north on Glen Cove (becomes Brewster St) for about 4½ miles to end of the road (at the fire station). Then turn right on Forest Ave and this store is on the right five lights down.

Garden Of Plenty
4 Wellwyn Road
516-482-8868
Hours: Daily 11:30 am to 9:30 pm
Chinese. Not pure vegetarian.
Menu: Has a good selection of vegetarian dishes. Fish Fantasy (made from bean curd), Snow White Chow Fun Rolls, Enoki Mushrooms and Sautéed Chinese Spinach.
Other Info: Full service, take-out. Accepts AMEX, MC, VISA. Price: $$.

The Health Nuts
45 Northern Boulevard
516-829-8400
Hours: Monday to Thursday, Saturday 9:30 am to 7 pm; Friday 9:30 am to 8 pm; Sunday 10 am to 5 pm
Natural Food Store and Gourmet Deli. Organic produce.
Menu: Soups, pasta, wraps, tofu & tempeh dishes and salads.
Comments: Vitamins, frozen foods, cosmetics, books and dietary products.
Directions: From LIE, take Exit #32 and go northwest on Little Neck Pkwy for 1 mile, then at Northern Blvd turn right and this place is a half-mile down.

**House of Dosas
416 South Broadway, Hicksville; 516-938-7517
Hours: Monday to Thursday 11 am to 9:30 pm Friday to Sunday 11 am to 10 pm
Pure Vegetarian authentic South Indian. Juice Bar.
Menu: Dosas (10 kinds) with homemade coconut chutney and sambar. Salads, rice dishes, curried vegetables and desserts. Almond or carrot halava. About 80% vegan.
Comments: Has only 20 seats. Very reasonably priced. Popular place. Plays pleasant Indian devotional music.
Other Info: Full service, take-out. Accepts MC, VISA. Price: $.
Directions: From LIE, take exit #41S. Take Rte 107 south 2 miles. When road forks after a mile take left road onto Broadway and this place is 1 miles down on right, opposite the Hicksville Motor Vehicle on the west side of the road. Half-mile south of Old Country Road.

HUNTINGTON

Straight from the Heart
80 East Main Street; 631-549-3750
Hours: Monday to Saturday 9:30 am to 7 pm Sunday 11 am to 6 pm
Natural Food Store and a good Café. Deli, Juice Bar, Bakery and Salad Bar. Organic produce. Pleasant staff. Has organic bulk goods.
Other Info: Accepts AMEX, MC, VISA.
Directions: On east side of Huntington Village on the main street in town. A little east of Park Ave.

Sweet Potatoes Organic Market
35 B Gerard Street; 516-423-6424
Web site: www.organicmarket.com
Hours: Monday, Tuesday, Wednesday, Saturday 9:30 am to 7 pm; Thursday & Friday 9:30 am to 8 pm; Sunday 12 noon to 6 pm
Natural Food Store and Café. Vegetarian Deli, Juice Bar, Vegan Bakery and Salad Bar. Organic produce.
Menu: Seitan dishes, daily soup, salads, burritos, sandwiches and tempeh & tofu dishes. Sweet Potato Salad is recommended. Mini-Zen Bowl with organic rice and vegetables is cheap. Vegan cookies, muffins, pies and a really good Couscous Mousse Cake. Fresh juices.
Comments: Relaxed, friendly atmosphere. Full service, take-out, catering, delivery.
Other Info: Accepts MC, VISA. Price: $.
Directions: Take Rte 25A, it then becomes Main

St in Huntington. At Wall St turn north and go 1 block, then turn right at Gerard and then this place is on the left not far from corner.

Tortilla Grill
335 New York Avenue
516-423-4141
Hours: Tuesday to Thursday, Sunday 11 am to 11 pm; Friday & Saturday 11 am to 12 pm; Closed Monday.
Mexican. Not pure vegetarian.
Menu: Vegetarian dishes are marked on the menu. Beans do not contain lard.
Other Info: Counter service, take-out. Cash only; no credit cards. Price: $.

ISLIP

Country Health & Diet Foods
484 Main Street (Rte 27A)
631-581-7722
Web site: www.countryhealthdiet.com
Hours: Monday to Saturday 10 am to 6 pm
Closed Sunday.
Natural Food Store and Deli. Organic foods, herbs, vitamins and minerals.
Menu: Just has ready-made sandwiches.
Other Info: Accepts AMEX, DIS, MC, VISA.
Directions: From Sunrise Hwy, take Exit #45 and go south on Commack Rd (becomes Nassau Ave) 1 mile, then turn right and this place is a quarter-mile down. This place is on the main street in town. Rear parking.

JERICHO

PureFood
36 Jericho Turnpike
516-939-2848; **fax:** 516 433-4286
email: PureFood@aol.com
Delivers Organic meals in Long Island. Vegan and Macrobiotic options.
Menu: Menu changes weekly. Butternut Squash Soup, Tofu Lasagna and Roasted Vegetables.
Comments: Uses organic produce. Meals are dairy-free. Does not contain chemicals, preservatives or refined sugar, and foods are low in saturated fats.
Other Info: Delivery only. Price: $$.

MANHASSET

Fresh Fields Whole Foods Market
2101 Northern Boulevard; 516-869-8900
Hours: Daily 8 am to 9 pm

Natural Food Store and Cafe. Deli, Bakery, Salad Bar and Juice Bar. Organic produce. Supermarket-type place. See Whole Foods Market information.
Directions: From LIE, take Exit #36 and go north on Searingtown Rd about 1 mile, then at Northern Boulevard turn left and this place is 1 block down. Across from the Americana Mall, on the border with Munsey Park.

MASSAPEQUA

Eden's Way Natural Foods
37 Broadway; 516-798-5670
Hours: Monday to Friday 10 am to 6:30 pm (until 8 pm Thursday); closed Sunday.
Natural Food Store. Decent selection of organic produce.
Menu: Has ready-made sandwiches.
Directions: From Sunrise Hwy, go north on Broadway and this place is 2 blocks down.

MEDFORD

Salad Bowl
1699 J Route 112; 516-475-1810
Hours: Daily 7 am to 6 pm
Natural Foods. Good selection of vegetarian dishes, but not all vegetarian.
Menu: Large selection of vegetarian and vegan dishes. Vegetable Lasagna, veggie burgers, soups (lentil, split pea, vegetable), Curried Chickpeas, Ratatouille, rice, Vegetable Cheese Casserole, Vegetarian Chili and Eggplant Parmigiana. Pita bread sandwiches with a choice of falafel, hummus or veggie burgers. Salads include Three Bean, Tofu with Raw Vegetables and Couscous. Has good desserts, including very good Cranberry Bread. Fresh juices. No alcohol.
Comments: Cooks and bakes everything on the premises. Fast service. Desserts contain honey and often eggs.
Other Info: Cafeteria style, counter service, take-out, catering. Price $-$$.
Directions: From LIE, take exit #64 and go south on Rte 112 and this place is 1½ mile down. From Sunrise Hwy, take Exit #53 and go north on Rte 112 and this place is about 1 mile down.

MERRICK

Trader Joe's
1714 Merrick Road, Merrick
516-771-1012; **Web site:** www.traderjoes.com
Natural Food Store.

MONTAUK, Suffolk County (at the end of the island)

Joni's
9 South Edison Plaza; 631-668-FOOD (3663)
Hours: Monday to Thursday 10 am to 9 pm; Friday & Saturday 10 am to 10 pm; Sunday 10 am to 7 pm
Natural Food Restaurant. Uses mostly organic produce.
Menu: Seasonal fruits, sandwiches, Coconut Bread, Tofu Stir-fry and non-dairy ice cream.
Other Info: Table service, take-out. Price: $.
Directions: This place is 1 mile west of the eastern end of Long Island, just south of Montauk Point State Park.

Naturally Good Foods & Café
38 South Etna Avenue, at South Essex Street
631-668-9030
Hours: Monday to Saturday 7 am to 6 pm (kitchen closes at 4 pm); Sunday 7 am to 3 pm
Natural Food Store and Café. Deli and Bakery. Organic produce
Menu: Breakfast and lunch dishes. Fresh baked goods. Fruit smoothies.
Comments: Herbal remedies, vitamins, natural cosmetic and grocery items.
Other Info: Non-smoking. Accepts credit cards. Price: $.
Directions: From Old Montauk Hwy, go north on Webster Rd 1 block, then at Webster Dr turn left and this place is a block down. This place is about 1 mile west of downtown Montauk, near Overlook Park.

MUNSEY PARK

Fresh Fields Whole Foods
2101 Northern Boulevard; 516-869-8900
Hours: Daily 8 am to 9 pm
Natural Food Store and Cafe. Deli, Bakery, Salad Bar and Juice Bar. Organic produce. Supermarket-type place. See Whole Foods Market information.
Directions: From LIE, take exit #36 and go north on Searingtown Rd about 1¼ mile. Then at Northern Blvd turn left and this store is on the left in the first building after the turn.

NORTHPORT

Organically Yours
114 Main Street; 631-754-2150
Hours: Monday to Friday 9:30 am to 7 pm; Sat-

urday 10 am to 6 pm; Sunday 12 am to 5 pm
Natural Food Store and Organic take-out Deli. Juice Bar. Vegan options. Organic produce.
Menu: Good soups (2 daily), whole grains dishes, and freshly made organic wraps including Soy Hummus and Black Bean wraps. At the juice bar there are fresh juices, protein shakes, smoothies, and organic tea and coffee.
Comments: Vitamins, herbs and natural beauty products. Uses organic produce in the deli.
Other Info: Counter service, take-out, delivery. Has just a few seats. Accepts MC, VISA. Price: $$.
Directions: From Fort Salonga (Rte 25A), go north on Reservoit Ave 1 mile, then at Main St turn left and this place is 2/3 mile down.

OCEANSIDE

Jandi's Nature Way
Great Lincoln Shopping Center, 24 Atlantic Avenue, at Longbeach Road; 516-536-5535
Hours: Monday, Tuesday, Wednesday, Friday 10 am to 7 pm; Thursday 10 am to 9 pm; Saturday 10 am to 6 pm; Sunday 11 am to 5 pm
Natural Food Store, Deli and Organic Juice Bar. Organic produce.
Menu: Has a selection of about 20 vegetarian dishes daily. Tofu dishes, vegetable dishes, sandwiches, salads and desserts. Organic fresh juices and wheatgrass.
Comments: Has a few tables to seat at. Fairly small natural food store with a good selection of items. Cooked food gets good recommendations. Counter service, take-out.
Directions: From Hwy 27, at Longbeach Rd go south and this store is about 1½ mile down on the right in the Great Lincoln Shopping Center.

Trader Joe's
3418 Long Beach Road
516-536-9163; **Web** site: www.traderjoes.com

PLAINVIEW

Dr B Well Naturally
8 Washington Avenue
516-932-9355; **fax:** 516-932-9366
Hours: Monday to Friday 9 am to 8 pm; Saturday 9 am to 7 pm; Sunday 9 am to 6 pm
Natural Food Store and Café. Organic Deli and Juice Bar. Bakery. Has an excellent organic produce section. Not pure vegetarian.
Menu: This place has a large selection of dishes in their deli. Tofu-dill Salad, baked goods, salads,

and Barbecued Tempeh. Daily lunch specials.
Comments: Has both indoor and outdoor seating. Has fat-free, gluten-free, salt-free, vegan, dairy-free and wheat-free options. Discount vitamins & herbs, homeopathic remedies, health & beauty aids, good selection of groceries and certified organic produce.
Other Info: Counter service, take-out, delivers. Accepts major credit cards. Price: $-$$.
Directions: From west Long Island Expressway take Exit #45. Go south on Manetto Hill Rd. Turn left at Washington and the store is on the right at the corner of Manetto Hill and Washington. From east LIE take Exit #48. Turn left on Round Swamp Rd. Bear right onto Old Country Rd. Turn right at Manetto Hill Rd, then right at Washington. The store is then on the right at the corner.

Hunan Cottage
135 Central Park Road
516-349-0390
Hours: Sunday to Thursday 11:30 am to 9:30 pm; Friday & Saturday 11:30 am to 10:30 pm
Chinese. Vegan options. Not pure vegetarian.
Menu: The separate vegetarian menu has over 20 dishes including mock "meat" dishes.
Comments: Casual place. Full service, take-out. Accepts AMEX, MC, VISA. Price: $$.

Trader Joe's
425 S Oyster Bay Road, Plainview
516-933-6900; **Web site:** www.traderjoes.com

PORT JEFFERSON

Tiger Lily Café
156 East Main Street
631-476-7080
Web site: www.tigerlilycafe.com
Hours: Monday to Saturday 9 am to 6 pm
Sunday 10 am to 5 pm
Gourmet Natural Foods. Juice Bar. Macrobiotic options. Not pure vegetarian.
Menu: Eggplant Baba Ghanouj Sandwich, Vegan Tofu Chicken Finger, Oriental dishes, brown rice, Tuscan Tofu Torta, Veggie-burger, vegetable wrap, falafel and desserts. Fresh juices, soy smoothies, cappuccino, espresso.
Other Info: Non-smoking. Cash only; no credit cards. Price $-$$.
Directions: This place is in the downtown. From E Broadway, go south on E Main St and this place in a block down. Note that E Main St is two block east of Main St.

PORT WASHINGTON

Twin Pines Co-op
382 Main Street
516-883-9777
email: pwtinpines@aol.com
Hours: Tuesday 12 noon to 5 pm; Thursday 10 am to 6 pm; Wednesday, Friday, Saturday 10 am to 5 pm; closed Sunday & Monday.
Natural Food Store.
Directions: From LIE, take exit #36 and go north on Searingtown Rd (becomes Port Washington Blvd) about 3 miles. At Main turn left (go west) and this place is on the left a little after a mile. Can park on the right at town dock.

RIVERHEAD

Green Earth Grocery
50 East Main Street
631-369 2233; **fax:** 631-369-1653
Hours: Monday to Friday 9:30 am to 6 pm; Saturday 10 am to 6 pm; Sunday 11 am to 4 pm
Natural Food Store and Café. Deli, Bakery and Organic Juice Bar with wheatgrass. Mainly Vegetarian (except tuna). Has a good selection of organic produce. Vegan and Macrobiotic options.
Menu: Good salads, sandwiches, pastas and vegetable dishes. Fresh baked goods included breads, cookies and muffins. Fresh juices, smoothies. Organic cappuccino and espresso.
Comments: Bulk foods and organic coffee. Does shipping. Everything is homemade on the premises.
Other Info: Non-smoking. Accepts AMEX, DIS, MC, VISA. Price: $-$$.
Directions: LIE to exit #72. Go east on Rte 25, which turns into Main St when it reaches Riverhead. Store is on left.

ROCKY POINT

Back to Basic Natural Food
632 Route 25A
631-821-0444
Hours: Monday to Thursday & Saturday 10 am to 6:30 pm; Friday 10 am to 7:30 pm; Sunday 11 am to 5 pm.
Natural Food Store. Organic produce.
Menu: Has ready-made sandwiches in the cooler.
Comments: Good selection of bulk items, vitamins, cheeses, spices, books, fruits & nuts and organic products.
Other Info: Accepts AMEX, MC, VISA.

RONKONKOMA

Buy Rite Health World (Cheese & Health Food)
299-10 Hawkins Avenue; 631-588-4180
Natural Food Store. Discount vitamins. Limited amount of organic produce.

SAG HARBOR, SUFFOLK COUNTY (in the Hamptons)

Provisions of Sag Harbor
Bay and Division streets; 631-725-3636
Hours: Daily 8:30 am to 6 pm
Natural Food Store and large Deli. Salad Bar and Juice Bar. Macrobiotic and Organic options. Organic produce.
Menu: Known for its wraps. Tempeh Reuben, Scrambled Tofu and Organic Vegetable Pot Pie. East-West Wrap is made of grilled tofu, sushi rice and marinated vegetables. Baby Buddha Bowl is brown rice, steamed greens with sea and root vegetables. Homemade chocolate chip and oatmeal raisin cookies (may have eggs, so ask). Fresh juices.
Other Info: Full service, counter service, take-out. Has seating. Non-smoking. Accepts AMEX, MC, VISA. Counter service, take-out. With plenty of seating. Price: $-$$.
Directions: From Route 27 (Montauk Hwy), at Sag Harbor Turnpike turn left and go 3¼ miles, then turn slight right on Main St (Rte 79) and go 1 mile, then at Long Island Ave turn right and at next corner, turn right onto Bay St (Rte 114) and go 1 block and this place is at the corner with Division.

SAYVILLE (Suffolk County, where ferries depart to Fire Island)

Cornucopia Natural Foods
39 North Main Street
631-589-9579
Hours: Monday to Friday 9 am to 7 pm; Saturday 10 am to 6 pm; Sunday 12 noon to 5 pm
Natural Food Store and Organic Deli. Juice Bar. Organic produce.
Menu: Ezekiel Roll with melted soy cheese, Lama Burger, Carrot Oat Burger, salads, sandwiches, soups, Tofu Cheesecake topped with organic blueberries and Chocolate Tofu Pie. Fresh juices.
Comments: Small, friendly place. Reasonably priced. Specializes in wheat-free, gluten-free and dairy-free dishes. Can make special orders. Open for over 25 years.
Other Info: Counter service, take-out. Has seating. Accepts AMEX, DIS, MC, VISA. Price: $.

Directions: On the main street in downtown Sayville.

SEAFORD

All Natural Health
3830 Sunrise Highway
516-785-5521; Web site: www.allnaturalusa.com
Natural Food Store.

SETAUKET

Wild by Nature Market
198 Main Street (Rte 25A)
631-246-5500; **fax:** 631-246-5276
Web site: www.wildnature.com
Hours: Monday to Saturday 8 am to 9 pm Sunday 8 am to 8 pm
Natural Food Store and Deli. Bakery. Organic produce. Not pure vegetarian.
Menu: Has a good selection of vegetarian dishes.
Comments: Vitamins, healing herbs, beauty products, homeopathic remedies and fresh flowers. Food is free of preservatives and artificial colors and favors.
Other Info: Accepts AMEX, MC, VISA. Counter service, take-out. Has seating.
Directions: This place is on the main street in town.

SHELTER ISLAND

Planet Bliss
23 North Ferrie Road (Route 114)
631-749-0053
Summer Hours: Wednesday to Monday 11 am to 10 pm
Café Hours: Monday, Wednesday, Thursday 12 noon to 3 pm, 6 pm to 9 pm; Friday & Saturday 12 noon to 3 pm, 6 pm to 10 pm; Sunday 11 am to 3 pm, 6 pm to 10 pm; closed Tuesday. Closed for the winter.
Natural Food Store and International Café. Juice Bar. Not pure vegetarian.
Menu: Salads, soba noodles, sandwiches and desserts. Fresh juices and smoothies. Has a Sunday brunch menu.
Comments: In an old Victorian house. Outdoor seating. Changing art display. 90% of the produce is organic. Relaxing atmosphere. Friendly place.
Other Info: Full service, take-out. Reservations are highly recommended. Accepts credit cards.
Directions: Shelter Island is at the east end of the Long Island. This place is on Rte 114, at the junction with Congdon Rd.

SOUTHOLD

The Natural Choice

56215 Main Road, Southold; 631-765-5153
Hours: Monday to Saturday 9:30 am to 5:30 pm
Closed Sunday.
Natural Food Store and Deli. Organic produce.
Menu: Veggie chili, soups, rice & bean salad, wraps and sandwiches.
Other Info: Counter service, take-out. Has three seats at the counter.
Directions: This place is on Hwy 25 in the middle of town.

ST JAMES

St James Natural Food

296 Lake Avenue; 631-862-6076
Hours: Monday to Saturday 9 am to 7 pm
Sunday 12 noon to 5 pm
Natural Food Store. Organic produce. Large selection of items.
Directions: From Rte 347, go north on Gibbs Pond (becomes Lake Ave S) and this place is 1¾ mile down.

SYOSSET

Long Island Health Connection

520 Jericho Turnpike; 516-496-2528
Hours: Monday to Saturday 9 am to 8 pm
Sunday 10 am to 6 pm
Natural Food Store and Deli. Vegan options. Juice Bar. Organic produce.
Menu: Has a wide selection of vegetarian dishes. Salads, soups, sandwiches, veggie burgers and main dishes. Fresh juices.
Comments: Vitamins, health foods and beauty products. Has a certified nutritionist.
Other Info: Full service, take-out. Accepts AMEX, MC, VISA. Counter service, take-out. Has a small seating area. Price: $.
Directions: From LIE, take exit #44 (from Northern Pkwy take exit #36) and go north on Seaford Oyster Bay Ewy, then take Rte 25 W exit (#14) towards Jericho, and merge onto Jericho Turnpike (Rte 25) going west and this place is a third-mile down.

WESTBURY

The Health Nuts

92 Old Country Road, Westbury
516-683-9177

Hours: Tuesday to Friday 9:30 am to 8 pm; Monday, Saturday 9:30 am to 7 pm; closed Sunday.
Natural Food Store and Gourmet Deli. Organic produce.
Comments: Vitamins, frozen foods, cosmetics, books and dietary products.
Other Info: Counter service, take-out. Has seating.
Directions: From Meadowbrook Pkwy, take Old Country Rd exit (#M1) and this place is a mile east on Old Country Rd.

**Zen Palate

477 Old Country Road, at Evelyn Ave
516-333-8686; Web site: www.zenpalate.com
Hours: Monday to Thursday 11:30 am to 10 pm
Friday to Sunday 11:30 am to 11 pm
Fully Vegetarian Asian. Mostly Vegan.
Menu: Has many mock "meat" dishes. Orange Sensation "Beef," Sesame Medallions, mock "chicken," Autumn Rolls and West Lake (steamed shiitake mushrooms in a wasabi sauce). Rice and noodle dishes.
Comments: Has a peaceful Zen Buddhism atmosphere. If you don't eat eggs you should see the warning about the Zen Palate restaurant in Manhattan. Well-designed place. Beautiful décor.
Other Info: Full service, take-out, catering. Non-smoking. Reservations recommended. Accepts AMEX, MC, VISA. Price: $$.
Directions: From the Long Island Exp going east, take exit #38 to the Meadowbrook Parkway. From the Meadowbrook Parkway, take exit M1 (E) for Westbury. Get on Old Country Rd going east and this place is about a half-mile down on the left. It is near the Roosevelt Fields Mall.

WEST HEMPSTEAD

Taj Mahal Restaurant

221 Hempstead Turnpike, between Cherry Valley Ave & Westminster Road
516-565-4607
Hours: Sunday to Thursday 11:30 am to 3 pm, 5 pm to 10 pm; Friday & Saturday 11:30 am to 3 pm, 5 pm to 11 pm
Indian. Not pure vegetarian.
Menu: Has a large selection of vegetarian dishes.
Comments: Relaxed, friendly atmosphere. Gets good recommendations. Good food and service. Not much ambiance.
Other Info: Full service, take-out. Accepts AMEX, MC, VISA. Price: $$.

North Carolina

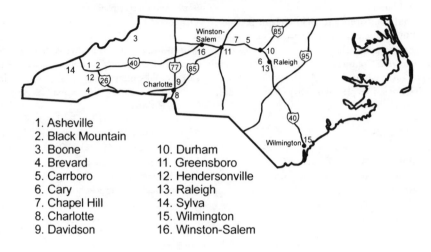

1. Asheville
2. Black Mountain
3. Boone
4. Brevard
5. Carrboro
6. Cary
7. Chapel Hill
8. Charlotte
9. Davidson
10. Durham
11. Greensboro
12. Hendersonville
13. Raleigh
14. Sylva
15. Wilmington
16. Winston-Salem

ASHEVILLE

Bargain Max
121 Sweeten Creek Road; 828-277-0805
Hours: Monday to Saturday 10 am to 6 pm
Closed Sunday.
Natural Food Store. Discounted health and organic foods.
Other Info: Accepts DIS, MC, VISA.

Café Max and Rosie's
52 North Lexington Avenue; 704-254-5342
Web site: www.maxandrosies.com
Hours: Mon to Sat 11 am to 5:30 pm; Closed
Sun. Psychic Fair every Saturday 2 pm to 5 pm
Vegetarian-friendly Natural Foods Restaurant. Macrobiotic and Vegan options. Not pure
vegetarian.
Menu: Tempeh Parmigiana Sandwich, salads,
Max's Favorite Veggie Burger, Finger Linkin' Not
Chicken, Club TLT (grilled tempeh with lettuce
and tomato), fried rice, Greek Salad, Grilled
Cheese, Brown Rice, Avocado Salad, Tempeh
Quesadilla, bagels and cream cheese, Middle Eastern Delight, Nachos Grande with homemade
salsa, Blackened Tofu, Veggie Pita and Bean Pita.
Fresh juices, smoothies and fresh fruit.
Comments: Relaxed place. Local organic produce
used when possible. Has a grand piano in the center of the dining room. Sells their own Café Max
& Rosie's cookbook. Vibrant paint-on-plywood

artwork. Has their entire menu on their Web site.
Other Info: Full service, take-out, catering. Nonsmoking. Price: $.
Directions: From I-240 loop, take Merrimon Ave
(US-25) exit (#5), and go south on N Lexington
Ave (US-25) a third-mile. Then at E Walnut St
turn right, then at the second street turn right
onto N Lexington Ave and this place is near the
turnoff.

Earth Fare and Café Terra
Westgate Shopping Center, 66 Westgate Parkway,
at Patton Ave and Westgate Parkway
704-253-7656; **Web site:** www.earthfare.com
Hours: Monday to Saturday 8 am to 9 pm
Sunday 9 am to 8 pm
Natural Food Store and Café. Deli, Juice Bar,
Bakery and Salad Bar. Organic produce.
Macrobiotic and Vegan options. Not pure vegetarian. Huge supermarket-type place.
Menu: Has a hot and cold buffet.
Comments: This is an impressive natural food
store with a massive selection. Highly recommended. Cooking classes and lectures. Books and
magazines.
Other Info: Counter service, take-out. Price: $$.
Directions: From I-240 loop, take exit #3B (Hwy
19) (Westgate-Holiday Inn) and this place in
parking lot on right near the exit. This place is
about a quarter-mile west of I-240 on Hwy 19, a
little north of the downtown.

French Broad Co-op
90 Biltmore Avenue, downtown; 828-255-7650; email: fbfc@fbfc.com; **Web site:** www.fbfc.com
Hours: Monday to Friday 9 am to 10 pm; Saturday 9 am to 7 pm; Sunday 12 pm to 8 pm
Natural Food Store. Large selection of organic produce. Supermarket-type place with a great selection.
Menu: Fresh breads daily, deli sandwiches and deli items.
Comments: Open to the public. Honors other food co-ops discounts to their members. Discounts for seniors on Mondays. Helpful staff. Has a farmer's market in their parking lot Saturday 8 am to 1 pm and Wednesday 4 pm to 7 pm from mid-April to mid-October.
Other Info: Accepts DIS, MC, VISA.
Directions: In downtown Asheville, two blocks south of Pack Square. From Rte 240 east, take Merrimon Ave exit (or Broadway depending on direction coming from), turn left on Broadway (south towards downtown) which becomes Biltmore at Vance Monument and then this place is on the left after 2 blocks. From Rte 240 west, take Patton Ave, then turn right at Biltmore Ave, Co-op is two blocks down on the left. This store's parking lot is at corner of Biltmore and Hillyard.

Heiwa Skokudo
87 North Lexington Avenue, downtown
828-254-7761
Hours: Monday to Saturday 11:30 am to 2:30 pm, 5:30 pm to 9:30 pm
Japanese. Not pure vegetarian.
Menu: Has vegetarian specials, vegetarian sushi, organic miso, tofu dishes and brown rice.
Comments: Make it clear you are vegetarian as some of the broths are not vegetarian.
Other Info: Accepts AMEX, DIS, MC, VISA.

Homestead Farms
Naples Road; 828-684-1155
Hours: Monday to Thursday 9 am to 6 pm; Friday 9 am to 4 pm; Sunday 9 am to 5 pm; closed Saturday.
Natural Food Store and Deli. Meat substitutes, good fruit jams.
Other Info: Counter service, take-out. Has seating.

**Laughing Seed Café
40 Wall Street
808-252-3445; **Web site:** www.laughingseed.com
Hours: Monday, Wednesday, Thursday 11 am to 9 pm; Friday, Saturday 11:30 am to 10 pm; Sun-

day 10 am to 9 pm; closed Tuesday.
Fully Vegetarian International. Bakery. Vegan and Macrobiotic options.
Menu: Has a web site that contains entire menu. Has a great selection of dishes. Kung Pao Tofu, quesadillas, Thai Red Curry, Wild Mushroom Enchiladas, The Florentine, Divinity Focaccia, Curried Mock Chicken Salad Sandwich, Basil Aioli, pizzas, The Mediterranean (artichoke hearts, calamata olives, roasted garlic), Greek salad, Pesto Penne Primavera, Mushroom Madness Pita, TLT Sandwich, Grilled Cheese Sandwich, Hummus Tahini, California Nori Roll, Harmony Salad, tempeh fajitas and pita sandwich. Homemade organic multi-grained breads The Harmony Bowl is good. There is the Vegetarian Combo, in which you can choose anything from two to five of any of the following dishes: Brown Rice, Tempeh, Tofu, Red Bean Chili, Steamed Vegetables, Potato Salad, Pinto Beans or Simple Salad. Fresh juices, smoothies, herbal teas and natural sodas.
Comments: Pleasant atmosphere and is a good dining experience. Indoor and outdoor seating. Good service. Has painted murals on the walls. Has a Kids menu. Mainly uses organic ingredients. In season their fruits, vegetables and herbs come from local organic farmers and are often picked the same day they are used. Items that take longer to prepare are marked. Soy mozzarella can usually be substituted for dairy cheese. The soy mozzarella contains a small amount of casein (milk). Baked desserts are naturally sweetened. Water is filtered. Mellow place.
Other Info: Full service, take-out. Non-smoking. Does not take reservations except for groups, which are suggested. Accepts AMEX, DC, DIS, MC, VISA. Price: $$. An 18% gratuity is added for parties of five or more.
Directions: Located in downtown Asheville. From I-240 loop, take Merrimon Ave (US-25) exit (#5), and go south on N Lexington Ave (US-25) a half-mile. Then at Patton Ave turn right and go a third-mile, at Haywood St turn right and go 2 blocks, then take the second left and bear left onto Wall St and this place is 1 block down.

Melanie's
32 Broadway; 828-236-3533
Hours: Wednesday to Friday 8 am to 2:30 pm (breakfast to 11:30 am); Saturday 8 am to 2:30 pm; Sunday Brunch 10 am to 2 pm; closed Monday & Tuesday.
Vegetarian friendly. Not pure vegetarian. Known for its breakfasts.

Salsa

6 Patton Avenue
828-252-9805
Hours: Mon to Thu 11:30 am to 2:30 pm, 5:30 to 9 pm; Fri & Sat 12 am to 3 pm, 5:30 pm to 9:30 pm
Mexican and Caribbean Natural Food Café. Vegan friendly. Not pure vegetarian.
Menu: Burritos, quesadillas, Azteca Pizza, enchiladas and many other vegetarian dishes. Can substitute soy cheese for milk cheese.

Souper Sandwich

Haywood Park Atrium, 46 Haywood Street
828-285-0003
Hours: Daily 8 am to 5 pm
Hot Bar and Salad Bar. All-you-can-eat Buffet.
Price: $.
Menu: Salad items, stuffed potatoes, pastas, soups and more.

BLACK MOUNTAIN

White Mountain Natural Foods

115 Black Mountain Avenue; 828-669-9813
Hours: Monday to Saturday 9 am to 6 pm
Closed Sunday.
Natural Food Store. No deli when I called but said may have one in the future.
Other Info: Accepts MC, VISA.
Directions: From I-40, take Black Mountain exit (#64) west, then go north a half-mile. At Vance Ave turn left and this place is 2 blocks down on right. This place is about 6 miles south of Asheville, about a half-mile west of Hwy 25.

BOONE

Angelica

506 West King Street; 828-265-0809
Hours: Daily 11 am to 9:30 pm
Vegetarian Restaurant. Vegan friendly.
Menu: Espinaca Grande (spinach salad with sautéed tempeh), salads, Nori Rolls, sautéed Tofu Vegetable Sandwich, burritos, quesadillas, enchiladas and good desserts. Fresh juices and smoothies.
Comments: Local organic produce used when possible. Uses whole grains.
Directions: It is in downtown Boone, near Appalachian State University on Hwy 321.

King Street Cafe & Smoothie Bar

454B West King Street, Boone
828-265-3434
Hours: Monday to Saturday 10 am to 8 pm

Closed Sunday.
Restaurant. Not pure vegetarian.
Menu: Sandwiches, pastas and smoothies.
Other Info: Accepts AMEX, MC, VISA.

BREVARD

Healthy Harvest

410 North Broad Street
inside College Plaza
828-885-2599
Hours: Monday to Saturday 9 am to 6 pm
Natural Food Store.
Directions: This place is on the main street in the downtown.

CARRBORO (near Chapel Hill)

Weaver Street Market and Carrboro Café

Carr Mill Mall
101 East Weaver Street, at N Greenboro
919-929-0010;
email: feedback@weaverstreetmarket.com;
Web site: http://www.weaverstreetmarket.com
Hours: Monday to Friday 9 am to 9 pm
Saturday & Sunday 9 am to 8 pm
Café opens at 7:30 am on the weekdays
Natural Food Store and Vegetarian-friendly Café.
Bakery and Salad Bar. Macrobiotic and Vegan options.
Menu: Has home baked breads, baked pastries, soups, ready-made sandwiches, salads with homemade dressings and desserts. Has a self-serve hot bar with vegan and vegetarian dishes. Vegetarian Chili, Tomato & Basil Soup, Pasta Salad, Rice & Beans Salad, Vegetarian Lasagna and Marinated Tofu Cutlets. Hummus, Eggplant & Sundried Tomato dip and Olive Caper Tapenade.
Comments: This is a small store, but it has good bulk items. Friendly place. Has good baked goods. Only sells organic and preservative free items in the store. Well-supplied market. Has indoor seating and outdoor patio dining. Salad bar items sold by weight.
Other Info: Buffet, take-out, catering, counter service. Has a nice lawn. Accepts MC, VISA.
Price: $$.
Directions: From I-40, take US-15/US-501 exit (#270) towards Chapel Hill/Durham, go south on Durham Chapel Hill Blvd (US-15) 5½ miles. Stay straight onto S Fordham Blvd for 1 mile (becomes Rte 54 Byp W), take Merrit Mill Rd towards S Greensboro St, turn left on Merritt Mill Rd and go 2 blocks, at S Greensboro St turn right and go ¾ mile.

CARY (5 miles west of Raleigh)

**Blue Moon Bakery & Café
Ashworth Village, 115-G West Chatham Street
919-319-6554; fax: 919-462-1673
Web site: www.bluemoonbakery.com
Hours: Monday to Friday 7 am to 6 pm;
Saturday 7:30 am to 5 pm; closed Sunday.
Vegetarian.
Menu: Many sandwiches including The Apollo
(feta and Greek salad sandwich), Asian Moon
Wrap (cellophane noodles and vegetables), Spicy
Black Bean Sandwich, Mushroom Cloud (grilled
Portabella Sandwich), Blue Moon BLT, vegetar-
ian hot dog, salads, soups, Planet Pasta and
Couscous Salad. Desserts such as cakes, pies, past-
ries and Pecan Pie Bars. Fresh juices, smoothies,
natural sodas, cappuccino, espresso. Local organic
produce used when possible.
Other Info: Full service, take-out. Price: $-$$.
Directions: From I-40, take Exit #291 towards
Cary, and go west on Cary Towne Blvd for 1 mile,
at Walnut St turn right and go 1½ mile, then
turn right onto S Academy (may have to go on
Dry Ave for a half-block) and go 6 blocks, then
at E Chatham St turn left and this place is 1 block
down. In the Ashworth Village shopping center,
right in downtown Cary.

Delhi Deli
Northside Station
329 North Harrison Avenue
919-460-1300
Hours: Monday to Friday 11 am to 3 pm, 5 pm
to 9 pm; Saturday & Sunday 11 am to 9 pm
South Indian Café. Mainly vegetarian. Not pure
vegetarian. Cheap Lunch Buffet.
Menu: Has a good selection of authentic South
Indian food. Vegetable Pakoras, soups, coconut
chutney, Bhel Puri, Dhokla, parathas, Masala
Dosa, Dahi Vada, chapatis, Poori, Sev Puri (puffed
rice with potatoes and cheese) and lassis.
Comments: Has very good food. Casual. Located
in a run down yogurt shop and totally lacks in
atmosphere with bare walls, a small seating area,
and Styrofoam cups and plates. No music. In a
little strip center. Food come standard a bit spicy
hot so you may want to ask that it isn't so. The
Masala Dosa is really hot. Friendly service.
Other Info: Counter service, take-out. Cash only;
no credit cards. Price: $.
Directions: From I-40, take the Harrison Ave
(#287) exit towards Cary and go 3 miles south.
The restaurant is on the right in a strip mall about
a quarter-mile before the train tracks.

Gaulart & Maliclet French Café
957 North Harrison Avenue; 919-469-2288
Hours: Monday 10:30 am to 2:30 pm; Tuesday
to Thursday 10:30 am to 9 pm; Friday & Satur-
day 10:30 am to 10 pm; closed Sundays.
International, French Café. Not pure vegetarian.
Menu: Has a good number of vegetarian dishes.
Has pizzas, salads, steamed vegetables, homemade
vegetarian soups and several other vegetarian
dishes. Three Steamed Vegetable Dish.
Comments: Casual atmosphere.
Other Info: Accepts MC, VISA. Price: $$.
Directions: From I-40, take exit #287, then go
south on Harrison Ave toward Cary and this place
is about 2½ miles, at Maynard Road. This place
is on the right, at corner of Harrison and Maynard.

Whole Foods Market
102B Waverly Place
919-816-8830; email: Cary@wholefoods.com;
Web site: www.wholefoodsmarket.com
Hours: Daily 7:30 am to 9 pm
Breakfast Bar opens daily at 7:30 am
Natural Food Store and Deli. Organic produce.
Supermarket-type place.

Woodlands
1305 Maynard Road; 919-467-6020
Hours: Monday 5 pm to 9 pm; Sunday, Tuesday
to Thursday 11:30 am to 3 pm, 5 pm to 9:30
pm; Friday & Saturday 11:30 am to 3 pm, 5 pm
to 10:30 pm
Vegetarian Indian. Vegan options. Mainly tradi-
tional South Indian cuisine.
Menu: Excellent dosas and vegetarian dishes. Rava
Masala Dosa is recommended. The lunch special
is good (dosa, eggplant curry, papadam, rice, chut-
ney, raita, dal). Samosas, pakoras, uthappam, co-
conut chutney (very good) and mango lassi.
Comments: Has some milks dishes, but nothing
with eggs. Service was quite good when I was
there. Popular with Indians. Low on ambience,
but high in food quality.
Other Info: Full service, counter service, take-
out, catering. Accepts MC, VISA.
Directions: From I-40, take exit #287 for
Harrison Avenue towards Cary, go west on
Harrison for 2 miles, at SE Maynard Rd turn right
(go north) and this place is near the Kroger.

CHAPEL HILL

Burrito Bunker
Amber Alley, 160½ East Franklin Street
919-932-9010

Hours: Monday to Saturday 11 am to 9 pm Closed Sunday. May be closed on Saturday.
Mexican Burrito Place. Not pure vegetarian.
Menu: Has a good a selection of vegetarian dishes. Chips & salsa, tacos, bean & rice, and bean burritos. Can choose between black and red beans. Guacamole, olives, cheese, sour cream and onions for additions.
Comments: No lard in the beans. Uses canola oil to cook the taco shells and chips. Really cheap burritos.
Other Info: Mainly take-out. No tables. Counter against one wall with a few stools. Price: $.
Directions: Located in downtown Chapel Hill in Amber Alley, between Franklin St and Rosemary St, near the parking garage. To get here you go thru alley off of Franklin Street and go up the steps on the other side. Then it is on the right. Some on-street parking available and there is a parking garage on Rosemary St.

Flying Burrito
746 Airport Road, at Hillsborough, half a mile from UNC; 919-967-7744
Hours: Monday to Friday 11:30 am to 2:30 pm, 5 pm to 10 pm; Sat & Sun 5 pm to 10 pm
Tex-Mexican. Not pure vegetarian.
Menu: Good Tex-Mex food. The Flying Vegetarian is half black beans and half rice. Burritos are the most popular dishes. Chips, guacamole and salsa. Can add black beans, sweet potatoes and guacamole to burritos. Good prices. Wins awards for being the best Mexican restaurant in the area.
Comments: Popular place with the locals. Is a popular bar scene at night. Casual, informal place. The hot salsa is really hot.
Other Info: Full service, take-out. Accepts MC, VISA.
Directions: From US 15-501 S, bear right onto Franklin St towards the downtown. Turn right onto Columbia St, which becomes Airport Rd. The restaurant is in a shopping plaza on the right.

Margaret's Cantina
Timberline Shopping Center, 1129 Weaver Dairy Road; 919-942-4745;
Web site: www.margaretscantina.com
Hours: Monday to Thursday 11:30 am to 2:30 pm, 5 pm to 9 pm; Friday 11:30 am to 2:30 pm, 5 pm to 10 pm; Saturday 5 pm to 10 pm; closed Sunday.
Mexican. Not pure vegetarian, but very veg friendly. Vegan options. Emphasizes healthy food.
Menu: Mexican Lasagna layered with corn tortillas, cheese, beans and hot salsa. Tempeh Enchi-

ladas, pitas and fajitas. Mediterranean dishes, Hummus, Greek salads, fried sweet potatoes with guacamole, nachos and Black Bean Chili. Greek quesadilla is made with spinach, tomatoes and cheese. Spicy Sopa Seca is a really hot dry soup. Organic brown rice. Cappuccino, espresso.
Comments: Uses butter, canola oil and olive oil for cooking. None of the salsas have meat stock in them. Outdoor dining. Popular place; lines on the weekend. Located next to two movie theaters. Reasonable prices. Good atmosphere and food.
Other Info: Full service, take-out. Accepts AMEX, DC, DIS, MC, VISA. Price: $-$$.
Directions: From I-40, take exit onto NC 86 south and take a left onto Weaver Dairy Road and go about a quarter-mile. Timberlyne is on the right.

Pepper's Pizza
Franklin Street, in the middle of town next to the Varsity Theater
919-967-7766; **Web site:** www.pepperspizza.com
Hours: Sunday to Thursday 11:30 am to 10 pm; Friday & Saturday 11 am to 12 midnight; Sunday 4 pm to 10 pm
Pizza. Vegan options. Not pure vegetarian.
Menu: Has several vegetarian toppings such as artichokes, sun-dried tomatoes, fresh zucchini, fresh spinach and mushrooms. Fresh salads. Can order slices of pizza.
Comments: Gets rated as the best pizza in Chapel Hill. Punk rock hang out. Funky atmosphere. Happening, trendy place. Can purchase uncooked dough and make your own pizzas at home. Friendly, efficient staff. Got award for having "Chapel Hill's Cleanest Men's Bathroom."
Other Info: Full service, take-out, delivery. Accepts MC, VISA.
Directions: Next to the Varsity Theater, between Columbia and Henderson Streets. From US 15-501 south bear right onto Franklin Street and this place is on the right. Some on-street parking is available, and an hourly lot is behind the restaurant (at Columbia and Rosemary).

Pyewacket
The Courtyard
431 West Franklin Street, at Robeson Street
919-929-0927; **email:** pyewacket@mindspring.com; **Web site:** www.pyewacketrestaurant.com
Hours: Monday to Thursday 5:30 pm to 9:30 pm; Friday & Saturday 5:30 to 10 pm; Sunday 5:30 pm to 9 pm
Natural Foods Restaurant. Mediterranean,

American, Asian.
Menu: The menu changes monthly. Use a lot of seeds and sprouts. "Morning Star" salad has apples, sunflower seeds, raisins, cheeses and salad items. The House plum dressing contains eggs (so be warned if you don't eat them). Has a good selection of vegetarian salads. Hummus, Cheese Quesadilla, Spanikopita, Indonesian Curried Rice, Lasagna, Thai Vegetables & Noodles, Sprouted Mushroom Sandwich is mushrooms, avocado and cheese on sunflower wheat bread. Lasagna. The salad with Lemon Tamari Dressing and bread is good. Fresh juices. No egg-free desserts.
Comments: Gets very high recommendations. Has a pleasant atmosphere. Comfortable and cozy place. Has a courtyard with fountains, gardens and statuary. Live music on the weekdays. Has several rooms. Has a patio in front facing Franklin Street. In the back is a glassed-in porch on a courtyard. Popular late night place with the hip. Used to be very vegetarian friendly, but no longer is that friendly.
Other Info: Full service, take-out. Accepts AMEX, DC, DIS, MC, VISA. Price: $$.
Directions: This place is in downtown Chapel Hill.

Silk Road Tea House

456 West Franklin Street; 919-942-1533
Hours: Tuesday to Sunday 3:30 pm to 12 am Closed Monday.
Middle Eastern Teahouse. Vegan friendly.
Menu: Turkish tea or coffee. Has over 70 teas. Just serves pastries and cookies, some of which are vegan.
Comments: Turkish atmosphere with rugs and artwork on walls. Relaxing, comfortable place. Plays world music. Helpful service. Happening atmosphere. Has low conches. Friendly staff. Place to hang out. Outdoor seating on the street.
Other Info: Counter service. Accepts DIS, MC, VISA. Price: $-$$.
Directions: From US 15-501 south, bear right onto Franklin St and continue into downtown. After the Columbia St intersection, on the right.

Thai Palace

1206 Raleigh Road, at NC 54; 919-967-5805;
Web site: http://thaipalace.citysearch.com/
Hours: Tuesday to Thursday, Sunday 5 pm to 9:30 pm; Friday & Saturday 5 pm to 10 pm; Closed Monday.
Thai. Not pure vegetarian.
Menu: Has a separate vegetarian menu. Most dishes can be made with tofu instead of meat.

Comments: A bit upscale. Uses fresh ingredients. Food gets rated as authentic and good.
Other Info: Full service, take-out, delivery. Accepts MC, VISA. Price: $$.
Directions: Take US 15-501 west from I-40 and take the NC 54 East exit. This place is in the Harris Teeter shopping center near the exit.

Whole Foods and The Penguin Cafe

81 South Elliott Road, at East Franklin, Chapel Hill; 919-968-1983
Web site: www.wholefoodsmarket.com
Hours: Daily 8 am to 9 pm;
Café Hours: Daily 7:30 am to 8 pm; Breakfast until 10:30 am on weekdays; Weekend Brunch until 2:30 pm.
Natural Food Store and Gourmet Deli. Salad Bar and Juice Bar. Supermarket-type place. Mostly Organic. Branch of Whole Foods Market.
Menu: Has a hot food counter with soups, vegetarian chili and other hot dishes. Fresh juice and smoothies. Espresso bar. Has a large amount of herbal hot and cold teas. Home baked breads.
Other Info: Cafeteria style, take-out. Has indoor and outdoor seating. Accepts AMEX, MC, VISA. Price: $$.
Directions: From I-40, take Rte 15/501 (exit #270) southwest towards Chapel Hill for about 1½ mile. At fork in road take right fork onto Franklin St and go a half-mile. At Elliot turn left and this place on left a block down.

CHARLOTTE

AJ Groceries

6140 East Independence Boulevard
704-563-6644
Indian Grocery Store.
Directions: Across from Rhodes Furniture (in Circuit City parking lot).

Berrybrook Farms Natural Foods Pantry

1257 East Boulevard, at Kenilworth Avenue
704-334-6528
Store Hours: Monday to Friday 9 am to 7 pm Saturday 9 am to 6 pm
Lunch Counter Hours: Monday to Saturday 11 am to 5 pm (4 pm on Saturday); closed Sunday.
Natural Food Store and Deli. Juice Bar. Not pure vegetarian, but mainly vegetarian. Vegan options. Organic produce.
Menu: Salads, soups, sandwiches, veggie burgers, tofu dogs, pizza with soy cheese and fresh juices. Specials change daily.
Comments: Food and service gets high recom-

mendations. Friendly place.

Other Info: Counter service, take-out only. Accepts DIS, MC, VISA. Price: $.

Directions: From I-277, take Kenilworth exit to East Blvd (going away from Charlotte). At East Blvd turn left. This place at intersection of East Blvd and Kenilworth. Across the street from a Circle K. From I-277, take Fourth St/NC-16 exit (#2A) towards Third St. At E 4th St/NC-16 turn left and go 1 block, at S McDowell St (NC-16) turn left and go a third-mile, at E Stonewall turn left (becomes Kenilworth Ave after a quarter-mile) and go 1¼ mile, at East Blvd turn right and this place is 1 block down at corner of Charlotte Drive.

Carolinas Medical Center

1000 Blythe Boulevard #506, Charlotte
704-355-2000

Hospital Cafeteria. Vegetarian-friendly. Not pure vegetarian.

Hours: 24 hours (vegetable section closes between 2:30 pm and 5:30 pm and at night)

Menu: The cafeteria serves vegetarian dishes such as black bean soup, vegetarian chili, veggie burgers and vegetable casserole.

Directions: Can get to this place by following the direction above for Berrybrook Farms.

Carolina Smoothies

1408 East Boulevard	704-358-0006
4517 Sharon Road	704-367-3435

Hours: Monday to Friday 8 am to 8 pm (until 9 pm on Friday)
Saturday & Sunday 9 am to 7 pm

Smoothie Bar. Fresh juices.

Menu: Great smoothies with fresh fruits, frozen yogurts and nutritional supplements. Peanut Butter Slam is chocolate, peanut butter, banana, soy milk and non-fat frozen yogurt. Light, healthy, good tasting food.

Home Economist Gourmet Market

5410 East Independence Blvd; 704-536-4663

Hours: Monday to Friday 9 am to 9 pm; Saturday 9 am to 8 pm; Sunday 11 am to 6 pm

Natural Food Store. Good selection of organic produce. Big place with a large selection of items.

Other Info: Accepts AMEX, MC, VISA.

Directions: From I-277, take the Independence Blvd exit and go southeast on Independence Blvd and this place is about 4 miles down.

House Of Chinese Gourmet

5622 Independence Boulevard; 704-563-8989

Hours: Monday to Thursday 11:30 am to 3 pm,

5 pm to 10 pm; Friday 11:30 am to 3 pm, 5 pm to 11 pm; Saturday 12 noon to 3 pm, 5 pm to 11 pm; Sunday 12 noon to 3 pm, 5 pm to 10 pm

Chinese. Not pure vegetarian. Vegan options.

Menu: Has over 20 vegetarian dishes. Soups, appetizers, tofu dishes and rice. Does not use MSG if requested.

Other Info: Full service, take-out. Accepts AMEX, MC, VISA. Price: $$.

India Palace

4515 East Independence Boulevard, at Sharon Amity; 704-568-7176

Hours: Thursday to Tuesday 11:30 am to 2:30 pm, 5 pm to 10 pm; Wednesday 5 pm to 10 pm

Indian. Lunch Buffet. Not pure vegetarian. Vegan options.

Menu: Has several vegetarian main dishes.

Comments: Good food and service.

Other Info: Full service, take-out, delivery. Accepts AMEX, DIS, MC, VISA. Price: $-$$.

International Groceries

5309-H East Independence Boulevard, beside Laser Quest; 704-531-7868

Indian and Middle Eastern Grocery Store.

Kelly's Café

3100 North Davidson Street, at East 34th Street
704-372-0103

Hours: Monday to Saturday 11 am to 10 pm
Sunday Brunch 11 am to 3 pm

Vegetarian International. Vegan options. Serves eggs. Not pure vegetarian.

Menu: Salads, sandwiches, main dishes, Portobello Stroganoff, Spinach Quesadillas (really good), burritos (recommended) and desserts. The Hummus Appetizer with artichoke hearts, Pimento Sandwich, pepper and olives is a full meal for some. Everything is homemade. The desserts are very good such as the Key Lime Pie.

Comments: Located in an arts district in an old restored house. Gets rated by some as the best vegetarian food in town. Friendly service and pleasant atmosphere. Everyone gives the place great reviews. Large portions. Everything is homemade. Reasonably priced.

Other Info: Reservations not necessary. Non-smoking. Cash only; no credit cards. Price: $-$$.

Directions: From I-85, take the Sugar Creek Rd exit (#41), then go south on Sugar Creek Rd for 1½ mile, at N Tryon St (NC-49, US-29) turn right (southwest) and go 1 mile, at 36th St turn left and go a half-mile, at N Davidson St turn right and this place is 2 blocks down at the corner of 34th St. Also from I-277, take exit #3C and go northeast on N Tryon St 1¼ mile, then at 30th St turn right and go a half-mile, then at N Davidson turn left and this place is a half-mile down.

La Plaz Cantina

1910 South Boulevard; 704-372-4168
Hours: Monday to Thursday 11:30 am to 2:30 pm, 5 pm to 10 pm; Friday 11:30 am to 2:30 pm, 5 pm to 11 pm; Saturday 4 pm to 11 pm; Sunday 4 pm to 10 pm
Mexican. Vegan options. Not pure vegetarian.
Menu: Tortillas, tamales and burritos. There is no lard or meat in the refried beans, black beans or rice. Non-alcoholic beer and wine. Veggie Black Bean Soups
Comments: Outside seating on patio. Friendly place.
Other Info: Full service. Accepts AMEX, DIS, MC, VISA. Price: $$.

The Peaceful Dragon

Mc Mullen Creek Market, 8324 Pineville Matthews Road No 509, Pineville; 704-544-1012; **Web site:** www.thepeacefuldragon.com
Hours: Lunch Monday to Friday 11:30 am to 3 pm, 5 pm to 9 pm; Monday to Friday select menu of sandwiches, salads and desserts; Saturday 11:30 am to 9 pm; Closed Sunday.
Full Vegetarian Asian. Mostly vegan. Asian grocery store.
Menu: Has good veggie dumplings, Silky Tofu, Kale, Veggie Ham Club Sandwich, Grilled Fish Steak, Cold Sesame Noodles and veggie burgers. Some desserts are ice creams (Ginger, Adzuki Red Bean, Green Tea), Mocha Cake and Mango Sorbets. Large selection of exotic teas.
Comments: Gets high recommendations. Dishes freshly made. Reasonable prices. No MSG. No unrefined sugar. Everything is homemade. Recommended.
Other features: Several classes are given here such as meditation, yoga, Tai chi, Kickboxing, Pakua, and Shaolin Kung Fu. Has a gift shops selling teapots, teas, CDs, Buddha statures, Feng Shui items, books, paintings, Tibetan prayers flags and much more.
Other Info: Reservations not necessary. Non-smoking. Accepts DIS, MC, VISA.
Directions: Next to Winn-Dixie. From I-485, take the NC-51 N exit (#64) towards Matthews, then go east on Pineville Matthews Rd (Rte 51) and this place is 1 mile down. This place is in the south part of town.

Talley's Green Grocery and Café Verde

Dilworth Gardens Shopping Center
1408-C East Boulevard, at Scott Avenue
704-334-9200; **Web site:** www.talleys.com
Hours: Monday to Saturday 7 am to 9 pm
Sunday 10 am to 7 pm
Natural Food Store and Restaurant. International. Salad Bar. Vegan options. Not pure vegetarian.
Large Natural Food Store and Deli. Salad Bar and Bakery. Has large grocery section, vitamin, vegetarian meat substitutes and natural medicines,
Menu: Has a large deli sections serving, soups, Lasagna, noodle dishes, veggie burgers, sandwiches, an excellent salad bar, sandwiches, steamed vegetables, pasta, tofu products, rice, desserts and other dishes. Has a great salad bar. Many different kinds of vegetarian sandwiches. Fresh juices.
Comments: It is quite a good place. Has weekly cooking classes and regular classes on Chinese medicine, meditation, alternative medicine, health subjects, acupressure, reflexology and other subjects. Regrettably serves meat. Have books and magazines. Recommended. It is one of the biggest natural food stores I have seen. Large produce departments. Basically has everything and is the size of regular supermarket. Have renetless cheeses.
Other Info: Cafeteria style, with a good amount of seating, take-out. Accepts AMEX, MC, VISA. Price: $-$$.
Directions: In the historic Dilworth section of Charlotte. From I-277, take Fourth St/NC-16 exit (#2A) towards Third St. At E 4th St/NC-16 turn left and go 1 block, at S McDowell St (NC-16) turn left and go a third-mile, at E Stonewall turn left (becomes Kenilworth Ave after a quarter-mile) and go 1¼ mile, At East Blvd turn left and this place is a block down on right in Dilworth Gardens Shopping Center.

**Woodlands

7128-A Albemarle Road
704-569-9193; **fax:** 704-569-9188
Hours: Tuesday to Thursday 11:30 am to 9:30 pm; Fri to Sun 11:30 am to 10 pm; closed Mon.
Fully Vegetarian South Indian.
Menu: Has a wide selection of vegetarian dishes. Dosas (a wide selection), Potato Bonda, samosas, Paneer Pakoras (very good), idly, uthappam, a good selection of rice dishes, Channa Batura, Poori Bhaji, Channa Masala, Vegetable Korma, Palak Paneer, Malai Kofta, Aloo Gobi, Indian breads, Mango Chutney, sambar, raita, salad, full

meal Woodland Special Dinner and South Indian Thali. Desserts such as gulabjumans, ice creams, Carrot Halava, Badam Halava. Mango lassi and chai.
Comments: Fairly efficient service. Good food. Has daily lunch specials.
Other Info: Full service, take-out. Price: $-$$.
Directions: From I-85, take West Harris Blvd exit, then go south for a few miles on West Harris Blvd, then at Albemarie Rd turn left and go a half-mile and this place is on the right in a small shopping plaza. From Independence coming from downtown Charlotte, turn left at Albemarie Road and go about 2 miles and this place is on the right about a half mile past W Harris Blvd. If you see the Wal-Mart on the left you went too far.

DAVIDSON

Home Economist Gourmet Market
261 Griffith Street
704-892-6191; **fax:** 704-892-8636
Hours: Monday to Saturday 9 am to 8 pm
Sunday 11 am to 6 pm
Natural Food Store and Deli.
Directions: From I-77, take Exit #30 towards Davidson/Davidson College and go east on Griffith St and this place is 1 mile down.

DURHAM

Anotherthyme
109 North Gregson Street; 919-682-5225
Hours: Monday to Friday 11:30 am to 2:30 pm; Monday to Thursday 6 pm to 9:30 pm; Friday & Saturday 6 pm to 10 pm; Sunday 6 pm to 9 pm
New American, Eclectic, International. Not pure vegetarian. No red meat is served.
Menu: Has vegetarian dishes, hummus, French Green Salad with cashews and avocado, Cheese Ravioli, veggie burritos and pastas. Fresh juices.
Comments: Managed by same people as Pyewacket in Chapel Hill. Food gets good recommendations. Good place for a romantic candle-lit dinner. A bit conservative. Good atmosphere. Gets mixed feelings about the service.
Other Info: Full service, take-out. Reservations may be a good idea on the weekends (may be full). Accepts AMEX, DIS, MC, VISA. Price: $$.
Directions: From Hwy 147 (Durham Freeway), take the Duke St exit and go north on Duke, after pasting Main Street, turn left onto Minerva Ave. Turn left at Gregson St and then this place is on the right before you reach Main Street. Can park in Brightleaf Square parking lot, across the street.

Blue Corn Mexican Restaurant
719 Ninth Street; 919-286-9600
Hours: Monday to Saturday 11:30 am to 9 pm Closed Sundays.
Mexican, Latin American. Vegetarian-friendly. Not pure vegetarian.
Menu: Has a good selection of vegetarian dishes. Vegetarian Fajita (sautéed zucchini, mushrooms, squash, peppers, onions with refried beans), Fried Plantains with Mango and Banana Sauce, Green Enchilada (spinach with corn enchilada), Spanish Rice and salads. Has several vegetarian choices for desserts such as Sopapilla (fried tortilla with cinnamon, honey & powdered sugar).
Comments: The food tastes really good. Not far from Duke University. Gets high recommendations. Good size portions. Interesting artwork and photographs on the walls.
Other Info: Accepts AMEX, DC, DIS, MC, VISA (at least $10). Price: $$.

China One
4325 Highway 55
919-361-3388; **Web site:** http://dinechina1.com/
Hours: Monday to Thursday 11 am to 2:30 pm, 4 pm to 10 pm; Friday 11 am to 2:30 pm, 5 pm to 10:30; Saturday & Sunday 11 am to 3 pm, 5 pm to 10:30 pm
Chinese. Vegan options. Not pure vegetarian. All-you-can-eat Buffet.
Comments: Popular, good place. Has authentic Chinese cuisine.
Other Info: Accepts AMEX, MC, VISA.

Durham Food Co-op
1101 West Chapel Hill Street; 919-490-0929
Hours: Monday to Saturday 10 am to 8 pm
Sunday 11 am to 7 pm
Natural Food Store. Organic produce. Free coffee for shoppers.
Other Info: Accepts AMEX, MC, VISA.
Directions: From I-85, take Gregson St exit, then go about 2 miles south on Gregson, at West Chapel Hill turn right. This place on left, at corner of Carroll and West Chapel Hill. From Hwy 147, take exit #13 and go west on Chapel Hill St and this place is a third-mile down.

Foster's Market
2694 Durham-Chapel Hill Boulevard, at Pickett Road, Durham; 919-489-3944
Web site: www.fostersmarket.com
Hours: Daily 7:30 am to 8 pm
Gourmet Store and Restaurant. Vegetarian-friendly. Not pure vegetarian.
Menu: Portobello sandwiches, salads, spinach

Ravioli and soups.
Comments: Has tables indoors and outdoors. Good place for a meal.
Other Info: Accepts AMEX, MC, VISA. Price: $.
Directions: From I-40, take the US 15-501 exit and go toward Durham. Go past South Square Mall and this place is on the left a little past the NC 751 overpass. On the border of Durham.

Greenhouse Café

2300 Chapel Hill Road, at Ward Street
919-489-5507
email: thegreenhousecafe@yahoo.com
Hours: Monday to Friday 11:30 am to 2:30 pm, 5:30 pm to 9 pm; Saturday 11:30 am to 2:30 pm, 6 pm to 9 pm; closed Sundays.
Vegetarian-friendly Café. New American. Vegan options. Not pure vegetarian.
Menu: Has a good selection of vegetarian dishes such as soups, a good variety of salads, sandwiches and main dishes. Parmesan Stuffed Mushrooms, Pumpkin Peanut soup, Greek Salad, Very Veggie Sub, Veggies over Rice, TLT (marinated tofu, lettuce, tomato on grilled herb bread; gets good ratings), Jerk Tofu with Coconut Jasmine Rice, Mushroom Veggie Burger, Mediterranean Pasta Salad, Black Bean Moussaka, Greek Salad and Linguine with Lemon Cream Sauce. Limited desserts and none for vegans.
Comments: Relaxing, cozy, comfortable, clean, casual place. Small seating area. Friendly service. A good choice for a nice meal. Gets good recommendations. Good, cheap food.
Other Info: Full service, take-out, catering. Accepts MC, VISA. Price: $-$$.
Directions: Next to the fire station. From I-85, take NC Hwy 147 exit (#172) and go south on Hwy 147 for 4 miles, take the Chapel Hill St exit (#13), then go west on W Chapel Hill St a half-mile, at Kent St turn left and go a third-mile, at Morehead Ave turn right and go a block, then at Chapel Hill Rd turn left (go southwest) and this place is ¾ mile down.

Pizza Inn (2 locations)

3906 Duke Street	471-1575
3648 Chapel Hill Boulevard	489-9109

Hours: Mon to Thur 11 am to 10 pm; Fri & Sat 11 am to 12 midnight; Sun 11 am to 11 pm
Pizza. Salad Bar. Not pure vegetarian.
Menu: Has pizzas, salads, soups and bread sticks. Has an inexpensive night buffet Monday to Wednesday.
Other Info: Accepts MC, VISA.

Saladelia Café

4201 University Drive; 919-489-5776
Hours: Monday to Thursday 10:30 am to 9:30 pm; Friday & Saturday 10:30 am to 10:30 pm; Sunday 11 am to 8 pm
Middle Eastern. Not pure vegetarian.
Menu: Has a good selection of vegetarian dishes. Hummus, Vegetarian Gyro, stuffed grape leaves, Eggplant Melt and good sandwiches.
Comments: Friendly staff. Sometimes has live jazz.
Other Info: Limited service, take-out. Accepts AMEX, DIS, MC, VISA. Price: $.
Directions: Take US 15-501 north to US 15-501 Business, then turn right onto Westgate Rd just after the underpass, follow Westgate till it ends, then turn left onto University. The restaurant is just past Pier One Imports on the right across from the South Square parking lot. Lots of parking available.

Wellspring Grocery (Whole Foods) and Penguin Cafeteria

621 Broad Street, between Main and Perry Streets
919-286-2290
Web site: www.wholefoodsmarket.com
Hours: Daily 9 am to 9 pm
Natural Food Store and Cafe. Deli, Bakery, Salad Bar and Juice Bar. Organic produce. Supermarket-type place. See Whole Foods Market on page WF.
Directions: From I-85, take Guess Rd exit south. Go right over tracks and get on Broad St and this place is on the right about 1½ mile down. From Durham Freeway (Hwy 147), take Swift Ave exit, then go north on Swift Ave a quarter-mile, going past Main and this place on left at Main and Broad.

GREENSBORO

Deep Roots Natural Market

3728 Spring Garden Street, between Wendover Avenue and Holden Road
336-292-9216
Web site: www.deeprootsmarket.com
Hours: Monday to Saturday 9 am to 8 pm
Sunday 12 noon to 7 pm
Natural Food Co-op. Organic produce.
Direction: Between Holden Rd and Wendover, not far from Old Cotton Mill Square. From I-40, take Wendover exit and go east at end of ramp onto Wendover Ave. Go about a mile and at Spring Gardens (first overpass) turn left. This place on left.

**Govinda's Vegetarian Restaurant

332 South Tate Street; 336-373-8809
Hours: Monday to Friday 11 am to 8 pm; Sunday Brunch 11 am to 2 pm; closed Saturday.
Fully Vegetarian International and Indian. Buffet. Vegan options.
Menu: Has rice dish, sandwiches and smoothies. Has Sunday brunch buffet with granola, scrambled tofu, vegan pancakes and more.
Comments: The food here is excellent and this place is highly recommended. Know the family who owns this place and they have been cooking gourmet food for years. Run by excellent people. Friendly, helpful service.
Other Info: Non-smoking. Buffet service, take-out. Accepts DIS, MC, VISA. Price: $.
Directions: From I-40, take the US-220 N exit (#122B) towards the Coliseum. Merge onto US-220 N (going northeast) and go 1 mile. Keep going straight onto Freeman Mill Rd and go 2½ miles, then take the Lee St exit, then turn left at W Lee St (US-29A) and go a third-mile, at Tate St turn right and go a half-mile and this place is on the left in a small downtown area near the university. This place is about ¾ mile from the Greenboro Coliseum.

Grape Vine Café and Juice Bar

Guilford Village, 435-B Dolley Madison Road
336-856-0070
Hours: Monday to Saturday 11 am to 8 pm (open to 8:30 pm); closed Sunday.
Fully Vegetarian International Natural Food Cafe. Mostly Vegan. Juice Bar.
Menu: Daily specials change daily. Soups, salads, sandwiches, burgers, chili, fresh baked bread, pita pockets, stews and main dishes. All vegan desserts. Non-alcoholic beer and wine. Fresh juices.
Comments: Pleasant café atmosphere. Art exhibits featuring local artists. Beautiful sunset views. Most food is vegan. Good vegan desserts. Has monthly theme dinner that features cuisines from around the world.
Other Info: Full service, cafeteria-style, take-out. Non-smoking. Accepts reservations but are not necessary. Accepts AMEX, DIS, MC, VISA. Price: $-$$.
Directions: From I-40, take the Guilford College/Jamestown exit (#213) and go northeast on Guilford College Rd for 2 miles (become College Rd), at Tomahawk Dr turn right and go a quarter-mile, then turn left at Dolley Madison Rd and this place is 100 yards down on the right side of the street behind the Pizza Hut, a half-mile before Friendly Ave, in the west part of town.

House of Health

1018 West Lee Street; 336-275-6840
Hours: Monday to Friday 10 to 6 pm; Sunday 10 am to 5 pm; closed Saturday
2500-A Battleground Avenue; 336-282-2010
Hours: Monday to Friday 10 am to 8 pm; Saturday 10 am to 6 pm; Sunday 11 am to 5 pm
Natural Food Store. Organic produce.
Other Info: Accepts AMEX, MC, VISA.

Jack's Corner Mediterranean Deli

1601 Spring Garden Street; 336-370-4400
Hours: Monday to Saturday 10:30 to 8:30 pm
Mediterranean Natural Foods Café. Vegan options. Not pure vegetarian.
Menu: Good amount of vegetarian dishes such as hummus and falafel. Has Mediterranean grocery items.
Comments: Good food and reasonable prices. Friendly place.
Other Info: Counter service, take-out. Accepts AMEX, MC, VISA.

**Joel's Natural Foods

Guilford Village Shopping Center
435 Dolley Madison Road, Suite C, Greensboro
336-855-6500
Hours: Monday to Friday 10 am to 9 pm; Saturday 10 am to 8 pm; Sunday 1 pm to 6 pm
Natural Food Store and Vegetarian Café. Organic produce.
Menu: Has a good selection of vegetarian items on the menu.
Comments: This place has a fair selection.
Other Info: Accepts AMEX, DIS, MC, VISA.
Directions: This place is next to the Grape Vine Café, above.

India Palace

413 Tate Street, near UNC; 336-379-0744
Hours: Daily 11:30 am to 3 pm, 5 pm to 10 pm
Indian. Vegan options. Not pure vegetarian.
Menu: Has a wide selection of vegetarian dishes such as soups, Indian breads, appetizers and main dishes.
Comments: Good food and prices. Uses a Tandoor over. Pleasant service.

HENDERSONVILLE

The Fresh Market

213 Greenville Highway
704-693-8223
Hours: Monday to Saturday 8 am to 9 pm
Sunday 10 am to 8 pm

Natural Food Store and Deli. Organic produce. **Other Info:** Counter service, take-out. Has a bench outside to sit at.
Directions: From I-26, take the US-64 exit (#18B) towards Hendersonville and go 2 miles southwest, at Church St (US 250) turn left and this place is a half-mile down.

Hendersonville Community Co-op–Life's Best Market
715-B Old Spartanburg Highway; 828-693-0505
Hours: Monday to Friday 9 am to 7 pm; Saturday 9 am to 6 pm; Sunday 12 noon to 5 pm
Natural Food Store and Deli. Organic produce.
Directions: From I-26, take Upward Road exit. Go right onto Spartanburg Hwy (176), then go for a while going over a bridge. At Old Spartanburg Hwy turn right. This place on left one block down.

RALEIGH

Dalat
Valley Shopping Center, 2109 Avent Ferry Road
919-832-7449
Hours: Mon to Thur 11 am to 3 pm, 5 pm to 9 pm; Fri & Sat 11 am to 3 pm, 5 pm to 10 pm
Vietnamese. Vegan-friendly.
Menu: Some vegetarian dishes.
Comments: Service and food is good. Low on décor. Popular place. One of the best Vietnamese places in town. Gets really good recommendations from customers.
Other Info: Accepts MC, VISA. Price: $.
Directions: Take the Beltline south to the Western Avenue East exit, then take Western to Avent Ferry Road. This place is in the lower level of the Mission Valley Shopping Center. Across from the Mission Valley Inn, near McKimmon Center and NCSU.

518 West Italian Café
518 West Jones, at Glenwood Avenue
919-829-2518
Hours: Mon to Thur 11:30 am to 2:30 pm, 5 pm to 9:30 pm; Fri & Sat 11:30 am to 2:30 pm, 5 pm to 10:30 pm; Sun 5 pm to 9:30 pm
Italian. Not pure vegetarian.
Menu: Pastas, pizzas, eggplant sandwich, calzones and salads.
Comments: A trendy, happening place. Popular with locals. Food gets good ratings. Very popular place and there can be a very long wait on Friday and Saturday nights. Has a kid's menu. Service is good, but can be a bit slow sometimes (especially

when crowded).
Other Info: Accepts AMEX, DC, DIS, MC, VISA. No reservations. Price: $$.
Directions: From I-440, take Glenwood Ave/Hwy 70 exit and go east on Glenwood Ave. At W Jones St (2 blocks after Peace St) turn left and this place is at the corner.

Harmony Farms
Creedmoor Crossing Shopping Center, 5653 Creedmoor Road; 919-782-0064
Hours: Monday to Friday 10 am to 7 pm; Saturday 10 am to 6 pm; Sunday 1 pm to 6 pm
Natural Food Store and Vegetarian-friendly Deli. Vegan options. Not pure vegetarian. Some organic produce.
Menu: Sandwiches, deli dishes and some hot dishes.
Comments: The Creedmoor Road location has a small restaurant.
Other Info: Accepts MC, VISA.
Directions: From I-440, take Glenwood Avenue exit (#7A) and then go northwest on Glenwood Ave past Crabtree Valley Mall about ¾ mile. At Creedmoor Road turn right and this place is 1 mile down in the Creedmoor Crossing Shopping Center.

Irregardless Café
901 West Morgan Street, near NCSU
919-833-9920
Web site: http://irregardless.citysearch.com/
Hours: Monday to Friday 11:30 am to 2:30 pm, 5:30 pm to 9:30 pm; Saturday 5:30 pm to 10 pm; Sunday 10 am to 2:30 pm
American. Not pure vegetarian. Vegan options marked on menu. Has a new menu daily.
Menu: Soups, homemade yogurt, hummus & hot pita, curried lentil, Asian Phyllo Pocket (tofu and stir-fry vegetables), Bean Burger, Swiss Cheese Sandwich, California Pocket Sandwich, Vegetable Chowder with Cheddar, several salads, Tabbouleh Salad Platter and Pasta Provencal (penne pasta with vegetables). Apple Crisp and Chocolate Chambord Pie for dessert. Sunny Pasta Sauté is pasta with artichoke hearts, tomatoes and other vegetables with a vinaigrette sauce. Spinach and Corn Enchiladas with ricotta cheese. Spinach Rollatini is pasta with spinach, mushrooms and three types of cheese. Fresh baked breads and good desserts. Locally roasted coffee. Cappuccino, espresso.
Comments: Phone 833-9920 to hear the menu of the day recording. Gets high ratings in local vegetarian food surveys and good reviews in local

publications. Casual, friendly, relaxed atmosphere. Live jazz music nightly six days a week. Pleasant place. Has two separate dining areas, one is casual and the other is more upscale with a piano players. Not as vegetarian friendly as it used to be. May have only one vegan main dish. **Other Info:** Full service, take-out. Non-smoking. Accepts AMEX, DC, DIS, MC, VISA. Price $$. **Directions:** From I-440, take the Hillsborough St exit (I-440) towards the downtown. After passing the NC State's campus go about ¾ mile, then bear right onto W Morgan St and this place is 2 blocks down on the right. Near Charlie Goodnight's Comedy Club, which is well-known.

Lilly's Pizza

1813 Glenwood Avenue, Five Points
919-833-0226
Hours: Sunday to Thursday 11 am to 10 pm Friday & Saturday 11 am to 11 pm
Gourmet Pizza. Vegetarian and vegan options.
Menu: Toppings include: soy mozzarella, broccoli, zucchini, spinach, eggplant, roasted peppers, artichoke hearts, pistachio nuts, pine nuts, sundried tomatoes, peaches, mandarin oranges and apples. Has a mushroom and feta pizza. Spinach, pesto and mozzarella calzone.
Comments: Free delivery and take-out. No atmosphere for eating at the place. Casual. Mainly just a take-out place. Pizza gets excellent ratings. Excellent service. Happening, hip place.
Other Info: Accepts AMEX, MC, VISA. Price: $.

Nur Grocery & Deli

2233 Avent Ferry Road; 919-828-1523
Hours: Daily 11 am to 9 pm
Middle-Eastern. Not pure vegetarian.
Menu: Pretty good falafel and good baklava.
Comments: Has a Middle Eastern grocery. Friendly staff. Reasonable prices.
Directions: Near Record Exchange in Mission Valley Mall

Second Nature Café

3201 Edwards Mill Road, at Duraleigh Road
919-571-3447
Hours: Monday to Friday 8:30 am to 9 pm; Saturday 8:30 am to 5 pm; closed Sundays.
Restaurant. Not pure vegetarian.
Menu: Has vegetarian and organic options. Soups, salads, veggie chili and sandwiches.
Comments: Relaxed place.
Other Info: Full service, take-out, delivery. Accepts DIS, MC, VISA.

Directions: From the I-440 Beltline, take the Glenwood Avenue west exit (US 70), go past Crabtree Valley Mall, then turn left at the first light onto Edwards Mill. Then this place is on the corner of Duraleigh and Edwards Mill next to Harris Teeter.

Simple Pleasures Market & Café

Glenwood Village Shopping Village
2923 Essex Circle
919-782-9227
Web site: http://simplepleasures.citysearch.com/
Store Hours: Monday to Saturday 10 am to 6 pm; Sunday 10 am to 3 pm
Café Full Lunch Hours: Monday to Friday 11 am to 2:30 pm; Saturday Brunch: 10 am to 2:30 pm; Sunday Brunch 10 am to 2 pm
Natural Food Store and Café. Not pure vegetarian. Gourmet foods.
Menu: Salads, soups, sandwiches, fries, Vegetable Plate, cheese quesadilla, Grilled Vegetable Sandwich and pastas. Gourmet coffees.
Other Info: Full service, take-out, catering. Accepts AMEX, DC, MC, VISA. Price: $-$$.
Directions: From I-440 Beltway, take the Lake Boone Trail exit (#5), then go east on Lake Boone Trail for 1½ mile, at Glenwood Ave turn slight right and this place is 1 block down in the Glenwood Village Shopping Village.

Sunflower's Sandwich Shop

315 Glenwood Street
at W Lane Street, downtown
Five Points neighborhood
919-833-4676
Hours: Monday to Friday 11 am to 3 pm; Saturday 11:30 am to 2:30 pm; closed Sundays.
Sandwich Shop. Not pure vegetarian.
Menu: Half of their menu is vegetarian. Homemade vegetarian soups, hummus, sandwiches and salads on the menu.
Comments: Pleasant atmosphere.
Other Info: Cash or check; no credit cards.
Directions: From the beltline (I-440), take Glenwood Avenue exit (#7), then go southeast on Glenwood Ave to the downtown and this place for 1½ mile down.

**Third Place Coffeehouse

1811 Glenwood Avenue
919-834-6566
Hours: Monday to Friday 6 am to 12 midnight Saturday & Sunday 7:30 am to 12 midnight
Vegetarian Coffeehouse. Vegan-friendly.
Menu: Has excellent coffee. Has good vegetarian

sandwiches such as hummus, peanut butter & honey and tabbouleh sandwiches. Organic corn chips. Vegan cookies. Cappuccino, espresso. **Comments:** Small, dimly lit place. Has comfortable couches. Has art by locals hung on the walls. Food and coffee gets really high ratings. Get rated by many as the best coffee shop in the triangle area. Excellent service. Good outdoor seating. Indoor seating at tables and couches. Interesting customers. Friendly place. Many people are of the opinion that this is the best vegetarian restaurant in the area. Recommended. Happening, cool place.
Other Info: No credit card; cash only.
Directions: From I-440, take Glenwood Ave exit (#7) southeast towards the downtown. This place is located at Five Points on the left.

Wellspring Grocery
Ridgewood Shopping Center
3540 Wade Avenue
919-828-5805
Web site: www.wholefoodsmarket.com
Hours: Daily 9 am to 9 pm
Café opens for breakfast at 7:30 am
Natural Food Store and Cafe. Juice Bar and Salad Bar.
Menu: Have a deli and a hot food counter with one or two entrees and a couple of soups. Really good vegetarian chili.
Comments: Gourmet and expensive. Price: $$.
Directions: From I-440 Beltline, take Wade Ave exit (#4A). This place is a half-mile east of I-440 in the Ridgewood Shopping Center, at corner of Ridge Ave and Wade Ave.

SYLVA

Lulu's on Main
612 Main Street
828-586-8989
Hours: Monday to Thursday 11 am to 8 pm; Friday Saturday 11:30 am to 9 pm; closed Sunday.
American Gourmet. Not pure vegetarian.
Menu: Has a vegetarian special nightly and several vegetarian dishes. Fresh grilled Portabella Mushrooms, Tofu Satay, vegetarian Black Bean Chili, organic Blue Chips & Salsa, Spinach Basil Pesto Pita, Hummus with Pita, Veggie Chef Salad, Tofu Nan, Black Beans & Saffron Rice, burritos and desserts.
Other Info: Reservations not necessary. Smoking permitted outside. Accepts DIS, MC, VISA. Price: $$.

WILMINGTON

Doxey's Market & Café
Landfall Shopping Center, 1319 Military Cutoff Road; 910-256-9952
Hours: Monday to Saturday 9 am to 7 pm; Saturday 12 noon to 6 pm; Soup and Salad Bar is open on Saturday, but the café is closed Saturday. Closed Sunday.
Natural Food Store and Café. Deli, Juice Bar and Salad Bar. Vegan friendly. Good selection of organic produce.
Menu: Soups, sandwiches, rice & bean, veggie chili and pastas dishes.
Comments: Friendly place.
Other Info: Accepts AMEX, DIS, MC, VISA. Has seating.
Directions: Just off Hwy 74/76 (Military Cutoff). This place on right in Landfall Shopping Center. Take I-40 until it ends (becomes NC Hwy 132) and follow signs to Wrightsville Beach, then take Eastwood Rd to Military Cutoff. This place then on left in Landfall Shopping Center. This place is 5 miles due east of downtown Wilmington.

Tidal Creek Food Co-op
4406 Wrightsville Avenue; 910-799-2667
Hours: Monday to Saturday 9 am to 8 pm Sunday 12 noon to 6 pm
Natural Food Store. Organic produce. Vegan-friendly.
Comments: Plans to get a deli in the future. Friendly place. Non-profit.
Other Info: Accepts AMEX, MC, VISA.
Directions: Take I-40 until it ends and it becomes College Rd (Hwy 132) and go about 5 miles south. At Wrightsville Ave turn right and this place is 2 blocks down on the left. This place is about 2 miles east of downtown Wilmington.

WINSTON-SALEM

Whole Foods Market
75 Miller Street; 336-722-9233
Hours: Daily 9 am to 9 m
Natural Food Store and Cafe. Deli, Bakery, Salad Bar and Juice Bar. Organic produce. Supermarket-type place. See Whole Foods Market information.
Directions: From I-40, take Stratford Road North ((#3B) and go a third-mile northeast on Stratford Rd, then at Miller St turn right and this place is a quarter-mile down.

North Dakota

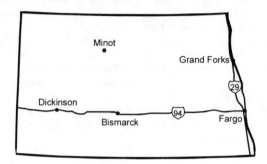

BISMARCK

Amazing Co-op
609 Memorial Highway; 701-775-4542
Hours: Monday to Friday 9 am to 8 pm; Saturday 9 am to 6 pm; Sunday 12 noon to 6 pm
Natural Food Store and Deli. Organic vegetables Wednesday to Friday.
Menu: Baked breads, soups (mostly vegan) and sandwiches. No meat in deli.
Other Info: Accepts MC, VISA.
Directions: From I-94, take Bismarck exit south into town about a third-mile. At E Divide Ave go west (turn left) towards the river and go about a mile. At Washington turn left (go south) and go about 1½ mile and at Memorial Hwy turn right. This place on left a half-mile down.

Earth Pantry
Kirkwood Mall Shopping Center
738 Kirkwood Mall
701-258-7987
Hours: Monday to Friday 10 am to 9 pm
Saturday 10 am to 7 pm
Sunday 12 noon to 6 pm
Natural Food Store. No produce.
Directions: This place off Bismarck Expressway in south Bismarck.

Green Earth Café
208 East Broadway Street
701-223-8646
Hours: Monday 7 am to 4 pm
Tuesday to Sunday 7 am to 9 pm
International Natural Foods. A coffeehouse-style place. Not pure vegetarian.

Menu: Veggie burgers, salads, sandwiches and a daily vegetarian special. Most of the baked goods contain eggs. Everything is freshly made.
Other Info: Limited service, catering, take-out. Price: $.
Directions: From I-94, get on I-194 (Exit #156) and go south a mile, then head east on Bus-Hwy 94 about 2 miles. Then at 2nd St turn left and go one block down, then at E Broadway Ave turn right and this place is right near the corner.

Terry's Health Products
801 East Main Avenue
701-223-1026
Hours: Monday to Friday 9 am to 6 pm
Saturday 9 am to 3 pm
Closed Sunday.
Natural Food Store.
Directions: From I-94, take Hwy 83 (#159) exit south about 1½ mile. At Main Ave turn left and this place on right.

DICKINSON

Natural Health
KDIX Radio Building
119 2nd Avenue West
701-225-6614
Hours: Monday to Friday 9:30 am to 6 pm
Saturday 9 am to 3 pm
Closed Sunday.
Natural Food Store. No produce.
Directions: From I-94, take Hwy 22 exit (#61) and go south on Hwy 22. At 2nd St turn left and go 1 block. Then at 2nd Avenue turn right and then this place is on the right.

FARGO

Swanson Health Products
109 North Broadway
701-293-9842
Hours: Monday to Friday 9 am to 6 pm
Saturday 9 am to 5 pm
Closed Sunday.
Natural Food Store. Organic produce (gets it on Thursday)
Other Info: Accepts MC, VISA.
Directions: From I-94, take University Drive exit (#351) north about 2 miles. At 2nd Avenue go east 7 blocks (half-mile), then at Broadway turn right. This place is one block down.

Tocchi Products
1111 2nd Avenue North
701-232-7700
Hours: Monday to Saturday 10 am to 6 pm (until 8 pm on Thursday); closed Sunday.
Natural Food Store. Seasonal limited organic produce.
Directions: From I-94, take University Avenue north exit and go about 2 miles north on University Ave to 13th Avenue south, where you turn right. This place is 1½ block east of University on 2nd Ave S.

GRAND FORKS

Amazing Grains Natural Food Market
214 Demers
701-775-4542; **Web site:** http://csf.colorado.edu/co-op/amazing.html
Hours: Monday to Saturday 9 am to 6 pm
Sunday 12 pm to 6 pm
Natural Food Store. Limited organic vegetables. Ready-made sandwiches. Baked goods. Baked bread Sunday.
Other Info: Accepts AMEX, DIS, MC, VISA.
Directions: From Hwy 2, go south on Bus-Hwy 81 a half-mile, then at 9th Avenue turn right and this place on right three blocks down.

MINOT

The Magic Mill
115 South Main
701-852-4818
Hours: Monday to Saturday 10 am to 5:30 pm
Closed Sunday.
Natural Food Store. Limited organic produce.
Directions: From Hwy 83, at Bardock go east two blocks, then at Main turn left and this place is three block down in the center of downtown, a little north of Trinity Hospital.

Oklahoma

1. Enid
2. Norman
3. Oklahoma City
4. Tulsa

NORMAN

Where Oklahoma University is located.

Dodson's Health Food

301 Main Street; 405-329-4613
Hours: Monday to Friday 9 am to 6 pm; Saturday 9 am to 6 pm; closed Sunday.
Natural Food Store. Has a decent selection of items. No deli.
Directions: From I-35, take Main St exit and then go east one mile and this place is on the left.

The Earth Natural Foods & Deli

309 South Flood Street; 405-364-3551
Hours: Monday to Friday 9 am to 7 pm; Saturday 9 am to 6 pm; Sunday 12 noon to 5 pm
Natural Food Store and Deli. No seating.
Directions: From I-35, go east on Main St towards the downtown about a mile. At Flood turn right and this place on left three blocks down.

OKLAHOMA CITY

Akin's Natural Foods Market

Mayfair Place Center, 2924 NW 63rd Street, at North May, near Lake Hefner; 405-843-3033
Hours: Monday to Saturday 9 am to 9 pm
Sunday 10 am to 6 pm
Natural Food Store and Deli. Juice Bar and Bakery. Has a large organic produce section.
Menu: Has a good selection of vegetarian dishes.
Comments: Has a good book section. Accepts AMEX, DIS, MC, VISA.
Directions: From I-44, take 63rd Street exit and go west on 63rd St. Then go about 3 miles down and this place is on the left in a small shopping center.

Gopuram Taste of India

4559 NW 23rd Street; 405-948-7373
Hours: Daily 11 am to 10 pm
Indian. Know for its vegetarian dishes. Not pure vegetarian. Vegan options.
Menu: North and South Indian. Has a selection of vegan and vegetarian dishes.
Comments: Vegetarian buffet every Wednesday night. Often has live sitar music in the evening. Upscale place.
Other Info: Full service, take-out, catering. Accepts AMEX, DIS, MC, VISA. Price: $-$$.

Grateful Bean Café

1039 North Walker Street, near the Federal Building; 405-236-3503
Hours: Monday to Friday 7 am to 5 pm
Closed Saturday & Sunday.
American. Not pure vegetarian.
Menu: Several vegetarian options on the menu. Has Bean Burger, Tofu Scramble and Powerhouse Veggie.
Other Info: Full service, catering, take-out. Accepts AMEX, DISC, MC, VISA. Price: $$.
Directions: This place is about a mile north of I-40 and a mile west of I-235. From I-235, take Exit 1E, then go west on NW 7th St 1¼ mile, then turn right at N Walker St and this place is 2½ blocks down.

Miriwa Restaurant

825 NW 23rd Street; 405-524-6158
Hours: Wednesday to Monday 11 am to 10 pm
Tuesday to 11 am to 3 pm
Chinese and Vietnamese. Not pure vegetarian.
Menu: Has a selection of vegetarian dishes.
Other Info: Accepts AMEX, MC, VISA.

Sala Thai
1614 NW 23rd Street; 405-528-8424
Hours: Monday to Friday 11 am to 9 pm; Saturday 5 pm to 10 pm; closed Sunday.
Thai. Vegan options. Not pure vegetarian.
Menu: Has a good selection of vegetarian dishes. Can make most dishes on the menu without meat. Salads, noodle dishes and rice dishes. Has a buffet.
Comments: Can have food on 1 to 5 scale of spicy hot. Has good-size portions. Gets good recommendations.
Other Info: Full service, take-out. No credit cards; cash only. Price: $$.

TULSA

Akin's Natural Foods Market
Newport Square Shopping Center, 3321 East 31st, at Harvard; 918-742-6630
Hours: Monday to Saturday 9 am to 8 pm
Sunday 12 noon to 6 pm
Directions: From I-44, get on US-64 going west towards Broken Arrow/Bartlesville, then take Harvard exit and go south on Harvard Ave about 1 mile, at 31st turn left and this place is a half-block down on left in Newport Square Shopping Center.
Fontana Shopping Center, 7807 East 51st, at Memorial; 918-663-4137
Hours: Monday to Saturday 9 am to 9 pm
Sunday 12 noon to 6 pm
Directions: This place is about 5 miles northwest of downtown Tulsa. From I-44 take Rte 97 north 5 miles. At 51st Street turn right and go about 2 miles. This place on right in Fontana Shopping Center. From I-64, take E 45th St (Rte 97) exit and go south 4 miles. At 51st Street turn left and go about 2 miles. This place on right in Fontana Shopping Center. From I-244, take exit 1A (W 51st St S, same as Gilcrease Exwy) and then go west on 51st St for 3 miles west and this place is on the left.
Natural Food Store. Organic produce. Supermarket-type place.

Bangkok Restaurant
3313 East 32nd Place; 918-743-9669
Hours: Monday to Saturday 11 am to 9 pm
Closed Sunday.
Thai. All-you-can-eat Buffet. Not pure veg.
Menu: Vegetables & Coconut Milk, curry vegetables, rice and Pad Thai Pak (oriental vegetables and ground peanuts). Any main dish on the menu can be made without meat.
Comments: No MSG. Full service. Accepts

AMEX, DC, MC, VISA. Price: $$.

Big Al's Subs & Health Foods
3303 East 15st Street
918-744-5080
Hours: Monday to Friday 10 am to 7 pm; Saturday 11 am to 4 pm; closed Sunday.
Deli. Vegetarian-friendly. Vegan options. Not pure vegetarian.
Menu: Has separate vegetarian menu. Has a good selection of vegetarian dishes. Sandwiches, Veggie Loaf, soups, salads, subs and burritos. Fresh juices and smoothies.
Other Info: Counter service, take-out. Has some seating. Non-smoking. Price: $.
Directions: This place is 4 blocks west of Tulsa State Fairground. From I-64, take 15th St exit and this place is about ¾ mile down on right, at junction with S Harvard Ave.

Casa Laredo
1114 East 41st; 918-743-3744
Hours: Monday to Saturday 11 am to 10 pm
Sunday 12 noon to 9 pm
Mexican. Not pure vegetarian.
Menu: Several vegetarian dishes on menu. Says lard and rice do not contain any meat products.
Comments: Good atmosphere. Friendly place. Live music six days a week.
Other Info: Accepts AMEX, DIS, MC, VISA. Full service, take-out. Price: $-$$.

Casa Laredo
6526 East 51st Street; 918-610-0086
Hours: Monday to Saturday 11 am to 10 pm
Closed Sunday.
Second branch of above.

Cedar's Deli
2606 South Sheridan Rd, at 26th Street
918-835-5519
Hours: Monday to Wednesday, Saturday 9:30 am to 5 pm; Thursday & Friday 9:30 am to 8 pm; closed Sunday.
Deli. Vegan options. Not pure vegetarian.
Menu: Vegetarian soups, sandwiches, falafel, Sampler Veggie Dinner, Lentil Soup and Cabbage Roll.
Comments: Has a selection of natural food items.
Other Info: Limited service, catering. Price: $.
Directions: From I-44, take Exit 51 for US-64 and go west on US-64 a half-mile, take Sheridan exit and then turn right at S Sheridan Rd (go north) and this place is 6/10 mile down on the left.

India Palace

6963 South Lewis Avenue
918-492-8040
Hours: Daily 11 am to 2:30 pm, 5 pm to 10 pm
Indian. Not pure vegetarian.
Menu: Has a large selection of vegetarian dishes.
Comments: Good food and atmosphere.
Other Info: Full service, take-out, delivery. Accepts AMEX, DIS, MC, VISA. Price: $$.

Wild Oats Market

1401 East 41st Street, at Peoria; 918-712-7555
Hours: Daily 8 am to 10 pm
Natural Food Store and Deli. Bakery. Organic produce. Supermarket-type place.
Directions: From I-44, take Riverside Dr (Exit 226A), at Riverside Dr go north about a mile, at 41st St turn right and this place is a half-mile down on left.

Ohio

1. Akron
2. Athens
3. Berea
4. Bevis
5. Canton
6. Cincinnati
7. Cleveland
8. Cleveland Heights
9. Columbus
10. Cuyahoga Falls
11. Dayton
12. Fairfield
13. Holland
14. Independence
15. Kent
16. Kettering
17. Lakewood
18. Miamisburg
19. Mayfield
20. Middleburg
21. Norwood
22. Oberlin
23. Solon
24. South Euclid
25. Springdale
26. Springfield
27. Tallmadge
28. Toledo
29. Troy
30. Upper Arlington
31. Willoughby
32. Yellow Springs
33. Youngstown

AKRON

Aladdin's Eatery
782 West Market
330-535-0110; Web site: www.alladinseatery.com
Middle Eastern. Not pure vegetarian. See Columbus.

Co-op Market
1831 West Market Street; 330-869-2590
Hours: Monday to Wednesday 9 am to 7 pm; Thur to Sat 9 am to 9 pm; Sun 12 noon to 6 pm
Natural Food Store.
Directions: From I-77, take White Pond exit (#132). Head north past railroad tracks for a half-mile. At Frank turn right and go a half-mile, then at Market (Rte 18) turn right and this place is on the right a half-mile down.

Mustard Seed Market
3885 West Market Street
330-666-7333; **Toll Free:** 888-476-2379

Store Hours: Monday to Thursday 9 am to 9 pm; Friday and Saturday 9 am to 10 pm; Sunday 10 am to 6 pm
Café Hours: Lunch: Monday to Saturday 11 am to 4 pm; Sunday Brunch 10:30 am to 3 pm
Dinner Hours: Monday to Thursday 4 pm to 8 pm; Friday and Saturday 4 pm to 9 pm
Large Natural Food Store and Café. Deli, Bakery and Juice Bar. Large organic produce section. Vegan and macrobiotic options. Not pure vegetarian, but is mostly.
Menu: Marks vegan and vegetarian dishes on menu. Has a good take-out section in the food store including a good salad bar, hummus sandwiches, cakes and much more. Soy cheese can replace regular cheese on request. Nachos, Grilled Portobello Mushrooms, Middle East Feast, selection of salads, rice, Vegetarian Tempeh Reuben, House Organic Greens, vegetarian wraps, Eggplant Napoleon, Nachos & Beans, Vegetarian Bean Enchilada, quesadilla, soups, Vegetarian Stir-fry, Macrobiotic Plate, organic brown rice and

vegetable of the day. Fresh juices.
Comments: This is a large supermarket type natural food store with a good-sized restaurant on the second floor. The organic produce section is like a large supermarket's produce section. Offers several classes on subjects such as cooking, aromatherapy, baking, massotherapy, Introduction to Feng Shui and several other subjects.
Other Info: Full service, take-out, catering. Accepts MC, VISA. Price: $$.
Directions: From I-77, take #136 for Rte 18 (Market St) and go east on Market St for a half-mile and this place on left in West Market Plaza.

ANDERSON (Cincinnati suburb)

Susan's Natural World
8315 Beechmont Avenue; 513-474-4990
Hours: Monday to Friday 10 am to 8 pm; Saturday 10 am to 6 pm; Sunday 12 noon to 5 pm
Natural Food Store and Restaurant. Juice Bar.
Menu: Two vegetarian soups daily. Sandwiches include: hummus, Garden Burger, Marinated Tofu Cutlet, Okara Burger Salad, Eggless Egg and vegetable sandwich. Sandwiches are served on a variety of organic breads and with chips. Seasonal fruits and salads. Fresh juices and smoothies (made with yogurt or flavored Spirutein). Organic coffee and herb teas.
Directions: From I-275, take Exit #65, then go west on Rte 125 and this place is 1¼ mile down.

ATHENS

Casa Nueva
4 West State Street
740-592-2016
Monday to Thursday 8 am to 2:30 pm, 5 pm to 9 pm (10 pm on Fridays); Saturday 9 am to 2:30 pm, 5 pm to 10 pm; Sunday 9 am to 2:30 pm; Serves breakfast or lunch until 4 pm
Mexican. Not pure vegetarian.
Menu: Has many vegetarian dishes. Daily brunch. Has a children menu.
Comments: Good food and breakfasts. Month long art exhibits. Local organic produce used when possible. Good place for people watching. Eclectic décor. Has a herb garden. Hardwood floor. Seating for 70 people. Comfortable, relaxed place. Visible kitchen. Has live music. Dancing.
Other Info: Full service, take-out. Does not accept reservations. Smoking allowed in bar. Accepts DIS, MC, VISA. Price: $$.
Directions: Court Street goes through the middle of Athens near the University. This place is on west State St, opposite the BP.

BEREA (Cleveland south suburb)

Nam Wah
392 West Bagley Road; 440-243-8181
Hours: Mon to Thur 11:30 am to 10 pm; Fri 11:30 am to 12 midnight; Sat 12 noon to 12 midnight; Sun 12 noon to 10pm
Chinese & Vietnamese. Not pure vegetarian.
Menu: Has a vegetarian menu including Lo Mien Curry, fried rice, noodles and several other dishes.
Other Info: Full service, take-out. Accepts AMEX, DC, MC, VISA. Price: $.

BEVIS (Cincinnati suburb)

Cincinnati Natural Foods
9268 Colerain Avenue; 513-385-7000
Hours: Monday to Friday 10 am to 8 pm; Saturday 10 am to 6 pm; Sunday 12 noon to 5 pm
Natural Food Store.
Other Info: Accepts AMEX, MC, VISA.

BLUE ASH (Cincinnati suburb)

Healthy's Health Food
9525 Kenwood Rd, Blue Ash; 513-984-1333
Hours: Monday to Friday 9:30 am to 7 pm; Saturday 9:30 am to 6:30 pm; closed Sunday.
Natural Food Store.

CANTON

Aladdin's Eatery
4633 Belden Village; 330-493-7700
Hours: Sunday to Thursday 11 am to 9:30 pm; Friday & Saturday 11 am to 11 pm
Middle Eastern. Not pure vegetarian. See Columbus.

Mulligan's
4118 Belden Village Street; 330-493-8239
Hours: Mon to Thur 11 am to 1 am; Fri & Sat 11 am to 2:30 am; Sun 11 am to 12 midnight
American. Vegan options. Not pure vegetarian.
Menu: Has a separate vegetarian menu. Soups, vegetarian chili, Gardenburgers (some contain eggs), pasta dishes, veggie hot dogs, Rice & Black Beans, salads, pastas and burritos.
Comments: Old-fashioned pub.
Other Info: Full service, take-out. Accepts AMEX, MC, VISA. Price: $.

CINCINNATI

Ambar India Restaurant
350 Ludlow Avenue, Clifton Heights

513-281-7000
Hours: Monday to Friday 11:30 am to 2:30 pm,
5 pm to 10 pm; Saturday 11:30 am 2:30 pm, 5
pm to 10:30 pm; Sunday 12:00 noon to 9 pm
North Indian. Not pure vegetarian
Menus: Has a good selection of vegetarian items
on the menu. Aloo Vindaloo (potatoes in a spicy
sweet sauce), vegetable samosa, Naan, vegetable
pakoras, paneer pakoras, Aloo Tikka, Assorted
Vegetable Platter, Rice Pilaf, Saag Choley (spinach and chickpea in tomato sauce), Malai Kofta,
Aloo Mattar and more. Has a Vegetarian Thali
meal.
Comments: Spicy, good food. Attentive service.
Bargain prices. Casual atmosphere. Has chandeliers and white tablecloths. They rate the food on
how spicy it is. Authentic décor with paintings.
Other Info: Full service, take-out, catering, delivery. Non-smoking. Accepts AMEX, DIS, MC,
VISA. Price: $$.
Directions: From I-75 S, take the US 52/Hppple
St Exit, (#3), then go towards US-27 S/US-127
S, turn left onto Hopple St, take a slight left onto
Martin Luther King Dr, Turn slight left onto
Clifton Colony Dr which becomes Morrison Ave,
turn right on Lowell Ave, turn left at Whitfield
Ave, then turn right at Ludlow Ave.

Arnold's Bar & Grill

210 East 8th Street
513-421-6234; **Web page:** http://cincinnati.com/
dining/arnolds/lunch.html
Hours: Monday to Friday 11 am to 1 am; Satur-
day 5 pm to 1 am; closed Sundays.
American Tavern. International, Italian. Vegetar-
ian options. Not pure vegetarian.
Menu: Has a selection of vegetarian soups and
specials. Greek Veggie Burger (during lunch),
Garden Burger (during lunch), salads, spaghetti
and other dishes. Fresh juices.
Comments: Old tavern. Uses fresh ingredients.
Outdoor courtyard dining. Sometimes has live
music.
Other Info: Full service, take-out. Reservations
suggested for groups. Accepts AMEX, DC, MC,
VISA. Price: $$.

Blue Gibbon

1231 Tennessee Avenue; 513-641-4100
Hours: Monday to Thursday 11 am to 10 pm;
Friday 11 am to 11 pm; Saturday 12 noon to 11
pm; Sunday 12 noon to 10 pm
Chinese. Vegan options. Not pure vegetarian.
Menu: Has several vegetarian dishes including
Szechuan String Beans, Bean Curd Home Style,
Vegetarian Delight, Eggplant & Green Beans,

Szechuan Broccoli, Sautéed Bean Sprouts and
several mock "meat" dishes.
Comments: Some of the mock meat dishes have
something to be desired.
Other Info: Accepts AMEX, DIS, MC, VISA.
Full service, take-out, catering, large banquet
room. Price: $$.

Boca

4034 Hamilton Avenue; 513-542-2022
Hours: Tuesday to Thursday 5:30 pm to 9:30
pm; Friday & Saturday 5:30 pm to 10:30 pm;
Sunday 10 am to 2 pm; closed Monday.
International. Vegan options. Not pure veg.
Menu: Has a good variety of vegetarian dishes
including Stomboki (marinated tofu with sesame
tamari), Corn & Potato Chowder, Lentil Veg-
etable Burger, Bowl of Steamed Vegetables, Avo-
cado & Spinach Salad, Homemade Granola, sal-
ads and Indian Spiced Vegetables.
Comments: Casual dining. Has a garden view
from many of the seats. Contemporary European
style décor. Has outdoor seating. Good place for
private parties.
Other Info: Full service, take-out. Non-smoking.
Accepts AMEX, MC, VISA. Price: $$.
Directions: Coming from north go south on I-
75 to I-74 west, take Springrove exit (#19) toward Elmore St, turn left at Springrove and go a
few blocks, then turn left on Hamilton Ave and
this place is 1½ block down. Coming from south
1-75, take Mitchell Avenue exit, take a right on
Mitchell, left on Springrove and right on
Hamilton Ave.

Cheng-I Cuisine

203 West McMillian Street; 513-723-1999
Hours: Monday to Saturday 11 am to 11 pm
Sunday 12 noon to 10 pm
Chinese. Not pure vegetarian.
Menu: Has a large vegetarian menu. Vegetarian
Spring Rolls.
Other Info: Full service, take-out, catering. Ac-
cepts DIS, MC, VISA. Price: $$.

Cincinnati Natural Foods and Red Apple Deli

6911 Miami Avenue, Madeira; 513-271-7777
Hours: Monday to Saturday 9:30 to 8 pm; Sat-
urday 10 am to 6 pm; Sunday 12 noon to 5 pm
Deli closes at 6 pm on weekdays.
Natural Food Store and Natural Food Cafe. Deli,
Juice Bar and Bakery. Mainly vegetarian. Vegan
friendly. Organic produce.
Menu: Barbecue Tofu, veggie Lasagna, veggie
burgers, several salads, vegetarian chili, Stir-Fry

Vegetables with Rice, Veal Cutlets (made of soy and wheat protein), Moroccan Chicken (soy protein), meatless "Sloppy Joes," Eggless Egg Salad, Black Bean Lasagna (really good), split pea soup, tofu noodle soup and other dishes.
Comments: Friendly place. Most dishes are sold by weight.
Other Info: Counter service, take-out. Has seating inside and five tables in the front of the store. Accepts AMEX, MC, VISA. Price: $.
Directions: From I-71 going south, take Montgomery exit (#12) and at Montgomery turn left (head east) and go a half-mile, at E Galbraith Rd turn right and go a third-mile, then at Miami Ave turn right and go 1¼ mile.

Cincinnati Natural Foods
9268 Colerain Avenue; 513-385-9622
Hours: Monday to Friday 10 am to 8 pm; Saturday 10 am to 6 pm; Sunday 12 noon to 5 pm
Natural Food Store. Friendly place.
Directions: From I-275, take Colerain exit and go south. This place on left a fourth of a mile south of Northgate Mall. Has a yellow sign with a red apple.

Clifton Natural Foods
169 West McMillan, Clifton Heights, near U of C; 513- 961-6111
Hours: Monday to Saturday 9 am to 8 pm Sunday 11 am to 5 pm.
Natural Food Store. Vegan options.
Menu: Falafel, hummus and ready-made sandwiches.
Other Info: Accepts MC, VISA.
Directions: From I-71, take Taft Rd exit (#3) and go west on W H Taft Rd (becomes Calhoun St) for 1 mile, at W Clifton Ave turn left and go 1 block, at W McMillan turn left and this place is 1 block down.

Floyd's Restaurant
129 Calhoun Street, Clifton Heights, near U of C; 513-221-2434
Hours: Monday to Friday 11 am to 2:30 pm, 5 pm to 9 pm; Friday & Saturday 5 pm to 10 pm; closed Sunday and Monday
Lebanese, Greek, Middle Eastern. Not pure veg.
Menu: Falafel, baba ghanouj, pita bread, lima beans with lemon and olive oil, tahini, hummus, salads and tabbouleh. Fresh juices.
Comments: No atmosphere. Gets rated by some as the best Lebanese food in Cincinnati.
Other Info: Full service, take-out. Price: $-$$. Cash only; no credit cards.

Healthy's Health Foods
9525 Kenwood Road; 513-984-1333
Hours: Monday to Friday 9:30 am to 7:30 pm; Saturday 9:30 am to 6:30 pm; closed Sunday.
Natural Food Store.
Directions: From I-71, take Pfeiffer Rd exit and go west on Pfeiffer. Then at Kenwood go south. This place on right.

**Manna Vegetarian Deli
3514 Erie Avenue, at Pinehurst; 513-321-5160;
Web site: www.healthymanner.com
Hours: Tuesday to Thursday 11 am to 7 pm; Friday 11 am to 3 pm; Sunday 12 am to 7 pm; Sunday Brunch 10 am to 2 pm; closed Monday & Saturday.
Vegetarian Deli. Vegan options. Use eggs in some dishes.
Menu: Soups, salads, sandwiches, Lasagna, mock "Chicken," mock "Meat Loaf" Sandwich, Vegetarian Meatballs, Veggie Barbecue (Vegan), Tofu Chicken Salad, Black Bean Burrito (vegan), Sesame Noodle (vegan) Hummus, Wild Rice, Sloppy Joe, Veggie Burgers, Candied Yams, Collard Greens, and Macaroni & Cheese Casserole (Vegan). Desserts such as apple pie, sweet potato pie and cheese pie. See full menu (http://www.healthymanna.com/id18.htm). Fresh juices and smoothies.
Comments: Got a good review in Cincinnati Enquirer (see review http://www.healthymanna.com/id48.htm). Has potted plants. Also sells supplements, herbal teas and vegetarian magazines and cookbooks. Dishes sold by weight. Price: $$.
Directions: From I-75, take Norwood Lateral Exit (Hwy 562), then take the Ridge Exit and turn right (eventually becomes Marburg), then turn left on Erie and this place is on your left. From I-71 going south get on Redbank Expressway and go 1½ mile, cross over Madison Rd, then at Brotherton Court turn left and go 1 block, then turn right on Erie and this place is 1¼ mile down. From I-71 going north, take Hwy 71N to the South Ridge exit, turn right (eventually becomes Marburg), then turn left onto Erie and then this place will be on your left.

Marx Hot Bagels
7617 Reading Road	513-821-0103
9701 Kenwood Road	513-891-5542
316 Northland Boulevard	513-772-3101
Hours: Daily 5:30 pm to 9 pm
Bagel Place. Not pure vegetarian.
Menu: Has around a dozen varieties of bagels and several vegetarian toppings.

Mayura Restaurant
3201 North Jefferson Avenue; 513-221-7125
Hours: Monday to Thursday 11:30 am to 2 pm, 5 pm to 9:30 pm; Friday & Saturday 12 noon to 2:30 pm, 5 pm to 10:30 pm; Sunday 12 noon to 3 pm, 5 pm to 9:30 pm
East Indian. Not pure vegetarian.
Menu: Has many vegetarian dishes. Pakoras, samosa, Vegetable Soup, Lentil & Spinach Soup, raita, Aloo Gobi, Mattar Paneer, Andhra Green Beans, Naan and Vegetarian Thali (rice, dal, salad, raita, vegetable subji, dessert).
Comments: This place is very popular so it is advised to arrive by 6:30 pm. Good atmosphere.
Other Info: Full service, take-out, catering. Reservations for parties of five or more. Accepts AMEX, DIS, MC, VISA. Price: $$.
Directions: Clifton by U of C turns into Jefferson further north.

Mullane's Parkside Café
723 Race Street; 513-381-1331
Hours: Monday to Friday 11:30 am to 10 pm; Saturday 5 pm to 11 pm; closed Sunday.
International. Vegetarian-friendly. Not pure veg.
Menu: Has a good selection of vegetarian dishes such as soup, sandwiches, Hummus & Vegetables, Vegetables with Curried Yogurt, Grilled Potatoes, salads, Spinach Sauté, Vegetable Sauté, Red Beans & Rice, pasta, veggie burger and bagels. The Raspberry Pie is really good
Comments: Has indoors and outdoors sidewalk seating. Romantic spot. Popular place. Wall has local artists' paintings on it. Excellent service.
Other Info: Accepts MC, VISA. Price: $-$$.
Directions: From I-75 going south, take the 7th St exit, then go east on 7th St for a half-mile, then turn left on Elm St and go 1 block, then turn right at Garfield and this place is 1 block down. From going north on I-75, take the 5th St exit, turn left on Elm St and then turn right on Garfield.

Myra's Dionysus Restaurant
121 Calhoun Street, Clifton Heights
513-961-1578
Hours: Monday to Thursday 10 am to 10 pm; Sat 10 am to 11 pm; Sun 5 pm to 10 pm
Greek and International. Vegetarian-friendly. Vegan options. Not pure vegetarian.
Menu: Has an excellent selection of good tasting vegetarian dishes. Spanikopita (spinach and feta in a pastry), delicious vegetarian soups such as Tomato Cilantro Soup, Greek Salad, Gado Gado (brown rice and peanut-ginger sauce with salad) and several vegan dishes. Its international menu

includes Mexican, Italian, Chinese, Middle Eastern, Indian, Turkish, Greek and Brazilian.
Comments: Has indoor and outdoor patio seating. Romantic, cozy atmosphere. Offbeat. Fairly good size portions.
Other Info: Full service, take-out, catering. No credit cards accepted. Price: $.
Directions: Across from the University of Cincinnati campus.

Pacific Moon Café
8300 Market Place Lane; 513-891-0091
email: info@pacificmooncafe.com;
Web site: www.pacificmooncafe.com
Hours: Sunday to Thursday 11 am to 10 pm; Friday & Saturday 11 am to 11 pm; Dim Sum Saturday & Sunday 10 am to 3 pm; delivers Monday to Friday 11 am to 2 pm & every evening 5 pm to 9:30 pm
Chinese. Not Pure Vegetarian.
Menu: Has a vegetarian section on the menu. Hot & Sour Ribs, Pepper Steak (mock "beef"), "Mock" Cashew Chicken, Hot & Sour Eggplant and Green Beans, Szechuan Vegetables and Green Beans. Fresh juices. Non-alcoholic beer and wine.
Comments: Upscale, but mellow, relaxed place. Live jazz on the weekends. There is outdoor seating next to a herb garden. "Best Chinese" according to Cincinnati Magazine, "Next best thing to China," The Cincinnati Enquirer, "Best Oriental," the Cincinnati Post. Gets rated as one of the best Chinese restaurants in the area.
Other Info: Full service, take-out, catering. Accepts AMEX, DC, MC, VISA. Price: $$-$$$.
Directions: In the Market Place of Montgomery. Across from Montgomery Square, behind Camargo Cadillac.

Planet Smoothie
4764 Cornell Road; 513-469-6221
Hours: Monday to Friday 7 am to 7 am; Saturday 10 am to 5 pm; closed Sunday.
Smoothie Bar.

Spatz Natural Life
607 Main Street, downtown; 513-621-0347
Hours: Monday to Friday 9 am to 6 pm; Saturday 9 am to 3 pm; closed Sunday.
Natural Food Store and Deli. Salad Bar. Vegan-friendly deli.
Menu: The lunch buffet changes daily. Serves vegetarian lunches with a variety of salads, vegan soups, vegetarian chili, Roasted Pepper Pasta, linguine, veggie Sloppy Joes, Pesto Pasta, Tofu & Rice, Black Bean Tortilla Loaf and Stir-fry Rice & Vegetables. Fresh juices.

Other Info: Price: $-$$.
Directions: From I-71, take Gilbert Ave/Reading Rd exit (#2) and go southwest on Gilbert Ave (US-22) for a half-mile, take a slight left onto E 8th St (US-22) and go 1 block, turn left at Sycamore St and go 2 blocks, at 6th St turn right and go 1 block and this place is near the corner of Main St.

Tandoor India Restaurant
8702 Market Place Lane, Montgomery Heights
513-793-7484; Web site: www.tandoor.com
Hours: Monday to Thursday 11:30 am to 2 pm, 5:30 pm to 9:30 pm; Friday & Saturday 11:30 am to 2 pm, 5:30 pm to 10:30 pm; closed Sun.
Gujarati and North Indian. Jain-style Vegetarian. Not pure vegetarian.
Menu: Has many vegetarian dishes including Malai Kofta, Mattar Paneer, Palak Paneer, Mushroom Mattar, Channa Masala, Bhindi Bhajee, vegetable samosa and Naan bread.
Comments: Has daily lunch buffet. East India specialties. From their Web site you can print coupons for various meal discounts.
Other Info: Full service, take-out. Accepts AMEX, DC, MC, VISA. Price: $$.
Directions: From I-275, take the Montgomery Rd exit. Go south on Montgomery and this place is on the left in Market Place, behind Camargo Cadillac, across from Montgomery Square.

Total Juice
631 Vine Street, near 6th Street
513-784-1666; **fax:** 513-784-1665
Hours: Monday to Friday 7 am to 5:30 pm; Saturday 11 am to 4 pm; closed Sunday.
Juice Bar and Café. Not pure vegetarian.
Menu: Has a wide variety of fruit and vegetable juices and smoothies such as Guava Oasis, Strawberry Passion and mango. Can add two nutritional additions such as brewer's yeast, wheatgrass or oat bran. Has a variety of wraps including Mediterranean Salad, Falafel Wrap, Stuffed Grape Leaves Wrap (vegan), bagels, Vegetarian Heaven Wrap (lentils, rice, olive oil), California Roll Wrap (sushi Asian type wrap) and salads. Wheatgrass. One vegetarian soup daily.
Other Info: Price: $.
Directions: Downtown near Fountain Square and Piatt Park.

Twin Pines Natural Foods Co-op
1051 North Bend Road, College Hill
513-681-3663
Hours: Daily 9 am to 8 pm
Natural Food Store. Organic produce.

Menu: Has falafel, baba ghanouj and a few other such dishes in cooler.
Other Info: Accepts MC, VISA.
Directions: From I-75 north to I-74 west and then exit at Colerain Avenue and turn left and go north. At North Bend Rd turn right and this place on right about 3 miles down.

**Ulysses Whole World Foods
209 West McMillan Street, Clifton Heights
513-241-3663
Hours: Monday to Saturday 11 am to 8 pm; 12 noon to 6 pm; closed Sunday,
Natural Food Store and Pure Vegetarian Deli. International. Vegan options.
Menu: Veggie burgers, homemade soups, veg BLT sandwich, garden salad, veg chicken sandwiches, several varieties of burritos, French fries, Fried Sweet Potatoes (recommended), quesadillas, veggie subs, Thai Veggie Stir-fry with Peanut Sauce, falafel, Seitan Sizzler (very good), Seitan Stir fry, vegetarian chili and desserts. The Radical Burger is good. Smoothies.
Comments: The most popular natural food store in the university area. Cincinnati Magazine rated it the best vegetarian restaurant in the area. Reasonably priced place. Service can be a bit slow.
Other Info: Deli and take-out only, limited catering. Has a few stools to seat at. Non-smoking. Does not take reservations. Price: $-$$.
Directions: This place is a half-block south of the University of Cincinnati campus. From I-71, take Taft Rd exit (#3) and go west on W H Taft Rd (becomes Calhoun St) for 1 mile, at W Clifton Ave turn left and go 1 block, at W McMillan turn left and this place is 1 block down. From I-75, take the Hopple Street exit (#2B), and go northeast on Clifton Ave ¾ mile. Then turn right on W McMillan and this place is on the right about ¾ mile down.

CLEVELAND

Aladdin's Eatery East Side
12447 Cedar Road, Cleveland Heights
216-932-4333; Web site: www.aladdinseatery.com
Hours: Sunday to Thursday 11 am to 10 pm Friday & Saturday 11 am to 11 pm
Mediterranean, Middle Eastern and Lebanese. Vegetarian friendly. Not pure vegetarian.
Menu: Homemade soups, salads and pita sandwiches.
Comments: Good service and food. Friendly place.
Other Info: Accepts AMEX, MC, VISA. Full service, take-out. Price: $.

Ali Baba Restaurant

12021 Lorain Road, west Cleveland
216-251-2040
Hours: Thursday to Saturday 11:30 am to 2 pm,
5 pm to 9 pm; closed Sunday to Wednesday.
Middle Eastern, Lebanese. Not pure vegetarian.
Menu: Has a vegetarian section on its menu.
Hummus, brown rice, falafel and baba ghanouj.
Comments: The food gets high ratings. No MSG,
preservatives, or artificial flavorings are added to
the food. Friendly place with good service.
Other Info: Full service, take-out, catering. Price:
$$. Cash only.

American Harvest Health Foods Market

Southland Shopping Center, 13387 Smith Rd,
west side of Cleveland; 440-888-7727
Hours: Monday to Saturday 9 am to 9 pm
Sunday 9 am to 6 pm
Natural Food Store and vegetarian Deli. Vegan-
friendly. Organic produce.
Menu: Soups, veggie pies, wraps, bean & rice
dishes and more.
Comments: Has a good selection.
Other Info: Accepts MC, VISA.
Directions: From 1-71, take the US-42 exit
(#234) towards Parma Hts/Strongsville, then go
northeast on Pearl Rd (US-42) for 2 miles, at
Smith road turn right and this place is on the left
in the Southland Shopping Center.

Cafe Tandoor

2096 South Taylor Road, 1/4 mile north of Ce-
dar Road in Cleveland Heights
216-371-8500
Hours: Monday to Saturday 11:30 am to 2 pm,
5:30 pm to 10 pm; Sunday 3 pm to 9 pm
Indian. Vegan-friendly. Not pure vegetarian.
Menu: Has around 20 vegetarian dishes
Comments: Clay oven. Good food and friendly,
efficient service. Popular place.
Other Info: Accepts AMEX, DIS, MC, VISA.
Price: $$.
Directions: Near University Circle concert halls.

Co-op Café

2130 Adelbert Road; 216-368-3095
Hours: Monday to Friday 8 am to 7:30 pm; Sat-
urday 10 am to 3 pm; closed Sunday.
Natural Foods Cafe. Vegan options. Not pure
vegetarian.
Menu: Soups, salads, sandwiches, Middle East-
ern dishes and Indian food. Powerburger, Tofu
Scramble, Tofu Ravioli, and Rice & Indian curry.
The Popeye Soup (yams, spinach and olive oil) is
worth trying. Fresh juices and smoothies.

Comments: Located in a fitness center, and is
open to members and non-members also. The
food is prepared at the Food Co-op, a few blocks
away.
Other Info: Limited service, take-out. Price: $.
Directions: From the I-71, take Chester Ave/US-
322 (#173) and go west 3 miles on Chester Ave,
at Euclid Ave (US-20) turn left and go a quarter-
mile, at Adelbert Rd turn right and this place is a
third-mile down. On the second floor in the 1-2-
1 Fitness Center, near University Circle.

Empress Taytu Ethiopian Restaurant

6125 St Clair Avenue, East Cleveland
216-391-9400
Hours: Tuesday to Saturday 5 pm to 10 pm
Closed Sunday & Monday.
Ethiopian Gourmet. Not pure vegetarian.
Menu: Split peas, stews, Lentils in Sauce and
Mixed Legumes. Dishes served with injera bread.
Yogurt and Mashed Bean appetizers.
Comments: Traditional Ethiopian foods. Seat-
ing on the food. There are no utensils, as you are
meant to eat the food by scooping it up with a
flatbread, traditional Ethiopian style. Gets a good
rating. Displays Ethiopian art and plays Ethio-
pian music. Usually busy on Friday and Saturday
nights. Has thatched dining areas with low carved
wood or basket furniture.
Other Info: Full service, take-out. Accepts
AMEX, DIS, MC, VISA. Price: $$.
Directions: Near University Circle.

Food Co-op

11702 Euclid Avenue; 216-791-3890
Hours: Monday to Saturday 9 am to 8 pm
Sunday 10 am to 6 pm
Natural Food Store and take-out Deli. Juice Bar
and Bakery. Organic produce.
Menu: Two soups, salads, sandwiches and about
10 main dishes.
Other Info: Accepts DIS, MC, VISA. Counter
service, take-out. No seating.
Directions: Near University Circle, 3 miles east
of the downtown. From I-90, take Martin Luther
King exit (#178) south and then go south to
Euclid and this place on right. This place is about
2 miles directly south of the exit.

Fulton Bar and Grill

1835 Fulton Road; 216-694-2122
email: thefulton@webtv.net
Web site: http://fultonohiocity.citysearch.com,
www.fultonbarandgrill.com
Hours: Daily 5 pm to 1 am
International. Vegetarian-friendly (at least 50%

of the dishes are vegetarian). Not pure veg.
Menu: Has several vegetarian options including Wild Mushroom & Goat Cheese Turnover, pasta, Roasted Asparagus & Fresh Mozzarella, Portobello Quesadilla, Pesto Pizza, interesting salads, Mid-east Platter (tabbouleh, hummus, baba ghanoush, pita), Roasted Vegetable and Tofu Raviolis (recommended).
Comments: Local organic produce used when possible. Got some good reviews in the local papers. Trendy, romantic place. Has a bright red ceiling and candles. Popular place.
Other Info: Accepts AMEX, MC, VISA. Price: $$-$$$.
Directions: From I-71 coming north, take Pearl Rd/Fulton Rd exit (#245), then got north on Fulton Rd and this place is 2 miles down. From I-71, take exit #171, then go west and this place is about 1 mile west of the exit.

Johnny Mango
3120 Bridge Avenue, at Fulton Avenue
216-575-1919
Hours: Monday to Thursday 11 am to 10 pm; Friday 11 am to 11 pm; Saturday 9 am to 11 pm; Sunday 9 am to 10 pm
International. Mexican, Thai, Jamaican. Vegetarian friendly (at least 50% of the dishes are vegetarian). Not pure vegetarian.
Menu: Tofu Miso Soup, breads, daily "Happy Beans" selection, homemade cornbread, black bean quesadillas, bean burritos, fresh breads and sandwiches. The Fried Plantains are very popular. Can get almost anything with seitan and tofu instead of meat.
Comments: Indoor and outdoor dining. Trendy, casual, inexpensive, happening place. Plays Island music. Nice décor. Gets recommended for vegetarian food. Popular. This place gets good ratings from customers.
Other Info: Full service, take-out. Reservations suggested for groups. Accepts AMEX, MC, VISA. Price: $$.
Direction: West side of Cleveland.

Nature's Bin Naturally
18120 Sloane Avenue, Lakewood; 216-521-4600
Hours: Monday to Friday 9 am to 8 pm; Saturday 9 am to 7 pm; Sunday 10 am to 6 pm
Natural Food Store and take-out Deli. Organic produce.
Comments: Gourmet food. One of the best natural food stores in northeast Ohio. Has the best selection of organic groceries and herbal supplement in the area. Has over 100 bulk food items. Founded in 1975 by Cornucopia, an organiza-

tion that gives support and employment to people with emotional and physical disabilities.
Other Info: Accepts DIS, MC, VISA.
Directions: From I-90, take Exit #164 towards McKinley/Lakewood, then go ¾ mile north on Riverside Dr, at W Clifton Blvd turn right and go a third-mile, then at Sloane Ave turn left and this place is a block down.

Peking Gourmet Chinese Restaurant
13955 Cedar Red, at Warrensville Center Road, in the suburbs of Cleveland near Cleveland Heights; 216-397-9939
Hours: Monday to Thursday 11:30 am to 10 pm; Friday to Saturday 11:30 am to 11 pm; Sunday 4 pm to 10 pm
Chinese. Not pure vegetarian.
Menu: Has a vegetarian menu. Steamed Broccoli & Wheat Pate, Seaweed Salad and non-cheesecake.
Comments: Family-run and operated place. Popular with the local college students. Good food and efficient service.
Other Info: Accepts AMEX, DC, MC, VISA. Price: $.

Saffron Patch
20600 Chagrin Boulevard; 216-295-0400
Hours: Sunday to Thursday 11:30 am to 2:30 pm, 5 pm to 9:30 pm; Fri & Sat until 10 pm
Indian. Vegan-friendly.
Menu: Has several vegetarian options.
Comments: Good food. Has a good Sunday brunch, which starts at noon. Large windows and white table clothes. Has woodcarvings on the shelves. Sitar background music. Some people believe this is the best vegetarian food in Cleveland.
Other Info: Accepts AMEX, DIS, MC, VISA.

***Soul Vegetarian Central
1791 Coventry Road, Coventry; 216-932-0588
Hours: Monday to Thursday 11 noon to 10:30 pm; Friday to Saturday 12 noon to 12:30 am; Sunday 10 am to 8 pm; Brunch 10 pm to 1 pm
Vegan Vegetarian Soul and International.
Menu: Mock "meat" dishes, soups, salads and several other vegetarian dishes. Kalebone, BBQ Roast, Pineapple Supreme, French fries, Lentil Burger, Battered Cauliflower, Macaroni & Cheese, Country Fried Steak, Stir-fried Rice, Tofu Salad, Tofu Sticks, Tofu Fillet, collard greens, Roast Sandwich, Kale Greens with Cornbread and Gyros. Smoothies. On Sunday mornings there is a vegan breakfast.
Comments: Pleasant atmosphere in a basic place.

The lady who runs this place is very pleasant and efficient. Gets good ratings from some of my friends. Has just a few tables. Mainly a take-out place. The prices are very reasonable. Does not use white sugar, additives or white flour. Wheat protein is used to make meat substitutes. Local organic produce used when possible. Uses ingredients that are free of preservatives and additives. Offers vegetarian cooking classes.
Other Info: Counter service, take-out, catering. Non-smoking. Accepts reservations, but they are not necessary. Price: $$.
Directions: This place is in east Cleveland. From I-90, take Chester Ave exit (#173B), then go south 3 miles on Chester Ave, at Euclid Ave turn left and go a half-mile, at Mayfield Rd (US-322) turn right and go 1¼ mile, then at Coventry Rd turn right and this place is 1 block down.

Shtick's Vegetarian Kitchen
11075 East Boulevard, in Gund Law School
216-231-0922
Hours: Monday to Thursday 7:30 am to 4 pm; Friday 7:30 am to 2:30 pm; closed Sat & Sun.
International. Not pure vegetarian. Price: $.
Menu: Good gazpacho, black bean burritos and curry vegetables. Daily specials.
Directions: It is in the Gund Law School, at the end of Case Campus Alley.

Tea House Noodles
1900 East 6th Street, between Euclid and Superior Avenues; 216-623-9131
Hours: Monday to Friday 10:30 am to 4 pm Closed Saturday & Sunday.
Asian. Chinese. Not pure vegetarian.
Menu: Has whole-grain brown rice, noodles dishes and Chinese vegetable dishes. Freshly made smoothies. Can add spirulina, ginseng and bee pollen. Has ginger, apple and carrot juices. Green tea.
Comments: Can get a bowl of Bok chow and shitake mushrooms for $3. It is a cheap, good valued place. No alcohol. Has only four tables.
Other Info: Accepts MC, VISA.

Webers Health Foods
18400 Euclid Avenue; 216-481-9544
Hours: Monday to Friday 9 am to 6 pm; Saturday 9 am to 2 pm; closed Sunday.
Natural Food Store.

Web of Life Natural Foods
Williamsburg Plaza
25923 Detroit Road, just west of Columber Westlake; 440-899-2882

Hours: Monday to Saturday 9 am to 9 pm
Sunday 10 am to 6 pm
Natural Food Store and take-out Deli. Smoothie Bar. Vegetarian. Mainly Vegan. Organic produce
Menu: MockTuna (chick pea and soy mayo), Split Pea Soup, vegan Chili Dogs, BBQ Seitan sandwich, whole grain breads, veggie Sloppy Joe, veggie hot dogs, Sweet Potato Fries, good salads, Oatscream frozen desserts and Vegan Haystacks (chocolate and coconut). Can make you own vegetable juice combinations. Great smoothies with ginseng, bee pollen and royal jelly.
Comments: The food here gets good recommendations. Bulk food. Has a library.
Other Info: Accepts DIS, MC, VISA.
Directions: This place is located in Western Cleveland. From I-90 take the Columbia Road exit (#159) and then go south on Columbia Rd a quarter-mile, then turn right (go west) on Detroit Road and this place is a third-mile down.

Wild Oats Market
27249 Chagrin Boulevard, Woodmere
216-464-9403
Hours: Monday to Saturday 7 am to 10 pm
Sunday 8 am to 9 pm
Natural Food Store and Cafe. Deli, Bakery, Salad Bar and Juice Bar. Organic produce. Supermarket-type place. See Wild Oats Market information.
Directions: From I-271, take the Chagrin exit (#29) and then go east on Chagrin Blvd and this place is a quarter-mile down.

Wild Oats Market
13130 Shaker Boulevard; 216-561-1630
Hours: Daily 8 am to 8 pm
Natural Food Store and Cafe. Deli, Bakery, Salad Bar and Juice Bar. Organic produce. Supermarket-type place. See Wild Oats Market information.
Directions: From I-71, take exit #247A and go east on I-490 towards Clark Ave for 2 miles where the highway ends. At E 55th St turn left and go a half-mile, at Woodland Ave turn right (OH Hwy 87) and go 1 mile, at Buckeye Rd turn slight right and go ¾ mile, at Shaker Blvd turn slight left and go 1½ mile, then at Shaker Square turn right and this place is a half-block down. This place is in east Cleveland.

CLEVELAND HEIGHTS

Nature's Bin Naturally
2255 Lee Road, Cleveland Heights
216-932-2462; fax: 216-932-4050
Hours: Monday to Friday 9 am to 8 pm; Saturday 9 am to 7 pm; Sunday 12 noon to 6 pm

Natural Food Store and Deli. Large organic produce section. Buffet.
Comments: Has a buffet, but it didn't have much of a selection when I went there. I can't really recommend it.
Other Info: Counter service, take-out. Has seating. Has parking in the back.

Tommy's
1824 Coventry Road, at Lancashire Blvd
Cleveland Heights; 216-321-7757
Web site: www.tammyscoventry.com
Hours: Monday to Thursday 7:30 am to 10 pm; Friday & Saturday 7:30 am to 11 pm; Sunday 9 am to 10 pm
Greek and International. Vegan options. Macrobiotic friendly. Not Pure Vegetarian.
Menu: Salads, sandwiches, hummus, Spinach Pies, falafel, veggie burger, Green Bean Bowl, Grilled Eggplant, baba ghanoush, tempeh burgers, Shitake Mushroom and desserts. Fresh juices. Known for its good milkshakes. Carob yogurt shake.
Comments: Some of the best vegetarian food in the city. Gets greats recommendations and wins awards for best vegetarian food in the Cleveland area. Shaded ceiling lights. Casual.
Other Info: Full service, counter service, take-out. Accepts AMEX, DIS, MC, VISA. Price: $$-$$$.
Directions: This place is in the Coventry Rd area of Cleveland Heights.

Yacov's Kosher Restaurant
13969 Cedar Road, Cleveland Heights
216-932-8848
Hours: Sun to Thur 11 am to 8 pm; Fri 11 am to 3 pm; Saturday open after sunset to 12 midnight.
Middle Eastern and Italian. Kosher. Vegan options. Not pure vegetarian.
Menu: Has a good selection of vegetarian dishes. Has falafel, Eggplant Parmesan and pizza. The food is really good.
Other Info: Cafeteria style, take-out. Price: $. Cash or local checks; no credit cards.

COLUMBUS

Aladdin's Eatery
2931 North High Street; 614-262-2414
Web site: www.aladdinseatery.com
Hours: Monday to Thursday 11 am to 10 pm; Friday & Saturday 11 am to 11 pm; Sunday 11 am to 9 pm
Middle Eastern. Not pure vegetarian.
Menu: Has several vegetarian options including many salads, vegetarian chili, Foole M Damas (fava beans with olive oil and tomatoes), tabbouleh, Falafel Salad, Almond Salad, Spinach Salad, Fruit & Nut Salad, good hummus, falafel, Lentil Soup and Lentil Chili. Fresh juices and smoothies.
Comments: Good Middle Eastern food. Small place, simple decor. Food does not contain artificial sweeteners and no additives. Good food and reasonable prices.

Beechwood Natural Foods
4185 North High Street; 614-262-0192
Hours: Monday to Friday 9:30 am to 7 pm; Saturday 9:30 am to 5 pm; closed Sunday.
Natural Food Store. Organic produce.
Menu: Has ready-made sandwiches.
Other Info: Accepts MC, VISA.
Comments: Has bulk items and a bookstand.

Benevolence
41 West Swan Street, near the North market
614-221-9330
Hours: Monday to Friday 11:30 am to 3 pm; Sat 8 am to 10:30 am, 11 am to 3 pm; closed Sun.
Restaurant. Not pure vegetarian.
Menu: Homemade soups, freshly baked breads, salads with great salad dressings and sandwiches.
Comments: Friendly, casual place. All dishes are freshly made daily. The seating is at long wooden communal tables. Pleasant, peaceful atmosphere. Quick service. Has a gift shop selling natural soaps, handmade jewelry and pottery. Very environmentally conscious.
Other Info: Full service, take-out (they prefer that you bring your own container). Accepts MC, VISA. Price: $.

Bexley Natural Market
508 North Cassady Avenue; 614-252-3951
Hours: Monday to Friday 10 am to 8 pm; Saturday 10 am to 6 pm; Sunday 11 noon to 5 pm
Natural Food Store. Organic produce.
Directions: From I-71, take I-670 east and exit at 5th Ave. Then at Cassady (first light) turn right.

The Blue Nile Ethiopian Restaurant
2361 North High Street; 614-421-2323
Web site: www.ethiopiancuisine.com
Hours: Tuesday to Friday 11:30 am to 3:30 pm, 5 pm to 10 pm; Saturday 12 noon to 3 pm, 5 pm to 10:30 pm; Sunday 12 noon to 3 pm, 5 pm to 9 pm; closed Monday.
Ethiopian. All-you-can-eat Buffet. Vegan friendly. Not pure vegetarian.
Menu: Has several vegetarian main dishes. Kik

Alcha (yellow split peas), collard greens and rice pudding.
Comments: Casual. Friendly service. Hip crowd. Food gets good ratings.
Other Info: Accepts AMEX, DIS, MC, VISA. Price: $.
Directions: It is a little north of the campus.

Clintonville Community Market (Calumet Natural Foods Co-op)
200 Crestview Road; 614-261-3663
email: edbain@hotmail.com; Web site: http://www.communitymarket.org/ccm
Hours: Monday to Saturday 7 am to 10 pm Sunday 9 am to 10 pm
Natural Food Store and take-out Deli.
Menu: Has salads and sandwiches.
Comments: Also called Calumet Natural Foods Co-op
Other Info: Accepts AMEX, MC, VISA. Counter service, take-out. No seating.
Directions: From I-71, take N Broadway exit (#114), then go east a third-mile on E North Broadway St, at Indianola Ave turn left and go ¾ mile, at Creatview Rd turn right and this place is a third-mile down.

**Dragonfly
247 King Avenue; 614-298-9986
email: info@dragonflyneov.com
Web site: www.dragonflyneov.com
Hours: Tuesday to Thursday 11:30 am to 10 pm; Friday to Saturday 11:30 am to 11 pm; Sunday 10:30 am to 3 pm, 5 pm to 9 pm; Organic Sunday Brunch 10:30 am to 3 pm; closed Monday.
Fully Vegetarian International Gourmet. Mostly Vegan. Organic Restaurant.
Menu: Nigiri Tofu (gets high recommendations), vegetable Jerk Pizza, Polenta Arepa (Grilled eggplant and vegetable with tofu sauce), Mush Tempura Yams, Spring Roll, Portabella Sandwich, Seitan Gyros, Brown Rice Casseroles, crepes and good desserts. The vegan Chocolate Mouse is very good.
Comments: Food gets really high recommendations as excellent food (also get some bad reviews). People say it is their favorite restaurant. Has alternative art gallery with paintings from local artists. Organic Sunday is 95% organic. Outdoor dining. Organic, preservative-free, whole foods. Modern dining room with a giant canoe hanging from the ceiling. Excellent service, but often a bit slow. Casual, friendly atmosphere. Has a good Web site.
Other Info: Full service, catering. Non-

smoking. Reservations for 6 or more. Accepts AMEX, MC, VISA. Price: $$.
Directions: One mile north of downtown Columbus, on the southeast corner of Neil and King. From I-71, take 5th Ave exit (#110A), then go west on E 5th Ave for 1½ mile, at Forsythe Ave turn right and go 2 blocks, then at King Ave turn left and go 1 block.

Firdous
3145 Kingsdale Center, Express counter at The North Market, in Upper Arlington
614-442-5555
Hours: Monday, Tuesday 11 am to 2 pm, 5 pm to 9 pm; Wednesday, Thursday, Sunday 11 am to 9 pm; Friday & Saturday 11 am to 10 pm
Middle Eastern. Vegan options. Not pure vegetarian.
Menu: Hummus, falafel, pita bread, tabbouleh (good) and a vegetarian lunch special.
Comments: Mixed opinions about the food. Some people think it is good and other feel that is no good and overpriced.
Other Info: Accepts AMEX, DIS, MC, VISA. Price: $-$$.

Flavors of India
North Market, 59 Spruce Street; 614-228-1955
Hours: Wednesday to Monday 11 am to 5 pm Tuesday to 11 am to 7 pm
Indian. Vegan options. Not pure vegetarian.
Menu: Channa Masala, Spinach Paneer, dal, basmati rice, Naan bread and other dishes. Has some really good mango lassi.
Comments: There is seating inside the market and also outside. Popular.
Other Info: Price: $. Cash only.

Nong's Hunan Express
1634 Northwest Boulevard, Upper Arlington neighborhood; 614-486-6630
Hours: Monday to Friday 11 am to 9:30 pm Saturday & Sunday 3 pm to 9:30 pm
Chinese, Thai, Vietnamese. Not pure vegetarian.
Menu: Has a large selection of vegetarian dishes.
Comments: Casual and laid-back place. No atmosphere and plain décor.
Other Info: Counter service, take-out. Accepts DIS, MC, VISA. Price: $$.

North Market
59 Spruce Street
614-463-9664; **Web site:** www.northmarket.com
Hours: Tuesday to Friday 9 am to 7 pm; Satur-

day 8 am to 5 pm; Sunday 12 noon to 5 pm; Sometimes open on Monday 9 am to 5 pm **Saturday Market** that has various restaurants, some co-ops, a bakery and organic produce stands. More upscale than normal farmers market. **Flavors of India** (see above), for cheap vegetarian plates and **Firdous Express** (see above) serves Greek falafel and hummus sandwiches.
Comments: Has a list of the merchant in the market on their Web site.
Directions: Walking distance form the convention center and Nationwide. There is a lot next door to park in, but you need to get your ticket validated by one of the shops in the market.

Nellie's Curry Pot
In the French Market, North of Street Route 161 off of Busch Blvd
Vegan-friendly Place. Many vegetarian main dishes. Inexpensive. Many items are low fat.

Not Guilty Cafe
Park Place Shopping Center, off N High Street, about 2 Miles N of I-270
Some vegetarian main dishes. Casual atmosphere. Inexpensive. Non-fat or very low fat fare. Very tasty food.

Raisin Rack Natural Food Market
618 West Schrock Road, Westerville
614-882-5886
Natural Food Store. Organic produce.
Directions: In a shopping center with Kinko's.

Sunflower Natural Foods
2591 North High Street; 614-263-2488
Hours: Monday to Saturday 9:30 am to 7 pm Sunday 12 noon to 6 pm
Natural Food Store. Organic produce.
Comments: Not such a big place.

Talita's
2977 North High Street
614-262-6000; Web site: www.talitas.com
Hours: Tuesday to Saturday 11 am to 10 pm Closed Sunday and Monday
Mexican. Not pure vegetarian.
Menu: Authentic Mexican food. Cheap veggie burritos, nacho with cheese, enchiladas, tacos, pizzas and salads.
Comments: Casual, friendly place. Good value. Has discount coupon on their web site. Price: $.

Tandori Chicken
Food Court, Lane Avenue Mall, 1677 Lane Av-

enue; 614-486-6288
Hour: Open during mall business hours Sunday buffet.
Indian. Vegan options. Not pure vegetarian.
Menu: About half the dishes on the menu are vegetarian. Good naan and dal. The combination plate is good.

**Udipi Café
Village Center
2001 East Dublin Granville Road, at Cleveland Avenue; 614-885-7446; **fax:** 614-885-7451
Hours: Daily 11:30 am to 10 pm
Fully Vegetarian Indian. Vegan options.
Other Info: Accepts MC, VISA.
Directions: From I-71, take Hwy 161/E Dublin Granville Rd (#117) and this place is about a 1½ mile down.

**Whole World Pizza and Bakery
3269 North High Street, in Clintonville
614-268-5751
Hours: Sunday to Thursday 10 am to 10 pm; Friday and Saturday 10 am to 11 pm; Sunday Brunch 10 am to 2 pm; closed Monday
Pure Vegetarian Natural Pizza Place. Vegan options.
Menu: Vegetarian soups, Broccoli Burger, wholewheat pizza, tofu dishes, salads, good soups, veggie burgers, Black Bean Nachos, Hummus Platter, Veggie Stir-fry, Broccoli & Cheese Soup, Tofu Sloppy Joe, Avocado Croissant, Spinach Rotoni Florentine, Potato Pancakes, "Bombay Burger," Greek Salad, cheese sub and other items. Some desserts are Chocolate Chip Cookies, and Lemon Squares. Uses homemade dressing. Some special pizza toppings are avocado, artichoke hearts, zucchini, tofu, alfalfa sprouts, broccoli and spinach. You can get either a white or wheat crust. During the Sunday brunch they serve scrambled tofu (topping such as mushroom, broccoli, provolone) and vegetable hash. Has a very good guacamole pizza.
Comments: Pizzas are made with whole-wheat, sugarless breads. Fresh vegetables are put on the pizzas. Small, happening place. Daily and weekly specials. Pizza can be ordered with or without cheese. Local organic produce used when possible. Has excellent Sunday brunches. Service is a bit slow. Several antique shops in the area. May use eggs in some of the dishes (check the mayonnaise), so you may want to check this.
Other Info: Non-smoking. Full service, take-out, catering. Accepts AMEX, DIS, MC, VISA. Price: $-$$.

Directions: From I-71, take N Broadway exit (#114), then go west on E North Broadway St for 1 mile, then at Broadway Place turn right and go 1 block, at Oakland Park Ave turn left and go 1 block, then at N High St (US-23) turn left and this place is a third-mile down.

**Woodlands Vegetarian Restaurant.
Olentangy Square Plaza, 816 Bethel Rd, off 315 N, near Ohio State University; 614-459-4101
Hours: Monday to Friday 11 am to 2 pm, 5 pm to 10 pm; Saturday 11 am to 3 pm, 5 pm to 10:30 pm; Sunday 12 noon to 8 pm
Vegetarian Indian. South Indian cuisine.
Menu: Has a wide selection of vegetarian dishes. Rice, dosas, idlys, curried vegetables, soups, vegetable pakoras and more.
Other Info: Full service, take-out, catering. Price: $-$$.
Directions: From OH Hwy 315, take the Bethel Rd exit, then go east on Bethel Rd and this place is a third-mile down.

CUYAHOGA FALLS

Nature's Goodness
1251 Main Street, at Howe Ave & Home Ave (a little north of Akron); 330-922-4567
Hours: Monday to Friday 10 am to 8 pm; Saturday 10 am to 6 pm; closed Sunday.
Natural Food Store and Deli. Organic produce.
Menu: Take-out vegan and vegetarian dishes. Soups, sandwiches, salads, tofu dishes and main dishes.
Other Info: Counter service, take-out. Has two little tables.
Directions: From OH Hwy 8, take Howe Ave exit, then go east on Howe Ave and this place is a quarter-mile down.

New Earth Natural Foods
1605 State Road, Cuyahoga Falls; 330-929-2415
Web site: www.newearthnaturalfoods.com
Natural Food Store. Organic produce. Has books. It is a fairly good size place. It has frozen natural food meals that you can microwave at the store.
Directions: This place is between downtown Akron and the Blossom Music Center.

DAYTON

Café Potage Restaurant
1301 Wayne Avenue, Dayton; 937-224-7687
Hours: Monday 11 am to 2:30 pm; Tuesday to Thursday 11 am to 9 pm (may be closed for din-

ner so best to check); Friday 11 am to 10 pm; Saturday 11 am to 10 pm; Sun 11 am to 2:30 pm
Restaurant. Not pure vegetarian.
Menu: About half the menu is vegetarian. Black Bean Burger, Curry Pumpkin Soups, veggie chili, pastas, Black Beans & Rice, Mexican Lasagna, veggie Lasagna, Ravioli and more.
Other Info: Accepts AMEX, MC, VISA. Price: $$.

Christopher's Restaurant
2318 East Dorothy Lane; 937-299-0089
Hours: Monday to Saturday 7:30 am to 9 pm
Closed Sunday.
Coffeehouse-type place. American. Not pure vegetarian.
Menu: Has several vegetarian dishes. Vegetarian soups, veggie Lasagna, veggie burgers and more.
Comments: Good food and cheap.
Other Info: Full service, take-out. Does not accept reservations. Accepts AMEX, DC, DIS, MC, VISA. Price: $$.
Directions: It is in a shopping center.

Dorothy Lane Market (2 locations)
2710 Far Hills Avenue; 513-299-3561
Washington Sq; 6177 Far Hills Ave; 513-434-1294; Web site: http://www.dorothylane.com/
Hours: Open 24 hours
Regular Supermarket with a Natural Food Section. Has a large organic produce section.

El Meson
903 East Dixie Drive, West Carrollton
937-859-8229
Web site: www.elmeson-macarema.com
Hours: Tuesday to Saturday 11 am to 2 pm, 5 pm to 9:30 pm (until 10 pm on Saturday)
Closed Sunday & Monday
Spanish/Latin-American. Good veg selection.
Menu: Vegetarian fajitas, Black Beans, veg tapas, pisto manchego and vegetarian tostones rellenos.
Comments: Pleasant, bustling atmosphere. Live harp-player or South American music on the weekends. Carved chairs, plants, cabana-style canopies and plants.

Euro Bistro
Page Manor Shopping Center, 5524 Airway Road
937-256-3444
Hours: Monday to Saturday 8 am to 3 pm
Closed Sunday.
Restaurant. Not Pure Vegetarian.
Menu: Homemade soups, salads, Veggie Lasagna, gourmet sandwiches and freshly baked breads.

Comments: Has outdoor seating in season.
Other Info: Limited service, take-out, catering.
Non-smoking. Price: $.

Healthy Alternatives
8351 North Main Street, 937-890-8000
Hours: Monday to Friday 10 am to 8 pm; Sunday 10 am to 6 pm; Sunday 12 noon to 5 pm
Natural Food Store.
Directions: From I-70, take Englewood exit (a little west of I-75) south to Main St. This place on right in Randolph Plaza.

Healthy Alternatives

Randolph Plaza
6204 Wilmington Pike, 937-848-8881
Hours: Monday to Friday 10 am to 8 pm; Saturday 10 am to 5 pm; Sunday 12 noon to 5 pm
Natural Food Store.
Directions: On east side of road, a fourth mile south of I-675 on Wilmington Pike

Little Saigon
1718 Woodman Drive, 937-258-8010
Hours: Monday to Saturday 11 am to 2 pm, 4:30 pm to 9 pm (until 10 pm); closed Sunday.
Vietnamese. Vegan-friendly.
Menu: Full page of vegan dishes on the menu.
Comments: Small. Very busy at lunch but quiet at dinner.

World of Natural Foods
Oakwood Plaza, 2314 Far Hills Avenue
937-293-8978
Hours: Monday to Saturday 10 am to 6 pm
Natural Food Store.
Directions: From Rte 48, take Kettering exit. Go north on Main St and this road becomes Far Hills Ave. This place is then on right in Oakwood Plaza.

FAIRFIELD (near Cincinnati)

Jungle Jim's Market
5440 Dixie Highway; 513-829-1919
Hours: Daily 8 am to 10 pm
International Food Store and large Deli & Bakery. Supermarket-type place. Has a large produce section. Has a large Indian, Asian and Italian section.
Comments: This place is huge. There are over 20,000 imported food items from 60 countries. The produce section is gigantic.
Directions: About five minutes from the north border of Cincinnati. From I-275, take exit #41 and go north on OH Hwy 4 (Springfield Pike,

then becomes Dixie Hwy) 3½ miles and then this place is on the right.

HOLLAND

The Grape Leaf Diner
909 S McCord Road, #6; 419-868-9099
Hours: Daily 11:30 am to 9 pm
Middle Eastern. Vegan options. Not pure vegetarian.
Menu: The vegetarian dishes are marked on the menu. Vegetarian Kebabs, Mushroom Sauté, falafel, Spinach Pie and several other dishes. Fresh juices.
Other Info: Full service, take-out, catering. Accepts AMEX, MC, VISA. Price: $-$$.

INDEPENDENCE

Aladdin's Eatery
6901 Rockside Road; 216-642-7550
Hours: Monday to Thursday 11 am to 10 pm; Friday & Saturday 11 am to 10:30 pm; Sunday 11 am to 9 pm
Middle Eastern. Not pure vegetarian. See Columbus.

KENT

Kent Natural Foods Co-op
151 East Main Street; 330-673-2878
Hours: Monday to Saturday 10 am to 6:30 pm
Closed Sunday.
Natural Food Store.
Menu: Has some ready-made dishes in their cooler such as sandwiches, pita roll-up, veggie pie, hummus, falafel and grape leaves.
Directions: This place on north side of road, east of Rte 43 on the main street of town. Main Street is Rte 59.

The Zephyr
106 West Main; 330-678-4848
Hours: Tuesday to Sunday for three meals
Closed Monday
Natural Foods Restaurant. Mostly Vegetarian.
Middle Eastern.
Menu: Salads, soups, falafel, veggie stir-fry, Middle Eastern dishes, veggie burgers, freshly baked desserts and other dishes.
Comments: Mainly a vegetarian restaurant except serves some seafood dishes.
Other Info: Full service, take-out, catering. Price: $.
Directions: This place is on the main street of Kent, right downtown.

KETTERING (near Cincinnati)

Kettering Hospital Cafeteria
3535 Southern Boulevard
937-296-7262; **Hospital number:** 937-298-4331
Hours: Daily for three meal
Mainly Vegetarian Cafeteria. Vegan options. Not pure vegetarian.
Menu: The menu changes regularly. Has a large selection of sandwiches and veggie burgers, freshly baked breads and desserts. Has a large salad bar with a good selection of dishes.
Other Info: Cafeteria style. Non-smoking. Price: $.

LAKEWOOD (Cleveland suburb)

Aladdin's Eatery
14536 Detroit Avenue
521-4005; **Web site:** www.aladdinseatery.com
Hours: Monday to Thursday 11 am to 10 pm; Friday & Saturday 11 am to 10:30 pm; Sunday 11 am to 9 pm
Middle Eastern. Not pure vegetarian. See Columbus.

Cornucopia Inc Natures Bin
18120 Sloan Avenue, near West Clifton
216-521-4600
Natural Food Store and Deli. Baked goods and a good bulk-food section. Organic produce.
Directions: This place is about 4 miles west of downtown Cleveland. From I-90, take exit #164 towards Lakewood/McKinley, then go north on Riverside Dr (OH Hwy 237) and go ¾ mile, at W Clifton Blvd (Hwy 237) turn right and go a half-mile, then at Sloane Ave turn left and go 1 block.

Doc Hebens Natural Food Market
11841 Detroit Avenue; 216-529-9170
Hours: Monday to Friday 10 am to 6 pm; Saturday 9:30 am to 5:30 pm; closed Sunday.
Natural Food Store.

MIAMISBURG

Sycamore Hospital Cafeteria
2150 Leiter Road; 937-866-0551
Hours: Daily for three meals
Vegetarian-friendly Hospital Cafeteria. Salad bar
Menu: The menu changes regularly. Vegetarian sandwiches, soups and hot dishes.
Other Info: Cafeteria style. Non-smoking. Price: $.

MAYFIELD

Aladdin's Eatery
755 Som Center Road; 440-684-1168
Web site: www.aladdinseatery.com
Middle Eastern. Not pure vegetarian. See Columbus.

MIDDLEBURG

American Harvest
Southland Shopping Center; 13387 Smith
440-888-7727
Hours: Monday to Saturday 9 am to 9 pm
Sunday 12 noon to 6 pm
Natural Food Store and Deli. Juice Bar.
Directions: From I-71, take Bagley Rd exit east. At Pearl turn left, then at Smith turn right. This place on right in Southland Shopping Center.

NORWOOD (near Cincinnati)

Wild Oats Market
2693 Edmonson Road; 513-531-8015
Hours: Monday to Saturday 8 am to 10 pm
Sunday 9 am to 9 am
Natural Food Store and Cafe. Deli, Bakery, Salad Bar and Juice Bar. Organic produce. Supermarket-type place. See Wild Oats Market information.

OBERLIN

Good Food Co-op
Oberlin College, Basement of Harkness; 440-775-6533; Web site: http://www.oberlin.edu/~gfc/
Hours: Monday 4 pm to 6 pm, Thursday 6:30 pm to 8:30 pm, Friday 4 pm to 6 pm; Saturday 10:30 am to 1 pm, Sunday 1 pm to 3 pm
Natural Food Store.
Directions: On the Oberlin College campus. Harkness is the second building to the west of the intersection of College and Professor Streets on the south side of College St.

SOLON (Cleveland suburb)

Mustard Seed Market & Café
6025 Kruse Drive; 440-519-FOOD
Natural Food Store and Café. See Akron for details. Not pure vegetarian.
Hours: Monday to Saturday 9 am to 9 pm
Sunday 10 am to 7 pm
Restaurant Hours: Monday 11 am to 3 pm (closed for dinner); Tuesday to Thursday 11 am

to 8 pm; Friday & Saturday 11 am to 9 pm
Sunday Brunch 10:30 pm to 3 pm
Menu: Has a good selection of vegetarian dishes.
Comments: Upscale design. Fresh juices.
Other Info: Full service, take-out. Has plenty of
seating.
Directions: From Hwy 422, take Som Center Rd
exit, then go south on Som Center Rd a quarter-
mile, then turn right at Solon Rd and go 1 block,
then turn right at Kruse Dr and this place is a
third-mile down. This place is about 7 miles
southeast of downtown Cleveland.

SOUTH EUCLID (Cleveland suburb)

Peking Gourmet and Chinese Restaurant

13955 Cedar Road; 216-397-9939
Chinese. Not pure vegetarian. See details in
Cleveland.

SPRINGDALE (north Cincinnati suburb)

Lu Lu's Rice & Noodles Shop

135 West Kemper Road, Springdale
513-671-4949
Hours: Monday to Thursday 11 am to 9:30 pm;
Friday & Saturday 11 am to 10 pm; closed Sun.
Asian, mainly Chinese and Thai. Not pure
vegetarian.
Menu: Singapore noodles, Pad Thai, noodles
dishes, tom yum soup and tofu dishes.
Comments: Very popular. Stops table seating a
half-hour before closing. Food gets high ratings.
Quick service. Price: $$.
Directions: In a shopping center in Tri County
Mall.

SPRINGFIELD (northeast Dayton)

Healthy Alternatives Natural

1195 Upper Valley Pike; 937-322-5559
Natural Food Store. See Dayton.

***Strange Brew Coffee House & Restaurant

227 East Cecil Street; 937-322-4233
Hours: Monday to Thursday 10 am to 12 mid-
night; Friday to Saturday 10 am to 3 am; Sunday
10 am to 10 pm
Fully Vegan Vegetarian Restaurant.
Menu: Romaine leaf salads, quesadillas made with
vegan cheese and sour cream, and several types of
sandwiches. The weekend brunch includes

tempeh sausage, tofu scrambles, pancakes, Gravy
& Biscuits and much more. For lunch and din-
ner there is mock egg salads, Chic-A-Pea No-
Pocket Platter, rice dishes, Boy Choy, Miso Soup,
mock tuna salad and Focaccia. Has over 100 dif-
ferent drinks including espressos, smoothies, hot
herbal teas and soda.
Comments: Everything freshly made. Gets good
recommendations. Live music on Friday and Sat-
urday nights. Uses fresh, mostly organic vegetar-
ian dishes. Has good Sunday breakfasts.
Other Info: Full service, catering. Accepts reser-
vations but are not necessary. Accepts cash and
checks. Price: $$.
Directions: This place is at the southeast corner
of North Limestone and East Cecil Streets. From
I-70, take Route 72-Cedarville/Springfield exit
(#54), then go north about 2½ miles, then turn
right at Cecil Street and this place is the first building on the right. Or from I-70, take exit #62 towards Springfield and go west on US-40 for 6½
miles, at Spring St turn right and go 2/3 miles,
then turn right at Cecil St.

TALLMADGE (Akron area)

Seven Grains Natural Market

92 West Avenue; 330-633-9999
Hours: Monday to Saturday 9 am to 8 pm
Sunday 10 am to 6 pm
Regular Supermarket and Natural Food Store.
Has a large selection of organic produce.

TOLEDO

Bassett's Health Foods

West Gate Shopping Center, 3301 West Central
Street, Suite 51; 419-531-0334
Hours: Monday to Friday 9:30 am to 9 pm; Sat-
urday 9:30 am to 8 pm; Sunday 11:30 am to 5
pm
Natural Food Store. Organic produce.
Directions: From I-475, take Secor exit north.
This place on right in West Gate Shopping Cen-
ter. At corner of Central and Secor.

Bassett's Health Foods

4315 Heatherdowns Boulevard, 419-382-4142
Natural Food Store. No produce.
Hours: Monday to Saturday 9:30 am to 8 pm
Sunday 11:30 am to 5:30 pm
Directions: From I-80/90, take exit #4, then go
north on Reynolds Rd. At Heatherdowns turn
right and this place on right.

The Beirut

4082 Monroe Street; 419-473-0885
Hours: Monday to Thursday 4 pm to 10:30 pm;
Friday & Saturday 4 pm to 11:30 pm; closed
Sunday.
Lebanese, Mediterranean, Italian and International. Not pure vegetarian.
Comments: Has vegetarian options such as vegetarian spaghetti, hummus and pizza.
Other Info: Full service, take-out. Accepts
AMEX, DIS, MC, VISA. Price: $$.

Phoenix Earth Food Co-op

1447 West Sylvania Avenue, between Jackman
Road and Willys Parkway; 419-476-3211
Hours: Monday to Friday 9 am to 8 pm (9 pm
on Thursday); Saturday 9 am to 7 pm; Sunday
11 noon to 5 pm
Natural Food Store. Has locally grown organic
produce.
Comments: Non-profit. Knowledgeable staff.
Friendly place. Books. Organizes potluck dinners.
Other Info: Accepts MC, VISA.
Directions: From I-75, take Phillips Ave exit
(#206) toward US-24, then go northeast on
Phillips Ave for ¾ mile, then at W Sylvania Ave
turn left and this place is a half-mile down. From
I-475, take Willis Parkway exit. Follow signs into
Willis. At Sylvania turn left and this place on left.

Tandoor Cuisine Of India

2247 South Reynolds Road; 419-385-7467
Hours: Tuesday to Sunday 11:30 am to 2:30 pm,
5 pm to 10 pm; closed Monday.
Indian. Vegan options. Not pure vegetarian.
Menu: Has a large selection of vegetarian dishes.
Comments: Uses clay oven to make naans, etc.
Other Info: Full service, take-out. Accepts
AMEX, MC, VISA.
Directions: It is one mile from exit #4 on the
Ohio Turnpike.

TROY

Cornerstone Natural Foods

110 East Main Street; 937-339-8693
Hours: Monday to Friday 9 am to 7 pm; Saturday 9 am to 6 pm; Sunday 1 pm to 5 pm
Natural Food Store.
Comments: Small place with a good selection of
goods.
Directions: From I-75, take Hwy 41 south for
about 2 miles (becomes also Main St). Go past
the circular intersections in the center of town
and this place is on the right after two blocks.

UPPER ARLINGTON (near Columbus)

Wild Oats Community Market

1555 West Lane Avenue, Lane Avenue Shopping
Center, Upper Arlington
614-481-3400; **Web site:** www.wildoats.com
Hours: Monday to Saturday 8 am to 9 pm
Sunday 8 am to 8 pm
Natural Food Store and Cafe. Deli, Bakery,
Salad Bar and Juice Bar. Organic produce. Supermarket-type place. See Wild Oats Market
information.
Directions: From I-71, take Hudson St exit
(#112), then go a quarter-mile west on E Hudson
St (US-23), at Summit St turn left and go 2/3
miles, at E Lane Ave turn right and this place is
2¾ miles down.

**Web of Life Natural Food Market

Williamsburg Plaza, 25923 Detroit Road, just
west of Columbia; 440-899-2882
Hours: Monday to Saturday 9 am to 9 pm
Sunday 10 am to 6 pm
Natural Food Store and Vegetarian Restaurant.
Mainly Vegan. Large selection of organic produce.
Menu: Has a wide selection of vegetarian dishes.
Comments: Recommended. Friendly place.
Directions: This place is a few miles northwest
of downtown Columbus.

WILLOUGHBY

***Just Natural Health Foods

38669 Mentor Avenue, at Kirtland Road
440-954-8638; **fax:** 440-954-8638; **Web site:**
www.justnaturalhealthfoods.com
Hours: Monday to Friday 9:30 am to 7 pm; Friday & Saturday 10 am to 5 pm; closed Sunday.
Restaurant closes a half-hour early.
Natural Food Store and Vegan Restaurant. Vegan-friendly. Macrobiotic options. Juice Bar.
Menu: Vegetarian breakfast, lunch and dinners.
Sandwiches, soups, salads and daily special.
Other Info: Counter service, take-out. Has a few
tables in front of the store. Price: $$. Accepts MC,
VISA.
Directions: Across from Andrew School for Girls.
From I-90 coming east, take Hwy 2 E exit (#185)
towards Palmersville, then go 4 miles east on Hwy
2, take the Hwy 640 E/Vine St exit towards
Willoughby and go 1 mile on Vine St (Hwy 640).
It then becomes Mentor Ave and then this place
is a half-mile down. From I-90 coming west, take
Exit #193 and this place is 2 miles northwest of
the exit.

Wooster Food Co-op

138 East Liberty Street; 330-264-9797
Hours: Monday to Saturday 10 am to 6 pm
Closed Sunday.
Natural Food Store. Organic produce.

YELLOW SPRINGS

Ha Ha Pizza

108 Xenia Avenue; 937-767-2131
Hours: Monday to Saturday 11:30 am to 9 pm;
Sunday 1 pm to 8 pm
Pizza. Vegetarian-friendly. Not pure vegetarian.
Menu: Offers whole-wheat pizzas. Soy cheese can
be put on the pizzas or in the calzones. Non-typical
vegetarian toppings are water chestnut,
tempeh, alfalfa sprouts, falafel, refried beans, banana,
broccoli, zucchini and eggplant. Also has
the normal toppings. Has a variety of calzones
such as Tofu, Pesto, Bean Burrito and Broccoli.
Comments: Uses extra virgin olive oil in sauces.
Other Info: Full service, take-out, catering. Price:
$.
Directions: On the main street of Yellow Springs.

**The Organic Grocery

230 Keith's Alley, just off Xenia Avenue
937-767-7215
Hours: Monday to Friday 9 am to 7 pm; Saturday
9 am to 7 pm; Sunday 11 am to 6 pm
**National Food Store and take-out Vegetarian
Deli.** Juice Bar. Vegan options. Organic produce.
Menu: Has sandwiches, vegetarian chili, hummus,
veggie sushi, falafel, curry vegetables, veggie
chili and more. Fresh juices.
Other Info: Counter service, take-out. No seating.
Non-smoking. Price: $.
Directions: From I-675, take Dayton/Yellow
Spring exit. Go south on Dayton/Yellow Springs
Rd eight miles to Yellow Springs. At Corry turn
right, then at Keith's Alley turn right. From I-70,
take US-68 S Exit (#52A) towards Xenia and this
place is 7 miles down.

Sunrise Café

259 Xenia Avenue
937-767-7211; **Web site:** www.sunrisecafe.com
Hours: Monday, Tuesday 10:30 am to 2 pm, 5:30
pm to 8:30 pm; Wednesday to Saturday 8 am to
2 pm, 5:30 pm to 9 pm; Sunday 9 am to 2 pm,
5:30 pm to 8:30 pm
Natural International, American. Vegan options.
Not pure vegetarian.

Menu: Has a good vegetarian section on the menu
including Sunrise Vegiburger, veggie soups,
Vegimelt, salads, pastas, Rice, Beans & Vegetables,
Thai Peanut Tofu and Tabbouleh. For breakfast
veggie sausage and multi-grain cereal with soy
milk.
Comments: Pleasant, restored 1940s diner. Everything
is homemade on the premises.
Other Info: Full service, take-out, catering. Non-smoking.
Accepts DIS, MC, VISA. Price: $-$$.
Directions: On the main street of Yellow Springs.

Winds Café & Bakery

215 Xenia Avenue; 937-767-1144
Hours: Tuesday to Saturday 11:30 am to 2 pm, 5
pm to 10 pm; Sunday Brunch 10 am to 2 pm;
closed Monday.
Natural Foods. Vegan options.
Menu: Has freshly baked breads, cakes and pastries.
Has several vegetarian options including
Scrambled Tofu, Stir-fried Tofu with Mushrooms,
Green Chilaquiles, French Lima Beans, Cheese
Ravioli, pastas, Organic Sandwich, muffins, cookies,
scones, sourdough and Focaccia. The menu
regularly changes. Fresh juices.
Comments: Some of the breads have eggs or dairy.
Breads can be served with olive oil.
Other Info: Full service, take-out. Accepts
AMEX, DIS, MC, VISA. Price: $$-$$$.
Directions: On the main street of Yellow Springs.

YOUNGSTOWN

Aladdin's Eatery

7325 South Avenue; 330-629-6450
Web site: www.aladdinseatery.com
Middle Eastern. Not pure vegetarian. See
Columbus.

Good Food Co-op

62 Pyatt Street; 330-747-9368
Hours: Monday to Saturday 10 am to 6 pm
Closed Sunday.
Natural Food Store. Organic produce and bulk
items.
Directions: From I-680, take Market St (Rte 7)
exit south. At Pyatt St turn left. This place on left
opposite Pyatt Street Market.

Health Food Center

265 Federal Plaza Way; 330-746-1515
Natural Food Store.

Oregon

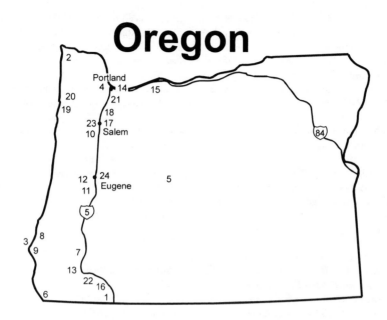

1. Ashland
2. Astoria
3. Bandon
4. Beaverton
5. Bend
6. Brookings
7. Canyonville
8. Coos Bay
9. Coquille
10. Corvallis
11. Cottage Grove
12. Eugene

13. Grants Pass
14. Gresham
15. Hood River
16. Jacksonville
17. Keizer
18. Lake Oswega
19. Lincoln City
20. Pacific City
21. Portland
22. Roque River
23. Salem
24. Springfield

ASHLAND

Ashland Bakery & Café
38 East Main Street; 541-482-2117
Winter Hours: Daily 8 am to 3 pm
Summer Hours: Daily 7 am to 8 pm
Café and Bakery. American. Living Foods and Vegan. Not pure vegetarian
Menu: Has many vegetarian options including soups, vegetarian Lasagna, Italian Vegetable soup, fresh baked goods, sandwiches and vegetarian chili.
Comments: Relaxed, casual place. Uses organic floor.
Other Info: Full service, take-out. Accepts MC, VISA. Price: $-$$.

Directions: From I-5, take exit #19 towards Ashland, then go south on S Valley View Rd a half-mile, at OR 99 turn left and this place is about 2 miles down. This place is in the middle of Ashland.

Ashland Community Food Store
237 North 1st Street, between A Street & B Street
541-482-2237; **email:** acfs@mind.net; **Web site:** www.acfs.org
Hours: Monday to Saturday 8 am to 9 pm
Sunday 9 am to 9 pm
Natural Food Store and Deli. Salad Bar and Bakery.
Comments: Does cooking classes.
Other Info: Counter service, take-out. Has a few

tables in the front and a few outside. Accepts DIS, MC, VISA.
Directions: From I-5 south, take Hwy 66 exit, coming off ramp turn left onto Siskiyou Blvd. At first street turn right and this place on left. From I-5 north, take Valley View exit #19 and off ramp turn right and go south a half-mile. At Hwy 99 turn left and go southeast 2 miles, at 1st St turn left and store on left.

Geppetto's
345 East Main Street
541-482-1138
Hours: Daily 8 am to 10 pm
Italian. Vegan options. Not pure vegetarian.
Menu: Has several vegetarian options including a selection of vegetarian pastas, veggie burgers and salads. The Eggplant Burgers are recommended. Has a daily vegetarian special, Tofu Burger, Cajun Burger. Pesto (ingredients come from own farm), Pasta with Sundried Tomato Sauce, Grilled Cheese Sandwich and Tofu Sausage Burger.
Comments: Friendly place. Full service, take-out. Accepts DIS, MC, VISA. Price: $-$$.

Greenleaf Restaurant
49 North Main Street; 541-482-2808
Mediterranean and International. Not pure vegetarian.
Comments: Good food and service.
Directions: At the Plaza, in the north end of downtown.

House of Thai
1667 Siskiyou Boulevard; 541-488-2583
Hours: Monday to Friday 11 am to 3 pm, 4 pm to 9 pm; Friday & Saturday 11 am to 3 pm, 4 pm to 10 pm; Sunday 4 pm to 9 pm
Thai. Not pure vegetarian.
Menu: Has a separate vegetarian menu.
Comments: It is considered to be a good place. Voted best Oriental restaurant in Ashland in 1992. Family managed.
Other Info: Full service, take-out, catering. Accepts MC, VISA. Price: $$.

Pilaf
10 Calle Guanajuato
541-488-7898; **Web site:** www.globalpantry.com
Hours: Tuesday to Saturday 11 am to 9 pm; Sunday 11 am to 4 pm; closed Monday.
Fully Vegetarian. Vegan options. Mediterranean, Middle Eastern and Indian food.
Menu: Pita and Panini sandwiches, salads, Greek Salad, hummus, Stuffed Grape Leaves, chapati,

dal, pakoras, falafel, Panini Veganini, Artichoke Panini, burritos, Mediterranean Sampler, Vegan Sampler (a great combination plate) and rice pudding. Has specials such as Lasagna, Whole Stuff Zucchini, Potato Moussaka and Sicilian Pasta. Cappuccino, espresso, chai and soy chai. Serves organic coffee.
Comments: Can dine on the balcony overlooking the creek. Well-designed dinning room with a fireplace. Pleasant atmosphere.
Other Info: Limited service, take-out, catering. Accepts MC, VISA. Price: $.
Direction: In Lithia Park on Ashland Creek. From I-5, take Exit #19 towards Ashland, then go south on Valley View Rd for a third-mile, then at Rte 99, turn left and this place is 2 miles down, near the intersection with Guanajuato Way.

ASTORIA

Community Store
1389 Duane Street
503-325-0027
Hours: Monday to Saturday 9 am to 6 pm Closed Sunday.
Natural Food Store and little Deli. Organic produce.
Other Info: Accepts MC, VISA.
Directions: From Hwy 30 (26/101 from south) follow signs to downtown Astoria. At 12th turn right in direction away from river and go 1 block. At Exchange turn left, then at 14th turn left and this place on left.

**The Columbia Café
1114 Marine Drive
503-325-2233
Hours: Sunday to Tuesday 8 am to 2 pm; Wednesday, Thursday 8 am to 2 pm, 5 pm to 8 pm; Friday & Sat 8 am to 2 pm, 5 pm to 9 pm
Vegetarian Natural Food Café. Vegan options. Not pure vegetarian.
Menu: Has many vegetarian options including bean burritos, crepes, homemade pasta and salads. Has several types of salsa. Fresh juices. Non-alcoholic beer.
Comments: Friendly place. Pleasant owner.
Other Info: Full service, take-out. Cash only; no credit cards. Price: $$.
Directions: From US 30 (26/101 from south) follow signs to downtown Astoria, then at 8th St (US 30) turn right and go 1 block, then at Commercial St (US 30) turn left and go a third-mile, at Marine Dr (US 30) turn a sharp left and this place is a quarter-mile down.

BANDON (on the Oregon coast between Brookings and Astoria)

**Mother's Natural Grocery
975 Highway 101
541-347-4086
Hours: Monday to Saturday 10 am to 6 pm
Closed Sunday.
Natural Food Store and Vegetarian Deli. Organic produce.
Menu: Three vegetarian soups daily, black bean burritos, veggie chili, several type of pita sandwiches, veggie Tofu Teriyaki, veggie Lasagna, salads and more.
Other Info: Counter service, take-out. Has several tables. Accepts MC, VISA.

BEAVERTON (POLAND SUBURB)

McMenamins Pub
2927 SW Cedar Hills Boulevard, by the mall
503-641-0151
Hours: Sunday to Thursday 11 am to 12 midnight; Friday & Saturday 11 am to 1 am
Tavern. Not pure vegetarian.
Menu: Has a good amount of vegetarian dishes on the menu. Pasta with Black Beans, Peanuts and Salsa, Paul's Famous Stir-fry and Spicy Tofu Burritos.
Other Info: Full service, take-out, catering. Non-smoking. Accepts AMEX, MC, VISA. Price: $.

Nature's Fresh NW (Wild Oats)
4000 SW 117th Street
503-646-3824
Hours: Daily 9 am to 9 pm
Natural Food Store and Cafe. Deli, Bakery, Salad Bar and Juice Bar. Organic produce. Supermarket-type place. See Wild Oats Market information.
Directions: From I-5, take Rte 217 exit and follow signs to Beaverton, then take Canyon exit and at Canyon turn left. At 117th turn right and this place on right. This place is about 5 miles west of downtown Portland.

Swagat Indian Cuisine
4325 SW 109th Avenue, at Beaverton–Hillsdale Highway; 503-626-3000
Hours: Daily 11:30 am to 2:30 pm, 5 pm to 10 pm
North and South Indian. Lunch buffet. Not pure vegetarian. See Portland for more information.
Menu: Has several vegetarian dishes. Fresh juices.
Comments: The lunch buffet is very popular. Friendly service. In a 50s style ranch house. Lunch

buffet is a good value. Food gets good ratings.
Other Info: Full service, take-out. Accepts AMEX, DC, DIS, MC, VISA. Price: $$.

Swagat's
2074 NW Lovejoy Street; 503-227-4300
Hours: Daily 11:30 am to 2:30 pm (lunch buffet), 5 pm to 10 pm
Indian. Inexpensive place. Not pure vegetarian.
Comments: Good service and a friendly atmosphere.
Other Info: Accepts AMEX, DIS, MC, VISA.

Trader Joe's
11753 SW Beaverton–Hillsdale Highway
503-626-3794

BEND

Devore's Good Food
1124 NW Neort; 541-389-6588
Hours: Monday to Saturday 8 am to 7 pm
Sunday 10 am to 6 pm
Natural Food Store and take-out Deli. Organic produce.
Menu: Soups, salads, casseroles, pizzas, veggie chili, sandwiches and hot dishes. Everything is made with organic produce.
Comments: Friendly place.
Other Info: Accepts MC, VISA. Counter service, take-out only.
Directions: From Hwy 97, go west on Greenwood (becomes Neort) and this place on right.

Nature's Fresh NW (Wild Oats)
2610 NE Highway 20, Bend; 542-389-0151
Hours: Daily 7 am to 10 pm
Natural Food Store and Cafe. Deli, Bakery, Salad Bar and Juice Bar. Organic produce. Supermarket-type place. See Wild Oats Market information.
Directions: From Hwy 97 (becomes NW 6th St), go west on US 20 and this place is 4½ miles down. This place is in east Bend.

Nature's
Wagner Payless Mall, 1950 NE 3rd Street
541-382-6732
Hours: Monday to Friday 9 am to 9 pm
Saturday & Sunday 9 am to 8 pm
Natural Food Store and Deli. Juice Bar.
Other Info: Counter service, take-out. Has seating. Accepts AMEX, MC, VISA.
Directions: 3rd Street is Hwy 97. This place on north side of road in Wagner Payless Mall.

BROOKINGS

Brooking Natural Food Co-op
511 Fern Ave (Mailing: PO Box 8051)
541-469-9551
email: prema@harborside.com
Natural Food Store. Organic produce.

CANYONVILLE

Promise Natural Food & Bakery
503 South Main
541-839-4167
Hours: Monday to Friday 9:30 am to 6 pm; Saturday 10 am to 5 pm; closed Sunday.
Natural Food Store. Bakery. Organic produce.
Other Info: Cash or check only; no credit cards.
Directions: From I-5, take exit #98 towards Canyonville/Days Creek, then go east on Canyonville Riddle Rd and go 2 blocks, at OR 99 (Main St) turn right and this place is 3 blocks down, at junction with 5th St.

COOS BAY (on the Oregon coast between Brookings and Astoria)

Coos Head Food Store
1960 Sherman Avenue, North Bend
541-756-7264
Hours: Monday to Friday 9 am to 7 pm; Saturday 10 am to 6 pm; Sunday 12 noon to 5 pm
Natural Food Store. Organic produce. Sells a good selection of vegetarian magazines.
Menu: Has Garden Burgers and burritos (only). Fresh juices including wheatgrass.
Other Info: Accepts AMEX, MC, VISA.
Directions: This place is a block south of North Bend Library on west side of road.

COQUILLE

Nosler's Natural Grocery
99 East 1st Street
541-396-4823
Hours: Monday to Friday 10 am to 6 pm (until 7 on Thursday); Saturday 12 noon to 5 pm; closed Sunday.
Natural Food Store and Deli. Organic produce.
Menu: Has a small selection of vegetarian dishes such as Boca Burger, sandwiches and Tofu Salad.
Other Info: Accepts MC, VISA. Counter service, take-out. Has a small seating area.
Directions: Take Rte 42 into Coquille and this place is at the corner of 1st Street, opposite the Safeway.

CORVALLIS

The Beanery
948 NW Circle Boulevard; 541-754-5916
500 SW 2nd Street; 541-753-7442
2541 NW Monroe Avenue; 541-757-0828
Hours: Daily 10 am to 9 pm
Coffeehouse. Not pure vegetarian.
Menu: Soups, salads, burritos, sandwiches, vegetarian Lasagna and desserts. Cappuccino, espresso.
Other Info: Counter service, take-out. Accepts DISC, MC, VISA. Price: $$.

Big River Restaurant & Bar
101 NW Jackson Street; 541-757-0694
Hours: Monday to Thursday 11 am to 2 pm, 5 pm to 9:30 pm; Friday 11 am to 2 pm, 5 pm to 11:30 pm; Saturday 5 pm to 11:30 pm; closed Sunday.
Restaurant. Not pure vegetarian.
Menu: Has a separate vegetarian menu. Roasted Summer Vegetables with Artichokes, squash, pizzas, Baby Beets with Vinaigrette Dressing and Organic Greens.
Comments: Upscale place. Accepts AMEX, MC, VISA.
Directions: This place is in the middle of town, next to the river. Coming into town on OR-34 coming west cross the river, at NW 2nd St (US 20) turn left and go 1 block, then at NW Van Buren Ave (OR 34) turn left and this place is 1 block down.

Cirello's Pizza
919 NW Circle Boulevard; 541-754-9199
Hours: Monday to Saturday 11 am to 10 pm; Sunday 4:30 pm to 9 pm; Delivery after 5 pm.
Italian. Vegan-friendly.
Menu: Gourmet veggie pizzas with special cheeses, artichokes and pesto. Fresh green salads.

First Alternative Co-op
1007 SE 3rd Street; 541-753-3115
email: firstalt@firstalt.com
Web site: www.firstalt.com
Hours: Daily 9 am to 9 pm
Natural Food Store and Deli. Organic produce, bulk grains, homemade breads. Good place to check the bulletin board for events.
Menu: Pre-made sandwiches, salads and hot dishes.
Other Info: Accepts AMEX, MC, VISA.
Directions: From I-5, take Hwy 34 exit west and drive to Corvallis. At 4th St turn left and this

place on left about 1 mile down. This place is about 8 miles from I-5.

**Interzone

1563 Monroe Street, at 16th; 541-754-5965
Hours: Monday to Friday 7 am to 12 midnight
Saturday & Sunday 8 am to 12 midnight
Vegetarian Coffeehouse. Vegan friendly.
Menu: Has Tempeh Turnovers, vegan pastries, salads, sandwiches, soups, scrambled tofu and much more
Comments: Friendly, casual place. Nice people.
Other Info: Cash only; no credit cards.
Directions: From coming into town coming west on OR 34, cross the bridge (becomes NW Harrison Blvd), then turn left at 4th St and go 3 blocks, then turn right at NW Monroe and this place is ¾ mile down (about 10 blocks).

**Nearly Normals

109 NW 15th Street
541-753-0791
Hours: Mon to Wed 8 am to 8 pm; Thur & Fri 8 am to 9 pm; Sat 9 am to 9 pm; closed Sun. Sunday for brunch in spring and summer
Full Vegetarian. Vegan options.
Menu: Full menu of vegetarian options with burritos, Italian Tofu Sandwich, Sun Burger, Tofu Burger, Curries, falafel, a couple soups, pastas, and Cheese Ravioli. Fresh juices. Has really good salads with tofu and homemade dressing. Freshly made desserts.
Comments: In a two story house near Oregon State University. Relaxed, friendly place. Comfortable atmosphere. Most likely the best vegetarian place in town. Local organic produce used when possible. Gets really high recommendations. Nice people.
Other Info: Limited service, take-out, catering. Cash only; no credit cards. Price: $-$$.
Directions: From coming into town coming west on OR 34, cross the bridge (becomes NW Harrison Blvd), then turn left at 4th St and go 3 blocks, then turn right at NW Monroe and this place is ¾ mile down (about 10 blocks), at corner of 15th St.

COTTAGE GROVE

Sunshine General Store

824 West Main Street
541-942-8836
Hours: Monday to Saturday 10 am to 7 pm
Closed Sunday.
Natural Food Store. Organic produce.
Other Info: Accepts MC, VISA.

Directions: From I-5, take exit #174 and follow signs to Rte 99. At Main St turn right and this place on right.

EUGENE

**Andrew Smash

840 Willamette Street
541-683-5667, 888-770-3707; email: 888-770-3707; Web site: http://www.andrewsmash.com
Fully Vegetarian Fast-Food.
Menu: Veggie burgers (both veggie and vegan), vegan soups and a vegan un-chicken patty option. Has a combo option, which is a burger, baked French fries and a drink. Fruit Smoothies, with or without dairy.
Comments: Colorful, brightly lit atmosphere. The staff is friendly and efficient.
Directions: Downtown area on Willamette Street.

Anitolio's

992 Willamette; 541-343-9661
Hours: Monday to Thursday 11:30 am to 9 pm; Friday 11:30 am to 3 pm, 5 pm to 10 pm; Saturday 11:30 am to 3 pm, 5 pm to 9 pm (Greek food only); Sunday 5 pm to 9 pm
Natural Foods Mediterranean. Not pure veg.
Menu: Has several vegetarian options including soups, salads and main dishes. Non-alcoholic beer.
Comments: Friendly management.
Other Info: Full service, take-out. Accepts MC, VISA. Price: $$.

The Beanery

2465 Hilyard Street, near the University of Oregon; 541-344-0221
Hours: Daily 6 am to 11 pm
152 W 5th Street; 541-342-3378
Web site: www.allannbroscoffee.com
Hours: Monday to Thursday 6 am to 9 pm; Friday & Sat 6 am to 10 pm; Sun 7 am to 9 pm
Coffee shop with a selection of vegetarian items. See description under Coravallis.
Menu: Garden Sandwiches, Tofu Burrito and other dishes.
Other Info: Accepts AMEX, MC, VISA.

Casablanca

5th Street Marketplace, 296 East 5th Avenue
541-342-3885
Hours: Daily 11 am to 6 pm
Middle Eastern. Vegan options. Not pure vegetarian.
Menu: Has many vegetarian options including hummus and falafel sandwiches.
Other Info: Cafeteria style, take-out. Price: $.

Cozmic Pizza
1432 Willamette Street
541-338-9333
Hours: Daily 11:30 am to 11 pm
Pizza Place. Mainly Vegetarian. Salad Bar. Not pure vegetarian.
Menu: Veggie pepperoni. Good lunch specials with vegetable and organic pizza by the slice. Good size salad bar.
Other Info: Accepts AMEX, MC, VISA.

**Friendly Foods
2757 Friendly Street; 541-683-2079
Hours: Monday to Saturday 8 am to 10 pm
Sunday 9 am to 10 pm
Natural Food Store and Vegetarian Deli. Organic produce.
Menu: Has a large variety of vegetarian dishes.
Other Info: Indoor and outdoor seating. Accepts AMEX, MC, VISA.
Directions: From I-5, take 30th Street exit and go west towards town. Road winds and becomes 29th, then 28th. Continue on 28th and at Friendly St turn right and this place on right near the turn.

The Glenwood Restaurant
Near the University of Oregon
1346 Alder Street   541-343-8303
Hours: Daily 7 am to 10 pm
2588 Willamette Street   541-687-8201
Hours: Daily 7 am to 9 pm
Hours: Alder Street place daily for 24 hours
Willamette place daily for three meals
California-style. Vegan options. Not pure veg.
Menu: Has a wide selection of vegetarian dishes including Scrambled Tofu, Fried Rice, Tofu Stir-fry, Tofu Burrito and salads.
Other Info: Take out. Accepts AMEX, DIS, MC, VISA. **Price:** $.

**Govinda's Vegetarian Buffet
270 West 8th Avenue; 541-686-3531
Hours: Monday to Friday 11:30 am to 2:30 pm, 5 pm to 8 pm; closed Sunday.
Fully Vegetarian International, American and Indian. All-you-can-eat salad and hot bar. Vegan options.
Menu: Lasagna, basmati rice, Vegetable subjis, enchiladas and desserts.
Comments: Recommended, very good place. Serves cafeteria style. Run by a Hare Krishnas.
Other Info: Counter service, take-out. Accepts AMEX, DIS, MC, VISA. **Price:** $-$$.
Directions: Take I-105 south until it end in the

city, then turn left at 7th Ave and go 4 blocks, then turn right at Charnelton and go 1 block, then turn left at W 8th Ave and this place is 1 block down.

***Herbie's Garden & Juice Bar
525 Willamette, Eugene; 541-284-2824
Hours: Monday to Friday 10 am to 7 pm; Saturday 10 am to 6 pm; closed Sunday.
Fully Vegan International. Mainly organic.
Menu: Soups, salads, sandwiches, wraps, veggie Philly Steak (made with homemade seitan), Herbieburger (black bean burger) and other dishes. Smoothies.
Comments: Has a pleasant décor with a fountain and plants. Friendly place.
Other Info: Full service, take-out. Non-smoking. Does not take reservations. Accepts AMEX, MC, VISA.
Directions: Right across the street from the main Post Office. At Willamette and Fifth. Take I-105 south until it ends in the city, then turn left at 7th Ave and 5 blocks, then turn left at Olive St and go 2 blocks, then at 5th turn left and this place is 1 block down at the corner.

**Holy Cow Café
222 East 13th Street, near University of Oregon
541-346-2562; **Web site:** http://
emufoods.uoregon.edu/holycow/index.html
Hours: Monday to Thursday 10 am to 7 pm; Friday 10 am to 3 pm; closed Sat & Sun.
Fully Vegetarian International. Mostly Vegan. Organic foods. Cafeteria-style Hot Bar with over 15 dishes. Salad Bar.
Menu: Has a large selection of vegetarian dishes that changes regularly. Thai Tofu, Mandarin Tofu, Roasted & Steamed Vegetables and Coconut Braised Vegetable Curry. Daily specials include vegetable Szechuan Tofu and Eggplant, veggie Mac and Cheese, Pad Thai Noodles, Indian Feast, Vegan Lasagna, enchiladas and Middle Eastern feast.
Comments: Organic restaurant located in a college student union food court. Compost project recycling with urban gardens and local farmers.
Other Info: Cafeteria-style, catering, take-out. Non-smoking. Accepts personal cheques.
Directions: In the EMU Student Union building on the University of Oregon campus. From Franklin Blvd. turn south on Agate St, turn right at 15th St, turn right at University St or at the street before. Parking meters available behind student union building. There is visitor parking on the south side of the building. There are also park-

ing meters on University St. Take I-105 south until it ends and then turn left at 7th St and go 2 blocks, the go south on Charnelton St for 6 blocks, then at 13th turn left and this place is about 7 blocks down.

Keystone Café
395 West 5th Street, downtown
541-342-2075
Hours: Daily 7 am to 3 pm. Breakfast all day.
Natural Food Restaurant and Organic Bakery. American. Not pure vegetarian
Menu: Breakfasts with whole-grain pancakes, potatoes, muffins and scones. Fresh juices.
Other Info: Full service, take-out. Price: $.
Directions: Take Hwy 105 south until it ends, then turn left at 7th Ave and go 3 blocks, then at Lincoln St turn left and go 3 blocks, then at 4th Ave turn left and go 1 block, then at Lawrence St turn left and this place is 1 block down at 5th Street.

Kiva
125 West 11th Avenue; 541-342-8666
Hours: Monday to Saturday 9 am to 8 pm
Sunday 10 am to 5 pm
Natural Food Store and Deli. Organic produce.
Menu: Salads, vegetarian sandwiches, tofu and tempeh dishes and other dishes.
Other Info: Accepts MC, VISA.
Directions: From I-5, take Downtown/Civic Center exit (I-115), at 7th Ave turn left and go 4 blocks. At Olive turn right and this place is on the right 4 blocks down, at the corner of 11th and Olive.

**The LocoMotive
291 East 5th; 541-465-4754
Web site: www.thelocomotive.com
Hours: Wednesday to Saturday 5 pm to 10 pm for dinner only; closed Sunday to Tuesday.
Fully Vegetarian International. Mostly Vegan.
Menu: Menu changes weekly. Soups, Spinach & Yogurt Soup, House Salad, Greek Salad, sandwiches, Black Bean Soup, burritos, Steamed Semolina, mashed potatoes & gravy, Pasta Paradiso, Sautéed Portobello Mushrooms, Couscous Stew and homemade breads. Some desserts are ice creams, sorbets, Brandy-Baked Apple, Cobbler du Jour and Baklava. Cappuccino, espresso.
Comments: Small European bistro-style place. Great place, a little upscale. White tablecloths. Family-owned and operated. Service is excellent. The owner is a nice guy. Considered to be the

best vegetarian restaurant in Eugene. Local organic produce used when possible.
Other Info: Full service, catering. Non-smoking. Reservations recommended for weekends. Accepts MC, VISA. Price: $$.
Directions: From I-5, take the #194B exit to Hwy 105, then go east on 7th Ave about 8 block, then turn left at High St and go 1 block, take a left at 5th Ave and this place is on your right. This place is across from the 5th Street Public Market.

**Lotus Garden
810 Charnelton, at 8th Avenue; 541-344-1928
Hours: Monday, Wednesday to Friday 11 am to 3 pm, 4:30 pm to 9 pm; Saturday 12 noon to 9 pm; Saturday 12 noon to 8 pm; closed Tuesday.
Fully Vegetarian Chinese. Traditional Szechuan and Hunan Vegan.
Menu: Has a large menu with mock "meat" dishes such as vegan "shrimp," mock "chicken," and Chinese vegetable dishes.
Comments: Gets good recommendations. Reasonably priced.
Other Info: Accepts DIS, MC, VISA. Price: $-$$.
Directions: Near downtown Eugene. From I-5, take the #194B exit to Hwy 105 and take it until it ends, then go east on 7th Ave 3 blocks, then turn right at Charnelton and this place is 1 block down at 8th Ave.

Mekala's Thai Restaurant
5th Street Marketplace, 296 East 5th Avenue
541-342-4872
Hours: Daily 11 am to 10 pm
Thai. Not pure vegetarian.
Menu: Has a good selection of vegetarian dishes. Fresh juices.
Comments: Pleasant atmosphere. A bit upscale, but the prices are reasonable. Gets great ratings. No MSG. Uses only canola oil for cooking.
Other Info: Full service, take-out, catering. Non-smoking. Accepts AMEX, MC, VISA. Price: $-$$.
Directions: Upstairs in the Fifth Street Public Market.

***Morning Glory Café and Bakery
450 Willamette Street; 541-687-0709
Restaurant Hours: Tuesday to Sunday 7:30 am to 3:30 pm
Coffee Hours: Monday to Saturday 6:30 am to 8 pm; Sunday 6:30 am to 6 pm
Vegan Bakery and Café. American, Kosher dishes.
Menu: Good baked goods, breads, Biscuits and

Gravy, sandwiches, salads, and BBQ Tofu. Fresh organic orange juice.
Comments: One of the better vegetarian restaurants in the country. Popular, friendly place. Good size portions.
Other Info: Full service, take-out. Cash only; no credit cards. Price: $.
Directions: Take I-105 until it ends, then go east on 7th Ave for 5 blocks, then at Olive St turn left and go 2 blocks, then at 5th Ave turn right and this place is 1 block down.

New Frontier Market
200 West Broadway; 541-345-1235
Hours: Monday to Thursday 7 am to 9; Friday 7 am to 10 pm; Saturday 8 am to 9 pm; Sunday 8 am to 8 pm
Natural Food Store and Deli. Organic produce.
Menu: Has a large amount of vegetarian dishes.
Other Info: Accepts AMEX, DC, DIS, MC, VISA.
Directions: The place is in downtown Eugene. From Rte 126, take Rte 99 S/Jefferson St exit towards City Center Mall/Fairgrounds, then go east on 7th Ave/Rte 99 for a quarter-mile, at Charnelton St turn right and go 2 blocks, then at Broadway turn right and this place is at the corner. Or take I-115 south until it end, then turn left at W 7th Ave and go 4 blocks, then at Charnelton St turn right and this place is 3 blocks down at W Broadway.

New Frontier Market – West
1101 West 8th Avenue; 541-345-7401
Hours: Monday to Friday 7 am to 12 midnight; Saturday 8 am to 12 midnight; Sunday 8 am to 11 pm
Natural Food Store and small Deli. Organic produce.
Other Info: Accepts AMEX, DC, DIS, MC, VISA.
Directions: From I-5, take exit #105 and go south into the city, then take Jefferson St (last exit) exit and get on Jefferson St and go 1 block. At 8th St turn right and then this place is 5 blocks down on corner of Van Buren and 8th St.

Oasis Fine Foods (Wild Oats)
2489 Willamette Street, at 24th
541-345-1014
Hours: Daily 8 am to 10 pm
Natural Food Store and Cafe. Deli, Bakery, Salad Bar and Juice Bar. Organic produce. Supermarket-type place. See Wild Oats Market information.

Comments: Has electric shopping carts.
Directions: From I-5, take 30th Avenue exit west (#189) towards South Eugene, then go west on 30th Ave 3½ miles (becomes Amazon Pkwy), at 29th turn left and go a third-mile, then at Willamette turn right and this place is a third-mile down on right.

Oasis Fine Foods (Wild Oats)
Oasis Plaza, 2580 Willakenzie Road
541-334-6382
Hours: Daily 8 am to 10 pm
Natural Food Store and Cafe. Deli, Bakery, Salad Bar and Juice Bar. Organic produce. Supermarket-type place. See Wild Oats Market information.
Directions: From I-5, take Belt Line Hwy (#195) west 1 mile to Coburg Rd exit. At Coburg Rd go south and this place on right a half-mile down. This place is in north Eugene.

Organically Grown Co-op
1800 Prairie Road, 503-689-5320
Natural Food Store.

**Pizza Research Institute
1328 Lawrence Street; 541-343-1307
Hours: Daily 5:30 pm to 9:30 pm
Vegetarian Pizza Place. Not pure vegetarian.
Menu: Has an excellent selection of vegetarian dishes. Has an excellent vegan pizza. Organic garden salads.
Comments: Good, friendly place. Makes their own totally vegan tofu topping, because they were not satisfied with what they can get outside.
Other Info: No credit card; cash only. Full service, take-out. Does not deliver.
Directions: From I-5, take I-115 west then south until it ends in the downtown. Then turn left on 7th and go 2 blocks, then turn right at Lawrence St (go south) and go 6 blocks, then turn left and make a quick right onto Lawrence and this place is a half-block down.

Red Barn
357 Van Buren; 541-342-7503
Hours: Monday to Saturday Daily 9 am to 9 pm Sunday 11 am to 6 pm
Natural Food Store. Has ready-made sandwiches. Organic produce.
Other Info: Accepts MC, VISA.
Directions: From I-5, take I-105/126 exit west, then take 6th St (Hwy 99) exit and bear right. At Blair turn right and this place on right at corner of 4th and Blair.

Sundance Natural Foods

728 East 24th, at Hilyard; 541-343-9142
Hours: Daily 7 am to 11 pm
Natural Food Store and mainly Vegetarian Deli. Salad Bar. Vegan friendly. Large place with a great selection.
Menu: Has an all-you-can-eat salad bar for $4.95. Soups and hot dishes.
Comments: Popular with the university students.
Other Info: Accepts AMEX, DC, DIS, MC, VISA.
Directions: This place is located near to the northeast corner of Amazon Park, near the University of Oregon in south Eugene. From I-5, take 30th Ave exit (#189) and go west on 30th Ave for 2 miles (a quick road). At Hilyard turn right and this place is 6 blocks down on right, at corner of 24th and Hilyard.

Wild Rose Market

5th Street Marketplace. 296 East 5th Avenue
541-484-7302
Hours: Daily 10 am to 6 pm
Natural Food Store with International foods. Vegan options. Not pure vegetarian
Menu: Has many vegetarian options including tortillas, salads, fresh soups, veggie burger, sandwiches and Gyros. Gourmet options. Fresh juices.
Comments: Reasonably priced. Good food.
Other Info: Counter service, take-out. Price: $.
Directions: From I-5, take the #194B exit to Hwy 105, then go east on 7th Ave about 8 blocks, then turn left at High St and go 1 block, take a left at 5th Ave and this place is on the left in the 5th Street Public Market.

GRANTS PASS

Farmer's Market

603 Roque River Highway; 541-474-0252
Hours: Monday to Saturday 8:30 am to 6:30 pm
Sunday 10 am to 5 pm
Natural Food Store. Organic produce.
Other Info: Accepts MC, VISA.
Directions: From I-5, take northern of two Grants Pass exits (#58), the get on 6th St and drive through town. Go over Roque River and when road divides stay left. This place on right after three traffic lights, a little past Herb's La Casita.

Sunshine Natural Food Market & Café

128 SW H Street, 541-474-5044
Hours: Monday to Saturday 9 am to 7 pm; Sunday 11 am to 4 pm; Salad Bar is only open on the weekdays.

Natural Food Store and Café. Deli, Bakery, Salad Bar and Juice Bar. Buffet Tuesday to Friday. Organic Salad Bar. Not pure vegetarian. Organic produce.
Menu: Has a good selection of vegetarian dishes. Has a good Soup and Salad Bar. Fresh juices.
Comments: Has no salad bar on the weekends, but has some ready-made dishes. Reasonably priced.
Other Info: Full service, buffet service, take-out. Price: $.
Directions: From I-5, take Hwy 199 exit (#55). Get on Hwy 199 (one way going west) and go 1½ mile, then at 7th turn left and go 3 blocks, then at H St turn right and this place is 1 block down on right.

GRESHAM

Nature's Fresh Northwest (Wild Oats)

2077 NE Burnside Road; 503-674-2827
Hours: Monday to Saturday 9 am to 10 pm
Sunday 9 am to 9 pm
Natural Food Store and Cafe. Deli, Bakery, Salad Bar and Juice Bar. Organic produce. Supermarket-type place. See Wild Oats Market information.
Directions: From I-84, take 238th Dr exit (#16) towards Wood Village, then go on 238th Dr for 1 mile, road becomes 242nd Dr and go another 2 miles, at NE Burnside St turn slight left and this place is 2 blocks down.

HOOD RIVER

China Gorge Restaurant

2680 Old Columbia River Drive
541-386-5331
Hours: Tuesday to Sunday 11 am to 9 pm
Closed Monday.
Chinese. Vegan options. Not pure vegetarian
Menu: Has a good selection of vegetarian dishes. Vegetarian Moo Shu, tofu dishes and rice.
Comments: Has a view of the Columbia River.
Other Info: Full service, take-out. Accepts AMEX, DIS, MC, VISA. Price: $$.

Wy'East Naturals

110 5th Street; 541-386-6181
Hours: Monday to Friday 7:30 am to 6:30 pm; Monday to Saturday 9 am to 5:30 pm; Sunday 10 am to 5 pm
Natural Food Store and Café. Deli, Bakery and Juice Bar. Organic produce.
Menu: Has a selection of vegetarian dishes. Or-

ganic salads, veggie burgers, sandwiches, wraps and soups. Fresh juices and smoothies.
Other Info: Counter service, take-out. Has a small amount of seating. Accepts AMEX, DIS, MC, VISA.
Directions: From I-84, take 2nd St exit (#63), then go south on 2nd 1 block. At Cascade turn right and go 3 blocks, then at 5th turn left and this place on the right near the corner.

JACKSONVILLE

Jacksonville Inn Restaurant
175 East California Street; 503-899-1900
Hours: Sunday to Thursday 5 pm to 9 pm
Friday & Saturday 5 pm to 10 pm
American. Not pure vegetarian.
Menu: Has a selection of vegetarian dishes. Pastas dishes are popular.
Comments: Well presented dishes. Good service. One of the best restaurants in the area. Upscale.
Other Info: Full service, take-out. Accepts AMEX, DC, DIS, MC, VISA. Price: $$-$$$.

Ruch Natural Foods
181 Upper Applegate Road
541-899-1519
Hours: Monday to Saturday 10 am to 7 pm
Sunday 10 am to 5 pm
Natural Food Store and Deli.
Menu: Veggie Lasagna, pizzas, soups and salads. Sandwich in the summer only.
Directions: Coming from Jacksonville on Hwy 238, when enter town at Upper Applegate Rd turn left and this place on left a quarter-mile down.

KEIZER

Thai Cuisine
4140 River Rd N; 503-393-6216
Hours: Monday to Friday 11 am to 2:30 pm, 5 pm to 9 pm; Saturday & Sunday 5 pm to 9 pm
Thai. Vegan options. Not pure vegetarian
Menu: Has a large amount of vegetarian dishes including Spring Rolls, vegetarian soups, tofu dishes and noodles dishes.
Other Info: Full service, take-out. Accepts MC, VISA. Price: $-$$.

LAKE OSWEGA (near Portland)

Nature's Fresh Northwest (Wild Oats)
17711 Jean Way; 503-635-8915
Hours: Daily 9 am to 10 pm

Natural Food Store and Cafe. Deli, Bakery, Salad Bar and Juice Bar. Organic produce. Supermarket-type place. See Wild Oats Market information.
Directions: From I-5, take Lower Boones Ferry Rd exit (#290), then go a half-mile northeast on Lower Boones Ferry Rd, at Jean Way turn right and this place is near the turn.

Trader Joe's
15391 Bangy Road
503-639-3238

LINCOLN CITY

Trillium Natural Foods
1026 SE Jetty Avenue
541-994-5665
Hours: Monday to Saturday 9:30 am to 7 pm
Sunday 11 am to 6 pm
Natural Food Store. Organic produce.
Directions: From Hwy 101, go east on East Devils Lake Road 1 block. At Jetty turn left and this place on right at corner near the factory stores.

MANZANITA

Mother Nature's Natural Foods
298 Laneda Avenue
503-368-5316
Hours: Monday to Saturday 10 am to 7 pm
Sunday 10 am to 5 pm
Natural Food Store. Juice Bar. Organic produce.
Menu: Pre-made sandwiches and other preparations. Fresh juices.
Other Info: Accepts MC, VISA ($10 or more).

NEWPORT
Good place for whale watching.

Oceana Natural Foods Co-op
159 SE 2nd Street
541-265-8285
Hours: Daily 8 am to 7 pm
Natural Food Store and Café. Deli and Juice Bar. All Organic Salad Bar. Vegan options. Not pure vegetarian. Organic produce.
Menu: Homemade soups, salads and sandwiches. Fresh juices.
Other Info: Counter service, take-out. Accepts AMEX, MC, VISA. Price: $.
Directions: From Hwy 101, go east onto Hwy 20 for 2 blocks, then at Benton turn left (go south) 2 blocks and this place at intersection of Benton and 2nd.

PACIFIC CITY

Grateful Bread Bakery
34805 Brooten Road; 503-965-7337
Hours: Thursday to Saturday 8 am to 5:30 pm; Sunday 8 am to 3:30 pm; closed Tues & Wed.
Restaurant. Not pure vegetarian.
Menu: Has a good selection of vegetarian dishes. Salads, several vegetarian soups and sandwiches. Veggie Chili, Corn & Cheese Soup and Minestrone Soup.
Other Info: Non-smoking. Accepts MC, VISA.

PORTLAND

Abou Karim
221 SW Pine (200 block, right next to the corner of Pine and SW 3rd Avenue), downtown
503-223-5058
Hours: Monday to Thursday 11 am to 2 pm, 5 pm to 9 pm; Friday 11 am to 2 pm, 5 pm to 10 pm; Saturday 5 pm to 10 pm; Sunday 5 pm to 9 pm
Lebanese, Middle Eastern. Vegan friendly. Not pure vegetarian.
Menu: Has over 10 vegetarian dishes. Eggplant stew, tabbouleh, falafel, Lentil soup, hummus, Eggplant Pate, vegetarian Shish-kabob, Eggplant Sandwich and more.
Comments: Good, well-priced food.
Other Info: Non-smoking. Accepts AMEX, MC, VISA. Price: $.

Assaggio
7742 SE 13th Avenue, at SE Lambert
503-232-6151
Hours: Tuesday to Thursday 5 pm to 9:30 pm; Fri & Sat 5 pm to 10 pm; closed Sun & Mon.
Italian. Vegetarian-friendly. Not pure vegetarian.
Menu: Has a good selection of vegetarian dishes. A good appetizer is fresh Asparagus, Roma Tomatoes and Olives. Excellent pastas with a variety of sauces.
Comments: One of the best Italian restaurants in Portland. Popular with locals. Romantic, popular place. Pleasant atmosphere.
Other Info: Non-smoking. Accepts AMEX, MC, VISA. Price: $$.

Bibo Juice
1445 NE Weidler; 503-288-5932
Directions: In the same building as Irvington Market.
622 SW Broadway, downtown, across from Nordstrom; 503-227-2334

Hours: Mon to Thur 7 am to 8 pm; Friday 7 am to 9 pm; Sat 8 am to 9 pm; Sun 8 am to 9 pm
Juice Bar.
Menu: A wide selection of juice and smoothies. Wheatgrass. Has some mixture such as Havana (coffee, banana, yogurt), Savannah (yogurt and peaches) and Astoria (blackberries, boysenberries, yogurt). Has nine different nutritional additions such oat bran, carbo boost and bee pollen.
Comments: Has outdoor dining. Popular place. Sometimes has live entertainment. The word "bibo" means "I drink" in Latin. Smoothies come in 24-ounce size and juices are 16 or 24 ounces.
Other Info: Accepts MC, VISA.

Café Lena
2239 SE Hawthorne Boulevard, at 23rd
503-238-7087
Hours: Tuesday to Thursday 8 am to 3 pm; Friday & Saturday 8 am to 4 midnight; Sun 8 am to 3 pm; closed Mon. Breakfast served until 3 pm.
American. Vegetarian and Vegan-friendly. Not pure vegetarian.
Menu: Ravioli of the day and pasta. Can get a set four-course vegetarian meal for $15. Vegan tofu scramble.
Comments: Popular for breakfast. Popular place with the artsy crowd. Friendly staff. Uses quality ingredients.
Other Info: Full service, take-out. Accepts MC, VISA. Price: $-$$.
Directions: In southeast Portland.

***Counter Culture
3000 NE Killingsworth Street
503-249-3799; email: matthew@counter-culture.com; Web site: www.counter-culture.com
Hours: Tuesday to Saturday 5 pm to 10 pm Saturday & Sunday 9 am to 2 pm
Vegan International.
Menu: Seitan with Corn Tortillas & Brown Rice, Coconut Noodles with Sesame Crusted Tofu, Mushroom Barley Risotto Cakes with Winter Greens, Potato Curry with Raita & Chapatis, Greek Salad, Couscous Salad, Mushroom Miso Soup, Stuffed Artichoke Florentine, Ginger Cakes and desserts. Samosa, Spring Rolls and curried lentils. Sweet potato ginger cakes with tofu sour cream is an excellent appetizer. "Tableside Aromatherapy" is samosas, roasted squash with tempeh, lentils, kale, quinoa pilaf and mint chutney. Has mainly vegan desserts, such as vegan Chocolate Toffee and Caramel Torte.
Comments: Offers cooking classes.
Other Info: Full service, take-out, catering. Res-

ervations suggested for dinner. Accepts AMEX, MC, VISA. Price: $$.
Directions: In northeast Portland. From I-5, take Portland Blvd exit (#304), then go west on Portland Blvd for 1 mile, at ML King Jr Blvd turn right and go a half-mile, at Killingsworth St turn left and this place is 1¼ mile down at 30th Ave.

**Daily Grind Natural Foods
4026 SE Hawthorne Boulevard, Hawthorne District; 503-233-5521
Hours: Monday to Friday 9 am to 9 pm Saturday & Sunday 10 am to 5:30 pm
Natural Food Store and Vegetarian Café. Deli, Bakery and Salad Bar. Organic produce.
Menu: Soups, salads, sandwiches, veggie burgers, Vegan Casseroles, mashed potatoes with gravy, and main dishes. Fresh juices.
Other Info: Limited service, cafeteria style, take-out. Accepts DIS, MC, VISA. Price: $. Pay by the pound.
Directions: This place is in southeast Portland. From I-84 going west, take 39th St exit (#2) and go south on 39th St 1½ mile, at Hawthorne turn left and this place is 1 block down on right. From I-84 going east, take 43rd St exit, then at second light turn left. Then at 39th turn left, then at Hawthorne turn left and this place is on the right 1 block down at 40th Ave.

**Dogs Dig Deli
212 NW Davis, Old Town Area
503-223-3362
Hours: Monday to Friday 9 am to 5 pm; Saturday 10 am to 2 pm; closed Sunday.
Vegetarian take-out Deli Fast Food. Breakfasts, Asian, Indian and South American. Very vegan-friendly.
Menu: Soups, salads, sandwiches, Avocado Sandwich, vegan burrito, grilled potatoes, hummus, tofu sandwiches, cookies. Granola and oatmeal for breakfast.
Comments: Pleasant dinning room with Maplewood tabletops. A popular, small place. Pleasant staff. Has a couple of table outside.
Other Info: Counter service, mainly take-out.
Directions: From I-5, take exit #301 towards Steel Bridge, then go west over the Steel Bridge, then at 3rd Ave turn left and go 3 blocks, then at Davis St turn left and this place is 1 block down.

Fellini
125 Northwest 6th Avenue
503-243-2120
Hours: Monday to Friday 11 am to 2 am

Closed Saturday & Sunday.
International, Asian, Mexican & Middle Eastern.
Menu: Has a selection of vegetarian dishes.
Comments: Often has live music. Accepts MC, VISA. Price: $$.

Food Front Cooperative Grocery
2375 NW Thurman Street, northwest side of Portland; 503-222-5658
Web site: www.foodfrontco-op.com
Hours: Daily 8 am to 9 pm
Natural Food Store and Deli. Good selection of organic produce.
Menu: Has a good selection of vegetarian dishes. Freshly baked breads, salads, sandwiches, soups, Veggie Lasagna, veggie chili and much more.
Comments: Has a good bulk food selection.
Other Info: Accepts MC, VISA.
Directions: From I-405, take Rte 30 exit and go west for a half-mile mile, then take Vaughn St exit, then at 23rd go south 1 block, then at NW Thurman St turn right and this place is a block down on right.

**Garden Café
Portland Adventist Medical Center
10123 SE Market Street; 503-251-6125
Restaurant open to the public hours: Monday to Friday for three meals 6:30 am to 6:30 pm Saturday & Sunday 11:15 am to 1:15 pm, 4:45 pm to 6:30 pm
Vegetarian Natural Foods. Salad Bar. Fresh Fruit Bar.
Menu: Soups, salads, a large variety of vegetarian sandwiches, mock "meat" sandwiches, and hot dishes. Option of around 15 vegetarian sandwiches.
Comments: Has comfortable indoor and outdoor seating. Very popular place. Reasonably priced. Seventh Day Adventist place.
Other Info: Counter cafeteria service, take-out, catering. Price: $.
Directions: This place is in east Portland. From I-205, take exit #18, then go east on Market St and this place is a half-mile down on the left.

Hands On Café
8245 NW Barnes
503-297-1480
Hours: Monday to Friday 11:30 am to 2 pm, 5:30 pm to 7:30 pm
Sunday 9:30 am to 1:30 pm
Menu: Has a selection of vegetarian dishes.
Comments: At the Oregon College of Arts and Crafts. Good lunch place. Price: $$.

Higgin's

1239 SW Broadway, at SW Jefferson
503-222-9070
email: Higgins@europa.com; Web site: http://
higgins.citysearch.com?
Hours: Mon to Fri 11:30 am to 2 am, 5 pm to
10:30 12 midnight; Sat & Sun 5 pm to 10:30 pm
International and Northwest. Vegetarian options.
Often use organic vegetables. Not pure veg.
Menu: Has a good selection of vegetarian dishes.
The menu changes seasonally. Root vegetables,
wintergreens and a rice dish. Vegetarian Penne.
Comments: Local organic produce used when
possible. Elegant, grand décor. Spacious, comfortable place. Open kitchen. Good place for private
parties. Granite and marble countertops. Is built
into a hill.
Other Info: Full service, take-out. Reservations
suggested. Smoking allowed in bar. Accepts
AMEX, DC, DIS, MC, VISA. Price: $$$.
Directions: This place is about a third-mile north
of the northeast corner of Portland State Univer-
sity, about a half-mile northeast of exit #2A on I-
405. From I-405, take Couch St exit (#2A) to-
wards Burnside St, then go north on 15th Ave
for 1 block, at Alder St turn left and go 1 block,
at 13th Ave turn right and go 2 blocks, at Salmon
St turn left (go east) and go about 7 short blocks,
then at Broadway turn right and this place is 2
blocks down.

India House

1038 Southwest Morrison, at SW 10th Avenue
503-274-1017
Hours: Monday to Thursday 11 am to 2:30
pm, 5:30 pm to 10 pm; Friday & Saturday 12
noon to 2:30 pm, 5:30 pm to 10:30 pm; closed
Sunday.
India. Good lunch buffet (three good vegetarian
choices). Not pure vegetarian.
Menu: Vegetable samosa, Bengan Bharta (egg-
plant), vegetable Korma (very good), Aloo Saag
and mango lassi.
Comments: Has very good Indian food. Popular
place. Some people believe this is the best Indian
restaurant in Portland. Can make the food really
hot (so you may want to be careful about this).
Good service and atmosphere. Authentic Indian
food. May want to be careful about the Vegetar-
ian Dinner Sampler for dinner (ask how long it
has been sitting); best to order something fresh.
Tablecloths on tables. Elegant place.
Other Info: Non-smoking. Accepts AMEX, DC,
DIS, MC, VISA. Price: $$.

It's A Beautiful Pizza

3341 SE Belmont; 503-233-5444
Hours: Sunday to Thursday 11 am to 10 pm
Friday & Saturday 11 am to 11 pm
Pizza. Not pure vegetarian.
Menu: Has topping such as shredded carrots,
peanuts, cilantro, roasted coconut, peanut-tamari
sauce and tofu. Calzone and salads.
Comments: Popular with the locals. The base-
ment can be a happening place at night. Has some
of the best pizzas in Portland. Has live music some
nights (Tuesday, etc.).
Other Info: Full service, take-out, delivers from
6 pm until closing (at least $15). Accepts AMEX,
MC, VISA. Price: $-$$.

Jarra's Ethiopian

1435 SE Hawthorne Boulevard
503-230-8990
Hours: Tuesday to Saturday 5 pm to 10 pm
Closed Sunday & Monday.
Ethiopian. Not pure vegetarian.
Menu: Has a selection of vegetarian dishes.
Comments: Has a good atmosphere. Ethiopian
décor with paintings and wildlife pictures of
Ethiopia. The food gets good ratings. Not cheap.
Other Info: No credit cards; cash only. Price: $$-
$$$.

Khun Pie's Bahn Thai

3429 SE Belmont Street; 503-235-1610
Hours: Tuesday to Thursday 6 pm to 9 pm; Fri
& Sat 6 pm to 9:30 pm; closed Sun & Mon.
Thai. Vegan options. Not pure vegetarian.
Menu: Has many vegetarian dishes.
Comments: Popular place.
Other Info: Cash only; no credit cards.

Laughing Planet Café

3320 SE Belmont
503-235-6472
Hours: Monday to Saturday 11 am to 10 pm
Sunday 11 am to 9 pm
**Vegetable and Vegan-friendly Café. Mainly a
Burrito Place.** Juice Bar. Not pure vegetarian.
Menu: Has burritos, soups, and baked good. A-
maze-in' Grace Quesadilla with Jack cheese, corn
and chilies. Vegan soups and chilis. Fresh juices.
Comments: It is a happening, interesting place.
Other Info: Non-smoking. Accepts AMEX, MC,
VISA.
Directions: From I-5, take Rte 99 exit (#300B)
towards Oregon City/US 26, then go east on SE
Belmont St and this place is 1½ mile down.

The Leaf & Bean Café
4936 NE Fremont, at NE 50th Avenue
503-281-1090
Hours: Monday to Friday 8 am to 8 pm
Saturday & Sunday 9 am to 8 pm
Vegetarian-friendly Restaurant. Not pure vegetarian.
Menu: Has homemade vegetarian and vegan soups. Salads and a good selection of vegetarian sandwiches such as the avo-vegetarian, which is avocado, cream cheese, cucumber and roasted red pepper.
Comments: Has a good selection of vegetarian dishes. A good place. Has won awards as best vegetarian food in Portland. Has a unique multi-colored façade. Can call ahead for take-out.
Other Info: Cash only; no credit cards.
Directions: In a northeast Portland, on the south side of Rose City Cemetery. From I-60, take 33rd Ave exit (#1), then go north on 33rd Ave for 1 mile, at Fremont St turn right and this place is 1 mile down.

Nature's Fresh NW (Wild Oats)
3535 15th Ave, at Fremont; 503-288-3414
Hours: Daily 9 am to 10 pm
Natural Food Store and Cafe. Deli, Bakery, Salad Bar and Juice Bar. Organic produce. Supermarket-type place. See Wild Oats Market information.
Directions: This place is in northeast Portland. From I-5, take Alberta St exit (#30) towards Swan Island, then go east on Alberta St for 1 mile, at ML King JR Blvd turn right and go ¾ mile, at NE Fremont turn left (go west) and this place is a half-mile down, at 15th Ave.

Nature's Fresh NW (Wild Oats)
Hillsdale Shopping Center, 6344 SW Capitol Highway; 503-244-3110
Hours: Daily 9 am to 10 pm
Natural Food Store and Cafe. Deli, Bakery, Salad Bar and Juice Bar. Organic produce. Supermarket-type place. See Wild Oats Market information.
Directions: From I-5, take Exit #297 towards Tervilliger Blvd, then go 2/3 mile north on Bertha Blvd, then turn right and this place is a quarter-mile down on right in Hillsdale Shopping Center.

Nature's Fresh Northwest (Wild Oats)
2825 East Burnside Street; 503-232-6601
Hours: Daily 9 am to 10 pm
Natural Food Store and Cafe. Deli, Bakery,

Salad Bar and Juice Bar. Organic produce. Supermarket-type place. See Wild Oats Market information.
Directions: This place is in east Portland. From I-5, take exit #302A towards Rose Quarter/City Center, then go east on N Weidler St (or any road) for a third-mile, at ML King JR Blvd turn right (go south) and go ¾ mile, at E Burnside St/US 30 turn left (go east) and go a third-mile, stay straight onto E Burnside St and this place is ¾ mile down.

Nature's Fresh NW (Wild Oats)
3016 SE Division Street; 503-233-7374
Hours: Daily 9 am to 10 pm
Natural Food Store and Cafe. Deli, Bakery, Salad Bar and Juice Bar. Organic produce. Supermarket-type place. See Wild Oats Market information.
Directions: From I-5, take exit #300B towards Oregon City (US 26), then go east on SE Belmont St for ¾ mile, at 20th Ave turn right and go a quarter-mile (south), at Hawthorne Blvd turn left and make a quick left onto 20th Ave and go a half-mile, at Division St turn left and this place is a half-mile down. From I-205, take Division St exit west and go about 50 blocks. This place on left.

New Seasons Market
7300 SW Beaverton & Hillsdale Highway
503-292-6838
Hours: Daily 8 am to 9 pm
Deli Hours: 8 am to 8 pm
Directions: This place is in southwest Portland. From I-405, take US 26 exit (#1D) towards Beaverton and go west on US 26 for 2¼ mile, then take exit #71B towards Sylvan, then go south on Scholls Ferry Rd for 2 miles, at Beaverton Hillsdale Hwy (Rte 10) turn slight right and this place is a quarter-mile down.
1214 SE Tacoma Street, 13th; 503-230-4949
Hours: Daily 8 am to 10 pm
Directions: This place is in south Portland. From I-5, take exit #299A towards Lake Oswego//Rte 43, then take Macadam Ave (Rte 43) south and go 2 miles, at Sellwood Bridge turn right and go over the bridge, road becomes Tacoma St and this place is a third-mile down.
5320 NE 33rd Avenue, Concordia area
503-288-3838
Hours: Daily 8 am to 10 pm
1453 NE 61st Ave, Hillsboro; 503-648-6968
Hours: Daily 8 am to 10 pm
Directions: From I-84, take NE Halsey St exit

(#4), then go west on Halsey St a half-mile, then turn left at 61st Ave and this place is near the corner.
Natural Food Store and Deli. Salad Bar. Organic produce.
Menu: Has a good selection of vegetarian dishes.
Other Info: Accepts MC, VISA.

Nicholas Restaurant
318 SE Grand Avenue, at Pine Street
503-235-5123
Hours: Monday to Saturday 10:30 am to 9 pm
Sunday 12 noon to 9 pm
Middle Eastern. Vegan and Vegetarian options. Not pure vegetarian.
Menu: Has a wide selection of vegetarian dishes. Veggie Kebab with rice, falafel, pizzas, fresh breads, hummus, grape leave and eggplant. The Vegetarian mezza is several different vegetarian dishes and it a good beginner dish to try. Good Turkish coffee.
Comments: Has really good food. No alcohol. Popular with the locals. Lacks atmosphere. Very good value. Can be a bit cramped because it is small and popular. Many people believe this is the best Middle Eastern food in Portland.
Other Info: Cash only; no credit cards. Price: $.
Directions: In southeast Portland.

Old Wives Tales
1300 East Burnside Street; 503-238-0470
Hours: Sunday to Thursday 8 am to 9 pm; Friday and Saturday 8 am to 10 pm; Good Sunday Brunch 8 am to 2 pm
Vegetarian-friendly Eclectic American. Specializes in vegetarian dishes. Vegan friendly. Not pure vegetarian.
Menu: Has a wide selection of vegetarian dishes. Has an excellent salad bar with homemade soups and breads. Soups, salads, sandwiches, tofu dishes, Black Bean Stew, mock chicken, Egyptian Loaf, mashed potatoes, tempeh burgers, rice noodles and Mexican dishes. Good dishes for children such as grilled cheese, steamed vegetables, burritos and noodle with cheese. Know for their Hungarian Mushroom Soup and an excellent salad bar. Fresh juices. Non-alcoholic beer and wine.
Comments: Good place for kids. Separate dining rooms for families and playroom for kids. Reasonably priced children meals. Friendly staff and good service.
Other Info: Full service, take-out. Reservations not necessary. Non-smoking. Accepts AMEX, DIS, MC, VISA. Price: $-$$.
Directions: In southeast Portland. From I-5, take

exit #302A towards City Center/Rose Quarter, then go east on N Weidler St for a third-mile, at ML King JR Blvd turn right and go ¾ mile south, at E Burnside St turn left and this place is a half-mile down, at 13th Ave.

The Paradox Palace Café
3439 SE Belmont; 503-232-7508
Hours: Monday to Wednesday 8 am to 9 pm
Thursday to Sunday 8 am to 10 pm
International. Mainly Vegetarian (about 90%). Vegan-friendly. Not pure vegetarian.
Menu: Has a large variety of vegetarian dishes. Sandwiches at cheap prices. Has breakfast meals with such dishes as Marinated Tofu, vegan French Toast and potatoes. Veggie burgers, salads, vegetarian Chili with Cornbread, veggie Lasagna, vegan Sloppy Joes, good bread, good Seitan Sandwich, Macaroni & Cheese and desserts. Vegan cookies and cakes. Barley coffee. Smoothies with yogurt or tofu.
Comments: Gets good recommendations. Relaxed, friendly, clean place. Good size portions. Popular with the locals; may have to wait for table. Interesting décor with treasure chests and urchin lamps. Good prices. The vegan burger may contain cheese.
Other Info: Cash only; no credit cards. Price: $.
Directions: From I-5, take OR Hwy 99E Exit (#300B) towards Oregon City (US 26), then go east on SE Belmont St and this place is 1½ mile down.

The People's Natural Food Store
3029 SE 21st Street, just south of Hawthorne Street, at Powell Blvd; 503-232-9051
email: peoples@eastsidewebsites.com
Web site: peoples@teleport.com
Hours: Daily 9 am to 9 pm
Nature Food Store. Organic produce.
Menu: Vegan Sushi, hummus and a large variety of ready-made sandwiches and salads in cooler.
Comments: There is an all-organic farmers market here on Wednesday from 2 pm to 7 pm.
Directions: From I-5, take Ross Island Bridge exit (#1A) and get on US 26 going east (becomes Powell Blvd), then go over Ross Island Bridge and go ¾ mile, then at 21st St turn left and this place is 2 blocks down.

Plainfield Mayur
852 SW 21st Street, Northwest Portland
503-223-2995; **Web site:** www.plainfields.com
Hours: Daily 5:30 pm to 10 pm
Indian. Vegan options. Not pure vegetarian.

Menu: Separate vegetarian menu includes samosas, soups, appetizers and main dishes. Malai Kofta, fresh Indian cheese with raisins and pistachios in a special spiced sauce.

Comments: Located in an historic Victorian mansion. Upscale. Considered to be one of the better Indian restaurants in the country. The Vegetarian Journal judged this place to be one of the best restaurants in this country. Wins awards as the best vegetarian restaurant in Portland. Elegant. Has silver ware and European crystal china. Has a private dining room for special events. Has excellent outdoor dining on the patio. Romantic. Popular with the locals. Good décor. Family owned and operated. Has Ayurvedic options. Some people think the place is not a good value for the money.

Other Info: Full service, take-out. Reservations recommended. Accepts AMEX, DIS, MC, VISA. Price: $$-$$$.

**The Purple Parlor

3560 North Mississippi Avenue
503-281-3560; email: eat@thepurpleparlor.com;
Web site: www.thepurpleparlor.com
Hours: Tuesday to Friday 7 am to 2 pm; Saturday & Sunday 8 am to 3 pm; closed Monday.
Fully Vegetarian Restaurant. Healthy dishes.
Menu: Tofu Scramble, freshly baked breads, vegan muffins, Rosemary Roasted Potatoes, Vegetables with Pesto over Polenta, Red Lentil Dal, homemade Bean Burger, Spiced Black Beans on a wheat Tortilla, Eggplant Sandwich, Pesto Polenta, Coconut Green Curry, Black-eyed Peas and Greens. Chocolate Cake (may contain eggs) and fresh fruit squares. Cappuccino, espresso.
Comments: In a beautifully renovated Victorian house. Can print a coupon to get a free coffee or espresso on their Web site. Dishes freshly prepared. Local organic produce used when possible. Coffeehouse atmosphere. Has patio seating outside.
Other Info: Full service, take-out. Non-smoking. Does not take reservations. Accepts MC, VISA. Price: $.
Directions: Between Skidmore and Fremont, a few blocks east of I-5. From I-5, take Alberta St exit (#303) towards Swan Island, then go east for 2 blocks, then at Albina Ave turn right going south (becomes Mississippi Ave) and this place is several blocks down.

Swagat's

2074 NW Lovejoy Street, at NW 21st Avenue, northwest Portland; 503-227-4300

Hours: Daily 11:30 am to 2:30 pm, 5 pm to 10 pm
Indian. Lunch buffet. Inexpensive place. Not pure vegetarian.
Menu: Has a good selection of vegetarian dishes. Dal, salads, Tandoori, vegetarian curried dishes, rice, Naan, Palak Paneer, papadam, dosa and vegetarian thalis. Mango lassi.
Comments: Good service and a friendly atmosphere. Good value for lunch; not as good for dinner. Has plenty of room.
Other Info: Full service, take-out. Accepts AMEX, DIS, MC, VISA. Price: $ for lunch; $$ for dinner.

Sweetwater's Jam House

3350 SE Morrison Street; 503-233-0333
Hours: Monday to Thursday 11:30 am to 12 midnight; Friday 11:30 am to 1 am; Saturday 5 pm to 1 am; Sunday 5 pm to 12 midnight Dinner stops one hour before closing.
Cajun & Creole, Caribbean. Not pure vegetarian.
Menu: Has a good selection of vegetarian dishes. Mashed potatoes, yams and plantains. Deep fried plantain slices.
Comments: Popular with the locals. Has outdoor dining. Happening place. Food usually gets good rating, but some people don't like the place.
Other Info: Smoking in bar. Accepts AMEX, MC, VISA. Price: $$-$$$.

Thai Orchid (several locations)

2231 West Burnside Street, northwest Portland 503-226-4542
10075 SW Barbur Boulevard, West Portland off I-5; 503-452-2544;
email: chamna.saenguraiporn@gte.net
Web site: http://thaiorchid2.citysearch.com/
Hours: Monday to Thursday 11:30 am to 2:30 pm, 4:30 pm to 10 pm; Friday 11:30 am to 2:30 pm, 4:30 pm to 11 pm; Saturday 12 noon to 11 pm; Sunday 12 noon to 10 pm
Thai. Not pure vegetarian.
Menu: The peanut sauces are recommended.
Comments: No MSG.
Other Info: Accepts AMEX, DIS, MC, VISA. Price: $-$$.

Thanh Thao Restaurant

4005 SE Hawthorne; 503-238-6232
Hours: Monday, Wednesday to Friday 11 am to 2:30 pm, 5 pm to 10 pm; Saturday & Sunday 11 am to 10 pm; closed Tuesday
Thai, Vietnamese. Vegan options. Not pure veg.
Menu: Has many vegetarian options including

mock "meat" dishes, soups, noodles dishes, Eggplant & Tofu (very good), appetizers and tofu dishes.

Comments: Sometimes has live entertainment. Sometimes service can be very slow. Food gets good recommendations. May have to wait to be seated on the weekends. Popular place. Friendly service. Modest décor. Lacks in atmosphere.

Other Info: Full service, take-out. Accepts DIS, MC, VISA. Price: $-$$.

Trader Joe's

4715 SE 39th Avenue; 503-777-1601
4218 NE Sandy Boulevard; 503-284-1694

Vita Café

3024 NE Alberta; 503-335-8233
Web site: www.vitacafe.citysearch.com
Hours: Monday to Thursday 11 am to 10 pm; Friday 5 pm to 11 pm; Saturday 8 am to 3 pm, 5 pm to 12 pm; Sunday 8 am to 3 pm, 5 pm to 11 pm; Breakfast on Weekends 8 am to 3 pm
International such as Asian, Mexican, American and Mediterranean. Mainly Vegetarian. Vegan friendly. Not pure vegetarian.
Menu: Has a large selection of vegetarian dishes. Boca Burger, French fries, White Miso Vegetable, soups, salads, sandwiches, Tofurky Sandwich, Sweet Potato Chips, Spicy Tempeh Sticks, Mushroom Tempeh Pate, Hot & Sour Coconut Soup, Curried Tofu & Rice, Asian Noodle Medley, Tempeh Sandwich, VRT Plate (vegetables, rice and tofu or tempeh), Thai Pasta, Mediterranean dishes, Greek Hummus Platter, Vegan Nacho, Bean Vegetarian Chili, Veggie Burrito with tofu or tempeh, quesadillas, Vegan Biscuits & Gravy, Granola and Morning Miso. Vegan hushpuppies with mango chutney and Mexican corncakes with vegan cheese are really good. Fried tempeh, mashed potatoes and almond gravy is really good
Comments: Local organic produce used when possible. All, homemade breads, sauces and desserts are egg- and dairy-free. Some interesting hip shops on Alberta Street. Food gets excellent ratings. Service does not always get good ratings. Often have to wait a while for your food (up to an hour). Reasonable prices. Good size portions. Seats around 90. Pleasant, happening atmosphere.
Other Info: Cash only; no credit cards.
Directions: In northeast Portland. From I-5, take Portland Blvd Exit (#304), then go east on Portland Blvd for 1 mile, at ML King JR Blvd turn right and go a half-mile, then at Killingsworth St turn left and go 1¼ mile, at 30th Ave turn right and this place is 3 blocks down.

ROGUE RIVER (near Grants Pass)

Rogue River Natural Foods

106 East Main Street; 541-582-3075
Hours: Monday to Friday 9:30 am to 6 pm; Saturday 9:30 am to 5 pm; closed Sunday.
Natural Food Store.
Menu: Ready-made sandwiches in cooler.
Directions: From I-5, take exit #48 and follow signs to Rogue River. At Main St turn left.

SALEM

India Palace Restaurant

377 Court Street NE; 503-371-4808
Hours: Mon to Fri 11:30 am to 2:30 pm, 5 pm to 9 pm; Sat & Sun 11:30 am to 3 pm, 5 pm to 9 pm
Indian. Vegan options. Not pure vegetarian.
Menu: Has several vegetarian options including vegetable curries, Naans, Indian breads and rice dishes.
Comments: Has a tandoori oven.
Other Info: Full service, take-out. Accepts MC, VISA. Price: $-$$.

Kwan's Cuisine

835 Commercial Street SE, at Mission
503-363-7711
Hours: Sunday to Thursday 11:30 am to 10 pm
Friday & Saturday 11:30 am to 11 pm
Vegetarian-friendly Chinese. Vegan options. Not pure vegetarian.
Menu: Has a special vegetarian section on the menu. Serves an assortment of mock "meat" dishes. Sautéed Vegetables, veggie chicken, BBQ Pork and other dishes. Fresh juices. Non-alcoholic beer and wine.
Comments: Some of the soups contain chicken broth, so you should ask about this. Food gets good ratings.
Other Info: Full service, take-out. Accepts AMEX, DC, DISC, MC, VISA. Price: $-$$.

La Margarita Company Restaurant

565 Ferry Street; 503-362-8861
Hours: Monday to Thursday 11 am to 2 pm. 5 pm to 9 pm; Friday & Saturday 11 am to 2 pm, 5 pm to 10 pm; Sunday 5 pm to 9 pm
Mexican with a French influence. Vegan-friendly. Not pure vegetarian.
Menu: Enchiladas, nachos, burritos, chila relenos and tacos. Rice, red or black beans with main dishes. Choice of salsa and sauces.
Other Info: Accepts AMEX, DC, DIS, MC, VISA. Price: $$.

**Lifesource Natural Foods
2649 Commercial SE; 503-361-7973
Hours: Monday to Friday 9 am to 9 pm; Saturday 9 am to 8 pm; Sunday 10 am to 7 pm
Natural Food Store and Vegetarian Deli. Bulk food. Organic produce.
Menu: Salads, soups (2 or 3), sandwiches, wraps, Vegetarian Lasagna and Vegetarian Chili.
Comments: Friendly place. Mostly everything in the store is vegetarian.
Directions: This place is in southwest Salem. From I-5 going south into Salem, take Salem Parkway exit (#260), then go southwest on Salem Pkwy for 3 miles, at Commercial St (Rte 99) turn slight right and go 2 miles (road becomes Front St and Rte 22, then Trade St), at Commercial St turn right and go 1½ mile, at corner of Culver Lane.

Macedonia Greek Cuisine
189 Libert Street NE; 503-316-9997
Hours: Monday to Thursday 11 am to 3 pm, 5 pm to 9 pm; Friday & Saturday 11 am to 3 pm, 5 pm to 10 pm; closed Sunday.
Greek. Not pure vegetarian. Price: $$.
Menu: Good selections of vegetarian cold dishes. Spinach pastry, Greek Salad, Eggplant Salad (Meltzanosalata), hummus, Yalantzi Dolmades (stuffed grape leaves) and more. Can get Combination Platter and can substitute the lamb with vegetarian dolmades.

The Off Center Café
1741 Center Street NE; 503-363-9245
Hours: Tuesday to Friday 8 am to 2:30 pm, 6 pm to 9 pm; Saturday & Sunday Brunch 7 am to 2 pm; Saturday & Sunday Dinner 6 pm to 9 pm; closed Monday.
Natural Foods Café type place. Vegan options. Not pure vegetarian.
Menu: Black Beans & Rice, Tofu & Rice and many other vegetarian dishes.
Comments: Friendly place. Good posters. Popular.
Other Info: Full service, take-out. Price: $$.
Directions: This place is near the center of town. From I-5, take Market St (OR Rte 213) exit (#256) towards Lancaster Mall, then go 1 mile west on Market St, at 17th St turn left (go south) and go ¾ mile, at Center St turn left and this place is a half-block down.

Salem Health Food Store
480 Center Street NE; 503-585-6938
Hours: Monday to Friday 10 am to 9 am; Saturday 10 am to 8 pm; Sunday 11 am to 6 pm
Natural Food Store. Organic produce.

SPRINGFIELD

Kuraya's Thai Cuisine
1410 Mohawk Boulevard; 541-746-2951
Hours: Mon to Thur 11 am to 9 pm; Friday & Sat 11 am to 10 pm; Sun 4:30 pm to 9 pm
Thai and & International. Vegan options. Not pure vegetarian
Menu: Has many vegetarian options.
Other Info: Full service, take-out, catering. Accepts MC, VISA. Price: $-$$.

Pennsylvania

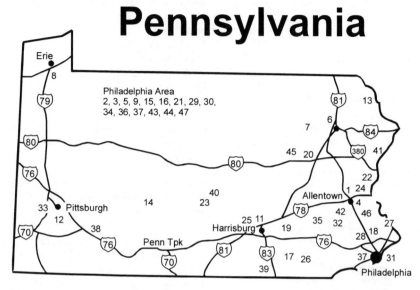

1. Allentown
2. Ardmore
3. Bala Cynwyd
4. Bethlehem
5. Bryn Mawr
6. Clarks Summit
7. Dallas
8. Erie
9. Fort Washington
10. Greensburg
11. Harrisburg
12. Homestead
13. Honesdale
14. Indiana
15. Jenkintown
16. Kimberton

17. Lancaster
18. Lansdale
19. Lebanon
20. Luzerne
21. Malvern
22. Marshall's Creek
23. Monroeville
24. Narberth
25. New Cumberland
26. New Holland
27. New Hope
28. North Wales
29. Paoli
30. Penndel
31. Philadelphia
32. Pine Forge

33. Pittsburgh
34. Plumsteadville
35. Reading
36. Southampton
37. Springfield
38. Stahlstown
39. Stoverstown
40. State College
41. Stroudsburg
42. Trexlertown
43. Wayne
44. West Chester
45. Williamsport
46. Willow Grove
47. Wynnewood

ALLENTOWN

Aladdin's
651 Union Boulevard
610-437-4023
Hours: Tuesday to Friday 11 am to 2 pm, 5 pm
to 10 pm; Saturday & Sunday 5 pm to 10 pm;
closed Monday
Middle Eastern.
Menu: Has a good selection of vegetarian dishes.
Comments: Good prices for lunch.

Garden Gate National Foods
17 South 9th Street; 610-433-8891
Hours: Monday, Tuesday, Wednesday, Friday 9
am to 9 pm; Wednesday 9 am to 6 pm; Saturday
9 am to 6:45 pm; Sunday 12 noon to 5 pm
Natural Food Store. Organic produce.
Menu: Has ready-made sandwiches.
Directions: From, I-78, get on US-22 and from
there take 7th St exit, if going west on US-22
from NYC keep left at fork in ramp and go 1
block, then at Mauchunk Rd turn left (becomes

7th St), at W Hamilton St turn right and go 4th blocks, then at 9th St turn left and this place is a half-block down.

Queen's Nutritional Products
1450 Pennsylvania Avenue; 610-691-6644
Hours: Monday to Saturday 9 am to 9 pm
Sunday 12 noon to 5 pm
Natural Food Store. Organic produce.
Comments: Helpful staff.

**Sign of the Bear
514 North Street Cloud Street; 610-429-8575
Hours: Monday to Wednesday 9:30 am to 7 pm;
Thursday & Friday 9:30 am to 8 pm; Saturday 9 am to 5:30 pm; closed Sunday.
Natural Food Store and Vegetarian Cafe.
Comments: Good selection in store. Good food in deli.
Directions: From I-78, take 15th St exit and go to Tilghman St and turn right. At Saint Cloud turn left and this place on right.

**Syb's West End Deli
2151 Liberty Street; 610-434-3882
Hours: Monday to Friday 7:30 am to 5:30 pm;
Saturday 7:30 am to 3 pm; Sun 7:30 am to 1 pm
Vegetarian. Vegan friendly.
Menu: Has vegan breakfasts. Vegetarian dishes are marked on the menu. At least three vegetarian daily specials. Real maple syrup.
Comments: Friendly place. Popular place on Sunday.
Directions: From I-78, get on US-22, then take Fullerton Avenue exit and go southeast on Fullerton for 1¼ mile, then at Tilghman St turn right and go ¾ mile, then at Grant St turn left and go 2 long blocks, then at W Liberty St turn right and this place is about a half-block down.

ARDMORE (5 mile west of Philadelphia)

All Natural Market
30 East Lancaster Avenue; 610-896-7717
Hours: Monday to Saturday 9 am to 9 pm; Saturday and Sunday 9 am to 6 pm; Deli closed an hour before the store.
Natural Food Store and Deli. Vegan options. Not pure vegetarian.
Menu: Soups, salads, sandwiches and main dishes. Fresh juices and smoothies.
Comments: Use 100% organic produce. Reasonably priced.
Other Info: Accepts MC, VISA. Price: $.
Directions: This place is on Rte 30, which is the main street coming through town. From Rte 1, take Lancaster Ave west and this place is about 2 miles down.

BALA CYNWYD (Philadelphia suburbs)

Healthwise
111 Bala Avenue; 610-668-9977
Hours: Monday 9 am to 1 pm, 4 pm to 8 pm;
Tuesday 9 am to 5 pm; Wednesday to Saturday 12 am to 5 pm; closed Sunday.
Natural Food Store.
Menu: Soups, salads, sandwiches and fresh juices.
Comments: Has a good selection of products. Good prices. Has Ayurvedic and alternative medicines. Good discounts on case orders.

**Main Line Health Food International & Carrot Bunch Restaurant
Bala Cynwyd Shopping Center, 51 East City Line Avenue; 610-664-5231
Hours: Monday to Friday 9:30 am to 8 pm; Saturday 9:30 am to 6 pm; closed Sunday.
Vegetarian Natural Food Place.
Menu: Has a large selection of vegetarian dishes.
Other Info: Full service, take-out. Non-smoking. Accepts MC, VISA. Price: $.
Directions: From I-76, take City Avenue exit (#33) and this place is right at the exit (south side).

BETHLEHEM

Green Café
22 West 4th Street
610-694-0192; Web site: www.thegreencafe.com
Hours: Tuesday to Saturday 11 am to 9 pm; Sunday Brunch 11 am to 3 pm; closed Monday
Natural Foods. International, American. Juice Bar. Macrobiotic and Vegan friendly. Buffet. Not pure vegetarian.
Menu: The menu changes regularly. Has a good variety of vegetarian dishes. Soups, African Peanut Soup, salads, falafel, rice dishes, Rice & Bean and samosas. Excellent Vegan Chocolate Cake.
Comments: Student's art on wall. Good food. Restaurant cooperative. Almost everything on the menu is vegan or can be made vegan. Casual, friendly place. Often uses organic ingredients. Food is freshly made on the premises.
Other Info: Full service, limited service, take-out. Non-smoking. No credit cards; cash only. Price: $-$$.
Directions: Near Lehigh University's main campus in south Bethlehem. Located near Godfrey

Daniels, a folk music place. From I-78, take Rte 412 exit (#21) towards Hellertown/Bethlehem, and go north on Rte 412 for 1 mile, then take a slight left onto E 4th St (Rte 412) and go 2¼ miles, then at Rte 378 (Wyandotte) turn left and go 1 block, then at 4th St turn left and this place is near the corner.

BRYN MAWR (6 miles west of Phila)

Arrowroot Natural Market
834 West Lancaster Avenue; 610-527-3393
Hours: Monday to Friday 9 am to 9 pm; Saturday 9:30 am to 6 pm; Sunday 10 am to 5:30 pm
Natural Food Store. Organic produce.
Menu: Has ready-made sandwiches.
Other Info: Accepts AMEX, DIS, MC, VISA.
Directions: From I-476, take the St David's exit to Rte 30. At Rte 30 go east for about 5 miles. This place is in the middle of town on Rte 30, which is the main street going through town, near the movie theater. From Rte 1, take Lancaster Ave west and this place is about 3 miles down.

CLARKS SUMMIT

Everything Natural
412 South State Street; 570-586-9684
Hours: Monday to Saturday 10 am to 8 pm
Closed Sunday.
Natural Food Store. Organic produce.
Comments: Only sells vegetarian items. Friendly, helpful staff.
Directions: From I-81, take exit #58 (Rte 6 & 11) and go northwest on Rte 6 towards Clark's Summit about 1½ mile. This place on the left in the downtown.

DALLAS

House of Nutrition
Route 309, North Dallas; 570-675-1413
Hours: Monday to Saturday Friday 10 am to 6 pm; Sunday 12 noon to 5 pm
Natural Food Store. Sometimes sells organic produce.
Comments: Good variety of products. Friendly place.

EASTON

Nature's Way
143 Northhampton Street; 610-253-0940
Hours: Monday, Wednesday, Thursday 9:30 am to 6 pm; Thursday & Friday 9:30 am to 8 pm; Saturday 9:30 am to 5 pm; Sun 12 noon to 4 pm

Natural Food Store. Has a good bulk section.
Directions: From I-78, take Easton exit and get on Hwy 611 going north, then at Larry Holmes Dr turn left. Then this place on right one block down. From I-22, take the N Riverside Dr exit and go south on N Riverside Dr a third-mile, then at Northhampton turn right and this place is 1 block down. This place is a quarter-mile west of the Delaware River.

ERIE

**Whole Foods Co-op
1341 West 26th Street, at Brown Avenue
814-456-0282; **fax:** 814-459-7079
email: ownership@wholefoodscoop.org
Web site: www.wholefoodscoop.org
Hours: Monday to Friday 9 am to 8 pm; Saturday 8 am to 8 pm; Sunday 11 am to 6 pm
Deli Hours: 11 am to 6 pm (may be closed on Sunday)
Natural Food Store and Vegetarian Deli. Vegan-friendly. Organic produce.
Menu: Menu changes daily. Stir-fries, Tomato & Rice Soup, Macaroni & Cheese, Red Lentil Corn Chowder, Shepherd Pie, Lasagna, enchiladas, Cabbage & Tofu over Rice, Vegan Quiche, Sesame Noodle, Italian Minestrone, Eggless Egg Salad, hummus, Three Beans with Rice, Chickenless Chicken Salad and sandwiches.
Comments: Local organic produce used when possible. Uses filtered water when cooking. Sells Honey House baked goods.
Other Info: Accepts DIS, MC, VISA. Has seating.
Directions: From I-90, take I-79 north and after you come into town, take the Rte 20 (26 St) exit (#43), and go east on 26th St and this place is 1½ mile down.

FORT WASHINGTON

Palace of Asia
285 Commerce Drive; 215-646-2133
Hours: Sunday to Thursday 11:30 am to 11 pm
Friday & Saturday 11:30 am to 12 midnight
Indian. Not pure vegetarian. See Lawrenceville, NJ.
Other Info: Full service, take-out. Accepts AMEX, DIS, MC, VISA. Price: $-$$.
Directions: Parking arranged for customers.

GREENSBURG (southwestern PA)

Natures Way Market
796 Highland Avenue; 724-836-3524

Hours: Monday to Friday 10 am to 6 pm (Wednesday closed 7 pm); Saturday 10 am to 5 pm; closed Sunday.
Natural Food Store.

HARRISBURG

Genesse Natural Foods
5405 Locust Lane; 717-545-3712
Hours: Monday, Tuesday, Saturday 10 am to 6 pm; Wednesday to Friday 10 am to 8 pm; closed Sunday.
Natural Food Store. Organic produce. Sells only vegetarian items.
Directions: From I-83, take Colonial Park exit and go to Prince St (few lights down). At Prince turn left, then at Locust Lane (at T intersection) turn left. This place on right a quarter-mile down.

Passage to India
525 South Front Street, adjacent to the Holiday Inn; 717-233-1202
Hours: Monday to Friday 11:30 am to 2:30 pm, 5 pm to 10 pm; Saturday 12 pm to 3:30 pm, 5 pm to 10 pm; Sunday 12 pm to 2:30 pm, 5 pm to 9 pm
Indian. Vegan options. Not pure vegetarian. Lunch buffet.
Menu: Has a wide selection of vegetarian dishes.
Comments: Can park in the Holiday Inn parking lot. Overlooks the Susquehanna River and has a nice view of the river. Voted best Ethnic and #1 Vegetarian Restaurant in area. 1994-1998 Readers Choice, Apprise Magazine.
Other Info: Full service, take-out, catering. Accepts AMEX, DIS, MC, VISA. Price: $$. Reservations recommended on the weekends.
Directions: Parking arranged for customers.

Raw-n-Natural
6075 Spring Road, Shermans Dale (State Routes 34 North and 850 West); 717-582-7767
Hours: Monday to Wednesday 10 am to 6 pm; Thursday 10 am to 8 pm; Friday 10 am to 4 pm; closed Saturday & Sunday.
Natural Food Store. Organic produce.
Comments: Has a good selection of products. Has cookbooks.

HOMESTEAD (southeast Pittsburgh suburb)

Curtis' Natural Foods Catering
120 East 9th Avenue
412-462-6688; Web site: www.curtisfoods.com
Vegetarian Catering.

Menu: Soups, salads, pastas, Veggie Chili, Lentil Spinach Soup, Black Bean Gazpacho, Chinese Noodles in Peanut Sauce, Anti-Chick Pasta Salad, Wheelin' Roasted Red Pepper Pesta Pasta, Basmati Rice, Dijon Lentil Salad, Garden Couscous Salad, Fireman's Bean & Rice, hummus and other dishes.
Comments: Got a good review in the Pittsburgh Post Gazette.

HONESDALE

Nature's Grace Health Foods and Deli
947 Main Street; 570-253-3469
Hours: Monday to Saturday 10 am to 6 pm (until 8 pm Friday); closed Sunday.
Natural Food Store and Deli. Vegan options. Not pure vegetarian.
Menu: Soups, salads, sandwiches, baked goods and burritos. Soft-serve frozen yogurt. Fresh juices.
Other Info: Counter service, take-out. Price: $.
Directions: Coming into Honesdale from Scranton on Rte 6 this place on left on Main St, right in the middle of town.

INDIANA (50 miles NE of Pittsburgh)

Vitamin Connection
1136 Philadelphia Street, at 11th Street
724-349-0535
Hours: Monday to Friday 10 am to 6 pm
Saturday 1 pm to 4 pm
Vitamin Store. Vitamins are discounted by 25-50% off retail.

JENKINTOWN

Fresh Fields (Whole Foods)
1575 Fairway Road
215-481-0800; fax: 215-481-0808
Hours: Monday to Saturday 8 am to 9 pm
Sunday 8 am to 8 pm
Natural Food Store and Cafe. Deli, Bakery, Salad Bar and Juice Bar. Organic produce. Supermarket-type place. See Whole Foods Market on page 666.

KIMBERTON

Kimberton Whole Foods & Sunflower Café
2140 Kimberton Road; 610-935-1444
Hours: Monday to Friday 8 am to 8 pm; Saturday 9 am to 6 pm; Sunday 10 am to 5 pm
Natural Food Store and Café. Deli. A full selec-

tion of organic produce.
Other Info: Counter service, take-out. Has seating. Accepts MC, VISA.
Directions: From I-76 east, take King of Prussia exit and head west on Rte 422, then take Rte 23 exit west. Then at Rte 112 turn left, then bear right onto Kimberton. This place is on the left a mile down.

LANCASTER

Lanvina Vietnamese Restaurant
1762 Columbia Avenue   717-393-7748
1651 Lincoln Highway E   717-399-0199
Hours: Mon to Fri for lunch and dinner 11 am to 2 am, 4:30 am to 9 am; Sat & Sun 11 am to 9 am
Vietnamese. Vegan options. Not pure vegetarian.
Menu: Has a large separate vegetarian menu. Spring Rolls, Rice Noodles, curry dishes, Vegetable Chow Mein, Lo Mein, soups and Fried Rice.
Other Info: Full service, take-out. Price: $.

LANSDALE

North Penn Health Food Center
1313 North Broad Street
215-855-1044
Hours: Monday to Saturday 9 am to 6 pm
Closed Sunday.
Natural Food Store.
Directions: From Rte 309, take Rte 63 exit. Rte 63 becomes Main. At Broad St go north and this place is on the right a mile down.

LEBANON (Pittsburgh southwest suburb)

Back to Basics
300 Mount Lebanon Boulevard
412-343-8156
Hours: Monday & Thursday 10 am to 8 pm; Tuesday, Wednesday & Friday 10 am to 6 pm; Saturday 10 am to 5 pm; closed Sunday.
Natural Food Store.

The Goodlife Market
1121 Bower Hill Road, southwest of the city
412-279-8499
Hours: Monday to Friday 10 am to 7 pm; Saturday 10 am to 5 pm; Sunday 12 noon to 4 pm
Natural Food Store and Deli. Juice Bar. Massage therapist at store.
Menu: Soups, sandwiches, veggie chili, Split Bean Soup, Bean Burger, Baco Burger, hummus, Beans & Rice, Spinach Pie and more.

Other Info: Counter service, take-out. Has counter seating and one table.
Directions: Across from St Claire Hospital.

LUZERNE

House of Nutrition
140 Main Street; 570-714-0436
Hours: Monday to Thursday 10 am to 8 pm; Friday & Saturday 10 am to 6 pm; Sunday 12 noon to 5 pm
Natural Food Store. Organic produce.
Directions: From I-81, take Wilkes Barre exit (#37), and get on Cross Valley (Rte 309 north), then take exit #6 (Luzerne). At light turn right onto Union St. At first light turn right and go over bridge, then take the immediate left. At stop sign turn left onto Main St and this place on left.

MALVERN

**SuTao Café
Great Valley Shopping Center, 81 Lancaster Ave; 610-651-8886
Web site: www.sutaocafe.com
Hours: Monday to Saturday 11:30 am to 9:30 pm; Sunday 12:30 pm to 8:30 pm; Buffet Lunch 11:30 am to 8:30 pm
Fully Vegan Chinese. Has American vegetarian selections. All-you-can-eat Buffet with hot dishes and a Salad Bar.
Menu: Over 50 items in a set menu. Sandwiches, veggie burgers, roll-ups, SuTao Roll-up with brown rice, soups, String Bean Rolls, Spicy Vegetable Rolls, Bean Burger (Curry Flavored), mock Tuna Salad Sandwich, SuTao veggie Seafood Sandwich, SuTao Burger (meat textured), Tofu in Shiitake Mushroom Sauce, mock shrimp dishes, Beef with Mushrooms, General Tsao's Chicken, Wanton Soup and much more. Good vegan ice cream.
Comments: Healthy, gourmet, oriental cooking. Has an informal eating area, a formal dining room and a party room. Casual place. Friendly staff. Nice atmosphere. Good prices.
Other Info: Full service, take-out, catering. Non-smoking. Reservations recommended. Accepts AMEX, DIS, MC, VISA.
Directions: SuTao Cafe is located in the Great Valley Shopping Center just off Lancaster Avenue, at corner of Rte 30 and Rte 401. From Rte 202 take Malvern exit, then take Route 29 south until it ends. Then turn right onto Rt. 30 going west. Before the first traffic light turn right into the Great Valley Center.

MARSHALL'S CREEK

Naturally Rite Restaurant and Natural Foods Market

Route 209; 570-223-1133
Store Hours: Monday to Saturday 9 am to 7:30 pm; Sunday 1 pm to 7:30 pm
Restaurant Hours: Monday, Wednesday, Thursday, Sunday 11 am to 9 pm; Friday & Saturday 11 am to 10 pm; closed Tuesday.
Natural Food Store and Restaurant. Health Clinic.
Menu: Has a large variety of vegetarian dishes. Pastas, French Fries, Sweet Potatoes, Grilled Vegetables and Garden Burger. Non-dairy ice cream. Fresh juices and flavored ice teas.
Comments: The restaurant has its own atmosphere separate from the store. Comfortable, small, relaxed place. Casual, informal. Has outdoors seating. Friendly service.
Other Info: Full service, take-out, catering. Non-smoking. Accepts AMEX, DIS, MC, VISA. Price: $$.
Directions: This place is on Rte 209 North going towards Fernwood. From I-80, take exit #52 (Marshall Creek). Go towards Marshall Creek and at Rte 209 turn right and then this place is 3 miles down on the right, about 2 minutes from the flea market.

Selene Co-op

305 West State Street; 610-566-1137
Hours: Monday & Tuesday 11 am to 6 pm; Wednesday to Friday 10 am to 7 pm; Saturday 10 am to 5 pm; closed Sunday.
Natural Food Store. Organic produce.
Menu: Has ready-made sandwiches and salads.

MONROEVILLE

**Udipi Café

4141 Old William Penn Highway; 412-373-5581
Hours: Wednesday to Sunday 11:30 am to 9 pm
Closed Tuesday.
Vegetarian Indian. Vegan friendly.
Menu: Has a good selection of South Indian dishes. Pakoras and Channa Masala.
Comments: Food can be quite spicy.
Other Info: Reservations not necessary. Non-smoking. No credit cards. Price: $-$$.
Directions: It is past the SV temple. From I-376 going east, take Business 22 exit (#6) (it comes after Churchill). At first traffic lights turn left onto Rodi Road, then turn right immediately onto Old William Penn Highway and go until you reach a

gas station on your left where the road forks. Take the right fork, the road winds and goes under I-376, at stop sign turn right and go 100 yards, then turn right onto the first road on the right. This road leads up a hill to the SV temple. At the temple (at the "Do Not Enter" sign), turn left. Turn right into the temple and park. From I-76 going west, take Rte 22 business exit, turn right at first traffic lights, then turn left at next traffic light onto Old William Penn Highway. Same as above.

NARBERTH

Narberth Natural Foods and Garden of Eatin'

231 Haverford Avenue; 610-667-7634
Store Hours: Monday to Saturday 10:30 am to 5 pm; **Restaurant Hours:** Monday to Saturday 11 am to 3 pm (on weekends until 4 pm) Closed Sunday.
Natural Food Store and Restaurant. Not pure vegetarian.
Menu: Has a good selection of vegetarian dishes. Soups, salads, sandwiches, pastas and hot dishes. Fresh juices.
Other Info: Full service, take-out. Accepts MC, VISA. Price: $.
Directions: From US Rte 1 going south, take US 1 S/City Ave exit (#33) on left, then turn right onto US 1/E City Ave and go 1 mile, at Conshohocken State Rd/Rte 23 turn right and go a half-mile, then stay straight and go onto E Montgomery Ave and go 1 mile, at Haverford Ave turn left and this place is a half-mile down.

NEW CUMBERLAND

**Avatar's Café & Juice Bar

321 Bridge Street; 717-774-2551
Web site: www.avatarsgrocerycafe.com
Hours: Tuesday to Friday 11 am to 3 pm, 5 pm to 9 pm; **Deli Hours:** Saturday 11 am to 2 pm
Closed Monday & Sunday.
Natural Food Store and Fully Vegetarian Café. Eclectic Gourmet Vegetarian.
Menu: Seitan Tempeh Loaf with Sweet Potatoes, Tofu Lasagna with homemade Red Sauce, Nasi Goreng (Indonesian Fried Rice with carmelized tofu) Adzuki Beans with Brown Rice and daily specials. Power House Sandwich (avocado, sprouts, veggies) is recommended. Good, big salads. Vegan chocolate cake, cardamom cake and maple walnut cake. Fresh juices, smoothies, wheatgrass juice.

Comments: Clouds painted on ceiling, walls pastel color, artwork and pillows. The café is located on the 2nd floor above Avatar's Natural Grocery. Open for 25 years. Pleasant atmosphere. Friendly service. Food gets high ratings.
Other Info: Full service, take-out. Non-smoking. Reservations suggested for parties of 5 or more. Accepts AMEX, DIS, MC, VISA.
Directions: From Pennsylvania Turnpike, take I-83 exit (#18) and go north on I-83 a quarter mile, then take the Limekiln Rd exit (18A). Then go east on Limekiln Rd (becomes Poplar) for ¾ mile, at Lewisberry Rd turn left and go a third-mile, at Old York Rd turn left and go a half-mile, then the road becomes Bridge road and this place is a quarter-mile down, next to a movie theater.

NEW HOLLAND

Community Natural Food Store
1065 West Main Street; 717-656-7222
Hours: Monday to Wednesday 9 am to 6:30 pm; Thursday 9 am to 8 pm; Friday 8 am to 8 pm; Saturday 9 am to 4 pm
Natural Food Store. Has a good selection of organic produce.
Menu: Has ready-made sandwiches.
Other Info: Accepts AMEX, MC, VISA.

NEW HOPE

New Hope Natural Market
415 B Old York Road; 215-862-3441
Hours: Monday to Friday 10 am to 7 pm; Saturday 10 am to 6 pm; Sunday 12 noon to 6 pm
Natural Food Store. Organic produce.
Menu: Has ready-made sandwiches.
Directions: This place at junction of Rte 202 and 179 (Old York Rd), about 1 mile west of the Delaware River.

NORTH WALES

Fresh Fields (Whole Foods)
1210 Bethlehem Pike
215-646-6300; fax: 215-542-2190
Hours: Monday to Saturday 8 am to 9 pm; Sunday 8 am to 8 pm
Natural Food Store and Cafe. Deli, Bakery, Salad Bar and Juice Bar. Organic produce. Supermarket-type place. See Whole Foods Market on page 666.
Directions: From Pennsylvania Turnpike, take Fort Washington exit, then go north on Rte 309 and this place is on the left about 5 miles down.

PAOLI

Arrowroot Natural Market
83 Lancaster Avenue;
610-640-2720
Hours: Monday to Friday 9 am to 9 pm; Saturday 9:30 am to 6 pm; Sunday 10 am to 4 pm
Natural Food Store and Café. Organic produce.
Menu: Has some ready-made sandwiches.
Comments: Has a homeopathic pharmacy and pharmacist. Used to have a café, but it was closed when I called, but may reopen.
Other Info: Accepts AMEX, MC, VISA.
Directions: This place is in the middle of Paoli on Rte 30. It is opposite a shopping center.

PENNDEL (10 miles west of Trenton)

The Natural Foods Store
131 Hulmeville Avenue
215-752-7268
Hours: Monday to Thursday 10 am to 6:30 pm; Friday 10 am to 7:30 pm; Saturday 10 am to 5:30 pm; Sunday 11 am to 4 pm
Natural Food Store. Good variety of products. Accepts MC, VISA.
Directions: From US Rte 1, take Bellevue Ave exit towards PA Rte 413, then go north on Bellevue Ave 1 block, at W Gilliam Ave turn left and go west a third-mile, at Hulmeville Ave turn right and this place is a third-mile down.

PHILADELPHIA
Ardmore, Bala Cynwyd, Jenkintown, Narbeth
There are several excellent vegetarian Chinese restaurants in Philadelphia. The China Town area is a few blocks east of Broad Street, a few blocks north of Market Street and south of Vine Street. www.veggiealert.com is a Philadelphia Web site.

Adobe Café
4550 Mitchell Street, at Leverington Avenue
215-483-3947
Hours: Monday to Thursday 5 pm to 10 pm; Friday 5 pm to 12 midnight; Saturday 5 pm to 12 midnight; Sunday 3 pm to 9:30 pm
Mexican, Southwestern. Not pure vegetarian.
Menu: Has a vegan section on the menu. Has a good selection of vegetarian dishes. Spicy seitan. Tofu and vegetable kebabs.
Comments: Outdoor covered patio dining. Friendly, attentive service. Big portions.
Other Info: Smoking at bar. Accepts AMEX, DIS, MC, VISA. Price: $.
Directions: In the Roxborough area.

**Arnold's Way and Vegetarian Café

4438 Main Street
215-483-2266; Web site: www.arnoldsway.com
Hours: Monday to Thursday 10 am to 5 pm;
Friday & Saturday 10 am to 6 pm; Sunday 11
am to 6 pm
Natural Food Store and Raw Food Deli. Juice
Bar. Vegan friendly. No produce. Has over 101
flavors of Banana Whips.
Menu: Specializes in raw foods featuring soups,
salads, raw veggie Steak, wraps fruit dishes and
seaweed wraps. Known for smoothies and raw
pies. Rawy Pies are ground raw vegetables and
wrapped in seaweed. Banana Whips come in a
wide assortment of flavors.
Comments: Uses over 1000 pounds of bananas a
week for banana whips, smoothies and shakes.
Friendly helpful staff. Only raw food restaurant
in Philadelphia.
Other Info: Counter service, take-out. Non-
smoking. Accepts reservations but not necessary.
Accepts AMEX, DC, MC, VISA.
Directions: From I-76 east, take exit #31
(Manyunk & Green Lane exit). At light turn right
and go over bridge, then at Main St turn right
and this place is 1 block down. Two minutes from
exit #31. From I-76 west, take Roxborough and
Manynk exit (#31), then at light turn left, then
at Main turn right and this place on right 1 block
down.

**The Basic Four Vegetarian Juice Bar

Reading Terminal Market, 12th and Filbert
Streets; 215-440-0991
Hours: Mon to Sat 11 am to 5 pm; closed Sun.
Vegetarian Sandwich Fast Food Place.
Menu: Great vegetarian hoagies and sandwiches.
The mixed vegetarian hoagie with veg corned-beef and
bologni is excellent. Veggie chicken hoagie is made
from soy. Tuna sandwich made with carrots.
Veggie Philly Steak, veggie burgers and good
Sweet-Potato Pie. Non-dairy cheesecake. Fresh
juices.
Comments: Can add either regular or soy cheese
to any sandwich. Service can be a bit slow (especially between 12 noon and 1:30 pm) because
the place is very popular. Open since 1981. This
is one of my favorites places and I have been here
many times. This place is highly recommended
for a quick meal.
Other Info: Counter style, take-out only. No seating. Price: $.
Directions: This place is a food stand in the
middle of the Reading Terminal Market, a few
blocks northeast of City Hall.

Cafette

8136 Ardleigh Street, at Hartwell Lane (at
Abington Avenue), Northwest Philadelphia
215-242-4220; fax: 215-242-4221
Hours: Mon 10:30 am to 4 pm; Tues to Sat 10:30
am to 4 pm, 4 pm to 9 pm; closed Sun.
American Restaurant. Not pure vegetarian.
Menu: Has some creative vegetarian dishes.
Jarlsberg Cheese Sandwich, Vegetarian Lasagna
and Vegetarian Chili.
Comments: The food gets high ratings. Has out-
door patio dining. Has live jazz.
Other Info: Reservations suggested for groups.
Cash only. Price: $-$$

**Center Foods & Café

1525 Locust Street; 215-732-9000
Hours: Monday to Friday 10 am to 7 pm; Satur-
day 10 am to 6 pm; closed Sunday.
Vegetarian.
Other Info: Take-out only on Saturday.

Charles Plaza

234-236 North 10th Street; 215-829-4383
Hours: Monday to Thursday 11:30 am to 10 pm;
Friday 11:30 am to 12 midnight; Saturday 1 pm
to 12 midnight; Sunday 1 pm to 10:30 pm
Chinese. Not pure vegetarian.
Menu: Soups, appetizers and mock meat dishes.
The Hot and Sour Soup is good. Has cheap lunch
specials that comes with soup and brown rice.
Fresh juices.
Comments: Formal dining. No MSG. This place
gets good recommendations from customers.
Other Info: Reservations required. Non-smok-
ing. Accepts AMEX, DIS, MC, VISA. Price: $$.

**Cherry Street Chinese Vegetarian

1010 Cherry Street, between Arch and Race
215-923-3663; fax: 215-923-4909
Hours: Mon to Fri 11:30 am to 10 pm; Sat 11:30
am to 11 pm; Sun 12:30 pm to 10 pm
Vegan Kosher Chinese. Macrobiotic options.
Menu: Has a large selection of dishes. The Dy-
nasty Mock chicken in a thick, spicy sauce is popu-
lar. Sesame Lemon Beef, Eggplant with Sauce,
General Tso Chicken, Bean Curd with Mixed
Vegetables, Sweet & Sour Pork, Vegetable Lo
Mein, Lemon Duck, Chicken with Walnuts and
Beef with Asparagus.
Comments: Excellent variety. Food is well pre-
sented. The meat substitutes are very authentic.
Good value. Friendly, efficient service.
Other Info: Full service, take-out, delivery. Has
an upstairs banquet room. Non-smoking. Accepts

AMEX, DC, DIS, MC, VISA. Price: $$.
Directions: Between 10th and 11th Streets in China Town.

Essene Natural Food Market and Café
719 South 4th Street, between Bainbridge and Fitzwater Streets; **Restaurant:** 215-928-3722; **Food Store:** 215-922-1146
Hours: Monday, Tuesday, Thursday, Saturday, Sunday 9 am to 8 pm; Wed, Fri 9 am to 9 pm
Natural Food Store and a Large Deli. Organic produce. Vegan and organic options. Juice Bar.
Menu: This place has a large selection of vegetarian dishes. Veggie burgers, noodles dishes, vegetables dishes, soups, salads, sandwiches, vegan enchiladas, pasta salad, Vegetable Lasagna, Tempeh Burgers, Macrobiotic Plate, Tofu Curry, Tofu Satay with peanut sauce, Lentil Cake with Cranberry Sauce, Grilled Vegetables and Tofu Burgers. Vegan cakes and many other baked desserts. Fresh juices.
Comments: The natural food store has a large selection of items. It is like a supermarket. Food is mainly sold by the pound.
Other Info: Counter service, take-out. Has plenty of seating. Accepts MC, VISA. Price: $$-$$$.
Directions: From Broad Street, go east on South St for 1 mile, then turn right at 4th St and this place is 3 blocks down. From going south on I-95, take S Columbus Blvd Exit (#16), then go on S Columbus Blvd a third-mile, at Washington Ave turn right and go a half-mile, at S 5th St turn right and go a half-mile, at Bainbridge St turn right and go 1 block, at S 4th St turn right and this place is 1 block down. This place is 3 blocks south of South St (in the middle of the main shopping area).

Fresh Fields (Whole Foods)
2001 Pennsylvania Avenue, 20th & Callowhill Streets; 215-557-0015; **fax:** 215-557-9521
Hours: Daily 8 am to 10 pm
Natural Food Store and Cafe. Deli, Bakery, Salad Bar and Juice Bar. Organic produce. Supermarket-type place. See Whole Food information.
Directions: From I-95 or after crossing the Benjamin Franklin Broad get on Vine St Exwy going west and go a half-mile, then take the PA 611/Broad Street exit, then go east on Vine St for 4/10 mile, then at N 20th St turn right and go 1 block, then turn left at Pennsylvania Ave and this place is at the corner.

Fresh Fields (Whole Foods)
929 South Street; 215-733-9788
Hours: Daily 8 am to 10 pm

Natural Food Store and Cafe. Deli, Bakery, Salad Bar and Juice Bar. Organic produce. Supermarket-type place. See Whole Foods Market information.
Directions: This place on South Street in the main shopping and tourist area.

**Govinda's Café
1408 South Street
215-985-9303
Hours: Monday to Thursday 11:30 am to 10 pm; Friday 12 noon to 12 midnight; Sunday 12 pm to 9 pm
Pure Gourmet Vegetarian International and Indian. Lunch and Dinner Buffet. Uses only natural ingredients. Buffet and Salad Bar.
Menu: The mock "shrimps" and "scallops" appetizers are authentic and great. Worth taking some to go. Pakoras, samosas, hummus, dal (lentil soup), exotic salads and pasta salad. Main dishes include Pepper Steak, Pasta Selerno, Sans Francisco Hills Kofta (vegetarian meatballs in marinara sauce with pasta), Mexico City Chili (chili with kidney and pinto beans in a spicy sauce with tofu), Steamed Vegetable Plate and Shrimp Fried Rice (mock shrimp with organic brown rice). You can get either brown or basmati rice. Stir-Fried Vegetables. Hawaiian Supreme (boy choy, dikon, snow peas, carrots, water chestnuts, broccoli with a sweet & sour sauce with rice) and Roma Eggplant Parmigiana. Vegan desserts such as chocolate cake and carrot cake.
Comments: Pleasant, friendly atmosphere. Everything is delicious. The food is great and the service is good. Highly recommended. Meet Hari, the manager, who is a good friend of mine. He is an incredibly nice guy. Classy place. Relatively unknown place because of its location. This restaurant used to be located in the middle of the main South Street tourist area and was very popular. Many of the customers may have wondered what happened to it (closed because of a fire and the high rents). The only problem with this place is that you have to be careful where you park, as your vehicle may get broken into. Do not leave any valuables visible. I am only saying this because the place is so good and I want you to come back (getting robbed may ruin the experience). As the area is scheduled for a major redoing by the city, the neighborhood should get much better.
Other Info: Full service, buffet service, take-out, catering. Non-smoking. Price: $$.
Directions: This restaurant is on South Street at the junction of Broadway and South Street. If

you are driving south from City Hall this place is a few shops to the right on South Street. South Street is one way coming onto Broadway. To park in front of the restaurant you need to go west on Lombard St (the street north of South St), then turn left at the next street (S 15 St), then turn left at the next street (South St) and this place is on the right at the end of the block.

***Harmony Chinese Vegetarian Rest.
135 North 9th Street
215-627-4520; **fax:** 215-627-7350
Hours: Sunday to Thursday 11:30 am to 10:30 pm; Friday & Saturday 11:30 am to 12 midnight
Fully Vegan Chinese.
Menu: Extensive Chinese vegan menu with over 100 items. House Wonton Soup and Yin & Yang Soup. Some appetizers are Spring Rolls and Spinach Dough Dumplings. Some main dishes are Hunan Beef, Sesame Chicken, General Tso's Chicken, Vegetarian Roasted Duck, Mongolian Pork, Tofu Hot Pot, Abalone Mushroom & Ham, Seaweed Roll, Fried Szechuan, Orange Beef (deep fried) and Mongolian Pork. The veggie ham is really good. Almond Tea is good.
Comments: Opened 1989. Chef/owner George Tang creates really excellent dishes. Excellent restaurant. Recommended place. Friendly, quick service. Pleasant atmosphere.
Other Info: Full service, take-out, catering, delivery. Non-smoking. Reservations recommended on weekends. Can be very busy on the weekends. Accepts AMEX, DIS, MC, VISA. Price: $$.
Directions: In Philadelphia's Chinatown at 9th and Cherry Streets. There's a parking lot on 9th and Arch Streets and one on 9th and Winter Streets (neither parking lot associated with restaurant).

***Kingdom of Vegetarians Restaurant
129 North 11th Street (between Arch & Race Street); 215-413-2290; **fax:** 215 413-2291
Hours: Daily 11 am to 11 pm
Fully Vegan Vegetarian Chinese. Hong Kong style. Kosher. All-you-can-eat Buffet.
Menu: Has a very large selection of vegetarian dishes (over 100 dishes). Wide array of gluten dishes. Has a large selection of reasonably priced lunch specials. Walnut Imitation Shrimp, soups, Dim Sum, Broccoli with Golden Mushroom, Stir-fry Rice Noodle, Sweet & Sour Spare Ribs, Spring Rolls, Steamed Spinach Dumplings and Jumbo Walnut Shrimp (fried mock shrimp, candied walnuts and broccoli). All-you-can-eat Dim Sum for a set price. Mongolian Pork, Lemon Chicken,

Fried Rice, noodles dishes. Buddha Rolls and Sesame Chicken are really good. Very good Won Ton Soup. Hot Jasmine Tea. Iced teas including Ginger Ice Tea. Vegan ice cream. Fresh juices.
Comments: Special Veggie Dim Sum for $10 per person. Good food and atmosphere. Several times each year has special parties where you pay $15 and get a 7-course meal. Friendly, efficient service. Service gets high ratings. Good size portions. Got good reviews in the Philadelphia Inquire and the Philadelphia Weekly.
Other Info: Full service, take-out. Non-smoking. Reservations required. Accepts AMEX, DIS, MC, VISA. Price: $-$$.
Directions: In Philadelphia's Chinatown, between Arch St and Race St, on 11th St.

Lemon Grass Thai Restaurant
3626-30 Lancaster Avenue; 215-222-8042
Hours: Monday to Thursday 11:30 am to 2 pm, 5 pm to 9 pm; Friday 11:30 am to 2 pm, 5 pm to 10 pm; Sat 5 pm to 10 pm; Sun 5 pm to 9 pm
Thai. Not pure vegetarian.
Menu: Has a separate vegetarian menu (may have to ask for it). The Lunch Special has a good selection of vegetarian dishes.
Comments: Has antique wooden carved sculptures. Often busy on weekend nights, so it may be a good idea to arrive early. Food gets good ratings.
Other Info: Full service, take-out. Reservations for parties of more than six (but not for less). Reservations suggested on weekends. Non-smoking. Accepts AMEX, DIS, MC, VISA. Price: $$.

**Magic Carpet Foods
36th & Spruce Streets, on the University of Pennsylvania's campus; 215-735-9211
Hours: Monday to Saturday 11 am to 2:30 pm
Vegan and Vegetarian Food Cart.
Menu: Slopping Joe made of veggie chili, cheese and tofu. Seizan is seitan peppersteak with vegetables and rice. Peanut Satay. Magic Meatballs is tofu meatballs and cheese with salad. Belladona.
Comments: Second Food Cart at Walnut and 34th. Good food and service. Good value. Food gets high recommendations. Price: $.

Mariposa Food Co-op
4726 Baltimore Ave; 215-729-2121; **Web site:** http://www.netaxs.com/~martink/mariposa.htm
Hours: Wednesday 3 pm to 9 pm; Thursday 1:30 pm to 9 pm; Saturday 12 noon to 4 pm
Natural Food Store.
Comments: Does not take cash. Payment must

be by check, money orders or food stamps. For travelers they give a one-month free membership. **Directions:** In west Philadelphia. From I-76/ Schykill Expressway, take South St exit and head west, then at Spruce St go west. At 47th turn left, then this place is at Baltimore Ave about 5 blocks down.

Minar Palace Indian Restaurant
1605 Sansom Street, between 16th & 17th Streets
215-564-9443
Hours: Mon to Sat 11 am 9 pm; closed Sunday.
Indian. Not pure vegetarian.
Menu: Has a good selection of vegetarian dishes. Saag Paneer, rice, dal and Vegetable Curry Platter.
Comments: Food gets high ratings. Fairly basic décor. Serves meals on plastic plates. Popular place.
Other Info: Full service, take-out, delivery, catering. Reservations suggested for groups. Accepts MC, VISA (minimum $15). Price: $-$$.

Natural Goodness Market & Café
2000 Walnut Street, at 20th; 215-977-7749
Hours: Monday to Friday 8 am to 8 pm; Saturday 10 am to 6 pm; Sun 12:30 pm to 5:30 pm
Natural Food Store and Restaurant. Mostly Vegan. Not pure vegetarian. Small selection of organic produce.
Menu: African Vegetables &Tempeh, soups, tofu salads, Seitan & Mushrooms, Vegan Reuben, sandwiches and daily specials. Fresh juices and smoothies.
Comments: Large herbal and homeopathic section. Has a small café.
Other Info: Limited service, take-out. Accepts MC, VISA ($10 minimum). Price: $.
Directions: From I-676E/US 30, take exit #38 towards Central Philadelphia, merge onto Vine St Exwy and go 100 yards, then take the 23rd St exit towards Ben Franklin Parkway, go left at fork in ramp, and go straight onto Winter St, at N 21st St turn right and go 2/3 miles, at Locust St turn left and go 1 block, at S 20th St turn left and go 1 mile.

**Nature's Harvest and Horizons Café
101 East Moreland Road, at York Road (Route 611) & Moreland Road (Route 63), Willow Grove, Montgomery County; 215-659-7705
Hours: Monday 11:30 am to 8 pm; Tuesday to Thursday 11:30 am to 9 pm; Friday & Saturday 11:30 am to 10 pm; Sunday 11 am to 6 pm
Café Hours: Tuesday to Thursday 11:30 am to

3:30 pm, 4:30 pm to 9 pm; Friday 11:30 am to 3:30 pm, 4:30 pm to 10 pm, Saturday 4:30 pm to 10 pm; closed Sunday & Monday.
Natural Food Store and Vegetarian Restaurant. Vegan options.
Other Info: Non-smoking. Accepts MC, VISA. Price: $$.

**Samosa Indian Vegetarian Cuisine
1214 Walnut Street, between 12th & 13th Streets
215-545-7776
Hours: Monday to Saturday 11 am to 3 pm, 5:30 pm to 9:30 pm; Sunday 12 pm to 3 pm
Vegetarian Indian. Vegan options. All-you-can-eat Buffet.
Menu: The buffet has vegetable soup, rice, Channa Masala, Palak Paneer, raita, dal and vegetable curry. Samosas, Indian breads and main dishes. Pickled vegetables and chilis. Homemade Kheer (rice pudding).
Comments: Good food. Friendly service. Reasonable prices. Popular place.
Other Info: Full service, take-out. Non-smoking. Reservations not accepted. Price: $-$$. Lunch $4.95, dinner $7.95 Buffet. Accepts MC, VISA.

**Samosa Indian Vegetarian Restaurant
1500 John F Kennedy Boulevard; 215-557-7740
Hours: Mon to Sat 11 am to 3 pm, 5:30 pm to 9:30 pm; Sun 12 noon to 3 pm, 5:30 pm to 9pm
Vegetarian Indian. Vegan options. Second branch of above.
Directions: This place is near the junction of Market Street and 15th St.

**Samosa Indian Vegetarian Restaurant
2 Penn Center Concourse; 215-557-7740
Hours: Mon to Sat 11 am to 3 pm, 5:30 pm to 9:30 pm; Sun 12 noon to 3 pm, 5:30 pm to 9 pm
Vegetarian Indian. Vegan options. Second branch of above.

Santa Fe Burrito Company
212 South 11th Street, between Walnut and Locust Streets; 215-413-2378
Hours: Monday to Saturday 11 am to 9 pm;
Delivery Hours: Monday to Saturday 4 pm to 8:30 pm; closed Sunday.
Mexican, Southwestern. Not pure vegetarian.
Menu: Veggie burrito, Black Bean Burrito. Mock Beef Burrito, Veggie Burger Burrito and mango juice. Wheat and white tortilla.
Comments: Casual place. Has Frequent Eater Card where get 10th burrito free.
Other Info: Counter service, take-out, delivery.

Free delivery for over $10. Non-smoking. Accepts AMEX, DC, DIS, MC, VISA. Price: $.

**Singapore Kosher Vegetarian Rest.

1006 Race Street, between 10th and 11th
215-922-3288
Hours: Mon to Thur 11:30 am to 10 pm; Fri & Sat 11:30 am to 11 pm; Sun 11:30 am to 10 pm
Fully Vegetarian Kosher Asian. Mostly vegan Chinese, Thai, Malaysian, Buddhist, Indian.
Menu: Has over one hundred items on the menu. Rainbow Chicken, Orange Beef, Vegetarian Roast Duck, Sesame Herbal Duck, General Tso's Mock Chicken (with broccoli), Hot & Sour Soup, Golden Shrimp, Golden Fish and Lechee Crispy Duck. Dumplings are good. Good asparagus and mushroom soup. Seitan Roast Duck with Chinese Vegetables (water chestnuts, taro root, carrots). Fresh juices.
Comments: Chosen as the best vegetarian restaurants in Philly Zagat Survey 1997 & 1999. Certified Kosher. Good service. Friendly, well-managed place. Gets really high recommendations. Food is good. Reasonably prices especially for lunch.
Other Info: Full service, take-out. Reservations suggested on weekends. Non-smoking. Accepts AMEX, DIS, MC, VISA. Price: $-$$.
Directions: In Chinatown.

Suburban Organics

856-427-0767; fax: 856-988-8002
email: suburbanorganics@bigplanet.com
Web site: www.suburbanorganics.com
Organic products delivery service. Delivers boxes of organic fruits, vegetables, coffee, breads and dairy produces.

Tandoor

106 40th Street, at Walnut Street (Sansom Street and Chestnut Street)
215-222-7122
Hours: Daily 11:30 am to 10:30 pm
Indian. Vegan options. Not pure vegetarian. All-you-can-eat Buffet.
Menu: The buffet has around nine vegetarian dishes. The lunch buffet is a real bargain. Authentic Punjabi food.
Comments: Good food. 20% discount with a student ID. Has Indian artifacts on the walls.
Other Info: Full service, take-out, delivery. Accepts AMEX, MC, VISA.

Weaver's Way Coop

559 Carpenter Lane; 215-843-2350
email: weaversw@weaversway.org
Web site: www.weaverway.org
Hours: Monday to Thursday 10 am to 8 pm; Friday 9 am to 8 pm; Saturday & Sunday 9 am to 6 pm
Natural Food Store and Deli. Organic produce.
Menu: Sandwiches, salads and prepared foods.
Directions: From I-76, take Lincoln Dr exit (#32), then go northeast on Lincoln Dr for 3 miles, then at McCallum St turn left and go 2 blocks, then turn left at Carpenter Lane and this place is halfway down block.

White Dog Café

3420 Sansom Street, between 34th & 35th Streets
215-386-9224; Web site: www.whitedog.com
Hours: Mon to Thur 11:30 am to 2:30 pm, 5:30 pm to 10 pm; Friday 11:30 am to 2:30 pm, 5:30 pm to 11 pm; Saturday 11 am to 2:30 pm, 5:30 pm to 11 pm; Sunday 11 am to 2:30 pm, 5 pm to 10 pm; Sat urday & Sunday Brunch 11 am to 2:30 pm
Organic Restaurant. Not pure vegetarian.
Menu: Organic Asian Cabbage and Fried Cashew Jasmine Rice.
Comments: Sidewalk café. Upscale casual. Eclectic atmosphere. Victorian era country style décor. Has live piano music. Has outdoor seating. Popular place and can be crowded.
Other Info: Accepts AMEX, DC, DIS, MC, VISA. Price: $$-$$$.
Directions: In the University City area, near University of Pennsylvania.

PINE FORGE

Gracie's New Age Eatery and 21st Century Café

Manatawny Road
610-323-4004
Hours: Thursday to Saturday 5 pm to 7:30
Natural Foods Restaurant. Not pure vegetarian.
Menu: Middle Eastern dishes, Ravioli, Saffron Curry, Black Bean Chili and more. Fresh juices, non-alcoholic beer.
Comments: Has outdoor dining on the terrace.
Other Info: Full service, take-out. Reservations suggested. Accepts AMEX, MC, VISA. Price: $$-$$$.
Directions: Parking arranged for customers.

PITTSBURGH

Pittsburgh Vegetarian Friendly Restaurant Reviews (http://www.pitt.edu/~animals/guide/loc.htm) Has a good list of vegetarian friendly restaurants in the Pittsburgh area. Includes restaurants not listed here.

Ali Baba Restaurant

404 South Craig Street, Oakland; 412-682-2829
Hours: Monday to Friday 11:30 am to 2:30 pm, 4 pm to 9:45 pm
Saturday & Sunday 4 pm to 9:45 pm
Middle Eastern. Vegan options. Not pure veg.
Menu: Has a variety of vegetarian dishes. Falafel, hummus, stuffed grape leaves (have to ask for vegetarian ones), Artichoke Salad, couscous, tabbouleh salad, Spinach Pie, salads, tahini and Syrian Soup. The couscous is really good. Regular and wheat pita.
Comments: In district of Oakland, east of the downtown. Quick, friendly service. Good value. Casual atmosphere.
Warning: The Rice with Pignola Nuts contains egg noodles.
Other Info: Full service, take-out. Accepts AMEX, DIS, MC, VISA. Price: $-$$.

Café Dejour

1107 East Carson Street; 412-488-9695
Hours: Monday & Tuesday 11:30 am to 3:30 pm; Wednesday to Saturday 11:30 am to 10 pm; closed Sunday.
Vegetarian-friendly Restaurant. Not pure veg.
Menu: Veggie burgers, veggie soups, sandwiches, salads and hot dishes.
Other Info: Cash only; no credit cards.

China Palace Chinese Restaurant

5440 Walnut Street
412-687-7423; **fax:** 412-687-5555
Hours: Mon to Thur 11:30 am to 10 pm; Fri & Sat 11:30 am to 10:30 pm; Sun 2 pm to 9 pm
Chinese. Not pure vegetarian.
Menu: Has a selection of vegetarian dishes.
Comments: Romantic, trendy place. Rated as one of the best Chinese places in the Pittsburgh area.
Other Info: Full service, take-out, free delivery within three miles. Accepts AMEX, DIS, MC, VISA. Price: $$.

Curtis' Natural Foods

120 East Ninth Avenue; 412-462-6688
Natural Food Restaurant. Not pure vegetarian.
Menu: Garbanzo soup, hummus, tahini, vegan Tofu-Vegetable Lasagna, Yellow Split Pea Soup,

Lentil Soup, baba ghanouj, Saffron Basmati Rice, Tabbouleh, Basmati Rice Salad, Un-Caesar Salad, Dijon Lentil Salad, Fireman's Beans & Rice, Southwestern Lentils & Rice, couscous, Artichick Pasta Salad, pastas and Tofu Cacciatore Bangkok cold noodles with Tempeh Curtis' Chili.
Comments: Pesto contains cheese and peanut noodles contain honey.
Directions: From I-279, take Exit #19, towards Perrysville Ave/US 19, go on Cemetery Lane, turn left at Perrysville Ave (US 19) and go 1¼ mile, turn slight right on Perry Hwy (becomes Township Rd) and go 1 block, at Glenmore Ave turn right and go a half-mile, at 9th St turn right and go 1 block, turn right at 8th Ave, at 12th St turn left and go 1 block, at 9th Ave turn right and this place is at the corner.

East End Food Co-op & Co-op Café

7516 Meade Street, in Point Breeze south of Pittsburgh; **Store:** 412-242-3598; **Café:** 412-242-7726; **email:** elcoop@idt.net
Web site: http://www.eastendfoodcoop.com/
Store Hours: 9 am to 8 pm
Café Hours: Daily 10 am to 7:30 pm
Natural Food Store and Organic Café. Vegan-friendly Deli. Juice Bar and Soup & Salad Bar. Vegetarian-friendly. Not pure vegetarian. Organic produce.
Menu: Has a good selection of vegan dishes. Tofu Burgers, Vegan Sea Burgers, Tofu Cashew Curry, Thai Sweet & Sour Tempeh, Vegetable Stir-fry, Pasta Primavera, Risotto Patties, Tofu Loaf with Gravy, Paella, mock Chicken Strips and salads. For brunch there is Scrambled Tofu, Roasted Potatoes and soy sausage.
Comments: Pay by weight. Lists ingredients and often marks vegan dishes. Good co-op. 20% discount on case on bulk orders. Arranges lectures. Besides food, also has recycled paper products and gardening supplies. One of the best selections of organic produce in Pittsburgh. Good bulk section.
Other Info: Limited service, take-out. Has seating for 20. Non-smoking. Accepts AMEX, DIS, MC, VISA.
Directions: This place is 5 miles east of downtown Pittsburgh. From I-376, take exit #9 (Edgewood), and at Braddock Ave turn right (go north). Go about 2 miles, at Meade St turn left and this place is one block down on the left. From I-376, take exit #11, then go northwest on Rte 8 for 1¾ miles, at Braddock Ave turn right and go 1 block, at Meade St turn left and this place is 1 mile down.

Fresh Fields (Whole Foods)

5880 Centre Avenue
Hours: Daily 9 am to 9 pm
Natural Food Store and Cafe. Deli, Bakery, Salad
Bar and Juice Bar. Organic produce.

Goldenseal

2731 Murray Avenue, east of downtown
412-422-7455
Hours: Monday, Wednesday, Friday, Saturday 9
am to 6 pm; Tuesday & Thursday 9 am to 7 pm;
closed Sunday.
Natural Food Store.
Comments: Has a large bulk herb and vitamin
section, and a very good health and beauty section. Tofu by the pound.

Jen's Juice Joint and Vegetarian Café

733 Copeland Street, Shadyside (east Pittsburgh
suburb); 412-683-7374
Hours: Monday to Saturday 8 am to 7 pm
Sunday 12 noon to 5 pm
Juice Bar and Deli. Vegetarian-friendly.
Menu: Fresh juices and supplements such as gin-
seng. Salads, vegetarian sandwiches and wraps.
Veggie Chickpea, chili, blue corn chips, grilled
cheese, Venice the Menace (grilled eggplant,
cheese, spinach and basil pesto), homemade soups
and soy hot dogs. Organic wheatgrass. Smoothies
and fruit shakes.
Comments: Has limited seating in the back and
outside front seating.
Other Info: Counter service, take-out. Price: $.
Directions: From I-376 W, take exit #8 towards
Squirrel Hill, then go northeast on Forward Ave
a quarter-mile, at Murray Ave turn left and go 1
mile, at Wilkins Ave turn left and go 1 block, at S
Negley Ave turn right and go a half-mile, at 5th
Ave turn left and go a quarter-mile, at S Aiken
Ave turn right and go a quarter-mile, at Elmer St
turn right and go 1 block, at Copeland St turn
right and this place is a half-block down.

Mad Mex (two locations)

370 Atwood Street, Oakland; 412-681-5656
7905 McKnight Road, North Hills
412-366-5656
Hours: Daily 11 am to 1 am
Tex-Mex, Mexican. Vegan options. Not pure veg.
Menu: Most of the dishes can be made vegetarian. Good burritos, Nachos with Soy Cheese, Rice
& Beans, tortillas, quesadillas, tacos, guacamole,
salsa and Grilled Portabella. Has soy sour cream
and soy cheese (supposed to be vegan).
Comments: Chips may be cooked in the same

oil as non-veg items. Happening, in place. At
night the lights are turned down and the music is
turned up loud. After 11 pm at night many of
the meals are half price. Food gets good recommendations.
Other Info: Full service, take-out. Reservations
not accepted. Non-smoking. Accepts AMEX,
DC, DIS, MC, VISA. Price: $$.

Pho Minh

4917 Penn Avenue; 412-661-7443
Hours: Monday, Wednesday, Thursday 11 am to
2 pm, 5 pm to 9 pm; Friday & Saturday 11 am
to 2 pm, 5 pm to 10:30 pm; Sunday 11 am to 10
pm
Asian, Vietnamese. Not pure vegetarian.
Menu: Has a good selection of vegetarian dishes.
Singapore Rice Noodle, Salad Rolls and curry
dishes. Fresh juices including coconut and lemon.
Comments: Small place with 10 tables. Cash
only; no credit cards. Price: $.

Roly Poly

705 Liberty Avenue; 412-281-5440
Hours: Monday to Friday 8:30 am to 7 pm
Closed Saturday & Sunday.
Deli. Vegetarian-friendly.
Menu: Has a selection of vegetable and cheese
tortilla wraps. Nut and Honey Wrap. Fresh juices.
Other Info: Cash only. Price: $.

Rustica Organic Gourmet Food Market

1105 East Carson Street, south side of Pittsburgh
412-381-0406
Hours: Monday to Friday 11 am to 6 pm; Satur-
day 11 am to 5 pm; closed Sunday.
Natural Food Store.
Comments: The store is small.

Spice Island Tea House

253 Atwood Street; 412-687-8821
Hours: Monday to Thursday 11:30 am to 9 pm;
Friday & Saturday 11:30 am to 10 pm; closed
Sunday.
Southeast Asian. Chinese, Thai, Indian, Burmese.
Not pure vegetarian.
Menu: Has a selection of vegetarian dishes.
Comments: Food gets good recommendations.
Other Info: Full service, take-out. Accepts
AMEX, DIS, MC, VISA. Price: $-$$.

Sree's Veggie Café

2107 Murray Avenue; 412-781-4765; email:
srees@srees.com; Web site: www.srees.com
Hours: Monday to Thursday 5:30 am to 8:30

pm; Friday & Saturday 5:30 am to 9:30 pm; closed Sunday.

Indian and Ayurvedic. Hyderabad Indian cuisine. Vegetarian and Vegan-friendly.

Menu: Dal, vegetable curries, Masala Dosa, Chickpea Potato, Coconut Chutney, basmati rice, tofu dishes, Indian breads, rice dishes and South Indian dishes. Has a set meal of rice, three vegetable or bean dishes and bread.

Comments: No MSG. Food freshly prepared. The owner and his wife are vegetarian. Regrettably uses Styrofoam cups and plastic utensils. Food gets good ratings. People like this place. Fast service. Not practically polite. Food gets good recommendations.

Other Info: Counter service, take-out, catering. Non-smoking. Price: $.

Directions: From I-376, take exit #8 towards Squirrel Hill/Homestead, then go a quarter-mile northeast on Forward Ave, at Murray Ave turn left and this place is a third-mile. This place is in east Pittsburgh.

Sree's Lunch at Carnegie Mellon U.

Trailer on Tech Street
Hours: Monday to Friday 11 am to 2 pm
Indian. Vegetarian and Vegan-friendly. Not pure vegetarian.
Comments: Inexpensive meals served from a truck.

Sree's Foods in Squirrel Hill

606 Main Street, Sharpsburg
412-781-4765; 800-3900-SREE (in Pittsburgh only)
email: sree@srees.com; Web site: www.srees.com
Hours: Only open Friday & Saturday 5:30 pm to 8:30 pm
Indian. Vegetarian and Vegan-friendly. Not pure vegetarian. See above.

Sweet Basil's Bar & Grille

5882 Forbes Avenue, Squirrel Hill
412-421-9958
Hours: Monday 11:30 am to 9 pm; Tuesday to Saturday 11:30 am to 10 pm; closed Sunday.
American Natural Foods Café. Vegan options. Not pure vegetarian.
Menu: Has vegetarian salads, sandwiches, pasta dishes, Roberta's Vegetable Salad, Grilled Vegetables (have them minus the mayo) and Three-Bean Vegetarian Chili.
Comments: Willing to prepare dishes as diners want.
Other Info: Accepts AMEX, MC, VISA. Price:

$-$$.
Directions: From I-376, take exit #8 towards Squirrel Hill/Homestead, then go a quarter-mile northeast on Forward Ave, at Murray Ave turn left and go a half-mile, then at Forbes Ave turn right and this place is 1 block down. This place is in east Pittsburgh.

Yacov's

2109 Murray Avenue, Squirrel Hill
412-421-7208
Hours: Sunday, Tuesday to Thursday 10:30 am to 8 pm; Friday 10:30 am to 2 pm; Saturday 7:30 pm to 11 pm; Sunday Brunch 10:30 am to 12 noon; closed Monday.
Mainly Vegetarian and Kosher Israeli. Not pure vegetarian (tuna).
Menu: Pizza, Portobello Hoagie, veggie meatball, veggie burger, falafel, hummus and other dishes. Some of the soups are vegetarian.
Comments: Friendly, helpful people. Recommended.
Other Info: Non-smoking. No credit cards. Price: $-$$.
Directions: From I-376, take exit #8 towards Squirrel Hill/Homestead, then go a quarter-mile northeast on Forward Ave, at Murray Ave turn left and this place is a quarter-mile down. This place is in east Pittsburgh.

**Zenith

86 South 26th Street, corner of Sarah Street
412-481-4833
Website: www.mamrama.net/zenith.htm
Hours: Wednesday to Saturday 11:30 am to 9 pm; Sunday brunch 11:30 am to 3 pm; closed Monday & Tuesday.
Fully Vegetarian International, Eclectic. Mostly Vegan.
Menu: The menu changes regularly. Most of the dishes can be made vegan. Shepherd's Pie and West African Ground Nut Stew. Has a separate menu for the Sunday brunch, which has a buffet with bread, fruits, salads and pastries. Sometimes has vegan Chocolate Mousse and Pina Colada Rice Pudding. Good selection of regular and herbal teas.
Comments: Zenith is a 4800 square ft industrial space that houses an antique store, art gallery and a vegetarian restaurant. Good, pleasant, friendly atmosphere. Place gets good ratings. Good size portions and a good value. Usually their desserts are not vegan and if they are they are labeled as such.
Other Info: Full service, catering. Accepts AMEX,

DIS, MC, VISA.
Directions: In south Pittsburgh, at the intersection of 26th and Sarah Street. From I-376, take Rte 885 exit (#7B) towards Glenwood, then at Hot Metal St go southwest over the bridge and go a half-mile, at E Carson St (Rte 837) turn right and go a quarter-mile, at S 26th St turn left and this place is a half-block down.

Zythos
2108 East Carson Street, south side of Pittsburgh
412-481-2234
Hours: Monday to Saturday 8 pm to 2 am
Mainly Vegetarian Restaurant. Techo Club. Not pure vegetarian.
Menu: Hummus, vegetarian grape leaves, wraps and beans (recommended).
Comments: Good service and atmosphere. Hip, techno & industrial bar.
Other Info: Accepts AMEX, DIS, MC, VISA.
Directions: In south Pittsburgh, at the intersection of 26th and Sarah Street. From I-376, take Rte 885 exit (#7B) towards Glenwood, then at Hot Metal St go southwest over the bridge and go a half-mile, at E Carson St (Rte 837) turn right and this place is 0.65 mile down. This place is ¾ mile due south of exit #5 on I-376.

PLUMSTEADVILLE (50 miles north of Philadelphia)

Plumsteadville Natural Foods, Inc
Plumsteadville Shopping Center, Route 611
215-766-8666
Hours: Monday to Thursday 9:30 am to 6:30 pm; Friday 9:30 am to 7 pm; Saturday 9:30 am to 5 pm; closed Sunday.
Natural Food Store. Organic produce.

READING

Dan's
1049 Penn Street, at 11th
610-373-2075
Hours: Tuesday to Friday 11:30 am to 1:30 am, 5 pm to 9 pm; Saturday 5 pm to 9 pm; closed Sunday & Monday.
American. Not pure vegetarian.
Menu: Menu changes seasonally. Has two vegetarian dishes daily. Some dishes are vegan.
Comments: Basement restaurant. Good place for special event. Helpful to vegetarian. Efficient friendly service.
Other Info: Accepts AMEX, DC, DIS, MC, VISA. Price: $$.
Directions: Parking arranged for customers.

Nature's Garden Natural Foods
Reading Mall, 4290 Perkiomen Avenue
610-779-3000
Hours: Monday to Saturday 9 am to 8 pm Closed Sunday.
Natural Food Store. Organic produce.
Menu: Has a large selection of vegetarian dishes. Soups, salads, sandwiches, veggie burgers, Tofu Hogie and hot main dishes. Fresh juices and smoothies.
Comments: Food is prepared fresh daily. Uses organic grains and beans.
Other Info: Limited service, take-out. Accepts MC, VISA. Price: $.

Sahara
334 Penn Street; 610-374-8500
Hours: Monday to Friday 11 am to 2:30, 5 pm to 10 pm; Saturday 11 am to 11 pm; closed Sun.
Middle Eastern, Lebanese. Vegan options. Not pure vegetarian.
Menu: Has a good selection of vegetarian dishes. Lentil soup, appetizers, falafel and hummus.
Comments: Sometimes has belly-dancer.
Other Info: Full service, take-out. Accepts AMEX, DC, DIS, MC, VISA. Price: $-$$.
Directions: Parking arranged for customers.

SOUTHAMPTON

**Blue Sage Vegetarian Grille
772 Second Street Pike, Southampton, Bucks County; 215-942-8888; www.bluesagegrille.com
Hours: Tuesday to Thursday 11:30 am to 3 pm, 5 pm to 9 pm; Friday & Saturday 11:30 am to 3 pm, 5 pm to 10 pm; closed Sunday & Monday.
Vegetarian New American. Gourmet food. 60% Vegan.
Menu: Thai Carrot Bisque, Hoisin BBQ Mushroom Caps, Bruchetta with White Bean Paté, spring rolls, Portobello Mushrooms, Risottos, vegan Thai Carrot Bisque, Black Bean Platter, Polenta Korma, Smash Plantain, baba ghanoush, Roasted Red Peppers and Smashed Plantain. Desserts such as Tangerine Sorbetto.
Comments: Good tasting creative cuisine. Small, nice place.
Other Info: Best to make reservations for parties of more than 4. Reservations suggested on the weekends. Non-smoking. Accepts AMEX, MC, VISA. Price: $$.
Directions: One-fourth mile north of Street Road. From coming west on US Rte 1, take PA-132/Street Rd exit and go 5 miles northwest on Street Rd, at 2nd St Pike/PA-232 turn right and this place is 1 long block down.

PENNSYLVANIA 519

SPRINGFIELD (Philadelphia suburbs)

Martindale's Natural Foods
Ye Olde Sproul Shopping Center, 1172 Baltimore
Pike & Route 320; 610-543-6811
Hours: Monday to Friday 9:30 am to 9 pm; Saturday 9 am to 7 pm; closed Sunday.
Natural Food Store. Organic produce. Has a good selection of organic produce. Vegan options.
Menu: Has vegan ready-made food in their cooler such as sandwiches and salads.
Comments: Helpful, friendly staff.
Directions: Next to the Springfield Mall.

STAHLSTOWN

***Maggie Mercantile
RD #1 Box 162C RT 711; 724-593-5056
Hours: Tuesday to Sunday 10 am to 6 pm (Friday until 8 pm); Sunday 11 am to 3 pm; closed Monday.
Natural Food Store and Vegan Café.
Menu: Has a wide selection of vegetarian and vegan dishes. The Sunday Buffet features a cuisine from various countries around the world.
Comments: New place.
Directions: From PA Turnpike, take Dunegon exit (#9), turn left and go ¼ mile, then turn left onto Rte 711 north and this place is about 3 miles down on the right. One story red building that has a truck in front with a sign that says Maggie.

STATE COLLEGE

The Granary
2766 West College Avenue; 814-238-4844
Hours: Monday to Saturday 10 am to 6 pm
Closed Sunday.
Natural Food Store. Has a small selection of organic produce.
Directions: From I-80, take Rte 26 south. This place is three miles south of the downtown.

STOVERSTOWN

Sonnewald Natural Foods
RD 1 Box 1510A, Lehman Road
717-225-3825
Hours: Tuesday to Thursday 10 am to 6 pm; Friday 10 am to 9 pm; Saturday 8 am to 5 pm; closed Sunday & Monday.
Natural Food Store. Supermarket-size place.
Comments: Will grind grains. Has free nutritional counseling.
Directions: From I-30, go south on Rte 616 for 2 miles. At light turn right in square and go about 2½ miles and at Lehman Rd turn right and this place is 150 yards down on left.

STROUDSBURG

Earthlight Natural Foods
829 Ann Street; 570-424-6760
Hours: Monday to Saturday 9:30 am to 6 pm
Sunday 12 noon to 4 pm
Natural Food Store. Organic produce.

Everybody's Café
905 Main Street; 570-424-0896
Hours: Sunday to Thursday 11 am to 9 pm
Friday & Saturday 11 am to 9:30 pm
Natural Foods European. Polish, Italian. Vegan options. Not pure vegetarian.
Menu: About a third of the menu is vegetarian. Has a good selection of vegetarian dishes. Mushroom Lasagna is very good. Mushroom Picata.
Comments: Creative dishes. Located in a large Victorian house.
Other Info: Full service, take-out, catering. Accepts AMEX, MC, VISA. Price: $-$$.
Directions: Parking arranged for customers.

TREXLERTOWN

Healthy Alternatives Food & Nutrition Center
7150 Hamilton Boulevard, near Allentown
610-366-9866
Hours: Monday to Wednesday 9:30 am to 6 pm; Thursday 10 am to 7 pm; Friday 10 am to 8 pm; Saturday 10 am to 4 pm
Natural Food Store. Has the biggest organic produce section in Lehigh Valley.
Menu: Soups, ready-made sandwiches, salads and hot dishes.
Comments: Good store. Has homeopathic medicines.
Directions: Near the Ames shopping center.

WAYNE

Fresh Fields (Whole Foods)
821 West Lancaster Ave, not far from Valley Forge
610-688-9400; **fax:** 610-688-9401
Hours: Monday to Saturday 8 am to 9 pm
Sunday 8 am to 8 pm
Natural Food Store and Cafe. Deli, Bakery, Salad Bar and Juice Bar. Organic produce. Supermarket-type place. See Whole Foods Market information.

Comments: Sandwiches, salads, soups and much more.
Directions: From Pennsylvania Turnpike, take I-202 exit south, then take Rte 252 south and go towards Paoli. At Rte 30 turn left and this place on the left 3 miles down.

WEST CHESTER

Great Pumpkin Health Foods
Market Street Plaza
607 East Market Street
610-696-0741
Hours: Monday to Friday 9 am to 8 pm
Saturday 9 am to 6 pm
Sunday 10 am to 3 pm
Natural Food Store. No produce.
Directions: Take Rte 3 (Market St), which is on the way out of town and this place is on the left.

Hunan Chinese Restaurant
Town and Country Shopping Center
1103 West Chester Pike
610-429-9999
Hours: Daily 11 am to 11 pm
Chinese. Not pure vegetarian.
Menu: Has a large vegetarian menu. Soups, appetizers, tofu and mock meat dishes, and vegetable dishes.
Comments: Food gets good ratings. Friendly service.
Other Info: Full service, take-out. Accepts AMEX, DIS, MC, VISA. Price: $-$$.

WILLIAMSPORT

Fresh Life
2300 East Third Street
570-322-8280
Web site: www.freshlife.com
Store Hours: Monday to Friday 9 am to 8 pm
Saturday 9 am to 5 pm
Closed Sunday.
Café Hours: Monday to Friday 9 am to 3 pm
Closed Saturday & Sunday.
Natural Food Store and Café. Deli, Bakery and Juice Bar. Organic produce.
Comments: Has a large selection of products in the store. Has seating.
Directions: This place is in southeast Williamsport. Take Rte 180 to 3rd St/Warrensville exit. Then go west on Sandhill Rd (becomes E 3rd St) and this place is 1 mile down.

WILLOW GROVE

**Nature's Harvest Market and Horizons Café
Moreland Plaza, 101 East Moreland Road
Store number: 215-659-7705; **Café number:** 215-657-2100
Store Hours: Monday 10 am to 8 pm; Tuesday to Saturday 10 am to 9 pm; Sun 11 am to 6 pm
Café Hours: Tuesday to Friday 11:30 am to 3 pm, 5 pm to 8:45 pm; Sat 11:30 am to 8:45 pm
Natural Food Store and Fully Vegetarian Cafe.
Fully Organic Juice Bar. Mostly Vegan.
Menu: Homemade soups, salads, sandwiches, Middle Eastern dishes, Seitan Steak Fajitas, Tofu Scallops Paulette (with pesto and grilled asparagus), Pecan & Baked Seitan, Sopa de Tortilla, Vegan Caesar Salad, Spicy Seitan Steak, Red Chili & Grilled Tofu, Jamaican BBQ Seitan Wings and Buffalo Wings (seitan). Vegan desserts such as Chocolate Mousse with raspberry sauce. Good barbeque sauce.
Comments: Everything freshly made. Good service and food. Creative cuisine. Friendly, knowledgeable staff. Restaurant gets very good ratings. Gourmet meatless cuisine. Use organic ingredients as often as possible.
Other Info: Full service, Limited service, takeout. Non-smoking. Reservations recommended on Friday and Saturday. Popular place. Accepts MC, VISA. Price: $$.
Directions: From PA Turnpike, take Rte 611 exit #27 to Willow Grove, then go south on Rte 611 for 2½ miles, then at Rte 63 turn slight right and this place is a quarter-mile down on the right. From Philadelphia, take Broad Street (611 North) 25 miles to Rt 63. Plenty of in-front parking. At junction of Rte 611 & Rte 63 in Moreland Plaza.

WYNNEWOOD

Fresh Fields (Whole Foods Market)
339 East Lancaster Avenue
610-896-3737; **fax:** 610-898-9129
Hours: Mon to Sat 8 am to 9 pm; Sun 8 am to 8 pm
Natural Food Store and Cafe. Deli, Bakery, Salad Bar and Juice Bar. Organic produce. Supermarket-type place. See Whole Foods Market information.
Directions: From Rte 1 (City Ave), go northwest on Rte 30 and this place is 1½ mile down on the right a little past Wynnewood Ave.

Rhode Island

1. Charlestown
2. East Greenwich
3. East Providence
4. Narragansett
5. Newport
6. Pawtucket
7. Providence
8. Smithfield
9. Wakefield
10. Warwick
11. Westerly
12. West Kingston

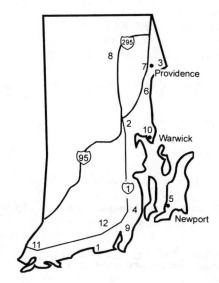

CHARLESTOWN

**Spice of Life
4820 Old Post Road; 401-364-2030
Summer Hours: Daily for lunch and dinner
Winter Hours: Sat & Sun 11 am to 5 pm
Vegetarian International, American Natural Foods. Juice Bar. Vegan options.
Menu: Soups, salads, sandwiches, burritos, wraps and smoothies. Chai Latte with soymilk.
Comments: Small, friendly place. The Fantastic Umbella Factory, a shopping complex with crafts and a garden, where Spice of Life is located is an interesting place.
Other Info: Full service, take-out. Reservations not accepted. Non-smoking. Cash only. Price: $-$$.
Directions: It is at the Fantastic Umbella Factory. This place is about 1 mile northeast of Ninigret National Wildlife Refuge and west of Fort Ninigret, just off of Rte 1.

EAST GREENWICH

Back to Basics Natural Foods Grocery
500 Main Street; 401-885-2679
Hours: Monday to Friday 9 am to 7 pm; Saturday 9 am to 6 pm; Sunday 12 noon to 5 pm
Natural Food Store. Organic produce.
Other Info: Accepts AMEX, DIS, MC, VISA.
Directions: From I-95, take Exit #9 and go south on Rte 4, then take the East Greenwich exit after

about a quarter-mile onto Division Rd. Go east on Division Rd for about 1¼ mile, take first left onto 1st Ave and go into town about 1 mile. Then at Main turn left. This place on right 3½ blocks down.

Pick Pockets Deli
431 Main Street; 401-884-0488
Hours: Monday to Saturday 10 to 8 pm
Sunday 10 am to 6 pm
Middle Eastern. Not pure vegetarian.
Menu: Hummus, baba ghanouj, falafel and stuffed grape leaves.
Other Info: Limited service, catering, take-out. No credit cards; cash only. Price: $$.

NARRAGANSETT

Crazy Burger
144 Boon Street, Narragansett; 401-783-1810
Hours: Monday to Friday 8 am to 8 pm; Saturday 8 am to 9 pm; closed Sunday.
American. Not pure vegetarian.
Menu: Has a selection of vegetarian dishes. Veggie soups, steamed vegetables, veggie burgers and other dishes.
Other Info: Accepts DIS, MC, VISA.

Food For Though
Mariner Square Mall
140 Point Judith Road #32
401-789-2445

Hours: Monday to Saturday 10 am to 6 pm (until 7 pm Friday); Sunday 12 noon to 5 pm
Natural Food Store.
Other Info: Accepts AMEX, MC, VISA.
Directions: From I-95, take Rte 4 south 15 miles and it becomes Rte 1. Then at Rte 108 go south about 1½ mile and it is past the Stop and Shop Mall (on right), on the left in Mariner Square Mall.

NEWPORT

Harvest Natural Foods
1 Casino Terrace; 401-846-8137
Hours: Monday to Saturday 9 am to 7 pm
Sunday 11 am to 5 pm
Natural Foods Store and Lunch Counter. Organic produce. Vegan options. Not pure veg.
Menu: Take-out meals at a lunch counter. All the soups are vegan. Vegetarian BLT, soups, salads, pastas, stir-fries, hummus and veggie sandwiches.
Other Info: Counter service, take-out. Accepts AMEX, DIS, MC, VISA. Price: $.
Directions: From I-95, take Rte 4 coming south or Rte 1 coming north, then go east on Rte 138 for 9 mile. Go over Jamestown Bridge and then Newport Bridge. After Newport bridge, take first exit, the Rte 238 S exit towards Scenic Newport and turn right onto Rte 138A (Rte 238, JT Connell Hwy) and it becomes Farewell St, at Thames St make a slight right and go a block. At Memorial Blvd turn left and go ¾ mile, at Bellevue Ave turn right and go a quarter-mile to Casino Terrace where you turn left into the Bellevue Shopping Center. It is a little past the Tennis Hall of Fame.

PAWTUCKET (It is a little north of Providence)

**Garden Grille Café and Juice Bar
727 East Avenue; 401-726-2826
Hours: Monday to Saturday 10:30 am to 9 pm
Sunday 11:30 am to 8:30 pm
Vegetarian Restaurant. Vegan options.
Menu: Salads, good selection of wraps, veggie burgers, Grilled Portobello Mushrooms, veg hot dogs, Vegetarian Chili, Tortilla Sandwiches, Asparagus Wrap, Sweet Potato Fries and Tofu Ravioli. Usually has three vegan soups daily. Dinner entrées (includes salad or soup) and nightly specials. Pizza made with soy cheese. Has a good Portobello Mushroom Sandwich. Daily and weekly specials. Vegan desserts including Praline "Cheese" Cake, Mud Pie and Chocolate Cinnamon Mousse Pie. Good variety of fresh juices and smoothies. Cappuccino, espresso.
Comments: One of the better places I visited in the country. Recommended. Relaxed, casual, pleasant atmosphere. The food is very good. The guy who manages the place is tuned on and helpful.
Other Info: Counter service, take-out, catering. Accepts AMEX, MC, VISA. Price: $-$$
Directions: Near Brown University. From I-95 going north, take Branch Ave Exit (#24) and merge onto Branch Ave, at Main St (Rte 1) turn left and go about one mile. At Lafayette St turn right and go a little less than a half-mile, At East Ave turn left and this place is in the middle of the block.

PROVIDENCE

Bread & Circus (Whole Foods)
261 Waterman Street, at Butler; 401-272-1690
Web site: www.wholefoodsmarket.com
Hours: Monday to Saturday 8:30 am to 10 pm
Sunday 8 am to 8:30 pm
Natural Foods Store and Deli. Good Salad Bar and Bakery. Excellent organic produce section. Macrobiotic and Vegan options. Not pure vegetarian. Supermarket-type place.
Menu: Assortment of vegetarian and vegan options in the deli and bakery. Cappuccino, espresso.
Comment: It is near Brown University.
Other Info: Counter service, take-out. Has no seating inside, but has seating outside during the summer. Accepts AMEX, DC, DIS, MC, VISA. Price: $.
Directions: From I-95, take I-195 exit. From I-195 take Gano St exit (#3), and at end of ramp turn right and go north on Gano St one mile. At Waterman turn right and this place is on the right after a half-mile.

Bread & Circus
University Heights Shopping Center
North Main Street & Dolyle Ave
Natural Food Store.
Comments: To open in May or June in 2002.

O-Cha
221 Wickendon Street; 401-421-4699
Hours: Sunday to Thursday 12 noon to 10 pm
Friday & Saturday 12 noon to 11 pm
Thai. Not Full Vegetarian.
Menu: Several vegetarian options. Peanut sauce Vegetables, mock "duck", noodle dishes and Sautéed Vegetables. Does not use MSG.
Other Info: Full service, take-out. Non-smoking. Accepts AMEX, MC, VISA. Price: $$.

India

1060 Hope Street   401-421-2600
123 Dorrance Street   401-278-2000
Hours: Sunday to Thursday 12 to 10
Friday & Saturday 12 noon to 11 pm
Indian. Not Pure Vegetarian.
Comments: Gets mixed reviews from customers.
Other Info: Non-smoking. Accepts AMEX, DC,
MC, VISA. Price: $$.

Taste of India

230 Wickenson Street;   401-421-4355
Hours: Mon to Sat 11:30 to 2:30, 5 pm to 10:30
pm; Sun 11:30 am to 2:30pm, 4:30pm to 9:30pm
Indian. Vegan options. Not pure vegetarian.
Menu: Separate vegetarian menu. Soups, appe-
tizers and several vegetarian main dishes.
Other Info: Full service, take-out. Non-smoking.
Accepts AMEX, MC, VISA. Price: $$.

SMITHFIELD

Food Work

Apple Valley Plaza, behind Apple Valley Mall
445 Putnam Pike; 401-232-2410
Hours: Monday to Saturday 10 am to 6 pm (un-
til 7 pm on Wednesday & Thursday)
Closed Sunday.
Natural Food Store. Organic produce.
Other Info: Accepts AMEX, DIS, MC, VISA.
Directions: From I-295, take exit #7 A or B. Get
onto Rte 44 and go west ¾ mile and this place is
on right in the Apple Valley Mall.

WAKEFIELD

Alternative Food Co-op

357 Main Street, Wakefield; 401-789-2240
Email: manager@alternativefoodcoop.com
Web site: www.alternativefoodcoop.com
Hours: Monday to Friday 8 am to 8 pm
Saturday & Sunday 9 am to 6 pm
Natural Food Store. Organic produce.
Other Info: Accepts MC, VISA.
Directions: From Providence take I-95 south, take
Exit #9 for Rte 4 south (exit forks to left), Rte 4
feeds into Route 1 after Wickford. Follow Route
1 South, past Route 138 take first Wakefield exit,
turn right (Tower Hill Road) at end of exit ramp,
(Dunkin Donuts is on left), which turns into
Main Street. Pass three traffic lights (road curves
left past Saab dealer). Co-op on right about ten
buildings down (across from Kenyon Ave).

Pick Pockets Deli

231 Old Tower Hill Rd, next to Dunkin Donuts
401-792-3360
Hours: Monday to Friday 10 am to 9 pm; Satur-
day 10 am to 7 pm; Sunday 11 am to 5 pm
Middle Eastern. Not pure vegetarian.
Menu: Hummus, baba ghanouj, falafel and
stuffed grape leaves.
Other Info: Counter service, catering, take-out.
Accepts AMC, VISA. Price: $$.

WARWICK

Village Natural

18 Post Road; 401-941-8028
Hours: Monday to Saturday 10 am to 6 pm
Sunday 12 noon to 5 pm
Natural Food Store. Organic produce only dur-
ing the summer.
Other Info: Accepts AMEX, MC, VISA.
Directions: From I-95, take exit for Rte 37 east
(#14W) and go east one mile, then at Post Rd go
northeast about 3 miles until it ends. When road
forks, go left and this place on left one block down.

WESTERLY

Allen's Health Food

Franklin Street; 401-596-5569
Hours: Monday to Thursday 9:30 am to 5:30
pm; Friday 9:30 am to 6 pm; Saturday 9:30 am
to 5 pm; closed Sunday.
Natural Food Store.
Directions: From I-95, take exit for Rte 49 (#92)
and go towards Pendleton Hill Rd and get on Rte
78 going east towards the ocean for about 5 miles
to Rte 1 (Franklin), then turn right and this place
is on the right.

WEST KINGSTON

The Alternative Food Cooperative

3362 Kingston Road
401-789-2240
Hours: Monday to Friday 9 am to 7 pm
Saturday & Sunday 9 am to 6 pm
Natural Food Store.
Directions: From I-95, take exit for Kingston (Rte
138) and University of Rhode Island. Go east on
Rte 138 about 7 miles. Store on right, a quarter-
mile west of Fairground Rd. This place is one
mile west of the entrance of URI campus.

South Carolina

1. Charleston
2. Columbia
3. Garden City
4. Greenville
5. Irmo
6. Lexington
7. Mount Pleasant
8. Myrtle Beach
9. North Charleston
10. North Myrtle Beach
11. Spartanburg
12. Walterboro
13. West Columbia

CHARLESTON

Angel Fish

Merchant Village Center
520 Folly Road
843-762-4722
Hours: Tues to Sun 11 am to 3 pm, 5 pm to 8 pm (until 9 pm on Fri & Sat) Closed Monday.
American Natural Foods. Vegetarian-friendly. Vegan options. Not pure vegetarian.
Menu: Salads, soups, pastas and other veg dishes. Usually no meat base in the soups. Fresh juices.
Comments: Comfortable atmosphere. Interesting design. Friendly service. Everything is freshly cooked.
Other Info: Full service, take out. Accepts AMEX, MC, VISA. Price: $$.
Directions: About a 15 minute drive south of the city. From Rte 30, take Exit #3 (Folly Rd, Rte 171), at Folly Rd turn right (go north) and this place is a third-mile down in Merchant Village Center.

Books, Herbs & Spices

1409 Folly Road
843-762-3025
Hours: Monday to Friday 10 am to 6 pm; Saturday 9:30 am to 5 pm; closed Sunday.
Natural Food Store.
Directions: From Hwy 17, take East Bay St exit, and follow signs to East Bay St. At East Bay turn right (go south). This place on left a mile south of Hwy 17, opposite Channel 5.

Doe's Pita Plus

334 East Bay Street #F; 843-577-3179
Hours: Daily 7:30 am to 4:30 pm
Middle Eastern. Not pure vegetarian.
Menu: Salads, sandwiches, hummus and stuffed grape leaves. Bakes own pita breads. Everything freshly made.
Other Info: Counter service, take-out. Price: $.

Earth Fare

South Windermere Shopping Center; 74 Folly Road Boulevard; 843-769-4800
Web site: www.earthfare.com
Hours: Monday to Saturday 8 am to 9 pm Sunday 9 am to 8 pm
Natural Food Store and Café. Deli, Bakery, Juice Bar and Salad Bar. Organic produce. Macrobiotic and Vegan options. It is a huge supermarket-type place. Not pure vegetarian.
Menu: Has a hot and cold buffet with a wide selection of vegetarian dishes. Good salad bar, vegan Potato Salad, Organic Black Beans, Oriental Noodles, falafel, Szechwan Tofu and Tofu Cottage Cheese.
Comments: This is an impressive natural food store with a massive selection. Recommended. Cooking classes and lectures. Books and magazines.
Other Info: Counter service, take-out. Accepts AMEX, DIS, MC, VISA. Price: $$.
Directions: This place is on the west side of the Rte 17 bridge, a mile southwest of the bridge. From Rte 30, take Exit #1 and go west on Rte 61 one mile. Then at Folly Rd Blvd (Savannah Hwy) turn right and this place is a half-mile down.

Health Nuts

Green Ridge Plaza, 2110 Greenridge Road, Suite E; 843-764-4956
Hours: Mon to Sat 10 am to 8 pm; closed Sun.
Sports Nutrition Store with a Juice Bar.
Menu: Sandwiches, big good salads, Hummus Sandwich and Baked Tofu Sandwiches.
Comments: Friendly place.
Directions: From I-26, take Exit #208 and go northeast for a mile and get on Rte 52 (turn left) going north and this place is ¾ mile down.

Horse & Cart Café

347 King Street, next to Marion Square
843-722-0797
Hours: Monday to Saturday 11 am to 7 pm
Closed Sunday.
American Restaurant and Bar. Not pure veg.
Menu: Salads and sandwiches. Veggie Sandwich, Mediterranean Salads and Burritos.
Comments: Stays open late for music (Irish music, drumming) and poetry readings. Friendly, very casual atmosphere. Good hang-out place.
Other Info: Full service, take-out. Accepts AMEX, MC, VISA. Price: $.

Mustard Seed

1220 Ben Sawyer Blvd, Suite M, in Mt Pleasant, north of historical district; 843-840-0050
1978 Maybank Highway; 843-762-0072
Hours: Monday to Thursday 5 pm to 9 pm
Friday & Saturday 5 pm to 10 pm
Restaurant. Not pure vegetarian.
Comments: Serves some healthy food. Good service. Price: $$.
Menu: Pastas, Veggie Lasagna (sometime) and salads.

Raspberry's Natural Food Store

1331 Ashley River Road, south of the downtown. 843-556-0076
Hours: Monday to Friday 9:30 am to 6:30; Saturday 9:30 am to 5:30 pm; Sun 1 pm to 6 pm
Natural Food Store and take-out Deli. Mainly vegetarian (serves tuna). Cooked dishes are all vegetarian. Organic produce.
Menu: Has a large amount of vegetarian dishes. Soups, salads, sandwiches and baked breads. Two vegan soups, vegan pastries and sandwiches.
Other Info: Accepts DIS, MC, VISA.
Directions: From I-26, take I-526 exit. From I-526, take Ashley River Rd (Rte 61) exit south and go east on Paul Cantrell Blvd one mile and road merges onto Ashley River Rd. This place then 1½ mile down on right.

***Soul Vegetarian

3225-A Rivers Avenue, North; 843-744-1155
Hours: Tuesday to Friday 11 am to 8:30 pm; Saturday & Sunday 8 am to 9:30 pm; Saturday & Sunday Breakfast 8 am to 11 pm; closed Mon.
Fully Vegetarian Soul and International. Mainly vegan. See Atlanta for details.
Menu: Herbed rice, vegan toasted Almond Ice Kream and much more.
Comments: This place is related to the other Soul Vegetarian Restaurant located around the country. There is honey in the BBQ sauce. The people who run this place are really nice.
Directions: From I-26 coming south, take Dorchester Rd (Rte 642, Exit #215), then at Dorchester Rd turn left and go one mile following the road around to the left, then at Rivers Ave (Rte78, Rte 52) turn right and this place is ¾ mile down.

COLUMBIA

***The Basil Pot

928 Main Street, right behind the state capitol building; 803-799-0928
Web site: www.metromark.net/basilpot.htm
Hours: Monday to Friday 8 am to 2:30 pm, 6 pm to 9 pm; Saturday 9 am to 2:30 pm, 6 pm to 9 pm; Sunday 9 am to 2:30 pm
Natural Foods Vegetarian-friendly Restaurant. Macrobiotic options. Not pure vegetarian.
Menu: Pizzas with Tempeh Sausage, salads, soups, Tofu Loaf, vegetarian chili, veggie burgers and baked goods (ingredients are listed). For breakfast there are Scrambled Tofu and non-dairy Blueberry Pancakes. Fresh juices.
Comments: Pleasant atmosphere. Plays classical music. Displays local art. Has plants.
Other Info: Full service, take-out. No credit cards: cash only. Price: $-$$.
Directions: From I-77, take Rte 277 west until it ends, then bear right onto Sunset Dr and go west a half-mile, then go south onto Rte 21 and after a mile its becomes Rte 176/Rte 21 S. Go straight 1½ mile (becomes Main St), then this place is 2½ blocks south of Rte 1.

Earth Fare

3312 Devine Street; 803-799-0084
Hours: Monday to Saturday 8 am to 9 pm
Sunday 9 am to 8 pm
Natural Food Store and Café. Deli, Juice Bar, Bakery and Salad Bar. Organic produce. Macrobiotic and Vegan options. It is a huge supermarket-type place. Not pure vegetarian.

Menu: Has a hot and cold buffet.
Comments: This is a large natural food store with a massive selection. Recommended. Cooking classes and lectures. Books and magazines.
Other Info: Counter service, take-out. Price: $$.
Directions: This place is a mile east of downtown Columbia, on Rte 76, just west of Rte 378. From I-77, take Exit #10 (Jackson Blvd, Rte 760) towards Fort Jackson. Go west on Rte 760 one mile, then at Rte 378/Rte 76 turn right and go a mile. When the road forks take Rte 76 left and this place is 100 yards down, between Ott Rd and Chatham Ave.

Nature's Way
1300 Augusta Road, a little off Highway 1
803-796-0768
Hours: Monday to Friday 8:30 am to 6 pm; Saturday 9 am to 5 pm; closed Sunday.
Natural Food Store.
Other Info: Accepts AMEX, MC, VISA.
Directions: Half a block from Triangle City area.

Nice-N-Natural
1217 College Street; 803-799-3471
Hours: Monday to Friday 11 am to 3:30 pm; Saturday 11 am to 3 pm; closed Sunday.
Natural Foods. Mostly Vegetarian. Vegan options. Not pure vegetarian.
Menu: A good selection of take-out soups, salads and sandwiches, veggie Reubenless Sandwich (recommended) and other dishes. A selection of fresh fruit salads. Fresh juices.
Other Info: Counter service, take-out. Does not accept credit cards. Price: $.
Directions: This place is in the center of town. From the junction of Rte 1 & Rte 21, go south on Rte 21 three blocks, then at College St turn left and this place is a block down, a little past Main St on the left.

Korean O-Bok Restaurant
1616 Decker Boulevard
803-787-1100
Hours: Tues to Thur 11 am to 9 pm; Fri & Sat 11 am to 10 pm; Sun 5 pm to 8 pm; closed Mon.
Korean. Not pure vegetarian.
Menu: Has a selection of vegetarian dishes. Bi Bim Bob is good.
Comments: Has good Korean foods. Some soups have bean paste base (other meat base), so best to ask about this. Meals come with a side dish so you may want to ask that no side fish dishes come with your meal.
Other Info: Accepts DIS, MC, VISA.

The Orient
Decker Plaza, 1735 Decker Blvd; 803-738-0095
Hours: Monday to Thursday 11 to 10 pm; Friday & Saturday 11 am to 10:30 pm; Closed Sun.
Chinese. Vegan options. Not pure vegetarian.
Menu: Has good selection of vegetarian dishes. Tofu dishes, Eggplant in Garlic Sauce, Tofu with Black Bean Sauce, Chinese Broccoli and many more vegetarian options.
Comments: Should ask for the vegetarian menu.
Other Info: Full service, take-out. Accepts MC, VISA. Price: $$.

Rosewood Market & Deli
2803 Rosewood Drive
803-765-1083; **Toll-free:** 888-203-5950
Web site: www.rosewoodmarket.com
Store Hours: Monday to Saturday 9 am to 9 pm
Sunday 10 am to 6 pm
Café Hours: Monday to Saturday 11:30 am to 2:30 pm, 5 pm to 7 pm
Natural Food Store and Café. Deli. Vegan and Macrobiotic options. Not pure vegetarian. Organic produce.
Menu: Main dishes, two soups, Barbeque Tofu, salads, couscous, pizzas, Carrot Raisin Salad, Split Pea Soup, Mexican Rice, BBQ Tofu, soy burgers, desserts and vegan baked goods.
Comments: Has a small café. Has daily vegetarian and macrobiotic dishes. Reasonably priced. Friendly place. Local organic produce used when possible.
Other Info: Limited service. Take-out deli. Has a few tables. Has outdoor seating. Accepts MC, VISA. Price: $.
Directions: From I-26 going east, take I-126 S exit and go 3½ miles and it ends and becomes Rte 76 (Rte 176 W, Rte 21 N) and go another half-mile, at Rte 48 S turn right and go 2½ miles, at Rte 16 turn left and this place is a mile down at junction of Rosewood (Rte 16) and Maple (opposite a shopping center).

Touch of India
14 Diamond Lane; 803-731-5960
Hours: Wednesday to Sunday 6 pm to 10 pm
Closed Monday & Tuesday.
Indian. Not pure vegetarian. Vegetarian buffet on Sunday.
Comments: Food gets high ratings.
Other Info: Accepts DIS, MC, VISA.

Yesterday
2030 Devine Street
803-799-0196; **Web site:** www.yesterdayssc.com

Hours: Sunday to Wednesday 11:30 am to 12 midnight; Thursday to Sat 11:30 am to 1 am. Tex-Mex. Vegan options. Not pure vegetarian. Menu: Black Bean Burger, vegan veggie burgers, Vegetarian Chili Meal (Black Bean Chili, flour tortillas, salad), nachos, pasta, Vegetable Platters, steamed broccoli, Baked Potatoes and other vegetarian dishes. Comments: Selected as one of the Top 500 Restaurant by Restaurant Hospitality Magazine. Relaxed, tavern atmosphere. Rustic décor. Senior citizen discount of 10% on entrees. Has indoor and outdoor dining on Santee Street. Parking is free for up to 1½ hours. Other Info: Full service, take-out, catering, delivery in local area. Accepts AMEX, DIS, MC, VISA. Price: $-$$. Directions: At "Friendly Five Point," on the corner of Devine Street and Harden Street, a few blocks from the U of South Carolina. From I-126, take Elmwood Ave exit and take Elmwood Ave until the road dead-ends, turn right at Bull Street, then turn left at Gervais St and go a couple blocks, then turn right onto Harden Street and this place is on the right. Parking lot in rear of the building where you can park for free when you get ticket validated in restaurant.

GREENVILLE

Cantinflas Gourmet Mexican and Vegetarian Restaurant

120 North Main Street; 864-250-1300
Hours: Monday to Thursday 11 am to 10 pm; Friday & Saturday 11 am to 11 pm; closed Sun. Mexican. Vegetarian friendly. Not pure veg. Comments: Friendly place. Other Info: Accepts AMEX, DC, MC, VISA.

Earth Fare

Lewis Plaza, 6 South Lewis Plaza, Augusta Road
864-250-1020
Hours: Monday to Saturday 8 am to 8 pm
Sunday 11 am to 6 pm
Natural Food Store. See Charleston, SC.
Other Info: Accepts AMEX, DIS, MC, VISA.

Gardner's Natural Market & Café

McAlister Market Place, 60 East Antrim Drive
Store number: 864-242-4856; Café number: 864-233-9258; Web site: www.gogarners.com
Hours: Monday to Saturday 9 am to 9 pm
Sunday 1 pm to 6 pm
Natural Food Store and Cafe. Deli, Juice Bar and

Bakery. Vegan options. Organic produce. Comments: It is the largest natural food store in Greenville. Other Info: Cafeteria style, take-out. Accepts DIS, MC, VISA. Directions: From I-85, take Laurens Rd exit (#48), and go north on Laurens Rd 2 miles. This place is the next right after Landwood Ave at E Antrim (can only turn right) and this place on right a quarter-mile down. This place is a quarter-mile southeast of junction of S Pleasantburg Dr & Laurens Rd.

India Palace

59 Liberty Lane
864-271-8875
Hours: Monday to Saturday 11:30 pm to 3 pm, 5 pm to 10 pm; Sunday 5 pm to 10 pm
Indian. Not pure vegetarian. Menu: Has a good selection of vegetarian dishes. Rice dishes, vegetables curries and appetizers. Other Info: Full service. Accepts AMEX, DIS, MC, VISA. Price: $-$$.

Pita House

495 South Pleasantburg Drive #B
864-271-9895
Hours: Mon to Sat 11 am to 9 pm; closed Sun. Mediterranean and Lebanese. Not pure veg. Menu: About half the menu is vegetarian. Hummus, baklava, Vegetarian Plate, falafel and baba ghanouj. Comments: The food is really good. Other Info: Full service, take-out. Reservations not accepted. Cash or check only. Price: $-$$.

SWAD Restaurant & Store

1421A Laurens Road
864-233-2089
Hours: Monday to Saturday 11 am to 8:30 pm
Closed Sunday.
Fully Vegetarian Indian. Bombay (Mumbai) and South Indian cuisine. Menu: Samosa, rice dishes, curried vegetables dishes and desserts. Comments: Reasonably priced. Also sells Indian spices and other items. The service is good and friendly. Other Info: Limited service, take-out. Accepts AMEX, DIS, MC, VISA. Price: $. Directions: From I-85, take Laurens Rd exit (#48), and go north on Laurens Rd for 2 miles. This place is a quarter-mile northwest of junction of S Pleasantburg Dr & Laurens Rd.

LEXINGTON

14th Carrot
5300 Sunset Boulevard; 803-359-2920
Hours: Monday to Saturday 9 am to 7 pm
Natural Food Store and Deli. Organic produce.
Menu: Not that vegetarian friendly when I called.
Other Info: Counter service, take-out. Has seating. Accepts AMEX, MC, VISA.

MOUNT PLEASANT

The Good Neighbor
Peach Orchard Plaza; 423 Coleman Boulevard
843-881-3274
Hours: Monday to Friday 10 am to 6 pm; Saturday 10 am to 5 pm; closed Sunday.
Natural Food Store and Juice Bar. Has fresh juices and smoothies.
Directions: From I-26, take Mt Pleasant exit (where I-26 ends), and go east on Business Hwy 17 and cross bridge into Mt Pleasant. Going over bridge (stay in right lane) and at fork go right onto Coleman Blvd. This place is then 1½ mile down on the right in the Peach Orchard Plaza.

MYRTLE BEACH

New Life Natural Foods
Plantation Point Plaza, 1209 38th Avenue, Hwy 17 Byepass; 843-448-0011
Hours: Monday to Saturday 9 am to 8 pm
Sunday 11 am to 6 pm
Natural Food Store and Café. International, Thai, Indian and Vietnamese. Deli and Juice Bar.
Other Info: Counter service, take-out. Has one table for seating.
Directions: From Hwy 501, go north on Bypass 12 (connects into Business 17). This place is a half-mile down on right in Galleria Mall.

NORTH CHARLESTON

Doe's Pita Plus
5134 North Rhett Avenue; 843-745-0026
Hours: Monday to Friday 8:30 am to 2:30 pm
Closed Saturday & Sunday.
Middle Eastern. Not pure vegetarian.
Menu: Salads, sandwiches, hummus and stuffed grape leaves. Bakes own pita breads.
Other Info: Counter service, take-out. Price: $.

NORTH MYRTLE BEACH

Harris Teeter Shopping Center
3320 Highway 17 S; 843-448-0011
Hours: Monday to Saturday 9 am to 8 pm
Sunday 11 am to 5 pm
Natural Food Store and small Deli. Juice Bar.
Organic produce.
Menu: Just serves sandwiches in the deli
Directions: From Hwy 501, take Rte 17 Bypass north 12 miles. This store on left in Harris Teeter Shopping Center.

SPARTANBURG

Garner's Natural Foods
Westgate Mall; 205 Blackstalk Road
864-574-1898; **Web site:** www.gogarners.com
Hours: Monday to Saturday 10 am to 9 pm
Sunday 1:30 pm to 6 pm
Natural Food Store. No produce.
Directions: From I-26, go north on US 29. This place is on left in Westgate Mall, at junction of I-26 and US 29.

Garner's Natural Foods
Hillcrest Mall; 1855 East Main Street (US 29)
864-585-1021; **Web site:** www.gogarners.com
Hours: Mon to Sat 9:30 am to 6 pm; closed Sun.
Natural Food Store and Café. Deli and Bakery.
Directions: From I-26, go north on US 29 (E Main St) about 5 miles and this place on right in Hillcrest Mall.

WALTERBORO

No Junk Julie's
301 Cooler's Dairy Road; 843-538-8809
Hours: Mon to Sat 9 am to 6 pm; closed Sunday.
Natural Food Store.
Directions: From I-95, take exit #57 and go toward Walterboro. At Robertson Blvd turn left, then turn left on Hwy 17A north. Bear right at fork. Turn left after Circle M Ranch (on left). At Cooler's Dairy Road (next street) turn left and the store is here.

WEST COLUMBIA

14 Carrot Whole Foods
Westland Square; 2250 Sunset Blvd
803-791-1568
Hours: Mon to Sat 9 am to 7 pm; Sun 1 pm to 6 pm
Natural Food Store. Organic produce and macrobiotic options.
Directions: From I-20, head east on I-26 and take Exit #110 (Hwy 378/Sunset Blvd) and turn left (go east). This place a mile down on left in Westland Square.

South Dakota

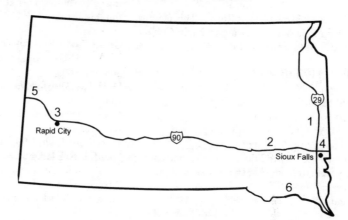

1. Brookings
2. Mitchell
3. Rapid City
4. Sioux Falls
5. Spearfish
6. Yankton

BROOKINGS

Nature's Paradise
1455 6th Street
605-697-7404
Hours: Monday to Saturday 10 am to 5:30 pm
Closed Sunday.
Natural Food Store. Organic produce.
Other Info: Accepts MC, VISA.
Directions: From I-29, take exit #132 and go west on 6th St one mile and this place is opposite a swimming pool.

MITCHELL

Wayne & Mary's
1313 West Havens
605-996-9868
Hours: Monday to Friday 9 am to 7 pm; Saturday 9 am to 5 pm; closed Sunday.
Natural Food Store. Limited organic produce in the summer.
Directions: From I-90, take Mitchell exit (#330). Go a mile north and at West Havens turn right and this place is on the right a fourth-mile down.

RAPID CITY

Hunan Chinese Restaurant
1720 Mt Rushmore Road
605-341-3888
Hours: Daily 11 am to 9:30 pm
Chinese. Not pure vegetarian.

Menu: Has a selection of vegetarian dishes. Vegetarian soups, appetizers and main dishes.
Other Info: Full service, take-out. Accepts AMEX, DIS, MC, VISA. Price: $$.

Staple and Spice
601 Mt Rushmore Road
605-343-3900
By corner of Saint Joseph and Mt Rushmore Road (Hwy 16)
Hours: Monday to Friday 9 am to 6 pm; Saturday 9 am to 5 pm; closed Sunday.
Natural Food Store.
Directions: From I-90, take exit 57 and take I-190 south and when it ends in 1½ miles it becomes West Blvd (then go 4 blocks further south), then at Saint Joseph turn left. This place is 2 blocks down on right side of road, at corner of Mount Rushmore Rd and St Joseph.

**Veggies
2050 West Main Street, #7
605-348-5019
Store Hours: Monday to Thursday 8 am to 8 pm; Friday 8 am to 3:30 pm; Sunday Bunch 10 to 3:30; closed Saturday.
Restaurant Hours: Monday to Thursday 11 am to 7 pm; Friday 11 am to 2 pm; Sunday 11 am to 2 pm
Natural Food Store with Vegan and Vegetarian Café. Juice Bar. All-you-can-eat Buffet. Fresh dishes.
Menu: One special vegetarian main dish daily,

veggie burger, Tofu Sandwich, soup of day, wraps and salads.
Comments: Seventh Day Adventist place. Friendly place.
Other Info: Limited service, buffet, take-out. Accepts MC, VISA. Price: $
Directions: West Main is Rte 79. This place is about a mile west of downtown Rapid City on Rte 79, 100 yards west of Rte 44.

SIOUX FALLS

East Dakotah Food Co-op
420 1st Avenue South
605-339-9506; **email:** rwb@dtgnet.com;
Website: http://w1.dtgnet.com/ednfci/
Hours: Monday to Friday 9 am to 7 pm; Saturday 9 am to 6 pm; Sunday 12 noon to 5 pm
Natural Food Store. Small amount of organic produce.
Directions: From I-29, take 12th St exit (#79) east and get on Rte 42 and go about 2½ miles east. At 1st Ave, turn right and this place on left, a block down.

SPEARFISH

Bay Leaf Café
126 West Hudson
605-642-5462; **Web site:** www.bayleafcafe.com
Hours: Monday to Thursday 11 am to 8 pm Friday & Saturday 11 am to 9 pm
Natural Foods Multi-ethnic Restaurant. Vegan options. Not pure vegetarian.
Menu: Good selection of vegetarian dishes. Vegan tempeh dishes, bean burrito, vegetarian soups, Black Bean Burger, Sautéed Tempeh & Vegetable and Garden Burgers. Cappuccino, espresso.
Comments: It is a good place. Mostly everything served is homemade.

Other Info: Full service, catering, delivery. Accepts AMEX, DIS, MC, VISA. Price: $-$$.
Directions: From I-90, take exit #12 towards Spearfish. At E Jackson Blvd go west towards town about ¾ mile. At Alt-Rte 14 (Main St) turn left and go two blocks. Then at W Hudson turn right and this place is a half-block down on the left.

Good Earth Natural Foods
138 East Hudson, Spearfish
605-642-7639
Hours: Monday to Saturday 9 am to 5:30 pm Closed Sunday.
Natural Food Store. Limited seasonal organic produce.
Directions: From I-90, take exit #12 towards Spearfish. At E Jackson Blvd go west towards town about ¾ mile. At 7th St, turn left (south) and go 2 blocks, then at Hudson St turn right and this place is one block down on right.

YANKTON

Body Guard
2101 Broadway Mall
605-665-3482
Hours: Monday to Saturday 8 am to 5:30 pm Sunday 11:30 to 5 pm
Natural Food Store and Café. Bakery. Vegan options. Not pure vegetarian.
Menu: Sandwiches, salads, veggie chili, pastas and other dishes.
Comments: Relaxed place. Sells bulk goods, vitamins and books.
Other Info: Limited service, take-out. Accepts AMEX, MC, VISA. Counter service, take-out. Has seating.
Directions: At 21st and Broadway at the Yankton Mall.

Tennessee

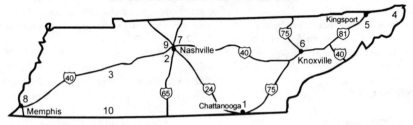

1. Chattanooga
2. Franklin
3. Hendersonville
4. Johnson City
5. Kingsport

6. Knoxville
7. Madison
8. Memphis
9. Nashville
10. Savannah

BARTLETT

Golden Garden
6249 Stage Road; 901-372-2012
Hours: Sunday to Thursday 11 am to 9:30 pm
Friday & Saturday 11 am to 10:30 pm
Chinese. Not pure vegetarian.
Menu: Mock "meat" dishes. Appetizers, soups and main dishes.
Comments: Should ask for the special vegetarian menu.
Other Info: Full service. Accepts AMEX, DC, DIS, MC, VISA. Price: $$.

CHATTANOOGA

**Country Life Natural Foods & Vegan Buffet
3748 Ringgold Road; 423-622-2451; **email:** countrylife@mindspring.com; **Web site:** http://www.outpostcenters.org/health/wildwood.html
Natural Food Store
Hours: Sunday to Thursday 9:30 am to 5:30 pm;
Restaurant Hours: Sunday to Thursday 11:30 am to 2:30 pm (Lunch only)
Closed Friday & Saturday.
Natural Food Store & Fully Vegan Restaurant.
All-you-can-eat Buffet. Salad Bar.
Menu: Menu changes daily. Corn bread, Brown Rice & Beans, Macaroni & Cheese and more.
Comments: Relaxing, tranquil, friendly, family atmosphere.

Other Info: Non-smoking. Buffet, take-out. Accepts reservations but not necessary. Accepts AMEX, DC, MC, VISA. Price: $-$$.
Directions: From I-24 coming west. Take the Germantown exit (#184) and go south 1 mile on S Germantown Rd, then at Ringgold Road turn left, and this place is 1 mile down on the right, between Blockbuster Video and Kingwood Pharmacy. From I-24, take Exit #181A, then take Rte 41 (Ringgold Rd) southeast and this place is about 1½ mile down. Plenty of parking near by.

India Mahal Restaurant
5970 Brainerd Road; 423-510-9651
Hours: Daily 11 am to 3 pm, 5 pm to 10 pm
Indian. Buffet. Not pure vegetarian.
Menu: Has more than 20 vegetarian dishes.
Other Info: Full service, take-out. Accepts DIS, MC, VISA. Price: $$.

GOODLETTSVILLE (10 miles north of Nashville)

Adventist Book Center
850 Conference Drive; 615-859-1125
Hours: Mon to Thur 8:30 am to 5 pm; Friday 8:30 am to 3 pm; Sun 12 noon to 5 pm; closed Sat.
Natural Food Store. Organic produce. Has a good selection.
Directions: From I-65, take Exit #97, then go east a quarter-mile, then turn right at Conference Dr and this place is a quarter-mile down.

HENDERSONVILLE

Four Seasons Produce
235 East Main Street; 615-264-0099
Hours: Monday to Thursday 8:30 am to 7 pm; Thursday 8:30 am to 4 pm; Sunday 10 am to 6 pm; closed Saturday
Natural Food Store. Organic produce.
Directions: This place is on Rte 31 (the main street going west-east through town) in the east part of town.

JOHNSON CITY

Natural Food Market
3211 People's Street, Suite 74
423-610-1000
Hours: Monday to Saturday 10 am to 8 pm
Closed Sunday.
Natural Food Store and Deli. Juice Bar.
Menu: Soups, salads, sandwiches, veggie chili and more.
Other Info: Counter service, take-out. Has counter seats and 5 tables. Friendly place.
Directions: From I-181, take exit #36 (Franklin St, Rte 381), then take Rte 381 south (turn right if going south/east on I-181, turn left if going north/west) and go a third-mile, then turn left and go a block, then turn left at People's St and this place is a half-mile down.

KINGSPORT

Good Food Grocery
138 Cherokee Street
423-246-3663
Hours: Monday to Saturday 10 am to 6 pm
Closed Sunday.
Natural Food Store.
Directions: From I-181, take US-11W Exit #55 then go east on US-11 a half-mile, then take ramp for Rte 36 S and go 1¼ mile south on Rte 36, then at Cherokee St turn right and this place is two blocks down.

KNOXVILLE

China Pearl
11248 Kingston Pike
Farragut (a little west of Knoxville)
865-966-6937
Hours: Daily 11 am to 10 pm
Chinese. Vegan friendly. Not pure vegetarian.
Menu: Has several vegetarian dishes. No MSG.
Other Info: Accepts AMEX, DIS, MC, VISA.

The Crescent Moon Café
705 Market Street; 865-637-9700
Hours: Monday to Friday 11 am to 2 pm
Closed Saturday & Sunday.
American Restaurant. Not pure vegetarian.
Menu: Has a selection of vegetarian dishes. Veggie chili, soups, sandwiches, salads and vegetarian specials (such as Portobello Mushroom dish).

Falafel Hut
601 James Agee Street (15th St), on UT campus
423-522-4963
Hours: Monday to Saturday 10:30 am to 9 pm
Closed Sunday.
Middle Eastern. Not pure vegetarian.
Menu: About half the menu is vegetarian. Soups, salads, bean soup, hummus and tabbouleh.
Other Info: Full service, take-out. Accepts AMEX, MC, VISA. Price: $-$$.

Kashmir India
711 17th Street, near Kingston Pike
865-524-1982
Hours: Sunday to Thursday 11:30 am to 3 pm, 5 pm to 10 pm; Saturday & Saturday 12 noon to 3 pm, 5 pm to 10:30 pm
Indian. Vegan options. Not pure vegetarian.
Menu: Has a wide selection of vegetarian dishes such as pakoras, samosas, Naans, Saag Paneer, Shahi Paneer Korma (good cheese dish) and thali meals. A favorite is the Vegetarian Platter. Mint chutney, sweet mango chutney and mixed pickle condiments.
Comments: Casual, small place. Plays Indian movies. Be careful where you park, because illegally parked cars are often towed.
Other Info: Full service, take-out. Accepts AMEX, DIS, MC, VISA. Price: $-$$.

King Tut's Grill
4132 Martin Mill Pike; 865-573-6021
Hours: Monday to Saturday 8:30 am to 10 pm
Closed Sunday.
Egyptian. Vegan options. Not pure vegetarian.
Menu: Has several vegetarian options including hummus, Greek Salad (request with no eggs), baba ghanouj, falafel sandwich (very good), Foule Mudammas Sandwich (fava beans with Egyptian salad on a pita), Lentil soup, Vegetable Platter and pasta.
Comments: Every night of the week there is a different special such as Pasta and Salad Night, Egyptian nights, etc
Other Info: Full service, take-out. Cash only. Price: $-$$.

Knoxville Food Cooperative

937 North Broadway Street, just off I-40
865 -525-2069; email: kcfc@esper.com
Web site: http://www.korrnet.org/kcfc/
Hours: Monday to Saturday 9 am to 9 pm
Sunday 12 pm to 7 pm
Natural Food Store. Organic produce. All vegetarian. Bulk food.
Comments: Non-members pay 10% over the price marked on the shelves. Pleasant service.
Other Info: Accepts AMEX, DC, DIS, MC, VISA.
Directions: Near the University of Tennessee. From I-640, take Broadway Exit #6 (Rte 441) south and then this place is on the right 2½ miles down. From I-40, take exit #387A and get on I-275 going north and go ¾ mile, then take East Baxter Ave exit (#1A). At Baxter Ave turn right and go a half-mile. At Stewart St turn right and go 1 block, at Cullen Pl turn left and go 1 block, at Irwin St turn left (becomes Caswell Ave), then at N Broadway St turn right and this place is in the middle of the block. Free parking. Illegally parked cars are often towed.

Natural Organic Foods

7025 Kingston Pike; 865-584-8422
Hours: Monday to Saturday 10 am to 6 pm
Closed Sunday.
Natural Food Store. Bulk foods.
Other Info: Accepts AMEX, MC, VISA.
Directions: From I-75/40, take exit #380. This place is one mile down on Kingston Pike on the left in West Hill Shopping Center.

Nature's Pantry – The Healthy Grocery

West Hill Shopping Center, 6600 Kingston Pike
865-584-4714
Hours: Monday to Saturday 9 am to 9 pm
Sunday 12 am to 6 pm
Natural Food Store. Organic produce Bulk food.
Other Info: Accepts MC, VISA.
Directions: From I-40, take exit #380 (West Hills exit). At Kingston Pike turn left going east. This place at the top of the hill 1½ mile down on the right.

Silver Spoon Café

7250 Kingston Pike, Suite 172, between the downtown and the university; 865-584-1066
Hours: Monday to Thursday 11 am to 10 pm;
Friday & Saturday 11 am to 11 pm; Sunday 10:30 am to 10 pm; Sunday Brunch 10:30 am to 2 pm
American and Italian. Not pure vegetarian.
Menu: Had several pure vegetarian main dishes,

salads and pastas. Non-alcoholic beer and wine.
Other Info: Full service, take-out. Accepts AMEX, DIS, MC, VISA. Price: $-$$.
Directions: At the Gallery.

Stir Fry Café

7240 Kingston Pike, Suite 128; 423-588-2064
Hours: Daily 11 am to 10 pm
Asian Food with an Americanized touch. Not pure vegetarian.
Menu: Most dishes are vegetarian. Tofu can be substituted for many of the meat dishes. Thai Bean Curd with peanut sauce, Red Curry with Tofu and other dishes.
Comments: Relaxed coffee shop type atmosphere. Make sure you make it clear you are a vegetarian.
Other Info: Accepts AMEX, DIS, MC, VISA.

Sunspot

1909 Cumberland Avenue; 865-637-4663
Hours: Daily 11 am to 10 pm
Vegetarian-friendly Restaurant. Not pure vegetarian.
Menu: Has a daily vegetarian special. Grilled Tofu Salad.
Comments: Makes an effort to give vegetarian what they want (vegetarian food). Not much of a selection, but the food is really good. Accepts AMEX, MC, VISA.

Time Out Ali Baba Delicatessen

8361 Kingston Pike; 615-693-1446
Hours: Sunday to Thursday 6:30 am to 11 pm
Friday & Saturday 6:30 am to 2 am
Vegan-friendly Middle Eastern. Mostly take-out. Not pure vegetarian.
Menu: Good hummus, tabbouleh and falafel.
Other Info: Cash only; no credit cards. Price: $.

The Tomato Head

12 Market Square, downtown, near the University of Tennessee; 865-637-4067
Web site: www.thetomatohead.com
Hours: Monday to Thursday 11 am to 9 pm;
Friday & Saturday 11 am to 10 pm; closed Sun.
Italian, and also Middle Eastern, South American and International. Vegan options.
Menu: Enchilada, Hummus Plate with vegetables, Bread & Tahini, sandwiches, salads, calzones, sandwiches, gourmet pizzas and hummus.
Comments: The dinning room is also used as an art gallery.
Other Info: Full service for dinner, limited service for lunch. Reservations not necessary. Non-smoking. Accepts AMEX, MC, VISA. Price: $-

$$.
Directions: From I-40, take Exit #388A on left towards downtown (US 441 S), merge onto Rte 158 W and go a third-mile. Take exit towards Summit Hill Dr, and go right onto E Summit Hill Dr and go 2 blocks, at S Gay St turn left and go 1 block, then at Wall Ave turn right and this place is a block down on the corner of Market Square.

MADISON (northeast Nashville suburb)

Sitar
116 21st Avenue N, at West End Avenue
615-321-8889
Hours: Mon to Sat 11:30 am to 3 pm, 5 pm to 10 pm; Sun 12 noon to 3 pm, 5 pm to 10 pm
Indian. Not pure vegetarian.
Menu: Has several vegetarian options. Soups, rice, dal, Naan, Spinach & Cheese, breads and vegetable curries.
Comments: One of the best Indian restaurants in the area. The lunch buffet is a very good value. The atmosphere and service is good.
Other Info: Full service, take-out, delivery. Accepts AMEX, DC, DIS, MC, VISA. Price Lunch: $, Dinner: $$.
Directions: Behind Fuddrucker's

Tennessee Christian Medical Center Cafeteria
500 Hospital Drive; 615-860-6600
Hours: Daily. No breakfasts on Sat and Sun
Vegetarian-friendly Seventh Day Adventist Cafeteria. Salad Bar. Not pure vegetarian.
Menu: Large salad bar. Quiche and burritos, among many options.
Other Info: Cafeteria-style, limited service, take-out. Price: $.
Directions: From I-65, take Old Hickory Blvd/Rte 45 exit #92 towards Madison. Take right fork in ramp and merge onto W Old Hickory Blvd and go 3 miles (becomes Rte 45). At Larkin Springs Rd (a half-mile past Randy Rd) turn right and go a half-mile. Then at Hospital Dr turn left and this place is down the block.

MEMPHIS

Brother Juniper's College Inn
3519 South Walker Avenue; 901-324-0144
Hours: Tuesday to Friday 7 am to 1 pm; Saturday 6:30 am to 12:30 pm; closed Sun & Mon.
American. Not pure vegetarian. Vegan options.
Menu: Salads, sandwiches, Granola, sandwiches, Greek Salad and Scrambled Tofu (recommended).
Comments: Known for its breakfasts. Friendly service. Good food. Saturday mornings are very busy, so you may want to arrive early.
Other Info: Full service, take-out, catering. Price: $.
Directions: Near the University of Memphis. From I-40 coming southwest into town, go straight onto Sam Cooper Blvd and go 3 miles west, then take Highland St exit (#7), at N Highland St turn left and go 2 miles, then at Walker Ave turn left and this place is near the corner.

The Golden Garden
6249 Stage Road; 901-372-2012
Hours: Sunday to Thursday 11 am to 9:30 pm Friday & Saturday 11 am to 10:30 pm
Chinese. Not pure vegetarian.
Menu: Has a separate vegetarian menu with over 70 dishes. Many mock "meat" dishes.
Comments: Friendly place.
Other Info: Accepts AMEX, MC, VISA.

**Jasmin's
3024 Coventon Pike, at Stage; 901-276-2722
Hours: Sunday, Tuesday to Thursday 11 am to 9:30 pm; Fri & Sat 11 am to 10 pm; closed Mon.
Vegetarian Chinese. Vegan-friendly. Price: $$.
Menu: Has a good selection of vegetarian dishes.

La Montagne Natural Food Restaurant
3550 Park Avenue; 901-458-1060
Web site: www.greenskies.net/lamontagne
Hours: Daily 11:30 am to 10 pm
Sunday Brunch
Natural Food Restaurant. International. Not pure vegetarian.
Menu: Tofitas Fajitas, pastas, veggie burgers, burritos and pizzas. Has daily special from different countries nightly. Espresso, cappuccino.
Comments: Named as one of the most romantic restaurants in Memphis. Gets really high recommendations. Has live music Friday and Saturday.
Other Info: Full service, take-out. Accepts MC, VISA. Price: $$.
Directions: Near the University of Memphis. From I-40 coming southwest in town go straight onto Sam Cooper Blvd and go 3 miles west, then take Highland St exit (#7), at N Highland St turn left and go 2 miles, then at Park Ave turn left and this place is a half-block down.

Saigon Le
51 North Cleveland Street, downtown
901-276-5326
Hours: Monday to Saturday 11 am to 9 pm

Closed Sunday.
Vietnamese, some Chinese. Not pure veg.
Menu: Has a large selection of vegetarian dishes.
Lemon Grass Tofu and vegetarian soups.
Comments: Popular during lunch.
Other Info: Accepts AMEX, MC, VISA.
Directions: Located near the Medical Center District.

Wild Oats Market
5022 Poplar Ave, at Mandihall; 901-685-2293
Hours: Monday to Saturday 8 am to 10 pm
Sunday 11 am to 9 pm
Large Natural Food Store and Vegan-friendly Restaurant & Deli. Bakery. Not pure vegetarian.
Menu: Veggie Burgers, Vegetable Stir-fry, Linguine, Vegan Lasagna, tempeh & tofu dishes, Oat Burgers and pastas. Fresh juices, smoothies, cappuccino, espresso.
Comments: This is a huge place with a large organic produce section. Whole grain bakery and a deli.
Other Info: Non-smoking. Cafeteria style, take-out. Accepts AMEX, DIS, MC, VISA. Price: $-$$.
Directions: From the east beltway I-240, take Exit #15 (Poplar Ave), then go west on Poplar Ave and this place is 2 miles down.

NASHVILLE

August Moon
4000 Hillsboro Pike; 615-298-9999
Hours: Sunday to Thursday 11 am to 10 pm
Friday & Saturday 11 am to 11 pm
Chinese Restaurant. Not pure vegetarian.
Comments: Voted as the best Chinese restaurant in Nashville. White tablecloth and cloth napkins. No MSG.
Other Info: Full service, take-out. Popular take-out place. Accepts AMEX, DC, MC, VISA.

Baja Burrito
722 Thompson Lane, at Bransford
615-383-2252; fax: 615-383-5021
Hours: Monday to Thursday 11 am to 8:30 pm; Friday & Saturday 11 am to 9 pm; closed Sun.
Mexican. Not pure vegetarian.
Menu: Burritos, tacos and salads. Burritos add-ons are rice, beans and other items. Salsa bar. The Sweet Baja Fruit Tea is recommended.
Comments: No lard in the beans or rice. Gets really good rating and is recommended. Very quick service. Reasonably placed. Good value. Very popular. Parking is hard to find, but you

can park across the street at 100 Oaks. Friendly staff. Cool Mexican décor. The owner, Troy, is a really nice guy.
Other Info: Accepts AMEX, DIS, MC, VISA. Counter service, take-out. Price: $.

Baraka Bakery & Restaurant
5596 Nolensville Road, at Old Hickory
615-333-9285
Hours: Monday to Saturday 10 am to 8 pm
Sunday 12 noon to 8 pm
Middle Eastern (Syrian-Lebanese). Not pure vegetarian.
Menu: Has falafel, hummus, baba ghanoush, tabbouleh and other vegetarian dishes. Freshly baked pita. Arabic coffee.
Comments: Casual place. Sells bulk lentils, basmati rice, olive oil, etc.
Other Info: Full service, take-out, delivery. Accepts AMEX, DC, DIS, MC, VISA.

Café Coco
210 Lousie Avenue; 615-321-2626
Hours: Daily 24 Hours
Coffee Shops, American. Not pure vegetarian.
Menu: Has a good selection of vegetarian dishes. Salads, pizzas, rice dishes, Italian sandwiches, wraps and more.
Comments: Has a front porch and yard that has tables with umbrellas. Casual, easygoing place. Good place to hang out. Food gets really good recommendations.
Other Info: Accepts AMEX, MC, VISA.
Directions: It is a block from Elliston Square.

Calypso Café
2424 Elliston Pl; 615-321-3878
Hours: Monday to Friday 11 am to 9 pm
Saturday & Sunday 11:30 am to 8:30 pm
Caribbean. Not pure vegetarian.
Menu: Has several good vegetarian dishes. Mixed Bean and Corn Salad, Black Beans and Calloloo (mustard greens and tomatoes).
Comments: Casual atmosphere. Many people feel it is one of the best places in town for vegetarian food. Food has an unique taste that some people may not like.
Other Info: Counter service, self-serve drinks, take-out, delivery. Accepts AMEX, MC, VISA. Price: $.

**Country Life Wholesale Food
1917 Division Street; 615-327-3695;
email: countrylife7@juno.com; Web site: www.countrylifewholesale-cooperative.com

Hours: Monday to Friday
Closed Saturday & Sunday.
Natural Food Store and Fully Vegetarian take-out Deli. Salad Bar. Seventh Day Adventist place. Vegan options.
Menu: Salad bar, soups and main dishes. Uses fresh vegetables and fruits.
Other Info: Cafeteria buffet style, take-out. Price: $.
Directions: From I-40 going south, take Exit #209 towards Broadway/US 70 S/US 431, At Broadway turn right and go a quarter-mile, then make a slight left and stay on Broadway and go a third-miles, then at Lyle Ave turn left and go a block, then at Division St turn right and this place at corner.

Harding Mall Health Foods
Harding Mall Shopping Center, 4050 Nolensville Pike Ste 115; 615-834-3770
Hours: Monday to Saturday 10 am to 8 pm
Sunday 1 pm to 6 pm
Natural Food Store.
Comments: Carries meat substitutes.

Royal Thai
204 Commerce Road   615-255-0821
210 Franklin Pike, Brentwood   615-376-9695
Hours: Monday to Saturday 11 am to 3 pm, 5 pm to 9 pm; closed Sunday.
Thai. Not pure vegetarian.
Comments: The food can be quite hot. Food can be mild, medium or hot if requested.
Other Info: Full service, take-out. Accepts AMEX, DIS, MC, VISA. Price: $$.

Sunset Grill
2001 Belcourt, at 21st Avenue, Hillsborough Village; 615-386-3663
Hours: Monday 4:45 pm to 1:30 am; Tuesday to Friday 11 am to 1:30 am; Saturday 4:45 pm to 1:30 am; Sunday 4:45 pm to 11 pm
Restaurant. Vegan friendly. Not pure vegetarian.
Menu: Has several vegetarian dishes and some vegan dishes. Daily Green Plate Special and pastas, veggie burger, Mediterranean Pasta, Veggie Voodoo Pasta and a daily vegetarian special.
Comment: Trendy, high-class, happening place. Star Sightings. Excellent service. Excellent outdoor patio dining. Gets really high recommendations. Popular place. Good for late night dining. Some people may think the place is a bit snooty.
Other Info: Full service, take-out. Accepts

AMEX, DC, DIS, MC, VISA. Price: $$$.
Directions: This place is in southwest Nashville near Vanderbilt University, between Bemont University and Peabody College. From I-65, take Wedgewood Ave Exit (#81). Go on Wedgewood Ave (turn right if coming west/south on I-65) and go 1½ mile, at 18th Ave S turn left and go 1 block, then at Belcourt Ave turn left and go 1 block, then at 20th Ave S turn left and this place is right at the corner.

Sunshine Grocery (Wild Oats)
3201 Belmont Boulevard
615-297-5100
Hours: Monday to Saturday 8 am to 9 pm
Sunday 10 am to 8 pm
Natural Food Store and Deli. Bakery and Juice Bar. Ethnic dishes. Not pure vegetarian. Fresh dishes and smoothies.
Comments: It is the largest natural food store in town. Good selection of organic produce. The food in the deli gets good recommendations. Food is freshly made.
Other Info: Counter service, take-out only. Accepts MC, VISA. Price: $.
Directions: This place is in south Nashville. From I-440, take 21st Avenue exit (#3) and head north towards city a quarter-mile. At Sweetbriar (first right) turn right and go 1 mile, then at Belmont turn right and go 1 mile (to second stop sign). This place on right in large purple building, near I-440.

Tin Angel
3201 West End Avenue
615-298-3444
Hours: Monday to Friday 11 am to 10 pm; Saturday 5 pm to 11 pm; Sunday 11 am to 3 pm
American. Vegetarian friendly. Not pure veg.
Menu: Has a good selection of vegetarian dishes such as Polenta Lasagna, vegetable quesadilla, salads, Eggplant Parmesan and Tour de France (pasta, white bean, vegetables),
Comments: One of the best vegetarian friendly places in Nashville. Romantic, upscale place with a bistro look with a fireplace and brick floors. Hip, casual place. Service and food is good. Friendly and efficient staff.
Other Info: Full service, take-out. Reservations not accepted. Accepts AMEX, DC, DIS, MC, VISA. Price: $$.
Directions: In the Hillsboro, West End area. From I-440, take Exit #1, then go southeast on W End Ave and this place is a mile down, at 32nd Ave.

Wild Oats Market

3909 Hillsboro Pike; 615-463-2480
Hours: Daily 8 am to 10 pm
Natural Food Store and Cafe. Deli, Bakery, Salad Bar and Juice Bar. Organic produce. Supermarket-type place. See Wild Oats Market information.
Directions: This place is in northwest Nashville about 1 mile southwest of I-440. From I-440E, take Exit #3 (Rte 431/Hillsboro Pike/21st Ave), then go southwest on Hillsboro Pike/21st Ave S (Rte 106) and this place is 1 mile down.

NEWPORT

The Mustard Seed

The Village Shopping Center, 331 Cosby Highway (Hwy 321); 423-623-4091
Hours: Monday to Thursday 10 am to 6 pm; Friday 10 am to 5 pm; closed weekends.

Natural Food Store. Seasonal produce. Trying to open a deli.
Directions: From I-40, take Newport/Garlinburg exit (#435). Take Hwy 321 northeast toward Newport 1½ miles. Go past three lights and this place on left in The Village Shopping Center.

SAVANNAH

Gina's Country Health and Vegan Shoppe

1315 Wayne Road
731-925-7220
Hours: Monday to Friday 9 am to 5 pm
Closed Saturday & Sunday.
Natural Food Store. Mainly vitamins.
Directions: This place is near the center of town on Hwy 64, which is the highway that goes west-east through town, near White St.

Texas

Amarillo (40)
3
(27)
25
17 Lubbock
10 19 7 (30)
2 20
Fort Worth (14) Dallas 16
12 4 9 (20)
1 24
11
El Paso 23
(20) (87) (45)
(10) 6
15 5 Austin
Houston 13
(35) (10)
San Antonio
21
(35)
Corpus Christi
8
18 22

1. Abilene
2. Addison
3. Amarillo
4. Arlington
5. Austin
6. Bryan
7. Colleyville
8. Corpus Christi
9. Dallas
10. Denton

11. El Paso
12. Fort Worth
13. Houston
14. Irving
15. Kerrville
16. Longview
17. Lubbock
18. McAllen

19. Plano
20. Richardson
21. San Antonio
22. South Padre Island
23. Waco
24. Waxahachie
25. Wichita Falls

ABILENE

Natural Food Center
2534 South 7th Street; 915-673-2726
Hours: Monday to Saturday 10 am to 6 pm; Saturday 10 am to 5 pm; closed Sunday.
Restaurant Hours: Monday to Friday 11 am to 2 pm; closed Saturday & Sunday.
Natural Food Store and Cafe. Vegetarian-friendly. Not pure vegetarian.
Menu: Mostly vegetarian. Soup, salads, sandwiches and hot main dishes.
Other Info: Accepts MC, VISA. Counter service, take-out. Has seating.
Directions: From Rte 83, take S 1st St (Hwy 84) exit and go east on S 1st St towards town 1½ mile, then at N Mockingbird Lane turn right and go south ¾ mile, then at S 7th St turn left and this place is a half-mile down.

ADDISON

Fresh Choice
4080 Belt Line Road, at Runyon Road
972-385-7353
Restaurant. See Austin.

AMARILLO

Eatrite Health Promotion Center & Back To Eden Restaurant
2425 West Interstate 40; 806-353-7476
Store Hours: Monday to Saturday 9 am to 6 pm Closed Sunday.
Restaurant Hours: 9 am to 4 pm
Natural Food Store and International Natural Foods Restaurant. Deli, Bakery, Salad Bar and Juice Bar. Not pure vegetarian.
Menu: Salads, homemade salad dressings, homemade soups, sandwiches and baked goods. Fresh juices and smoothies.
Other Info: Limited service, take-out, catering. Accepts AMEX, DIS, MC, VISA. Price: $-$$.
Directions: From I-40, take Georgia exit (#68) and this place is 2 blocks east of S Georgia St right next to highway. Has a painting with fruits and vegetables on it.

ARLINGTON

Good Health Place
Pecan Plaza, 2503 South Cooper Street
817-265-5261

Hours: Monday to Saturday 9:30 am to 6:30 pm **Natural Food Store.**
Directions: From I-30, take Cooper exit south. This place on left in Pecan Plaza about 3 miles south. From I-20, take S Cooper Exit (#449) and go north on S Cooper and this place is 2 miles down on the right.

Whole Foods Market
801 East Lamar Boulevard
817-461-9362; **fax:** 817-461-1688
Hours: Daily 9 am to 9 pm
Natural Food Store and Cafe. Deli, Bakery, Salad Bar and Juice Bar. Organic produce. Supermarket-type place. See Whole Foods Market information.
Directions: From I-30, take Ballpark Way exit (#29), then get on E Lamar Blvd (if coming west on I-30 turn right at Ballpark Way at end of ramp), then turn left at E Lamar) and go west for 1½ mile, and this place at intersections with Madison Dr.

AUSTIN

Bamboo Garden
625 West Ben White Boulevard, Travis Heights
512-444-7988; **fax:** 512-444-6022; **Web site:** http://bamboogarden.citysearch.com/
Hours: Daily 11 am to 10 pm
Asian, Chinese. Vegan options. Not pure vegetarian.
Menu: Has a good selection of vegetarian dishes.
Other Info: Full service, take-out, delivery. Accepts AMEX, DC, MC, VISA.

Bangkok Cuisine
9041 Research Boulevard (183 & Burnet Road)
512-832-9722
Hours: Daily 11 am to 3 pm, 5 pm to 10 pm
Thai. Not pure vegetarian. Lunch buffet with some vegetarian dishes.
Menu: Has a separate vegetarian menu. Homemade raspberry tea.
Comments: Fried vegetarian dishes are usually cooked in the same oil as the non-vegetarian dishes. Food can be very hot, so you may want to ask that it is less spicy.
Other Info: Accepts AMEX, DIS, MC, VISA.

**Bouldin Creek Coffeehouse & Café
1501 South 1st Street
512-416-1601
Hours: Monday to Thursday 7 am to 10 pm; Friday 7 am to 12 midnight; Saturday 9 am to 12

midnight; Sunday 9 am to 10 pm
Vegetarian Coffee Shop. Vegan-friendly.
Menu: Has a good selection of vegan dishes. Vegan dishes are marked on the menu. Baked oatmeal. Smoothies. Hummus, tofu scramble, Bean & Rice, vegetable plate, vegetarian Sloppy Joe, Greek Salad and Portobello Mushroom.
Comments: Has a variety of outdoor seating such as a deck out back. Pleasant, laid-back, sociable, comfortable place. Has games piled up that you can play. Sometimes has live music on the back deck. A bit of a romantic spot. Gets good ratings. Quick, good, friendly service. Very nice people. Accepts MC, VISA.
Directions: From I-35, take Exit #233 and go west on E Riverside Dr 1 mile, then at Barton Strings Rd turn left and go a quarter-mile, then at S 1st St turn left and this place is ¾ mile south on 1st St.

Brick Oven Restaurant
1608 West 35th Street; 512-453-4330
Hours: Monday to Friday 11 am to 2 pm, 5 pm to 10 pm; Saturday 5 pm to 10 pm; Sunday 5 pm to 9 pm
Italian, Pizza. Not pure vegetarian.
Menu: Has really good pizzas.

Casa de Luz
1701 Toomey Road; 512-476-2535
Hours: 11:30 am to 2 pm, 6 pm to 8 pm Saturday & Sunday Brunch Buffet 11:30 am to 2 pm
Macrobiotic International Restaurant. Mainly Vegan, 90% Organic. Different nights have different theme.
Menu: Menu changes daily. Soups, salads, brown rice, raw vegetables, steamed greens, beans, sauces, buckwheat pancakes, tofu dishes, All American (Okara Burgers with yam fries) and Guatamalan (tortilla with tofu stir-fry). Vegan desserts.
Comments: Friendly, peaceful atmosphere. Food gets high ratings. Often uses organic ingredients. Has indoor and outdoor dining on the patio. Has a large communal dining table. Interesting, casual place. Usually plays relaxing music. Non-profit organizations with classrooms, an auditorium and gardens. Yoga and massage on-site. Has classes on Tai Chi, natural cooking, Sufism and other subjects. The Sunday brunch is recommended. Price: $$.
Directions: From I-35, take Exit #233 and go west on E Riverside Dr 2 miles until it deadends, then at S Lamar Blvd turn left and go 1 block, then at Tommey Rd turn right and this place is a

half-mile down. Near Zilker Park in central Austin. It is next to the south side of Town Lake Park.

Central Market
4001 North Lamar Boulevard
512-206-1000; fax: 512-206-1010
Hours: Daily 9 am to 9 pm
Natural Food Store and Deli. Juice Bar. Organic produce. Not pure vegetarian.
Menu: Has a café that serves macaroni and cheese, salads, sandwiches and peanut butter & jelly sandwich.
Comments: Has a large produce section. Has all kinds of things. Tuesday evening is kid's night. Often has live entertainment. Can get a massage here. Restaurant gets good recommendations. Accepts AMEX, MC, VISA.
Directions: This place is 3 miles north of the downtown. From I-35, take Exit #238B towards US-290/Houston, then go west on E Koenig Lane for 1 mile, at Guadalupe St turn left and go a half-mile, at W 51st St turn right and go 2 blocks. Then at N Lamar Blvd turn left and this place is 1 mile down. From I-35, take exit #236B and go west on E 45th St 2¼ miles, then at N Lamar turn left and this place is ¾ mile down.

China Palace
6605 Airport Boulevard, at Highway 290 (Yellow Brick Road Center); 512-451-7104
Hours: Daily 11 am to 2:30 pm, 4:30 pm to 10 pm
Chinese. Not pure vegetarian.
Menu: Good selection of vegetarian dishes.
Comments: Has vegetarian lunch and dinner buffets. Has different dining rooms.
Other Info: Accepts MC, VISA. Price: $-$$.

Eastside Café
2113 Manor Road
512-476-5858; fax: 512-477-5847; Web site: http://eastsidecafe.citysearch.com/
Hours: Monday to Friday 11 am to 10 pm
Saturday & Sunday 10 am to 10 pm
International. Not pure vegetarian.
Menu: Has some vegetarian dishes. Pasta, Pesto Ravioli, Artichoke Manicotti, Chips & Salsa, salads, Garden Burger and Roasted Vegetable Enchiladas.
Comments: In an old house with several rooms. Has outdoors dining. Elegant, casual place. Service can be a bit slow. Food generally gets good ratings. Their Web site has their menu on it. Grows much of the produce that they use.
Other Info: Accepts AMEX, DC, DIS, MC,

VISA. Price: $$-$$$.
Directions: From I-35, take Exit #236A and go southeast on E Dean Keeton St a half-mile and it meets Manor Rd and then it is 1 block down.

Frank & Angies' Pizza
508 West Avenue; 512-472-3534
Web site: http://frankandangies.citysearch.com/
Hours: Monday to Saturday 11 am to 10 pm
Sunday 5 pm to 10 pm
Italian and Pizza. Vegan options. Not pure vegetarian.
Menu: Very good New York style pizzas, salads and good Focaccia vegetarian sandwich. The Holy Cannoli dessert is eggless. Veggie meat balls and veggie Lasagna.
Comments: Eclectic music played. Casual, cozy atmosphere. Has a shaded patio next to Shoal Creek.
Other Info: Full service, take-out, delivery (call 494-1500). Price: $.

Fresh Choice Restaurant
9761 Great Hills Trail; 512-795-9200; fax: 512-795-9075; Web site: www.freshchoiceinc.com
Hours: Sunday to Thursday 11 am to 9 pm
Friday & Saturday 11 am to 10 pm
Fast-food Health Food. Vegetarian-friendly. Large Salad Bar. All-you-can-eat buffet.
Menu: Has a large selection of items in their salad bar. Baked potatoes, pizzas and some vegetarian soups.
Other Info: Full service, take-out. Non-smoking. Reservations not accepted. Accepts AMEX, MC, VISA. Price: $.
Directions: This place is about 6 miles north of downtown Austin. From I-35, take Hwy 183 northwest about 4 miles. This place is then a half-mile west of Hwy 183 on Great Hills Trail. Has a parking lot.

Juice Joint
1625 Barton Springs Road; 512-494-1767
Web site: http://juicejoint.citysearch.com/
Hours: Monday to Friday 9 am to 8 pm
Saturday & Sunday 9 am to 8 pm
Juice Bar.
Menu: Fresh juices and smoothies. Apple, mango, watermelon, pineapple, grapefruit, berries, orange, peach, banana and cantaloupe juices. Mineral shot, spirulina and guarana. Vegan cookies and frozen fruit bars.
Other Info: No credit cards.
Directions: From I-35, take Exit #233B A and go west on E Riverside Dr 1 mile, then turn left

on Barton Springs Rd and go west and this place is about 1½ mile down. It is a half-mile east of Zilker Park in central Austin. It is a quarter-mile south of Town Lake Park.

Kerbey Lane Café
2700 South Lamar Boulevard; 512-445-4451
Hours: Daily for 24 hours
American, Mexican. Vegetarian-friendly.
Menu: Black Bean Tacos, veggie burgers, Cheese Quesadillas, interesting salads and more.
Comments: Uses locally grown produce. Have other locations in Austin. Gets mixed reviews, some very good and some very bad.
Other Info: Full service, take-out. Accepts AMEX, DIS, MC, VISA. Price: $
Directions: Parking arranged for customers.

**Little Bombay
9616 North Lamar #195, at Burnet Road
512-339-0808
Hours: Tuesday to Saturday 11:30 am to 9:30 pm; closed Monday.
Fully Vegetarian Indian. South Indian fast-food.
Menu: Has some North and South Indian food. Samosas, dosas, Bombay Chat, Dahi Batata Pooris, coconut chutney and more. Mango lassi and chai tea (masala tea).
Comments: Busy place.
Other Info: Counter service, take-out. Order at the counter and then the food is brought to you. Can call ahead and just come and pick up your order. Price: $. Accepts AMEX, DIS, MC, VISA.
Directions: This place is about 5 miles north of downtown Austin. From I-35, take Exit #243 for W Rundberg Lane, then go west on W Rundberg Lane 1 mile, then at N Lamar Blvd turn right and this place is a third-mile down.

**Madras Pavilion
9025 Research Boulevard, Suite 100 (Burnet & Hwy 183); 512-719-5575
Web site: www.madras-pavilion.com
Hours: Monday to Thursday 11:30 am to 3 pm, 5:30 pm to 9:30 pm; Fri 11:30 am to 3 pm, 5:30 pm to 10 pm; Sat & Sun 11:30 am to 10 pm
Pure Vegetarian Indian. Vegan-friendly. Not pure vegetarian. All-you-can-eat Buffet. Kosher.
Menu: Masala Dosa, curried vegetables, samosas, Panir Pakora, coconut chutney, Coconut & Yogurt Curry, Palak Panir and good South Indian Thalis.
Comments: Basic décor. Friendly, helpful service. Good food. Reasonable prices. There are also branches in Richardson and Houston.
Other Info: Accepts AMEX, DIS, MC, VISA.

Price: $.
Directions: From I-35, take Exit Research Blvd/ Hwy 183 (#239) and then go northeast on Research Blvd (Hwy 183) and this place is 3 miles northeast of the exit.

Magnolia Café
2304 Lake Austin Boulevard, at Upson Street
512-478-8645
1920 South Congress Avenue; 512-445-0000
Hours: Daily for 24 hours
American, Mexican. Not pure vegetarian.
Menu: Has a good selection of vegetarian dishes. Spinach Lasagna, burritos, enchiladas, Love Veggies and several salads.
Comments: Comfortable, casual place. Usually has a line for brunch. Reasonable prices. Pleasant atmosphere. Very good, friendly service.
Other Info: Full service, take-out. Reservations not accepted. Accepts AMEX, DIS, MC, VISA.
Price: $.
Directions: Parking arranged for customers.

**Mother's Café and Garden
4215 Duval Street, in a small shopping center
512-451-3994; **email:** camalan@netport.com;
Web site: http://motherscafe.citysearch.com/
Hours: Mon to Fri 11:30 am to 10 pm; Sat & Sun 10 am to 10 pm; Sat & Sun Brunch 10 am to 3 pm
Fully Vegetarian American and Mexican. Vegan-friendly.
Menu: Has a large menu. BBQ Tofu, Mushroom Stroganoff, stir-fries, Spinach Mushroom Enchiladas, Spicy Tofu, homemade Bueno Burger, Artichoke Enchiladas with black olives, Spinach Salad, pastas, fajitas, Artichoke Bisque, Enchiladas Verdas, guacamole, soups, Zucchini Poblano (very good), Vegetarian Spinach Lasagna (very good), veggie burgers and salads. Free chips and salsa. Good selection of desserts (50% vegan). Fresh juices and good smoothies.
Comments: Plant-filled indoor garden dining room with a fountain. Has outdoor seating. Located in the historic Hyde Park neighborhood. Great atmosphere. Mellow guitar music played. Sometimes there is live classical guitar music on Friday and Saturday. Good place. Has a weekend brunch.
Warning: Has eggless noodles (so may have to ask for them).
Other Info: Full service, take-out. Has a lunch counter for quick service. Non-smoking. Reservations recommended for groups of 6 or more. Accepts DC, DIS, MC, VISA. Price: $-$$.
Directions: Coming north on I-35 (stay on lower level), take 38½ Street Exit (#237), go west (left)

to second light, then at Duval go north (turn right) and this place is at southeast corner of 43rd & Duval. Coming south on I-35, take exit for Airport and 38½ St (#237A), at Airport turn right, then make quick left onto 45th and go to second light (¾ mile), then at Duval turn left and this place is 2 blocks down at 43rd. Parking arranged for customers.

**Mr Natural
1901 E Cesar Chavez Street, at Chicon
512-477-5228
Hours: Monday to Saturday 9 am to 7 pm
Closed Sunday.
Natural Food Store and small Vegetarian Restaurant. Vegetarian. Mexican. Juice Bar and whole-wheat Bakery. Mainly Vegan.
Menu: Has a wide selection of dishes. Veggie burgers, Breakfast Tacos with veggie sausage, Zucchini Poblano, Sunflower Tofu Tamales, Carne Guisada, soups, Tofu Pumpkin Pie, veggie tamales, homemade tortillas and Vegetarian Fajitas. The lunch plate is a really good deal. Smoothies. The Spinach and Pineapple Drink is interesting.
Comments: The food gets really high ratings. Friendly, casual place. Once a month has vegetarian breakfast buffet. Most of the cakes, cookies and breads are egg- and dairy-free. Some desserts are wheat-free. The neighborhood is not very good.
Other Info: Cafeteria style, take-out. Accepts MC, VISA. Price: $.
Directions: Near the University of Texas.

Pho Cong Ly
8557 Research Boulevard, at Peygin
512-832-5595
Hours: Daily 10 am to 9 pm
Vietnamese. Vegetarian-friendly.
Menu: Soups, noodles soups and other dishes.
Comments: A bit of a formal place. Good service. Exotic cuisine.

Red River Café
2912 Medical Arts Street; 512-474-8609
Hours: Monday to Friday 7 am to 8 pm
Saturday & Sunday 8 am to 5 pm
Coffeeshop. Vegetarian-friendly. Not pure vegetarian.
Menu: Has a selection of vegetarian dishes. Salads, tacos, veggie burger, Garden Club Sandwich, veggie tacos, chips with homemade salsa and French Veggie Pita. Fresh squeezed orange juice.
Comments: Good place to hang out. Good food.

Nice artwork on walls. Friendly, quick service. Popular place so it pays to get here early for the weekend brunch. Has outdoor patio seating. Reasonable prices.
Directions: Located a block from the University of Texas. Has parking facilities.

Shanghai River
Village Shopping Center
2700 West Anderson Lane (Northwest), between Burnet Road and Mopac
512-458-9598; **fax:** 512-458-2460; **Web site:** http://shanghairiver.citysearch.com/
Hours: Daily 11:30 am to 2:30 pm, 4:30 pm to 9:30 pm
Chinese. Vegan options. Not pure vegetarian. Daily lunch and dinner buffet.
Menu: Has a vegetarian buffet on Wednesday, Friday and Sunday nights. Has a selection of mock meat dishes. Spring rolls, soups, vegetarian sushi and eggless fortune cookies.
Comments: Good food. Traditional décor.
Other Info: Full service, take-out, catering, delivery. Has a Banquet Room that seats 175 people. Accepts AMEX, DC, MC, VISA. Price: $.
Directions: Across from The Cinema Four, about a half-mile from North Cross Mall.

Souper Salads (several locations)
4211 South Lamar (S)   512-441-6958
10710 Research, Ste 125 (NW) 512-343-0807
2438 W Anderson (N)   512-451-9320
6700 Middle Fiskville Road   512-453-7687
Salad Bar. Not pure vegetarian.
Menu: Many salad items, baked potatoes and sandwiches. Usually has one vegetarian soup.
Comments: All breads may have eggs in them.

Sun Harvest (Wild Oats)
2917 West Anderson Lane
512-451-0669; **fax:** 512-451-5805
Hours: Daily 8 am to 10 pm
Natural Food Store and Cafe. Deli, Bakery, Salad Bar and Juice Bar. Organic produce. Supermarket-type place. See Wild Oats Market information.
Directions: It is three blocks west of the Northcross Mall, about 3 miles north of the downtown. From I-35, take exit #241 and go west on Hwy 183 (Research Blvd) for 3 miles, then go south on N Mo Pac Exwy for 1 mile, take Far West Blvd exit, then turn right onto Executive Center Dr and go 2 blocks, at Wood Hollow Dr turn right and go 1 block, at Spicewood Springs Rd turn right (becomes W Anderson Lane) and this place is a half-mile down.

Sun Harvest (Wild Oats)
4006 South Lamar
512-444-3079; fax: 512-444-6597
Hours: Daily 8 am to 10 pm
Natural Food Store and Cafe. Deli, Bakery, Salad Bar and Juice Bar. Organic produce. Supermarket-type place. See Wild Oats Market information.
Directions: From I-35, take exit #230 towards US 290/Ben White Blvd, then go west on E Ben White Blvd (becomes US 290) for 2½ miles, take Lamar Blvd/West Gate Blvd then go north (take a slight right) onto S Lamar Blvd and this place is a third-mile down.

Thai Kitchen (three locations)
3437 Bee Caves Road; 512-328-3538
3009 Guadalupe, north end of Drag
512-474-2575
803-A E William Cannon Drive; 512-445-4844
Hours: Mon to Sat 11am to 2:30pm, 5pm to 9:45pm; Sun 11:30am to 2:30pm, 5 pm to 9:30pm
Thai. Vegan friendly. Not pure vegetarian.
Menu: Has over 20 vegetarian main dishes.
Comments: Good food. Hot spices. Casual atmosphere. Remind them to not use fish sauce. Has artworks and photos from Thailand. Efficient service.
Other Info: Accepts AMEX, MC, VISA. Price: $-$$.

Threadgill's World Headquarters
301 West Riverside Drive, at Barton Springs
512-472-9304
6416 North Lamar Blvd; 512-451-5440
Hours: Monday to Thursday 11 am to 10 pm; Friday 11 am to 12 midnight; Saturday 10 am to 12 midnight; Sunday 10 am to 9:30 pm
Southern, American, Soul. Vegetarian-friendly.
Menu: Has a Vegetable Plate. Salads.
Comments: Sometimes has live entertainment. Has a children's menu. Food gets very mixed reviews from customers, some very bad and other very good.
Other Info: Non-smoking. Accepts MC, VISA. Price: $-$$
Directions: Parking arranged for customers.

**Veggie Heaven
1914 A Guadalupe Street, at M L King JR Blvd
512-457-1013; Web site: www.veggieheaven.org
Hours: Monday to Friday 11 am to 9 pm
Saturday & Sunday 12 noon to 9 pm
Fully Vegetarian Chinese. Mostly Vegan.
Menu: A great selection of vegetarian dishes with over 50 dishes. Variety of vegan dishes including

wraps, salads, veggie buns, noodle entrées and rice. Protein 2000 (mock breaded chicken), Spicy Soybean Tofu, Eggplant Tofu, Lucky Seven, Five Star (mock fish), "Mt Everest" (wrap made of avocados, vegetable kebabs, alfalfa, mushrooms and cream cheese with barbecue-flavored sauce in a tortilla wrap) and Spicy Soybean Tofu.
Comments: Relaxed place. Good, fast service. Recommended. Very reasonably priced. Has pictures of each dish. A young crowd. Popular with students at the University of Texas. Got good reviews in the local newspapers. I really liked this place. The spring rolls were excellent. Very good food. Has its own parking lot. Friendly, helpful, cool staff. A bit like a fast-food place. Smallest place. Has Tai Chai and massage next door. The Web site has a complete menu on it.
Other Info: Full service, take-out. Non-smoking. Accepts reservations, but not necessary. Accepts MC, VISA. Price $-$$.
Direction: At Guadalupe and 20th Street, across from the Dobie Mall. Close to downtown, across from the University of Texas on the "The Drag." Has its own parking lot. From I-235, take MLK Boulevard exit (#235A) towards State Capitol/E 15th St, and go west a half-mile on MLK Blvd St (can also go west on E 15th St), then at Guadalupe turn right and this place is the third building down on the left.

**West Lynn Café
1110 West Lynn Street
512-482-0950; email: camalan@inetport.com;
Web site: http://westlynn.citysearch.com/
Hours: Monday to Thursday 11:30 am to 10 pm; Friday 11:30 am to 10:30 pm; Saturday 11 am to 10:30 pm; Sunday 11 am to 9:30 pm; Saturday & Sunday Brunch 11:30 am to 3 pm
Fully Vegetarian International. Asian, Italian, Southwestern, Thai, Mexican, Indian. Vegan options.
Menu: Has over fifty dishes. Pizza Portobello, Fettuccine al Greco, Thai Red Pepper Curry, Chile Relleno, Eggplant Parmesan, pastas, Caribbean Stir-fry, salsa, soups, curry dishes, pizzas and egg-free desserts. Fresh juices, cappuccino, espresso.
Comments: Award winning building design. In an interesting historic area near the downtown. Upscale place. Gourmet vegetarian. Good place for a romantic dinner. The food gets excellent ratings. Judged to be one of the best vegetarian restaurants in the US. Owned by the same people as Mother's Café. Got great reviews in the local papers. Friendly, helpful service.
Other Info: Full service, take-out. Non-smoking. Accepts AMEX, DC, DIS, MC, VISA. Price: $-

$$.

Directions: On southwest corner of W 12th St and West Lynn St. Take 12th St west from Lamar and this place is at the 1st traffic light west of Lamar. In a historic neighborhood near the downtown. From I-35, take #235A exit for MLK Blvd/ 15th and go west on 15th St for 1½ mile (becomes Enfield Rd), at Lorrain St turn left and go 1 block, at W 13th St turn right and go 2 blocks, at W Lynn St turn left and this place is 1 block down.

Wheatsville Food Co-op

3101 Guadalupe; 512-478-2667; **email:** wheats@io.com; **Web site:** www.wheatsville.com
Store Hours: Daily 9 am to 11 pm
Deli Hours: Daily 9 am to 9 pm.
Natural Food Store and Café. Deli. Has a great selection of organic produce (good prices). Large supermarket-style place.
Menu: Rice & Beans, pizzas, tamales, salads, sandwiches, tacos, Potato Artichoke Salad, Sweet Potatoes, Greek Salad, hummus, Garbanzo Bean Salad, Tofu Salad Sandwich, mushroom tamales and tabbouleh. Eggless cookies. Sandwiches have a choice of breads or rolls. Fresh juices and smoothies.
Comments: You can eat at the tables outside. Café is reasonably priced. Has recycling facilities. Membership at the Co-op is $15 per year and $70 for a lifetime. Non-members pay 7% extra. They offer massages. Price: $.
Warning: You should ask for vegan mayo if you do not eat eggs.
Directions: From I-35, take 38th St exit (#237B) and go 1 mile west. At Guadalupe turn left and this place is 7 blocks down on left. From I-35 coming north, take exit #236A towards 26th-32nd Sts, take 26th St ramp, merge onto E Dean Keeton St (becomes E 26th St) and go ¾ mile, take a slight right onto San Jacinto Blvd and go a quarter-mile, then take a slight left onto E 30th St and go a half-mile, at Guadalupe St turn right and this place is 1 block down.

Whole Foods Market

9607 Research Boulevard, Suite 300
512-345-5003; **fax:** 512-476-5704;
Web site: www.wholefoods.com
Hours: Daily 8 am to 10:30 pm
Natural Food Store and Cafe. Deli, Bakery, Salad Bar and Juice Bar. Organic produce. Supermarket-type place. See Whole Foods Market information.
Directions: From I-35, head northwest on Hwy 183 (#240B) and go 4 miles, take exit for Great Hills Trail/TX Rte 360 and go straight onto Research Blvd for ¾ mile and this place on the right in a shopping center. At intersection of Route 183 & Route 360.

Whole Foods Market

601 North Lamar, Suite 1000
512-476-1206; **fax:** 512-476-5704
Web site: www.wholefoods.com
Hours: Daily 8 am to 10 pm
Natural Food Store and Cafe. Deli, Bakery, Salad Bar and Juice Bar. Organic produce. Supermarket-type place. See Whole Foods Market information.
Directions: From I-35, take exit #234B towards 2nd-4th Sts/1st St and then go west on 1st St for 1 mile, then at Trinity St turn right and go 1 block, at 2nd St turn left and go a half-mile, at San Antonio St turn right and go 2 blocks, at W 4th turn left and go 3 blocks, at Rio Grande St turn right and go 2 blocks, at W 6th St turn left and this place is 3 blocks down at the corner with N Lamar.

World Beat Café

600 West Martin Luther King Jr Boulevard, at Nueces Street; 512-236-0197
Hours: Mon to Wed 11 am to 8 pm; Thur to Sat 11 am to 10 pm; Sun 12 noon to 8 pm
African, Ethiopian, Nigerian. Vegetarian friendly. Not pure vegetarian.
Menu: Has a selection of vegetarian dishes. Vegetables dishes, rice, Yam Fufu, fried plantains and veggie burgers. The "Beat Platter" is rice, fried plantains, stir-fried vegetables and black-eyed peas.
Comments: Uses tropical vegetables. Dim lights with a low ceiling. Has good size portions. Has African Nights, where there is traditional African music and dancing. Friendly, casual atmosphere. Food gets good ratings. Has African masks on one of the walls. Plays African music (also has a large screen TV).
Other Info: Accepts AMEX, MC, VISA. Price: $.
Directions: Near the University of Texas.

BRYAN

Smetana Grocery

7700 West Highway 21; 979-775-9337
Hours: Monday to Thursday 6 am to 11 pm; Fri & Sat 6 am to 12 midnight; Sun 7 am to 11 pm
Natural Food Store and Deli.
Directions: This place is going west toward Caldwell on Hwy 21, west of Rte 6.

COLLEYVILLE

Healthy Approach Market
5100 Highway 121 North, at Glade Road
817-399-9100
Hours: Monday to Saturday 9 am to 9 pm
Sunday 11 am to 7 pm
Natural Food Store. Juice Bar.
Comments: Good selection of products.
Directions: From the 820 loop, take Grapevine
Hwy exit (Hwy 26), and go north on Hwy 26.
Go 3 miles into Colleyville (road becomes
Colleyville Blvd). This place on left in Kroger
Shopping Center.

CORPUS CHRISTI

Sun Harvest Farms (Wild Oats)
1440 Airline Road
361-993-2850; fax: 361-993-6187
Hours: Daily 9 am to 9 pm
Natural Food Store and Cafe. Deli, Bakery,
Salad Bar and Juice Bar. Organic produce. Supermarket-type place. See Wild Oats Market
information.
Directions: From I-37, take Padre Island Dr (Hwy
358) east for about 6 miles and this place at corner of Padre and Airline.

DALLAS
Denton, Fort Worth, Irving, Plano, Richardson
and Waxahachie

Café Greek
12817 Preston Road, at LBJ Freeway
972-934-9767
Hours: Monday 11:30 am to 2:30 pm; Sunday,
Tuesday to Thursday 11:30 am to 2:30 pm, 5
pm to 9 pm; Friday & Saturday 11:30 am to 2:30
pm, 5 pm to 10 pm
Greek. Vegan options. Not pure vegetarian.
Menu: Has falafel, salads, hummus, baba
ghanoush, tabbouleh, Spanikopita, feta cheese and
more.
Comments: Good food and service.
Other Info: Full service, take-out. Accepts
AMEX, DIS, MC, VISA. Price: $-$$.
Directions: Has a parking lot.

California Pizza Kitchen
5505 Belt Line Road   972-490-8550
8411 Preston Road   214-750-7067

Chow Thai
5290 Belt Line Road, in Addison
972-960-2999

Hours: Monday to Friday 11 am to 10 pm
Saturday & Sunday 5 pm to 10 pm
Thai. Not pure vegetarian.
Menu: Has a large selection of vegetarian dishes.
Other Info: Accepts AMEX, DIS, MC, VISA.
Price: $$.
Directions: Has a parking lot.

Cosmic Café
2912 Oak Lawn, just south of Cedar Springs
214-521-6157
Hours: Mon to Thur 11 am to 11 pm; Fri & Sat
11 am to 11:30 pm; Sun 12 noon to 10 pm
Indian and International. Coffeehouse type place.
Menu: Good amount of vegan dishes. Good ve-
gan desserts. Herbal tea.
Comments: Pleasant atmosphere. Has outdoors
patio dining. Bohemian atmosphere. Service can
be slow. Are usually willing to accommodate
vegans. Formerly call Cosmic Cup. Has a drum
and dance circles every Tuesday night (around 30
or 40 people come). Indian tabla music and po-
etry readings.
Other Info: Reservations not accepted. Smoking
on patio. Price: $-$$. Accepts AMEX, MC, VISA.
Directions: From I-35E, take Oak Lawn Ave exit
(#430A), at Oak Lawn Ave go northeast and this
place is ¾ mile down. This place is a 1½ mile
northwest of downtown Dallas. Has a parking
lot.

Dream Café
2800 Routh Street #170, at Laclede Street
214-954-0486
Hours: Daily 7 am to 10 pm
New American. Health Foods. Vegan options.
Vegetarian-friendly. Not pure vegetarian. Often
uses organic vegetables.
Menu: Has a changing "Planet Earth" vegetarian
meal for dinner, which can be made vegan if requested. Pizzas.
Comments: Gets good recommendations. Has
outside patio dining. Children friendly place with
a box of toys for the kids to play with. Popular
place.
Other Info: Full service, take-out, delivery. Reservations suggested for groups. Non-smoking except on the patio. Accepts AMEX, DC, DIS, MC,
VISA. Price: $$.
Directions: Near downtown in the Quadrangle.
On the main street of the Routh Street area north
of the downtown. Has a parking lot.

Farmers' Market
Pearl Expressway between Central Expressway and
Harwood Street

Largest city market in the country. Over 1000 farmers spread over four blocks.
Hours: Daily from sunrise to sunset.

Follow Your Heart

Plaza of the Americas food courtyard, lower level 600 North Pearl, Suite G103, at San Jacinto Street downtown; 214-953-0411
Hours: Daily 8 am to 3 pm
Mainly Vegetarian (serves tuna) International Health Food. Juice and Smoothie Bar. Mostly Vegan.
Menu: Has sandwiches, main dishes and a daily special. Amigo Lasagna (Spanish Vegetable Lasagna), Italian Rice Balls, Veggie Enchiladas, Veggie Hummus Wrap, Frijoles (with low-fat mozzarella), lentil soup, Rice & Beans, cucumber-tomato salad, Thai Tofu with Noodles & Peanut Sauce, tabbouleh, Penne Pasta with Mushrooms, Curried Tofu with Vegetables and Texas Chile over Brown Rice. Fresh juices and smoothies. No alcohol.
Comments: Has outside seating. Healthy food. Fast, friendly service. Next to ice skating rink. Staff may not be totally reliable about what dishes are vegan.
Warning: The quiche contains egg-white.
Other Info: Counter service, takeout, catering. Non-smoking. Accepts reservations but not necessary. Accepts AMEX, DC, DIS, MC, VISA. Price: $-$$.
Directions: Located in the arts district of downtown Dallas. From the intersection of Pearl & San Jacinto, go east on San Jacinto. Take an immediate right into The Plaza of the America's parking garage. Bring parking ticket for validation and free parking inside Plaza Tower. Take elevator down to the lower level and this place on your right hand side next to the ice skating rink.

**Francis Simun's Bakery

3106 Commerce Street, at Hall Street
214-741-4242
Hours: Monday to Friday 6:30 am to 5 pm; Saturday 9 am to 2 pm; closed Sunday.
Vegetarian Bakery. Vegan options.
Menu: Has a good selection of vegan organic muffins, scones and other baked items. Fresh juices.
Other Info: Full service, take-out, catering. Non-smoking. Accepts AMEX, DC, DIS, MC, VISA. Price: $-$$$.
Directions: In the Deep Ellum area, east of the downtown. Has street parking.

Fresh Choice

601 15th Street; 972-881-9792
Web site: www.freshchoiceinc.com
Hours: Sunday to Thursday 11 am to 9 pm
Friday & Saturday 11 am to 10 pm
Italian and Pizza. Vegan options. Not pure vegetarian. See Austin for details.
Other Info: Accepts AMEX, DIS, MC, VISA.
Directions: Parking arranged for customers.

Fresh Start

4108 Oak Lawn Avenue; 214-528-5535
Hours: Monday to Friday 7:30 am to 7:30 pm; Saturday 9 am to 6 pm; Sunday 12 noon to 6 pm
Natural Food Store. Sports Supplements.
Directions: From I-35E, take Tollway North exit (#429) and go north on Dallas North Tollway for 1¼ mile, take Lemmon Ave exit, at Lemmon Ave turn right and go 1 mile, at Oak Lawn Ave (TX-289) turn left and this place is a half-mile down. Has a parking lot. This place is about 1½ mile due north of the downtown.

**The PenDragon Café

5601 Sears Street, at Greenville Avenue
214-821-3340
Hours: Tues to Thur 11 am to 9 pm; Fri & Sat 11 am to 2 am; closed Sun and Mon.
Vegetarian American and International. Serves dairy but no eggs.
Menu: Soups, salads, sandwich, quesadilla, Fried Eggplant Sandwich, fried Zucchini, Grilled Cheese Sandwiches, French fries and more.
Other Info: Accepts AMEX, DC, DIS, MC, VISA. Full service, take-out. Price: $$.

India Palace

12817 Preston Road, at LBJ
972-392-0190
Hours: Mon to Thur 11:30 am to 2:30 pm, 5:30 pm to 10 pm; Fri 11:30 am to 2 pm, 5:30 pm to 11 pm; Sat 12 noon to 3 pm, 5:30 pm to 11 pm; Sun 12 noon to 3 pm, 5:30 pm to 10 pm
Indian. Not pure vegetarian.
Menu: Has a vegetarian thali. Whole-wheat Indian breads.
Comments: One of the best Indian places in Dallas.
Other Info: Reservations recommended. Accepts AMEX, MC, VISA. Price: $$.
Directions: Has a parking lot.

Jamba Juice

70 Highland Park Village, at Preston Road and Mockingbird Lane; 214-219-3338

Hours: Monday to Friday 7 am to 9 pm; Saturday 8 am to 9 pm; Sunday 10 am to 7 pm
Juice Bar.
Menu: Fresh juices and smoothies. Soups, salads and sandwiches.
Comments: Good service. Noodles often contain eggs.
Other Info: Non-smoking. Accepts MC, VISA. Price: $.
Directions: From I-35E coming north, take Dallas North Tollway exit (#429D) and go north for 2½ miles, take Mockingbird Lane exit, then at Mockingbird Lane turn right and this place is a half-mile down. Has a parking lot. This place is about 2½ miles north of downtown Dallas.

**Kalachandji's Restaurant
5430 Gurley Avenue, in east Dallas
214-821-1048; fax: 214-660-0579
Hours: Tuesday to Friday 11:30 am to 2 pm, 5:30 pm to 9 pm; Saturday 12 noon to 3 pm, 5:30 pm to 9 pm; Sunday 5:30 pm to 9 pm; closed Mon.
Fully Vegetarian International and Indian. Vegetarian Buffet and Salad Bar.
Menu: The menu changes daily. Curried vegetable dishes, Lasagna, quiche, enchiladas, homemade soups (different one daily), steamed vegetables, special spiced rice, homemade breads and Eggplant Curry. For desserts there is halava, burfi, gulabjamun and more. House Tamarind Tea is excellent. No alcohol.
Comments: Outdoor courtyard with trees, flowers and fountains. Excellent décor. Glass-topped tables, a small fountain, and stained-glass insets in the walls. Managed by the Hare Krishnas. Has a good, peaceful atmosphere and the food is great. Highly recommended. Reasonably priced. No preservatives. Has an Indian gift shop connected. Peaceful place. Beautiful décor. Popular with visiting musicians who have left autographed pictures (Annie Lennox and the B-52s). Connected to a Hare Krishna temple, but there is no proselytizing in the restaurant. Has a beautiful temple room that is worth seeing.
Other Info: Buffet, catering, cafeteria style. Non-smoking. Accepts reservations but not necessary. Accepts MC, VISA. Price: $-$$.
Directions: In east Dallas, at corner of Gurley and Graham, 2 blocks north of I-30. From I-30 coming from west, take Exit #48, go west 2 blocks on Service Road and turn right on Gurley and this place is 2 blocks down. Plenty of parking available on street. From I-30 coming from east, turn left at Grand Ave and go 1 block, at Fairview Ave turn left and go 2 blocks, at Gurley turn right and this place is half-way down the block.

Queen of Sheba
3527 McKinney, at Lemmon Avenue
214-521-0491
Hours: Sunday to Friday 11 am to 10:30 pm
Saturday 11 am to 11 pm
Ethiopian, Italian, American. Not pure vegetarian.
Menu: Has a vegetarian section on menu. Buffet has Italian dishes on Monday and Tuesday, American on Wednesday and Thursday, and Ethiopian on Friday.
Comments: Gets some high recommendations. Friendly staff. Very popular on Friday and Saturday nights. Good food. Nice, romantic atmosphere.
Other Info: Full service, take-out. Accepts AMEX, DC, DIS, MC, VISA. Reservations recommended. Price: $-$$.

Roy's Nutrition Center
130 Preston Royal Shopping Center, at Preston Road and Royal Lane; 214-987-0213
Hours: Sunday to Thursday 9 am to 10 pm; Friday 9 am to 3:30 pm; closed Saturday.
Natural Food Store and Deli. Juice Bar, Bakery and good Salad Bar. Vegetarian-friendly deli. Not pure vegetarian.
Menu: Soups, salads, sandwiches, Stir-fry Vegetables, Rice and Lasagna. Fresh juices.
Other Info: Counter service, take-out. Accepts AMEX, DIS, MC, VISA. Price: $.
Directions: From coming north on I-35E into Dallas, take Exit #429D and go north on Dallas North Tollway for 6½ miles, take Royal Lane exit, then turn right (go east) onto Royal Lane and this place is a third-mile down in Preston Royal Shopping Center. This place is about 6 miles due north of downtown Dallas.

**Sankofa Vegetarian Café
1908 Martin Luther King Boulevard, at Interstate 45 and Harwood; 214-421-0013
Hours: Tuesday to Friday 11 am to 8 pm; Saturday 11 am to 6:30 pm, 8 am to 12 midnight; Sunday 8 pm to 12 midnight
Vegetarian Restaurant. Juice Bar.
Menu: Good soups, salads, tacos, mock chicken, spaghetti, veggie burgers, Beans & Rice, Black Bean Burgers on whole-grain bun and veggie chili. The mock meat dishes are very good. Fresh juices and smoothies. No alcohol.
Comments: Has live music performances and poetry readings.
Other Info: Full service, take-out, private parties, catering. Non-smoking. Accepts AMEX, MC, VISA. Price: $.

Directions: From I-45, take exit #283 for MLK Blvd and this place is right next to the exit.

Whole Foods Market and The Bluebonnet Café

2218 Lower Greenville Avenue, at Belmont
214-824-1744; 214-824-1744
Hours: Daily 8 am to 10 pm
Natural Food Store and Cafe. Deli, Bakery, Salad Bar and Juice Bar. Organic produce. Supermarket-type place. See Whole Foods Market information.
Menu: Veggie burger, Black Beans & Rice, soups, Tempeh Burger, Black Bean Tamales and much more.
Comments: Very good food.
Directions: In the Greenville area, near Southern Methodist University, north of the downtown. From I-75, take Mockingbird Lane exit east. At Greenville turn right and this place on left. From I-30, take Barry Ave exit (#48A), then go northwest on S Barry Ave (becomes S Munger Blvd) for 1½ mile, at Greenville Ave turn right and this place is ¾ mile down. This place is 1 mile northeast of downtown Dallas.

Whole Foods Market

11661 Preston Road, Suite 224, Preston Forest Village; 214-361-8887; **fax:** 214-361-9169
Hours: Daily 8 am to 10 pm
Natural Food Store and Cafe. Deli, Bakery, Salad Bar and Juice Bar. Organic produce. Supermarket-type place. See Whole Foods Market information.
Directions: From Dallas North Tollway, take Forest Lane exit and go a half-mile west on Forest Lane, at Preston Rd (TX-289) turn right and this place is 1 block down. This place is 7 miles north of downtown Dallas.

Whole Foods Market

7205 Skillman Street, at Kingsley
214-341-5445; **fax:** 214-341-3350
Hours: Daily 8 am to 9 pm
Natural Food Store and Cafe. Deli, Bakery, Salad Bar and Juice Bar. Organic produce. Supermarket-type place. See Whole Foods Market information.
Directions: From I-635, take Skillman exit (#16), go southwest on Skillman and this place is 2 miles down on right. This place is about 5 miles north of downtown Dallas.

ZuZu Handmade Mexican Food (several locations in the Dallas area)

Espartaco Borga, 2651 North Harwood, Suite 200, Dallas   214-521-4456
4866 Belt Line Road, Dallas 972-960-6900
North International Parkway 214-638-6105

2651 North Harwood Street   214-871-2706
6423 Hillcrest Avenue   214-521-4456
223158 Arapaho Village Center, Richardson
972-437-6114
Tex-Mex. Not pure vegetarian.
Menu: Has bean burritos, chips and salsa.
Comments: Uses chicken broth in rice.
Other Info: Accepts AMEX, DC, DIS, MC, VISA. Price: $.

DENTON

Cupboard Natural Foods and Café

200 West Congress Street, at Elm Street
940-387-5386
Hours: Monday to Saturday 9 am to 9 pm
Sunday 11 am to 5 pm
Natural Food Store, Café and Deli. Vegetarian friendly.
Menu: Has a good selection of vegetarian and vegan dishes. Several salads, soups, sandwiches, Tomato Basil Soup, seven-grain bread, Veggie Wrapper (black beans, avocado, cheese and cilantro pesto in a large tortilla) and frozen yogurt. Fresh juices, smoothies and Ginger Peach Tea. No alcohol.
Comments: Nice, friendly atmosphere. Plays new-age music. Small place with around 10 tables.
Store: Has a good selection of herbs, natural foods, cosmetics, candles, greeting cards and other items.
Other Info: Reservations not accepted. Nonsmoking. Accepts AMEX, DC, DIS, MC, VISA.
Directions: From I-35, take exit #469 towards US-380/Decatur, then turn right onto W University Dr (US 380) and go east 2¼ miles, at N Elm St (US 377) turn right and go ¾ mile north, at Congress St turn right and this place is right at the corner. Has a parking lot.

The Greenhouse

600 North Locust Street, at Congress Street
940-484-1349
Hours: Mon to Thur 11 am to 10 pm; Fri & Sat 11 am to 11 pm; Sun 12 noon to 9 pm
Restaurant. Not pure vegetarian.
Menu: Nachos, salads, sandwiches, pastas and more.
Other Info: Reservations recommended for parties of six or more. Accepts AMEX, DIS, MC, VISA. Price: $-$$.
Directions: Has a parking lot.

Mr Chopsticks

1120 West Hickory, at Welch Street
940-382-5437
Hours: Monday to Saturday 10 am to 10 pm

Sunday 11:30 am to 9 pm
Thai and Southeast Asia. Not pure vegetarian.
Menu: Has a wide selection of vegetarian dishes.
Comments: Good about accommodating vegetarians.
Other Info: Limited service, take-out. Accepts MC, VISA. Price: $.
Directions: Has a parking lot.

Healthy Foods and Vitamins
824 West University Drive; 940-382-8816
Natural Food Store.

EL PASO

Lee Trevino Vitamin Expo
1840 North Lee Trevino Drive, Suite 704
915-599-1778; **fax:** 915-599-4248
Hours: Monday to Saturday 10 am to 7 pm
Closed Sunday.
Natural Food Store.

Montana Vitamin Expo
6590 Montana Avenue, Suite G
915-779-6527; **fax:** 915-772-9921
Hours: Monday to Saturday 10 am to 7 pm
Closed Sunday.
Natural Food Store.

Sun Harvest Farms (Wild Oats)
6100 North Mesa Street, at Balboa
915-833-3380; **fax:** 915-833-3138
Hours: Daily 8 am to 10 pm
Natural Food Store and Cafe. Deli, Bakery, Salad Bar and Juice Bar. Organic produce. Supermarket-type place. See Wild Oats Market information.
Directions: From I-10, take Sunland Park Dr exit (#13) and go northeast 1½ mile. At North Masa turn left. At Balboa (next light) turn right and this place on left in a shopping plaza.

FORT WORTH

Fresh Choice
3010 South Hulen Street; 817-738-9878
Hours: Sunday to Thursday 11 am to 9 pm
Friday & Saturday 11 am to 10 pm
Restaurant. Not pure vegetarian. See Austin.

Hot Damn, Tamales
3404 West Seventh Street; 817-335-5610
Web site: www.hotdamntamales.com
Hours: Monday to Friday 11 am to 6 pm; Saturday 11 am to 4 pm; closed Sunday.
Mexican. Not pure vegetarian.

Menu: Has gourmet tamales. Cheese and Mushroom Tamales, salads and Spinach Mushroom Enchilada Casserole.
Comments: Displays paintings and sculptures by Eric Whitney.
Other Info: Non-smoking. Accepts DIS, MC, VISA. Price: $.
Directions: Near the Fort Worth Arts Districts. Has a parking lot.

Jamba Juice
400 Main Street, Fort Worth; 817-870-1001
Hours: Monday to Friday 7 am to 9 pm; Saturday 8 am to 10 pm; Sunday 10 am to 7 pm
Juice Bar. Not pure vegetarian.
Menu: Fresh juices and smoothies. Soups, salads and sandwiches.
Comments: Good service. Noodles often contain eggs.
Other Info: Non-smoking. Accepts MC, VISA. Price: $.
Directions: This place is a few blocks east of Fort Worth Shopping Mall. Has a parking lot. From I-30, take US 287 exit (#15B) towards I-35W/Downtown and go 1 mile west on ML King Freeway, then take TX-280 Spur west for a quarter-mile, take E 4th St exit and merge onto E 4th St and go 1 block, at Jones St turn right and go 2 blocks, at 2nd St turn left and go 3 blocks, at Houston St turn left and go 1 block, at W 3rd St turn left and this place is 1 block down.

Maharaja
6308 South Hulen Street, at Oakmont Trail
817-263-7156
Hours: Daily 11:30 am to 2:30 pm, 5:30 pm to 10 pm; Monday to Thursday 11 am to 10 pm; Friday 11 am to 10:30 pm; Saturday 11:30 am to 10:30 pm; Sunday 11:30 am to 10 pm
Indian. Good lunch buffet. Not pure vegetarian.
Comments: Some people really like this place. Good place for a special event.
Other Info: Non-smoking. Accepts AMEX, DC, DIS, MC, VISA. Price: $$.
Directions: In a shopping center near Old Granbury Road, around two miles south of Hwy 820.

Ray's Health Foods
5437 South Hulen Street; 817-370-7611
Hours: Monday to Saturday 10 am to 6 pm
Closed Sunday.

Sunflower Shoppe
5817 Curzon Street, at Camp Bowie Boulevard
817-738-9051

Hours: Monday to Saturday 9 am to 9 pm
Sunday 11 am to 7 pm
Natural Food Store and Café. Juice Bar.
Menu: Has a limited selection of vegetarian
dishes. Sandwiches and tabbouleh. Fresh juices
and smoothies.
Other Info: Non-smoking. Reservations not accepted. Accepts AMEX MC, VISA. Price: $.
Directions: From I-30 west, take Camp Bowie
exit (#9) and go south on Camp Bowie a half-
mile. Then at Curzon turn left and this place on
right corner. Has a parking lot.

HOUSTON

A Moveable Feast

Echo Lane Shopping Center, 9341 Katy Freeway,
at Echo Lane (I-10); 713-365-0368
Hours: Monday to Saturday 9 am to 9 pm
Closed Sunday.
Natural Food Store and large Restaurant. South-
ern and Tex-Mexican. Macrobiotic and Vegan
options. Not pure vegetarian. Vegan friendly Deli.
Organic produce.
Menu: Has a daily special and a Macrobiotic Plat-
ter (rice and vegetables) daily. Blue Corn Enchi-
ladas with Black Beans, Vegetarian Barbecue
Seitan, Meatless Happy Burgers, Pita Pizza, Chili
Tempeh Burgers, Cheeseless Florentine Lasagna,
Vegetarian Chicken Steak, Vegan Spinach Enchi-
ladas, Roasted Potato Sticks, Pimento cheese-less
Sandwich, South Plate (has mock fried chicken),
Vegetarian Fajitas, Veggie Chili, Happy Burgers,
and Cheeseless Spinach Enchiladas. The Eggplant
Sandwich and Potato Wedges are very good. The
Cream Herb Salad Dressing is popular. Fresh
juices, smoothies and organic coffee.
Comments: Casual, upscale. Creative cuisine.
Very busy place. Good bulletin board. There is a
farmer's market on Saturday mornings.
Other Info: Full service, take-out, catering, de-
livery. Accepts AMEX, DIS, MC, VISA. Price:
$-$$.
Directions: From I-10, take exit #758 and this
place is right at the exit. This place is about 7
miles west of downtown Houston.

**Anand Bhavan

6662 Southwest Freeway, in Bellaire
713-977-0150
Hours: Daily 11 am to 9 pm
Lunch Buffet 11 am to 3 pm
Fully Vegetarian Indian. Some American dishes.
Lunch Buffet.
Menu: South Indian dishes such as masala dosa

and sambar.
Comments: Has outdoor seating.
Other Info: Full service, take-out. Accepts MC,
VISA. Price: $.
Directions: This place is just outside the 610
South loop on the corner of Hwy 59 and
Hillcroft. It is about 7 mile west (a little south)
of downtown Houston. Parking arranged for
customers.

Ashoka Indian Cuisine

3640 Hillcroft, at Richmond
713-977-1272
Hours: Mon to Fri 11am to 2:30pm, 5:30pm to 10pm;
Sat & Sun 12 noon to 3pm, 5:30pm to 10pm
Indian. Vegetarian-friendly. Lunch Buffet.
Menu: Has a wide selection of vegetarian dishes.
Salads, fruit salads, dal, Navaratna Korma, Saag
Paneer, rice dishes, chutneys, raita, curried veg-
etables and Kheer (rice pudding dessert). Lassi.
Other Info: Full service, take-out, delivery. Ac-
cepts AMEX, DIS, MC, VISA.

Baba Yega Restaurant

2607 Grant Street; 713-522-0042
Hours: Monday to Thursday 11 am to 10 pm;
Fri & Sat 11 am to 11 pm; Sun 11 am to 10 pm
American Natural Foods. Not pure vegetarian.
Menu: Has a good selection of vegetarian dishes.
Avocado, cheese and spout sandwich. Veggie
burgers with cheese, avocado and sprouts. Pastas.
Sunday brunch buffet.
Comments: This place gets high recommenda-
tions. Relaxed, pleasant atmosphere. Has good
outdoor dining on a beautiful patio. Has a par-
rot. Good staff. Good place for a special event.
Other Info: Accepts AMEX, DC, DIS, MC,
VISA. Price: $.

Bombay Palace

4100 Westheimer Suite 107
713-960-8472; fax: 713-963-8061
Hours: Mon to Sat 11 am to 2:30 pm, 5 pm to
10:30 pm; Sun 11 am to 3 pm, 5 pm to 11 pm
Indian. All-you-can-eat Lunch Buffet. Not pure
vegetarian.
Menu: The buffet has good vegetarian dishes.
Tandoor breads.
Comments: Generally has good service and at-
mosphere. Some people don't like this place.
Sometimes has live entertainment.
Other Info: Full service, take-out, catering, de-
livery. Reservations suggested. Non-smoking.
Accepts AMEX, DC, MC, VISA. Price: $$.
Directions: Parking arranged for customers.

**Bombay Sweets Vegetarian Rest.
5827 Hillcroft Street; 713-780-4453
Hours: Daily 11 am to 9:30
Vegetarian Indian Sweets and Snack.
Other Info: Counter service, take-out. Has seating. Accepts AMEX, MC, VISA.

California Pizza Kitchen
1705-A Post Oak Road
713-963-9262; Web site: www.cpk.com

Cedar's
4703 Richmond Avenue; 713-572-9445
Hours: Monday to Saturday 11 am to 9:30 pm
Sunday 11:30 am to 8 pm
Middle Eastern Cafeteria. Not pure vegetarian.
Menu: Has a vegetarian buffet. Salads, hummus, steamed asparagus, potatoes, cauliflower, falafel and more. Strong Turkish Coffee and Passion Fruit Tea.
Comments: Serves fresh, good food.
Other Info: Accepts AMEX, DIS, MC, VISA. Price: $.

Mekong
3241 Southwest Freeway, at Buffalo Speedway
713-669-9375
Hours: Monday to Friday 11 am to 3 pm, 5 pm to 9:30 pm (until 10:30 Saturday); Saturday 11 am to 10:30 pm; Sunday 12 noon to 9:30 pm
Vietnamese. Thai also. Not pure vegetarian.
Menu: Has vegetarian tofu dishes. Vegetable Stir-fries with Tofu.
Comments: Has outdoor dining. Romantic place. Has nice antique pieces, hardwoods and artwork. Price: $$.
Directions: Across from the Compaq Center.

Empress of China
5419-A West Farm Road 1960; 281-583-8021
Hours: Monday to Saturday 11 am to 2 pm, 5 pm to 10 pm; closed Sunday.
Chinese. Vegan-friendly. Not pure vegetarian.
Comments: Typical Chinese place for lunch and an elegant place in the evening. Upscale. Excellent atmosphere. Does vegetarian banquets. Gets some high ratings. Received CitySearch award for best Chinese restaurant.
Other Info: Full service, take-out, catering. Reservation recommended, especially on the weekends and holidays. Generally gets good ratings. Accepts AMEX, DIS, MC, VISA. Price: $$.

**Garden Bistro
9013 Westheimer Road; 713-783-6622
Hours: Daily 11 am to 3 pm, 5:30 to 9:30 pm

Vegetarian Asian. Vegan friendly.
Menu: Dumplings, brown rice, mock beef dishes, eggplants dishes, Garden Fried Rice, mock shrimp, Corn & Miso Soup and other dishes. Soy ice cream. Fried Yams or Bananas. No alcohol.
Comments: Good place. Helpful, knowledgeable staff. Gets some good ratings. Reasonable prices. Good size portions. Friendly service.
Other Info: Full service, take-out, delivery. Reservations not necessary. Non-smoking. Accepts AMEX, DIS, MC, VISA. Price: $-$$.
Directions: This place is a block east of Columbia Medical Center. From I-610, take exit #9A towards San Felipe Rd/Westheimer Rd, and go onto the W Loop Freeway S for a half-mile, at Westheimer Rd turn right (go west) and this place is 4 miles down. This place is 8 miles west of downtown Houston. On Westheimer at Fondren. Convenient parking available at all times.

Gourmet India
13155 Westheimer Road, at Eldridge
281-493-5435
Hours: Mon 11 am to 2:30 pm, 5:30 pm to 10 pm; Tues to Thur 11:30 am to 2:30 pm, 5:30 pm to 10 pm; Fri 11 am to 2:30 pm, 5:30 pm to 11 pm; Sat 12 noon to 3 pm, 5:30 pm to 11 pm; Sun 12 noon to 3 pm, 5:30 pm to 10 pm
Indian. Not pure vegetarian.
Menu: Has a selection of vegetarian dishes. Dal, Channa Masala, rice dishes, Mango lassis. Homemade mango or pistachio ice creams. Rice pudding and Gulabjamun.
Other Info: Accepts AMEX, DIS, MC, VISA. Price: $-$$.

Happy Vegetarian Market
6131 Wilcrest Drive, at Harwin
281-879-8989
Vegetarian Asian Food Store.
Directions: From I-10, take Sam Houston Tollway W south 4 miles, then take Westheimer Rd/Richmond Ave exit and go a half-mile south on Beltway 8/W Sam Houston Pkwy, at Westheimer Rd turn right and go west ¾ mile, at Wilcrest Dr turn left (go south) and this place is 1½ mile down. This place is 9 miles west (a little south) of downtown Houston.

Hobbit Café
2243 Richmond Street, between Kirby and Greenbrair; 713-526-5460
Hours: Mon to Thur 11 am to 9:30 pm; Fri & Sat 11 am to 10:30 pm; Sun 11:30 am to 9 pm
International. Not pure vegetarian.

Menu: Has several vegan dishes. Mushroom and Spinach Enchiladas, soups, sandwiches, salads, Black Bean Burger and a good Soy Burger. The Black Bean Nachos are very good. Fruit salad with yogurt and honey. Fresh juices and smoothies. **Comments:** Has a pleasant dining area on the porch under an oak tree. Tolkien-related décor. Tudor-style place. Laid-back, relaxed place. Pleasant atmosphere. In general gets really high recommendations. Has got some really good reviews. **Other Info:** Accepts AMEX, DIS, MC, VISA. Price: $$.
Directions: From I-45, take US 59 (#46B) exit towards Jackson/Freeport and go south on US 59 for 2½ miles, take Shepherd Dr exit towards Green Briar Dr, at S Shepherd Dr turn right and go 2 blocks north, at Portsmouth St turn left and go 1 block, at S Sandman St turn right and go 1 block, at Richmond Ave turn left and this place is 3 blocks down. This place is 3 miles southwest of downtown Houston.

Irma's Restaurant
22 North Chenevert Street, at Ruiz Street, downtown; 713-222-0767
Hours: Monday to Friday 8 am to 3 pm
Closed Saturday & Sunday
Mexican. Not pure vegetarian.
Menu: Spinach Enchiladas. Fresh-squeezed Lemonade.
Comments: Good atmosphere. Food gets high ratings.
Other Info: Full service, take-out, catering. Accepts AMEX, DC, MC, VISA. Price: $.

Jamba Juice
1151 Uptown Park Boulevard; 713-621-9694
Hours: Monday to Friday 7 am to 9 pm; Saturday 8 am to 9 pm; Sunday 10 am to 7 pm
Juice Bar.

**Madras Pavilion
3910 Kirby Drive, Suite 130, at US Highway 59 713-521-2617
Web site: www.madras-pavilion.com
Hours: Daily 11:30 am to 10 pm
Fully Vegetarian South Indian. Lunch Buffet.
Menu: Naans, soups, dosas, uthappam, curries, Indian breads, Palak Panir, Channa Masala, Malai Kofta, Rava Masala Dosa, Rava Idly, Vegetable Korma, Tamarind Rice, Vegetable Pallav Rice, creamed spinach, sambar and desserts. Has a first class lunch buffet with a good selection of dishes. Madras coffee.
Comments: Recommended place. Pleasant atmo-

sphere. Also has other branches in Dallas and Austin. Won CitySearch award for best vegetarian restaurant in Houston. Popular lunch buffet. Food usually gets good reviews. Lunch buffet is a good value. Usually plays South Indian music. Popular place and it can often be crowded. Service gets very mixed opinion (some people think it is very bad).
Other Info: Full service, buffet, take-out. Price: $-$$.
Directions: From I-45, take TX-288/US 59 exit (#46B) and go towards Victoria (west) for 2½ miles, take exit towards Kirby Dr and this place is a block north of US 59 on Kirby. This place is 3 miles southwest of downtown Houston.

**My Lien Vegetarian Restaurant
11528 C Bellaire Boulevard; 281-530-3838
Hours: Sunday, Monday, Wednesday, Thursday 11:30 am to 9:30 pm; Friday & Saturday 9 am to 10 pm; closed Tuesday.
Vegetarian Vietnamese and Chinese. Mainly vegan.
Menu: Has a large selection of traditional dishes with mock meats. Good food. Price: $$.

Naturally Yours Café
4830 Almeda Road, at Rosedale; 713-520-7694
Hours: Monday to Friday 11 am to 8 pm; Saturday 12 noon to 6 pm; closed Sunday.
Natural Pharmacy and Natural Food Café. Mainly vegetarian. Not pure vegetarian.
Menu: Has mostly vegetarian and vegan dishes. Veggie burgers, Portobello Burgers, salads, VLT (soy bacon) Sandwich, Sautéed Orgnanic Vegetables, French fries, soups, fresh fruit salads, veggie-Chicken Salad, Gravy Burgers and brown rice. Smoothies and herbal teas.
Comments: Has outdoor dining.
Warning: There is a dangerous dip in the driveway of the front parking. Also has parking in the back on the side.
Other Info: Reservations not necessary. Nonsmoking. Accepts AMEX, DIS, MC, VISA.
Directions: From I-45, take Rte 288/US-59 exit (#46B) towards Lake Jackson/Victoria and get on US-59 going towards Victoria and go ¾ mile, then take the Fannin St exit and go on Fannin St 1/10 mile, at Wentworth St turn left and go 1 block, turn left at San Jacinto St and go 1 block, at Wentworth St turn right and go a half-mile, at Almeda Rd turn right and this place is 1 block down, at corner with Arbor St. In the Third Ward area. This place is 2 miles south of downtown Houston.

**Quan Yin

10804-E Bellaire Boulevard; 281-498-7890
Hours: Tuesday to Thursday 11 am to 9 pm; Friday 11 am to 10 pm; Saturday 10 to 10 pm; Sunday 10 am to 9 pm; closed Monday.
Vegetarian Vietnamese, Asian, Chinese.
Menu: Has a wide selection of vegetarian dishes. Has mock meat and fish dishes. Fish Ball Soup, Sweet & Sour Soup, Vegan Shark Fin Soup, To Fu Stew, Spring Rolls, Stir-fry Vegetables, Vegan Jellyfish Salad, Roasted Duck, Chicken Fried Steak, Vegan Fish with Sweet & Sour Sauce, Water Crest Soup, Vietnamese Rice Combination, Pork Chops, Spare Ribs and Braised veggie Fish. Fresh juices, Soy Bean Drink, Salted Lemonade, ice tea and non-alcoholic beer.
Comments: Run by the religious group, The International Supreme Master Ching Hai Meditation Association. No MSG. Good food. The food gets very good recommendations.
Other Info: Full service, take-out. Reservations not accepted. Accepts MC, VISA. Price: $$.
Directions: From Sam Houston Tollway W, take exit towards Bellaire Blvd, at Bellaire Blvd turn right and this place is ¾ mile down. At the corner of Bellaire and Wilcrest in Southwest Houston. Parking arranged for customers.

Red Pepper Restaurant

5626 Westheimer; 713-622-7800
Hours: Daily 11 am to 10 pm
Chinese. Not pure vegetarian.
Menu: Has a large selection of vegetarian dishes. Red Pepper's Bean Curd, Spinach Soup, mock Fish (black mushrooms wrapped in bean curd skins), Spinach in Garlic Sauce, Dry Bean Curd, and Peking Duck.
Comments: A bit formal; but can dress casually.
Other Info: Full service, take-out. Accepts AMEX, DC, MC, VISA. Price: $$.

Redwood Grill

4611 Montrose Boulevard; 713-523-4611
Hours: Monday to Thursday 11 am to 2:30 pm, 5 pm to 10 pm; Fri 11 am to 2:30 pm, 6 pm to 11 pm; Sat 5:30 pm to 10 pm; Sun 6 pm to 9 pm
New American. International, Eclectic, Mexican, French, Asian. Not pure vegetarian.
Menu: Salads, pastas, Spinach Salad and other dishes.
Comments: Upscale.
Other Info: Full service, take-out, delivery. Non-smoking. Accepts AMEX, DC, DIS, MC, VISA. Price: $-$$.
Directions: On southeast side of Hwy 59.

Seekers Natural Foods and Vitamins

9336 Westview Drive; 713-461-0857
Natural Food Store and Restaurant. 80 item Salad Bar. Macrobiotic options. Not pure veg.
Menu: A large variety of salad items. Spring Rolls, Veggie Burger and Lasagna. Fresh juices and smoothies.
Comments: Does not use salt or white sugar. Often uses organic produce in the salad bar.
Other Info: Full service, take-out. Accepts AMEX, MC, VISA. Price: $.
Directions: From I-610, take exit #6 towards Bellaire Blvd, turn left at Bellaire Blvd and the place is 1¼ mile down on the left. This place is 5 miles southwest of downtown Houston.

**Shri Balaji Bhavan

5655 Hillcroft Avenue; 713-783-1126
Hours: Wednesday to Monday 11 am to 9:30 pm; closed Tuesday.
Fully Vegetarian South Indian. Mostly Vegan. Udupi style cooking.
Menu: Masala Dosa, samosa and Vegetarian "Thali" meal. The Shri Balaji Bhavan's special crêpe dishes and boiled rice patties are good.
Comments: Food served on banana leaves.
Other Info: Counter service, take-out. Non-smoking. Accepts reservations but not necessary. Accepts DIS, MC, VISA.
Directions: At Southwest Freeway and Hillcroft. 1½ block north of the freeway (on the right). From I-610, take US 59 exit (#8A) towards Victoria and go 2 miles west, then take Hillcroft Ave exit and stay straight onto Southwest Freeway for a third-mile, at Hillcroft Ave turn right and this place is a third-mile down.

Souper Salad

5460 Weslayan	713-660-8952
1574 W Gray	713-524-3536
2435 Post Oak Blvd	713-961-4047
6516-J Westheimer	713-785-0536
7469 SW Fwy	713-981-1800
4884 Beechnut	713-664-4992
2414 University Blvd	713-521-3963
7504 Fm 1960 Roadwest	281-807-4500
6783 Highway 6 North	281-345-4770
14714 Memorial Drive	281-597-0571

Web site: www.suppersalad.com

Sunshine New Body Health Food

4915 MLK; 713-643-2884
Hours: Monday to Friday 10 am to 6 pm
Closed Saturday & Sunday.
Natural Food Store and Deli.

**The Spice Vegetarian Restaurant
2241 Richmond Avenue; 713-529-3100
Hours: Monday to Saturday 11 am to 3 pm, 5
pm to 9:30 pm; closed Sunday.
Vegetarian Thai.
Other Info: Full service, take-out. Accepts
AMEX, MC, VISA.

Thai Pepper
2049 West Alabama Street; 713-520-8225
Hours: Monday to Thursday 11:30 am to 10:30
pm; Friday 11:30 am to 11 pm; Saturday 5:30
pm to 11 pm; Sunday 5 pm to 10 pm
Thai. Not pure vegetarian.
Menu: Willing to substitute meat for vegetables.
Comments: Gets good ratings. Will convert meat
dishes to vegetarian. Said to be the best Thai food
in Houston.
Other Info: Full service, take-out. Accepts
AMEX, DC, DIS, MC, VISA. Price: $-$$.

**Udupi Café
Shepherd Plaza
2121 Richmond Avenue, at Shepherd Drive
713-521-3939
Hours: Monday to Friday 11 am to 3 pm, 5 pm
to 10 pm; Saturday & Sunday 11 am to 10 pm
Vegetarian Indian. Vegan friendly. All-you-can-
eat Buffet.
Menu: Curried vegetables, uthappam, idlies,
dosas, Coconut Rice, Palak Paneer, Samba Vada
(fried lentil donuts), Gobi Manchurian (fried cauliflower), raita and many other dishes. Mango
Lassi. The pickled lemon chutney is good. No
alcohol.
Comments: Popular place. Good food. Helpful,
quick service. This place generally gets very good
reviews.
Other Info: Accepts AMEX, MC, VISA. Price:
$$.
Directions: From I-45, take Rte 288/US 59 (exit
#46B) and go southwest on US 59 for 2½ miles,
take Shepherd Dr exit towards Greenbriar Dr, at
S Shepherd turn right and go 2 blocks, at Ports-
mouth St turn left and go 1 block, at Sandman St
turn right and go 1 block, at Richmond Ave turn
left and this place is at the corner. The place is
about 3 miles southwest of downtown Houston.

***Tien Ren Vegetarian Restaurant
7549 Westheimer Road
713-977-3137; **fax:** 713-977-3775
Hours: Tuesday to Thursday 11:30 am to 9:30
pm; Friday & Saturday 11:30 am to 10 pm; Sun-
day 11:30 am to 9 pm; closed Monday.

Fully Vegan Chinese. All-you-can-eat weekday
Lunch Buffet.
Menu: Has more than 100 dishes. Mock seafood
dishes, Eggless Foo-Young, Black Pepper Vegan
Steak, Vegan Peking Duck, Emerald Tofu, Pine
Nut Soy Fish, Moo-Shu Vegetables, Vegan cook-
ies and Pumpkin Pie.
Comments: Clean, friendly place. No MSG. No
animal products including dairy and eggs. Food
gets high ratings. Creative dishes. Has soybean
and wheat-gluten dishes.
Other Info: Full service, take-out. Non-smoking.
Reservations recommended. Accepts AMEX,
MC, VISA. Price: $.
Directions: Westheimer at Hillcroft. From I-610,
take exit #9A towards FM-1093/Westheimer Rd
and at Westheimer Rd turn right (go west) and
this place is 2½ miles down. This place is 7 miles
west of downtown Houston.

Whole Foods Market
11145 Westheimer, at Wilcrest
713-784-7776; **fax:** 713-954-3768
Hours: Daily 9 am to 10 pm
Natural Food Store and Cafe. Deli, Bakery, Salad
Bar and Juice Bar. Organic produce. Super-
market-type place. See Whole Foods Market
information.
Directions: From Sam Houston Tollway, take exit
towards Westheimer Rd/Richmond Ave, turn
right (go west) at Westheimer and this place is 1
mile down. This place is 8 miles west of down-
town Houston.

Whole Foods Market
6401 Woodway #149
713-789-4477; **fax:** 713-789-9419
Hours: Monday to Saturday 8 am to 10 pm
Sunday 9 am to 10 pm
Natural Food Store and Cafe. Deli, Bakery, Salad
Bar and Juice Bar. Organic produce. Super-
market-type place. See Whole Foods Market
information.
Directions: From I-610, take exit #10 towards
Woodway Dr/Memorial Dr, then take a slight
right (go west) onto Woodway Dr and this place
is 2¾ miles down on the left. This place is about
7 miles west of downtown Houston. From I-10,
take South Ross exit and go south 2 miles. At
Woodway turn left and this place on left.

Whole Foods Market
4004 Bellaire Boulevard, West University Place
713-667-4090; **fax:** 713-667-4013
Hours: Daily 9 am to 10 pm

Natural Food Store and Cafe. Deli, Bakery, Salad Bar and Juice Bar. Organic produce. Supermarket-type place. See Whole Foods Market information.
Directions: From I-610, take exit #6 towards Bellaire Blvd, turn left onto Bellaire Blvd and go 1 mile, at Weslayan St turn left and this place is near the corner. This place is 5 miles southwest of downtown Houston.

Whole Foods Market
2955 Kirby Drive
713-520-1937; **fax:** 713-520-0265
Hours: Monday to Saturday 8 am to 10 pm
Natural Food Store and Cafe. Deli, Bakery, Salad Bar and Juice Bar. Organic produce. Supermarket-type place. See Whole Foods Market information.
Directions: From I-45, take Rte 288/US 59 (exit #46B) and go southwest on US 59 for 2½ miles, take Kirby Drive exit, turn right (go north) at Kirby Dr and go a half-mile and this place is at junction with Steel St. This place is about 3 miles southwest of downtown Houston.

Ziggy's Health Grill
2320 West Alabama Street
713-527-8588, 713-527-8589
Hours: Monday to Friday 11 am to 9 pm
Saturday & Saturday 9 am to 9 pm
American Fast Food Restaurant. Not pure vegetarian.
Menu: Veggie burgers and quesadillas.
Comments: Has outdoor seating.
Other Info: Full service, take-out, delivery. Non-smoking. Accepts AMEX, DC, DIS, MC, VISA.

IRVING

**Sai Krishna
2836 O'Connor Road, at Rochelle Boulevard
972-257-9726
Hours: Sunday to Thursday 11:30 am to 3 pm, 6 pm to 9 pm
Friday & Saturday 11:30 am to 10 pm
Vegetarian Indian. Lunch Buffet.
Menu: Soups, Indian breads, rice dishes, Masala Dosas, Vegetable Curry, Curried Potatoes and Gulabjamun.
Comments: Small place. Pleasant atmosphere.
Other Info: Reservations recommended, especially on the weekends. Non-smoking. Price: $. Accepts AMEX, MC, VISA.
Directions: From I-35, take exit #433A and get on TX Hwy 183 going west for 5 miles, take

O'Connor Rd exit and merge onto W Airport Freeway, at N O'Connor Rd turn right and this place is a half-mile down. Has a parking lot. This place is about 8 miles northwest of downtown Dallas.

KERRVILLE

HEB Supermarket has organic produce.

Kerrville Health Foods
130-B West Main Street; 830-896-7383
Hours: Monday to Friday 9 am to 6 pm; Saturday 9:30 am to 5 pm; closed Sunday.
Natural Food Store. No produce.
Directions: From I-10, take Kerrville exit to Main St. This place is 2 blocks past HEB Supermarket.

LONGVIEW

Jack's Natural Food Store
1614 Judson Road; 903-753-4800
Hours: Monday to Friday 9 am to 6 pm; Saturday 9 am to 5 pm; closed Sunday.
Natural Food Store and Café. Deli and Juice Bar. No produce.
Directions: From I-20, take Rte 31 exit (#589) towards downtown Longview and go 6 miles, at US-80 turn right, then at TX Hwy 502 Spur turn left and this place is 1½ mile down. Or from I-20, take Estes Parkway exit north. Estes becomes High St, then Judson. This place on right about 7 miles down.

Jack's Natural Food Store
2199 Gilmer Road; 903-759-4262
Hours: Monday to Saturday 9 am to 6 pm
Deli Hours: 10:30 am to 3 pm
Closed Sunday.
Natural Food Store and Cafe. Deli and Juice Bar. Organic carrots only.
Other Info: Accepts AMEX, MC, VISA.
Directions: From I-20, take Hwy 259 north, then at Hwy 281 Loop turn left, then at Gilmer Rd (Hwy 300) turn left and this place is a third-mile down on right.

LUBBOCK

The Alternative Food Company
2611 Boston Avenue; 806-747-8740
Hours: Monday to Saturday 9 am to 6 pm
Closed Sunday.
Natural Food Store and Café. Juice Bar. Organic produce.

Menu: Has a good selection of vegetarian dishes.
Other Info: Accepts AMEX, MC, VISA.
Directions: From I-27, take 34th St exit and go west 1¼ mile. At Boston turn right and this place on right a half-mile down.

MCALLEN

Sun Harvest Farms (Wild Oats)
2008 North 10th Street
956-618-5388
Hours: Daily 8 am to 9 pm
Natural Food Store and Cafe. Deli, Bakery, Salad Bar and Juice Bar. Organic produce. Supermarket-type place. See Wild Oats Market information.
Directions: From US 83, go north on TX Hwy 336 (also becomes 10th St) and this place is 2½ miles down.

PLANO (Dallas suburb)

Akbar
301 West Parker Road, at Alma Drive, in Ruisseau Village
972-423-3007
Hours: Daily 11:30 am to 2:30 pm, 5:30 pm to 10 pm
Indian. Weekend Buffet. Vegan options. Not pure vegetarian.
Menu: Has a good selection of vegetarian dishes. Baigan Burtha (peas, carrots and onions in a curry sauce), salads, rice dishes, raita, naan bread and Gulabjamun.
Comments: Has a nice décor with a collection of Indian musical instruments. Has white tablecloths and fancy tableware.
Other Info: Non-smoking. Accepts AMEX, DC, DIS, MC, VISA. Price: $-$$
Directions: Has a parking lot.

Smoothie Factory
910 West Parker Road, Suite 170, at Alma Drive
972-398-1807
Hours: Monday to Friday 7 am to 9 pm; Saturday 8 am to 8 pm; Sunday 10 am to 6 pm
Smoothies Place.
Menu: Fresh juices and over 20 variety of smoothies. Smoothies can be made with sherbet or without it. Can be made with sugar or honey. Uses frozen fruits. Can add supplements such as herbs, Echinacea and others. Also sells supplements.
Other Info: Non-smoking. Price: $.
Directions: In a shopping center.

Whole Foods Market
2201 Preston Road, Suite C, Plano
972-612-6729; fax: 972-867-0414
Hours: Daily 8 am to 10 pm
Natural Food Store and Cafe. Deli, Bakery, Salad Bar and Juice Bar. Organic produce. Supermarket-type place. See Whole Foods Market information.
Directions: From I-635, take Preston exit north and go about eight miles and this place on left. From I-75, take Park exit and go west on Park about 5 miles. This place at junction of Park and Preston, across from Wal-Mart on northwest side of road. This place is 15 miles north of downtown Dallas.

RICHARDSON (Dallas suburb, 10 miles northeast)

Asia World Supermarket
400 North Greensville Avenue, at Belt Line Road
972-497-9356
Hours: Daily 9 am to 9 pm
Deli Hours: 9 am to 7 pm
Asian Market and Asian Deli.
Comments: Has a wide variety of fresh vegetables. Good prices. Has a large variety of Asian foods. Has tofu and soy products.
Other Info: Non-smoking. Accepts MC, VISA.

**Food for Thought
581 West Campbell Road; 972-889-3663
Web site: http://www.fftdallas.com/
Hours: Tuesday to Sunday 11:30 am to 2:30 pm, 6 pm to 10 pm; Friday to Sunday 11:30 am to 2:30 pm, 6 pm to 10:30 pm
Vegetarian North and South Indian. Lunch Buffet with over 30 dishes.
Menu: Samosas, pakoras, dosas, vegetables dishes, Mulligatawny Soup, Cream of Mushroom Soup and Rava Kichadi (cream of wheat and vegetables). Fresh juices, Mango Lassi and chai tea. No alcohol.
Comments: Good food. Service is not perfect. Pleasant décor.
Other Info: Full service, take-out, catering. Non-smoking. Reservations not accepted. Accepts AMEX, DC, DIS, MC, VISA. Price: $.
Directions: From US 75, take exit #26 towards Campbell Rd, then at E Collins Blvd turn right and go a quarter-mile, at Alma Rd turn left, then at E Collins Blvd turn left and go ¾ mile, at W Campbell Rd turn left and go 1 mile and this place is 1 block past Nantucket Drive. West of the freeway. In a nondescript shopping center. Has a parking lot.

**Gopal – Fine Indian Vegetarian Cuisine
758 South Central Expressway
972-437-0155
Vegetarian Indian. Lunch and Dinner Buffet.
Comments: Inside Continental Inn Motel.
Other Info: Full service, take-out. Price: $-$$.

***International Buddhist Progress Society
1111 International Parkway #300, 2nd floor (northwest corner of Arapaho & International)
972-907-0588
Hours: Monday to Friday 11:30 am to 1:30 pm
Saturday & Sunday 12 noon to 1:30 pm
Vegan Chinese Buddhist. Buffet.
Menu: Has a good selection of tofu and vegetable dishes.
Comments: Pleasant atmosphere. Has a nice temple on the 3rd floor. Gets good recommendations.
Other Info: Non-smoking. Accepts AMEX, DIS, MC, VISA. Price: $-$$.
Directions: From US-75, take exit #25 towards Arapaho Road, at Jackson St turn right and go two blocks, at N Greenville Ave turn left and go a half-mile, at E Arapaho Rd turn right and go 1 mile east, at International Pkwy turn left and this place is 1 block down. Has a parking lot.

Macro Broccoli
580 West Arapaho Road, Suite 406, at Hampshire, Richardson; 972-437-1985
Warning: I was not able to contact this place, but have included it because it is (or was) a good place.
Hours: Monday to Thursday and Saturday 11 am to 7 pm; Friday 11 am to 9 pm; Sunday Brunch 11 am to 2 pm
Natural Foods Restaurant. Japanese and American. Macrobiotic. Vegan and macrobiotic options. Mostly vegetarian (serves fish).
Menu: Over 100 items on the menu. Menu changes daily. Most of the dishes are vegan and macrobiotic. Two soups daily. Good Miso Soup, Indian Tofu Stew, Meatless Loaf, Cauliflower Fettuccine, "Salmon" Croquettes, brown rice, salads, Red Lentil Soup, Black Bean Stew, Lasagna, Chalupas, Vegetable Garbanzo Soup, vegetable pies, Blanched Vegetables with tofu dressing, pasta dishes, Chickpea Croquets, Broccoli Quiche, Vegetable Stew, steamed vegetables, Tofu Burgers, baked goods and other dishes. Carob Mousse Cake and Blueberry Cobblers. Free Bancha Tea with meals. No alcohol.
Comments: Rated as one of the better vegetarian restaurants in the US. Has two common tables.

Small place. Very casual. Reasonable prices. Good food. No eggs, sugar, artificial color or flavoring, yeast, dairy or preservatives. Basic décor. Friendly service. Mostly uses organic produce. Local organic produce used when possible. Sometimes has cooking classes. Has frozen main dishes to take home. Has literatures that you can read on vegetarianism and holistic medicine. Low-fat and low-sodium. Has free 30-minute macrobiotic consultations. Have fish, but it is cooked separately.
Other Info: Cafeteria style, buffet style, take-out. Non-smoking. Accepts MC, VISA. Price: $-$$.
Directions: From US 75, take Arapaho Rd exit (#25), then at Arapaho Rd turn left (go west) and go ¾ mile. In the back of Camelot Village and is hard to see from the street. Has a parking lot. This place is 12 miles northeast of downtown Dallas.

**Madras Pavilion
101 South Coit, #359, at Beltline; 972-671-3672
Web site: www.madras-pavilion.com
Hours: Monday to Friday 11:30 am to 3 pm, 6 pm to 10 pm
Saturday & Sunday 11:30 am to 10 pm
Vegetarian South Indian. Kosher. Lunch Buffet.
Menu: Has a popular daily lunch buffet until 3 pm. Lentil soup, naan, dal, vegetable dishes, sambar, samosa, Paneer Pakoras, Medhu Vada, rasam, uthappam and bonda. Desserts such as kulfi.
Comments: Good service. Has a private room for special events.
Other Info: Reservations not accepted. Non-smoking. Accepts AMEX, DIS, MC, VISA. Price: $-$$.
Directions: In the Dallas Metroplex at southwest corner of Beltline & Coit. From I-75, take Coit Rd exit (#8B), then go west on Coit Rd and this place is 2½ miles down. Has a parking lot.

Souper Salad
760 South Central Expressway, Richardson
972-699-7756
Hours: Monday to Saturday 10 am to 9 pm
Sunday 11 am to 8:30 pm
Soup and Salad Place. Not pure vegetarian.

**Suma Veggie Café
800 East Arapaho Drive, #120, at Bowser Road
972-889-8598
Hours: Monday to Friday 11 am to 2 pm, 5 pm to 9 pm; Saturday 12 noon to 9 pm; closed Sun.
Vegetarian Chinese. Pure Vegan. All-you-can-eat Lunch Buffet.

Menu: Has over 75 dishes on the menu. A variety of soups such as Hot & Sour Soup, Bean Curd with Cabbage, Vegetarian Chicken, Veggie Shrimp, Sweet & Sour Pork, Veggie lo Mein, Fried Rice, wontons, Eggplant Curry, Orange Chicken, Veggie Pork & Zucchini, Beef Fried Noodles, pasta, Veggie Ham, Curry Veggie Chicken, Kung Pao, veggie Sweet & Sour Chicken and Veggie Shrimp lo Mein. No alcohol.
Comments: Laid-back, casual family-run place. Ingredients are often organic. No MSG, eggs, animal products, artificial coloring, preservatives or dairy. Good food. Reasonable prices. Gets very good reviews. Has good-size portions. The lunch buffet is a real bargain. Sells frozen mock meats made from wheat gluten and mushrooms that can be brought home. Popular with the Dallas Vegetarian Lunch Group.
Other Info: Non-smoking. Accepts AMEX, DIS, MC, VISA. Price: $-$$.
Directions: From I-75, take Exit #26 Arapaho Rd, then go east on Arapaho Rd and this place is ¾ mile down at the corner of N Bowser Rd. Has a parking lot.

**Udipi Café

35 Richardson Heights Village, at Central Expressway and Spring Valley Court
Richardson (corner of Beltline and Central)
972-437-2858
Hours: Wednesday to Monday 11:30 am to 9:30 pm; closed Tuesday.
Vegetarian Indian. South Indian Restaurant. Lunch Buffet.
Menu: Gobi Manchurian, soups, dosas (over 10 varieties), palao rice dishes, rava masala dosa, sambar, coconut chutney, idly, dal, Lemon Rice, uthappam and vada. No alcohol.
Comments: This is a good place.
Other Info: Accepts MC, VISA. Price: $-$$.
Directions: From Central Exwy, take Exit #24 and this place is right next to the exit. Has a parking lot.

***Veggie Garden

516 West Arapaho Drive, #112; 972-479-0888
Hours: Monday to Friday 11:30 am to 2:30 pm, 5 pm to 9 pm; Sat & Sun 11 am to 9 pm
Pure Vegan Vegetarian Chinese. All-you-can-eat Lunch Buffet.
Menu: Eggless Eggrolls, spring rolls, Hot & Sour Soup, mock meat dishes (fish, chicken, pork, squid, beef & shrimp), rice and vegetables dishes, Fried Tempura lo Mein, brown rice, Tofu with Brown Sauce, Eggplant with Basil, Stir-fried Broc-

coli, Orange-flavored Shrimp and Stir-fried Vegetables. Fried ice cream (nondairy and dairy versions). No alcohol.
Comments: Friendly service. Good size portions. Good place. Nice atmosphere. No preservatives, MSG, food coloring, or animal products. Uses tofu, soy and TVP (textured vegetable protein). Good value lunch buffet.
Other Info: Non-smoking. Price: $-$$. Accepts MC, VISA.
Directions: From I-75, take Exit #26 Arapaho Rd, then go west on Arapaho Rd and this place is a half-mile down Has a parking lot.

Whole Foods Market

60 Dal-Rich Village, Coit & Belt Line
972-699-8075; **fax:** 972-699-9419
Hours: Daily 8 am to 10 pm
Natural Food Store and Cafe. Deli, Bakery, Salad Bar and Juice Bar. Organic produce. Supermarket-type place. See Whole Foods Market information.
Directions: From I-75, take Coit Rd exit (#8B), then go north on Coit Rd and this place is 2½ miles down. Or from I-75, take Beltline exit and go west and this place is on Coit Rd, about two miles down on the left.

SAN ANTONIO

Adelante

21 Brees Street; 210-822-7681
Hours: Tuesday to Saturday 11 am to 9 pm
Sunday 9 am to 2 pm
Tex-Mex. Health food. Not pure vegetarian.
Menu: Good vegetarian tamales with rice, beans and low sodium beans. Enchiladas (good spinach one), guacamole, tacos and Vegetable Combo Plate. No lard in the beans.
Comments: Does not use lard and red meat. Casual, popular place. Nice atmosphere. Gets good recommendations. Has good service. Interesting décor with hand-painted lamps. Has a good magazine rack. Good place for kids.
Other Info: No credit cards: only cash. Price: $.
Directions: In Alamo Heights off the Austin Highway.

Boardwalk Bistro

4011 Broadway, at Hildebrand, Alamo Heights
210-824-0100
Hours: Monday 11 am to 3 pm; Tuesday to Thursday 11 am to 10 pm; Friday & Saturday 11 am to 11 pm; closed Sunday.
International. French, Greek, Mediterranean,

Spanish, Mediterranean, American. Not pure vegetarian.
Menu: Has a large vegetarian menu. Garden Pizza, bagel, Grill Tofu Caesar (see warning below, ask take out), Veggie Burger, Vegetarian Lasagna and Prosciutto Wrapped Asparagus.
Comments: Has outdoor dining. Has live entertainment. Romantic spot.
Warning: There are anchovies in the Caesar salad.
Other Info: Accepts AMEX, DC, DIS, MC, VISA. Price: $$.
Directions: Parking arranged for customers.

Espuma Coffee & Tea Emporium
928 South Alamo Street, in the King William area, a little south of the downtown.
210-226-1912
Hours: Monday to Thursday 7 am to 7 pm; Friday 7 am to 12 midnight; Saturday 7 am to 10 pm; Sunday 8 am to 5 pm
Coffeehouse. Not pure vegetarian.
Menu: Has a selection of sandwiches. Grilled Veggie Pita Hummus Wrap with yogurt sauce. Mozzarella, tomato and pesto sandwich. Granitas is a coffee slush. Cappuccino, espresso.
Comments: Has live music on Friday. Displays local artists' work. Outdoor dining. Good atmosphere.
Other Info: Accepts MC, VISA. Price: $.
Directions: In the Riverside area.

Fiesta Patio Café
1421 Pat Booker Road; 210-658-5110
Hours: Monday to Thursday 11 am to 8:30 pm; Friday & Saturday 11 am to 9 pm; closed Sun.
Mexican Natural Foods. Vegan options. Not pure vegetarian.
Menu: Homemade salsa and tacos. Spanish style whole-grain brown rice.
Comments: Does not use lard in food. Uses peanut oil for cooking. Food does not contain MSG or artificial ingredients. Sells natural cheeses and alfalfa sprouts. Sometimes uses organic vegetables.
Other Info: Full service, take-out. Accepts AMEX, MC, VISA. Price: $.

Formosa Garden
1011 NE Loop 410, at Nagadoches
210-828-9988
Hours: Daily 11 am to 2:30 pm, 5 pm to 10 pm
Chinese. Not pure vegetarian.
Menu: Has a selection of vegetarian dishes. Most dishes can be made without meat.
Comments: One of the best Chinese places in San Antonio.
Other Info: Accepts AMEX, DIS, MC, VISA.

Gini's Homecooking & Bakery
7214 Blanco Street, just north of Loop 410
210-342-2768
Hours: Monday to Friday 7 am to 9 pm; Saturday 8 am to 9 pm; Sunday 9 am to 4 pm
Low-fat American. Natural Foods. Not pure vegetarian. Know for vegetarian meals.
Menu: Freshly baked bread, Vegetable Platter, Earth Burger, vegetarian soups and salads. Cookies, pies, fresh fruits and fresh juices.
Comments: Healthy food. Gets high recommendations.
Other Info: Full service, take-out. Non-smoking. Accepts AMEX, MC, VISA. Price: $-$$.
Directions: From I-410 Loop, take Blanco Rd exit (#19), then go north on Blanco Rd and this place is a half-mile north.

India Oven
1031 Patricia Drive, near the airport
210-366-1030; **Web site:** www.indiaoven.com
Hours: Daily 11 am to 2:30 pm, 5 pm to 10 pm
Indian. Vegan options. Not pure vegetarian.
Menu: Has a selection of vegetarian dishes. Eggplant & Potato, Aloo Mattar, Saag Paneer, Navratan Korma, Chickpea dish, Potato & Spinach and rice dishes. Has a vegetarian combination plate.
Comments: Plays authentic music.
Other Info: Full service, take-out, catering. Reservations not accepted. Accepts AMEX, DC, DIS, MC, VISA. Price: $$.
Directions: Parking arranged for customers.

Liberty Bar
328 East Josehpine Street
210-227-1187
Hours: Monday to Thursday 11:30 am to 10:30 pm; Friday & Saturday 11:30 am to 12 midnight; Sunday 10:30 am to 10:30 pm
American. Not pure vegetarian.
Menu: Has sandwiches, salads, pastas, Portobello Mushroom Sandwich, Zucchini Sandwich and more.
Comments: This place gets good reviews. Good food and service. Eclectic décor.
Other Info: Accepts AMEX, MC, VISA. Price: $$.

Simi's India Cuisine
4535 Fridericksburg Road, Suite 109
210-737-3166
Hours: Monday to Friday 11 am to 2:30 pm, 5:30 pm to 10 pm
Saturday & Sunday 12 noon to 3 pm, 5:30 pm to 10 pm

Northern Indian (Punjabi). Vegetarian-friendly. Vegan options. Has a good size lunch buffet. **Menu:** Saag Paneer (spinach and homemade cheese), samosas and Rasmalai (homemade cheese, cooked down milk & pistachios) and Pistachio Ice Cream. No alcohol.
Comments: Elegant décor. There is an Indian grocery next door. If you want your food spicy hot you may have to ask for it.
Other Info: Accepts AMEX, MC, VISA. Price: $$.
Directions: In a strip center across the street from Crossroads Mall.

Sun Harvest Farms (Wild Oats – Callaghan)
8101 Callaghan Road
210-979-8121; **fax:** 210-375-2093
Hours: Daily 8 am to 10 pm
Natural Food Store and Cafe. Deli, Bakery, Salad Bar and Juice Bar. Organic produce. Supermarket-type place. See Wild Oats Market information.
Directions: From I-10, take Callaghan Rd exit, then go on McDermott Frwy (US 87), then go east on Callaghan Rd and this place is 1 block down. This place is about 1 mile due north of where I-10 and I-410 Loop meet. This place is about 5 miles northwest of downtown San Antonio.

Sun Harvest Farms (Wild Oats – Nacogdoches)
2502 Nacogdoches Road
210-824-7800; **fax:** 210-820-0349
Hours: Daily 8 am to 9 pm
Natural Food Store and Cafe. Deli, Bakery, Salad Bar and Juice Bar. Organic produce. Supermarket-type place. See Wild Oats Market information.
Directions: From I-410 Loop, take Nacogdoches Rd exit (#23), then go north on Nacogdoches and this place is a quarter-mile down. This place is about 5 miles north of downtown San Antonio.

Sun Harvest Farms (Wild Oats – San Antonio)
17700 US Highway 281 N, #200
210-499-1446; 210-402-3191
Hours: Daily 8 am to 9 pm
Natural Food Store and Cafe. Deli, Bakery, Salad Bar and Juice Bar. Organic produce. Supermarket-type place. See Wild Oats Market information.
Directions: From TX-1604 Loop, go south on

San Pedro Ave and go ¾ mile, at Donella Dr turn left and go 1 block, then at San Pedro Ave turn left and this place is a third-mile down. This place is ¾ mile south of the intersection of Hwy 281 and TX-1604 Loop, about 10 miles due north of downtown San Antonio.

Thai Kitchen
445 McCarty Road; 210-344-8366
Hours: Monday to Saturday 11 am to 2:15 pm, 5 pm to 9:30 pm; closed Sunday.
Thai and Chinese. Not pure vegetarian.
Menu: Has a selection of vegetarian main dishes. Soups, appetizers, Hot & Sour Soup, noodle dishes, curry vegetables, Spring Rolls and Bean Curd.
Other Info: Full service, take-out. Accepts AMEX, DC, DIS, MC, VISA. Price: $-$$.

Twin Sisters Bakery & Café
124 Broadway Street, near the downtown
210-354-1559
Hours: Monday to Saturday 7 am to 3 pm
Closed Saturday & Sunday.
6322 North New Braunfels Avenue, in Alamo Heights; 210-822-0761
Hours: Monday to Saturday 7 am to 9 pm
Sunday 9 am to 2 pm
American, Mexican Natural Foods. Bakery & Deli. Macrobiotic and Vegan options. Vegetarian-friendly. Not pure vegetarian.
Menu: Has a good selection of vegetarian dishes. Baked goods, good soups, salads, pizzas, pastas, quesadillas, Avocado Sandwiches, Corn Tortillas and Mexican dishes. For breakfast has tacos and oatmeal. Fresh juices.
Comments: The owners call this place a "herbally influenced restaurant." Casual place. Has live music most Friday evenings. Mellow place.
Other Info: Full service, take-out, delivery. Accepts MC, VISA. Price: $-$$.

Viet-Nam Restaurant
3244 Broadway Street, at Mulberry Street
210-822-7461
Hours: Daily 11 am to 10 pm
Vietnamese. Not pure vegetarian.
Menu: Has a selection of vegetarian dishes. Can make most of the dishes without meat. Clay pot specials. Sweet jasmine tea.
Comments: Has outdoors dining. Popular place. Review of the place at http://theweeks.org
Other Info: Accepts AMEX, MC, VISA. Price: $.
Directions: North of the downtown in Alamo Heights

Volare Gourmet Pizza & Pasta

5054 Broadway Street, at Barilla Street
210-828-3354
Hours: Monday to Thursday 11 am to 2:30 pm,
4:30 pm to 10 pm; Fri to Sun 11 am to 10 pm
Italian and Pizza Restaurant. Not pure veg.
Menu: Has a selection of vegetarian dishes. Pizza
with artichoke hearts, zucchini, spinach, eggplant
and mushrooms. Sells individual slices of pizza.
Comments: Has an outdoor patio. Has only two
tables inside.
Other Info: Full service, take-out, delivery. Accepts AMEX, MC, VISA. Price: $.

Whole Foods Market

255 East Basse, Suite 130, in Alamo Heights
neighborhood
210-826-4676; fax: 210-930-3388
Hours: Daily 8 am to 10 pm
Natural Food Store and Cafe. Deli, Bakery,
Salad Bar and Juice Bar. Organic produce. Supermarket-type place. See Whole Foods Market
information.
Comments: Has an area where they do professional massage. Most likely has the best selection
of organic produce in the area.
Directions: From Hwy 281, take Jones
Maltsburger exit. This place is next to the exit on
the right in Quarry Market shopping center. This
place is about 5 miles north of downtown San
Antonio.

Zuni Grill

511 Riverwalk Street; 210-227-0864
Web site: banguets@joesfood.com
Hours: Sunday to Thursday 7:30 am to 9:30 pm;
Friday & Saturday 7:30 am to 10:30 pm
Southwestern American. Vegan options. Not pure
vegetarian.
Menu: Has vegan soups and several vegetarian
dishes. Pizza, Blue Corn Nachos, Spinach Salad,
Guacamole Salad and sandwiches.
Comments: Has indoor and outdoor seating.
Other Info: Full service, take-out, catering. Accepts AMEX, DIS, MC, VISA. Price: $$.
Directions: This place is one block from the San
Antonio Convention Center. It is in the middle
of the Riverwall Tourist area.

SOUTH PADRE ISLAND

Naturally's

5712 Padre Boulevard; 956-761-5332
Hours: Monday to Saturday 9:30 am to 5 pm
Sunday 11 am to 5 pm
Natural Foods International Deli. Juice Bar and
Salad Bar. Mostly Vegetarian. Organic produce.
Menu: Daily soups, a wide variety of salad items,
Vegetable Stew with injera bread, pastas, tofu hog
dogs, Chili Pie, Spinach Enchiladas, Polenta with
marinara sauce and tempeh burgers. Fresh juices.
Non-alcoholic beer.
Comments: Friendly place. Has vitamins and
grains.
Other Info: Full service, take-out. Price: $.
Directions: After crossing the bridge at Port Isabel,
turn right and go north on Padre Blvd and this
place is about 2 miles down.

WACO

Waco Health Foods

1424 Lake Air Drive; 254-772-5743
Hours: Tuesday to Saturday 9 am to 6 pm
Closed Sunday & Monday.
Natural Food Store.
Directions: From I-35, take Valley Mills Dr exit
west. At Lake Air Dr turn right and this place is
on the left.

WAXAHACHIE (DALLAS SUBURB)

Kirkpatrick's

207 South College Street; 972-937-0010
Natural Food Store.

WICHITA FALLS

Sunshine Natural Foods

2907 Bob Street; 940-767-2093
Hours: Monday to Friday 9 am to 6 pm; Saturday 10 am to 5:30 pm; closed Sunday.
Natural Food Store and Deli. Salad Bar.
Directions: From Hwy 281, take Kell Hwy (Hwy
82) and go 1½ mile, then take Kemp Blvd
exit and then this place is in the Parker Square
Shopping Center.

Utah

1. Alta
2. Cedar City
3. Draper
4. Holladay
5. Layton
6. Logan
7. Midvale
8. Moab
9. Murray
10. Ogden
11. Park City
12. Provo
13. Salt Lake City
14. Springdale
15. Torrey

ALTA

Shallow Shaft
Little Cottonwood Canyon, PO Box 8029
801-742-2177; **Web site:** www.shallowshaft.com
Hours: Daily in the summer 6 pm to 10 pm
Other times Thursday to Sunday 6 pm to 10 pm
Outside of the summer it is a good idea to call or
Check web site about opening hours.
Regional Northwest and Southwest. Slightly
vegetarian friendly. Not pure vegetarian.
Menu: Menu changes regularly. Has pastas,
Sautéed Mushroom Caps, salads, veggie pizzas and
vegetables dishes.
Comments: Local organic produce used when
possible. Dishes are mostly baked, sautéed in ol-
ive oil or broiled. Has got some good reviews in
newspapers and restaurant sites. Willing to work
with you.
Other Info: Accepts AMEX, MC, VISA. Price:
$$-$$$.

CEDAR CITY

Sunshine Health
111 West 535 South; 435-586-4889
Hours: Monday to Saturday 9 am to 6 pm
Closed Sunday.
Natural Food Store. Organic produce.
Directions: From I-15, take Rte 14 exit east. Then
at Main St go south and this place is on the right
in Renaissance Square.

DRAPER

Cowboy Grub
372 East 12300 S, Draper; 801-572-5566
Hours: Monday to Friday 11 am to 10 pm; Saturday 11 am to 11 pm; closed Sunday.
Tex-Mex Restaurant. Good Salad Bar. Bakery.
Menu: Steamed Veggie Plate, veggie sandwich,
sandwiches and salad items. Over 40 items in salad
bar (over half are fresh veggies). Homemade dressings. Has a children's menu.
Comments: Pleasant atmosphere and good service. Has a children's playroom and crayons at
the tables. Good value. Price: $$.
Directions: Take 12300 S Exit (#294), and go
east on E 12300 S and this place is a half-mile
down.

HOLLADAY

Great Harvest Bread Company
4667 South 2300 E; 801-277-3277
Hours: Daily 7 am to 6 pm
Bakery. Has a variety of breads made from whole
Montana red wheat. Stoneground at this place.

LAYTON

Great Harvest Bread Company
96 North Main; 801-543-0304
Bakery. Has a variety of breads made from whole
Montana red wheat. Stoneground at this place.

LOGAN

Angies
690 North Main; 435-752-9252
Hours: Sunday to Thursday 6 am to 10 pm
Friday & Saturday 6 am to 11 pm
American Family Restaurant. Vegan options. Not
pure vegetarian.
Menu: Has several vegetarian options including
a variety of wraps, Veggie Club Sandwich with
Avocado, Garden Burgers and Breakfast Veggie
Skillet.
Comments: Helpful and efficient place.
Directions: This place is on the main street in
town. It is at the corner of E 700 N on Hwy 91.

Shangri-La Health Foods
438½ North Main Street; 435-752-1315
Hours: Monday to Saturday 9 am to 6 pm
Closed Sunday.
Natural Food Store. Has books and appliances.
Directions: Take Hwy 91 south into Logan and
it becomes Main St. This place in Albertson's
shopping center, at junction of W 400 North
(Hwy 89) and Main St.

Straw Ibis Market and Café
52 Federal Avenue, between 1st & 2nd, run off
of Main Street; 435-753-4777
Hours: Monday to Saturday 6 am to 9 pm
Sunday 8 am to 6 pm
Natural Food Store and Café. Deli, Bakery and
Juice Bar.
Menu: Has a great selection of vegetarian dishes.
Quesadilla, Hummus Sandwich, Taco Loca (rice,
beans, vegetables), an assortment of wraps, soups
and a daily vegetarian special.
Comments: Friendly, helpful place. Best place in
town to eat.
Other Info: Counter service, take-out. Has seat-
ing. Accepts AMEX, MC, VISA.
Directions: This place on Federal, a half-block
east of Main St (Rte 89) and a half-block north
of Tabernacle Park, between W 100 N & W 200
N.

MIDVALE

Good Earth Natural Foods
7206 South 900 East; 801-562-2209
Hours: Monday to Saturday 9 am to 8 pm
Closed Sunday.
Natural Food Store. Organic produce.
Other Info: Accepts AMEX, MC, VISA.
Directions: From I-15, take W 7200 S exit, then

go east on W 7200, then at 900 East go east 2
miles. Then at S 900 E turn right and this place
is a quarter-mile down, on the west side of the
road. From I-215, take Exit #9, and go south on
Union Park Ave a half-mile and this place is at
Fort Union Blvd intersection.

MURRAY (Salt Lake City suburb)

Wasatch Broiler
4927 South State Street; 801-266-3311
Hours: Monday to Thursday 11 am to 9 pm; Fri
& Sat 11 am to 10 pm; Sun 11 am to 9 pm
American. Not pure vegetarian.
Menu: Has several vegetarian options including
Vegetable Pasta, Veggie Stir-fry Rice, pita bread
and green salads. Vegetables are steamed or grill,
and not fried.
Comments: Uses only fresh, low-fat ingredients,
with little salt and sugar. Modern decor.
Other Info: Full service, take-out. Accepts
AMEX, DIS, MC, VISA. Price: $.

OGDEN

**Bright Day Natural Foods
952 28th Street; 801-399-0260
Hours: Monday to Saturday 9:30 am to 6 pm
Closed Sunday.
Natural Foods Vegetarian Restaurant.
Menu: Has soups, salads, sandwiches and hot
main dishes.
Directions: This place is a half-mile north of 32nd
St, at Jackson Ave. From I-15, take Rte 79 E/31st
St exit (#344), then go east on 32nd St 1 mile, at
Wall Ave turn left and go a block, then at Patterson
St turn right and go a half-mile, at Washington
Blvd (Rte 89) turn left and go 1 block, at 30th St
turn right and go a half-mile, at Madison Ave
turn left and go a block, at Darling St turn right
and go 2 blocks, at Monroe Blvd turn left and go
2 blocks, at Kershaw St turn right and go 2 blocks,
at Quincy Ave turn left and go 1 block, at 28th
St turn right and go 1 block, at Fowler turn left
and this place is right there.

Down To Earth Natural Foods
5418 South 1900 West, Roy; 801-728-0234
Hours: Monday to Saturday 9 pm to 8 pm; deli
closes at 6 pm; closed Sunday.
Natural Food Store and Deli. Juice Bar. Organic
produce.
Menu: Pastas, salads, sandwiches, soups, tofu
dishes and hot dishes.
Other Info: Counter service, take-out.

Directions: From I-15, take Exit #346 and go west on Wilson Lane a half-mile, then at S 1900 W turn left.

Great Harvest Bread Company

272 Historic 25th Street   801-394-6800
4848 Harrison Boulevard   801-476-4605
Bakery. Has a variety of breads made from whole Montana red wheat. Stoneground at this place.

Harvest House Natural Foods

500 South State Street; 801-621-1627
Hours: Monday to Friday 9 am to 6:30 pm
Saturday 9 am to 5 pm
Restaurant Hours: 11:30 am to 4 pm
Closed Sunday.
Natural Food Store and Cafe. Deli and Juice Bar.
Menu: Has a decent selection of vegetarian dishes.
Other Info: Accepts AMEX, MC, VISA.
Directions: From coming from south on I-15, take UVSC exit (#272) and turn right. From coming from north, at exit ramp turn left and go east on W 1200 a quarter-mile, then bear right onto W 1300 S St and go 1½ mile, then at State St turn left heading north and this place is at junction of 500 South on the left 1½ miles down.

Main Street Pizza & Noodle

2388 North 4350 W, Ogden; 801-732-1940
Hours: Tuesday to Thursday 5 pm to 8 pm; Friday & Saturday 5 pm to 9 pm; closed Sunday and Monday
Italian, Pizza. Not pure vegetarian.
Menu: Has several vegetarian options including calzone, vegetarian pizzas, Focaccia Pizza (three cheeses, olive oil, fresh basil & tomatoes with no sauce), vegetarian gourmet pizzas, garlic bread, salads and vegetarian oriental stir-fry.
Comments: Fresh ingredients. Happening, comfortable place. Cool décor.
Other Info: Counter service, take-out. Order at counter, get a number and food is delivered to your table. Accepts AMEX, DIS, MC, VISA.
Price: $.
Directions: Across the street from Plain City Elementary.

PARK CITY

Evening Star Dining

268 Main Street; 435-649-5686
Hours: Daily 8 am to 430 pm, 5:30 pm to 11 pm
International. Not pure vegetarian.
Menu: Sautéed Vegetables, fresh baked breads,

Portobello Mushrooms, Vegetable Lasagna, pasta dishes, homemade Bean Burger and homemade desserts.
Comments: Often uses organic, healthy ingredients. Creative dishes. This place becomes Morning Ray Cafe for breakfast & lunch. See above.
Other Info: Non-smoking. Accepts AMEX, MC, VISA. Price: $$.
Directions: This place is on the main street of town.

Fairweather Natural Foods

1270 Ironhorse (just off Bonanza); 435-649-4561
Hours: Monday to Friday 9 am to 7 pm; Saturday 10 am to 6 pm; Sunday 12 am to 6 pm
Natural Food Store and Deli. Organic produce.
Menu: Organic soups, salads and sandwiches.
Comments: Groceries, herbs, supplements and body care items.
Other Info: Accepts DIS, MC, VISA.
Directions: From I-80, take Hwy 224 exit toward Park City Ski Area. Go 5 miles and at Iron Horse Drive turn left, then turn into the last driveway on left.

Leger's Produce

1351 Kearns; 435-649-5678
Hours: Daily 8:30 am to 3:30 pm
Sandwich Deli Place. Not pure vegetarian.
Menu: Veggie sandwiches with Haas avocados, lettuce, tomatoes, sprouts and cheese.
Comments: Specializes in huge sandwiches. A half sandwich is about the size of a full sandwich in a normal restaurant. Can call in an order and it will be ready when you arrive.
Other Info: Counter service, mainly take-out. Price: $.

Main Street Pizza & Noodle

530 Main Street
435-645-8878
Hours: Sunday to Thursday 11:30 am to 10:30 pm; Friday & Saturday 11:30 am to 11:30 pm
Italian, Pizza. Not pure vegetarian.
Menu: Has several vegetarian options including calzone, vegetarian pizzas, Focaccia Pizza (three cheeses, olive oil, fresh basil and tomatoes with no sauce), gourmet vegetarian pizzas, garlic bread, salads and vegetarian Oriental Stir-fry.
Comments: Fresh ingredients. Happening, comfortable place. Cool décor.
Other Info: Counter service, take-out. Order at counter, get a number and food is delivered to your table. Accepts AMEX, DIS, MC, VISA.
Price: $.

Morning Ray Café
268 Main Street
435-649-5686
Web site: www.themorningray.com
Hours: Sunday to Wednesday 8 am to 10 pm
Thursday to Saturday 7 am to 2 am
Coffee Shop and Dinner place at night. Mostly organic and vegetarian. Not pure vegetarian.
Menu: Homemade granolas, bagels (gets bagels from excellent H&H Bagels in New York), Bean Burger, Home Fries, veggie sandwich, breads, Falafel Plate, veggie Reuben and desserts. Coffee, espresso.
Comments: Organic ingredients used whenever possible. Becomes Evening Star Dining for dinner. Popular with the locals. Service can be slow.
Other Info: Full service, take-out, bakery counter. Price: $ for lunch, $$ for dinner.
Directions: This place is on the main street in town.

Nacho Mama's
1821 Sidewinder Drive, in Prospector Square
435-645-8226
Hours: Daily 5 pm to 10 pm (sometimes to 12 midnight)
Mexican, Southwestern. Not pure vegetarian.
Menu: Spinach Enchiladas (with spinach, peppers and cream cheese), Cheese Enchiladas, Vegetarian Burritos, cheese quesadillas, tacos, enchiladas, tostadas and salads.
Comments: Vegetarian-based sauces. Popular with the locals. Can be very busy during the skiing season. Veggie burrito is a bargain. Has pool and foosball tables.
Other Info: Accepts AMEX, DIS, MC, VISA. Price: $-$$.

PROVO

Bombay House
463 North University Avenue; 801-373-6677
Hours: Monday to Saturday 4 pm to 10:30 pm
Closed Sundays.
Indian. Not pure vegetarian.
Menu: Has a wide variety of vegetarian dishes such as samosa, rice dishes, curry dishes, and naan. For desserts there is Kulfi and Gulabjamun. Mango lassi.
Comments: Food gets great ratings from customers. Excellent, friendly and attentive service. Authentic music.
Other Info: Full service, take-out. Accepts AMEX, DC, MC, VISA.

Good Earth Natural Foods & Café
1045 South University Avenue
801-375-7444
Hours: Monday to Saturday 9 am to 8 pm
Closed Sunday.
Natural Food Store. Organic produce. Has good selection of organic produce, bulk foods and other items. Price: $.
Directions: This place is in south Provo. S University Ave is Hwy 189. From I-15, take exit for Hwy 189 (#266), then go north on Hwy 189 (University Ave) and this place is one mile down.

SALT LAKE CITY

Bangkok Thai
1400 South Foothill Drive, #210
801-582-THAI (8424)
Web site: www.bangkokthai.com
Hours: Monday to Thursday 11:30 am to 2:30 pm, 5 pm to 9:30 pm; Friday 11:30 am to 2:30 pm, 5 pm to 10 pm; Saturday 12 pm to 10 pm; Sunday 5 pm to 9 pm
Thai. Vegan options. Not Full Vegetarian.
Menu: Has a separate vegetarian menu with over 40 dishes. Seasonal Eggplant or Squash, Gang ka Ree, Chef's Special Tofu, Bangkok Thai Fried Rice Noodles, Lemon Grass Stir-fry, Kao Pad Ga Prow, Lad Nar Noodles and Pad Tofu. Woon Sen Kai has eggs in it.
Comments: Many of the dishes on the menu can be made vegetarian or vegan on request. Uses vegetable stock in the soups. Can be a bit crowded, so you may have to wait for a seat. On "Meatless Mondays" all vegetarian entrees at discount prices. Should make it clear when ordering that you want vegetarian food. Has exotic oriental style décor. Flowers, plants, tapestries, antiques and sculptures. Seats 100. Relaxed place. Good place for a special event. Has outdoors seating on the balcony. Offer discount coupons on their web site. Has gotten a good rating in Zagat Guide and won various awards for best Thai and Asian food in Salt Lake City. Has won awards for best vegetarian food in Utah.
Other Info: Full service, take-out, catering. Reservations suggested. Non-smoking. Accepts AMEX, DC, DIS, MC, VISA. Price: $$.
Directions: From downtown take E 400 South Road going east, then get on E 500 South St, then get on Foothill Dr (Rte 186) going southeast and this place is ¾ mile down on the second floor of Foothill Village. This place is 4 miles east of the main downtown area.

Bombay House

1615 Foothill Drive; 801-581-0222
Hours: Monday to Saturday 4 pm to 10 pm
Closed Sunday.
Indian. Not pure vegetarian. Indian food store
next door.
Menu: Has a large variety of vegetarian dishes
including a variety of rice dishes, Indian breads,
Naans, Saag Panir, Aloo Mattar and curry dishes.
Mango lassi and rose milk. Non-alcoholic beer
and wine.
Comments: Gets high recommendations for hav-
ing really good food. It seems like most people
enjoy it. Romantic, elegant place. Has nice paint-
ings on the walls. Has a large aquarium with exotic fish. Popular place. One of the best places in
the Salt Lake City for Indian food.
Other Info: Full service, take-out. Reservations
suggested for groups. Accepts AMEX, DC, DIS,
MC, VISA. Price: $-$$.
Directions: In Lamplighter Square.

Cedar's of Lebanon

152 East 200 South; 801-364-4096
Web site: http://cedarsoflebanon.citysearch.com/
Hours: Monday to Thursday 11:30 am to 10 pm;
Friday 11:30 am to 11 pm
Saturday 12 noon to 3 pm, 5:30 pm to 11 pm;
Sunday 12 noon to 3 pm, 5 pm to 11 pm
Middle Eastern, Lebanese. Not pure vegetarian.
All-you-can-eat Buffet.
Menu: Has several vegetarian options including
stuffed grape leaves, several salads, couscous,
hummus, falafel, tabbouleh, baba ghanouj,
mousaka and more. Cheese Beurek is feta cheese
with phyllo dough, rice and a choice of salad or
soup.
Comments: All-you-can-eat lunch buffet with a
good selection of vegetarian dishes. Nice Arabian
carpets. Live music and belly dancing on Friday
and Saturday nights. Does not use canned vegetables. Does not deep-fry anything. Uses olive
oil and sesame seed oil. Casual place. Not high
on décor.
Other Info: Full service, take-out, catering. Private room for parties. Accepts AMEX, DC, DIS,
MC, VISA. Price: $-$$.

Cowboy Grub

2350½ Foothill Drive; 801-466-8334
Hours: Monday to Thursday 11 am to 10 pm;
Friday & Saturday 8 am to 11 pm; closed Sun.
Tex-Mex Restaurant. Good Salad Bar. In-house
bakery.
Menu: Steamed Veggie Plate, veggie sandwich,

sandwiches and over 40 items in salad bar (over
half are fresh veggies). Homemade dressings. Has
a children's menu.
Comments: Pleasant atmosphere and good service. Has a children's playroom and crayons at
the tables. Good value.
Other Info: Accepts AMEX, DIS, MC, VISA.
Price: $$.
Directions: From I-80, take Exit #130, then go
northwest on Foothill Dr (Rte 186) and this place
is about ¾ mile down. Right behind K-Mart.

***Evergreen House

755 South State Street; 801-328-8889
Hours: Monday to Saturday 12 noon to 9 pm
Closed Sundays.
Fully Vegan Chinese.
Menu: Serves good tasting Chinese mock meat
dishes. All entrées, soups and desserts are vegan
(except fortune cookies). Spring Rolls, Curry Po-
tato, Mock Chicken (very good), Black Pepper
Soy Bean (good) and udon & rice noodle dishes.
The special Golden Nuggets gets bad rating from
some.
Comments: Run by a very pleasant, hard-work-
ing woman known as Ms Tuo. This Chinese res-
taurant scores low on atmosphere but high on
taste and value. No alcohol.
Warnings: The fortune cookies usually contain
egg.
Other Info: Full table service, take-out.
Directions: In a strip mall on State Street. From
I-80, take Exit #310 and go 1 mile east on W
600 S, then at S State St turn left and this place is
1½ block down, across from Sears.

Free Wheeler Pizza

1624 South 1100 E	801-486-3748
853 East 400 S	801-322-3733

Hours: Monday to Thursday 11 am to 11:30 pm;
Fri & Sat 11 am to 1 am; Sun 11 am to 11 pm
Pizza. Not pure vegetarian.
Menu: Some special vegetarian toppings are pea-
nuts, broccoli, red peppers, almonds, zucchini,
spinach, walnuts, pesto and almonds. Whole-
wheat, sourdough crusts.
Comments: Pizzas get mixed opinions; some
people love them and other hate them.
Other Info: Full service, take-out, delivery. Ac-
cepts AMEX, DIS, MC, VISA. Price: $-$$.

Great Harvest Bread Company

5592 South Redwood Road	801-966-9699
905 East 900 S	801-328-2323
3414 Bengal Boulevard	801-944-1744

Bakery.

Menu: Good varieties of breads made from stone-ground (on premises) 100% whole Montana red wheat.

Guru's

912 East 900 S; 801-355-4878

Hours: Monday to Thursday 11 am to 10 pm; Friday & Saturday 11 am to 11 pm; closed Sunday.

American, Asian, Health Food. Not pure veg.

Menu: Salads, pastas, rice dishes, burritos, pasta and tacos. No alcohol or coffee.

Comments: Very popular place with various classes of people. Food gets really high rating. Outdoor dinning and sidewalk café. Popular with locals. Has TVs hanging from the ceiling with images of nature with no sound. Good service, food and atmosphere. Good selection of dishes. Reasonably priced. Good for people on a budget.

Other Info: Counter service, take-out. Order meal at counter and a server brings it to you. Price: $.

Directions: This place is a half-block west of Washington Square Park in the middle of the downtown area. From I-15, take Exit #309 and go east on E 900 S for 2 miles and this place is near the junction of E 900 S and S 900 E.

India Unlimited

1615 South Foothill Drive; 801-583-3300

Hours: Monday to Thursday 11 am to 8 pm; Friday & Saturday 11 am to 8:30 pm; closed Sunday.

Indian Grocery Store. Good gourmet store.

Comments: Spices, Maharishi Ayurvedic products, chutneys, pickles, condiments and classical Indian music tapes & CD's. Cooking classes. Friendly, helpful staff.

Directions: North side of Lamplighter Square.

Koko Kitchen

702 South 300 E; 801-364-4888

Hours: Monday to Friday 11 am to 8 pm; Saturday 11:30 am to 8 pm; closed Sunday.

Japanese. Vegan options. Not pure vegetarian.

Menu: Authentic Japanese food. Has several vegetarian and vegan dishes. Vegetables over Rice, steamed vegetables and noodle salad.

Comments: Gets really high ratings. Most people enjoy this place. Outdoor dining in the backyard. Sidewalk Café. Small, popular place. Friendly, excellent service.

Other Info: Counter service, take-out, delivery (up to 3 pm for orders of at least $20), catering. Place order and they call your name when ready.

Accepts AMEX, DIS, MC, VISA. Price: $-$$.

Directions: This place is in the center of town. From I-15, take exit #310 and go east on E 600 S about 1½ mile, then turn right at S 300 E and this place is one block down.

Long Life Vegi House

1353 East 3300 S; 801-467-1111

Hours: Monday to Thursday 11:30 am to 9:30 pm; Friday to Saturday 11:30 am to 10:30 pm; Sunday 5 pm to 9:30 pm

Mainly Vegetarian Chinese and also Vietnamese, American. Vegan options. Serves shrimp dishes.

Menu: Makes mock "meat" dish from soy products and wheat gluten. Good Spring Rolls, Lemon & Cashew Chicken, Eggplant with Spicy Garlic Sauce, Sweet & Sour Pork, Vegetarian Kung Pao Chicken and pot stickers. The Garlic Eggplant and Asparagus dish is good. Non-alcoholic beer.

Comments: Food get high recommendations. No MSG. Has another branch in California. Relaxed, casual atmosphere. First-class service.

Other Info: Full service, take-out. Accepts MC, VISA. Price: $$.

Directions: From I-15, take Exit #306, then go east about 2 miles on E 3300 S and this place is a half-block past S 1300 E.

Oasis Café

151 South 500 East; 801-322-0404

Hours: Monday to Thursday 7 am to 9 pm; Friday 7 am to 9:30 pm; Saturday 8 am to pm; Sunday 8 am to 9 pm

Vegetarian-friendly American & Middle Eastern, also International. Not pure vegetarian (serves seafood). Everything can be made vegetarian.

Menu: Homemade granola, Eggplant Ravioli, Portobello Mushroom Rueben, salads, sandwiches, Roasted Vegetables and hummus. Fresh juices.

Comments: Pleasant, comfortable, relaxed setting. Gets great reviews from the newspapers and customers. "Best Patio Dining" City Weekly. "Best Vegetarian" & "Best Weekend Brunch" Salt Lake Magazine. Has dining in a courtyard, which has a small fountain in the center. Street-side sitting. Has fireplaces. Vegan dishes are marked on the menu. Excellent, friendly, efficient service. Good music and nice décor. Sometimes has live music. Has the excellent Golden Braid bookstore (worth checking out) next to it.

Other Info: Full service, take-out, catering. Non-smoking. Reservations not necessary. Accepts

AMEX, MC, VISA. Price: $$$.
Directions: This place is in the center Salt Lake City. From I-15, take Exit #311 and then go east on E South Tampa for about 1½ mile. At S 500 E turn right and this place is 1½ block down.

***Sage's Café
473 East Broadway; 801-322-3790; **Email:** ian@ sagescafe.com; **Web site:** www.sagescafe.com
Hours: Wednesday to Friday 11 am to 10 pm; Saturday & Sunday 9 am to 11 pm; breakfast served until 5 pm; Lunch Buffet Monday to Friday 11 am to 4 pm
Fully Vegan Gourmet. Mostly organic. About 50% organic in the winter and 80% organic in the summer.
Menu: Vegan Philly "Cheese Steak," hummus, nachos, Seasoned Potato Wedges, Soup of the Day, Sautéed Spinach Salad, Oriental Soba Salad, burritos, Spicy Black Bean Burger, Tempeh Fillets, pastas, Steamed Vegetable Plate, Raw Plate, sandwiches and a daily special. Serves good breakfasts that include home-style hash browns, Tofu Scramble, French Toast (dipped in tofu batter), veggie sausage and breakfast burritos. Delicious desserts such as cookies, cakes, pies and soy ice cream. Fruit smoothies, soy shakes, soy milk, soy floats, chai and espresso. Makes own root-beer and gingerale.
Comments: Good, reasonably priced food. Unique décor. Fast service. Cozy, comfortable, friendly place. Environmentally conscious and recycles when possible. Turns waste into compost in community gardens. Offers a discount to bring own containers for take-out dishes. Uses fresh and organic produce when possible. If you fill out their online survey you can get 25% off your next meal. Has plenty of natural light and greenery.
Specials: Brunch on the weekends. Wednesday 6 pm to 10 pm is all-you-can-eat pizza night. Thursday night is a five-course International meal.
Coupon: Can print a coupon from their Web site to get a house-brewed rootbeer, ginger beer or 100% fresh squeezed lemonade with a purchase of a sandwich, large salad or entrée.
Other Info: Full service, catering and take-out. Non-smoking. Does not take reservations. Accepts AMEX, MC, VISA, Personal Cheques. Price: $-$$.
Directions: In the heart of downtown Salt Lake City (near corner of 500 E 300 S). From I-15, take Exit #311 and go east on W 200 S into town, then at S 500 E turn right and go one block, then turn right at E Broadway and this place is near the corner. Street parking.

Star of India
177 East 200 South; 801-363-7555
Hours: Monday to Thursday 11:30 am to 2:30 pm, 5:30 pm to 10 pm; Friday & Saturday 11:30 am to 10:30 pm; Sunday 2 pm to 10 pm
North Indian, Tandoori. Has an inexpensive lunch buffet. Not pure vegetarian.
Other Info: Full service, take-out. Accepts AMEX, DC, DIS, MC, VISA. Price: $-$$.

Wild Oats Community Market
1131 EWilmington Ave, at 2250S
801-359-7913
Hours: Monday to Saturday 8 am to 10 pm Sunday 10 am to 8 pm
Directions: From I-80, take 700 E (7th) exit. Go east and this place is on the right. Going west, turn left and go under overpass and this place on right.
645 East 400 S; 801-355-7401
Hours: Monday to Saturday. 8 am to 10 pm Sunday 10 am to 9 pm
Natural Food Store and Cafe. Deli, Bakery, Salad Bar and Juice Bar. Organic produce. Supermarket-type place. See Wild Oats Market information.

SPRINGDALE (Zion National Park Area)

Zion Pizza & Noodles
Zion National Park Town Center; 435-772-3815
Summer Hours: Daily 4 pm to 10 pm
Winter Hours: Daily 4 pm to 9 pm
Italian. Not pure vegetarian.
Menu: Several types of vegetarian pizzas and stir-fry pastas with vegetables.
Other Info: Full service, take-out. Cash only; no credit cards. Price: $$.

TORREY

Capitol Reef Café
360 West Main Street
801-425-3271
Hours: Daily 7 am to 9 pm
Closed for winter.
Natural Foods. Not pure vegetarian.
Menu: Has a good selection of vegetarian dishes that include salads, sandwiches, Mushroom Lasagna, pastas, Stir-fry Vegetables and other dishes. Fresh juices, cappuccino, espresso.
Comments: It is next to an Inn, a few miles from Capitol Reef Natural Park.
Other Info: Full service, take-out. Price: $$.
Directions: On east side of town.

Vermont

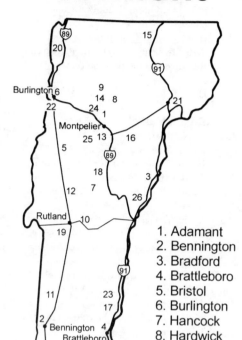

9. Johnson
10. Killington
11. Manchester
12. Middlebury
13. Montpelier
14. Morrisville
15. Newport
16. Plainfield
17. Putney
18. Randolph
1. Adamant   19. Rutland
2. Bennington   20. Saint Albans
3. Bradford   21. Saint Johnsbury
4. Brattleboro   22. South Burlington
5. Bristol   23. Springfield
6. Burlington   24. Stowe
7. Hancock   25. Waitsfield
8. Hardwick   26. White River Junction

ADAMANT

Adamant Co-op
Center Road; 802-223-5760
Hours: Monday to Friday 9:30 am to 6 pm; Saturday 10 am to 3 pm; Sunday 10 am to 1 pm
Natural Food Store. Organic produce.
Other Info: Accepts MC, VISA.
Directions: Coming into Adamant from Montpelier, at fork go right onto Center Rd. Go 5 miles and this place is in Adamant at crossroad on the right.

BENNINGTON

Blue Benn Diner
102 Hunt Street; 802-442-5140
Hours: Monday & Tuesday 6 am to 5 pm; Wednesday to Friday 6 am to 8 pm; Saturday 6 am to 4:30 pm; Sunday 7 am to 4 pm
American and Mexican Food. Not pure veg.
Menu: Some vegetarian dishes including salads and quiche.

Comments: Diner car restaurant. Reasonably priced. Good desserts.
Other Info: Full service, take-out. Non-smoking. Cash only. **Price:** $.

Spice & Nice
223 North Street; 802-442-8365
Hours: Monday to Saturday 9 am to 5:30 pm Sunday 11 am to 4 pm
Natural Food Store. Organic produce.
Directions: This place is on Rte 7 (North St), about a half-mile north of the junction of Rte 9 and Rte 7, the center of Bennington.

BRADFORD

South End Market
South Main Street, next to library
802-222-5701
Hours: Monday to Saturday 8 am to 6 pm Closed Sunday.
Natural Food Store. Organic produce.
Directions: From I-91, take Bradford exit (#16)

and go west (north on Rte 25) about a half-mile. Then turn left at 25B and after entering Bradford Village, at 25B turn left and this place on left.

BRATTLEBORO (southeastern Vermont, just over the Massachusetts and New Hampshire borders)

Brattleboro Food Coop
2 Main Street
802-257-1841
email: preorder@sover.net
Web site: www.brattleborofoodcoop.com
Hours: Monday to Saturday 8 am to 9 pm
Sunday 9 am to 9 pm
Food Store Store and Café. Deli, Bakery, Salad Bar and Juice Bar. Organic produce and bulk food.
Menu: Salad items, soups, ready-made salads and main dishes. Fresh juices and smoothies.
Comments: A big place with a good selection of items. Has an excellent deli section.
Other Info: Counter service, take-out. Seating in the café.
Directions: From I-91, take exit #1, then turn right (or left if you are southbound) onto Canal Street (Rte 5, becomes Main Street). This place is a mile northeast, on the left at intersection, in the Brookside Shopping Plaza.

**Common Ground
25 Elliot Street
802-257-0855
Summer Hours: Daily 11 am to 2 pm, 5 pm to 9 pm; Winter Hours: Monday to Saturday 5 pm to 9 pm; Sunday Brunch 11 am to 2 pm
Fully Vegetarian International Restaurant. Vegan friendly. Mexican, American. Vegan options. Completely organic produce. Serve eggs during Sunday brunch, but not on other days
Menu: Seitan sandwiches, soups, Miso, veggie burger, burritos, salads, Cashew Burger (recommended), Seaweed Salad and stir-fries. Fresh juices.
Comments: Cooperative restaurant owned by the workers. Has a good variety of vegetarian meals. First-class service. Open since the early seventies. In the evening there is dancing with various bands. Uses organic foods and local produce. Very friendly, helpful people. Recommended.
Other Info: Full service, take-out. Non-smoking. Reservations not necessary. No credit cards; cash only. Price: $-$$.
Directions: From I-91, take exit #1, then turn right (or left if you are southbound) onto Canal Street (Rte 5, becomes Main Street) and go a mile

northeast into town. When the road turns left (a block from the river) go two blocks, then at Elliot St turn left and this place is on the left 100 yards down.

Northeast Cooperatives, Inc
PO 8188, Quinn Road, Brattleboro, VT 05304
802-257-5856; fax: 802-257-7039
email: necoop@northeastcoop.com
Web site: http://www.northeastcoop.com
Resource and distribution center.

BRISTOL

Bristol Market
28 North Street
802-453-2448
Hours: Monday to Saturday 9 am to 7 pm
Sunday 10 am to 6 pm
Natural Food Store and Deli. Bakery and Juice Bar.
Menu: Vegetarian Lasagna, an assortment of sandwiches, seitan and tempeh dishes, Eggless Egg Salad, hummus, Sautee Vegetables, salads, soups and much more.
Comments: Friendly, helpful people.
Other Info: Accepts MC, VISA.
Directions: Has a good selection in the deli. On north side of street, a block from the main intersection in town.

BURLINGTON

**Healthy Living
4 Market Street
802-863-2569
Hours: Daily 8 am to 8 pm
Sunday Brunch 9 am to 1 pm
Natural Food Store and Vegetarian Deli. Salad Bar. Good selection of organic produce.
Menu: Has a good selection of vegetarian dishes. Scrambled Tofu and vegan pancakes for Sunday brunch. Sandwiches, salads, soups, veggie Lasagna and veggie chili.
Comments: Good service. From Monday to Saturday the hot deli bar is fully vegetarian and mostly vegan. On Sunday during the brunch there are some real meat items.
Directions: Conveniently located in the downtown. From I-89, take Exit #14 (S Burlington). Then go west on Rte 2 (follow signs to downtown Burlington). After a mile take a slight left (follow road) onto Main Street. Go another mile and this place is on left, at the first street past the Barnes & Noble.

India House Restaurant
207 Colchester Avenue
802-862-7800
Hours: Sunday to Thursday 11:30 am to 2:30 pm, 5 pm to 9 pm; Friday and Saturday 11:30 am to 2:30 pm, 5 pm to 10 pm
Indian. Not pure vegetarian. Vegetarian options.
Other Info: Full service, take-out. Reservations suggested for groups. Non-smoking. Accepts AMEX, DC, MC, VISA. Price: $$.

Onion River Coop
82 South Winooski Avenue; 802-863-3659
email: orc@together.net
Web site: www.onionriver.org
Hours: Daily 9 am to 9 pm
Natural Food Store and Cooperative. Deli. Excellent selection of organic produce.
Menu: Has a wide selection of vegetarian dishes.
Other Info: Accepts DIS, MC, VISA.
Directions: From I-89, take Exit #14 (S Burlington). Then go west on Rte 2 (follow signs to downtown Burlington).

HANCOCK

Sweet Onion Inn
Route 100, PO Box 66; 802-767-3734, 800-897-6490: **email:** sweeto@madriver.com
Web site: www.sweetonioninn.com
Bed & Breakfast. Fully Vegetarian Breakfasts and Dinners.
Comments: Rooms with bath with breakfast and dinner are $135. Has nearby hiking trails and waterfalls. Located in the Green Mountains.

HARDWICK

Buffalo Mountain Co-op
14 North Main Street (Rte 15); 802-472-6020
Hours: Monday to Thursday, Saturday 9 am to 6 pm; Friday 10 am to 7 pm; Sunday 10 am to 3 pm
Natural Food Store. Organic produce.
Comments: Sometimes has soups and sandwiches.
Other Info: Accepts MC, VISA.
Directions: This place in on east side of the main street in downtown Hardwick.

JOHNSON

Roo's Natural Foods
Main Street; 802-635-1788
Hours: Monday to Friday 10 am to 5:30 pm;

Saturday 11 am to 4 pm; closed Sunday.
Natural Food Store. Organic produce.
Comments: The French Press Café, in the same building, serves sandwiches and salads.
Other Info: Cash only; no credit cards.
Directions: This place in the same building as the French Press Café. In the center of town in a large yellow house, a block from Grand Union.

KILLINGTON

Hemingway's
Route 4, PO Box 337; 802-422-3886
Hours: Tuesday to Sunday 6 pm to 10 pm
Closed Monday.
New American, Italian, French. Good vegetarian options. Not pure vegetarian.
Menu: Has a set four-course vegetarian meal. The meal changes regularly. An example meal is Asparagus Flan with Tomato Fondue, Vegetable Strudel, Wild Mushroom Risotto, grilled vegetables, Leek Flan, crepes, Sushi Rolls, fresh fruit soup and many more vegetarian options.
Comments: In a nicely designed 19th century mansion. Good, romantic atmosphere. Voted to be one of the top 25 restaurants in the country by Food & Wine magazine. In a beautiful location at the food of Killington mountain. Has a garden view. Chandeliers, artwork, fireplace. Has several dining rooms. Good place for a special event. Can get vegan, low-fat and wheat-free meals, but you should call in advance for special needs.
Other Info: Reservations suggested on weekends. Full service. Reservations suggested. Non-smoking. Accepts AMEX, MC, VISA. Price: $$$-$$$$. $50 for a vegetarian meal.

MANCHESTER

Bagel Works
Routes 11 & 30; 802-362-5082
Hours: Monday to Thursday 6 am to 5 pm
Friday to Sunday 6 am to 6 pm
Bagel Deli. Vegan options. Not pure vegetarian.
Menu: Over 15 varieties of bagels. Toppings include tofutti spread, cream cheese and salads. Vegan soups. Uses all natural ingredients that don't contain preservatives. Fresh juices.
Other Info: Counter service, take-out. Cash only; no credit cards. Price: $.

Village Fare
Union Street; 802-362-2544
Hours: Tuesday to Sunday

Closed Monday.
Gourmet Café. Not pure vegetarian.
Menu: Has vegetarian soups, salads, sandwiches and main dishes. Order at counter.

MIDDLEBURY

Middlebury Natural Foods Co-op
1 Washington Street; 802-388-7276
Hours: Monday to Saturday 8 am to 7 pm
Sunday 9 am to 5 pm
Natural Food Store. Organic produce.
Other Info: Accepts AMEX, MC, VISA.
Directions: From Rte 7, at traffic circle go east on Washington and this place on left.

Nature's Market
303 Center Hill Road; 802-362-0033
Hours: Monday to Saturday 11 am to 6 pm
Sunday 11 am to 5 pm
Natural Food Store. Organic produce.
Other Info: Accepts MC, VISA.

New Morning Natural Foods
Route 11 & 30 (road is both); 802-362-3602
Hours: Monday to Saturday 9 am to 6:30 pm
Sunday 11 am to 5 pm
Natural Food Store. Organic vegetables.
Menu: Has some ready-made sandwiches in their cooler.
Other Info: Accepts MC, VISA.
Direction: On the main street coming through town.

Storm Café
3 Mill Street; 802-388-1063
Hours: Tuesday to Saturday 11 am to 3:30 pm, 4 pm to 6 pm; closed Sunday & Monday.
American. Not pure vegetarian.
Menu: Veggie Lasagna, veggie chili, a selection of vegetarian soups, salads and sandwiches. Small menu.
Comments: Uses organic produce in some dishes. In basement of Frog Hollow Mill. Interesting setting for a meal.
Other Info: Full service, take-out. Non-smoking. Accepts MC, VISA. Price: $$-$$$.

Tully & Maries
5 Bakery Lane; 802-388-4182
Hours: Sunday to Thursday 11:30 am to 9 pm
Friday & Saturday 11:30 am to 10 pm
International Restaurant. Not pure vegetarian.
Menu: Has a good selection of vegetarian dishes. Veggie Burger, veggie chili, Black Bean Burger,

veggie soups, sandwiches and salads.
Other Info: Full service, take-out. Non-smoking. Accepts AMEX, MC, VISA. Price: $$-$$$.

Up For Breakfast
4935 Main Street, Route 7A
802-362-4204; **email:** info@upforbreakfast.com;
Web site: www.upforbreakfast.com
Hours: Monday to Friday 7 am to 12 noon
Saturday & Sunday 7 am to 1 pm
Restaurant. Vegetarian-friendly Breakfast Place. Juice Bar. Not pure vegetarian.
Menu: Veggie sausages, salads, sandwiches and fresh juice.
Comments: Got good reviews in USA Today, Yankee Magazine, Providence Journal, Gourmet Magazine and others. Price: $$.

MONTPELIER

Hunger Mountain Coop
623 Stone Cutters Way; 802-223-8000
email: info@hungermountain.com
Web site: www.hungermtncoop.com
Hours: Daily 8 am to 8 pm
Natural Food Store and Café. Deli, Bakery and Salad Bar. Organic produce. Supermarket-type place. Coffee Bar.
Menu: Soups, salads, sandwiches, veggie Lasagna, veggie chili, organic cheeses and baked goods.
Comments: One of the largest selections of organic produce in New England. Has a beautiful view overlooking the Winooski River. Has seating. Friendly place.
Other Info: Accepts MC, VISA.
Directions: On Granite Street Extension, on the river next to Allen Lumber. From I-89, take Montpelier exit (#8) onto Memorial Dr. At Main Street (1 miles down at light) turn left and go one block. Then at Stonecutter's Way (first right) turn right and this place on right.

State Street Market & The World Wide Wrap
20 State Street, at Main Street; 802-229-9353;
The Wrap number: 802-229-6112
Store Hours: Monday to Thursday 10 am to 6:30 pm; Friday 10 am to 7 pm; Saturday 10 am to 6 pm; Sunday 11 am to 5 pm
The Wrap Hours: Monday to Friday 10 am to 6 pm; Saturday 11 am to 6 pm
Natural Food Store and International Deli. Salad Bar. Macrobiotic and Vegan options. Not pure vegetarian.
Menu: Organic buffet. Soups, salads, sandwiches,

Tofu Lasagna, vegetarian chili, Veggie Sushi and hot dishes. Fresh juices and smoothies.
Comments: Has a large buffet bar. Popular place. The World Wide Wrap is in the back of State Street Market.
Other Info: Buffet, take-out. Cafeteria style, take-out. Accepts AMEX, MC, VISA. Price: $.
Directions: From I-89, take Montpelier exit onto Memorial Dr. At Main St (at light 1 mile down), turn left and go a third-mile. At State St (next light) turn left and this place on left 100 yards down.

MORRISVILLE

Appletree Natural Foods
Munson Avenue; 802-888-8481
Hours: Monday to Friday 9 am to 6 pm; Saturday 9:30 am to 6 pm; closed Sunday.
Natural Food Store. Limited organic produce.
Directions: From Rte 15, turn at blinking light in Morrisville (left from west, right from east), then turn left into the Pricechopper/McDonald's parking lot. At Munson turn right (road between Pricechopper & McDonald's), and at strip mall turn left and this place there.

NEWPORT

Newport Natural Foods Bakery and Café
66 Main Street
802-334-2626
Hours: Monday to Friday 9 am to 5:30 pm; Saturday 9 am to 5 pm; Sunday 11 am to 4 pm
Natural Food Store and mainly Vegetarian Café. Deli and Bakery. Organic produce.
Menu: The menu changes daily. Salads, soups, sandwiches, fresh baked goods, veggie chili, veggie Lasagna and various hot dishes. Good selection to choose from.
Comments: Friendly, good people.
Other Info: Cafeteria style, take-out. Accepts AMEX, MC, VISA. Price: $.
Directions: From I-91, take downtown Newport exit (#27) and go about 3 miles to the downtown. When roads ends (crosses river) turn left onto Main St and this place on right a half-mile down.

PLAINFIELD

Winooski Valley Co-op
135 Main Street, behind the fire station.
802-454-8579
Hours: Monday to Saturday 10 am to 7 pm (un-til 9 pm Tuesday & Thursday) Sunday 10 am to 2 pm
Natural Food Store. Organic produce.
Comments: Has a play area for the kids.
Other Info: Accepts MC, VISA.
Directions: From Rte 2 in Plainfield, at blinking light bear right into town. At fork bear left and this place on left a couple hundreds yards down behind the fire station.

PUTNEY

Putney Food Coop
8 Carol Brown Way, PO Box 730
802-387-5866
Web site: www.putney.net/coop/
Hours: Monday to Saturday 7:30 am to 8 pm Sunday 8 am to 8 pm
Natural Food Store and Café. Deli. Organic produce.
Menu: Soups, salads, sandwiches, pesto filled pretzels, hot dishes and daily specials. Fresh baked goods.
Other Info: Accepts AMEX, MC, VISA.
Directions: From I-91, take exit #4 for Rte 5 north and this place near exit.

RANDOLPH

White River Co-op
3 Weston Street
802-728-9554
email: amymcd1@juno.com
Hours: Monday to Friday 9 am to 6 pm; Saturday 10 am to 4 pm; closed Sunday.
Natural Food Store.
Comments: Friendly place.
Directions: From I-89, take Exit #4, then take Rte 66 west for about 3 miles, then at Rte 12 go south for a half-mile. At Weston St (second right after train tracks) turn right and this place on right 50 yards down.

RUTLAND

Rutland Area Co-op
77 Wales Street
802-773-0737
Hours: Monday to Saturday 9 am to 7 pm Sunday 11 am to 4 pm
Natural Food Store and Deli. Organic produce.
Menu: Has some ready-made sandwiches in their cooler.
Other Info: Accepts MC, VISA.
Directions: From Rte 7 going south from Burl-

ington, at West St (Rte 4 business) turn right. At Court St (2 blocks down) turn left. At Washington (2 blocks down), turn right and go one block. At Wales turn right and this place is first building on left. Can park in first parking lot for co-op.

Sunshine Natural Market & Deli
42-44 Center, downtown Rutland
802-775-2050
Hours: Monday to Saturday 9 am to 7 pm
Sunday 11 am to 5 pm
Natural Food Store and Deli. Organic produce.
Menu: Has some ready-made sandwiches in their cooler.
Other Info: Accepts AMEX, DIS, MC, VISA.
Directions: From Rte 7 going south from Burlington, at West St (Rte 4 business) turn right. At Court St (2 blocks down) turn left. At Washington (2 blocks down), turn right and go one block. At Wales turn right and this place is at corner of Wales and Center St.

SAINT ALBANS

Rail City Market
8 South Main Street
802-524-3769
Hours: Monday to Saturday 9 am to 6 pm
Closed Sunday.
Natural Food Store. Limited organic produce.
Other Info: Accepts DIS, MC, VISA.
Directions: From I-89, take exit #19, then go west on Tangleweed Dr (only direction you can go) for 1½ mile, at Main St (Rte 7) turn right (go north) towards St Albans business district. This place a mile down on left across from park (south end), at intersection with Rte 36.

SAINT JOHNSBURY

Natural Provisions
130 Railroad Street
802-748-3587
Hours: Monday to Friday 8:30 am to 6 pm
Saturday 8:30 am to 5 pm
Sunday 10 am to 4 pm
Natural Food Store. Organic produce.
Other Info: Accepts AMEX, DIS, MC, VISA.

SOUTH BURLINGTON

Healthy Living Natural Foods
4 Market Street; 802-863-2569
Hours: Daily 8 am to 8 pm
Natural Food Store and Deli. Juice Bar. Organic

produce.
Directions: From I-89, take Exit #14, then go east on Rte 2, then at Dorset St (first right turn) turn right and go a third-mile, then at Market St turn right and this place is near turnoff. Near University Mall.

Moon Meadow Organic Market
150 Dorset Street, #C7
802-862-9000
Hours: Monday to Saturday 9 am to 8 pm
Sunday 10 am to 6 pm
Natural Food Store and Deli. Juice Bar, Organic produce.
Menu: Has a good selection of vegetarian dishes. Has soups, pastas, wraps, hummus, sandwiches and salads.
Other Info: Counter service, take-out. Has 4 tables.
Directions: From I-89, take Exit #14, then go east on Rte 2, then at Dorset St (first right turn) turn right and this place is a half-mile down, just past the University Mall.

SPRINGFIELD

Springfield Food Co-op
76 Chester Road
802-885-3363
Hours: Monday to Saturday 9 am to 6 pm
Sunday 11 am to 4 pm
Natural Food Store. Organic produce.
Other Info: Accepts AMEX, MC, VISA.
Directions: From I-91, take exit #7 (Springfield). Take Rte 11 west 4 miles into Springfield and go toward the downtown and bear left staying on Rte 11. This place on left in front of Tire Warehouse.

STOWE

Miguel's Stowe Away
3148 Mountain Road
802-253-7574
Hours: Monday to Friday 5:30 pm to 10 pm; Saturday 12 noon to 3 pm, 5 pm to 10 pm; Sunday 12 noon to 3 pm, 5 pm to 10 pm
Mexican and American. Not pure vegetarian.
Menu: Organic brown rice, Rice & Beans, burritos, Roasted Vegetables, vegetarian chili and more.
Comments: Good Mexican selections. Fireplace. Has outdoor seating. Often uses organic ingredients.
Other Info: Full service, take-out. Non-smoking. Accepts AMEX, DC, DIS, MC, VISA. Price: $.

WAITSFIELD

Sweet Pea Natural Foods
Village Square
Route 100
802-496-7763
Hours: Monday to Saturday 8:30 am to 6 pm
Sunday 11:30 am to 5 pm
Natural Foods Store and Vegetarian Deli.
Organic produce.
Menu: Soups, salads, veggie chili, pastas, Sesame
Noodles, tempeh and tofu dishes, sandwiches,
fresh breads and daily specials.
Comments: Has 20 seats. Local organic produce
used when possible.
Other Info: Accepts MC, VISA. Price: $.
Directions: This place is in the center of town
on the left coming from I-89 on Rte 100
south.

WHITE RIVER JUNCTION

Upper Valley Food Co-op
49 North Main Street; 802-295-5804
Hours: Monday to Saturday 9 am to 8 pm
Sunday 11 am to 7 pm
Natural Food Store and Deli. Local organic produce. Best selection of produce around.
Menu: Ready-made sandwiches, salads and two
soups
Other Info: Accepts DIS, MC, VISA. Counter
service, take-out. Has seating.
Directions: From I-91, take exit #11 (White River
Junction/Rte 5) and go north (east) on Rte 5 (left
from north, right from south). A little past third
light at fork (after 1.5 miles) go right down a small
hill onto N Main St and this place is a quarter-
mile down (second driveway on left). In a large
yellow building.

Virginia

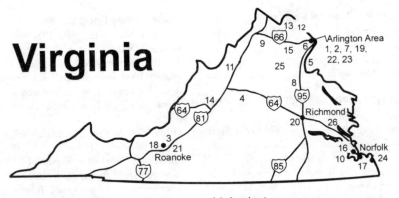

Alexandria

Bilbo Baggins Restaurant

208 Queen Street; 703-683-0300;
Hours: Sunday to Thursday 11:30 am to 2:30 pm, 5:30 pm to 10 pm; Friday & Saturday 11:30 am to 2:30 pm, 5:30 pm to 10:30 pm; Sunday Brunch 11:30 am to 2:30 pm
American, Italian. Not pure vegetarian.
Menu: Salads, pastas, sandwiches and Vegetarian Plate. Cappuccino, espresso. Non-alcoholic beer and wine.
Comments: Comfortable atmosphere.
Other Info: Full service, take-out, catering. Reservations suggested for groups. Accepts AMEX, DC, DIS, MC, VISA. Price: $$-$$$.
Directions: This place is in downtown Alexandria, a few blocks west of the Potomac River, near the corner of N Lee St and Queen St.

Bombay Curry Company

3102 Mt Vernon Avenue
703-836-6363
Hours: Monday to Saturday 11:30 am to 2:30, 5:30 pm to 10 pm
Sunday 11:30 am to 2:30 pm, 5:30 pm to 9 pm
Indian. Not pure vegetarian.

Menu: Bombay Curry, curry vegetables, rice dishes and Vegetarian Thali.
Other Info: Full service. Accepts DC, DIS, MC, VISA. Price: $$.

Cash Grocer

1315 King Street, at West Street; 703-549-9544
Hours: Monday to Saturday 10 am to 6:30 (until 8 pm Thursday); closed Sunday.
Natural Food Store. Organic produce.
Menu: Has ready-made sandwiches and salads in cooler.
Other Info: Accepts AMEX, MC, VISA.

Fresh Fields (Whole Foods) (Annandale)

6548 Little River Turnpike
703-914-0040; **fax:** 703-914-8803
Hours: Monday to Saturday 8 am to 9 pm
Sunday 8 am to 8 pm
Natural Food Store and Cafe. Deli, Bakery, Salad Bar and Juice Bar. Organic produce. Supermarket-type place. See Whole Foods Market information.
Directions: From I-395, take Duke St (Rte 236, exit #3B) exit west. Go west on Duke St and it becomes Little River Turnpike. This place is two miles down on right in Pinecrest Plaza.

Healthways Natural Foods
1610 Belle View Boulevard; 703-660-8603
Hours: Monday to Friday 10 am to 7 pm (until
8 pm on Thursday); Saturday 10 am to 6 pm;
Sunday 12 noon to 5 pm
Natural Food Store. Organic produce.
Other Info: Accepts MC, VISA.

Mediterranean Bakery and Café
352 South Pickett Street; 703-751-1702
Hours: Monday to Saturday 8 am to 8 pm
Sunday 8 am to 6 pm
Middle Eastern, Mediterranean, Lebanese Natural Foods. Vegan-friendly. Not pure vegetarian.
Menu: Falafels, hummus, a selection of salads,
spinach pies, baba ghanouj, tahini and Greek
Salad.
Comments: Mediterranean décor with terra cotta
canopy and arches. There is a large Middle Eastern grocery here that has Greek and Italian items.
Other Info: Counter service, take-out. Accepts
AMEX, DC, DIS, MC, VISA. Price: $-$$.
Directions: Coming from Maryland on the Capital Beltway (I-495), take the Van Dorn St (Rte
613) exit, turn left onto S Van Dorn St and it
becomes S Van Dorn St. Then at Edsall Rd turn
right, then at S Pickett St turn left, then this place
is in the Trade Center Shopping Village.

Pita House
407 Cameron Street; 703-684-9194
Hours: Monday to Saturday 11 am to 10 pm
Sunday 12 noon to 8:30 pm
Authentic Lebanese. Vegan options. Not pure
vegetarian.
Menu: Has several vegetarian dishes. Veggie Delight is fried cauliflower with eggplant, tomatoes
and lettuce on a pita bread. Baba ghanouj, hummus, falafel and Moujadra Bel Riz (lentils and
rice with onions),
Comments: Small place. Family owned and operated. Good food. Friendly, casual place. Has
tablecloths on tables at night. Accepts AMEX,
DIS, MC, VISA.
Directions: From I-495 coming from Maryland,
take exit for Rte 193 and get on George Washington Memorial Pkwy and go 15 miles, then get
on N Washington St, At Queen St turn left, at N
Pitt St turn right and then at Cameron St turn
left.

ARLINGTON (west DC suburb)

Bombay Curry House
2529 Wilson Boulevard; 703-528-0849
Hours: Daily 11 am to 3 pm, 5 pm to 10 pm

Indian. Not pure vegetarian.
Menu: Has several vegetarian dishes.
Other Info: Reservations suggested for groups.
Accepts AMEX, DC, DIS, MC, VISA. Price: $-
$$.
Directions: Parking arranged for customers.

Café Dalat
3143 Wilson Boulevard, 3100 Block at the
Clarendon Metro; 703-276-0935
Hours: Sunday to Thursday 11 am to 9:30 pm
Friday & Saturday 11 am to 10:30 pm
Vietnamese Café. Vegan options. Not pure veg.
Menu: Has a page on the menu of vegetarian
dishes. Hot and Sour Soup, vegan spring roll and
vegan Vegetarian Curry.
Comments: Friendly, good service. Food is good.
Reasonable prices. Has outdoors seating.
Other Info: Accepts MC, VISA. Price: $.
Directions: Across from the Clarendon Metro
station. From I-66, take Arlington Blvd exit, take
Rte 237 (10th Street) ramp and go straight onto
10th St (Rte 237) for a third of a mile. At Washington Blvd turn right. Then at Highland St turn
right, at Wilson Blvd turn left and this place is a
block down on right.

China Gourmet Café
2154 Crystal Plaza Arcade; 703-415-0300
Hours: Monday to Friday 11 am to 8 pm; Saturday 11 am to 6 pm; closed Sunday.
Chinese. Vegan options. Not pure vegetarian.
Menu: Has a selection of vegetarian dishes.
Other Info: Limited service, take-out. Price: $.
Directions: Underground in Crystal City Plaza.

Delhi Dhaba
2424 Wilson Boulevard; 703-524-0008
Hours: Sunday to Thursday 11 am to 10 pm
Friday & Saturday 11 am to 11 pm
Indian. Buffet. Not pure vegetarian.
Menu: Has a wide selection of vegetarian dishes.
Alu Began (eggplant, potato) is good.
Comments: All-you-can-eat buffet on Sunday.
Good food. Reasonable prices. Has outdoor seating. Plastic plates and forks.
Other Info: Cafeteria service, take-out, delivery.
Order dishes at counter and food is brought to you.
Accepts AMEX, DC, DIS, MC, VISA. Price: $.
Directions: Free parking for customers.

Fresh Fields (Whole Foods)
2700 Wilson Boulevard
703-527-6596; **fax:** 703-527-6588
Hours: Daily 8 am to 10 pm
Natural Food Store and Cafe. Deli, Bakery, Salad

Bar and Juice Bar. Organic produce. Supermarket-type place. See Whole Foods Market information.
Directions: This place is about 1 mile west of downtown Arlington. From Rte 495, take I-66 (US-50) east, then take Fairfax Dr exit. Take N Fairfax Dr (Rte 237), then go right onto 10th St N (Rte 237 E), at Wilson Blvd turn left. Go straight onto Clarendon Blvd. Then at N Danville St turn left.

Kabab Masala

305 North Glede Road; 703-522-6666
Hours: Sunday to Thursday 11 am to 11 pm
Friday & Saturday 11 am to 2 am
Indian. Vegan options. Not pure vegetarian.
Menu: Has a large selection of vegetarian dishes.
Other Info: Full service, take-out. Accepts AMEX, DC, DIS, MC, VISA. Price: $.

Lebanese Taverna

5900 Washington Boulevard; 703-241-8681
Hours: Monday to Saturday 11:30 am to 2:30 pm, 5 pm to 10 pm; Sunday 4 pm to 9:30 pm
Middle Eastern, Lebanese, American. Not pure vegetarian. Not vegan friendly.
Menu: Has a vegetarian section on the menu. Sandwiches and vegetarian main dishes.
Comments: Very popular place. Has got many good reviews in the media. Good place for a group. Good value.
Other Info: Full service, take-out, catering. Reservations necessary for groups. Accepts AMEX, DC, DIS, MC, VISA. Price: $-$$.
Directions: Parking arranged for customers.

Madhu Ban

3217 North Washington Blvd; 703-528-7184
Hours: Monday to Saturday 10 am to 10 pm
Sunday 12 noon to 10 pm
South Indian. Some American dishes. Daily Lunch Buffet. Vegan friendly. Not pure veg.
Menu: Has a wide variety of vegetarian dishes. Soups, salads, masala dosa, rice & curry dishes, and desserts. Non-alcoholic beer and wine.
Comments: Reasonable prices. Good value.
Other Info: Full service, take-out, catering. Reservations not accepted. Non-smoking. Accepts MC, VISA. Price: $-$$.
Directions: From George Washing Memorial Pkwy, take I-66 E (US 50) exit and keep right at fork in ramp and merge onto Arlington Blvd, then take the Washington Blvd ramp towards Claredon. Get on Washington Blvd. Parking arranged for customers.

Salai Thai

2900 North 10th Street
703-465-2900
Hours: Monday to Thursday 11 am to 10 pm; Friday & Saturday 11:30 am to 11 pm; Sunday 12 noon to 10 pm
Thai. Vegan options. Not pure vegetarian.
Menu: Has a separate vegetarian menu.
Other Info: Accepts AMEX, MC, VISA.

**Saran Foods

5151 North Lee Highway
703-533-3600; **fax:** 703-533-3616
Hours: Tuesday to Thursday 11 am to 9:30 pm; Friday & Saturday 11 am to 10 pm; Sunday 11 am to 9 pm
Lunch Buffet 11:30 am to 3 pm; closed Monday.
Vegetarian Indian. Lunch Buffet.
Menu: Basmati Rice, Vegetable Biryani, dosas, Aloo Tikki, Dal Makhni, Channa Masala, Palak Paneer, Palak Matar, Shahi Paneer, Malai Kofta, Navrattan Korma, pakoras, idlies, sambar, Indian breads. uthappam and Saran Thali (three curries, samosas, tikki, sambar, dal, salad, raita, white rice, roti, papadam & dessert). Gulabjamun and Rasmalai. Mango lassi and chai.
Comments: Basic place with 10 tables.
Other Info: Non-smoking. Price: $.
Directions: Can take George Washington Memorial Pkwy, then take Rte 123 N exit toward Chain Bridge/Washington. Then from there get on Rte 29, where this place is located. It is about 3 miles west of the GW Memorial Pkwy and a mile north of I-66.

The Uncommon Market

1041 South Edgewood Street
703-521-2667; **fax:** 703-553-0739
email: mailto:arlcoop@aol.com;
Web site: http://members.aol.com/arlcoop/
Hours: Monday to Saturday 9 am to 9 pm
Sunday 9 am to 6 pm
Natural Food Store. Organic produce.
Comments: Gets ready-made sandwiches delivered on Thursdays.
Other Info: Accepts MC, VISA.
Directions: From I-66 going toward DC, take exit for Glebe Road going South toward Washington Blvd, cross Rte 50, then at South 7th St (say 244) turn left and go 4 block, then at South Walter Reed Dr turn right and go four blocks, at Columbia Pike turn left and go a block, then at South Edgewood turn right and this place is a block down.

BLACKBURG

Annie Kay's Whole Foods
301 South Main Street; 540-552-6870
Hours: Monday to Friday 9 am to 8 pm; Saturday 9 am to 6 pm; Sunday 12 noon to 6 pm
Natural Food Store.
Comments: Has books, herbal remedies and other dishes.
Directions: From I-81, take Virginia Tech exit. Follow signs towards Virginia Tech. At Hwy 460 go north towards Blackburg. Take Business District exit to South Main and this place is on the right.

Eats Natural Foods Co-op
1200 North Main Street; 540-552-2279
Hours: Monday to Saturday 10 am to 8 pm Sunday 12 noon to 6 pm
Natural Food Store. Small, good selection of organic produce.
Comments: Good selection of bulk goods and other items. Good prices.
Other Info: Accepts DIS, MC, VISA.
Directions: From I-81, take southern Christiansburg exit towards Blackburg on Hwy 460. Take the bypass road after town, then take Prices Fork Rd and go in direction of downtown for 2 miles. When the road ends, then turn left onto Main St and this place is 1¼ mile down on the right.

Gillie's
153 College Avenue Northwest; 540-961-2703
Hours: Monday to Saturday 7 am to 9 pm Sunday 8 am to 2 pm
Vegetarian International. Vegan friendly.
Menu: Has soups, salads, sandwiches and hot dishes. Breads are freshly baked on the premises.
Comments: Often very popular on the weekends.
Directions: From I-81, take southern Christiansburg exit towards Blackburg on Hwy 460. Take the bypass road after town, then take Prices Fork Rd and go in direction of downtown for 2 miles. When the road ends, then turn right onto Main St and this place is 3 blocks down on the right.

CHARLOTTESVILLE

**Integral Yoga Natural Foods
923 Preston Avenue, near Washington Park
434-293-4111
Hours: Monday to Saturday 9:30 am to 8 pm Sunday 11 am to 6 pm
Natural Food Store and Vegetarian Deli. Juice Bar. Vegan options.
Menu: Has many vegetarian dishes. Sandwiches, Indian dishes, knishes, hummus, pasta dishes, Lasagna (often), soup of the day, Mexican dishes and daily specials. Non-alcoholic beer and wine.
Comments: Sells by the pound. Friendly place.
Other Info: Self-serve, take-out. Has seatings. Accepts MC, VISA. Price: $.
Directions: From Rte 29 (Emmet St), take Barracks Rd (Rte 654) exit, then go southeast on Barracks Rd ¾ miles, then bear right on Preston Ave and this place is 1 mile down on the left in the Preston Plaza, which is between Barracks Road Shopping Center and Historic District. This place is 1 mile northwest of the downtown.

Ming Dynasty
1417 Emmet Street; 434-979-0909
Hours: Sunday to Thursday 11:30 am to 10 pm Friday & Saturday 11:30 am to 11 pm
Chinese. Vegan-friendly. Not pure vegetarian.
Menu: Has a large selection of vegetarian dishes. Fried Rice, Spring Rolls, tofu dishes, Rice Noodles, and an assortment of mock meat and fish dishes.
Comments: Good vegetarian selection. Lunch buffet is 75% vegetarian.
Other Info: Full service, take-out. Accepts AMEX, MC, VISA. Price: $$.

Rebecca's Natural Food
1141 Emmet Street; 434-977-1965
Hours: Monday to Friday 9 am to 8 pm Saturday & Sunday 10 am to 6 pm
Natural Food Store. Organic produce.
Other Info: Accepts MC, VISA.

**Veggie Heaven
923 Preston Avenue; 804-296-9739
Hours: Monday to Friday 11 am to 8 pm; Saturday 11 am to 5 pm; closed Sunday.
Vegetarian International, Middle Eastern, European Restaurant. Full Deli, Juice Bar and Salad Bar. Macrobiotic and Vegan options.
Menu: Has a wide selection of vegetarian dishes. Sandwiches, salads, soups and daily specials. Has organic salads and fresh juices.
Other Info: Counter service, take-out, catering. Reservations not necessary. Non-smoking. Accepts DIS, MC, VISA.

Whole Foods Market
1416 Seminole Trail
804-973-4900; **fax:** 804-973-4650
Hours: Monday to Saturday 9 am to 9 pm Sunday 9 am to 8 pm

Natural Food Store and Cafe. Deli, Bakery, Salad Bar and Juice Bar. Organic produce. Supermarket-type place. See Whole Foods Market information.
Directions: From I-64, take 250 east exit and go north on Rte 29 (becomes Seminole Trail). This place on the left in a small shopping center opposite the Fashion Square Mall.

DALE CITY

The Natural Grocer
14453 Potomac Mills Road; 703-494-7287
Hours: Monday to Friday 10 am to 8 pm; Saturday 10 am to 6 pm; closed Sunday.
Natural Food Store. No produce.
Directions: From I-95, take exit #156, then follow signs to Potomac Mills. Then take Dale Blvd west 1 mile, then turn right at Birchdale Ave and go a half-mile. This place is in the Potomac Festival Shopping Center behind Day's Inn Hotel.

FAIRFAX

Healthway Natural Foods
10360 Lee Highway; 703-591-1121
Hours: Monday to Wednesday, Friday 10 am to 7 pm; Thursday 10 am to 8 pm; Saturday 10 am to 6 pm; Sunday 12 noon to 5 pm
Natural Food Store. Organic produce.
Menu: Has several types of ready-made sandwiches.
Other Info: Accepts DIS, MC, VISA.
Directions: From Rte 66, take Rte 123 toward Fairfax. This place is on the left a block past the intersection of Rte 123 and Lee Highway.

Woodlands Vegetarian Indian Restaurant
4078 Germantown Road
703-385-1996
Hours: Daily 11:30 am to 10 pm
Vegetarian Indian.
Other Info: Reservations are suggested. Non-smoking. Accepts MC, VISA.

FALLS CHURCH (west DC suburb)

Fresh Fields (Whole Foods)
7511 Leesburg Pike
703-448-1600; fax: 703-847-1441
Hours: Monday to Saturday 8 am to 10 pm
Sunday 8 am to 9 pm
Natural Food Store and Cafe. Deli, Bakery, Salad Bar and Juice Bar. Organic produce. Super-market-type place. See Whole Foods Market information.

Directions: From I-66, take Rte 7 (Leesburg Pike, 66A) west towards Tyson's Corner. This place on left a mile down the road, a little past Pimmet Drive.

Kennedy's Natural Foods
West End Shopping Center, 1051 West Broad Street; 703-533-8484
Hours: Monday to Friday 9 am to 7 pm; Saturday 10 am to 6 pm; closed Sunday.
Natural Food Store and Café. Deli, Bakery and Juice Bar.
Menu: Sandwiches, salads, tofu dishes, 2 vegetarian soups daily (usually) and other dishes.
Other Info: Counter service, take-out. Has seating. Accepts AMEX, MC, VISA.
Directions: From I-66, go east on Rte 7 and this place on right in West End Shopping Center.

Panjshir Restaurant
924 West Broad Street; 703-536-4566
Hours: Monday to Saturday 11 am to 2 pm, 5 pm to 11 pm; closed Sunday.
Afghan. Not pure vegetarian.
Menu: Has several vegetarian dishes. Pumpkin and eggplant dishes. The Kadu (sautéed pumpkin with tomato & yogurt) is very good.
Other Info: Full service, take-out. Accepts AMEX, DC, MC, VISA. Price: $$.
Directions: Parking arranged for customers.

FREDERICKSBURG

Pantry Shelf Natural Foods
811 Sophia Street; 540-373-2253
Hours: Monday to Thursday, Saturday 10 am to 6 pm; Friday 10 am to 7 pm; closed Sunday.
Natural Food Store. Organic produce.
Comments: Has a good selection of books.
Other Info: No credit cards.
Directions: From I-95, take exit #130 and go east on Rte 3 (Plank Rd) for 1½ mile, then take a slight left onto William St and go 1½ miles, at Sophia St turn right and this place is 2 blocks down.

FRONT ROYAL

Better Thymes
411-C South Street; 540-636-9209
Hours: Monday to Wednesday 9 am to 6 pm; Thursday & Friday 9 am to 8 pm; Saturday 9 am to 5 pm; Sunday 12 noon to 5 pm
Natural Food Store and take-out Deli. Organic carrots only.

Menu: Has good selection of soups, sandwiches and salads.
Other Info: Accepts AMEX, MC, VISA. Counter service, take-out. No seating.
Directions: From I-66, take Front Royal exit. Go south on Rte 340 to Rte 55 east. This place in first shopping center on the right.

HAMPTON

Rajput Indian Cuisine
9 East Queens Way; 757-723-2377
Hours: Monday to Thursday 11:30 am to 2:30 pm, 5 pm to 10 pm; Friday & Saturday 11:30 am to 2:30 pm, 5 pm to 11 pm; Sunday 12 noon to 10 pm
Indian. Vegetarian friendly. Not pure vegetarian.
Menu: Has a good selection of vegetarian dishes.
Comments: Has a nice décor. Food gets high ratings. Good service.
Other Info: Accepts AMEX, MC, VISA.

HARRISONBURG

Kate's Natural Products
451 University Boulevard; 540-433-2359
Hours: Monday to Saturday 9 am to 6 pm Closed Sunday.
Natural Food Store and Deli. Organic produce.
Menu: Has soups, salads, sandwiches and hot dishes (changes daily). Has a decent selection.
Other Info: Counter service, take-out. Has a few tables.
Directions: From I-81, take exit #247 and go southeast on Hwy 33 a half-mile. Turn right at the second light onto University Blvd and this place on right 1 mile down. From I-81, take VA Hwy 659/Port Republic Rd exit (#245), then go 1 mile on VA Hwy 331 (University Blvd).

HERNDON (DC suburb near Arlington)

A Little Place Called Siam
328 Elden Street
703-742-8881
Hours: Monday to Saturday 12 noon to 10 Sunday 12 noon to 9:30 pm
Southeast Asian, Thai. Vegan options. Not pure vegetarian.
Menu: Has a large selection of vegetarian dishes.
Comments: Has outdoor dining.
Other Info: Full service, take-out. Reservations suggested for groups. Accepts AMEX, DC, DIS, MC, VISA. Price: $-$$.
Directions: Parking arranged for customers.

Hard Times Café
394 Elden Street
703-318-8941; **fax:** 703-318-8942
Hours: Monday to Thursday 11 am to 11 pm; Friday & Saturday 11 am to 12 midnight; Sunday 12 noon to 11 pm
American. Not pure vegetarian.
Menu: Veggie Mac (chili on spaghetti), veggie chili and salads.
Comments: Live country music. Has outdoor seating. Good place for a private party.
Other Info: Full service, take-out. Accepts AMEX, MC, VISA. Price: $.
Directions: Free parking for customers.

Harvest of India
364 Elden Street; 703-471-8149
Hours: Daily 11:30 am to 2:30 pm, 5:30 pm to 10 pm
North Indian. Not pure vegetarian. Vegan-friendly.
Menu: Has several vegetarian dishes. Samosas, pakoras, Malai Kofta and Indian breads.
Comments: Good food. Good place for a private party.
Other Info: Full service, take-out. Accepts AMEX, DC, DIS, MC, VISA. Price: $-$$.
Directions: Parking arranged for customers.

The Tortilla Factory Restaurant
648 Elden Street; 703-471-1156
Hours: Monday to Thursday 11 am to 9:30 pm Friday & Saturday 11 am to 10 pm Sunday 12 noon to 9 pm
Mexican. Vegan options. Not pure vegetarian.
Menu: Has a good selection of vegetarian dishes and indicates them on the menu. Vegetarian Mexican Lasagna, fajitas, cheese enchiladas, black bean burritos, tacos and guacamole. Refried and black beans are vegan. Non-alcoholic beer and wine.
Comments: Uses canola oil in cooking.
Other Info: Full service, take-out, catering. Accepts AMEX, DIS, MC, VISA. Price: $$.

LEESBURG

Andy's Pizza & Subs
9F Catoctin Circle SW; 703-771-0277
Hours: Monday to Thursday 11 am to 10 pm; Friday & Saturday 11 am to 11 pm; Sunday 12 noon to 9 pm
Italian, Pizza, American and Deli. Vegan options. Not pure vegetarian.
Menu: Pizzas, pastas and subs.

Comments: Small relaxed place.
Other Info: Accepts MC, VISA. Full service, take-out, delivery. Price: $.
Directions: At corner of Catoctin Circle and King Street.

LEXINGTON (between the Blueridge and Allegheny Mountains)

**Blue Heron
4 East Washington; 540-463-2800
Hours: Monday to Thursday 11:30 am to 2:30 pm; Friday & Saturday 11:30 am to 2 pm, 5:30 pm to 9 pm; closed Sunday.
Fully Vegetarian Natural Food Store. Vegan friendly.
Menu: Grilled Tofu Sandwich, Spicy Fried Noodles, Triple Goddess Burger (popular), soups, pastas, salads and sandwiches. The Dinner menu has five main dishes that change weekly. There is a vegan special each night for dinner. Hot and cold herbal teas.
Comments: Uses locally grown organic produce whenever possible. Food freshly prepared. Wood floors, old brick and good art. Comfortable place. Food is nicely presented. Small, friendly place. Candlelight dinners on Friday and Saturday evenings.
Other Info: Full service, take-out. Non-smoking. Reservations recommended for dinner, no reservations at lunchtime. No credit card. Accepts personal checks.
Directions: Located in historic downtown Lexington. From Main St (which is one way) turn right onto Washington St, and this place is immediately on your left.

Rockbridge Food Co-op's Healthy Foods
110 West Washington Street; 540-463-6954
Hours: Monday to Thursday 9 am to 6 pm; Friday 9 am to 8 pm; Saturday 9 am to 5 pm
Deli Hours: Monday to Friday 11 am to 2 pm
Natural Food Store and Juice Bar.
Menu: Sandwiches and sometimes soups and salads. Fresh juices and smoothies.
Other Info: Accepts DIS, MC, VISA.
Directions: From I-81, take Lexington exit and follow signs towards Lexington Visitor Center. This store is on the left a little past the Visitor Center.

LYNCHBURG

Fresh Air Natural Foods
Forest Plaza Shopping Center, 3225 Old Forest Road; 434-385-9252

Hours: Monday to Friday 10 am to 8 pm; Saturday 10 am to 5 pm; closed Sunday.
Natural Food Store. Organic produce (comes in on Wednesday).
Directions: Take Rte 29 to Hwy 501 north. After pasting Hwy 221, a quarter-mile later bear right onto Old Forest Rd and this place is 1 mile northeast on the right in the Forest Plaza Shopping Center.

MANASSAS

Healthway Natural Foods
10778 Sudley Manor Drive; 703-361-1883
Hours: Monday to Thursday 10 am to 7 pm; Friday 10 am to 8 pm; Saturday 10 am to 6 pm; Sunday 12 noon to 5 pm
Natural Food Store. Has a small selection of organic produce.
Other Info: Accepts DIS, MC, VISA.
Directions: From Rte 66, take exit #47 and go south on Rte 234 and this place is 1 mile down on right in the Bull Run Plaza Shopping Center.

NEWPORT NEWS

Nawab
Oyster Point Square, 11712 Jefferson Avenue
757-591-9200; **Web site:** www.nawabonline.com
Hours: Daily 11:30 am to 2:30 pm, 5 pm to 10 pm
Menu: Has a selection of vegetarian dishes.

NORFOLK

Health Food Center
1701 Colley Avenue (has a juice bar) (Ghent Area)
757-625-6656
Hours: Monday to Friday 10 am to 7 pm; Saturday 10 am to 6 pm; **Juice Bar Hours:** 10 am to 4 pm; closed Sunday.
Natural Food Store and Juice Bar. Serves just juices and smoothies.
7639 Granby Street; 757-625-7283
700 North Military Highway, Suite 2018
757-461-2883
Natural Food Store.

HealthQuest
2000 Colonial Avenue; 757-461-0026
1094 Military Highway
222 West 21st Street, Suite B; 757-622-0191
Natural Food Store.

Nawab Indian Cuisine
888 North Military Highway
757-455-8080; **Web site:** www.nawabonline.com

Hours: Monday to Thursday 11:30 am to 2:30 m, 5 pm to 10 pm; Friday 11:30 am to 2:30 pm, 5 pm to 10:30 pm; Sat 12 noon to 3 pm, 5 pm to 10:30 pm; Sun 12 noon to 3 pm, 5 pm to 10 pm **Indian.** Daily Lunch Buffet. Vegan options. Not pure vegetarian.
Menu: Has a selection of vegetarian dishes.
Comments: Authentic décor. Nice atmosphere. White tablecloths.
Other Info: Full service, take-out. Accepts AMEX, DIS, MC, VISA. Price: $$.
Directions: Parking arranged for customers.

Whole Foods Co-op
119 West 21st Street; 757-626-1051; **email:** wholefoodscoop@hotmail.com; **Web site:** home.att.net/~coop21, http://wholefoodsco-op.hypermart.net/
Hours: Monday to Thursday, Saturday 10 am to 6 pm; Friday 10 am to 7 pm; closed Sunday.
Natural Food Store and Deli. Juice Bar. Organic produce. Over 200 herbs and spices.
Menu: Serves fresh juices and sandwiches.
Directions: From I-64, take I-564/Granby St exit (#276) towards Naval Base, then go south on Granby St (Rte 460 W) for 3½ miles (towards the downtown), then at W 21 St turn right and this place is at the corner.

RADFORD

Annie Kay's Whole Foods
601 3rd Street; 540-731-9498
Hours: Monday to Friday 9 am to 7 pm; Saturday 9 am to 6 pm; closed Sunday.
Natural Food Store. Organic produce.
Other Info: Accepts MC, VISA.
Directions: From I-81, take Radford exit. Get on Tyler and go north toward town about 3 miles. At Norwood (becomes 1st St) turn left and go 1 mile, then at Wadsworth turn left and go 2 blocks. This place on right at corner of 3rd and Wadsworth.

RESTON

Fresh Fields (Whole Foods)
11660 Plaza America Drive
703-736-0600; **fax:** 703-736-0674
Hours: Monday to Saturday 8 am to 9 pm Sunday 9 am to 8 pm (closes at 9 pm in summer)
Natural Food Store and Cafe. Deli, Bakery, Salad Bar and Juice Bar. Organic produce. Supermarket-type place. See Whole Foods Market information.

Directions: From Dulles Tollroad (267) going west, take exit #12 (Reston Parkway). At Sunset Hill (next street) turn right going east. At the third traffic light, after about 2 miles, turn right onto Plaza America Drive. This place is then in a shopping center on the right after a quarter-mile.

RICHMOND

Café Indochine
2923 West Cary Street; 804-353-5799
Hours: Monday to Saturday 5 pm to 9:30 pm Closed Sunday.
Vietnamese, French. Vegan options. Not pure vegetarian.
Menu: Has a good selection of vegetarian dishes. Vegetable wraps, Portobello Tofu and Pasta Indochine.
Comments: Creative dishes. Elegant décor. Has stained-glass chandeliers. Friendly, efficient service. Staff willing to substitute tofu or bean-curd in most dishes. Good place for a special event.
Other Info: Full service, take-out, catering. Accepts AMEX, MC, VISA. Price: $$.

Café Mandolin
1309 West Main Street; 804-355-8558
Hours: Tuesday to Friday 11:30 am to 2 pm, 5:30 pm to 9:30 pm; Saturday 5:30 pm to 9:30 pm
International, Eclectic. Not pure vegetarian.
Menu: Has a good selection of vegan dishes. Grilled Tempeh and Vegetable Filet. Polenta and Portobello Mushrooms.

Cary Street Café
2631 West Cary Street, in the Carytown district. 804-353-7445
Hours: Daily 11 am to 2 am
Restaurant. Not pure vegetarian.
Menu: Good amount of vegetarian dishes. ELT is an eggplant, lettuce and tomato sandwich. Basmati rice with Summer Squash Cakes, hummus sandwiches and Black Bean Burritos (very good).
Comments: Plays Grateful Dead music, among other things. Casual, friendly place. Has outdoor dining. Sidewalk café. Has live music every day and a full bar. Popular place.
Other Info: Counter service, take-out. Accepts AMEX, MC, VISA. Price: $$.
Directions: From I-95, take I-195 S (toll road) (exit #79) and go 3 miles south, take Rosewood Ave exit, take a slight right onto Rosewood Ave, then take an immediate right onto McCloy St and go 1 block, then at Grayland Ave turn right and go 2 blocks, at S Sheppard St turn left and go

1 block, then at W Cary St (VA Hwy 147) turn right and this place is a quarter-mile down. This place is about 1 mile west of the main downtown area.

Christopher's Runaway Gourmay Lunch Cart (four locations)
MCV Campus
10th & Main
9th & Main
11th & Main
Downtown
Sidewalk cart with some vegetarian dishes. Pesto Pasta.

Ellwood Thompson's Natural Market and The Café
4 North Thompson Street; 804-359-7525
Web site: www.ellwoodthompsons.com
Hours: Monday to Saturday 8 am to 9 pm
Sunday 9 am to 8 pm
Natural Food Store and Cafe. Deli, Salad Bar and Juice Bar. Vegan options. Not pure vegetarian.
Menu: Have good vegetarian selections. The menu changes regularly. Roast Sweet Potatoes, Grilled Sweet Peppers and Mushroom Tart. Fresh juices.
Comments: The chef is a graduate of The Culinary Institute of America and a registered dietitian. Good food. Reasonably priced. Has a vegetarian take-out dinner special (can check their Web site to see what it is). The Web site also lists a recipe of the day.
Other Info: Counter service, take-out, catering. Accepts MC, VISA. Price: $.
Directions: From I-95, take I-195 S (Powhite Parkway, toll road) (exit #79) and go 3 miles southeast, then take Cary St (VA Hwy 147) exit, keep left at fork and merge onto Cameron St and go 1 block, at Cary (VA Hwy 147) turn left, then at Thompson turn left and this place is 1 block down on left in a shopping center next to Blockbuster Video.

Farouk's House of India
3033 West Cary Street, in the Carytown area.
804-355-0378
Hours: Daily 11:30 am to 3 pm, 5 pm to 10 pm
Indian. Not pure vegetarian.
Menu: Has a lunch buffet and a good amount of vegetarian options for dinner. Basmati Rice, Kofta Malai, curry dishes and Mango Lassi.
Comments: Food gets good ratings.
Other Info: Full service, take-out. Accepts

AMEX, DC, DIS, MC, VISA. Price: $-$$.
Directions: Parking arranged for customers.

Good Foods Grocery
Stony Point Shopping Center
3062 Stony Point Road
804-320-6767
Hours: Monday to Saturday 9 am to 9 pm
Store closed Sunday. Café closed Saturday & Sunday.
Natural Food Store and Café. Deli and Bakery. Organic produce.
Other Info: Counter service, take-out. Has seating.
Directions: From I-195 south, take Powhite Parkway exit, then take Forest Hill Ave south exit. At Forest Hill Ave turn right and go west for 2 miles, at Rte 678 turn right and go northwest a third-mile and this place is in the Stony Point Shopping Center. This place is about 5 miles west of downtown Richmond.

Good Foods Grocery
Gayton Crossing Shopping Center, 1312 Gaskins Road, at Gayton Rd; 804-740-3518
Hours: Monday to Saturday 9 am to 9 pm
Closed Sunday.
Natural Food Store and Café. Deli and Bakery. Organic produce.
Directions: From I-64, take Gaskins Rd south exit (#180) and go south 2½ miles and this place on right. This place is about 5 miles northwest of downtown Richmond.

**Harrison Street Coffee Shop
402 North Harrison Street
804-359-8060
Hours: Monday to Friday 8 am to 5 pm
Saturday & Sunday 10 am to 3 pm
Fully Vegetarian. Mostly Vegan.
Menu: The menu changes daily and there is around 10 main dishes. Fajita, Tex-Mex Tofu Steak Sandwich and much more. Has a good selection of coffees.
Comments: Has live music sometimes on Wednesday nights. New place.
Other Info: Counter service, take-out. Non-smoking. Accepts MC, VISA.
Directions: On Harrison Street between Grace and W Franklin Streets, 1½ block south of VCU's Siegel Center (basketball arena). From I-64, take Rte 1 exit (#76) and go south on Rte 1 for a quarter-mile, then at Grace St turn right and go 4 blocks, then at Harrison St turn left and this place is 1 block down.

Hole in the Wall

307 North Laurel Street; 804-225-7103
Vegetarian-friendly Restaurant and Bar. Not pure
vegetarian.
Menu: Emphasis on vegetarian dishes. Basmati
rice,
Comments: Happening place. Live entertainment. Avant-garde bands. Full bar.
Other Info: Accepts AMEX, MC, VISA. Price:
$-$$.
Directions: From I-64, take Rte 1 exit (#76) and
go south on Rte 1 for a quarter-mile, then at Grace
St turn right and this place is 2 blocks down at
corner with Laurel. Parking arranged for customers.

Ipanema

917 West Grace Street; 804-213-0170
Hours: Monday to Friday 11 am to 3 pm, 5:30
pm to 11 pm; Sat 11 am to 3 pm; closed Sun.
Mostly Vegetarian Restaurant. Vegan friendly.
Not pure vegetarian.
Menu: The menu changes daily. Stuffed Porto-
bello Mushroom, sweet potato fries and salads.
Comments: Casual, friendly place. Very good
food.
Other Info: Smoking allowed everywhere. Ac-
cepts MC, VISA. Price: $$.
Directions: From I-64, take Rte 1 exit (#76) and
go south on Rte 1 for a quarter-mile, then at Grace
St turn right and this place is 3 blocks down.

Palani Drive

401 Libbie Avenue, west side of Richmond
804-285-3200
Hours: Daily 10:30 am to 10 pm
International Restaurant. Healthy foods. Not
pure vegetarian.
Menu: Good wraps, quesadillas, soups and sal-
ads. Fresh juices. Smoothies with ginseng, bee
pollen, oat bran, soy protein and gingko biloba.
Wheat grass. Palani Powerman Smoothie (pine-
apple, orange, banana, mango and whey protein)
is good.
Comments: Has gotten awards for best vegetar-
ian food in the area. Has outdoor dining. Hap-
pening place.
Other Info: Accepts AMEX, MC, VISA. Counter
service, take-out. Price: $.
Directions: This place is about 2 miles west of
the downtown. From I-95 going south into town,
take I-64 exit (#79) and go west on I-64 for 1
mile, take US 33/Staples Mill Rd exit (#185) and
stay left at fork in ramp and merge onto Staples
Mill Rd and go 1 mile, at Broad St turn right and

go 1 mile, then turn left onto Libbie Ave and this
place is 1¼ mile down.

Panda Garden

935 West Grace Street; 804-359-6688
Hours: Daily 11 am to 11 pm
Chinese. Not pure vegetarian.
Menu: Has a wide selection of vegetarian and very
good mock meat dishes. Mock chicken dish is
good.
Comments: Reasonable prices.
Other Info: Accepts AMEX, DIS, MC, VISA.
Price: $.

Strawberry Street Café

421 North Strawberry Street, on the east side of
Monroe Park; 804-353-6860
Hours: Monday to Thursday 11:30 am to 3 pm,
5 pm to 10:30 pm; Friday & Saturday 11 am to
12 midnight; closed Sunday.
Vegetarian-friendly American. All-you-can-eat
Salad Bar. Not pure vegetarian.
Menu: Has a good amount of vegetarian and ve-
gan dishes. Has good salads and soups.
Comments: Well-known place. Trendy, popular,
happening place. Place gets good reviews. Good
service.
Other Info: Accepts MC, VISA. Price: $$.
Directions: Next to Strawberry Street Market.

The Village Café

1001 West Grace Street; 804-353-8204
Hours: Daily 8:30 am to 2 am
Vegetarian-friendly American. Full Bar.
Menu: Falafel, hummus, veggie burgers, pastas,
salads, Soy burgers, baked potatoes, spaghetti and
pizzas.
Comments: Bar-type atmosphere. Happening
place. Hip crowd. Very popular during the school
year at night. Good food and atmosphere.
Other Info: Accepts AMEX, DIS, MC, VISA.
Price: $-$$.
Directions: Near Virginia Commonwealth Uni-
versity.

The White Dog

2329 West Main Street; 804-340-1975
Hours: Tuesday to Thursday, Sunday 5 pm to 11
pm; Friday & Saturday 5 pm to 12 midnight.
Vegetarian-friendly American Restaurant. Not
pure vegetarian.
Menu: Has a good selection of vegetarian dishes.
Has a daily vegetarian special. Mashed potatoes,
breads, salads, pastas and more
Comments: Laid-back place. Good food.

Friendly, efficient service. Nice atmosphere. The place gets good reviews from customers.

Other Info: Accepts AMEX, MC, VISA. Price: $$-$$$.

Directions: From I-95 coming south, take I-195 S exit (#79) and go south on I-195 for 1 mile, take Hamilton St exit towards Rte 33/Rte 250/Broad St, stay right at fork in ramp and merge onto N Hamilton St and go 2 blocks, at W Broad St turn left (go east) and go ¾ mile, at Rte 161/N Blvd turn right and go 2 blocks, at Strawberry St turn right and go 1 block, at Park St turn left and make a quick right onto Strawberry St and go south a half-mile, then at W Main St turn right and this place is near the corner.

ROANOKE

**Eden's Way Vegetarian Kitchen
106 Church Avenue, SE; 540-344-3336

Hours: Monday to Friday 11 am to 3 pm, 5 pm to 8 pm; closed Saturday & Sunday.

Vegetarian International Restaurant and Natural Food Store. Juice Bar. Mostly Vegan.

Menu: Homemade vegetarian dishes. Non-dairy Cheese Lasagna, quiche, Au Gratin Potatoes, Pecan Meatloaf, Vegetarian Chix Salad, sandwiches, falafel, soups, wraps, salads, whole-grain breads, and Garden burgers. Bakes own whole-grain breads and desserts.

Comments: Homemade eggless mayo, mustard, ketchup and a variety of non-dairy salad dressings. Indoor garden café; also has sidewalk dining tables. Carryout next to café and health food store. Good service. Pleasant atmosphere. Good size portions. Low-fat food.

Other Info: Full service, take-out. Non-smoking. Accepts reservations but not necessary. Accepts AMEX, DIS, MC, VISA. Price: $.

Directions: From I-81, get onto I-581, exit downtown, go to 3rd light, turn right on Church. Next to all-night parking. Or take 220, then take Eastward exit on Elm, go 2 lights then turn left, then go 2 lights then turn left.

Market Square
Downtown Roanoke

Permanent farmer's market with local fresh produce.

Roanoke Natural Foods Co-op
1319 Grandin Road SW; 540-343-5652

Hours: Monday to Friday 9 am to 7 pm; Saturday 8 am to 9 pm; Sunday 12 noon to 6 pm

Natural Food Store. Organic produce.

Hours: Has a good selection of vegetarian dishes.

Soups, Lasagna, sandwiches and tofu dishes.

Other Info: Counter service, take-out. Has seating. Accepts AMEX, MC, VISA.

Directions: From I-581, take US 11 exit (#5) towards the Downtown, keep left at fork in ramp and merge onto US 11/US 20 Bus and go a third-mile, at US-11 S turn right and go west and this place is about 2½ miles down on Grandin Rd. Across the street from Grandin Theater.

Wildflour Market & Café and Baker (three Roanoke locations)
1212 4th Street SW   540-343-4543
Towers Mall   540 344-1514
7770 Williamson Road, Hollins 540-362-1812

Website: www.wildflour.baweb.com

Hours: Monday to Friday 11 am to 8 pm; Saturday 11 am to 5 pm; closed Sunday.

Natural Foods. Vegan options. Not pure vegetarian.

Menu: Soups, salads, sandwiches, baked goods and dessert. Rice and Beans, burritos, Lasagna, quesadillas and veggie burgers. Cappuccino, espresso.

Comments: Each branch of this restaurant has a daily vegetarian special and a bakery. Small place. Food gets really high ratings.

Other Info: Full service, take-out, catering. Accepts AMEX, DIS, MC, VISA. Price: $-$$.

SPRINGFIELD

Fresh Fields (Whole Foods Market)
8402 Old Keene Mill Road
703-644-2500; **fax:** 703-644-7447

Hours: Monday to Saturday 8 am to 9 pm Sunday 8 am to 8 pm

Natural Food Store and Cafe. Deli, Bakery, Salad Bar and Juice Bar. Organic produce. Supermarket-type place. See Whole Foods Market on page 666.

Menu: Salads, soups, breads and more.

Directions: From I-95, take Springfield exit (#169A) and go west on Old Keene Mill Rd for about 3 miles, and this place on right at junction with Rolling Rd.

Healthway Natural Foods
6402-4 Springfield Plaza
703-569-3533

Hours: Monday to Friday 10 am to 7 pm (until 8 pm Thursday); Saturday 10 am to 6 pm; Sunday 12 noon to 5 pm

Natural Food Store. No produce.

Directions: From I-95, take Old Kilmer Rd. This place on right in Springfield Plaza.

Taj Mahal

7239 Commerce Street; 703-644-2875
Indian. See Washington DC

VIENNA

**Amma Vegetarian Kitchen

344 Maple Avenue East; 703-938-5328
Web site: www.image-in-asian.com/amma/
Hours: Mon to Fri 11:30 am to 2:30 pm, 5:30
pm to 9:30 pm; Sat & Sun 11:30 am to 10 pm
Fully Vegetarian South Indian.
Menu: South Indian dishes including Masala
Dosas, Idly, sambar, coconut chutney, Aloo Matar, uthappam and lassis.
Comments: Food gets high ratings. Quick service. Good value. Casual, no-frills place with plastic utensils. Busy during lunch.
Other Info: Full service, cafeteria, take-out. Accepts reservations but not necessary. Accepts
AMEX, DIS, MC, VISA. Price: $.
Directions: From 495 Beltway, take #11B (Rte
123/Chain Bridge Rd) exit and then take Route
123 south towards Vienna, Tyson's Corner. Rte
123 (Chain Bridge Rd) after a couple miles become Maple Ave, then this place is another half-
mile down.

Fresh Fields (Whole Foods Market)

143 Maple Avenue East
703-319-2000; fax: 703-319-2001
Hours: Monday to Saturday 8 am to 10 pm
Sunday 9 am to 9 pm
Natural Food Store and Cafe. Deli, Bakery, Salad
Bar and Juice Bar. Organic produce. Supermar-
ket-type place. See Whole Foods Market on page
666.
Directions: From I-66, take Vienna/Natalie St
exit east. Then at Maple turn right (going east).
This place on the right five blocks down. From
495 Beltway, take #11B (Rte 123/Chain Bridge
Rd) exit and then take Route 123 South towards
Vienna/Tyson's Corner. Rte 123 (Chain Bridge
Rd) after a couple miles become Maple Ave, then
this place is another mile down.

Panjshir II Restaurant

224 West Maple Avenue; 703-281-4183
Hours: Monday to Saturday 12 noon to 2:30 pm,
5 pm to 11 pm; Sunday 5 pm to 11 pm
Afghan. See Fall Church.
Comments: Good value. Good place for private
parties.
Other Info: Full service, take-out. Accepts
AMEX, MC, VISA. Price: $-$$.

Directions: From 495 Beltway, take #11B (Rte
123/Chain Bridge Rd) exit and then take Route
123 south towards Vienna/Tyson's Corner. Rte
123 (Chain Bridge Rd) after a couple miles become Maple Ave, then this place is another 1¼
mile down. Parking arranged for customers.

**Sunflower Vegetarian Restaurant

2531 Chain Bridge Road, at 123 & Nutley Street,
near McDonald's; 703-319-3888
Hours: Monday to Saturday 11:30 am to 10 pm
Sunday 12 noon to 10 pm
Fully Vegetarian International, Japanese, Chi-
nese and Continental. Mostly Vegan. Macrobiotic
options.
Menu: Wide amount of good dishes including
many mock meat dishes. General Tao's Surprise,
Cold Soba Salad, Miso Soup, Organic Spinach
Spaghetti, Tomato Tofu, Eggplant in Chili Sauce,
Lily Flower Soup, Seaweed Salad. Spring Rolls,
Macrobiotic Tofu, homemade Tofu Burgers, rice
dishes, Wakame Soup, noodle dishes, Asparagus
Rolls, Sunflower Forest and Sunflower Satisfac-
tion. The Fried Chicken appetizer is very good.
Vegan desserts such as Tofu Pumpkin Pie. Organic tea, fresh juices and non-alcoholic beer.
Comments: Very nicely decorated. Has sunflow-
ers all over the restaurant, on the walls pens, cups,
clock and garden. Helpful, friendly, fast service.
Considered by many to be the best vegetarian
restaurant in the DC area. Lists all ingredients at
back of menu. Has a sister restaurant "Helianthus"
in New York City. Has about 20 tables. This place
comes highly recommended.
Other Info: Full service, take-out. Non-smoking.
Does not take reservations. Accepts AMEX, DC,
DIS, MC, VISA. Price: $$.
Directions: Capital Beltway (495) to I-66 West,
then take Exit #62 North to Nutley Street. Turn
left at 4th traffic light onto Chain Bridge Road,
and this place is about 50 yards after turn on left.

VIRGINIA BEACH

Azar's Natural Foods Market & Café

108 Precott Avenue; 757-486-7778
Hours: Daily 11 am to 8:30 pm
Middle Eastern Café and part Middle Eastern
Food Store. Not Pure Vegetarian.
Other Info: Full service, take-out. Accepts
AMEX, MC, VISA.

Bangkok Garden Restaurant

4000 Virginia Beach Boulevard; 757-498-5009
Hours: Monday to Thursday 11 am to 10 pm;

Friday & Sunday 11 am to 10:30 pm; Sunday 12 noon to 9 pm

Thai. Vegan options. Not pure vegetarian.
Menu: Has a separate vegetarian menu.
Comments: Has traditional artifacts decorating the restaurant.
Other Info: Full service, take-out. Reservations suggested for groups. Non-smoking. Accepts AMEX, DIS, MC, VISA. Price: $$.
Directions: Parking arranged for customers.

Eat To Live
2372 Virginia Beach Boulevard; 757-431-0199
Hours: Monday to Friday 11 am to 7 pm; Saturday 12 noon to 7 pm; closed Sunday.
International Restaurant. Vegetarian-friendly.
Menu: Has a good selection of vegetarian dishes.

Fresh Fair Café
700 19th Street, at Cypress Ave; 757-491-5383
Hours: Monday to Saturday 6:30 am to 9 pm
Closed Sunday.
Natural Foods Cafe. Juice Bar.
Menu: Has several vegetarian dishes. Sandwiches, salads, soups, pasta salads and fresh juices.
Other Info: Full service, take-out. Price: $.
Directions: Take I-264 east until it ends and go 1 block, then at Cypress Ave turn right and go 2 blocks, then at 19th turn right and this place is at the corner.

Fresh Market & Deli, Inc.
744 Hilltop North; 757-491-0904
Hours: Monday to Friday 9 am to 9 am; Saturday 10 am to 8 am; closed Sunday.
Gourmet Food Store and Deli. High quality vegetables and fruits.
Menu: Has some vegetarian sandwiches, salads and soups.

Health Food Centers (two locations)
5312 Kempsriver Drive, Suite 105
757-523-8961
4572 Virginia Beach Boulevard, #3B
757-499-0002
Natural Food Store.

HealthQuest (three locations)
928 Diamond Spring Road; 757-671-1775
1650 General Booth Boulevard, Suite 107
757-721-1059
Natural Food Store.

Heritage Health Food Store and Café
314 Laskin Road (Hwy 58); 757-428-0500
Hours: Monday to Saturday 10 am to 7 pm (un-

til 9 pm on Friday); Sunday 12 noon to 7 pm
Natural Food Store and Café. Deli. Vegan options. Not pure vegetarian. Good selection of organic produce.
Menu: Soups, salads, sandwiches and desserts. Fresh juices and smoothies.
Comments: Has a good selection of foods free of sugar, wheat or dairy. Friendly, nice staff.
Other Info: Counter service, take-out. Accepts AMEX, DIS, MC, VISA.
Directions: Take I-264 east until it end and go straight towards the ocean a half-mile, at Pacific Avenue turn left and go north ¾ mile, then at Laskin turn left and this place is at the corner.

Terranova Natural Food Store
Hilltop Square Shopping Center, 550 First Colonial Road, Suite 309, corner of Laskin Road and First Colonial; 757-425-5383
Hours: Monday to Saturday 9:30 am to 7:30 pm
Sunday 12 noon to 6 pm
Café Hours: Monday to Friday 10 am to 4 pm
Café closed Saturday & Sunday.
Natural Food Store and Deli. Organic produce. Not pure vegetarian.
Menu: Has a good selection of vegetarian dishes. Sandwiches, salads, soups, veggie chili, veggie Lasagna and hot dishes. Fresh juices and smoothies.
Comments: Creative foods.
Other Info: Full service, take-out. Price: $. Accepts MC, VISA.
Directions: From I-264, take First Colonial Rd North exit (#21) and go north on First Colonial Dr a half-block and this place is on the right in the Hilltop Square Shopping Center.

Virginia Garden
3640 Dam Neck Road, Suite 24
757-427-0378
Natural Food Store. Organic produce.

WARRENTON
A half-hour from Shenandoah National Park.

The Natural Marketplace
5 Diagonal Street; 540-349-4111
Hours: Monday to Wednesday, Friday 9 am to 6 pm; Thursday 9 am to 7 pm; Saturday 9:30 am to 5 pm; closed Sunday.
Natural Food Store and Deli. Juice Bar. Organic produce.
Menu: Has a selection of vegetarian dishes.
Other Info: Counter service, take-out. Seating.
Directions: From I-66, take Gainesville/Rte 29 exit south and go about 12 miles. At Rte 29/211

Business Route turn right. At Bob's Big Boy turn left. This place is 3 blocks down on the left corner of Waterloo and Diagonal, a quarter mile down in a yellow house.

WILLIAMSBURG

Chea Trinh
Williamsburg Shopping Center, 157 Monticello Avenue, at Richmond Road; 757-253-1888
Hours: Daily 11:30 am to 3 pm, 5 pm to 10 pm
Vietnamese. Not pure vegetarian. Take-out.
Menu: Has a good selection of vegetarian dishes.
Other Info: Full service, take-out. Price: $$.
Accepts AMEX, MC, VISA.

Health Shelf
Williamsburg Shopping Center
159½ A Monticello Ave
757-229-1240
Natural Food Store.
Comments: Not a very big place but has a decent selection.
Directions: From I-64, take VA Hwy 143 exit (#238) towards Colonial Williamsburg and get on Hwy 143, at VA Hwy 132 turn right (go southwest) and go 1¼ mile, at US-60 turn right (go west) and go 1¼ mile, at Richmond Rd (Rte 162) turn left and go a third-mile, at Monticello Ave turn right and this place is 1 block down.

Washington DC

WASHINGTON DC SUBURBS

Maryland: Adams Morgan, Bethesda, Capital Heights, Chevy Chase, College Park, Frederick, Gaithersburg, Greenbelt, Kensington, Langley Park, Laurel, Mt Rainer, Olney, Riverdale, Rockville, Silver Spring, Spencerville, Takoma Park, Wheaton and White Oaks.
Virginia: Alexandria, Arlington, Fairfax, Falls Church, Herndon, Loton, Springfield, Sterling, Vienna and West Vienna.

Addis Ababa Ethiopian Restaurant
2106 18th Street NW, in Adams Morgan
202-232-6092
Hours: Daily 11 am to 2 am; Saturday & Sunday Ethiopian Vegetarian Buffet 11 am to 3 pm
Ethiopian. Not pure vegetarian.
Other Info: Accepts AMEX, MC, VISA.

**Amma Vegetarian Kitchen
3291 M Street NW, 2nd Floor, Georgetown
202-625-6625
Hours: Mon to Thur 11:30 am to 2:30 pm, 5:30 pm to 10 pm; Fri 11:30 am to 2:30 pm, 5:30 pm to 10:30 pm; Sat 11:30 am to 4 pm, 5:30 pm to 10:30 pm; Sun 11:30 am to 4 pm
Fully Vegetarian. Mainly East Indian.
Menu: Has a wide selection of vegetarian dishes. Soups, salads, curries, breads, Palak Paneer (spinach and fresh cheese), Rice Pulao, appetizers, Malai Kofta, and Aloo Chole (chickpeas and potatoes over rice). South Indian dishes like Masala Dosa, Idly and others. Gulabjamun and Ras Malai. Mango lassi and salty lassi.
Comments: Gets good ratings. Popular place. Has gotten many good reviews in newspapers. Good atmosphere. Good place for a special event. Good value. Reasonably priced. Dosas contain butter and dal (lentil) and sometimes contains cream. Pleasant, cozy atmosphere. Basic place that uses plaster utensils and Styrofoam plates.
Other Info: Full service, counter service, cafeteria style, take-out. Accepts reservations but not necessary. Accepts AMEX, MC, VISA. Price: $-$$.

Directions: In Georgetown at the western end of M Street, three blocks east of Key Bridge Parking arranged for customers.

Asia Nora
2213 M Street NW; 202-797-4860; **fax:** 202-797-1300; **Web site:** www.noras.com
Hours: Monday to Thursday 5:30 pm to 10 pm; Fri and Sat 5:30 am to 10:30 pm; closed Sun.
New American, Asian and International. It is registered as 100% organic. Vegan options. Not pure vegetarian.
Menu: The five-course vegetarian sampler is $40, but it is good for two people. Soups, salads and main dishes. Grilled Spring Asparagus Nori Roll (vegetarian sushi and wasabi). The miso soup is good. Fresh juices.
Comments: Gets high recommendations. It is an upscale place and formal. Most people wear a suit and tie, but there is no dress code. Asia Nora has dark walnut tables, fancy architecture, and low lighting. Restaurant Nora is a well-lit room with Amish quilts. One of better restaurants in DC.
Warning: Many of the dishes use fish sauce, so you should ask about this.
Other Info: Full service, take-out. Accepts MC, VISA. Price: $$$.
Directions: From Potomac: Follow Massachusetts Avenue into town through Sheridan Circle. At the first light after the circle, take a right onto 23rd Street. Follow 23rd Street to M Street. Asia Nora is to your left, a half-block down, but M street is one-way heading to your right. You can follow 23rd past M Street, take a left on L Street, then left on 22nd Street, and finally left on M Street. Asia Nora will now be on the right hand side of the street halfway down the block. Has detailed directions on their web site from Annapolis, Maryland, Dulles, Potomac and National Airport. Parking arranged for customers.

Bacchus
1827 Jefferson Place NW, Dupont Circle
202-785-0734
Hours: Monday to Thursday 12 noon to 2:30

pm, 6 pm to 10 pm; Friday & Saturday 12 noon to 2:30 pm, 6 pm to 10:30 pm; closed Sunday. **Lebanese, Middle Eastern.** Not pure vegetarian. **Comments:** Authentic décor. Has tapestries. Seats 60. Good place for special event. **Other Info:** Reservations suggested. Accepts AMEX, MC, VISA. Price: $$-$$$. **Directions:** From Dupont Circle go two block southeast on Connecticut Avenue, then turn left on Jefferson Place and this place is on the left, a half-block down. Parking arranged.

Bombay Club

815 Connecticut Avenue NW, #302, between H & I Streets; 202-659-3727
Hours: Monday to Thursday 11:30 am to 2:30 pm, 6 pm to 10 pm; Friday 11:30 am to 2:30 pm, 6 pm to 11 pm; Saturday 6 pm to 11 pm; Sunday 11:30 am to 2:30 pm, 5:30 pm to 9 pm **Indian.** Cuisines from all over India. Not pure vegetarian.
Menu: Has a selection of vegetarian dishes.
Comments: Upscale with fancy dinning room and patio. Popular place. British colonial mood. People dress formal here. Authentic décor with murals. Good place for special event. Live piano music.
Other Info: Full service, take-out. Accepts AMEX, DC, MC, VISA. Price: $$.
Directions: This place is at the northeast corner of Lafayette Park, right in front of the White House. Parking arranged for customers.

Burrito Brothers

1524 Connecticut Avenue, NW; 202-332-2308
Directions: This place is just northwest of Dupont Circle.
205 Pennsylvania Avenue, SE; 202-543-6835
Directions: East of the White House.
Hours: Daily 8 am to 10 pm
Pennsylvania Ave place closed on Sunday.
Mexican. Not pure vegetarian.
Menu: California-style burritos. Has low fat ones.
Comments: The tortillas and beans are lard-free.
Other Info: Limited service, take-out. Price: $.

Café Asia

1134 19th Street NW; 202-659-2696
email: cafeasia@cafeasia.com
Web site: www.cafeasia.com
Hours: Monday to Saturday 11:30 am to 10 pm Closed Sunday.
Asian. Not pure vegetarian.
Menu: Vegetarian sushi and tofu dishes. Good desserts.
Comments: Popular place during lunch. Good

food. Upscale. Unique art deco décor. Happening place. Good place for a special event. Good value.
Other Info: Full service, take-out, catering. Reservations suggested for groups. Accepts AMEX, DC, DIS, MC, VISA. Price: $-$$.
Directions: From VA take 395 north over the 14th street Bridge. Then at K street turn left (west), at 18 street turn right, then at M St turn left, then at 19th Street turn left and this place is on the right side. (19th street is one way). Parking garages on left and right sides of street. Take Hwy 66 east to Washington DC and then go over the Key Bridge, then go right at end of bridge and go on K street NW, then at 18th Street turn left, at M Street turn left, then turn left on 19th Street. By Metro Rail get off at Dupont Circle, take Dupont Circle exit toward M Street, walk past M street and this place is before L Street.

City Lights of China

1731 Connecticut Avenue NW, between R & S Streets, Dupont Circle; 202-265-6688
Hours: Monday to Thursday 11:30 am to 10:30 pm; Friday 11:30 am to 11 pm; Saturday 12 noon to 11 pm; Sunday 12 noon to 10:30 pm
Chinese. Vegan options. Not pure vegetarian.
Menu: Hunan and Szechuan cuisine. Has a separate vegetarian menu that you should ask for. Has a wide variety of vegetarian dishes. Soups, appetizers, main dishes and mock meat dishes.
Comments: Is a large popular place located in a basement.
Other Info: Full service, take-out. Accepts AMEX, DC, DIS, MC, VISA. Price: $$-$$$.
Directions: From Dupont Circle, go northwest on Connecticut Avenue four blocks and this place is on the right. Near the Dupont Circle Metro stop.

***Delights of the Garden

2616 Georgia Avenue NW, near Howard University; 202-319-8747
Web site: www.epiphanybooks.com
Hours: Monday to Wednesday 12 am to 8 pm; Thursday to Saturday 11 am to 11 pm; Sunday 12 pm to 7 pm; Sunday Brunch.
Fully Vegan. Vegetarian, specializing in raw food. Also has some cooked foods.
Menu: Mainly raw food menu. The Side Sampler Plate is worth checking out. It contains kush, vegetables, seaweed, nutmeat (paste made from whole-wheat bulgur), chips & salsa, sunflower seeds, hummus and barbecue sauce. Kush is a dish like tabbouleh or rice, but it is soaked spiced raw

bulgur. Vegan Banana Bread, Tofu Dogs, Pita Bread Sandwiches, veggie burgers, veggie tuna, BBQ Nutmeat and Seaweed Salad. Fresh juices.
Comments: Relaxed, casual place. One of the best pure vegetarian restaurants in DC. It is a small place without much seating. Delights of the Garden started as an all-raw foods restaurant, but has added cooked food to the menu. Good food. Have their own cookbook. Has unique mock meats. Their motto is "Good Food for Good People."
Other Info: Full service, counter service, take-out. Non-smoking. Accepts reservations but not necessary. Cash only; no credit cards. Price: $-$$.
Directions: It is opposite Howard University's School of Business. Independence Avenue to 7th Street uptown. 7th Street turns into Georgia Ave.

****Everlasting Life Coop and Eternity Juice Bar**

2928 Georgia Avenue, NW, near Howard University; 202-232-1700
Web site: www.everlastinglife.net
Hours: Monday to Saturday 9 am to 9 pm Sunday 11 am to 9 pm
Natural Food Store and Fully Vegetarian Cafe. Juice Bar. Organic produce. Specializes in Raw Cuisine.
Menu: Has raw (emphasis on) and cooked foods. Soups, Live Stir-fry, Mung Bean Salad, Tofu Salad, pasta salad (with organic noodles), Couscous Salad, Tofu-seaweed Salad, Mock Chicken Salad, sandwiches, Stir-fry Vegetables, fresh fruit salad, Pickled Beets, cornbread, Bean Curd Salad, Mushroom Salad, Carrot Supreme and Vegan soft-serve ice cream. Fresh juices, wheatgrass juice and smoothies. The Cashew Nog (soy milk, ground cashews, coconut milk) is popular.
Comments: The restaurant is very good. The co-op has good organic produce and bulk food sections. Largest coop in DC. Relaxed place.
Other Info: Full service, take-out. Accepts AMEX, MC, VISA.
Directions: This place is about a 1½ mile north of where I-395 ends in DC, on the northeast corner of Howard University. From I-495, take Georgia Ave exit in Silver Spring and go south towards DC. At 16th turn right, then at Upshur St NW turn left, then at Georgia Ave NW turn right and this place is on your right at Columbia Rd.

Fasika's Ethiopian Restaurant

2447 18th Street NW, between Columbia & Belmont Roads, Adams Morgan
202-797-7673

Hours: Monday to Thursday 5 pm to 11:30 pm; Friday 5 pm to 1 am; Saturday 12 noon to 1 am; Sunday 12 noon to 11:30 pm
Ethiopian. Vegan options. Not pure vegetarian.
Menu: Has a vegetarian menu. Salads, bean dishes and vegetables dishes.
Comments: Gets good ratings. Has live jazz on Friday and Saturday.
Other Info: Full service, take-out, delivery. Accepts AMEX, DC, MC, VISA. Price: $$.
Directions: This place is about a mile southeast of the National Zoological Park, about a mile north of Dupont Circle. From Dupont Circle, go northwest of Dupont Circle a half-mile, then make a slight right onto Columbia Rd NW and go a third-mile, then at Belmont Rd NW turn right, then a block down at 18th St NW turn left and this place is a half-block down on the left.

Fresh Fields

4530 40th Street NW, Tenley Circle
202-237-5800
Hours: Monday to Saturday 8 am to 10 pm Sunday 8 am to 9 pm
Natural Food Store and Cafe. Deli, Bakery, Salad Bar and Juice Bar. Organic produce. Supermarket-type place. See Whole Foods Market information.
Directions: From I-495, take River Rd (Rte 190 south) exit and go toward DC for about 7 miles. Then make a slight left onto Chesapeake St NW, then at Wisconsin Ave turn right, at Brandywine St turn left, then at 40th St turn right. This place near junction of 40th and Wisconsin, a block north of where River Rd meets Wisconsin.

Fresh Fields

2323 Wisconsin Avenue NW, Georgetown
202-333-5393; **fax:** 202-333-5392
Hours: Daily 8 am to 10 pm
Natural Food Store and Cafe. Deli, Bakery, Salad Bar and Juice Bar. Organic produce. Supermarket-type place. See Whole Foods Market information.
Directions: From Dupont Circle, go southwest on Massachusetts Ave, then turn left at Observatory Lane. At the light, Wisconsin Ave, turn left, and this place on left. From I-495, take River Rd southeast into DC for about 7 mile, then take a slight right onto Wisconsin Ave.

Fresh Fields

1440 P Street, NW, near Logan Circle/Dupont Circle; 202-332-4300; **fax:** 202-265-0061
Hours: Monday to Saturday 8 am to 10 pm

Sunday 8 am to 9 pm
Natural Food Store and Cafe. Deli, Bakery, Salad Bar and Juice Bar. Organic produce. Supermarket-type place. See Whole Foods Market information.
Directions: From Dupont Circle, go east on P St NW one mile.

Food for Thought
In the Black Cat Club, 1811 14th Street, NW
202-797-1095
Black Cat Club number: 202-667-4900
Hours: Monday to Thursday 8 pm to 1 am; Friday & Saturday 7 pm to 2 am; closed Sunday.
American Natural Foods. Mostly Vegetarian. Vegan options. Not pure vegetarian.
Menu: Has a wide selection of creative vegetarian dishes. Soups, salads, sandwiches, main dishes, daily specials and desserts. Fresh juices.
Comments: Live music daily. Good value.
Other Info: Full service, take-out. Non-smoking. Accepts AMEX, DC, DIS, MC, VISA. Price: $$
Directions: This place is about 1 mile north of the main downtown area.

Good Health Natural Foods
325 Pennsylvania Avenue SE; 202-543-2266
Hours: Monday to Saturday 9:30 am to 7 pm
Closed Sunday.
Natural Food Store and Deli. Juice Bar. Macrobiotic options. Vegan options. Not pure vegetarian.
Menu: Soups, salads, sandwiches, veggie burgers, hijiki and bean soups. Has a take-out section with ready-made dishes.
Other Info: Counter service, take-out only. Accepts MC, VISA. Price: $.
Directions: Across from the Library of Congress, about 3 blocks southeast of the Capital building.

Harmony Café
3287½ M Street NW, Georgetown
202-338-3881
Hours: Monday to Saturday 11:30 am to 11 pm
Sunday 5 pm to 11 pm
Asian. Vegetarian Friendly. Not pure vegetarian.
Menu: Most dishes can be made vegetarian. Has a good selection of mock meat dishes and good tofu dishes.
Comments: Has a nice décor with ornately carved wooden chairs.
Other Info: Accepts DIS, MC, VISA. Price: $$.
Directions: This place is about 2 blocks north of Georgetown University Hospital, about a mile east of the Potomac River.

Honest to Goodness Burritos
15th and K Streets, NW; 202-276-1799
Hours: Monday to Friday 11 am to 2:30 pm
Closed Saturday & Sunday.
Vegetarian-friendly Lunch Cart with burritos. Not pure vegetarian.
Comments: Burrito are made fresh, so may have to wait about five minutes. Very popular. Price: $.

**Indian Delight
Union Station Mall, 50 Massachusetts Avenue NE, near the White House; 202-842-1040
Hours: Monday to Saturday 10 am to 9 pm
Sunday 12 noon to 6 pm
Fully Vegetarian Indian. Mostly Vegan.
Menu: Soups, salads, curried dishes, rice dishes, desserts and daily specials.
Comments: Authentic Indian food. Low on atmosphere. Located in a typical food court in a not-so-typical mall that is part of a train and metro station
Other Info: Counter service, take-out. Non-smoking. Accepts reservations, but not necessary. No credit cards. Price: $.
Directions: This place is at Union Station, a quarter-mile north of the Capital building. Red line metro stops here.

**Indian Delight
1100 Pennsylvania Avenue NW, near the White House; 202-371-2295
Pure Vegetarian Indian. Branch of the one described above. Vegan friendly.
Comments: The Pennsylvania branch is in an old post office. Price: $.

Juice Joint Café
1025 Vermont Avenue NW; 202-347-6783
Hours: Monday to Friday 7:30 am to 4 pm
Closed Saturday & Sunday.
Juice Bar.
Menu: Salads, soups, sandwiches, wraps and stir-fries. Fresh juices and smoothies.
Other Info: Non-smoking.
Directions: Take subway to McPhearson Square.

Julia's Empañadas
2452 18th Street NW, at Columbia Road, Adams Morgan; 202-328-6232
Hours: Sunday to Thursday 10 am to 10 pm
Friday & Saturday 10 am to 3 am
1000 Vermont Avenue NW, Logan Circle
202-789-1878
Hours: Monday to Friday 10 am to 6 pm

1410 U Street; 202-387-4100
Hours: Daily 10 am to 6 pm
1221 Connecticut Avenue NW, Dupont Circle
202-861-8828
Latin. Not pure vegetarian.
Menu: Vegetarian-style empanadas. Spinach, broccoli and cheese empañadas.
Other Info: Limited service, take-out. No credit cards. Price: $$.

Lebanese Taverna
2641 Connecticut Ave NW, at Woodley Rd, Woodley Park area
202-265-8691; **fax:** 202-265-8681
Hours: Monday to Thursday 11:30 am to 2:30 pm, 5:30 pm to 10:30 pm; Friday & Saturday 11:30 am to 3:30 pm, 5:30 pm to 11:30 pm; Sunday 5 pm to 10 pm
Lebanese, Middle Eastern, Mediterranean, American. Not pure vegetarian.
Menu: Has a full page of vegetarian dishes on the menu. Falafel, hummus, tabbouleh, Taverna's Bread (cooked in wood-burning oven) and more.
Comments: Friendly service. Good food. One of the best Middle Eastern places in DC. Gets good reviews from the food critics. Wood-burning pizza oven. Good place for a special event. Has outdoor seating. Good value. This place is quite happening on weekend evening (loud).
Second Branch: Has a branch at 5900 Washington Boulevard, Arlington, 703-241-8681.
Other Info: Outdoor Café. Full service, take-out. Accepts AMEX, DC, DIS, MC, VISA. Price: $$.
Directions: This place is 1¼ mile northwest of Dupont Circle on Connecticut Ave. You can get here by taking the Connecticut Ave exit from I-495 and this place is about 6 miles south on Connecticut. Woodley Park–Zoo Metro stops near here. Parking arranged for customers.

Miss Saigon
3057 M Street NW, Georgetown
202-333-5545
fax: 202-333-6459
Hours: Monday to Friday 11:30 am to 10:30 pm
Saturday & Sunday 12 noon to 11 pm
Vietnamese. Not pure vegetarian.
Menu: Has a page of vegetarian dishes on the menu.
Other Info: Full service, take-out, delivery. Reservations suggested. Accepts AMEX, DC, MC, VISA. Price: $-$$.
Directions: This place is 6 blocks east of Key Bridge on M Street (main street in Georgetown), between 30th and 31st Streets.

Naturally Yours
2029 P Street NW; 202-429-1718
Hours: Monday to Saturday 10 am to 8 pm
Sunday 10 am to 5 pm
Natural Food Store and Juice Bar. Organic produce. Does not have a deli. Everything in the store is vegetarian.
Menu: Has ready-made sandwiches and ready-made dishes such as mock chickens and hummus in their coolers. Fresh juices and power shakes.
Comments: The produce section is not very big. Fairly good selection in store.
Other Info: Accepts AMEX, MC, VISA.

Oodles Noodles
1120 19th Street; 202-293-3138
Hours: Monday to Thursday 11:30 am to 3 pm, 5 pm to 10 pm; Friday & Saturday 11:30 am to 3 pm, 5 pm to 10:30 pm; closed Sunday.
Asian including Chinese, Japanese, Thai, Vietnamese and Indonesian. Not pure vegetarian.
Menu: Has a good selection of Asian noodle dishes.
Other Info: Accepts AMEX, DC, MC, VISA. Price: $$.
Directions: This place is 5 blocks due south of Dupont circle on the right.

People Garden Coop
3155 Mount Pleasant Street NW
202-232-4753
Hours: Monday to Thursday 9 am to 9 pm; Fri & Sat 9 am to 8 pm; Sun 10 am to 8 pm
Natural Food Store and Deli. 90% Vegan & Organic. Juice Bar. Organic produce. Not pure vegetarian (sometimes serves chicken or turkey products).
Menu: Has vegan and vegetarian salads and main dishes. Falafel, dolma, spring rolls, soups, Veggie Stew, sandwiches, salads and more. Fresh juices and smoothies.
Comments: Friendly place. Has bulk foods.
Other Info: Counter service, take-out. Has seating during the day for lunch.
Directions: This place is about a half-mile east of the National Zoological Park. From I-495 take Rte 29 S (Colesville Rd) exit and go south on Colesville Rd for 2½ miles, at 16th St turn left and go 5 miles, then at Lamont St turn right, then make a sharp left onto Mt Pleasant St, and this place is near the corner.

Red Sea Ethiopian Restaurant
2463 18th Street NW, between Columbia & Belmont Roads, Adams Morgan

202-483-5000
Hours: Sunday to Thursday 11:30 am to 10 pm
Friday & Saturday 11:30 am to 11 pm
Ethiopian. Vegan options. Not pure vegetarian.
Menu: Has several authentic Ethiopian vegetarian dishes.
Comments: Uses native herbs and spices. Has outdoor seating. Good place for a group. This is the most famous of the several Ethiopian restaurants in the Adam Morgan area.
Other Info: Full service, take-out. Reservations suggested. Accepts AMEX, DC, DIS, MC, VISA. Price: $$.
Directions: This place is about a mile southeast of the National Zoological Park and about a mile north of Dupont Circle. From Dupont Circle, go northwest of Dupont Circle a half mile on Connecticut, then make a slight right onto Columbia Rd NW and go a third-mile, then at Belmont Rd NW turn right, then a block down at 18th St NW turn left and this place is a half-block down on the left.

Restaurant Nora

2132 Florida Avenue, NW, between Connecticut & Massachusetts, Dupont Circle
202-462-5143; **fax:** 202-234-6232
Hours: Monday to Thursday 6 pm to 10 pm; Friday & Saturday 6 pm to 10:30 pm; closed Sunday.
Natural International and New American. Organic and biodynamic. Not pure vegetarian.
Menu: Menu changes daily. Same as Asia Nora above. Has a nightly Organic Vegetarian Plate. Has a good selection of vegetarian salads, appetizers and main dishes. Fresh juices.
Comments: Formal, but can dress fairly casual. In a romantic carriage house. Food and service gets great ratings. Good, upscale décor. Good place for a special event.
Other Info: Full service. Reservations recommended. Accepts MC, VISA. Price: $$$-$$$$.
Directions: Follow Massachusetts Avenue into town through Sheridan Circle. At the first light after the circle, take a left onto Florida Avenue. Go one block on Florida. Nora's on the right hand side at the corner of Florida and R Street. Valet parking available.

Ruppert's

1017 7th St NW, between New York Avenue & L Street; 202-783-0699
Hours: Tuesday and Wednesday 6 pm to 10 pm; Thursday 11:30 am to 2:30 pm, 6 pm to 10 pm; Friday and Saturday 6 pm to 11 pm

New American. Vegan options. Uses organic produce. Not pure vegetarian.
Menu: Has two vegan appetizers, a vegan main dish and a vegan sorbet on the menu. The menu changes nightly. Bakes four kinds of breads daily. They do not use butter or milk in their cooking. Has some innovative recipes and exotic vegetables. Semolina with fresh herbs.
Comments: It is a fancy place, but the exterior doesn't show it. High priced. Usually uses locally grown produce. Good place for special event. Luxury, downtown institution. Warm, relaxed atmosphere. One of the owners is a vegan.
Other Info: Full service, take-out. Reservation suggested. Accepts AMEX, DC, DIS, MC, VISA. Price: $$-$$$.
Directions: This place is about 1½ mile northeast of the Capital building. Take I-395 north into DC, take the exit going towards Massachusetts Ave, merge onto 2nd St, then make an immediate left onto Massachusetts Ave and go 5 blocks, then turn right onto 7 St and go a block and this place is just past New York Avenue. Parking arranged for customers.

Sala Thai

2016 P Street NW, Dupont Circle
202-872-1144
Hours: Sunday to Thursday 10 am to 10 pm
Friday & Saturday 10 am to 11 pm
Thai. Vegan friendly. Not pure vegetarian.
Comments: Has a separate vegetarian menu. Willing to make any dish vegetarian. Ask for the non-fish vegetarian sauce. Friendly service. Nice, casual atmosphere. Reasonable prices.
Other Info: Full service, take-out, delivery. Accepts AMEX, DC, MC, VISA. Price: $-$$.
Directions: This place is two blocks west on P St. Parking arranged for customers.

Secret of Nature Health Food

3923 South Capitol Street, SW; 202-562-0041
Hours: Monday to Friday 9 am to 7 pm; Saturday 9 am to 6 pm; closed Sunday.
Natural Food Store & Café. Macrobiotic and Vegan options. Not pure vegetarian.
Menu: Has a large variety of vegetarian dishes including soups, salads, sandwiches and more. Fresh juices.
Other Info: Counter service, take-out, catering. Price: $.
Directions: This place is in southeast DC on other side of the river. From I-495 get on I-295 going north, take Portland Street exit, stay right at fork in ramp and go straight on Malcolm X Ave SE,

then turn left to get on S Capitol St SW ramp, then stay left at fork and this place is about a half-mile down.

Senbeb Co-op

5924 Georgia Avenue, NW; 202-723-5566
Hours: Monday to Saturday 10 am to 8 pm
Sunday 12 noon to 5 pm
Natural Food Store and Vegan-friendly Deli. Not pure vegetarian.
Comments: This store is vegan friendly.

Skewer's

1633 P Street, NW
202-387-7400; **fax:** 202-667-8642
Hours: Daily 11 am to 11 pm
Middle Eastern. Vegan options. Not pure veg.
Menu: Falafel, hummus and vegetable kebabs.
Comments: Has outdoor seating. Good value.
Other Info: Full service, take-out, delivery. Accepts AMEX, MC, VISA. Price: $$.

***Soul Vegetarian Café

2606 Georgia Avenue NW
202-328-7685 (SOUL)
Web site: www.kingdomofyah.com/sv.htm
Hours: Monday to Saturday 11 am to 9 pm
Sunday Brunch 11 am to 3 pm
Vegan Soul Food. African, American, Italian, Middle Eastern.
Menu: Gravy Burger, Liberia Burger (made with black eye peas), battered baked fries, Lasagna, tacos, Vegan Pizza, Stir-fries, Collard Greens & Corn, vegan Macaroni & Cheese, BBQ Tofu Sub, Tofu Cheesecake, Carrot Cake, vegan ice cream, Sweet Potato Pie, and Vegan Cinnamon Buns. Smoothies, soy milk and soy shakes. Has take-out juices in the cooler.
Comments: Basic décor. Part of a chain of Soul vegetarian restaurants. This is a small place. Has gotten high rating from several people I know.
Other Info: Counter service, take-out. Three tables. Accepts MC, VISA. Price: $-$$.
Directions: From I-95, go east on I-695, then take I-295 (Baltimore–Washington Parkway) going south. Bear right onto Rte 50 (follow sign to Washington) and go 4 miles, at N Capitol St turn right and go a half-mile, turn right onto S St, then turn left onto N Capitol St, at Rhode Island Ave (Rte 1) turn left and go a half-mile, at Florida Ave turn right and go a third-mile, Then turn right onto Georgia Ave (Rte 29) and this place is a half-mile down. Opposite Howard University School of Business. It is about 1½ mile directly north of where I-395 ends in DC.

Taj Mahal

1327 Connecticut Avenue, NW; 202-659-1544; **email:** orgmail@washingtonpost.com
Web site: http://yp.washingtonpost.com/E/V/WASDC/0003/04/23/
Hours: Monday to Saturday 11:30 am to 2:30 pm, 5:30 pm to 10 pm; Sunday 5:30 pm to 10 pm; **Buffet Lunch:** Monday to Friday 12 noon to 2 pm
Indian. Vegan options. Not pure vegetarian.
Menu: Has a selection of vegetarian dishes such as soups, appetizers, main dishes and desserts. Vegetable Korma, Shahi Paneer, Channa Masala, Bengan Bharta, Matar Pulao, Mango Chutney, Indian breads, Vegetable Biryani and lassis.
Comments: Oldest Indian restaurant in DC; open since 1965. Has menu on Web site. Food gets mixed reviews.
Other Info: Full service, take-out. Accepts AMEX, DIS, MC, VISA. Price: $$.
Directions: This place is on Connecticut Ave, a block southeast of Dupont Circle on the left side.

Teaism

20009 R Street NW, near Dupont Circle
202-667-3827; **fax:** 202-667-3286
email: info@teaism.com
Hours: Monday to Friday 8 am to 10 pm; Saturday 9:30 am to 10 pm; Sunday 9:30 am to 9:30 pm; Sat & Sun Brunch 9:30 am to 2:30 pm
Japanese, Asian Tea Room. Not pure vegetarian.
Comments: Good atmosphere. Has outdoor dining. Has a large selection of teas. No alcohol. Seats 35.
Other Info: Accepts AMEX, MC, VISA. Price: $-$$.
Directions: Between Connecticut and 21st Street on R St. From Dupont Circle go northeast on Connecticut Ave, then turn right onto R St NW and this place is near the corner on right. This place is a block from Dupont Circle metro stop.

Wrap Works

1601 Connecticut Ave NW; 202 265-4200
Hours: Sunday to Thursday 11 am to 11 pm
Friday & Saturday 11 am to 12 midnight
Has some vegetable wraps. Not pure vegetarian.

Yes Organic Market

658 Pennsylvania Avenue
202-546-9850
Hours: Monday to Saturday 8 am to 9 pm
Sunday 9 am to 7 am
Natural Food Store. Organic produce.
Other Info: Accepts MC, VISA.

Yes! Natural Gourmet

3425 Connecticut Avenue NW
202-363-1559
Hours: Monday to Saturday 8 am to 9 pm
Sunday 9 am to 8 pm
Natural Food Store and take-out Deli. Juice Bar.
Menu: Soups, salads and sandwiches. Fresh juices.
Other Info: Counter service, take-out. No seating. Accepts AMEX, MC, VISA. Price: $.
Directions: From I-495, take Connecticut exit south and go five miles. This place on left, a half-mile south of Connecticut and Livingston, near the zoo. Close to Cleveland Park metro stop.

Yes Natural Gourmet

1825 Columbia Road NW
202-462-5150
Hours: Monday to Saturday 9 am to 8 pm
Sunday 12 noon to 6 pm
Natural Food Store and Deli. Juice Bar.
Directions: From I-495, take Connecticut Ave exit south. At Calvert turn left and at Columbia turn right. This place on right. From Dupont Circle go northeast a little less than a half-mile on Connecticut Ave, then make a slight turn and this place is 4/10 mile down the road.

Zed's Ethiopian Cuisine

3318 M Street, NW
202-333-4710
Hours: Sunday to Thursday 11 am to 10 pm
Friday & Saturday 11 am to 11 pm
Ethiopian. Vegan options. Not pure vegetarian.
Menu: Has several vegetarian dishes.
Comments: No utensils used; uses injera bread to eat food. Authentic, good food. Good value.
Other Info: Reservations suggested for groups. Accepts AMEX, DC, DIS, MC, VISA. Price: $-$$. Full service, take-out.
Directions: On the main street in Georgetown.

Zorba's Café

1612 20th Street, NW
202-387-8555
Hours: Monday to Saturday 11 am to 11 pm
Sunday 11:30 am to 10 pm
Greek, Mediterranean. Vegan options. Not pure vegetarian.
Menu: Falafel, hummus, Spanakopita and more dishes.
Comments: Good value. Has outdoor patio seating. Relaxed, pleasant atmosphere.
Other Info: Deli style, take-out. Accepts AMEX, MC, VISA. Price: $$.
Directions: This place is a half-block north of the Dupont Circle Metro station. From Dupont Circle go a block west on Massachusetts Ave and make a right on 20th St and this place is a block down.

Washington

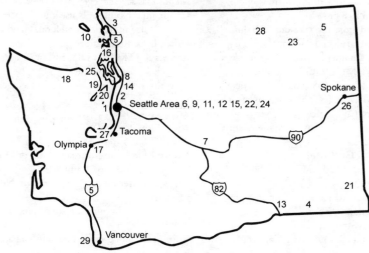

1. Bainbridge Island
2. Bellevue
3. Bellingham
4. College Place
5. Colville
6. Eastsound
7. Ellensburg
8. Everett
9. Federal Way
10. Friday Harbor
11. Gig Harbor
12. Issaquah
13. Kennewick
14. Kirkland
15. Mountlake Terrace
16. Mount Vernon
17. Olympia
18. Port Angeles
19. Port Townsend
20. Poulsbo
21. Pullman
22. Redmond
23. Republic
24. Seattle
25. Sequim
26. Spokane
27. Tacoma
28. Tonasket
29. Vancouver

BAINBRIDGE ISLAND

Natural Gourmet
Harold's Square; 206-842-2759
Hours: Monday to Saturday 9:30 am to 6 pm
Sunday 10 am to 5:30 pm
Natural Foods. Not pure vegetarian. Vegan
options.
Menu: Soups, salads, sandwiches and main dishes.
Fresh juices, cappuccino, espresso.
Other Info: Limited service, take-out. Accepts
MC, VISA. Price: $.

BELLEVUE

India Gate
3080 48th Avenue SE
425-747-1075; **fax:** 425-747-1076
Hours: Mon to Sat 11 am to 2:30 pm, 5 pm to
10 pm; Sun 12 noon to 2:30 pm, 4 pm to 9 pm
Indian. Lunch Buffet. Mainly North Indian. Not
pure vegetarian.

Comments: Has a wide selection of vegetarian
dishes. Good Indian food. Food gets good recommendations. Good value.
Other Info: Full service, take-out, delivery. Non-
smoking. Accepts AMEX, DC, DIS, MC, VISA.

Juice Plant
Key Tower
601 108th Avenue NE
425-467-0202
Hours: Monday to Friday 7 am to 5 pm
Closed Saturday & Sunday.
Juice Bar. Vegetarian. See Seattle.
Menu: Fresh juices and smoothies. Salads, baked
potatoes, veggie chili, veggie Lasagna, Toca Sand-
wich and veggie sandwiches.
Other Info: Accepts AMEX, DIS, MC, VISA.
Counter service, take-out. Has 3 tables.
Directions: From I-405, take NE 8th St exit
(#13A), and then go west on NE 8th St 2 blocks,
then at 108th Ave NE turn left and this place is 1
block down.

Moghul Palace

10301 NE 10th Street; 425-451-1909
Hours: Monday to Saturday 11:30 am to 2:30 pm, 5 pm to 10 pm; Sunday 5 pm to 10 pm
Indian. Vegan-friendly. Not pure vegetarian.
Menu: Has a large selection of vegetarian dishes.
Comments: Friendly service. Willing to make changes to dishes. Upscale atmosphere. This place gets high ratings. Good value.
Other Info: Non-smoking. Accepts AMEX, DIS, MC, VISA. Price: $$.
Directions: Free parking for customers.

Nature's Pantry

10200 10th Street, NE; 425-454-0170
Hours: Monday to Friday 9 am to 7 pm; Saturday 9:30 am to 6 pm; Sunday 11 am to 5 pm
Juice Bar closes a half hour before the store.
Directions: In downtown Bellevue. From 405 Freeway, take West NE 8th St exit and go west on NE 8th St a half-mile, then at 102nd turn right. This place at 10th and 102nd.
Cross Roads, 15600 8th Street #15, NE 425-957-0090
Hours: Monday to Thursday 9 am to 7 pm; Fri & Sat 9 am to 8 pm; Sun 11 am to 6 pm
Directions: From I-520 E, take Rte 148 exit south and bear right at exit. Go straight and at NE 8th turn left. Go past 156th and make left at next light. Drive through parking lot and this place in on left across the parking lot.
Natural Food Store and Vegan-friendly Café. Deli and Juice Bar. Supermarket-size place. Not pure vegetarian. Large selection of organic produce.
Menu: Salads, sandwiches, organic salads, noodles dishes, pastas and other dishes. Fresh juices.
Other Info: Accepts MC, VISA. Limited service, take-out. Price: $.

Public Market

Crossroad Mall, NE 8th and 156th Avenue NE
Variety of food booths, many with vegetarian dishes. Has Indian, Middle Eastern, Chinese, Italian and pizza places.
Directions: From I-405, take NE 8th St exit (#13A), and then go east on NE 8th St and this place is about 3 miles down on NE 8th St.

Raga

556 108th Avenue NE; 425-450-0336
Hours: Daily 11:30 am to 2:30 pm (Lunch Buffet), 5 pm to 10 pm
Indian. Some American dishes. Mainly vegetarian all-you-can-eat Lunch Buffet.
Menu: Has a good vegetarian section on their menu.

Comments: Good food. Food gets good ratings.
Other Info: Full service, take-out, delivery. Non-smoking. Accepts AMEX, DC, MC, VISA. Price: $-$$.
Directions: Free parking for customers.

Thai Chef

1645 140th Avenue, NE; 206-562-7955
Hours: Daily 11 am to 2:30 pm, 5 pm to 9:30 pm
Thai. Vegan options. Not pure vegetarian.
Menu: Has a wide selection of vegetarian dishes such as soups, appetizers and main dishes.
Other Info: Full service, take-out. Accepts AMEX, MC, VISA. Price: $$.

The Thai Kitchen

14115 20th Street, NE
425-641-9166; **fax:** 425-746-6743
Hours: Daily 11 am to 10 pm
Thai. Vegan options. Not pure vegetarian.
Menu: Has many vegetarian options including Springs Rolls, Tofu with Peanut Sauce, soups, Tofu & Spinach with Peanut Sauce, Hot and Sour Soup and rice dishes.
Warning: Make sure you request that no oyster sauce is added to a dish.
Other Info: Full service, take-out. Reservations suggested for groups. Non-smoking. Accepts AMEX, MC, VISA. Price: $.
Directions: Parking arranged for customers.

BELLINGHAM

Community Food Co-op

1220 North Forest; 360-734-8158
Hours: Daily 8 am to 9 pm
Café Hours: 8 am to 8 pm
Natural Food Store and Cafe. Deli. Organic produce. Supermarket-size place.
Menu: Has a wide selection of vegetarian dishes.
Comments: Inside the store is the Swam Café.
Directions: From I-5, take Lakeway exit (#253), then go west on E Holly St ¾ mile (bears to right). At State St turn left and go 1 block, then at Chestnut turn left and go 1 block, then at Forest turn left and this place on right.

Old Town Café

316 West Holly Street; 360-671-4431
Hours: Monday to Saturday 6:30 am to 3 pm Sunday 8 am to 2 pm
Natural Foods. Vegan options. Mostly Organic. Not pure vegetarian.
Menu: Soups, salads, sandwiches, Scrambled Tofu, veggie burgers and main dishes. Fresh juices, cappuccino, espresso.

Comments: Shares tips between everyone on the staff. Local produce used when possible. Recycles. Serves breakfasts and lunches.
Other Info: Full service, take-out. Non-smoking. Price: $.
Directions: From I-5, take Exit #253 towards Lakeway Dr and go on Lakeway Dr east for ¾ mile (becomes Holly St after third-mile), then at Cornwall Ave turn left and this place is at the corner.

Maharaja
3930 Meridian Street #J
360-647-1589; **fax:** 360-671-7698
Hours: Daily 11 am to 10 pm
Indian. Vegan options. Not pure vegetarian.
Menu: Has a large selection of vegetarian dishes.
Other Info: Full service, take-out, delivery. Accepts AMEX, DIS, MC, VISA. Price: $$.
Directions: Parking arranged for customers.

Terra Organica
929-A North State Street; 360-715-8020
Hours: Daily 9 am to 9 pm
Café Hours: Monday to Saturday 8 am to 6 pm
Natural Food Store and Cafe. Organic produce (all produce is 25% off on Sunday)
Hours: Sandwiches, soups, salads, pasta salad and more. Fresh juices and smoothies.
Comments: Most of the food in the store are organic. Conscious of getting ethical products. The food is good.
Other Info: Counter service, take-out. Order at counter and food can be brought to table.
Directions: On North State St, 3 blocks south of Bellingham Hotel. From I-5, take Exit #253 towards Lakeway Dr and go on Lakeway Dr east for ¾ mile (becomes Holly St after a third-mile), then at N State St turn left and this place is a third-mile down.

COLLEGE PLACE

HIS Garden & Bakery
28 SE 12th Street, near S College Ave
509-525-1040; **Web site:** http://www.freshweb produce.com/hisgarden/
Hours: Sunday to Thursday 7:30 am to 6 pm; Friday 10 am to 4 pm; Sunday 9 am to 5 pm; closed Saturday.
Natural Food Store and Deli. Organic produce. Bakery (some items are wheat-free).
Menu: Good selection of vegetarian dishes. Eggless Egg Salad, Tofuky Sandwich, Chick-pea Tuna, Vegan dips, salads, vegetarian soups, pizza and veggie chili (sometimes).

Comments: Friendly place. Accepts AMEX, MC, VISA.
Directions: From US-12, go south on Gose St (becomes N College Ave) and this place is about 1½ mile down, at the junction with SE 12 St.

Ivy Tea Room
30 SE 12th; 509-525-4752
Hours: Monday to Friday 10 am to 5 pm; Sunday 12 noon to 5 pm; closed Saturday.
Café style Restaurant. Not pure vegetarian.
Menu: Has a good selection of vegetarian dishes. Has a large variety of teas.
Comments: Pleasant atmosphere.
Directions: From US-12, go south on Gose St (becomes N College Ave) and go about 1½ mile, at SE 12 St turn left and this place is immediate near the corner.

**Walla Walla College Cafeteria
32 SE Ash; 509-527-2732
Cafeteria Hours: Monday to Friday 7 am to 1:30 pm, 4:30 pm to 7 pm (Friday closes at 6:15 pm); Saturday 8:30 am to 9:15 am, 12:15 noon to 1:15 pm, 5:15 pm to 6:30 pm; Sunday 10 am to 1:30 pm, 4:30 pm to 6:15 pm
Fully Vegetarian University Cafeteria. Vegan options.
Menu: Has Mexican foods, sandwiches, salads, steamed vegetables, scrambled tofu and main dishes. Desserts sweetened with dates. The Vegan Section is only open for lunch time. Vegan desserts.
Comments: Walla Walla College is a Seventh-day Adventist school and the school cafeteria is fully vegetarian. Really nice people. There is also a snack bar that is open at different hours than the cafeteria.
Other Info: Cafeteria service, take-out. Limited hours in summer. Price: $.
Directions: From WA-125 coming from Oregon, turn left at S College Ave and this place is 1½ mile down.

COLVILLE

**North Country Co-op
282 West Astor; 509-684-6132
Hours: Monday to Friday 9 am to 6 pm (until 7 pm in Summer); Saturday 10 am to 5 pm; closed Sunday.
Natural Food Store and Vegetarian Deli. Bakery. Organic produce.
Menu: Mainly only has vegetarian dishes. Two soups, three main dishes, baked breads, sandwiches and salads. One or two vegan dishes daily.

Other Info: Counter service, take-out. Has seating upstairs and downstairs. Accepts MC, VISA.
Directions: From Rte 395 when it comes into town it becomes Main St. At 2nd go west 1 block, then at Wynn turn left and go 1 block, then at Astor turn right and this place on right at end of block.

EASTSOUND

Orcas Home Grown Market
North Beach Road; 360-376-2009
Hours: Daily 8 am to 9 pm
Natural Food Store and Deli. Bakery and Juice Bar. Deli is mainly vegetarian. Organic produce
Menu: Salads, sandwiches, soups and vegetarian specials.
Other Info: Counter service, take-out. Accepts MC, VISA.
Directions: Take ferry from Anacortes. At Orcas landing, take Horseshoe Highway into Eastsound. This place in downtown on the right.

ELLENSBURG

Valley Café & Take-out
105 West 3rd Avenue; 509-925-3050
Hours: Sunday to Thursday 11 am to 8:30 pm
Friday & Saturday 11 am to 9 pm
Northwestern. Not pure vegetarian.
Menu: Has some vegetarian dishes such as pastas and salads. Use vegetarian stocks in vegetable soups.
Comments: Art deco place. Foods are freshly prepared.
Other Info: Full service, take-out. Accepts AMEX, DIS, MC, VISA. Price: $-$$.

EVERETT

The Sister
2804 Grand; 425-252-0480
Hours: Monday to Friday 7 am to 4 pm
Closed Saturday & Sunday.
American. Not pure vegetarian.
Menu: Salads, soups, hummus, sandwiches, bagels and homemade veggie burgers.
Comments: Family owned and operated. Displays local artwork.
Other Info: Limited service, take-out. Accepts MC, VISA. Price: $.

**Sno-Isle Natural Food Co-op
2804 Grand Avenue; 425-259-3798
email: awinters@u.washington.edu
Hours: Monday to Saturday 8 am to 8 pm

Sunday 12 noon to 6 pm
Natural Food Store and Vegetarian Deli. Mainly organic and vegetarian. Organic Juice Bar. Vegan options. Organic produce.
Menu: Two soups daily, salads, sandwiches and many other dishes. Fresh juices and smoothies.
Comments: Everything made on premises. 6000 square foot place.
Other Info: Counter service, take-out. Accepts AMEX, DIS, MC, VISA.
Directions: From I-5, take downtown Everett exit (#194). Take Pacific Ave west about a mile, then at Grand Ave turn right and this place on left 3 blocks down.

FEDERAL WAY (Whidbey Island)

Marlene's Market & Deli
31839 Gateway Center Boulevard S
253-839-0933
Hours: Monday to Friday 9 am to 9 pm; Saturday 9 am to 8 pm; Sunday 10:30 noon to 6 pm
Natural Foods Store and Cafe. Deli and Juice Bar. Espresso Bar serves organic coffee. Not pure vegetarian. Organic produce.
Menu: Has a good selection of vegetarian soups, salads, Everyday Veggie and hot dishes. Fresh juices and smoothies.
Comments: Pleasant atmosphere. Limited service, take-out. Accepts MC, VISA. Price: $.
Directions: From I-5, take middle Federal Way exit (#143), then go west on S 320 St a quarter-mile, then turn right at 23rd Ave S (second right) and go a block and turn right and this place is a quarter-mile down. This place is just off west side of I-5 in Gateway Center (has blue tile roofs).

**Blueberry Jazz
5438 South Woodard Ave (525 and Woodard), Freeland, WA
360-331-4950; Web site: www.blueberryjazz.com
Summer Hours: Wednesday to Saturday 11 am to 2 pm, 5 pm to 8 pm; closed Sunday to Tuesday. Closes for the winter.
Bakery Hours: Monday to Saturday 7:30 am to 11:30 pm
Fully Vegetarian International Gourmet. Bakery. Mostly Vegan. Fine gourmet vegetarian cuisine offered in four courses.
Menu: Menu changes according to season. Meals are multi-course. Baked goods and desserts. Veggie burgers, BBQ Chicken, Oriental Mock Chicken Salad, Mushroom Burger, Teriyaki Veggie Burger, Tuno Cakes Holmes Harbor, Taco Salad, Roasted Eggplant Pita, soups, Broccoli Swiss Pie with Carrot Glaze, French fries, Eggplant Gorganzola,

Pasta Primavera and Broccoli Swiss Pie with Carrot Glaze. Has selection of desserts. An example meal is Baby Spinach Salad, Italian Polenta Plank, Eric's Portobello Wellington with mushroom pecan stuffing, and ice cream.
Comments: Has nice grounds with a fishpond and a great view of Holmes Harbor. Friendly staff. Good, well-presented food. Quiet, peaceful atmosphere.
Other Info: Full service, counter service, takeout. Non-smoking. Reservations recommended. Accepts MC, VISA and checks. Price: $$.
Directions: From Seattle, head north towards Mukilteo and go across the Clinton Ferry to Freeland. Go two blocks past traffic light, then turn right and this place is on the left.

GIG HARBOR

Whole Foods Market
3122 Harborview Drive; 253-851-8120
Hours: Monday to Saturday 9:30 am to 6 pm
Closed Sunday.
Natural Food Store. Small place. Organic produce.
Directions: In downtown Gig Harbor.

ISSAQUAH

PCC Issaquah
1810 12th Avenue; 425-369-1222
Web site: www.pccnaturalmarkets.com
Hours: Daily 6 am to 10 pm
Natural Food Store and very large Deli. Organic produce.
Menu: Salads, sandwiches, Roasted Portobello Mushrooms, tabbouleh, Mediterranean Sampler, baked goods, desserts and main dishes.
Comments: Known to have the most organic produce in the area.
Other Info: Counter service, take-out, catering. Accepts DIS, MC, VISA.
Directions: From I-90 take exit #15, then go south on Renton Issaquah Rd for a quarter-mile, then turn left and this place is a third-mile down in a shopping center.

KENNEWICK

Highland Healthfood Superstore
101 Vista Way; 509-783-7147
Hours: Monday to Thursday 9:30 am to 8 pm;
Friday 9:30 am to 3 pm; Sunday 12 noon to 5 pm; closed Saturday.
Natural Food Store.
Other Info: Accepts MC, VISA.

Directions: From I-82, take Hwy 395 (exit #113) north for 3½ miles, then at Vista Way turn right and this place is a quarter-mile down on right.

KIRKLAND (Seattle suburb)

**Café Happy
102 Kirkland Avenue; 425-822-9696
Hours: Daily 10 am to 8:30 pm
Vegetarian Chinese. Vegan friendly.
Menu: Soups, stir-fry dishes, Sesame Cake Steamed Buns, sandwiches and many mock meat dishes. Ice cream. Espresso, pearl tea.
Comments: Run by a Taiwanese family who are very friendly. Choose what to order from pictures posted on the wall. Good food.
Other Info: Full service, take-out. Non-smoking. No credit cards.
Directions: In downtown Kirkland. From I-405, take exit #18 for Kirkland and go west on NE 85th St for 1 mile to downtown Kirkland, then turn left at Lake St and go 2 blocks, then turn left at Kirkland Ave and this place is right at the corner.

PCC Kirkland
10718 NE 68th Street; 425-828-4622
Web site: www.pccnaturalmarkets.com
Hours: Daily 8 am to 10 pm
Natural Food Store and Cafe. Deli and Bakery. Organic produce. Supermarket-type place.
Menu: Salads, sandwiches, Roasted Portobello Mushrooms, tabbouleh, Mediterranean Sampler, baked goods, desserts and main dishes.
Other Info: Counter service, take-out, catering.
Directions: From I-405 coming north, take NE 70th Place exit (#17). At stop sign turn left, then at NE 70th turn left (becomes NE 68th St) and this place is ¾ mile down on right in Houghton Village Shopping Center. From I-405 south, take NE 70th Place exit (#17). At NE 70th Place turn left. Same as above.

Shamiana (two branches)
10724 Northeast 68th Street, Kirkland
425-827-4902; **fax:** 425-828-2765
Directions: In the same shopping center as Puget Consumers Coop Kirkland. Free parking for customers.
Hours: Monday 5 pm to 9:30 pm; Tuesday to Thursday, Sunday 11 am to 2:30 pm, 5 pm to 9:30 pm; Friday & Saturday 11 am to 2:30 pm, 5 pm to 10 pm
2255 NE 65th Street, West side of town, by University of Washington, just north of town.
206-524-3664

Hours: Tuesday to Thursday, Sunday 11 am to 2:30 pm, 5 pm to 9:30 pm; Friday & Saturday 11 am to 2:30 pm, 5 pm to 10 pm; closed Mon. **Indian and Pakistani Region Food.** Lunch Buffet. Vegan options. Not pure vegetarian. **Menu:** Has a good selection of vegetarian dishes. Eggplant dishes, dal, chapati, Matar Paneer, Eggplant Bartha, Samosas, Saag (pureed spinach with coconut milk), vegetable curry and various chutneys. Non-alcoholic beer. **Comments:** Elegant place. Nice decor. Vegetarians pay less for lunch buffet than the meat buffet. Has artifacts from India and Pakistan on walls including Indian cooking utensils. This place is unique in that is run by a husband and wife who are not Indians, the husband grew up in India as his father worked for the US government in India. Owned by extremely friendly people. **Other Info:** Full service, take-out. Non-smoking. Accepts AMEX, MC, VISA. Price: $$.

MOUNTLAKE TERRACE

Manna Foods
21705 66th Avenue West; 425-775-3479
Natural Food Store. Limited produce section.
Comments: Very reasonable prices.

MOUNT VERNON

The Deli Next Door
202 South First Street; 360-336-3886
Hours: Monday to Saturday 9 am to 8 pm
Sunday 9 am to 6 pm
Natural Food Store and Deli. 50% vegetarian. Not pure vegetarian.
Menu: Salads, sandwiches and special dishes. Fresh juices.
Other Info: Limited service. Price: $.

OLYMPIA

Blue Heron Bakery
4935 Mud Bay Road NW; 360-866-2253
Natural Bakery. Not pure vegetarian.
Menu: Has a good selection of breads such as toasted blue corn and ten grain. Has a chocolate chip cookies and vegan fudge bar.
Comments: Use natural sweeteners such as turbinado sugar.
Directions: It is in the South Sound, a little west of Evergreen State College. From Hwy 101, take Mud Bay Rd exit towards Evergreen State College and this place is a third-mile west on Mud Bay Rd.

Olympia Food Co-op
3111 Pacific Avenue SE; 360-956-3870
Hours: Daily 9 am to 9 pm
Natural Food Store and Salad & Soup Bar. Organic produce. Vegan options. Not pure veg.
Menu: The menu changes regularly. Has several vegetarian and vegan dishes. Tofu Sandwich, sandwiches, salads, Nori Rolls, soups, Pesto Pasta and Tempeh. Fresh juices.
Comments: Often uses organic ingredients. This and the Olympia West Side are run by the same people.
Other Info: Cafeteria style, take-out. Has a few tables to sit at. Cash only; no credit. Price: $.
Directions: This place is about 2 miles east of downtown Olympia. From I-5 north, take exit #107 (Pacific Ave) and go west on Pacific Ave a quarter-mile. Then turn left at Lansdale and this place is at the corner of Lansdale and Pacific.

Olympia West Side Food Co-op
921 North Rogers; 360-754-7666
Hours: Daily 9 am to 8 pm
Natural Food Store and Deli. Pre-made sandwiches and salads that they sell in their cooler.
Directions: This place is in western Olympia on the west side of the lake, about 1½ mile due north of where Hwy 101 and I-5 split. It is at the intersection of Bowman and Rogers.

Proffitt's Café
406 4th Avenue; 360-357-8187
Hours: Daily 8 am to 2 pm
Natural Foods. Vegan options. Not pure vegetarian.
Menu: Tabbouleh Sandwich, hummus, salads and Garden Burger. Cappuccino, espresso.
Comments: Casual, cozy place.
Other Info: Counter service, take-out. Accepts MC, VISA. Price: $$.
Directions: From I-5, take exit #105 towards State Capitol/City Center, Then go north on E Bay Dr (becomes Plum St) for a half-mile, at State Ave turn left and go a quarter-mile, at Adams St turn left and go 1 block, then turn left and this place is near the corner.

Saigon Rendez-Vous
117 West 5th Avenue; 360-352-1989
Hours: Monday to Saturday 10:30 am to 10 pm
Sunday 11:30 am to 9 pm
Chinese and Vietnamese. Vegan options. Not pure vegetarian.
Menu: Has a good selection of vegetarian dishes including many mock meat and seafood dishes.

Has a separate vegetarian menu with over 50 dishes. Hot & Sour Soup, Wonton Soup, Soy Chicken with Broccoli, Tofu with Lemon Grass, rice and much more.
Comments: Uses soy as a meat substitute.
Other Info: Full service, take-out. Accepts DIS, MC, VISA. **Price:** $-$$.

Urban Onion

116 Legion Way, downtown Olympia
360-943-9242; **Email:** uomgr@caterforme.com (can make reservations by email)
Web site: www.city-olympia.com/urbanonion
Hours: Monday to Wednesday 7 am to 9 pm; Thursday 7 am to 10 pm; Friday 7am to 11 pm; Saturday 8 am to 11 pm; Sunday 8 am to 9 pm
Health Food. Vegetarian-friendly.
Menu: Has a selection of healthy vegetarian dishes. Salads, sandwiches, soups, tabbouleh, homemade bread, Green Salad (with sprouts, cabbage, carrot), Veggie Stir-fry with Fried Rice, hash browns, lentil soup, Sautéed Vegetables, Steamed Brown Rice with Indonesian Peanut Sauce, Cheese & Walnut Ravioli, Rice & Bean Enchilada and UO Nut Burger. Blue Corn Chips with salsa and cheese dip. Hummus and Vegetable Plate with pita bread. Has good homemade Lemon-Tahini dressing and you can take a container home with you. Desserts. Fresh juices, cappuccino, espresso.
Comments: Has high ceilings with elegant booths and tables. Has outdoor courtyard seating overlooking the park. Can add tofu or textured vegetable protein to most dishes. Good size portions.
Other Info: Full service, take-out, catering. Accepts AMEX, MC, VISA. **Price:** $$.
Directions: Located in the historic Hotel Olympian opposite Sylvester Park. From coming from I-5 North into town, take exit #105 B (City Center Exit) to Plum Street and go north towards the Olympia city center. At the third stoplight, turn left at Legion Way and this place is 6 blocks down in the lobby of the Hotel Olympian on the right at corner of Legion Way and Washington St. From coming from south on I-5, take exit #105 to Plum Street. Then, follow the directions above. Can park for 90 minutes in the free parking zones near the restaurant.

**Voyeur Vegetarian Café

404 East 4th Street; 360-943-5710
Hours: Daily 11:30 am to 12 midnight
Vegetarian Restaurant.
Menu: Has a good selection of vegetarian dishes. Soups, sandwiches and salads.
Other Info: Full service, take-out. Accepts

AMEX, MC, VISA.
Directions: From coming from I-5 North into town, take exit #105 B (City Center Exit) to Plum Street and go north towards the Olympia city center about ¾ mile, then turn left at 4th St and this place is 4 blocks down. From coming from south on I-5, take exit #105 to Plum Street. Then, follow the directions above.

PORT ANGELES

Café Garden

1506 East First Street; 360-457-4611
Hours: Sunday to Thursday 6:30 am to 8 pm
Friday & Saturday 6:30 am to 9 pm
Ethnic. Vegan options. Not pure vegetarian.
Menu: Has several vegetarian dishes. Salads, Stir-fry and pastas.
Other Info: Accepts DIS, MC, VISA. **Price:** $$.

PORT TOWNSEND

Coho Café

1044 Lawrence Street; 360-379-1030
Hours: Wednesday to Sunday 5 pm to 9 pm
Closed Monday & Tuesday.
Restaurant. Not pure vegetarian.
Menu: Has a vegetarian and vegan special daily such as Roasted Pumpkin.

The Food Co-op

1033 Lawrence Street
360-385-2883; **email:** organic@ptfoodcoop.com
Hours: Monday to Saturday 8 am to 9 pm
Sunday 9 am to 7 pm
Natural Food Store and Deli. Local produce whenever possible.
Menu: Has a good selection of vegetarian dishes. Soups, sandwiches, salads and hot dishes.
Comments: Friendly place.
Other Info: Accepts MC, VISA.
Directions: From Rte 20 drive into Port Townsend and road becomes Sims. At Hamson turn left, then at Lawrence turn right and this place is 2 blocks down on the right at corner of Lawrence and Pope.

Khu Larb Thai

225 Adams Street; 360-385-5023
Hours: Sunday, Wednesday to Thursday 11 am to 8:30 pm; Friday & Saturday 11 am to 9:30 pm; closed Monday.
Thai. Vegan options. Not pure vegetarian.
Menu: Has a good selection of vegetarian dishes. Sweet & Sour Vegetable, tofu dishes and curry vegetables.

Warning: Make sure you request that none of the dishes contain fish sauce.
Other Info: Accepts MC, VISA. Price: $$.

The Salad Café
634 Water Street; 360-385-6532
Hours: Daily 7 am to 2 pm
Natural Foods. Vegan options. Not pure veg.
Menu: Tofu & Vegetables, quesadillas, Tofu Reuben Sandwich, Blintzes, soups and salads. For breakfast there is oatmeal, Sauté Tofu and Tofu Scramble,
Other Info: Full service, take-out. Accepts AMEX, MC, VISA. Price: $-$$.
Directions: From Rte 20 drive into Port Townsend and road becomes Sims, then this place is at the junction of Sims (Rte 20) and Quincy, a block from the water.

POULSBO

Central Market
20148 10th Avenue; 360-779-1881
Hours: Daily for 24 hours.
Regular Supermarket. Has organic produce and a natural food section.
Directions: Take Bainbridge Island/Seattle ferry. After getting off ferry go right on Hwy 305 and after about 10 miles this store is on the right.

PULLMAN

Swilly's
200 NE Kamaken Street; 509-334-3395
Hours: Mon to Fri 11 am to 2 pm, 5 pm to 9:30 pm; Saturday 5 pm to 9:30 pm; closed Sun.
International. Greek, Italian, Southwest, Italian, Middle Eastern. Vegan friendly. Not pure veg.
Menu: Has many vegetarian dishes. Veggie burgers, soups, salads, veggie wraps, pastas, and lunch and dinner specials. Desserts.
Comments: Interesting seasoning. Reasonable prices. Casual place.
Other Info: Full service, take-out. Reservations accepted on weekends. Accepts AMEX, MC, VISA. Price: $$-$$$.

REDMOND

Minklen's Green Earth Nutrition
125 Airport Way; 425-226-7757
Hours: Monday to Friday 9 am to 7 pm; Saturday 9:30 am to 6 pm; closed Sunday.
Natural Food Store.
Other Info: Accepts AMEX, DC, DIS, MC, VISA.

**Pabla Indian Cuisine
Fred Meyer Shopping Plaza, 364 Renton Center Way SW; 425-228-4625; **email:** pabla@pabla.org
Web site: www.pabla.org
Hours: Daily 11 am to 3 pm (Lunch Buffet), 5 pm to 10 pm
Vegetarian Indian. Punjabi. Excellent all-you-can-eat Lunch Buffet. Vegan friendly. Connected to an Indian Grocery Store.
Menu: Has over 90 dishes on the menu. Spicy Salad, samosas, basmati rice, lentil dal, Eggplant Bhartha (spicy eggplant stew), Channa Masala, yogurt raita, mint chutney, various rice dishes, naan bread and various Indian desserts.
Comments: Food gets high ratings. Has a second branch in downtown Seattle that serves meat.
Other Info: Accepts AMEX, DC, DIS, MC, VISA. Price: $-$$.

REPUBLIC

Ferry County Co-op
34 North Clark Street; 509-775-3754
Hours: Monday to Friday 7:30 am to 5:30 pm (until 6 pm in spring); Saturday 10 am to 4 pm; closed Sunday.
Natural Food Store and Cafe. Deli and Bakery. Limited organic produce.
Menu: Baked goods, soups, sandwiches, salads, pasta salad, rolls and fresh soup.
Other Info: Accepts MC, VISA.
Directions: From Rte 20, go north on Clark and this place on right one block down in the middle of the downtown.

SAN JUAN ISLAND

**Town House Bed & Breakfast
392 Little Road (was 1230), Friday Harbor
360-378-5464, 800-858-4276
Web site: http://www.san-juan-island.com/
Bed and Breakfast. Vegetarian Breakfasts. Breakfast can be made Vegan. Gourmet.
Menu: Moroccan Pie, Fruit filled Blintzes, Baked Hash Brown, Polenta with Mushroom Sauce, Sweet Nut Tamele, Quinoa Pilaf (a South American grain), apricot-orange couscous, fresh fruits and much more.
Comments: Breakfasts are served on fine china, with silver, crystal and antique linens. Vegan diets can be catered to with advance notice.
Bed & Breakfast: Queen Anne style B&B, on 10 acres overlooking San Juan Valley. Adult only Bed and Breakfast. Has just two large suites with private baths and private sitting rooms. Has luxury rooms. Good place for a special event.

SEATTLE

Antique Sandwich Company
5102 North Pearl; 253-752-4069
Hours: Monday to Saturday 7 am to 7:30 pm
Sunday 8 am to 7:30 pm
Sandwich Shop. Not pure vegetarian.
Menu: Has sandwiches, vegetarian soups, black bean burritos, hummus pita, Spinach Lasagna, veggie chili and salads. Fresh juices, milk shakes and espresso.
Comments: Has antique tables and chairs. Has live music. Also sells Third World items.
Other Info: Accepts AMEX, MC, VISA.
Directions: From I-5, take Swift Ave exit (#161) towards Albro Place, then go east on S Eddy St, at Beacon Ave turn left and go a third-mile, at S Orcas St turn right and go 1½ miles, at 51st Ave turn left and this place is a third-mile down.

***Araya's Vegetarian Place
4732 University Way NE; 206-524-4332
Hours: Monday to Saturday 12 noon to 9:30 pm
Sunday 5 pm to 9:30 pm
Lunch Buffet Hours: Monday to Saturday 11:30 to 3:30 pm
Vegan Thai. Buffet. One is vegan and the other serves meat. All you can eat lunch buffet Monday to Saturday.
Menu: Stir-fries, soups, curry dishes and other dishes. The Hot and Sour Soup is really good. Thai Iced Tea with coconut milk.
Comments: Food gets really high ratings. Has got several awards for best vegan restaurant. All-you-can-eat brunch lunch buffet on Saturday. Interesting décor. Acoustic guitar and poetry on Sunday evening.
Other Info: Full service, take-out, delivery. Non-smoking. Accepts AMEX, MC, VISA. Price: $-$$.
Directions: In the University District. From I-5, take Exit #169 towards NE 45th St, then go east on 45th St and go 4 blocks, at 11th Ave turn left and go 1 block, at 47th St turn right and go 2 blocks, then at University Way turn left and this place is a half-block down. Free parking.

Bahn Thai Restaurant
409 Roy Street; 206-283-0444
Hours: Monday to Friday 11:30 am to 3 pm, 4:30 pm to 9:30 pm; Saturday 3 pm to 10 pm; Sunday 3 pm to 9:30 pm
Thai. Vegan options. Not pure vegetarian.
Menu: Has a selection of vegetarian dishes. The coconut ice cream is very good.
Comments: Romantic atmosphere. Thai paint-

ings and subdued lighting. Reasonable prices. Friendly, quick service.
Other Info: Full service, take-out. Accepts AMEX, DIS, MC, VISA. Price: $.
Directions: Near the Seattle Center. Parking arranged for customer.

**Bamboo Garden
364 Roy Street, at Nob Hill Avenue North, between 3rd & 4th Avenues; 206-282-6616
Hours: Daily 11 am to 10 pm
Fully Vegetarian Chinese. Mainly Vegan.
Menu: Has a large selection of over 100 vegetarian dishes including hot pots and sizzling plates. Sesame Chicken, Szechwan Chicken, Corn Chowder Soup, Bok Choy, Buddha's Imperial Feast, Mu Shu Pork, Ruby Princess (mock chicken, asparagus with a spicy sauce), Stir-fried Vegetables & Mock Chicken, Duck Noodle Soup, Sweet & Sour Chicken (very good), Fried Tofu Nuggets and Mandarin Chicken (a favorite).
Comments: Food gets high ratings. Well-priced. No eggs or dairy product are used, except there are eggs in the fortune cookies. Service gets mixed rating, but usually gets a high rating.
Warning: Fortune cookies contain eggs.
Other Info: Full service, take-out. Accepts AMEX, DIS, MC, VISA. Price: $-$$.
Directions: Located a block north of the Seattle Center, not far from the Space Needle. A little north of Seattle Center and Queen Anne. From I-5, take Seneca St exit (#165), then go northwest 1 mile on 4th Ave, at Broad St turn slight right and go 1 block, at 5th Ave N turn left and go a third-mile down, then at Roy St turn left and this place is 2 blocks down.

***Café Ambrosia
2501 Fairview Avenue, E, at Nob Avenue North 206-325-7111; email: info@cafeambrosia.com; Web site: www.cafeambrosia.com
Hours: Tuesday to Thursday 5 pm to 9 pm; Friday & Saturday 5 pm to 10 pm; Sunday Brunch 10 am to 2 pm, 5 pm to 9 pm; closed Monday.
Fully Vegan. Health Food.
Gourmet Vegetarian International. Most food is organic. Upscale Vegan Organic Restaurant.
Menu: Has a large menu with over 100 dishes. Spring Rolls, Fingerling Potato and Mushroom, Stuffed Mushrooms, Mediterranean Napoleon, special salads, Spinach & Asparagus Salad, Boy Choy, Asparagus & Snow Peas, Grilled Vegetable Kebabs, sizzling plates, Asian Noodle Stir-fry, noodles dishes, Grilled Polenta Safari, Pan-fried Rice Noodles, Herbed Soy Cutlet, Asian Napoleon, Mediterranean (spinach tortilla with

hummus), Fall Celebration of Squash, Garden Paella, mock salmon (very good), Brazilian Black Bean Stew, Francis' Ambrosia Burger (made of oatmeal, potato, walnut, onion), couscous, Carrot Ginger Soup, Angel Hair Pasta With Wild Mushrooms, Veggie Kebabs and Ruby Princess (mock chicken with asparagus). Lemon Custard and Apple Joy for desserts. Buddha's Imperial Feast is very good. Brunch menu includes Tofu-Tempeh Sausages, Mediterranean Scrambled Tofu, pancakes, French toast, Mushroom Crepes and waffles.

Comments: View of Lake Union. Food gets good ratings. Place is popular at night, so you may want to arrive early to get a seat. Good, quick service. Well-presented meals. Reasonable prices. Upscale with white tablecloths. On the shore of east Lake Union. Plays classical music.

Warning: The fortune cookies contain eggs.

Other Info: Full service, take-out. Banquet facilities. Accepts AMEX, MC, VISA. Price: $$.

Directions: At Roanoke, on the east shore of Lake Union. Driving South on I-5, take Exit #168A after crossing the Ship Canal Bridge. At the light, make a right turn onto Roanoke Street. Driving North on I-5 take Exit #168A, at stop sign, turn left onto Lakeview Blvd. At second traffic light turn left onto Roanoke Street. Go down hill toward Lake Union. At the bottom of the road, follow the bend to your left. The restaurant is to your immediate right after you make the turn in the road. Free parking lot in front of restaurant.

Café Counter Intelligence

2219 2nd Avenue; 206-441-8075
Hours: Monday to Friday 7 am to 4 pm; Saturday 9 am to 2 pm; closed Sunday.
Natural Foods. Not pure vegetarian.
Menu: Soups, salads and sandwiches.
Other Info: Full service, take-out. Price: $

**Café Flora

2901 East Madison Street, at 29th Street
206-325-9100
Web site: www.cafeflora.com
Hours: Tuesday to Friday 11:30 am to 10 pm; Saturday 9 am to 2 pm, 5 pm to 10 pm; Sunday 9 am to 2 pm, 5 to 9 pm; closed Monday.
Mainly Vegetarian International. Mexican, Indian, Japanese. Vegan options. Gourmet. Not pure vegetarian (serves fish). Gourmet food.
Menu: The menu changes weekly. About half the menu is vegan (less during the weekend brunch). Oaxaca Tacos, Portobello Wellington, Grilled Pasta Napoleon, Soba Salad, Indian Chickpea Stew, Coconut Tofu with Sweet Chili Sauce,

Nutburger and Grilled Nutburgers Crepes. Smoked Mushroom and Spinach Salad, Soba Salad, Caesar Salad, Ginger Pesto Samosas, Quesadilla Verde, Cheese & Fruit Plate, pizza, fajitas, Sweet Potato Fritters, falafel sandwich, Curryburger, Steamed Vegetables, Mashed Potatoes, Coconut Tofu, soups and Reuben Sandwiches. Vegan desserts. Fresh juices. Rosemary Lemonade is recommended. Non-alcoholic beer.

Comments: Pleasant atmosphere. Good size portions. Vegan items are marked on the menu. Very popular place. Especially busy in the early evenings. Good location with a beautiful setting. Beautiful décor. Indoor patio with a skylight with shrubs and a fountain. Has works of local artists on the walls. Elegant. Has a fountain and a stone floor. This place gets really good ratings for food and service. Gets excellent reviews. Many people consider that this place has the best vegetarian food in Seattle. Plays classical music. Can be busy on weekend nights and you may have a short wait for a table. Organic produce used when possible. Creative and thoughtfully presented dishes. Good place for a special event.

Other Info: Full service, take-out. Reservations for large parties only. Non-smoking. Reservation only for parties of 8 or more. Accepts MC, VISA, personal cheques. Price: $$.

Direction: This place is 2½ miles east of downtown Seattle in the Madison Valley neighborhood, at the corner of East Madison and 29th Avenue East, between Martin Luther King Way and Lake Washington Blvd. Has guest parking next to the restaurant on 29th Avenue E. There is an additional lot marked with a large Cafe Flora sign east of the restaurant on E Madison St. No 11 bus from downtown stops just outside the entry of the restaurant. From I-5 north, take the Madison Street exit (#164 A), at Madison turn right and go east (away from downtown) about 2 miles, and this place is on the southeast corner of 29th Avenue and E Madison. From I-5 south, take left exit to Hwy 520, then take immediately first right, which is the Montlake Blvd exit. After exiting, get into right lane and go straight through the intersection and road becomes Lake Washington Blvd, road winds through the arboretum for about 1 mile, then turn right onto East Madison Street and this place is one long block down on the left.

Café Venus

609 Eastlake Avenue E
206-624-4516
Web site: www.cafevenus.com
Hours: Monday to Friday 11 am to 10 am Saturday & Sunday 6 pm to 11 am

Vegan and Vegetarian-friendly Restaurant. Not pure vegetarian.
Menu: Grilled Vegetables, pizza, Planetary Salad (grilled vegetables, roasted polenta and walnuts), Stuffed Mushrooms, Asparagus Ravioli, pasta and other dishes.
Comments: Has live music on Saturday and Sunday nights. Has a full bar. Happening place. Place gets high ratings. Good staff. Good place to hang out. Good food. Sociable, pleasant atmosphere.
Other Info: Accepts MC, VISA.
Directions: From I-5, take Exit #167 towards Mercer St/Seattle Center, and this place is right next to the exit (on the west side).

**Carmelita

7314 Greenwood Ave, N, between 73rd & 74th; 206-706-7703; Web site: www.carmelita.net
Hours: Tuesday to Sunday 5 pm to 10 pm Closed Monday.
Fully Vegetarian International, Mediterranean. Vegan options. Organic produce.
Menu: Soups, Chickpea Croquette, pizzas, special salads, pasta dishes, White Salad, Butternut Squash, Tomato & Goat Cheese Tartlet, Ravioli, baba ghanoush, Chickpea Pizza, Antipasto Platter, Grilled Tofu, Japanese Eggplants, Portabella Mushroom Roulade, Roasted Vegetables, homemade pesto, Roasted Tofu Cullets, North African Ragout, Grilled Marinated Vegetables, Baked Corn Empanadas and other gourmet dishes. Non-alcoholic beer and wine.
Comments: Upscale. Seasonal dishes using local produce. Outdoor garden dining. Beautiful décor. Family owned and operated. Seats around 100. Has an outdoor patio garden. Friendly, helpful staff. Food gets very high ratings. Creative dishes. Popular place. Very good service. Happening place.
Other Info: Reservation suggested. Non-smoking. Accepts MC, VISA. Price $$.
Directions: In the Phinney Ridge area. From I-5, take N 85th St exit (#172) towards Aurora Ave, then go west on N 85th St, at Aurora Ave (WA 99) turn left and go a quarter-mile, at N 80th St turn right and go a half-mile, at Greenwood Ave turn left and this place is a third-mile down.

Cyclops Café

2421 1st Avenue; 206-441-1677
Hours: Sunday to Wednesday 4 pm to 10 pm Thursday to Saturday 4 pm to 11 pm
Café. Not pure vegetarian.
Menu: Hummus, Penne with Eggplant, Crackerbread Pizza, salads, soups and Root-Vegetable Gratin with goat cheese. Green Curry

Noodle with Crispy Tofu. Espresso.
Comments: Pleasant, eclectic atmosphere. Hip, happening place. Loud music. Creative dishes.
Other Info: Full service, take-out. Price: $$.
Directions: From I-5, take the Seneca Ave exit (#165), then go west on Seneca St for a third-mile, at 1st Ave turn right and this place is ¾ mile down.

Essential Baking Company

1604 North 34th Street
206-545-3804
Hours: Monday to Friday 6 am to 6 pm; Saturday 8 am to 6 pm; Sunday 8 am to 4 pm
Organic Bakery and Café. Mainly vegetarian.
Menu: Organic breads, sandwiches, fruit salads, soups, Russian Borscht, sweet potatoes, grilled vegetables with hummus, baba ghanoush, Marinated Artichokes & Vegetables and salads. Organic juices and organic sodas.
Directions: In Seattle's Gas Works Park in Fremont. From I-5, take #169 towards 45th St/50th St, then go on Roosevelt Way a third-mile, at Campus Pkwy turn right and go 1 block, at 9th Ave turn left and go 50 yards, then at 40th St turn right and go 2 blocks, at Pacific St turn slight left and go 1 mile (roads becomes 34th St) and this place is at corner of Woodlawn Ave N.

***Globe Café and Bakery

1531 14th Avenue; 206-324-8815
Hours: Tuesday to Sunday 7 am to 4 pm Sunday and Tuesday open in evening for Poetry reading (only serves baked goods)
Closed Mondays.
Vegan Café and Bakery.
Menu: Biscuits and Gravy gets high rating and is very popular. Hot Tofu Sandwich, Scrambled Tofu, Saffron Rice, salads, corn bread, Rice & Thick Gravy, Rice & Black Beans, penne pasta with red sauce, Veggie Stir-fry, home-fries, Tofu Fajitas with grilled sweet peppers, Vegan French toast and pancakes. Very good baked goods. Several types of vegan cakes and cookies. Cinnamon rolls. Fresh juices, espresso, soy latte.
Comments: Funky, casual coffeehouse. Monthly art shows. Sometimes has acoustic music or poetry readings. Has good food. Worker owned. Has outdoor seating.
Other Info: Limited service, take-out. Non-smoking. No credit cards; cash only. Price: $.
Directions: Located on South Capitol Hill, between Pike and Pine. From I-5, take Olive Way exit (#166), then at Melrose Ave go east, then at E Pike St turn left and go 2/3 mile, at 14th Ave turn left and this place is a little down the block.

***Good Morning Healing Earth

901 NE 55th Street, a half-block west of Roosevelt
206-523-8025
Hours: Tuesday to Thursday 11 am to 9 pm; Friday to Sunday 8 am to 9 pm; closed Monday.
Fully Vegan. Whole-grain and mainly organic.
Menu: Soups, salads, sandwiches, veggie burgers, Seitan Sloppy Joe, stir-fry dishes, Home Fries, Rice & Beans, Rice with Tofu, Lemon Tahini Salad Dressing, pasta dishes, Beat Loaf (brown rice, corn meal and vegetables) with Red Sauce, and Hot & Spicy BBQ Seitan Sandwich. Good vegan pumpkin pie. Colombian corn pudding. Homemade vegan ice cream. Vegan Raspberry Chocolate Cake. Fresh juices.
Comments: Has indoor and outdoor seating. Good atmosphere. Small, funky place. Only four tables. Helpful staff. Good size portions. Organic produce used when possible. Cooks with whole-grains. Sometimes has live music. Quiet, friendly, comfortable place. Has eclectic art.
Other Info: Full service, take-out. Non-smoking. No credit cards. Accepts reservations but not necessary. Price: $-$$.
Directions: One block west of Roosevelt in the University district of Seattle. From I-5, take Ravenna Blvd exit (#170) towards NE 65th St, then go east on Ravenna Blvd 2 blocks, then turn right at Roosevelt Way and go a quarter-mile, then at NE 55th St turn right and this place is 1 block down.

Gordito's

213 North 85th Street; 206-706-9352
Hours: Wednesday to Monday 10:30 am to 9 pm
Closed Tuesday.
Mexican. Salad Bar Not pure vegetarian.
Menu: Has a selection of vegetarian and vegan dishes. Has good tofu burritos. Fajita taco, spinach burrito, Enchilada Plate and salads.
Comments: Popular, good place. Friendly fast-serve place. Beans do not contain lard and there is no chicken stock in rice. Good size portions.
Other Info: Counter service, take-out. Order food at counter and then servers brings food when done.

**Gravity Bar

Broadway Market on Capitol Hill
415 Broadway E, Capitol Hill, between Harrison & Republican Streets
206-325-7186; Web site: www.gravitybar.com
Hours: Sunday to Thursday 10 am to 10 pm
Friday and Saturday 10 am to 11 pm
Mainly Vegetarian Restaurant. Macrobiotic and Vegan options. Many of the dishes are organic. Juice Bar. Not pure vegetarian (serves tuna)
Menu: Has a large menu with a selection of macrobiotic and raw foods. Vegan burger, soups, sandwiches, a good selection of salads, pizza and main dishes. Brown Rice and Steamed Vegetables with fried Tofu (a favorite), Thai Green Lotus Plate, Alamo Wrap (black beans, lemon tahini, cabbage & salsa), Barbecued Vegetable Roll-up, Hummus Sandwich, Un-Sushi Roll (whole-wheat chapati filled with sun-dried tomato, avocado, rice and cucumber with a Kimono dip) and Spirulina Soup with miso. Fresh juices and wheatgrass. Grass Hopper (pineapple, mint & wheatgrass) is a favorite. Has excellent smoothies.
Comments: Casual, hip, eclectic atmosphere. Food gets high ratings. Good juice bar. Friendly, helpful staff. Have another branch downtown. Service can be a bit slow. Reasonably priced.
Other Info: Full service, take-out. Accepts MC, VISA. Price: $-$$.
Directions: In the Broadway Market on Capitol Hill. From I-6, take the Olive Way exit (#166), then go on Olive Way for a half-mile, at Broadway turn left and this place is 2 blocks down.

**Green Cat Café

1514 East Olive Way (Denny Way), at Crawford Place, between Belleville & Denny; 206-726-8756
Hours: Daily 7 am to 4 pm
Fully Vegetarian. Vegan options.
Menu: Morning Bowl is maple almond granola with vanilla yogurt and fresh fruit. A selection of several salads, sandwiches, wraps, pasta dishes, Huevos Rancheros, rice dishes, blue corn chip nachos with black bean chili and tofu scramble (very good). Pan-Asian Portobello Salad, Linguini Putanesca Pasta, rice noodles, Asian Salad, brown rice, Curried Tofu Stir-fry, Spiced Tofu Scramble with Vegetables, Vegetable Curry, Rosemary-roasted Red Potatoes, Buddha Bowl (vegetables, brown rice with peanut or lemon-tahini sauce) Open-face Cheese &, Avocado Sandwich. Vegan Sandwich (12-grain bread with potato, sprouts, seeds, cucumber, tomato, carrot) and Santa Fe Steam Roller (whole-wheat tortilla with brown rice, black bean chili, blue corn chip). Fresh juices and smoothies. Ginger Blast (fresh ginger, a lemon juice shot, honey with cayenne). Mojo Wonder Juice. Cappuccino, espresso.
Comments: Vegan dishes are marked on the menu. Reasonable prices. Good portions. Popular place with young people. Lunch is popular. Casual. Friendly staff. Relaxing, pleasant atmosphere. Has outdoor dining. Sidewalk café. Good value. Busy place. Place gets high ratings.

Other Info: Full service (night time), counter service (day time, order at counter and food is brought to you), take-out. Has a few seats on the outdoor patio. Non-smoking. Accepts MC, VISA. Price: $.
Directions: On Capitol Hill between I-5 and Broadway Avenue. Hard to find a parking spot. May have to park blocks away. From I-5, take the Olive Way exit (#166), then go east on Olive Way and this place is 2 blocks down.

***Hillside Quickie and Vegan Sandwich Shop

4106 Brooklyn Avenue NE, at 41st Street (U-District); 206-632-3037
Hours: Monday to Friday 11 am to 8 pm; Saturday 10:30 am to 8 pm; closed Sunday.
Fully Vegan Sandwich Shop Café.
Menu: Large variety of sandwiches including Crazy Jamaican Burger, TLT and Flaming BBQ Burger. Soups, salads, Tofu dishes and tempeh & seitan dishes. Desserts.
Comments: Great atmosphere Plays reggae music. Gets good sunlight.
Other Info: Counter service, take-out. Non-smoking. Accepts reservations but aren't necessary.
Directions: From I-5, take 45th Street Exit (#169). Then go east on 45th St for 3 blocks, at Roosevelt Way turn right and go 2 blocks, at 42nd St turn left and go 3 blocks, then turn right at Brooklyn and this place is 1 block down on corner on the left, at 41st St.

The Hi Spot Café

1410 East 34th Avenue, at East Union Street
206-325-7905; **Web site:** www.hispotcafe.com
Breakfast Hours: Daily 8 am to 2 pm
Lunch Hours: Daily 11:30 am to 2 pm
Baked Goods & Espresso Hours: Monday to Friday 7 am to 4 pm
Saturday & Sunday 8 am to 4 pm
American Natural Foods. Coffeehouse. Vegan options. Not pure vegetarian.
Menu: Soups, salads, sandwiches, scrambled tofu, burritos and good Grilled Veggie Sandwich. Fresh juices, cappuccino, espresso.
Comments: Located in a Victorian house. Has outdoor patio dining. Bakery with whole-grain, low-sugar, low-salt pastries. No cellular phones allowed. Cozy, pleasant atmosphere. Candlelit with fresh flowers. Good service and food. Can be busy during lunch and weekend and you may have to wait for a seat. Good value. Has menu on Web site.

Other Info: Full service, take-out. Non-smoking. Accepts DIS, MC, VISA. Price: $.
Directions: This place is about 2 miles due west of exit #165 on I-5. From I-5, take the Seneca St exit (#165), then go west on 5th Ave 1 block, at Spring St turn left and go 1 block, at 7th Ave turn right and go 1 block, at Madison St turn left and go ¾ mile, go straight onto E Union St and go 1¼ mile, then turn left at 34th Ave and this place is at the corner.

**Honey Bear Bakery

17171 Bothell Way NE, Lake Forest Park
206-366-3330
Vegetarian Restaurant. Mostly Organic.
Menu: Homemade soups, salads, sandwiches, Black Bean Chili and organic whole-wheat baked goods. Fresh juices, espresso.
Comments: Seattle institution. Pleasant atmosphere. Good bakery with some vegetarian choices for lunch. Good value.
Other Info: Full service, take-out. Non-smoking. No credit cards. Price: $.
Directions: In the Wallingford area. From I-5, take Exit #175 towards 145th St/Rte 523, then go west on NE 145th St/Rte 523 for 1½ mile, then turn left at Bothell Way and this place is 1½ mile down. Parking arranged for customers. This place is in north Seattle.

India House

4737 Roosevelt Way, NE, at 50th Street
206-632-5072
Hours: Tuesday to Thursday 11:30 am to 2 pm, 5 pm to 10 pm; Friday 11:30 am to 2 pm, 5 pm to 10:30 pm; Sat 11:30 am to 2 pm, 5 pm to 10:30 am; Sun 12 noon to 3 pm, 5 pm to 10 am
Indian. Vegan options. Not pure vegetarian.
Menu: Has a large vegetarian menu.
Comments: Has an elegant Indian décor with artifacts and paintings.
Other Info: Full service, take-out. Accepts AMEX, DC, DIS, MC, VISA. Price: $-$$.

Juice Plant

999 3rd Avenue; 206-622-7938
Hours: Daily 7 am to 5 pm
Health Food Restaurant and Juice Bar. American and some International. Not pure vegetarian.
Menu: Organic fresh juices. Has a small menu including salads, sandwiches, breads, energy bars (such as: spirulina, ginseng), swamp chips (potatoes, carrots, beets & yams) and muffins.
Directions: This place is 1 mile northwest of

where I-5 and I-90 meet. From I-5, take Seneca St exit (#165), then go northwest on 5th Ave, then turn right at Madison St (go east) and then this place is 2 blocks down at the corner of 3rd Ave.

Julia's

1714 North 44th Street, Wallingford area
206-633-1175
Hours: Monday 7 am to 3 pm; Tuesday to Thursday 7 am to 9 pm; Fri to Sun 7 am to 10 pm
Vegetarian-friendly Restaurant. Not pure veg.
Menu: Has several types of salad including Soba Noodle Salad with Tofu Steak, Greek Spinach and Julius Caesar Salad. For dinner there is soups, Grilled Marinated Shitake Mushrooms with feta cheese, Black Bean Cakes, Stir-fry Vegetables over Brown Rice and Venetian Herbed Polenta. For lunch there is Garden Burgers, Hummus Sandwich, Black Bean Burrito, Corn Tortillas Sandwich and vegetable soup. During breakfast there is a Tofu Breakfast Special (scrambled tofu with mushrooms and scallions, pan-fried potatoes, whole-wheat toast) and Sautéed Vegetables. Fresh juices.
Comments: One of the most popular places in Seattle. Happening place. Has hanging plants and wood tables. Has a good selection of vegetarian dishes for dinner, but not such a good selection for lunch.
Warning: Curried Cauliflower Soup contains chicken stock.
Other Info: Reservations suggested for Sunday brunch, and Friday and Saturday night.
Directions: From I-5, take exit #169 towards 45th St/50th St, then go west on 45th St for ¾ mile, at Densmore Ave turn left and go 1 block, at 44th St turn left and this place is at the corner.

Kokeb Ethiopian Restaurant

926 12th Avenue
206-322-0485
Hours: Monday to Saturday 5 am to 9 pm
Closed Sunday.
Ethiopian. Not pure vegetarian.
Menu: Has a selection of vegetarian dishes.
Comments: On weekends at 10 pm this place becomes a dance hall with live African music. Good, friendly service.
Other Info: Full service, take-out, delivery. Non-smoking. Accepts AMEX, MC, VISA. Price: $-$$.
Directions: A little east of Seattle University. Free parking.

Madison Market

1600 East Madison Street, at 16th Avenue East
206-329-1545; Web site: http://www.delicious-online.com/retailers/centralcoop/, www.madisonmarket.com
Hours: Daily 7 am to 12 midnight
Deli Hours: 8 am to 10 pm
Natural Food Store and Deli. Large selection of organic produce. Juice Bar.
Menu: Has a large selection of vegetarian dishes in the deli.
Comments: Central Co-op operates under the name of Madison Market. Friendly place. Offers discounts on cases.
Other Info: Counter service, take-out. Has a small counter area for seating. Accepts AMEX, MC, VISA.
Directions: From I-5, take Seneca St exit (#165), then go south a few blocks, then turn left at Madison St and this place is 1 mile northeast, at corner of Denny and 12th.

Neelam's Authentic Indian Cuisine

4735 University Way NE; 206-523-5275
Hours: Sunday to Thursday 11:30 am to 3 pm, 5 pm to 10 pm
Friday & Saturday 11:30 am to 3 pm, 5 pm to 10:30 pm
Indian. Not pure vegetarian.
Menu: Samosas, basmati rice, Malai Kofta, Baigan Bhartha (roasted eggplant curry) and curry dishes.
Comments: Good value. Food can be quite spicy hot, so you may want to ask them to cool it.
Other Info: Non-smoking. Accepts DIS, DC, MC, VISA.
Directions: In the University District. Free parking for customers.

New Orleans Creole Restaurant

114 South First Avenue South; 206-622-2563
Hours: Monday to Thursday 11 am to 11 pm; Friday & Saturday 11 am to 2 am; closed Sunday (sometimes open for brunch).
Creole, Cajun. Vegan options. Not pure veg.
Menu: Has a vegetarian section on the menu. Has a vegetarian Gumbo Soup (okra soup). Vegetarian eggplant dish. Red Beans and Rice. Veggie Sauté.
Comments: Located in historic Pioneer Square. Has outdoor seating. Has live jazz and blues music nightly.
Other Info: Full service, take-out. Accepts AMEX, DC, MC, VISA. Price: $$.
Directions: Parking arranged for customers.

PCC (Puget Consumer Coop) Fremont

716 North 34th Street; 206-632-6811
Web site: www.pccnaturalmarkets.com
Hours: Daily 7 am to 11 pm
Natural Food Store. Organic produce. Supermarket-size place.
Menu: Has a large selection of pre-made sandwiches and wraps. Organic Mashed Potatoes with Mushroom Gravy. Can prepare box lunches. Sandwiches and salads.
Comments: Freshly baked bread section.
Other Info: Counter service, take-out, catering.
Directions: From I-5, take Exit #167 towards Seattle Center/Mercer St, then go northwest on Westlake Ave for a half-mile around the water, then keep going north on Westlake Ave, at 4th Ave turn right and go over bridge and road becomes Fremont Ave and go 1 more block, at 34th St turn right and this place is 1 block down. Or from I-5, take NE 45th St exit, then go west on 45th, then at Stone Way turn left, then at N 34th St turn right. This place on right a little before Fremont Ave.

PCC Greenlake

7504 Aurora Avenue North; 206-525-3586
Web site: www.pccnaturalmarkets.com
Hours: Daily 8 am to 11 pm
Natural Food Store and Café. Deli, Bakery and Juice Bar. Organic produce.
Directions: From I-5, take 50th St exit, then go west on Aurora Ave N by going on overpass. At the fork just before overpass drive up incline to left, at Aurora Ave (Hwy 99), turn right and this place is on the right, a little north of corner of Winona Ave N and Aurora Ave, opposite Aurora Cycle. To get to store parking lot turn right at Winona and parking lot on left.

PCC Ravenna

6504 20th NE; 206-525-1450
Web site: www.pccnaturalmarkets.com
Hours: Daily 9 am to 9 pm
Natural Food Store and Café. Deli, Bakery and Juice Bar. Organic produce.
Directions: From I-5, take Ravenna Blvd exit (#170) towards 65th St exit, then at NE 65th St go ¾ mile, then at 20th Ave NE turn left and this place is at the corner on right.

PCC View Ridge

6514 40th Avenue; 206-526-7661
Web site: www.pccnaturalmarkets.com
Hours: Daily 7 am to 10 pm
Natural Food Store and Café. Deli, Bakery and Juice Bar. Organic produce.

Directions: From I-5 south, take NE 65th St/Ravenna exit. At 65th St turn right and go 1¾ mile and this place is on corner of 65th and 40th Ave on the left. From I-5 north, take NE 71st St/NE 65th St exit (#171). At Roosevelt Ave (stop sign) turn right, then at NE 65th go 1¾ mile.

PCC Seward Park

5041 Wilson Avenue S; 206-723-2720
Web site: www.pccnaturalmarkets.com
Hours: Daily 7 am to 10 pm
Natural Food Store.
Directions: From I-90 west, take Rainer Ave exit, then go south on Rainer Ave about 2 miles, at Genesee turn left, at 50th Ave South turn right (roads become Wilson Ave South) and this place on right. From I-5, take Swift Ave (#161) towards Albro Place, then go east on S Eddy St a quarter-mile, at Beacon Ave turn left and go a third-mile, at S Orcas St turn right and go 1.35 mile, at 48th Ave turn left and go a quarter-mile, at S Dawson turn right and go 1 block, at 50th St Ave turn left and this place is 1 block down (about a half-mile west of the water). This place is about 1½ mile northeast of the exit.

PCC West Seattle

2749 California Avenue SW; 206-937-8481
Web site: www.pccnaturalmarkets.com
Hours: Daily 7 am to 10 pm
Natural Food Store and Café. Deli, Bakery and Juice Bar. Organic produce. Natural Food Store.
Directions: This place is in west Seattle. From I-5, take West Seattle Freeway exit (exit #163 going north, exit #163A going south) and go west 2 miles, then take Admiral Way exit. At California Ave SW turn left and this place is 1 block down on right.

Pepe's on University Way

4535 University Way NE, between 45th and 47th
206-633-3544
Hours: Daily 11 am to 9 pm
Mexican Fast Food. Not pure vegetarian.
Menu: Has a good selection of vegetarian dishes. Veggie burritos, bean and cheese burritos, rice and tortillas.
Comments: Says they have no lard in the beans or meat products in the rice.
Other Info: Accepts MC, VISA.

Rainbow Grocery

417 15th Avenue East, at East John Street
206-329-8440
Hours: Daily 8 am to 9 pm
Natural Food Store. Juice and Soup Bar. Organic

produce.
Menu: Has soups and deli items in their cooler. Fresh juices.
Other Info: Accepts MC, VISA.
Directions: From I-5 south, take Olive Way exit east (#166) and go ¾ mile (becomes John). At 15th turn left and this place is 2½ blocks down on left, between Harrison and Republican Streets. From I-5 north, take Denny Way exit east, at John turn left, then at 15th turn left.

Rover's
2808 East Madison Street, at 28th Avenue, Madison Valley; 206-325-7442
Web site: www.rovers-seattle.com
Hours: Tuesday to Saturday 5:30 pm to 9:30 pm
Gourmet French. Not pure vegetarian.
Menu: Has prix-fixe five course vegetarian meals daily. An example meal is Vine-Ripe Tomato, Vegetable Medley, Micro Greens with Balsamic Infusion, Wild Mushrooms & Goat Cheese Tart, Roasted Parsnip Flan & Celeriac Perigord Truffle Potage, Spice Infused Pinot Noir Sorbet, Glazed Mushrooms in Phyllo with Matsutake Mushroom Rogout and a selection of desserts. Has a Local Cheese Plate.
Comments: Excellent service. Elegant décor. Flowers on tables. Very good food. Good experience. Got number one rating in ZAGAT Restaurant Guide. Considered to be one of the top restaurants in Seattle. Worth the splurge. Outdoor dining. Romantic place. Notable Chefs. Has outdoor seating.
Other Info: Reservations are required. Non-smoking. Accepts AMEX, DC, MC, VISA. Price: $$$$. $70 for five-course meal.
Directions: In Madison Valley.

Sabra Mediterranean Sandwich Shop
1916 Pike Place, #14; 206-441-4544
Hours: Monday to Saturday 11 am to 5:30 pm Closed Sunday.
Mediterranean. Vegetarian-friendly. Not pure vegetarian.
Menu: Salads, pita sandwiches, falafel, hummus, tabbouleh, baba ghanoush, Eggplant stuffed with Zucchini, Red Lentil Soup and more.
Comments: Not much seating.
Directions: In Pike Place Market in the Soames Dunn Building.

**Silence-Heart-Nest Restaurant
5247 University Way NE, U-district
206-524-4008
Hours: Monday, Tuesday, Thursday to Saturday 11 am to 9 pm; Sun 9 am to 2 pm; closed Wed.

Fully Vegetarian Western-style. Asian, Indian, American. Vegan friendly.
Menu: Has a large menu. Samosas, veggie burgers, curries, salads, chapati, masala dosa, dal, hummus wraps, salads, raita, mashed potatoes with mushroom gravy, brown basmati rice, whole-wheat chapatis and chutneys (tamarind raisin is good). Good desserts. Has vegan desserts such as vegan chocolate pudding. Vegan dishes are marked with a (V) on the menu.
Comments: Pleasant, peaceful atmosphere. Reasonably priced. Good, friendly service. Popular place. Offers free meditation classes. Has hanging plants. Waitresses dress in saris. Has outdoor dining. Run by followers of the Indian guru Sri Chinmoy. Plays New Age or Indian music.
Warning: The Neat Loaf contains eggs.
Other Info: Full service, take-out. Non-smoking. Price: $.
Directions: In the University District near the University of Washington. From I-5 going north, take exit #169 towards NE 45th St/50th St, keep left in fork in ramp, then merge onto 7th Ave for 1 block, at 50th St turn right and go 4 blocks, at 11th Ave turn left and go 1 block, at NE 52nd St turn right and go 3 blocks, at University Way turn left and this place is 50 yards down.

Sit & Spin
2219 4th Avenue, between Bell & Blanchard Streets; 206-441-9484
Hours: Sunday to Thursday 9 am to 12 am Friday & Saturday 9 am to 2 am
American Café. Rock Club. Vegan options. Not pure vegetarian.
Menu: Hummus sandwich, Black Bean Burritos, vegetarian chili, soup, pizzas and sandwiches. A large selection of fresh juice and smoothies. Cappuccino, espresso.
Comments: Live arts center, Laundromat, rock bar and café. Laid-back, trendy place. Has outdoor seating. Good value. Has board games. Live music. Plays rock, hip, techno and alternative rock. Often have to be 21 for live music. Can see their schedule at: http://seattle.citysearch.com/profile/10796492/
Other Info: Limited service, take-out. Price: $.
Directions: In downtown Seattle. From I-5, take the Seneca St exit (#165), then go 3 blocks west on Seneca St, than at 4th Ave turn right and this place is two-third mile down. Parking arranged for customers.

Sound View Café
1501 Pike Place #501; 206-623-5700
Hours: Monday to Friday 8 am to 5 pm; Satur-

day 8 am to 5:30 pm; Sunday 9 am to 3:30 pm **95% Vegetarian Natural Foods.** Vegan-friendly. **Menu:** Has a large amount of vegetarian dishes. Sandwiches, salads, Tofu Scrambled (very good), pasta salads and veggie enchiladas. **Comments:** Very friendly place. **Other Info:** Cafeteria style, take-out. Non-smoking. Accepts AMEX, DIS, MC, VISA. Price: $. **Directions:** In downtown Seattle. From I-5, take the Seneca St exit (#165), then go 6 blocks west on Seneca St, then turn right on 1st Ave and go 3 blocks, then at Pike St turn left and this place is 50 yards down. Parking arranged for customers.

Stalk Exchange

Green Lake/Greenwood/Phinney Ridge
6710 Greenwood Avenue N, at 67th Street
206-782-3911
Hours: Wednesday to Friday 10 am to 3 pm, 5 pm to 9 pm; Saturday 9 am to 3 pm, 5 pm to 9 pm; Sunday Brunch 9 am to 3 pm; closed Monday & Tuesday
American Coffeehouse. Mainly Organic. Vegetarian-friendly. Not pure vegetarian.
Menu: Has a decent selection of vegetarian dishes. Soups, salads, Nutty Brie, Mashed Potatoes, Jasmine Rice and assorted Vegetable Plate. Good homemade breads.
Comments: Has a fireplace. Good dining experience. Has outdoor dining. Local organic produce used when possible. Food generally gets good ratings. Comfortable, relaxing place. Popular for weekend brunch.
Other Info: Accepts MC, VISA. Price: $$-$$$.
Directions: In the Phinney Ridge neighborhood. From I-5, take exit #169 towards 45st/50st and this place is 1½ mile northwest of the exit on the other side of Green Lake.

Still Life In Fremont

709 North 35th Street, between Aurora & Fremont Avenue; 206-547-9850
Hours: Daily 7:30 am to 10 pm
Vegetarian friendly Eclectic Coffeehouse. Vegan options. Not pure vegetarian.
Menu: Emphasizes vegetarian food. Has several vegan and vegetarian dishes. Homemade good soups, vegan chili, salads, sandwiches, Vegetable Pie, fresh breads, pizzas and vegetarian main dishes. Cappuccino, espresso.
Comments: Has plenty of windows, art on the walls and mismatched wooden furniture. Popular place. Place gets high ratings. Good value. Post ingredients of soups on blackboard menu. Friendly, personal, relaxing, causal place. Often

has live music. Can call to find out special dishes of the day.
Other Info: Non-smoking. Price: $-$$.
Directions: From I-5, take Exit #167 towards Seattle Center/Mercer St, then go northwest on Westlake Ave for a half-mile around the water, then keep going north on Westlake Ave, at 4th Ave turn right and go over bridge and road becomes Fremont Ave and go 1 more block, at 35th St turn right and this place is near the corner. Can be hard to find parking in the area.

**Sunlight Café

6403 Roosevelt Way NE, at 64th
206-522-9060
Hours: Monday to Friday 10 am to 9 pm; Saturday and Sunday 10 am to 9 pm; Saturday & Sunday Brunch 10 am to 2 pm
Fully Vegetarian. Mainly American and some International. Vegan options.
Menu: Has many vegan dishes such as sautéed vegetables and desserts. Lasagna, Brown-rice Salad, cheese enchiladas, veggie burgers, soups, steamed vegetables & rice, Stir-fries, Hummus Pita Sandwich, Vegetable Tofu Sauté, and Nutburgers. Has eggless waffles with maple syrup and fresh fruit. Fresh juices, organic espresso and herbal teas. Yogi tea is very good.
Comments: Friendly, quick service. Oldest vegetarian place in town. Casual, leisure place. Good value. Very busy for Saturday and Sunday brunches. Simple décor. The sunny southern room is a good place to sit. Has local artwork on the walls.
Other Info: Reservations not required. Non-smoking. Full service, take-out. Accepts MC, VISA. Price: $-$$.
Directions: From I-5, take Ravenna Blvd exit (#170) towards NE 65th St, then go east on 65th St for 2 blocks, at Roosevelt Way turn right and this place is 1 block down. This place is a few blocks southeast of the exit.

***Teapot Vegetarian House

125 15th Avenue East; 206-325-1010
Hours: Daily 11:30 am to 10 pm
Fully Vegan. Asian including Chinese, Thailand, Japanese, Singapore, Indonesian. Pareve/Kosher certified.
Menu: Has a wide selection of vegan dishes. Has a good selection of mock meat dishes including mock chicken, seafood, duck and beef. Spring Rolls, steamed dumplings, Szechuan Soup, Miso Soup & "Shark Fin," Hot & Sour Soup and Avocado Nori Rolls. The Crispy Mandarin Beef is

good. Sesame Crisp Appetizers is sweet gluten sheets with caramel sauce. Bo Bo Platter ($12) is a selection of the appetizers. The Diamond Vegetarian Meal consists of Rice Soup, Tofu Prawns in spicy tomato sauce, vegetable chow mein and pot stickers. Sizzler Plate with tofu and mushrooms. Vegan desserts.

Comments: Uses fresh ingredients. Family owned and operated. Pleasant dining room with plants and a small pond in the middle.

Warnings: The fortune cookies have eggs in them.

Other Info: Full service, take-out. Non-smoking. Accepts MC, VISA.

Directions: From I-5 coming north, take exit #164B towards 4th Ave and merge onto I-90 going west where it dead ends and turns to the right taking you onto 4th Ave going north for a third-mile, at S Jackson St turn right and go a half-mile, at 12th Ave turn left and go 2 blocks, at E Yesler Way turn right and go 2 blocks, then at 15th Ave turn left and this place is halfway down the block. This place is ¾ mile northeast of where I-5 meets I-90.

Union Bay Café

3515 NE 45th Street; 206-527-8364
Hours: Tuesday to Sunday 5 pm to 10 pm Closed Monday.
Northwest and Italian. 40% Vegetarian.
Menu: Has several vegan dishes. Always has two main vegetarian dishes and several appetizers. Grilled Focaccia Bread and eggplant spread. Portobello Mushroom Chops with seasonal vegetables, roasted potatoes, pumpkin soup, Autumn Salad (mixed greens, goat cheese, hazelnuts), Buckwheat Crepe, Wild Rice & Gorgonzola, pasta dishes and Capelli d'Angeli (pasta dish with olives and sun-dried tomatoes).
Comments: White tables clothes and candles on tables. Nice décor. Vegetarian dishes are marked on the menu. Pastas don't contain eggs.
Other Info: Accepts AMEX, MC, VISA.

**Vita Bar

8334 Rainer Avenue S
206-760-7800; **email:** vita-bar@consultant.com
Hours: Monday to Friday 9 am to 7 pm; Saturday 11 am to 5 pm; closed Sunday.
Mainly Vegetarian.
Menu: Has breakfast, lunch and dinner menus. Red Bean and Rice, Stir-fry, soups, salads and Soy Ice Cream. Fresh juices.
Comments: The lady who runs this place is really nice. Friendly, casual place.
Directions: This place is in southeast Seattle.

From I-5, take ML King Way exit (#157), then go north on ML King Jr Way a half-mile, at S Ryan Way turn right and go a half-mile, at 51st Ave turn left (go north) and go ¾ mile, road become Rainier Ave and this place is half-mile down.

Whole Foods Market

1026 NE 64th Street, between Roosevelt Way and 12th Avenue, Roosevelt Square
206-985-1500
Hours: Daily 8 am to 10 pm
Natural Food Store and Cafe. Deli, Bakery, Salad Bar and Juice Bar. Organic produce. Supermarket-type place. See Wild Oats Market information.
Directions: From I-5, take the Ravenna Blvd exit (#170) towards NE 65th St, then go east on 65th St for 2 blocks, at Roosevelt Way NE turn right and this place is a half-block down.

SEQUIM

Khu Larb Thai II

120 West Bell Street; 360-681-8550
Hours: Tuesday to Sunday 11 am to 2:30 pm, 4:30 pm to 8:30 pm; closed Monday.
Thai. Not pure vegetarian. See Port Townsend, WA.
Other Info: Accepts AMEX, MC, VISA.

Sunny Farms Country Store

261461 Highway 101, corner of Mill Road, near Cosco; 360-683-8003
Hours: Daily 8 am to 7 pm
Natural Food Store and Deli. Organic produce.
Comments: Grows much of their organic produce. Friendly place.
Other Info: Accepts MC, VISA. Counter service, take-out.
Directions: About a mile west of Sequim on Hwy 101.

SPOKANE

China Best

226 West Riverside, downtown
509-455-9042
Hours: Monday to Friday 11 am to 2 pm, 4:30 pm to 8:30 pm; Sunday 5 pm to 8:30 pm
Chinese. Vegan options. Not pure vegetarian.
Menu: Has over twenty vegetarian dishes. Has some good tofu dishes.
Comments: Each dish is freshly prepared.
Other Info: Full service, take-out. Accepts AMEX, DIS, MC, VISA. Price: $$.

Lorien Herbs & Natural Food Inc
414 East Trent Avenue
509-456-0702
Hours: Monday to Friday 10 am to 6 pm; Saturday 10 am to 5 pm; Sunday 12 noon to 4 pm
Natural Food Store. Good selection of organic produce.
Directions: From I-90, take Division St exit (#281) north, then go north on Division St (US 2) a half-mile, At E Trent Ave (Rte 290) turn right and this place on right a third-mile down. This place is a few blocks south of Ganzaga University.

Mizuna
North 214 Howard Street, downtown
509-747-2004
email: dining@mizuna.com
Hours: Mon 11:30 am to 2:30 pm; Tues to Thur 11:30 am to 2:30 pm, 5 pm to 9 pm; Fri to Sat 11:30 am to 2:30 pm, 5 pm to 9:30 pm (open for drink until 12 midnight); closed Sun.
Vegetarian-friendly International. Vegan friendly. Not pure vegetarian (serves fish).
Menu: Stir-fries, salads, sandwiches (during lunch only), Vegetable Curry and much more. Fresh juices, cappuccino, espresso. Non-alcoholic beer and wine.
Comments: Has living music in the evening. Classic guitar and Celtic harp music. Local organic produce used when possible.
Other Info: Full service (for dinner), limited service (for lunch). Accepts AMEX, MC, VISA. Price: $$-$$$.
Directions: From I-395, take Maple St exit (#280) towards Lincoln St, then go north on Walnut St a third-mile, at W 1st Ave turn right and go a third-mile, at Lincoln St turn left and this place is 3 blocks down.

Niko's
West 725 Riverside; 509-624-7444
Hours: Mon 11 am to 2 pm, 5 pm to 9 pm; Tues & Wed 11 am to 9 pm; Thur & Friday 11 am to 10 pm; Sat 5 pm to 10 pm; closed Sun.
Middle Eastern, Greek. Not pure vegetarian. All-you-can-eat Lunch Bar.
Menu: Has a wide selection of vegetarian dishes.
Other Info: Full service. Price: $$.

The Onion
302 West Riverside, downtown; 509-747-3852
7522 North Division Street; 509-482-6100
Hours: Sunday to Thursday 11:15 am to 11:30 pm; Friday & Saturday 11:15 am to 1 am
Vegetarian-friendly Restaurant. Not pure veg.
Menu: Garden Burger, Boca Burger Deluxe, Chinese Noodles, salads, Cheese Quesadilla, Baked Potatoes, spaghetti, nachos and fettuccine.
Comments: Good service. Fun place.
Other Info: Accepts AMEX, DIS, MC, VISA.
Directions: From I-395, take Division St/US 2 N exit (#281), then go north on Division St for a third-mile, at W Spraque Ave turn left and go 2 blocks, at N Bernard turn right and go 1 block, at W Riverside Ave turn left and this place is at the corner.

Pilgrim's Nutrition
210 North Howard Street; 509-747-5622
9616 East Sprague Avenue, Suite B
509-924-7781
9118 East Spraque Avenue; 509-928-1741
4750 North Division Street, Suite 172
509-489-1112
14700 East Indiana Avenue; 509-924-2889
Hours: Monday to Saturday 10 am to 9 pm
Sunday 10 am to 6 pm
Natural Food Store.

TACOMA

Marlene's Market & Deli
Best Plaza
2951 South 38th Street
253-472-4080
Hours: Monday to Friday 9 am to 8 pm; Saturday 9 am to 7 pm; Sunday 11 am to 6 pm; Deli closes an hour before the store.
Natural Food Store and Café. Deli, Bakery and Juice Bar. Large selection of organic produce. Supermarket-size place. See Federal Way, WA.
Comments: Large selection of natural grocery items. Has organic clothing.
Directions: From I-5 take 38th St W exit (#132), then take 38th St west down a small hill for a half-mile and this place on right in Best Plaza.

**Quickie Too: A Vegan Café
1324 South Martin Luther King Avenue
253-572-4549
Hours: Monday, Wednesday, Thursday, Friday, Sunday 11 am to 8 pm
Closed Tuesday and Saturday.
Vegetarian Restaurant. Mainly vegan and organic.
Menu: Salads, sandwiches, veggie steak on wheat sub roll, Jamaican Spiced Tempeh Sub, Mama African Burger, Cascadian Farm organic French Fries, spaghetti and garlic bread. Has tempeh, seitan and tofu subs and sandwiches.

Comments: Simple décor. Their sandwiches get excellent ratings.
Directions: In the Hillside neighborhood. From I-5, take S 38th St exit (#132) towards Gig Harbor (Rte 16), then go north on Spraque 1 mile, at S 12 St turn right and go a half-mile, at ML King JR Way turn right and this place is 1 block down. This place is about 1 mile northwest of where I-5 and I-705 meet.

Westgate Nutrition Center

5738 North 26th Street
253-759-1990
Hours: Monday to Friday 9 am to 6 pm; Saturday 10 am to 5 pm; Sunday 12 noon to 5 pm
Natural Food Store.
Directions: Near Point Defiance Park. Close to corner of Pearl St and N 26th.

Whole Foods Market

6810 27th Street West
253-565-0188
Hours: Monday to Friday 10 am to 6 pm; Saturday 10 am to 5:30 pm; closed Sunday.
Natural Food Store.
Directions: From I-5, take Bremerton/Gig Harbor exit (Hwy 16), then go west on Hwy 16 about 4 miles, then take 19th St (TCC) exit, then go west on 19th St for 1 mile, then at Mildred turn left and go a half-mile south. When Mildred curves road becomes 27th and then this store is a quarter-mile down on left at curve. Has a blue awning and is behind Paragon Plaza. This place is on the west side of Fircrest Golf Club.

TONASKET

Okanogan River Co-op

21 W 4th Street; 509-486-4188
Summer Hours: Monday to Friday 9 am to 7 pm; Saturday 10 am to 5 pm; Sunday 12 noon to 4 pm; **Deli Counter Hours:** 11 am to 1 pm, then has ready-made dishes in cooler.
Natural Food Store and very Vegetarian-friendly Cafe. Deli and Juice Bar. Mostly vegetarian.
Menu: Sandwiches, soups, salads and hot dishes.
Comments: Very seldom makes non-vegetarian dishes.
Directions: From Rte 97 (becomes Main St), at 4th St turn west and this place is 3 blocks down on left.

VANCOUVER

Nature's Marketplace (Wild Oats)

8024 East Mill Plain Boulevard
360-695-8878; **fax:** 360-694-0764
Hours: Daily 8 am to 9 pm
Natural Food Store and Cafe. Deli, Bakery, Salad Bar and Juice Bar. Organic produce. Supermarket-type place. See Wild Oats Market information.
Menu: Has salads, pizza, baked potatoes and veggie sushi.
Comments: Offers massages.
Directions: From 205 north, take Mill Plain exit (#28) and go west on Mill Plain Blvd and this place is 1½ mile down in Garrison Square Mall, at corner of Garrison and Mill Plain Blvd.

West Virginia

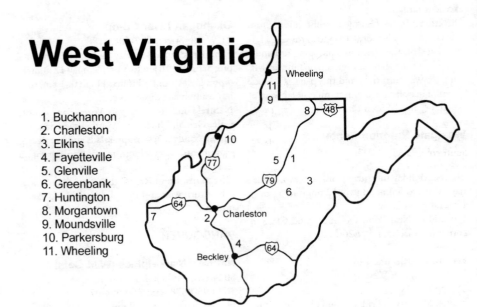

1. Buckhannon
2. Charleston
3. Elkins
4. Fayetteville
5. Glenville
6. Greenbank
7. Huntington
8. Morgantown
9. Moundsville
10. Parkersburg
11. Wheeling

BUCKHANNON

Molly's Pantry Inc
39 College Avenue
304-472-5099
Hours: Monday to Saturday 9 am to 5 pm
Closed Sunday.
Natural Food Store.
Directions: From I-79, take exit #99 (Rte 33 east for 15 miles to Buckhannon). Take a slight right at Main St and go east about a mile, then at Florida St (three blocks east of Rte 4) turn right. This place is then ¾ mile down at College and Florida.

ELKINS
Krogers carries some organic produce.

Good Energy Foods
100 3rd Street
304-636-5169
Hours: Monday to Saturday 9 am to 5:30 pm
(until 6:30 pm on Friday)
Natural Food Store. No produce.
Comments: In a historic building.
Other Info: Accepts AMEX, DIS, MC, VISA.
Directions: Hwy 33 becomes Randolph Ave in Elkins. From Rte 33 going north turn left onto 3rd St and this place is three blocks down. It is in the historical area of the town.

FAYETTEVILLE

Healthy Harvest
309 North Court Street; 304-574-1788
Hours: Wednesday to Saturday 11 am to 6 pm
Closed Sunday, Monday, Tuesday.
Natural Food Store. Juice Bar.
Directions: From Rte 19, at traffic light go south at Court St (Rte 16). This place is on right 150 yards down.

GLENVILLE

Country Life
211 North Lewis Street; 304-462-8157
Hours: Monday to Thursday 10 am to 6 pm
Friday 10 am to 4 pm
Closed Tuesday, Saturday, Sunday.
Natural Food Store.
Directions: From I-79, take Burnsville exit. Go west on Rte 5 for 35 miles. After entering Glenville turn left at T intersection and store is a quarter-mile down on the right.

GREENBANK

Sweet Thyme Inn
Route 92/28, PO Box 85
304-456-5535; **email:** info@sweetthymeinn.com;

Web site: www.sweetthymeinn.com
Hours: Daily for three meals. Must be reserved in advance
Hotel and International Vegetarian Restaurant. Mainly Vegan.
Menu: Mushrooms and Seitan Stroganoff, French Onion Soup, Spinach and Portobello Mushroom Salad, Ravioli, Asparagus Risotto and Pine Nuts, Roasted Veggie Brochettes, Southern Baked Patties and Corn & Potato Chowder. For breakfast there is Potato-Kale Croquettes and Biscuits & Southern Gravy.
Comments: This restaurant is in a hotel, in which comfortable rooms begin at around $80. Local organic produce used when possible. Price: $$.
Advance reservations are necessary and they ask for a minimum of six people if you are not staying in the inn.
Directions: Green Bank (off Rte 28) is just across from the border of the western Virginia border, near the Monongahela National Forest. From Route 92/28 watch for Inn sign on right just before BP station.

HUNTINGTON

Nawab Indian Cuisine
4th Avenue, at 7th Street; 304-525-8600
Hours: Daily 5 pm to 10 pm
Indian. Not pure vegetarian.
Menu: Has a good selection of vegetarian dishes.
Other Info: Accepts AMEX, DIS, MC, VISA.

MORGANTOWN

Maxwell's
1 Wall Street
304-292-0982
Hours: Monday to Thursday 11 am to 8 pm; Friday & Saturday 11 am to 9 pm; Sunday Brunch 11 am to 1:45 pm
Restaurant. Vegan options. Not pure vegetarian.
Menu: Has a large selection of vegetarian dishes. Mushroom Burgers, salads, stir-fry, tofu sandwich and vegetarian sandwiches.
Comments: Marks the vegetarian dishes on the menu. Every Thursday is pasta night.
Other Info: Full service, take-out. Accepts MC, VISA. Price: $-$$.
Directions: Downtown, next to the waterfront. From I-79, take Rte 19 (#152) exit towards Westover/Morgantown. Go west on Rte 19 for 2½ miles and after crossing the bridge, Rte 19 turns north going along the river. This place is then about a quarter-mile down on the left.

**Mountain People's
1400 University Avenue
304-291-6131
Web site: www.mountaincoop.com
Hours: Monday to Friday 9 am to 8 pm
Saturday & Sunday 10 am to 6 pm
Natural Food Store and Fully Vegetarian International Restaurant. Deli. Has organic produce. Vegan friendly.
Menu: Vegetarian soups, salads, Strudel, Pot Pie, Lasagna, sandwiches, Black Bean & Sweet Potato Chili, hummus, fresh baked bread and pies. Diner Specials on Wednesday & Thursday 5 pm to 8 pm (a main dish and either a soup or side salad) for $7.
Comments: Relaxed, casual place. The restaurant is connected to a co-op natural food store.
Other Info: Cafeteria style, take-out. Has around four tables to seat at. Non-smoking. Reservations not necessary. Accepts DIS, MC, VISA. Price: $
Directions: This place is next to the University of West Virginia. From I-79, take Rte 19 (#152) exit towards Westover/Morgantown. Go west on Rte 19 (becomes Beechurst) for 2½ miles and after crossing the bridge Rte 19 turns north going along the river. Go north on Rte 19 (becomes University Ave) and this place is then about a quarter-mile down (2 blocks) on the left, at University and Fayette St.

Sunflowers
1137 Van Voorhis Road
304-598-0668
Hours: Monday to Saturday 10 am to 7 pm
Sunday 1 pm to 5 pm
Natural Food Store.
Directions: From Rte 19 after crossing bridge into town go southeast about 1½ mile, then turn left at Patteson Dr and go 1½ mile east, then turn left at Van Voorhis Rd and go north and this place is ¾ mile down.

MOUNDSVILLE

**Palace of Gold Restaurant
RD1 NBU #24
Palace of Gold Number: 304-843-1812
Temple Number: 304-843-1600
Palace of Gold Hours: October to March 10 am to 5 pm; April to September 10 am to 8 pm
Fully Vegetarian Indian and International. Vegan options.
Menu: Has a good selection of vegetarian dishes. Veggie burgers, curried vegetables, steamed vegetables, several rice dishes, dal, soups, salads &

great salad dressings, Lasagna, pastas, Curd Dishes and some excellent desserts.

Comments: This restaurant is in basement of the Hare Krishna Palace of Gold. The Palace of Gold was built in honor of his Divine Grace AC Bhaktivedanta Swami Prabhupada, the founder of the Hare Krishna movement. It is a stunningly beautiful building with a gold-plated dome. The service is good and the atmosphere is peaceful and spiritual. The food is great and the place is recommended. Down the hill from the Palace of Gold is an interesting Hare Krishna Temple and a guest house for overnight stays.

Snack Bar: There is also a snack bar in the guest house next to the temple that serves snacks, pizzas and sandwiches.

Other Info: Full service, take-out. Accepts MC, VISA. Price: $-$$.

Directions: This place is located on the ISKCON (Hare Krishna) farm a few miles east of Moundsville, about ten miles south of Wheeling, WV. You can call 304-843-1600 to get directions from various locations. From I-70, get on I-470 (in Wheeling if coming from west on I-70), then take exit number #2 and go south on Hwy 88 about 7 miles, then in Moundsville turn left onto Rte 250 and go east 2 miles, when you see the sign for Palace of Gold turn left and this place is 5 miles down on the right. This restaurant is in the beautiful golden domed Palace of Gold.

PARKERSBURG

Mother Earth
1638 19th Street
304-428-1024
Hours: Monday to Saturday 9 am to 7 pm Closed Sunday.
Natural Food Store. Organic produce.
Other Info: Accepts MC, VISA.
Directions: From I-77, head west on Rte 50 into Parkersburg about 2 miles. At Plum Ave turn right and go about a mile to 19th Street. At 19th St turn left and this place is a block down.

WHEELING

Health Nuts
1908 Market Street
304-232-0105
Hours: Monday to Saturday 10:30 am to 6:30 pm; closed Sunday.
Natural Food Store. No produce.
Directions: This place at north end of Center Market, a block from Ohio Valley Hospital. From I-470, take US Rte 250 (#1 or #2) exit toward Wheeling/Moundsville and after about a half-mile take Rte 2 N (18th St) exit. At 18th St turn left and then at Chapline St make a slight left turn and go one block. At 20th St turn right and at the next block turn right and this place is one block down.

Wisconsin

1. Ashland
2. Cumberland
3. Gay Mills
4. Green Bay
5. La Crosse
6. Lake Delton
7. Lake Geneva
8. Luck
9. Madison
10. Manitowoc
11. Menomonie
12. Milwaukee
13. Mount Horeb
14. New Richmond
15. Oshkosh
16. Rice Lake
17. Richland Center
18. River Falls
19. Sheboygan
20. Sparta
21. Spring Green
22. Steven's Point
23. Superior
24. Trempealeau
25. Viola
26. Viroqua
27. Wauwatosa
28. Wisconsin Dells

ASHLAND

Black Cat Coffee House
211 Chapple Avenue; 715-682-3680
Hours: Monday to Friday 7 am to 10 pm; Saturday 8 am to 10 pm; closed Sunday.
American. Not pure vegetarian.
Menu: Has a good selection of vegetarian dishes. Pizzas, a variety of veggie sandwiches, hummus and salads.
Comments: Good place to hang out. Friendly place.
Other Info: Full service, take-out. Price: $.

Chequamegon Co-op
215 Chapple Avenue; 715-682-8251
Hours: Mon to Sat 9 am to 8 pm; closed Sun.
Natural Food Store.
Directions: From the junction of Rte 13 and Rte 2 (next to the water) this place is 6 blocks southwest. Coming into town on Rte 13, turn left (go southwest) onto Rte 2 and go 6 blocks, at Chapple Ave turn left and this place is a block down at junction with Main St.

CUMBERLAND

Island City Food Co-op
1155 6th Avenue
715-822-8233
Hours: Monday to Friday 10 am to 5:30 pm
Saturday 10 am to 3 pm
Closed Sunday.
Natural Food Store.
Directions: This place is a half-mile west of the downtown on Hwy 63. Signs for this place on highway.

GAY MILLS

Kickapoo Exchange Food Co-op
209 Main Street
608-735-4544
Hours: Monday to Saturday 10 am to 6 pm
Closed Sunday.
Natural Food Store. Organic produce.
Directions: This place is on the south side of the main street in town.

GREEN BAY

**Kavarna
112 South Broadway; 920-430-3200
Hours: Mon to Thurs 9 am to 11 pm; Fri & Sat 9 am to 12 midnight; Sun 9 am to 6 pm
Fully Vegetarian.
Menu: Pasta salads, Black Bean Burger, veggie pitas, salads, two kinds of vegetarian soups and more. Vegan brownies.
Comments: Good, relaxing atmosphere. Has live bands at night. Has board games to play. Food gets good ratings.
Other Info: Counter service, take-out. Order at counter then food is brought to table. Accepts MC, VISA.

Z Harvest
2475 University Avenue; 920-468-1685
Hours: Monday & Tuesday 11 am to 3 pm; Wednesday to Saturday 11 am to 9 pm; closed Sunday.
American Restaurant. Not pure vegetarian.
Menu: Has a good selection of vegetarian dishes. Portobello Sandwich, Black Bean Burger, veggie burger and salads.
Other Info: Reservations recommended on weekends. Non-smoking. Accepts AMEX, DIS, MC, VISA.

LA CROSSE

People's Food Coop
315 South 5th Avenue; 608-784-5798
Hours: Monday to Friday 7 am to 8 pm; Saturday 7 am to 7 pm; Sunday 8 am to 6 pm
Natural Food Store and a small Café. Deli and Bakery. Vegan options. Organic produce.
Menu: Salads, vegetarian soups, sandwiches and daily specials.
Other Info: Accepts MC, VISA.
Directions: In downtown La Crosse. From I-90, take Hwy 16 exit south (it becomes Losey Blvd). At Main St turn right and go 2 blocks, then at 5th Ave turn left and this place is two blocks down on left.

LAKE GENEVA

The Cactus Club
430 Broad Street; 262-248-1999
Hours: Sunday to Thursday 11 am to 9 pm
Friday & Saturday 11 am to 10 pm
Southwestern. Not pure vegetarian.
Menu: Black bean burrito, Stir-fries, vegetable burrito, Gardenburger, vegetable fajita and more.
Other Info: Full service, take-out. Reservations necessary for groups. Accepts AMEX, DIS, MC, VISA. Price: $$.
Directions: Parking arranged for customers.

LUCK

Nature's Alternative Co-op
241 Main Street; 715-472-8084
Hours: Monday to Friday 9 am to 5 pm (until 6 pm Thur & Fri); Sat 9 am to 3 pm; closed Sun.
Natural Food Store. Organic produce.
Directions: From Rte 48, go south on Main St. This place is 1½ block down on right.

MADISON

Blue Plate Dinner
2089 Atwood Avenue; 608-244-8505
Hours: Monday to Thursday 7 am to 9 pm; Friday 7 am to 10 pm; Saturday 7:30 am to 10 pm; Sunday 7:30 am to 10 pm
American. Vegan options. Not pure vegetarian.
Menu: Has several vegetarian sandwiches and usually there is a vegetarian special. Artichoke Sandwich, Black Bean Burger, soups, Grilled Eggplant and a daily vegetarian dinner special. Cappuccino, espresso.
Comments: Has a 1950s atmosphere with art-décor design and big band music.
Other Info: Full service, take-out. Accepts MC, VISA. Price: $-$$.

Canterbury Booksellers & Coffeehouse
315 West Gorham Street; **Store number:** 608-258-9911; **Café number:** 608-441-9917
Hours: Monday to Saturday 9 am to 7 pm
Sunday 11 am to 6 pm
Menu: Has a decent selection of vegetarian dishes. The menu changes regularly. Veggie burgers, soups, Tofu Sandwich and salads.
Warning: The vegetarian chili may have meat in it.

Caspian Café
University Square Mall, 17 University Square
608-259-9009
Hours: Monday to Friday 11 am to 5 pm
Middle Eastern, Persian. Not pure vegetarian.
Menu: Falafel, hummus, grape leaves and tabbouleh.
Other Info: Full service, take-out. Cash only. Price: $-$$.
Directions: Parking arranged for customers.

Himal Chuli

318 State Street; 608-251-9225
Hours: Monday to Saturday 11 am to 9 pm
Sunday 11 am to 8 pm
Nepalese. Not pure vegetarian.
Menu: Has a vegetarian section on the menu.
Known for Momocha Dumplings stuffed with
vegetables with a peanut sauce. There is a vegan
special with brown rice, lentil soup and vegetables.
Comments: Friendly, attentive service.
Other Info: Limited service, take-out. No credit
cards; cash only. Price: $-$$.

Husnu's

547 State Street; 608-256-0900
Hours: Daily 11 am to 11 pm
Mediterranean, Italian, Turkish. Not pure
vegetarian.
Menu: Falafel, couscous, hummus, eggplant and
other dishes. Non-alcoholic beer.
Other Info: Full service, take-out. Accepts MC,
VISA. Price: $-$$.

**JC Turtle

At Library Mall on weekdays
On Saturday at corner of North Pinckney and
East Main, near Capital Square
Organic Vegetarian Cart serving breakfast.
Comments: Uses eggs in some of the dishes. Pur-
chases produce every morning at local farmer's
markets during season.

LuLu's Deli and Restaurant

2524 University Avenue; 608-233-2172
Hours: Monday to Wednesday 11 am to 9 pm;
Thursday to Saturday 11 am to 9:30 pm; closed
Sunday.
Middle Eastern. Vegan options. Not pure veg.
Menu: Falafel, hummus, baba ghanouj and other
vegetarian dishes. Non-alcoholic beer and wine.
Other Info: Full service, take-out. Accepts MC,
VISA. Price: $-$$.

**Magic Hill Natural Foods

2862 University Avenue, west of Capital Square.
608-238-2630
Hours: Monday to Friday 8 am to 9 pm
Saturday & Sunday 9 am to 8 pm
Natural Food Store and Vegetarian Deli. Bak-
ery, Salad Bar and Juice Bar. Organic produce.
Menu: Has a good selection of vegetarian dishes.
Comments: Fairly big place that has organic
products, bulk grains & spices and gourmet
products.

Other Info: Accepts AMEX, MC, VISA. Counter
service, take-out. Has a few tables.
Directions: This place is near the southwest corner of the university. From I-90, take US-51 exit
(#132) towards Madison/De Forest. Go southwest on US-51 for 4 miles, then turn right onto
E Washington Ave/US-151 and go another 4
miles. US-151 become Blair St (US-151), then
follow US-151 into town (street names changes
several times) for 2 more miles, then at S Park St
turn right and go third-mile, then at Spring St
turn left and go 2 blocks, at N Mill St turn right
and go 3 blocks, at Spring St turn left and go 1
block, at N Charter St turn right and go a quarter-mile, at University Ave make slight left and
go third-mile, at Campus make slight right and
go 1.3 miles west (becomes University Ave) and
this place is near junction with Ridge St.

Mifflin Street Community Coop

32 North Bassett Street; 608-251-5899
email: dawn@terracom.net;
Web site: http://www.sit.wisc.edu/~mifflin/
Hours: Monday to Friday 10 am to 9 pm
Saturday & Sunday 10 am to 8 pm
Natural Food Store. Organic produce.
Menu: Has ready-made sandwiches.
Other Info: Accepts MC, VISA.
Directions: This place is in the downtown area.
From I-90/94, take John Nolen Drive north
(#263) 2 miles. Then take Broom St exit and go
northwest 5 blocks. At Mifflin St turn left and go
1 block. This place on left at intersection of Bassett
and Mifflin.
Parking: There are five free parking spots in front
of the store. Store will reimburse customers for
one hour of parking in any downtown ramp with
a minimum purchase of five dollars. Ask cashier
for parking coupon when making a purchase.

North Farm Co-op

204 Regas Road
608-241-2667; Web site: www.northfarm.com
Natural Food Store. Organic produce.
Hours: Monday to Friday 8 am to 5 pm
Closed Saturday & Sunday.
Natural Food Store. No produce.
Directions: From Hwy 51, get off at Milwaukee
St. If going north on Hwy 51 at end of ramp
turn left and go under overpass for a quarter-mile.
At Regas Rd, just past the main Madison Post
Office, turn right and go 1½ block. Go past a
stop sign and bear right. This place on left and
has a green awning.

Sunporch Café Restaurant and Café
Lakepoint Commons, 2701 University Avenue
608-231-1111
Hours: Monday 7 am to 2 pm; Tuesday to Saturday 7 am to 4 pm; Sunday 8 am to 3 pm
Restaurant. Vegan options. Not pure vegetarian
Menu: Has many vegetarian dishes. Menu changes with the season. Pasta dishes, veggie burgers, Scrambled Tofu, soups, sandwiches, pita sandwiches and salads.
Other Info: Full service, take-out, catering. Reservations suggested for groups. Accepts AMEX, MC, VISA. Price: $$.
Directions: This place is at the southwest corner of the University of Wisconsin. From I-90, take US-51 exit (#132) towards Madison/De Forest. Go southwest on US-51 for 4 miles, then turn right onto E Washington Ave/US-151 and go another 4 miles. US-151 become Blair St (US-151), then follow US-151 into town (street names changes several times) for 2 more miles, then at S Park St turn right and go third-mile, then at Spring St turn left and go 2 blocks, at N Mill St turn right and go 3 block, at Spring St turn left and go 1 block, at N Charter St turn right and go quarter-mile, at University Ave make slight left and go third-mile, at Campus make slight right and go 1.3 miles west and this place is one block after it becomes University Ave, at the junction with University Bay Dr (also Farley Ave on south side).

Sunroom Café
638 State Street, near the university
608-255-1555
Hours: Monday to Saturday 7 am to 9:30 pm
Sunday 9 am to 9:30 pm
Ethnic European-style Cafe. American, Mexican. Not pure vegetarian.
Menu: Has several vegetarian dishes. Gourmet desserts. During breakfast there is Mushrooms & Tomatoes in a sauce and Scrambled Tofu. Lunch and dinner has salads, pastas and sandwiches. Veggie Burgers, one or two soups and veggie chili. Fresh juices, cappuccino, espresso.
Comments: Has a view of the street from the upstairs seating. Good food.
Other Info: Full service, take-out. Accepts MC, VISA. Price: $$.
Directions: On the university campus.

Whole Foods Market
3313 University Avenue (University Plaza)
608-233-9566; fax: 608-233-8066
Hours: Daily 8 am to 9 pm
Natural Food Store and Cafe. Deli, Bakery, Salad Bar and Juice Bar. Organic produce. Supermarket-type place. See Whole Foods Market on page 666.
Directions: From I-90, take exit for Highways 12/14 in Madison and go about 6 miles. Take Midvale Blvd exit (#258) and turn right off exit (go north towards downtown). Take Midvale for 2 miles to University, then turn right and this place is on the right 3 blocks down.

Williamson (Willy) Street Food Coop
1221 Williamson Street
608-251-6776; email: willst@willystcoop.com;
Web site: www.willystcoop.com
Hours: Daily 8 am to 9 pm
Natural Food Store and Deli. Vegan Bakery and Coffee Bar. Has a large selection of organic produce.
Menu: Homemade soups and salads, and organic salad bar. Fresh juices.
Comments: Friendly place. Been open over 20 years. There is a good vegetarian Southeast Asian restaurant next door also worth checking out.
Other Info: Counter service, take-out. Has seating. Accepts AMEX, MC, VISA.
Directions: This place is between the two lakes, off Hwy 151, 4 miles west of I-90. From I-94, get on Rte 30 going west for 3 miles, then take US-151 (S Washington Ave) exit towards State Capitol, merge onto E Washington Ave and go west 2 miles, at S Baldwin St turn left and go a quarter-mile, at E Wilson St turn right and go 1 block, at S Few turn left and this place is a block down at corner with Williamson St.

MANITOWOC

Manitowoc Food Co-op
713 Buffalo Street; 414-684-3000
Hours: Monday, Thursday, Friday 9 am to 7 pm; Tuesday, Wednesday 9 am to 5 pm; Saturday 9 am to 3 pm; closed Sunday.
Natural Food Store.
Directions: From I-43, take US-10/Rte 42/CR-JJ exit (#152) and go east (becomes Rankin St) for about 4 miles. At N 9th St (can also turn right at Maritime Dr) turn right and go south 1½ mile. Then at Buffalo turn left and this place on right 1 block down.

MENOMONIE

Menomonie Market Co-op
1309 North Broadway; 715-235-6533
Hours: Monday to Friday 9 am to 7 pm; Satur-

day 9 am to 5 pm; Sunday 12 noon to 5 pm
Natural Food Store and small Deli. Organic produce.
Menu: Menu changes daily. Sandwiches, salads, soups, veggie chili, burritos, enchiladas and other dishes.
Other Info: Accepts MC, VISA.
Directions: From I-94, take exit #41 (Hwy 25) and go south on Hwy 25 (turns into Broadway). This place is on the right 1 mile south of I-94.

MILWAUKEE

Abu's Jerusalem Restaurant
1978 North Farwell Avenue; 414-277-0485
Hours: Monday 11 am to 4:30 pm
Tuesday to Sunday 11 am to 9:30 pm
Middle Eastern. Not pure vegetarian.
Menu: Has a wide selection of vegetarian dishes. Has hummus, falafel, tabbouleh, chili, Spinach Pies, eggplant and baba ghanouj.
Comments: Rated as a good middle-eastern place. Pleasant place. Good service.
Other Info: Full service, take-out. Price: $-$$.

Au Bon Appetit
1016 East Brady Street; 414-278-1233
Hours: Tuesday to Thursday 5 pm to 9 pm; Friday & Saturday 5 pm to 10 pm; closed Monday & Sunday.
Lebanese. Vegan options. Not pure vegetarian.
Menu: Has a good selection of vegetarian dishes. Falafel, hummus, soup, tabbouleh, baba ghanouj, Couscous and Lentil Soup. Fresh juices. Lebanese coffee.
Comments: Food gets good recommendations.
Other Info: Full service, take-out, catering. Accepts MC, VISA. Price: $$.

Beans & Barley Café
1901 East North Avenue, at Oakland Avenue
414-278-7878; **Menu Info:** 414-278-7800
Web site: www.beansandbarley.com
Hours: Monday to Saturday 9 am to 9 pm; Sunday 9 am to 8 pm; Breakfast 9 am to 11 am
Natural Food Store and Restaurant. Deli, Grocery Store and Bakery. International including Middle Eastern & Mexican. Vegan options. Not fully vegetarian but has a good selection.
Menu: Daily soup and salad specials. TLT (tempeh, lettuce and tomato), sandwiches, Vegetarian Chili, Guacamole & Chips, Hummus & Vegetable Pocket, stir-fry dishes, Tempeh Reuben, Rice of the Day, Tofu Burger, veggie burrito, Grilled Vegetable Sandwich, tostadas, quesadillas,

Artichoke Parmesan Sandwich and soy burgers. Fresh juices.
Comments: Uses as much as possible locally grown organic vegetables. Uses fresh ingredients. Prices are reasonable. Good food and service. Friendly atmosphere. Restaurant seats 80 people. The deli is not so well supplied. The store has a good selection of items. Especially busy on weekend breakfasts.
Comments: High ceiling and large plate glass windows.
Other Info: Full service, take-out. Reservations not necessary. Non-smoking. Accepts DIS, MC, VISA. Price: $-$$.
Directions: From Hwy 43, take North Ave exit (#73C) and go east on North Ave about 2 miles towards the lake. This place on right at corner of Oakland and North. It is 4 blocks west of Veterans Park. This place is a mile north of the main downtown area.

**Bombay Sweets
3401 South 13th Street; 414-383-3553; **Web site:** www.milwaukeefoods.com/bombaysweets
Hours: Daily 11 am to 9 pm
Vegetarian Indian. Vegan options.
Menu: Has 60 vegetarian dishes. Indian breads, Bhel Poori, Samosa Chat, Aloo Tikki Chat, a selections of dosas, Parathas, Vegetable Biryani, Rice Pulao, Mattar Paneer, Channa Masala, Aloo Gobi and Indian desserts.
Comments: Pretty good place. Price: $.
Directions: From Hwy 94, take Holt Ave exit (#314A) and go west on Holt ¾ mile. Then at 13th St turn right and this place is then a half-block down on the west side of the street.

Brewed Awakening
1208 East Brady Street; 414-276-BREW (2739)
Hours: Monday to Friday 7 am to 12 midnight
Saturday & Sunday 9 am to 12 midnight
Coffee Shop. Vegan friendly. Not pure veg.
Menu: Vegetarian Chili, soups, sandwiches, bagels and baked goods. Has really good coffee.
Other Info: Inside area is non-smoking. Accepts AMEX, MC, VISA.

Carini's La Conca D'Oro
3468 North Oakland Avenue; 414-963-9623
Hours: Tuesday to Thursday 11 am to 10 pm; Friday 11 am to 11 pm; Saturday 4 pm to 11 pm; Sunday 4 pm to 9 pm; closed Monday.
Italian. Not pure vegetarian.
Menu: Has a vegetarian buffet Wednesday to Friday. Several types of pastas, Eggplant Parmesan

Sandwich and Pasta Con Broccoli E Cavolfiore. Melenzane Spiedini is eggplant stuffed with cheese and breadcrumbs with a tomato sauce.
Comments: A bit upscale.
Other Info: Full service, take-out. Reservations suggested on weekends. Accepts AMEX, DIS, MC, VISA. Price: $$-$$$.

Casablanca
730 West Mitchell Street
414-383-2363
Hours: Tuesday to Saturday 11 am to 9 pm
Sunday 12 noon to 6 pm
Lunch Buffet: Tuesday to Friday 11 am to 3 pm
Closed Monday.
Middle Eastern. All-you-can-eat Vegetarian Lunch Buffet.
Menu: Hummus, falafel, stuffed grape leaves, tabbouleh, baba ghanoush and more.
Comments: Very good value. Accepts MC, VISA. Price: $.
Directions: From I-94, (Hwy 41) take W Lapham Blvd Exit (#312B), then go 2 blocks west on W Lapham Blvd, then at 7th St turn right and go 1 block, then at W Mitchell St turn right and this place is a half-block down. This place is in south Milwaukee.

Health Hut
2225 South 108th Street
414-545-8844
Hours: Monday to Friday 9:30 am to 8 pm
Saturday 9 am to 4 pm
Natural Food Store.
Comments: Good selection of organic produce, bulk foods, natural products and meat substitutes.

In Good Health Café
Manchester Mall, 220 Oak Street, Grafton
262-376-9020, 888-414-9500;
email: Customer_Service@aliveandhealthy.com;
Web site: www.aliveandhealthycom
Hours: Monday to Friday 10 am to 7 pm
Saturday 10 am to 3 pm
Natural Foods Store and Cafe. Salad Bar. Organic dishes.
Comments: Has Ayurvedic and homeopathic remedies.
Directions: This place is 15 miles north of Milwaukee. From Hwy-43, take Exit 89 (CR-C) toward Cedarburg, then go west on CR C for a quarter-mile, at N Port Washington Rd turn right and go 1 mile, at Lakefield Rd turn left and go 2 miles, at Green Bay Rd turn right and go ¾ mile and this place is in the Manchester Mall.

Milk'n Honey Natural Foods
10948 West Capital Drive, near Hwy 100
414-535-0203
Hours: Monday to Friday 10 am to 7 pm; Saturday 9 am to 4 pm; Sunday 10 am to 5 pm
Natural Food Store. Limited organic produce. Has some baked goods.
Other Info: Accepts AMEX, MC, VISA.
Directions: From Hwy 45, take Capitol Drive Exit #44 (Hwy 190) and go east a half-mile. This place is on left. This place is 6 miles northwest of downtown Milwaukee.

Outpost Natural Foods
100 East Capitol Drive, near 1st Street
414-961-2597
email: outpost@execpc.com
Web site: www.outpostcoop.com
Hours: Daily 8 am to 9 pm
Natural Food Store and Deli. Bakery, Salad Bar and Juice Bar. Organic produce.
Menu: Soups, Roasted Red Pepper Stew, Spinach & Tomato, Herb Vegetable Pie, Red Bean & Gumbo, Roast Potatoes & Vegetables, sandwiches and salads.
Comments: Best place in town for organic vegetables and fruits.
Other Info: Accepts DIS, MC, VISA.
Directions: From I-43, take Capitol Drive exit and go east on E Capitol Dr and this place is 9 blocks down on left after 3 traffic lights. This place is 3 miles north of downtown Milwaukee.

West Bank Café
732 East Burleigh Street; 414-562-5555
Hours: Sunday to Thursday 5:30 pm to 9:30 pm
Friday & Saturday 5:30 pm to 10 pm
Vietnamese, French, Chinese, American. Vegan options. Not pure vegetarian.
Menu: Has a wide selection of vegetarian dishes.
Comments: Good food and value.
Other Info: Accepts AMEX, MC, VISA. Price: $-$$.

MOUNT HOREB

General Store Co-op
517 Springdale Street; 608-437-5288
Hours: Monday to Friday 10 am to 6 pm
Saturday 10 am to 4 pm
Natural Food Store. Organic produce.
Comments: Member owned and operated place. Local artisans display their artwork, jewelry and pottery.
Directions: From Highways 151/18, take Busi-

ness 151/18 and it becomes Springdale Street. This place is in the center of town.

NEW RICHMOND

Nature's Pantry Co-op
258 South Knowles Street; 715-246-6105
Hours: Monday to Friday 9 am to 5 pm
Saturday 9 am to 1 pm
Natural Food Store.
Directions: Take 65 north into downtown New Richmond and this place is at the second intersection on the right, at the corner of South Knowles and 3rd.

OSHKOSH

Kitchen Korner Health Food
463 North Main Street; 920-426-1280
Hours: Monday to Friday 9 am to 6 pm
Saturday 9:30 am to 4 pm
Natural Food Store. Limited organic produce.
Directions: From Hwy 41, take Hwy 45 north into town, then at Church Ave turn right and this place is five blocks down at the corner North Main.

RICE LAKE

Main Street Market
1 South Main Street; 715-234-7045
Hours: Monday to Saturday 10 am to 5:30 pm
Closed Sunday.
Natural Food Store and Deli. Organic produce.
Menu: Has some soups, salads and sandwiches.
Comments: Has cooking classes.
Directions: From Hwy 53, take north Rice Lake exit (Hwy 48), and make a right (if coming north) at exit ramp towards Rice Lake. Go about 1¼ mile to Main St and turn right (go south). Go about 8 blocks (to second traffic light) and this place at corner of Main and Messenger.

RICHLAND CENTER

Pine River Food Co-op
134 West Court Street; 608-647-7299
Hours: Monday to Friday 9 am to 6 pm
Saturday 10 am to 4 pm
Natural Food Store. Some organic produce.
Comments: Local organic produce used when possible.
Directions: From Hwy 14, go east on Court St and this place is one block down on left. This place is in the center of town.

RIVER FALLS

Whole Earth Grocery
126 South Main Street; 715-425-7971
Hours: Monday to Friday 9 am to 7 pm
Saturday & Sunday 9 am to 4 pm
Natural Food Store. Organic produce.
Directions: From I-94, take Hwy 35 exit (#4) and go south on Hwy 35 toward downtown River Falls about 5 miles, then just north of town at the fork in the road, take the right one onto N Main St. This place is about 2 miles down on the right.

SHEBOYGAN

Nature Best Health Food Store
809 Riverfront; 920-452-6176
Natural Food Store.

Weather Center Café
809 Riverfront; 920-459-9283
Hours: Monday to Thursday 7:30 am to 7 pm; Friday 7:30 am to 8 pm; Saturday 9 am to 8 pm; Sunday 10 am to 5 pm
Vegetarian-friendly Restaurant. Not pure veg.
Menu: Vegan Wrap, soups (all vegetarian) and veggie sandwiches.
Comments: Friendly place. Counter service, take-out.

SPARTA

Beaver Creek Community Cooperative
127 North Water Street; 608-269-9770
Hours: Monday to Friday 10 am to 6 pm; Saturday 9 am to 5 pm; closed Sunday.
Natural Food Store. Organic produce.
Directions: From I-90, take Exit #25, and go north on Hwy 27 for 1½ miles, then at Hwy 16 turn right and go east a half-mile, then turn right onto Rte 21 (Water St) and this place is 5 blocks down at the junction with E Main St.

SPRING GREEN

Spring Green General Store & Café
137 South Albany Street
608-588-7070
Hours: Monday to Friday 9 am to 6 pm; Saturday 8 am to 6 pm; Sunday 8 am to 4 pm
Cheese Warehouse and Natural Foods Restaurant. Vegan options. Not pure vegetarian.
Menu: The menu changes daily. Mexican dishes, Italian dishes, Sweet Potato Soup, raita and Veg-

etable Stir-fry. Cappuccino, espresso.

Comments: In a cheese warehouse near the Wisconsin River. During the summer mainly uses locally grown produce. Has a special breakfast on the weekends.

Other Info: Limited service, take-out. Accepts MC, VISA. Price: $.

Directions: From Hwy 14, go south on Rte 23 for ¾ mile, then at E Jefferson St turn right and this place is 1 block down in a blue building.

STEVEN'S POINT

Steven' Point Food Co-op

633 2nd Street, at 4th Street; 715-341-1555

Hours: Monday to Friday 9 am to 8 pm (until 7 pm Tuesday); Saturday 9 am to 5 pm; Sunday 10 am to 4 pm

Natural Food Store and take-out Deli. Organic produce. Bakery.

Menu: Sandwiches, hummus and ready-made salads.

Comments: Has a large amount of items in the store. Everything is prepared the night before.

Other Info: Accepts MC, VISA. Dishes in cooler, take-out only. No seating.

Directions: From I-39, take Exit 161 and go south on 2nd St 1¼ mile. This place is at the junction with 4th Ave.

SUPERIOR

Commonhealth Food Co-op Outlet

1505 North 8th Street; 715-392-1476

Natural Food Store.

Directions: From I-35, take Hwy 535 S exit and go south 1 mile on Hwy 535 into town. When it gets to Hwy 53 exit, then go south on Hammond Ave 4 block, then at N 8th St turn right and this place is one block down.

TREMPEALEAU

The Trempealeau Hotel Restaurant

150 Main Street; 608-534-6898; Web site: http://trempealeauhotel.com/dining.html

Summer Hours: Daily 11 am to 10 pm

Winter Hours: Thursday to Sunday 11 am to 9 pm

Menu: Has several vegetarian dishes, which are marked on the menu. Spinach Lasagna, Vegetable Stew and salads.

Comments: Good hiking and biking along the Mississippi River and in Perot State Park.

Warning: Walnut Veggie Burgers and Fettuccine

Pasta contain eggs.

Other Info: Reservations recommended, especially in the summer. Non-smoking. Accepts MC, VISA.

Directions: This place is on the main street in town in downtown Trempealeau.

VIOLA

Viola Natural Food Co-op

Commercial Drive, PO Box 243; 608-627-1476

Hours: Monday to Friday 12 noon to 6 pm; Saturday 12 noon to 4 pm; closed Sunday.

Natural Food Store. A small place.

Directions: Drive north on Hwy 131 into Viola. At Commercial Drive turn right. This place three buildings down on left.

VIROQUA

Viroqua Co-op

303 North Center Street

608-637-7511

email: ufcoop@frontiernet.net

Hours: Monday to Friday 8 am to 7 pm; Saturday 9 am to 7 pm; Sunday 11 am to 5 pm

Natural Food Store. Locally grown organic produce in season. Organic dairy products.

Directions: This place is behind Nelson's Agri-Center, a block north of Hwy 56 and a block east of Hwy 14.

WAUWATOSA (4 miles west of Milwaukee)

Outpost Natural Foods

7000 West State Street

414-778-2012

email: outpost@execpc.com

Web site: www.outpostcoop.com

Hours: Daily 8 am to 9 pm

Natural Food Store and Deli. Bakery, Salad Bar and Juice Bar. Organic produce.

Comments: Best place in town for organic vegetables and fruits.

Other Info: Counter service, take-out. Has a seating area. Accepts DIS, MC, VISA.

Directions: From I-94 E, take Exit #307A (this place is 1 mile directly north of this exit) towards 68th St/70th St and go straight onto W Kearney St for 1 block, then at S 70th St (north) turn left and go a quarter-mile, then at W Mt Vernon Ave turn left and go 1 block, at 71st St turn right and go one block, then at W Blue Mound Rd (US-18) turn right and go 1 block, then at N 70th St turn left and this place is ¾ miles down.

WISCONSIN DELLS

**Cheese Factory Restaurant
521 Wisconsin Dells Parkway, Lake Delton
608-253-6065
Web site: http://www.cookingvegetarian.com/cheesefactoryrestaurant.htm
Summer Hours: Wednesday to Monday 9 am to 9 pm; closed Tuesday.
Winter Hours: Thursday to Sunday 9 am to 9 pm; closed Monday to Wednesday.
Vegetarian International. Gourmet. Not pure vegetarian.
Menu: Soups, salads, sandwiches, veggie burgers, pastas, Veggie Chicken Sandwich, Lasagna, Chicken Tofu Ramano, Thai Stir-fry, Baked Idaho Potatoes, Fruit & Cheese Plate, Chinese Stir-fry Vegetables, Sicilian "Meatball" Pasta, gourmet pizzas, Seitan Fajita, Bean Burrito and hummus sandwiches. For dessert there is Carrot Cake and Key Lime Pie.
Comments: Has a beautiful garden outside. Has own Cheese Factory cookbook. Has menu on web site. Good original soda fountain. Good food.
Warning: Some of their noodles contain eggs; so may want to ask about this. Mushroom Stroganoff served on egg noodles. Spanikopita contains eggs. Cheeses that they use are not always rennet free.
Other Info: Full service, take-out, catering. Reservations necessary for groups. Accepts AMEX, MC, VISA. Price: $$.
Directions: From I-90/94, take Exit #92 and go north on Hwy 12 and this place is about 2 miles north in downtown Lake Delton, at the junction of Rte 12 & Wisconsin Dells Parkway. Parking arranged for customers.

**The Secret Garden Café
In The White Rose B&B Inn, Wisconsin Dells
910 River Road; 608-254-4214, 800-482-4724
Web site: www.thewhiterose.com
Hours: Monday, Wednesday to Friday 9 am to 9 pm; Saturday & Sunday 8 am to 9 pm
Fully Vegetarian International.
Menu: Home fried potatoes, Lasagna, Moussaka, Thai Stir-fry, quesadilla, Macho Nachos, gourmet pizzas and Mediterranean Pizza.
Comments: Has indoor seating and outdoor seating under a 100 year old oak tree. Located in a Victorian mansion. Bed and Breakfast. Sister restaurant is Cheese Factory Restaurant in Lake Delton.
Other Info: Full service, counter service, take-out, catering. Reservations recommended. Accepts AMEX, MC, VISA.
Directions: From I-90, take Exit #87 for Wisconsin Dells, then go 1½ mile east towards town on Rte 13 and this place is next to the river on River Road. One block north of Broadway on River Road. In the "White Rose Bed & Breakfast." Parking across the street.

Wyoming

1. Casper
2. Cheyenne
3. Cody
4. Jackson Hole
5. Lander
6. Laramie
7. Riverton
8. Sheridan
9. Wilson

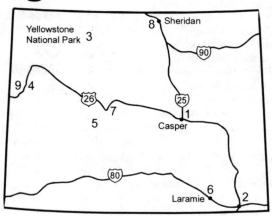

CASPER

Alpinglow Natural Foods
242 South Wolcott, Casper; 307-234-4196
Hours: Monday to Friday 9:30 am to 6 pm; Saturday 9 am to 5 pm; closed Sunday.
Natural Food Store and Juice Bar.
Menu: Soups, salads and sandwiches. Fresh juices and smoothies.
Other Info: Counter service, take-out. Has some seating.
Directions: From I-25, take Center St exit (#188) and go south ¾ mile. At Midwest turn left and it becomes E 2nd St. This place is a half-block down on the left at the corner of Midwest and South Wolcott.

CHEYENNE

Dynasty Café
600 West 19th Street; 632-4888, 632-2088
Hours: Monday to Saturday 11 am to 10 pm
Closed Sunday.
Chinese & Vietnamese. Vegan options. Not pure vegetarian.
Menu: Has several vegetarian options.
Comments: Good sized portions. Reasonably priced. Good tasting food.

Twin Dragons
1809 Carey Avenue; 307-637-6622
Hours: Monday to Saturday 11 am to 10 pm

Sunday 11 am to 9 pm
Mandarin Chinese. Not pure vegetarian.
Menu: Has separate vegetarian section on the menu. Chow Mein, rice dishes and tofu dishes.
Other Info: Full service, take-out. Accepts AMEX, DIS, MC, VISA. Price: $.

CODY

Hong Kong Restaurant
1244 Sheridan Avenue
307-527-6420
Summer Hours: Daily 11 am to 9:30 pm
Winter Hours: Monday to Saturday 11 am to 8:30 pm; closed Sunday.
Chinese. Not pure vegetarian
Menu: Has several vegetarian dishes including rice, tofu and vegetable dishes.
Comment: Vegetarian items are marked on the menu.
Other Info: Full service, take-out. Accepts DC, MC, VISA. Price: $-$$.
Directions: Five blocks from historical area.

Whole Foods Trading Co
1239 Rumsey Street; 307-587-3213
Hours: Monday to Saturday 9:30 am to 5:30 pm
Closed Sunday.
Natural Food Store. No produce.
Directions: From Rte 14 (Sheridan Ave), at 12th St go north one block and turn right and this place on right a half-block down.

JACKSON HOLE

Bagel Jacks
145 North Glenwood; 307-733-9148
Hours: Daily 6:30 am to 4 pm
American and International. Vegan options. Not pure vegetarian.
Menu: Bagel and veggie soups.
Comments: This restaurant is in a building built in 1911. Has hardwood floors.
Other Info: Full service. Reservations recommended. Accepts AMEX, MC, VISA. Price: $.

Chinatown Restaurant
850 West Broadway Street; 307-733-8856
Hours: Monday to Friday 11 am to 9:30 pm
Saturday & Sunday 5 pm to 9:30 pm
Chinese Restaurant. Not Pure Vegetarian.
Menu: Has a separate vegetarian section on the menu.
Other Info: Accepts AMEX, MC, VISA.

Harvest Organic Foods
130 West Broadway Street; 307-733-5418
Winter Hours: Monday to Saturday 8:30 am to 6 pm; Sunday 9 am to 4 pm
Summer Hours: Monday to Saturday 7 am to 8 pm; Sunday 9 am to 4 pm
Café Hours: Monday to Saturday 8:30 am to 3 pm; Sunday 9 am to 12 noon
Natural Food Store and Restaurant. Deli, Bakery, Salad Bar and Juice Bar. Organic produce.
Menu: Has organic soups, veggie chili, salads, Mexican Plate, Indian Plate, stir-fry vegetables, Garden Burger and more. Organic salad bar.
Other Info: Accepts MC, VISA.
Directions: Broadway is Rte 89. This place is two blocks from the town-square in the middle of town.

LANDER

The Golden Corral
400 North Federal; 307-856-1152
Hours: Sunday to Thursday 11 am to 9 pm
Friday & Saturday 11 am to 10 pm
American. Not pure vegetarian.
Menu: Has baked potatoes and a large salad bar.
Other Info: Full service, take-out. Price: $-$$.

The Magpie
159 North 2nd Street; 307-332-5565
Hours: Monday to Friday 7 am to 6 pm
Saturday 7 am to 2 pm
Closed Sunday.

International. Vegan friendly. Not pure vegetarian.
Menu: Menu changes daily. There are two or three vegetarian dishes daily. Roasted Vegetable, veggie chili, vegetarian soups and pastas.
Other Info: Accepts cash and checks.
Directions: From Rte 287 coming west into town, after pasting Rte 789 go west a half-mile, then at N 2nd St turn left and this place is a half-block down.

LARAMIE

Jeffrey's Bistro
123 East Ivinson Avenue; 307-742-7046
Hours: Monday to Wednesday 11 am to 7 pm;
Thursday to Saturday 11 am to 9 pm; closed Sun.
International, American. Emphasis on vegetarian dishes. Vegan options. Not pure vegetarian.
Menu: Has a selection of vegetarian and vegan dishes. Soups, pastas, veggie burgers, salads and steamed vegetables.
Comments: Pleasant, casual place.
Other Info: Full service, take-out. Accepts AMEX, MC, VISA. Price: $.
Directions: From I-80, take 3rd St (Rte 287) exit north, at Ivinson Ave turn left and go west two blocks. Ivinson is a block north of Rte 30.

Overland
100 East Ivinson Avenue; 307-721-2800
Hours: Sunday to Thursday 11 am to 8 pm
Friday & Saturday 11 am to 9 pm
American and International. Not pure vegetarian.
Menu: Has a selection of vegetarian dishes. Fettuccine Pasta, Chinese Stir-fry, Greek Pasta Manicotti, salad, Rice & Bean and Tomato Garlic Pasta.
Comments: Casual place.
Other Info: Full service, take-out. Accepts AMEX, DIS, MC, VISA. Price: $$-$$$.

Sweet Melissa Vegetarian Café
213 South 1st Street; 307-742-9607
Hours: Monday to Saturday 11 am to 9 pm
Vegetarian Restaurant. Vegan options.
Menu: Soups, salads, sandwiches, Lentil Loaf, falafel, tortilla chips, Pot Pie, Mashed Potatoes and desserts.
Other Info: Full service, take-out. Cash and checks only; no credit cards.
Comments: Good, friendly place. Nice people.
Directions: From I-80, take the US-287/3rd St exit (#313) towards Ft Collins, CO, then go north

on 3rd St (US 287) and this place is 1 mile down, then at N Iverson turn left and this place is 2 blocks down on 1st St.

Whole Earth Grainery
111 Ivinson Avenue, Laramie; 307-745-4268
Hours: Tuesday to Saturday 11 am to 6 pm
Closed Sunday.
Natural Food Store.
Comments: Friendly store.
Directions: From I-80, take 3rd St (Rte 287) exit (#313) north about a mile, at Ivinson turn left. This place on right two blocks down.

RIVERTON

Wind River
221 East Main Street, Riverton; 307-856-0862
Hours: Monday to Saturday 10 am to 5:30 pm
Closed Sunday.
Natural Food Store. Organic produce.
Other Info: Accepts MC, VISA.
Directions: This place in the middle of town on Rte 26, which is also East Main, between 2nd & 3rd Streets. It is across from Ace Hardware.

SHERIDAN

Golden China Restaurant
In the Brundage and Coffeen shopping center
307-674-7181
Chinese. Not pure vegetarian.

Nanci's Natural Food
38 South Main Street
307-674-8344
Natural Food Store.
Directions: On the main street in town, near Loucks St.

WILSON

Here and Now Natural Foods
1925 North Moose Wilson Road
307-733-2742
Hours: Monday to Saturday 4 pm to 6 pm
Closed Sunday.
Natural Food Store. No produce. Delivers.
Directions: From Hwy 22, go north on Teton Village Rd (also N Moose Wilson Rd). This place is on the left a half-mile down. Teton Village ski area is down same road.

Ingredients and Chemicals That May Contain Meat, Fish, Egg or Dairy

This section contains a list of ingredients to look out for. It also contains a list of foods that would normally be considered vegetarian, but may contain meat, fish or egg products.

Acid casein	Milk	Bread and cereal enrichment.
Activated carbon	Vegetable (within USA) or animal (cow bone)	Sugar processing and water purification.
Adipic acid (Hexanedioic Acid)	Synthetic, may contain extremely low amount of meat products	Processed food to impart a tart flavoring.
Adrenaline	Adrenal glands of hogs, cattle and sheep	Medicine.
Albumen	Egg white, blood, vegetable tissues Usually derived from egg whites	Baked goods, cakes, cookies, pastries, candies and cosmetics.
Albumin	Made from blood, eggs, cow's milk or vegetable	To add texture or to thicken food.
Allantoin	Cows, most mammals, many plants (especially comfrey)	Cosmetics, creams and lotions.
Ambergris	Whale intestines, synthetic or vegetable	Used in making perfumes and as foods flavoring.
Amino acid	Animal, vegetable, synthetic and bacterial	
Anchovies	Small, silvery fish	Worcestershire sauce.
Animal shortening	Lard, butter, suet	Pie crust, cookies, refried beans, flour tortillas and crackers.
Arachidonic Acid	Usually from animal liver	Creams and lotions to cure eczema and rashes in skin. A liquid unsaturated fatty acid in fat of animals and humans.
Artificial coloring	Usually synthetic, vegetable, insects	An additive to give color to food. Not found naturally in food.
Artificial flavor	Usually synthetic, vegetable, animals	An additive that is used to replace natural flavors. Not found naturally in food.
Benzoic Acid	Animals, berries	Deodorants, mouthwashes and aftershave lotions.
Beta-carotene) (Provitamin A)	Mainly synthetic or vegetable	Dairy products, cheese, ice cream, vegetables, cereals, beverages and sweets. A food colorant.
Biotin (B factor)	Usually bacterial and vegetarian	Dietary supplements, cosmetics and shampoos.
Bone Char	Animal bone ash	Charcoal to filter sugar to make it white.
Calcium stearate	Usually animal (cow or hog), vegetable-mineral	Vanilla, salad dressing, garlic salt and dry molasses. An additive to keep dry ingredients from sticking together or to get ingredients to mix together.
Cane Sugar (Sucrose)	Vegetable. Animal bones are often used as a filter while processing it	Natural sugar. Florida Crystal Sugar and Jack Frost Sugar are not processed with animal bones.
Capric acid (N-decanoic Acid)	Vegetable or animal	Ice cream, baked goods, sweets, beverages and artificial flavorings. An element in some fats used to make synthetic flavoring. red lollipops and food coloring.

Caprylic Acid	Cow's or goat's milk	Coconut oil, palm oils, perfumes & soaps.
Carmine (Cochineal or Carminic Acid)	Red coloring made from insects	Candies, frozen pops, bottled juice, red apple sauce, colored pasta, "natural" cosmetics and shampoos.
Carotene. Provitamin A Beta Carotene	Animal, plants	Coloring in cosmetics and vitamin A.
Casein	Milk protein	Added to dairy products such as cottage cheese, "non-dairy" creamers, cream cheese, sour cream, cheese. Added to imitation and soy cheese, breads and cereals. Cosmetics and hair preparations.
Carbohydrate	Vegetable or animal (insects)	Cornstarch and glucose.
Carmine	Animal (insects)	Juices, dairy products, ice creams, fruit fillings, pudding and baked goods. Food coloring made from female beetles.
Clarifying agent	Animal (egg, gelatin, fish bladder), milk, mineral	Used to help filter out small particles out of liquids to make the liquid clear.
Cochineal	Animal, insects	Juices, ice cream, fruit fillings, yogurt, pudding and sweets.
Cysteine (L-cysteine)	Human hair	Baked goods, breads, food supplements. It is an amino acid that is produced by the human body. Hair care products and creams.
Cystine (L-cystine)	Human hair, horsehair	Food supplements. It is an amino acid that is produced by the human body. Animal bones may be use to filter it.
Dextrose (glucose, corn sugar)	Vegetable	
Diglyceride	Animal (cow or hog), vegetable	Baked goods, peanut butter, chewing gum, whipped topping, sweets, drinks, ice creams and shortening. Used to mix ingredients that normally don't mix together, such as water and oil.
Disodium inosinate	Animal (meat or animal), vegetable, fungal	Canned vegetables, spreads, powdered soups and sauces. A flavor enhancer.
Dough Conditioner	Usually mineral, but sometimes animal, vegetable or synthetic	Helps to make dough easier to handle. Such as glyceryl monostearate, potassium bromate, locust (carob) bean gum, monocalcium sulfate, benzoyl peroxide and calcium sulfate.
Duodenum Substances	Digestive tracts of cows and pigs	Vitamin tablets and medications.
Emulsifier	animal (cow, hog, eggs, milk), vegetable, synthetic	Processed foods, peanut butter, candies, dairy products, baked goods, soft drinks, chocolate and ice creams. It is used to keep unlike ingredients mixed together. Lecithin, mono- and diglycerides, calcium stearoyl, polysorbate and monostearate.
Enzyme	Animal (cow, hog), eggs, vegetable, fungal or bacterial	Cheese and baked goods. Protein added to food to change it. Rennet, which is used in the process of making cheese, may be derived from either an animal or vegetarian source. Examples are rennet, papain, pectinase, lactase, trypsin, protease and lipase. Pipsins, lipases, trypsins usually come from animals.

Folic acid (pteroyl glutamic acid, folacin)	Usually synthetic or fungal; could be animal, vegetable	Enriched food such as baked goods and macaroni. B-vitamin complex.
Fat	Animal (cow or hog), vegetable	Tallow, lard, soybean oil & cocoa butter.
Fatty acid	Animal (cow or hog), vegetable, synthetic	Used in lipsticks, food, cosmetics, detergents and soap.
Flavor enhancer	Animal (meat or fish), vegetable	Monosodium glutamate, disodium guanylate, disodium inosiante and soy sauce. It gives food a flavor, but has little or no flavor itself.
Foaming agent	Usually animal or dairy-mineral	Sodium caseinate. Used to make food foam.
Gelatin	Hooves, cartilage, bones of animal	Jellybeans, marshmallows, yogurts, ice cream, cakes and frosted cereals. Shampoos and cosmetics, coating on pills and capsules. On photographic film. Used as a thickener.
Glucose (Dextrose)	Fruits or animal tissues	Soft drinks, frosting, candies and baked goods.
Glycerin. Glycerol	Byproduct of soap manufacturing (usually is animal fat)	Cosmetics, foods, toothpastes, mouthwashes, ointments, chewing gum, medicines and soaps.
Glycerides (Mono-, Di-, Tri-glycerides)	Animal fat (cow, hog), vegetable, synthetic	Processed foods, baked goods, peanut butter, jelly, ice cream, chocolate, chewing gums, candies, beverages, shortening and whipped toppings. Used to mix ingredients that normally don't mix together, such as water and oil. Most of them are vegetarian, but some may be animal-based.
Glycerol (Glycerin, Glycerine)	Usually vegetable, may be animal (cow, hog)	Candies, baked goods, marshmallows, sweets and soft drinks. Preservative that helps retain moisture.
Guanine	Scales of fish	Shampoo, nail polish & other cosmetics.
Invert sugar (Colorose, Inversol)	Vegetable. May be processed with cow bones. If derived from sugar beets, it is not usually processed with cow bones	Baked goods and candy. Often non-vegetarian.
Insulin	From hog pancreas.	Used by millions of diabetics daily. Alternatives: synthetics, vegetarian diet and nutritional supplements, human insulin grown in a lab.
Isinglass	Fish	Alcoholic beverages (white wine and chardonnay) and some jelly deserts.
Isopropyl Palmitate		Complex mixtures of isomers of stearic acid and palmitic acid. (See Stearic Acid.)
Keratin	Usually animal (chicken, hair and nails of)	What the amino acid tyrosine is often made from.
Lac-resin (shellac)	Animal (insect secretion)	Candy, fruit, pills. Combined in making wax.
Lactic acid	Animal, milk	Pickles, frozen desserts, fruit preserves, candy, olives, yogurt, cheese, sauerkraut and chewing gum and foods produced by fermentation. Skin fresheners. Sometimes in beer.

Lactose (saccharum lactin)	Milk sugar from mammals	Used to sour milk, medicinal diuretics, laxatives baked goods, medicines and baby formulas.
Lactylic stearate	Salt of stearic acid from tallow	Dough conditioner.
Lanolin	Fat from sheep's wool	Chewing gum, cosmetics and ointments.
Lard	Fat from abdomen of a pig	Tortillas (sometimes), refried beans, processed foods, chewing gum, some baked goods and piecrust (sometimes). It is sometimes used in the production of maple syrup, but not usually by the larger producers. Shaving creams, soaps, cosmetics.
Lanolin	Oil glands of sheep, extracted from their wool.	Skin care products, cosmetics and some medicines.
Lecithin	Phospholipids from plants, animal tissues or egg yolk. Mainly from eggs and soybeans. Usually vegetarian.	Baked goods, margarine, soft drinks, chocolate, candy, cereal, vegetable oil sprays and cosmetic. Lipsticks, hand creams, lotions, soaps, shampoos, medicines and eye creams. Waxy substance.
Linoleic Acid	An essential fatty acid.	Cosmetics and vitamins.
Lipase	Enzyme from the tongue and stomach of animals (hog, cow), fungal	Cheese, ice cream, chocolate, cream and margarine. Used in making cheese and digestive aids.
Luetein	Yellow coloring from marigolds or egg yolks	Food coloring for processed foods.
Magnesium stearate	Animal (cow, hog)-mineral, vegetable-mineral	Sugarless gum, candy and pills. Used as a preservative or to mix ingredients that normally don't mix together, such as water and oil.
Maple syrup	Vegetable, may be processed with an extremely small amount of animal (cow or hog) or with butter. This is usually now only done by traditional, smaller producers. Most larger producers use a compound from a synthetic source to reduce foaming.	Pancake syrup, candy, cereal. Holsum, Spring Tree and Maple Groves do not use animal-derived products to process their maple syrup.
Methionine	Usually from egg and casein (dairy)	Texturizer and for freshness in potato chips. It is an essential amino acid.
Modified starch	Vegetable	Pie filling, gravies, desserts and sauces. Corn that has been altered. Animal products are used in making oleic, which is often used in making adipic acid, which is used to alter corn to make starch.
Monoglyceride	Animal (cow or hog) fat or vegetable	Baked goods, peanut butter, chewing gum, whipped toppings, sweets, drinks, ice cream, shortening, margarines, cake mixes, candies and in cosmetics. Used to mix ingredients that normally don't mix together, such as water and oil.
Myristic acid (n-tetradecanoic)	Usually animal (cow or sheep)	Processed foods, baked goods, ice cream, candy, cocoa flavoring, butter, chocolate, gelatin desserts and butterscotch. Component of fats used in food.

Natural coloring	Usually vegetable, animal (insects)	Processed foods, baked goods, beverages, candy, cereal, ice cream, pasta, dry mixes, margarine.
Natural flavoring	Vegetables, animal (meat, fish, eggs, milk)	Processed foods, baked goods, drinks, salad dressing and cereals. An additive to give flavoring to food.
Nutritive sweetener	Vegetable, animal (insect), synthetic	Sucrose, molasses, aspartame, dextrose, corn syrup, fructose and honey. Sweeteners that have more than two calories per gram.
Oleic acid (oleinic acid)	Animal tallow, vegetable fats and oils	Cheese, candy, synthetic butter, beverages, baked goods, ice cream, vegetable fats, oils, soaps, lipsticks, cosmetics and nail polish. Fats that bind or flavor food.
Olestra (Sucrose polyester, Olean)	Vegetable, synthetic. Often gotten from inedible tallow.	Tortilla chips, potato chips, cheese puffs, crackers, lipsticks, nail polish, creams. The sucrose used to process it may be filtered by cow bones. A fat substitute. Derivatives: Oleyl Oleate, Oleyl Stearate.
Palmitic acid (n-hexadeconoic)	Animal (cow, hog fats), vegetable oils, palm oil. Usually non-vegetarian.	Baked goods, cheese and butter flavoring shampoos, shaving soaps, creams. Helps ingredients that don't normally mix together, such as water and oil. Derivatives: Palmitate, Palmitamine, Palmitamide.
Pepsin	Enzyme from a pig or cow stomachs	Rennet to make cheese, digestive aids and vitamins. An enzyme that helps break down proteins. A clotting agent.
Polypeptides	Obtained from slaughterhouse wastes.	
Polysorbate	Animal, vegetable, synthetic	Baked goods, gelatin products, chocolate, ice cream, candy, soft drinks, nondairy creamer, salad dressing, spreads, artificial toppings, pickles and cosmetics. Used to mix ingredients that normally don't mix together, such as water and oil. Derivatives of fatty acids.
Processing aid	Animal (cow, hog), egg, milk, vegetable, synthetic, mineral	Sugar, juice, beer, wine. Something added to foods during processing, and then is mostly or completely removed. It can be used to get rid of unwanted flavoring or coloring or aid in filtering.
Propolis	Resinous substance that comes from bees	Supplements and found in "natural" toothpastes
Protease	Animal, vegetable, fungal, bacterial	Rennin, papain, lactase, pepsin, bromelain, trypsin. Dough conditioning, beer. A general term for enzymes that break down proteins.
Rennet	Animal (usually cow Enzyme from calves' stomachs), vegetable, bacteria, molds	Cheese, custard. Rennet is used in the processing of cheese. In many soy cheese brands.
Rennin	Animal (usually cow), vegetable, bacteria, molds	Cheese, custard. Rennin is used in the processing of cheese.
Resinous Glaze	Excretion of certain insects.	Candy glaze, in hair lacquer.

Simplesse	Milk, egg	Ice cream, yogurt, margarine and salad dressings. Fat substitute. Egg may be used to process it.
Sodium stearoyl lactylate	Animal-mineral (cow, hog), milk, vegetable-mineral.	Baked good mixes, pudding mixes, pancake mixes, instant rice, coffee whiteners, shortenings, margarine, dehydrated fruits or vegetables. Used to condition dough or to mix ingredients that normally don't mix together, such as water and oil.
Stearic acid (n-octadecanoic)	Animal (cow, stomachs of pigs, and sometimes from dogs and cats from animal shelters), vegetable	Food flavoring, chewing gum, soaps, deodorants, creams, cosmetics and hairspray.
Steroids, Sterols	Animal glands, vegetable.	In creams, lotions, hair conditioners. Used in hormone preparation.
Sucrose (sugar)	Vegetable; may have been processed by using cow bone filter.	
Surface-active agents (surfactants, such as sorbitan monostearate)	Animal, vegetable, synthetic.	Processed foods, cheeses, peanut butter and salad dressing. A general term for a food additive to process them.
Surface-finishing agents	Animal, vegetable, synthetic	Fruits and baked goods. Beeswax, shellac wax, gum acacia, carnauba wax and paraffin. Put on food to make it look shiny. Normally vegetarian.
Suet (Tallow)	White fat from kidneys and loins of animals	Margarine, shortening, pastries, cake mixes, cooking oils, soaps, candles, cosmetics, rubber, waxed paper & crayons.
Tallow (Suet fatty acid, Stearic Acid)	Fat from cattle, sheep, sometimes vegetable	Margarine, shortening, pastries, cake mixes, cooking oils, soaps, candles, cosmetics, rubber, waxed paper and crayons. Animal fat that is used to make baked goods more fluffy or to reduce the foam during the production of maple syrup, yeast and beet sugar.
Tyrosine (L-tyrosine)	Animal (chicken feathers)	Dietary supplements, suntan products. It is an amino acid that is produced by and needed by the body.
Urea, Carbamide	Excreted from urine and body fluids. Synthetically.	In hair colorings, deodorants, mouth washes shampoos, hand creams. Browning agents for food such as pretzels. Derivatives: Imidazolidinyl Urea, Uric Acid
Vitamins (choline, biotin, inositol, riboflavin, etc.)	Animal, vegetable.	Vitamins may come from an animal or vegetarian source. Best to get vegetarian vitamins at health food stores.
Vitamin A (A1, retinal)	Egg yolks, fish liver oil, vegetables, carotene in carrots, wheat germ oil, and synthetics.	Supplements, "natural" cosmetics. Skim milk, milk, dietary infant formula, margarine, certain cheeses. Hair-dyes, cosmetics, creams, perfumes. Exist in milk, fish oil and eggs. Yellow and orange vegetables contain an ingredient that is transformed into this vitamin.

Vitamin B12	Found in all animal products. Usually animal source, synthetic form is vegan	Fortified foods and supplements.
Vitamin D-3	Fish liver oil, milk, egg yolk, etc. Vitamin D-3 is always from an animal source.	Fortified foods and supplements. A vitamin needed for bone and teeth development.
Vitamin D-2	Yeast, plants, animal fats, mineral sources, synthetics, vegetarian vitamins, exposure of skin to sunshine.	Many other vitamins can come from animal sources.
Vitamin D-1	Produced by human skin when exposed to the sun, animal, vegetable; usually from animals	Cosmetics, lotions, creams.
Wax	Vegetable, animal (insect- or cow), synthetic; usually vegetarian.	Put on vegetables and fruits as a protective coating. Candy, chewing gum.
Whey	Watery liquid that separates from milk	Cakes, breads, cookies, candies, crackers. In cheese-making.

Vegetarian & Alternative Web Sites

These are some of the sites that I have viewed in my travels through the Internet while doing this book. These sites are definitely worth visiting. You can also visit our own site at www.vegetarian-restaurants.net, which has a wide assortment of links and an excellent list of vegan, vegetarian, vegetarian-freely restaurants and natural food stores. Our site also has a list of updates to this book, which can be printed out and used in your travels.

Restaurants and Natural Food Stores

City Search (www.citysearch.com) – This site put out by Microsoft has an good selection of vegetarian restaurants grouped by major cities. List restaurants by cuisine (vegetarian, vegan, health food), but it is not very clear how vegetarian-friendly the restaurant are. It is a relatively up-to-date and descriptive site. Also it has reviews written by customers, which are often worth reading.

Co-op Directory (http://www.columbia.edu/~jw157/food.coop.html)

Co-op Directory for USA and Canada (www.praireenet.org/co-op/directory)

Co-op Links (http://csf.colorado.edu/co-op/)

Co-op Link (www.newleafcoop.com/link.htm)

Happy Cow's Global Guide to Vegetarian Restaurants (www.happycow.net) – Happy Cow has a good list of vegetarian restaurants and natural food stores. One of the top-five best lists of vegetarian restaurants on the Internet.

JewishVegan Kosher Restaurants (www.jewishvegan.com/restaurant.html) – Has a list of kosher vegetarian restaurants. Has single vegan and vegetarian listings.

Earthrise (http://www.earthrise.com/ERParNAmerica.html) – This site has a list of around 10,000 natural food stores and nutrition centers across the USA. The site also discusses products produced by Earthrise.

Restaurantrow.com (www.restaurantrow.com) – 110,000 restaurants in 47 countries.

TimeOut (www.timeout.com) – Has a good list of vegetarian site for several major cities.

Trader Joe's (www.traderjoes.com) – Has a list of Traders Joe's markets around the country.

VegDining (www.vegdining.com) – Has a list of over 1,000 vegetarian restaurants around the world. This is the best and is the most up-to-date site on the subject. They offer the VegDining Discount Card with which you can get discounts at selected vegetarian restaurants.

VegEats! (www.VegEats.com) – Has a fairly good list of vegetarian-friendly and vegan-friendly restaurants. Has vegan recipes and an excellent list of links to sites that lists vegetarian restaurants. Also presented are links to vegan and vegetarian recipe web sites. In six languages: English, German, Spanish, French, Italian and Portuguese.

Vegetarian in Paradise Yellow Pages (www.vegparadise.com) – This is an excellent site that has a large amount of interesting reviews of vegetarian restaurants in the Los Angeles area, an excellent link section, a list of vegetarian foods available from various airlines and more. Definitely worth checking out.

The Vegetarian Travel Guide (www.vegetarianusa.com) – Has a good selection of links to co-ops, natural food stores, vegetarian restaurants, vacation places, alternative sites and vegetarian groups across the US.

World Guide to Vegetarianism (http://old.veg.org/Guide) – Has a list of vegetarian and vegetarian-friendly restaurants, natural food stores and organizations.

Whole Foods Markets (www.wholefoodsmarket.com) – Has a list of Whole Food Markets. Can order natural products and organic foods online.

Wild Oats (www.wildoats.com) – Has a list of the Wild Oats markets around the country.

Zagat (www.zagat.com) – Has a good list of vegetarian restaurants in selective city with good reviews.

Farmers Markets

California Farmers' Markets (www.farmernet.com) – Has a list of farmers' Markets in Southern California.

Seasonal Produce and Farmers Markets (www.seasonalchef.com) – Has a list of the largest farmers markets in California, and the rest of the United States.

USDA Farmers Market (www.ams.usda.gov/farmersmarkets/map.htm) – Has a list of farmers markets in the US.

Magazines and Newsletters

Just Eat an Apple (http://www.sunfood.net/jeaa/jeaamenu.html) – Articles about raw food diet.

Inner Self Magazine (www.InnerSelf.com) – Has thousands of articles, links and more.

Natural Resource Directory (www.nrd.com) – Directory of services and resources. It is divided into the following categories: Environmentally and Socially Responsible Resources, Health, Fitness and Bodywork, Natural Remedies and Products, Natural Food Markets and Vegetarian-friendly Restaurants.

New Age Directory.Com (www.newagedirectory.com) – Lists events free online. Has an event calendar, links and offers mini web pages.

Natural Florida (www.FloridaNaturally.com) – Has information, resources, phone numbers and addresses in reference to natural living, health, vegetarian restaurants and natural food stores in South Florida.

Natural Hawaii (www.NaturalHawaii.com) – Has information, resources, phone numbers and addresses in reference to natural living, health, vegetarian restaurants and natural food stores in Hawaii.

Natural Yellow Pages (www.NaturalYellowPages.com) – Is an international source of information, resources, phone numbers and addresses in reference to natural living, health, vegetarian restaurants and natural food stores.

All Raw Times (www.rawtimes.com) – Has information about raw foods diets.

Vegetarian Baby and Child (www.vegetarianbaby.com) – Information for vegetarian parents of children under three.

Vegetarian Journal Vegetarian Resource Group (VRG) http://www.vrg.org/journal(www.vrg.org/journal/address.htm) – Published by the Vegetarian Resource Group, which is a non-profit organization dedicated to educating the public on vegetarianism and related subjects. Has vegetarian articles, vegan recipes, nutritional information and list vegetarian events.

Vegetarian Times' The Virtual Vegetarian (www.vegetariantimes.com) – Vegetarian Times' web site. Has links to other vegetarian sites.

Veggie Life (www.veggielife.com) – Has articles grouped into various subjects.

Veg News (www.vegnews.com) (408 358-6478; fax 408 358-7638; email: editor@vegnews.com) – This is one of the most popular vegetarian web sites.

Recipes

Recipes by Mollie Katzen (www.molliekatzen.com) – This site is done by the author of Moosewood Cookbook.

FatFree (www.fatfree.com) – Has a list of over 2,000 low-fat and fat-free vegetarian recipes. Has frequently asked question (FAQ) the subject.

International Vegetarian Union Recipes (http://www.ivu.org/recipes/) – Has thousands of vegetarian recipes. Over 1780 of them are vegan. Recipes are divided by cuisine.

Veggies Unite! (www.vegweb.com) – Has over 2,000 recipes and links to vegetarian sites.

Information

EatVeg (www.eatveg.com) – Has vegetarian information with an emphasis on organic raw foods. Has an assortment of links.

Famous Veggie (www.famousveggie.com) – Famous vegetarian personalities, past and present. Has vegetarian quotes. Articles, recipes, a chat room, nutrition information, stories of vegetarians and vegetarian links.

Feng Shui Warehouse (www.fengshuiwarehouse.com) – Has Feng Shui products and a Feng Shui directory that includes workshops and consultants. Free catalog (800) 399-1599.

Garden of Health (www.gardenofhealth.com) – Living food subjects, organic foods and nutritional information. List of links.

Holistic Health Yellow Pages (www.findhealer.com) – Alternative health directory with many health articles and physicians who practice holistic health. Numerous links on the holistic subject.

Holistic Web Directory (www.123relax.com) – Has thousands of articles on holistic subjects. A natural directory of health professionals. Discussion board in which questions can be asked to health professionals.

Is It Veggie (www.isitveggie.com) – This is an excellent site that lists what products are vegetarian and vegan by manufacturers in the UK. Also has some links to interesting articles.

Vegetarianism History (http://www.ivu.org/history) The International Vegetarian Union (www.ivu.org) – Has some interesting articles and links.

Gene-Watch (www.gene-watch.org/) – This site discusses genetically engineered food. Organized by Dr Martin Tietel who is author of the book "Genetically Engineered Foods: Changing the Nature of Nature."

Going Vegetarian (http://www.vegsoc.org/newveg) – Site of UK Vegetarian Society. Vegetarian information.

Good Stuff Online (www.goodstuffonline.com) – Vegetarian recipes, nutritional information, cookbook reviews and a link to purchase cookbooks.

GoVeg.com (www.meatstinks.com) – Has an assortment of information about how meat stinks. This site is put out by Peta.

Green People (www.greenpeople.org) – Searchable database of vegetarianism, eco-friendly products, organic foods, pet supplies, baby products, beauty products, hemp, health products and recycled products.

Hippy Land (www.hippy.com) – Has a list of links in relation to vegetarianism, organic farming, vegetarian restaurants and vegetarian organizations. Also has hippy information.

Living and Raw Food (www.living-foods.com) – Raw food site with a good amount of information, articles and recipes. Has a list of vegetarian books on the subject, raw food restaurants and links in reference to raw and living foods.

Loma Linda University Vegetarian Food Guide (http://www.llu.edu/llu/nutrition/vegguide.html) – Vegetarian research done by Seventh Day Adventist University Hospital helped establish a vegetarian food guide.

The Natural Center for the Preservation of Medicinal Herbs (www.ncpmh.org) – Discusses wild medicinal herbs, the problems with preserving them and what can be done to help. By herbalist and author Tim Blakely.

PCRM Physicians Committee for Responsible Medicine (www.pcrm.org) – PCRM is a nonprofit organization founded in 1985 that is connected with 5,000 physicians. Promotes preventive medicine and a vegetarian diet. Challenges government dietary recommendations and is against animal experimentation.

Planet Veggie (http://www.planetveggie.com/) – Has a lot of information about vegetarianism.

Questions and Answers on Vegetarian Nutrition (http://members.aol.com/sauromalus/vegnutr.htm) – Information about vegetarian nutrition. Discusses how diet is important in disease prevention.

US Soyfoods Directory (www.soyfoods.com) – List a new recipe each month.

SoyStache (www.soystache.com) – Information about famous vegetarians, recipes, a large list of links, and environmental and health facts.

Thinktwice Global Vaccination Institute (www.thinktwice.com) – Has articles that deal with the potential side effects of vaccinations.

Mundo Vegetariano (www.mundovegetariano.com) – Spanish language site with a wide assortment of vegetarian subjects and links to vegetarian sites.

Vegetarian Dogs (www.vegetariandogs.com)

Vegetarian Pages (www.veg.org) – Has some articles and links in reference to vegetarian subjects.

Veggie Guides (www.vegetarianguides.com) – Has a list of vegetarian guides.

The Veggie Place (www.veggieplace.com) – Has information about vegetarianism, animal rights and the environment. Articles and vegetarian recipes.

Veggies Unite (www.vegweb.com) – Has some interesting articles, recipes, discussions groups and over 4,000 recipes. Has a large amount of links to other vegetarian sites and information. Has a vegetarian guide for around the world. **Vegetarian Glossary** (www.vegweb.com/glossary) is a good glossary of vegetarian related things.

Vegigirl's Guide to Ethical Protein (www.vegigirl.com) – Has a list of vegetarian meat substitutes, nutritional information, foods that contain animal products and some links.

Vegetarian Pages (http://www.veg.org/veg/) – This is a major site with a list of vegetarian links.

VegFamily (www.vegfamily.com) – Subtitled Vegan Parenting Online, this site is for vegan parents.

VegSource—Your Friendly Vegetarian Resource! (www.vegsource.com) – Has many articles by famous people in the vegetarian and medical field and lists over 5,000 recipes. Founded by Jeff and Sabrina Nelson of Chatsworth, California. Has book reviews and the Veg Source Discussion Boards. Has a good set of vegetarian links. This is a very good site and is worth visiting.

Vegan Sites

Vegan Action (www.vegan.org) – Has information on veganism. News stories, interviews, editorials, a community directory, recipes and items to buy at the Vegan Street Market. It has a list of animal derived items. Copies of The Vegan News and vegan clothing.

Vegan.com: Disparaging Meat Since 1997 (www.vegan.com) – Vegan Foundation web site that provides vegan news, links, recipes, resources and articles about vegan, vegetarianism and anti-meat issues. A typical issue will have a feature article of interest to vegans, nutrition information, recipe of the month and events.

Vegetarian Organizations

The International Vegetarian Union (IVU) (www.ivu.org) – Has been promoting vegetarianism since 1908. This site can be viewed in various languages such as French, Italian, Spanish, Japanese, Chinese and German. Has an excellent set of links.

Asian Vegetarian Union (http://www.ivu.org/avu/) – Promotes vegetarianism in Asia.

European Vegetarian Union (http://www.ivu.org/evu/) – Promotes vegetarianism in Europe.

EarthSave (www.earthsave.org) – EarthSave is a

worldwide organization that promotes a plant-based diet to save the earth. Has information about the organization and articles.

Food for Life Global (www.ffl.org) –The largest vegetarian food relief program with branches all over the world. This Hare Krishna organization distributes millions of spiritual vegetarian meals each year to needy people. Has information about this program.

Mothers for Natural Law (www.safe-food.org) – Founded in 1996, this organization deals with genetic engineering. Has information on genetically engineered crops and organizes a campaign to label GE foods.

North American Vegetarian Society (NAVS) (http://mars.superlink.com/user/dupre/navs/index.html) (www.navs-online.org) – Has articles, a list of their events and links.

Vegan Outreach (www.veganoutreach.org) – This is an organization dealing with veganism.

VivaVegie Society, New York City (www.vivavegie.org) (http://www.southwind.net/~ebase/Orgs/VivaVeg/VivaV.html) – This group engages in vegetarian street advocacy. They make annual appearances at festivals in New York.

Vegetarian Youth Network (http://www.geocities.com/Rainforest/vines/4482/index.html) – This is a support group for vegetarian teens. It is run by and for youths.

Vegetarian Organizations USA

Boston Vegetarian Society (www.bostonveg.org) – Organizes the Boston Vegetarian Food Festival.

Chicago Vegetarian Society (www.chicagovegetariansoc.org) – Information about their events and links to other sites.

Southern California Vegetarians (www.socalveg.org)

Vegetarian Society of Colorado (www.vsc.org) – Has a list of Colorado restaurants, vegetarian links, articles and other subjects.

Vegetarian Society of New Mexico (www.unm.edu) – Has a good list of vegetarian restaurants in New Mexico.

Vegetarian Information, San Francisco Bay Area (www.VegInfo.com)

Vegetarian Web Directories

4Vegetarians.com (www.4vegetarians.com) – One of the web guides presented by 4anything.com is devoted to vegetarian subjects. It is subdivided into various vegetarian categories.

Vegetarian Cuisine about.com (http://vegetarian.about.com) – About.com has a large assortment of subjects, one of which is vegetarianism. The vegetarian section is compiled by Tif-

fany Refior and it is has a good selection of links to articles, recipes, restaurant sites and shopping suggestions.

Animal Rights Organizations

Animal Concerns Community (www.AnimalConcerns.org) – Has animal articles, educational and government resources, and a list of links to animal related sites.

Animal News (www.animalnews.com) – Has a wide selection of animal articles and animal links.

Animal Rights Resource Site (ARRS) (http://www.envirolink.org/arrs/index.html) – Has a good amount of articles on Animals Rights and vegetarianism.

The Ark Trust, Inc. (www.arktrust.org) – National non-profit organization dedicated to animal protection. Their site has information about their activities and has animal-friendly links.

Farm Animal Reform Movement (FARM) (http://members.gnn.com/FARM/, http://www.farmusa.org) – Advocates animal rights and a vegetarian diet. Their motto is, "Promoting plant-based solutions for the future of the planet." Organizes campaigns such as Great American Meatout, National Veal Ban Action, Industry Watch and World Farm Animals Day. Founded in 1981.

Farm Sanctuary (www.farmsanctuary.org) – A national, nonprofit organization dedicated to rescuing and protecting farm animals.

People for the Ethical Treatment of Animals (PETA) (www.peta-online.org, www.peta.org) – Largest animal rights organization in the world. Has a site worth visiting with over 20 sites that are linked together. Deals with cruelty to animal. List news events, PETA Poll, Frequently Asked Questions, links to other PETA sites and links to vegetarian web resources. Has an excellent list of ingredients derived from animals that is definitely worth visiting (http://www.peta-online.org/mc/facts/fsm16.html).

United Poultry Concerns (www.upc-online.org)

Annieappleseedproject (www.annieappleseedproject.org) – Has a good list of links in reference to alternative medicine, therapies, clinics (including cancer clinics) and various other subjects.

Mail Order Companies Food Shopping Online

ABC Vegetarian On-Line Store (www.vegefood.com) – Vegetarian on-line food store. Also includes vegetarian recipes and articles.

A Different Daisy (www.differentdaisy.com) – Has over 700 products at this online vegan store.

Asian Gourmet Gift Basket (www.asiangourmet baskets.com) (Toll free 877 981-5581; fax 303 975-5199, Vickie Inc, PO Box 620745, Littleton, CO 80162) – Has tofu, authentic Asian sauces and exotic ingredients.

Dining by Design (www.diningbydesign.com; phone: 402-327-8880; fax: 402-327-8496; email: karmyn@diningbydesign.com) – Delivers vegan or vegetarian foods to your door coast to coast. Foods fit various special nutritional needs. A selection of international cuisines.

EthicalShopper.com (www.EthicalShopper.com) – An online shopping source for environmentally-friendly products.

Funtimes.com (www.funtimes.com/healthexpo) – Has alternative health products and foods.

Healthshop.com (www.healthshop.com) – Has more than 6,000 natural vitamins, herbs, supplements and personal care products.

Heartland Products (http://chiana.trvnet.net/~hrtlndp/) – Non-leather source for men's and women's shoes, belts, jackets, wallets, brief cases and baseball gloves. Also has hemp products.

Lori's Earth Friendly Products (www.earth-friendly.com) – Kosher vegetarian products, vegan products and organic cotton clothing.

The Mail Order Catalog for Healthy Eating (www.healthy-eating.com) Box 180, 413 Farm Road, Summertown, TN 38483 (800 695-2241; 931-964-2241). Has a good selection of natural food products including soy foods, tofurky, vegetarian meat substitutes, vegetarian food items, vegetarian cookbooks and other alternative health titles, and half-price alternative and vegetarian books.

Pangea Vegan Products (www.veganstore.com) (800-340-1200, 2381 Lewis Avenue, Rockville, Md 20851) – Sells vegan items including non-leather shoes, belts, buttons, shirts, stickers and vegan cruelty-free body care products.

Penn Herb Company, Ltd (www.pennherb.com) – Herbal remedies for various ailments.

Vegan Essentials (www.veganessentials.com) – On-line shopping company offering vegan products certified by Vegan Action. Sells home goods, household products, body care items, hemp, clothing, jewelry, shoes and more.

Vegan Gift Baskets (www.vegangiftbaskets.com) – Vegan gift baskets, with a choice of baked goods, candies, nuts and pretzels. They donate a portion of profits to PETA.

Vegan Street (www.veganstreet.com) (773 252-0026) – Has vegan sayings on clothing, vegan hemp, bags and other items.

Vegetarian Image (www.vegetarianimage.com) – Vegetarian-saying T-shirts, necklaces and buttons.

TheVegetarianSite (www.thevegetariansite.com)

– Animal-free products such as shoes, vegan personal care products, vegan books and hemp items.

Vegetarian Store (www.vegetarianstore.com) – Sells soy-based meat alternatives, dairy alternatives and various vegetarian food products.

Organic

BioDemocracy/Organic Consumers Association (www.purefood.org) – Information on organic standards, toxic foods, food irradiation, genetically engineered foods and various animal disease.

Florida Organic Growers and Farmers Association (www.foginfo.org).

Gardens Alive (www.gardens-alive.com) – Sells products for organic farming.

Go Organic Campaign (www.go-organic.com/)

Master Composter (www.mastercomposter.com) – Information on do-it-yourself organic framing.

Northeast Organic Farmers Association of Massachusetts (www.nofa.org)

Organic Alliance (www.organic.org) – An organization dedicated to spreading information on the benefits of organic farming.

National Organic Program (www.ams.usda.gov/nop/)

Organic Consumers Association (www.organic consumers.org, email: campaign@organic consumers.org) – National organic organization dedicated to maintaining high organic standards.

Organic Essentials (www.organicessentials.com)

Organic Gardening magazine (www.organic gardening.com)

Organic Links (www.linksorganic.com)

Organic Trade Association (www.ota.com)

Seeds of Change (www.seedsofchange.com) – Sells certified organic vegetable seeds and organic foods.

USDA's National Organic Program (http://www.ams.usda.gov/nop)

Vegetarian Singles and Dating

Concerned Singles Newsletter (www.concerned singles.com) (413-445-6309, Box 444-VT, Lenoxdale, MA 01242) – Links single vegetarians and persons concerned with the environment.

Green Singles Newsletter (www.GreenSingles.com) – Connects single vegetarian, and also those interested in animal rights and the environmental.

Green Singles NATURAL Friend (www.natural-friends.com) – Links singles interested in the environment.

Veggie Date (www.veggiedate.com) – Vegetarian singles dating and networking service.

Vegetarian Matchmakers (www.veggiematch makers.com) – Leading vegetarian & vegan matchmaker service in the UK. Been doing it since 1980.

Organic Produce

The organic produce industry is a $6 billion-a-year business. Around 10,000 farms nationwide claim to be organic. There are 6,600 Certified Organic farms in the US. Organic farming is beneficial to the lakes, rivers and wildlife because they do not use chemicals and synthetic herbicides. Organic agriculture does not use toxic fertilizers and pesticides, which pollute the groundwater, which is a major source of drinking water. It also causes rivers and lakes to be less polluted. Organic farming keeps the topsoil on the fields and helps keep it from eroding away, which increases the quality of the soil.

Organic food is grown without using any synthetic pesticides, herbicides, insecticides, gungicides, fertilizers and hormones. No artificial flavors or colors have been added.

Farms using organic farming techniques use nontoxic methods such as mechanical weeding, pruning, covering plants, mulching, using beneficial insects such as ladybugs (that eat other insects), rotating crops and planting more resistant varieties of crops. They may use botanical pest-control agents derived from plants and mild soap sprays if needed.

Many organic farmers do not use any pesticides at all. They use high quality natural fertilizers (such as cow manure) and other natural methods, which enable them to grow high quality, healthy plants. In this way, their plants are much more resistent to insects.

The pesticides used in organic farming are usually better for the environment, but are not necessarily less dangerous to humans. I spent some time on a farm that was doing organic farming, and I observed that they were spraying the vegetables with pesticides. I asked about this and was told that unless the vegetables were sprayed with pesticides that insects would eat them all up. I then asked whether the spray was less dangerous to humans and was told that there was a good chance that it was not.

The difference between organic pesticides and what is normally sprayed on crops is that non-organic pesticides are derived from chemical sources and not from natural or herbal sources (the sources that were used until the 1940s in the US and presently used in organic farming). Examples of natural pesticides used are chrysanthemum flower and nicotine from crushed tobacco. Pesticides used in organic farming are better for the environment, and are therefore much better for humans in the long run, but its safety to human is not necessabry better in all case, but it often is better. Just because fruits and vegetables are organic does not mean they should not be washed thoroughly to get rid of pesticides, as other produce would be washed.

There is a difference between "natural" and "organic" foods. Natural foods are minimally processed and do not contain artificial ingredients, preservatives and chemicals that are usually added to process the food. Certified organic foods are grown according to certain strict standards.

Organic farming methods are usually more labor intensive than conventional farming, so the cost of organic farming will usually be more, which may affect the end price of the produce. Also certain organic foods cost more because the demand exceeds the supply. As the supply increases, the price will most likely go down.

Rules to Be Known as Organic

On December 20, 2000, the U.S. Department of Agriculture released its ruling on what is the U.S. standard on organic produce. It made a decision on what would be defined as "organic." This ruling replaces any definition that individual states had had in defining organic produce and set a national standard. Foods that meet the new federal standards can bear the seal "USDA Organic." The Agriculture Secretary Dan Glickman called the rules "the strictest, most comprehensive organic standards in the world." The ruling can be seen on the USDA Web site at: www.ams.usda.gov/nop.

No prohibited substances are allowed to be used on the land within three years of harvesting organic produce. Farmers must keep detailed records on the methods and materials that are used in their organic farming. Organic farms must be inspected each year by a third-party certifier.

It is best that organic seeds are used, but non-organic seeds can be used under certain conditions.

Crop pests, insects, diseases and weeds should be stopped as much as possible by pulling weeds or by biological methods (e.g., lady-bugs).

Crop rotation must be done. Organic farming uses crop rotation, so insects have a problem finding the crops. If a crop is planted in the same soil, it gives insects a chance to find them and destroy them.

Natural pesticides are allowed, as well as a list of synthetic pesticides (sometimes dangerous ones) and herbicides. Certain synthetic substances can be used if natural methods don't work.

Genetic engineering (man-made alterations of natural food), sewage sludge and irradiation cannot be used.

To be listed as an organic dairy farmer, there are requirements for housing, grazing and veterinary practices. How the manure is handled is regulated so runoff does not pollute waterways. There are also rules on how the dairy products should be processed and packaged.

Organic Product Labeling

There are several rules that processed foods must pass to be certified as organic. When food is processed both the processing plant and the finished product must be certified as organic. The finished products are then labeled by the percentage of organic ingredients that they contain. Only certified products can be labeled as organic. The name of the certifier must be listed on products that are more than 70% organic. A USDA seal can appears on products that are more than 95% organic. The seal is green and white and says "USDA Organic."

The identity and percentage of organic ingredients must be listed on food packaging. If a label says "100% organic" or "organic," the product must contain only organically produced raw or processed substances, excluding water or salt. If a product is 95% to 100% organic, it can be labeled "organic" on the front page. If a product is made from 70% to 95% organic ingredients, it can say "made with organic ingredients" on the front of the package. If a product is less than 70% organic, it cannot use the term "organic" on the main label. It can only list organic ingredients on the ingredient panel.

Genetic Engineering

Genetic engineering is when the genes of unrelated plants and animals are combined to produce combinations of plants, such as between viruses and vegetables or fish and strawberries. Many people believe that genetic engineering is dangerous, unpredictable, and can reduce the nutritional value of food. Quite frankly, who would think any different? Of course, many people do. Often no proper tests have been done to judge the safety of genetically altered foods, so in many cases there is no proof that they are not bad for humans.

The British Medical Association has asked for a moratorium on commercial growing of genetically engineered crops. Many countries throughout the world have banned genetic engineered crops. Regrettably, America is not one of them.

This process can hurt organic farming because pollen from these crops can blow onto neighboring farms.

Hare Krishna Temples

At all Hare Krishna (ISKCON) temples there are weekly Sunday Vegetarian Feasts during which a good tasting vegetarian meal is served. There is also chanting of the holy names of the Lord (Hare Krishna) and a *Bhagavad Gita* class during which philosophy is discussed. It is definitely worth checking out.

For an up-to-date list of Hare Krishna restaurants and templea see www.iskcon.org or www.krishna.com.

Canada

Ashcroft, BC – Saranagati Dhama, Box 99, Ashcroft, BC 250-453-2397
Email: devadevi@wkpowerlink.com
Calgary, Alberta – 313 Fourth Street NE
403-265-3302
Edmonton, Alberta – 9353 35th Avenue
403-439-9999;
Email: jsharma@mail.awinc.com
Montreal, Quebec – 1626 Pie IX Boulevard
514-521-1301
email: iskconmontreal@sprint.com)
*Ottawa, Ontario – 212 Somerset St, E
613-233-1884;
102623.2417@compuserve.com)
Regina, Saskatchewan –1279 Retallack St
306-525-1640)
* **Toronto**, Ontario – 243 Avenue Rd
416-922-5415
Email: Toronto@iskcon.net
* **Vancouver**, B.C. – 5462 S.E. Marine Drive, Burnaby; 604-433-9728
Email: jaygo@direct.ca;
Govinda's Restaurant: 604-433-2428
Email: jaygo@direct.ca

USA

Alachua Florida – PO Box 819
904 462-2017; Email: alachua@pamho.net
Atlanta, Georgia – 1287 Ponce de Leon Ave, NE
404-378-9234
Email: 76415.175@compuserve.com
Austin, Texas – 1810 San Gabriel St
512-320-0372; Email: iskconaustin@cs.com
Baltimore, Maryland – 200 Bloomsbury Ave, Catonsville; 410-744-4069
Berkeley, California – 2334 Stuart St
510-540-9215; Email: Berkeley@com.org

Boise, Idaho – 1615 Martha St
208-344-4274
Boston, Massachusetts – 72 Commonwealth Ave
617-247-8611; Email: premananda@juno.com
Carriere, Mississippi (New Talavan)
31492 Anner Road
601-749-9460; Email: talavan@inbop.com
Chicago, Illinois – 1716 W Lunt Ave
773-973-0900; Email: chicago@iskcon.net
*Dallas, Texas – 5430 Gurley Ave
214-827-6330; email: txkrishnas@aol.com
*Denver, Colorado – 1400 Cherry St
303-333-5461; Email: nmd@com.org
*Detroit, Michigan – 383 Lennox Ave
313-824-6000; Email: fmansion@flash.net
Gainsville, Florida – 214 NW 14th
352-336-4183; Email: krishna@afn.org
Gurabo, Puerto Rica – Rte 181
PO Box 1338, Bo. Sta., Rita
787-737-3917
Hartford, Connecticut
1683 Main St, East Hartford
860-289-7252; Email: bhaktirasa@poboxes.com
Hillsborough, North Carolina
1032 Dimmocks Mill Rd
919-732-6492
Email: bkgoswami@compuserve.com
*Honolulu, Hawaii – 51 Coelho Way
808-595-3947
Email: iskconhawaii@ureach.com
Houston, Texas – 1320 W 34 St
713-686-4482; Email: hktv@starmail.com
Kansas City, Missouri – Rupanuga Vedic College, 5201 The Paseo
816-361-6167, 800 340-5286
Email: rvc@rvc.edu
*Laguna Beach, California – 285 Legion St
949-494-7029; Email: tuka@rupa.com
Long Island, New York – 197 S Ocean Ave, Freeport
516-223-4909; Email: nimainitai@aol.com
*Los Angeles, California – 3764 Watseka Ave
310-836-2676; Email: nirantara@juno.com
*Miami Beach, Florida – 2445 Collins Ave
305-442-7218; Email; nirantara@juno.com
Moundsville, West Virginia (New Vrindavan) – RD No 1, Box 319, Hare Krishna Ridge
304-843-1600; Email: palaceofgold@juno.com
Mulberry, Tennessee – Murari Project, Rt. No 1,

Box 146-A
615-759-6888
Email: 104400.3353@compuserve.com)
New Orleans, Louisiana – 2936 Esplanade Ave
504-486-3583; Email: rrk196820@cs.com
*New York, New York – 305 Schermerhorn St,
Brooklyn
718-855-6714; Email: dayananda@msn.com
New York, New York – 26 Second Avenue
212-420-1130; Email: dayananda@msn.com
Philadelphia, Pennsylvania – 51 W Allens Lane
215-247-4600; Email: vrndavana@netreach.net
*Philadelphia, Pennsylvania – 1408 South St
215-985-9335
Email: savecows@aol.com
Port Royal, Pennsylvania – RD No 1, Box 839
717-527-4101; Email: acyutadasi@acsworld.net
Phoenix, Arizona – 100 S Weber Dr, Chandler
602-705-4900
Email: 105613.1744@compuserve.com
Portland, Oregon –2353 SE 54th Ave, Portland
503-236-0417
Email: portland_krishna@hotmail.com
Queens, New York – 114-37 Lefferts Blvd
848-9010; Email: sunandanadas@hotmail.com)
San Diego, California – 1030 Grand Ave, Pacific
Beach
858-483-2500; Email: newgovardhan@cs.com
San Jose, California – 2990 Union Ave
408-559-3197
Seattle, Washington – 1420 228th Ave, SE,
Issaquah
425-391-3293; Email; haribol@iskcon.net
Spanish Fork, Utah – 8628 S State Rd
801-798-3559; Email: carudask@burgoyne.com

St Louis, Missouri – 3926 Lindell Blvd
314-535-8085; Email: surapala@pamho.net
Tallahassee, Florida – 1323 Nylic St
850-224-3803
Email: haridas.thakur.hdg@pamho.net
Topanga, California – 20395 Callon Drive
Towaco, New Jersey – PO Box 109
973-299-0970
Email; mrugesh_shroff@merck.com
*Tuscon, Arizona – 711 E Blacklidge Drive
520-792-0630
Email: 105613.1744@compserve.com
Washington DC – 10310 Oaklyn Drive, Poto-
mac, Maryland
301-299-2100; Email: potomac@pamho.net

* Vegetarian Restaurant in the temple. For more
details see section under state and city in this book.

Hare Krishna Restaurants
Alachua, Florida – Govinda's 14603 Main St
904-462-450
Eugene, Oregon – Govinda's Vegetarian Buffet,
270 W 8th
503-686-3531
Gainesville, Florida – Vegetarian Palace, 2106 SW
34th St
353-378-2955
Greensboro, North Carolina – Govinda's 332
South Tate St
336-373-8809
San Juan, Puerto Rico – Gopal, 201B Calle
Teuan, Viejo, San Juan
787-724-0229

Famous Vegetarians

In the Past

Louisa May Alcott, writer
Clara Barton, nurse and the first president of the American Red Cross
Charles Darwin, author and scientist
Leonardo da Vinci, artist
Isadora Duncan, dancer
Thomas Edison, inventor
Albert Einstein, physicist
Ben Franklin, American statesman, philosopher and scientist
Mahatma Gandhi, Indian independence leader
Jerry Garcia, musician, member of Grateful Dead
Sylvester Graham, inventor
John Harvey Kellogg, physician and scientist
Linda McCartney
John Milton, writer
Sir Isaac Newton, physicist
Plato, physicist and writer
AC Bhaktivedanta Swami Prabhupada, founder of ISKCON (International Society for Krishna Consciousness)
Pythagoras, Greek philosopher
Swami Satchidananda, spiritual leader
Albert Schweitzer, musician, physician, Nobel Peace Prize winner
George Bernard Shaw, writer and Nobel Prize Laureate in Literature
Mary Wollstonecraft Shelly, English novelist
Percey Bysshe Shelley, English poet
Upton Sinclair, author
Isaac Bashevis Singer, writer & Nobel Prize winner
Socrates, Greek philosopher
Benjamin Spock, author and pediatrician
Henry David Thoreau, writer
Leo Tolstoy, author
Voltaire, French writer
HG Wells, author
John Wesley, religious leader

Present Vegetarians

Henry (Hank) Aaron, Major League baseball player
Bryan Adams, musician
Maxine Andrews, singer with Andrews Sisters
Bob Barker, TV personality
Kim Basinger, actress
Jeff Beck, musician
Cindy Blum, opera singer
Surya Bonaly, Olympic figure skater
David Bowie, musician
Boy George, musician
Berke Breathed, cartoonist
Christie Brinkley, model
Roger Brown, professional football player
Ellen Burstyn, actress
Peter Burwash, tennis pro, Davis Cup winner
Andreas Cahling, bodybuilder
Chris Campbell, Olympic medallist in wrestling
Deepak Chopra, medical doctor and author
Skeeter Davis, country singer
Joe Elliot, guitarist with Def Leppard
Melssa Etheridge, rock singer
Peter Falk, actor
Peter Gabriel, musician
Sara Gilbert, actress
Elliot Gould, actor
Darah Hanah, actress
Richie Havens, musician
Doug Henning, magician
Dustin Hoffman, actor
Desmond Howard, Heisman trophy winner and professional football player

Orlando Area Parks

It is standard at Walt Disney parks to have an ingredient list of each dish served at the snack booths and fast service places, that you can request to see.

Except for several of the restaurants, you cannot make a reservation at Walt Disney World restaurants. But you can request Priority Seating in advance to reserve a seat in many of the restaurants. It is advised to request Priority Seating at least 24 hours in advance, but it is a good idea to make arrangements a week in advance for a special vegetarian request. Priority Seating requests can be made 120 days in advance. At Victoria & Albert's Chef's Table reservations can be and should be made 180 days in advance.

To make a vegan or special request, call the main Walt Disney World number 407-824-2222 and they will transfer you to whatever restaurant you want. Ask to speak directly with the chiefs, who are happy to help you with your special meal. This should be done at least a week in advance.

People who have special dietary needs usually can bring a cooler into the parks. It is best to confirm this in advance at the main number.

Most of the places have relaxed dress code. At Victoria & Albert's there is a dress code.

Magic Kingdom

There are three fresh fruit and vegetable stands in the park: one on Main Street, one at Mickey's ToonTown Fair and one at Liberty Square. The fruits are pre-washed and ready to eat. You can also get carrot sticks, pickles, juices, Powerade and fresh fruit cups.

Cinderella's Royal Table, Fantasyland, has a character buffet breakfast, with Cinderella herself there. They have a Vegetable Plate (pasta and vegetables), Gus's Artichoke and Spinach Dip with homemade pita chips and salad. If you call them at least a week in advance they can arrange a vegan breakfast with vegan pancakes, granola, fresh fruit and

veggie sausages. The breakfast potatoes contain bacon, so should be avoided.

Tony's Town Square Restaurant has an Eggplant and Portobello dish, cheese Ravioli, pizzas and several pasta dishes. Hard pastas at Tony's are vegan. They are willing to work with you to prepare you a pure vegetarian meal.

The Plaza Restaurant, Main Street, has a good veggie sandwich on multigrain bread. **Crystal Palace**, Main Street, has a buffet lunch, served by Winnie the Pooh and associates.

Cosmic Ray's Starlight Café, in Tomorrowland, has Boca Burgers (comes with either French fries or carrots), Vegetable Soup and Greek Salad.

Plaza Pavilion has pizzas and salads.

Columbia Harbour House, at the entrance of Fantasyland, has a hummus sandwich, Garden Salad and a vegan chili, French fries and fresh apple pie.

Liberty Square Potato, in Liberty Square, has baked white and sweet potatoes. Next to the potato wagon is a fruit and vegetable stand.

Epcot

Has two annual food festivals. The **Food and Wine Festival**, in autumn, features the various cuisines from over 30 countries. During the **Food Among the Flowers Festival** in the springtime there are mid-Saturday brunches and quest speakers.

The **Garden Grill Restaurant**, in Future World, has Farmer Mickey and other Disney characters. Has an all-you-can-eat meal. Has a Vegetarian Platter, couscous with grilled vegetables. The buffet has good sunflower bread. If you call a week in advance it may be possible to get a vegan breakfast.

Electric Umbrella, Innoventions East, Future World, has hummus and tabbouleh wraps, French fries and fruit salad. Has a view of the dancing waters of the Fountain of

Nation.

Pure and Simple, Wonder of Life, Future World, has pizza, Roasted Vegetable Salad, baked potatoes, veggie wrap and fat-free frozen yogurt.

Coral Reef Restaurant, in the Living Seas, has a phyllo dough strudel filled with cheese and roasted vegetables with lentil salad. Has a giant saltwater aquarium with over 5,000 fish in it.

The **Sunshine Season Food Fair** has several food shops. The **Pasta and Potato** has good Vegetable Lasagna, Eggplant Parmesan, Portobello Mushroom Wrap, a garden salad and baked potatoes.

L'Originale Alfredo di Roma Ristornate, Italy Pavilion, World Showcase, is an expensive place with a selection of pastas and salads. The hard pasta doesn't contain eggs, but the Fettuccine pasta contains eggs.

Marrakesh Restaurant, Morocco Pavilion, World Showcase, has Jamina's Salad Plate (vegetable couscous, and Moroccan salads). It has an exotic décor, belly dancers and musicians. It is expensive.

Cantina de San Angel, Mexico Pavilion, at World Showcase, has the Plato Combination (bean burrito, a quesadilla and bean taco) at a reasonable price.

San Angel Inn Restaurante, Mexico Pavilion, World Showcase, is a romantic place with candlelit tables and a unique village design. Has a vegetarian Combination Plate (an enchilada, black bean burrito and sautéed vegetables) and Rice & Beans (no lard). It is expensive.

Les Chefs de France Restaurant, France Pavilion, World Showcase, has Grilled Vegetable Sandwich, Plat Vegetarien (a gratin of eggplant, zucchini & tomato with a cheese topping), Tarte a la tomate (tomato and goat cheese on a crust) and sorbets made with fresh fruits.

Tangierine Café has a Mediterranean Vegetarian Platter with hummus, tabbouleh and salads. Ask to have the mayonnaise removed from the lentil salad. Has Moroccan breads and a dairy-free almond pastry.

Disney–MGM Studios

Echo Park Produce, next to Echo Lake,

has a selection of fresh fruits and cut fruits.

50's Prime Time Café, near Echo Lake, plays TV vintage sitcoms and Cousin Bill and Sister Sue serves the guests. Has Penne Pasta, Boca Burger, Vegetable Soup, Vegetable Lasagna and Tofutti. The onion rings have eggs in their bread sauce.

Hollywood Brown Derby, Sunset Boulevard, has a good grilled Portobello Mushroom Sandwich and a salad.

Next to it is **Starring Rolls Bakery**, at Sunset Blvd and Hollywood, which has baked goods and some fresh fruits.

Rosie's All-American Café, Sunset Boulevard, has a Boca Burger. Next door is **Catalina Eddie's** that serves pizzas. **Sunset Market Ranch**, Sunset Boulevard, has baked potatoes. **Anaheim Produce**, Sunset Boulevard, has a selection of fresh produce.

At **Sci-Fi Dine-in Theater Restaurant**, Commissary Lane, you eat in a 1950s car watching science fiction films clips and cartoons. The servers wear roller skates. Has Boca Burgers, pasta and a Vegetable Club sandwich (Portobello mushroom with roasted vegetables & cheese).

Toy Story Pizza Planet, near New York Street, has pizzas and salad.

Mama Melrose's Ristorante Italiano, New York Street, has a selection of pizzas and pastas. The Roasted Panino is grilled eggplant, tomatoes, yellow squash, zucchini and cheese sandwich.

Disney's Animal Kingdom

Rainforest Café, Entrance Plaza, has an interesting design with the appearance of a rainforest. Has good size portions. Has Rainforest Natural Burger, pastas, pizza and Portobello Mushroom sandwiches (normally comes with egg mayonnaise). The Paradise Plate is a fruit plate (the muffins contain eggs).

Pizzafari, Safari Village, has Hot Vegetable Sandwich, salad and pizzas.

At **Chip 'n' Dale's Cookie Cabin**, Camp Minnie-Mickey, the Butter and Sugar cookie and Macadamia Nut cookie do not contains egg, but contain milk products.

Best of the Best in Asia, Asia, has a vegan Rice Bowl and roasted (in the husk) corn on the cob.

There is a **fruit stand** next to the entrance of Kilimanjaro Safaris, near the entrance of Africa, which has fresh fruits and freshly squeezed juices.

Tusker House, in Harambe Village, has the Marinated Vegetable Sandwich (Portobello mushrooms, zucchini and yellow squash). Vegetables are cooked separate from meat products. Breads here contain eggs. Has mashed potatoes, sautéed vegetables and macaroni & cheese. The rice contains chicken stock.

Downtown Disney

FoodQuest and Wired Wonderland Café, on the 5th floor of the DisneyQuest Arcade, has a vegetarian vegetable soup, Portobello Mushroom Sandwich, a veggie wrap, pizza, Spinach and Artichoke dip with chips.

Planet Hollywood has Garden Burgers, pasta and wood-stove pizzas.

Wolfgang Puck Café has Macaroni and Cheese, pizzas and pastas.

Rainforest Café has Rainforest Natural Burger, pastas, pizza and Portobello Mushroom sandwiches (normally comes with egg mayonnaise). The Paradise Plate is a fruit plate (the muffins contain eggs).

House of Blues has Portobello Mushroom Sandwich, corn bread, mashed potatoes, sweet potatoes and sautéed vegetables. The Beans n' Greens contains ham.

Gourmet Pantry Deli has ready-made sandwiches, salads and pastas. Has a cheese and tabbouleh sandwiches. The gourmet jellybeans don't contain gelatin. The rice crispy treat do.

All the pastas at the **Portobello Yacht Club** contain eggs.

Disney Resort Restaurant

California Grill, Disney Contemporary Resort, is an upscale place that has a great view of the night fireworks at the Magic Kingdom. It also has some vegetarian options such as Vegetarian Unplugged, which is an assortment of dishes. Has several vegetarian options for dinner. Price: $$$-$$$$.

Artist Point, Disney's Wilderness Lodge, has some exotic vegetarian dishes and are more than willing to work with you. Price: $$$$.

Victoria & Albert's, Disney's Grand Floridian Resort & Spa, was rated as the top restaurant in Orlando and one of the top ten in the country by Zagat Guide. Has a seven-course vegetarian meal and with 24-hour advance notice can make a vegan meal. Price is around $100 for a meal.

Universal Orlando

Most of the places have a relaxed dress code.

Universal Studios

There is a **fruit stall** in front of the Café La Bamba.

Beverly Hill Boulangerie has the Health Sandwich (avocado & cheese on a oat bun) and salad.

Lombard's Landing (407-224-6400) has Garden Burgers (bun and maybe the burger contain cheese), Five Cheese Ravioli, pasta and a Fruit Plate. Takes reservations and gets good ratings. There is a good view of the Dynamite Nights Stuntacular that begins just before the park closes.

The **Classic Monster's Café** has good cheese and vegan pizzas.

Café La Bamba has corn-on-the-cob, baked potatoes, tacos and salads.

Islands of Adventure

There are not many vegetarian options here.

Confisco Grille has Spanakopizza (flatbread with feta cheese, olives & spinach), Grilled Vegetable Muffuletta (grilled vegetables with gouda cheese in a sesame roll) and a Mediterranean Platter. Various characters such as Spiderman and Woody Woodpecker visit the place.

Enchanted Oak Tavern, at The Lost Continent, has baked potatoes and roasted corn-on-the-cob.

Café 4's, at the Marvel Super Hero Island, has pizzas.

Pizza Predattoria, at Jurassic Park, has pizzas.

Mythos, The Lost Continent of Adventure, has pizza and pasta. It has a great décor with carvings of the Greek gods. Upscale design with crystal chandeliers. Popular place.

Port of Entry Fruit Stand, Port of Entry Islands of Adventure, has an assortment of fruits and drinks.

CityWalk

The CityWalk is a 30-acre area outside the entrance to Universal. There are about a dozen theme restaurants at this place.

Emeril's is an expensive high-class place. The owner and chef is Emeril Lagasse, one of the top chefs in the country. It has wood-stove cooked pizzas. During the high season you have to make a reservation weeks in advance. Has vegetarian Ravioli, Roasted Vegetable Plate and organic smashed potatoes.

Pastamoré Italiano has pizza, spaghetti, Five Cheese Ravioli and vegan antipasto salad.

Marketplace Café has pizza and Italian Veggie Sandwich

Hard Rock Café has a veggie burger (their own recipe), pasta, salads and baked potato.

Bob Marley–A Tribute to Freedom is a replica of Bob Marley's home in Jamaica. Has Natty Dread Jamaican vegetable potties with yucca fries. Has salads, chips & salsa and Cheddar Cheese Fondue. Has live reggae bands and a dance floor.

Jimmy Buffett's Margaritaville has Macaroni & Cheese and a Spinach Tortilla Wrap.

NBA City has pizzas.

Latin Quarter has a Cheese Tortilla and pizza,

Nascar Café has pizzas and spaghetti.

More Information (suggested reading)

For more details on vegetarian eating in Orlando, Walt Disney World and Universal Orlando I would highly suggest you get the book by Susan Shumaker and Than Saffel called Vegetarian Walt Disney World and Greater Orlando. It is an extremely detailed book with information on vegetarian eating at most of the restaurants at Walt Disney World and Universal Orlando. Besides the restaurant information they also give very useful tourist information about the parks and give recommended schedules to help enjoy your trip to Walt Disney World. They have useful maps of the parks and Orlando area.

VARIOUS CUISINE RESTAURANTS

Flying

When you reserve a long-distance flight, you should reserve a vegetarian meal at the same time. It is a good idea to call a few days before your flight departure and reconfirm your vegetarian meal. Also when you check in you should confirm that they have it recorded that you are to receive a vegetarian meal. Regrettably, even after reconfirming a vegetarian meal, sometimes the correct number of vegetarian meals do not get on the plane.

It is often possible to get a vegetarian meal even if you did not order one. If you do not receive your ordered vegetarian meal, it is a good idea to talk to the airline staff. Often a meal of side dishes from the extra first-class and coach meals can be quite a good vegetarian meal. One advantage of ordering a vegetarian meal is that you usually receive it before the other meals are served. If you would like more information, you can check out the Vegetarian in Paradise site (www.vegparadise.com), which lists many of the selections that various airlines offer vegetarians.

Some airlines have several vegetarian options. About 50% of the requested special meals are vegetarian meals.

Taking the Train

If you give 72-hour-advance notice for trips on Amtrak's overnight trains and long-distance passenger trains, you can often get decent vegetarian meals. A typical vegetarian meal is peas, corn on the cob and a choice of Sweet Potato Casserole or Garlic Mashed Potatoes. You can sometimes get Penne Pasta Primavera or veggie burgers at lunchtime.

There are two dining cars—first-class and coach—on overnight trains. On first-class there is a vegan dinner of Vegetarian Lo Mein and a Vegetable Spring Roll if requested. Stir-fried Vegetables over Rice and vegetarian Lasagna can be gotten in coach.

Call 800-USA-RAIL to request a special Amtrak meal. Call 877-SKIP I-95 to request a special meal for the Auto Train that goes from Lorton, Virginia (just south of Washington DC) to just north of Orlando.

Chinese

Egg roll wrappers are made of wheat flour and egg. Spring roll wrappers are usually made of wheat flour and water. Often Chinese soups contain a non-veg base; egg drop soup often contains chicken stock, and hot & sour soup often has a beef base. Ask whether the broth contains any meat products (be specific as possible).

Sometimes noodle and rice dishes, such as Chinese fried rice, contain a meat broth even if they are listed on the "vegetarian menu." Many Chinese dishes contain oyster sauce (real), a thick, dark brown sauce. Often Chinese consider oyster sauce to be vegetarian, so it could be possible to be told a dish is vegetarian, while it contains non-veg oyster sauce.

Often noodles can contain eggs and if you ask if it is vegetarian you will be told that it is vegetarian. This is even true in vegetarian restaurants. If you do not eat eggs, you should ask if the noodles contain eggs. You should ask your question several times and should make sure your server understands what you are saying. Sometimes Chinese servers will agree with you to be polite and not really understand what you are saying. So you may want to have them repeat what you just said.

Often fortune cookies contain eggs, even in a vegan or vegetarian restaurant.

Greek and Middle Eastern

Whole grains and legumes are staples of the Greek and Middle Eastern diet. Vegetarian and salad dishes usually make up a good portion of the menu. Some common vegetarian dishes are falafel (deep-fried chickpea or fava bean balls spiced with garlic, cilantro and cumin), hummus (mashed, creamy chickpeas and tahini), vegetarian stuffed grape leaves and tabbouleh (salad of bulgur wheat, tomatoes, onions and parsley with lemon juice), and baba ghanoush (roasted eggplant dip). Pita sandwiches stuffed with falafel, salad, tahini or hummus are popular.

Dolmadakia, or dolma, is a salty stuffed grape leaf; the vegetarian version is traditionally served cold, while a meat dolma is usually served hot. A typical Greek entree is fava, yellow split peas with onions and garlic. The grains in couscous may be cooked in a chicken or lamb stock.

Greek rice is often cooked in a chicken stock; so you may want to ask about this. You may also want to ask about whether the falafels are cooked in oil that is also used in cooking any meat products.

Indian

Indian cuisine is often vegetarian-friendly. Over 50% of all Indians do not eat meat and eggs, but they do eat dairy products. Many dishes contain milk, cheese or ghee (clarified butter). Indian breads are often topped with butter. Indian dishes are often cooked in ghee, which is clarified butter, so if you are a vegan you may want to ask whether preparations are fried in ghee or vegetable oil.

A potential problem with Indian restaurants is that it can be difficult to get a straight answer about what dishes contain animal products. I often ask several times to confirm that a dish is vegetarian. Indian servers often just give you a token yes to everything you say, just to be polite. Unless you ask the manager or owner, it can be difficult to get a straight answer about whether a dish is vegetarian. Even then I may be doubtful. This is a major reason, if you are a serious vegetarian, to avoid Indian restaurants that serve meat.

Naan bread sometimes contains eggs or yogurt in the dough, so you may want to ask about this. Mulligatawny, a spicy lentil soup, often contains pieces of chicken and a meat broth.

Italian

The main thing to look out for is eggs in the pastas and meat broth in the sauces. Traditional hard pastas, made with semolina wheat flour and water, are 100 percent vegan. Many hand- or house-made fresh pastas (Ravioli or Fettuccine) contain eggs. Minestrone is vegetable pasta soup that often contains chicken or beef stock. Marinara sauce is typically vegetarian, but Bolognese sauce contains meat. Puttanesca sauce often contains anchovies. Risotto, an Italian rice dish, often contains a meat broth.

Japanese

Sushi bars often have a vegetarian sushi (made with avocado, pickled vegetables (oshinko) and vegetable nori maki) such as kappa maki (contains sticky rice and cucumber). Japanese dishes may contain dashi, a broth usually containing bonito (fish). Dashi is often in miso soup and hijiki (a mild black seaweed dish).

Vietnamese

Sometimes dishes that are listed as vegetarian contain fish. Often a fish sauce is mixed with different dishes. Fish sauce is called nuoc mam (anchoy-based). Vietnamese spring rolls often come with this sauce. Peanut sauce, used as a dressing on noodle dishes and salads, often contains fish. You should make clear that no fish sauce is used in any dishes. It is not good enough to ask if a dish is vegetarian; you should ask that it does not contain fish or fish sauce.

Thai

Many Thai dishes are vegetarian. They often cook with a fish sauce called nam pla, which can often be removed. Coconut milk is often used in preparations instead of dairy milk. Thai food can be cooked extremely hot, so you may want to request a more mild spicing.

Mexican

Rice may be cooked in chicken broth and beans are often cooked with lard. Cal-Mex cuisine is more likely to be vegetarian. A typical Cal-Mex meal often contains rice, salad or bean burritos. Flour tortillas sometimes contain lard, while corn tortillas normally don't, but corn tortillas may be deep-fried in lard. It is important to ask what cooking fat is used. Sauces often contain meat stocks.

Spanish

Spanish cuisine is frequently confused with Mexican or other Latin American cooking. Spanish dishes are usually mild and closer to the foods of Mediterranean France and Italy.

Spanish rice is often made with a chicken stock base, and may contain fish or meat. Spanish cuisine is usually low-fat.

French

Quiche Lorraine contains eggs and often bacon. French Onion soup often contains a beef stock. In French cooking there is often a meat glaze on vegetables. Breads often contain eggs.

Ethiopian

Ethiopian style cooking includes several well-cooked spicy stews called wots. They are served with injera, a flat pancake type bread. The teff (a native grain of Ethiopia) injera gets some high recommendations. They serve another injera made of teff, millet, corn and barley. Some dishes served are Pumpkin Wot (pumpkin stew), Tomato Fit-Fit (cold tomato stew), Yemisir Wot (spiced red pepper sauce and lentil stew), Yatakilt Alitcha (steam vegetables), Collard Greens and Yater Alitcha (yellow split pea stew with ginger and garlic). Yemiser Wot is a spiced lentil stew. Baklava is an Ethiopian dessert. Meals often end with a cup of spiced tea (cloves).

Most places have traditional Ethiopian low tables. Eating is done by using a piece of injera to scoop up the food. Food is spiced with red hot pepper, cardamom, curry, coriander, ginger, cumin, fresh herbs and shallots.

Gursha is an Ethiopian custom of putting portions of food in another person's mouth. There is an Ethiopian saying: "Those who eat from the same plate will not betray each other."

Veggie Burgers

Veggie burgers made by various companies and homemade ones made in restaurants sometimes contain eggs. Also in restaurants veggie burgers may be cooked on the same grill as meat burgers, so you may want to ask about this.

The original **Garden Burger** does not contain eggs, but most of the other varieties of the veggie burgers made by Garden Burger do contain eggs.

Most of the veggie meats including their veggie burger and veggie sausages made by **Morning Star** contain eggs.

Baco has a vegan burger that doesn't contain eggs. Some of their mock meat items do contain eggs such as their chicken nuggets and veggie sausage.

It seems that **Vyes** products in general don't contain eggs. Their veggie burger and hot dogs don't contain eggs.

Smart mock deli meats do not contain eggs. The **Sunshine Burger** doesn't contain eggs. The **Light Life** veggie burger and veggie hot dogs don't contain eggs.

Ordering out

Speaking Vegetarian by Bryan Geon (Pilot Books, 1999) is a foreign-phrase book written for vegetarians. It lists valauble phrases such as "I do not eat meat, chicken or fish" in several languages.

FRENCH Je ne mange pas de viande, de poulet ou de poisson.

ITALIAN Non mangio carne, pollo o pesce.

SPANISH No como carne, pollo o pescado.

Vegetarian and Vegan Organizations

ARIZONA

Jewish Vegetarians of Arizona
PO Box 32842, Phoenix, AZ 85064
602-840-7142

CALIFORNIA

Vegetarian Life, Special Interest Group of MENSA
PO Box 3425, Shell Beach, CA 93448, San Francisco; 805-937-1863

East Bay Vegetarians
8716 Seneca, PO Box 5450, Oakland, CA 94605
510-562-9934

San Francisco Vegetarian Society
PO Box 2510, San Francisco, CA 94126
415-273-5481; email: contact@sfvs.org;
Web site: www.sfvs.org
Arranges potluck dinners. Has links on their web site to other Bay Area vegetarian groups.

Bay Area Jewish Vegetarians
303 Adams Street, #201, Oakland, CA 94610
510-465-0403
email: bajv@ivu.org; Web site: www.ivu.org/bajv

Club Veg of San Diego
5663 Balboa Ave, PMB 334; San Diego, CA 92111
760-757-1033; Web site: www.clubveg.net

California FarmerMarket Directory
Northern & Southern edition. 800-952-5272.

Sacramento Vegetarian Society
PO Box 163583, Sacramento, CA 95816
916-554-7090

California Vegetarian Association
PO Box 6213, Thousand Oaks, CA 91359
818-377-4090, 805-529-7519

Southern California Vegetarians
Los Angeles, CA; 310-289-5777; email: info
@SoCalVeg.org; Web site: http://aouie.net/veg/

CONNECTICUT

Hartford Vegetarian Society
PO Box 271502, West Hartford, CT 06127
203-666-5872
c/o Leslie Gordon, Noah Webster House
227 South Main, West Hartford, CT 06107
203-521-5362

FLORIDA

Vegetarians of South Florida
Environmental Center, 1101 SW 104th Street
Miami, FL 33176; 305-347-2600

Vegetarian Singles Club
16750 NE 10th Avenue, North Miami Beach, FL 33162; 305-949-0950

GEORGIA

Vegetarian Society of Georgia
Box 2164, Norcross, GA 30091
707-662-4019; email: vsg@vegsocietyofga.org
Web site: www.vegsocietyofga.org

HAWAII

Gentle World
PO Box 238
Kapaau, HI 96765
808-884-5551
Vegan commune and publishing company.

KANSAS

Vegetarians of Kansas City
PO Box 7782, Shawnee Mission, KS 66207
816-464-1310; Contact: JoAnn Farb
Monthly potluck. Sponsor special events.

MAINE

Maine Vegetarian Resource Network
Shari Greenfield, RFD 2, Box 194
Belfast, ME 04915
207-338-1861; email: sharig@ctel.net

658 VEGETARIAN ORGANIZATIONS

MARYLAND

Vegetarian Society of Maryland, Inc.
PO Box 1478
Bowie, MD 20717
301-249-7926

Vegetarian Resource Group (VRG)
PO Box 1463
Baltimore, MD 21203
410-366-8343, fax: 366-8804
Web site: http://envirolink.org/arrs/VRG/home.html
Publish bi-monthly Vegetarian Journal.

Farm Animal Reform Movement (FARM)
10101 Ausburton Lane
Bethesda, MD 20824, 301-530-1737
email: farmofarmusa.org
Web site: www.farmusa.org
Organizers of The Great American Meatout & other events.

MASSACHUSETTS

Boston Vegetarian Society
PO Box 38-1071, Cambridge, MA 02238-1071
Contact: Evelyn B. Kimber, 617-424-8846
email: president@bvs.org, ekimber@juno.com
Has regular potlucks and meetings. Founded in 1986.

Vegetarian Resource Center (VRC)
PO Box 38-1068, Cambridge, MA 02238-1068
617-625-3790, fax: 617-357-2596
Contact: Maynard S. Clark
Maynard@vegetarian.org
email: vrc@tiac.net / info@vegetarian.org
Web site: http://www.tiac.net/users/vrc/vrc.html

MIT Vegetarian Support Group
PO Box 1068, Cambridge, MA 02238
617-424-8846
Informal student organization. Free membership.
Organize events and potlucks.

New England Anti-Vivisection Society (NEAVS)
333 Washington Street, Suite 850, Boston, MA 02108; 617-523-6020
email: info@ma.neavs.com
Web site: www.neavs.org
Publishes "Vegetarian Dining in the Boston Area".

MICHIGAN

Michigan Vegetarian Society
PO Box 258, Clawson, MI 48017

Vegans in Motion
2593 Columbia Ave, Berkley, MI 48072
email: vim@all4vegan.net
Website: www.all4vegan.net/vim.htm

The Vegetarian Lifestyle
VINE - Vegetarian Information Network & Exchange
Box 2224, Ann Arbor, MI 48106
734-428-3426; email: veginfo@tc3net.com or vineinfo@yahoo.com
VINE meets the first Wednesday of every month.

PeaceMakers Vegetarian Outreach and Support Center
14425 East Jefferson (at Chalmers)
contacts: Linda Means
810-731-0551; email: means@gmr.com
Tom Milano: 313-331-9300

Michigan Vegetarian Society
PO Box 60066, Roseville, MI 48066-6006
313-774-1161

MINNESOTA

EarthSave - Minnesota
5025 Morgan Avenue S, Minneapolis, MN 55419; 612-926-5023

Vegetarian Society for Earth
c/o Cheri Sundin, Peace of Green
619 Mall Germain, Saint Cloud, MN 56301
612-356-7387.

MISSOURI

Missouri Vegetarian Society
PO Box 2345, Overland, MO 63114
314-429-2786

NEW JERSEY

Shore Vegetarians
Maria Hidalgo Dolan, PO Box 221
Allenwood, NJ 08720
908-899-9000

Vegetarian Families of the Shore
1475 W Front St, Lincroft, NJ 07738
908-458-5435

Central Jersey Vegetarian Group
Stacey Walder, PO Box 952, Manville, NJ 08835
908-281-9563

Vegetarian Society of South Jersey
PO Box 272, Marlton, NJ 08053
609-234-7615; email: vssj@hotmail.com; Web
site: http://123easy.com/vssj/vssj.html, http://
www.vssj.com/vssjie.html
Has a dinning guide on web site for South Jersey.

NEW MEXICO

The Vegetarian Lifestyle
Vegetarian Society of New Mexico
Karen Schwartz, PO Box 81963
Albuquerque, NM 87198
Web site: www.unm.edu/~patric/vsnm.html

Vegetarian Society of New Mexico
PO Box 94495, Albuquerque, NM 87199
email: Info@vsnm.org; Web site: www.vsnm.org
Has a list of vegetarian and vegetarian-friendly
restaurants on their web site.

NEW YORK

Big Apple Vegetarians
Contact: Jean Thaler, 125 Ocean Pkwy. Apt. #3A
Brooklyn, NY 11218; 718-855-6030
Social group with monthly events in the Big
Apple!

Club Veg: Triple Cities
PO Box 625, Westview Station, Binghamton, NY
13905; 607-655-2993
email: triplecities@clubveg.org
Web site: www.clubveg.org/triplecities/
Contact: Amie Hamlin
607-724-1691; email: amieha@aol.com
Web site: http://www.netcom.com/~byb/
clubveg/clubveg.html

Farm Sanctuary
PO Box 150, Watkins Glen, NY 14891
607-583-2225
Farm Sanctuary is a 175-acre farm that is houses
rescued cattle, goats, turkeys, pigs and other animals. Open May 1 to October 31. To get there
from Watkins Glen, follow Route 409 West to
Route 23 for 8 miles. Turn left on Aikens Road

and follow for one and a half miles to the Farm
Sanctuary.

Jewish Vegetarian Society
Judah Grosberg, PO Box 144, Hurleyville, NY
12747; 914-434-6335

North American Vegetarian Society
PO Box 72, Dolgeville, NY 13329
Contact: Brian Graff
518-568-7970
Web site: http://mars.superlink.com/user/dupre/
navs/index.html Web site: www.navs-online.org

Vegan Society of Queens
150-39 75th Avenue, #2A,
Flushing, NY 11367

Vegetarian Society of New York
PO Box 1518, New York, NY 10028
212-535-9385

Vegetarian Youth Network
PO Box 1141, New Paltz, NY 12561
email: VYNet@mhv.net
Web site: http://www.geocities.com/RodeoDrive/
1154/
Support network for vegetarian teens. Run by
vegetarian youth.

Vegetarian Singles
PO Box 300412, Brooklyn, NY 11230-0412
718-437-0190; fax: 718-633-9817
Web site: www.veggiesingles.com

VivaVegie Society, Inc.
PO Box 294, Prince Street Station
New York, NY 10012-0005
212-414-9100
email: vivavegie@triroc.com; vivavegi@novalink.
com
Web site: www.earthbase.org/vivavegie/; http://
www.southwind.net/~ebase/Orgs/VivaVeg/
VivaV.html;

NORTH CAROLINA

Triangle Vegetarian Society
PO Box 3364, Chapel Hill, NC 27515
919-489-3340; Web site: http://www.trinet.com
/tonc/tvspage.html
Sponsor vegetarian potlucks and dinner outings.
There are some interesting reviews of restaurants
on North Carolina on the Triangle Society web
site (www.trianglevegsociety.org).

Western N. Carolina Vegetarian Society
Sandi Annable, PO Box 368
Cullowhee, NC 28723

Very Vegetarian Society
c/o Anne & Wesley Weaver, 620 Bellview Street
Winston-Salem, NC 27103; 910-765-2614

OHIO

Vegetarian Club of Canton
Box 9002, Canton, OH 44711
330-823-2158

Cincinnati Vegetarian Resource Group
Susan Huskin, Box 31455, Cincinnati, OH
45231; 513-542-6810

Vegetarian Society–Greater Dayton Area
PO Box 750742, Dayton, OH 45475-0742
937-885-1432; email: vsgda@yahoo.com

Vegetarian Society of Toledo & NW Ohio
Attn Hal Hamer, Box 12485, Toledo, OH 43606
419-536-4073

Vegetarians of Greater Youngstown
Bill & Marianne Whitehouse, 1631 Price Road
Youngstown, OH 44509; 330-799-7237

Vegetarian Connection
4826 Ridgebury Boulevard, Lyndhurst, OH
44124; 216-381-1385

OKLAHOMA

Vegetarians of Oklahoma City
c/o Carolyn McGarraugh, 7724 NW 20
Bethany, OK 73008; 405-789-3506

Vegetarians for Life
409 NW 33rd Street
Oklahoma City, OK 73118
405-524-7989

OREGON

Corvallis Vegetarians
John Donell, 45 NW 16th Street, #303 Corvallis
Plaza Apts, Corvallis, OR 97330
503-753-2265

Portland Vegetarians
PO Box 19521, Portland, OR 97219
503-295-9798, 503-223-5596

Umpqua Valley Vegetarian Society
Sandy Itzkowitz, 2165 NW Watters Street
Roseburg, OR 97470; 503-672-5897

RHODE ISLAND

Rhode Island Vegetarian Society
Rhode Island Vegetarian Society
Karen Iacobbo, Box 716, N, Scituate, RI 02857
401-421-6193

Rhode Island Animal Rights Coalition
PO Box 28514, Providence, RI 02908
401-783-1574

SOUTH CAROLINA

Clemson Vegetarian Group
Margaret OReilly
PO Box 33131
Clemson, SC 29633
803-653-3329

Friends of the Earth Vegetarian Society
PO Box 763, Clemson, SC 29633

Greenville Vegetarian Assoc.
Dawn Wells, 10 Terramont Drive
Greenville, SC 29615

South Carolina Vegetarian Society
Attn. Carol Cassetti - Pres, Box 1093
Lexington, SC 29072; 803-957-8155.

Kindred Spirits Vegetarian Collective
1914 Huntington Place, Rock Hill, SC 29732
803-328-5977

TENNESSEE

Vegetarian Assoc of West Tennessee
901-683-VEGE

East Tennessee Vegetarian Society
PO Box 1974, Knoxville, TN 37901
865-689-2446; Web site: www.korrnet.org/etvs/

Tennessee Vegetarian Society
PO Box 854, Knoxville, TN 37901
423-558-VEGE

Veganooga
PO Box 854
Knoxville, TN 37901
423-267-VEGE

VEGANET
PO Box 321
Knoxville, TN 37901
423-558-VEGE
National.

TEXAS

Texas Vegetarian Society
c/o Joe Dinoffer, 5416 Gurley Avenue
Dallas, TX 75223
214-823-3078

Vegetarian Society of Houston
2476 Bolsover #231, Houston, TX 77005; 713-880-1055; Web site: www.vshouston.org

UTAH

Vegetarian Voice of Utah
PO Box 2762
Salt Lake City, UT 84110-2762
Web site: www.vegetarianvoice.com

VERMONT

Vermont Vegetarian Society
c/o Judy Miner, RR 1 Box 1797
N Ferrisburg, VT 05473
802-453-3945.

WASHINGTON

EarthSave: Seattle
PO Box 9422 Seattle, WA 98109; 206-781-6602
Web site: http://seattle.earthsave.org/
Has a monthly potluck dinner.

WASHINGTON DC

Vegetarian Society of DC
PO Box 4921, Washington, DC 20008
Voice Mail: 202-362-VEGY (8349);
email: vsdc@vsdc.org
Web site: www.vsdc.org
Oldest vegetarian society in the US. Founded in 1927.

Raw Foods Vegetarian Club
7627 16th Street NW
Washington, DC 20012-1405
202-726-5671; email: rawvegfood@aol.com
Contact: Robert Jordan
Hold regular potluck dinners.

WISCONSIN

Wisconsin Vegetarian Society
PO Box 241, Neenah, WI 54957-0241
Contact: Trish Tucker-Keyes

Please check out our web site at **www.vegetarian-restaurants.net** for a more detailed list of vegetarian, vegan, animal rights and evironmentally-friendly organizations. If you would like to be included in this list, please contact us at **veggierestaurants@hotmail.com.**

NATURAL FOOD STORE MAJOR CHAINS

Whole Foods Market
(www.wholefoodsmarket.com)
Natural Food Store. There is a fairly large selection of Whole Foods Markets across the country. They are usually large supermarket size places with a large deli, salad bar and a large selection of organic produce.
Menu: Usually has a wide selection of vegetarian dishes in their deli. Grilled Tofu, rice dishes, noodle dishes, baked sweet potatoes, root vegetables, tofu dishes, roasted potatoes and noodles with peanut dressing. Sandwiches, large selection in salad bar, pizzas and baked goods (some vegan). Items range from $2.99 to $6.99 per pound. Sandwiches and hot dishes. Salad and soup bar. Fresh juices and smoothies.
Comments: Usually service is efficient and friendly, more so than most places. Recommended.
Other Info: At most of the places you order at the deli counter. Most places also have a self-serve salad bar. Most places have several tables to eat at. Accepts all major credit cards, ATM and debit cards.

Wild Oats (www.wildoats.com)
Natural Food Store. These places are usually large, well-stocked natural food stores. They usually have a large produce section, often as large as most grocery stores. Has a large salad bar, a large selection of hot items in its deli and hot fresh pizza. Usually they have an excellent selection of goods.
Menu: Dishes served varies from store to store Dishes are freshly made. Have a good selection of vegetarian dishes. Some examples of dishes served are: veggie burgers, macro platter, vegetarian soups, salads, tofu dishes, steamed vegetables, whole-wheat pizza, sandwiches, Bowl of Plenty (steamed vegetables on rice), Save-the-Chicken Salad Sandwich, Tempeh Seitan, Tofu Foo Young, Tofu Fried Rice, Tofu Stroganoff, veggie tamales, Roasted Rosemary Tempeh, barbecue tempeh, Veggie Reuben, Spinach Lasagna, Three Bean Chili, enchiladas, vegetable burrito and organic rice. Have desserts such as brownies. Fresh juices, cappuccino, espresso. Items range from $2.99 to $5.99 per pound.
Comments: Most places have special events such as yoga, fitness, Feng Shui, cooking classes, massage classes and more. Some of the places have a newsletter that describes the monthly events offered. Usually service is efficient and friendly, more so than most places. Recommended. They often prepare foods using local organic produce.
Owned by Wild Oats: Ideal Market, Colorado; Henry's Marketplace, California; Nature's: A Wild Oats Market, Oregon & Washington; People's Market, Illinois; Sun Harvest Farms, Texas; Vitamin Expo, Texas. Most of these places are large natural food stores. The Vitamin Expo stores in Texas are not usually so big.
Other Info: Counter service, take-out, catering. Non-smoking. Accepts AMEX, DIS, MC, VISA. Prices: $-$$.

Trader Joe's
Web site: www.traderjoes.com
Natural Food-type Store.
Comments: This is one of the best natural food type stores that you will find. Most of these places are big and have an excellent selection of items. Organic whole-wheat spaghetti, 100% pure Italian olive oil, organic canned soups, Trader Joe's juices and much more. Many of the items are Trader's Joe own brands, which are usually first-class. Recommended. Definitely worth visiting.

Glossary

Amino acids – Amino acids are the building blocks of protein and they also have other uses.

Antioxidants – Photochemicals that are present in plants that help the body get rid of free radicals.

Adzuki beans – Small, brown sweet bean. Used in Japanese cooking.

Agar-agar – A clear, flavorless odorless sea vegetable. It is freeze-dried, sold in sticks, flakes or powder. It is a natural thickener and is a good substitute for gelatin.

Arame – A thin, spaghetti like, dark brown sea vegetable rich in calcium, iron and other minerals.

Beta-carotene – It is a substance found in deep orange, yellow and red vegetables and fruits. It is believed that it protects against cancer and heart disease.

Bean thread noodles – Translucent cellophane noodles threads made from green mung beans starch. Can also be deep-fried.

Bulgur – Cracked hulled and parboiled wheat.

Canola oil – Rapeseed oil. Lower in saturated fat than other oils.

Carob – Used like cocoa powder in baked goods, but does not contain caffeine, and is lower in fat.

Cheese – Dairy cheeses. Hard, aged cheeses often contains animal rennet. Cheeses that do not contain rennet are often made with chymosin (a bacteria), that may be listed as enzymes. Kosher cheeses are made with vegetarian rennet because Jewish dietary law does not allow the mixing of dairy and meat. Soy and nut cheeses often contain a milk protein called casein.

Cholesterol – Cholesterol is a waxy substance that can often be found in the arteries of a person who is diseased. If there is too much cholesterol in a person's diet there may be a hardening of the arteries which can cause heart disease. Cholesterol is made by the liver and is only found in animal foods such as meat, eggs and dairy products. Plant foods do not contain cholesterol. The body does not need any cholesterol since the body can produce all that it needs. A diet with a low level of saturated fats and cholesterol is healthiest, and this diet can help reduce the chance of coronary artery disease, high blood pressure, diabetes and cancer.

Complementary proteins – Refers to the practice of eating foods in the correct combination in order to optimize the correct intake of essential amino acids. This combination of food is believed to form a "complete protein." At the present time this practice is no longer considered to be valid by most experts.

Co-op – A Co-op is a group that purchases food in bulk to distribute it to its members at discount prices. They often specialize in selling organic produce and natural foods. Some co-ops have their members pay a monthly fee and others require them to put in a certain amount of hours of work and in return they receive a lower price on goods sold by the co-ops.

Curry – Spicy India and Thai dishes. Dishes that contain curry powder, which is a mixture of spices.

Egg Replacer – Powdered combination of starches and leavening agents that bind cooked and baked foods instead of eggs. Sold in health food stores.

Cyanocobalamin – This is a form of vitamin B12 that is believed to be the best form for absorption by the human body.

Enzymes – Proteins added to foods to modify them. May be derived from animal, vegetable, bacterial or fungal sources. Often enzymes used to make cheeses are derived from animal products. Examples of enzymes are rennet (animal), pectinase (fruit), protease (animal, lactase, fungal), papain (vegetable), lipase (animal, fungal) and trypsin (animal).

Essential amino acids – Amino acids that are not manufactured by the body and have to be gotten from food.

Feta cheese – Soft, tangy cheese made from cow's or goat's milk. Used in Greek and other Mediterranean cuisines.

Fiber – Fiber or roughage is only found in plants, and is not found in animal products. A vegetarian diet is a good source of fiber.

Free radicals – Molecules that cause damage to the body's cells.

Fruitarian – People who only eat fruits and apparent vegetables that are actually classified as fruits such as avocados, nuts, seeds, eggplant, zucchini and tomatoes.

Garam masala – A Indian blend of ground, dry-roasted spices. Typically it includes cumin, black pepper, cloves, cardamom, fennel, dried chilies, cinnamon, nutmeg, coriander and other spices.

Gelatin – A tasteless, clear thickening agent usually made from animal products. There are also often vegetarian gelatin that is made from plant gums. Some kosher gelatins are animal-free. Sometimes you will see kosher gelatin listed on a yogurt package, but the yogurt label does not say the yogurt product is kosher. The gelatin is kosher (is not meat and milk mixed together or is made from fish), but if it is a meat derived gelatin and it is mixed with the yogurt than the yogurt product is not kosher nor is it fit for a vegetarian.

Gluten – a protein complex made from grains, found in a high level in wheat and in lesser amounts in rye, barley, oats and spelt. It is mixed with water and spices and is often used in vegetarian meat substitutes. It can be used to make bread rise as a leavening agent.

Hijiki (hee-jee-kee) – A black sea vegetable that is sold in strands. Expands five times after it is soaked and cooked.

Hydrogenated Fat – This is vegetable oil that has been hardened. Corn oil can take a stick shape such as margarine. It is used in baking and in peanut butter. Hydrogenated fats can produce cholesterol and may increase the chance of coronary artery disease.

Jalapeno chili – Dark green chili pepper that are one or two inches long. Can be extremely hot.

Lacto Ovo Vegetarian – A lacto-ovo vegetarian does not eat meat, fish or poultry, but eats eggs and milk. They eat eggs and products made with eggs in them, yogurt, cheese, milk and ice creams.

Lacto Vegetarian – A lacto vegetarian does not eat meat, fish, poultry or eggs, but includes dairy products in their diet. They will eat milk, yogurt, cheese and ice cream that does not include eggs. They would avoid ice cream that contains eggs, veggie burgers that contain eggs, and baked goods and pancakes that contain eggs.

Legumes – Plants that produce seed pods that break on both sides when ripe. Some examples are beans, soybean, peas, peanuts and lentils.

Light olive oil – Filtered olive oil that is lighter in color and flavor than regular olive oil. Good for baking and cooking. Good to use for high-heat frying.

Macrobiotic – Macrobiotic takes into consideration the concept of yin and yang, which is applied to the acid and alkaline qualities in foods, to get a neutral pH diet. This food is often prepared in a Japanese-style. It recommends using local foods. Macrobiotic diets are often vegetarian, but some of them may contain seafood in their diet. In this diet all other meat products are

excluded, as are eggs and dairy products. They also do not eat "nightshade vegetables" (potato, pepper and eggplant), refined sugar and tropical fruits.

Mung beans – A bean that has a yellow flesh and black, yellow or green skin. Often used for sprouting. Used in Indian cooking to make a healthy bean soup.

Natural Foods – Foods that generally have had minimal processing, and do not contain chemical additives, preservatives, artificial colors or flavoring. Natural foods are usually more nutritious because they are less processed and do not contain potentially harmful ingredients. There is no legal definition of the words "natural food." A natural breakfast cereal would use whole grains and contain more fiber, minerals and vitamins than normal cereals. Foods used in natural foods are often organically grown and usually contains less sodium. Foods that are sweetened will usually only have the minimum sweetener. They will often use fruit juice to sweeten them instead of refined sugar. Does not use nitrites or monosodium glutamate.

Nutritional yeast – A variety of brewers (inactive) yeast that has a cheesy/nutty flavor that is rich in minerals and vitamins. Like brewer's yeast, but tastes good. Added to soups and casseroles or put on spaghetti and toast.

Organic – No prohibited substances allowed to be used on the land within three years of harvesting organic produce. It is best that organic seeds are used, but non-organic seeds can be used under certain conditions. Crops pests, insects, diseases and weeds should be stopped as much as possible by pulling weeds or by biological methods (lady-bugs). Certain synthetic substances can be used if natural methods don't work. Crop rotation must be done. Crop waste and animal goods should be used, and certain permitted synthetic materials. Genetic engineering, sewage sludge and irradiation cannot be used.

Phyllo dough – Thin pastry layers used in Middle Eastern and Greek dishes.

Pure Vegetarian – One who does not consciously eat meat, fish, poultry or eggs. A pure vegetarian will never eat meat under any circumstances. They will also avoid products that have meat products in them such as cheese made with the rennet of a cow's stomach, products that contain animal gelatin, refried beans with lard in them, candies that contain eggs and other ingredients derived from meat products, marshmallows made with eggs, and baked goods that contain eggs.

Protein – Protein is nitrogen-containing compounds that become amino acids when they are digested. Amino acids make up protein and they make up the basic structure of every cell. They make up antibodies, enzymes and hormones.

Raw foods diet – A diet in which primarily only uncooked food is eaten. One who follows this type of diet believes that cooking changes food in a negative way and makes it less nutritional; dimishing the vitamin and mineral contents of the food.

Rennet – An enzyme that is used as a starter to curdle milk to make cheese. It is usually made from the stomach lining of calves, pigs and lambs. It may also be made from a vegetarian substance.

Rice Milk – This is a rice-based beverage that can be used as a substitute for dairy milk on cereal, etc. It is often fortified with nutrients. It comes in a variety of flavors including plain, carob or vanilla.

Rice – There are several varieties of rice.

Basmati Rice – A creamy white, aromatic, nutty tasting, long-grain rice that is grown in the foothills of the Himalayan mountains in India and Pakistan. Brown basmati, or Texmati is a cross between basmati and long-grain brown rice.

Brown Rice – Unpolished, whole, natural brown rice that has higher nutritional value than white rice, but some people will not like its taste as much. It is higher in fiber, phosphorus, B-vitamin, linoleic acid, iron and protein than white rice.

Refined White Rice – Rice that is dehulled, refined (the bran and germ is removed) and polished.

Enriched White Rice – Rice that has been refined and then sprayed with a vitamin solution, and then coated with protein, which makes it more nutritious, but it is still not as good as brown rice.

Long-grain Rice – Long grain rice that is fluffy and separates nicely when cooked.

Jasmine Rice – Aromatic rice from Thailand.

Japanica Rice – A short-grain black rice with a sticky texture that originated in Japan. It is usually mixed with brown rice in dishes.

Wehani Rice – It is derived from rice from India and is grown in California. It has large grains and taste like brown rice and has the texture of wild rice.

Sushi Rice – A short-grain rice that has a sticky texture. It is often used in sushi and nori rolls.

Wild Rice – It is dark brown, longer than long-grain rice and slender. It is not really rice but is the seed of an aquatic grass. It is usually grown in patties and is grown in Minnesota (mainly),

Michigan, Wisconsin, the Rocky Mountain area and California.

Saffron – Comes from autumn crocus. Gives food a yellow color. Has unique pleasant taste. Relatively expensive.

Sea Salt – Salt that comes from the sea. Sun baked or baked in a kiln. Does not contain sugar, chemicals or other additives. High in trace minerals.

Seitan – Boiled or baked wheat protein (gluten). A meat-like, high-protein, chewy dough-like food that has the texture and taste of meat. It is often used as a meat substitute. It is served fried, stir-fried or baked. Has no saturated fat or cholesterol.

Soy Cheese – This is imitation dairy cheese that is made of soybean. A person who is a vegan may want to check the label for casein, which is a protein derived from milk.

Soy Milk – It is extracted from soybeans and is rich creamy milk. It can be used for many things that cow milk is used for on cereal or in coffee. It is often fortified with vitamins and minerals. It cannot be called milk on the package because the USDA only permits lactational liquid from a mammal to be called milk. It has a nutty flavor. Soy milk is an excellent source of protein and is high in vitamin B. Ingredients such as job's tears or carrageenin are often added to it to give it a feel like cow's milk in the mouth.

Soy Sauce – Salty liquid that is derived from drained off soybean miso. Imitation soy sauces are also chemical hydrochloric acid extraction or imitation sauces flavored with corn sauce. Shoyu is derived from compressed soybean and then is fermented for four to six months. Tamari is similar in taste to shoyu, but doesn't contain wheat.

Strict vegetarian – One who does not consciously eat meat, fish or poultry. A pure vegetarian will never eat meat under any circumstance. They will also avoid products that have meat products in them.

Tamari (tuh-MAH-ee) – Brewed soy sauce that contains no sugar.

Tandoori – Indian style of cooking that uses a round-topped clay and brick tandoor oven. Food is baked over direct heat.

Tempeh – Fermented whole soybean. It is made from cooked soybeans that are hulled and then compressed into cakes and then fermented for 24 hours. It is often mixed with grains and then combined with a mold culture. Often made into mock meat substitutes or tempeh burgers. It is made with a culture called rhizopus, which is grown on hibiscus leaves. It is a traditional Indonesian food that is usually mixed with rice. It can be fried or baked. It is high in B vitamin and protein. It is rich in fiber. It is sold in the refrigerated or frozen food section. Like cheese and other fermented products a little mold on the surface is harmless and can just be cut off.

Textured vegetable protein (TVP) – It is compressed soy flour, which usually comes in a dry granules or chunks that look like ground beef after it is rehydrated. Rehydrated it can have the texture and look of meat.

Tofu – Soybean curd (looks like white cheese) made by curdling and then pressing out the liquid in soy milk making a solid block. It is high in protein, low in sodium, and is a good source of B-vitamins and iron. Depending on how much of the water has been pressed out of the tofu it will be different degrees of hardness. It can be soft or firm. Hard tofu is often used in stir-fries. Middle firm tofu can be used in baked goods and as an egg replacer. Soft tofu can be used in sauces, puddings and custards. If the curdling agent is made from a calcium compound it is a good source of calcium. A four-ounce serving of tofu contains just six grams of fat and is low in saturated fat. The softer the tofu, the lower the fat content. Tofu is used by many Asian cultures. Tofu should be kept refrigerated unless it is packaged tightly. You need to check its expiration date on the package. Once the package is opened tofu should be rinsed and covered with water to store it. The water should be changed daily and the tofu should be used within a week. It can be kept for up to five months when frozen.

Vegan – One who does not eat any animal products including meat, fish, eggs and dairy, or foods that contain any of these products. They also do not use any non-food items that contain products from animals including wool from sheep, leather and silk. Vegans often do not eat honey, because bees may be killed while harvesting it.

Veggie Burger – Veggie burgers are made from soy protein, vegetables, rice, grains or fiber. Some brands contain eggs, dairy or cheese. They can be grilled, baked or micro-waved.

Vegetarian – One who does not eat meat or fish. Some vegetarian also do not eat dairy products because they do not eat any animals byproducts.

Wheatgrass – Young green grass sprouts of wheat. Considered to be very healthy. Made into juice.

Middle Eastern Food

Baba Ghannouj – Baked eggplant dip with lemon, garlic and herbs.

Baklava – Fillo pastery (phyllo dough) in layers with honey and walnut.

Couscous – Pasta made from semolina flour.

Dolmades – Rice, tomatoes, herbs wrapped in grape leaves with olive oil, lemon and garlic.

Emjedrah – Lentil and rice spread.

Falefel – Deep-fried chickpeas shaped into croquettes.

Foule Muddammas – Traditional Egyptian fava bean dip with diced garlic and olive oil, lemon, peppers and parsley.

Garbanzo Salad – Chickpeas with parsley, scallions, olives, vinegar and oil.

Greek Salad – Feta cheese, cucumber, tomato, olives, onion and peppers with an olive oil, fresh lemon and oregano dressing.

Gyros (vegetarian) – Flat pita bread sandwich with seitan, cheese, tomato, lettuce and onion.

Hummus – Pureed, mashed garbanzo beans (chickpea) dip or spread that contains garlic, lemon juice and tahini (sesame seed butter). A spicy paste made from chickpeas and sesame butter. Popular in Israel and the Middle East.

Moussaka – Eggplant and chickpeas.

Mediterranean Salad – Red and green cabbage, onion, carrots with olive oil, parsley, vinegar dressing and dill.

Muhablea – Milk pudding cooked in rose water and topped with shredded coconut and cinnamon.

Mujadara – Rice and lentils.

Pita Bread – Flat bread.

Roz Whaleeb – Rice pudding with walnuts, raisins, cinnamon and honey.

Saganaki – Feta cheese sautéed in olive oil until golden brown. Served with olives, peppers, tomatoes and cucumber.

Sargali – Fillo pastry filled with almond, honey and nutmeg.

Spanakopita – Fillo dough with spinach and green onions. Baked in an oven until golden brown.

Spinach Fatayer - Spinach, tomato, onion, lemon, olive oil and spices baked inside pita dough.

Skoradelea Garlic Dip – Diced potatoes with olive oil, garlic and fresh herbs.

Tabbouleh Salad – Salad of bulgur wheat, tomatoes, onions and parsley with lemon juice

Tahini (tah-HEE-nee) – A thick nut butter paste made of ground sesame seeds.

Tzatziki – Yogurt, cucumber, dill and garlic.

Indian

Indian cooking often contains hot red or green chilis and onions.

Achar – Hot spicy pickle in oil. A favorite is Mango Achar.

Alu – Potato.

Alu Paratha – Flat bread stuffed with spiced potatoes.

Bhaji – Sautéed spinach and chickpeas with spices.

Basmati rice (bahs-MAH-tee) – Delicate long-grain rice with a nutty flavor. It is aged to enhance its aroma and nutlike flavor.

Batakanu Sak – Potatoes cooked in gravy with mild sauce.

Bengan Bharta – Baked eggplant sautéed with tomatoes and spices.

Bhindi – Ladies' finger, okra.

Biryani – Mild fancy rice; sometimes served with a sauce.

Bonda – Spicy potato balls.

Bombay Bhaji – Puree of vegetables served with flat bread.

Cardamom – Aromatic spice used in Indian cooking. Comes in a pod containing a small black or brown seeds. Considered to be a special spice.

Chaas – Buttermilk with powdered cumin and mint.

Chai – Indian spiced tea.

Channa – Chickpeas (garbanzo beans). Light-brown beans with a nutty flavor

Channa Masala – Chickpeas (garbanzo beans) with spices and usually with onions.

Channa Dal – Split yellow lentils soup.

Chapati – Unleavened Indian bread.

Chawal – Seasoned basmati rice.

Chutney – Chutney is a jam-like dipping sauce, often sweet and spicy hot, but also can be salty. Usually accompanies main dishes. Coconut, mango and tamarind chutneys are common. Sweet chutney is made with fruit, sugar, chili and spices.

Coconut Chutney – Fresh creamy coconut based chutney is a South Indian dish that is used as a dip for dosa, idly, etc.

Coriander seed – Dried, ripe fruit of the coriander plant, a relative of parsley. Coriander leaves are also known as cilantro.

Curd – Yogurt.

Dahi – Yogurt.

Dal – Spiced lentil soup

Dal Vada – Deep-fried savory made of yellow lentils and spices.

Dhokla – Steamed chickpea bread topped with cilantro and sometimes green chili peppers.

Dosa – Large paper-thin pancake (crepe) made of a mixture of fermented rice and bean flours. Cooked on a grill until they are crisp and airy. They are then wrapped in a large cone. Often filled with potato curry (masala dosa). Usually served with sambar (spicy lentil soup) and coconut chutney. A basic South Indian food.

Ful-Gobhi – Cauliflower and green peas.

Gajar – Carrots.

Ghee – Clarified butter used in cooking. To make ghee you cook a pound or more of butter. As it cooks the solids come to the top and they are scrapped off. When all the solids are gone and the butter is clean the finished product is called ghee.

Gobhi – Cauliflower.

Gulab Jamun – Fried milk pâté dumplings in golden syrup. Very rich and sweet.

Halava (Halwa) – A sweet made of wheat, butter and sugar. It is a little like cream of wheat.

Idly (Idli) – Steamed dumplings made of ground, fermented rice flour or with lentil dhal, usually eaten with coconut chutney. Savory and mild.

Jeera – Cumin.

Kaju – Cashew.

Khichdi – Lentils mixed with rice and various vegetables. This is a common dish in India.

Kheer – Rice pudding with dry fruits in milk

Kofta – Fried vegetable ball.

Lassi – Sweet or salty yogurt drink. Often made with fresh fruit.

Makhani – Cooked in a rich butter sauce.

Mango Kufi – Mango ice cream.

Masala Chai – Indian tea cooked with cardamom, ginger and milk.

Masala Dosa – A dosa that is wrapped around a savory filling of potato and usually onion. Usually spiced with turmeric and mustard seed.

Masala Poori – Seasoned, puffed, whole-wheat bread.

Mattar – Peas.

Mattar Pulao – Fried rice with peas.

Moong Dal – Green lentil soup.

Namkin – Package spicy snack. General word for snack.

Naan – Leavened bread baked in Tandoor oven. Sometimes contains eggs.

Nimbu Paani – Fresh lemonade drink.

Paani – Water.

Papad (Pappadam) – Crisp lentil cracker appetizer. Thin bean lentil wafers.

Pakora – Pieces of vegetable or paneer (curd) dipped in spiced chickpea batter and deep-fried. Served with a chutney.

Palak – Spinach.

Paneer –Homemade soft cheese. Pot cheese.

Pappadam (papar) – Fried lentil flour wafer.

Paratha – Indian flatbread that is often stuffed with potato or cheese. Rich, soft Indian flatbread; served hot.

Piaz – Onions.

Pista – Pistachio.

Poori (Puri) – Deep-fried flat bread; served hot.

Poori Bhaji – Puffed whole-wheat bread with potato and vegetables.

Pulao – High quality rice dish often mixed with vegetables or paneer.

Raitha – Yogurt and shredded vegetable (often cucumber) salad.

Rajma – Red kidney beans in a richly seasoned gravy.

Rava Dosa – A dosa made of semolina and fermented lentils like a traditional crepe.

Roti – Flat whole-wheat bread.

Sabji (Sabzi) – A vegetable dish. Dishes that are mainly vegetables are called a sabji.

Sak (sag) – Spinach.

Sambar – Thin lentil and vegetable sweet and sour soup used for dipping. Served with South Indian dishes such as dosa, idly, etc.

Samosa – A deep-fried crisp turnover stuffed with vegetables. Savory pastries that are usually filled with spicy potatoes and green peas.

Sev Puri – A mixture of potatoes, garbanzo beans, yogurt and chutney in a fried bread.

Tandoori – Baked in a clay oven.

Thali – Vegetarian meal which includes a variety of preparations; often it is all-you-can-eat and you can ask for free refills.

Uppuma – Savory, spicy semolina; rich and mild.

Uttapam – Thick lentil crepe often topped with a variety of vegetables.

Vada (Urid) – Savory, lentil doughnut.

Asian

Daikon – Long, white radish, used in Japanese cuisine as a garnish. It is a digestive aid.

Ginger – Golden-colored pungent, root vegetable used as a spice in Asian and Indian cooking. Can give food a spicy hot taste.

Hiziki – A noodle-shaped, blue black sea vegetable that has a strong, nutty aroma. Hiziki contains fourteen times more calcium than milk.

Kombu – Dark green sea vegetable.

Kukicha tea – Roasted twigs, stems and leaves of Japanese tea bush. It is a digestion aids and is high in calcium. Also called Bancha Tea.

Miso – Protein rich fermented soybean paste which also contains salt and miso starter (a mold culture called koji), and then aged for one to three years. It may also contain barley or rice. It may have water added and is often used to flavor soups. It can be used as seasoning. The darker types tend to have a stronger flavor and be saltier than lighter colored ones. Aids circulation & digestion.

Nori (NOH-ree) – Paper-thin, crispy black or dark purple sheets made from sea vegetable. Used to wrap around sushi. High in vitamins and minerals. Nori turns green when roasted.

Soba – Noodles made from buckwheat flour or buckwheat and whole wheat flour.

Tamari – The liquid that rises during the process of making miso. There are also imitation chemically processed varieties.

Wakame – Long, thin, green sea vegetable. Tastes sweet and has a delicate texture. High in protein and iron.

Index

Books Published by Spiritual Guides

For details and updates check our website at: **www.spiritualguides.net or www.vegetarian-restaurants.net**

India: A Practical Guide by Jada Bharata, John Howley

This book gives a detailed explanation of places in India, including: temples, forts, beaches, holy places, palaces, wildlife parks, the Himalayan mountains, museums and much more. It has easy to understand introductional information, so is very useful for a first time visitor to India or Southeast Asia. It has 196 maps. Contains detailed practical information including: hotels, restaurants, travel information, in all price ranges. Also it has sections on health, history, festivals, what to bring, and religious information. Over 500 towns and cities listed, and thousands of places described.

INDIA, published by Spiritual Guides, is an invaluable asset for a person planning to make a visit to India. It is very detailed and covers most of the major places covered in other travel books written on India, plus many other places. The practical advice on India is very helpful and is written in a street-smart manner. This book explains how to to have a pleasant and inexpensive trip to this exotic country.

Price: $20; ISBN Number: 0-9653858-4-1; Pages 1093

Holy Places and Temples of India

Detailed descriptions of holy places and temples in Inda. Lists over 30 holy places, 200 temples and has 63 maps. Extenisve accommodations, good list of vegetarian restaurants, transportion, and much more.

Price $15; ISBN 0-9653858-0-9; Pages 672

Vrindavan and Braja Mandala by Jada Bharata Dasa

Vrindavana is the land of Krishna. For a devotee of Krishna this is the most important place in the world to visit. This is the place where Krishna appeared on this earth and where He had many of His pastimes.

Many places are listed in this book such as: Vrindavana, Mathura, Govardhana Hill, Radha Kunda, Gokula, the twelve forests of Vrindavana. Also listed is Uchagrama, the village of Lalita Sakhi; Prema Sarovara; Sanket, where Radha and Krishna would meet; Javat, the village where Radharani lived after She got married; Raval, where Radharani appeared; Baldeo, where there is an ancient Deity of Balarama; and Kamyavana, which has many important places in it.

There is also much practical information in this book. There is a list of places to stay and eat at while in Vrindavana. There is also travel information for within Braja and travel information telling how to get to Vrindavana. There is also a good section on where to shop in Vrindavana and a health section.

There are also sections on Delhi and Jaipur.

Price: $12; ISBN 0-9653858-1-7 Pages 505

Sri Navadvipa and Jagannatha Puri by Jada Bharata Dasa

Contains a detailed description of Mayapur and the Navadvipa Dhama area. Included in this book are most of the major places that are visited on Navadvipa Dhama Parikrama. All the nine islands are described. It also describes Gaura Mandala or the places that Lord

Caitanya and his associates had their pastimes, in Bengal and Bangladesh.

There is also a section about Jagannatha Puri. A short section on Calcutta is included as most people going to Mayapur will pass through Calcutta. Included are what each place is and what its significance is, stories about the places, maps, and descriptions of how to get to the places.

There is also a lot of practical information in this book. There is a list of places to stay and eat at while in Mayapur, Jagannatha Puri and Calcutta. Also travel information is included and valuable practical hints.

Price: $10 ISBN 0-9653858-2-5 Pages: 264

Hinduism, What It Really Is, Sanatana Dharma, Vastu Sastra, Vedic Astrology and Gemology

This book is an easy to understand definition of Hinduism written for the beginner. A section of this book is on this web site. Besides the basics of Hinduism, there are also sections on Vedic astrology, gemology and Vastu Sastra. Many of the important Hindu gods are described and there are some beautiful line drawings of many of the gods. Such important questions are answered such as: What is the meaning of OM and who are Krishna, Vishnu, Hanuman and Brahma? Some subjects described are yoga, temple worship, Indian festivals, karma, temple design, Buddhism, important temples, Vedic marriages, Siva-lingas, cows and important holy places. At the end of the book is a glossary where many of the words used in Hinduism are defined.

The astrological and gemology section are written in an easy to understand way, so it will be very useful to the beginner. In many cases when one goes to an astrologer various terms are often used and often a beginner may have no idea what the astrologer is talking about. Therefore many of the terms are described in easy to understand English.

In the gemological section there are descriptions of the astrological uses of the gems, how they benefit a person, who should wear each particular gem, and what is a good or bad gem. There are also some useful terms described in reference to gemology.

Vastu Sastra is the Vedic or Indian science of building. By building a house under the rules of Vastu Sastra it can influence the fortunes of the residents. This book gives some ideas how one should build a house in a way that will have a positive influence on the people living in it. It also describes how the things should be placed in the inside of the house. There is also a description of what decisions should be made before a house should be purchased.

PRICE: $9.95 ISBN 0-9653858 PAGES: 250